WELSH LITERATURE

The literature of Wales is one of the oldest continuous literary traditions in Europe. The earliest surviving poetry was forged in the battlefields of post-Roman Wales and the 'Old North' of Britain, and the Welsh-language poets of today still write within the same poetic tradition. In the early twentieth century, Welsh writers in English outnumbered writers in Welsh for the first time, generating new modes of writing and a crisis of national identity which began to resolve itself at the end of the twentieth century with the political devolution of Wales within the United Kingdom. By considering the two literatures side by side, this book argues that bilingualism is now a normative condition in Wales. Written by leading scholars, this book provides a comprehensive chronological guide to fifteen centuries of Welsh literature and Welsh writing in English against a backdrop of key historical and political events in Britain.

GERAINT EVANS grew up in a Welsh-speaking community in north Wales and studied at the universities of London, Swansea, and Cambridge. After teaching Celtic Studies at the University of Sydney, he returned to Wales where he is now Senior Lecturer in English at Swansea University and a member of the Centre for Research into the English Literature and Language of Wales (CREW). His research interests include modernism, Welsh writing in English, and the history of the book in Britain.

HELEN FULTON trained as a Celticist at the University of Oxford and did postdoctoral research in medieval Welsh poetry at the Centre for Advanced Welsh and Celtic Studies in Aberystwyth. She taught at the University of Sydney before returning to the UK where she held chairs of medieval literature at the universities of Swansea and York. She is now Professor of Medieval Literature at the University of Bristol. She has published in both Welsh and English and specializes in the politics of literary production in medieval Wales and England.

THE CAMBRIDGE
HISTORY OF
WELSH LITERATURE

*

Edited by
GERAINT EVANS
Swansea University
HELEN FULTON
University of Bristol

CAMBRIDGE
UNIVERSITY PRESS

CAMBRIDGE
UNIVERSITY PRESS

University Printing House, Cambridge CB2 8BS, United Kingdom

One Liberty Plaza, 20th Floor, New York, NY 10006, USA

477 Williamstown Road, Port Melbourne, VIC 3207, Australia

314–321, 3rd Floor, Plot 3, Splendor Forum, Jasola District Centre,
New Delhi – 110025, India

79 Anson Road, #06–04/06, Singapore 079906

Cambridge University Press is part of the University of Cambridge.

It furthers the University's mission by disseminating knowledge in the pursuit of
education, learning, and research at the highest international levels of excellence.

www.cambridge.org
Information on this title: www.cambridge.org/9781107106765
DOI: 10.1017/9781316227206

First published 2019
3rd printing 2019

Printed in the United Kingdom by TJ International Ltd. Padstow Cornwall

A catalogue record for this publication is available from the British Library.

Library of Congress Cataloging-in-Publication Data
NAMES: Evans, Geraint, editor. | Fulton, Helen, date, editor.
TITLE: The Cambridge history of Welsh literature / edited by Geraint Evans, Helen Fulton.
DESCRIPTION: Cambridge, United Kingdom ; New York, NY: Cambridge University Press,
2018. | Includes bibliographical references and index.
IDENTIFIERS: LCCN 2018023254 | ISBN 9781107106765 (alk. paper)
SUBJECTS: LCSH: Welsh literature – History and criticism. | English literature – Welsh
authors – History and criticism. | Wales – In literature. | Bilingualism in literature.
CLASSIFICATION: LCC PB2206 .C36 2018 | DDC 891.6/609–dc23
LC record available at https://lccn.loc.gov/2018023254

ISBN 978-1-107-10676-5 Hardback

Contents

Contents

PART VI
AFTER DEVOLUTION

Maps

Contributors

SUSAN ARONSTEIN is Professor of English and Honors at the University of Wyoming. She is the author of *Hollywood Knights: Arthurian Cinema and the Politics of Nostalgia* (2005) and *British Arthurian Narrative* (2012) as well as the co-editor of *Disney's Middle Ages: A Fairy Tale and Fantasy Past* (2012). Her articles on medieval Arthurian romance, medieval film, medievalism, and Disney have appeared in numerous books and journals, including *Exemplaria, Prose Studies, Assays, Cinema Journal, Theatre Survey, Women's Studies,* and *Studies in Medievalism.*

WILLIAM CHRISTIE is Professor and Head of the Humanities Research Centre at the Australian National University and a Fellow of the Australian Academy of the Humanities. He was foundation president of the Romantic Studies Association of Australasia (2010–2015) and is the author of *Samuel Taylor Coleridge: A Literary Life* (2006) – awarded the NSW Premier's Biennial Prize for Literary Scholarship in 2008 – *The Letters of Francis Jeffrey to Thomas and Jane Welsh Carlyle* (2008), *The Edinburgh Review in the Literary Culture of Romantic Britain* (2009), *Dylan Thomas: A Literary Life* (2014), and *The Two Romanticisms, and Other Essays* (2016). Recent research includes an Australian Research Council project entitled 'An Open University: Public Lecturing in the Romantic Period' and a network of scholars exploring cultural relations between China and the West in the modern world. For many years president of the Dylan Thomas Society of Australia (1998–2005), he is also the author of *Under Mulga Wood* (2004), an award-winning imitation of Dylan Thomas's *Under Milk Wood* that has enjoyed performances around Australia and has been broadcast on ABC national radio.

MARY-ANN CONSTANTINE is Reader at the University of Wales Centre for Advanced Welsh and Celtic Studies. She works on the literature and history of Romantic-period Wales and Brittany, and has a particular interest in travel writing and in the cultural politics of the 1790s. With Dafydd Johnston, she was general editor of the ten-volume series *Wales and the French Revolution* (2012–2015). Other publications include *The Truth Against the World: Iolo Morganwg and Romantic Forgery* (2007) and the co-edited volume *Enlightenment Travel and British Identities: Thomas Pennant's Tours in Scotland and Wales* (2017). Recent research includes a book about the Welsh Tour, 1760–1820.

MICHELLE DEININGER is Co-ordinating Lecturer in Humanities in Continuing and Professional Education at Cardiff University. Michelle completed her AHRC- funded doctoral thesis at Cardiff University, which mapped a tradition of the female-authored short story in Wales. She has published a number of articles and book chapters and her recent research includes a monograph, *Scholarship and Sisterhood: Women, Writing and Higher Education.*

ELIZABETH EDWARDS is Research Fellow at the University of Wales Centre for Advanced Welsh and Celtic Studies, Aberystwyth. Her publications include *English-Language Poetry from Wales 1789–1806* (2013) and *Richard Llwyd: Beaumaris Bay and Other Poems* (2016). Recent research includes a monograph on eighteenth-century women's writing.

ALICE ENTWISTLE is Professor of Textual Aesthetics and Contemporary Poetry at the University of South Wales. Research projects include critical monographs on the work of bilingual Welsh poet Gwyneth Lewis and the Belfast-based writer Ciaran Carson.

GERAINT EVANS is Senior Lecturer in English at Swansea University. His research interests include literary modernism, Welsh writing in English, and the history of the book in Britain, often with a focus on the languages and cultures of Wales and their interaction with England and with international English culture.

HELEN FULTON is Professor of Medieval Literature at the University of Bristol. She has published widely on medieval Welsh and English literatures, including Arthurian literature, political poetry, and urban culture. She is a Fellow of the Learned Society of Wales and of the Society of Antiquaries. Recent publications include the edited collection *Urban Culture in Medieval Wales* (2012) and the co-edited volume *Anglo-Italian Cultural Relations in the Later Middle Ages* (2018).

KATIE GRAMICH is Professor of English Literature at Cardiff University. She specializes in modern literature from Wales, women's writing, poetry, and translation. Her monographs *Twentieth-Century Women's Writing in Wales: Land, Gender, Belonging* (2007) and *Kate Roberts* (2011) are both published by the University of Wales Press. Recent research includes an edition and translation of the work of the fifteenth-century poet, Gwerful Mechain.

MELINDA GRAY completed her PhD in the Department of Comparative Literature at Harvard University. Her research focuses on cultural relationships between Wales, England, and North America in the late nineteenth century.

TUDUR HALLAM is Chair and Professor of Welsh at Swansea University. His publications include a book on literary theory and canon formation, *Canon Ein Llên: Saunders Lewis, R. M. Jones ac Alan Llwyd* (2007) and a study of Saunders Lewis's poetics as playwright, *Saunders y Dramodydd* (2013). In 2016–2017, he was a Fulbright visiting professor at the University of Houston, based at Arte Público Press.

E. WYN JAMES was formerly professor in the School of Welsh at Cardiff University and co-director of the university's Centre for Welsh American Studies. He is an authority on Welsh literature and culture of the modern period and has published widely in areas relating to religion, identity, gender studies, folklore, and book history. Particular research interests include the anti-slavery movement and the Welsh diaspora in Patagonia. Professor James has held visiting fellowships at the universities of Harvard and Cambridge and is a Fellow of the Learned Society of Wales.

DAFYDD JOHNSTON is Director of the University of Wales Centre for Advanced Welsh and Celtic Studies in Aberystwyth. Formerly Professor of Welsh at Swansea University, he led the AHRC-funded project based there which produced the online edition of the poetry of Dafydd ap Gwilym (www.dafyddapgwilym.net) and was main editor of the print volume, *Cerddi Dafydd ap Gwilym* (2010). Among his recent publications is *The Literature of Wales* (2017).

DAVID KLAUSNER is Professor Emeritus of English and Medieval Studies at the University of Toronto, where he teaches Old and Middle English and Middle Welsh. His publications include the volumes in the series Records of Early English Drama for Herefordshire, Worcestershire, and Wales, and he is completing the research for the North Riding of Yorkshire.

STEPHEN KNIGHT is Honorary Professor in Culture and Communication at the University of Melbourne. He previously held professorial chairs at the universities of Sydney and Cardiff. He has published extensively on Welsh and English literature from the Middle Ages to the present day.

LLŶR GWYN LEWIS studied at Cardiff and Oxford before completing a doctorate on the work of T. Gwynn Jones and W. B. Yeats. Following periods as a lecturer in Welsh at Swansea and Cardiff universities, he now works as resource editor at the Welsh Joint Education Committee in Cardiff. He has published articles, poetry, and fiction in periodicals including *Llên Cymru*, the *International Journal of Welsh Writing in English*, *Ysgrifau Beirniadol*, *Poetry Wales*, *Taliesin*, and *O'r Pedwar Gwynt*.

DIANA LUFT is a Wellcome Trust Research Fellow at the University of Wales Centre for Advanced Welsh and Celtic Studies in Aberystwyth, where she is editing the corpus of medieval Welsh medical texts.

SEÁN AERON MARTIN completed an MA in History at Bangor University in 2017. His MA dissertation explored Euroscepticism in Britain during the early 1990s. His PhD at Bangor University, funded by the Great Heritage Project, examines the politics of nuclear power and nuclear landscapes in north Wales.

CATHERINE MCKENNA is Margaret Brooks Robinson Professor of Celtic Languages and Literatures at Harvard University. She is one of the editors of the standard edition of the Poets of the Princes (*Cyfres Beirdd y Tywysogion*) and has also written on Welsh narrative prose and on the structure of some medieval Welsh manuscripts.

JAMIE MEDHURST is Reader in Film, Television and Media and co-director of the Centre for Media History at Aberystwyth University. He is also lead editor of the journal *Media History*. He has published widely on broadcasting history, including *A History of Independent Television in Wales* (2010). He is writing a book on the early years of television and the BBC and is leading a Leverhulme Trust Research Project on 'Television and Society in Wales in the 1970s'. Jamie sits on advisory boards for the Wales National Broadcast Archive and the 'BBC Connected Histories' project.

PAUL O'LEARY is the Sir John Williams Professor of Welsh History at Aberystwyth University. He writes on migration, urban development, and interactions between Wales and the wider world. He is co-editor of the *Welsh*

History Review and co-founder of the Ireland–Wales International Research Network. Among his publications are *Immigration and Integration: the Irish in Wales, 1798–1922* (2000) and *Claiming the Streets: Processions and Urban Culture in South Wales, c. 1830–1880* (2012). He also co-edited *A Tolerant Nation? Revisiting Ethnic Diversity in a Devolved Wales* (2015).

KATHARINE K. OLSON received a joint PhD in History and Celtic Studies from Harvard University. She subsequently held the Sir John Rhys Scholarship in Celtic Studies at Jesus College, Oxford, and postdoctoral fellowships from the British Academy and Harvard University. Formerly Lecturer in Medieval and Early Modern History at Bangor University, she is Assistant Professor of History at San José State University (California State University) in California and an Honorary Research Associate of Bangor University. Research projects include a major monograph on religion, culture, and Reformation in Wales and the Marches for Oxford University Press and the British Academy.

ANGHARAD PRICE is Professor of Welsh at Bangor University and has published widely on modern Welsh literature, especially in comparative contexts. Her study of the early career of T. H. Parry-Williams, *Ffarwél i Freiburg* (2013), won the Ellis Griffith Prize and was shortlisted for the Wales Book of the Year award in 2014.

ROBERT RHYS taught Welsh-language literature at Swansea University until his retirement in 2018. He has published books on the nineteenth-century authors James Hughes and Daniel Owen as well as a study of the early poetic development of Waldo Williams. He has edited two volumes of critical essays on Welsh-language poets of the twentieth century. With Alan Llwyd, he produced an annotated edition of the poems of Waldo Williams, *Cerddi Waldo Williams, 1922–1970* (2014).

EURYN RHYS ROBERTS is Lecturer in Medieval and Welsh History at Bangor University. He was a contributor to the Polish National Science Centre-funded project 'Imagined Communities: Constructing Collective Identities in Medieval Europe' from 2013 to 2016. His recent research is on Welsh identity in the period between the Norman and Edwardian conquests.

LISA SHEPPARD is Lecturer in Welsh at Cardiff University. Her research examines the contemporary literature of Wales in both Welsh and English, with a particular focus on how the relationships between different linguistic and ethnic communities in Wales are portrayed. Her monograph *Y Gymru 'Ddu' a'r Ddalen 'Wen'* (2018) examines the depiction of multiculturalism in contemporary Welsh fiction.

M. WYNN THOMAS is Professor of English and Emyr Humphreys Professor of Welsh Writing in English, Swansea University. A Fellow of the British Academy and a Fellow of the Learned Society of Wales, he has published over two dozen books on the poetry of Walt Whitman and on the two literatures of Wales. His most recent publications are *Cyfan-dir Cymru* (2017) and *All That Is Wales* (2017), Welsh Book of the Year 2018.

DIANA WALLACE is Professor of English Literature at the University of South Wales. Her publications include *Sisters and Rivals in British Women's Fiction, 1914–39* (2000), *The Woman's Historical Novel: British Women Writers, 1900–2000* (2005), *Female Gothic Histories: Gender, History and the Gothic* (2013), and *Christopher Meredith* (2018). She edited Hilda Vaughan's *Here Are Lovers* (1926) for Honno's Welsh Women's Classics series.

ANDREW WEBB is Senior Lecturer at Bangor University, where he specializes in Welsh Writing in English. His monograph *Edward Thomas and World Literary Studies* was published in 2013.

MARI ELIN WILIAM is Lecturer in Modern History at Bangor University. She specializes in post-1945 Wales and has published on the history of Welsh devolution. Her recent research is on identity and modernization, particularly in north-east Wales.

CHRIS WILLIAMS is Head of the College of Arts, Celtic Studies and Social Sciences at University College Cork. Previously he was Professor of History and Head of the School of History, Archaeology and Religion at Cardiff University. His most recent publication is 'A Question of "Legitimate Pride"? The 38th (Welsh) Division at the Battle of Mametz Wood, July 1916' (*Welsh History Review*, 2017), and he continues to work digitally on the cartoons of J. M. Staniforth (1863–1921) at www.cartoonww1.org.

GRUFFYDD ALED WILLIAMS is Emeritus Professor of Welsh at Aberystwyth University. He has published widely on Welsh medieval and renaissance literature. His recent publications include *Dyddiau Olaf Owain Glyndŵr*, winner of the Literature Wales creative-non-fiction prize in 2016, also published in an English version, *The Last Days of Owain Glyndŵr* (2017). In 2017 he published in the journal *Llên Cymru* a study of Anglo-Welsh cultural interaction at Lleweni, Denbighshire, home of the Salusbury family during the Tudor and early Stuart period.

KEVIN WILLIAMS is former Professor of Media and Cultural History at Swansea University. His main research area is the history of mass communication, including print and broadcast media. He has published widely on these topics and on the media in Wales.

MARK WILLIAMS is Associate Professor in Global Medieval Literature and Fellow and Tutor in English at St Edmund Hall, University of Oxford. He is the author of *Fiery Shapes: Celestial Portents and Astrology in Ireland and Wales, 700–1700* (2010) and *Ireland's Immortals: A History of the Gods of Irish Myth* (2016). Recent research includes a book of essays on magic and enchantment in medieval Irish and Welsh literature.

Acknowledgements

The ideas which made it possible for us to imagine this book have been collecting in our conversations for decades, and many of them are witness to the debts which we all accumulate to friends and colleagues. The editors would like in particular to thank Professor M. Wynn Thomas, who supported this project from the beginning and whose enthusiasm and scholarship have helped to open up literary studies in Wales and make possible the previously unimaginable.

Some specific acknowledgements are due in relation to individual chapters: Dr Edwin Richard Hustwit (Chapter 1); Thomas Owen Clancy (Chapter 2); Georgia Henley and Owain Wyn Jones (Chapter 5); Huw Pryce, Jerry Hunter, Daniel Huws, the Centre for the Study of the Book at the University Oxford, Bangor University, and St John's College, Oxford (Chapter 8); Peredur Lynch and M. Paul Bryant-Quinn (Chapter 9); Jane Aaron (Chapter 28); and Aberystwyth University (Chapter 32).

The editors would like to thank the Faculty of Arts at the University of Bristol and the College of Arts and Humanities at Swansea University for support to produce and edit this volume. Special thanks are owed to two people: our research assistant, Huw Edwardes-Evans, whose hard work, eye for detail, and grace under pressure greatly assisted the editorial process; and Giles Darkes, who designed and produced the maps.

Finally, we would like to thank Ray Ryan at Cambridge University Press for his patience and advice, and for his vision in commissioning this volume.

Abbreviations

AHRC	Arts and Humanities Research Council (UK)
BBCS	*Bulletin of the Board of Celtic Studies*
BL	British Library, London
CMCS	*Cambrian* [formerly *Cambridge*] *Medieval Celtic Studies*
GPC	*Geiriadur Prifysgol Cymru*, Dictionary of Welsh
Mod. W.	Modern Welsh
MW	Middle Welsh
n.d.	no date (of publication)
NLW	National Library of Wales, Aberystwyth
plu.	plural
RED: Wales	*Records of Early Drama: Wales* (Toronto: University of Toronto Press, 2005)
s.a.	Latin *sine anno*, 'without date' (of publication)
s.l.	Latin *sine loco*, 'without a place' (of publication)
s.n.	Latin *sine nomine*, 'without a name' (of publisher)
STC	*A Short-Title Catalogue of Books Printed in England, Scotland and Ireland, and of English Books Printed Abroad 1475–1640*, edited by A. W. Pollard and G. R. Redgrave; rev. 2nd edn, ed. W. A. Jackson, F. S. Ferguson, and K. F. Pantzer, 3 vols. (London: The Bibliographical Society, 1986–1991)
THSC	*Transactions of the Honourable Society of Cymmrodorion*
TNA	The National Archives, Kew
W.	Welsh
Wing	*A Short-Title Catalogue of Books Printed in England, Scotland, Ireland, Wales, and British America, and of English Books Printed in Other Countries, 1641–1700*, compiled by Donald Goddard Wing, rev. 2nd edn, ed. John J. Morrison, Carolyn W. Nelson and Matthew Seccombe, 4 vols. (New York: Modern Language Association of America, 1972, 1982, 1988, 1998)

Glossary of Welsh Literary Terms

awdl, plu. *awdlau*
Any long poem, written in *cynghanedd*, which uses the traditional strict metres. This term also applies to the poem which is normally required in the competition for the chair in modern *eisteddfodau*.

bro, plu. *broydd*
A richly connotative term for 'environ, region, valley, neighbourhood'.

brut, brud
A chronicle which derives from or which continues Geoffrey of Monmouth's *Historia Regum Britanniae*. The term *brud* also refers to prophecy in Welsh.

canu rhydd
Poetry or song composed in free metre (non-syllabic). It became popular in the late Middle Ages and especially after the decline of the bardic order.

cynfardd, plu. *cynfeirdd*
The poets of the earliest period whose work has survived, including Taliesin and Aneirin, whose work is placed in the sixth century by the *Historia Brittonum*.

cynghanedd
An intricate system of consonantal repetition and internal rhyme which was codified over centuries and which is normally required in every line of strict-metre poetry.

cywydd
One of the most popular of the twenty-four metres practised by the professional poets of medieval Wales, particularly associated with the period after the Poets of the Princes, that is, *c.* 1300–1500. The *cywydd* today is a verse

paragraph of rhyming couplets, written in *cynghanedd*, where each line is of seven syllables and the final syllables in each rhymed couplet must be stressed and unstressed. There is a competition for the best *cywydd* at the National Eisteddfod.

cywyddwr, plu. cywyddwyr
The poets of the period after the Poets of the Princes who mostly composed in the *cywydd* metre.

eisteddfod, plu. eisteddfodau
Originally an assembly of poets, the modern eisteddfod is a competitive cultural festival for literary, musical and other disciplines. The National Eisteddfod takes place every year during the first week of August.

englyn, plu. englynion
One of the most popular of the traditional metres for *cynghanedd* poetry, of which there are a number of variations. Verses are usually of three or four lines.

englyn unodl union
The most popular form of the *englyn*, a four-line single-rhymed stanza in full *cynghanedd* with a syllable count of ten, six, seven and seven.

gogynfardd, plu. gogynfeirdd
The Poets of the Princes, who flourished between the first half of the twelfth and the second half of the fourteenth century, but excluding those later poets who used the *cywydd* metre

hengerdd
The poetry of the *cynfeirdd*, a term which was originally used to denote the work of the sixth-century poets mentioned in the *Historia Brittonum*, including Taliesin and Aneirin, but now used for all the early poetry before the *gogynfeirdd*.

hir-a-thoddaid
One of the twenty-four traditional metres for poetry written in *cynghanedd*, it forms the first two lines of the popular *englyn unodl union*.

Mabinogi, Mabinogion
The Four Branches of the *Mabinogi*, *Pedair Cainc y Mabinogi*, are the four traditionally related tales at the heart of the group of medieval Welsh prose tales which were collected and translated in the nineteenth century by Charlotte Guest, who adopted the scribal neologism

'Mabinogion' as a collective term. The form *Mabinogi* generally refers to the Four Branches, while the form *Mabinogion* refers to all eleven tales collected and published by Guest.

pryddest

A long poem not written in full *cynghanedd*. In modern *eisteddfodau* the *pryddest* is the name of the poem which is normally required in the competition for the Crown.

uchelwr, plu. *uchelwyr*

Literally 'high men' (noblemen), this term was used to describe the medieval Welsh gentry, especially the class of landowners and administrators which emerged after the fall of the princes in 1282.

Maps

PICTS

North Sea

Din Eidyn (Edinburgh)
STRATHCLYDE
GODODDIN
BERNICIA
Lindisfarne
Bamburgh
NORTHUMBRIA
RHEGED
Carlisle
Penrith
Catraeth
DEIRA
CUMBRIA
York
ELMET
LINDSEY

IRISH KINGDOMS

Irish Sea

ISLE of MAN

Degannwy
Aberffraw
Dinas Emrys
GWYNEDD
Chester
Pengwern
Oswestry
MERCIA
EAST ANGLIA
Llanbadarn Fawr
CEREDIGION
POWYS
BRYCHEINIOG
DYFED
ERGYNG
GLYWYSING
GWENT
Gloucester
Cirencester
ESSEX
London
KENT
Bath
WESSEX
SUSSEX
DUMNONIA

English Channel

CORNWALL

ESSEX	English kingdoms
⬚	Approximate extent of English kingdoms
POWYS	British kingdoms
—	Course of Offa's Dyke

0		100 miles
0		160 kms

1 Britons and Saxons in Wales and the Old North, *c.* 600

xxii

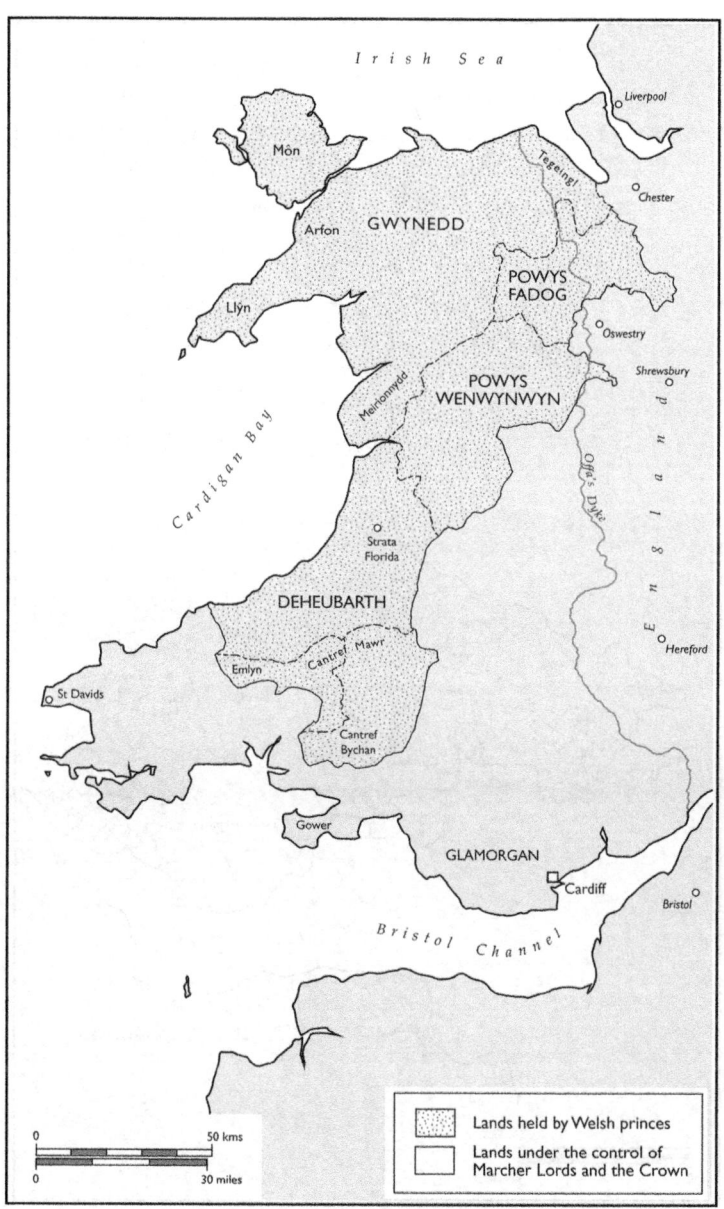

2 The lands of the Welsh princes before 1284

3　The Principality and the Marcher Lordships, *c.* 1400

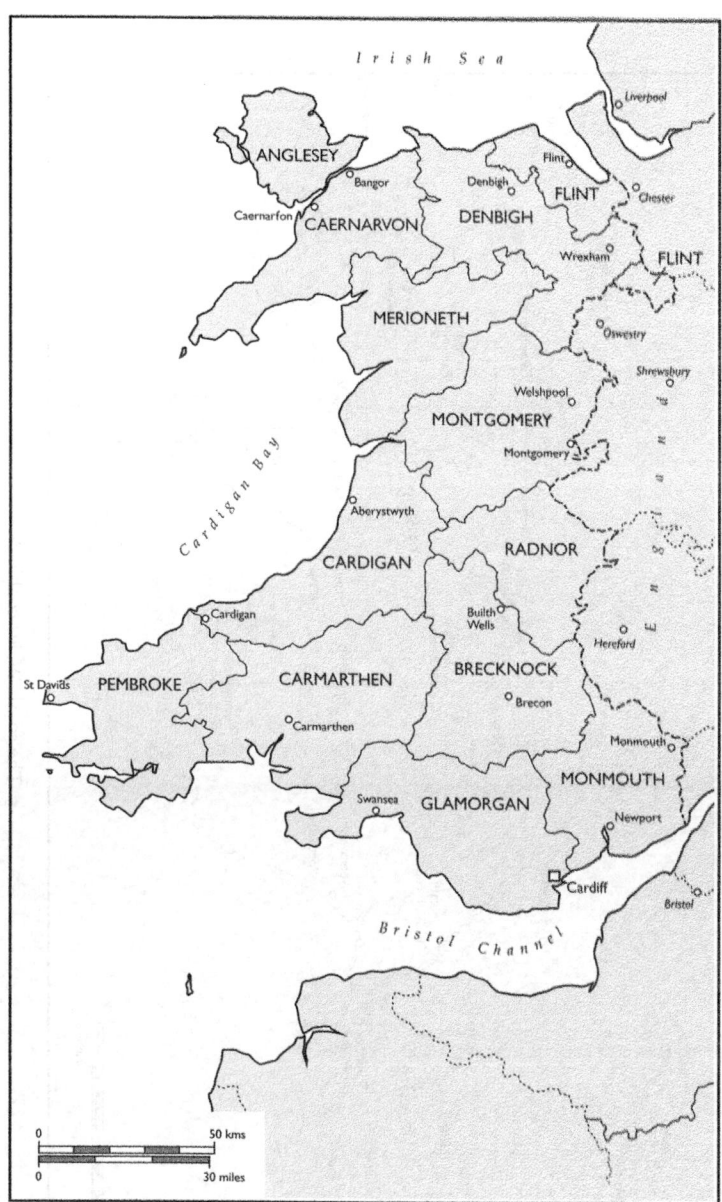

4 The shires of Wales after the Acts of Union, *c.* 1550

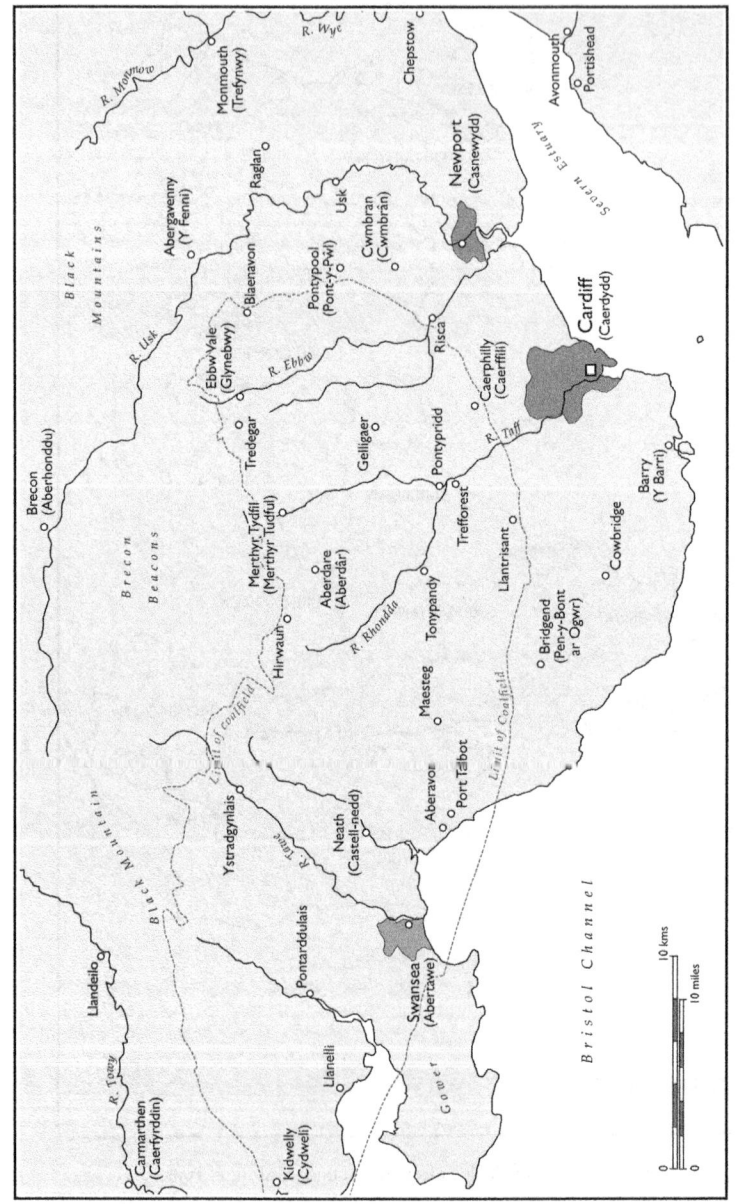

5 The south Wales coalfields

6 The counties of Wales before 1974

7 The counties of Wales, 1974–1996

8 The local authority areas of modern Wales

Introduction

GERAINT EVANS AND HELEN FULTON

The last book to be called *A History of Welsh Literature* was published in 1955, and its title signified the literature of Wales written in Welsh. The volume was a translation into English, by H. Idris Bell, of the literary history published two years earlier, *Hanes Llenyddiaeth Gymraeg hyd 1900*, by Thomas Parry, one of the foremost medieval scholars and literary critics of his day. The literature of Wales is one of the oldest continuous literary traditions in Europe and Parry's history was understandably designed to focus attention on the medieval centuries, on religious writing, and on the eisteddfod tradition. It dealt exclusively with literature written in Welsh and it stopped at the end of the nineteenth century, although Bell added to his translation a brief appendix on twentieth-century trends.

Parry's history, valuable though it remains as a work of scholarship, suggests the reasons why a new literary history for Wales is needed. It was also in 1955 that Cardiff was proclaimed the capital city of Wales and in the six decades since then the political situation of Wales, and consequently its cultural preoccupations, have changed in ways that Parry could not have imagined. Principally, the political devolution of Wales in 1999 and the establishment of firstly a National Assembly and more recently a Welsh Government (Llywodraeth Cymru), which is located in Cardiff, has changed the social and cultural landscape of Wales almost beyond recognition. Secondly, and just as significantly, the language movement in Wales has led to substantial institutional support for the Welsh language and a culture of bilingualism that has shaped generations of writers and audiences since the middle of the twentieth century. As cultural production in Wales has changed, so have perceptions of Wales's cultural heritage: the Middle Ages, though undoubtedly a golden age for Welsh literature, are increasingly received via modern remediations, while the importance of religion – particularly Nonconformist religion – as an agent of both linguistic preservation and cultural conservatism in Wales needs to be balanced against the economic consequences of industrialization in the nineteenth and twentieth centuries and its collapse in the twenty-first.

This new *History of Welsh Literature* offers a comprehensive, multi-authored critical survey of the literature of Wales from the earliest centuries to the present day. It is the first substantial single-volume account of Welsh literature in both languages, and as such it recognizes its responsibility to canon formation and the shaping of cultural identity. While taking full account of the older canon, as marked out by Parry and his predecessors, this book aims to identify a new modern canon which includes writing in both languages addressed to a range of audiences in Wales and beyond. Written at a time when the study of medieval literature was at the heart of the university curriculum, Thomas Parry's literary history inevitably suggested that the golden age of Welsh writing was in the past. This new volume celebrates the grandeur of the past but also imagines a literature of Wales which has a golden future.

The main aim of the book is to formalize the recent turn in Welsh scholarship towards adopting a single, holistic view of Wales's cultural past and present by balancing the two literatures of Wales – in Welsh and English – within a coherent historicized vision. In order to do this, we have included chapters at the beginning of each section which provide some historical background and we apply modern paradigms of cultural theory including postcolonial and gendered readings of key texts and literary developments. The book attempts to dismantle a simple binary between 'literature' and 'writing' in all its forms and resists a privileging of 'literature' while still engaging with the idea of a canon and the forces by which canons are created. The book is written in English in order to address an international audience and to locate our discussion of Welsh literature, in both languages, in the field of comparative literature. As a complement to this outward-looking focus, we are closely engaged with the politics of language and cultural production within Wales itself, looking at the processes by which the cultural practices of Welsh-language society gradually became comprehensible to, and shared with, an English-speaking public.

The structuring rationale of the book is chronological and contextual. Starting with the vitality of medieval Welsh literature, whose echo is still heard by contemporary writers and film-makers, the book considers a series of key periods in the literary history of Wales including moments of social and political change, when the economics of cultural production demanded modernization and a re-evaluation of the past. The sixteenth-century Acts of Union coincided with the Reformation, inspiring a Tudor sensibility in Welsh writing that led directly to the antiquarianism of the eighteenth and nineteenth centuries. Industrialization in south Wales and the creation of 'the valleys' sparked a new awareness of Wales's vulnerability to external forces and legitimated Welsh writing in English. In the long post-industrial decades of the twentieth century, literary voices spoke of decline, as if all of Wales had once been down the mines, before the contemporary drama of devolution, on the cusp of the new century, released the possibility of a multicultural future for a multilingual Wales.

The contextualizing argument of the book has three aspects. Firstly, it promotes literature as a significant medium of political expression and change. Just as canon formation is a kind of nation building, Welsh literary texts, from the medieval to the modern, work through the problems and challenges of representing a nation that is not a state. In the literatures of both languages, speaking for the nation means, very often, articulating resistance to the idea of England as the colonizing and imperial power, a resistance that is often problematic and self-defeating. From the earliest poetry of Taliesin and Aneirin, forged in the battlefields of post-Roman Wales and the 'Old North' of Britain, to the passionate rhetoric of Saunders Lewis in the mid-twentieth century, the push of the Welsh against English power is matched by the pull of hegemonic safety and set off-balance by the factionalism within Wales itself. The heroic battle of the men of Gododdin in sixth-century north Britain pitted the British against each other as much as against the Anglo-Saxons, while the long controversy following the publication of Caradoc Evans's collection of short stories, *My People* (1915), points to a deep and longstanding cultural divide within modern Wales. The origins of this can be traced to Nonconformist religion and the social changes wrought by industrialization in the late nineteenth century, resulting in the competing needs of rural and urban environments, one largely Welsh-speaking and the other mainly English-speaking. With the slow march towards devolution at the end of the century, after a close-won referendum that displayed the reality of a politically divided nation, writers began to find new subjects for a politically engaged literature, especially inequalities of class, race, and gender which, while certainly not confined to Wales, nonetheless had a distinctive Welsh articulation. The industrial novels of the early twentieth century champion the working classes and express the predominantly socialist and patriarchal politics of the steel and mining areas, while practices of writing and publishing result in the systematic exclusion of women's voices in any great number until later in the century.

A second aspect of the book's focus has to do with the economics of cultural production, without which literature, in any language, cannot survive. From the Tudor prohibition of printing presses in Wales to the establishment of Welsh-medium education and media in the twentieth century, the means by which literary texts are reproduced and disseminated have had a direct impact on the form and content of the literature of Wales. To some extent, Welsh culture has always been a 'survivor' culture, that is, a culture that has had to be flexible in devising the means of ensuring its own continuity, and most chapters in the book reflect this in various ways. In the medieval centuries, patronage from the church and secular lords was the only means by which literature could be produced and preserved: without the regional princes before 1282 and the *uchelwyr* (gentry) after 1282, who supported the poets and native Welsh culture throughout the centuries of Norman and English rule more or less up to the introduction of printing, the medieval heritage of Wales is likely to have been very small indeed.

Similarly, the humanists and antiquarians of the sixteenth to eighteenth centuries were instrumental in preserving the medieval literary past while recording the preoccupations of the present and nurturing a poetic tradition that could be traced back to Taliesin. Even the Puritan-leaning Nonconformist chapels made a strong contribution to literary production in the form of sermons, biographies, commentaries, and especially hymns which provided a popular connection to music and poetry. In the modern period, the emergence of publishing houses and literary periodicals in Wales, along with the rise of film and broadcasting, has generated a significant increase in the quantity and range of cultural production in both languages, and while funding remains an issue, particularly from the public sector, the contemporary literary scene is relatively buoyant. Perhaps the most significant element in the cultural production of Wales since the eighteenth century has been the eisteddfod, the tradition of annual literary competitions which, emerging from a somewhat obscure medieval past, was appropriated and rejuvenated by Iolo Morganwg into a cultural celebration that remains highly influential as a literary barometer. The National Eisteddfod has created a unique culture of literary prizes for writing in Welsh and maintains a particular power in the economy of literary publishing and canon formation.

Finally, this book looks squarely at the politics of language as a key determiner of literary production and one of the most defining markers of Welsh cultural life since the late Middle Ages. By considering the two literatures side by side, as part of a singular history and under the single rubric of 'Welsh literature', the book argues that bilingualism, always present in Wales, is becoming widely recognized as its normative condition. Bilingualism has not always been seen as an unmixed blessing, and there are many in Wales who fear it is merely a phase that will give way to a final collapse of the Welsh language; however, there are many others who look to examples from Europe and further afield and see that bilingualism can be a stable and long-term state that is good for both languages. The beginnings of Welsh writing in English can be traced back at least to the fifteenth century, when Welsh and English speakers were co-located in many areas of the March of Wales in the east and south of the country. Writing in English became a more powerful literary movement in the nineteenth century, mainly as a result of industrialization, and was fully established as an economically and culturally significant literature by the twentieth century. Originally called 'Anglo-Welsh' literature, a term that was generally disliked by writers on both sides of the hyphen, it was reconceived as 'Welsh writing in English' towards the end of the century, and this term has now become standard. There remains the problem of what 'Welsh' writing means, whether in Welsh or in English. For the purposes of this book, we have tended to think about textual identity rather than the social identity of writers and have generally included texts which engage directly with Welshness in one way or another, whether written inside or outside Wales, and whether the author identifies as Welsh or not.

Part I of the book, 'Britain, Wales, England', covers the largest period of time, from the emergence of Wales as a clearly defined territory in the aftermath of the Saxon invasions and settlements of the fifth and sixth centuries, through the period of Norman settlement and the creation of the Welsh March, beyond the Edwardian conquest of 1282 and through to the end of the fifteenth century, and to the end of the *medium aevum*, the time between the classical world and the modern. This is a rich period of Welsh literature, with the earliest surviving poetry, attributed to Taliesin and Aneirin, reaching back to a time as distant from Chaucer as we are now. The texts of the earliest *hengerdd* (old poetry) mark the recorded beginnings of an unbroken, living poetic tradition that stretches back almost to the post-Roman period. With the earliest poetry surviving in a language which is still recognizable to speakers of Welsh today, this is one of the literary glories of Europe. This section of the book also discusses medieval prose texts including histories and considers the extraordinary collection of prose tales which we now know as the *Mabinogion*. Towards the end of the period of Welsh independence there is a period of complex court poetry known as *gogynfeirdd* poetry, which is some of the most linguistically complex poetry in the language. These court poets rapidly disappeared in the years after 1282, and a new kind of poetry gradually emerges, written by professional poets, and often praising the *uchelwyr* or gentry class, who became the new literary patrons after the suppression of the princely dynasties. The period of the *cywyddwyr*, poets who wrote mainly in the *cywydd* metre, spans the last three centuries of this opening section and includes the work of some of the greatest of the medieval Welsh poets, including Dafydd ap Gwilym, Iolo Goch, and Guto'r Glyn.

Part II, 'After the Acts of Union', describes a period of rapid change for Welsh poets and scribes. The Acts of Union coincide with the tumult of the Reformation, and the end of traditional bardic culture overlaps with the rise of printing and the change to vernacular worship. The concerns and challenges of European humanism are visible in every aspect of the cultural life of Wales, and the production of a Welsh translation of the Bible in a Tudor state which promoted vernacular worship would have a lasting effect on linguistic survival. The decade of the 1540s sees the first appearance of printing in Welsh, an innovation which will also have a profound impact. The leading figure in this, as in so much else during this century of change, is William Salesbury, who exemplifies the humanist ideal in Welsh life, writing books which cover the full range of humanist learning, translating the New Testament and other religious texts into Welsh, and publishing books in London in Welsh and in English.

In the early sixteenth century, the bardic tradition overlaps with the rise of antiquarian writing and some of the most significant figures, such as Edmwnd Prys and William Salesbury, combine poetry and manuscript production with serious interests in translation, genealogy, and Latin learning. In this period many parts of the March of Wales, now incorporated into English counties, were still largely Welsh speaking so that Welsh life and culture was visible over a far larger area than the new Tudor maps might indicate. In the mid-sixteenth century, it is possible that there were more Welsh speakers living in London than in any one of the Welsh towns, while prominent writers such as Maurice Kyffin and Wiliam Llŷn, the most famous Welsh poet of his day, both lived in Oswestry, which, though technically in England, was still a largely Welsh-speaking town.

The first examples of Welsh writing in English are to be found in the Tudor period, often linked with the Welsh in London. This is partly because of the importance of London for trade, education, and printing, but despite this innovation it is literature in Welsh, and literacy in Welsh, that will continue to be the dominant force in Wales until the late nineteenth century. But in the centuries that follow the Reformation, the pace of change in the ideas which dominate Welsh life and literary production will increase. This is the period covered by Part III, 'Revolution and Industry', when new ideas flood into Wales relating to the Enlightenment, to the Romantic movement, and to political revolution. All of these find a platform in literary writing, where new forms of expression begin to emerge. Popular poetry and travel writing become more prominent and the patterns of literary production and consumption begin to change, in the country as well as in the towns. The unusually high literacy rate in eighteenth-century Wales, a phenomenon which is linked to the rise of Nonconformist religion, produces a new kind of serious but genuinely popular poetry in the form of Welsh hymns. Other forms of printing, such as broadsheet ballads, also appeal to popular tastes, and throughout Wales and England, following the lapse of the Licensing Act in 1695, there was an explosion of provincial printing. The first significant centre of Welsh book production outside London is Amwythig, or Shrewsbury, another former Marcher town where Welsh had lingered; however, by the second quarter of the eighteenth century, printing in Wales itself was properly established with locally produced books competing for the first time with Welsh books from the London trade. A huge amount of Welsh-language printing would now transform Welsh literary life over the next two centuries.

Part IV, 'The Transition to Modernity', shows how secular fiction becomes much more significant as the nineteenth century develops, with representations of Wales and Welsh life beginning to appear more frequently in English and Welsh texts. As the twentieth century begins, there is change everywhere. A renaissance in Welsh-language poetry sweeps away the didactic mediocrity of most nineteenth-century verse as writers such as T. Gwynn Jones rediscover the glories of the medieval bardic tradition, reinventing the art of *cynghanedd* and inspiring a whole generation of young writers. Looking back now at the first half of the twentieth century, it is hard not to see it as a golden age of Welsh poetry when writers such as R. Williams Parry, Gwenallt, and Waldo Williams created a new canon of Welsh poetry in response to the challenges of the modern world while Kate Roberts recorded the dreams and hardships of working people in the finest Welsh short stories of the century.

At the same time there was a profusion of Welsh writing in English, with new periodicals helping to create new markets for writing which captures the reality of industrial life in a colonial economy. Periodic literature in Welsh, which had been enormously strong in the nineteenth century, continued to thrive, and alongside the new magazines in English, such as *Wales* and *The Welsh Review*, writers working in both languages found ready outlets for poetry and short stories, two forms which came to dominate Welsh literary production. In the decades between the wars, a new generation of writers started to sell books about Welsh life, in Wales but also in London and New York. Rhys Davies supported himself as a professional writer in London for half a century and, while Dylan Thomas captured many of the headlines, writers such as Geraint Goodwin, Margiad Evans, Idris Davies, and Dorothy Edwards were all quietly establishing an international audience for literature from Wales.

After two world wars the Wales which emerges into the 1950s was changed almost beyond recognition. The apparent certainty of the industrial economy began to fade, and this is reflected in the literature of the period. Many more writers in English were being published from London, while for writers working in Welsh the third quarter of the century was a time when the yearning for self-determination finally began to feel like a possibility. At the same time, new kinds of emancipation brought unprecedented levels of mobility and the rural heartland of Welsh-language culture began to feel the threat of the outside world. Meanwhile, the world of Welsh poetry was as brilliant as ever, with the renaissance sparked by T. Gwynn Jones still producing new generations of strict-metre poets who invigorated the eisteddfod culture and kept the old traditions feeling fresh and new. Poets such as Dic Jones, Alan Llwyd, and Gerallt Lloyd Owen continued to write poems which captured the aspirations of the nation, and with the rise of Welsh broadcasting a new era of mass communication created something which seemed unlikely in the modern world: a popular weekly radio programme with a national following in which teams of poets competed at different kinds of poetic composition.

Part V, 'The Path to Nationhood in the Late Twentieth Century', examines the last decades of the century when Welsh literary life was vibrant, in both languages, although the idea of the full-time writer continued to change rapidly as the major publishing houses of London and New York sought new ways to maximize their market share in a shrinking world. Small Welsh publishing houses such as Poetry Wales Press, Gomer Press, and Barddas offered an alternative to metropolitan or university publishers, but the pull of the older paradigms of difference remained strong.

The first writer to unite fully the two literatures of Wales in a single body of work emerged at this time, and he was one of the great poets of the twentieth century. R. S. Thomas already had an international reputation as an English-language poet when he began writing prose in Welsh in the 1970s and 1980s and associating himself more closely with Welsh-language culture and with what Emyr Humphreys called 'the Taliesin tradition'. Living close to the sea in Sarn-y-Plas on the Llŷn peninsula, 'R.S.' became the first writer in Wales whose international stature as a poet in English was matched by his stature as a cultural ambassador for the Welsh language.

As the century drew to a close, the political yearning for national self-determination took an unusual turn. The growing sense of a shared European identity aligned with the political and economic identity of the European Union, made Westminster seem less and less relevant and, in the end, the grip of colonial rule which had held on to Wales for centuries slipped quietly away. Part VI, 'After Devolution', shows that when devolution finally came in 1999, the new century immediately brought a rejuvenated cultural confidence to writers in Wales. Poets such as Menna Elfyn were writing in Welsh and translating their own work into English, while Gwyneth Lewis took the next step and wrote original poetry in both languages. Other writers followed, including Fflur Dafydd and Owen Martell, and with the new millennium has come a new paradigm of literary production in which the dragon's 'two tongues' speak together.

With the emergence of Cardiff as a political capital and a major centre for theatre and television, and with the rise of decentralized new media, small publishing houses, and self-publishing, writers are moving between these different channels to create new kinds of literary careers. Welsh writing today makes a significant contribution, as economic and cultural capital, to the cultural industries of Wales, which include theatre, film, television, and digital media, as well as fiction and poetry, all in both languages. The role of national bodies such as the Welsh Arts Council, Welsh Books Council, Literature Wales, and the National Theatre Wales in promoting a Welsh culture which is both distinctive and heteroglossic remains crucial to the vitality of Welsh writing.

In a chronological history such as this, the temptation to write in a teleological mode is strong: has Welsh literature finally arrived at the place where it has been heading since the days of Taliesin and Aneirin? But the ending of this book is not the end of the story. As with all living histories, there is no point of closure, no *telos* that satisfies the need for an ending: there will always be more to come. The literature of Wales has shadowed the nation's politics since the Middle Ages. Today, a flourishing multicultural literature, in all its forms, continues to describe the state of the nation.

PART I

*

BRITAIN, WALES, ENGLAND

Britain, Wales, England, *c.* 600–1450

EURYN RHYS ROBERTS

On 22 April 1445 Edward ap Dafydd, the head of the Bryncunallt household in the lordship of Chirk (in north-east Wales), died of a mortal illness. Soon afterwards, his death was the subject of a poignant elegy by Guto'r Glyn (*fl. c.* 1435–90), one of fifteenth-century Wales's foremost poets.[1] Words of sorrow and the poet's anguish echo through the poem. For Guto'r Glyn, Edward ap Dafydd was both a pillar of local society and a cultivated patron, a man who had been able to put his rebel associations and family links with Owain Glyn Dŵr behind him. In this post-Glyn Dŵr world, Edward ap Dafydd emerges from his obituarist's elegy as a paragon of learning. He was, we are told, a man who combined a delight in language with an expertise in both civil and canon law. It is a measure of Edward ap Dafydd's learning that he is compared favourably with Gildas, the sixth-century historian-cum-prophet who had, by Guto'r Glyn's day, come to represent a model of saintly wisdom.

At first sight it may seem surprising that a Welsh poet of the fifteenth century should choose to invoke the name of Gildas. After all, in the *De excidio Britanniae* ('The Ruin of Britain') (probably written between AD 530 and 545), Gildas was highly critical not only of the political leaders of his own day but of the fawning court poets who apparently upheld their wicked rule. Yet at a deeper level, this allusion is not as puzzling as it may seem. More than anything perhaps, the comparison of Edward with Gildas attests to a deeply-rooted pride in the literary and intellectual traditions of Wales. The vigorous Latin of Gildas's tirade against his fellow-Britons and Guto'r Glyn's consummate mastery of the poetic craft testify in their different ways to the vitality of British and Welsh literary culture over a period of nearly a thousand years.

At our starting point around the year AD 600, Wales, or those parts of Britain that were soon to become Wales, may still be characterized as 'sub-Roman'; by the year 1450, Wales was firmly on the road to closer political, social, and economic integration with England. Viewed in retrospect, this period falls into three main phases: the slow emergence of Wales as a geopolitical unit during the early medieval period; the two centuries separating the coming of the Normans in 1066 and the Edwardian conquest of 1282; and, finally, a prolonged period of adjustment interspersed by episodes of crisis and conflict. The aim of this historical introduction is to paint the main outlines with a broad brush and to introduce as much factual detail as is necessary to demonstrate the influences and environments which shaped the literature of medieval Wales.

From Gildas to Gruffudd ap Llywelyn: Kingship and Competition

The great transition from Roman to medieval Wales began with the end of Roman military and governmental power in Britain in the early fifth century. British territorial communities occupied much of the island, far beyond the boundaries of what is now modern Wales, and shared a language and culture. The British rulers denounced by Gildas commanded lands along the western coast of Britain from Cornwall to Anglesey. Despite the controversy over the interpretation and dating of much of the *hengerdd*, the early vernacular poetry referring to the Britons of Wales and the 'Old North', it is clear that the cultural affinities of the northern Britons connected them to a larger whole. In the regions of Gododdin, Rheged, and Strathclyde, territories extending across modern Cumbria, the Pennines, and the Lowlands to Edinburgh, the British of the north identified themselves with their countrymen in Wales.[2]

The end of Roman imperial power in Wales and western Britain presents a picture of both collapse and continuity. By the end of the sixth century, the lands of the former Roman diocese of *Britanniae* ('the Britains') were a long way from the complexity and prosperity of the late Roman world. The diverse regional effects of 'romanization' on Wales probably explain the differences between the seemingly substantial kingships which emerged in the north and west and the more numerous and territorially smaller rulerdoms of the south-east which are recorded in the charter material copied in the Book of Llandaff (*Liber Landavensis, c.* 1120–34). By the seventh century, Wales, or most of what would become Wales, was divided loosely into rulerdoms of differing size and dynastic origins. In the ninth century the balance of power and political geography roughly corresponded to the four corners of Wales: Gwynedd in the north, Powys in the central eastern region, Dyfed in the south-west, and Gwent in the south-east.

It would be wrong to suppose that the Anglo-Saxon conquest of eastern Britain was sudden and irresistible. In the early seventh century, Cadwallon of Gwynedd (d. 634) could raid far into Northumbria at the head of a military alliance with the still-pagan Mercians. Though the tables had turned by the middle of the seventh century, with the emerging power of Mercia now the dominant partner, it is clear that ethnic and religious differences were no barrier to military co-operation. In this period too, the expanding Anglo-Saxon kingdoms contained large numbers of Britons, setting in train the largely hidden process of the 'anglicization' of the British areas of western and northern England.[3] However, the Britons of the west would continue to speak a variety of the same language, Brittonic, that was once spoken throughout large parts of Britain, a language that became known in Wales as Cymraeg.

It was not until the eighth century that a clear boundary between the Britons of Wales and their English neighbours emerged (though in places it would remain uncertain for centuries). Under their king Offa (d. 796), the Mercians gave the border region with Wales a measure of definition with the construction of Offa's Dyke, the most impressive earthwork in Europe from the period. By the eighth century, the Britons of Wales (or, as we can now call them, the Welsh) had been politically and territorially confined. Yet the consciousness of their British inheritance would continue to run like a silver thread through the literary culture of Wales beyond the period of this discussion. Their perception of unjust disinheritance at the hands of the Saxons, which had begun with Gildas, became hard-wired into the Welsh sense of nationality in the medieval period.

During the ninth and tenth centuries, the whole of Wales, apart from the very south-east, fell into the hands of the descendants of Merfyn Frych (d. 844). Merfyn, originally, it would seem, from the Isle of Man, was able, during the second quarter of the ninth century, to assume the kingship of Gwynedd in the north, and his descendants, later called the 'Merfynion' (or alternatively the 'Second Dynasty of Gwynedd'), would come to dominate Wales, on and off, until the Edwardian conquest of 1282–3. While Anglo-Saxon raids into Wales, including from truncated Mercia, continued into this period and are a major concern in the Welsh chronicles, the period was also marked by co-operation with and submission to the Anglo-Saxons on their borders, most noticeable during the reign of Athelstan (d. 939) in England and Hywel Dda's ('the Good') (d. 950) hegemony in Wales. But as the great prophetic poem *Armes Prydein* ('The Prophecy of Britain') attests, not everyone in Wales welcomed the overlordship of the newly united kingdom of England.

By the eleventh century, new dynasties had emerged to challenge the Merfynion, and it was individuals from these families who would do much to shape subsequent events during the eleventh century. This was the context in which Gruffudd ap Llywelyn (d. 1064) came to power, a ruler who was extraordinarily successful in expanding his authority over the whole country, and his reign was in a way the apogee of native Welsh power. Gruffudd makes his first appearance in the Welsh chronicles in 1039, when he is named as the successor to Iago ab Idwal (d. 1039), king of Gwynedd. We are not told whether Gruffudd's rise to power in the north owed anything to violence; however, what we can say with some certainty is that when his ambitions turned to south Wales, he pursued them largely by military means, launching attacks on the rulers of Deheubarth until he achieved mastery of the south in 1055. During the remaining nine years of his life, Gruffudd's attentions were very much drawn eastwards towards England. By the 1050s Gruffudd had become a force to be reckoned with and a potentially useful ally for those engaged in the power struggles of Edward the Confessor's reign. In 1056, Gruffudd was recognized as Edward's under-king in Wales and his territorial conquests along the Anglo-Welsh border were acknowledged.

In the 1060s, however, Gruffudd became a target of Harold Godwinesson, the powerful Earl of Wessex. Advancing from Gloucester at the end of 1063, Harold, at the head of a highly mobile force of cavalry, bore down upon Gruffudd as he celebrated Christmas at his court in Rhuddlan. Though Gruffudd managed to escape by sea, his court and most of his fleet were destroyed. From this point onwards there was no turning back. For a kingship ultimately based on military success, the 1063–4 campaigns of Harold Godwinesson were a mortal blow to Gruffudd's prestige. With support ebbing away and the royal coffers significantly diminished, Gruffudd's fate was sealed. No single source lays out for us in one clear sequence the events leading up to the murder of Gruffudd. All we can say with any certainty is that Gruffudd was killed through the treachery of his own men. His severed head was presented to the English, and, in recognition of his victory, Harold ordered for it to be delivered to Edward the Confessor along with the figurehead of Gruffudd's ship. With the death of Gruffudd ap Llywelyn in 1064, Wales was, as we know with hindsight, on the brink of dramatic transformation.

Welsh Rulers, Marcher Lords, and English Kings

The advent of the Normans arguably marks more of a break in the history of Wales than any other event between the collapse of the Roman imperial system and the profound changes set in train at the end of the eighteenth century by large-scale industrialization. One historian's claim that 'The Normans made the Welsh a European people' is not without justification.[4] But it should also be emphasized that the Welsh themselves were not without enterprise, and, from the start of the twelfth century, native rulers demonstrated their own appetite for aggressive expansion and a willingness to embrace new cultural influences and practices. The survival and adaptability of native Welsh power culminated in the thirteenth century with the attempts, and eventual failure, of the princes of Gwynedd to create an enduring native principality of Wales.

Wales did not have to wait long before it felt the aftereffects of the battle of Hastings in 1066. In an attempt to secure a restless and porous frontier zone, William the Conqueror created three new earldoms, Hereford, Chester, and Shrewsbury, lining the Anglo-Welsh border with a strong Norman presence. By the early 1090s, it seemed as if much of Wales had undergone a Norman takeover. In 1093, the death of Rhys ap Tewdwr, king of Deheubarth, at the hands of the Normans of Brycheiniog opened up the relatively rich lands of the south-west, hitherto spared conquest and settlement. Though it would prove premature to speak of the 'fall of the kingdom of the Britons', it was clear that the Normans had introduced a dangerous new dynamic to Welsh politics.[5] It is Rhigyfarch ap Sulien (d. 1099), in his finely crafted Latin lament, who perhaps best captures the 'shock and awe' effect of the *adventus Normannorum*: 'One vile Norman intimidates a hundred natives with his command, and terrifies (them) with his look.'[6] Under the able leadership of men such as Gruffudd ap Cynan (d. 1137), king of Gwynedd, the early Norman advances in northern and central Wales were gradually reversed in the opening decades of the twelfth century, but many more of these inroads were not reversed, especially in the fertile southern lowlands. The long-lasting and ambiguous duality between native Wales (*pura Wallia*) and the Norman-controlled March of Wales (*marchia Wallie*) was the legacy of this unfinished conquest.

The political history of twelfth-century Wales can be divided into two broad periods, the first coinciding with the reign of Henry I (1100–35) and the Welsh recovery of the years 1135–55, and the second marked by the attempts of Henry II (d. 1189) to restore the *status quo ante* 1135 and the emergence in native Wales of a series of effective and ambitious rulers. During the reign of Henry I, the emergent powers in native Wales, particularly the ruling dynasties of Gwynedd and Powys, were recognized, and major changes were effected in Norman-controlled Wales through the use of 'feudal' forms of control. With the death of Henry I in 1135, the Anglo-Norman world was plunged into civil war. This in turn led to revolts in many parts of Wales and a dramatic redrawing of the political map. By the middle of the twelfth century, native rule had been restored to over half of the surface area of Wales, and from this territorial basis would coalesce three major polities: Powys, Deheubarth, and Gwynedd. Though overshadowed by the changes initiated by the native rulers of the thirteenth century, under princes such as Owain Gwynedd (d. 1170) and Rhys ap Gruffudd (the Lord Rhys, d. 1197), native Wales underwent a measure of territorial consolidation and governmental 'modernization'. However, the speed with which Henry II was able to re-impose royal supremacy reveals how fragile the Welsh *revanche* really was. So far as Henry was concerned, control and submission rather than the conquest of native Wales was the order of the day. This was achieved by means of military campaigns, military service, extracting tribute, and public rituals of submission.

For the Welsh princes, establishing a workable relationship with the king did not necessarily diminish their status within native society. This was the period of the *gogynfeirdd*, the 'quite early poets' who sang the praises of the princes and celebrated their battles, whether against rivals within Wales or against external forces. The greatest native rulers of the period also sought to secure their supremacy over native society through the assumption of assertive titles proclaiming Wales-wide authority (as in several of Owain Gwynedd's *acta*), and through the acceptance of client status *vis-à-vis* the king (as in the case of the Lord Rhys's appointment as justiciar in south Wales by Henry II).

The twelfth and especially the thirteenth century were also times of striking cultural accommodation and socio-economic change. Through the establishment of castle-boroughs, the Normans quickened the tempo of economic change, with towns such as Brecon and Cardiff becoming important centres of exchange and specialization. The process of Europeanization was also at work in the Welsh church. In the ecclesiastical sphere, subjugation was effected through the appointment and control of bishops, the establishment of new diocesan structures, and the acknowledgement of Canterbury's primacy. New influences also prevailed in the monastic sphere, first of all with the impact of Benedictine monasticism, then as a result of Cistercian and Augustinian foundations in Wales, and ultimately, in the thirteenth century, through the arrival of the mendicant orders. The Cistercians, in particular, were much favoured by native Welsh rulers, and in turn their monasteries, such as those at Strata Florida in west Wales and Valle Crucis and Strata Marcella in the north-east, became important centres of literary as well as spiritual and agricultural activity.

Assimilation of new influences had its military dimension too, as can be seen from the castles built from the early twelfth century onwards by the native princes. Military and aristocratic life was also a focal point of linguistic exchange. Words such as *pali* ('brocaded silk') and *glaif* ('spear; sword'), both Welsh derivations from Old French (*paile/palie*; though Middle English may have been the conduit for *glaive*), were incorporated into court poetry and native prose tales. Translators and interpreters were likewise in demand in such a linguistically mixed society. Those who moved between these different linguistic worlds might also adopt a second, less culturally distinctive, name in addition to their Welsh name, or could have the cognomen *Sais* (lit. 'Englishman/Saxon'; also 'English-speaker') denoting their familiarity with the language and customs of the English. As the literature of the period testifies, the process of borrowing did not flow in only one direction. The appearance of Geoffrey of Monmouth's *Historia Regum Britanniae* ('History of the Kings of Britain'), in around 1138, is a strikingly popular example of the literary adaptation of Welsh historical material for the international Latin stage. And it was another epitome of this frontier world, Gerald of Wales (d. *c.* 1223), who, in aiming his *Descriptio Kambriae* ('The Description of Wales', 1194), at an international audience, penned the first sustained ethnographic description of Wales and the Welsh. If the twelfth and thirteenth centuries marked an important stage in the external perception of the 'otherness' of Welsh native society, it was also an age in which Wales was increasingly drawn – through conquest and cultural change – into the ambit of Latin Christendom and learning.

By the end of the twelfth century, a state of uneasy equilibrium had emerged in Wales between those areas under native Welsh rule and those subject to Anglo-Norman (or English as we can now call them) control. The delicate balance would remain roughly unchanged until the Edwardian conquests of 1277 and 1282–3. Yet two contrary trends can be discerned during the last century of Welsh independence. On the one hand, the princes of Gwynedd aspired to be recognized as princes of all Wales, thus turning a loose hegemony over native Wales into a homage-based principality to be held under the feudal superiority of the English Crown. On the other hand, as English governmental practices became more bureaucratic and integrative, so did the nature of royal overlordship become more exacting and intrusive. The eventual conquest of Wales by Edward I may be said to have ensued as a result of this contradiction – conflict was bound to erupt sooner or later. Indeed, it is not unreasonable to suppose that the creation of a native principality of Wales by the princes of Gwynedd made the Edwardian conquest more, not less, likely; while conversely, it might be suggested that the changes effected in the governance of native Wales eased its eventual incorporation into the English realm.

The image of thirteenth-century Wales as an 'Age of the Two Llywelyns' is an attractive one. Under Llywelyn ab Iorwerth (d. 1240) and then his grandson Llywelyn ap Gruffudd (d. 1282), native Wales underwent a measure of 'state-building' such as it had hitherto never known.[7] Though the death of Llywelyn ab Iorwerth functioned as a brake on the hegemonic ambitions of the Gwynedd dynasty, under the terms of the Treaty of Montgomery of 1267 Llywelyn ap Gruffudd was granted by Henry III the title 'prince of Wales' and the right to the fealty and homage of all save one of the other native rulers of Wales. This new hierarchical structure of power, however, did not last long: by 1277 it had been dismantled, and before the end of 1282 its prince had been killed. The prince's repeated failure to pay homage to the new king, Edward I, led to a declaration of war in 1276, and the defeat and demolition of Llywelyn's wider principality in 1277. When a Welsh revolt against royal oppression and mismanagement broke out in 1282, Llywelyn soon put himself at its head. The result, however, was never in question. On 11 December 1282, Llywelyn was slain by the English in an ambush in mid-Wales, and by the summer of 1283 Edward's forces had taken control of Gwynedd. Before the end of the year, the prince's brother, Dafydd ap Gruffudd, had been executed at Shrewsbury, and the younger members of the Gwynedd dynasty, along with the regalia and relics of Welsh princely rule, removed and taken to England. Edward I, it seemed, had achieved a 'final solution of the Welsh problem'.[8]

Late Medieval Wales: Coexistence and Crisis

The framework of Welsh politics and political allegiance was permanently recast by the Edwardian conquest and its subsequent legal settlement. The broad outlines of the new order were established by the statute issued at Rhuddlan in March 1284, which laid down the new administrative and legal provisions for the governance of the conquered territories of native Wales. The Edwardian settlement was underpinned by the most impressive and best-documented castle-building programme in medieval history. Castles such as Caernarfon and Conwy were designed to keep the Welsh in check and underscore the imperial pretensions of the king. With new borough towns established in their shadow, they were intended as centres of both civil and military authority.[9] While the tentacles of royal government did not extend into the Marcher lordships, Edward used his power to create new lordships, such as Chirk and Dyffryn Clwyd, and attempt to define the status of existing ones vis-à-vis the Crown. The scale and speed of the Edwardian conquest of Wales was remarkable. It is little wonder that some contemporaries proclaimed that an old empire – the Arthurian monarchy of the whole of Britain – had been revived, though in the memorable phrase of one modern medievalist the Edwardian settlement of Wales might more aptly be termed 'the first colonial constitution'.[10]

The Edwardian conquest also ushered in a new era of social and cultural realignment. With the demise of the old ruling elites, the Welsh squirearchy or *uchelwyr* (literally, 'high men') now looked to the new political order for social advancement. Though the top posts in the royal administration in Wales remained largely closed to Welshmen throughout the fourteenth century, opportunities were available further down the 'colonial' hierarchy. These natural leaders of local society assumed cultural leadership as well, becoming patrons of the court poets and of literary production more generally. This cross-current is exemplified most conspicuously, perhaps, by the career of Rhydderch ab Ieuan Llwyd (d. *c.* 1400). Side by side with the various posts that he held under the English justiciars of south Wales during the 1380s and 1390s went his lavish patronage of poets in his native Ceredigion. An expert in Welsh law, Rhydderch was also the man for whom the literary anthology known as *Llyfr Gwyn Rhydderch* ('The White Book of Rhydderch') was probably written. While young, Rhydderch ab Ieuan was the subject of a *marwnad ffug*, or pseudo-elegy, by the greatest Welsh poet of the day, Dafydd ap Gwilym (d. *c.* 1350), whose poetic style bespeaks both the confidence of the *uchelwyr* and an openness to innovation. Nor did these men limit their cultural diet to native literature; an upsurge in the translation and adaptation of French and Latin works into Welsh testifies to broader literary tastes and a European outlook.

Yet, as with nearly every other corner of fourteenth-century Europe, it was also a period of deepening crisis in Wales. Although some thrived in the new political climate, there were many others who were left frustrated and bitter. Despite instances of successful integration, the basic division between colonizer and colonized in post-conquest Wales was unmistakable. Different laws and customs, especially concerning land tenure and inheritance, served to deepen the ethnic cleavage, expressed most explicitly, perhaps, by the administrative division of some lordships into Englishries and Welshries. In parts of

Wales, too, the legacy of conquest was keenly felt by those who had been driven off their lands to make way for the new settlers from England. It could also be a dangerous and frightening place for the colonists, especially when wider upheavals had repercussions on law and order in Wales (as they did in the reign of Edward II, and later with the granting of the Principality to Edward the Black Prince). The panic engendered by the outbreak of anti-English violence in the 1340s can be gauged by the letters sent to the Black Prince by the English burgesses of north Wales. Those of Caernarfon, for example, complained to the Prince in early 1345 that the Welsh had become so 'cruel and malicious towards the English . . . that they [the burgesses] dare not go anywhere for fear of death'.[11]

The cataclysms, firstly, of famine in the early fourteenth century, and of the visitation of plague from mid-century onwards, further intensified this climate of resentment. The plague popularly known as the Black Death first reached Wales in 1349, and further outbreaks of the great pandemic followed during the 1360s. In the words of the poet Llywelyn Fychan, 'It caused grief and fury everywhere' (*llwyr y gwnâi alar a llid*).[12] It is little wonder, then, that some in Wales harboured messianic hopes of deliverance. During the 1360s and 1370s, the hopes of some were focused on Owain ap Thomas ap Rhodri, or Owain Lawgoch as he was known (d. 1378), the grandson of Llywelyn ap Gruffudd's youngest brother. As the military commander of a company of Welshmen in French service, and a man of impeccable dynastic credentials, he was a logical choice, but his plans came to nothing: he was assassinated in 1378 by an agent of the English government. Soon the tensions latent in Wales at the end of the fourteenth century converged with devastating effect around the figure of Owain Glyn Dŵr (d. *c.* 1415), who rebelled against the newly-crowned Henry IV in 1400.[13]

The decision to proclaim Owain ap Gruffudd Fychan, or Owain Glyn Dŵr as he came to be known, as the prince of Wales had a national, redemptive, dimension. Along with the air of mystery which surrounds its leader, it is this element that gives the revolt its undoubted imaginative appeal to modern eyes. Yet, prior to the outbreak of the revolt, Owain Glyn Dŵr's personal history seems to have followed much the same pattern of co-operation as that of other Welshmen of comparable status. Though sprung from the princely lineages of Powys and Deheubarth, he had trained at the Inns of Court in London and had seen military service in Scotland. Helped by his in-laws, the Hanmer family, he seems to have moved easily in English aristocratic circles, and, as the lord of three middle-sized estates, he was also comfortably well-off. How and why he decided on unleashing the sudden fury of revolt has to remain a matter of speculation.

The history of a long guerrilla war does not lend itself to a tidy narrative of events. The revolt arose in the first instance out of a local quarrel between Owain and his English neighbour, Reginald, Lord Grey of Ruthin. Yet, like a brush fire, the revolt began to spread quickly, igniting underlying tensions with destructive force. Initial attacks were focused on the English plantation boroughs of north-east Wales and the northern March. For some two years, however, the future of the revolt remained in the balance. The English government was able to stabilize the situation for a short while, but from the summer of 1402 the initiative had moved to the rebels, with Glyn Dŵr's adherents appearing in areas hitherto untouched by the revolt. Owain was also aided by political rivalries in England, which did much to hamper the English government's response.

During the next two years, the revolt would acquire an international dimension. A Franco-Welsh treaty was concluded in July 1404, and in the summer of 1405 Owain's army was bolstered by a sizeable French expeditionary force. Owain's quasi-messianic pretensions, reflected in the so-called Tripartite Indenture of 1405, now went as far as proposing the dismemberment of the English realm, with the creation of a much-enlarged Wales and the division of England north and south. His authority was also displayed vividly in his great seal, which shows him enthroned holding a sceptre and bears the legend: *Owenus Dei gratia princeps Wallie* ('Owain, by the grace of God prince of Wales'). What began as a rebellion with 'fire and sword' (*ferro et flamma*) quickly found its institutional expression in ambitious proposals such as the creation of universities and the metropolitan status and independence of St David's.[14]

Before the end of 1406, however, there were signs that the power behind the programme for an independent principality of Wales was waning. It had become a long war of attrition, waged in a poor, rural, and plague-ridden country. As French support lapsed, so also did Henry IV's position in England improve. The English government could now make its vast superiority in material resources and manpower tell. The fall of two great castles in 1408, Aberystwyth and Harlech, destroyed any remaining semblance of Owain's princely authority. The immediate rebel threat would continue, and Owain Glyn Dŵr would remain at large, but by 1409 it can be said that the uprising had failed, and by 1415 that English authority throughout Wales had been successfully reimposed. Whether the end of the Glyn Dŵr revolt heralds the beginning of 'modern Wales' may be a moot point, but that it put paid to any notions of an independent native principality is not to be doubted.

This historical overview ends as it began in the decades following the Glyn Dŵr revolt. Contemporaries, and in their wake later commentators, bewailed its destructiveness. The delicate ethnic and social fabric of post-conquest Wales had been torn asunder by over a decade of war. Yet, as the career of Edward ap Dafydd of Bryncunallt illustrates, men who had imperilled their own and their family's fortunes by defecting to Glyn Dŵr's cause were soon enough reconciled to the king and restored to their positions as pillars of local society. Despite the penal laws which were issued against the Welsh in the wake of the rebellion, it was not long before Welshmen of note were enjoying lucrative office, purchasing lands in the boroughs, and securing letters of denizenship. Further opportunities arose with the resumption of warfare with France and the ensuing Wars of the Roses. The Welsh court poetry of the fifteenth century – for all its tendency to express anti-English sentiment – became increasingly preoccupied with men who sought a far richer prize, the power to put a Welsh king on the throne of England.

Notes

1. See *Guto'r Glyn.net*, www.gutorglyn.net (accessed 8 August 2017), no. 104.
2. The modern words *Cymru* (Wales), *Cymry* (the Welsh), *Cymraeg* (Welsh language), and 'Cumbria', the modern English county, are all related to an earlier unattested form, **com-brogī*, meaning people who share the same territory, 'fellow countrymen'. This period of British history has been charted most recently by Thomas Charles-Edwards, *Wales and the Britons, 350–1064* (Oxford: Oxford University Press, 2012). See also Wendy Davies, *Wales in the Early Middle Ages* (Leicester: Leicester University Press, 1982).
3. For the anglicization of the heartlands of the former diocese of *Britanniae*, see Nick Higham, ed., *Britons in Anglo-Saxon England* (Woodbridge: Boydell Press, 2007); Charles-Edwards, *Wales and the Britons*, 421–2.
4. Gwyn A. Williams, *When Was Wales? A History of the Welsh* (Harmondsworth: Penguin, 1985), 62.
5. *Brut y Tywysogyon, or The Chronicle of the Princes, Peniarth MS. 20 Version*, ed. and trans. Thomas Jones (Cardiff: University of Wales Press, 1952), 19 (*s.a.* 1091–3).
6. Michael Lapidge, 'The Welsh-Latin Poetry of Sulien's Family', *Studia Celtica* 8–9 (1973–4): 68–106 (90–1).
7. Some of the ways in which Gwynedd in the thirteenth century developed state-like features are discussed by David Stephenson, *The Governance of Gwynedd* (Cardiff: University of Wales Press, 1984), reissued as *Political Power in Medieval Gwynedd: Governance and the Welsh Princes* (Cardiff: University of Wales Press, 2014).

8. R. R. Davies, *Conquest, Co-existence, and Change: Wales 1063–1415* (Oxford: Oxford University Press, 1987), reissued as *The Age of Conquest: Wales 1063–1415* (Oxford: Oxford University Press, 1991, 2000), 349.

9. On the borough towns established by Edward, see M. W. Beresford, *New Towns of the Middle Ages: Town Plantation in England, Wales and Gascony* (London: Lutterworth, 1967).

10. Helen Maud Cam, *Law-Finders and Law-Makers in Medieval England: Collected Studies in Legal and Constitutional History* (London: Merlin Press, 1962), 133. For Edward's own enthusiasm for the mythological past, and its use more generally by the English to claim the domination of Britain in the twelfth and thirteenth centuries, see R. R. Davies, *The First English Empire: Power and Identities in the British Isles 1093–1343* (Oxford: Oxford University Press, 2000), 4–53.

11. *Calendar of Ancient Correspondence Concerning Wales*, ed. J. Goronwy Edwards (Cardiff: University of Wales Press, 1935), 231.

12. *Galar y Beirdd: Marwnadau Plant / Poets' Grief: Medieval Welsh Elegies for Children*, ed. and trans. Dafydd Johnston (Cardiff: Tafol, 1993), 52–3.

13. The standard account of the rebellion is by R. R. Davies, *The Revolt of Owain Glyn Dŵr* (Oxford: Oxford University Press, 1995).

14. *The Chronicle of Adam Usk, 1377–1421*, ed. and trans. C. Given-Wilson (Oxford: Oxford University Press, 1997), 144.

2

Britons and Saxons: The Earliest Writing in Welsh

HELEN FULTON

In 1868, the Scottish historian and antiquarian William Forbes Skene published an edition and translation of early Welsh poetry from four manuscripts which he called *Four Ancient Books of Wales*. Though these manuscripts are not particularly ancient relative to those of classical literature (the earliest of Skene's four manuscripts dates to the mid-thirteenth century), they contain the oldest surviving versions of literature in Welsh, some of them dating back to at least the ninth century. Skene's edition was instrumental in bringing early Welsh literature to the attention of historians, philologists, and literary scholars and led ultimately to the first scholarly editions of Welsh poetry in the early twentieth century.[1]

Much of the material in the four manuscripts alludes to the early history of Wales and its British neighbours to the north, in the regions of what are now northern England and the lowlands of Scotland. Running throughout the earliest strand of Welsh literature, with echoes continuing late into the Middle Ages, is the dominant theme of the often antagonistic relationships between these British peoples as they competed for land and power. Their regional battles were complicated by the presence of the incoming Saxons, whose settlements between the sixth and eleventh centuries gradually eroded British territories in the north and along what is now the border between Wales and England. The genres of court poetry and saga poetry, which dominate Welsh literature throughout the early Middle Ages, repeat elegaic themes of heroic defeat, loss of land, and dispersal of people, while praise poems to great leaders, historical and legendary, attempt to balance the scales in favour of Welsh tenacity and survival. The earliest writing in Welsh is not without interest (or value) to students of British history and the Anglo-Saxon settlements, but its literary qualities separate it decisively from the discourse of history and draw us into an imagined world of Christian warriors and kings, the psychogeography of territories and place-names, the uncanny operations of the supernatural, and the 'emotional communities' of pre-Norman Wales.[2]

The Latin Tradition in Wales

Before looking in more detail at Skene's 'four ancient books', we should note that, well before the Norman conquest, Wales had a culture of writing based mainly in religious centres where Latin manuscripts were copied and circulated. One of the most important surviving texts about the early history of Britain, the *Historia Brittonum* ('The History of the Britons') was written in Gwynedd, north Wales, in A D 829–30, in the early years of the reign of Merfyn Frych. Merfyn and his son, Rhodri Mawr, created a dynasty which was to dominate Welsh politics until the English conquest of Gwynedd in 1282. His court at Aberffraw, on the island of Môn (Anglesey), lay on the major sea routes between Britain, Ireland, and the continent, fostering a literate culture in touch with wider intellectual trends. The mixture of historical events, legendary heroes, and supernatural marvels which forms the *Historia Brittonum* was the product of knowledge, belief, and oral tradition accumulated at Merfyn's court.[3]

Though few manuscripts from Wales written in Latin before 1000 have survived, and those mainly in English monastic libraries, the evidence of later copies and allusions to books that must have existed in Wales indicate the extent of what has been lost.[4] One of the most significant monastic schools in post-Roman Wales was at Llanilltud Fawr (Llantwit Major in the Vale of Glamorgan), named after its founder St Illtud and very likely the place where Gildas, the sixth-century writer of *De excidio Britanniae* ('The Ruin of Britain'), received his training.[5] Latin charters survive from the neighbouring monastery at Llancarfan, while the scriptorium at St David's in west Wales produced genealogies of Welsh princes as well as copies of Latin texts. Probably the largest and most active scriptorium was at Llanbadarn Fawr near Aberystwyth, led first by Sulien (1011–91), bishop of St David's, and then by his two sons, Rhigyfarch and Ieuan, both of whom wrote texts in Latin which have survived.[6] They owned a library of Latin books that included works by influential writers such as Virgil, Ovid, Lucan, and Aldhelm.[7]

Another significant survival of Latin writing in Wales is the *Liber Landavensis* ('The Book of Llandaff'), a large compendium of charters, saints' lives, and other material relating to the diocese of Llandaff, near Cardiff.[8] It was compiled after 1120 (with later additions) with the aim of raising the status of Llandaff in order to support its claims to lands and other privileges under the early Norman lords of south Wales. Written mainly in Latin by a number of different hands, the manuscript also contains sections in Welsh, notably the *Braint Teilo* ('Right of Teilo'), a catalogue of rights and privileges that had been granted to the diocese before the Norman settlements.

As evidenced by the Book of Llandaff, the culture of Latin writing in Wales produced the earliest surviving remnants of writing in Welsh, mainly in the form of Old Welsh glosses and marginalia in Latin manuscripts. Some of the most important survivals, linguistically at least, are the marginal comments in Welsh about land disputes which were written into the eighth-century Book of St Chad (also known as the Lichfield Gospels), probably written in the monastery at Llandeilo Fawr in south-west Wales.[9] The longest amount of text surviving in Old Welsh is the Computus fragment (*c.* 850 x 910), comprising twenty-three lines of commentary on calculating the date of Easter.[10] The most interesting survivals from a literary point of view are two poems in Old Welsh written into the spaces of a Latin versification of the Gospels by the fourth-century commentator Juvencus (Cambridge, Cambridge University Library MS Ff.4.42). The manuscript, heavily glossed in a number of different hands, dates from the second half of the ninth century and the poems, one of three stanzas and the other of nine, are written in a hand of about the same period.[11] Composed as *englynion* (that is, a group of stanzas in the *englyn* metre), the longer poem is religious and the shorter one seems to be more secular and heroic in content, evoking a warrior context.

The Black Book of Carmarthen

Returning now to Skene's 'four ancient books', these date from the thirteenth and fourteenth centuries and contain, among later works, what survives of the poetry of the *cynfeirdd*, or 'early poets', an eighteenth-century term referring to poets composing in Welsh before the Norman conquest. Modern critics call their poetry *hengerdd*, 'old poetry'. The oldest surviving manuscript written entirely in Welsh is *Llyfr Du Caerfyrddin* ('The Black Book of Carmarthen', Aberystwyth, National Library of Wales MS Peniarth 1), of about 1225 x 1250, containing a selection of poetry composed or first written down at various periods between the ninth and twelfth centuries, a selection which presumably represents the eclectic choice of the manuscript's scribe or patron.[12] There are praise poems and elegies to princes of south Wales exemplifying the conventions of twelfth-century court poetry, some religious and proverbial items, and a group of poems associated with early Welsh traditions of Arthur and the prophet Myrddin, who was to become the

'Merlin' of Geoffrey of Monmouth's *Historia Regum Britanniae* (*c.* 1138) and *Vita Merlini* (*c.* 1150).[13]

One of the most interesting poems in the manuscript is the group of seventy-three verses known as *Englynion y Beddau* ('The Stanzas of the Graves'), probably dating to the ninth century.[14] Each verse commemorates the burial places of fallen heroes, bringing together a host of legendary names from early Welsh literature, many of them known from other contexts. One of them, Geraint son of Erbin, is also the subject of another sequence of *englynion* in the Black Book and reappears as the hero of his own Welsh prose romance, having first been adapted into French romance as the hero of Chrétien de Troyes' twelfth-century verse narrative, *Erec et Enide*.[15] Arthur himself is listed as one of the fallen heroes of the Stanzas of the Graves, but the location of his grave is described as *anoeth byd* ('a wonder of the world'), meaning that it is unknown and undiscoverable.

A characteristic of the poems in the Black Book, like most of the *hengerdd*, is that the literary tradition of which they are a part encompasses not just Wales, in its modern geographical form, but also the areas of southern Scotland and northern England which were inhabited by speakers of Brittonic languages closely related to Welsh who formed a distinctive cultural and linguistic community across a wide region of early Britain. A continuous traffic of people, poets, and traditions in both directions between the 'Old North' (in Welsh, 'Yr Hen Ogledd') and Wales during the period of the English settlements accounts for the northern locations of many early Welsh heroes and their exploits, including Myrddin, who declares in a sequence of verses known as the *Afallennau*, literally 'Apple Trees', that he fought at the battle of Arfderydd (thought to be Arthuret in northern Cumbria where a battle was fought in A D 573) and then lived as a wild man in Coed Celyddon, the Forest of Caledonia.[16]

The Book of Aneirin

The second of Skene's 'four ancient books' is *Llyfr Aneirin* ('The Book of Aneirin', Aberystwyth, National Library of Wales, Cardiff MS 2.81), dated to about 1260.[17] A colophon at the beginning of the book says: 'hwn yw e gododin. Aneirin ae cant' ('This is "The Gododdin". Aneirin sang it'). Written in two hands and associated with one of the Cistercian abbeys under the patronage of the princes of Gwynedd, either Aberconwy or Strata Marcella, the small manuscript contains a long sequence of elegies – known as

Y Gododdin ('The Gododdin') – and several shorter pieces about the British kingdoms of the Old North: Strathclyde, Cumbria and, in particular, Gododdin.[18]

Though the manuscript was written in the thirteenth century and is transmitted through the medium of Middle Welsh, its contents have been copied from much earlier exemplars, now lost. The poetry contains linguistic forms dating from the seventh to early twelfth centuries, that is, Old Welsh forms with a considerable smattering of the Brittonic language that preceded Old Welsh.[19] Most of the manuscript comprises what is taken to be *Y Gododdin* itself, a collection of stanzas in the *awdl* metre commemorating individual heroes or, in some cases, the whole warband of the men of Goddodin who fought and died at the battle of Catraeth.[20] The two scribes of the manuscript, known as A and B, have each provided a different version of *Y Gododdin* based on different exemplars, with the (incomplete) B-text containing the more archaic material. Of the surviving *awdlau* as we have them, 62 are unique to the A-text, 21 are unique to the B-text, and 17 are common to both (with a further three or four stanzas repeated as variants within the B-text).[21]

Gododdin is the Welsh form of the tribal name that appears in Latin as Votadini, those peoples who lived around the modern city of Edinburgh (which appears as Din Eidin in the poem) until the conquest of the Gododdin kingdom by the English of Northumbria, probably in the seventh century.[22] Catraeth, where the battle described in the poem took place, can be identified on linguistic grounds with Catterick in Yorkshire, 167 miles south of Edinburgh, a region occupied in the early sixth century by the Anglians of Deira who are named in the poem as the principal enemies of the men of Gododdin. A number of the warriors are called 'Dewr daen' ('scatterer of the Deirans');[23] others are killers of 'Saeson' ('the Saxons'), or 'Lloegrwys' ('the men of England').

The standard account of the historical context of the poem, based on references in the poem itself and the few historical sources for the period (none of which mentions a battle at Catraeth), assumes that the men of Gododdin and their British allies in the northern territories launched a military offensive at Catraeth against the Anglians of Bernicia and Deira who were threatening their southern borders.[24] In this scenario, the battle at Catraeth is dated to *c*. 600, shortly before the two Anglian kingdoms were united into Northumbria in 605 under the rule of the Bernician king Aethelfrith. A second and quite different scenario has been proposed by one of the poem's editors, John Koch, who has challenged this nationalistic picture of the British versus the English, arguing instead that the battle of Catraeth took place between two bi-ethnic armies each comprising Britons and Anglians. Following a complex reconstruction of the geopolitics of the Old North, Koch proposes a date for the battle of Catraeth of about 570.[25] Thomas Owen Clancy has proposed a more streamlined explanation, that various battle-leaders, whether British or English, routinely made opportunistic raids on other territories and the battle of Catraeth was likely to have been one such raid, involving British and English on both sides.[26]

The precise political situation is difficult to reconstruct from the available evidence which simply points to various hostile interactions among British and Anglo-Saxon tribes of the Old North in the late sixth and early seventh centuries, as Bernicia and Deira gradually expanded their territories into the British regions of Gododdin, Rheged (in the area of modern Cumbria and Lancashire), and Elmet (around the modern city of Leeds in south Yorkshire). The historical significance of the battle of Catraeth is also difficult to gauge, given its absence from the historical record. Most critics have read the A- and B-texts together as a single narrative about the battle at Catraeth, with the army of the Gododdin feasting at Din Eidyn before marching to the battle-field where they were brutally cut down by a superior force of Anglians (with or without support from other British tribes). Certainly many of the *awdlau* in the A-text support this reading, with a number of stanzas beginning with the same phrase, 'Gwŷr a aeth gatraeth' ('Men went to Catraeth'), to introduce an elegy for a fallen warrior, as in this example:

> Gwŷr a aeth Gatraeth, oedd ffraeth eu llu,
> Glasfedd eu hancwyn a gwenwyn fu,
> Trychant trwy beiriant yn catáu,
> A gwedi elwch tawelwch fu.
> Cyd elwynt lannau i benydu,
> Dadl ddiau angau i eu treiddu.[27]

> (Warriors went to Catraeth, their host was swift,
> Fresh mead was their feast and it was bitter,
> Three hundred fighting under command,
> And after the cry of jubilation there was silence.
> Though they went to churches to do penance,
> The certain meeting with death came to them.)

However, this modern assumption of a 'Catraeth Legend' underpinning the poem has created an apparently seamless plot for a poem which is by no means coherent or easily explicable in narrative terms.[28] The B-text, representing the oldest strand of the poem, while evidently focused on the men of Gododdin, scarcely mentions Catraeth as a place of particular importance, though the few references that do appear in the B-text seem to support the A-text narrative of a military expedition to a place called Catraeth.

When the poem (or some version of it) was first composed is another matter for speculation. It may have happened quite shortly after the battle took place, and the expressions of sorrow regarding the deaths of so many men from Gododdin certainly strike the reader as authentically recent. According to Koch's understanding of the language and transmission of Y Gododdin, a written text of the poem, based on oral transmissions of earlier elegies, must have existed by the middle of the seventh century, with the B-text preserving some of its oldest linguistic forms. Koch agrees with A. O. H. Jarman that the poem was circulating in Strathclyde, the neighbouring British territory, at some time before the fall of Din Eidin (possibly in 638) and that some of the other poetic material found in the Book of Aneirin was added at that point.[29] Whereas Jarman proposed a largely oral transmission of the poem from Gododdin to Strathclyde and thence to Wales, Koch believes there were written versions in circulation in Strathclyde from about 638 until the mid-ninth century, and that an archaic written text was first brought to Wales around 655 or 656 (the ancestor of the A-text and part of the B-text).[30] Another written version remained in Strathclyde until the 870s before transmission to Wales, more or less unchanged, as the most archaic stratum of the B-text.[31]

The possible contemporaneity of Y Gododdin is strengthened by the fact that its supposed composer, Aneirin, was almost certainly a sixth-century poet. The Historia Brittonum, written or compiled in Gwynedd in 829–30, refers to a group of British poets active at the time of King Ida of Northumbria (as Bede called him), who ruled Bernicia from 547 to 559, and at the time of Maelgwn Gwynedd, the north Welsh prince who died in 547.[32] Among this group of five poets, two have poetry attributed to them in early Welsh manuscripts: Aneirin and Taliesin. The poet Aneirin is named four times in the Book of Aneirin as the author of Y Gododdin, and although none of these attributions occurs in the oldest layer of the text, they do suggest that, when written versions began circulating in Strathclyde in the mid-seventh century, the poem was regarded as the authentic work of Aneirin, a sixth-century poet. A few later references in the poem suggesting that Aneirin himself was present at the battle are likely to be literary flourishes added for dramatic effect in performances of the poem when it reached Wales.

While attempts to reconstruct the historical and political context of *Y Gododdin* as a sixth-century text are to some extent necessary for a detailed understanding of this archaic and many-layered poem, it should also be read as a piece of thirteenth-century literature which scribes and their patrons believed was worthy of preservation and circulation. It constituted a powerful memorial to a series of British heroes from the past, whose names are listed one after the other, with brief details of their courage in battle, like epitaphs on a war memorial. The language of warrior heroism, a dense texture of epithets and tags such as 'golden-torqued', 'attackers', 'shattered his shield', 'bull of combat', 'spear-shafts', 'a host of horsemen', along with such tropes as the rush to battle, repayment of the lord's hospitality, refusal to flee or show mercy, and lives willingly short-lived, constructs an aristocratic warrior ideology in which actions speak far more loudly than words and death is the surest route to fame and glory. These were the men who were the ancestors of the present-day Welsh, especially the men of Gwynedd, who traced their origins to Cunedda, a legendary leader from Gododdin who settled in Gwynedd in the first half of the fifth century. The story of the men of Gododdin was therefore a story for the men of Gwynedd, evoking cultural memories of their heroic origins and the ancient struggle against the Saxons, a struggle that was to end in Gwynedd in 1282 with the death of the last prince of Wales, Llywelyn ap Gruffudd.

The Book of Taliesin

The third of the 'four ancient books of Wales' is *Llyfr Taliesin* ('The Book of Taliesin', Aberystwyth, National Library of Wales MS Peniarth 2).[33] Written by a single hand, that of a professional scribe working in one of the monastic scriptoria of Wales, the manuscript has been dated to the first half of the fourteenth century, but much of its contents are considerably earlier. Apart from one religious piece in Latin, the manuscript is entirely in Welsh, containing a total of sixty-one poems which were probably copied directly from one or more existing exemplars. The title, the Book of Taliesin, was probably given to the manuscript by one of its early owners, perhaps the great book collector of the seventeenth century, Robert Vaughan, who kept the manuscript in his library at Hengwrt near Dolgellau in north-west Wales.

The poetry in the manuscript, though written entirely in the *awdl* metre, is very varied in its style and contents, encompassing religious, prophetic, and legendary material along with praise poems and references to international heroes such as Alexander the Great. As in the Black Book of Carmarthen, the poetry of the Book of Taliesin is of varying and uncertain dates, much of it pre-1100, though transmitted through a thirteenth-century orthography which shows very few traces of Old Welsh forms. If there is any coherence to the collection at all, it is the figure of Taliesin himself, appearing in various guises as a heroic poet of sixth-century north Britain, a prophet and riddle-maker, and a court poet composing verse comparable to that of the twelfth- and thirteenth-century 'poets of the princes'.[34] In many of the poems, the element of performance is explicit: the narrator, sometimes but not always named as Taliesin, often speaks in the first person or addresses his audience directly, speaking as a character rather than as a professional poet.

We have already seen that the name of Taliesin was included with that of Aneirin in a list of British (that is, Welsh) poets active in the mid-sixth century, and among the poems in the Book of Taliesin is a group of twelve that refer to a sixth-century historical context in Wales and the Old North of Britain.[35] Eight of them are praise poems to Urien of Rheged, whose kingdom may have extended from beyond the Solway Firth over modern Cumbria and Lancashire and, possibly, as far east as Catraeth (Catterick) in Yorkshire; a ninth addresses Gwallawg, the leader of Elmet, a territory just to the south of Rheged. These nine poems are found in a single group in the manuscript (nos. 34–42, using Marged Haycock's numbering).[36] Dotted about elsewhere are a further three which seem to belong to a similar historical context: no. 13, also to Gwallawg, no. 26, in praise of Cynan Garwyn, ruler of Powys in north-east Wales in the late sixth century, and no. 48, an elegy to Urien's son Owain, placed among a small group of elegies to famous heroes. These twelve 'historical' poems were edited as a collection by Ifor Williams who made a case for them as the authentic compositions of the historical sixth-century court-poet Taliesin.[37]

Though we have little evidence on which to base a historicized narrative around these twelve poems, a number of them are composed in praise of historical figures, especially Urien of Rheged and his son Owain. We know from the *Historia Brittonum* that Urien was a major battle-leader who fought with his sons against Theodric of Bernicia. He succeeded in besieging his opponents for three days and nights in the island of Metcaud (Lindisfarne), but was then treacherously murdered by Morgant, a rival British prince, a death that was lamented in another group of poems, the Llywarch Hen cycle, discussed below. In Taliesin's poetry, Urien is a hero of the British in their territorial struggles against rival enemies, variously figured as English or other British leaders, calling on his allies to slaughter the usurpers. One of the most famous of Taliesin's poems, 'Gwaith Argoed Llwyfain' ('The Battle of Argoed Llwyfain'), creates a dramatic scene in which Urien and Owain exchange insults with a rival leader, Fflamddwyn, literally 'flame-bearer'. The poem is quoted here in full because of its narrative force:

> E Bore duw sadwrn kat uawr a uu.
> or pan dwyre heul hyt pan gynnu.
> dygrysswys flamdwyn yn petwar llu.
> godeu a reget y ymdullu.
> dyuwy o argoet hyt arvynyd.
> ny cheffynt eiryos hyt yr vn dyd.
> Atorelwis flamdwyn vawr trebystawt.
> A dodynt yg gwystlon a ynt parawt.
> Ys attebwys. Owein dwyrein ffossawt.
> nyd dodynt nyt ydynt nyt ynt parawt.
> A cheneu vab coel bydei kymwyawc
> lew. kyn as talei o wystyl nebawt.
> Atorelwis vryen vd yr echwyd.
> o byd ymgyfaruot am gerenhyd.
> dyrchafwn eidoed oduch mynyd.
> Ac am porthwn wyneb oduch emyl.
> A dyrchafwn peleidyr oduch pen gwyr.
> A chyrchwn fflamdwyn yn y luyd.
> A lladwn ac ef ae gyweithyd.
> > A rac gweith argoet llwyfein
> > bu llawer kelein.
> > > Rudei vrein rac ryfel gwyr.
> > A gwerin a grysswys gan einewyd.
> > Armaf y blwydyn nat wy kynnyd.
>
> > > Ac yny vallwyf y hen
> > > ym dygyn agheu aghen.
> > > ny bydif ymdyrwen
> > > na molwyf vryen.[38]

(There was a great battle, Saturday morning,
From the time the sun rose till it set.
Fflamddwyn came on, in four war-bands.
Goddau and Rheged were mustering,
Summoned men, from Argoed to Arfynydd:
They were given not one day's delay.
Fflamddwyn shouted, big at boasting:
'Have my hostages come? Are they ready?'
Answered Owain, bane of the East:
'They've not come, are not here, are not ready,

And a cub of Coel's line must be pressed
Hard before he'd render one hostage.'
Shouted Urien, lord of Yrechwydd:
'If a meeting for peace-talk's to come,
Let our shield-wall rise on the mountain,
And let our faces lift over the rim,
And let our spears, men, be raised high,
And let us make for Fflamddwyn amidst his warbands,
And let us slay him and his comrades.'
  Before Argoed Llwyfain
  There was many a dead man.
    Crows grew crimsoned from warriors.
And the war-band charged with its chieftain:
For a year I'll shape song to their triumph.

And until I die, old,
By death's strict demand,
I shall not be joyful
Unless I praise Urien.)[39]

Although there is no historical evidence for a battle at Argoed Llwyfain, it is intriguing to speculate that 'Fflamddwyn' may have been a nickname for one of the English leaders, perhaps even Theodric of Bernicia himself.[40] Fflamddwyn is mentioned again in another of the poems, the plangent 'Marwnad Owain' ('Elegy to Owain'), a lament for the loss of a great soldier in which the poet claims that Owain slew Fflamddwyn and 'thought it no more than sleep'.

As in the case of Aneirin's work, reconstructions of such an archaic historical context can only be speculative. Cynan Garwyn (or Cynan ap Brochfael) is known from early Welsh genealogies; Gwallawg and Urien are both named in the ninth-century *Historia Brittonum* as allies against the Bernicians; Taliesin and Aneirin are also mentioned there. But to what extent the Taliesin poems to sixth-century heroes, as they have survived in the Book of Taliesin, can be regarded as sixth-century poems is debatable; they are probably best regarded as thirteenth-century transmissions of court poetry celebrating a heroic past whose memory would have appealed to the princes of Wales before and after the Norman conquest.

Apart from the 'historical' Taliesin poems, the Book of Taliesin contains more than twenty prophetic and supernatural pieces, including the well-known Arthurian poem called 'Preiddeu Annwn' ('The Spoils of Annwn', that is, the Otherworld). One of the longest and most significant poems is that which calls itself *Armes Prydein* ('The Prophecy of Britain'), which foretells the arrival of a great host of British warriors and their allies to drive out the hated Saxons and restore British sovereignty over the Island of Britain. Set in an identifiably historical context of tenth-century Britain, the poem is a cry of resistance to the hegemony of English overlords and the heavy taxes imposed on the Welsh people, and a rejection of the pro-English policies of Welsh princes such as Hywel Dda (d. 950). Amongst dramatic images of the bloody uprising that will take place, the poet invokes Myrddin as his authority for the coming slaughter of the Saxon enemy:

> [E]f gyrhawt allmyn y alltuded.
> nys arhaedwy neb nys dioes dayar . . .
> . . . Kymry a Saesson kyferuydyn
> y am lan ymtreulaw ac ymwrthryn.
> o diruawr vydinawr pan ymprofyn.
> Ac am allt lafnawr a gawr a gryn.
> Ac am Gwy geir kyfyrgeir y am peurllyn.
> A lluman adaw agarw disgyn.
> A mal [bwyt] balaon Saesson syrthyn.
> Kymry kynyrcheit kyfun dullyn.[41]

> (Foreigners will be driven into exile,
> None will receive them, no land is theirs . . .
> . . . Welshmen and Saxons will meet in combat,
> On all sides struggling and grappling together
> Of mighty war-bands as they test their strength,
> And on the slope blades, battle-cries, close combat,
> On Wye's banks cry countering cry round bright water,
> And banners abandoned and savage assault,
> And as food-stuff for wolves the Saxons will fall.
> Welsh lords as one band will marshall their ranks.)

The poem is propelled by images of Welsh unity as a political and martial force, though Wales was far from being a single nation but rather a collection of princedoms constantly in contention among powerful lords, both Welsh and English. The prophecy of a Welsh return to the sovereignty of Britain, later called the 'prophecy of Merlin', was integral to the Welsh sense of their own history and is used in *Armes Prydein*, as in later texts, as a call to arms at a historical moment of hegemonic competition involving not only the Welsh and English but also the Irish and the Vikings.[42] *Armes Prydein* is the earliest, but not the last, call by Welsh poets to throw off English oppression and assert 'the immemorial claims of the Britons to Britain'.[43]

The Llywarch Hen Poems

The latest of Skene's four manuscripts is the *Llyfr Coch Hergest* ('The Red Book of Hergest', Oxford, Jesus College MS 111), written somewhere between 1382 and 1408. A massive anthology of Welsh poetry, prose, prophecies, medical texts, and histories, the Red Book was commissioned by a nobleman, Hopcyn ap Tomas ab Einion of Ynysforgan, in south Wales, and mostly written by a scribe called Hywel Fychan.[44] Most of the texts can be dated somewhere between the twelfth and fourteenth centuries and include the prose tales of the *Mabinogion*, translations of the French Charlemagne legends, and a large corpus of poetry in the *awdl* metre.

Among this material is a group of earlier poems in the *englyn* metre that belong to the *hengerdd*, composed at various times between the eighth and tenth centuries and referring to a pre-Norman political context on the borders of Wales and England. Known as *englynion chwedlonol*, or 'saga *englynion*', these poems are thought to represent the surviving elements of one or more lost prose sagas recounting the adventures of Welsh heroes and their families in the struggles against the English on their borders in the eighth and ninth centuries. The Red Book contains the most complete extant collection of saga *englynion*, written into a section of the manuscript copied by its main scribe, Hywel Fychan.[45]

The Red Book saga *englynion* can be grouped into a number of related strands which seem to represent various lost prose tales. The most distinctive cycle, and the one which Ifor Williams used as a title for the whole set of *englynion*, is the story of Llywarch Hen ('the Old') and his sons, all of whom were killed in battle leaving Llywarch to mourn them and his own old age. Two of the sequences of stanzas concern Gwên, the youngest of Llywarch's twenty-four sons and the last one to die, who engages in a dialogue with his father about the nature of courage before he goes into battle. The poem captures brilliantly – and poignantly – the generational difference of attitude between father and son: while Llywarch insists on death rather than dishonour, Gwên defines honour more pragmatically. Though he cannot promise not to flee in the heat of battle, he declares he will not call for help by blowing on the horn given to him by the great hero Urien:

[LLYWARCH:]   Y corn ath rodes di vryen.
                ae arwest eur am y en.
                chwyth yndaw oth daw aghen.

[GWÊN:]   Yr ergryt aghen rac *angwyr* lloegyr
          ny lygraf vym mawred.
          ny duhunaf rianed.[46]

([LLYWARCH:]) The horn which Urien gave you
          with its band of gold around its mouthpiece –
          blow on it if you come to have need.

[GWÊN:]   Despite battle-horror before the warriors of
           England
          I will not mar my greatness.
          I will not awaken maidens.)

In the next sequence, Llywarch laments the death of Gwên and we learn that Gwên was as courageous in battle as Llywarch would ever have wished, outperforming the the deeds of his other sons:

      Gwen wrth lawen yd welas neithwyr
      [yr] athuc ny techas.
      oer adrawd ar glawd gorlas . . .

      . . . Gwen wrth lawen yd wyliis neithwyr
      ar ysgwyt ar y *gnis*.
      kan bu mab ymi [nyt egis] . . .

      . . . Pedwarmeib ar hugeint am bwyat.
      eurdorchawc tywyssawc cat.
      oed gwen goreu mab oe dat.[47]

      (Gwên by Llawen kept watch last night.
      Despite the onslaught he did not retreat.
      Sad is the tale on the green bank . . .

      . . . Gwên by Llawen kept watch last night
      with his shield against his chin.
      Since he was my son he did not escape . . .

      . . . I had twenty-four sons,
      a gold-wearing, princely troop.
      Gwên was the best of his father's sons.)

In the following sequences, Llywarch mourns his other sons, especially Pyll ('though both the host of England and many from afar might have come to Wales, Pyll would have taught them sense') and Maen, both given the epithet '[g]wyn' ('fair'). Not all the stanzas fit into a clear narrative, and it is likely that the cycle includes stanzas from other narrative strands inspired by the main story of Llywarch and his son Gwên.[48]

The references to Urien of Rheged in another sequence of verses recall the heroic poetry of Taliesin. While Taliesin described the battle feats of Urien and his son Owain, the Red Book *englynion* are mainly concerned with the death of Urien in battle, continuing the mood of mourning that dominates the entire collection. In some of the verses, a narrator laments the death of his lord, Urien, against whom he was obliged to fight in a factional conflict which set one group of British against another. Riding back from the battle, the narrator, on the winning side, carries with him the head of Urien, taken from the battlefield, and expresses his broken-hearted sorrow at the death of a man who was once his lord:

> Penn a borthaf yn aghat vy llaw.
> llary ud llywyei wlat.
> penn post prydein ry allat.
>
> Penn a borthaf am porthes.
> neut atwen nat yr vy lles.
> gwae vy llaw llym digones.[49]
>
> (I carry a head in the grasp of my hand
> of a generous lord – he used to lead a country.
> The chief support of Britain has been carried off.
>
> I carry a head which cared for me.
> I know it is not for my good.
> Alas, my hand, it performed harshly.)

Other verses describe the burial of Urien, the mourning of his sister Efrddyl, and miscellaneous memories of Urien's great leadership and prowess in battle. A final sequence provides a nostalgic description of the court of Urien and Owain, once a centre of warrior activity and now deserted and ruined: 'Many a lively hound and spirited hawk were fed on its floor before this place was ruins.'[50]

Like Urien, Llywarch Hen appears to have been a historical person, though less well-attested than Urien. Llywarch's name is found in genealogies of the sixth-century leaders of north Britain, descended from the same line as Urien, that is, from Coel, one of the dynastic ancestors of the kings of Gwynedd. The verse cycles about Llywarch and Urien are therefore consciously anachronistic, recreating a sixth-century world of brutal territorial battles among British and English warlords in the context of contemporary eighth- and ninth-century struggles of the Welsh in Powys with the Mercians on their borders.

A third cycle of *englynion*, known as 'Canu Heledd' ('The Song of Heledd'), has a more substantive narrative framework than the other two and is more clearly linked to a ninth-century political context in Powys. The implied narrative context of the verses concerns the death of Cynddylan, a historical ruler of Powys. A number of the verses seem to be in the voice of Cynddylan's sister Heledd, who laments the loss of her family and of Cynddylan's stronghold in Pengwern (part of the kingdom of Powys, now in modern Shropshire) in the mid-seventh century, when the Mercians expanded their borders to the north and west. In the view of Ifor Williams, the first scholarly editor of the Llywarch Hen cycle, this seventh-century context was refracted through a ninth-century lens at a time when the border was again in a state of violence caused by pressure from the Mercians.[51] However, Jenny Rowland has argued that the historical Cynddylan reigned in Powys before the events described in the verse cycle and that he was likely to have been allied with Penda of Mercia, not crushed by the Mercians as the Heledd verses suggest.[52] It is likely, then, that Canu Heledd is a fictional account based on past events, particularly the loss of Pengwern and the death of Cynddylan as a famous Powys king. Legends of the past have been recreated in the present as a vehicle for the expression of grief and loss in ninth-century Powys.

The figure of Heledd is described as the daughter of Cyndrwyn, known in historical sources as a member of one of the ruling dynasties of Powys in the seventh century. Like the character of Llywarch, Heledd is the last survivor of her family and the bulk of the verses are laments (in her own voice or that of other narrators) for the loss of Cynddylan and his siblings, along with mournful contemplations of the ruins of their courts, particularly that of Pengwern (supposedly located in the vicinity of modern Shrewsbury).[53] A sequence of sixteen verses, each beginning 'Stafell Cynddylan . . . ' ('the hall of Cynddylan . . .'), creates a remorseless rhythm of anguish for the fallen hero and what his death means for those left behind:

> Stauell gyndylan neut athwyt heb wed.
> mae ym bed dy yscwyt.
> hyt tra uu ny bu dollglwyt.
>
> Stauell gyndylan y *digarat* heno.
> gwedy yr neb pieuat.
> o wi a angheu byrr ym gat.[54]

(The hall of Cynddylan – you have become bereft of form.
Your shield is in the grave.
While he was alive there was not a broached gate.

The hall of Cynddylan is abandoned tonight
after he who owned it.
Oh death, why does it leave me behind?)

The loss of place is felt almost as acutely as the loss of family, and repeated images of destroyed towns and lands laid waste are witness statements to the very real aftermath of warfare among Welsh and English along the borders of Wales in the ninth century.

It is conventional to understand the Llywarch Hen *englynion* as they were first described by Ifor Williams, that is, as verse remnants of lost prose sagas of Wales (on the model of those Old Irish prose sagas which also contain extensive verse elements). The historicity of most of the characters suggests a background of legendary tales of former rulers and heroes, and the evidence of the Welsh Triads supports the likelihood that a large body of story material was once in circulation but is no longer extant. The verses are incontrovertibly spoken 'in character', that is, by a narrator who claims to have some personal connection with the events described, in contrast to more formal bardic praise poetry (invariably composed in the *awdl* rather than *englyn* metre).

However, it has to be admitted that attempts to reconstruct what might have been the original narratives surrounding the *englynion* are faltering at best and hamstrung by the impossibility of reconciling the various pieces of the jigsaw puzzle into coherent narratives. Assuming the *englynion* did originally form part of prose narratives, these are no longer within our reach. Alongside a certain proportion of linked verses suggestive of a narrative context, there are many others which appear to be random additions, later accretions, or independent compositions, which tend to work against the theory of 'saga poetry'.[55] Among the more obviously independent poems is the group of penitential stanzas which use images of the natural world to reflect on the difficulties of the human condition. In 'Claf Abercuawg' ('The Sick Man (or Leper) of Abercuawg', a modern title) the narrator speaks 'in character' as a warrior lord debilitated by illness, but there is no indication of his identity or a larger narrative framework:

Llem awel llwm benedyr byw.
pan orwisc coet teglyw
haf. teryd glaf wyf hediw.

Nyt wyf anhyet. milet ny chatwaf.
ny allaf darymret.
tra vo da gan goc canet.[56]

(Piercing is the wind; bare ? . . ..
When the woods put on the fair colour of summer.
I am ?feverishly ill today.

I am not active. I do not keep a host,
I cannot go about.
While it pleases the cuckoo let it sing.)

Another gnomic poem, 'Eiry Mynydd' ('Mountain Snow'), so named after its
opening phrase repeated in each of thirty-five stanzas, expresses the despair of
a man who knows he is too old to love or to fight, but again, there are no
clear connections between this 'character' and other story material:

Eiry mynyd, hyd ar dro;
chwerdyt bryt wrth a garo;
kyt dywetter wrthyf chwedyl,
mi a atwen veuyl lle y bo . . .

. . . Eiry mynyd, hyd mywn brwyn;
oer micned, med ygherwyn;
gnawt gan bob anauus gwyn.[57]

(Mountain snow, stag roaming.
The heart laughs at what it loves.
Though a tale be told to me,
I know disgrace wherever it be . . .

. . . Mountain snow, stag in rushes;
Marshes freezing, mead in cask.
Common for the injured to moan.)[58]

A close analogy to the tenuous narrative structure of the Llywarch Hen
poems is provided by the Myrddin (Merlin) verses which are found in the Red
Book and also in the Black Book of Carmarthen: though these *englynion*
clearly allude to known legends about Myrddin, it is difficult if not impossible
to shape these surviving *englynion* into a coherent narrative structure which
makes sense of all of them at the same time.[59] Similarly, many of the poems in
the Book of Taliesin are spoken 'in character' (by Taliesin or someone else)
but do not seem to be part of a narrative sequence. Other analogies can be
found further afield, in the lyric poetry of Old English for example, some of

which are in the form of poems spoken 'in character' but are not necessarily regarded as being part of lost sagas. Old English lyrics from the tenth-century Exeter Book, such as *The Wanderer, The Seafarer, The Wife's Lament, The Ruin,* and *Wulf and Eadwacer,* express emotions of longing and grief similar to those of the Welsh *englynion,* suggesting comparable literary traditions in pre-Norman England and Wales among societies shaped by a warrior elite, a plunder economy, a penitential religion, and a class of clerics familiar with classical Latin models of elegy and works such as Boethius's *De Consolatione Philosophiae.* Although the Old English poems have distinct narrative voices and contain some narrative detail, again like the Welsh, they are usually read as dramatic monologues drawing on a shared knowledge of existing legends and a particular view of providence and the afterlife.[60] It is not impossible to read the Welsh *englynion* in the same way; neither can we ignore the likely influences from Latin literary and philosophical traditions. The most that can be said is that the group of Llywarch Hen *englynion* call on an assumed knowledge of people and events from the British past which are remembered in a lyrical and fictionalized form. It is certainly possible to imagine the *englynion* being sung or recited as stand-alone pieces, rich with allusion to a shared cultural history, in the manner of eighteenth-century ballads.

Perhaps the most obvious feature of the *englynion,* and one which unifies them as a group, is their very explicit use of emotion to animate and propel the verses, in striking contrast to the naturalistic style of the surviving Welsh prose narratives and in contrast to the more contrived rhetoric of bardic poetry. Grief for the loss of a child, despair at the powerlessness of advancing age, pride in past achievements, the horror of large-scale death in battle, the pain of conflicting loyalties, nostalgia for lost places – these emotions, expressed simply and directly by various narrators, are the actual subjects of the poetry, not so much the people or the events themselves. While the surviving prose narratives of Wales build chains of action in a largely chronological sequence, implying causation through juxtaposition, the *englynion* alternate continuously between past and present, using emotion to manage memories of trauma and construct emotional communities of the victims of territorial war. Unlike bardic poetry such as *Y Gododdin,* with its socialized emotions conveying the formal and masculinist response to the death of heroes as something to celebrate, the *englynion* imagine the possibility that other kinds of emotion might be equally appropriate. Through each narrator, whose 'character' is defined by their suffering, the uninhibited expression of negative emotions is presented as a legitimate and necessary response to the destruction of a social order. Yet these emotions are, nevertheless, neither universal nor uniquely individual but a product of their social context. In their emotional honesty, the poems acknowledge a truth not mentioned by Taliesin or Aneirin, that territorial war – the very political and economic basis of the early medieval order – incurs a personal cost to humanity, male and female, high and low, that not even the grace of God can mitigate.

Notes

1. Some of the early Welsh texts in Skene's edition had already appeared in print, in the large anthology called *Myvyrian Archaiology of Wales*, ed. Owen Jones, Edward Williams [Iolo Morganwg], and William Owen Pughe, 3 vols. (London, 1801–7), though this work is less reliable than that of Skene.

2. The term 'emotional community' comes from an article by Barbara Rosenwein, who defines it as a social community which shares 'systems of feeling'. See Barbara H. Rosenwein, 'Worrying about Emotions in History', *American Historical Review* 107, 3 (June 2002): 821–45, especially p. 842; and her more recent book, *Emotional Communities in the Early Middle Ages* (Ithaca, NY: Cornell University Press, 2006), 23–5.

3. Attributed to a monk, Nennius, the *Historia Brittonum* remains a major source for early British history and its cultural traditions, including Arthurian folk legends. For the Latin text and English translation, see *Nennius, British History and the Welsh Annals*, ed. and trans. J. Morris, History from the Sources: Arthurian Period Sources 8 (London: Phillimore, 1980). For an authoritative study of the text, see Thomas Charles-Edwards, *Wales and the Britons, 350–1064* (Oxford: Oxford University Press, 2012), 437–67.

4. For a survey of Latin literature in Wales, see Patrick Sims-Williams, 'The Uses of Writing in Early Medieval Wales', in *Literacy in Medieval Celtic Societies*, ed. Huw Pryce (Cambridge: Cambridge University Press, 1998), 15–38. See also Michael Lapidge and Richard Sharpe, *A Bibliography of Celtic-Latin Literature 400–1200* (Dublin: Royal Irish Academy, 1985).

5. Ceri Davies, *Welsh Literature and the Classical Tradition* (Cardiff: University of Wales Press, 1995), 9.

6. Ibid., 16; Michael Lapidge, 'The Welsh-Latin Poetry of Sulien's Family', *Studia Celtica* 8–9 (1973–4): 68–106; Sarah Zeiser, 'Bragmaticus omnibus Brittonibus: David, Sulien, and an Ecclesiastical Dynasty in Conquest-Era Wales', *Proceedings of the Harvard Celtic Colloquium* 31 (2011): 305–20; Sarah Zeiser, 'Latinity, Manuscripts, and the Rhetoric of Conquest in Late Eleventh-Century Wales' (PhD diss., Harvard University, 2012).

7. Sims-Williams, 'Uses of Writing', 23.

8. *The Text of the Book of Llan Dâv*, ed. J. Gwenogvryn Evans (Aberystwyth: National Library of Wales, 1979). See Wendy Davies, *An Early Welsh Microcosm: Studies in the Llandaff Charters* (London: Royal Historical Society, 1978); John Reuben Davies, *The Book of Llandaf and the Norman Church in Wales* (Woodbridge: Boydell and Brewer, 2003).

9. Dafydd Jenkins and Morfydd E. Owen, 'The Welsh Marginalia in the Lichfield Gospels. Part I', *CMCS* 5 (1983): 37–66; 'Part II: The Surrexit Memorandum', *CMCS* 7 (1984): 91–120.

10. Ifor Williams, 'The Computus Fragment', *BBCS* 3 (1926–7): 245–72.

11. The verses have been edited by Helen McKee, *The Cambridge Juvencus Manuscript glossed in Latin, Old Welsh, and Old Irish: Text and Commentary* (Aberystwyth: CMCS Publications, 2000); see also Helen McKee, 'Scribes and Glosses from Dark Age Wales: The Cambridge Juvencus Manuscript', *CMCS* 39 (2000): 1–22. The manuscript is available online: 'Cambridge Juvencus', http://cudl.lib.cam.ac.uk/view/MS-FF-00004–00042/1 (accessed 17 August 2017).

12. The manuscript is available online: 'Black Book of Carmarthen', www.llgc.org.uk/blackbook (accessed 17 August 2017).

13. The poetry in the Black Book has been edited in Welsh by A. O. H. Jarman, *Llyfr Du Caerfyrddin* (Caerdydd: Gwasg Prifysgol Cymru, 1991). For a description of the manuscript and its contents, see Jarman, '*Llyfr Du Caerfyrddin*: The Black Book of Carmarthen', *Proceedings of the British Academy* 71 (1986): 333–56; Daniel Huws, *Medieval Welsh Manuscripts* (Cardiff: University of Wales Press, 2000), 70–2. For discussions of the early Arthurian and Myrddin poems, see Rachel Bromwich, A. O. H. Jarman, and Brynley F. Roberts, eds., *The Arthur of the Welsh: The Arthurian Legend in Medieval Welsh Literature* (Cardiff: University of Wales Press, 1991). The poetry of the Black Book has been translated by John K. Bollard, 'Myrddin in Early Welsh Tradition', in *The Romance of Merlin: An Anthology*, ed. Peter Goodrich (New York: Garland, 1990), 13–54.

14. For the text and translation, see John K. Bollard, ed. and trans., and Anthony Griffiths, photographer, *Englynion y Beddau: The Stanzas of the Graves* (Llanrwst: Gwasg Carreg Gwalch, 2015). On the significance of the stanzas, see Thomas Jones, 'The Black Book of Carmarthen "Stanzas of the Graves"', *Proceedings of the British Academy* 53 (1967): 97–137.

15. The *englyn* sequence, 'Gereint Fil' Erbin', is edited in Jarman, *Llyfr Du Caerfyrddin*, 48–9, and translated by Joseph P. Clancy, *Medieval Welsh Poems* (Dublin: Four Courts Press, 2003), 107–8.

16. On the tradition of the 'two Merlins' described by Geoffrey of Monmouth – the boy prophet in the *Historia Regum Britanniae* and the northern warrior in *Vita Merlini* – whom Gerald of Wales named Merlinus Ambrosius (W. Myrddin Emrys) and Merlinus Sylvester (W. Myrddin Wyllt, 'the wild')

respectively, see Oliver J. Padel, 'Geoffrey of Monmouth and the Development of the Merlin Legend', *CMCS* 51 (2006): 37–65; *Trioedd Ynys Prydein: The Triads of the Island of Britain*, ed. and trans. Rachel Bromwich, 4th edn (Cardiff: University of Wales Press, 2014), 458–62.

17. The manuscript has been printed in facsimile, *Llyfr Aneirin: Facsimile*, ed. Daniel Huws (Aberystwyth: Llyfrgell Genedlaethol Cymru, 1989). The manuscript is also available online: 'Llyfr Aneirin', www.llgc.org.uk/book ofaneirin (accessed 17 August 2017).

18. For modern editions of the poem, see *Aneirin: Y Gododdin*, ed. and trans. A. O. H. Jarman (Llandysul: Gomer Press, 1988); and *The Gododdin of Aneirin: Text and Context from Dark-Age North Britain*, ed. and trans. John T. Koch (Cardiff: University of Wales Press, 1997). Other important editions are *Canu Aneirin*, ed. Ifor Williams (Caerdydd: Gwasg Prifysgol Cymru, 1938), the first scholarly edition of the poetry in Welsh only; and *The Gododdin: The Oldest Scottish Poem*, trans. K. H. Jackson (Edinburgh: Edinburgh University Press, 1969), which provides an annotated translation of the poem without the original Welsh. For a description of the manuscript, see Huws, *Medieval Welsh Manuscripts*, 72–7. A translation of the A and B versions of *Y Gododdin* in the order of the manuscript has been made by Joseph P. Clancy in *The Triumph Tree: Scotland's Earliest Poetry AD 550–1350*, ed. T. O. Clancy (Edinburgh: Canongate, 1999) and with revisions in Clancy, trans., *Medieval Welsh Poems*, 45–76.

19. John Koch's edition of the poem attempts to reconstruct what is likely to have been its earliest written form in Archaic Neo-Brittonic of the mid-seventh century. For a comprehensive evaluation of linguistic aspects of dating early Welsh poetry, see Patrick Sims-Williams, 'Dating the Poems of Aneirin and Taliesin', *Zeitschrift für Celtische Philologie* 63 (2016): 163–234.

20. Though *Y Gododdin* is treated by most editors and translators as a single poem, with variants, accretions, and unrelated material attached to it, nothing in the manuscript points conclusively to this. The difficulty in knowing exactly how to retrieve the poems from the manuscript (i.e. how to, and whether to, combine the various poems into one or more larger texts) has exercised many critics, most trenchantly Brendan O Hehir in his article 'What Is the *Gododdin*?', in *Early Welsh Poetry: Studies in the Book of Aneirin*, ed. Brynley F. Roberts (Aberystwyth: National Library of Wales, 1988), 57–97.

21. These figures are calculated from the edition of the poem by Jarman. Scribe A copied about 88 stanzas and Scribe B about 42 stanzas. There are in addition a small number of interpolated stanzas that belong to other traditions.

22. An entry in the Irish annals records 'the siege of Etin' in AD 638, taken by some historians to mark the final stage in the conquest of Gododdin by King Oswald of Northumbria, though this is not certain. See David N. Dumville,

'The Origins of Northumbria: Some Aspects of the British Background', in *The Origins of Anglo-Saxon Kingdoms*, ed. Steven Bassett (Leicester: Leicester University Press, 1989), 213–22.

23. *Aneirin: Y Gododdin*, ed. and trans. Jarman, stanzas 59–61.

24. This historical context is proposed in detail by Jackson, *The Gododdin: The Oldest Scottish Poem*, 3–13, and *Aneirin: Y Gododdin*, ed. and trans. Jarman, xvii–xxiv.

25. An alternative date for the battle of *c.* 540 was proposed by David Dumville, though his main argument is that there is too little evidence to establish a date with any reliability. See 'Early Welsh Poetry: Problems of Historicity', in *Early Welsh Poetry*, ed. Roberts, 1–16, and further comments by Koch, ed. and trans., *The Gododdin of Aneirin*, xvii–xviii. On the historical background more generally, see Charles-Edwards, *Wales and the Britons*, 365–78.

26. See Thomas O. Clancy, 'The Kingdoms of the North: Poetry, Places, Politics', in *Beyond the Gododdin: Dark Age Scotland in Medieval Wales*, ed. A. Woolf (St Andrews: Committee for Dark Age Studies, University of St Andrews, 2013), 153–76, especially p. 163.

27. Text and translation from *Aneirin: Y Gododdin*, ed Jarman, 6–7.

28. Philip Dunshea, 'The Meaning of *Catraeth*: A Revised Early Context for *Y Gododdin*', in *Beyond the Gododdin*, ed. Woolf, 81–114.

29. An extraneous stanza in the manuscript refers to a different battle, one at Strathcarron, which can be dated to 642. The Strathcarron stanza is likely to be contemporary with the battle, indicating the way in which the text developed by accretion over time and its likely path of transmission around northern Britain before coming to Wales. See Charles-Edwards, *Wales and the Britons*, 367–70; *The Triumph Tree*, ed. Clancy, 114.

30. *The Gododdin of Aneirin*, ed. and trans. Koch, lxxxix–xc. See also Thomas Charles-Edwards, 'The Authenticity of the Gododdin: An Historian's View', in *Astudiaethau ar yr Hengerdd, Studies in Old Welsh Poetry*, ed. R. Bromwich and R. B. Jones (Cardiff: University of Wales Press, 1978), 44–71.

31. *The Gododdin of Aneirin*, ed. and trans. Koch, cvii–cx. Koch divides the B-text into later (B^1) and earlier (B^2) recensions. See his stemma of recensions on p. lxxi.

32. The relevant passage from *Historia Brittonum* can be found in *Nennius: British History and the Welsh Annals*, ed. and trans. J. Morris, History from the Sources: Arthurian Period Sources 8 (London: Phillimore, 1980), section 62. See also the discussion in *The Gododdin of Aneirin*, ed. and trans. Koch, cx–cxi.

33. For a full account of the manuscript, see *Legendary Poems from the Book of Taliesin*, ed. and trans. Marged Haycock, 2nd edn (Aberystwyth: CMCS Publications, 2015), 1–9, and the conspectus on 558–9. See also Haycock's edition of religious verse from the Book of Taliesin, *Blodeugerdd Barddas o Ganu Crefyddol Cynnar* (Cyhoeddiadau Barddas, 1994) and her edition and translation of the prophecies, *Prophecies from the Book of Taliesin* (Aberystwyth: CMCS Publications, 2013). A digitized version of the

manuscript is available via the website of the National Library of Wales, 'Llyfr Taliesin', www.llgc.org.uk/bookoftaliesin (accessed 17 August 2017).

34. Not all the surviving material about Taliesin, or written in his voice, appears in the Book of Taliesin: for example, the dialogue between Myrddin and Taliesin which appears in the Black Book of Carmarthen is not included in the Book of Taliesin. Haycock has suggested that some of the legendary poems are relatively late and that, in view of some striking linguistic similarities, they may in fact have been composed by one of the *gogynfeirdd*, Prydydd y Moch (*fl. c.* 1174/5–*c.* 1220). See *Legendary Poems*, ed. and trans. Haycock, 27–36.

35. Charles-Edwards, *Wales and the Britons*, 378–80.

36. *Legendary Poems*, ed. and trans. Haycock, 558–9.

37. *The Poems of Taliesin*, ed. Ifor Williams and trans. J. E. Caerwyn Williams (Dublin: Dublin Institute for Advanced Studies, 1968). Most of the 'authentic' poems have been translated by Joseph P. Clancy in *The Triumph Tree*, ed. T. O. Clancy, and in *Medieval Welsh Poems*, 39–44. On the poem to Cynan Garwyn and the historical context see Patrick Sims-Williams, 'Powys and Early Welsh Poetry', *CMCS* 67 (2014): 33–54, and Marged Haycock, 'Living with War: Poets and the Welsh Experience, *c.* 600–1300', in *Kings and Warriors in Early North-West Europe*, ed. Jan-Erik Rekdal and Charles Doherty (Dublin: Four Courts Press, 2016), 24–87.

38. Williams and Williams, *The Poems of Taliesin*, 6–7 (no. VI).

39. Clancy, trans., *Medieval Welsh Poems*, 42–3. The last four lines form a coda which is also attached to the other poems to Urien.

40. The suggestion that 'Fflamddwyn' might refer to Theodric was made by William Forbes Skene himself in *The Four Ancient Books of Wales* (Edinburgh: Edmonston and Douglas, 1868), vol. I, 232. For further comments on the name, see *Trioedd Ynys Prydein*, ed. and trans. Bromwich, 353. Fflamddwyn is generally assumed to be English, though Thomas O. Clancy sounds a note of caution on this ('Kingdoms of the North', 174, n. 57).

41. *Armes Prydein: The Prophecy of Britain*, ed. Ifor Williams, trans. Rachel Bromwich (Dublin: Dublin Institute for Advanced Studies, 1972), ll. 28–9 and ll. 54–61. The translation given here is by Clancy, *Medieval Welsh Poems*, p. 116.

42. Thomas Charles-Edwards suggests that *Armes Prydein* may have been composed by a poet from Gwynedd in about 939, and that its political purpose was to reject English lordship (and those Welsh princes who supported the English) in support of the anti-English Viking leader, Olaf Guthfrithsson of Dublin. See *Wales and the Britons*, 519–35.

43. Ibid., 535.

44. The Red Book has been described by Huws, *Medieval Welsh Manuscripts*, 79–83. See also Chapter 7 in this volume.

45. The saga *englynion* were edited in Welsh by Ifor Williams, *Canu Llywarch Hen* (Caerdydd: Gwasg Prifysgol Cymru, 1935, repr. 1990). The standard edition is now that of Jenny Rowland, ed. and trans., *Early Welsh Saga Poetry: A Study and Edition of the* Englynion (Cambridge: D. S. Brewer, 1990). See also *A Selection of Early Welsh Saga Poems*, ed. Jenny Rowland (London: Modern Humanities Research Association, 2014); and Clancy, trans., *Medieval Welsh Poems*.

46. Rowland, ed. and trans., *Early Welsh Saga Poetry*, 405 and 469. For a detailed reading of the poem, see Charles-Edwards, *Wales and the Britons*, 668–74.

47. Rowland, ed. and trans., *Early Welsh Saga Poetry*, 406–8 and 469–70.

48. Rowland distinguishes between those poems to Llywarch's sons which are 'full poems with a narrative purpose' and later 'antiquarian listing poems' in which the names of the sons are listed together in groups (ibid., 39).

49. Ibid., 421 and 478.

50. Ibid., 481, verse 48; Welsh text, 426.

51. Williams, *Canu Llywarch Hen*, lxxiii–iv. For an account of the relations between English and Welsh in this period, see Charles-Edwards, *Wales and the Britons*, 419–28.

52. Rowland, ed. and trans., *Early Welsh Saga Poetry*, 125–36. See also John T. Koch, *Cunedda, Cynan, Cadwallon, Cynddylan: Four Welsh Poems and Britain 383–655* (Aberystwyth: Centre for Advanced Welsh and Celtic Studies, 2013).

53. The story of Heledd has been discussed by Marged Haycock, 'Hanes Heledd Hyd Yma', in *Gweledigaethau: Cyfrol Deyrnged yr Athro Gwyn Thomas*, ed. Jason Walford Davies (Cyhoeddiadau Barddas, 2007), 29–60. On the wider folk-tale elements, see Andrew Welsh, 'Branwen, Beowulf, and the Tragic Peaceweaver Tale', *Viator* 22 (1991): 1–13.

54. Rowland, ed., and trans., *Early Welsh Saga Poetry*, 432 and 485.

55. Such difficulties led Patrick Ford, in his edition and translation of the Llywarch Hen cycle, to argue that the *englynion* were not the remnants of prose sagas but rather individual poems of generic types, such as elegies, praise poems, and gnomic poems. See *The Poetry of Llywarch Hen*, ed. and trans. Patrick K. Ford (Berkeley: University of California Press, 1974); for Rowland's counter-arguments, see *Early Welsh Saga Poems*, 8–11.

56. Rowland, ed. and trans., *Early Welsh Saga Poetry*, 448 and 497. See also Rowland's discussion of the poem, 190–200.

57. Nicolas Jacobs, ed., *Early Welsh Gnomic and Nature Poetry* (London: Modern Humanities Research Association, 2012), no. II, stanzas 6 and 15.

58. Clancy, trans., *Medieval Welsh Poems*, 111–12.

59. See also Jarman, 'The Merlin Legend and the Welsh Tradition of Prophecy', in *The Arthur of the Welsh*, ed. Bromwich *et al.*, 117–45. It is striking that the name Llallawg and its diminutive Llallogan, the 'Lailoken' of the Myrddin legend, occur in the Llywarch Hen sequence (Rowland, ed. and trans., *Early*

Welsh Saga Poetry, 415, verses 7 and 8, translation at 474), one of a number of cross-story allusions in the *englynion* that work against the theory of self-contained sagas.

60. On the Old English elegies, see Andy Orchard, 'Not What it Was: The World of the Old English Elegy', in *The Oxford Handbook of the Elegy*, ed. Andy Orchard and Karen Weisman (Oxford: Oxford University Press, 2010), 101–17. On connections between Old English and Welsh lyrics, see P. L. Henry, *The Early English and Celtic Lyric* (London: Allen and Unwin, 1966); Sarah Higley, *Between Languages: The Uncooperative Text in Early Welsh and Old English Nature Poetry* (University Park, PA: Pennsylvania State University Press, 1993, repr. 2010).

3

Magic and Marvels

MARK WILLIAMS

The supernatural has long coloured the Wales of the imagination. Stirred by Wales's linguistic difference and dramatic landscape, many writers in English have projected supernatural allurements and terrors onto an imagined version of the country.[1]

This association has licensed both fascination and dismissal. The most famous example is provided by Matthew Arnold, who coined the phrase Celtic 'natural magic' in his 1867 publication, *On the Study of Celtic Literature*, the influence of which was in inverse proportion to its author's actual expertise. By this phrase Arnold actually meant a supposedly 'Celtic' gift for depicting nature with a sense of pristine force, but later writers picked the concept up and applied it to the wealth of fantastical incident in medieval Welsh and Irish literature, intensifying the stereotype of the 'mystical' Celt.[2] This last had a dubious racial dimension too in that the 'Celt', barely competent to govern his own affairs, was typically contrasted with the stolid, practical 'Teuton', natural wielder of imperial power. Followers of Arnold located the value of the medieval literature of Wales (and Ireland) in the fantastical, but, like him, they saw those literatures as fugitive from narrative logic and authorial control.

All this might be put down to the condescension of an imperial state towards its oldest colony, but an air of Celtic 'unreason' has continued to attach to critical discussions of the supernatural in Welsh literature, which to this day are notable for a lack of conceptual precision. To take a common example, a certain strand of magic in French and English romance is sometimes said to be 'Celtic' in origin: Corinne Saunders argues that such romance is 'coloured by the characteristic style of Celtic poetry', pigeonholed as 'dream-like and irrational'.[3] And yet that very quality is not well understood, even in relation to Welsh literature itself. The upshot is that we still await a thorough investigation of what Welsh writers of the Middle Ages were doing when they brought supernatural wonders into their texts, and it would be desirable for Celtic scholars (that is, scholars studying the Celtic languages and their written records) to attempt the kinds of sophisticated studies of the magical and marvellous which have been done for English and French medieval literature, shaking off Arnold's ghost.[4] Some potential lines of investigation are outlined towards the end of this chapter.

Magic Between Fiction and Reality

In general it may be said that Welsh supernaturalism has both points of contact with and intriguing differences from the magical in other medieval literatures.[5] Fruitful work has recently been done on the complex relationship between literary and historical magic, emphasizing that, as a perennial dimension of human culture, medieval people saw magic as a dubious force, characteristically opposed to the licit power of miracles, which were the province of God and the saints. 'Natural' magic – which involved knowledge of herbs and stones and the movement of the heavenly bodies – was potentially allowable, though the border between it and demonic magic – which was thought to depend on the agency of evil spirits – was not always clear.[6] Behind all of it lay the occult sciences of alchemy, astrology, and evocation which were transmitted to western Europe from Arabic sources from the eleventh century onwards.

In contrast to some other European lands, it is not straightforward to compare fictional and historical magic in Wales. The difficulty is that our evidence for practical conjuring is late (largely post-Reformation), while the most spectacular instances of magic in the literature are all essentially early (high medieval). A good example of the former is the early modern manuscript Aberystwyth, National Library of Wales MS Peniarth 171, in mixed English and Welsh, which details magical practices of the kind standard across Europe; it shows that some Welshmen in the seventeenth and eighteenth centuries were well aware of classic texts on hermetic thought such as Heinrich Cornelius Agrippa's *Three Books of Occult Philosophy*. Such late texts give us little insight into the practical magic of the medieval period, and this is confirmed by Richard Suggett's survey of references in Welsh to magical practitioners from the sixteenth century onward. He notes that the evidence suggests that the structure of popular occult categories was changing at the time, visible in the importation of English loanwords such as *wits* ('witch').[7] Medieval conventions about magic and the real-life individuals who practised it were clearly being superseded. We can only catch glimpses of such persons: it seems, for example, that medieval Welsh courts had people who performed magic tricks, as we know English and French ones did. The *Trioedd Cerdd*, for example, refer to the 'magician' (*hudol*) as one of the three kinds of lower-status 'scurrilous poets', and this almost certainly refers to the kind of person known in English as a 'juggler' or 'tregetour' ('illusionist').[8] They were clearly not of high status.

One thing which does seem clear, and to have a distinctly Welsh dimension, is that the supernatural was closely associated with persons thought to be capable of foretelling the future or offering supernatural insight into the present, and that these individuals were themselves associated with the professional poets.[9] Marged Haycock has demonstrated how rich the vocabulary was in this sphere, and how widely spread out in time.[10] From the Old Welsh period, there is some suggestive early terminology for those who made prognostications and prophecies. The early political prophecy *Armes Prydein* ('The Prophecy of Britain'), written *c.* 930, instructs its readers to rely on the authority of its vision of the future and to avoid the *llyfrawr*. This might be an archaic plural of *llyfr* (book), but more likely represents a borrowing of Latin *librarius* (copyist), which is widely attested with the extended meaning 'one who possesses occult knowledge derived from books, a sage, soothsayer'.[11] Tellingly, the *llyfrawr* is paired in the same line with the 'greedy poet', suggesting an early link between the native tradition of prophetic poetry and those who possessed occult insights derived from books. Another glimpse of learned prophetic personnel – also operating somewhere between poetry and magic – is afforded by the term *sywedydd* (learned soothsayer, augur); this could refer to the canonical learning of a saint but was used more often to imply prognosticatory ability, as was *dewin*, from Latin *divinus*, which came to imply seership.[12] There were other native terms such as *darogenydd*, used to refer to practitioners skilled in the prophetic poetry which formed a popular and prominent sub-genre in the later Middle Ages; from the fifteenth century there is evidence that some Welsh learned poets had become familiar with astrology and were prepared to allude to it in verse.

All this suggests that, to the extent that the typically male tradition of learned magic was found in medieval Wales, it was focused through the prophetic function of the learned poets. There are hints, however, of divinatory activities taking place lower down the social scale: this presumably is the context of Gerald of Wales's famous twelfth-century anecdote about *awenyddion* (inspired ones) – consultant diviners who prophesied in a seizure-like trance in response to their questioners, and whose dark meanings had to be pieced together by those who listened to them.[13] Strikingly, Gerald himself is prepared, after some debate, to attribute the powers of *awenyddion* to divine grace.

Such other pieces of evidence as there are belong to the realm of folktale, and these shed an uncertain light at best on actual practice. A classic example of the latter is Walter Map's story in *De nugis curialium* of the ghost of a Welsh *maleficus* – a 'wizard' or 'sorcerer' – which carries on committing murder by black magic after his death until finally destroyed by an English knight.[14] The anecdote may hint at English stereotyping of the Welsh as preoccupied by and proficient in magic – it is common across Europe to find that lowland dwellers suspect the inhabitants of mountainous, less fertile areas nearby of witchcraft – but it tells us nothing about historical practice. This general dearth of early evidence contrasts sharply with the spectacular prominence of the supernatural in early Welsh literature, where it intersects with the demonic, otherworldly, and divine; it is to a brief survey of the terminology pertaining to these that we now turn.

First, what distinction is to be drawn between magic and the other term in the chapter title, 'marvel'? Briefly, a marvel is something *seen*: the term derives from Latin *mirabilium*, itself derived from verbs of looking on in wonder. It is something mysterious that appears before the eye, beyond the norm of experience, certainly, but potentially perfectly natural.[15] The marvel, in this sense, simultaneously poses a hermeneutic problem and offers its solution. Magic, on the other hand, must by its nature be supernatural, and characteristically it eludes or tricks the eye; it is frequently something one sees which is not really there or which possesses only a shadowy or evanescent existence, and which is potentially demonic. Both magic and marvel are distinct from a third term, *miraculum*, the miracle, which is a manifestation of the power of God.

It is worth asking at the outset whether these two ideas map onto native concepts. *Mirabilium*, as we shall see later in this chapter, does indeed occur in a Cambro-Latin context. But for native terminology, we have to turn to the greatest work of medieval Welsh prose, the Four Branches of the *Mabinogi*.[16] In the First Branch, *Pwyll Pendeuic Dyuet* ('Pwyll Prince of Dyfed'), the hero Pwyll goes to sit upon the mysterious *gorsedd Arberth*, a mound which bestows upon any nobleman sitting there one of two things: 'either his receiving of blows, or else he would see a wonder' (*a'y ymriw neu archolleu, neu ynteu a welei rywedawt*).[17] The phrasing underlines that Middle Welsh *rywedawt* (Mod. W. *rhyfeddod*), 'prodigy, marvel, singularity', is here explicitly *something seen* in the same way as Latin *mirabilium*, though the word's actual etymology denotes overwhelming potency.

Pwyll has wonders aplenty: he immediately sees the beautiful Rhiannon, who becomes his wife, riding by the mound. (One wonders who would have inflicted the 'blows' had Pwyll had worse luck.) Rhiannon's horse seems to be uncatchable, and at this point, as soon as Pwyll ceases to watch and tries to intervene, marvel crucially modulates into magic. Pwyll says: 'There is some magic significance there' (*y mae yno ryw ystyr hut*), using one of the two classic terms for magic in Welsh.[18] This noun, *hud* (MW *hut*), is often collocated with another, *lledrith* (in MW usually *lleturith*), and together they denote the memorable literary magic associated with the semi-mythological characters of the Four Branches, and often with other figures, especially in the work of the *cywyddwyr*, the court poets of the Welsh gentry.

Both terms are etymologically significant. *Hud* (with its associated verb *hudaw*, 'to enchant') has no Irish cognate but is distantly related to the Norse word *seiðr*, apparently a type of magic particularly associated with women. *Lled(f)rith*, on the other hand, is less mysterious but more complex. The second element is an otherwise unattested **brith*, cognate with Irish *bricht* (spell, enchantment), while the first – not apparently altering the meaning greatly – is *lled* (semi-, rather).[19] The two words, whatever may have been any original distinctions in meaning, are effectively synonyms. As the *-f-* was often lost, a third term probably influenced the semantic range of *lled(f)rith*: this was *rhith*, 'shape, form', regularly used in the Four Branches and elsewhere for the outer appearance of an object or person manipulated by magic. (The related verb *rhithyaw* denotes precisely that action.) We will encounter all these terms again in the next section.

Arthurian Wonders

Marvels per se enter Welsh literature with the ninth-century *Historia Brittonum*, which concludes with a section listing *mirabilia* in three groups, those of Britain, Anglesey, and Ireland. They are basically topographical: eye-catching examples include the altar of St Illtud, which supposedly floated in the air, the hot springs of Bath, and the sixty islands of Loch Lomond, each with an eagle's nest. (Note that the last two are awe-inspiring and mysterious, but not supernatural.) The *Historia* is originally the work of a Welsh-speaking cleric based in Gwynedd and writing in Latin in 829–830, though it survives in successive versions; the *mirabilia* section is found in only two of these. It provides a compressed history of the Britons as a people and of an already remote past. The *mirabilia* section, however, is strikingly oriented towards south Wales and adjacent border country, in a manner that suggests access to local knowledge of this area on the part of the author; some of the marvels seem suggestively connected to the world of *Culhwch ac Olwen*, the oldest work of Arthurian prose, perhaps composed in the middle of the eleventh century and also a southern work. Two of the British marvels in the *Historia* are specifically Arthurian: the first is *Carn Cabal*, a cairn of stones bearing the paw-print of Arthur's dog Cafal; the other is the Grave of Amr, Arthur's son, the dimensions of which mysteriously fluctuate. All this strongly suggests the presence of a rich body of local onomastic folklore, in which significant features in the landscape came to be associated with the figures of a legendary past.

More difficult instances of the magical and marvellous are to be found in the so-called early Arthurian poems. Two of these – the most substantial – are important for our purposes: both are clearly non-historical and of uncertain date, being preserved in later manuscripts. One, known as *Pa gur* from its first line (*Pa gur yv y porthaur*, 'what man is the gatekeeper?') survives in the thirteenth-century *Llyfr Du Caerfyrddin* ('The Black Book of Carmarthen'); the other, *Preiddeu Annwn* ('The Spoils of Annwn', that is, of the Otherworld) is preserved in Aberystwyth, National Library of Wales MS Peniarth 2, the so-called Book of Taliesin, which dates from the first quarter of the fourteenth century. The dating of Welsh verse on linguistic grounds is not as yet a precise science, and *c.* 1150 is normally offered as a cut-off date by which these poems must have been composed; technically this would allow for the influence of Geoffrey of Monmouth's *Historia Regum Britanniae* (*c.* 1138) on the poems, but there are no convincing signs of this, and they may in fact be very much older, perhaps dating back to the early 900s, or even earlier.[20]

The scenario of *Pa gur yv y porthaur* is one well attested in Welsh and Irish literature: the difficult gatekeeper who prevents or challenges individuals who want to enter a hostile stronghold, in this case Arthur and 'the best men in the world', who are attempting to enter the fortress of one Awarnach.[21] Arthur's companions are an eclectic group of human beings apparently augmented by magical powers and peculiarities. One, named Anguas (Mod. W. *Anwas*) is termed *edeinawc* (the winged); while this might be a reference to supernatural speed, it could equally have been intended to be taken literally. Another of Arthur's companions is Cai, termed 'Cai the Fair' (*Cei guin*) and 'the Tall' (*hir*). Oddly, he is given no special abilities in *Pa gur*, but from later sources we know that he was supposed to have possessed the ability to generate great natural heat, to go without sleep and hold his breath under water for nine days and nights, and to make himself as tall as a large tree when he so desired.[22]

The wrangling dialogue between Arthur and the intractable porter hints at a legendary (and basically northern British) landscape populated by non-human or semi-human creatures: the poem is set in a world of heroic adventure in which both good and hostile parties possess supernatural attributes. In a telling moment, we learn that Arthur (or Cai) has been fighting 'dog-heads' (cinbin) in Edinburgh: these presumably are a local version of the cynocephali who had been a classic feature of European lore about 'monstrous races' since the ancient world.[23] It is striking that even in this early source the peopling of the landscape of Britain with supernatural creatures clearly owed at least as much to the international culture of Latin learning as it did to some supposedly Celtic past. The nineteenth-century notion of a specifically Celtic supernaturalism is strongly undercut by evidence such as this for the naturalization of international ideas in Welsh (and Irish) literature.

Similarly striking is the mention of mysterious hostile women in the poem, of whom Cai is said to have slain nine. The word used here is guiton (Mod. W. gwiddon), and though this now means 'witch', it may be misleading to translate it so in a medieval context, for these women appear to be Amazons rather than workers of spells. They are a classic example of the lack of precision already lamented: a comparative analysis of the 'warrior witch' theme in Welsh and Irish literature is earnestly to be desired, for the idea is a relatively common one within those two literatures but is strikingly unlike the usual depiction of the witch outside them.[24] The number nine seems to be significant: in the tale of Peredur vab Efrawc ('Peredur son of Efrog'), one of the three continental-style romances in the collection known today as the Mabinogion, the hero also fights the nine witches of Gloucester (naw gwidon ... Kaer Loyw); nine witches also appear in the seventh-century Breton Latin Life of Saint Samson, which presumably either reflects a still older insular tradition or was itself the original source for this curious theme.[25]

The theme of nine women brings us to our other early Arthurian poem, Preiddeu Annwn, in which we hear of an otherworldly cauldron warmed by the breath of nine maidens.[26] This is one of the most atmospheric but also elliptical of all medieval Welsh poems; the name means 'The Spoils of the Otherworld' (or 'Inworld', or 'Un-world'), and it depicts a disastrous raiding adventure made over the sea by Arthur and his followers upon a series of seven mysterious fortresses. The poem's most recent editor and translator, Marged Haycock, notes that it provides a 'glittering kaleidoscopic view of the Otherworld', but its supernatural sights tend to be as opaque as they are evocative. To choose a representative example, of one otherworldly fortress, *Caer Rigor*, we hear the following:

> Echwyd a muchyd kymyscetor;
> gwin gloyw eu gwirawt rac eu gosgor[27]

(Fresh water and jet are mixed together;
Sparkling wine is their drink, set in front of their battalion.)

Haycock brilliantly notes that, in the Middle Ages, jet was supposed to catch fire when placed in water, so the image may be of an otherworldly feast, flickeringly illuminated by a suitably outlandish light.[28] If this is magic, then the audience of this poem must have been formidably tolerant of allusive learning.

Poems such as *Pa gur* and *Preiddeu Annwn* point to a flourishing body of Arthurian tradition which has not survived and whose relation to what has come down to us is uncertain. *Pa gur* is most obviously akin to a tale already mentioned, *Culhwch ac Olwen* (c. 1050), the first monument of Welsh literary prose and the first Arthurian tale in any language; a number of characters appear in both. It is with this text that the magical and marvellous enter Welsh narrative in a spectacular manner. Tonally very varied, *Culhwch* is a literary rather than oral tale, but it is clearly close to the oral storytelling tradition and to folklore.

One minor figure in *Culhwch* is worth particular attention. This is Menw son of Teirgwaedd (perhaps 'Little One, son of Three Cries'), and I foreground him here because he is the earliest attested magician in Welsh vernacular literature.[29] In Triad 27 he is described as one of the Island of Britain's 'Three Enchanters' (*Tri Lleturithavc*), and this is entirely consonant with his role in *Culhwch*, though he is not explicitly described as such in that text.[30] Menw embodies several characteristics which become key conventions in the depiction of the Welsh literary magician: he is the proto-wizard of Welsh tradition, an important comparandum for the better-known Gwydion and Math of the Fourth Branch of the *Mabinogi*. Menw's signal characteristics are three in number. Firstly, his magic transforms outer appearances; secondly, it can be self-applied but can also be performed upon others; finally, and most crucially, he has in his repertoire a radical form of magic which involves transformation into animal form, with far-reaching consequences.

In *Culhwch* we are first told that Menw's pre-eminent talent is invisibility. Arthur includes him in the band of heroes who help his nephew Culhwch for precisely this reason: ' . . . o delhynt y wlat aghred mal y gallei yrru lleturith arnadunt, hyt nas gwelei neb vynt ac vyntvy a welynt pawb' (' ... if they should come to a heathen land he would be able to cast a spell upon them, so that no one might see them and they might see everyone').[31] Later he is able to defuse the ferocity of a supernatural guard dog. This affinity with animals reappears in Menw's final feat in the tale, in which he shapeshifts into bird form in order to scout out whether the monstrous boar Twrch Trwyth has a special comb and pair of shears stuck in the bristles between his ears, the obtaining of which is a crucial goal of the quest. All does not go according to plan:

> Ac ymrithaw a oruc Menw yn rith ederyn, a disgynnu a wnaeth uch penn y gwal, a cheissaw ysglyffaw un o'r tlysseu y gantaw. Ac ny chauas dim, hagen, namyn un o'e wrych. Kyuodi a oruc ynteu yn wychyrda, ac ymysgy-tyaw hyt pan ymordiwedawd peth o'r gwenwyn ac ef. Ac odyna ny bu dianaf Menw uyth.[32]

> (And Menw transformed himself into the form of a bird and swooped down above the boar's lair and tried to snatch one of the treasures from him. And he got nothing, however, apart from one of his bristles. Utterly enraged, the boar arose and shook himself so that a bit of the poison got him. And thence-forth Menw was never physically well.)

Here we have a significant inaugural sounding of the theme that magic is desperately dangerous – especially in its most extreme form, shapeshifting – and that over-reaching leads the magician into disaster.

The Great Enchanters

The themes perceptible in the magic of Menw son of Teirgwaedd – a minor player in *Culhwch ac Olwen* – are magnificently developed in the greatest monument of medieval Welsh prose, the Four Branches of the *Mabinogi*, and especially in its three magicians, Llwyd son of Cil Coed, Math son of Mathonwy, and Gwydion son of Dôn. It is to them that we turn for the remainder of this chapter.

Earlier it was remarked that the lack of detailed engagement with magic in medieval Welsh literature is a peculiarity of the field, and nowhere is that lack more apparent than in relation to the Four Branches. Despite a luxuriant and growing body of scholarship, as yet no one seems to have asked whether the author of these famous tales had a 'theory of magic', by which I mean a coherent imaginative conception of how enchantment works and where its potentials and limitations lie.[33] (This is another hangover of the Arnoldian view that Celtic literature intrinsically privileges imagination over logic.) In my view there is some evidence that the author *did* have such a theory – that he was not merely rehearsing themes from traditional, orally transmitted stories but had brooded upon literary magic with his characteristic sober thoughtfulness.[34] It is conceivable that he expected his audience to think similarly deeply about it – and to be disturbed.

Like Menw, the enchanters of the Four Branches are all men: the enchantresses ubiquitous in medieval English and continental literature are alien to Welsh tradition. Rhiannon, it may be protested, has distinct magical characteristics, but these consist of supernatural accoutrements – an uncatchable horse and a bottomless bag. (The first may not even be under her control: it is possible that the audience was supposed to understand that she *cannot* stop, unless asked to do so with a particular formula, and is in fact labouring under some kind of paternal curse or prohibition.) Aranrhod too seems at first sight to have some kind of magical power: consumed with shame and bitterness, she is able to 'fix a fate' upon her son Lleu, that he may have neither a name, nor weapons, nor a wife of human stock. The short-circuiting of these prohibitions drives the plot of the middle section of the Fourth Branch: that so much ingenuity has to be expended in the process shows that they have genuine binding force. The fact that Culhwch's stepmother is also able to issue a similarly binding prohibition – that the boy may marry no woman but Olwen – in closely similar language suggests that malevolent maternal magic was a Welsh literary topos, one clearly related to the international theme of the jealous stepmother, but with only two examples it is difficult to get a sense of how this was imagined to work. Aranrhod is certainly a powerful personage, but there is no sign that Culhwch's stepmother is supposed to have more than ordinary powers. And even Aranrhod is twice unable to see through her brother Gwydion's magic when it is in front of her or all around her, strongly suggesting that her magical abilities – if such they are – belong in a different category from his. (We might compare Manawaydan in the Third Branch, who is shrewd enough to detect magical transformation and so is able to use his enemy's strength against him.)

The magic done by the enchanters of the Four Branches has several signal features. As with Menw, it involves the manipulation of how things look and can be self-applied; animal transformation is its most extreme and perilous manifestation. The author seems to have conceptualized magic as a body of skilled techniques (the word used is *kelfydodeu*, 'arts') which are somehow 'gone into' – a metaphor which seems to suggest that a particular mental state must be cultivated.[35] This (I note in passing) reflects the author's keen interest in the indirect but nonetheless palpable depiction of the processes of thinking, rumination, and inner change.

Further, all three magicians also deploy a *hutlath* ('magic wand') and the use of this object is intriguing. It appears to be a tool for serious magic, as transformation into or out of animal form almost always explicitly involves being 'struck' (*taraw*) by a magician's wand, while merely changing appearances – making one person temporarily look like another, or altering their apparent age – never does.[36] The magic wand is a conspicuously international concept, attested as far back as Homer; it is the embodiment of the magician's power. Magicians in Irish saga also use wands, often of yew or rowan, and once again this is an area where the interplay between native and international conventions would repay investigation.[37]

But it is animal transformation – the kind of magic which requires a wand – which provides the clearest evidence for the author's careful thinking about magic. In the Fourth Branch, in which shapeshifting is most insistently thematized, he uses two terms to conceptualize the process. These are *rith* (Mod. W. *rhith*), 'outward form', and *anyan* (*anian*), 'instinct, inner nature', the latter deriving from Latin *ingenium*.[38] The former is related to one of the most common verbs in the *Mabinogi* (and in Welsh generally) for the changing of things into different shapes by enchantment, (*ym*)*rithyaw*. These two terms provide a revealing key enabling us to weigh up the various transformations in the cycle. The Four Branches' most spectacular – and grotesque – shapeshifting sequence is the three-year transformation of the brothers Gwydion and Gilfaethwy into pairs of male and female animals; this is Math son of Mathonwy's punishment upon them for the rape of his footholder Goewin. Math explicitly frames this punishment in terms of *rith* and *anian*:

> mi a wnaf ywch gerdet y gyt, a'ch bot yn gymaredig, ac yn un anyan a'r gwyduilot yd ywch yn eu rith, ac yn yr amser y bo etiued udunt wy, y uot ywchwitheu.[39]

> (I shall make you journey together, and be each other's mates and of the same nature as the wild animals in whose forms you will be, and at the time when they should have offspring, you yourselves will have offspring.)

It is important to note that if one is given the outer form of an animal, plus the inner nature of an animal, then one *simply is that animal*. The brothers' human consciousness is not merely hidden behind an animal form but suspended altogether. This is a very different and more radical take on magical metamorphosis from that attested in other works of the central Middle Ages. To take two examples from within a century of the Four Branches' likely composition, we might compare the enchanted wolf of Marie de France's *Bisclavret*, or Gerald of Wales's famous anecdote of the werewolves of Ossory; in each case, the animals are humans whose minds are unaltered beneath their transformed outer shapes; Gerald's werewolves can reveal their human bodies by peeling back their wolf-pelts.[40] The author of the Four Branches makes plain that this is not the case for Gwydion and Gilfaethwy.

The question must therefore be asked: where does the brothers' punishment actually lie? It is common in scholarship on the Four Branches to note that their transformation is fitting, in that (in a sense) it involves making them simultaneously violate the Levitical taboos against incest, sodomy, and bestiality.[41] But we are explicitly told that they have the inner nature of animals for the duration of their metamorphosis, and for an animal merely to be itself is not a punishment. The answer, I think, is that the punishment starts when the transformation stops: it inheres in the shame the brothers feel forever afterwards. Math says as much, pinpointing the brothers' great shame (*kywilyd mawr*) at having borne offspring to each other.[42] Math's own magical powers, too, seem to involve the preparation of names, and the names he gives to the three animal-children – Bleiddwn, Hyddwn, and Hychddwn Hir – memorialize their parents' disgrace by containing the nouns for the animals into which they were transformed.

Rhith and *anian* give us powerful tools for analysing the magical transformations in the Four Branches. There is no space here to explore these in detail, but several incidents in the text become even more subtle and intriguing if viewed in this light. The wife of the enchanter Llwyd uab Cil Coed in the Third Branch, *Manawydan uab Llyr* ('Manawydan son of Llŷr'), is pregnant in both her human form and when enchanted into the shape of a mouse: this becomes an essential plot point. From this we can conclude that magic cannot uncreate a human soul, even in a foetus; the woman's *anian* shows through her enchanted *rhith*. (It also showcases the author's remarkable gift for thematic foreshadowing: did the audience remember this incident and wonder what would have happened to the male bodies of Gwydion and Gilfaethwy had Math turned them back *while pregnant*? Magic in the *Mabinogi* takes us to some perverse places.) *Rhith* and *anian* also help us with the less extreme branch of magic in the tales, that of disguise. It is clear that merely changing someone's appearance – as Arawn, Llwyd, and Gwydion all do – is a skin-deep alteration and the inner nature remains unchanged. The author highlights this fact when Gwydion changes himself and his nephew Lleu into the form of 'two young lads' as part of a cunning scheme. Lleu actually is a young lad, but Gwydion's expression is 'more serious than that of the boy' (*yn prudach ... noc un y guas*), highlighting his maturity and cunning.[43] The inner shows through the outer.

Crucially, to give Math – always the arch-enchanter of Welsh tradition – the ability to transform both *rhith* and *anian* is to ascribe to him an alarming degree of power. This should be placed against the background of the upsurge of interest among thinkers across western Christendom in questions of essence, selfhood, and supernatural transmogrification, which, as Caroline Walker Bynum has shown, was a phenomenon of the twelfth and thirteenth centuries.[44] The proliferation of theological anxieties was in part a response to the rediscovery of Ovid's *Metamorphoses*, in which gods, humans, animals, trees, and stones interchange in a manner profoundly disturbing to the medieval mind; part of the response was an imaginative willingness to explore the relationship to Christian truth of human-like, hybrid, and mutated beings.

As concepts, *rhith* and *anian* map precisely onto the terms 'accident' and 'substance' which were to become fundamental to debates in scholastic philosophy in the century after the Four Branches' likely composition. Christian theology needed a theory of metamorphosis because the central ritual of the religion, the Eucharist, depended on the consecrated bread and wine continuing to look, feel, and taste unchanged while being inwardly and literally transformed in their essence into Christ's flesh and blood. The Aristotelian concepts of substance (essential nature) and accidents (sense-percepts) could be used to explain transubstantiation by asserting that God allowed the accidents of the Eucharistic gifts to remain unchanged while transforming their substance. The crucial point is that this was a divine prerogative: demons, and magicians aided by demons, were acknowledged to be able to alter the accidents of objects and persons, but only God was able to alter their inner essence. And yet this is precisely the power which Math is shown to possess.

All this underscores the point that the author of the Four Branches was conspicuously interested in theorizing magic. In doing so, he – writing somewhere in Wales around the year 1100 – managed to anticipate the terms of an anxious debate about metamorphosis which soon engaged some of the finest theological minds in Christendom. This owed much to his characteristic thoughtfulness, and it may be down to him that metamorphosis evidently became a significant intellectual concern among Welsh literary men at the time. Most famously, a pervasive interest in changes of shape is visible in the poems in the voice of the so-called 'legendary Taliesin' – himself a shapeshifting transmigrant – many of which may be late twelfth-century and thus almost certainly postdate the Four Branches.

What is certainly clear is that shapeshifting was an important inherited motif in Welsh tradition, even if the author of the Four Branches made it a preoccupation. So much is suggested by the Triads, one of which runs as follows:

> Teir Prif Hut Enys Prydein:
> Hut Math mab Mathonwy (a dysgavd y Wydyon vab Don),
> a Hut Vthyr Benbragon (a dysgavd y Venw vab Teirgwaed),
> a Hut Gwythelin Gorr (a dysgavd y Goll vab Kollurewy y nei).[45]

> (Three Great Enchantments of the Island of Britain:
> The Enchantment of Math son of Mathonwy [which he taught to Gw(y)dion son of Dôn], and the Enchantment of Uthyr Pendragon [which he taught to Menw son of Teirgwaedd], and the Enchantment of Gwythelyn the Dwarf [which he taught to Coll son of Collfrewy his nephew]).

This list of enchanters is textually split: the clauses in brackets are missing in the version in one of the manuscripts, Aberystwyth, National Library of Wales MS Peniarth 16. Rachel Bromwich made the persuasive suggestion that the shorter form of this triad (in Peniarth 16) is the older and that, in each case, *hut* means not 'magical teachings' but 'act of magic' and refers in each case to shapeshifting, two of the acts being known: that performed by Math upon Gwydion and Gilfaethwy, and that undergone by Uthr Pendragon in order to sleep with Eigr (Igraine) and so father Arthur. Gwythelyn the Dwarf is otherwise unknown to us.[46] The name of the enchanter Menw hints intriguingly that dwarves were associated with magic in Wales, if the name is indeed cognate with Irish *menb* (little); we also have Eiddig *Gor* (the dwarf), attested elsewhere in the Triads as one of a trio of warrior-magicians, the others being Math and Menw.

Math comes first in the triad quoted above, which underscores that he and Gwydion are the archetypal enchanters in Welsh tradition. One telling detail is that there is a clear power differential between the two, and that Gwydion's magic seems to develop in the course of the Fourth Branch. He begins by being capable of creating illusions or temporary transformations – as when he fashions shields out of toadstools – but he only performs transformations into or out of animal shape after he has himself been transformed. He gains the ability to effect permanent metamorphoses – Math's specialty – in the course of the story, and on this point it should be noted that it is not wholly clear whether or not the magic wand he uses to transform Lleu back into human form is actually Math's own. (The Middle Welsh phrase *y hutlath* is ambiguous: 'his magic wand' or 'the magic wand'.) Math sends Gwydion off sympathetically upon his quest to recover Lleu, and it is conceivable that we are supposed to imagine that the master has given his pupil his own wand, symbolic embodiment of his capacity for radical, metamorphic magic. This is the form of enchantment which is the most theologically dubious: elsewhere it is the prerogative of God, who is said in *Culhwch ac Olwen* to have transformed a king into a boar, the Twrch Trwyth, as a punishment for his sins; we might also compare the dialogue poem *Ymddiddan Arthur a'r Eryr* ('Dialogue of Arthur and the Eagle'), composed at some point before 1150, in which Arthur encounters the soul of his nephew Eliwlad, mysteriously incarnated as an eagle. The eagle is keen to bestow Christian instruction upon the hapless Arthur, suggesting that it is God himself who is responsible for his transformed state.[47]

A second case study from the Fourth Branch is revealing here, and this is the haunting story of the creation of Blodeuwedd by Math and Gwydion to be a wife for Lleu Llaw Gyffes:

> 'Ie,' heb y Math, 'keisswn ninheu, ui a thi, oc an hut a'n lledrith, hudaw gwreic idaw ynteu o'r bloden.' Ynteu yna a meint gwr yndaw ac yn deledi-whaf guas a welas dyn eiroet. Ac yna y kymeryssant wy blodeu y deri, a blodeu y banadyl, a blodeu yr erwein, ac o'r rei hynny, asswynaw yr un uorwyn deccaf a thelediwaf a welas dyn eiroet.

> ('Aye,' said Math, 'let us attempt, you and I, by means of our magic and enchantment, to conjure a woman into being for him out of flowers.' Lleu then was a fully grown man and the handsomest lad that anyone had ever seen. And then they took the flowers of the oak, and the flowers of the broom, and the flowers of the meadowsweet, and out of those they conjured up the single most beautiful and best-endowed maiden anyone had ever seen.)

The flowers that the two enchanters gather to create Blodeuwedd are a literalization of the tropes of feminine beauty in Welsh tradition: hair is frequently 'as yellow as the broom' – Olwen in *Culhwch* is described in precisely this way – while meadowsweet has the creamy softness of female skin.[48] And yet they also have an intriguing kinship with the wider European tradition of 'natural magic' which frequently used plants for their supposed magical properties.

If we take the creation of Blodeuwedd seriously – as thoughtful early twelfth-century listeners might well have done – then its implications are unsettling. As seen, medieval thinking about the supernatural drew a fundamental distinction between natural and demonic magic, and here the ambiguity of Math and Gwydion's act of creation is most apparent. Welsh literary magic never explicitly features the conjuration of spirits, and yet what precisely *is* Blodeuwedd, ontologically speaking? Were they to hear the story, the churchmen who were involved in condemning magical practitioners elsewhere in Europe at the time of the Four Branches' composition might have had little hesitation in classifying her as an evil spirit animating a temporary body. Her adultery with Gronw Pebr and her attempt on her husband's life would have aligned her with *succubi*, demonic spirits taking the form of women and a demonstrable focus of contemporary anxieties.[49] The creation of automata of various kinds was commonly ascribed to medieval magicians.

Theologically speaking, this is the only orthodox way in which the creation of Blodeuwedd might be explained; but once again the author of the Four Branches seems to have been prepared to contemplate more radical possibilities, namely that pre-Christian magicians like Math and Gwydion might have been capable of creating a human soul. This is duly foreshadowed earlier in the text in Math's transformation of Gwydion and Gilfaethwy's three animal-children into human form: their metamorphosis is not a disenchantment, like that of their parents, for they have never been human; indeed, in terms of human biology their conception would have been impossible. But nothing in the text suggests that, once transformed, they are anything other than normatively human, in which case Math has *created three human souls* by magic. With the creation of Blodeuwedd, the enchanters are once again ascribed literally divine powers. It is telling that the verb used for summoning Blodeuwedd into being – *asswynaw*, Mod. W. *aswyno* – is unique in the Four Branches; it is uncommon with this meaning elsewhere, but the related verb *swynaw* is used by the thirteenth-century court poet Prydydd y Moch to denote acts of creation by God himself.[50]

Conclusion

The inhabitants of medieval Wales, like people everywhere, enjoyed tales in which fantastical elements were to the fore; these form a significant but still largely unexamined and untheorized area of the literature. The Victorian view that magic, or 'wonder', is an especially Celtic literary phenomenon cannot be sustained, but there are certainly elements in the Welsh depiction of supernatural incidents which are distinctive.

Two observations can be made in conclusion. Firstly, magic is figured as autochthonous and to do with the past: the most elaborated examples of Welsh literary magic involve personnel from native traditions about the legendary inhabitants of the 'Old North' and the pre-Saxon, pre-Roman world of the Four Branches. Magic in Welsh writing is mysterious and extreme, but by and large it is not exotic, in the way that it often is in English and continental romance. Again, in contrast to other European literary traditions, Welsh magic makes strikingly little use of elaborate 'technology' – it is short on magic rings, girdles, books, and the like. Such examples as there are seem to possess an uncanny, archaic quality, with a particular prominence given to cauldrons and hanging bowls, the 'cauldron of rebirth' in the Second Branch, *Branwen uerch Lyr* ('Branwen daughter of Llŷr') – a kind of resurrection machine – being the most signal example.

Secondly, magic is rarely happy or whimsical; rather, its atmosphere is melancholy and its consequences dismaying. I mentioned Menw son of Teirgwaedd as the prototype enchanter in Welsh prose, and his permanent crippling by the Twrch Trwyth is symbolic of this dimension of magic, as a force which causes more problems than it solves, not least for the magician himself. Magic is also often strikingly concrete, solid enough to have practical and legal consequences within the world of the stories. As seen, the author of the Four Branches – undoubtedly the most magic- and marvel-filled tales in Welsh tradition – is a master at the depiction of magic in this ironic, provocative vein. His thinking about magic is extraordinarily searching and reflective, and consists of more than the mere framing of inherited supernatural incidents within a graceful style. His writing showcases what Corinne Saunders has called the 'edginess' of the occult sciences, which can span the divine and the demonic, in that he deliberately leaves open the possibility that supernatural skill might allow the enchanter a godlike level of power, presciently anticipating anxieties which were to become widespread among European men of learning in the twelfth century. Magic in the *Mabinogi* arcs towards unhappiness; it is typical of its author that unorthodox theological possibility is so elegantly held in tension with depictions of social catastrophe.

Notes

1. John Cooper Powys is only the most famous example; it has been a particularly strong tendency in children's literature, not least Alan Garner's celebrated *The Owl Service* (London: Collins, 1967).

2. Matthew Arnold, *On the Study of Celtic Literature* (London: Smith Elder, 1867), quoted from *Lectures and Essays in Criticism: The Complete Prose Works of Matthew Arnold*, ed. R. H. Super, 11 vols. (Ann Arbor, MI: University of Michigan Press, 1960–77), III, 291–386. There is a substantial literature on this essay and its ideological content, but see especially Rachel Bromwich, *Matthew Arnold and Celtic Literature: A Retrospect, 1865–1965* (Oxford: Oxford University Press, 1965) and W. E. Buckler, 'On the Study of Celtic Literature: A Critical Reconsideration', *Victorian Poetry* 27, 1 (Spring 1989): 61–76.

3. Corinne Saunders, *Magic and the Supernatural in Medieval English Romance* (Cambridge: Cambridge University Press, 2010), 180–1.

4. Not least from Saunders herself; but see also Geraldine Heng, *Empire of Magic: Medieval Romance and the Politics of Cultural Fantasy* (New York: Columbia University Press, 2003); Helen Cooper, *The English Romance in Time: Transforming Motifs from Geoffrey of Monmouth to the Death of Shakespeare* (Oxford: Oxford University Press, 2004); Carolyne Larrington, *King Arthur's Enchantresses: Morgan and her Sisters in Arthurian Tradition* (London: I. B. Tauris, 2006); J. Wade, *Fairies in Medieval Romance* (Basingstoke: Palgrave Macmillan, 2011).

5. See my pilot essay 'Magic in Medieval Wales and Ireland', in *The Routledge History of Medieval Magic*, ed. Sophie Page and Catherine Rider (London and New York: Routledge, forthcoming).

6. R. Kieckhefer, *Magic in the Middle Ages* (Cambridge: Cambridge University Press, 1989), denies the validity of this distinction at all.

7. Richard Suggett, *A History of Magic and Witchcraft in Wales* (Stroud: History Press, 2008), 25.

8. *Gramadegau'r Penceirddiaid*, ed. G. J. Williams and E. J. Jones (Cardiff: University of Wales Press, 1934), 136, 151.

9. See in particular Aled Llion Jones, *Darogan: Prophecy, Lament and Absent Heroes in Medieval Welsh Literature* (Cardiff: University of Wales Press, 2013), though note Dafydd Johnston's constructively critical review of Jones's Darogan, *CMCS* 67 (Summer 2014): 90–3.

10. Marged Haycock, 'Literary Criticism in Welsh before *c.* 1300', in *The Cambridge History of Literary Criticism*, vol. II: *The Middle Ages*, ed.

A. Minnis and I. Johnson (Cambridge: Cambridge University Press, 2005), 336–7.

11. *Armes Prydein: The Prophecy of Britain from the Book of Taliesin*, ed. Ifor Williams, trans. Rachel Bromwich (Dublin: Dublin Institute for Advanced Studies, 1972), 14–15; for *librarius/llyfrawr*, see T. Jones *et al.*, 'Nodiadau Cymysg', *BBCS* 11 (1944): 137–8.

12. Mark Williams, *Fiery Shapes: Celestial Portents and Astrology in Ireland and Wales, 700–1700* (Oxford: Oxford University Press, 2010), 87–90.

13. See Gerald of Wales, *The Journey Through Wales and the Description of Wales*, trans. Lewis Thorpe (Harmondsworth: Penguin, 1978), I.5

14. Walter Map, *De nugis curialium: Courtiers' Trifles*, ed. and trans. M. R. James, rev. C. N. L. Brooke and R. A. B. Mynors (Oxford: Oxford University Press, 1983), II.27: 202–3.

15. For these categories in medieval English chronicles, see Carl S. Watkins, *History and the Supernatural in Medieval England* (Cambridge: Cambridge University Press, 2007), especially p. 18.

16. The Four Branches are discussed further in Chapter 4.

17. *Pedeir Keinc y Mabinogi*, ed. Ifor Williams (Caerdydd: Gwasg Prifysgol Cymru, 1930, 1951), 9. All references to the Four Branches are from this edition.

18. *Pedeir Keinc*, ed. Williams, 10.

19. *Pedeir Keinc*, ed. Williams, 63, 247; for further etymology, see B. Maier, 'Dead Men Don't Wear Plaid: Celtic Myth and Christian Creed in Medieval Irish Concepts of the Afterlife', in *Writing Down the Myths*, ed. Joseph Falaky Nagy (Brepols: Turnhout, 2013), 109–36 (117).

20. See Patrick Sims-Williams, 'The Early Welsh Arthurian Poems', in *The Arthur of the Welsh: The Arthurian Legend in Medieval Welsh Literature*, ed. Rachel Bromwich, A. O. H. Jarman and Brynley F. Roberts (Cardiff: University of Wales Press, 1991), 33–72 (37–40); also the useful bibliographic guide to the poem in J. T. Koch, 'The Celtic Lands', in *Medieval Arthurian Literature: A Guide to Recent Research*, ed. N. J. Lacy (New York: Garland, 1996), 239–322, at 262.

21. The poem is edited by A. O. H. Jarman in *Llyfr Du Caerfyrddin* (Caerdydd: Gwasg Prifysgol Cymru, 1982), no. 31, pp. 66–8.

22. *Culhwch and Olwen: An Edition and Study of the Oldest Arthurian Tale*, ed. Rachel Bromwich and D. Sion Evans (Cardiff: University of Wales Press, 1992), ll. 266–73.

23. Sims-Williams ('The Early Welsh Arthurian Poems', 42–3) suggests that the figure named Gwrgi Garwlwyd ('rough-grey man-dog') in the poem was himself imagined as a *cynocephalus*.

24. We might compare Scáthach, Cú Chulainn's instructress in arms; Irish saga and romantic tale is rich in monstrous, physically imposing women, and how they should be classified and compared is not as yet at all clear.

25. *Historia Peredur vab Efrawc*, ed. G. W. Goetinck (Cardiff: University of Wales Press, 1976), 29.17.

26. *Legendary Poems from the Book of Taliesin*, ed. and trans. Marged Haycock, 2nd edn (Aberystwyth: CMCS Publications, 2015), 435.

27. *Legendary Poems*, ed. and trans. Haycock, 436.

28. *Legendary Poems*, ed. and trans. Haycock, 445.

29. In Latin we might point to the *magi* ('sorcerers') surrounding the tyrant Vortigern in *Historia Brittonum*; these seem fairly clearly to be a topos borrowed from Irish hagiography.

30. He was a reasonably well-known figure; in *Breudwyt Ronabwy* ('The Dream of Rhonabwy'), he is one of Arthur's forty-two counsellors and was mentioned by the poets Cynddelw, Dafydd ap Gwilym, and Iolo Goch; see P. C. Bartrum, *A Welsh Classical Dictionary: People in History and Legend up to about AD 1000* (Aberystwyth: National Library of Wales, 1993), 472.

31. *Culhwch and Olwen*, ed. Bromwich and Evans, ll. 408–11, my translation.

32. *Culhwch and Olwen*, ed. Bromwich and Evans, ll. 1030–5, my translation.

33. One of the only pieces to do so as yet is Pierre-Yves Lambert, 'Magie et pouvoir dans la quatrième branche du *Mabinogi*', *Studia Celtica* 28 (1994): 97–107.

34. The author (and a single author is assumed for the Four Branches) is generally taken to have been a man, but note A. Breeze, 'Did a Woman Write the Four Branches of the Mabinogi?', *Studi Medievali* 38, 2 (1997): 679–705.

35. *Pedeir Keinc*, ed. Williams, 70.

36. See, for example, *Pedeir Keinc*, ed. Williams, 65, 75, 76, 90.

37. Circe uses a magic wand or staff in *Odyssey* 10: 238, to change Odysseus's men into pigs.

38. My ideas about the importance of *rhith* and *anian* to the magic of the Four Branches have been further developed by Angela Grant in 'Magical Transformation in *Pedeir Keinc y Mabinogi* and *Hanes Taliesin*' (M.Phil. diss., University of Oxford, 2010).

39. *Pedeir Keinc*, ed. Williams, 75.

40. See the seminal discussion by Caroline Walker Bynum, 'Metamorphosis, or Gerald and the Werewolf', *Speculum* 73, 4 (1998): 987–1013.

41. See, for example, Michael Cichon, 'Eros and Error: Gross Sexual Transgression in the Fourth Branch of the *Mabinogi*', in *The Erotic in the Literature of Medieval Britain*, ed. Amanda Hopkins and Cory James Rushton (Woodbridge: D. S. Brewer, 2007), 105–15; Roberta L. Valente, 'Gwydion and Aranrhod: Crossing the Borders of Gender in *Math*', *BBCS* 35 (1988): 1–9; K. Millersdaughter, 'The Geopolitics of Incest: Sex, Gender

and Violence in the Fourth Branch of the *Mabinogi'*, *Exemplaria* 14, 2 (2002): 271–316.

42. *Pedeir Keinc*, ed. Williams, 76–7.

43. *Pedeir Keinc*, ed. Williams, 81.

44. See Bynum's classic study *Metamorphosis and Identity* (New York: Zone Books, 2001), which incorporates material about the werewolves of Ossory.

45. *Trioedd Ynys Prydein: The Triads of the Island of Britain*, ed. and trans. Rachel Bromwich, 4th edn (Cardiff: University of Wales Press, 2014), 61. The Triads are lists of story motifs and characters in groups of three, many of them dating from the thirteenth century.

46. Bromwich suggests he may be the same as the 'Gwidolwyn the Dwarf' mentioned in *Culhwch* as the possessor of a set of bottles that act as the magical equivalent of thermos flasks.

47. Marged Haycock, 'Ymddiddan Arthur a'r Eryr', in *Blodeugerdd Barddas o Canu Crefyddol Cynnar*, ed. Haycock (Christopher Davies: Llandybie, 1994), 297–312.

48. *Culhwch and Olwen*, ed. Bromwich and Evans, l. 490 (p. 18).

49. Map, *De nugis*, II. 11–13, 158–9; Saunders (*Magic and the Supernatural*, 115) gives other instances.

50. *Legendary Poems*, ed. and trans. Haycock, 28; e.g. *Duw o Nef ry-th-swynas* ('God from Heaven has created you').

4

Commemorating the Past After 1066: Tales from *The Mabinogion*

DIANA LUFT

The collective title *Mabinogion* normally refers to the group of eleven medieval Welsh prose texts believed to be (more or less) native compositions. The title became standardized following the publication by Lady Charlotte Guest of the texts and translations in the mid-nineteenth century, where she referred to the tales as 'the Canon of Welsh Romance', however erroneous or idiosyncratic that usage may be.[1] The group comprises the tales known as the Four Branches of the *Mabinogi* (*Pwyll Pendeuic Dyuet*, 'Pwyll Prince of Dyfed', *Branwen uerch Lyr*, 'Branwen daughter of Llŷr', *Manawydan uab Llyr*, 'Manawydan son of Llŷr', and *Math uab Mathonwy*, 'Math son of Mathonwy'); the three so-called 'romances' (*Gereint uab Erbin*, 'Geraint son of Erbin', *Peredur*, and *Owein neu Iarlles y Ffynnawn*, 'Owain, or the Lady of the Fountain'); and four other tales: *Culhwch ac Olwen*, 'Culhwch and Olwen', *Breudwyt Maxen*, 'The Dream of Maxen', *Cyfranc Lludd a Llefelys*, 'The Adventure of Lludd and Llefelys', and *Breudwyt Ronabwy*, 'The Dream of Rhonabwy'.[2] Guest also included a twelfth tale in her collection, *Hanes Taliesin* ('The Story of Taliesin'), the late medieval folktale about the sixth-century poet Taliesin.[3]

Of all medieval Welsh prose texts, these tales known as the *Mabinogion* have received the greatest amount of scholarly attention since the publication of Guest's translation. This attention has resulted in a wealth of different, often competing interpretations of the texts, a variety made possible by the fact that, despite more than a century of scholarship, there is little concrete information upon which to base an analysis of the tales. The basic facts of their composition – the who, when, where, or why – remain the subject of debate. We do not know who wrote the texts, or who read them (or listened to them read aloud), although more is known about the scribes and patrons of later manuscript copies.[4] We do not know with any certainty when or where the texts were produced. Earlier theories which favoured a pre-Norman composition date and a southern origin for the Four Branches have been superseded by analyses which argue for a later date, from the late twelfth to the mid thirteenth century, and a northern milieu.[5] There is a general consensus that *Culhwch ac Olwen*, the Arthurian adventure tale, is the oldest of the tales: some scholars prefer the date of *c.* 1100 favoured by the text's editors, while others argue for a date in the mid to late twelfth century, and others again place the text later still, in the first half of the thirteenth century.[6] Some scholars suggest that *Breudwyt Ronabwy*, another early Arthurian story, dates from the time of Madog ap Maredudd (d. 1160), during whose reign in Powys the events of the story are supposed to take place; others place the composition later, proposing a range of dates from the early thirteenth to the beginning of the fourteenth century.[7] A number of scholars have associated some of the tales with Llywelyn ap Iorwerth (d. 1240), the great prince of north Wales who negotiated a treaty with King John and married his daughter.[8] Perhaps the best that can be said is that the tales, in the form in which they have survived, are likely to have been compiled and perhaps written down at various times during the period between the Norman conquest of 1066 and the conquest of Wales by Edward I in 1282.

To what extent are they to be read as entertainment, and to what extent are they didactic, to be understood as mirrors for princes, or codes of behaviour?[9] Would the characters and themes have been already familiar to a medieval audience? Would the stories have resonated with allusions dating back to a mythic past, or were they novel? Scholars do not agree on how to read these texts at the most basic level. For example, are we to understand the First Branch as a sort of *Bildungsroman*, charting the main character's development from 'nice but dim' into a wise and successful leader, as Catherine McKenna has argued, or is it simply a joke that someone so lacking in common sense is called 'Pwyll' (literally 'sense')?[10] Is *Gereint uab Erbin* an essentially misogynistic text, or is it about performing masculinity?[11] While all can agree that *Breudwyt Ronabwy* is a satire, there is disagreement as to what or who is the subject of the author's barbs. Is it a literary satire, poking fun at the over-wrought romances of the day, or is the target political, comparing contemporary figures unfavourably with the giants of the past, or is it a send-up of the literature of dreams and their learned interpretations, or is the critique aimed at Welsh pretensions that a *mab darogan*, or son of prophecy, will arise to lead the nation back to its former glory?[12] Or is it ultimately an almost postmodern story about the failure of stories, the inadequacy of language and the impossibility of communication?[13] Does the massive list of 800 names that bisects *Culhwch ac Olwen* represent a flourish of learned allusions, or is it the result of the exuberance of the storyteller, or is it simply meant to be ridiculous?[14]

The Critical Tradition

In the absence of such basic information, scholars have tended to look for clues in the texts themselves to make inferences about the historical facts of their composition and have interpreted episodes in the texts as echoes of actual events which can help date and locate them.[15] The faint traces of a Norman or Anglo-Norman presence in most of the tales have prompted some recent postcolonial approaches to the texts, exploring the likely impact of the Norman settlements in Wales. Analysis of the power relations between different actors in the texts has demonstrated the deep anxiety about sovereignty that underlies them, a concern with shifting borders, uncertain alliances, and the machinations of foreign colonialist polities. The Four Branches, it has been argued, are pervaded by a sense of loss, with stark images of the depopulation of Wales in the Second and Third Branches reflecting anxieties about the passing of Welsh political and cultural power.[16] In the Second Branch, the story of Branwen daughter of Llŷr, set in an apparently remote pre-Saxon past, the Welsh king, Branwen's brother Brân (or Bendigeidfran, literally 'Bran the Blessed'), is forced to wage war against the king of Ireland, decimating Wales in the process. In the Third Branch, Manawydan, another son of the dynastic ancestor Llŷr, must use his wits to save the land of Dyfed in south Wales from a plague-like curse which renders the land empty and barren. The tale of *Peredur*, an adaptation of the twelfth-century French romance of *Perceval* by Chrétien de Troyes, has been characterized as a hybrid text which, while drawing on the French cultural sources of the Anglo-Norman colonizers of twelfth-century Wales for its material, manages to subvert that material in its presentation of Arthur's court as the representative of a foreign power.[17] Lacking a definite context in which to interpret the texts, scholars have turned to studies of myth and folklore to try to assign meaning to the characters and episodes in them in one of the oldest critical approaches to the *Mabinogion*. Many early critics assumed that there was a 'Celtic' stratum underlying the texts in some earlier form, looking to Ireland and its older, more authentically Celtic traditions for analogues which might explain some of their more perplexing elements.[18] The heroes of the three French-inspired tales, Owain, Geraint, and Peredur, are united by their reliance upon female support, often of a supernatural kind, to gain their positions of power, as is Pwyll, the prince of Dyfed, in the First

Branch. This narrative theme has been interpreted as a version of the Celtic 'sovereignty goddess' motif, wherein a king gains temporal power through uniting with a goddess figure, the exchange being signposted by the goddess proffering a drink to the newly appointed king.[19] As a number of critics have pointed out, however, arguing against the 'sovereignty goddess' theory, many of the episodes can just as readily be explained by the exigencies of the plot.[20]

In a similar vein, many of the characters of the Four Branches have been regarded as representatives of earlier Celtic gods and goddesses, their attributes and actions explained by their relationship to continental Celtic deities. The figure of Rhiannon, for example, the mysterious but determined woman who marries Pwyll in the First Branch, has been interpreted as a reflex of the Celtic horse-goddess, Epona. Her magically accelerating horse and her later punishment whereby she is made to act as a horse and carry guests to the court on her back seem to cement her association with horses, while her marriages to two successive kings of Dyfed, Pwyll and then Manawydan (in the Third Branch), have been explained as a sovereignty motif.[21] The implication of this type of interpretation is that a number of Iron Age 'Celtic' associations were remembered and still held some sort of significance for the authors and/or the audiences of these tales. In fact, the association of Rhiannon with Epona is tenuous, and the logic of the story can, once again, account for many of these elements: what would Rhiannon ride if not a horse? What is more humiliating than having to bear guests to the court on one's back?[22] Some scholars have traced the folk-tale elements of the texts, identifying international motifs which might elucidate some of the more perplexing episodes.[23] Others have sought to find traces of ancient historical events in the texts in an attempt to explain them.[24] These approaches are united by their assumption that the texts need explication through reference to outside sources, as they are not intelligible on their own. A rival tendency, meanwhile, has emphasized the structural coherence of the texts, their quality and entertainment value, insisting that they do not need such explications.[25]

In the absence of an agreed interpretative framework for the texts, scholars have searched for sources and analogues for events related in them, in the expectation that such sources and analogues will help either to explain the events or to dismiss them as the products of those sources. A particular focus of interest has been the three Welsh texts from the *Mabinogion*, sometimes called the 'romances', which correspond to three twelfth-century verse romances written in French by Chrétien de Troyes. *Peredur*, as we have seen, corresponds to Chrétien's *Perceval*, the Welsh *Owein neu Iarlles y Ffynnawn* to Chrétien's *Yvain*, and *Gereint uab Erbin* to Chrétien's *Erec et Enide*. The similarities between the two groups of tales have been generally understood as the result of the French and Welsh authors drawing on a common store of Celtic story material, thus maintaining the independence of the Welsh tales as wholly native compositions, but more recently the Welsh tales have been regarded as more or less loose adaptations of Chrétien's works.[26]

A related scholarly tendency has attempted to throw light on the texts by examining evidence for the appearance of their characters in other genres of Welsh texts, such as poetry and the Triads, in an attempt to ascertain whether the authors of the *Mabinogion* were presenting familiar characters in a familiar way, or whether they were introducing new characters and novel situations. It is unclear, for example, whether the allusions in the Four Branches to individual triads which do not appear in the collection known as *Trioedd Ynys Prydein* ('Triads of the Island of Britain') preserve material which has not survived or whether the author has made them up, and if so, to what end.[27] The reference to the slaying of Dylan in the Fourth Branch as the victim of 'trydyd anuat ergyt' ('one of three unfortunate blows') looks, on the surface, very much like a triad. It is echoed in other sources, such as the poem 'Marwnat Dylan Eil Ton' ('The Death of Dylan Eil Ton'; his name means literally 'sea son of wave'), which also recounts the death of Dylan on the seashore by a blow.[28] But no such triad exists in the surviving collections. *Breudwyt Maxen* presents its title character Maxen as a romantic hero, while Geoffrey of Monmouth's *Historia Regum Britanniae* ('History of the Kings of Britain', *c.* 1138) paints him (Maximianus) as a villain who despoiled Britain of her youth and left her open to attack.[29] What are we to make of the references to characters from the Four Branches in Welsh court poetry, where the details do not necessarily match up with our expectations?[30] Arianrhod was apparently known to fifteenth- and sixteenth-century poets as Math's original virgin footholder, without whom he cannot live, whereas in the Fourth Branch she is called to stand in for Goewin, Math's footholder, who is raped by Gilfaethwy thus rendering her unqualified for the job. Ian Hughes suggests that the poets' version of Arianrhod may be drawn from an oral version of the tale, which may have differed significantly from the version preserved in the *Mabinogion*.[31] But if this oral version differs so greatly from the medieval text, then to what extent are we talking about the same story? How many Fourth Branches might there be?

The Manuscript Tradition

One piece of contextual evidence which may help to address some of the unanswerable questions about the *Mabinogion* is the manuscripts in which the texts have been preserved.[32] But the manuscript tradition of the *Mabinogion* is relatively poor. All the texts in this group survive in the mid-fourteenth-century White Book of Rhydderch (NLW, MSS Peniarth 5 and 4) and the Red Book of Hergest (Oxford, Jesus College, MS 111), which was written in the years after 1382, except *Breudwyt Ronabwy* which survives only in the Red Book. While it is agreed that these manuscripts contain copies of the texts made many years after they were originally composed, it is difficult to theorize about their original manuscript contexts because there are so few earlier copies surviving, and only in fragments. There are no copies of either *Culhwch ac Olwen* or *Breudwyt Ronabwy* besides those of the White and Red Books before the seventeenth century. *Cyfranc Lludd a Llefelys*, which gives a dramatic account of dangerous threats to pre-Saxon Britain during the reign of King Lludd son of Beli, is found embedded in four of the six versions of *Brut y Brenhinedd* ('Chronicle of the Kings'), the thirteenth-century Welsh translation of Geoffrey of Monmouth's *Historia Regum Britanniae*, but there are no independent copies of it besides the White and Red Books until the eighteenth century. A single leaf of the Second Branch and a single leaf of the Third Branch survive as Aberystwyth, National Library of Wales, MS Peniarth 6, parts i and ii. These are in the hand of the same scribe and were originally part of the same late thirteenth-century manuscript, indicating that the Four Branches, at least, were conceived of as a united collection before the White Book. Two fragments of two early fourteenth-century copies of *Gereint uab Erbin* form Peniarth 6iii and Peniarth 6iv. These were originally two separate manuscripts, and there is no indication of what their other contents might have been.[33] A fragment of *Owein neu Iarlles y Ffynnawn* fills a single quire of the late fourteenth-century Oxford, Jesus College, MS 20, where it is preceded by a collection of *hengerdd* (early poetry) and followed by religious texts and a copy of *Seith Doethion Rhufein*, a translation of the Latin wisdom text *The Seven Sages of Rome*. It is uncertain whether this fragment was originally intended to be included in this manuscript: Daniel Huws notes that it is in the hand of a different scribe and describes it as an 'addition'.[34]

Breudwyt Maxen is found in the late thirteenth-century manuscript Peniarth 16v along with a copy of *Proffwydoliaeth Fyrddin* ('The Prophecy of Merlin'), a translation of the prophecies of Merlin which form Book 7 of Geoffrey's *Historia*. These works may be united by their Galfridian subject matter.

The juxtaposition of the two texts suggests that the title character of *Breudwyt Maxen* is indeed to be associated with Geoffrey's account of that king's deeds, despite the differences in these sources. Lastly, *Peredur* survives in two earlier manuscripts: the late thirteenth-century Peniarth 7 and the early fourteenth-century Peniarth 14iv.[35] In the former, the text precedes a collection of Charlemagne material (translated from French into Welsh) and a series of texts known as *Ystoria Addaf* ('The Story of Adam'), which relates a history of salvation. In the latter, *Peredur* is once again associated with *Ystoria Addaf*, appearing at the end of a collection of mostly religious texts (the exception being *Proffwydoliaeth Fyrddin*). It may well be that the survival of *Peredur* in these two manuscripts is by chance, the result of their production in a monastic milieu with access to Latin and French texts and an interest in both religious and romance subject matter.[36] Or it may be the case that romances such as *Peredur* and the Charlemagne material are to be read as part of the salvation history that fills the rest of these manuscripts. In both cases, the heroes are presented as extending the scope of God's salvation by defeating the non-Christian occupiers of distant lands. Whatever the reason for the inclusion of *Peredur* in these two manuscripts, these copies offer a context for understanding the text in a different way from how they are presented in the White and Red Books, a context which is lacking for the other *Mabinogion* texts.

By the same token, later copies of the *Mabinogion* texts are also of little help in the reconstruction of earlier manuscript contexts because, with the exceptions of *Owein neu Iarlles y Ffynnawn* and *Breudwyt Maxen*, transmission is in a straight line from either the White Book or the Red Book. All later copies of the Four Branches, *Gereint uab Erbin*, *Peredur*, *Culhwch ac Olwen*, *Breudwyt Ronabwy*, and *Cyfranc Lludd a Llefelys* can be traced to these two sources. This may be a boon for editors of the texts, but for those wishing to understand their significance to different audiences over time, it is problematic. The source of three early modern copies of *Owein neu Iarlles y Ffynnawn* is unclear (NLW, MSS Llanstephan 171, Llanover B 17, and Cwrtmawr 20). All three copies differ from the White and Red Book versions by omitting any reference to Owain's lion, suggesting that they descend from an earlier version that also omitted these sections.[37] A fourth early modern copy (NLW, MS Llanstephan 58) seems to represent a version of an oral retelling of the tale.[38] It is unclear whether this version is descended from an older version than any of the others, or a different version, although it does contain the lion episodes that feature in the White and Red Book versions. Lastly, it is unclear whether the copy of *Breudwyt Maxen* found in London, British

Library, MS Additional 31055 in the hand of the antiquarian Thomas Wiliems of Trefriw (d. *c.* 1622) is taken from the Red Book or the White Book or from another source.[39]

The *Mabinogion* and the Matter of Britain

The manuscript evidence for the *Mabiniogion* texts before they were anthologized in the White and Red Books provides few clues to help us understand how they should be read. But those two anthologies can themselves offer indications as to how the patrons and scribes of the manuscripts regarded the texts at the end of the fourteenth century.[40] The content of the manuscripts, and the way in which the material is organized within them, points to a strong interest in the early history of Britain as a record of the history of the Welsh people themselves. The tales of the *Mabinogion*, with their accounts of ancestral dynasties, supernatural powers, and the great British king Arthur, were central to this history.

It is generally accepted that the collection known as the *Mabinogion* is a modern invention rather than a reflection of their original status as separate tales: Sioned Davies points out, for example, that while the Four Branches form a close group, the rest of the texts in the collection 'vary as regards date, authorship, sources, content, structure, and style'.[41] But although the texts could not have been produced as a unified collection by their original authors, the scribes of the White and Red Books apparently did consider them to be a group, with the possible exception of *Breudwyt Ronabwy*. In the White Book, a group of eight texts comprising the Four Branches, *Peredur*, *Breudwyt Maxen*, *Cyfranc Lludd a Llefelys*, and *Owein neu Iarlles y Ffynnawn* appears between folios 171 and 242, all in the hand of a single scribe (Scribe D). This group is followed by a copy of the Triads and *Bonedd y Saint* ('Genealogy of the Saints'), in the hand of the same scribe, then a group comprising a collection of *hengerdd*, *Geraint uab Erbin*, and *Culhwch ac Olwen* in the hand of a second scribe (Scribe E), with additions by Scribe D.[42] These texts treating the matter of Britain are grouped together, in the same way that other texts treating the matter of France are grouped together earlier in the manuscript (that is, the collection of Charlemagne texts in the hand of Scribe B which fills folios 66–117). In the Red Book of Hergest, all of the *Mabinogion* texts are found together between folios 154 and 205 of the manuscript, with the exception of *Breudwyt Ronabwy*, which appears earlier.[43] Like the White Book, the Red Book is a planned collection produced on commission for a wealthy patron. Its contents are arranged thematically: it begins with the *brutiau*, the Welsh chronicles, the great compiled history of Britain that starts with the siege of Troy, before moving on to the matter of France with a collection of Charlemagne texts. These are followed by a collection of wisdom texts, triads, and proverbs, and then come the *Mabinogion* texts, followed by texts of practical instruction. It seems that for the compilers of these two great manuscripts, the texts of the *Mabinogion* did, for the most part, form a group, despite their disparate origins.

Furthermore, in the Red Book, some of the *Mabinogion* texts are arranged in a chronological fashion so as to trace the fortunes of the British king, Beli son of Manogan, and his immediate descendants. In the Red Book, the *Mabinogion* section begins with two of the Arthurian tales inspired by Chrétien de Troyes, *Owein neu Iarlles y Ffynnawn* and *Peredur*. These are followed by *Breudwyt Maxen*, *Cyfranc Lludd a Llefelys*, and the Four Branches, which form a tight group united by their chronology. *Breudwyt Maxen* is a confusing case, as it seems to contain characters from two different time periods. The title character is a version of the Roman Magnus Maximus who was proclaimed emperor in 383.[44] He sets out in pursuit of a woman who appears to him in a dream and who turns out to be Elen, daughter of Eudaf son of Caradog. These characters of Maxen, Eudaf, and Elen appear in Geoffrey of Monmouth's *Historia* as Maximianus, Octavius, and Octavius's unnamed daughter, the first two being the 99th and 98th kings of the Britons according to Geoffrey's version of British history. Upon his entry into Britain, the Welsh Maxen is described as seizing control of the island from Beli and returning it to Eudaf. This Beli is Geoffrey's Heli, the 79th king of Britain, who, following Geoffrey's chronology, must have been long dead by the time the events in *Breudwyt Maxen* are supposed to have taken place.[45]

The reference to Beli in *Breudwyt Maxen* may cause a disjunction between the characters within the text, but it serves to link the tale with the one that follows it, *Cyfranc Lludd a Llefelys*. This tale describes events during the reign of Lludd son of Beli, who appears in Geoffrey's *Historia* as Lud, Geoffrey's 80th king of Britain.[46] The Four Branches appear to take place during the reign of Beli's son Caswallawn, Geoffrey's Cassibellaunus, the 81st king of Britain, who succeeds his brother Lud. The Second Branch is concerned with the children of Penardun, the daughter of Beli son of Mynogan, namely Brân (Bendigeidfran), Branwen, and Manawydan (the children of Llŷr), and Nysien and Efnysien (by a different father, Euroswydd). In this story, Caswallawn seizes power from his nephew Brân while the latter is away fighting in Ireland, disenfranchising Brân's son Caradog.[47] Caswallawn is mentioned again in the Third Branch, when Pryderi goes to Oxford to pay homage to him.[48] This tightly knit group of tales is followed by two more Arthurian texts, *Geraint uab Erbin* and *Culhwch ac Olwen*. The presence of Arthur in these two texts indicates that, chronologically, they take place after the other group.

Whatever their original settings, *Breudwyt Maxen*, *Cyfranc Lludd a Llefelys*, and the Four Branches form an identifiable group in the Red Book, following a chronology based on the reigns of the kings Beli, Lludd, and Caswallawn. This chronology is not integral to the texts themselves and, indeed, causes several problems. The disjunction caused by the presence of Beli in *Breudwyt Maxen* has been mentioned above. Further problems arise with this ordering of the texts. According to the genealogies, Brân's son Caradog is the father of Eudaf and the grandfather of Elen, who appear in *Breudwyt Maxen*.[49] As Rachel Bromwich has pointed out, according to Geoffrey's *Historia*, Beli had originally come to power by ousting Eudaf from the throne. In defeating Beli and returning rule of the Island of Britain to Eudaf, Maxen restores the throne to the descendants of Caradog, who had been ousted by Caswallawn in the Second Branch.[50] As things stand in the Red Book, this restoration occurs before the ousting that it is meant to remedy, and the tale of Caradog's descendants (Eudaf and his daughter Elen) precedes that of Caradog himself. Following the chronology of the characters of the texts according to the genealogies and the logic of the stories themselves, the Four Branches should come first, then *Breudwyt Maxen* and then *Cyfranc Lludd a Llefelys*. The arrangement of the texts in the Red Book does not follow this chronology; rather, it adheres to the timeline of the kings who appear in Geoffrey's *Historia*.

This timeline, however, is not necessarily of Geoffrey's invention and is likely to have its roots in native Welsh tradition. The Triads, for example, many of them predating Geoffrey's *Historia*, refer to Lludd and Caswallawn as the sons of Beli, as do the sixth-century poems of Taliesin.[51] Nevertheless, the chronological arrangement in the Red Book suggests that the texts are being presented by the compiler(s) of this manuscript as a version of British history. The Red Book begins with the collection of historical texts built around *Brut y Brenhinedd* ('The Chronicle of the Kings'), the thirteenth-century Welsh translation of Geoffrey's *Historia*. This is the central historical narrative of medieval Wales, whose key themes of the loss of sovereignty in Britain and the hopes of its restoration under a prophesied ruler, though not the products of Geoffrey's imagination, receive their most enduring form in his work.[52] The texts of the *Mabinogion* echo these themes. Like Geoffrey's *Historia*, the *Mabinogion* presents a past where British kings ruled over the entire Island of Britain.[53] Like the *Historia*, the tales treat the themes of loss of sovereignty and its restoration under rightful leaders. Episodes in the *Mabinogion* have echoes in Geoffrey's work. At the end of the Second Branch, Brân's men travel to London and bury his head under under the White Hill in one of the three 'fortunate concealments' of the Island of Britain.[54] The Triad which this action references states further that Brân's head is buried with its face towards France, and that it was Arthur who dug up the head, unhappy that another king should be responsible for the protection of the land.[55] The king's physical body (or his head at least) seems to be guarding the kingdom. This episode is echoed in the *Historia* in the preservation of the body of Geoffrey's penultimate king Cadwallawn, whose corpse is enbalmed in bronze and set upon a statue of a horse. This rather macabre monument was erected over the western gate of London 'in order to cause fear and terror amongst the Saxons'.[56] The idea seems to be similar to that which motivates the interment of Brân's head: the physical presence of the king will offer protection from, in the case of Cadwallawn, an imminent threat. According to Geoffrey, Cadwallawn's son Cadwaladr is warned against pursuing the kingship of Britain by an angelic voice which advises him to go to Rome instead. The voice prophesies that the Britons will never regain control of Britain until Cadwaladr's bones are brought back from Rome, when the bones of all the saints of Rome which had been hidden for fear of the pagans would be revealed.[57] In this case, the burial of the rightful heir in another country ensures that foreign invaders will gain the upper hand.

The echo of these episodes in the Second Branch lends credence to them, not necessarily as actual historical events, but as statements of the right of British kings to the land. The invocation of 'Ynys Prydein' in the *Mabinogion*, the mythical ideal of an Island of Britain united under a single British king, echoes Geoffrey's frequent allusions to that same political entity, but in contrast to Geoffrey's vision of the island united under its Norman masters, the *Mabinogion* affirms the uniting of the peoples of the island under British dominion.[58] In this way, the *Mabinogion* texts offer an alternative history to Geoffrey's version. While not replicating Geoffrey's account of British history, they support the ideas behind it by offering a variant set of events that take place within the same political and geographical framework. History, or rather that singularly Welsh combination of history and prophecy known as *brud*, was one of the chief concerns of the patron of the Red Book, Hopcyn ap Tomas, who is referred to as 'maister of Brut' in a letter sent in 1403. The letter recounts that Hopcyn was summoned by Owain Glyn Dŵr when the latter was in Carmarthen, as he wanted to know 'how and what maneer hit schold be falle of him'.[59] *Brud* had come to mean prophecy by this time, but the concept derives from the prophecies that are an integral part of *Brut y Brenhinedd*, in which the outcomes of the future depend on the moral behaviour of the actors of the past.[60] Hopcyn's mastery of *brud* is a mastery of history as well as prophecy. It is very likely, then, that his interest in the *Mabinogion* was a product of his interest in British history. Whatever the original purpose of these texts, it seems that by the fourteenth century they had been co-opted into the dominant historical narrative of the day, that of Geoffrey's *Historia*, and turned into a narrative of the return of power to the Welsh.

Though their precise historical contexts and purposes cannot be retrieved, the tales of the *Mabinogion* remain a significant witness to Welsh political and narrative concerns after the coming of the Normans. The greatness of Arthur as a British overlord is affirmed in *Culhwch ac Olwen*, the earliest vernacular account of Arthur's leadership, while Arthur's subsequent appropriation by Norman kings and French story-tellers is satirized in *Breudwyt Ronabwy*. The adaptations of Arthurian tales from the romances of Chrétien de Troyes (along with the translations of French Charlemagne stories found alongside the *Mabinogion* in the Red Book of Hergest) suggest the increasing Welsh interest in the cultural traditions of their Norman and English neighbours. Above all, the Four Branches and the tales of British history reclaim a lost past, confirmed by Geoffrey of Monmouth's *Historia Regum Britanniae*, in which Welsh kings ruled over the whole Island of Britain, their power made manifest through supernatural events.

Though the context and arrangement of the *Mabinogion* in the White Book and Red Book manuscripts suggest something of their continuing importance for fourteenth-century patrons and readers, this does not move us further towards dating or localizing the texts in their earlier forms. It does not go any distance towards filling the information void in which they seem to exist. This void may be frustrating for those who seek concrete answers to the questions raised here. But it also offers a space for many competing analyses to coexist and the possibility for further interpretation. While scholars may be no closer to apprehending the original functions of the *Mabinogion*, the texts remain immensely meaningful, enriched by over 150 years of scholarship.

Notes

1. *The Mabinogion: From the Llyfr Coch o Hergest and Other Ancient Welsh
   Manuscripts*, ed. and trans. Lady Charlotte Guest, 3 vols. (London: Longman,
   Orme, Brown, Green, & Longmans; Llandovery: W. Rees, 1849). The Welsh
   texts and English translations first appeared as a seven-volume series
   between 1838 and 1845 and were reissued as a three-volume set in 1849.
   The English translations, without the Welsh texts, first appeared as a single
   volume in 1877 and were reissued in 1906 (London: J. M. Dent, 1906). Guest's
   quotation comes from the 1906 volume, xviii.

2. The form *mabinogion* occurs only once in the manuscript sources and is
   assumed to be a false plural, a scribal error for the form *mabinogi* which occurs
   several times in the Four Branches and is already a plural form. Its precise
   meaning is obscure, but it is almost certainly connected to the Welsh word
   mab (boy, son). See Diana Luft, 'The Meaning of *Mabinogi*', *CMCS* 62 (2011):
   57–79; Helen Fulton, 'Cultural Meanings in the *Mabinogi*', in *Origins and
   Revivals: Proceedings of the First Australian Conference of Celtic Studies*, ed.
   G. Evans, B. Martin, and J. Wooding (Sydney: Centre for Celtic Studies,
   University of Sydney, 2000), 437–52. By convention, *Mabinogion* is used by
   modern editors and translators to refer to the eleven tales as a group (following
   the lead of Lady Charlotte Guest), while *Mabinogi* refers only to the Four
   Branches which are related textually as a coherent set of tales. The standard
   translation of *The Mabinogion* is by Sioned Davies (Oxford: Oxford University
   Press, 2008), with earlier translations by Gwyn Jones and Thomas Jones
   (London: Dent, 1949) and Jeffrey Gantz (Harmondsworth: Penguin, 1976).

3. For a discussion and translation of *Hanes Taliesin*, see *The Mabinogi and Other
   Medieval Welsh Tales*, trans. Patrick K. Ford (Berkeley and Los Angeles:
   University of California Press, 1977).

4. For theories about the author of the Four Branches, see Sioned Davies,
   'Pedeir Keinc y Mabinogi: A Case for Multiple Authorship?', in *Proceedings of the
   First North American Congress of Celtic Studies*, ed. G. MacLennan (Ottawa:
   University of Ottawa, 1988), 443–59; Sioned Davies, 'Written Text as
   Performance: The Implications for Middle Welsh Prose Narratives', in
   Literacy in Medieval Celtic Societies, ed. Huw Pryce (Cambridge: Cambridge
   University Press, 1998), 133–48; Ned Sturzer, 'Inconsistencies and Infelicities
   in the Welsh Tales', *Studia Celtica* 37 (2003): 127–42; Andrew Breeze,
   The Origins of the Four Branches of the Mabinogi (Leominster: Gracewing, 2009).

5. For the southern-origin theory, see *Pedeir Keinc y Mabinogi*, ed. Ifor Williams,
   2nd edn (Cardiff: University of Wales Press, 1951). For the northern-origin
   theory, see Brynley F. Roberts, 'Where Were the Four Branches of the
   Mabinogi Written?', in *The Individual in Celtic Literatures*, ed. Joseph

Falaky Nagy (Dublin: Four Courts Press, 1991), 61–73, and Patrick Sims-Williams, 'Clas Beuno and the Four Branches of the Mabinogi', in *150 Jahre 'Mabinogion': deutsch-walisische Kulturbeziehungen*, ed. Bernhard Maier and Stephan Zimmer (Tübingen: Max Niemeyer, 2001), 111–27. On issues of dating, see Simon Rodway, 'The Where, Who, When and Why of Medieval Welsh Prose Texts: Some Methodological Considerations', *Studia Celtica* 41 (2007): 47–89, and his *Dating Medieval Welsh Literature: Evidence from the Verbal System* (Aberystwyth: CMCS Publications, 2013). For a useful summary of the arguments, see *Math uab Mathonwy*, ed. Ian Hughes (Dublin: Dublin Institute for Advanced Studies, 2013), xv–xxi.

6. *Culhwch ac Olwen: An Edition and Study of the Oldest Arthurian Tale*, ed. Rachel Bromwich and D. Simon Evans (Cardiff: University of Wales Press, 1992), lxxxi, and Thomas Charles-Edwards, 'The Date of *Culhwch ac Olwen*', in *Bile ós Chrannaib: A Festschrift for William Gillies*, ed. Wilson McLeod *et al.* (Ceann Drochaid: Clann Tuirc, 2010), 45–56. For later dates see Simon Rodway, 'The Date and Authorship of *Culhwch ac Olwen*: A Reassessment', *CMCS* 49 (2005): 21–44, and his *Dating Medieval Welsh Literature*, 168–70.

7. See Thomas Charles-Edwards, 'The Date of the Four Branches', *THSC* (1970–1971): 263–98 for the first position. For various later dates, see Ceridwen Lloyd-Morgan, '*Breuddwyd Rhonabwy* and Later Arthurian Literature', in *The Arthur of the Welsh: The Arthurian Legend in Medieval Welsh Literature*, ed. Rachel Bromwich, A. O. H. Jarman, and Brynley Roberts (Cardiff: University of Wales Press, 1991), 183–208; Helen Fulton, 'Cyd-destun Gwleidyddol *Breuddwyt Ronabwy*', *Llên Cymru* 22 (1999): 42–56; Helen Fulton, 'Originating Britain: Welsh Literature and the Arthurian Tradition', in *A Companion to British Literature*, ed. Robert DeMaria, Heesok Chang, and Samantha Zacher (Oxford: Wiley-Blackwell, 2014), 308–22.

8. Brynley Roberts, for example, argues that Elen's request for the founding of the cities of Caernarfon, Carmarthen, and Caerleon as her bride price in the tale *Breudwyt Maxen* reflects Llywelyn ap Iorwerth's interest in those three centres. See his edition of the text, *Breudwyt Maxen Wledic* (Dublin: Dublin Institute for Advanced Studies, 2005), lxxviii–lxxxvi. For other associations of the tales with Llywelyn ab Iorwerth, see Susan Aronstein, 'When Arthur Held Court in Caer Llion: Love, Marriage, and the Politics of Centralization in *Gereint* and *Owein*', *Viator* 25 (1994): 215–28; Helen Fulton, 'Magic and the Supernatural in Early Welsh Arthurian Narrative: *Culhwch ac Olwen* and *Breuddwyd Rhonabwy*', *Arthurian Literature* 30 (2013), 1–26.

9. For such readings, see Andrew Welsh, '*Manawydan fab Llyr*: Wales, England and the "New Man"', in *Celtic Languages and Celtic Peoples: Proceedings of the Second North American Congress of Celtic Studies, 1989*, ed. Cyril J. Byrne, Margaret Harry, and Pádraig Ó Siadhail (Halifax: D'Arcy McGee Chair of

Irish Studies, St Mary's University, 1992), 369–82; Catherine McKenna, 'Learning Lordship: The Education of Manawydan', in *Ildánach Ildírech: A Festschrift for Proinsias Mac Cana*, ed. John Carey *et al.* (Aberystwyth: Celtic Studies Publications, 1999), 101–20; Catherine McKenna, 'Revising Math: Kingship in the Fourth Branch of the *Mabinogi*', *CMCS* 46 (2003): 95–118; Helen Fulton, 'The *Mabinogi* and the Education of Princes in Medieval Wales', in *Medieval Celtic Literature and Society*, ed. Helen Fulton (Dublin: Four Courts Press, 2005), 230–47.

10. Catherine McKenna, 'The Theme of Sovereignty in *Pwyll*', *BBCS* 29 (1980–81): 35–52.

11. See Helen Roberts, 'Court and *Cyuoeth*: Chrétien de Troyes' *Erec et Enide* and the Middle Welsh *Gereint*', *Arthurian Literature* 21 (2004): 53–72, and Helen Fulton, 'Gender and Jealousy in *Gereint uab Erbin* and *Le Roman de Silence*', *Arthuriana* 24.2 (2014): 43–70, for this interpretation.

12. See J. K. Bollard, 'Traddodiad a Dychan yn *Breuddwyd Rhonabwy*', *Llên Cymru* 13 (1980): 155–63; Edgar Slotkin, 'The Fabula, Story, and Text of *Breuddwyd Rhonabwy*', *CMCS* 18 (1989): 89–111; and Lloyd-Morgan, '*Breuddwyd Rhonabwy* and Later Arthurian Literature' for the literary satire; Fulton, 'Cyd-destun Gwleidyddol *Breudwyt Ronabwy*', for the political target; Dafydd Glyn Jones, 'Breuddwyd Rhonabwy', in *Y Traddodiad Rhyddiaith yn yr Oesau Canol*, ed. Geraint Bowen (Llandysul: Gwasg Gomer, 1974), 176–9, and Fulton, 'Originating Britain', for the last theory.

13. Sarah Higley, 'Perlocutions and Perlections in the Dream of Rhonabwy: An Untellable Tale', *Exemplaria* 2 (1990): 537–61.

14. See Doris Edel, 'The Catalogues in *Culhwch ac Olwen* and Insular Celtic Learning', *BBCS* 30 (1983): 253–67, for the first interpretation; Sioned Davies, 'Performing *Culhwch ac Olwen*', *Arthurian Literature* 21 (2004): 27–51, for the second; and Joan Radnor, 'Interpreting Irony in Medieval Celtic Narrative: The Case of *Culhwch ac Olwen*', *CMCS* 16 (1988): 41–59, and Ned Sturzer, 'The Purpose of *Culhwch ac Olwen*', *Studia Celtica* 39 (2005): 145–67, for the third. See also Kirstie Chandler, 'The Humour in *Breuddwyd Rhonabwy*', *Studia Celtica* 36 (2002): 59–71, for similar concerns about *Breudwyt Ronabwy*.

15. For criticism of this methodology, see Rodway, *Dating Medieval Welsh Literature*, 4–9.

16. Patricia Clare Ingham, 'Marking Time: *Branwen, Daughter of Llyr* and the Colonial Refrain', in *The Postcolonial Middle Ages*, ed. Jeffrey Jerome Cohen (New York: St Martin's Press, 2000), 225–46; Catherine McKenna, 'The Colonization of Myth in *Branwen uerch Lyr*', in *Myth in Celtic Literatures*, ed. Joseph Falaky Nagy (Dublin: Four Courts Press, 2007), 105–19; Jon Kenneth Williams, 'Sleeping with an Elephant: Wales and England in the Mabinogion', in *Cultural Diversity in the Middle Ages*, ed.

Jeffrey Jerome Cohen (New York: Palgrave Macmillan, 2008), 173–90; Michael A. Faletra, *Wales and the Medieval Colonial Imagination: The Matters of Britain in the Twelfth Century* (New York: Palgrave Macmillan, 2014), 178–80.

17. Susan Aronstein, 'Becoming Welsh: Counter-Colonialism and the Negotiation of Native Identity in *Peredur vab Efrawc*', *Exemplaria* 17 (2005): 135–68. See also Natalia Petrovskaia, 'Dating *Peredur*: New Light on Old Problems', *Proceedings of the Harvard Celtic Colloquium* 29 (2009): 223–43.

18. On the Celtic aspects of these texts, see W. J. Gruffydd, *Math vab Mathonwy: An Inquiry into the Origins and Development of the Fourth Branch of the Mabinogi with the Text and a Translation* (Cardiff: University of Wales Press, 1928); W. J. Gruffydd, *Rhiannon: An Inquiry into the First and Third Branches of the Mabinogi* (Cardiff: University of Wales Press, 1953); Proinsias MacCana, *Branwen Daughter of Llŷr: A Study of the Irish Affinities and of the Composition of the Second Branch of the Mabinogi* (Cardiff: University of Wales Press, 1958); Patrick K. Ford, 'Prolegomena to a Reading of the Mabinogi: *Pwyll* and *Manawydan*', *Studia Celtica* 16–17 (1981–2): 110–25; Patrick K. Ford, '*Branwen*: A Study of the Celtic Affinities', *Studia Celtica* 22–23 (1987–8): 29–41.

19. Rachel Bromwich, 'Celtic Dynastic Themes and the Breton Lays', *Études Celtiques* 9 (1960): 439–74; Glenys Goetinck, *Peredur: A Study of Welsh Tradition in the Grail Legends* (Cardiff: University of Wales Press, 1975).

20. See, for example, Natalia Petrovskaia, *Medieval Welsh Perceptions of the Orient* (Turnhout: Brepols, 2015), 163–5. For a more general critique of the idea of the sovereignty goddess and the ubiquity of its application, see Erica Sessle, 'Exploring the Limitations of the Sovereignty Goddess through the Role of Rhiannon', *Proceedings of the Harvard Celtic Colloquium* 14 (1994): 9–13.

21. The classic discussion of Rhiannon as a figure from early Celtic mythology is by Gruffydd, *Rhiannon*. See also his earlier work, *Folkore and Myth in the Mabinogion* (Cardiff: University of Wales Press, 1958).

22. See Ronald Hutton, 'Medieval Welsh Literature and Pre-Christian Deities', *CMCS* 61 (2011): 57–85, for a treatment of the idea that the characters of Welsh tales were based on Celtic deities; and Jessica Hemming, 'Ancient Tradition or Authorial Invention? The "Mythological" Names in the Four Branches', in *Myth in Celtic Literatures*, ed. Nagy, 83–104, for a discussion of the non-mythological origin of many of the names in the Four Branches.

23. W. J. Gruffydd, 'The Mabinogion', *THSC* (1912–13): 14–81; K. H. Jackson, *The International Folk Tale and Early Welsh Tradition* (Cardiff: University of Wales Press, 1961); Juliette Wood, 'The Calumniated Wife in Medieval Welsh Literature', *CMCS* 10 (1985): 25–38; Andrew Welsh, 'The Traditional Narrative Motifs in *The Four Branches of the Mabinogi*', *CMCS* 15 (1988): 51–62; Andrew Welsh, 'Traditional Tales and the Harmonizing of Story in *Pwyll*

Pendeuic Dyuet', *CMCS* 17 (1989): 15–41; Andrew Welsh, 'Branwen, Beowulf, and the Tragic Peaceweaver Tale', *Viator* 22 (1991): 1–13; Joseph Falaky Nagy, 'Folklore Studies and the Mabinogion', in *150 Jahre 'Mabinogion'*, ed. Maier and Zimmer, 91–100.

24. John Carey, 'A British Myth of Origins?', *History of Religions* 31 (1991): 24–38; John T. Koch, 'A Welsh Window on the Iron Age: Manawydan, Mandubracius', *CMCS* 14 (1987): 17–52; John T. Koch, 'Brân, Brennos: An Instance of Early Gallo-Brittonic History and Mythology', *CMCS* 20 (1990): 1–20.

25. Tony Hunt, 'The Art of *Iarlles y Ffynnawn* and the European *Volksmärchen*', *Studia Celtica* 8–9 (1973): 107–20; J. K. Bollard, 'The Structure of the Four Branches of the *Mabinogi*', *THSC* (1974–75): 250–76; J. K. Bollard, 'The Role of Myth and Tradition in the Four Branches of the *Mabinogi*', *CMCS* 6 (1983): 67–86; Ceridwen Lloyd-Morgan, 'Narrative Structure in *Peredur*', *Zeitschrift für Celtische Philologie* 38 (1981): 187–231; R. M. Jones, 'Narrative Structure in Medieval Welsh Prose Tales', in *Proceedings of the Seventh International Congress of Celtic Studies*, ed. D. Ellis Evans (Oxford: Oxford University Press, 1986), 171–98; Sturzer, 'Inconsistencies and Infelicities'.

26. For the common source theory, see *Owein, or Chwedyl Iarlles y Ffynnawn*, ed. R. L. Thomson (Dublin: Dublin Institute for Advanced Studies, 1968) and references therein, and Constance Bullock-Davies, *Professional Interpreters and the Matter of Britain* (Cardiff: University of Wales Press, 1966). For the Welsh texts as adaptations of the French, see Tony Hunt, 'Some Observations on the Textual Relationship of *Li Chevaliers au Lion* and *Iarlles y Ffynnawn*', *Zeitschrift für Celtische Philologie* 33 (1974): 93–113; A. H. Diverres, '*Iarlles y Ffynnawn* and *Le Chevalier au Lion*: Adaptation or Common Source?', *Studia Celtica* 16–17 (1981–2): 144–62; Carl Lindahl, 'Yvain's Return to Wales', *Arthuriana* 10 (2000): 44–56; Erich Poppe, '*Owein, Ystorya Bown*, and the Problem of "Relative Distance": Some Methodological Considerations and Speculations', *Arthurian Literature* 21 (2004): 73–94; and Ceridwen Lloyd-Morgan, 'Migrating Narratives: *Peredur, Owain*, and *Geraint*', in *A Companion to Arthurian Literature*, ed. Helen Fulton (Oxford: Wiley-Blackwell, 2009), 128–41.

27. Rachel Bromwich, 'Trioedd ynys Prydein and the Chwedlau', in *Trioedd Ynys Prydein*, ed. and trans. Rachel Bromwich, 4th edn (Cardiff: University of Wales Press, 2014), lxix–lxxx.

28. *Math uab Mathonwy*, ed. Hughes, lxxiii–lxxvi, 71–2.

29. *Breudwyt Maxen Wledic*, ed. Roberts, lxiii–lxiv. See also John F. Matthews, 'Macsen, Maximus, and Constantine', *Welsh History Review* 11 (1982): 431–48; and Patrick Sims-Williams, 'Some Functions of Origin Stories in Early Medieval Wales', in *History and Heroic Tale: A Symposium*, ed. Tove Nyberg *et al.* (Odense: Odense University Press, 1985), 97–131. For

Geoffrey's account of Maximianus, see *History of the Kings of Britain: An Edition and Translation of the De gestis Britonum [Historia Regum Britanniae]*, ed. Michael D. Reeve, trans. Neil Wright (Woodbridge: Boydell Press, 2007), Book 5, 98–110.

30. Ian Hughes, 'The Four Branches of the *Mabinogi* and Medieval Welsh Poetry', *Studi Celtici* 4 (2006): 154–93.

31. *Math uab Mathonwy*, ed. Hughes, lxxii, and his 'The King's Nephew', in *150 Jahre 'Mabinogion'*, ed. Maier and Zimmer, 55–66.

32. For a discussion of the manuscript tradition, see Thomas Charles-Edwards, 'The Textual Tradition of Medieval Welsh Prose Tales and the Problem of Dating', in *150 Jahre 'Mabinogion'*, ed. Maier and Zimmer, 23–40.

33. Daniel Huws, *Medieval Welsh Manuscripts* (Cardiff: University of Wales Press, 2000), 245; see also Huws's forthcoming work, seen in draft, *A Repertory of Welsh Manuscripts and Scribes* (2 vols., unpublished), 'Peniarth 6'.

34. Huws, *Repertory*, 'Jesus 20'.

35. For a treatment of the relationship between these versions, see Brynley F. Roberts, '*Peredur son of Efrawg*: A Text in Transition', *Arthuriana* 10 (2000): 57–72, and Peter Wynn Thomas, 'Cydberthynas y Pedair Fersiwn Ganoloesol', in *Canhwyll Marchogion: Cyd-destunoli Peredur*, ed. Sioned Davies and Peter Wynn Thomas (Caerdydd: Gwasg Prifysgol Cymru, 2000), 10–50.

36. Daniel Huws, 'Y Pedair Llawysgrif Canoloesol', in *Canhwyll Marchogion*, ed. Davies and Thomas, 3–4.

37. *Owein*, ed. Thomson, x.

38. Sioned Davies, '"O Gaer Llion i Benybenglog": Testun Llanstephan 58 o *Iarlles y Ffynnon*', in *Cyfoeth y Testun: Ysgrifau ar Lenyddiaeth Gymraeg yr Oesoedd Canol*, ed. R. Iestyn Daniel *et al.* (Caerdydd: Gwasg Prifysgol Cymru, 2003), 326–48. For an edition of the text, see R. L. Thomson, *Iarlles y Ffynnon: The Version in Llanstephan MS 58*', *Studia Celtica* 6 (1971): 57–89.

39. *Breudwyt Maxen Wledic*, ed. Roberts, xiv.

40. For a discussion of the Four Branches in the context of the White Book see Catherine Mckenna, 'Reading with Rhydderch: Mabinogion Texts in Manuscript Context', in *Language and Power in the Celtic World*, ed. Anders Ahlqvist and Pamela O'Neill (Sydney: Celtic Studies Foundation, University of Sydney, 2011), 205–30.

41. *Mabinogion*, trans. Davies, x.

42. Huws, *Medieval Welsh Manuscripts*, 231.

43. Daniel Huws, 'Llyfr Coch Hergest', in *Cyfoeth y Testun*, ed. Daniel *et al.*, 5. See Catherine McKenna, '"What Dreams May Come Must Give Us Pause": *Breudwyt Ronabwy* and the Red Book of Hergest', *CMCS* 58 (2009): 69–99, for a reading of that text in the context of its place in the Red Book.

44. *Breudwyt Maxen Wledic*, ed. Roberts, xliii.

45. 'Ac y goresgynnws er enys e dreis y ar Veli vab Manogan a'e veibeon ac a'e gyrrws wynt <ar vor>' ('and he seized the island by force from Beli son of Manogan and his sons and he drove them upon the sea'), *Breudwyt Maxen Wledic*, ed. Roberts, 7. For Geoffrey's Heli, see *History of the Kings of Britain*, ed. Reeve, trans. Wright, Book 3, 66–7.

46. *Cyfranc Lludd a Llefelys* ed. Brynley F. Roberts (Dublin: Dublin Institute for Advanced Studies, 1975).

47. 'Onyt goresgyn o Gaswallawn uab Beli Ynys y Kedyrn, a'y uot yn urenhin coronawc yn Llundein' ('except that Caswallawn son of Beli has seized the Isle of the Mighty, and is the crowned king in London'), *Branwen uerch Lyr*, ed. Derick Thomson (Dublin: Dublin Institute for Advanced Studies, 1961), 15.

48. 'A minheu a af y hebrwng uy gwrogaeth y Gaswallawn uab Beli hyt yn Lloegyr' ('and I will go to England to convey my homage to Caswallawn son of Beli'), *Manawydan uab Llyr*, ed. Ian Hughes (Cardiff: University of Wales Press, 2007), 2.

49. P. C. Bartrum, *A Welsh Classical Dictionary: People in History and Legend up to about AD 1000* (Aberystwyth: National Library of Wales, 1993), 114. See also Dafydd Glyn Jones, 'Bonedd yr Arwyr', in his *Agoriad yr Oes* (Talybont: Y Lolfa, 2001), 158–79.

50. Rachel Bromwich, 'Dwy Chwedl a Thair Rhamant', in *Y Traddodiad Rhyddiaith*, ed. Bowen, 143–75.

51. See *Trioedd Ynys Prydein*, ed. and trans. Bromwich, 305–6 and 416–17, and P. C. Bartrum, 'Was There a British "Book of Conquests"?', *BBCS* 23 (1986): 1–5, for the relationship between Geoffrey's kings and those found in the Triads and genealogies. On Taliesin as a sixth-century poet, see Chapter 2 in this volume.

52. Brynley Roberts, 'Geoffrey of Monmouth and Welsh Historical Tradition', *Nottingham Medieval Studies* 20 (1976): 29–40, and his 'Geoffrey of Monmouth, Historia Regum Britanniae and Brut y Brenhinedd', in *The Arthur of the Welsh*, ed. Bromwich et al., 97–116. See also Chapter 5 in this volume for a discussion of the reception of Geoffrey's *Historia* in Wales.

53. For a treatment of the importance of the idea of the Island of Britain, see Sims-Williams, 'Some Functions of Origin Stories', 110–19.

54. 'Wynt a doethant hyt yn Llundein, ac a gladyssant y penn yn y Gwynuryn. A hwnnw <uu y> trydyd matcud ban gudywyt, a'r trydyd anuat datcud pann datcudywyt; cany doey ormes byth drwy uor y'r ynys honn, tra uei yn y cud hwnnw' ('they came to London and buried the head at the White Hill. And that was one of the three fortunate concealments when it was hidden, and one of the three unfortunate disclosures when it was disclosed; because no oppressor would ever

come over the sea to this island while it was in that hiding place'), *Branwen uerch Lyr*, ed. Thomson, 17.

55. *Trioedd Ynys Prydein*, ed. and trans. Bromwich, 94.
56. 'Yr aruthred ac ouyn y'r Saesson' ('terror and fear to the Saxons'), *Brut Dingestow*, ed. Henry Lewis (Caerdydd: Gwasg Prifysgol Cymru, 1942), 204. Geoffrey of Monmouth uses a similar phrase, *in terrorem Saxonibus*, 'to intimidate the Saxons' (*History of the Kings of Britain*, ed. Reeve, trans. Wright, Book 11, 276–7).
57. *Brut Dingestow*, ed. Lewis, 206; *History of the Kings of Britain*, ed. Reeve, trans. Wright, Book 11, 278–9.
58. For this view of Geoffrey's purpose, see R. William Leckie, *The Passage of Dominion* (Toronto: University of Toronto Press, 1981), and Faletra, *Wales and the Medieval Colonial Imagination*.
59. Hopcyn ap Tomas and the Red Book are discussed in Chapter 7 of this volume. See also Prys Morgan, 'Glamorgan and the Red Book', *Morgannwg* 21 (1978): 42–60. On this particular episode, see Helen Fulton, 'Owain Glyndŵr and the Prophetic Tradition', in *Owain Glyndŵr: A Casebook*, ed. Michael Livingston and John K. Bollard (Liverpool: University of Liverpool Press, 2013), 475–88.
60. For discussions of *brut / brud*, see Jerry Hunter, *Soffestri'r Saesson* (Caerdydd: Gwasg Prifysgol Cymru, 2000), 78–107; Aled Llion Jones, *Darogan: Prophecy, Lament and Absent Heroes in Medieval Welsh Literature* (Cardiff: University of Wales Press, 2013), 2–4.

5

Court Poetry and Historiography Before
1282

CATHERINE MCKENNA

Overview

During the 1090s, Welsh aristocrats and clerics came to feel threatened by the new Norman ascendancy in Britain more keenly than they had at any previous point during the thirty years or so that had elapsed since the Battle of Hastings. Wales had for centuries before the arrival of the Normans experienced pressure from Anglo-Saxon kingdoms to the east, and throughout the eleventh century had suffered the depredations of Vikings. Nor did the Normans ignore Wales entirely during their first years in Britain: from the late 1060s, William the Conqueror had instituted powerful earldoms on the Welsh border for the dual purpose of controlling Welsh aggression and establishing bases from which further conquest might be effected. The Normans made significant advances into Wales in the following years; William himself asserted his theoretical authority over Wales in 1081, when he visited St Davids, in west Wales, on what was euphemistically described as 'pilgrimage'.[1] But after the death in 1093 of Rhys ap Tewdwr, ruler of Deheubarth, Norman efforts to subjugate Wales intensified. More castles were constructed, more boroughs established, more ecclesiastical foundations redefined as subsidiaries of Norman monasteries in England. Violence and oppression rose to new levels, if we are to judge by Rhigyfarch ap Sulien's Latin lament, or by the laconic entry in one chronicle for 1093: 'And then fell the kingdom of the Britons.'[2] The tide turned, however, after Henry I died in 1135. During the Anarchy of Stephen's reign (1135–54), native Welsh rulers recovered a good deal of territory. And although Stephen's successor, Henry II, eventually secured the submission of the most powerful Welsh princes, the native aristocracy would remain in control of west Wales north of the Teifi, for all practical purposes, until late in the thirteenth century.

This period between 1135 and the final conquest of Wales by Edward I in 1282–3 has often been described as a golden age of Welsh native culture, and of literature in particular. Some scholars have located the composition of the Four Branches of the *Mabinogi*, for instance, in the reign of Stephen (see Chapter 4 in this volume). The date of the Four Branches must remain a matter of debate. It is certain, however, that this 150-year period saw the emergence of a class of professional poets devoted to supporting the native princes in their efforts to resist further encroachment of their territories and authority by the English king, as well as in their efforts to establish pre-eminence among their fellow Welsh rulers. Often looking back to poets whom they believed to have sung the praises of the heroes of the 'Old North' in the era that preceded the Anglo-Saxon conquest of England and the origins of the Welsh principalities of Gwynedd, Powys, and Deheubarth, the court poets of the twelfth and thirteenth centuries self-consciously located themselves in a tradition of immemorial antiquity. The *beirdd y tywysogion*, or 'poets of the princes', were doing much more than simply maintaining or reviving an ancient cultural practice, however. Rather, the twelfth and thirteenth centuries saw the formation of a cultural marketplace in which the poets were indispensable to the princes' prestige. Competing with one another for the patronage of the most powerful rulers, the poets also encouraged the princes to compete for their services. Some of the poets carved out enduring places for themselves and their families in a dynasty's *curia*. The poets of this period appear to have developed a self-regulating professional organization for the maintenance of poetic standards, an order in which only one poet in a district, it would seem, bore the title *pencerdd*, or 'chief of song'.[3]

The period 1135–1282 was one in which Norman incursion posed contin-uous and significant challenges to Welsh political autonomy. At the same time, however, contact with the Marcher lords and the English Crown introduced the Welsh princes and their courts to a great variety of new cultural forms and practices in the spheres of law, diplomacy, warfare, architecture, music, literature, and the staging of royalty, among others. These novel symbolic systems were useful to the Welsh princes in their dealings with the English. They also offered them instruments for the devel-opment and performance of expanded power and authority among their Welsh peers. During this period, Gwynedd, Powys, and Deheubarth – and in the thirteenth century, Gwynedd in particular – emerged as the dominant political entities in what had been 'a country of many kings, many dynasties, many kingdoms'.[4] The rulers of these territories drew not only upon linguistic and cultural traditions that united the Welsh but also upon newly imported modes of representation in consolidating their power. The court poets were their partners in both aspects of the enterprise, the traditional and the innovative, the native and the imported.

The cultural institutions that the poets of this period built in symbiotic collaboration with their princes were products of their particular historical moment. After the conquest of 1283, and especially after the Acts of Union in the sixteenth century, praise poetry would be just one among a wide variety of modes available to poets. It would remain important to the poet's goal of securing patronage, and to the patron's sense of himself as a Welsh gentleman in the world, but after the conquest it would no longer be fundamental to the fabric of society, as it was during the period when 'the texture of over-kingdoms and princely authority was [being] woven more tightly'.[5]

Welsh historiography too came of age during the period between the advent of the Normans and the Edwardian conquest of Wales in 1282. Annalistic records were maintained in Wales from as early as the eighth century, but the period between 1135 and the end of Welsh independence saw the emergence of a more narrative historiography, and of history written in the vernacular. Influenced by the power of Geoffrey of Monmouth's story-telling in *Historia Regum Britanniae* ('History of the Kings of Britain'), or *De Gestis Britonum* ('Of the Deeds of the British'),[6] Welsh writers showed an increasing interest in shaping the story of the era from a distinctively Welsh perspective. In the later Middle Ages, scribes would build comprehensive histories for Wales extending from the Creation to the end of Welsh independence. These compilations comprised a summary of biblical history, a version of the Troy story based on the account attributed to Dares Phrygius, Geoffrey's *Historia* in translation (known in most versions as *Brut y Brenhinedd*, 'Chronicle of the Kings'), and the *Brut y Tywysogion* ('Chronicle of the Princes'), which covers the period from the end of Geoffrey's *Historia* down to the death of Llywelyn ap Gruffudd in 1282. The impulse to build this extensive narrative first manifested itself shortly after the end of our period, in the middle of the fourteenth century. However, Geoffrey's book was received enthusiastically in Wales from at least the end of the twelfth century, and it encouraged reflection not only on the story it tells of Britain between the arrival of Brutus and the death of Cadwaladr in 681 but also on the subsequent history of Wales; it would seem to have been the catalyst for the creation of the *Brut y Tywysogion*. This period also saw the production of the first biography in Welsh, an encomiastic account of the life of the twelfth-century prince

Gruffudd ap Cynan of Gwynedd, composed in Latin in the late twelfth century and translated into Welsh in the thirteenth.[7]

In certain respects, the tradition of court poetry and the development of a narrative and vernacular historiography in twelfth- and thirteenth-century Wales are parallel cultural phenomena arising out of the same social and historical circumstances. Both embody the renewed cultural confidence of much of the period; both reflect a growing sense of Wales as an integral entity, the remnant of the 'true' Britain and its heir. Both the bardic tradition and the historiographic tradition recognize the threat posed to Welsh culture by Anglo-Norman encroachment, but both also adapt some of the strategies of that oppositional culture – its genres, rhetorical modes, stories, and records – in the recuperation of a distinctive Welsh identity. Nevertheless, poetry and historiography are products of different, if interconnected, intellectual and social orders. The poetry is the product of a class of secular professionals about whose literacy we know virtually nothing. Its language is Welsh, with the exception of an occasional phrase of ecclesiastical Latin, such as *Dominus Deus*. The poets and their poems belong to the world of princely courts. The annals, chronicles, and other materials that constitute medieval Welsh historiography, on the other hand, are the work of Christian clerics working in ecclesiastical foundations. They develop through the self-conscious production of contemporary or retrospective written records of significant events and through the sharing and exchange of such documents in highly literate environments. Until well into the thirteenth century, the language of these records was Latin.

One important point of connection between poetry and historiography in twelfth- and thirteenth-century Wales stands out, however, and that is the Cistercian monastic order that established thirteen houses in Wales during our period. Although the earliest patrons of these monasteries were Norman lords, it was not long before many of them came under the patronage of Welsh princes. These religious houses emerged as centres of the 'golden age of Welsh native culture' mentioned earlier. The ties between the monasteries and the dynasties that provided them with land, support, and protection were strong. Princes visited these foundations and undoubtedly brought members of their entourages with them, including perhaps their court poets. Through these connections, monastic communities, like court poets, came to be invested in the aspirations of the local aristocracy and interested in their conflicts. It was in the Cistercian monastery of Strata Florida that the chronicle eventually translated into Welsh as *Brut y Tywysogion* was compiled, drawing on material from other Cistercian houses and thus creating a national narrative out of multiple local records. It was also at Strata Florida, we have reason to believe, that the most important written record of court poetry was produced, the Hendregadredd manuscript (Aberystwyth, NLW, MS 6680B). The scribes at Strata Florida may well have gathered poems from the records and memories of Cistercian monasteries in various parts of the country in the same way that they gathered materials for their chronicle.

Historiography

Historical records were maintained in Wales from at least as early as the eighth century, during the period when Welsh society and institutions were establishing themselves following centuries of incremental loss of British territory to the Anglo-Saxons. It was in the ecclesiastical foundation of St Davids that historiographical materials from northern Britain, Ireland, and elsewhere were first gathered, and contemporary events were recorded there for several hundred years. These St Davids annals, known as the *Annales Cambriae*, purport to document events beginning in the mid-fifth century but were in fact maintained as a record of contemporary events only from the late eighth century.[8] Surviving versions of these annals suggest in their differences something about the movement of historiographical texts from scriptorium to scriptorium in the British archipelago and beyond, enabling the absorption of materials that filled in the record prior to the time at which it was begun, and the extension of a chronicle beyond the date at which it had originally concluded. All versions of the *Annales Cambriae* reflect the use of earlier Irish and British chronicles as sources. Several of them incorporate material derived from such sources as the Bible and Isidore of Seville's chronicles to fill in the early historical record, and some extend the original chronicle well into the thirteenth century with entries that sometimes reveal knowledge of and interest in the Anglo-Norman world, both within Wales and beyond. The English influence in these thirteenth-century versions of *Annales Cambriae* undoubtedly reflects the Norman control of St Davids from fairly early in the twelfth century, but it also suggests familiarity with the interweaving of British and English history in the writing of Geoffrey of Monmouth.

The appearance and rapid transmission in Wales of Geoffrey of Monmouth's *Historia Regum Britanniae* had a tremendous influence on history writing in Wales. It has been shown, for example, that Version C of the *Annales Cambriae* recasts some of the early material concerning the sixth- and seventh-century struggle in northern Britain between Britons and Anglo-

Saxons to make it conform to Geoffrey's account of the period.[9] And one manuscript of Welsh Latin annals contains a copy of Geoffrey's *Historia* as well. These are just two indications of the eagerness with which Geoffrey's approach to historiography – descriptive, rhetorical, chronologically comprehensive, and shaped by a strong sense of the rhythm of British history – was received in Wales.

Geoffrey's book appeared in the late 1130s, quite near the beginning of the period of Welsh resurgence. The question of its relationship to its sources is far too complicated for discussion here. However, in a survey of Welsh historical writing, two things are important about his work. The first is that he manifestly drew upon sources that survive, such as Gildas's sixth-century polemic on *The Ruin and Conquest of Britain*[10] and the ninth-century *Historia Brittonum*,[11] as well as sources that do not survive in the form in which he knew them, such as genealogies and king lists. He exhibits a knowledge of Welsh tradition that is preserved elsewhere in poetry, saints' lives, the Triads, and the narratives of the *Mabinogion*. Thus, we know that sources for the history of Britain and of Wales existed in the twelfth century and were available to Geoffrey, however unlikely it may be that the 'ancient book in the British tongue' that he claims as his single source ever existed.

Geoffrey's book was received enthusiastically in Wales. By the middle of the thirteenth century, three separate translations into Welsh of Geoffrey's Latin book had been produced, and additional translations would be made in the fourteenth century. The various translations were sometimes combined, creating additional versions of the Welsh book known as *Brut y Brenhinedd*. All of this activity bears ample witness to the importance accorded to Geoffrey's book. We have twenty-six full or fragmentary manuscript texts of *Brut y Brenhinedd*, a very large number indeed considering that many more are likely to have disappeared given the poor rate of survival of medieval Welsh manuscripts. At least four of these belong to our period, loosely speaking,[12] and a number of others to the first half of the fourteenth century.[13]

Several Welsh Latin chronicles, notably the B Version of *Annales Cambriae* and the text known as the *Cronica de Wallia*, provide a glimpse into another major development in medieval Welsh historiography. These texts appear to have been compiled not at St Davids, but in one or more Cistercian monasteries.[14] Kathleen Hughes believed that Strata Florida, founded in 1164, was the centre of activity for the B Version, while David Dumville has argued for Neath, but they agree on the Cistercian provenance of the text as it stands and are also in agreement about the centrality of Strata Florida to the *Cronica de Wallia*.[15]

These two texts attest to a shift in the centre of gravity of medieval Welsh historiography to the Cistercian monasteries, institutions that were, as we have seen, involved in the politics and the bardic culture of the period. Cistercian historiography in Wales reflects that same close association with the cultural resurgence of the twelfth and thirteenth centuries; Kathleen Hughes wrote of the B Version of *Annales Cambriae* that from 1189 to 1263, 'they speak with the voice of independent Wales',[16] and the *Cronica de Wallia* covers only that period, commencing at 1190 and ending at 1266. The annals of Cistercian provenance draw in places upon materials from several different houses, each of which held records concerning the aristocratic families of its own geographical area. The network of monasteries of the order allowed each to concentrate on the political concerns of its patrons and its enemies, and also made possible the assembly of the varied records thus compiled into a chronicle of Welsh Wales.

It was also in a Cistercian monastery, almost certainly Strata Florida, that a Latin chronicle very like the *Cronica de Wallia*, combined with a version of the St Davids chronicle that underlies the extant versions of *Annales Cambriae*, was translated into Welsh, and a tradition of vernacular historiography established. That Welsh adaptation of a now lost text is known as *Brut y Tywysogion*, or the Chronicle of the Princes. It exists in two versions, representing two separate translations into Welsh. The Latin source of this new chronicle was also combined with sources for English history, and that too was translated into Welsh, producing a text known as *Brenhinedd y Saesson* ('Kings of the English').[17]

Strictly speaking, these vernacular chronicles do not belong to our period. *Brut y Tywysogion* and *Brenhinedd y Saesson*, and undoubtedly their common Latin source, all originally terminated at 1282, the year of the death of Llywelyn ap Gruffudd and the end of Welsh independence. They commence in 681 with the departure from Britain of Cadwaladr ap Cadwallon, who is the last of the British kings according to Geoffrey's *Historia Regum Britanniae*. It is apparent from this chronology that this set of vernacular accounts and their Latin source are retrospective documents, intended to recount the history of the Welsh people from the moment at which they lost any claim to sovereignty over the whole of Britain, down to the moment of their forfeiture of political autonomy even in Wales.

It is equally apparent that *Brut y Tywysogion* and *Brenhinedd y Saesson* take Geoffrey's *Historia* as foundational and paradigmatic. They build upon his history of British Britain by attaching to it the annalistic materials that had accumulated in Wales from the eighth century on, and they emulate it by establishing a coherent chronology that constitutes a national history of sorts. There are tremendous differences between the *Historia* and *Brut y Tywysogion*. Geoffrey's sources are famously elusive, and there is good reason to believe that much of his narrative is pure invention. Each of the Welsh chroniclers, on the other hand, from the first eighth-century compilers of the *Annales Cambriae* down to the translators who produced *Brut y Tywysogion*, has been shown to have searched archives and borrowed manuscripts in order to amass the most comprehensive record possible. It can hardly be proven that at no point in this process did a scribe record a misreported, misunderstood, or purely fictional event, but the work of making the chronicles was a work of compilation by successive generations of diligent scribes, rather than the enterprise of a single author with an overarching rhetorical purpose like Geoffrey's.

Nevertheless, *Brut y Tywysogion* attests to the tremendous influence that Geoffrey had on monastic learned communities, on their sense of the structure of history and their taste in storytelling. For here and there in the chronicles, and increasingly in the accounts of later years, there is a narrative flair to certain episodes that suggests the development of a more rhetorical and ample approach to the writing of history.

The vernacular historiography that emerged in the thirteenth and fourteenth centuries did not speak to the international audience that the Cambro-Norman Gerald of Wales reached with his twelfth-century Latin accounts of Wales and its people, the *Itinerary Through Wales* and *Description of Wales*.[10] Together with the poetry and the narrative prose that were gathered in the great manuscript books of the fourteenth and fifteenth centuries, however, it would serve the citizens of the post-conquest principality as an essential constituent of sustained Welsh identity.

Court Poetry

It is more difficult to say when Welsh poetry was first recorded in writing than it is to estimate when the maintenance of a written historical record began. The oldest surviving book in Welsh, the Black Book of Carmarthen, is an eclectic anthology of poetry, and it dates from about 1250. It is likely that most of the poems in the Black Book were copied from earlier manuscripts, but it is possible that at least some of them were written from memory or dictation.[19] While the origins of a written tradition of Welsh poetry remain unclear, there is no doubt that the canon of poetry associated with the twelfth- and thirteenth-century Welsh princes is in large measure defined by a single book, the Hendregadredd manuscript, compiled in the fifty years or so after 1282. Hendregadredd is a planned anthology of court poetry. It opens with an elegy for Gruffudd ap Cynan of Gwynedd, who died in 1137; he is the earliest of the princes celebrated in the collection, and thus the period stretching from his reign to the death of Llywelyn ap Gruffudd in 1282 has been defined as the era of the *beirdd y tywysogion*, or 'poets of the princes', who are sometimes referred to as the *gogynfeirdd*, or 'somewhat early poets' (although the latter term includes some fourteenth-century poets as well). Gruffudd ap Cynan was also the first Welsh ruler to be celebrated in a biography, as has already been noted. It is not insignificant that this figure occupies such an important position in both the poetic and the historiographical traditions. He died at the beginning of the Welsh cultural resurgence of the twelfth century, and his elegy was inscribed in Hendregadredd soon after the downfall of the last native prince of Wales, who was also the prince of Gwynedd. In both the historiographical and poetic genres, Gruffudd ap Cynan stood simultaneously for the primacy of Gwynedd and the dignity of Wales.

There are indications that the tradition of praise poetry for Welsh rulers had its beginnings before the middle of the twelfth century: the Black Book of Carmarthen contains two courtly praise poems addressed to aristocrats of the early twelfth century. Indeed, it has been suggested that the tradition of praise poetry in Britain can be traced back at least as far as the sixth century: twelve poems associated with the northern British leader Urien Rheged and his son Owain in the fourteenth-century Book of Taliesin are regarded by some scholars as authentic survivals from that period. However, the twelfth and thirteenth centuries undoubtedly saw a tremendous upsurge in the amount of poetry produced for the courts of princes. Far more verse survives from that period than from earlier – about 12,600 lines, attributed to thirty-four named poets. Their surviving verse consists overwhelmingly of eulogies of living lords and elegies for lords who have died, along with a few poems for their wives or daughters and some occasional poems arising out of the relationship of a particular poet and a particular patron. Poems in praise of God and the Christian saints also constitute a significant proportion of their poetry. This, at any rate, is the nature of the poetry preserved in Hendregadredd and in the late fourteenth-century Red Book of Hergest, our other main source of Welsh court poetry. It has been argued, however, that some of the legendary and prophetic poems attributed to Taliesin in the fourteenth-century Book of Taliesin are the work of twelfth- and thirteenth-century court poets adopting the persona of that early medieval bard. This suggests that the court poets composed in a variety of modes, although praise poetry was their bread and butter, and the work most highly valued by the compilers of the Hendregadredd manuscript.

The praise poetry is conventional in both form and content, but at its best far from stale and predictable. The most skilled of the poets of the princes combine phrases that echo the *hengerdd* ('ancient poetry') of Aneirin and Taliesin, stock images that princes would have learned to recognize and expect, and fresh new metaphors. Thus, in an *awdl* in praise of Madog ap Maredudd of Powys, the poet Cynddelw (*fl. c.* 1155–95) refers, as does *Y Gododdin*, attributed to Aneirin, to the drink that a worthy martial leader provides to his retinue. He describes his lord as an 'eagle', employing one of the more frequently occurring metaphors in court poetry, but also, start-lingly, as 'the swirling of water around the feet of a seagull on the shore'.[20] The poets concentrate on the patron's martial valour and military achieve-ments, which keep his people safe. They also celebrate his generosity and hospitality, to all of his followers and especially to his poet. These are the principal themes and values of the praise poetry. Subsidiary topics are the prince's noble lineage, and the fairness and firmness of his rule. For the most part, elegies for patrons who have died are similar in tone to eulogies of living princes: they celebrate his victories and ignore any military setbacks he may have suffered; they rejoice in the suffering inflicted on enemies while eliding the inevitable suffering of his own people in warfare; they make token gestures of sorrow at the lord's passing and offer a cursory prayer for the welfare of his soul, but the focus is on the prince's life, rather than his death.

This is because the elegies are court poems, not personal lyrics, and their function was to present the dead prince to his heirs and rivals as a model of good lordship. This is apparent even in the elegy by Bleddyn Fardd (*fl. c.* 1268–83) for Llywelyn ap Gruffudd, the last native Welsh prince, who was killed in 1282: in the opening lines, he advises Dafydd, Llywelyn's surviving brother, against rash or haughty behaviour in the perilous circumstances of the moment. With Dafydd's death the following year, however, the implications of the fall of the Gwynedd dynasty threaten to overwhelm Bleddyn, and he laments that 'I have lost every friend and every lord that I loved' (line 7).[21] The greatest exception to the conventional elegy is the powerful *marwnad* com-posed for Llywelyn ap Gruffudd by Gruffudd ab yr Ynad Coch (*fl. c.* 1277–83). That poem envisions Llywelyn's death as violent, bloody, and irremediable, as dire as Arthur's death at Camlann, and catastrophic in its consequences for the future of Wales:

> Poni welwch-chwi hynt y gwynt a'r glaw?
> Poni welwch-chwi'r deri'n ymdaraw?
> Poni welwch-chwi'r môr yn merwinaw—'r tir?
> Poni welwch-chwi'r gwir yn ymgyweiriaw?
> Poni welwch-chwi'r haul yn hwylaw—'r awyr?
> Poni welwch-chwi'r sŷr wedi r'syrthiaw?
> Poni chredwch-chwi i Dduw, ddyniadon ynfyd?
> Poni welwch-chwi'r byd wedi r'bydiaw?[22]

> (See you not the rush of wind and rain?
> See you not the oaks lash each other?
> See you not the ocean scourging the shore?
> See you not the truth is portending?
> See you not the sun hurtling the sky?
> See you not that the stars have fallen?
> Have you no belief in God, foolish men?
> See you not that the world is ending?)[23]

This elegy by Gruffudd ab yr Ynad Coch does not appear in the Hendregadredd anthology of court poetry; our only medieval manuscript source for that poem is the late fourteenth-century Red Book of Hergest. However, it has been argued that the text of the poem in a seventeenth-century manuscript was copied from quires of the Hendregadredd manuscript that have since been lost.[24] Its absence from Hendregadredd serves to remind us of the uncertain prospect of long-term survival that attended any poem intended primarily for performance.

Poems addressed to God constitute the majority of the poems of a religious nature that have survived. These too are public court poems, as is apparent in both their content and their elaborate forms. The typical *awdl i Dduw* praises God in much the same manner as a prince would be praised, for his salvific activity and his generosity to his people and his poet. Court laws dating from the time of the princes stipulate that a poet called upon to perform should begin with a poem about God, and then present a poem for the king or prince.[25] Most of the surviving poems to God were in all likelihood composed for performance at court in fulfilment of this protocol. Other poems with religious content, including poems celebrating the Welsh saints Dewi, Cadfan, and Tysilio, are also structured as eulogies, both of the saints themselves and of the ecclesiastical foundations associated with them at St Davids, Tywyn, and Meifod respectively. These would have been performed at those institutions under the patronage of the abbot or the local prince.

The courtly nature of all the poetry of the princes – eulogies, elegies, hymns to God – is mirrored in its elaborate forms: the poems are highly wrought artefacts, designed to dazzle. They were composed by poets not only gifted but trained. The two forms that they employ are the *awdl* and the *englyn*. The former is an open-ended sequence of couplets linked to one another by a single end-rhyme that may be sustained for 100 lines or more. It is more common for a long *awdl* to comprise several monorhyming sections, joined by a device known as *cymeriad*, which links the opening of one rhyming section to the end of the preceding one by the repetition of a word. The couplets constituting an *awdl* are of various shapes, and the poets combine them not only for variety but also to structure their poems. The *englyn*, on the other hand, is a stanza. Although there are three-line *englyn* forms, it is the various kinds of four-line *englyn* that are employed in the court poetry of the twelfth and thirteenth centuries. There has been much debate concerning the functions and relative status of *awdlau* vs *englynion*, to use the plural forms of *awdl* and *englyn*; the most that can be said with confidence is that the *awdl* appears to have been regarded as a more elevated form.

The strict ornamental patterns of consonants constituting the *cynghanedd* of fourteenth- and fifteenth-century *cywydd* poetry had not developed fully in our period. However, what would come to be called *cynghanedd sain* is very common. A line of nine syllables is divided into three parts, of which the first two rhyme, while the third is bound to the second by alliteration, as when Cynddelw describes Madog ap Maredudd as "I'wrł gr*ug*, yng ng*oddug*, yng ng*oddaith*' ('the roar of heather in tumult, on fire').[26] Even apart from this specific pattern, the poets are generally extravagant in their use of internal rhyme and alliteration.

These forms and modes of ornamentation are particularly appropriate to the public function of true court poems, but we see them employed as well in other kinds of occasional pieces. Fewer of these have survived than of eulogies and elegies for princes and other eminent persons, which were the poems most likely to be recorded and anthologized, as they constituted an important element in the histories of dynasties, principalities, and Wales as a whole. Nevertheless, we catch a glimpse here and there of the practice of composing poems in praise of noblewomen, which were most likely per-formed in their private quarters rather than in the main hall of a court.[27] There are also poems attributed to two of the Welsh princes themselves, Hywel ab Owain Gwynedd (d. 1170) and Owain Cyfeiliog of Powys (d. 1197).

Hywel is the purported author of a number of poems celebrating the glories of Gwynedd and its women, and Owain of a single extended *awdl* in praise of the men of his retinue. It has been suggested that Owain's poem may in fact have been composed for him by his court poet, Cynddelw Brydydd Mawr, and Hywel may have had help with his charming lyrics as well.[28] It is likely to have been their association with the princes, though, that accounts for the inclusion of these poems in the Hendregadredd anthology, where they afford a glimpse into an aristocratic world in which the elaborate forms of court poetry could also be employed in *jeux d'esprit*. The reputation of the afore-mentioned Cynddelw as 'the great poet', if that is what his epithet *prydydd mawr* refers to, may account for the survival of a touching series of three *englynion* on the death of his son Dygynnelw, a unique example of the forms and modes of court poetry adapted to more personal lyric purposes.

It is very likely that the court poets also composed poems in forms other than those they employed in their eulogies and elegies, but nevertheless for the audiences of the princely courts. Marged Haycock has shown that many of the poems in the early fourteenth-century Book of Taliesin, a book written while the Hendregadredd manuscript was still being added to, are probably the work of court poets. She has made a detailed case for Prydydd y Moch, an important Gwynedd poet of the last quarter of the twelfth century and first quarter of the thirteenth, as the author of a number of poems whose speaking persona is the legendary and archetypal poet Taliesin. These are poems that put on display esoteric knowledge of various kinds – knowledge of Welsh legendary tradition, of scripture, of classical literature, and of Christian apocrypha. They abound in riddles and in boasts about the spiritual powers of the poet. Many of these poems employ shorter lines than those found in the eulogies and elegies, and typically a single rhyme is sustained over a shorter course of lines than would be expected in an *awdl*. It is thought that they may have served as general entertainment at courtly gatherings that included not only the resident prince and his retinue, but also ambassadors and visitors from other parts of Wales.[29]

It is, however, the public praise poetry of the medieval court poets that has survived in the greatest quantity, not only because it was the stock in trade of the court poets, but also because it played a significant role in the political culture of twelfth- and thirteenth-century Wales. The poets were publicists for ambitious princes and contributed to the coalescence of power in Gwynedd, Deheubarth, and Powys – and eventually in Gwynedd above all. They also contributed to the emergent sense of overarching Welsh identity by defining their patrons and their language in opposition to the *Saeson*, the

English. The princes depended upon the verbal skill of their poets as they depended upon their own martial skills, and those of their followers, to advance their ambitions. For example, on at least one occasion, Prydydd y Moch, court poet to Llywelyn ab Iorwerth of Gwynedd, served Llywelyn as ambassador to Rhys Gryg, a southern prince of much less extensive power, in order to cement the alliance between the two princes. For the occasion, he composed and undoubtedly performed a poem of extravagant praise for Rhys that also describes Llywelyn as the greatest king since Arthur and promises that Rhys's own fame and glory will be enhanced by welcoming Llywelyn's poet into his court.[30]

The poets depended on the patronage of the princes, but their skills were valuable to those princes, and thus highly marketable. Cynddelw was a native of Powys and served as court poet to the last prince of a united Powys, Madog ap Maredudd. In an elegy for Madog, who died in 1160, Cynddelw laments the invasion by Gwynedd of the cantref of Edeirnion; it would not have happened had Madog been alive, he insists.[31] Yet it was not long before Cynddelw found himself in the court of Owain Gwynedd, prince of north Wales. He composed eulogies for Owain and one for his son, the poet-prince Hywel. He also composed an elegy for Owain, who died in 1170. Then at some point he moved south, to the court of the Lord Rhys of Deheubarth, the most powerful Welsh lord of the final quarter of the twelfth century. One would like to imagine that he was present at that court in 1176 when the Lord Rhys held a competition during his Christmas feast at which the best poet was awarded a chair. It was poets from Gwynedd who won that competition, according to *Brut y Tywysogion*,[32] and Cynddelw might have been considered a Gwynedd poet if he had spent a decade or more at the court of Owain and his sons.

Whether he participated in that feast or not, Cynddelw is an excellent example of the aggressive competitiveness of Welsh bardic culture in the time of the princes. He certainly claims to have won a chair in poetic contention, and thereby to have acquired the right to take on students; in fact, he claims it is customary for him to triumph in such contentions.[33] Like other poets, he advertises his poetic skill within his poems, as though inviting members of his audience to bid for his services, and disparages the abilities of his fellow poets: 'Shut up, bards, it's a bard you hear,' he commands in a poem composed for the Lord Rhys.[34]

The poets are sufficiently confident in the value of their cultural capital to challenge their princely patrons when they feel themselves underappreciated. Prydydd y Moch, court poet to three generations of Gwynedd princes, warns one of them not to let his poems be treated 'like pearls before swine', and he counsels another not to 'trample on his own cloak' by disregarding the profit that his poet's service brings him.[35]

Welsh court poetry of the twelfth and thirteenth centuries was intended for oral performance. Its contemporary cultural power was a function of the interplay of personalities, reputations, and the political moment in which it was performed at a princely court. Subsequently preserved in anthologies like the Hendregadredd manuscript and the Red Book of Hergest, it became for posterity something different: a record of the triumphs and losses of the final centuries of an independent Wales, and a window into the aristocratic life of that era. The Cistercian order, so central to the tradition of Welsh historiography, played an important part in this phase of the tradition of court poetry as well. It was at the Cistercian monastery of Strata Florida that the Hendregadredd manuscript was compiled over the course of several decades. A single scribe laid it out, leaving space for additional poems by each of the poets to whom he had assigned a gathering, and nineteen later contributors added systematically to his collection.[36] Their work is analogous to that of the historians who gathered material from annals maintained at various monasteries of the order and combined them, also at Strata Florida, into the inclusive Latin chronicle that underlies the *Brut y Tywysogion*. Like that comprehensive national history, the collected poetry of the princes was central to the national identity that the Cistercians sought to develop and to sustain.

Conclusion

Medieval Welsh historiography developed in a monastic milieu. Its original language was Latin, a vernacular historiography emerging only in the later thirteenth century; its sources were, for the most part, written and included texts of international provenance. The literary culture that produced the court poetry of the twelfth and thirteenth centuries was different in almost every respect. It had deep roots in a vernacular and largely oral tradition of legendary history; it required of its practitioners the ability to skilfully manipulate the lexical and phonological resources of the Welsh language within the confines of a restrictive metrical structure. We do not know a great deal about the training of a poet, but allusions in the poetry suggest a system in which the craft was taught by a recognized poet to the students that he took on, rather than within the institutional framework of a school as such.

Nevertheless, the cultural worlds of historiography and court poetry intersected. Poets and clerics belonged to different branches of a class of learned men closely associated with the aristocracy. Poets would have accompanied their patrons on visits to monasteries that they protected and supported, as the poems on ecclesiastical foundations suggest. It may have been through such contacts with clerics that they acquired the biblical learning displayed in the Taliesin poems and familiarity with some of the basic ideas disseminated in school texts – such as the notions of the five ages of the world, or the four elements – that find their way into the court poetry. Familiarity on the part of monastic historians with the traditions of court poetry is suggested by the encomiastic death notices that occur, although not in abundance, in *Brut y Tywysogion*. The most extravagant of these celebrates the Lord Rhys ap Gruffudd of Deheubarth, who died in 1197. In one version of *Brut y Tywysogion*, the eulogy in prose is followed by an elegy in Latin verse, a collocation that emblematizes both the close association of, and the differences between, the worlds of historiography and vernacular poetry.

It is no accident that the two traditions meet in connection with the Lord Rhys. It was he, as has been noted, who convened an assembly of poets and musicians to compete for prizes at his Christmas feast in 1176. He was also the effective founder, in 1165, of the Cistercian monastery of Strata Florida, where both *Brut y Tywysogion* and the Hendregadredd anthology of court poetry would be compiled in the years after the conquest of 1283. One of the great figures of the Welsh cultural resurgence, the Lord Rhys played a significant role in establishing the institutions within which both historiography and poetry could flourish and survive.

Notes

1. *Brut y Tywysogyon, or The Chronicle of the Princes: Red Book of Hergest Version*, ed. and trans. Thomas Jones (Cardiff: University of Wales Press, 1955), 30–1.
2. Ibid., 32–3. For an edition and translation of the lament of Rhigyfarch ap Sulien, see Michael Lapidge, 'The Welsh-Latin Poetry of Sulien's Family', *Studia Celtica* 8–9 (1973–4): 68–106, at 88–93; and more recently, Sarah Zeiser, 'Latinity, Manuscripts, and the Rhetoric of Conquest in Late Eleventh-Century Wales' (PhD diss., Harvard University, 2012), 332–6.
3. Dafydd Jenkins, '*Bardd Teulu* and *Pencerdd*', in *The Welsh King and His Court*, ed. T. M. Charles-Edwards *et al.* (Cardiff: University of Wales Press, 2000), 162–6.
4. R. R. Davies, *Conquest, Co-existence, and Change: Wales 1063–1415* (Oxford and New York: Oxford University Press, 1987), 14.

5. Ibid., 13.

6. *The* Historia Regum Britannie *of Geoffrey of Monmouth*, ed. Neil Wright and Julia Crick, 5 vols. (Cambridge: D. S. Brewer, 1984–91).

7. See *Vita Griffini Filii Conani: The Medieval Latin Life of Gruffudd ap Cynan*, ed. and trans. Paul Russell (Cardiff: University of Wales Press, 2005); and *Historia Gruffud vab Kenan*, ed. D. Simon Evans (Cardiff: University of Wales Press, 1977).

8. On these earliest Welsh annals, see Kathleen Hughes, 'The Welsh Latin Chronicles: "Annales Cambriae"and Related Texts', The Sir John Rhŷs Memorial Lecture, 1973 (London: Oxford University Press, 1974), also published in *Proceedings of the British Academy* 59 (1973): 233–58. See also David N. Dumville, 'The Welsh Latin Annals', in *Histories and Pseudo-Histories of the Insular Middle Ages* (Aldershot: Variorum, 1990), vol. III, 461–7. See *Annales Cambriae*, ed. John (ab Ithel) Williams (London: Longman, Green, Longman, and Roberts, 1860).

9. Hughes, 'The Welsh Latin Chronicles', 243.

10. See *Gildas: The Ruin of Britain and Other Works*, ed. and trans. Michael Winterbottom (London: Phillimore, 1978).

11. See *Nennius: British History and the Welsh Annals*, ed. and trans. J. Morris, History from the Sources: Arthurian Period Sources 8 (London: Phillimore, 1980).

12. These are Aberystwyth, NLW MS Peniarth 44; NLW Llansteffan MS 1; NLW MS 5266B (the Dingestow manuscript); and NLW MS Peniarth 21. See Owain Wyn Jones, 'Historical Writing in Medieval Wales' (PhD diss., Bangor University, 2013), 37, nn. 28–31; and Daniel Huws, 'Table of Welsh Vernacular Medieval Manuscripts', in *Medieval Welsh Manuscripts* (Cardiff and Aberystwyth: University of Wales Press and National Library of Wales, 2000), 58.

13. NLW MS 3036B (Mostyn 117); NLW Peniarth MS 45; Cardiff, Central Library MS 1.363 (Hafod 2); British Library, Cotton MSS, Cleopatra B.v. See Owain Wyn Jones, 'Historical Writing in Medieval Wales', 37–8, nn. 30–2; and Huws, 'Table of Welsh Vernacular Medieval Manuscripts', 59. For an overview of *Brut y Brenhinedd*, see *Brut y Brenhinedd, Llanstephan MS. 1 Version, Selections*, ed. Brynley F. Roberts (Dublin: Dublin Institute for Advanced Studies, 1971), xxiv–xxxix.

14. Hughes, 'The Welsh Latin Chronicles', 247–9.

15. Ibid., 257; Dumville, 'The Welsh Latin Annals', 464.

16. Hughes, 'The Welsh Latin Chronicles', 250.

17. *Brut y Tywysogion, Red Book Version*, ed. and trans. Jones; also *Brut y Tywysogion, or the Chronicle of the Princes, Peniarth MS 20 Version*, ed. and trans. T. Jones (Cardiff: University of Wales Press, 1952); and *Brenhinedd y Saesson, or the Kings of the Saxons: BM Cotton MS. Cleopatra B.v and the Black Book of*

Basingwerk, NLW MS. 7006, ed. and trans. T. Jones (Cardiff: University of Wales Press, 1971). *Brenhinoedd y Saeson, 'The Kings of the English', AD 682–954: Texts P, R, S in Parallel*, ed. D. N. Dumville, Basic Texts for Medieval British History 1 (Aberdeen: University of Aberdeen Department of History, 2005).

18. Gerald of Wales, *The Journey Through Wales and the Description of Wales*, trans. Lewis Thorpe (Harmondsworth: Penguin, 1978).

19. This possibility is discussed by Huws in 'Five Ancient Books of Wales', in *Medieval Welsh Manuscripts*, 71–2. There is further discussion of non-written sources in Paul Russell, 'Scribal (In)consistency in Thirteenth-century South Wales: The Orthography of the Black Book of Carmarthen', *Studia Celtica* 43 (2009): 168 and 170; and Nerys Ann Jones, 'Ffynonellau Canu Beirdd y Tywysogion', *Studia Celtica* 37 (2003): 100–1.

20. *Gwaith Cynddelw Brydydd Mawr, I*, ed. Nerys Ann Jones and Ann Parry Owen, Cyfres Beirdd y Tywysogion, vol. III (Caerdydd: Gwasg Prifysgol Cymru, 1991), no. 1, ll. 14, 18, 26. All translations are mine unless otherwise indicated.

21. *Gwaith Bleddyn Fardd a Beirdd Eraill Ail Hanner y Drydedd Ganrif ar Ddeg*, ed. Rhian M. Andrews *et al.*, Cyfres Beirdd y Tywysogion, vol. VII (Caerdydd: Gwasg Prifysgol Cymru, 1996), no. 52, l. 7.

22. Thomas Parry, ed., *The Oxford Book of Welsh Verse* (Oxford: Clarendon Press, 1962), 47–8.

23. Joseph P. Clancy, trans., *The Earliest Welsh Poetry* (London: Macmillan, 1970).

24. Dafydd Johnston, 'Bywyd Marwnad: Gruffudd ab yr Ynad Coch a'r Traddodiad Llafar', in *Cyfoeth y Testun: Ysgrifau ar lenyddiaeth Gymraeg yr Oesoedd Canol*, ed. R. Iestyn Daniel *et al.* (Caerdydd: Gwasg Prifysgol Cymru, 2003), 200. Also, Johnston, review of *Gwaith Dafydd Benfras ac Eraill o Feirdd Hanner Cyntaf y Drydedd Ganrif ar Ddeg*, ed. N. G. Costigan (Bosco) *et al.*, Cyfres Beirdd y Tywysogion vol. VI, *Llên Cymru* 21 (1998): 196–7; and Huws, 'The Hendregadredd Manuscript', in *Medieval Welsh Manuscripts*, 226.

25. *The Law of Hywel Dda: Law Texts from Medieval Wales*, ed. and trans. Dafydd Jenkins (Llandysul: Gomer Press, 1986), 20.

26. *Gwaith Cynddelw Brydydd Mawr, I*, ed. Jones and Parry Owen, no. 7, l. 9.

27. *The Law of Hywel Dda*, ed. and trans. Jenkins, 20.

28. Gruffydd Aled Williams, 'Owain Cyfeiliog: Bardd-dywysog?', in *Beirdd a Thywysogion: Barddoniaeth Llys yng Nghymru, Iwerddon a'r Alban*, ed. Brynley F. Roberts and Morfydd E. Owen (Caerdydd: Gwasg Prifysgol Cymru a Llyfrgell Genedlaethol Cymru, 1996), 180–201; see also Gruffydd Aled Williams, 'Canu Owain Cyfeiliog', in *Gwaith Llywelyn Fardd I ac Eraill o Feirdd y Ddeuddegfed Ganrif*, ed. Kathleen Anne Bramley *et al.*, Cyfres Beirdd y Tywysogion, vol. II (Caerdydd: Gwasg Prifysgol Cymru, 1994), 199–206.

29. *Legendary Poems from the Book of Taliesin*, ed. and trans. Marged Haycock, 2nd edn (Aberystwyth: CMCS Publications, 2015), 25–40.

30. Especially ll. 91–102; *Gwaith Llywarch ap Llywelyn 'Prydydd y Moch'*, ed. Elin M. Jones and Nerys Ann Jones, Cyfres Beirdd y Tywysogion, vol. V (Caerdydd: Gwasg Prifysgol Cymru, 1991), no. 26.
31. *Gwaith Cynddelw Brydydd Mawr, I*, ed. Jones and Parry Owen, no. 8, ll. 65–8.
32. *Brut y Tywysogion: Red Book Version*, ed. and trans. Jones, 166–7.
33. *Gwaith Cynddelw Brydydd Mawr, I*, ed. Jones and Parry Owen, no. 21, ll. 182–7; and *Gwaith Cynddelw Brydydd Mawr, II*, ed. Jones and Parry Owen, Cyfres Beirdd y Tywysogion, vol. IV (Caerdydd: Gwasg Prifysgol Cymru, 1995), no. 6, ll. 236–7.
34. *Gwaith Cynddelw Brydydd Mawr, II*, ed. Jones and Parry Owen, no. 10, l. 16.
35. *Gwaith Llywarch ap Llywelyn 'Prydydd y Moch'*, ed. Jones and Jones, no. 8, ll. 13–14; no. 2, ll. 59–60.
36. Huws, 'The Hendregadredd Manuscript', 199–218.

6

The Aftermath of 1282: Dafydd ap Gwilym and his Contemporaries

DAFYDD JOHNSTON

The death of Llywelyn ap Gruffudd at the hands of the English in 1282 brought to an end the kingdom of Gwynedd's resistance to Edward I, marking the final demise of the independent Welsh princes. This turning point in Welsh political history also demarcates the boundary between two periods in the history of Welsh poetry, distinguished by a change in patronage. Until 1282–3 poets had been maintained at the courts of the princes with duties and privileges defined by the native laws. The loss of royal patronage meant that poets had to turn to patrons from the lower ranks of the Welsh nobility, and this change was one of the factors which eventually led to a new poetic style in the period under consideration in this chapter and the next.

The new patrons belonged to a class known in Welsh as *uchelwyr* (literally 'high men'), a term denoting freemen possessing land through inheritance, usually rendered in English as gentry or nobility. The poets of this period are therefore known as *beirdd yr uchelwyr*, in contrast to *beirdd y tywysogion*, the poets of the princes. However, there was some degree of continuity of patronage, since a few of the *uchelwyr* were descended from royal lineages and others belonged to families which had served the princes and probably also patronized poets (most notably the numerous descendants of Ednyfed Fychan, minister to Llywelyn Fawr of Gwynedd, who married a daughter of the Lord Rhys of Deheubarth).

The loss of the royal courts, although undoubtedly traumatic at the time, was by no means an unmitigated disaster for the poets, since their new patrons were a much more numerous class than the princes, and they seem to have regarded patronage of traditional praise poetry as a means of demonstrating their standing as leaders of Welsh society, albeit on a much more local scale than their royal predecessors. Because it was no longer possible for a poet to be maintained as a permanent member of any court, poets travelled around the country much more than their predecessors had done, visiting a series of patrons on extensive journeys sometimes lasting several months. In addition to their secular patrons they would also have visited religious houses, particularly the Cistercian abbeys which provided another element of continuity from the age of the princes.[1]

The new towns of Wales established in the aftermath of the Edwardian conquest of 1282 have often been regarded as islands of Englishness from which the native Welsh were excluded. Whilst this may be true of towns with a strong military presence, such as some in the recently subdued region of Gwynedd, understanding of the ethnic composition of urban populations is now more nuanced, and it is recognized that the towns did play a significant role in Welsh culture.[2] Dafydd ap Gwilym's comic account of his unfortunate encounter with three English merchants in an urban tavern is sometimes cited as evidence that the towns were a hostile environment for the Welsh, but it might also indicate that poets did visit the towns and found ready audiences there.[3] Nevertheless, the poets' primary base of patronage continued to be the gentry whose wealth and power derived from their rural estates, and much of the praise poetry to them celebrated a pastoral ideal in opposition to urban mercantilism.

Although this chapter will highlight new literary developments, the contrast between the two periods should not be overstated. There were many aspects of continuity in both poetry and prose, and some of the supposedly innovative features which became apparent in the fourteenth century, such as use of European literary conventions, can in fact be traced back well into the thirteenth century. An instructive material witness to that continuity is the Hendregadredd manuscript, originally a retrospective compilation of the poetry of the age of the princes made around 1300, probably at the Cistercian abbey of Strata Florida, an undertaking continued by a second generation of scribes, before the manuscript moved to a local nobleman's house where visiting poets seem to have utilized blank spaces to add pieces in both the old style and the new.[4]

It might be argued that literature itself was a key element of continuity after the Edwardian conquest, providing the Welsh nobility with a sense of cultural identity which to some extent compensated for the loss of political sovereignty. If that was so, then the poets may have represented a vestige of national unity, traversing as they did an otherwise fragmented country and performing their compositions in a standardized literary language and a style redolent of the former royal courts. But on the other hand, many of those who patronized the poets had a vested interest in the new political regime, holding offices in local government in the service of absent English lords and raising troops for the king's foreign wars. There was thus a potential clash between their political and their cultural loyalties, and the heroic ideals inherited from a poetic tradition which celebrated resistance to the Saxon invaders became increasingly anachronistic.

As a result of the influx of settlers in the wake of the Edwardian conquest, English and French became much more widespread in Wales, and those *uchelwyr* who held administrative offices would certainly have been bilingual or even trilingual. This multilingual environment left its mark on the new poetry of the fourteenth century, which is studded with loanwords. It also led to an increase in translation activity, and most of the prose literature of the fourteenth century is translated from French or Latin. Translation of French romances had already begun under the patronage of the princes in the thirteenth century, stimulated by contact with the Normans of the Marcher lordships, and the contrast between the two periods is less marked in the case of prose than in the case of poetry.

The Welsh version of the story of Beves of Hampton, *Ystorya Bown de Hamtwn*, dates from the thirteenth century, and the first part of the Charlemagne cycle, *Cronicl Turpin*, was translated for Prince Gruffudd ap Maredudd of Deheubarth.[5] Translations of other parts of that cycle followed in the early fourteenth century, and references in the poetry to heroes such as Roland, as well as to heroes of romances of which no Welsh translation has survived, such as Fulke Fitz Warin, suggest widespread familiarity with the material of European romance. Towards the end of the century, the Greal legends were translated from two French romances, *La Queste del Saint Graal* and *Perlesvaus*, to form the longest of all Middle Welsh prose works.[6] An influential work translated from Latin was *Kedymdeithyas Amlyn ac Amic*, the story of two faithful friends which provided an exemplary model of male companionship.[7] A set of popular *exempla* associated with the Seven Sages of Rome was adapted into Welsh around the middle of the fourteenth century, and unusually for prose works of this period, it is attributed to a named author, Llywelyn Offeiriad (Llywelyn the Priest).[8]

Manuscripts of the fourteenth century also contain a range of functional texts which formed an integral part of the literary culture of the period, encompassing religion, history, medicine, law, heraldry, husbandry, and travel writing. A programme of translations of religious works seems to have begun in the thirteenth century in response to the decrees of the Fourth Lateran Council of 1215 which sought to raise educational standards amongst churchmen and laity, promoted in Wales especially by the Dominican Friars. The fruits of this programme, including a Welsh version of the *Elucidarium* by Honorius of Augustodunum and several saints' lives, are preserved primarily in two manuscript collections of the mid-fourteenth century, one copied by an anchorite at Llanddewifrefi,[9] and the other, Peniarth 5, part of the White Book of Rhydderch. Historiography also features prominently in manuscripts, playing a vital role in maintaining a sense of nationhood, and it was in the fourteenth century that translations of Geoffrey of Monmouth's *Historia Regum Britanniae* were combined with two other texts, *Ystorya Dared* on the Trojan war which preceded Aeneas's coming to Britain, and the chronicle of the age of the Princes, *Brut y Tywysogion*, to produce a complete history of the Welsh nation. The other type of text which accounts for a substantial proportion of the contents of Welsh manuscripts in this period is the law of Hywel Dda.[10] Aspects of the native laws continued to be operative in some areas of Wales until the Acts of Union, particularly with regard to landownership, so these texts would have had some practical purpose, but they also seem to have been valued by patrons as an expression of cultural identity.

Evidence for poetry composed in the decades immediately following the Edwardian conquest of 1282 is scarce, and although loss of manuscripts may have been a factor, there undoubtedly was a decline in bardic activity resulting from the crisis of patronage. When poetry does reappear a generation or so later, most of it is highly traditional in content and style. This should not be regarded simply as literary inertia, but rather as a deliberate assertion of cultural continuity in a period of complex political loyalties. The importance of continuity is evident in the work of Gwilym Ddu, a poet from Arfon in the heart of the old kingdom of Gwynedd, whose elegy to Trahaearn Brydydd Mawr depicts his fellow-poet as successor to a bardic tradition stretching back through the masters of the age of the princes to the legendary figures of Myrddin and Taliesin.[11] Gwilym's only known patron was Sir Gruffydd Llwyd, great-grandson of Ednyfed Fychan and a prominent servant of the Crown in Gwynedd. When Sir Gruffydd was imprisoned by the king for eighteen months in 1316–18 for unclear reasons (possibly to do with a projected pan-Celtic uprising against the English), Gwilym composed two poems portraying him as leader of his people in war and peace, whilst avoiding any specific reference to his political allegiances.[12]

The fourteenth-century poets who continued to use the traditional poetic style are sometimes known as later *gogynfeirdd*, a term primarily used to denote the Poets of the Princes. This bardic conservatism had its adherents in all parts of Wales, including Casnodyn of Glamorgan, poets such as Llywelyn Brydydd Hoddnant whose work was preserved in the Hendregadredd manuscript in Ceredigion, and Gruffudd ap Maredudd of Anglesey. The characteristic features of this poetry are the use of the monorhyme *awdl* metres with heavy ornamentation involving internal rhymes, archaic vocabulary with extensive compounding, and loose syntax based on parallel phrases, all of which combine to create an impressively elevated but rather ponderous poetic style.

Gruffudd ap Maredudd (*fl.* 1366–82) was the last great exponent of the old style, and the substantial body of his work preserved in the Red Book of Hergest displays a remarkable consistency of style and vision across a range of poetic genres, including eulogy and elegy, courtly love poems, satirical invective, and religious verse.[13] He appears to have relied on the patronage of a single extended family in his native Anglesey, the Tudors of Penmynydd, another branch of the descendants of Ednyfed Fychan and one which seems to have remained loyal to some ideal of political independence. In an elegy to Goronwy ap Tudur in 1382, he makes a telling comparison with the loss of Llywelyn, the last prince of Gwynedd, who died exactly one hundred years earlier.[14] And Gruffudd ap Maredudd's most politically significant poem is his address to Owain Lawgoch, last direct descendant of the royal line of Gwynedd, urging him to return from his exile in the service of the king of France to reclaim his patrimony.[15] Drawing on the language of prophecy to inspirational effect, this poem is powerful evidence that Gruffudd ap Maredudd's conservatism was much more than just a matter of literary fashion. His style was particularly suited to long poems which approached their subject from multiple angles, building a composite picture in the manner of a mosaic. Such is his celebration of the Rood at Chester,[16] and his stately elegy to a young woman called Gwenhwyfar, one of the high points of fourteenth-century Welsh poetry, in which he adopts the persona of the lamenting lover in order to express her family's grief.[17]

Use of the old *awdl* metres did not necessarily entail a conservative poetics. Even in the period soon after the Edwardian conquest, there are instances of bold innovation which anticipate the work of Dafydd ap Gwilym and his contemporaries. Gruffudd ap Dafydd ap Tudur is a particularly interesting figure in this respect, although unfortunately only five of his poems have survived.[18] There is reason to believe that he had been a member of Llywelyn ap Gruffudd's court at Abergwyngregyn in Gwynedd, and that one at least of his poems was composed not long after Llywelyn's death in 1282. He is the author of the earliest definite example of a request poem, asking for the gift of a bow, and also of a poem of thanks for the gift of a belt, two genres which were soon to become extremely popular. But it is his two love poems which are of most interest. One is a complaint addressed to a girl who refuses to reply to his pleas, in which he urges her to follow the example of Adam and Eve by making free love in a woodland setting. This is one of Dafydd ap Gwilym's favourite themes, and Dafydd must have known this poem since he reused a couplet from it. The other love poem makes even bolder play with the conventions of courtly love by presenting a court case in which the poet formally accuses a girl of having killed him by rejecting his love. The girl then makes her defence, stating quite simply that she cannot have killed him because he stands alive in court. This self-mocking take on the motif of the mortally wounded lover is striking evidence of the literary sophistication of audiences in north-west Wales in the late thirteenth century.

Another innovative poet of the early fourteenth century was Casnodyn, although the mixture of old and new modes amongst his twelve surviving poems defies easy categorization.[19] A native of west Glamorgan, his poetry pays a great deal of attention to travel, both around Wales and on pilgrimage to Jerusalem (in preparation for which he composed a lengthy *awdl* seeking the blessing of the Trinity), and he is the first to fully reflect the new bardic itinerancy. In his love poems addressed to noble women, he twice uses a device known from the *rhieingerddi* of the previous age, sending a horse as a love-messenger (a device used later in the century by Hywel ab Einion Lygliw and Gruffudd ap Maredudd). Casnodyn's love poems belong in the tradition of the *rhieingerdd* in that they functioned as praise for noble women and their families, but he added a more personal element and sought to persuade one young lady, a certain Awd of Llandeilo Fawr, to come to a tryst with him in the woods.

An aspect of Casnodyn's work which some modern readers find shocking is a viciously misogynistic verse attacking a woman called Nest.[20] Such satires actually feature quite prominently in the collection of contemporary poetry in the Red Book of Hergest, perhaps reflecting the compilers' tastes, and many poets of the fourteenth century composed such verse, whether as entertainment or in deadly earnest. They are generally regarded as a legitimate part of the bardic repertoire, the poet being able to curse and harm by his satire as well as being able to bless and safeguard by his praise. However, the predilection for satire was a cause of concern for some critics, who sought to maintain moral standards by setting out rules regarding the style and content of poetry in bardic grammars which constitute the earliest literary theory in Welsh.[21]

The precise authorship of the grammars is still unclear, but it is fairly certain that the fourteenth-century versions were the work of churchmen.

The earliest, probably dating to the 1320s, is attributed to a priest called Einion Offeiriad, and that seems to have been revised soon afterwards by Dafydd Ddu of Hiraddug, a canon in the diocese of St Asaph. Although not members of the professional bardic order, both Einion and Dafydd Ddu were accomplished poets. Einion's well-crafted eulogy to Sir Rhys ap Gruffudd suggests that he enjoyed the patronage of that powerful nobleman, whilst Dafydd Ddu was the author of didactic religious verse, and both are credited with devising new metres.[22] Their grammars are unlikely to have been used as textbooks for bardic education (although gradually adapted for that purpose in the fifteenth and sixteenth centuries), but nevertheless they are of great interest as an indication of how the bardic order responded to the crisis of patronage in the early fourteenth century.

The linguistic content of the grammars, covering syllables and parts of speech, was derived from the standard Latin works of Priscian and Donatus, scarcely adapted to the Welsh language. The section on poetic craft set out the traditional *awdl* metres, augmented to reach the ideal number of twenty-four, and metrical faults to be avoided. The most original part of the work, and the one which most clearly reveals the authors' idealistic philosophy, is the section detailing the virtues for which different people should be praised, ranging from God, Mary, and the saints, through the various ranks of ecclesiastics and laymen, including women and unmarried girls. This is followed by a series of statements on the nature of poetry, mainly in triadic form and based on a tripartite classification of types of poet with a strong moral bias. The highest grade is the *prydydd*, a bardic teacher whose main function was to praise virtuous people. Next is the *teuluwr*, a pupil of the *prydydd* whose poetry was meant primarily to entertain. The lowest grade is the *clerwr*, who is portrayed as a scurrilous purveyor of artless and immoral invective. This classification bears little relationship to the realities of bardic practice, since most of the major poets of the fourteenth century produced poems typical of all three grades, but it does suggest how the poets sought to maintain their traditional high status by emphasizing on the one hand the intricacies of their specialist craft and on the other the moral distinction between them and unqualified versifiers, whilst at the same time ensuring that their work had a broad appeal as entertainment. All this is very relevant to the emergence of the *cywydd* as the favoured metre of the *teuluwr*.

The examples of metres and metrical faults given in the various versions of the grammars provide an intriguing glimpse of a new kind of poetry, and it is here that we find the earliest examples of the *cywydd* metre, or the *cywydd deuair hirion* to give it its full name. The rudimentary form of those examples suggests that it began as a low-status metre, but by the middle of the century it had been tightened up by Dafydd ap Gwilym and his contemporaries into a metre which was sufficiently intricate to demonstrate a poet's technical artistry and yet flexible enough to be a vehicle for narrative, description, and lyric poetry. The essential features are couplets of seven-syllable lines, one ending with a stressed syllable and the other with an unstressed one, as seen in this example from a *cywydd* by Dafydd ap Gwilym addressing a seagull:

> Dilwch yw dy degwch di,
> Darn fal haul, dyrnfol heli. (DG.net 45.3–4)
>
> (Your beauty is without blemish,
> a piece like the sun, gauntlet of the brine.)

The key advantage of the *cywydd* over the monorhyme *awdl* was that the end-rhyme changed with every couplet, making far less demand on a poet's lexical resources and leading to a much lighter style.[23] The earliest *cywyddau* have only intermittent ornamentation within the line, but full *cynghanedd* soon became a requirement in every line. Meaning literally 'harmony', *cynghanedd* consists of a combination of alliteration and internal rhymes. It had been a feature of Welsh poetry since the earliest period, developing gradually over several centuries, but it was only towards the end of the age of the princes that it began to be treated as a rule-based system. *Cynghanedd* has an intrinsic appeal to the ear which would surely have been enhanced by the musical accompaniment on the harp or crwth.[24] It is also a very effective rhetorical device in the hands of an accomplished practitioner, underlining the meaning by binding words together and giving the line a memorably finished quality. Here are examples of the four main types of *cynghanedd*, all by Dafydd ap Gwilym. The simplest type is *cynghanedd lusg*, in which a word within the line rhymes with the penultimate syllable of the final word (both rhymes underlined here):

Harddwas teg a'm anrhegai   (*DG.net* 32.9)

Cynghanedd draws involves repetition of a sequence of consonants at the beginning and end of the line:

Gorllwyn ydd wyf ddyn geirllaes   (*DG.net* 111.1)

In *Cynghanedd groes* the repeated sequence fills the two halves of the line:

Lawlaw â mi, lili môr   (*DG.net* 45.8)

Cynghanedd sain combines rhyme and alliteration:

A'r byd yn hyfryd yn haf   (*DG.net* 34.8)

The style of the fourteenth-century *cywydd* was also elevated by extensive use of compound words and parenthetical phrases known as *sangiadau* which could extend syntax over several lines creating a polyphonic effect within the sentence. But on the other hand the *cywydd* often featured touches of ordinary speech, exclamations, curses, and English loanwords, so that again a balance was struck between artistry and plainness, between high and low styles.

Dafydd ap Gwilym is generally credited with popularizing the *cywydd* in the 1330s and 1340s through his bold and witty love poetry, but in fact several other poets were producing similar poems around the same time, and given the nature of the material it is extremely difficult to date individual poems. Dafydd tends to overshadow his contemporaries because far more of his poems have survived. The most recent edition of his poetry accepts 147 poems as his genuine work, but more than double that number are attributed to him in manuscripts, and his name seems to have been synonymous with a certain type of love poetry.[25]

Dafydd ap Gwilym was a native of north Ceredigion, and a number of his poems are located in his native parish of Llanbadarn Fawr near Aberystwyth, including one in which he depicts himself eyeing up the girls during a church service. The few dateable references in his poems cluster in the 1340s, and there is reason to believe that his career was relatively short. He was of noble stock and may not have depended on poetry for his living as bardic professionals did. However, he clearly was thoroughly trained in the poetic craft and produced *awdlau* in the traditional style, some of the stylistic features of which he transferred to the *cywyddau* which make up the bulk of his output.

In addition to his contribution to the early development of the *cywydd*, Dafydd ap Gwilym was also the first Welsh poet to make extensive use of themes and motifs from European literature (although as already noted such elements were already present in Welsh poetry a generation or so earlier). The only foreign author that he specifically acknowledges as a literary model is the Latin poet Ovid. Although he refers several times to 'the book of Ovid' ('llyfr Ofydd'), and to himself as 'Ovid's man' ('dyn Ofydd'), it is far from certain that he was familiar with Ovid's poetry. The significance of these references lies rather in the type of love poetry represented by Ovid in Medieval Europe, a playful and often cynical version of *amour courtois* without any of the high-minded idealism originally associated with that literary mode. It is likely that Dafydd knew the influential French work *Le Roman de la Rose*, and he certainly shared the spirit of its late thirteenth-century continuation by Jean de Meun.[26] Sexual gratification is always the ultimate aim of the persona which Dafydd adopts in his poetry, although frustrated desire is the dominant emotion.

Some of Dafydd's poems relate to anonymous girls who can be seen as common types in particular literary genres, such as the coy country girl in the *pastourelle* and the easily seduced *bourgeoise* in the *fabliau*. Two girls are identified by name and each forms the subject of a number of Dafydd's poems. Although there is strong evidence that they really did exist, they can also be seen to fit into a literary matrix. Dyddgu was the daughter of an identifiable Ceredigion nobleman, and in his poems to her Dafydd adopts the role of the unrequited lover vainly admiring from afar. Morfudd is known to have been the wife of a merchant in Aberystwyth, and a group of at least thirty of Dafydd's poems depict his tempestuous relationship with her beginning before her marriage and continuing well after it. This is the love triangle so common in the *fabliaux* in which a young wife is married to an older husband who jealously guards her against a predatory lover. Much of the humour of Dafydd's poetry involves mockery of the jealous husband or self-mockery of the poet's failed attempts to outwit him.

His enforced separation from both Dyddgu and Morfudd gave rise to one of Dafydd's most characteristic genres, the *llatai* or love-messenger poem in which a creature is sent to his beloved. The motif of the love-messenger was common enough in Welsh and other literatures, but Dafydd's unique contribution to the genre was to focus attention on the messenger itself and to invest it with symbolic significance. So the seagull represents the beauty of the girl in the coastal castle to whom it is sent, the skylark is a symbol of the transcendent power of song, and the wind traversing the world unconstrained is a focus for the earthbound poet's yearning for free access to his beloved. These and other creatures are memorably described both through objective observation and by using a poetic technique known as *dyfalu* (literally 'riddling'), a kaleidoscopic series of imaginative comparisons, one or sometimes two to a line, which is one of the most attractive features of medieval Welsh poetry, used extensively in poems of request and thanks for gifts from the fourteenth century onwards.

Some of Dafydd ap Gwilym's finest poems are based on a single extended image or conceit, a technique which is quite unusual in Welsh poetry and one which he used to explore the complexities of sexual love. His love for a girl is likened to an unruly foster son which has taken possession of his heart,[27] and in another poem to a hare constantly eluding the hunter and darting back to its lair.[28] His long courtship of Morfudd is likened to a farmer's care for his crop which is ultimately destroyed by a sudden rainstorm.[29] And Morfudd herself is compared to the sun, her radiant beauty flitting between clouds and disappearing at the end of the day into her husband's house.[30]

Another conventional theme of European love literature which Dafydd ap Gwilym made very much his own is the woodland bower (*y deildy*) as the ideal setting for the lovers' tryst. This too gave ample opportunity for appreciative description, some of it elaborately metaphorical, as when the grove where he receives a *llatai* sent by Morfudd is portrayed as a church in which the birds celebrate a mass which is far superior to the imperfect performance of the human priest.[31] The implication here and in numerous other poems is that the natural world is blessed by God, and furthermore that sexual love in such a setting is also divinely sanctioned. But the forces of the natural world also hinder the fulfilment of love in a series of comic poems which show Dafydd frustrated by things like a full moon, which deprives him of the cover of darkness for his nocturnal escapades, and a sudden mist, which prevents him from finding a girl in the woods. Metaphorical comparisons are here used as a satirical device to express antipathy, whilst also conveying a sense of wonder at the sinister beauty of a world transformed. In a dazzling sequence of images stretching over thirty lines the mist becomes amongst many other things a roll of parchment, a bird-net, a blanket, a spider's web, cambric cloth, and a coat of armour.[32]

Outdoor lovemaking, both real and literary, was dependent on the seasons, and this is a major theme in Dafydd ap Gwilym's poetry, partly a reflection of folk customs marking the turning points of the year. The duality of the natural world is again evident in the contrast between celebration of summer and complaint about the rigours of winter.[33] In European love literature, the seasonal theme is essential to the genre known as the *reverdie* responding to the rebirth of nature in early summer. Dafydd's inventive treatment of convention is evident in his version of the *reverdie*, 'Cyngor y Bioden' ('The Magpie's Advice').[34] Adopting the persona of a love-stricken poet, Dafydd tells how in a woodland grove on an early April day he was inspired by the new life all around him to feel rejuvenated and sing of the joys of love, until interrupted by the harsh voice of a magpie telling him that he is too old for all that and ought to be keeping warm by the fireside. Dafydd responds by abusing the magpie as a bird of ill omen, but he has no answer to the magpie's final advice that he might as well become a hermit. Like many of Dafydd ap Gwilym's poems, this is rich in ambiguity and can be interpreted in several different ways. On a superficial reading it appears to be an amusing comic piece, complete with entertaining dialogue, in which the poet is made to look very foolish (perhaps a precursor of the April fool). But on another level it can be seen to make serious points about the passage of time and man's relationship with nature. In the natural world life follows the cycle of the seasons, but for the human subject time is linear and any sense of rejuvenation by identification with nature is mere self-deception.

A heightened sense of mortality is a characteristic of the poetry of the mid-fourteenth century, predating the Black Death but certainly intensified by its arrival in 1349. A rather bizarre sub-genre which arose in this period is the mock-elegy composed while the subject was still alive but with as much expression of grief as the genuine *marwnad*. The practice is proved by the existence of elegies by poets to one another (such as Dafydd ap Gwilym and Madog Benfras), presumably meant as an elaborate tribute, and in other cases it can be suspected on the basis of dates (for instance Dafydd ap Gwilym's elegy to Rhydderch ab Ieuan Llwyd, owner of the White Book of Rhydderch).[35] Even the most passionate outpourings are not beyond suspicion, such as the elegy by Llywelyn Goch ap Meurig Hen to Lleucu Llwyd, a married woman from Meirionethshire, which is one of the outstanding love poems of the period.[36] Based on the serenade genre, the poet addresses Lleucu in the grave as a lover would appeal to a girl to let him into her house. This declaration of undying devotion ranks with Gruffudd ap Maredudd's elegy to Gwenhwyfar in its painful awareness of the fragility of human beauty.

Llywelyn Goch's poem is a valuable reminder that the creative use of literary conventions seen in the work of Dafydd ap Gwilym is also well attested by his contemporaries. For the witty trickery of the *fabliau*, we have Madog Benfras's account of how he gained access to his lady's chamber by disguising himself as a saltman.[37] Gruffudd Gryg has *llatai* poems every bit as inventive as those of Dafydd ap Gwilym, composed whilst on pilgrimage to Santiago, in which he sends both the moon and a wave as messengers to his love at home in Anglesey.[38] Gruffudd ab Adda's address to a birch tree erected as a maypole in the town of Llanidloes, complaining that it had been taken from its natural environment where it provided shelter for lovers, engages with cultural tensions between town and country. Iolo Goch utilized the dialogue between the body and the soul, normally a religious genre, as a device to narrate a bardic circuit traversing the country.[39] Iolo Goch of Denbighshire (*fl.* 1345–97) was the most significant of Dafydd ap Gwilym's younger contemporaries, and he seems to have been primarily responsible for establishing the *cywydd* metre as an acceptable medium for praise poetry.

It may have been Dafydd ap Gwilym who first used the *cywydd* for praise of a patron in four poems which he composed to Ifor Hael (Ifor the Generous, an epithet which Dafydd bestowed upon him) of Glamorgan, probably in the 1340s. These boldly proclaim an intimate friendship with his patron, even using some of the motifs of love poetry, and they may reflect an ideal of male bonding which was common in the late Middle Ages. They did have some influence on later praise poetry as the relationship between poet and patron shifted to a much more equal footing than had been the norm in the age of the princes. However, it was Iolo Goch who transferred much of the language, style, and social ideals of traditional eulogy to the *cywydd*, thus making it an acceptable medium in the eyes of those who held the purse-strings. In fact the key text may be one which had no patron in the normal sense. Soon after 1347, Iolo composed a *cywydd* to King Edward III praising his military successes in Scotland and France and drawing on the prophecy known as 'The Six Kings to follow John'.[40] Although the poem addresses the king directly, it would surely not have been performed in his presence and is more likely to have been political propaganda aimed at promoting recruitment of troops from Wales for the war in France, perhaps patronized by a nobleman involved in recruitment such as Sir Rhys ap Gruffudd.

Iolo Goch went on to use the *cywydd* for eulogies and elegies to the Tudor family of Anglesey, patrons of the arch-traditionalist Gruffudd ap Maredudd. His elegy to Tudur Fychan of Penmynydd (d. 1367) is a potent combination of old and new, portraying Tudur as the protector of the native Welsh of Gwynedd, filling the gap left by the princes whom his ancestors had served.[41] That elegy concludes with a bleak vision of Anglesey bereft of its leader, but Iolo subsequently praised four of Tudur's sons together in an exuberant *cywydd* which exemplifies the value of family unity amongst the *uchelwyr* for the local community, the brothers being the four pillars of the island.[42] Iolo lived through a period in which many communities were in danger of collapse in the wake of the Black Death, and it is not surprising that social stability is a major issue in his poetry. This is key to understanding a poem which is unique in the Welsh bardic tradition in that it celebrates the humble ploughman.[43] Iolo's poem is far less radical than it might appear, since it promotes the interests of landowners (in this case probably the church in the diocese of St Asaph) by praising the ploughman for accepting his lot without complaint and fulfilling his duty to feed the rest of society, at a time when many of the labouring class were taking advantage of the scarcity of labour to demand greater freedom.

A classic celebration of the paternalistic social order, and a poem in which the *cywydd* form is integral to the vision, is Iolo Goch's depiction of Owain Glyn Dŵr's court at Sycharth.[44] Composed in the 1390s, when Glyn Dŵr was still a loyal servant of the Crown, having distinguished himself in the Scottish wars, the poem shows him as a prosperous gentleman living on his country estate in the marcher region near Oswestry. The wooden house on a mound surrounded by a moat, with tiled roof and chimney, was typical of architectural fashions in English gentry houses of the period, and everything on the surrounding estate was in its proper place to sustain the domestic economy – the mill, dovecot, fishponds, rabbit and deer parks, and arable land. Cooperation is a pervasive theme, the reciprocal greeting between poet and patron, the services performed by bondmen collaborating in the system of co-tillage, and the family relationships of husband and wife with children arranged in pairs. These mutual bonds are mirrored by the architecture of the house itself and reinforced by numerical symbolism of binary pairs and multiples. The couplet structure of the metre is part of this pattern, corresponding to the pairs of roof beams which are called 'couples', and the *cynghanedd* within each line can be seen to reflect the theme of binding (the root *cyngan* being used to convey architectural symmetry). The connection between poetry and architectural construction is made elsewhere, but nowhere are the two crafts linked in such suggestive detail as they are here:

> Cyplau sydd, gwaith cwplws ŷnt,
> Cwpledig pob cwpl ydynt;
> Clochdy Padrig, Ffrengig ffrwyth,
> Clostr Wesmustr, clostir esmwyth;
> Cynglynrhwym pob congl unrhyw,
> Cangell aur, cyngan oll yw.

> (There are rafters fashioned in couples,
> every couple is coupled together;
> Patrick's bellhouse, French fruit,
> Westminster's cloister, a comfortable enclosure;
> each corner bound in the same way,
> golden chancel, it is entirely symmetrical.)

Iolo Goch's depiction of Sycharth might appear to be a rather complacent idealization, but awareness of the forces which threatened to undermine this harmonious construct, as attested elsewhere in his poetry, can help to sharpen our response. Since the middle of the century, mortality rates had threatened the future of communities, and indeed the continuity of the family unit itself seemed to be at risk. The old social bonds which ensured a plentiful supply of labour for landowners' estates were breaking down. And ethnic tensions always threatened to erupt into violence, as they did on a grand scale under Glyndŵr's leadership in September 1400. Three years later this splendid house was burnt to the ground by Prince Henry. Iolo's poem is the best evidence we have both for the material existence of Glyndŵr's court and for the social vision which informed it.

Notes

1. Dafydd Johnston, 'Monastic Patronage of Welsh Poetry', in *Monastic Wales: New Approaches,* ed. Janet Burton and Karen Stöber (Cardiff: University of Wales Press, 2013), 177–90.

2. See Helen Fulton, ed., *Urban Culture in Medieval Wales* (Cardiff: University of Wales Press, 2012).

3. 'Trafferth mewn Tafarn' ('Trouble at an Inn'); text and translation are available in the online edition of Dafydd ap Gwilym's poetry, *Dafydd ap Gwilym.net* (2007), www.dafyddapgwilym.net (henceforth *DG.net*) (accessed 17 October 2017), poem 73.

4. See Daniel Huws, *Medieval Welsh Manuscripts* (Cardiff: University of Wales Press, 2000), 193–226.

5. *Ystorya Bown de Hamtwn*, ed. Morgan Watkin (Caerdydd: Gwasg Prifysgol Cymru, 1958); *Ystorya de Carolo Magno*, ed. Stephen J. Williams (Caerdydd: Gwasg Prifysgol Cymru, 1930). See also Helen Fulton, 'Translating Europe in Medieval Wales', in *Writing Europe, 500–1450: Texts and Contexts*, ed. Aidan Conti *et al.* (Cambridge: D. S. Brewer, 2015), 159–74.

6. *Ystoryaeu Seint Greal*, ed. Thomas Jones (Caerdydd: Gwasg Prifysgol Cymru, 1992).

7. *Kedymdeithyas Amlyn ac Amic*, ed. Patricia Williams (Caerdydd: Gwasg Prifysgol Cymru, 1982).

8. *Chwedleu Seith Doethon Rufein*, ed. Henry Lewis (Caerdydd: Gwasg Prifysgol Cymru, 1958).

9. *The Elucidarium and Other Tracts in Welsh from Llyvyr Agkyr Llandewivrevi*, ed. J. Morris Jones and John Rhŷs (Oxford: Oxford University Press, 1894).

10. For a general introduction to the law of Hywel Dda, see T. M. Charles-Edwards, *The Welsh Laws* (Cardiff: University of Wales Press, 1989).

11. *Gwaith Gruffudd ap Dafydd ap Tudur, Gwilym Ddu o Arfon, Trahaearn Brydydd Mawr ac Iorwerth Beli*, ed. N. G. Costigan *et al.* (Aberystwyth: Canolfan Uwchefrydiau Cymreig a Cheltaidd, 1995), poems 6–9.

12. Morgan T. Davies, 'The Rhetoric of Gwilym Ddu's *Awdlau* to Sir Gruffydd Llwyd', *Studia Celtica* 40 (2006): 155–72.
13. *Gwaith Gruffudd ap Maredudd*, ed. Barry J. Lewis and Ann Parry Owen, 3 vols. (Aberystwyth: Canolfan Uwchefrydiau Cymreig a Cheltaidd, 2003, 2005, 2007).
14. Ibid., vol. I, poem 6 (ed. Lewis), ll. 33–6.
15. Ibid., vol. III, poem 1 (ed. Parry Owen). Owain Lawgoch was assassinated by the English in France in 1378.
16. Ibid., vol. II, poem 1 (ed. Lewis); for an English translation see Barry J. Lewis, *Welsh Poetry and English Pilgrimage: Gruffudd ap Maredudd and the Rood of Chester* (Aberystwyth: Canolfan Uwchefrydiau Cymreig a Cheltaidd, 2005).
17. *Gwaith Gruffudd ap Maredudd*, ed. Lewis and Parry Owen, vol. III, poem 5 (ed. Parry Owen).
18. *Gwaith Gruffudd ap Dafydd ap Tudur*, ed. Costigan *et al.*, poems 1–5.
19. *Gwaith Casnodyn*, ed. R. Iestyn Daniel (Aberystwyth: Canolfan Uwchefrydiau Cymreig a Cheltaidd, 1999).
20. Ibid., poem 12.
21. For the texts of the various grammars, see *Gramadegau'r Penceirddiaid*, ed. G. J. Williams and E. J. Jones (Caerdydd: Gwasg Prifysgol Cymru, 1934).
22. *Gwaith Einion Offeiriad a Dafydd Ddu o Hiraddug*, ed. R. Geraint Gruffydd and Rhiannon Ifans (Aberystwyth: Canolfan Uwchefrydiau Cymreig a Cheltaidd, 1997).
23. Dafydd ap Gwilym did choose to compose two monorhyme *cywyddau* (*DG. net*, poems 32 and 34), but this never caught on.
24. On the musical background to the poetry, see Sally Harper, 'Dafydd ap Gwilym, poet and musician', *DG.net*, www.dafyddapgwilym.net/essays/ sally_harper/index_eng.php (accessed 17 October 2017).
25. *DG.net*. For a selection of other poems attributed to Dafydd ap Gwilym in manuscripts see Helen Fulton, ed., *Dafydd ap Gwilym: Apocrypha* (Llandysul: Gomer Press, 1996). The edition of Dafydd's work by Thomas Parry assigns 146 poems to Dafydd, excluding his debate with Gruffudd Gryg (*Gwaith Dafydd ap Gwilym*, ed. Thomas Parry (Caerdydd: Gwasg Prifysgol Cymru, 1952)). Translations of the entire corpus of Dafydd's poetry are available at *DG.net*. Other translations include those by Gwyn Thomas, trans., *Dafydd ap Gwilym: His Poems* (Cardiff: University of Wales Press, 2001) and R. M. Loomis, trans., *Dafydd ap Gwilym: The Poems* (Binghamton, NY: Center for Medieval and Early Renaissance Studies, State University of New York, 1981).
26. On the European background to Dafydd ap Gwilym's work, see Helen Fulton, *Dafydd ap Gwilym and the European Context* (Cardiff: University of Wales Press, 1989) and Huw M. Edwards, *Dafydd ap Gwilym: Influences and Analogues* (Oxford: Oxford University Press, 1996).

27. 'Y Mab Maeth' ('The Foster-son'), *DG.net*, poem 77.

28. 'Serch fel Ysgyfarnog' ('Love like a Hare'), *DG.net*, poem 75.

29. 'Hwsmonaeth Cariad' ('The Husbandry of Love'), *DG.net*, poem 109.

30. 'Morfudd fel yr Haul' ('Morfudd like the Sun'), *DG.net*, poem 111.

31. 'Offeren y Llwyn' ('The Woodland Mass'), *DG.net*, poem 39.

32. *DG.net*, poem 57.

33. The contrast is most explicit in 'Mis Mai a Mis Tachwedd' ('May and November'), *DG.net*, poem 33.

34. *DG.net*, poem 36.

35. *DG.net*, poem 10.

36. *Gwaith Llywelyn Goch ap Meurig Hen*, ed. Dafydd Johnston (Aberystwyth: Canolfan Uwchefrydiau Cymreig a Cheltaidd, 1998), poem 12.

37. *Gwaith Madog Benfras ac Eraill o Feirdd y Bedwaredd Ganrif ar Ddeg*, ed. Barry J. Lewis (Aberystwyth: Canolfan Uwchefrydiau Cymreig a Cheltaidd, 2007), poem 44.

38. *Gwaith Gruffudd Gryg*, ed. Barry J. Lewis and Eurig Salisbury (Aberystwyth: Canolfan Uwchefrydiau Cymreig a Cheltaidd, 2010), poems 6 and 7.

39. *Iolo Goch: Poems*, ed. and trans. Dafydd Johnston (Llandysul: Gomer Press, 1993), poem 14.

40. Ibid., poem 1.

41. Ibid., poem 4.

42. Ibid., poem 5.

43. Ibid., poem 28.

44. Ibid., poem 10.

7

Literary Networks and Patrons in Late Medieval Wales

HELEN FULTON

The late fourteenth and fifteenth centuries were a golden age of manuscript production in Wales. Only a handful of manuscripts containing Welsh survive from the period before 1250; between then and 1400, more than eighty surviving manuscripts were compiled, and a further sixty between 1400 and 1500; it is likely that many more were written which have not survived.[1]

When manuscripts began to be preserved, it was largely because they were functional, with the earliest surviving manuscripts of the mid-thirteenth century containing historical chronicles and copies of the Welsh legal texts known as the 'Laws of Hywel Dda'. On the other hand, there are a few manuscripts from the late thirteenth and early fourteenth centuries which are entirely literary, preserving an older tradition of poetry, prophecy, and history. What is perhaps the oldest manuscript written in Welsh, the Black Book of Carmarthen (*Llyfr Du Caerfyrddin*), dating from *c.* 1250, contains only literary works, particularly early poetry about Arthur and about Myrddin, the bard and prophet presented to Latin readers by Geoffrey of Monmouth as Merlin.[2]

The aim of this chapter is to describe the links between manuscript production and patrons, both religious and secular, in Wales in the fourteenth and fifteenth centuries. Patrons, poets, and scribes, working in religious institutions and gentry houses, together formed material and semiotic networks which were responsible for the circulation, preservation, and transmission of cultural knowledge in Welsh. In other words, poets and patrons, manuscript books, and the buildings in which they were made interacted in a social network that resulted in a particular form of cultural production, a 'making of knowledge'.[3] This network became increasingly important as the spread of the English language in Wales, especially in the regions of the March, gathered pace during the fifteenth century. As Welsh poets became more politicized following the rebellion of Owain Glyn Dŵr in 1400 and the subsequent factionalism exacerbated by the Wars of the Roses, the support of powerful patrons among the gentry, themselves interconnected with monastic institutions and with each other, became the key to the survival of the Welsh traditions of prose and court poetry up until the Reformation.

Manuscripts and Monasteries

Like other areas of Europe, Wales shared in the revival of monasticism that began in the late eleventh century. From that time, a web of monastic houses, starting with Benedictine and Cluniac orders and soon followed by Cistercians, Franciscans, and Dominicans, spread throughout Wales with a particular concentration in the Anglo-Norman regions to the east, south, and south-west of the country.[4] While some of these foundations represented the steady march of Norman colonization, others, particularly those of the Cistercians, engaged with native Welsh rulers in the twelfth century and located themselves in the heart of the independent territories in the west and north. By 1201, there were thirteen Cistercian houses in Wales, supported by mainly Welsh but also some Norman lords whose extensive benefactions 'probably doubled the amount of land under ecclesiastical control in Wales'.[5]

In return for this substantial material support, the Cistercian monasteries took over from the older Welsh foundations the task of copying and record-ing the cultural heritage preserved in the Welsh language.[6] Though we do not have a complete record of which manuscripts were written or copied in which monasteries, some of the earliest surviving historical and literary manuscripts can be associated with one or more of the Cistercian abbeys. Cardiff, Central Library MS 2.81, more commonly known as the Book of Aneirin (*Llyfr Aneirin, c.* 1260), containing the early Welsh poem *Y Gododdin*, was probably copied at Aberconwy, a monastery on the north coast sup-ported by the princes of Gwynedd, while Aberystwyth, National Library of Wales (NLW) MS Peniarth 2, the Book of Taliesin (*Llyfr Taliesin*), dating from the first half of the fourteenth century, is likely to be a product of one of the Cistercian houses in south-east or mid-Wales.[7]

The fourteenth and fifteenth centuries saw a resurgence of cultural pro-duction supported by the new gentry of Wales, the *uchelwyr*. As Dafydd Johnston has pointed out in Chapter 6 of this volume, these patrons, inherit-ing the task of literary preservation from the vanished class of independent princes after 1282, embraced literary patronage as an expression of their social status. The patrons of Welsh culture were both lay and ecclesiastical, work-ing in collaboration with monastic scriptoria which could provide the materials and expertise for book production. From the late fourteenth century, there is increasing evidence that gentry households kept their own libraries and, in some instances, supported clerically trained scribes to copy and translate manuscripts in-house. This practice of secular production suggests the emergence of a new element in the manuscript network, namely a commercial market among the *uchelwyr* for books in Welsh, perhaps encouraged by the growth of urban trade in Wales after the Edwardian conquest of 1282.[8]

The case of the vernacular historical chronicle, *Brut y Tywysogyon* ('Chronicle of the Princes'), provides an interesting example of the networks of monastic communication and lay patronage across Wales which facilitated the spread of culturally significant texts. The *Brut*, a continuation of Geoffrey of Monmouth's *Historia Regum Britanniae* ('History of the Kings of Britain') (*c.* 1138), from the death of the last British king Cadwaladr to the death of the last Welsh prince, Llywelyn ap Gruffudd in 1282, originated as a Latin chronicle at the Cistercian abbey of Strata Florida. Though the Latin text does not survive, two vernacular versions of the *Brut* circulated widely, indicating its popularity with Welsh patrons in the fourteenth century. According to Daniel Huws, 'The earliest surviving manuscript of one version, NLW MS Peniarth 20, was written at the Cistercian abbey of Valle Crucis about 1330, and that of the other, NLW MS Peniarth 18, probably at Strata Florida, in the middle of the fourteenth century.'[9] In other words, monastic scribes at both these houses, despite their being on opposite sides of the country (Valle Crucis is near Wrexham in north-east Wales while Strata Florida is near Aberystwyth in west Wales), shared in a regular system of manuscript exchange based partly on a desire to increase their respective libraries but also on commissions from patrons willing to support the recording of Welsh history as a form of nation building.

Further evidence for this and similar networks comes from scribal hand-writing. For example, NLW MS Peniarth 18, the Strata Florida manuscript of the *Brut*, is one of a group of manuscripts written by the same scribe, who identified himself in one of his manuscripts as 'the Anchorite of Llanddewibrefi', a village with a collegiate church about ten miles from Strata Florida. This group of manuscripts is associated with the scriptorium at Strata Florida which, perhaps more than any other Cistercian abbey in the fourteenth century, engaged with the Welsh literary tradition.[10] Its abbots were Welshmen, rather than Englishmen, who supported manuscript production on behalf of lay patrons and also provided patronage to Welsh poets as a signal of their own status, resulting in praise poems such as that to

Llywelyn Fychan ap Llywelyn, abbot of Strata Florida from 1344 to 1380, by Llywelyn Goch ap Meurig Hen (*fl. c.* 1350–90).[11]

Strata Florida is the likely location for the compilation of the Hendregadredd manuscript (Aberystwyth, NLW MS 6680B) in the early fourteenth century. One of the most important anthologies of Welsh court poetry composed before 1282, the manuscript was planned by one scribe and copied by nineteen other distinctive hands, suggesting, as Daniel Huws says, 'a large and settled community'.[12] Moreover, this monastic community operated as part of a local network with a neighbouring gentry family living at Parcrhydderch in the parish of Llangeitho which, like Llanddewibrefi, was about ten miles from Strata Florida. Ieuan Llwyd ap Ieuan (*fl. c.* 1332–43) and his wife Angharad were patrons of Welsh writing, as was their son Rhydderch ap Ieuan Llwyd (*c.* 1325–*c.* 1400), and all three were the subjects of praise poetry addressed to them by professional court poets.[13] At some stage during Ieuan's lifetime, in the second quarter of the fourteenth century, the Hendregadredd manuscript was kept in his home at Parcrhydderch where the last layer of additions was added to it in a variety of hands. The poems copied into the manuscript at Ieuan's house are not the work of early court poets, like the rest of the manuscript, but are contemporary verses of the fourteenth century, many of them addressed to Ieuan and his family. It seems most likely, then, that the Hendregadredd manuscript, perhaps commissioned by Ieuan Llwyd to be written at Strata Florida, later became a kind of visitor's book in his house where visiting poets, including Dafydd ap Gwilym, inscribed verses in their own hands.

The significance of the Parcrhydderch family as patrons of Welsh culture is affirmed by their association with another major anthology of Welsh literature, the White Book of Rhydderch (*Llyfr Gwyn Rhydderch*, c. 1350), originally a single book but now preserved in two separate manuscripts (Aberystwyth, NLW MSS Peniarth 4 and Peniarth 5).[14] The White Book is a substantial compendium, written entirely in Welsh, containing many of the canonical texts of medieval Welsh literature, including the earliest surviving texts of most of the prose narratives known collectively as the *Mabinogion*.[15] There are also some popular texts translated from Latin and French, including adaptations of the Charlemagne legends and a Welsh version of a lost Anglo-Norman text of the romance of Bevis of Hampton, called in Welsh *Ystorya Bown de Hamtwn*.[16] The majority of the texts are religious, including some saints' lives and popular stories from biblical apocrypha, alongside proverbs and triads. The White Book, as it survives, contains very little poetry apart from a few anonymous verses associated with the Merlin (Welsh Myrddin) tradition.[17]

Like the Hendregadredd manuscript, we can assume that the White Book was written at Strata Florida: its five scribal hands, one of which belongs to the Anchorite, suggest a monastic community working to a commission from their neighbouring patron, Rhydderch ap Ieuan Llwyd. The contents of the anthology, mixing religious and secular texts, original and translated tales, and prose and poetry, indicate an intention to record a representative selection from the Welsh popular literary tradition as it was understood in the mid-fourteenth century. The inclusion of translations of French romances shows that this was not an antiquarian endeavour but a desire to own a book which would be read by the family, used to entertain guests, and perhaps lent to other gentry and religious houses to be copied. Most strikingly, the manuscript contains a later addition of four short stanzas (englynion) by Dafydd ap Gwilym, written in to a blank space by someone with access to the manuscript at the end of the fourteenth century, perhaps at the request of Rhydderch.[18]

While there were likely to have been close links between Strata Florida and Parcrhydderch, this model of a lively network of monastic scribes and gentry patrons was not confined to west Wales. There are some small but significant material links between the family at Parcrhydderch and another gentry house across the country, that of Hopcyn ap Tomas ab Einion of Ynysforgan near Swansea in west Glamorgan, south Wales. A patron of Welsh literature, Hopycn ap Tomas commissioned the manuscript anthology known as the Red Book of Hergest (Llyfr Coch Hergest, Oxford, Jesus College, MS 111), compiled at some time between 1382 and 1408, the year of Hopcyn's death.[19] The largest of all the medieval Welsh manuscripts, the Red Book is a vast anthology of material, virtually all of it in Welsh, including the major historical chronicles, prose tales, romances, translations of French romance and Latin religious texts, a large collection of hengerdd (early poetry), and an unrivalled collection of 'poetry of the princes' (from the twelfth to fourteenth centuries) written in the older metres of awdl and englyn. A conspicuous absence from this massive literary canon is poetry from Hopcyn's own time written in the cywydd metre, the new form popularized by Dafydd ap Gwilym and his contemporaries in the early fourteenth century.[20] Perhaps, as Daniel Huws speculates, the exclusion of such verse was deliberate since 'Hopcyn was conservative in taste', or he may have made a separate collection of cywydd poetry which is now lost.[21]

The Red Book of Hergest, compiled for Hopcyn ap Tomas in south Wales, and the earlier White Book of Rhydderch, compiled for Rhydderch ab Ieuan Llwyd in west Wales, have a particular connection which hints at the kind of networks operating among patrons and scribes. One of the scribal hands appearing in the White Book has been identified as that of the main scribe of the Red Book, a man whose name we happen to know: Hywel Fychan ap Hywel Goch. Several manuscripts copied by Hywel survive – all of them associated with Glamorgan, where Hopcyn ap Tomas lived – and in one of them he left a colophon giving his name and describing himself as a scribe working for Hopcyn ap Tomas: 'o arch a gorchymun y vaester nyt amgen Hopkyn uab thomas uab einawn' ('at the request and command of his master, no other than Hopcyn ap Tomas ab Einiawn').[22] In the White Book, a few lines of Hywel's writing fill a gap left by one of the five main scribes while writing out the text of *Culhwch ac Olwen*, presumably because at that point he found that 'his exemplar was defective or illegible'.[23]

At some stage, then, Hywel Fychan, the scribe of Hopcyn ap Tomas, had access to the White Book, originally commissioned by Rhydderch ab Ieuan Llwyd, and to another exemplar, which he used to fill in the gap left by the White Book scribe. This exemplar may well have been the Red Book itself which also contains a text of *Culhwch ac Olwen*, but where, in that case, did Hywel get his material to write the Red Book? His immediate source was not the White Book, judging by a close comparison of the texts they share in common, particularly the Four Branches of the *Mabinogi*.[24] The current consensus is that both books, the Red and the White, were copied independently from an earlier common source;[25] however, this theory presupposes that yet a third large anthology of medieval Welsh poetry and prose was in circulation somewhere between south and west Wales, of which no trace survives. There are also very considerable differences between the two anthologies in terms of their contents, with the White Book favouring religious material while the later Red Book contains far more material and is in general more concerned with secular and historical texts. A common source therefore seems unlikely. A stronger possibility, and one supported by manuscript evidence, is that several shorter manuscripts in circulation among gentry houses provided both Hywel Fychan and the compiler of the White Book with their material, each having access to a different set of manuscripts with some texts in common, particularly the *Mabinogion* prose tales and the Charlemagne romances.[26] This would account for some of the differences between the two anthologies, such as the absence of the prose tale *Breudwyt Ronabwy* ('The Dream of Rhonabwy') from the White Book but not from the later Red Book, and the lacuna in the White Book text of *Culhwch ac Olwen* which Hywel knew how to fill from whatever sources he had used to copy the Red Book.

More interesting is the evidence provided by the Red Book and the White Book concerning the mobility of scribes and manuscripts: Hywel must have known the White Book existed in west Wales and either Hywel himself or the White Book (or both) must have travelled between south and west Wales around the year 1400, indicating the networks of contacts among the *uchelwyr*. Furthermore, it seems likely that Hywel, though clerically trained, was a professional lay scribe working in the homes of patrons such as Hopcyn ap Tomas, rather than in a monastic scriptorium, suggesting a productive network of exchange between patrons, scribes, and religious foundations.[27] The fact that at least two poets, Dafydd y Coed (*fl.* 1380) and Llywelyn Goch ap Meurig Hen, whose work is preserved in the Red Book, sang praise poems to both Rhydderch ab Ieuan Llwyd and Hopcyn ap Tomas provides a further point of contact between these two patrons and their manuscripts, despite their geographical distance from each other.[28]

It is also noteworthy that a number of surviving manuscripts containing the Welsh laws were copied by some of the same scribes who also wrote literary manuscripts, such as the Book of Taliesin scribe who also copied law texts (London, British Library MS Cotton Cleopatra A.xiv) and a version of the Welsh romance *Gereint vab Erbin* (surviving as a fragment in Aberystwyth, NLW MS Peniarth 6 part iv from the first half of the fourteenth century).[29] All these connections indicate a dynamic communication network which depended on the mobility of poets, scribes, and manuscripts and on the commitment of patrons to Welsh literary culture, past and present. By the late fourteenth century, the *uchelwyr* were not only supporting manuscript production in the monastic houses of Wales but were also commissioning lay scribes to create books for personal use in their libraries at home. This pattern of secular book production was to continue in the fifteenth century, with poets themselves increasingly producing holograph copies of their work.

Factionalism and Political Poetry in the Fifteenth Century

The court poets of the fifteenth century relied increasingly heavily for patronage on the leading families of the March of Wales, both long-standing *uchelwyr* and more recent English families who intermarried with their Welsh neighbours. In many respects, they continued the literary traditions established by the generations of poets composing after 1282, using the metres of the *englyn, awdl,* and *cywydd* and deploying distinctive genres such as eulogy, elegy, religious poetry, and poems of request and thanks. What seems new in the fifteenth century are the closer links between poets and their patrons, with many of the poets composing to generations within the same family, spending time at their mansion houses, and compiling manuscripts of their own work at or near these places of patronage. What is new, too, is a clear poetic engagement with the politics of the age, often expressed through an allegiance to particular patrons, partisan calls to arms, and dramatic prophecies of triumph and disaster.[30]

From the time of the rebellion of Owain Glyn Dŵr in 1400 and during the violent factionalism of the Wars of the Roses, Welsh poets and writers became more politicized, converting older traditions of praise and prophecy into expressions of support for one or other of the two factions of Lancaster and York and finally uniting in their support for Henry Tudor whom they regarded as a true Welshman. The rebellion of Owain Glyn Dŵr, sparked off by a land dispute between Owain and his English neighbour, Sir Reginald Grey of Ruthin, in north-east Wales and fuelled by wider discontent surrounding the deposition of Richard II in 1399 and his replacement by Henry IV, polarized Wales and had severe consequences for the political and cultural stability of the country.[31] One of the consequences of the rebellion was a temporary lull in literary production in Wales. Very little seems to have been produced during the years of the rebellion and immediately afterwards, and even the voices of the poets were temporarily silent.[32] Owain's main strategy had been the destruction of the borough towns along with their surrounding farmland and religious buildings, a process exacerbated by English military reprisals. The result was a drastic decline in secular and ecclesiastical revenues, leading to the loss of both literary patrons and the means to produce manuscripts. Furthermore, punitive statutes and ordinances which were issued by the Crown against the Welsh following the rebellion effectively excluded the *uchelwyr* from those senior levels of public life which they had previously occupied. There was little, then, for the poets to celebrate in the early decades of the fifteenth century.

Owain Glyn Dŵr himself had been a notable patron of poets who visited his house at Sycharth in north-east Wales and sang his praises before the outbreak of the rebellion. Composing in the late fourteenth century, Iolo Goch sang of Owain's proud lineage, his fine house, and his generosity to poets, describing him as an armed knight, 'brenin ar y barwniaid' ('king over the barons'), as he set off to fight for Richard II in Scotland in 1385.[33] In the same year or thereabouts, Gruffudd Llwyd celebrated Owain's safe return from the Scottish campaign, comparing him to three romance heroes: Uthr Pendragon, the father of Arthur; Owain ab Urien, the northern British hero; and 'Ffwg', that is, Fulke Fitz Warin, a Norman Marcher lord whose family had inspired an Anglo-Norman romance which was clearly known in Wales.[34] Both Iolo Goch and Gruffudd Llwyd emphasized Owain's military prowess, linking him with heroes of the past and drawing on the bardic images and conventions of the *cynfeirdd*, the early poets of pre-Norman Wales. To Iolo Goch, Owain is 'dwyn paladr, gwaladr gwiwlew' ('bearing a spear, fine bold lion'), 'cannwyll brwydr' ('candle of battle'),[35] 'llew Prydain, llaw Peredur' ('lion of Scotland, Peredur's hand'), 'llithio'r brain, llethu Brynaich' ('feeding the crows, overpowering the Scots').[36] To Gruffudd Llwyd, Owain is comparable with the ancient battle-leaders of Britain, Caw, Bran, Beli, Constantine, and Arthur.

When Owain's name begins to reappear in praise poetry after about 1415, it is not as a great battle hero but rather as the illustrious ancestor of many of the leading families of Wales. He is positioned as a lasting exemplar of the virtues of the *uchelwyr* and the guarantor of their legitimacy as the nobility of Wales. Owain's legacy therefore resided with the families who could trace their descent from him and who became the subjects of much of the praise poetry of the later fifteenth century. Two families in particular were closely connected to Owain and his descendants, the Hanmers and the Pulestons (Welsh Pilstwn). Both families had moved into Maelor Saesneg, the area south of Chester, after the Edwardian settlement of 1284 when the new county of Flint (into which the old Welsh commote of Maelor Saesneg was now absorbed) was established. Servants of the Crown, these families, like the Normans before them, married into local Welsh families and contributed to the support of Welsh culture, including patronage of the poets. Owain Glyn Dŵr's wife was Margaret Hanmer, daughter of Sir David Hanmer, a judge in the Court of the King's Bench under Richard II; Owain's sister, Lowri, married Robert Puleston; his daughter Catrin married Edmund Mortimer, whose elder brother Roger was the 4th Earl of March, after Edmund had been captured by Owain and converted to the cause of the rebellion.

From these family interconnections stemmed some of the finest Welsh praise poetry of the fifteenth century. In his elegy for Siôn ap Madog Pilstwn (*fl. c.* 1450–1465), Guto'r Glyn calls him '[c]âr Owain' ('Owain's kinsman'), implying the connective similarities between Owain Glyn Dŵr, Siôn, and the popular romance heroes of the time:

Brawd Otwel a Bwrd ytoedd,
Brawd er cael ffawd Ercwlff oedd;
Alecsander i Wrecsam
Yn iacháu rhwng iawn a cham;
Troelus neu Ector eilwaith
Trefor a dwy Faelor faith.[37]

(He was the brother of Otiel and Bors,
a brother to enjoy the valour of Hercules;
an Alexander to Wrexham
judging correctly between right and wrong;
another Troilus or Hector
of Trefor and the two great Maelors.)

Writing in praise of Siôn ap Madog Pilstwn's son, another Siôn, the poet
Tudur Aled (*fl. c.* 1465–*c.* 1525) refers to a number of his ancestors including
Owain Glyn Dŵr. The poet uses conventional imagery of heroism and
military prowess to praise a man of considerable standing in the region of
Gwynedd:

Eithr llew coch wrth ddryllio caith
Amlwg oeddud, mal goddaith;
Gŵr wyd a ddwg ar dy ddart
Arfau Owain i'r fowart.[38]

(You were but a red lion shattering churls,
visible, like a bonfire;
you are a man who bears on your spear
the arms of Owain in the forward line.)

In a praise poem to Siôn Hanmer (d. 1480), grandson of Sir David Hanmer
and a leading Lancastrian in north Wales during the middle decades of the
century, Guto'r Glyn compares him to the Nine Worthies, the group of nine
battle-leaders, pagan and Christian, which included Hector, Alexander the
Great, Arthur, and Charlemagne, who were frequently evoked in medieval
literature as paragons of chivalry and military might. Guto describes Siôn as
'ysgwier fal rhwysg Owain / Gwŷr a meirch ac aur a main' ('an esquire with
power like Owain in terms of men and horses and gold and stones'),
comparing him to his uncle, Owain Glyn Dŵr.[39] This comparison suggests
that Siôn, the 'Nine Worthies in one', was as effective in rallying support for
the Lancastrians as Owain had been in raising his rebellion against the English
king.

While Owain Glyn Dŵr and his rebellion were not openly discussed in the public poetry of the Welsh bards in the early fifteenth century, other events soon intervened to provide material for poets addressing politically engaged patrons. When the Wars of the Roses began in earnest, with the battle of St Albans in May 1455, the leading families of Wales had already formed their allegiances, based to a large extent on where they lived and under whose lordship, and on the personal loyalties they had established as fighting men during the wars in France in the 1420s and 1430s. Although it is an over-simplified division, it is broadly the case that the eastern and southern areas of Wales around the March were largely Yorkist while the areas further west and in the north were more inclined to support the Lancastrian cause. During these turbulent decades of civil war, patrons of Welsh poetry wanted to hear about the triumphs and aspirations of whichever party they supported, and although the poetry of the period is by no means entirely political, with occasional verse, religious verse, love poetry, satire, and praise of noble patrons continuing to be popular, there is nevertheless a strong strain of political and prophetic poetry which characterizes the work of many of the fifteenth-century poets.

One of the most significant patrons of Welsh poets in the middle decades of the fifteenth century was William Herbert (c. 1423–69), lord of Raglan castle near Abergavenny, who was knighted by Henry VI in December 1452 and created Earl of Pembroke by Edward IV in September 1468.[40] Loyal to Henry VI while he was king, Herbert was nevertheless a Yorkist supporter and was one of the key campaigners responsible for putting Edward IV on the throne in March 1461. Throughout that decade, he was given authority over most of Wales where he worked tirelessly (and ruthlessly), deploying his family and allies to secure the country against the Lancastrian rebels led by Jasper Tudor. In his court at Raglan, William Herbert provided support for many of the leading poets of the time who sang effusive praise to the most powerful Welshman of their day. One poet in particular, Hywel ap Dafydd ab Ieuan ap Rhys (fl. c. 1450–1480), or 'Hywel Dafi' as he was known, seems to have been connected with Raglan as one of its regular poets, where he not only sang praise poems to Herbert but also engaged in poetic debates or ymrysonau with other poets such as Guto'r Glyn (c. 1435–1490) and Bedo Brwynllys (fl. c. 1460) who were part of the same literary circle at Raglan. Though no manuscripts from Raglan survive, as far as we know, there is evidence that William Herbert did commission manuscripts: London, British Library MS Royal 18. D.ii, containing copies of John Lydgate's Troy Book and Siege of Thebes, was presented to Edward IV by Herbert and his wife, Anne Devereux, who are depicted at the beginning of the book kneeling before the king.[41]

Among his many patrons, who included the Vaughan and Scudamore families, Hywel Dafi composed a number of praise poems to William Herbert. In one, he opens with a formal greeting to the lord of Raglan:

> Hardd Wiliam, hoyw urddolwaed,
> Herbard, ystiward, nos daed,
> Arglwydd Rhaglan, seithran serch,
> Hyd yno hwde annerch.[42]
>
> (Splendid William Herbert of vibrant honourable blood,
> steward, good evening to you,
> lord of Rhaglan, seven servings of love,
> take a greeting there.)

In another poem, written after William's elevation to the peerage as Earl of Pembroke, Hywel links William together with Edward IV as the protectors of Wales:

> Yrl Wiliam, ŵyr Lywelyn,
> A geidw'r tir ac Edwart ynn. (no. 69, ll. 11–12)
>
> (Earl William, Llywelyn's grandson,
> who guards the land and Edward for us.)

Perhaps the most famous of the poets who sang to William Herbert was Guto'r Glyn, whose praise poems to many families on both sides of the Wars of the Roses illustrate the essentially economic basis of the relationship between poets and patrons. On the one hand, we find Guto singing to families such as the Pulestons, supporters of Jasper Tudor and the Lancastrian party in Wales, and the Talbots, the earls of Shrewsbury, who were loyal to Henry VI; on the other hand, Guto addressed praise poems to prominent Yorkist families such as the Trefors and William Herbert.[43] One of his most famous poems hails the achievement of Herbert in capturing Harlech castle from the Lancastrians in 1468, the deed that won him his earldom from Edward IV:

> Bwriaist – ergydiaist godwm –
> Ben Carreg Cennen i'r cwm.
> Ni ddaliawdd ei chlawdd achlân
> Ywch, Harddlech, mwy no chorddlan.
> Ni'th ery na thŷ na thŵr
> Na chan caer na chwncwerwr.[44]

(You cast – you encompassed a fall –
the top of Carreg Cennen down into the valley.
Its dyke, Harlech's, did not stand up at all
to you, any more than a sheep-fold.
Neither house nor tower can withstand you
nor a hundred fortresses nor a conqueror.)

Later in the same poem Guto refers to Herbert as 'brenin ein iaith' ('king of our nation', literally, 'tongue' or 'language'), urging him to use his status to unite Wales against the factionalism that was tearing it apart.

On the other side of the political divide, the great hero of the Welsh Lancastrians was Jasper Tudor, half-brother of Henry VI and uncle to the young Henry Tudor whose father Edmund had died before he was born. During the reign of the Yorkist king Edward IV, Jasper led a sustained resistance in Wales with the support of the French and, after Edward's renewed kingship in 1471, carried Henry Tudor off to Brittany with him to live in exile until 1485 when Henry, supported by large numbers of disaffected Yorkists, returned to Britain, via Wales, to challenge Richard III. After the triumph of Bosworth, Jasper Tudor served Henry VII, who created him Duke of Bedford, and lived until 1495, a Lancastrian who brought to life the new royal dynasty of the Tudors.

Praise poems were addressed to Jasper by one of the foremost poets of the fifteenth century, Lewys Glyn Cothi (fl. 1447–89), a prolific poet who sang to many of the leading Welsh gentry in both north and south Wales.[45] Though Lewys acknowledged the remarkable leadership of William Herbert in one or two poems, his greatest allegiance was to Jasper and the noble Welsh families who fought for the Lancastrian cause. Referring to the period immediately following the battle of Mortimer's Cross in February 1461, when the Lancastrians under Jasper Tudor were defeated and his father, Owain Tudur, was executed, Lewys describes the main players in this dramatic moment of history:

Henri frenin ffordd ydd êl hinon
ef â â'r gware, ef a'r goron.
Edwart dywysog heb dretusion
a geidw'r ynys â gwayw dur union.
Siasbar yn drydydd, Penmynydd Môn,
a ennill y gwr, myn llaw Garon.
Harri o Ritsmwnt o Gaerllion
ar ôl ei ewythr â i Liwon.
Marchog o'r gardr fal yr oedd Meirchion

yw Siasbar a gâr ei ragorion;
yn farc y'i gelwir o hyn i Fôn,
yn ddug y'i gelwir yn dda'i galon.[46]

(May king Henry go forth in fair weather,
he goes with the game, he and the Crown.
Prince Edward, without treaties,
keeps the island with a straight steel spear.[47]
Jasper's the third, of Penmynydd in Môn,
who gets the man, by the hand of St Caron.
Henry of Richmond follows his uncle
from Chester to Llifon.[48]
A Knight of the Garter like the other knights
is Jasper who loves his privileges;
he will be called a hallmark from here to Môn,
he will be called a duke whose heart is good.)

Manuscript Production in the Fifteenth Century

In terms of cultural production, the century is marked by a decisive shift towards secular manuscript copying and book production in the homes of leading Welsh families. It is not until the mid-fifteenth century that collections of poetry by fourteenth- and fifteenth-century poets, composing particularly but not exclusively in the *cywydd* metre, begin to survive in substantial amounts. In many cases, these manuscripts were written by the poets themselves, copying out their own work alongside the work of earlier poets. NLW MS Peniarth 54, dating from about 1480, contains a large number of Dafydd ap Gwilym's poems together with substantial work by poets of the second half of the century, contemporary with the manuscript itself, including Huw Cae Llwyd (*c.* 1431–*c.* 1505), Hywel Dafi (*fl. c.* 1450–1480), and Hywel Swrdwal (*fl. c.* 1430–1475). According to Daniel Huws, 'A remarkable fact about this contemporary poetry is that most of it has every appearance of being autograph.'[49] Other autograph copies of poems are found in NLW MS Peniarth 60 (*c.* 1510), while MS Peniarth 67 (*c.* 1485) is entirely in the hand of Hywel Dafi. Lewys Glyn Cothi is another poet who took care to record his verse in his own hand: most of his work survives either in his own hand or in manuscripts that he owned.[50] It appears, then, that from the middle of the century the poets were taking charge of their own work and writing it down themselves as a more permanent record of their art, to be kept in the libraries of their patrons.

Large anthologies similar to the Red Book of Hergest – though not quite so large – continued to be produced in the March of Wales during the fifteenth century, probably by clerically trained scribes but not by clerics in monasteries. Two such books, NLW MS Peniarth 50 (c. 1445) and MS Peniarth 26 (c. 1456), are trilingual manuscripts containing a variety of texts in Welsh, English, and Latin. Peniarth 50 has a title, 'Y Cwta Cyfarwydd', or 'the informative little [book]', and contains mainly history and prophecy, including the well-known English prophecies 'Cock in the North', 'When Rome is Removed', and those attributed to John of Bridlington. The manuscript is written in one hand over a period of time, suggesting the same kind of house scribe as Hywel ap Fychan, and interestingly it seems to have been compiled in Glamorgan, like Hywel's Red Book of Hergest. We can therefore assume that Peniarth 50 was the product of another gentry household in Glamorgan around the middle of the fifteenth century, and one closely involved in the politics of the Wars of the Roses, as expressed through the medium of prophecy.

NLW MS Peniarth 26 can be located in or near the town of Oswestry, on the border with England. Oswestry was one of a number of Welsh towns which were the objects of praise by the cywyddwyr, drawing on a classical tradition of the praise of cities.[51] Though the town was situated within an English Marcher lordship owned by the earls of Arundel, it was prized by the Welsh urban community as a place of architectural, commercial, and religious significance in the region. Guto'r Glyn called it 'Llundain gwlad Owain' ('the London of Owain [Glyndŵr's] land'),[52] and Tudur Aled referred to 'gorchestol gaer a chastell' ('[its] imposing fortress and castle'), which, along with the town walls and gates, could be seen from afar by approaching travellers.[53] The manuscript is a genuine anthology containing a variety of genres such as history, astronomy, poetry, and, like Peniarth 50, prophecy in Welsh and English, including 'Cock in the North' and two versions of 'When Rome is Removed'. In both manuscripts, the main focus of the Welsh prophecies is the return of Welsh sovereignty over the island of Britain, a trope going back to the earliest stratum of Welsh poetry and re-energized during the Wars of the Roses when Welsh poets looked for a mab darogan, a 'son of prophecy', who would fulfil the nation's ambitions to see a Welshman on the throne of England. Edward IV in some respects satisfied this ambition, with his Mortimer lineage which could trace its descent from the Welsh princes, but it was Henry Tudor, whose Welshness could be in no doubt, who increasingly became the focus of Welsh political hopes.

The interest in prophecy during the Wars of the Roses indicated by these two manuscripts is amply reinforced by the court poets, many of whom included prophetic poetry, *canu brud*, in their repertoire. A poet particularly associated with prophecy is Dafydd Llwyd of Mathafarn (*fl. c.* 1400–1490) who spoke from a predominantly Lancastrian position and anticipated the triumph when Henry Tudor, grandson of Owain Tudur, would take the throne and unite the nation:

> Penadur o Dudur daid
> Yw'r eryr, ŵr oreuraid,
> Owain fwyn, awen o Fôn
> A gwncweria gan coron;
> Hwn yw fo yn ôl hun faith
> A wna'n hynys yn uniaith.[54]

> (The eagle is a chieftain, a golden man,
> grandson of noble Owain Tudur,
> the Anglesey inspiration
> who will conquer a shining crown.
> He is the man who, after a long sleep,
> will make our island into a single nation.)

The reference to a 'long sleep' recalls the legend of Arthur and even, perhaps, Owain Glyn Dŵr, both of them popularly thought to be sleeping in another world, waiting for their return; and the image of 'our island' as one nation alludes to Welsh claims to sovereignty over the whole island of Britain by ancient right. These allusions, implying that Henry Tudor will be the *mab darogan* returning to restore British rule, are characteristic of medieval Welsh prophecy as a form of political propaganda.

Angled towards one faction or the other, *canu brud* was popular with patrons whose families participated in the civil war. One such family were the Vaughans (Welsh Fychan) of Tretower and Hergest on the March of Wales. Thomas Vaughan of Hergest, near Kington in Herefordshire, was a half-brother of William Herbert and a Yorkist supporter who died with William at the battle of Edgecote in 1469. Both Hergest and another family seat at Tre'rtŵr (Tretower, near Crickhowell in Powys), where Thomas's older brother Sir Roger Vaughan (Syr Rhosier Fychan) lived, were significant centres of poetic patronage throughout the later fifteenth century. Sometime after Richard III's successful challenge for the throne in 1483, Lewys Glyn Cothi composed a praise poem to Sir Roger Vaughan's son Thomas who had

supported Richard's claim. Celebrating Richard's success, Lewys positions
Thomas as his right-hand man:

> Y Brenin Rhisiart, barnai'n wresog,
> yw tarw cryfraisg tyrau Caerefrog.
> A faidd dyn heddiw faedd danheddog,
> na llu o Gaer-wysg na Lloegr ysgog?
> A oes Wyddel gwyllt na swyddog – na llu
> na bo'n crynu, unben coronog?
>
> Ni wn a oes dyn o hyn i Stog,
> na neb yn Nyfnaint na bo'n ofnog.
> Y llew a aned aeth yn llwynog
> i gadw'r deÿrnas gwedy'r draenog,
> a'r gŵr o Dre'rtŵr, tiriog – benadur,
> i faedd hen Arthur a fydd nerthog.
>
> Syr Tomas, curas y gwŷr caerog,
> asur yw ei helm a sêr hoelog,
> a mwg o rubi ar helm gribog
> ac ymyl ei ŵn lliw'r melynog;
> aur Rhisiart y sydd ar osog – rhyfel,
> aur yn fur uchel a'i roi'n farchog.[55]

> (King Richard, he made quickfire decisions,
> is the mighty bull of the towers of York.
> Will a man dare today to confront a spiked boar,
> or stir up a host from Exeter or England?
> Is there a wild Irishman, or a magistrate, or a host
> who would not tremble, a crowned lord?
>
> I doubt there is a man from here to Stoke
> or anyone in Devon who would not be afraid.
> Born a lion, he went as a fox
> to guard the realm after the hedgehog,
> and the man from Tretower, a landed chieftain,
> is old Arthur's boar who will be strong.
>
> Sir Thomas, breastplate of the men in fortresses,
> azure is his helmet and studded with stars,
> and the glow of rubies on a crested helmet,
> and the border of his cloak the colour of a goldfinch;
> it is Richard's gold on the hawk of war,
> gold in a high wall and he gives it as a knight.)

In terms of patronage and manuscript transmission among families of *uchelwyr*, it is noteworthy that this poem by Lewys Glyn Cothi is one of two *awdlau* he composed to Thomas Vaughan of Tretower and his sons that Lewys himself wrote into the Red Book of Hergest during the reign of Richard III (1483–85).[56] At some stage during the fifteenth century, the Red Book had travelled from Glamorgan to one or both of the seats of the Vaughan family at Hergest and Tretower, with the former giving the manuscript its name. The Red Book therefore contains praise poems to at least two sets of patrons associated with the anthology, Hopcyn ap Tomas of Ynysforgan who commissioned the manuscript and the Vaughan families of Hergest and Tretower who were later owners of it.[57] There was also a White Book of Hergest (now lost), another anthology containing Welsh prose and verse (including a collection of poems by Dafydd ap Gwilym), much of it in the hand of Lewys Glyn Cothi himself. Lewys's praise poems to Thomas Vaughan of Hergest and his son Watcyn ap Tomas written into this manuscript in Lewys's hand suggest that it was the Vaughans of Hergest who commissioned the lost White Book as a companion volume to the Red Book.[58]

Conclusion

Welsh writing of the fourteenth and fifteenth centuries is characterized by the co-operation between monasteries and gentry families in preserving texts and by the increased exposure of writers and patrons to cultural and linguistic trends beyond the borders of Wales. By the fifteenth century, manuscript production was moving from the monasteries to gentry houses, and poets themselves were increasingly writing out their own poetry and that of their contemporaries. Prose writing in Welsh, especially the functional texts preserving laws, history, medicine, and religious material, remained the work of professional scribes commissioned by gentry families to provide manuscripts for their libraries. Literary patronage among the *uchelwyr* was energized by the senior roles held by many of them in the English government of Wales after 1284 and by war service under English and Marcher lords during the Hundred Years War and the Wars of the Roses. These experiences not only exposed many of the *uchelwyr* and their writers to new cultural influences but inspired them to value and preserve the literature of their own nation.

Late medieval literature in Welsh is dominated by the work of the court poets who, like their predecessors, formed a significant part of cultural and political life in Wales. The tradition of Welsh court poetry evident from the earliest records of the *cynfeirdd* singing before 1066 and flourishing during the generations of *gogynfeirdd* who sang to the independent princes of Wales before 1282 survived into the late Middle Ages and up until the Acts of Union in the early sixteenth century. The poets themselves were highly conscious of their status, established through regular challenges and public competitions.[59] Although their most common metre was the *cywydd*, the late medieval bards also made conscious use of the *awdl*, associated with the poetry of the princes, to compose their most formal praise poetry. Alongside the new popular genres of love poetry, nature poetry, urban satire, and political prophecy, their staple forms were those of their predecessors: praise poetry, eulogies, poems of request and thanks, and poems celebrating martial heroism in the wars in France and the civil war in Wales and England, all addressed to patrons who represented the most prominent and politically engaged families in Wales. Many of the poets looked outside their own tradition as well and were influenced by French traditions circulating in Wales, as is evident from the Welsh translations of French romances and the frequent poetic references to romance heroes such as Bevis, Charlemagne, Guy of Warwick, and many others.

This chapter has been able to mention only a small number of the dozens of court poets we know to have been composing and singing to patrons in late medieval Wales. Though following strict metrical forms and the rules of *cynghanedd* and including traditional tropes and imagery, the poetry speaks to us in the varied, lively, and individual voices of those who composed it, aware that they had been trained into a centuries-old tradition of poetry. The key to this long tradition and its continued transmission after the Reformation was the role played by its patrons, first the princes and noble families of Wales and the March who provided patronage for poets and support for the preservation and collection of literary manuscripts, and later the antiquarians of the sixteenth and seventeenth centuries who ensured the literature was passed on. The network of knowledge exchange formed by patrons, scribes, and poets has resulted in a rich legacy of poetry and prose from late medieval Wales.

Notes

1. Daniel Huws, *Medieval Welsh Manuscripts* (Cardiff and Aberystwyth: University of Wales Press and National Library of Wales, 2000), 36–7, 40. These figures are based on Huws's table of manuscript production on pp. 58–64. See also Patrick Sims-Williams, 'The Uses of Writing in Early Medieval Wales', in *Literacy in Medieval Celtic Societies*, ed. Huw Pryce (Cambridge: Cambridge University Press, 1998), 15–38.

2. On the poetry from the Black Book of Carmarthen, see Chapter 2 in this volume.

3. This quote, and the term 'material semiotics', comes from John Law, 'Actor Network Theory and Material Semiotics', in *The New Blackwell Companion to Social Theory*, ed. Bryan S. Turner (Oxford: Wiley-Blackwell, 2009), 141–58 (154).

4. For an account of these foundations, see F. G. Cowley, *The Monastic Order in South Wales, 1066–1349* (Cardiff: University of Wales Press, 1977). The website *Monastic Wales* provides a useful map and description of all the monastic houses of Wales, www.monasticwales.org/listsites.php (accessed 17 August 2017).

5. R. R. Davies, *Conquest, Coexistence, and Change: Wales 1063–1415* (Oxford: Oxford University Press, 1987), 197.

6. Dafydd Johnston, 'Monastic Patronage of Welsh Poetry', in *Monastic Wales: New Approaches*, ed. Janet Burton and Karen Stöber (Cardiff: University of Wales Press, 2013), 177–90.

7. *Legendary Poems from the Book of Taliesin*, ed. and trans. Marged Haycock (Aberystwyth: CMCS Publications, 2007). See also Chapter 2 in this volume.

8. On the towns of Wales, see *Boroughs of Mediaeval Wales*, ed. Ralph A. Griffiths (Cardiff: University of Wales Press, 1978); *Urban Culture in Medieval Wales*, ed. Helen Fulton (Cardiff: University of Wales Press, 2012).

9. Huws, *Medieval Welsh Manuscripts*, 76; see also 47. On *Brut y Tywysogyon* and its relationship to Geoffrey's *Historia Regum Britanniae* (*c.* 1138) and other Welsh chronicles, see Brynley F. Roberts, 'Geoffrey of Monmouth, *Historia Regum Britanniae* and *Brut y Brenhinedd*', in *The Arthur of the Welsh: The Arthurian Legend in Medieval Welsh Literature*, ed. Rachel Bromwich *et al.* (Cardiff: University of Wales Press, 1991), 97–116; J. Beverley Smith, 'Historical Writing in Medieval Wales: The Composition of *Brenhinedd y Saesson*', *Studia Celtica* 42 (2008): 55–86.

10. On the significance of Strata Florida, see Helen Fulton, 'Ceredigion: Strata Florida and Llanbadarn Fawr', in *Europe: A Literary History*, ed. David Wallace, 2 vols. (Oxford: Oxford University Press, 2016), I, 438–54.

11. *Gwaith Llywelyn Goch ap Meurig Hen*, ed. Dafydd Johnston (Aberystwyth: Canolfan Uwchefrydiau Cymreig a Cheltaidd, 1998), no. 2. The poem thanks God for sparing the life of the abbot after a serious illness.

12. Huws, *Medieval Welsh Manuscripts*, 252. For a detailed description of the manuscript, see Huws, *Medieval Welsh Manuscripts*, 193–226. Catherine McKenna has written about the contents of the Henregadredd manuscript in Chapter 5 of this volume.

13. The family of Ieuan Llwyd is described in *Gwaith Llywelyn Brydydd Hoddnant, Dafydd ap Gwilym, Hillyn ac Eraill*, ed. Ann Parry Owen and Dylan Foster Evans (Aberystwyth: Canolfan Uwchefrydiau Cymreig a

Cheltaidd, 1996), 6–13; see also Huws, *Medieval Welsh Manuscripts*, 216–18 and 249–52.

14. The two manuscripts are slightly damaged and incomplete; for a full description, see Huws, *Medieval Welsh Manuscripts*, 227–68. Huws also sets out the evidence which links the White Book with Rhydderch ab Ieuan Llwyd (247–9).

15. For a diplomatic edition of sections of the White Book, see *Llyfr Gwyn Rhydderch: Y Chwedlau a'r Rhamantau*, ed. J. Gwenogvryn Evans and Bobi Jones (Cardiff: University of Wales Press, 1977). The White Book lacks one of the eleven tales of the *Mabinogion*, namely *Breudwyt Ronabwy* ('The Dream of Rhonabwy'). The term 'Mabinogion' was first used by Lady Charlotte Guest as an umbrella title for her edition and translations of all the tales which she published in seven volumes between 1838 and 1845; see Chapter 4 of this volume.

16. Translations into Welsh from French and Latin texts form a significant part of the canon of medieval Welsh literature. For an overview, see Helen Fulton, 'Translating Europe in Medieval Wales', in *Writing Europe, 500–1450: Texts and Contexts*, ed. Aidan Conti *et al.* (Cambridge: D. S. Brewer, 2015), 159–74; see also Ceridwen Lloyd-Morgan, 'French Texts, Welsh Translators', in *The Medieval Translator II*, ed. Roger Ellis (London: Centre for Medieval Studies, Queen Mary and Westfield College, University of London, 1991), 45–63.

17. Huws speculates that the White Book may have originally contained a substantial collection of poetry by the *gogynfeirdd*, the 'poetry of the princes'. See *Medieval Welsh Manuscripts*, 227–68. Later copies of the White Book also indicate that it originally contained most of the saga *englynion* associated with Llywarch Hen. See Jenny Rowland, ed. and trans., *Early Welsh Saga Poetry: A Study and Edition of the* Englynion (Cambridge: D. S. Brewer, 1990), 393–402.

18. Huws, *Medieval Welsh Manuscripts*, 255. The *englynion* appear on fol. 65v of NLW MS Peniarth 5; they have been edited by R. G. Gruffydd, 'Englynion y Cusan by Dafydd ap Gwilym', *CMCS* 23 (1992): 1–6.

19. For what is known of Hopcyn's life, see Brynley F. Roberts, 'Hopcyn ap Tomas ab Einion', in *Oxford Dictionary of National Biography* (Oxford: Oxford University Press, 2004), online edition, www.oxforddnb.com/view/article/48547.

20. The metrical form of the *cywydd* is described by Dafydd Johnston in Chapter 6 of this volume.

21. Huws, *Medieval Welsh Manuscripts*, 82–3. We can surmise from poetic references that Hopcyn probably owned a considerable library of books: see Christine James, 'Hopcyn ap Tomas a "Llyfrgell Genedlaethol" Ynysforgan', *THSC* 13 (2007): 31–57.

22. The colophon is cited in full by Brynley F. Roberts, 'Un o Lawysgrifau Hopcyn ap Tomas o Ynys Dawe', *BBCS* 22 (1967): 223–7.

23. Huws, *Medieval Welsh Manuscripts*, 252. Hywel's writing occurs on fol. 83v of NLW MS Peniarth 4.

24. Though the texts of the Four Branches and the Welsh romances in the Red Book and the White Book are very close, there are sufficient differences of spelling and lexis to indicate that the former was not directly dependent on the latter. See the discussion in *Owein, or Chwedyl Iarlles y Ffynnawn*, ed. R. L. Thomson (Dublin: Dublin Institute for Advanced Studies, 1968), xii–xvi. Jenny Rowland has also argued that the Red Book is not a direct copy of the White ('The Manuscript Tradition of the Red Book *Englynion*', *Studia Celtica* 18–19 (1983–4): 79–95).

25. Huws, *Medieval Welsh Manuscripts*, 255.

26. These earlier manuscript sources are likely to include NLW MS Peniarth 6, from the second half of the thirteenth century, and NLW MS Peniarth 7 from *c.* 1300. For a discussion of manuscripts earlier than the White Book which contain fragments of the *Mabinogion*, see Huws, *Medieval Welsh Manuscripts*, 245–6.

27. The likelihood that Hywel was a professional lay scribe was suggested by Gifford Charles-Edwards, 'The Scribes of the Red Book of Hergest', *National Library of Wales Journal* 21, 3 (1979–80): 246–56.

28. Parcrhydderch, in the parish of Llangeitho, is about sixty miles from Ynysforgan in west Glamorgan. Little is known about Dafydd y Coed, but he was evidently active in the second half of the fourteenth century. For his poems to Rhydderch and Hopcyn ap Tomas, see *Gwaith Dafydd y Coed a Beirdd Eraill o Lyfr Coch Hergest*, ed. R. Iestyn Daniel (Aberystwyth: Canolfan Uwchefrydiau Cymreig a Cheltaidd, 2002), no. 1 and no. 3. Llywelyn Goch ap Meurig Hen is thought to have been active between *c.* 1350 and *c.* 1390. For his poems to Rhydderch and to Hopcyn, see *Gwaith Llywelyn Goch ap Meurig Hen*, ed. Johnston, no. 4 and no. 6.

29. *Legendary Poems*, ed. and trans. Haycock, 1–2.

30. The standard work of reference on Welsh poetry of the fourteenth and fifteenth centuries is Dafydd Johnston, *Llên yr Uchelwyr: Hanes Beirniadol Llenyddiaeth Gymraeg, 1300–1525* (Caerdydd: Gwasg Prifysgol Cymru, 2005). For older surveys in English, see A. O. H. Jarman and Gwilym Rees Hughes, eds., *A Guide to Welsh Literature*, vol. II: *1282–1550*, rev. Dafydd Johnston (Cardiff: University of Wales Press, 1997); H. I. Bell, The *Development of Welsh Poetry* (Oxford: Clarendon Press, 1936). A large selection of late medieval Welsh court poetry has been translated into English by Joseph P. Clancy, *Medieval Welsh Poems* (Dublin: Four Courts Press, 2003).

31. The most authoritative account of the rebellion, its causes and its aftermath, is R. R. Davies, *The Revolt of Owain Glyn Dŵr* (Oxford: Oxford University Press, 1995).

32. According to Dafydd Johnston, only two poets are known to have sung about the events of the Glyn Dŵr rebellion at the time, Madog ap Gronw Gethin and Llywelyn ab y Moel. See Johnston, *Llên yr Uchelwyr*, 232. Gruffydd Aled Williams describes Owain's relationship with his praise poets in *Owain y Beirdd* (Aberystwyth: Prifysgol Cymru, 1998).

33. From the poem 'Praise of Owain Glyndŵr', line 14, in *Iolo Goch: Poems*, ed. and trans. Dafydd Johnston (Llandysul: Gomer Press, 1993), no. 9. See also Dafydd Johnston's Chapter 6 in this volume, where he discusses Iolo's poem to Owain's house at Sycharth.

34. Gruffudd's poem has been edited in *Gwaith Gruffudd Llwyd a'r Llygliwiaid Eraill*, ed. Rhiannon Ifans (Aberystwyth: Canolfan Uwchefrydiau Cymreig a Cheltaidd, 2000), no. 11. Gruffudd also composed a second praise poem to Owain (no. 12) as well as a eulogy to Rhydderch ab Ieuan Llwyd (no. 13).

35. Johnston, ed. and trans., *Iolo Goch: Poems*, no. 9, lines 37 and 54.

36. Ibid., no. 8, lines 55 and 79.

37. *Guto'r Glyn.net*, no. 72, ed. and trans. R. Iestyn Daniel, www.gutorglyn.net/gutorglyn/poem/?poem-selection=072, ll. 17–22. Siôn's wife Alswn belonged to the Trefor family; the 'two great Maelors' are Maelor Gymraeg and Maelor Saesneg, the two easternmost areas of the county of Flintshire in north-east Wales.

38. *Gwaith Tudur Aled*, ed. T. Gwynn Jones (Caerdydd: Gwasg Prifysgol Cymru, 1926), vol. I, no. XLII, ll. 25–8, my translation.

39. *Guto'r Glyn.net*, no. 75, ed. and trans. Alaw Mai Edwards, www.gutorglyn.net/gutorglyn/poem/?poem-selection=075, ll. 39–40.

40. For an account of the life of William Herbert, see Ralph A. Griffiths, 'Herbert, William, First Earl of Pembroke (c. 1423–1469)', in *Oxford Dictionary of National Biography* (Oxford: Oxford University Press, 2014), online edn, www.oxforddnb.com/view/article/13053 (accessed 17 August 2017).

41. There is some doubt as to whether the manuscript was presented to Edward IV or to Henry VI before the events of 1461. For a description of the manuscript, see Kathleen L. Scott, *Later Gothic Manuscripts, 1390–1490*, 2 vols. (London: Harvey Miller, 1996), II, 282–4.

42. *Gwaith Hywel Dafi*, ed. A. Cynfael Lake, 2 vols. (Aberystwyth: Canolfan Uwchefrydiau Cymreig a Cheltaidd, 2015), II, no. 66, ll. 1–4.

43. The names of Guto'r Glyn's patrons can be retrieved from the index in *Gwaith Guto'r Glyn*, ed. John Llewelyn Williams and Ifor Williams (Caerdydd: Gwasg Prifysgol Cymru, 1939), 377–81; see also the list of patrons in the online edition of his poems, *Guto'r Glyn.net*, www.gutorglyn.net/gutorglyn/patron-list.

44. *Guto'r Glyn.net*, no. 21, ed. and trans. Barry J. Lewis, ll. 21–6, www.gutorglyn
    .net/gutorglyn/poem/?poem-selection=021 (accessed 17 August 2017).
45. Johnston, *Llên yr Uchelwyr*, 244–7.
46. *Gwaith Lewys Glyn Cothi*, ed. Dafydd Johnston (Caerdydd: Gwasg Prifysgol
    Cymru, 1995), no. 11, ll. 9–20, my translation.
47. Edward was the son of Henry VI, killed at Tewkesbury in 1471.
48. Henry, the son of Edmund Tudor, was the nephew of Jasper Tudor. Henry's
    title was Earl of Richmond before he was crowned as Henry VII. Llifon is a
    region of Môn (Anglesey).
49. Huws, *Medieval Welsh Manuscripts*, 95.
50. E. D. Jones, 'A Welsh *Pencerdd*'s Manuscripts', *Celtica* 5 (1959): 17–27.
51. Helen Fulton, 'The *Encomium Urbis* in Medieval Welsh Poetry', *Proceedings of
    the Harvard Celtic Colloquium* 26 (2006): 54–72.
52. From the poem 'Moliant i Groesoswallt', ed. Eurig Salisbury, *Guto'r Glyn.net*,
    no. 102, line 21. For other praise poems to Oswestry, see Helen Fulton,
    'Trading Places: Representations of Urban Culture in Medieval Welsh
    Poetry', *Studia Celtica* 31 (1997): 219–30.
53. *Gwaith Tudur Aled*, ed. Jones, no. LXV, l. 6.
54. *Gwaith Dafydd Llwyd o Fathafarn*, ed. W. Leslie Richards (Caerdydd: Gwasg
    Prifysgol Cymru, 1964), no. 8, ll. 95–100, my translation.
55. *Gwaith Lewys Glyn Cothi*, no. 130, ll. 13–30, my translation.
56. The second poem is in *Gwaith Lewys Glyn Cothi*, no. 131.
57. Prys Morgan has argued that the Red Book passed to the Vaughan family as
    part of the spoils of the Wars of the Roses, appropriated by the Yorkist
    Vaughans from the Lancastrian descendants of Hopcyn ap Tomas. Morgan
    also speculates that the Red Book may have gone first to Tretower, where
    Lewys Glyn Cothi copied in his poems to that family, and then to Hergest.
    See Prys Morgan, 'Glamorgan and the Red Book', *Morgannwg: Transactions of
    the Glamorgan Local History Society* 22 (1978): 42–60.
58. The White Book of Hergest, dated *c.* 1470, was lost in a fire in London in the
    early nineteenth century, but its contents had been copied out by the
    antiquarian scholar John Davies of Mallwyd (*c.* 1567–1644) and survive in
    London, British Library MS Additional 14871 (formerly BL MS 20), *c.* 1617
    (containing the poems by Lewys Glyn Cothi) and in NLW MS Peniarth 49
    (containing mainly poems by Dafydd ap Gwilym). The poems by Lewys to
    the family at Hergest that survive from the White Book of Hergest include
    Gwaith Lewys Glyn Cothi, nos. 125 and 127. The two poems to the family at
    Tretower mentioned above (nos. 130 and 131) were copied by Lewys into
    both the Red Book and the White Book.

59. The poets regularly challenged each other in the form of *ymrysonau*, debates or arguments conducted by a pair of poets alternating across a series of poems. Formal competitions or *eisteddfodau* were held on occasion; the earliest recorded *eisteddfod* was held in Aberteifi (Ceredigion) in 1176 with further meetings held in 1451 and 1523, the last of these organized by Tudur Aled and others specifically to reform and regulate the craft of bardic poetry. For further details, see Hywel Teifi Edwards, *The Eisteddfod*, Writers of Wales (Cardiff: University of Wales Press, 1990).

PART II

*

AFTER THE ACTS OF UNION

8

The Acts of Union: Culture and Religion in Wales, c. 1540–1700

KATHARINE K. OLSON

In 1450, the late medieval British Isles were culturally and politically divided. English lordship extended over a wide range of diverse laws, languages, and institutions which in many areas existed alongside native Welsh customs. During the period c. 1450–1700, the British Isles experienced long-term, multi-faceted change as a more centralized British state emerged. With the end of the Wars of the Roses and the accession of Henry Tudor (Henry VII) to the throne in 1485, the Tudor period witnessed English attempts to consolidate political, legal, and administrative power and to promote uniformity in the peripheries of Ireland, Wales, and Scotland. The cultural impact of the extension of English governance was felt most keenly in these areas, where increasing centralization had long-term repercussions for the future of the native Celtic languages, society, and culture.

By the middle of the fifteenth century, Wales began to experience a significant revival and recovery in the aftermath of the devastation left by the revolt of Owain Glyn Dŵr. The reorientation of the Acts of Union of 1536 and 1542–3 was to have far-reaching consequences for politics, administration, law, society, and culture in Wales. The Tudor Reformations likewise brought significant changes in the experience of worship to Wales, though the nature of religious change was slow and tortuous, stretching into the seventeenth century and beyond. The period from c. 1450 is remarkable for its profound developments experienced by the Welsh with regard to culture, society, religion, and identity.

In the fifteenth century, Wales did not exist as a political unit. From the Statute of Rhuddlan in 1284 to the Act of Union of 1536, those areas known collectively as Wales today were divided into the Principality and the March. The former comprised the shires of Cardigan and Carmarthen in south Wales and those of Anglesey, Merioneth, and Caernarfon in the north (a feudal demesne of the Crown), while in the north-east, Tegeingl and Maelor Saesneg (Flint) were ultimately placed under the authority of the justice of Chester. The March – a patchwork of separate lordships and jurisdictions held of the Crown whose autonomous privileges were staunchly guarded by their Marcher lords – was concentrated in the south and east of Wales, though it extended westward into Pembrokeshire.[1]

The development of landed estates in Wales continued apace in the latter half of the fifteenth century and into the sixteenth, with land tenure, office-holding, and lineage determining the rise of many families. The Stradling and Mathews families of Glamorgan and the house of Dinefwr, among others, thrived in the south. In the north, dominant landholding families included the Mostyns, the Wynns of Gwydir, and the Gruffydds of Penrhyn, while new families like the Bulkeleys of Baron Hill were in the ascendant. The gentry also played a significant role in the Principality and the March in the maintenance of order and administration in local communities in the absence of effective and powerful central government and administration. While revenue continued to be collected by the crown and lords in the Principality and Marcher lordships, in practical terms little control was exercised by the centre. Land, lineage, marriage, and opportunity paved the way to power for local gentry families across Wales, as the examples in Cardiganshire and Carmarthenshire of men like Rhys ap Thomas and Gruffydd ap Nicholas certainly demonstrate.

The Wars of the Roses of the second half of the fifteenth century saw Wales embroiled on both sides of the conflict. Though the allegiances of individual lords fluctuated, the Principality and the Duchy of Lancaster lordships generally supported the Lancastrians while the House of York won the support of much of the remainder of the March.[2] Welsh hopes were revived in the person of Henry Tudor, earl of Richmond. He was the grandson of Owen Tudor (d. 1461) of Penmynydd on Anglesey and Catherine of Valois, the widow of Henry V (d. 1422), and the son of Margaret Beaufort (d. 1509) and Edmund Tudor (d. 1456). Born in Pembroke in 1457, months after the death of his father, Henry Tudor came to be seen as the *mab darogan* (son of prophecy) and the fulfilment of Welsh prophetic and political ambitions to restore the Welsh to their rightful place on the British throne. Following Henry's victory at Bosworth Field on 22 August 1485 against the forces of Richard III, he was crowned king, and those with Welsh links who had supported him were rewarded with money, lands, and titles. Having married Elizabeth of York, a descendant of Llywelyn ab Iorwerth (d. 1240) of Gwynedd, Henry – who claimed descent from Cadwaladr himself – appositely named his first-born son Arthur. His reign prompted Welshmen to seek new opportunities, patronage, and preferment in London and at the Tudor court.[3]

The Act of Union and Its Consequences

Under Henry VIII, significant efforts were made to improve royal control of administration and law and order in the peripheries, including Wales, where social turbulence seemed to be endemic. These efforts took on a new significance with the king's break with Rome in the early 1530s. In a vigorous attempt to deal with problems of law and order, Rowland Lee, bishop of Coventry and Lichfield, was appointed the new lord president of the Council in the Marches of Wales in 1534; he sought to reduce law-lessness and criminality in the Marches with a firm hand.[4]

Most notably, the year 1536 saw the passage of 'An Act for laws and justice to be ministered in Wales in like form as it is in this realm,' better known as the Act of Union of 1536 (27 Henry VIII, c.26).[5] Said to be motivated by the king's 'singular zeal Love and Favour' for Wales, it created a single legal, administrative, and political unit of 'England and Wales', abolishing at a single stroke the Marcher lordships. Some of these lands were joined to existing English or Welsh counties, and others were made into new shires or counties in Wales (Denbigh, Brecknock, Glamorgan, Montgomery, Radnor, and Monmouth, with the last of these granted special status), all with their respective shire towns. In line with this reorganization, the Welsh were granted parliamentary representation; every shire was given one member (Monmouthshire two), as were the shire towns. In a significant move, those born in Wales were to have all 'Freedoms Liberties Rights and Privileges and Laws' of the 'naturally born [English]' for the first time. In so doing, the Act brought to the Welsh gentry new economic and legal benefits as well as a long-demanded equality with the English in terms of the law.[6]

There was a price to pay for these privileges. For those gentry and free-holders holding office in Wales, knowledge of English was to be mandatory; no person who spoke Welsh alone could hold or enjoy office unless they knew and utilized the English tongue in their offices. In addition, the Act stated the intent 'utterly to extirp all and singular the sinister Usages and Customs' which differed from those of his realm and had led to 'great discord', instead promoting 'amicable Concord and Unity' with the use of a single tongue. English land tenure, not Welsh, was to be used, and other customs found in the Marcher lordships were to be discouraged.[7] The 1536 Act was followed in 1543 by what is commonly known as the Second Act of Union (34 & 35 Henry

VIII, c.26). It was presented in the preamble as an act for 'good Rule and Order' so that Henry's Welsh subjects might 'grow and arise to more Wealth and Prosperity'.[8] At the heart of this statute was a range of administrative, judicial, and legal reforms. The Council in the Marches of Wales, based at Ludlow, was strengthened; it now functioned on a statutory basis.[9] In addition, the Court of Great Sessions was established in Wales, which was to have four judicial circuits, each of which encompassed three shires (not Monmouthshire). The statute suppressed what were some of the oldest laws and customs in Wales relating to property and inheritance, those which 'heretofore in divers parts of Wales hath been used and accustomed' (that is, gavelkind or partible inheritance), replacing them with English tenure according to common law.[10]

While the Act of Union of 1536 was indeed significant, assessing its shorter- and longer-term impact on Welsh culture and identity is not unproblematic. It did not yield immediate results for Welsh culture, society, and identity, nor were these static. Change was of long duration, as J. Goronwy Edwards has argued, and more complex.[11] Indeed, to a degree, the Act 'simply recognised existing trends and gave statutory recognition to changes that had already taken place',[12] whilst others were happening gradually or had yet to occur. The Act of Union did, however, in Glanmor Williams's words, represent a 're-orientation' which redefined both jurisdictional and administrative boundaries, thereby establishing a more unified system of justice, law, and administration, as well as providing the Welsh with a new and improved legal status.[13] Nevertheless, as Peter Roberts has suggested, 'It would be foolish to consider these measures as expressing a consistent and single-minded "Tudor policy towards Wales" and its language and culture, or to assume that their cultural impact was invariably what they intended.'[14] Similarly, while traditional accounts of the Act of Union have focused on the anglicization of the gentry, a 'two-way process of accul-turation of Welsh and English elements' has also been posited, suggesting that, prior to the Act of Union, society in Wales had experienced both anglicizing and 'cymricizing' tendencies.[15] Moreover, if Tudor legislation sought in theory to unify the disparate parts of the realm under one common language, law, religion, and custom, then the reality was more complex. Toleration extended to a 'certain cultural pluralism' in practice, particularly in terms of the Welsh language, and more so in the case of Wales than Ireland.[16]

The Act of Union and Literary Activity

While its effects on the Welsh language, culture, and society in Wales are notable, in some ways the Act recognized longer-term trends. In late medieval Wales, Welsh served as a predominant medium for daily life, courtship, law, native poetry, prose, devotions, and more. Yet Wales had long been a 'linguistically mixed society' as well, comprising English, French, Latin, and Flemish speakers, together with a Welsh nobility and gentry which had frequently intermarried with English-speaking families.[17] While daily interactions in Welsh were common, knowledge of Latin and English for administration was also important. To a degree, then, the Act of Union merely confirmed existing late medieval practice and trends towards a bilingual and even multilingual gentry and office-holders.

However, the devaluing of the Welsh language and its replacement with English in the public sphere, for administrative, business, education, and other uses, ultimately diminished Welsh-language literary learning and oral culture. English was elevated and seen by the ambitious and aspiring as a language of opportunity and advancement, and while literacy in English expanded in the period 1536–1660, literacy in Welsh did not.[18] The 1536 Act arguably encouraged the native gentry to act as 'anglicizing influences', using English as a language of correspondence, personal accounts, and advancement.[19] With time, some reoriented their cultural priorities and outlook towards England. Others persisted in speaking the language, acting as bardic patrons and encouraging others actively to use Welsh; in 1606–1607, Sir John Wynn of Gwydir urged his daughter-in-law to learn Welsh on account of the fact that it would 'serve her turn well and be no burden'.[20]

By the early Stuart period, the cultural and social priorities and horizons of many Welsh gentry were in the process of a transition which ultimately led them to look increasingly towards England for advancement, direction, and daily life. An English education could have cultural repercussions on the outlook of the gentry and act as an anglicizing influence, bringing with it English fashions, ideas, language, connections, and an English viewpoint, as in a case from the 1630s. William Wynn of Glyn in Merioneth gave life advice to his son Cadwaladr, who was away at university in Oxford, counselling him to 'Speake no Welsh to any that can speake English, noe not to your bedfellows, and thereby you may attaine ... and freely speak the Englishe tongue perfectly.' His father preferred that he keep company with 'studious, honest Englishmen than with many of your own countreymen who are more prone to be idle and riotous than the English'.[21] By the eighteenth century a proportion of the gentry in Wales used English as their first language, and their knowledge of the Welsh tongue declined or even disappeared, and with it, their support of Welsh culture, poetry, and identity.

Whereas Wales in 1450 had possessed a robust and vibrant literary tradition and bardic order, supported by both their traditional *uchelwyr* patrons and the patronage of new families of English descent, the bardic order demonstrated signs of gradual decline in the later sixteenth and seventeenth centuries. The Act of Union of 1536 itself did not signal the immediate demise of native poetry or the bardic order in Wales, but it gave impetus to the gradual anglicization of the gentry. It also removed a major source of literary patronage in the form of the dissolved monasteries. It officially promoted English to the premier language in Wales in public life, gradually eroding the role of Welsh language learning, the literary language, and oral culture. Indeed, provisions for uniformity of law and custom and the end of native inheritance laws also meant a devaluing of pedigrees and the traditional role of the poet as genealogist, which had implications for native kinship and the family. Over time, bardic standards and traditional patronage inevitably declined, along with literacy in Welsh.

Social and economic problems in early modern Wales also had cultural implications. The Tudor period experienced an increasing gulf between the rich and the poor. A variety of factors, including price inflation, a steady increase in population, poor weather, bad harvests, and famines like those of the 1580s and 1590s, insufficient resources and food supply all contributed to the problem of poverty in early modern Wales.[22] Likewise, the dissolution of the monasteries caused the stoppage of many traditional institutional channels of monastic aid to the poor and the loss of a significant source of traditional bardic patronage. Problems of vagrancy and poverty had significant repercussions for the native poets and performers and their livelihoods in the form of Tudor vagrancy legislation. Begging without a licence was effectively outlawed in 1531, and five years later the 'Act for Punyshment of Sturdy Vacabundes and Beggars' classed wandering minstrels and poets with vagrants, rogues, and vagabonds as subject to being duly punished. The 1572 Vagrancy Act specifically defined unlicensed entertainers (including minstrels) as vagabonds, which had a significant effect on their ability to make a living, and also redefined their remuneration as begging. After 1536, their names appear among lists of beggars and vagabonds brought to trial in the Court of Great Sessions. One Denbighshire case in the 1550s of 'Vagabonds Cawllyng themselyffes mynstrelles', for example, resulted in the prosecution of three fiddlers, three harpers, two crowders, a dancer, several poets, and other allegedly unsavoury characters.[23] An association between the native poets, libel, and Catholicism was assumed by some contemporaries, as in Gaelic Ireland. A damning report on the state of religion in north Wales during Elizabeth's reign linked the poets to Catholic sympathies and practices like pilgrimages, while the 'Welsh libel' which circulated in 1601 sought to provoke rebellion against the Protestant English.[24]

For the humanists and antiquarians of early modern Wales, the professional poets functioned as the main, often secretive, repositories and custodians of the ancient learning and language of Wales. Some of the established gentry families and patrons of poets, such as the Wynns of Gwydir, show a continued interest in history, genealogy, ancestry, the antiquities, and heraldry, entertaining poets generously at their *plastai* (mansion houses). At the same time, families in the ascendant commissioned noble pedigrees and praise poetry to legitimate their newfound social and economic status. These 'new' men as well as established families enlisted herald poets like Siôn Tudur to research their pedigrees and create lengthy, colourful rolls containing the full pedigrees and heraldry of their families; one fine example is the 25-foot-long roll created in about 1570 by the poet Wiliam Cynwal (d. 1587 or 1588) for David Salusbury of Llanrhaeadr.[25] But some of the poets themselves complained of 'unworthy praise' and a 'bardic office that is without nobility', saying that men who once sang to princes, lords, bishops, earls, barons, prelates, and other noble patrons were now condemned to turn low-born men into gentry and give them noble pedigrees; worse than this, much of the blame for the state of things was laid at the door of the poets.[26] Similar sentiments were voiced in a satire by Edmwnd Prys around the year 1580; he questioned whether praising 'mean and strengthless men' as if they were warriors and putting their pedigrees to verse with flattery was fitting.[27]

The infamous tale of the late sixteenth-century professional poet Meurig Dafydd and his ill-fated visit to Beaupré Hall (Glamorgan) has often been used to illustrate the early modern decline of the bardic order. According to the story, the esquire William Basset of Bewper was presented by Meurig Dafydd (*fl.* 1580–1593) with a praise poem in his honour. Having read the poem, Basset asked whether a copy existed. When told this was the only copy, he paid the poet a noble and destroyed the poem in the fire, saying: 'By my honesty I swear that if there be no copy of this extant, none shall there ever be.'[28] While a sad commentary on the standards of contemporary poetry, it should not be taken to reflect an overall decline in standards and bardic patronage, though it suggests the increasing prevalence of written transmission of poetry. The rich and varied strict-metre poetry of Siôn Tudur, for example, was of a high standard. He enjoyed the patronage of many, including the Mostyns of Talacre (Flintshire), the Salusburys of Lleweni, Rug, and Bachymbyd, the Wynns of Gwydir, the Prys family of

Plas Iolyn, the Trefors of Trefalun, and the Bulkeleys of Porthaml. Other contemporary poets of note included Wiliam Llŷn, Siôn Brywnog, Wiliam Cynwal, and Siôn Phylip. Free-metre verse flourished, including carols and *cwndidau*, many on religious themes, while interest in and demand for traditional strict-metre elegies, eulogies, and religious poetry for saints' days, holidays, and other time-honoured themes remained. But the cultural reorientation of the gentry and their gradual anglicization had begun.

The last person to earn his living as a professional poet, John Davies (Siôn Dafydd Laes), died in 1695. However, as Daniel Huws has reminded us, it is unwise to take this as a *terminus ad quem* for Welsh poetry. Rather, after 1700 and into the nineteenth century poetry continued to be produced and copied.[29] Some Welsh gentry, including families like the Mostyns, Wynns of Gwydir and Foelas, Lloyds of Rhiwedog, Prices of Newtown, Salusburys of Lleweni, Dwnns of Ystrad Merthyr, Wyns of Twr, Bulkeleys of Porthaml, and Vaughans of Porthaml (Breconshire), remained steadfast patrons into the seventeenth century, as a selection of surviving court books from *c.* 1550 to *c.* 1650 demonstrates, and sometimes beyond. These families hailed from across Wales: Montgomeryshire, Denbighshire, Merioneth, Anglesey, Caernarvonshire, Pembrokeshire, Carmarthenshire, Breconshire, and Flintshire, though mostly from the north.[30] Traditional praise poems were still in demand, as well as elegies and genealogies commissioned for funerals.[31] Poets including the herald Rhys Cain still embarked on bardic circuits, as his itinerary (*c.* 1600) around north Wales and the Marches attests.[32] In Merioneth, where the remarkable Phylip family of Ardudwy produced poets until 1677 and support of the bardic order appears to have endured almost the longest, bards and minstrels were made welcome in the houses of some twenty gentry families as late as the end of the eighteenth century.[33] Nonetheless, by *c.* 1640 there was a clear decrease in the places visited on the once-crowded *cwrs clera* (bardic circuit) as well as a sustained decline in bardic learning and literacy and thus of the quality of the poetry itself.[34]

Reformation, Dissent, and the Vernacular

The Tudor Reformations did not prompt armed resistance or revolt in Wales as they did in England. It has been suggested that Welsh anticlericalism, loyalty to the Tudor dynasty, memories of the Glyndŵr revolt, economic opportunities for the Welsh gentry, and a general apathy towards religious practice imposed from outside may all have played a role in this.[35]

The response in Wales was very likely due to a complex combination of factors, but it was not entirely apathetic: some popular discontent was apparent.[36] The Henrician and Edwardian Reformations had limited popularity and success overall and did little to transform the traditional beliefs of the majority of the Welsh. Even under Elizabeth, the implementation and reception of Protestant reforms was hardly thoroughgoing, and popular beliefs and practices such as devotions to the saints, pilgrimages, vigils at holy wells, and the use of rosaries continued. Indeed, the idea that the Welsh people were spiritually backward and in need of reform persisted in both Protestant and Catholic confessional rhetoric. However, according to Glanmor Williams, by 1603 'at least among the educated and literate minority' the Reformation was 'ensured', and 'bearing fruit'.[37]

The local gentry in particular played a part in the religious leanings of local communities, especially their own households and tenants. Their complex loyalties and implementation (or lack thereof) of reforms helped to shape local responses to Protestant reforms. By the 1580s, the Elizabethan settlement had been publicly embraced by most of the gentry of the highest rank, but many families in Wales remained Catholic, including the Somersets of Raglan, earls of Worcester, and the Herberts of Powys Castle. The Wynns of Gwydir and the Stradlings of St Donats offered literary patronage to Catholic writers whilst publicly embracing the settlement. The numbers of missionary priests actively ministering to Catholics and encouraging conversion in Wales peaked during the Elizabethan period.

Religious dissent in early modern Wales was not limited to Catholics. Although Puritanism did not gain a real foothold in Wales until the middle of the seventeenth century, an early exponent was the outstanding Puritan martyr John Penry (1559–93).[38] The Puritans were ultimately more successful in those counties, towns, and ports which were on trade routes to England. These areas boasted more substantial numbers of English speakers, had a goodly distribution of English-language books, higher literacy rates, an emphasis on the reading of the Bible and authority of the Word, and more frequent sermons – providing fertile ground for the growth of Puritanism. Archbishop Laud sought in the 1630s to discourage the growth of Puritanism in England and Wales and promote religious uniformity.[39] Despite this, the first Nonconformist church in Wales, the Llanfaches congregation, was established in 1639 as a 'church within a church', whose members still retained ties with the established church.[40]

It was not until the 1640s that calls for religious reforms grew louder, and the godly Reformation in Wales gained further support in terms of both funds and personnel. Some notable Welsh Puritans who emerged in the 1630s and 1640s included the gifted preacher Walter Cradock (d. 1659), William Erbury (d. 1654), Vavasor Powell (d. 1670), and the talented Morgan Llwyd (d. 1659).[41] Puritanism in Wales was not one unified entity from the 1640s onwards but a myriad of radical sects which held differing ideas and doctrines, including the Welsh Congregationalists, Presbyterians, Fifth Monarchists, and Baptists, the Congregationalists being the most numerically visible of these. Herefordshire-born John Miles established the first Baptist church in Wales at Ilston (Gower) in 1649, and more churches followed in the border counties and parts of south Wales. The Quakers likewise emerged in Wales during the Interregnum as an influential radical sect, especially in border areas. Roman Catholics and Quakers experienced the worst excesses of intolerance, and large numbers of Quakers departed for America in the 1680s in order to escape religious persecution and worship freely in Pennsylvania, William Penn's New Jerusalem.[42] With the Toleration Act of 1689, the end of the seventeenth century ultimately saw the weakening of the Anglican Church in Wales as dissent experienced 'a modest and encouraging growth' in the decades before the Methodist Revival, particularly amongst urban communities in south Wales and the border counties.[43]

Though religion and religious practice were sites of contention, they were undoubtedly the most important domain for the ultimate survival of the Welsh language in early modern Wales. By the 1540s, genuine efforts had begun by humanists and early reforming Protestants to confront problems of language and literacy in a largely monoglot, Welsh-speaking society. Multilingualism in Welsh, Latin, and increasingly English for administrative purposes was reasonably common amongst the small minority of late medieval clergy and the laity who were literate, but as little as 10 per cent and as much as 20 per cent of the general population may have been literate at this time, including a minority literate only in Welsh.[44] Literacy in the English tongue was on the rise, especially in towns, and it was increasingly to become the language of administration. The hope for Protestant reformers was that the Welsh, 'a poore people not obstinate to hear, nor dull to understand ... but for want of knowledge now a long time seduced', would be transformed by the pure light of the gospel.[45]

In the 1560s, Elizabeth supported the translation of the scriptures into both Welsh and Irish in order to aid in the development of Protestantism in those areas where English was not the prevailing language. In Wales, the 1563 Act of Parliament for 'the translating of the Bible and Divine Service into the Welsh tongue' (5 Eliz. I, c.28) owed much to the steadfast campaigning of William

Salesbury (1520–84) and members of the House of Commons.[46] This Act marked the elevation of Welsh to official status as a language of worship in parishes where Welsh was spoken. While the original intent was to have both the Bible and Book of Common Prayer prepared by St David's Day (1 March) 1567, the Welsh translation of the Book of Common Prayer (*Lliver gweddi gyffredin*) by William Salesbury appeared in May 1567 and the New Testament (*Testament Newydd ein Arglwydd Jesu Christ*), translated mainly by Salesbury together with Richard Davies, bishop of St David's, appeared in October of that year. It was William Morgan (1545–1604) who completed the translation of the entire Bible in 1588, a remarkable and erudite accomplishment; its expense and size, however, meant that it was best suited for parish churches rather than private homes. In 1620, the bishop of St Asaph, Richard Parry, and Dr John Davies of Mallwyd translated the Authorized Version of the Bible into Welsh, while the 'familiar friend', the more affordable five-shilling *Y Beibl Bach* ('the little bible') of 1630, was designed for family and private use in terms of size and price.[47]

The transition in Wales to a print culture was a gradual and tortuous one. Between 1546 and 1660, a total of slightly more than a hundred known Welsh books had been printed, mainly in London but also in continental cities such as Milan and Paris. For the illiterate and the semi-literate in Wales, the oral transmission of religious ideas and concepts in understandable Welsh to a largely monoglot Welsh-speaking population remained central to Protestant and Catholic efforts. Free-metre poetry (*canu rhydd*) – especially the *cwndidau* of south-east Wales and the *halsingod* of south-west Wales – was therefore an especially important medium for religious education and reforms. The works of Protestant poets like the metrical psalms of Edmwnd Prys (d. 1621) and the collection of Welsh poetry, *Cannwyll y Cymry* ('The Welshman's Candle'), of the Old Vicar (Rhys Pritchard, d. 1644) Llandovery, circulated in written form, achieving great popularity based on their ability to communicate key religious teachings in simple and memorable ways.[48] For the Catholics, the oral transmission and recitation of poetry and prose played an important role in ministry, education, and conversion. For example, the *carolau* (carols) of the martyred schoolmaster Richard White (d. 1584) or original works like those of the missionary priest Robert Gwyn (*fl. c.* 1568–1600) were intended to be read or recited aloud in recusant circles and households; the language is colloquial and the content simple and intelligible to all. Yet while the long-term impact of print and the role of the Welsh-language Bible and other key texts is evident, it was far from immediate. Rather, while print was significant, 'oral transmission was still of the utmost significance'.[49] The 1670s and final decades of the seventeenth century are, however, notable for the burgeoning numbers of Welsh-language books published concerned with religion; the seventy years following the Restoration saw the publication of approximately 545 Welsh books, printed mainly in London and Shrewsbury.[50] Indeed, it was only during the period 1660–1730 that Wales 'moved from an oral culture to a print culture' as a result of the 'first intensive campaign to disseminate the cardinal doctrines of the Protestant Reformation by means of printed books in Welsh'.[51]

Religion, Identity, and the Past

The period *c.* 1450–1700 witnessed the definition and redefinition of Welsh identity along cultural, constitutional, historical, and confessional lines. In the later Middle Ages, a strong sense of the mythical past and origins of the Welsh and their language as descendants of the ancient Britons is evident in contemporary poetry, prose, and discourse. The myth of Trojan origins and the British inheritance owed much to the *Historia Regum Brittaniae* (*c.* 1138) of Geoffrey of Monmouth and his description of the period from the arrival of Brutus and the Trojans in Britain to the death of Cadwaladr in 682, though its roots were older still. The sins of the British, loss of the kingship of Britain, and the enduring hope for a return to their ancient sovereignty in the figure of the *mab darogan* were all combined in the Welsh historical consciousness and had 'specific political ends'.[52] Indeed, the articulation of present dynastic loyalties was also linked by the Welsh to the myth of Trojan origins and British inheritance. In Maurice Kyffin's *The Blessedness of Brytaine* (1587), Elizabeth was praised as a 'Blessed Branch of Brutus Royall Race' and Welsh poets were urged to praise this lineage: 'Pencerddiaid [chief poets], play an Auncient Harp, and Crowde: Atceiniad [reciter], sing her prayses pearcing lowd.'[53] The Stuarts were commended by writers like John Davies of Hereford (d. 1618) for their noble lineage and descent from Brutus and Arthur. The accession of James I, a descendant of Owen Tudor, was seen as the fulfilment of a prophecy by Merlin which seemed to position James as the first king of British descent since the death of Brutus who would restore the British line and kingdom.[54] However, after 1603, with the union of the crowns, a shifting political landscape and priorities meant that the idea of a distinct Welsh national identity and exclusive claim to British history and the British tongue did not hold their former sway. Indeed, after the events of the 1640s, the previous connection of the royal dynasty with Welsh identity and history was largely severed.

The development of a unique national identity and consciousness, based on a shared past, is apparent amongst the Welsh humanists of the sixteenth century, underpinned by the conventional vision of a glorious past stretching back to ancient Troy. The so-called myths of Samothes, Brutus, Joseph of Arimathea, and Ysgolan, based on the works of the pseudo-Berosus, Geoffrey of Monmouth, and William of Malmesbury, were central to this vision. The first three of these myths provided a providential, indeed 'extraordinarily exalted lineage' to the history of the Welsh language, stretching back to Hebrew, Greek, and Latin antiquity.[55] This Welsh past was also distinguished by high learning – books written in the Welsh tongue – including (according to Protestant humanists) a copy of the Scriptures. The fourth myth, that of Ysgolan, destroyer of the treasures of learning, gave a rationale for why none of these splendid books survived.[56] Welsh humanists, regardless of their religious beliefs, sought to defend the part played by Brutus in their exalted history from attacks like those of Polydore Vergil and William Camden, and showed staunch dedication and loyalty to their native language and history, seeking to preserve and strengthen it. These efforts included the translation of key religious texts into Welsh (for example, by Sir John Prise, William Salesbury, and William Morgan), the compilation of dictionaries and grammars (Thomas Wiliems, John Davies, and Gruffydd Robert), the collection of antiquities, genealogies, and heraldry, and the writing and publication of histories of Wales, its counties, and families (Sir John Prise, David Powel, Humphrey Llwyd, Rice Merrick).

Religion, the past, and national identity were intertwined for the Welsh. If, during the reign of Mary Tudor (1553–1558), Protestantism was merely *ffydd Saeson* (the faith of the English), some hundred years later it was presented in very different terms, as *ffordd yr hen Gymry* (the way of the old Welsh).[57] Indeed, it has been argued that peaceful Welsh responses to the Elizabethan Reformation were partly due to the success of Protestant humanists in 'naturalizing the reform movement in the native tradition'.[58] For early Welsh Protestant humanists like William Salesbury, their staunch support of the Welsh tongue and nation went hand in hand with belief in God, loyalty to the king, and support of a unified realm. In his 1547 book *Oll Synnwyr Pen Kembero Ygyd* ('The Sum of a Welshman's Wisdom'), Salesbury urged his fellow Welshmen to wish for the gospel in the Welsh tongue, as it had existed centuries ago at the time of their 'ancestors, the Old Britons'. He also invoked the authority of ancient poets, including Merddin Embris (Merlin Ambrosius), Taliesin, and Merlin Wyllt.[59] The British past and key figures like Taliesin were also invoked in support of the Catholic cause by contemporary poets; religious and ethnic tensions came to the fore in a 'Welsh libel' in verse by Edward Dafydd circulated in 1601, for example. Composed to provoke rebellion against the Protestant English, it called upon the Welsh to rise up against the Saxons, who were accused of killing Christ.[60]

Finally, Welsh poetry, prose, and other evidence suggest that there was a successful diffusion of ideas, in oral and written forms, among the Welsh populace concerning their glorious, shared British past and the workings of prophecy. For example, the popular belief in a prophecy by Merlin concerning the Welsh and how they would rule the realm of Britain again was a matter of contention in a 1551 inquiry into the devoutly Protestant bishop of St David's, Robert Farrar (d. 1555). Farrar was accused by a number of lay witnesses of referring to forbidden prophecies during a sermon, and of stirring up enmity and 'hatred' between the Welsh and the English. In his sermon, Farrar said: 'Welshmen are more gentle [than the English]. And no marvayle, for sumtyme ye were britannes, and had this Realme yn governaunce. And yf the prophesye of Merlyn be true, ye shall have it agayne.'[61]

The sense of Welsh identity which emerged after 1450 was based largely on *iaith* ('language', but also 'nation'), law, custom, and on a shared sense of the storied past of Wales. In this context, the accession of the Tudor dynasty to the throne in 1485 was seen by many in Wales as the fulfilment of ancient prophecy. This experience of a separate Welsh identity did not cease with the union of England and Wales in 1536, even though the Act had profound repercussions for the constitutional and cultural development of Wales, which lost its centuries-old structure of Marcher lordships and Principality and found itself re-imagined as the west wing of England. Communities were no longer distinguished by native or Marcher laws and customs (the old Welshries and Englishries), and some areas with large numbers of Welsh speakers (such as Oswestry) were geographically redefined as being in England. Peter Roberts has argued that a paradox is apparent with respect to the Act of Union and the Welsh national consciousness: it 'emerged from the imperial programme of the Tudors strengthened rather than undermined'.[62] Nevertheless, the complex longer-term repercussions of the Act of Union, Tudor policy, and religious reform were to have a profound effect on the literary articulation of a distinct Welsh identity and the construction of the past in the seventeenth century and beyond.

Notes

1. Glanmor Williams, *Renewal and Reformation: Wales, c. 1415–1642* (Oxford: Oxford University Press, 1987), 31. On the formation and customs of the March, see R. R. Davies, *Lordship and Society in the March of Wales, 1282–1400* (Oxford: Clarendon Press, 1978).

2. On Wales and the Wars of the Roses, see H. T. Evans, *Wales and the Wars of the Roses*, 2nd edn (Stroud: Sutton, 1998).

3. On Henry Tudor and Wales, see Ralph A. Griffiths and Roger S. Thomas, *The Making of the Tudor Dynasty* (Gloucester: Alan Sutton, 1985); Glanmor Williams, *Harri Tudur a Chymru / Henry Tudor and Wales* (Cardiff: University of Wales Press, 1985); S. B. Chrimes, *Henry VII*, 2nd edn (New Haven: Yale University Press, 1999).

4. The Council in the Marches of Wales was first established by Edward IV in the 1470s to manage his significant landholdings in the March, and the Council was continued by Henry VII. Rowland Lee was stridently anti-Welsh and 'an extreme punisher of offenders'. See J. Gwynfor Jones, ed., *Wales and the Tudor State: Government, Religious Change and the Social Order 1534–1603* (Cardiff: University of Wales Press, 1989), 176–8.

5. On the Act of Union, see *Statutes of Wales*, ed. Ivor Bowen (London and Leipsic: T. Fisher Unwin, 1908); J. G. Edwards, *The Principality of Wales, 1267–1967: A Study in Constitutional History* (Caernarfon: Caernarvonshire Historical Society, 1969); Peter R. Roberts, 'The "Act of Union" in Welsh History', *THSC* (1972–3), 49–72; Williams, *Renewal and Reformation*.

6. Peter R. Roberts, 'Tudor Legislation and the Political Status of "The British Tongue"', in Geraint H. Jenkins, ed., *The Welsh Language Before the Industrial Revolution* (Cardiff: University of Wales Press, 1997), 126.

7. *Statutes*, ed. Bowen, 75–93.

8. Ibid., 101.

9. The Council held civil and criminal jurisdiction and judicial and administrative powers over the neighbouring English border shires and Wales.

10. The borough towns of Wales were able to maintain their privileges, rights, and customs specified by charter, with some qualifications, provided they used English law. *Statutes*, ed. Bowen, 102–4, 122–3.

11. Edwards, *The Principality of Wales*, 35–9.

12. W. S. K. Thomas, *Tudor Wales* (Llandysul: Gomer Press, 1983), 58.

13. Williams, *Renewal and Reformation*, 274–5.

14. Roberts, 'Tudor Legislation', 123.

15. Ibid., 123–4.

16. Peter R. Roberts, 'Tudor Wales, National Identity, and the British Inheritance', in *British Consciousness and Identity: The Making of Britain,*

1533–1707, ed. Brendan Bradshaw and Peter R. Roberts (Cambridge: Cambridge University Press, 1998), 13.

17. Llinos B. Smith, 'The Welsh Language Before 1536', in *The Welsh Language Before the Industrial Revolution*, ed. Jenkins, 27–35.

18. Richard Suggett and Eryn White, 'Language, Literacy, and Aspects of Identity in Early Modern Wales', in *The Spoken Word: Oral Culture in Britain, 1500–1850*, ed. Adam Fox and Daniel Woolf (Manchester: Manchester University Press, 2002), 53, 63.

19. Geraint H. Jenkins, Richard Suggett, and Eryn White, 'The Welsh Language in Early Modern Wales', in *The Welsh Language Before the Industrial Revolution*, ed. Jenkins, 79.

20. *Calendar of Wynn of Gwydir Papers, 1515–1690*, ed. John Ballinger (Aberystwyth: National Library of Wales, 1926), no. 430.

21. *Calendar of the Clenennau Letters and Papers in the Brogyntyn Collection*, National Library of Wales Journal Supplement series IV, Pt 1, ed. T. Jones Pierce (Aberystwyth: National Library of Wales, 1947), no. 444.

22. The Welsh population, for example, grew from an estimated 278,000 in 1536 to an estimated 405,000 in 1630. Meanwhile, the increased demand for food and rise in land values contributed to inflation; the price of grain increased threefold between 1540 and 1639. Williams, *Renewal and Reformation*, 381–2.

23. NLW, Great Sessions Records, Wales 4/1/2/36. See also Richard Suggett, 'Vagabonds and Minstrels in Sixteenth-Century Wales', in *The Spoken Word*, ed. Fox and Woolf, 138–72.

24. BL, Lansdowne MS. 11, fol. 10; TNA, SP15/127/258, fol. 61v; R. Geraint Gruffydd, 'Awdl Wrthryfelgar gan Edward Dafydd', *Llên Cymru* 5 (1959): 155–63; 8 (1964): 65–91.

25. Bangor University Archives, BMSS/119. See also M. Siddons, *The Development of Welsh Heraldry*, 4 vols. (Aberystwyth: National Library of Wales, 1991–2007).

26. *Gwaith Siôn Tudur*, ed. Enid Roberts, 2 vols. (Caerddydd: Gwasg Prifysgol Cymru, 1981), I, poem 151, ll. 606–9.

27. Thomas Parry, *A History of Welsh Literature*, trans. H. I. Bell (Oxford: Clarendon Press, 1955), 207.

28. John Stradling, *The Storie of the Lower Borowes of Merthyrmawr*, ed. Henry J. Randall and William Rees, South Wales and Monmouthshire Record Society Publications 1 (Cardiff: William Lewis, 1932), 70–1.

29. Daniel Huws, *Cynnull y Farddoniaeth* (Aberystwyth: Canolfan Uwchefrydiau Cymreig a Cheltaidd, 2004), 11.

30. Ibid., 35–6.

31. Suggett and White, 'Language, Literacy, and Aspects of Identity', 57.

32. NLW MS Peniarth 178, ii, 56–72; Huws, *Cynnull y Farddoniaeth*, 11.

33. Jenkins *et al.*, 'The Welsh Language in Early Modern Wales', 79.

34. Ibid., 80.
35. Glanmor Williams, *Wales and the Reformation* (Cardiff: University of Wales Press, 1997), chapter 2.
36. Katharine K. Olson, '"Slow and Cold in the True Service of God": Popular Beliefs and Practices, Conformity, and Reformation', in *Christianities in the Early Modern Celtic World*, ed. Robert Armstrong and Tadhg Ó hAnnracháin (London: Palgrave, 2014), 92–107.
37. Williams, *Wales and the Reformation*, 396.
38. Lloyd Bowen, *The Politics of the Principality: Wales, c. 1603–1642* (Cardiff: University of Wales Press, 2007), 212. See also J. Gwynfor Jones, *Crefydd, Cenedlgarwch a'r Wladwriaeth: John Penry (1563–1593) a Phiwritaniaeth Gynnar* (Caerdydd: Gwasg Prifysgol Cymru, 2014).
39. T. Richards, *The Puritan Movement in Wales, 1639 to 1653* (London: National Eisteddfod Association, 1920), 25–7; Bowen, *Politics of the Principality*, chapter 5.
40. Geraint H. Jenkins, *The Foundations of Modern Wales: Wales 1642–1780* (Oxford: Oxford University Press, 1992), 44; R. Geraint Gruffydd, *'In That Gentle Country': The Beginnings of Puritan Nonconformity in Wales* (Bridgend: Evangelical Library of Wales, 1976).
41. Geraint H. Jenkins, *Protestant Dissenters in Wales, 1639–1689* (Cardiff: University of Wales Press, 1992), 10–13.
42. Richard Allen, *Quaker Communities in Early Modern Wales: From Resistance to Respectability* (Cardiff: University of Wales Press, 2007).
43. Jenkins, *Foundations of Modern Wales*, 197.
44. Glanmor Williams, 'The Early Stuart Church', in *The Welsh Church from Reformation to Disestablishment, 1603–1920*, ed. G. Williams *et al.* (Cardiff: University of Wales Press, 2007), 15; W. P. Griffith, *Learning, Law, and Religion: Higher Education and Welsh Society, c. 1540–1640* (Cardiff: University of Wales Press, 1989), 109.
45. 7 October 1567. D. Matthew, 'Some Elizabethan Documents', *BBCS* 6 (1931–3), 78.
46. Roberts, 'Tudor Legislation', 141, 143; *Statutes of the Realm*, ed. Alexander Luders et al., 11 vols. (London: Dawsons of Pall Mall, 1810–1828), IV, Pt i, 2457; *Statutes of Wales*, ed. Bowen, 149–51. See also Chapter 12 in this volume.
47. Garfield Hughes, ed., *Rhagymadroddion 1547–1659* (Caerdydd: Gwasg Prifysgol Cymru, 1976), 122–5.
48. T. H. Parry-Williams, *Canu Rhydd Cynnar* (Caerdydd: Gwasg Prifysgol Cymru, 1932); 'Hopcyn' (Lemuel J. Hopkin James) and 'Cadrawd' (T. C. Evans), *Hen Gwndidau, Carolau, a Chywyddau, Being Sermons in Song in the Gwentian Dialect* (Bangor: Jarvis & Foster, 1910).
49. Jenkins *et al.*, 'The Welsh Language in Early Modern Wales', 93.

50. Jenkins, *Foundations of Modern Wales*, 85, 202–3; Eiluned Rees, *The Welsh Book Trade Before 1820* (Aberystwyth: National Library of Wales, 1988), vi. Provincial printing spread rapidly following the collapse of the Crown Privilege in the 1690s. The first legal printing in Wales is not recorded until 1718.

51. Jenkins, *Foundations of Modern Wales*, 204.

52. J. Beverley Smith, *Yr Ymwybod â Hanes yng Nghymru yn yr Oesoedd Canol / The Sense of History in Medieval Wales* (Aberystwyth: Coleg Prifysgol Cymru / University College of Wales, 1991), 2–3; see also Brynley F. Roberts, 'Geoffrey of Monmouth and the Welsh Historical Tradition', *Nottingham Medieval Studies* 20 (1976): 29–40.

53. Kyffin's poem was composed in the aftermath of the Babington Plot against Queen Elizabeth which involved two Welshmen. See Maurice Kyffin, *The Blessedness of Brytaine, or a Celebration of the Queenes Holyday, 1587* (facsimile, London: Honourable Society of Cymmrodorion, 1885), sig. B, B4. Thomas Churchyard's *The Worthines of Wales* (London: G. Robinson for Thomas Cadman, 1587) offered another statement of steadfast loyalty in the same year.

54. For statements of this kind by men such as George Owen and Sir William Maurice of Clenennau, both squires and antiquarians, see George Owen, *The Description of Penbrokeshire*, ed. H. Owen, 4 vols. (London, 1902–1936), I, 263; *Clenennau Letters and Papers*, ed. Pierce, 134–5. See also John Davies, *Microcosmos: The Discovery of the Little World, with the Government Thereof* (Oxford: Joseph Barnes, 1603); Roberts, 'Tudor Wales', 39–41.

55. R. Geraint Gruffydd, 'The Renaissance and Welsh Literature', in *The Celts and the Renaissance: Tradition and Innovation*, ed. Glanmor Williams and Robert Owen Jones (Cardiff: University of Wales Press, 1990), 19–20. See also J. E. Caerwyn Williams, *Geiriadurwyr y Gymraeg yng Nghyfnod y Dadeni* (Caerdydd: Gwasg Prifysgol Cymru, 1983).

56. Ceri Davies, *Latin Writers of the Renaissance* (Cardiff: University of Wales Press, 1981); Ceri Davies, ed., *Rhagymadroddion a Chyflwyniadau Lladin, 1551–1640* (Cardiff: University of Wales Press, 1980; R. Brinley Jones, *The Old British Tongue: The Vernacular in Wales, 1540–1640* (Cardiff: University of Wales Press, 1970).

57. Jenkins, *Foundations of Modern Wales*, 174; see also *Hen Gerddi Gwleidyddol, 1588–1660* (Cardiff: Cymdeithas Llên Cymru, 1901).

58. Roberts, 'Tudor Wales', 20.

59. William Salesbury, *Oll Synnwyr Pen Kembero Ygyd* [1547], in *Rhagymadroddion*, ed. Hughes, 9–16.

60. It was the Jews who were usually accused of killing Christ in pre-modern popular traditions; see for example TNA, SP15/127/258, fol. 61v; Gruffydd, 'Awdl Wrthryfelgar gan Edward Dafydd', 155–63; 8 (1964), 65–9.
61. British Library, Harleian MS 420, fols. 90a, 93a.
62. Roberts, 'Tudor Wales', 8.

9

Welsh Humanism After 1536

ANGHARAD PRICE

Circumstances had not been propitious for the advent of humanism in post-1536 Wales. Europe's major vernaculars had come to rival Latin and Greek as vehicles of learning and culture,[1] and to the sensitized few, if Welsh was to assume its rightful place alongside other modern languages, it urgently needed to respond to the challenges posed by print technology, by advancements in scholarship and by tumultuous changes in religion and politics. But there was a distinct sense of foreboding as the very foundations of Welsh literature seemed to be crumbling. The social order that had sustained it throughout the Middle Ages was slowly changing: Henry VIII's split with Rome had created religious and social unease in a country where papal authority had remained unquestioned for centuries, whilst Thomas Cromwell's dissolution of the monasteries brought actual material disarray, including the dissipation of Welsh manuscripts containing a rich and varied body of medieval literature. (There were forty-six monasteries in Wales during the 1530s, and all had been decimated a decade later.)[2] The professional bardic order, guardian of traditional poetics and learning, had been in gradual decline since the late fifteenth century,[3] and by the middle of the sixteenth its insistence on oral transmission seemed strangely at odds with the advancement of print culture. (An extended and fascinating poetic debate took place between poets William Cynwal and Edmwnd Prys with the more traditional Cynwal resisting the flattening tendencies of print, whilst Oxford-educated Prys advocated its democratic values.)[4] Despite innovations in strict-metre poetry by poets such as William Midleton, Tomos Prys and Edmwnd Prys himself (who adapted the *awdl-gywydd* form for his metrical versions of the Psalms), many literary forms that had served Welsh society throughout the medieval period seemed outdated. And whilst strict-metre verse was still being commissioned well into the seventeenth and even the eighteenth century, the professional poets could no longer depend entirely on the patronage of the Welsh gentry as it slowly embraced the literary forms favoured at the Tudor court, including its preference for free-metre verse and colloquial registers.[5]

Most importantly of all, the illustrious literary Welsh language seemed to be under threat. Even if the daily lives of most ordinary – monoglot – Welshmen had been untouched by the Acts of Union of 1536 and 1542–3, their gradual impact on Welsh society would be far-reaching,[6] as the status and prestige of Welsh in public life came to be undermined by the decree that 'none should hold public office in Wales unless he spoke English'.[7] London became the centre of gravity, and because the Welsh ruling classes were encouraged 'to take an active role in the process of anglicization',[8] the traditional professional poets found it increasingly difficult to make a living solely from their craft. As the English Reformation advanced under Edward VI, anglicization extended even to the Sabbath, with Archbishop Cranmer's 1549 Act of Parliament ordering the replacement of the Latin liturgy by readings from the English Book of Common Prayer. For the first time, the English language was regularly heard at church services throughout Wales. Though no active attempts were made to prevent the use of Welsh on a day-to-day basis, 'officially its status was lowered to that of a dialect',[9] and English came to dominate legal, political, administrative, and even religious life in Wales.

It seemed only a matter of time before Welsh literature and learning succumbed to the same transmutation, for the Welsh language had no civic institutions to ensure its viability in the modern world: there was no Welsh university to project the glories of the past into a literate future, there was no centre of print culture to act as focal point for its standardization, and neither princely court, civic theatre nor urban literary establishment promoted its enrichment and eloquent use. In short, at a time when other vernaculars were playing a crucial role in advancing the cause of Europe's emerging nations, no structure existed in the Wales of 1536 that would create and maintain the intellectual and cultural life of a vital modern language.

This unpromising state of affairs was overturned by a small number of individuals who not only ensured the viability of Welsh literature in the challenging years after 1536 but brought it into fruitful contact with the learning and culture of European humanism. By the time of Henry VIII's death in 1547, a handful of Welshmen, trained in the *studia humanitatis* at Oxford and Cambridge, belonging to both sides of the religious divide and sharing a profound concern for the welfare of their native tongue (as well as for the souls of their compatriots), had opened a new and illustrious chapter in the history of Welsh letters.

The main, and perhaps most adventurous, protagonist in this remarkable episode was William Salesbury (c. 1507 – c. 1586). Described as 'the ear and mouthpiece of the Renaissance and Reformation in Wales',[10] his vision of Wales's needs, and the steps he took to meet them, are credited by one leading historian of the period as being 'the primary reason why Wales retained an individual literature and culture of her own after the sixteenth century'.[11] Salesbury was a scholar of widespread interests and immense energy, and from the beginning dedicated his life to bringing humanist learning and the Protestant faith to the people of Wales, and to making the Welsh language 'the peer of those modern languages which had already undergone that transforming process'.[12]

It is generally assumed, despite scant concrete evidence, that Salesbury first came into contact with humanist ideas at Oxford (he is said to have studied, possibly law, at Broadgates Hall).[13] It was at Oxford that he advanced his knowledge of both classical and modern languages, and where he familiarized himself with the printing press (which had been in use in the city since the late fifteenth century). And it was there, almost certainly, that he converted from Catholicism to Protestantism, though the actual circumstances of his conversion remain nebulous. After Oxford, during the late 1520s, Salesbury spent time in London, not only commencing legal studies at Thavies Inn – another important centre of humanist activity – but also working at John Waley's press in Foster Lane, and Nicholas Hyll's in St John's Street. Here, Salesbury initiated his life's work in creating and nurturing the relationship between the printing press and his beloved Welsh language, spurred on by the belief that 'it was urgently necessary to give vernaculars the respect and cultivation that they needed in order to advance the cause of Protestantism'.[14]

It is no coincidence that Salesbury's first books were a dictionary and a collection of proverbs, both typical products of vernacular humanism. Published in early 1547, they share with John Prise's *Yny lhyvyr hwnn* of 1546–7 the honour of being the first three books printed in Welsh. This alone represented some achievement. Licences to print books were not granted to Welsh publishers until the early eighteenth century, and in the meantime, the work of London's English printers had to be keenly overseen. The books then had to be transported back to Wales and distributed amongst the literate few. Even then, on account of the scattered rural population and the difficulty of transportation and communication, they would be slow to make an impact.

In view of this, Salesbury's vision and achievement are truly remarkable, his individual published output representing a substantial portion of all Welsh books to appear in the sixteenth century. In the five years between 1547 and 1552, for example, he published four books in Welsh and three in English.[15] A closer look at these, the very earliest products of Welsh publishing, yields fascinating insights into the concerns and aspirations of the first Welsh humanists during the tumultuous years following 1536. Indeed, Salesbury himself embodies their remarkable deftness in advancing the cause of the Welsh vernacular whilst at the same time complying with the political realities of post-1536 Wales.

The pioneering dictionary of 1547 is a case in point. Despite being called *A Dictionary in Englyshe and Welsh*, it is in fact a Welsh–English lexicon, containing a list of Welsh words with their English equivalents and including a guide on how to pronounce English (a source of valuable information about early modern English phonetics). Its professed aim was to teach English to the Welsh, but its deeper motivation is more complex. The dictionary had been approved for publication in 1544 by Henry VIII, the privilege of printing it signed in late 1546.[16] The dictionary itself is preceded by a dedicatory letter to the king whose obsequious tone has provoked the ire of some modern commentators, in particular its claim that the dictionary represented a valuable tool in ensuring the spread of English throughout the Tudor realm. As a recently converted Protestant, however, Salesbury's deference to the head of the new church was to be expected, and in ensuring the king's support for a work published in a language other than the official language of the realm, he was also exercising all necessary caution.

Indeed, the apparent compliance with Henry's desired 'communion of one tonge' is deceptive. As a product of a polyglot Tudor humanism for whom languages were not mutually exclusive, Salesbury's approach was subtler. In the first place, as he stressed in his Welsh preface, there were many advantages, both scholarly and spiritual, to be gained from acquiring the powerful English language which was 'adorned with all manner of good learning'. (The word *dysc* ('learning') appears – in some form or other – countless times in the preface.) Moreover, to realize what had been achieved in English might become a motivation to attempt the same in Welsh, as demonstrated so brilliantly by Salesbury himself who went on to publish a series of pioneering Welsh books, both original and translations, revealing a more progressive approach to the Welsh language than his dedicatory letter would have us believe.

The remainder of the preface is spent – rather tellingly – on instructing the Welsh reader as to how to use a dictionary. Principles of equivalence are explained, as is the rule of alphabetical order (including a warning against the 'deceptiveness' of Welsh mutations in this respect), and Salesbury concludes with a warning to his fellow Welshmen that English pronunciation was not always phonetic. Indeed, his advice to his readers was to go to England and ask for guidance, casually revealing the fluidity of movement in 1547 between the two countries that made up the Union. The list of words within the dictionary itself is also illustrative, showing a willingness to embrace contemporary dialect forms and borrowings from English, and containing fascinating references to mid-sixteenth-century culture (e.g. 'doublet', 'satin of Bruges', 'witchcraft', 'historiographer', and 'Latinist'). Also making use of vocabulary lists kept in the manuscripts of Welsh bards, this rudimentary dictionary prepared the way for the more sophisticated work of later lexicographers such as Henry Salesbury, author of 'Geirva Tavod Cymraec', and Thomas Wiliems, author of the Latin–Welsh 'Thesaurus Linguae Latinae et Cambrobrytannicae', both of which were substantial works of humanist scholarship, though they remained unpublished. Their manuscripts were in fact placed in the care of John Davies, Rector of Mallwyd, who incorporated them into his own monumental two-part Welsh–Latin *Dictionarium Duplex* of 1632, deemed to be the crowning glory of Welsh lexicography in the early modern period. There is, however, a certain urgency to William Salesbury's early, if ramshackle, dictionary which is lacking in the later works: whilst Wiliems's and Davies's aim was to make the study of Welsh vocabulary a matter of European scholarly interest (hence their choice of Latin as a medium), Salesbury's target audience was the literate public: his work was aimed at satisfying the immediate linguistic, spiritual, and educational needs of his fellow Welshmen.[17]

If the preface to Salesbury's dictionary is characteristic of early Welsh humanism, his preface to the second of his 1547 publications, a collection of proverbs, is yet more so. Entitled *Oll Synnwyr Pen Kembero Ygyd* ('The Sum of a Welshman's Wisdom', literally 'all the sense of a Welshman's head'), the collection includes some 900 Welsh proverbs[18] taken from a manuscript written in the hand of the distinguished sixteenth-century poet (and friend of Salesbury) Gruffudd Hiraethog, whose own work was based on late medieval collections. The Salesbury–Hiraethog partnership is highly emblematic: on the one hand we have the professional poet's custodianship of the Welsh language and its traditional poetic forms, and on the other, the humanist's desire to bring it into a fruitful dialogue with other scholarly and literary traditions – both vernacular and classical – by means of the printing press, as well as to make it available to the Welsh people at large.

In his preface Salesbury both acknowledges his debt to Gruffudd Hiraethog (declaring that he himself had merely 'lifted the lid' on the poet's work) and establishes a relationship with fellow humanists such as John Heywood, Polydore Vergil and 'Erasmus Roterodamus' who had themselves published similar collections (Erasmus being singled out for particular praise).[19] Proverbs were seen not only as eloquent expressions of ancient wisdom, but also, in Salesbury's words, as containing 'the soul of the language'. In a passage of copious Ciceronian rhetoric which embodies his own ideals of Renaissance eloquence, he thanks Hiraethog for his work in preparing the groundwork for the present collection, and develops the architectural analogy further by likening proverbs to structural elements in the construction of a house.[20] Other Welsh poets, however, are chastised for keeping their learning hidden in manuscripts,[21] and Salesbury stresses again the need to bring the nation's treasures to light by means of the printing press. Most urgently of all, he advocates the enrichment of the contemporary vernacular – the language of selling, eating, and drinking – by bringing it into contact with the new learning. In an oft-quoted statement, Salesbury's humanist invective reaches its peak as he warns his fellow Welshmen of the perils of failing to cultivate their own vernacular:

> If you do not wish to become worse than animals (who were not born to understand like humans), insist on learning in your language: and if you do not wish to be more unnatural than any other nation under the sun, love your language and those who love it.[22]

A final ringing call pervades Salesbury's extraordinary foreword to *Oll Synnwyr Pen Kembero Ygyd*, namely his command to his fellow countrymen, for the sake of their own souls, to make a barefooted pilgrimage to the king himself and demand to have the Scriptures in their own language.[23] Salesbury was aware that vernacular translations of the Scriptures had already been published throughout Europe, crowned by Luther's German translation of the Bible in 1534, and he fully realized 'that to make Protestantism work it needed to be presented in the tongue of the people of Wales'.[24]

He soon initiated that process himself by translating into Welsh extracts from the Epistles and Gospels contained in the English Book of Common Prayer (1549) and publishing them in a volume entitled *Kynniver Llith a Ban*, in 1551. Welsh translations of the Paternoster, the Creed, and the ten commandments had already been published in 1546–7 under the title *Yny lhyvyr hwnn*, attributed to Sir John Prise (1502–55), a high-ranking Tudor civil servant who had safeguarded important Welsh manuscripts following the dissolution of the monasteries (which he himself had administered). Salesbury's translations were, however, more substantial and scholarly and represent the first Welsh scriptural translations to be made directly from Greek and Hebrew in consultation not only with other humanist translations but also with earlier Welsh adaptations.[25]

In his extensive Latin preface to *Kynniver Llith a Ban*, in which he asks the Welsh bishops to authorize the use of his translation, Salesbury outlines his humanist *ad fontes* methodology. But the translation itself is also notable for the gracefulness of its expression and Salesbury's mastery over the Welsh language, in particular his extensive vocabulary and his fine ear for rhythm and euphony; the marginal glosses reflect his efforts accurately to convey the original wording in Hebrew and Greek (as well as to ensure comprehension across Wales by including dialect variants). His scholarliness had its drawbacks, however, and Salesbury's 'dignifying' Latinization of Welsh, in terms of lexicon and syntax, impedes the text's readability: the spelling of common Welsh words is defamiliarized in an attempt to demonstrate their Latin etymology (e.g. *eccleis* for *eglwys*), or when the Latin plural suffix *-ae* is used instead of the usual *-au*. In the interest of enrichment, Salesbury varies the translation of Greek words by alternately using Welsh words of Celtic and Latin origin, and even varies the spelling of single Welsh words (e.g. *Deo; Dew; Dyw*). He delights in neologizing and also makes use of archaic Middle Welsh spelling, words and syntax, though this might be due, in part, to his use of older (pre-Reformation) translations, some of which he would have known by heart. Another linguistic quirk resulting from his attempt to assert the dignity of the Welsh language was the omission of the nasal mutation (e.g. 'vy-popul', as opposed to 'vy mhobl'), which he seems to have regarded as lacking in grace.

These peculiarities, inconsistent and often incongruent with contemporary Welsh, may have been responsible for the fact that *Kynniver Llith a Ban* seems not to have been extensively used in Welsh church services following its publication in 1551, though a more likely explanation is the death of the Protestant Edward VI and the coronation of the Catholic Queen Mary two years later. During Mary's five-year reign, Salesbury kept a low profile, presumably in his native area of Llansannan,[26] but following Elizabeth I's succession he re-emerged, along with his friend and fellow Protestant humanist Bishop Richard Davies of St Asaph,[27] to undertake further scriptural translation into Welsh. Under Davies's considerable influence (and aided by other highly placed Welshmen at the queen's court), Elizabeth's government was persuaded to pass the law of 1563 which not only directed the urgent translation of the Bible and the Book of Common Prayer into Welsh but made it compulsory reading in areas where Welsh was widely spoken. In terms of the use of the Welsh language in the public domain, this act was perhaps as beneficial as the 1536 Act of Union had been detrimental.

Salesbury embarked on the work at Davies's palace at Abergwili, the translation of the Prayer Book emending and extending the work already accomplished in *Kynniver Llith a Ban*, whilst Richard Davies himself translated parts of the New Testament. Thomas Huet, Precentor of St David's, translated the book of Revelation, whilst Salesbury undertook to translate the rest, now in consultation with Beza's recently published Latin translation as well as the English Great Bible. High standards of post-Reformation scholarship were maintained throughout, and word-for-word fidelity to the original was amplified by marginal notes and parenthetical synonyms and insertions. At best, both Davies's and Salesbury's attempts produced an elegant and memorable translation (creating a literary idiom that inflects Welsh prose writing well into the twentieth century), though Salesbury's linguistic quirks still marred the text's readability, provoking irritation amongst contemporaries such as Maurice Kyffin (1555–98) who complained that 'a true Welshman's ear' could not bear to listen to it.[28]

Both the *Lliver Gweddi Gyffredin* and the *Testament Newydd* appeared within six months of each other from Henry Denham's press in 1567. A lengthy preface to the New Testament, entitled 'Epistle at y Cembru', was used by Davies, the ardent Protestant humanist, to advance the theory that Protestantism represented the true and original religion of the Welsh, brought to the Britons at the dawn of Christianity by Joseph of Arimathea (a theory later summarized in Archbishop Parker's *De Antiquitate Britannicae Ecclesiae etc.* of 1572).[29] This early form of Protestantism, writes Davies, had been corrupted by Augustine's 'English' form of Roman Catholicism, its early manuscripts – including the Scriptures in Welsh – destroyed through wars and neglect. Davies's argument was reinforced by Salesbury himself in his dedication to Queen Elizabeth, in which he portrays this New Testament as the reincarnation of the 'ancient scriptures' of the true faith of Wales, thus inverting the widely held view of Protestantism as an English newcomer.

Sadly, the Davies–Salesbury partnership did not survive the translating of the Bible in its entirety (it broke down due to a disagreement about one word, according to Sir John Wynn of Gwydir). The only remaining works known to have been produced by Salesbury, the energetic and impetuous humanist polymath, were a herbary, never published, and a treatise on rhetoric published posthumously. In the meantime, the urgent task of translating the whole Bible was placed in the capable hands of William Morgan, himself a learned humanist who had been instructed in Hebrew at Cambridge by the renowned Protestant scholar Antoine Meillet. Morgan – later made bishop of St Asaph – edited the versions of his predecessors and completed the translation of the entire Bible by *c.* 1587, spending the next year in London overseeing its passage through the printing press. It was finally published in late 1588 and is prefaced by Morgan's expression of gratitude to both Elizabeth I and John Whitgift for their support. This Welsh Bible, Morgan assured the queen and the archbishop of Canterbury, was a necessary means of securing religious uniformity, for 'unless religion is taught in the vulgar tongue, not knowing its sweetness and value, no one will undergo any trouble for the sake of acquiring it'. Its effect, as it turned out, extended far beyond the religious sphere, for Morgan's 1588 Bible is the one publication now credited with having ensured the very survival of the Welsh language – and its literature – into modernity.

Certainly, William Morgan's translation owes a huge debt to Salesbury's momentous and remarkable groundwork. But his own learning should not be underestimated, nor his creative and imaginative approach to translation, as well as his sheer literary flair. In fact, he succeeded in creating a scholarly translation that nevertheless exploited the riches of his native bardic tradition and also made use of the suppleness of contemporary colloquial Welsh (though inevitably, perhaps, tending towards north Welsh patterns). He consulted the newest scholarship in scriptural translation, including Beza's 1582 Greek New Testament and Latin translation, and translated the Old Testament directly from Hebrew (in consultation with the Geneva Bible of 1560 and the Bishops' Bible of 1568).

Even at the time of its publication, the 1588 Bible was greeted with unanimous praise, celebrated by contemporary poets such as Siôn Tudur and Siôn Mawddwy, and commended by fellow Protestant humanists such as Huw Lewys who, in his preface to his own translation of Miles Coverdale's *A Most Spyrytuall and Most Precious Pearle*, extolled Morgan for not only bringing 'this treasure, the true and pure word of God to light', but also for 'restoring to a dissipated, almost annihilated language its due respect and dignity'.[30]

Further revision to Morgan's Bible was carried out by two great scholars in the early seventeenth century, Richard Parry and the aforementioned John Davies of Mallwyd, whose 1620 edition became the basis for the 1630 'Beibl

Bach'. This brought Salesbury and Morgan's words to the common Welsh people and provided them with a rich and supple literary language that more than adequately responded to the demands of theology and literature for the next three centuries. Later scholars may have criticized Morgan's conservative adherence to literary as opposed to spoken forms, objecting in particular to his use of 'abnormal' subject-verb sentence structure (denigrated as translatese), as opposed to the more 'natural' verb-initial order.[31] But all in all, the 1588 Bible was an outstanding humanist accomplishment, its linguistic effects far-reaching and its influence on the literature of subsequent centuries – both sacred and secular – immeasurable.

The exceptional status of the Bible, and the natural authority assumed by the state-sanctioned publications of Salesbury, Morgan, and their fellow Protestants should not, however, obscure the achievements of the Catholic humanists of Wales who faced almost insurmountable difficulties in publishing their own brand of humanist literature in Welsh. Several of them had taken leading roles in the Marian Reform movement of 1553–8 but had fled to the continent soon after Elizabeth's accession to the throne and the subsequent passing of the Acts of Uniformity. During their lifelong exile, these Oxbridge-educated scholars, like their Protestant counterparts, succeeded in bringing their own form of humanism, inflected by their experiences on the continent and by post-Tridentine doctrine, to bear on sixteenth-century Welsh letters.[32] Their literary activities and aspirations reveal quite clearly that reinvigorating the Welsh vernacular was of central importance to scholars on both sides of the religious divide, and that both Catholic and Protestant humanists shared a passionate desire to make the Welsh language a vehicle for learning, as well as for spiritual salvation.

Indeed, the most important text produced by the Welsh exiles in Italy reveals that shared inheritance in striking fashion. This is the momentous, innovative, and beautifully written grammar of Welsh composed by Gruffydd Robert (c. 1527–98) and published at Vicenzo Girardone's press in Milan from 1567 onwards. Research newly conducted by M. Paul Bryant-Quinn at the Biblioteca Ambrosiana in Milan, in which fresh information about Gruffydd Robert's life and work have emerged, confirms that he was a native of Caernarvonshire, had studied at Oxford, and had enjoyed a successful ecclesiastical career during Queen Mary's reign, before fleeing to the continent soon after Elizabeth's succession. In 1561 he matriculated at Louvain, before advancing to Rome a year later where he joined the community of Welsh and English exiles at the English Hospice (later called the 'English College'). By 1565, his abilities had brought him to the attention of

Archbishop Carlo Borromeo who appointed him Canon of Milan Cathedral. Borromeo was a leading Tridentine reformer and an avid promoter of Renaissance learning and the arts, and Gruffydd Robert's Welsh grammar bears all the hallmarks of the humanist environment within the archbishop's household. Reminiscent of Castiglione's *Il Cortegiano* (1528), it takes the Platonic form of a dialogue and is set, in Raphaelesque style, against the backdrop of the dappled shade of an Italian vineyard. Here, the two interlocutors, 'Gr' and 'Mo', start longing for things Welsh, thinking of what one might achieve 'for the benefit of Wales to pass the time in pleasure and joy, whilst sheltering from the midsummer haze'.[33]

The grammar's opening dedication to William Herbert, Earl of Pembroke, had already introduced the question of language. It is imaginatively written as a monologue spoken by the Welsh language, personified as a wandering scholar who laments his neglect at the hands of the Welsh people. Distinctly echoing the sentiments of Protestant humanists such as William Salesbury, the Welsh language demands the respect given to other European vernaculars:

> Seeing myself disregarded and neglected for many long years by all in the land of the Welsh, and without any fruitful writings [in me] that would serve to educate my people in learning and skill, I saw well to travel the countries of Europe and to discover if other languages were as unheeded and as unbeneficial to their speakers as I was.[34]

Having travelled through Spain, France, Flanders, and Germany, and throughout Italy as far as Calabria, and enquiring in each place about the state, privileges, and fate of their respective vernaculars, the neglected Welsh language comes to the conclusion that it 'could not see nor hear of any language that was not greatly appreciated by its natural speakers'.[35] It was time for the Welsh to follow the example of their European counterparts.

This concern sets the scene for the grammar proper, and in the opening dialogue 'Gr' and 'Mo' immediately turn their attention to the Welsh language, and to the pressing need to cultivate it. They set about analysing, classifying, and developing aspects of Welsh syntax, vocabulary, orthography, pronunciation, and even metrics, intelligently adapting the grammars written by Renaissance scholars such as Pietro Bembo to an analysis of modern Welsh.[36] Though manifesting a historical understanding of language, Robert's emphasis throughout is on the living vernacular – another feature which he shares with William Salesbury. He takes a liberal approach to language, discussing colloquialisms, dialect variations, and borrowings from other languages, and introducing neologisms (some still in use in present-day Wales), in a fresh and invigorating way, his immense humanist achievement all the more remarkable in that it was secured without the benefits of consultation with fellow scholars, or a large body of native speakers, or indeed any manuscript sources.

The very survival of Robert's work is miraculous, and there is little doubt that its impact was limited by its author's religious affiliation, by the book's being produced a thousand miles from Wales, and by the lack of a Welsh university – or indeed any cultural or educational establishment – that might have capitalized on its scholarship. Gruffydd Robert died in obscurity in Milan on the eve of the seventeenth century. But his work had made a deep impression on a small but significant number of Welsh humanists, gaining the praise of Catholics and Protestants in equal measure. Maurice Kyffin, the zealous Protestant translator of Jewel's *Apologiae pro Ecclesiae Anglicanae*, commended the Milanese Welsh grammar for being 'so pure, so brilliant, and so wonderful in expression that one could not wish for greater perfection' (this in a foreword to an anti-Catholic tract).[37] And it is similarly telling that the only copy now kept at the National Library of Wales originally belonged to John Dee, Queen Elizabeth I's Welsh astronomer.

As a grammar, Robert's achievement represents the apogee of Welsh vernacular humanism after 1536, its humanist conception reflected not only in its subject matter but also in its written style: Robert's elegant, idiomatic, and supple prose is a joy to read, impressively combining classical rhetorical features with spoken patterns and introducing a modern, vigorous prose idiom over twenty years before the appearance of Morgan's 1588 Bible. (It also contains the only example of a Welsh humanist translation of a classical text, namely Cicero's *De Senectute*.)

Other Welsh grammars appeared over the following decades, a striking example being that written by the gifted polyglot, Siôn Dafydd Rhys of Anglesey, who had himself spent most of the 1560s in Italy (where he also authored two grammars of Greek and Latin, as well as a guide to Italian pronunciation). His grammar of Welsh, entitled *Cambrobryttanicae Cymraecaeve linguae institutiones et rudimenta* (1592), is prefaced by a lively and censorious introduction in which he, too, bemoans the disrespect shown to the contemporary Welsh language. He extols Gruffydd Robert's grammar as an example to be followed and calls its author a 'great aristocrat of learning'.[38] Unlike his hero, however, and despite his own evident genius as a writer of copious, if earthy, idiomatic Welsh prose, Rhys composed his own grammar through the medium of Latin, his concern being less with describing and enriching the language for daily use than with bringing it to the attention of fellow scholars across Europe. In this respect, his work shows similarities to the dictionaries of Thomas Wiliems and John Davies, as well as to the latter's own grammar of Welsh (written in Latin), *Antiquae linguae Britannicae . . . rudimenta* (1621), deemed by many to be the crowning glory of Welsh humanist scholarship.[39] Again, though Davies acknowledges his debt to Gruffydd Robert, his own (more conservative) concern is with the literary language as embodied in old manuscripts, and his work lacks the immediacy of Salesbury and Gruffydd Robert's adventurous forays into the contemporary vernacular.

Gruffydd Robert's fellow Catholic exiles in Italy manifested a similar spirit of adventure (it is no coincidence that an important study of their literary activities bears the Italian title, *Avventure Linguistiche del Cinquecento.*)[40] Their distance from Wales and the Welsh language, and the physical and legal impediments they faced in attempting to produce their own form of Welsh Catholic humanism, lends their linguistic and literary enterprises a precarious ardency. No figure embodies this more plainly than that of Morys Clynnog. Like Robert himself, Clynnog was a native of north-west Wales and was educated at Christ Church, Oxford. Following Queen Mary's coronation in 1553, he became a leading member of Archbishop Pole's household in Lambeth Palace, rising to the position of bishop of Bangor in 1558. Indeed, he was on his way to Rome to receive the pope's blessing on his appointment when the strange coincidental death of Pole and Mary on the same day obliged him to remain in exile for the rest of his life (first at Louvain, and then, like his friend Gruffydd Robert, from 1562 in Rome).

By 1575 Clynnog had been elected the first rector of the English College at Rome, though he was soon made to resign his post, accused of exacerbating 'national' differences between Welsh and English students. His writings certainly reveal an impassioned mix of frustrated patriotism and fierce religious zeal, and throughout his long years of exile, Clynnog maintained a rhetorically powerful – though politically fruitless – correspondence with the papal authorities in which he urged the Vatican to make north-west Wales a centre of military intervention against the heretical Queen Elizabeth. These missives to the pope are significant in that they are characterized by both the methods and the preoccupations of post-1536 Welsh humanism. In attempting to convince the Vatican to land its naval army on the banks of the Menai Straits, Clynnog stressed time and again the discrete linguistic and religious identity of Catholic Wales (as opposed to Protestant England), always referring in a scholarly way to ancient manuscripts to substantiate his claims. These old writings, he wrote, showed quite clearly that the Welsh expected salvation from Rome, thus 'tying their minds to the Papal army'.[41] Conscious that his Protestant compatriots were successfully using the printing press to advance their own religious cause, Clynnog also attempted to create, from Italy, a body of Catholic Reformation literature in Welsh. In 1568 he had already succeeded in publishing his own Welsh adaptation of a Latin catechism by the Jesuit, Diego de Ledesma, entitled *Athrawaeth Gristnogawl*,[42] which is one of the few Counter-Reformation publications known to have reached Welsh readers,[43] and throughout the 1570s he continued to seek papal patronage for the printing of Welsh texts in Italy (with a view to smuggling them back to Wales). Indeed, he wielded the influence of fellow Welshman, Owen Lewis of Anglesey, the Vatican's *Referendarius* for all matters related to England and Wales, in requesting some 200 pieces of papal gold to pay for the printing in Italy of three Welsh translations as an 'antidote' to Protestant publications.[44] Regrettably, these translations are no longer to be found, though the recent uncovering at the Bibliothèque Mazarine in Paris of a 1612 Welsh translation by Rhosier Smyth, friend of Clynnog, suggests that further discoveries cannot be discounted.[45] Owen Lewis's later attempt to persuade the Vatican to change the name on a tomb in Rome bears similar traces of Welsh humanist thought. The tomb in question had been previously dedicated to the Saxon king, Caedwalla. Now, Lewis and his fellow Welshmen in Rome wished to see the name changed to that of the seventh-century British king, Cadwaladr. This was neither a small act of pedantry nor an attempt to gain petty advantage over the English exiles in Italy ('national' tensions were ongoing). On the contrary, the presence of Cadwaladr's remains in Rome was of crucial importance to the Welsh Catholics' religious ambitions and was also symptomatic of their humanist concern with historiography.

Geoffrey of Monmouth's twelfth-century *Historia Regum Britanniae* (translated into Middle Welsh as *Brut y Brenhinedd*) had been a highly influential pseudohistory of the kings of Britain throughout the medieval period. In the sixteenth century, against the scepticism of contemporary historians such as Polydore Vergil, author of *Anglica Historia*, Geoffrey's text re-emerged at the hands of the Welsh humanists – on both sides of the religious divide – as a key means of authenticating Welsh identity in the years following 1536. For Protestants, such as John Prise and the historian and cartographer Humphrey Llwyd,[46] as well as Salesbury, Davies, and Morgan, as mentioned earlier, Geoffrey's text pointed to the existence of ancient Welsh scriptural texts, now lost, which expressed the early Protestantism of ancient Britain. (It also served, conveniently, to validate the Tudor dynasty's claim to the British throne.) The Welsh Catholic humanists, by contrast, exploited the *Historia* in order to strengthen the long-standing historical and religious ties between Wales and Rome. A renewed claim for Cadwaladr's 'presence' in 1580s Rome reinvigorated the belief that therein lay the salvation of the Welsh, for in the *Historia* Merlin had prophesied that the ancient Britons would again rule the British Isles when Cadwaladr's bones were returned. Now that the Welsh exiles in Rome had located those sacred bones, the kingdom of Britain could be freed from the yoke of Protestant (and English) rule. The changing of the name on Caedwalla's tomb had both religious and political repercussions, and it is fascinating to see how the Welsh Catholics used historiography to undermine the political and religious status quo in post-1536 Wales, whilst the Protestants used the same approach to consolidate it.

Owen Lewis's plan, for better or for worse, was never implemented, and it is tempting, with Protestant-inflected hindsight, to view the activities of the Welsh Catholic exiles of the sixteenth century as a mere footnote in the history of Welsh humanism, or at best as humanist potential unfulfilled (nothing embodies this more poignantly, perhaps, than the drowning of Morys Clynnog in an attempt to return home to Wales during the 1580s). But to quantify their success – or not – in terms of books published or impact made is to fail to see the scope and ambition of the humanist enterprise they shared with their Protestant counterparts. As R. Geraint Gruffydd notes, the Protestant and Catholic humanists of Wales, as a group, were 'apart from religious division . . . remarkably homogenous', sharing not only a vision of Wales's glorious past but also 'the determination that the glory should be restored'.[47]

Indeed, to view the whole humanist endeavour of post-1536 Wales in quantitative terms would be misleading. True, the narrow focus on linguistic and religious matters (at the expense of more wide-ranging interests in fields such as drama, or the natural sciences) is lamentable; the emphasis on translation, as opposed to the authoring of original works, disappointing. But to compare the achievements of Welsh humanism with those of the urban societies of larger European nations would be meaningless. Welsh humanist scholars, whether Protestant or Catholic, had neither a printing press, nor a university, nor indeed any national institution to call their own, yet they succeeded in bringing their language into productive interplay with Europe's other modern vernaculars. Through the vibrancy and eloquence of their writings, they created a firm linguistic basis on which later generations of writers could capitalize. Their vision and dedication, along with the astonishing quality of works of grammar, lexicography, rhetoric, and theology, produced against all odds, had far-reaching implications. At precisely the moment when Wales's political identity was being subsumed into Tudor England, the Welsh humanists made their own vernacular a powerful means of expressing cultural sovereignty. Motivated by a knowledge of past glories, and a conviction of present-day distinctiveness, they used their beloved Welsh language to construct a 'national community of honour' that could, in its own limited but crucial way, 'confront other nations on equal terms'.[48]

Notes

1. Warren Boutcher, 'Vernacular Humanism in the Sixteenth Century', in *The Cambridge Companion to Renaissance Humanism*, ed. Jill Kraye (Cambridge University Press, 1996), 191.

2. Glanmor Williams, 'Wales and the Reformation', in *Wales Through the Ages*, ed. A. J. Roderick (Llandybïe: Christopher Davies, 1960), vol. II, 25.

3. G. J. Williams, *Agweddau ar Hanes Dysg Gymraeg*, ed. Aneirin Lewis (Caerdydd: Gwasg Prifysgol Cymru, 1985), 34.

4. See Ceri W. Lewis, 'The Decline of Professional Poetry', in *A Guide to Welsh Literature c. 1530–1700*, ed. R. Geraint Gruffydd (Cardiff: University of Wales Press, 1997), 40–3. See also Jerry Hunter, 'Cyfrinachau ar Dafod Leferydd: Ideoleg Technoleg yn yr Unfed Ganrif ar Bymtheg', in *Chwileniwm: Technoleg a Llenyddiaeth*, ed. Angharad Price (Caerdydd: Gwasg Prifysgol Cymru, 2002), 36–53.

5. See Thomas Parry, *Hanes Llenyddiaeth Gymraeg hyd 1900* (Caerdydd: Gwasg Prifysgol Cymru, 1953), 128–31.

6. W. Ogwen Williams, 'The Union of England and Wales', in *Wales Through the Ages*, ed. Roderick, Vol. II, 21 and following.

7. Ibid., 20.

8. Geraint H. Jenkins, Richard Suggett, and Eryn M. White, 'Y Gymraeg yn y Cyfnod Modern Cynnar', in *Y Gymraeg yn ei Disgleirdeb: Yr Iaith Gymraeg cyn y Chwyldro Diwydiannol*, ed. Geraint H. Jenkins (Caerdydd: Gwasg Prifysgol Cymru, 1997), 78.

9. Prys Morgan, *A Bible for Wales* (Aberystwyth: Gwasg Cambria, 1988), 21.

10. R. Brinley Jones, *William Salesbury*, Writers of Wales (Cardiff: University of Wales Press, 1994), 11.

11. Glanmor Williams, 'The Achievement of William Salesbury', *Welsh Reformation Essays* (Cardiff: University of Wales Press, 1967), 191.

12. R. Geraint Gruffydd, 'The Renaissance and Welsh Literature', in *The Celts and the Renaissance: Tradition and Innovation*, ed. Glanmor Williams and

Robert Owen Jones (Cardiff: University of Wales Press, 1990), 19. There is no doubt that Salesbury, alongside his humanist education, had an intimate knowledge of the rich bardic tradition of his native Denbighshire. Cf. G. J. Williams, 'Traddodiad Llenyddol Dyffryn Clwyd a'r Cyffiniau', *Transactions of the Denbighshire Historical Society* 1 (1952): 20–32.

13. Cf. James Pierce, *The Life and Work of William Salesbury: A Rare Scholar* (Talybont: Y Lolfa, 2016), 31–2.

14. Brinley Jones, *William Salesbury*, 8–9.

15. These are (i) a guide in English to the pronunciation of Welsh, partly designed to help anglicized Welshmen rediscover their roots; (ii) an English translation of Linacre's *De Sphaera*; and (iii) an anti-Catholic doctrinal tract entitled *The Baterie of the Popes Botereulx*.

16. Pierce, *The Life and Work of William Salesbury*, 89.

17. See Branwen Jarvis, 'Welsh Humanist Learning', in *A Guide to Welsh Literature c. 1530–1700*, ed. Gruffydd, 135–41.

18. Salesbury published a second, corrected and amplified version of this collection of proverbs in 1567 ('Crynodab or Diarebion Sathredig . . .'), though only one copy of that edition has survived.

19. See Garfield H. Hughes, ed., *Rhagymadroddion 1547–1659* (Caerdydd: Gwasg Prifysgol Cymru, 1976), 14.

20. Ibid., 13.

21. Ibid., 10.

22. Ibid., 11.

23. Ibid., 12.

24. Brinley Jones, *William Salesbury*, 38.

25. The sources used by Salesbury are listed in Isaac Thomas, *William Salesbury a'i Destament* (Caerdydd: Gwasg Prifysgol Cymru, 1967).

26. Pierce, *The Life and Work of William Salesbury*, 187.

27. Glanmor Williams, 'Bishop Richard Davies (?1501–1581)', *Wales and the Reformation* (Cardiff: University of Wales Press, 1997), 155–90.

28. Maurice Kyffin, *Deffyniad Ffydd Eglwys Loegr* (1595). Quoted in Hughes, ed., *Rhagymadroddion*, 92.

29. See Saunders Lewis, 'Damcaniaeth Eglwysig Brotestannaidd', in *Meistri a'u Crefft*, ed. Gwynn ap Gwilym (Caerdydd: Gwasg Prifysgol Cymru, 1981), 116–39.

30. Huw Lewys, *Perl Mewn Adfyd* (1595). Quoted in Hughes, ed., *Rhagymadroddion*, 100.

31. Oliver Currie, 'Reappraising the Role of Sixteenth-Century Bible Translations in the Development of Welsh Literary Prose Style', *Translation Studies. Special Issue: Translation in Wales* 9, 2 (2016): 152–67.

32. See Angharad Price, *Gwrthddiwygwyr Cymreig yr Eidal* (Caernarfon: Gwasg Pantycelyn, 2005).

33. Gruffydd Robert, *Gramadeg Cymraeg*, ed. G. J. Williams (Caerdydd: Gwasg Prifysgol Cymru, 1939), 1–2.

34. Ibid., opening dedication.

35. Ibid.

36. Cf. T. Gwynfor Griffith, 'Italian Humanism and Welsh Prose', *Yorkshire Celtic Studies* 6 (1953–8): 1–26.

37. Kyffin, *Deffynniad Ffydd Eglwys Loegr*. Quoted in Hughes, ed., *Rhagymadroddion*, 92.

38. Siôn Dafydd Rhys, *Cambrobryttanicae Cymraecaeve linguae institutiones et rudimenta* (1592).

39. John Davies, *Antiquae Linguae Britannicae . . . Rudimenta* (1621).

40. T. Gwynfor Griffith, *Avventure Linguistiche del Cinquecento* (Florence: Le Monnier, 1961).

41. See T. J. Hopkins and Geraint Bowen, 'Memorandwm Morys Clynnog at y Pab Gregori XIII yn 1575', *Cylchgrawn Llyfrgell Genedlaethol Cymru* 19, 1 (1965): 1–34.

42. See M. Paul Bryant-Quinn, 'To Preserve our Language: Gruffydd Robert and Morys Clynnog', *Journal of Welsh Religious History* 8 (2000): 17–34.

43. There is some evidence that a Catholic printing press was secretly set up in a cave on the Great Orme, near Llandudno. Cf. R. Geraint Gruffydd, *Argraffwyr Cyntaf Cymru: Gwasgau Dirgel y Catholigion adeg Elisabeth* (Caerdydd: Gwasg Prifysgol Cymru, 1972).

44. See R. Geraint Gruffydd, 'Dau Lythyr gan Owen Lewis', *Llên Cymru* 2 (1952–3): 36–45.

45. See also Geraint Evans, 'A Lost Seventeenth-Century Welsh Book Rediscovered in Paris', *THSC* 15 (2009): 28–40; and Geraint Evans, 'The Authorship of *Drych Cydwybod* [?1616]', *THSC* 17 (2011): 1–13.

46. John Prise's *Historiae Brytannicae Defensio*, published posthumously in 1573, was composed in defiance of Polydore Vergil's *Anglica Historia*. See the edition and translation by Ceri Davies, *Historiae Britannicae Defensio, A Defence of the British History* (Oxford: Bodleian Library, 2015). A more sustained challenge to Vergil was posed by Humphrey Llwyd's *Cronica Walliae* (1559) and his *Commentarioli Britannicae Descriptionis Fragmentum* (1568), which served as a basis for David Powel's *The Historie of Cambria* of 1584, the first printed history of Wales. A more cautious approach to Geoffrey's *Historia* may be found in the chronicle written by the Tudor soldier, Elis Gruffydd, *Cronicl o Wech Oesoedd* (1552).

47. Gruffydd, 'The Renaissance and Welsh Literature', 19.

48. Caspar Hirschi, *The Origins of Nationalism: An Alternative History from Ancient Rome to Early Modern Germany* (Cambridge University Press, 2012), 14.

10

Drama and Performance in Medieval and Early Modern Wales

DAVID N. KLAUSNER

The survival of documentary evidence for performance traditions in early Wales is irregular at best; Welsh archives were never kept with the care that was lavished on materials held by English administrative bodies, and in many ways we are fortunate that anything survives at all. The records of the Welsh Court of Great Sessions, which frequently recorded performers in the context of their brushes with the legal system, provide a good example. When the Court was abolished in 1836, the records were entrusted to the care of those who had charge of them at the time (usually a town clerk). However, no funding was provided for their storage, so they were for the most part kept in wholly unsuitable spaces, afflicted by damp, rodents, insects, and general neglect. In some jurisdictions they were simply discarded or sold to make paper or to line collars.[1] With these strictures in mind, it would be unwise to treat the following commentary as exhaustive or terminal; though suggestive, absence of evidence cannot be taken as evidence of absence.

Biblical Plays

The earliest records of non-liturgical drama in the British Isles date from the second half of the fourteenth century. A few fragments of what appear to be play-texts are of earlier date, and Chaucer's note that the randy clerk Absolon in 'The Miller's Tale' 'pleyeth herodes upon a scaffold hye' implies an audience familiar with biblical plays on the slaughter of the innocents, as well as with fixed scaffold staging.[2] There are no records in Wales of either civic biblical drama, such as was staged regularly in York, Chester, or Coventry, or of parish plays, for which there is ample documentary evidence in England. There is, however, evidence of a dramatized Crucifixion that antedates virtually all of the English material.

In 1320, the newly appointed bishop of Hereford, Adam Orleton, made a thorough visitation of the ecclesiastical houses under his jurisdiction. This included the small Benedictine priory of St Mary, Abergavenny, Monmouthshire, and Orleton recorded the results of his visitation in his register, in the form of a letter to the priory. He found that the priory had not been subject to episcopal visitation in the previous forty years, and that strict observance of the Benedictine Rule had seriously fallen off; that despite its income being sufficient to support thirteen monks, the priory housed at most five or six; that no prior had been properly appointed by election, but that one of the monks, Fulk Gastard, had taken on the position of prior dative, and had himself been guilty of alienation of goods and 'many vices of incontinent living'.[3]

The monks were found to be neglecting the rule of silence, to be eating meat on fast days, to be neglecting the night offices, and to be playing forbidden games with dice and knuckle-bones. Most heinous, however, was their participation in some form of mimetic entertainment:

> & quosdam ipsorum spectaculum / suorum corporum
> facientes & aliquociens quod non sine cordis amaritudine
> referimus nudi extensis brachiis cum baculis & ligatis ad
> modum crucifixi stramine vel alio aliquo ad modum corone /
> capitibus eorum superposito de ipsorum dormitorio
> nocturno tempore descedentes & sic incedentes. ac
> ludentes coram sociis suis / & aliis inibi morantibus
> & alia enormia facientes que ad presens / propter
> ipsorum enormitatem nimiam subticemus /

> (and some of them make a spectacle of their bodies and
> sometimes – which we did not learn without bitterness of
> heart – they come down naked from their dormitory at
> night, with arms stretched out with rods and tied in the
> manner of someone crucified, with straw or something
> else in the manner of a crown put upon their heads, and
> walk in that way and play before their fellows and others
> staying there and do other outrageous things, about which
> we are silent because of their excessive outrageousness.)[4]

Although Orleton does not explicitly name it as such, it seems very likely that what the bishop is describing is a Crucifixion pageant of some kind; he does not call it by such terms, but it is extremely unlikely that he would have had the vocabulary to do so.

First, it is useful to note that the description of the event, though hardly a model of clarity from our point of view, contains a level of detail unusual in a visitation letter. It seems clear that the brothers were miming the Crucifixion ('extensis brachiis cum baculis & ligatis ad modum crucifixi'), using such props as a crown of thorns ('stramine vel alio aliquo ad modum corone'), and playing ('ludentes') before an audience from both within and without the priory ('coram sociis suis / & aliis inibi morantibus'). What other details can be gleaned from this brief description? Orleton's description, disingenuous though it may be, does give us some hints as to the nature of the event. The pageant, if it was such, may well have been staged without words, since the description concentrates on the action and gives no suggestion of any textual impropriety nor, for that matter, of any text at all. We are also given some information on the physical aspects of the event. The rods (presumably wooden) which formed the cross-pieces of the improvised cross (or crosses) to which the participant's (or participants') arms were tied and the straw (or 'alio aliquo', that is, some similar material) from which the crown of thorns was fashioned both suggest the use of familiar local materials as properties. The brothers' nakedness may well have horrified Orleton, but his implication that it was both sexual and irreverent is unsupported in the evidence he provides. It seems possible that what is being described is costuming, that is a form of dress such as a loincloth appropriate both to the mimetic action and to distinguish the participants from the spectators. Although this is less clear, it seems unlikely that the event was presented as a part of the liturgy, since Orleton makes no comment about the profaning of the divine office. Most important, the fact that the event takes place before the participants' fellows and others staying there identifies it as a performance, with a clear distinction made between participants and audience.

Orleton's visitation was made on 25 September, hardly an appropriate time of year for a Crucifixion pageant, so it seems very likely that Orleton did not actually see the events he describes. The verb he uses is 'referimus' – 'we learned' of the pageant or, perhaps more accurately, 'we were told'. The bishop's evidence is very unlikely to have involved the direct experience of the performed Crucifixion, and it is virtually certain that he based his letter on third-party reports.

The Abergavenny Crucifixion pageant, striking though it may be, is followed by a substantial gap in the evidence for drama in early Wales. The earliest play-texts in the Welsh language are a nativity play and a passion play at least a century and a half later. A considerable degree of popularity is suggested by their survival in at least a dozen manuscripts. These manuscripts date from the mid-sixteenth century at the earliest, though the differences between the manuscripts suggest that a considerable period of time has passed since the plays' composition and first writing down, an event which I would date sometime in the second half of the fifteenth century. The plays as they have come down to us demonstrate several of the characteristics we would normally associate with a text intended for dramatic performance: there are speech headings throughout identifying speakers, and several characters – especially the Messenger who links the sections of the plays together – speak to the audience in ways familiar from English plays, telling them at the beginning to shut up and listen, and occasionally interpreting events on stage. Both plays are structurally unlike the biblical plays of Chester and York, in that they are presented as continuous rather than as discrete episodes. In this they are closer to the plays of the Cornish *Ordinalia*, although the Cornish plays are much more extensive and are driven by elaborate stage directions.

There is also one thing we expect to find in a play that is missing. The nativity play provides an example. Herod takes leave of his Queen, travels to Bethlehem, and surveys the slaughter of the innocents all in the space of eight lines:

EROD

Vy mrenhines ayr i ffen
mi af oddyma i veddlem
i ddala meibon giwdi
trigwchi yngharisalem
A wneythochir gorchymyn
a roes i atochi bob vn
moyswch imi gar ymron
y meibon rwy ni mofyn

Y KENADWR

May nhwy yma gar ych bron
ysawl ysy yn sygno i bron
o vewn i oedran dwyflwydd
yn ych gwydd yn ddimryson

(HEROD

My golden-haired queen,
I shall go from here to Bethlehem,
to catch the children of Judea,
remain thou in Jerusalem.
Have you done the command
which I gave each one of you?
Bring here before me
the children that I seek.

THE MESSENGER

They are here before you
Those that suck the breast,
within two years of age
before you, without question.)[5]

The actual slaughter of the innocents appears to have taken place between the lines of the play. The York Cycle, for example, takes a whole play to present the action that here is glossed over. This is consistent throughout the two Welsh plays: in the passion play, it is not even clear exactly where the Crucifixion takes place. This lack of concern with the action of the play suggests a mode of performance that has essentially eliminated action, that is, a *tableau vivant*, a sequence of largely static stage pictures involving text, but little or no action.

Morality Plays and Dialogues

The genre of morality play, in which a representative human figure, styled as Everyman, Mankind, or Humanum Genus, is tested in an allegorical battle for his soul between the forces of good and evil, was popular in England in the later fifteenth and early sixteenth centuries, but the only surviving Welsh morality play, *Y Gwr Kadarn* ('The Strong Man'), is very different from the English plays.[6] It begins in the mode of the English *Castle of Perseverance*, with the eponymous Strong Man presenting himself as the servant of Master Mundus, the World, who is the source of his wealth and power. In a debate with a Priest, the Strong Man learns of the fickleness of Mundus, that his generosity may end and the Strong Man's wealth and power may be taken away. Learning that he will shortly die, the Strong Man repents and dies, blessed by the Priest. So far, the play is similar to *Castle*, especially in that play's debates between Humanum Genus and his Good Angel. The Welsh play, however, continues with the seduction of the Strong Man's wife by his erstwhile Servant. After their marriage, the Servant becomes tyrannical, and the Wife concludes the play repenting her foolish marriage. This combination of morality and the marital admonition of an interlude is not found in any of the English plays, and the two halves of the Welsh play do not seem entirely comfortable together.

A dialogue-debate play, *Ymddiddan yr Enaid ar Korff* ('Dialogue of the Soul and the Body') is the most fully theatrical of the surviving plays from the late Middle Ages, including not only frequent direct address to the audience but also a number of stage directions.[7] The dialogue indicated in its title widens into a verbal battle between the devil and the Archangel Michael for man's body and soul. Following this debate, an Angel appears and describes to a Strong Man (perhaps with reference to the morality play) the fate of body and soul after death. Although much of this material is part of the common

European tradition of body / soul debates, the Welsh play is the most consciously theatrical of the large body of examples.

Troelus a Chresyd

A five-act tragedy, *Troelus a Chresyd* is the sole Welsh play that seems to imply a measure of familiarity with London's professional theatre.[8] Copied between 1613 and 1622 by the well-known antiquarian John Jones of Gellylifdy, Flintshire, the single manuscript gives no indication of the play's date, and it appears to be a product of either the late sixteenth or the early seventeenth century; if the latter, it might well be a product of the vogue for plays dealing with the Troy story that produced, among others, Shakespeare's *Troilus and Cressida*. The Welsh play could not be more different from Shakespeare's. Based on Chaucer's *Troilus and Criseyde* and its continuation, Robert Henryson's *Testament of Cresseid*, the play's five acts follow the five books of Chaucer's poem, with the events of the *Testament* forming a conclusion to Act 5. The play is marked by a number of elaborate stage directions, and these include information rare in early modern play-texts. When Kressyd is brought before the Trojan council, the stage direction for Troilus reads, 'ac ar hynn mae yn syrthio mewn kariad' ('and now he falls in love').[9] One stage direction confirms the dramatic nature of the text, although John Jones simply calls it 'hanes' ('story, tale'). Immediately before Diomede's final rejection of Kressyd, the stage direction reads: 'Diomedes ar ys ystaeds, a Chressyd yn dyfod yno' ('Diomede on the stage, and Kressyd coming there').[10] Extensive descriptions of costume for the colloquy of the planets in Act 5 derive entirely from Henryson's text and seem closer to the costume directions found in court masques than those of London's professional theatres. No evidence has been found indicating that the play was ever performed in the seventeenth century, and it may have been closet drama or intended only for reading, though it was mounted in 1954 at the Ystradgynlais National Eisteddfod.[11]

Travelling Players

One form of drama found with some frequency in England, the performance in a private house by a company of travelling players, is especially rare in Wales, and a document describing such a performance emphasizes just how unusual it was. In 1654, a small company of three players performed in a house called Derwyn Fechan in the parish of Dolbenmaen, just at the foot of the Llŷn peninsula on the road from Caernarvon to Harlech. The house still stands, but nothing is known of the play that was performed. What brings the occasion to our notice is that during the performance an affray broke out among the spectators. The fight had nothing to do with the play but centred on the disputed use of a bridge over a local stream that gave access to public grazing land. The case was remitted to the Caernarvonshire Quarter Sessions, and a number of the witnesses' depositions survive. Since the witnesses were all part of the audience for the play, some descriptions of the play are included. One Moris ap William David gave the following statement:

> vpon munday the 29th day of may last past at night was
> at the dwelling house of Hu<ghe> ap William ap Evan of
> Derwynfechan where was then present the said Hughe
> ap William ap Evan & Elline his wife & all ye family: &
> three straungers two of them men & one ladde which
> three this deponent saw act an enterlu<de> the night
> aforesaid: all three beinge disguised & some tymes one
> of them in womeans apparel all three at seuerall tymes
> apperinge in seuerall changes of apparel after divers
> sorts & in ye shape of others some tymes in blacke some
> tyme<s> in redde & some tymes in all other Collours yet
> this deponent knoweth the actors were the three
> straungers whoe Continued thus acting; and diliueringe
> seuerall parts by heart for an houre or two together in
> the presen<ce> of Hugh ap William ap Evan & Elline;
> Entringe into one roome & thence departing into another
> roome as their seuerall partes required . . .[12]

It is clear what is being described here. Moris saw a play which involved several of the norms for a small travelling company: a doubling scheme in which each actor would play several parts indicated by changes of costume, a boy to play women's parts, entrances and exits. What is so striking about Moris's deposition, however, is his evident pride at having figured it all out. They may have changed their apparel, he notes, but we knew that it was the same three actors. Moris's deposition provides a strong indication of just how unusual such a performance was for rural Wales. Where had these travelling players come from? England? Doubtful – unlike the border country of the Marches, west Wales on the far slopes of Snowdonia was almost entirely Welsh-speaking with the exception of a few anglophone communities like Beaumaris. An English-language play in Derwyn Fechan would simply not have found an audience. This would be particularly true in a rural village community like Dolbenmaen, and we can deduce the nature of the community from the depositions. The play is seen as a pleasant and unusual diversion, but what really exercises the audience is the concern over grazing rights that leads to the affray. The depositions are in English, but this was a requirement of the court – one of the provisions of Henry VIII's Welsh Act of Union of 1541 was the insistence that all matters brought before the courts of Great Sessions or Quarter Sessions be in English, with the provision for translators where necessary. So Moris ap William David may well have given his evidence in Welsh, but there is no way we can know this, since had he done so it would have been brought forward to the court in English. Dolbenmaen was not an English-speaking parish, and it is very likely that the play, whatever it may have been, was in Welsh.

Evidence for English travelling companies performing in Wales is very sparse, in part because the primary source for such events lies in the household accounts of the gentry, and these are extremely rare in Wales. Two brief examples, however, are found in the accounts of Sir Thomas Aubrey of Llantrithyd, Glamorgan, just east of Cowbridge. Sir Thomas paid the King's Players a substantial 20s. early in 1622, and 5s. to an unidentified 'company of players' in the village of St Nicholas, just west of Cardiff.[13]

Interludes / *Anterliwtau*

The term 'interlude' was common in sixteenth-century England referring to dramatic performance, and it appears occasionally in Welsh sources as well before its adoption in Welsh for the 'anterliwt' tradition of the eighteenth century.[14] A group of men from Churchstoke, Montgomeryshire, appeared at the Hereford consistory court in 1589 to answer the charge of 'setting forthe of enterludes on the sabothe daye'.[15] James Whitelocke, a magistrate on the Chester circuit, noted in his journal in 1621 that he and his fellow justices had been entertained at Ruthin with 'an enterlude'.[16] A tidbit of further information on the writing of plays in Welsh is found in a letter which, unfortunately, can be neither dated nor localized, in which a schoolmaster complains to a pupil's father that, rather than translating his Latin exercises, he 'misemploy'd his time in composeing something, which they call an interlude'. Although the interlude Whitelocke saw would probably have been in English, the errant student might well have been composing in Welsh, since his schoolmaster further complains that he was wont to 'trifle away his usefull houres in welch rimeing'.[17]

A volume of the poetry of Rhys Cain (National Library of Wales, MS. Peniarth 68) contains on its next-to-last page the final quatrain of an 'interlude', identified as such in a following note, 'Ag velli y terfyna yr holl Enterlvwt gynta' ('And thus ends the whole of the first interlude'). The writer identifies himself as Thomas Aspull, clerk, and notes that he finished writing the interlude on 22 October 1582. The paper of the final two pages of the manuscript is quite different from that of the rest of the volume, so it appears that the bulk of the play was lost before the two parts were bound together.

Finally, NLW 5269 contains (ff. 531–34v) a 214-line fragment of an *anterliwt* of Argolws and Simoniax dating from the middle of the seventeenth century, thus anticipating the popular Welsh tradition of *anterliwtau* by half a century. The surviving part of the text requires four actors and might resemble the Dolbenmaen play of 1654.[18]

School Plays

Almost simultaneous with the Derwyn Fechan play, a series of plays were presented in the highly anglicized borough of Beaumaris, Anglesey, that were without question not in Welsh. Under the direction of the Rev. William Williams, the Beaumaris School mounted productions of at least two plays from printed sources, one of them, *The Rebellion of Naples, or The Tragedy of Massenello*, probably by Thomas Bayly, youngest son of Lewis Bayly, bishop of Bangor. *Massanello* was printed in 1649, and Williams produced it in 1652. He wrote a prologue for the performance that he copied into his commonplace book.[19] *Massanello* seems a dangerous choice for a school play three years after the execution of Charles I, for it is unashamedly royalist in sentiment, as the opening dumb show demonstrates:

> there appears a Vision of little Boyes: One whereof,
> King-like, in War-like state, ascends the Throne; after that,
> a Company of Beggar-boyes pull down the King, throwing
> him to the ground, snatching away his Crown, Globe and
> Scepter, who lies in a trance; the Beggar-boyes all in clusters
> get up into, and upon the Throne: The Throne breaks, it
> thunders and lightens, and they all run away. After that,
> melodious musick; the King rises up, stands dejectedly,
> whil'st a throne descends from above, with a Crown, Globe
> and Scepter in it; he assaies the Crown, and settles it upon
> his head; he takes the Globe and Scepter in his hands, and
> seats himself in the Throne: It rains first wheat, and then
> gold upon his head; he ascends up, and vanisheth.[20]

The story of the fisherman Massenello's rebellion and rise, only to be driven mad by the acquisition of power, is also an odd choice for a school play, requiring two onstage beheadings: 'He thrusts out his head, and they cut off a false head made of a bladder fill'd with bloud. Exeunt with his body.'[21]

In 1655, Williams chose a somewhat more suitable play, Thomas Randolph's pastoral comedy *The Muses' Looking Glass*, which had been printed in 1638.[22] Again, it is a curious choice for a school: the player Roscius presents the extremes of Vice and Virtue as binary pairs, opting in the end for 'golden Mediocritie', the 'mother of vertues'.[23] As with *Massenello*, Williams recorded his verse prologue in his commonplace book, hinting that he may have faced some adverse reactions to *Massenello* a few years earlier:

> And 'cause it is a very daungerous age
> Hating all sorts of plots, therefore our stage,
> To please all jealous Auditors, hath got
> A pleasant Comedie without a plot.[24]

Williams indicates in his prologue that he played Roscius himself, 'Though I a player personate this day. . . '[25]

Documentary Evidence

Our understanding of drama in early Wales can be expanded beyond these surviving play-texts and prologues by documentary evidence, consisting of administrative or legal documents in which the performance of a play is usually of secondary or background interest. So a dispute over the ownership of the bells in the priory church of Abergavenny came before the Court of Augmentations in 1537. The townspeople claimed that the bells belonged to the town, and had been paid for by the citizenry, despite their hanging in the priory church. John ap polle ap John gave evidence that

> he was one of them with one Ienky da blether Iohn bengreth Thomas coke Ienkyn ap gwillim llwelyn vynneth and William ap polle ap Ieuan that went aboute into the countrie with games and playse to gather money to pay for the foresaid belles.

Maredudd ap polle ap John, John ap polle's brother, declared that 'he neuer sawe no man pay any thynge for the same belles but only the towne and the countrie that they gate apon theym with games and plays'.[26] Research on late medieval drama in England has shown that plays, both religious and secular, formed a major part of parish fund-raising, and this seems likely to be a Welsh reference to such an undertaking.[27] The records of the Court of Augmentations do not give any information on when the bells might have been purchased, but the ages of the two brothers whose depositions form a major part of the evidence were eighty and eighty-eight respectively. It seems likely that the events they describe occurred at least forty and as much as sixty years earlier, so that the 'games and plays' they describe would likely have taken place in the late fifteenth century.

Records of the Court of Great Sessions and episcopal consistory court books refer occasionally to local performance venues or to performance events. The bulk of these references are found in the Marches, especially in the area of Maelor Saesneg in eastern Flintshire. They may constitute further evidence of English-style parish drama. A matrimonial dispute in the village of Penley, Flintshire, recorded in 1570 by the Chester consistory court took place 'after the play was done', and a witness's deposition to the Court of Great Sessions in 1591 terms the green at Burgedin, Montgomeryshire, a 'pleing place'.[28] A Tallarn Green, Flintshire, assault case in 1608 notes that the disagreement took place in 'an Arbor or play place'.[29] There is no doubt that the phrase 'playing place' is ambiguous and might refer to a variety of sporting events, but the designation of the Tallarn Green site as an 'Arbor or play place' would seem to make it unsuitable for football or other games. It should also be noted that 'playing places' used for performance are common in England, and one of these, the quarry at Shrewsbury, is no more than fifteen miles from the three towns in the Welsh records.[30]

A particularly problematic document involving the performance of a play comes from the Court of Star Chamber in 1604. The bill of complaint, entered by John Vaughan of Westminster, lists a number of charges brought against a group of men in Llanelli, Carmarthenshire. Under the leadership of Phillip Bowen and his son, David Phillip Bowen, the group is described as 'Men of contentious spirittes, lewde liues and evell conversacons', and they are accused of a series of assaults and affrays directed especially at English new-comers, and leading to the attempted murder of a customs official. The climax of their crime spree is a bit of a surprise:

> the said Phillippe Bowen being Cheiftaine and Ringleader
> vnto all the reste coulde not be satisfied onelye with Causing
> a moste profaine and scurrilous stage playe to be acted and
> played vpon or aboute the twentieth daye of Maye last within
> the perishe Churche of Llanelly aforesaid to the great dishonor
> of god the prophayninge of his Temple the breache of your

Maiesties laws and the grievous offence of manye trewe
Christian protestantes and loyall Subiectes . . .[31]

The description in the bill of complaint gives us very little useful information about the event; if it caused offence to 'many trewe Christian protestantes', then it would seem to have been a Catholic or anti-Protestant play, perhaps containing some of the material which so exercised Christopher Goodman in his criticisms of the Chester plays, or the sort of recusant polemic that initiated a Star Chamber case against Sir John Yorke in 1609.[32] More questions remain than answers, however: if the Llanelli play were sectarian, how did it come to be played in the parish church? And most simply, what was a group of thugs (as they appear to have been) doing putting on a play? Star Chamber documents are often unreliable in the stories they tell, since the Court was frequently used by the litigious to harass neighbours and enemies. Although the plaintiff in this case did have a Welsh name, his London residency may suggest that this is not merely a case of local feuding and his complaint may have been entirely legitimate.

The use of municipal buildings for stage performances was a common procedure in England, allowing civic control of both the performances and their content. Few civic records survive in Wales, however, and significant evidence is found only in the Common Attorneys' account books for Swansea. These contain regular receipts between 1617 and 1634 from 'stage players' for the re-glazing of broken windows in the town hall. Unfortunately, the accounts give no hint of what manner of performance might so regularly break the windows. Travelling professional players appear only very rarely in Welsh sources; the parlous state of Welsh roads, the relative poverty of Welsh towns, and the difficult terrain would not have made Wales an attractive prospect for touring. Swansea, on the other hand, could be reached easily by sea and traded regularly with English towns like Barnstaple and Bristol.[33] This might represent a possible route for the players who visited Swansea on such a regular basis.[34]

Robert Bulkeley of Dronwy, Anglesey, kept a daily journal through the 1630s and noted his attendance at four plays. Bulkeley had been sent off to Oxford but returned to Anglesey after his father's death to run the estate, remaining there for the rest of his life. His journal cites plays in villages like Bodedern, Llanddeusant, and Pont yr Erw, and at the non-specific 'the schoole'.[35] All these entries are a bit ambiguous ('to a play at . . .'), referring perhaps to cards or gambling. The entry for 7 September 1633, however, is unambiguous, for Bulkeley says that he 'rid to the schoole to heare a play'.[36]

Oxford-trained, Bulkeley wrote his journal in English, but the plays he heard must have been in Welsh; English-language plays in the villages of north-west Anglesey would not have attracted an audience.

Household Drama

A genre of drama entirely in English is represented by performances in the homes of the gentry and aristocracy. These performances were usually occasional in nature: wedding masques were performed for both the Salusbury household at Lleweni, Denbighshire, in 1586 and 1595, and the Myddelton family at Chirk, Denbighshire, in 1634 and 1641; the Salusbury masques included a performance for the installation of John Egerton, second earl of Bridgewater, as Lord President of the Council of the Marches.[37] Masques and plays for such occasions were often written by a member of the household: Sir Thomas Salusbury, in particular, wrote a masque for the wedding of Sir Thomas Myddelton's eldest daughter in 1641. Salusbury's manuscripts also include several uncompleted play-texts as well as a five-act drama, *Love or Money*. Unlike the occasional pieces, there is no record of any performance of this play, and it must be considered closet drama.[38]

Bardic Performance

Public or semi-public performance by Welsh-language poets is documented largely within the poetry itself, as well as in such regulatory texts as the so-called 'Statute of Gruffudd ap Cynan'.[39] The Statute has no real connection with the twelfth-century Gwynedd ruler, Gruffudd ap Cynan, but is a product of the two *eisteddfodau* held in Caerwys, Denbighshire, in 1523 and 1567, assembled for the first and revised for the second of these occasions. The document attempts on the one hand to codify the training of poets by defining with some precision what must be learned for attaining professional status at several different levels, and on the other hand to define and regulate proper conduct by poets towards their patrons.[40] While only limited conclusions can be drawn from the Statute concerning the details of bardic performance, one mode can be reconstructed rather more clearly. The Statute and its ancillary documents mention the performance of *cyff clêr* ('butt of bards') in which a senior poet is 'roasted' (mocked playfully) by a number of his students. The documentary sources note that a *cyff clêr* is most commonly held at a marriage feast, and a complete set of *cyff clêr* poems survives from the wedding of Wiliam Lloyd ap Elisau to Elizabeth verch Owen ap Siôn which took place at Rhiwedog, Merioneth, on 20 October 1555.[41] The senior poet was Gruffudd Hiraethog, and roast was conducted by his students, Lewis ap Edward, Siôn Tudur, and Simwnt Fychan. The poems are off-colour, verging on the obscene, and rely extensively on double-entendre and other forms of word play. Significantly, the poems' punning implies an understanding of both Welsh and English, so a bilingual audience must have been anticipated.

Public Revels

English towns and villages present us with a wealth of public revelry. Even many small villages appointed a summer king to lead the celebration of planting or harvest, while larger towns had a whole year of celebratory events, both secular and sacred.[42] Evidence of such performative traditions in Wales is much more limited, but it is not certain whether this indicates an absence of such traditions or the absence of documentary sources. One single document suggests that the latter might be the case. In 1585 Richard Price of Beaumaris, Anglesey, was relieved of his burgage fine of 10s. by unanimous vote of the city council in view of the fact that 'he is lord of the mery pastymes'.[43] Although this document might suggest that our ignorance of such positions in other Welsh towns is a product of document loss, it is worth bearing in mind that Beaumaris was a highly anglicized borough, and that if we were to seek English traditions in the principality, Beaumaris would be the first place to look.

The haphazard survival of documentary evidence makes it difficult to draw broad conclusions about drama and performance in early Wales. Nonetheless, some things seem reasonably clear. Welsh antiquaries like John Jones (the copyist of *Troelus a Chresyd*) were heavily involved in the collection and preservation of manuscripts from a relatively early period, certainly from the second half of the sixteenth century, so it is unlikely that we have lost a large repertoire of Welsh-language plays. The survival of at least a dozen copies of the nativity and passion plays would support such a conclusion. The Dolbenmaen interlude and the Anglesey plays that Robert Bulkeley attended speak to the existence of local performances of Welsh drama, since they took place in predominantly Welsh-speaking locales. We need to be wary of drawing conclusions from references to local 'playing places', since the bulk of these occur in towns near the English border, especially in Montgomeryshire and Flintshire, where local performances may well have been influenced by English practice. For the same reason, it is inadvisable to draw conclusions about performance in one Welsh county from the Great Sessions records of another as a way of compensating for the often considerable differences in the survival of records. So, for example, we cannot draw conclusions about Caernarvonshire, where very limited records survive, from the much more complete records of Flintshire or Denbighshire.[44]

Some isolated records may, however, indicate more extensive performance occasions for which we have no other sources. These would include the window-breaking players in the Swansea town hall, the – possibly recusant – play in Llanelli parish church, and the interlude players who performed before Sir James Whitelocke and his fellow Chester circuit justices in Ruthin. It is not possible to determine the language of these performances, though it seems likely that the Ruthin performance would have been in English. No such question arises with 'Troelus a Chresyd' or the household plays of the Salusburys and Myddeltons. These, however, were all based firmly on English models and tell us little about Welsh performance.

The evidence for drama and dramatic performance in early Wales is not extensive, but it paints a canvas broad enough to indicate its own insufficiencies. The existence of play-texts in both Welsh and English as well as documented performances in Welsh-speaking areas confirm the performance of plays in both languages. Performance records from Swansea to Anglesey to the towns of the Flintshire march describe a broad geographical spread. Documents like the witness statements at the Dolbenmaen affray suggest strongly that some forms of performance common in England, such as small companies of travelling players, were unusual in Wales, at least in west Wales. The history of the Welsh archives tells us unequivocally that much has been lost and that the performance records that do survive represent but a fraction of the whole. Largely for economic reasons, Wales was never a hotbed of dramatic performance; but neither was it a land without drama.

Notes

1. The sad story of the treatment of the records of the Court of Great Sessions is told by Glyn Parry, in *A Guide to the Records of Great Sessions in Wales* (Aberystwyth: National Library of Wales, 1995), xl–xlix.
2. See the early fourteenth-century 'Interludium de Clerico et Puella', in British Library, MS. Add. 23986; J. A. W. Bennett and G. V. Smithers, eds., *Early Middle English Verse and Prose*, 2nd edn (Oxford: Oxford University Press, 1968), 196–200. Geoffrey Chaucer, *The Riverside Chaucer*, ed. Larry Benson (Boston: Houghton Mifflin, 1987), 71, l. 3384.

3. David Klausner, ed., *Records of Early Drama: Wales* (London and Toronto: The British Library and University of Toronto Press, 2005), 378 (hereafter *RED: Wales*).

4. Klausner, *RED: Wales*, 216 (text), 378 (translation).

5. Gwenan Jones, ed., *A Study of Three Welsh Religious Plays* (Bala: The Bala Press, 1939), 148–9, ll. 227–34.

6. Sarah Campbell, '"The Strong Man" and its Contexts: An Edition, Translation and Study of a Medieval Welsh Morality Play' (PhD diss., Catholic University of America, 2004).

7. Jones, *Three Welsh Religious Plays*, 238–59.

8. *Troelus a Chresyd o Lawysgrif Peniarth 106*, ed. W. Beynon Davies (Caerdydd: Gwasg Prifysgol Cymru, 1976).

9. Ibid., 58.

10. Ibid., 127. The word *ystaeds* is clearly an English borrowing, and this is its first use in Welsh.

11. Gwyn A. Williams, '*Troelus a Chresyd*: A Welsh Tragedy', *THSC* (1957), 37.

12. Klausner, *RED: Wales*, lxxiii, 65; Gareth Haulfryn Williams, '*Anterliwt Derwyn Fechan, 1654*', *Caernarvonshire Historical Society Transactions* 44 (1983): 53–8.

13. Lloyd Bowen, ed., *Family and Society in Early Stuart Glamorgan: The Household Accounts of Sir Thomas Aubrey of Llantrithyd, c. 1565–1641* (Cardiff: South Wales Record Society, 2006), 47, 55.

14. Nicholas Davis, 'The Meaning of the Word "Interlude": A Discussion', *Medieval English Theatre* 6, 1 (1984): 5–15; Darryll Grantley, *English Dramatic Interludes, 1300–1580* (Cambridge: Cambridge University Press, 2004).

15. David N. Klausner, ed., *Records of Early English Drama: Herefordshire and Worcestershire* (Toronto: University of Toronto Press, 1990), 235–6.

16. Klausner, *RED: Wales*, 130.

17. Ibid., 271–2.

18. Gruffydd Glyn Evans, 'Yr Anterliwt Gymraeg', *Llen Cymru* 1 (1950–1): 83–96; 2 (1953): 224–31.

19. NLW MS 15, 140A; Klausner, *RED: Wales*, 43–4.

20. TB, *The Rebellion of Naples, or The Tragedy of Massanello* (London: 1649), Wing B199, 2–3.

21. Ibid., 73.

22. Thomas Randolph, *The Muses' Looking Glass* (London: 1638), STC 20694.

23. Wing 1534:09, 77–8.

24. Klausner, *RED: Wales*, 44, ll. 34–7.

25. Ibid., 45, l. 5.

26. Ibid., 218–19.

27. Alexandra F. Johnston and Wim Hüsken, eds., *English Parish Drama*, Ludus 1 (Amsterdam: Rodopi, 1996).

28. Klausner, *RED: Wales*, 197, 225.

29. Ibid., 199.
30. J. A. B. Somerset, ed., *Records of Early English Drama: Shropshire* (Toronto: University of Toronto Press, 1994), 387.
31. Klausner, *RED: Wales*, 99.
32. Elizabeth Baldwin, Lawrence M. Clopper, and David Mills, eds., *Records of Early English Drama: Cheshire Including Chester*, 2 vols. (London and Toronto: The British Library and University of Toronto Press, 2007), I, 143–8; G. W. Boddy, 'Players of Interludes in North Yorkshire in the Early Seventeenth Century', *North Yorkshire Record Office Publications* 7, 1 (1976): 95–130.
33. E. A. Lewis, *The Welsh Port Books (1550–1603)*, Cymmrodorion Record Series 12 (Cardiff: University of Wales Press, 1927), 12–13; David N. Klausner, 'English Economies and Welsh Realities: Drama in Medieval and Early Modern Wales', in *Authority and Subjugation in Writing of Medieval Wales*, ed. Ruth Kennedy and Simon Meecham-Jones (New York: Palgrave Macmillan, 2008), 213–29.
34. David N. Klausner, 'Plays and Performing in South Wales', *Early Theatre* 6, 2 (2003): 57–72.
35. Klausner, *RED: Wales*, 48–51.
36. Ibid., 50.
37. Ibid., 141–50, 153, 155–6; David N. Klausner, 'Family Entertainments among the Salusburys of Lleweni, Denbighshire, and their Circle, 1595–1641', *Welsh Music History / Hanes Cerddoriaeth Cymru* 6 (2004): 129–54. Egerton's appointment was also celebrated at Ludlow Castle with a performance of Milton's 'Comus'.
38. Klausner, *RED: Wales*, cxiv, 141–50, 153, 155–6. The masque is found in British Library, Egerton MS 2623, art. 13; Salusbury's unfinished plays and the closet drama, 'Love or Money' are in NLW MS 5390D, 59–67, 337–78, and 69–109 respectively.
39. Klausner, *RED: Wales*, 159–65, 172–6, 349–56, 360–4. See also David N. Klausner, 'The Statute of Gruffudd ap Cynan / Statud Gruffudd ap Cynan', *Welsh Music History / Hanes Cerddoriaeth Cymru* 3 (1999): 282–98.
40. David N. Klausner, '"The Statute of Gruffudd ap Cynan": A Window on Medieval Welsh Bardic Practice', in *Gablánach in Scélaigecht: Celtic Studies in Honour of Ann Dooley*, ed. Joanne Findon, Sarah Sheehan, and Westley Follett (Dublin: Four Courts Press, 2013), 265–75.
41. Klausner, *RED: Wales*, 210–14 (text), 372–6 (translation).
42. Ronald Hutton, *The Rise and Fall of Merry England: The Ritual Year, 1400–1700* (Oxford: Oxford University Press, 1994).
43. Klausner, *RED: Wales*, 42. This document is a particularly good example of the haphazard nature of the survival of such records. Only nine small fragments survive of the Beaumaris council order and minute book, and only

one of these preserves the full text of a council order (Bangor, University of Wales Library, General Collection 478B).

44. References to performance occur mostly in the court's gaol files (Great Sessions 4) which include witnesses' depositions. These files survive in bulk (though not complete) for Flintshire (1542 on) and Denbighshire (1545 on). The relevant files are listed in Parry, *Guide to the Records*, 103–10 (Flintshire) and 111–17 (Denbighshire). Only one set of gaol files for 1622 survives for Caernarvonshire, then nothing until 1718 (Parry, *Guide to the Records*, 176).

Tudor London and the Origins of Welsh Writing in English

GERAINT EVANS

Amongst the hundreds of Welsh love poems which survive from the late fifteenth century in the *cywydd* metre, there is one which is an intriguing witness to the co-existence of manuscript and print. The poem is attributed to Bedo Brwynllys (*fl.* 1469) and it is well attested, surviving in seven manuscripts dating from the early sixteenth to the early eighteenth centuries.[1] In this poem, as in many others of the genre, a male poetic persona describes the beauty of a young woman who has been seen, or perhaps secretly observed, at a fair: 'Gwelais mewn ffair ddisgleirddyn' ('I saw at a fair a beautiful young woman').[2] But in the second half of the *cywydd*, as praise gives way to hyperbole, there is an extended description of the maiden's features in terms of the latest printing at Westminster:

> Dilwch yw d'ael, du o lir,
> Dawn popi'n duo papur.
> Ni liwiodd du ar liain,
> Nid mwy o'r fath, dim mor fain.
> Copi wrth brint y capel,
> Campus bwyth cwmpas y bêl;
> Crest o'r inc, croes Duw ar wen,
> Cryn lath arwydd cron lythyren.[3]

> (Your eyebrows are dustless and black as the cloth of Liere,
> the essence of poppy, which blackens paper.
> Black never coloured linen paper
> quite so well, so finely.
> A copy after the print of the chapel,
> excellent reward, this perfect sphere;
> a crest of ink, God's cross on whiteness,
> the symbol of a round letter.)

The poem lists a series of images relating to ink, paper and printing type, and the reference to 'print y capel' seems to point to William Caxton's first premises in one of the chapels of Westminster Abbey, from where he published the first book printed in England, *Dictes or Sayengis of the Philosophers*, in November 1477.[4]

This poem might be the earliest surviving reference in Welsh to the new phenomenon of printing and to the explosion of print technology in the late fifteenth century in which, for the first time, near-identical copies of texts were being produced in quantities limited only by economic expediency and distributed to a readership which was larger than a social community. There would be no printing in Welsh until the 1540s, but the cultural awareness of the latest developments in technology and commodity consumption is as sharp in Welsh as it is in any of the countries which were affected by the printing revolution in fifteenth-century Europe.

The Origins of Welsh Writing in English

The traditional view in the mid to late twentieth century was that the Anglo-Welsh novel, as it was generally called, was a nineteenth-century phenomenon which came to fruition in the early twentieth century. The work most often cited in reference books as the first Anglo-Welsh novel is T. J. Llewelyn Pritchard's *Twm Shon Catti*, first published in 1828. But thanks to the pioneering work of Jane Aaron on the nineteenth century and Moira Dearnley on the eighteenth, we now have a much better understanding of how much fiction was produced in English which deals with Wales and Welsh life before 1900.[5] Moira Dearnley's work lists about fifty novels printed before 1800, and there are much larger numbers from the nineteenth century. In fact, literary works in English which deal with Wales and Welsh life go back at least to the sixteenth century, and it is hard to construct a theoretical framework in which they are typologically different from works written in English from or about Wales in the early twentieth century.

For poetry, the origins of Welsh writing in English seem to begin with the 'Hymn to the Virgin' by Ieuan ap Hywel Swrdwal (*c.* 1430–*c.* 1480). The poem can be dated to the early 1470s and its popularity throughout the early modern period is attested by the large number of manuscript copies which have survived. The poem is written in English in the style and metre of a Welsh *awdl*, with an attempt to reproduce the poetic effects of *cynghanedd* in English. The poem consists of thirteen stanzas and a total of ninety-six lines, and is addressed to the Virgin Mary:

O michti ladi, owr leding, tw haf
       At hefn owr abeiding:
    Yntw ddy ffest efrlasting
    I set a braents ws tw bring.

 O mighty lady, our leading, to have
       At heaven our abiding:
    To bring us to the everlasting feast
    You planted a branch [of Jesse's tree].[6]

This remarkable poem is the first known attempt to reproduce the poetic effects of *cynghanedd* in English. It was written by a Welsh poet who was studying at Oxford and whose poetry in Welsh is also attested in the manuscript record. This poem therefore represents a number of the key features of Welsh writing in English as it has come to be defined: there are textual features which are recognizably Welsh, it is written in an English which is inflected by Welsh or by English speech in Wales, the constructed audience includes both Welsh and non-Welsh speakers, and the author's literary output straddles more than one language or discursive field.

It also seems historically appropriate that this poem has survived from the decade before the Tudor period, when Welsh literary production in London, in manuscript and print, starts to become more significant. The text of this extraordinary poem became better known after the publication of the pioneering anthology *Anglo-Welsh Poetry, 1480–1980*, which was edited by Raymond Garlick and Roland Mathias. The anthology was designed to build on and illustrate the historical argument which Raymond Garlick had first explored in 1970 in his equally important *Introduction to Anglo-Welsh Literature*, which had been commissioned for the Writers of Wales.[7] This radical idea, that Welsh writing in English, as it came to be called later in the century, might have coexisted with literature in Welsh since before the Tudors, did not immediately appeal to everybody. Critics for whom Welsh writing in English was defined by the industrial literature of the south-east were wary of anything which might seem to minimize the historical significance of the 'first flowering' of early twentieth-century writing. But the argument proposed by Garlick and Matthias was impossible to ignore and very soon a new historical perspective opened up.

One aspect of the history of poetry in Wales which the work of Garlick and Mathias explored was the antiquity of the poetic conversation between the two languages which is exemplified in the tradition of writing *cynghanedd*, and particularly of writing *englynion*, in English. With the example of Ieuan ap

Hywel Swrdwal before them, critics began to notice a number of examples from later centuries. The practice is often linked to the genre of humour, although one of the first poems published by the young Robert Graves was an entirely serious *englyn* called 'The Will o' the Wisp', which appears without attribution in the 'Note on Welsh Metrics' in his father's anthology, *Welsh Poetry Old and New in English Verse* (1912). The poem begins: 'See the gleam in the gloaming–out yonder / It wand'reth bright flaming', faithfully deploying the metrical demands of the *englyn*.[8] One of the best *englyn* poems in English, and one of the most quoted, is by Waldo Williams, whose mastery of *cynghanedd* in Welsh perhaps gave him an advantage:

> Yes, Idwal, it is oddish; – it is strange;
> It is true outlandish,
> Not a fowl nor yet a fish:
> An englyn writ in English.[9]

The Welsh in Tudor London

The late survival of the manuscript tradition in Wales can be seen as a reflex of the late appearance of print. By the time the first Welsh printed books appeared in London in the late 1540s, all book production in Britain was controlled by the Crown and there would be no officially sanctioned printing in Wales until the early eighteenth century.[10] The granting of the Stationers' Charter in 1557 further concentrated printing in London, although a decree of Star Chamber in 1586 made an exception of the monopoly for Cambridge and Oxford. A few Welsh books would be printed in Oxford and a small number of recusant texts were printed in France and Italy, but the overall pattern would remain unchanged until the early eighteenth century, when the lapse of the 1662 Licensing Act in 1695 saw a sudden explosion of provincial printing in Wales and the Marcher towns and throughout England.[11] This gave a greater significance to London for Welsh people and Welsh culture than might otherwise have been the case, and it also helped to preserve the culture of manuscript production in Wales, a culture which was the dominant form for the preservation and transmission of written texts well into the sixteenth century and which was still an active part of Welsh literary life when the antiquarian scholars of the eighteenth century began to publish the *editiones principes* of medieval Welsh literature.

A large number of Welsh speakers lived in Tudor London, more, perhaps, than in any of the towns in Wales. In Welsh culture and in the Welsh textual experience of town life after 1485, London is a constant presence, and it could hardly be otherwise because London was already the metropolis of Britain, the centre of government and trade and the only major centre of printing. With a growing population in 1547 of between 55,000 and 70,000, it was perhaps the twelfth largest town in Europe, and for size and wealth it already had no British competitors. Yet by 1600 London would have a population of some 200,000.[12] In the sixteenth century the Welsh gentry found patronage at court, while others found employment in the city of London or the Inns of Court, and all were exposed to reform and to the humanist books and ideas which helped to support it.

Increasing numbers of Welsh people had been attracted to London since the coronation of Henry Tudor as Henry VII of England in 1485. A number of Welshmen are recorded as serving in the royal household, perhaps 170 in the period 1500–49, and we have a valuable account of Welsh life in London in the early sixteenth century in the work of Elis Gruffudd, whose chronicle contains a portrait of Welsh life in early Tudor London.[13] The diocese of London continued to attract Welsh clerics throughout the sixteenth century, and from the reign of Edward VI, the period which saw the beginnings of Welsh printing, Welshmen became more influential at the centre of power.[14] William Thomas (d. 1554), for example, was an informal royal tutor and clerk of the Privy Council, 1550–53, and Sir Thomas Parry (c. 1515–60) was one of the anglicized Welsh gentry who flourished in the middle decades of the century. Three days after Elizabeth's accession, Parry was made controller of the queen's household and a member of the privy council. His son, also called Sir Thomas Parry, became ambassador to France from 1602 to 1606 and a privy councillor under James I.[15]

This was a period of rapid population growth. Between 1541 and 1582, the population of London grew from fewer than 50,000 to about 112,000, and by the end of the century it would reach 200,000. Outside London, of course, town life was still far being a universal experience. In the 1540s only about 10 per cent of the population of Britain lived in towns containing 2,000 inhabitants or more, and in the later sixteenth century Carmarthen, the largest town in Wales, was the only Welsh town with a population of this size. Other significant towns in Wales were Brecon, which was somewhat smaller than Carmarthen, and Caernarfon and Denbigh which had barely a thousand inhabitants each.[16] Estimates of the Welsh population in London in the mid sixteenth century vary from around 1 to 3 per cent of the total population, although Emrys Jones, the historian of the Welsh in London, argues that one reading of the figures for 1582 suggests that the Welsh element of the population was around 6,300 individuals, which would be closer to 6 per cent of the total population. Even the more conservative of the estimates makes it clear that there would have been significant numbers of Welsh people in London in the 1540s and 1550s, when Welsh printing began. This is not to suggest that even several thousand Welsh speakers scattered throughout a large, cosmopolitan city like London could in any sense replicate the linguistic dynamics of any of the small, Welsh-speaking towns in Wales, but the figures are nevertheless significant, particularly for the development of Welsh writing in English.

It seems that the Welsh were not identified with any particular region of the city of London, and in some ways this is not surprising as the Welsh presence in London was so well established in the late Middle Ages that by the early modern period they were fully assimilated into London life. In attempts to identify the locations of the London Welsh in the sixteenth century, for example, there is little mention of the diocese of Holborn, where William Salesbury lived in the 1540s and early 1550s, first at Thavies Inn and then later at Ely Rents, the tenements fronting Holborn which were part of Ely House, the London residence of the bishop of Ely.[17] One piece of topographical evidence is interesting, however. Emrys Jones attempts to estimate the origins of the Welsh in London by county of origin, and in the middle of the sixteenth century he puts Denbighshire – Salesbury's home county – first, with neighbouring Flintshire a close second.[18]

This history of expansion and social mobility after 1485 created a sense of identity with London and of kinship with the Tudors which persisted for Welsh readers well into the eighteenth century. One of the most amusing and outspoken books of Welsh history published in that century was written by a silk mercer and minister from Hereford called Simon Thomas. *Hanes y Byd a'r Amseroedd* ('A History of the World and the Times') first appeared in 1721 and went through at least five editions before 1800. This is how it delineates the 'Welshness' of the future Henry VII of England:

> Ein Cyd wladwr *Harry*, (yr hwn nid oedd etto ddim on *Iarll*, efe meddaf) oedd o ran ei fam, yn perthyn i dylwyth brenhinol Lloegr; eithr o ochr ei Dâd, *Cymro* ydoedd. Canys ei Dâd cu *Owen ap Tudur* oedd o Hiliogaeth hên Dywysogion Cymru.[19]

> (Our compatriot Harry, (he who was as yet merely an Earl, I say) was, through his mother, related to the royal family of England; but on his father's side, he was a Welshman. Because his grandfather Owen ap Tudur was a descendant of the old Princes of Wales.)

Welsh Books and English Books in Tudor London

There was at least one attempt to print examples of Welsh speech before the publication of the first Welsh printed book *Yn y lhyvyr hwnn* ('In This Book'), which appeared in London in 1546. This is in a work by Andrew Borde called the *First Book of the Introduction of Knowledge*, a guide to the languages, customs, and countries of Europe and the Near East for English merchants and travellers, which:

> dothe teache a man to speake parte of all maner of languages, and to know the usage and fashion of all maner of countreys. And for to know the moste parte of all maner of coynes of money, the whych is currant in every region.[20]

Of the Celtic languages, there are guides to Cornish, Welsh, and Irish, following the descriptions of Cornwall, Wales, and Ireland. The book begins with England and Cornwall followed by Wales, Ireland, and Scotland and as a general guide to the English empire just a few years after the first Act of Union, Borde says that:

> [while there are many languages] in Englande the walshe tongue is [used] in wales . . . [also] The Cornyshe tonge in Cornwall, and Irish in Irlande, and French in the English pale.

The Welsh chapter contains 164 lines including 24 lines of poetry. There are Welsh words and phrases in 44 of these lines, all with English translations, making it one of the longest linguistic guides in the book. Borde makes it clear that he is describing what the language might sound like to an English speaker, so that they might learn to say some of the phrases:

> Who so wyl lerne to speake some Welshe Englyshe and Welshe foloweth. And where that I do not wryte true welshe I do write it that every man may rede it & understand it without any teachynge.

Like most of the chapters, the section on Wales begins with a comic portrait of the country in pentameter couplets.[21] This includes references to a number of popular markers of Welsh identity, real or imagined, such as patronymics, the use of harps and a fondness for prophesy. The most interesting part of the Welsh chapter, however, is the section of phrases for travellers, which contains what may be the first examples of Welsh to be printed. The orthography suggests that these phrases were collected by the author as spoken forms, which he transcribed using English conventions. There are standard greetings and some useful questions for travellers:

Is this the ryght way to the towne
Ayhon yoo yr forth yr dre (ll. 130–1)

Hostes geve me a rekening
Vey leetowraac mee imi gyfry (l. 152)

Syr can you speke any welshe
Sere auedorowgh weh gamraac (ll. 113–14)

Ye syr I can speke some welshe
Ede oh sere medorabeth dyck (ll. 115–16)

So by the 1540s Wales was already being written about in English travel
writing which recognized the Welsh language as the key indicator of
national identity, and soon after Borde's book was published in London,
Welsh writers, publishing in London or, less often, in Oxford, were drawn
into the textual experiences of a multilingual diaspora and found themselves writing in more than one language for more than one kind of
audience.

One of the most significant of these early Welsh writers in English is
Humphrey Llwyd (1527–68), the antiquary and map maker. Llwyd was born
in Denbigh and educated at Brasenose College, Oxford, becoming MA in
1551.[22] In 1553 he entered the service of Henry Fitzalan, twelfth earl of Arundel,
and despite spending periods of time back in Wales, he remained a member
of Arundel's household for the rest of his life. Llwyd was an important Welsh
antiquary and map maker, whose *Cambriae typus* was printed by Ortelius in
Antwerp and reprinted as many as fifty times between the appearance of
Theatrum orbis terrarum in 1573 and George Horn's *Accuratissima orbis antiqui
delineatio* in 1741. Two manuscripts in Welsh survive in Llwyd's hand, both
genealogical works which are indebted to Gruffudd Hiraethog, but his
contribution to Welsh writing in English could hardly be more significant.
His extraordinary manuscript history of Wales, *Cronica Walliae*, was completed *c.* 1559 and copies survive in NLW MS Llansteffan 177 and BL MS
Cotton Caligula A vi.[23] Early in the history he describes his project:

Because I have taken in hande to wrrite the lives and actes of the kinges and
princes of Walles whiche ruled that countrey from Cadwalader to Lhewelyn
sonne of Gruffith ap Lhewelyn, which was the laste of the Britishe bloodde
that had the governaunce of Wales, I thinke hit nessessarie to sette furthe the
perfecte discription of the countrey as hit was in the olde tyme and as hit is at
thees dayes and therby the readere may the more playnely and easely
understande the woorke following.   (fol. 2r)

Llwyd's description of Wales is explicitly addressing a non-Welsh or a Welsh diaspora readership. He is deliberately doing this in English and he is consciously interpreting the history of the country for an outsider subject position. Later in the chronicle, he describes himself as a pioneer in the field:

> I was the first that tocke the province in hande to put thees thinges into the Englishe tonge. For that I wolde not have the inhabitantes of this Ile ignorant of the histories and cronicles of the same, wherein I am sure to offende manye because I have oppenede ther ignorance and blindenes thereby.
>
> (fol. 24r)

Llwyd's description of himself as the pioneer of Welsh anglophone writing is probably more significant than has been acknowledged, and his construction of a non-Welsh audience is particularly interesting, though, as we shall see, William Salesbury had already done something very similar. Humphrey Llwyd's complete manuscript was unpublished at his death and the first full edition appeared as recently as 2002, but his work had an extraordinary afterlife through its incorporation into *The Historie of Cambria, Now Called Wales*, one of the foundational works of Welsh history, which was also written in English and published in London in 1584.[24] *The Historie of Cambria* contained the largest sections of Llwyd's *Cronica Walliae* to be published before Ieuan M. Williams's edition of the manuscript was published in 2002, and it was to be the most influential book of Welsh history for 300 years. Like some of William Salesbury's Welsh books from the middle years of the century, it contains an eight-page preface 'To the Reader', but the book is fronted by a dedicatory epistle to Sir Philip Sidney 'Written by 'Dauid Powel' from 'my lodging in London the 25. of March 1584', it is a lovely example of a formal dedication within the tradition of English humanist writing and, like other English texts by sixteenth-century Welsh writers such as Humphrey Llwyd, William Salesbury and John Penry, it uses the conventions of English writing to argue the cause of Wales:

> To the right worshipful Sir Philip Sydney knight. It is the maner of most writers (Right worshipfull) in dedicating of their bookes, to praise and extoll the vertues and noble qualities of such men as they choose to be patrons of their works, whereby to winne some credit and countenance to themselves: the which thing I see to be doone by a great number of writers (as well strangers and countreymen) who have set out the praise and commendation of your noble gifts.

There are a number of other writers who wrote in English about Wales and Welsh life during this period, including Maurice Kyffin, Thomas Churchyard, and John Penry. Maurice Kyffin (c. 1555–98) seems to have been a member of a landed family from Oswestry, which was a largely Welsh-speaking town in the middle of the sixteenth century. He studied with Wiliam Llŷn, the most famous Welsh poet of his day, who also lived in Oswestry, and in the late 1570s Kyffin lived in London, where he knew John Dee. His best-known Welsh work is *Deffynniad Ffydd Eglwys Loegr* (1595), a translation of Bishop Jewel's *Apologia* for the faith of the Church of England. *Deffynniad Ffydd* is a classic of Welsh prose, but Kyffin also wrote a long poem in English in celebration of Elizabeth's thirty years as queen of England. *The Blessednes of Brytaine* was published in London in 1587, with a second edition appearing a year later. The poem celebrates the unity and 'inestimable benefits' of Britain at a time when the country was under constant threat, and like other books of the time it contains a fine preface of dedication, this one being to 'The Right Honorble and Renouned in all Heroicall Vertues, Sir Robert Devreux Knight, Erle of Essex'.

Alongside a number of histories and chronicles, Thomas Churchyard (c. 1523–1604) published an antiquarian description of Wales in English verse called *The Worthines of Wales* (1587). Churchyard had a long career as a soldier, and as he was born in Shrewsbury he would have grown up amongst speakers of Welsh, although *The Worthines of Wales* is written for a non-Welsh or diaspora audience. His descriptions of towns in the March of Wales is particularly interesting and perhaps confirms the idea that London's connections with Welsh-speaking Wales in the sixteenth century often meant a connection with the March and with the eastern counties of Wales which bordered England.

Another interesting writer, who worked in a very different field, is John Penry (1562/3–93), the martyr of Welsh congregationalism as he is sometimes remembered, or John of Wales as Thomas Nashe called him, slightingly, in one of the anti-Martinist tracts. Penry's *Treatise Containing the Aequity of an Humble Supplication* (1587) is one of three treatises about Wales, essentially petitions for royal support, which were printed by him in Oxford and on secret presses in London or elsewhere in the late 1580s before he moved to Edinburgh in the early 1590s.[25] What is interesting about John Penry, from the point of view of Welsh writing in English, is that everything he wrote about Wales is written in English, with the polemical purpose of addressing a non-Welsh audience whose sympathy was being courted for political and social change. By tradition Penry is thought to have been born and raised at Cefn Brith on Mynydd Epynt in Brecknockshire, which would make him another writer from the Welsh-speaking heartland of the March. Penry's complaint, like Salesbury before him, was concerned with the necessity of Welsh-language provision for preaching and ministry in Wales. Despite writing in English, there is no doubt of his proficiency in Welsh because one of his notebooks has survived amongst the Ellesmere manuscripts in the Huntingdon library and sections of his diary entries are in Welsh:

> The 12 moneth December 1592.
> 18. u du Robert [Harries] am lawer o nos grouso mawr.[26]
>
> (18th. To the house of Robert [Harries] for much of [the] night[.]
> A great welcome.)

And three nights later, on 21 December 1592, he records:

> 21. ni a swperasam yn hu Willam Sunmer.
>
> (21st. We had supper at the house of William Sunmer.)

Penry wasn't totally convinced about the usefulness of the Welsh New Testament of 1567 but 'swperasam' is a form that might not look out of place in Salesbury's classically inflected translation.

William Salesbury

The most significant Welsh literary figure in the mid sixteenth century is William Salesbury (*c.* 1520–*c.* 1580), the pioneer of Welsh book production in London in the years before Elizabeth's excommunication in 1570. Salesbury's early career in London is bounded by two events: the publication of *Yn y lhyvyr hwnn* ('In This Book') in 1546 and the accession of Queen Mary in 1553, which brought to an end state support for vernacular printing. Between these two events Salesbury wrote, edited, or published eight books, covering the full range of humanist thought, including lexicography, rhetoric, the law, history, proverbial wisdom, and astronomy. His later career included the first Welsh translation of the New Testament and a Welsh botanical manuscript which remained unpublished until the late twentieth century.

From the first appearance of Welsh printing in 1546 until the death of Edward VI in 1553, William Salesbury wrote or published at least eight works in Welsh and English, one of which, *Kynniver Llith a Ban*, also includes a substantial 'Dedication to the Bishops' in Latin.[27] Of these eight works, seven were published and one remained in manuscript – Salesbury's translation into Welsh of *Tabulae de schematibus et tropis* ('Tables of Schemes and Tropes'), a work on rhetoric by Petrus Schade, commonly known as Petrus Mosellanus, which was first published in Antwerp in 1533.[28] Salesbury's early works are:

1 *A Dictionary in Englyshe and Welshe* (1547)
   [N. Hill for] 'J[ohn] Waley'. STC 21616.
2 *Oll Synnwyr Pen Kembero Ygyd* ('The Sum of Welsh Wisdom') [1547?]
   'Nycholas Hyll'. STC 12403.9.
3 *The Description of the Sphere or the Frame of the Worlde* (1550)
   'R[obert]. Wyer'. STC 20398.7 and 20399. (Thavies Inn)
4 *A Brief and a Playne Introduction* (1550)
   [R. Grafton for] 'Roberte Crowley'. STC 21614. (Thavies Inn)
5 *Ban Wedi i Dynny. . .o Gyfreith Howel Dda*
   ('An Excerpt Taken from the Law of Hywel') (1550)
   [R. Grafton for] 'Roberte Crowley'. STC 21612. (Ely Rentes)
6 *The Baterie of the Popes Botereulx, Commonly Called the High Altare* (1550)
   [R. Grafton for] 'Roberte Crowley'. STC 21613. (Ely Rentes)
7 *Kynniver Llith a Ban* ('As Many Readings and Excerpts') (1551)
   [?R. Grafton for] 'Roberte Crowley for William Salesbury'.
   STC 2983 [=21617]. (Ely Rentes)
8 Llyfr Rhetoreg Petrus Mosellanus
   ('The Book of Rhetoric of Petrus Mosellanus') (1552)
   Cardiff MS 2.39 (formerly Cardiff MS 21).

At least three of these works were to play a significant role in the establishment of Welsh as an institutional language in the middle decades of the sixteenth century. *A Dictionary in Englyshe and Welshe* (1547) and *A Brief and a Playne Introduction* ... *[to]* ... *the Brytysh Tongue* (1550) are important linguistic works which provided practical assistance to non-Welsh-speaking clergy in Wales in the early years of vernacular worship, while *Kynniver Llith a Ban* (1551) provided a Welsh translation of the 'epistles and gospels' of the 1549 English Prayer Book.[29] The compulsory use of the English Prayer Book and its revised successor of 1552 marked the beginning of a crucial period of linguistic history in which vernacular worship in Wales (and for many, therefore, vernacular literacy) would have been in English had there not been Welsh translations available and sufficient official support to allow their use. While it is difficult to know how extensively *Kynniver Llith a Ban* was used in Welsh churches, its importance was that it provided the only alternative to English worship in Welsh parishes prior to the publication of the

Welsh New Testament and Book of Common Prayer in 1567, both of which were also translated by William Salesbury and printed in London.[30] Beyond these two books in 1567, Salesbury was also a major contributor to the Welsh Bible of 1588. He collaborated on the translation of the Old Testament, and his New Testament of 1567 was largely incorporated into that edition, with some emendation and changes to orthography.[31]

Another way in which Salesbury's early books are significant in the history of the literature of Wales is that he is a literary pioneer in two languages. He writes in Welsh for a Welsh audience, he writes in English for an English audience, and he writes in a mixture of the two languages for a bilingual audience. It is widely acknowledged that Salesbury's biblical translations laid the foundations for modern Welsh prose, but some of his English texts are also wonderful examples of English humanist prose. One of the most interesting of the English texts by Welsh writers from Elizabeth's reign is Salesbury's preface of dedication to Elizabeth in the Welsh New Testament of 1567. There is a lot of front matter in the *Testament Newydd*, in the three languages of Wales: Welsh, Latin, and English, and Salesbury's English preface is less well known than his Welsh address to the reader, which has been widely reproduced. The Welsh preface was included, for example, in the 1850 reprint of Salesbury's *Testament* from which the English preface was silently omitted.[32] Here is the opening section:

When I call to remembrance as well the face of the corrupted Religion in England at what tyme Paules churcheyarde in the Citie was occupied by makers of alabaster images to be set up in Churches, and they of Pater noster rowe earned their lyuing by makyng of Pater noster bedes only, they of Aue lane by sellyng Aue bedes, of Crede lane by makyng of Crede bedes: as also the vaine Rites crepte into our country of Wales, whan in steade of the lyuyng God men worshipped dead images of wood and stones, belles and bones, with other such vncertain reliques I wot what, and with all consider our late general reuolt from Goddes most holy worde once receaued, and dayly heare of the lyke inforced vppon our brethern in forain countryes, hauing most piteousely susteined great calamities, bitter afflictions, and merciles persecutions: vnder which verye many doe yet styll remaine: I can not, most Christian Prince, and gracious Soueraine, but euen as dyd the poore blynde Bartimeus, or Samaritane lepre to our Sauiour, so com I before your maiesties feete, and there lying prostrate not onely for my self, but also for the delieuery of many thousandes of my countrey folkes from the spirituall blyndnes of ignoraunce, and fowl infection of olde Idolatrie and

false superstition, most humbly, and dutifully to acknowlege your incomparable benefite bestowed vpon vs in graunting the sacred Scriptures the verye
remedie & salue of our gostly blyndnes and leprosie, to be had in our best
knowen tongue: which as far as euer I can gather (thoughe Christs trewe
Religion sometyme floorished among our Auncesters the old Britons) yet
were neuer so entierlye and vniuersallye had, as we now (God be thanked)
haue them.[33]

This is a perfect example of an English renaissance preface. It contains
elements of formal praise, complex syntax, syntactical balancing, and a
wide range of ornamental and rhetorical features. It is a beautiful early
example of Welsh writing in English, no less perfect than the Welsh
preface to the reader, but undeservingly less well known. In the Welsh
preface, the reader is apparently being addressed by Richard Davies,
the bishop of Menevia or St David's: 'Richard can ras Dyw Episcop
Menew, yn damuno adnewyddiat yr hen ffydd catholic a gollauni
Euangel Christ i'r Cembru oll'[34] ('Richard by the grace of God
Bishop of Menevia wishing a renewal of the old catholic faith and
the light of Christ's Gospel to all Welsh people'). The preface which
follows this greeting, however, was probably also written by William
Salesbury. The Parker Library in Corpus Christi College, Cambridge,
holds a number of Salesbury items, including some letters from
Salesbury to Parker, and in their copy of the Welsh New Testament
of 1567 there is a marginal Welsh note on this page, in a contemporary
hand, which claims that this section was in fact written by Salesbury.

Another example of Salesbury writing in English gives us a rare excur-
sion into comedy. There isn't much comedy in the Welsh Reformation, so
the comic tale of the Clerk of the Court from Salesbury's *Playne and
Familiar Guide* [*to Welsh*] (1550, 1567) also deserves to be better known.
The *Guide* was written to provide help with pronunciation of Welsh for
non-Welsh clerics in Welsh livings whose work included the reading of
prayers and scriptures from the newly printed Welsh editions. It was first
issued in 1550, when Salesbury published *Kynniver Llith a Ban*, and it was
reissued in 1567 to coincide with the publication of his translation of the
New Testament. This anecdote about the hapless clerk is one of the
earliest comic anecdotes in the canon of Welsh writing in English and
while it predates the comic genius of Gwyn Thomas, Rhondda by about
400 years, it shares his manner of affectionate observation. After the
discussion of the individual letters and sounds there is a section on the
use of abbreviations:

For I do remember that once a Clarke (beyng but a yong beginner) at an Assise in our country holden at Denbygh, redde a mans name (being short written) *Eden ap Iorum*, where he should have read it *Eden-yuet ap Yorvverth*. And so the Cryer called styll *Eden ap Iorum* come into the court, or lose x pound: that thou shalt lose, for thou wast sene here euen now.

And true it was, for the person that was so oft and so loud called, stood styll all thys whyle euen at the Cryers backe, and answered not at all (being so straungely misnamed) untyl he had wel-most lost amerciament. At whych feate the gest at the last perceyved, was there no small laughter of all the whole Court.[35]

The Seventeenth Century

Later in the sixteenth century, and into the seventeenth, the number of Welsh people in London continued to rise and publishing in London became an established part of Welsh literary production. The growing significance of printing in London was not challenged until the collapse of the Crown copyright led to an explosion of provincial printing, a change which also coincided with a rapid decline in the production of literary manuscripts in Wales.

Of the many literary texts in English which were written by Welsh writers or which represent Wales and Welsh life in the seventeenth century, three are worth noting here as they extend the generic range of texts which have been discussed. One interesting dramatic work which dates from well before the closure of the theatres in 1642 and which was re-published in 1663, after the Restoration, is *The Valiant Welshman*, 'Written by R. A. Gent', which portrays 'The True Chronicle History of the Life and Valiant deeds of Caradoc the King, King of Cambria, now called Wales. As it hath beene sundry times acted by the Prince of Wales his seruants.' The first edition to survive was 'Imprinted by George Purslowe for Robert Lownes' and was 'solde at his shoppe at the little north dore of Paules'. The title page is dated 1615 and the book was entered into the Stationers' Register on 21 February of that year. The work has been attributed to Robert Armin (1563–1615), and while there is no certainty about this attribution, Armin is credited with a variety of publications from the 1590s onwards. Interestingly, the play has a significant clown part, and although not Welsh, Armin was a famous comic actor who would have been familiar with the representation of Welsh characters on the London stage. He first created many of Shakespeare's later comic characters, including the clown Feste in *Twelfth Night* and Touchstone in *As You Like It*. The play *The Valiant Welshman* deals with the heroism of Caradoc, who intervenes in the civil wars of prehistoric Wales fought between Octavian and the usurper Monmouth. The King of Britain then solicits Welsh help against the invading Romans, so Caradoc leaves his own wedding feast and performs valiantly against the improbably hapless Roman army.

Another interesting writer from the early seventeenth century is David Lloyd (1597–1663) who was educated at Oxford and became dean of the cathedral at St Asaph. His best-known work, a mock epic entitled *The Legend of Captain Jones* (1631), is referenced in Andrew Marvell's *The Rehearsal Transprosed* (1673), suggesting that forty years after it first appeared it was still a byword for comic exaggeration. There were a number of seventeenth-century editions, and the 1663 edition was issued with a frontispiece which depicts the brave Captain on horseback, in full armour on an armoured horse, armed with a sword and a lance. In the 1671 edition there is a larger folding frontispiece in which the mounted hero is single-handedly attacking an elephant of war whose castle carries a fierce-looking bowman. *The Legend* tells the story of an Elizabethan soldier who performs spectacular and improbable feats of arms, and it is particularly interesting in the history of the two literary languages of Wales because it may have begun as a parody of 'Awdl foliant Rhisiart Siôn o Fuellt', 'An awdl in Praise of Rhisiart Siôn of Buellt', by Siôn Tudur, a prominent Welsh poet who later lived in the diocese of St Asaph. It has also been suggested that it may satirize the boastful accounts of Captain John Smith's exploits in the Americas, which were published in London in the 1620s and 1630s.

Although the novel is a relatively late development in Welsh writing, one of the earliest English novels on a Welsh theme appeared in London in 1678. The anonymous *Tudor: A Prince in Wales* was published by 'H.H. for Jonathan Edwin, at the Sign of the Three Roses on Ludgatehill'. The novel fictionalizes the life of Owen Tudor, the grandfather of Henry VII of England, and the book appears to have been an original French composition, published in Paris in 1677 as *Tideric, Prince de Galles*. A racier English version appeared in 1751, 'Printed for William Owen, at Homer's Head, near Temple Bar', in which the title has been improved to *The Life and Amours of Owen Tideric*, 'First wrote in French, and published many Years since at Paris, and now [newly] translated into English'. It is interesting to speculate whether the nonconformist and Puritan readership of Simon Thomas's *Hanes y Byd a'r Amseroedd* (1721), which was so full of praise for Owen Tudor's Welsh ancestry, had any interest in the 'life and amours' of the Welshman who married 'Catharine, Princess of France'.

Conclusion

From the early Tudor period onwards, there is a wide range of texts written in English by Welsh authors while an equally significant number of non-Welsh authors begin to write in English about Wales and Welsh life, or to incorporate Welsh characters into their work. These texts cover the full range of literary and historical production: poetry, drama and fiction, history, biography and politics, travel and topography. All these genres are visible in the manuscript and print record before 1700, and while the production and consumption of literature in Welsh continues to be dominant in Wales until the nineteenth century, Welsh writing in English is now an established part of the literature of Wales. It is also in the seventeenth century, when Welsh literature and English literature begin to intersect and overlap in ever more complex ways, that we see a number of English writers living in Wales without writing about Welsh life and we also see some Welsh writers living their lives in Wales while participating in the literary culture of England. One example of the former type of writer is Jeremy Taylor (d. 1667), the English divine, whom Samuel Coleridge placed alongside Shakespeare, Milton, and Bacon as 'the four great geniuses of our older literature'.[36] Taylor was chaplain to the Carbery household at Gelli-Aur, the Golden Grove estate near Llandeilo in Carmarthenshire, where many of the works for which he is remembered were written. These include *The Rule and Exercises of Holy Living* (1650), *The Rule and Exercises of Holy Dying* (1651), and *Sermons Preached at Golden Grove* (1651).

The best-known examples of the second type of writer mentioned above are probably the great metaphysical poet Henry Vaughan (1621–1695) and his twin brother Thomas Vaughan (1621–1666), the alchemist and poet. Henry Vaughan was born at Newton, Scethrog, in the Usk valley, and while it is likely that he grew up speaking Welsh as well as English, he may have had little knowledge of traditional Welsh bardic practices, despite living much of his life in Wales. In his small volume of poems *Olor Iscanus: A Collection of Some Select Poems and Translations* (1651), he famously describes himself as 'Mr Henry Vaughan *Silurist*', which may have been an antiquarian way of trying to suggest that although he was Welsh, he was not 'a Welsh writer'.

Our view of the early history of Welsh writing in English has broadened and changed considerably in the last fifty years. Despite the pioneering work of early twentieth-century scholars such as W. J. Hughes, who had tried to stimulate interest in the earlier centuries of Welsh writing in English by publishing lists of English texts about Wales from before 1830,[37] the apparent newness of the young writers of the 'first flowering' of 'Anglo-Welsh literature', and the context of modernity in which they worked, created a hegemonic disinclination to look back beyond Allen Raine and Caradoc Evans into the centuries of complementary, multilingual literary production which form such a rich part of the history of Wales. But with the impetus of new scholarship in the 1970s and 1980s, the paradigm shifted. Critics such as M. Wynn Thomas began to reinvent the field as Welsh writing in English and began to write comparatively about writers in both languages, and to look back to writers from earlier centuries. In so doing, they began to locate the literature of Wales in the comparative context of other world literatures because, like Humphrey Llwyd, they 'wolde not have the inhabitantes of this Ile ignorant of the histories and cronicles of the same'.

Notes

1. The MSS listed in the National Library of Wales Index to Welsh Poetry in Manuscript (MALDWYN) are London BL Add MS 29, London BL Add MS 31094, Cardiff MS 7, Cardiff MS 26, Oxford Jesus College MS 14, Aberystwyth NLW MS Peniarth 76 and Aberystwyth NLW MS Peniarth 112.
2. P. J. Donovan, ed., *Cywyddau Serch y Tri Bedo* (Caerdydd: Gwasg Prifysgol Cymru, 1982), 15–16, l.1; my translation.
3. Donovan, ed., *Cywyddau Serch y Tri Bedo*, 15–16, ll. 51–8.
4. This reading of the poem was first suggested by Ifano Jones in his pioneering study *Printers and Printing in Monmouthshire and Wales* (Cardiff: William Lewis, 1925), 1; on Bedo Brwynllys see also Dafydd Johnston, *Llên yr Uchelwyr: Hanes Beirniadol Llenyddiaeth Gymraeg 1300–1525* (Caerdydd: Gwasg Prifysgol Cymru, 2015), 318–19 and 335.
5. Jane Aaron, *Nineteenth-Century Women's Writing in Wales: Nation, Gender and Identity* (Cardiff: University of Wales Press, 2007); Moira Dearnley, *Distant Fields: Eighteenth-Century Fictions of Wales* (Cardiff: University of Wales Press, 2001). See also Chapter 17 in this volume for an account of some of these early novels written in or about Wales.
6. Raymond Garlick and Roland Mathias, eds., *Anglo-Welsh Poetry, 1480–1980* (Bridgend: Poetry Wales Press, 1984), 45–8.
7. Raymond Garlick, *An Introduction to Anglo-Welsh Literature* (Cardiff: University of Wales Press, 1972).
8. Alfred Perceval Graves, *Welsh Poetry Old and New in English Verse* (London: Longmans, Green, 1912), 139.

9. Alan Llwyd and Robert Rhys, eds., *Waldo Williams: Cerddi 1922–1970* (Llandysul: Gwasg Gomer, 2014), 405.

10. For a full discussion and catalogue of the early Welsh printed books, see Eiluned Rees, *Libri Walliae: A Catalogue of Welsh Books and Books Printed in Wales 1546–1820* (Aberystwyth: National Library of Wales, 1987) and Charles Parry, *Libri Walliae: Supplement to the Catalogue of Welsh Books and Books Printed in Wales 1546–1820* (Aberystwyth: National Library of Wales, 2001).

11. For a concise account of publishing throughout England and Wales, see John Feather, *A History of British Publishing*, 2nd edn (Abingdon: Routledge, 2006).

12. See Penry Williams, *The Later Tudors: England 1547–1603* (Oxford: Clarendon, 1995), 10–11, and A. L. Beier and R. Finlay, eds., *London 1500–1800: The Making of a Metropolis* (London: Longman, 1986), 2–10.

13. See Jerry Hunter, 'Taliesin at the Court of Henry VIII: Aspects of the Writing of Elis Gruffydd', *THSC* 10 (2004): 41–56; see also Thomas Jones, 'A Welsh Chronicler in Tudor England', *Welsh History Review* 1 (1960): 1–17.

14. Emrys Jones, *The Welsh in London 1500–2000* (Cardiff: University of Wales Press on behalf of the Honourable Society of Cymmrodorion, 2001), 19–24.

15. See Jonathan Hughes, 'Sir Thomas Parry', in *Oxford Dictionary of National Biography* (Oxford: Oxford University Press, 2014), online edition, www.oxforddnb.com/view/article/21433 (accessed 17 August 2018).

16. Jones, *The Welsh in London*, 36.

17. See Geraint Evans, 'William Salesbury and Welsh Printing in London Before 1557', in *Authority and Subjugation in Writing of Medieval Wales*, ed. Ruth Kennedy and Simon Meecham-Jones (London: Palgrave Macmillan, 2008), 251–66.

18. Jones, *The Welsh in London*, 10–12.

19. S[imon] T[homas], *Hanes y Byd a'r Amseroedd* (London: D. Lloyd, 1721), 143; my translation.

20. For an account of this book and an edition of the Welsh sections, see Geraint Evans, 'Wales and the Welsh Language in Andrew Borde's *Fyrst Boke of the Introduction of Knowledge*', *Studia Celtica* 42 (2008): 87–104.

21. This is reminiscent of Caxton's *Descrypcyon of Englonde* (1480), STC 13440a, where most of the section on Wales is in verse: 'Wales now is called wallia / And somtyme it heet cambria . . .'

22. R. Brinley Jones, 'Humphrey Llwyd (1527–1568)', in *Oxford Dictionary of National Biography* (Oxford: Oxford University Press, 2004).

23. The text quoted here is taken from Ieuan M. Williams's edition, *Humphrey Llwyd, Cronica Walliae* (Cardiff: University of Wales Press, 2002).

24. David Powell, *The Historie of Cambria, Now Called Wales* (London: R. Newberie and H. Denham, 1584).

25. John Penry, *A Treatise Containing the Aequity of an Humble Supplication. . . in the Behalf of the Countrey of Wales* (Oxford: Joseph Barnes, 1587); all three

treatises have been edited in David Williams, ed., *Three Treatises Concerning Wales* (Cardiff: University of Wales Press, 1960).

26. See *The Notebook of John Penry, 1593*, ed. Albert Peel, *Camden Society*, 3rd series, LXVII (London: Royal Historical Society, 1944); my translations.

27. See also the section in the Introduction regarding the 'Dedication to the Bishops' in John Fisher, ed., *Kynniver Llith a Ban* (Cardiff: University of Wales Press, 1931), xxiii–xxvi.

28. Salesbury's work was not published in the sixteenth century but survives in Cardiff MS 2.39 (formerly Cardiff MS 21), and in later copies; see R. Brinley Jones, *William Salesbury*, Writers of Wales (Cardiff: University of Wales Press, 1994), 33.

29. The Act of Uniformity was passed on 21 January 1549 for the use of the Book of Common Prayer from Whitsuntide 1549. The Second Act of Uniformity was passed in April 1552 for the use of the 1552 Prayer Book from November 1552. Both Acts also made church attendance compulsory. See Glanmor Williams, *Wales and the Reformation* (Cardiff: University of Wales Press, 1997), 163–6.

30. See Isaac Thomas, 'Translating the Bible', in *A Guide to Welsh Literature c. 1530–1700*, ed. R. Geraint Gruffydd (Cardiff: University of Wales Press, 1997), 154–75.

31. See Chapters 9 and 12 for a fuller account of this and other aspects of William Salesbury's career.

32. *Testament Newydd William Salesbury* (Caernarfon: Robert Griffith, 1850).

33. *Testament Newydd* (London: Henry Denham for Humfrey Toy, 1567), sig. ai^r–ai^v.

34. *Testament Newydd* (1567), sig. Aiii^r; my translation.

35. William Salesbury, *A Playne and Familiar Introduction, Teaching How to Pronounce the Letters in the Brytishe Tongue* (London: Henry Denham, 1567). The orthography and punctuation are reproduced as printed. This section is mostly set in black letter but with the names, here given in italics, printed in roman type.

36. See Logan Pearsall Smith, ed., *The Golden Grove: Selected Passages from the Sermons and Writing of Jeremy Taylor* (Oxford: Clarendon Press, 1930), xiii.

37. W. J. Hughes, *Wales and the Welsh in English Literature* (Wrexham: Hughes and Son, 1924).

12

Bibles and Bards in Tudor and Early Stuart Wales

GRUFFYDD ALED WILLIAMS

In both England and Wales, the religious changes of Henry VIII's reign had linguistic implications with the official sanction of an English Bible and initial moves – such as Archbishop Thomas Cranmer's *Litany* of 1544 – to introduce English into public worship. After Henry's death in 1547 and the accession of Edward VI, reformist tendencies and linguistic innovation gathered momentum; under Cranmer's leadership the promotion of English as the language of liturgy culminated in the provision of the Book of Common Prayer in 1549. In the Celtic-speaking peripheries of the realm, the emergence of an exclusively anglophone church was inevitably problematic. In Cornwall the Western Rebellion of summer 1549 – though primarily fuelled by religious conservatism and economic grievances – had a linguistic dimension. Rejecting the new order of service the rebels declared that 'we the Cornyshe men (wherof certen of us understande no Englysh) utterly refuse thys newe Englysh'.[1] In Wales, with its large monoglot Welsh-speaking population, disquiet with religious changes was not expressed in physical action, but the Glamorgan poet Tomas ab Ieuan ap Rhys probably voiced the perception of many of his compatriots when he disparaged the new religion as *ffydd Saeson* ('the faith of the English').[2]

There was clearly a need for the authorities to take realistic cognizance of the linguistic situation in Wales if the new religion were to achieve more than a passive and unenthusiastic acceptance. But little over a decade after the 1536 'Laws in Wales Act', which declared a united polity dominated by English, the politico-religious establishment may have been reluctant to adopt such an approach. It was left to a committed Protestant layman – William Salesbury, born in Llansannan, Denbighshire, in about 1520 – to show the way in this respect. Exposed to Protestant religious influences during his Oxford student days, Salesbury's reformist tendencies may have been further honed during a subsequent period in London at the Inns of Court. Issuing from a line of leading patrons of Welsh poetry – he came from a cadet branch of the

Salusbury gentry family of Lleweni near Denbigh – and thoroughly immersed in Welsh literary culture, he was also fully acquainted with the culture and values of Renaissance humanism. A polymath with a formidable linguistic armoury – according to Thomas Wiliems, another Welsh humanist, Salesbury knew Hebrew, Greek, Latin, English, French, German 'and other languages' apart from his native Welsh[3] – he was also acutely aware of the potential of the printing press as an agent to propagate the new learning and religion. As early as December 1545, together with the London printer John Waley, he was granted a privilege to print a dictionary in English and Welsh and unnamed translations. Later, his association with another London printer – the fervently Protestant Robert Crowley – advanced Salesbury's literary career and religious ideals.[4]

In 1547 Salesbury published *A Dictionary in Englyshe and Welshe* – a work meant to aid Welshmen to 'spedly learne the englyshe tongue' – and the same year probably saw the publication of his *Oll Synnwyr pen Kembero ygyd* ('The Sum of a Welshman's Wisdom'), a proverb collection assembled by Salesbury's friend, the poet Gruffudd Hiraethog. Salesbury's preface to the collection – a publication inspired by his admiration of Erasmus's *Adagia* and other Renaissance proverb collections – has been described as 'the manifesto of the Renaissance and Welsh Protestant humanism'.[5] Apart from earnestly advocating the cultivation and embellishment of Welsh as a vehicle for learning, Salesbury passionately urged his readership – mostly, probably, Welsh clergy and gentry – to persuade the authorities to sanction a Welsh Bible:

> Pererindotwch yn droednoeth, at ras y Brenhin ae Gyncor y ddeisyf cael cennat y cael yr yscrythur lan yn ych iaith er mwyn y cyniuer ohanoch or nyd yw n abyl, nac mewn kyfflypwriaeth y ddyscy Sasnaec.[6]

> (Go on barefooted pilgrimage to his grace the king and his council to entreat permission to have the holy scripture in your language for the sake of those among you who are not able nor likely to learn English.)

Faced with a complacent ecclesiastical establishment, the impatient Salesbury took the initiative, publishing a Welsh translation of the liturgical Epistles and Gospels, *Kynniver Llith a Ban*, in 1551 (a work printed by Robert Crowley, who had in 1550 printed two Protestant polemical works and a manual of Welsh pronunciation by Salesbury). In a Latin dedication to the four Welsh bishops and the bishop of Hereford (whose diocese then had a significant Welsh-speaking population), Salesbury urged them to submit his work to scholars for scrutiny and, if commended, to authorize its use.[7] He emphasized that his work was a strict translation, not a paraphrase, paying due regard to the Greek fountainhead and also to Hebrew in connection with portions of Matthew's gospel. Modern textual analysis of Salesbury's renderings has confirmed his claims to scriptural fidelity: not only did he often fine-tune the Great Bible readings of the Book of Common Prayer by reference to Erasmus's Greek Testament, the Vulgate, and reformist translations by Luther, Tyndale, and Coverdale, but he also on occasion opted for his own independent interpretations.[8] Faced with the challenge of augmenting Welsh vocabulary to cope with the demands of scripture, Salesbury excelled at the coining of neologisms but also had occasional recourse to terms employed in medieval Welsh religious texts. *Kynniver Llith a Ban* displayed some of the traits evident in his later translations: a scholarly devotion to copiousness and verbal variety, orthographic peculiarities such as a predilection for Latinate forms like *Deo* (for *Duw*), *popul* (*pobl*), and *eccleis* (*eglwys*) coupled with the retention of some features of Middle Welsh orthography, a reluctance to indicate initial mutations, and the listing of lexical variants as marginalia. Though such features might have confounded readers, Salesbury's versions in essence displayed a fluent mastery of Welsh literary prose. The extent of the practical use of *Kynniver Llith a Ban* during the remainder of Edward VI's reign is unknown, but it was employed to some extent as a stopgap text during the early years of Elizabeth's restoration of Protestantism.

During the reign of the Catholic Mary, Salesbury lay low in Wales: a tradition – embedded in Welsh Protestant mythology – that he embarked on a translation of the New Testament whilst in hiding is unlikely. The accession of Elizabeth in 1558 and a Protestant church settlement brought new opportunities. The appointment of Richard Davies – latterly a Protestant exile in Frankfurt – as bishop of St Asaph in 1560 and of St David's in 1561 provided Salesbury with an influential ally to press the authorities for a Welsh Bible and liturgy. Their efforts culminated in 1563 in 'An Act for the translating of the Bible and the Divine Service into the Welsh Tongue' (5 Eliz. I, c.28),[9] probably steered through the Commons by Humphrey Llwyd, MP for Denbigh, and through the Lords by Bishop Davies.[10] It commanded the Welsh bishops and their Hereford counterpart to arrange for the translation of the whole Bible and Book of Common Prayer by 1 March 1567 for use in churches 'where the Welsh tongue is commonly used'. In 1564 Richard Davies invited Salesbury to his episcopal palace near Carmarthen to further the project. The Welsh Book of Common Prayer (with an accompanying complete Psalter) – all Salesbury's work – appeared in May 1567 and was followed in October by the New Testament. Salesbury contributed some 80 per cent of the latter, all apart from five epistles – 1 Timothy, Hebrews, James, and 1 and 2 Peter – translated by Richard Davies, and Revelations translated by Thomas Huet, precentor of St David's. The Testament's pre-liminary matter included a long and subsequently influential 'Epistle to the Welsh' by Davies, a fervent apologia for Protestantism perceived not as an innovation, but as a restoration of the true scriptural religion allegedly introduced to the Britons by Joseph of Arimathea.[11] The editorial work on both the Prayer Book and the Testament was undertaken by Salesbury and it was he who oversaw the printing of both volumes – funded by Humfrey Toy, a London bookseller with Carmarthen affiliations – at Henry Denham's press in St Paul's churchyard.

The 1567 translations reflected the advance of biblical scholarship since the publication of *Kynniver Llith a Ban*. The 1563 Act had explicitly commanded translation of the Bible and Prayer Book 'as is now used within this Realm in English', implying that the Great Bible was the intended scriptural exemplar. But the 1567 translators were aware that the Great Bible had been superseded in terms of accuracy by the more literal Geneva English Bible of 1560 produced by William Whittingham and his exiled collaborators. It replaced the Great Bible as the touchstone for the 1567 translations; other relevant works like Theodore Beza's Latin translation of 1556 and editions of the original scriptural texts by Robert and Henri Estienne and Sebastian Münster were also consulted. The claim on the Testament's title page that it was 'Drawn ... word for word from the Greek and Latin' ('Gwedy ei dynnu ... air yn ei gilydd o'r Groec a'r Llatin') reflected the translators' quest for accuracy. The indefatigable Salesbury in particular strove to keep abreast with the latest biblical scholarship. The Testament contained minor revisions of his Prayer Book renderings, attributable to his having consulted Beza's 1565 Greek and Latin Testament, probably whilst in London during the few months between the appearance of the two Welsh publications.[12]

The 1567 translations were triumphs of scholarship and were inherently highly accomplished examples of Welsh prose, which significantly enhanced the lexicon of the language and elevated its status. But, thanks to Salesbury – whose editorial hand was evident throughout both publications – their usefulness was impaired by the accentuated display of features evident in *Kynniver Llith a Ban*, Latinate or archaic spellings, a reluctance to indicate the mutations of Latin-derived words, and a confusing degree of lexical variety. Criticism of such features must have preceded publication, probably reflecting the reception of *Kynniver Llith a Ban*. In his *A playne and a familiar Introduction* published in May 1567, Salesbury referred to criticisms 'that I had peruerted the whole orthographie of the tonnge'[13] and, significantly, inserted a preliminary sheet in the Prayer Book entitled 'An explanation of certaine wordes being quareled withall', defending forms such as the Latinized *Vy-popul* (for *fy mhobl*) which he claimed served 'to saue the word the les maimed'.[14] That Salesbury's Welsh perplexed both clergy and congregations is suggested by the criticism of the Puritan John Penry who asserted that the Testament was 'most pitifully euill read of the reader, and not vnderstoode of one among tenne of the hearers';[15] similarly, the more mainstream Maurice Kyffin declared that the printed word of the Testament was such that 'the ear of a true Welshman could not bear to hear it'.[16] Significantly, Salesbury and Davies did not produce a complete Welsh Bible as stipulated in 1563. Sir John Wynn of Gwydir claimed that they had started to translate the Old Testament but that a quarrel between them 'for the general sense and etymology of one word' aborted the project.[17] Modern scholarship has doubted this explanation, speculating that such a quarrel, if it occurred, arose from tension between Davies's outright evangelizing mission and Salesbury's adherence to what he considered to be linguistic and literary embellishment.[18]

It was the personal initiative and perseverance of William Morgan, a native of Penmachno, Caernarvonshire – a Cambridge doctor of divinity – which led to the first complete Welsh translation of the Bible, a work he accomplished whilst vicar of Llanrhaeadr-ym-Mochnant, Denbighshire. His initial intention had been to translate the Pentateuch only, but he was encouraged and helped financially by John Whitgift, Archbishop of Canterbury, to proceed with the whole Bible.[19] After Morgan had spent a year in London at the home of Gabriel Goodman, the Ruthin-born dean of Westminster, supervising its printing, the Bible was published in November 1588, the Privy Council decreeing that it be placed in every parish church by the Christmas following.

Morgan was well placed to take advantage of advances in international biblical scholarship; Christopher Plantin's Antwerp polyglot Bible (1568–73), Tremellius's Latin Old Testament (1575–9, with London editions in the 1580s), and the 1582 edition of Beza's Greek New Testament were all works he consulted, though not uncritically.[20] In a Latin dedicatory epistle addressed to Queen Elizabeth, he generously hailed his predecessors Davies and Salesbury; whilst expressly praising Salesbury for his service to the church, he also claimed to have purged his Testament of its faulty mode of writing.[21] Whilst Morgan's New Testament largely reproduced Salesbury's wording – it has been estimated that three-quarters of the translation was unchanged[22] – the orthography was normalized, Latinate forms and archaic vocabulary pruned, and lexical variety curtailed; similar changes also featured in Morgan's revision of Salesbury's Psalter. In translating the texts of the Old Testament and Psalter, Morgan sought to convey the exact meaning of the Hebrew, successfully reconciling this aim with producing a readily comprehensible Welsh version whose vocabulary, though containing many neologisms, drew both on contemporary colloquial Welsh usage – including a limited use of English borrowings – and on the traditional literary lexicon of the professional bards. Morgan's Bible was a literary masterpiece, combining scriptural fidelity with a felicitous and dignified use of Welsh sensitively deployed in cadenced sentences. Unlike the 1567 translations Morgan's Bible was well received, receiving plaudits in a number of bardic eulogies: Siôn Tudur praised Morgan for his 'flowing Welsh ([C]ymraeg rwydd) . . . which perfectly kept the rule of grammar', whilst Owain Gwynedd hailed 'the great feat of Doctor Morgan' (*mawrgamp y Doctor Morgan*) in channelling the virtue of Hebrew to 'our language'.[23] Morgan's achievement gained him promotion to the see of Llandaff in 1595 followed by translation to St Asaph in 1601, three years before his death. In his later years he continued his scholarly labours, producing a revised version of the Welsh Book of Common Prayer in 1599;[24] he also produced a revised version of the New Testament, but the manuscript was lost when the printer Thomas Salisbury fled London during the plague of 1603.

The publication of the English Authorized Version of 1611 made a revised Welsh Bible a desideratum. It was published in 1620, the work of Bishop Richard Parry – William Morgan's successor at St Asaph – and his brother-in-law and chaplain Dr John Davies, vicar of Mallwyd in Merioneth.[25] Davies had been William Morgan's protégé: tutored by him whilst he worked on the 1588 Bible at Llanrhaeadr-ym-Mochnant, Davies termed Morgan his 'Gamaliel' and, after graduating at Oxford, followed his mentor to Llandaff and St Asaph, assisting him with the revised Prayer Book of 1599 and the lost revised Testament. In an introduction to the 1620 Bible, Parry explained his desire to emulate the success of the English Authorized Version; some of the revised translations of 1620 inevitably reflect its influence – in the case of the Old Testament it has been estimated that about a third of the new translation displayed affinity with the authorized version[26] – but Parry and Davies's strict scholarly adherence to the principle of fidelity to the original languages also often led them to reject its renderings. Davies was thoroughly acquainted with the classical language of the bards whom he extensively patronized, publishing the best pre-modern grammar (1621) and dictionary (1632) of Welsh, works based on bardic linguistic usage.[27] It was he who ensured the conformity of the 1620 Bible with the norms – in many respects conservative – of the bardic language, ironing out some of the colloquialisms used by Morgan in 1588 and 1599, substituting forms such as *na allei* for *na alle*, *titheu* for *tithe*, and *â* for *aiff*. Parry and Davies's 1620 Bible represented the apogee of the tradition of Welsh scriptural translation initiated by Salesbury and his collaborators and advanced by Morgan; standing on the shoulders of their predecessors – and not a little indebted to them – Parry and Davies produced a masterly work of polished literature. This was essentially the Bible that was familiar to Welsh speakers until its replacement by the New Welsh Bible in 1988.

It was fortunate that, at a time when English became embedded in the religious sphere in England, Wales was endowed with men of learning, vision, and energy who eventually secured a parallel role for Welsh in religion. It must be emphasized, however, that they did not labour within a uniformly favourable ideological context. The palpably nationalist English Tudor state – into which Wales was wholly incorporated by the 1536 and 1542 'Laws in Wales' Acts – instinctively favoured a polity unified by the use of English. Given this background, it is not surprising that proponents of a Welsh Bible and liturgy encountered not only apathy but also obstinate opposition. Significantly, probably following a proviso added in the House of Lords, the 1563 Act authorizing the translations stipulated that an English Bible and Prayer Book were to be placed in churches alongside the projected Welsh volumes so that those who did not understand English 'may by conferring both Tongues together, the sooner attain to the Knowledge of the English Tongue'.[28] William Salesbury, in a preface to his manual on Welsh pronunciation *A playne and a familar Introduction* (1567), related how some opponents of the Welsh New Testament and Prayer Book had approached their publisher, Humfrey Toy, 'some saying wyth *Iudas* the Traitor, what needed thys waste? For when ye haue all done, there is fewe or none that can read it'.[29] Despite Whitgift's support, a residual opposition to the concept of a Welsh Bible in some quarters was indicated in William Morgan's dedicatory epistle to the Queen in his 1588 translation. He cited those who favoured the imposition of English on the Welsh as an alternative to providing them with scriptural translations, castigating their belief that denying a vernacular Bible would encourage the learning of English.[30] Maurice Kyffin's introduction to *Deffynniad Ffydd Eglwys Loegr* (1595), a translation of Jewel's *Apologia Ecclesiae Anglicanae*, indicated that such attitudes occurred in church circles, citing an ecclesiastic who in a church council opposed the printing of Welsh, favouring the promotion of English and the abandonment of Welsh, and asserting that a Welsh Bible would do no good but much harm. Kyffin's rejoinder is famous, 'A alle Ddiawl ei hun ddoedyd yn amgenach?' ('Could the Devil himself say otherwise?').[31] However, despite their passionate commitment to the promotion of Welsh for religious purposes, men like Salesbury, Morgan, and Kyffin did not waver in any way in their loyalty to the Tudor state; nor did they oppose their compatriots' acquisition of English. Ironically, in view of their achievements and the intransigence with which they had to contend, both Salesbury and Morgan voiced support for the concept of a realm united by a knowledge of English, Salesbury explicitly commending the 1536 'Laws in Wales' Act and the underlying principle of its 'language clause':

> that they that be vnder dominion of one most gracious Hedde and kynge shal vse also one language and that euen as theyr hertes agree in loue and obedience to your grace [Henry VIII] so may also theyr tongues agree in one kynd of speche & language ... [32]

Such was the prevalence of Welsh in Tudor Wales that even the passionate protagonists of its use for religious purposes – all deeply attached to the language and thoroughly versed in its literary culture – could not foresee the potential perils of bilingualism or, indeed, of political union under the English Crown.

The translation of the Bible and Book of Common Prayer into Welsh embedded Protestantism in the national fabric of Wales. Culturally, too, the consequences were immense. The translations perpetuated the Welsh language by elevating its status and ensuring that it came to serve what was for centuries a core aspect of national life. They endowed the language with a greatly enhanced lexicon enriched by numerous neologisms to exactly convey scriptural meaning, but they also perpetuated some conservative features deriving from the language of the bards which still characterize standard Welsh today. The enhanced language was well fitted to become the medium of a rich new tradition of prose writing on religious and theological matters, one to which Anglican, Puritan, and Nonconformist authors ultimately contributed. The Bible's influence on subsequent Welsh imagination – intensified by the evangelical religious ferment of the eighteenth century – can scarcely be overemphasized.[33]

****

If the Welsh Bible and liturgy were the most prominent facets of cultural innovation in sixteenth-century Wales, the forces of cultural continuity and conservatism were best exemplified by the age-old bardic tradition, famously described by Sir Philip Sidney:

> In Wales, the true remnant of the ancient Britons, as there are good authorities to show the long time they had poets, which they called 'bards', so through all the conquests of Romans, Saxons, Danes and Normans . . . yet do their poets even to this day last – so as it is not more notable in soon beginning than in long continuing.[34]

Bardic activity, typified by visits to gentry homes on the 'three special feasts' (*Tair Gŵyl Arbennig*) of Christmas, Easter, and Whitsuntide to declaim *cywyddau* and *awdlau* of praise composed in strict *cynghanedd* or, when occasion demanded, to present elegies for the departed, did indeed continue as a prominent feature of gentry cultural life in Tudor Wales.

Unlike their Irish contemporaries, the bards of Tudor Wales were never subjected to penal strictures or persecution.[35] But the sixteenth century witnessed attempts by the English state to extend an arm's-length control over the bards and the associated profession of musicians, both groups being probably suspected as potential threats to the social order and confused with the age's multiplying throng of vagrants. The immediate regulatory agents were Welsh gentry representatives of royal authority, mostly patrons of the poets themselves and occasionally amateur practitioners of the bardic art. Two attempts at regulation were associated with the small borough of Caerwys in Flintshire, which hosted *eisteddfodau* – primarily concerned with the assessment of candidates for bardic and musical degrees – in 1523 and 1567.[36] The prime movers and likely direct organizers of these gatherings were members of the Flintshire gentry family of Mostyn, who owned property in Caerwys; they probably sought to emulate the Dutton family in neighbouring Cheshire, empowered by the Crown to license minstrels who were thereby exempted from the provisions of the vagrancy acts.[37] Significantly, Richard ap Hywel of Mostyn served as sheriff of Flintshire in 1523, and his grandson, William Mostyn, formerly sheriff of both Denbighshire and Flintshire, was sheriff of Caernarvonshire in 1567. The Mostyns were aided by fellow members of the north Wales gentry official class, among them their kinsmen. In 1523 Richard ap Hywel was assisted by Sir William Gruffydd, chamberlain of north Wales, and Sir Roger Salusbury, steward of Denbigh. In 1567 those sitting in judgement with William Mostyn – all specifically authorized by royal commission – included a member of the Council of the Marches, the lawyer Dr Ellis Price; of the twelve active commissioners eleven were justices of the peace, nine had held shrievalties, and five had served as members of parliament.

The royal commission for the 1567 eisteddfod – granted, interestingly, when Sir Henry Sidney, father of Sir Philip, was president of the Council of the Marches – indicates the motives which prompted the event:

> Wheras it is come to the knowledge of the Lorde President and other our said Cunsaill in our marches of wales that vagraunt and idle persons naming theim selfes mynstrelles, Rithmers, and Barthes, are lately growen into such an intollerable multitude within the principalitee of north wales, that only gentlemen and other by theire shameles disorders are oftentymes disquieted in theire habitacions/ But also thexpert mynstrelles and musicions in tonge and Connyng therby much discouraged to travail in thexercise and practize of theire knowledges and also not a litle hyndred in theire Lyvinges and prefermentes.[38]

The interests of the state with respect to social order and the class interest of gentry patrons are here presented as coinciding with bardic concerns relating to the selectiveness and material rewards of their profession. The bards undoubtedly colluded with officialdom in connection with both Caerwys *eisteddfodau*: Tudur Aled, the leading poet of his day, and the gentleman poet Gruffudd ab Ieuan ap Llywelyn Fychan acted as expert advisors at the 1523 eisteddfod, and the 1567 commission provided for the summoning of 'expert men in the said facultie of the welshe musick' to aid the commissioners. De facto submission to quasi-state regulation is demonstrated by the only two bardic licences to have survived, that of Gruffudd Hiraethog (1546) and of Simwnt Fychan (1567): these documents explicitly state that their grantors were authorized by commissions of Henry VIII and Elizabeth.[39]

The keystone of Tudor bardic regulation was the Statute of Gruffudd ap Cynan.[40] Invested with status by its alleged connection with an ancient prince – it embodied a claim that Gruffudd (c. 1055–1137) had held an eisteddfod in Caerwys – it is likely that the Statute, despite traces of ancient content, was in reality compiled by the promoters of the 1523 Caerwys eisteddfod to validate their regulatory authority. It stipulated technical requirements for the various bardic degrees, that of *pencerdd* ('chief poet') and three subsidiary pupillary grades, those of *disgybl pencerddaidd*, *disgybl disgyblaidd*, and *disgybl ysbas*, who were to be instructed and overseen by bardic teachers of *pencerdd* status. It ordained standards of bardic morality, proscribing the harassment of women, gambling, composition of scurrilous and blasphemous verse, participation in affrays and murder, and consort with thieves. Significantly, the Statute urged obedience to established authority: the bards were enjoined not to follow 'the customs of vagabonds' (*arveroedd vakbwns*), and 'to render true service to all of the prince's loyal subjects and his officials to strengthen and assist them'. It also sought to regulate the bards' relations with patrons, stipulating times for visits to their homes – principally the three 'special feasts', local saints' feasts, and the celebration of nuptials – and also the number of bards allowed to visit patrons of various income levels. It stipulated the fees payable to each grade of poet on the special feasts, and ordained that a regulatory eisteddfod be held every three years. The Statute – in some respects the equivalent of a guild charter and in minor points of detail possibly influenced by such documents – outlined an ideal order: though not without influence – its authority being cited in connection with the 1567 eisteddfod and occasionally by poets – parts of the Statute remained a dead letter, none more so than the stipulation regarding triennial *eisteddfodau*. In practice the old custom of awarding bardic degrees at nuptial feasts persisted during the sixteenth century, being merely supplemented by the Caerwys *eisteddfodau* which in some cases confirmed degrees previously conferred at nuptials.

Bardic activity during the sixteenth century was widespread and its output prolific. As many as seventeen bards graduated at the 1567 Caerwys eisteddfod, including four who were granted the highest degree of *pencerdd*, and seven who were awarded the next degree of *disgybl pencerddaidd*.[41] The extant output of these two grades of poets amounts to over 1,300 *cywyddau* and *awdlau* – poems of substantial length – apart from hundreds of shorter *englynion*.[42] But such figures greatly underestimate contemporary bardic output: the eisteddfod was confined to the bardic province of Aberffraw, comprising only the north Wales counties. If more Welsh poetry has survived from the sixteenth century than from any previous era, its overall quality is inferior to the poetry of the preceding two centuries. Of sixteenth-century professional bards, only Wiliam Llŷn, awarded the miniature silver chair as the best poet at the 1567 eisteddfod – he excelled at evoking earthly transience with great epigrammatical force in his elegies – and, possibly, Siôn Tudur of St Asaph and Siôn Phylip of Ardudwy stand comparison with their leading medieval counterparts. Though bardic output was quite diverse, including examples of love poetry, satire, bardic contentions, religious poems, and varied occasional verse, its staple productions were eulogies and elegies addressed to gentry patrons. Although generally technically proficient in terms of *cynghanedd*, the poetry inclined to well-trodden paths, relying on the stock sentiments of eulogy couched in conventional imagery. Some fine individual poems of their type notwithstanding, this poetry generally bore a worn and tired aspect, intensified sometimes by an overload of leaden genealogical detail. William Salesbury's mid-century report of the thoughts of an exiled young Welsh gentleman he met in St Paul's Churchyard is significant: Salesbury's acquaintance complained of the imaginative uniformity of contemporary Welsh poetry, claiming that much of it gave the impression of issuing from the same heart, of following an identical pattern, or being cast from the same mould ('mor gwbl gyffelyp ei dychymig a mal tarddent or vn galon ne petit yn ei llûnio wrth yr vn patrwn ne eu bwrw yny'r vn volt').[43] A lack of individuation was certainly apparent in much sixteenth-century Welsh poetry. Strong poetic personalities were rare: the most prominent – like the buccaneering gentleman poet Thomas Prys of Plas Iolyn or the combative archdeacon of Merioneth, Edmwnd Prys – were figures outside the ranks of the professional bards.

The patrons of poetry included university-educated humanists. These admired the linguistic expertise of the professional bards yet did not desist from criticizing aspects of contemporary bardism and proposing remedies for its perceived deficiencies. William Salesbury's manuscript *Llyfr Rhetoreg* (1552) – a translation of a work by Petrus Mosellanus – was intended to address the criticism voiced by his London friend by encouraging the bards to embellish their poetry with rhetorical figures. In a poetic debate lasting from 1580 to 1587 – generating fifty-four poems and almost 5,500 lines – the Cambridge-educated Edmwnd Prys levelled a humanist critique at Wiliam Cynwal, a professional bard and 1567 Caerwys graduate.[44] Charging Cynwal and his ilk with displaying excessive flattery in their eulogies and with peddling false pedigrees – Cynwal was an expert herald and genealogist – Prys urged a new poetics to replace mendaciously-inclined eulogy. He advocated the composition of divine verse based on the Bible, probably anticipating the Welsh translation of his friend William Morgan; he also favoured the popular Renaissance genre of scientific verse, being probably familiar with Guillaume Du Bartas's encyclopaedic scientific epic *La Sepmaine* (1578). Dismissive of Cynwal's bardic degree, Prys urged the bards to seek university learning and acquire languages, the prerequisites of a new poetry. A defensive Cynwal's retort was to dismiss Prys as a mere interloper lacking a bardic degree; ignoring his adversary's wider concerns about the matter of poetry, he sharply advised him to return to his priestly duties. Another humanist who tried to encourage bardic innovation was Siôn Dafydd Rhys, a medical graduate of Siena University who published works on Italian, Latin, and Greek in Italy before producing a Welsh grammar in 1592. In an open letter addressed to the bards (1597), he urged them to widen Welsh poetic matter to embrace the gamut of Renaissance learning, drawing on the works of natural philosophers, mathematicians, astronomers, astrologers, and metaphysicians.[45] The practicality of these humanist critics' agenda was debatable given the realities of the Welsh cultural context: their preferred poetic modes predicated a new type of poet far removed by way of training, economic circumstances, and outlook from the Welsh professional bards of their day. An issue too – acknowledged by Prys when debating with Cynwal – was the dominance of *cynghanedd* in high-status Welsh poetry. Though a skilled *cynghanedd* poet himself, it is significant that, in his Welsh metrical psalter of 1621 – the best contemporary example of the biblically based poetry he favoured – Prys resorted to more flexible free-metre verse which eased adherence to scriptural verity. The humanists' ambitious promptings fell on stony ground: even amateur gentry and clergy poets, free of the economic constraints which inclined the professional bards towards eulogy, produced very little by way of genuinely innovative verse.

Towards the end of our period, there were indications that traditional bardism was increasingly pressurized.[46] Poets often complained of declining patronage: not all such references should be taken at face value – contrasting the generosity of the particular patron being addressed with an alleged general decline in patronage became almost a topos of eulogy – but in aggregate they are probably significant. Other factors also made for difficulties. The inflation of the times – between 1540 and 1640 money declined to a fifth of its value – may have sapped both patronage and bardic incomes: poets bemoaned *byd drud* ('the expensive world'). The increasing mobility of the gentry drawn by the attractions of urban life was also disadvantageous. Morys Berwyn (d. 1615) complained of gentry absences around Conwy at the New Year, a traditional season for bardic circuits; former patrons and their wives had gone to London and Chester and their children away to school. There are poems urging patrons to return from these English cities, from Wiltshire, and even from Wolverhampton. Other poems suggest that the bards suffered from changing literary tastes and faced competition from free-metre poets: Edwart ap Raff (d. 1606) bemoaned the *cywydd*'s lack of popularity compared to 'foolish' carols, a sentiment later echoed by Rhisiart Phylip (d. 1641) who complained that both the *englyn* and the *cywydd* were now expiring ('Darfod ... mae'r ddau') being displaced by songs in free metre (*dyriau*). There are indications, too, that by the last decade of the sixteenth century bardic organization was disintegrating. Siôn Dafydd Rhys, in his 1592 grammar, complained of the bards' decline in status 'without *eisteddfodau* worth mentioning, nor indeed privileges and degrees as before' ('heb nag Eistedhbhfôdeu [wiw sôn am danynt] ganthynt, na chwaith Breinieu na Gradheu bhal gynt').[47] That the bards themselves felt the need for regulation is indicated by a *cywydd* by Siôn Mawddwy addressed to the Pembrokeshire antiquarian George Owen asking him to intercede to demand another eisteddfod to restore lost bardic prestige. Similar representations may have prompted an unsuccessful petition addressed in 1594 to the president of the Council of the Marches by twelve north Wales gentlemen calling for a commission to hold an eisteddfod like those held at Caerwys, where 'all the persons within wales professinge any of the said sciences musicke or poetrie' could be summoned.[48] An unknown poet addressing the translator Rowland Vaughan of Caer-gai in Merioneth *c.* 1650, in a *cywydd* significantly entitled *Marfolaeth holl Brydyddion Cymru* ('The Death of All the Poets of Wales') lamented that both *eisteddfodau* and nuptial feasts where bards were graduated were no more.[49]

More than any other factor, however, it was the progressive anglicization of the gentry class which undermined bardic culture. This trend was often deplored in poems from the end of the sixteenth century onwards. 'Wales has become English' ('Aeth Cymru'n Seisnig') bemoaned Huw Llŷn (*fl.* 1560–1600) in an elegy to a Pembrokeshire patron. Addressing the scholar Dr John Davies of Mallwyd in 1627, Rhisiart Phylip characterized Welsh as being then 'cold and thin and disregarded' ('Weithian oer a thenau wyd, / Iaith ddi-stôr, fo'th ddi'styrwyd'), with children 'prattling the language of the English' ('A'th blant . . . Aeth i sisial iaith Saeson'). Even when the gentry still spoke Welsh, the progressive anglicization of their literary tastes boded ill for the bards. Such a process is demonstrated by the case of the Salusbury family of Lleweni near Denbigh, kinsmen of William Salesbury. Though by origin English settlers, they had long assimilated culturally and were leading patrons of Welsh bards for generations.[50] Sir John Salusbury (?1566–1612) continued his family's generous patronage, welcoming numerous bards to Lleweni at the traditional seasons.[51] But Sir John – who married an English wife and who spent much time in London – also had English literary interests; he wrote English verse himself, employed the English poet Robert Chester, and knew Ben Jonson and, probably, Shakespeare.[52] A further stage in the process of acculturation was apparent in the career of his son and heir Sir Henry Salusbury (1589–1632). Bardic visits to Lleweni during his time appear to have been very infrequent. His literary tastes were overwhelmingly

English: an English poet like his father, it was a sign of the times that he was moved, in 1623, to address in verse John Hemings and Henry Condell, Shakespeare's former colleagues, in celebration of their publication of the famous First Folio.[53] It was a new age, far removed from the heyday of the Welsh bards.

Notes

1. Anthony Fletcher and Diarmaid MacCulloch, *Tudor Rebellions*, 5th edn (Harlow: Pearson Longman, 2008), 152.
2. 'Hopcyn' (Lemuel J. Hopkin James) and 'Cadrawd' (T. C. Evans), *Hen Gwndidau, Carolau a Chywyddau, Being Sermons in Song in the Gwentian Dialect* (Bangor: Jarvis and Foster, 1910), 33.
3. Thomas Parry, 'Tri Chyfeiriad at William Salesbury', *BBCS* 9 (1937–9): 109.
4. Geraint Evans, 'William Salesbury and Welsh Printing in London before 1557', in *Authority and Subjugation in Writing of Medieval Wales*, ed. Ruth Kennedy and Simon Meecham-Jones (New York: Palgrave Macmillan, 2008), 251–66; Peter W. M. Blayney, *The Stationers' Company and the Printers of London* (Cambridge: Cambridge University Press, 2013), vol. II, 637–9.
5. Saunders Lewis, 'Damcaniaeth Eglwysig Brotestannaidd', in *Meistri'r Canrifoedd: Ysgrifau ar Hanes Llenyddiaeth Gymraeg gan Saunders Lewis*, ed. R. Geraint Gruffydd (Cardiff: University of Wales Press, 1973), 127.
6. William Salesbury, *Oll Synnwyr pen Kembero ygyd*, ed. J. Gwenogvryn Evans (Bangor and London: Jarvis & Foster and Dent & Co., 1902), sig. A.iii.
7. William Salesbury, *Kynniver Llith a Ban*, ed. John Fisher (Cardiff and Oxford: University of Wales Press Board and Humphrey Milford, Oxford University Press, 1931), unfoliated preliminaries.
8. Isaac Thomas, *Y Testament Newydd Cymraeg 1551–1620* (Caerdydd: Gwasg Prifysgol Cymru, 1976), 70–125; Isaac Thomas, *Yr Hen Destament Cymraeg 1551–1620* (Aberystwyth: Llyfrgell Genedlaethol Cymru, 1988), 42–63.
9. Ivor Bowen, *The Statutes of Wales* (London and Leipsic: T. Fisher Unwin, 1908), 149–51.
10. R. Geraint Gruffydd, 'Humphrey Lhuyd a Deddf Cyfieithu'r Beibl i'r Gymraeg', *Llên Cymru* 4 (1956–7): 114–15.
11. Lewis, 'Damcaniaeth Eglwysig Brotestannaidd', 116–39.
12. The 1567 translations are fully discussed in Thomas, *Y Testament Newydd Cymraeg*, 151–355. For English discussions of the Book of Common Prayer and Psalter, see R. Geraint Gruffydd, 'The Welsh Book of Common Prayer, 1567', *Journal of the Historical Society of the Church in Wales* 17, 22 (1967): 43–55, and Gwilym H. Jones, 'The Welsh Psalter, 1567', *Journal of the Historical Society of the Church in Wales* 17, 22 (1967): 56–61.

13. William Salesbury, *A playne and a familiar Introduction teaching how to pronounce the letters in the Brytishe tongue* (London: Henry Denham, 1567), sig. Aii^v.

14. William Salesbury, *Llyfr Gweddi Gyffredin 1567*, facsimile, ed. Melville Richards and Glanmor Williams (Cardiff: University of Wales Press, 1965), sig. *j^v.

15. David Williams, *John Penry: Three Treatises Concerning Wales* (Cardiff: University of Wales Press, 1960), 56.

16. W. Prichard Williams, ed., *Deffynniad Ffydd Eglwys Loegr* (Bangor: Jarvis & Foster, 1908), [x].

17. J. Gwynfor Jones, ed., *The History of the Gwydir Family and Memoirs* (Llandysul: Gomer Press, 1990), 61–2.

18. Thomas, *Y Testament Newydd*, 302.

19. William Morgan, *Y Beibl Cyssegr-lan 1588*, facsimile (Aberystwyth: National Library of Wales, 1987), sig. *ij^v.

20. See Thomas's discussions, *Y Testament Newydd*, 302–55; Thomas, *Yr Hen Destament*, 134–254.

21. Morgan, *Y Beibl Cyssegr-lan*, sig. *iii.

22. Thomas, *Y Testament Newydd*, 321.

23. For poems quoted, see R. Geraint Gruffydd, '*Y Beibl a droes i'w bobl draw*': *William Morgan yn 1588* (London: The British Broadcasting Corporation, 1988), 37, 42.

24. Discussed by Thomas, *Y Testament Newydd*, 356–67.

25. On the 1620 Bible, see further Thomas, *Y Testament Newydd*, 368–420; Thomas, *Yr Hen Destament*, 255–98.

26. Thomas, *Yr Hen Destament*, 295.

27. On Davies see Ceri Davies, ed., *Dr John Davies of Mallwyd: Welsh Renaissance Scholar* (Cardiff: University of Wales Press, 2004).

28. On the proviso see Gruffydd, 'Humphrey Lhuyd', 115, n. 2.

29. Salesbury, *A playne and a familiar Introduction*, sig. Aii^v.

30. Morgan, *Y Beibl Cyssegr-lan*, sig. *iii.

31. Williams, *Deffynniad Ffydd Eglwys Loegr*, [xiv].

32. William Salesbury, *A Dictionary in Englyshe and Welshe moche necessary to all suche Welshemen as wil spedly learne the englyshe tongue* (London: John Waley, 1547), dedication to Henry VIII, sig. [Aii].

33. See, e.g., Derec Llwyd Morgan, *Y Beibl a Llenyddiaeth Gymraeg* (Llandysul: Gwasg Gomer, 1998).

34. Gavin Alexander, ed., *Sidney's 'The Defence of Poesy' and Selected Renaissance Literary Criticism* (London: Penguin Books, 2004), 6.

35. J. E. Caerwyn Williams and Patrick K. Ford, *The Irish Literary Tradition* (Cardiff: University of Wales Press, 1992), 176–7.

36. Gwyn Thomas, *Eisteddfodau Caerwys / The Caerwys Eisteddfodau* (Cardiff: University of Wales Press, 1968); Enid Roberts, 'Eisteddfod Caerwys 1567', *Transactions of the Denbighshire Historical Society* 16 (1967): 23–61.

37. Elizabeth Baldwin, Lawrence M. Clopper, and David Mills, eds., *Records of Early English Drama: Cheshire including Chester*, 2 vols. (London and Toronto: The British Library and University of Toronto Press, 2007), I, xxxi–xxxii, 37–8, 41–4.

38. David Klausner, ed., *Records of Early Drama: Wales* (London and Toronto: The British Library and University of Toronto Press, 2005), 170 (henceforth abbreviated to *RED: Wales*).

39. T. H. Parry-Williams, ed., *Rhyddiaith Gymraeg: Y Gyfrol Gyntaf, Detholion o Lawysgrifau, 1488–1609* (Caerdydd: Gwasg Prifysgol Cymru, 1954), 46–7; Klausner, ed., *RED: Wales*, 181–2.

40. For texts see Klausner, ed., *RED: Wales*, 159–65, 172–6. For trenchant commentary on the Statute's significance, see Eurys I. Rowlands, 'Nodiadau ar y Traddodiad Moliant a'r Cywydd', *Llên Cymru* 7 (1962–3): 238–43.

41. D. J. Bowen, 'Graddedigion Eisteddfodau Caerwys, 1523 a 1567 / 8', *Llên Cymru* 2 (1952–3): 129–34; Klausner, ed., *RED: Wales*, 176–81.

42. Figures compiled from MALDWYN, the National Library of Wales's online index to Welsh poetry in manuscript, http://maldwyn.llgc.org.uk (accessed 17 August 2017).

43. W. Alun Mathias, 'Llyfr Rhetoreg William Salesbury', *Llên Cymru* 1 (1950–1): 266.

44. Gruffydd Aled Williams, ed., *Ymryson Edmwnd Prys a Wiliam Cynwal* (Caerdydd: Gwasg Prifysgol Cymru, 1986); Gruffydd Aled Williams, 'The Poetic Debate of Edmwnd Prys and Wiliam Cynwal', in *The Renaissance and the Celtic Countries*, ed. Ceri Davies and John E. Law (Oxford: Blackwell Publishing, 2005), 33–54.

45. Thomas Jones, ed., *Rhyddiaith Gymraeg, Yr Ail Gyfrol: Llawysgrifau a Llyfrau 1547–1618* (Caerdydd: Gwasg Prifysgol Cymru, 1956), 159.

46. Poetry quotations here and in the following paragraph are from D. J. Bowen, 'Y Cywyddwyr a'r Dirywiad', *BBCS* 29 (1980–2): 453–96.

47. Joannes Davides Rhæsus [= Siôn Dafydd Rhys], *Cambrobrytannicæ Cymraecæve Lingvae Institvtiones et Rvdimenta* (London: Thomas Orwin, 1592), sig. **4^{v}.

48. Klausner, ed., *RED: Wales*, 31–3; D. J. Bowen, 'Ail Eisteddfod Caerwys a Chais 1594', *Llên Cymru* 3 (1954–5): 139–61.

49. Bowen, 'Ail Eisteddfod Caerwys', 161.

50. John Rowlands, 'A Critical Edition and Study of the Welsh Poems Written in Praise of the Salusburies of Lleweni' (D.Phil. diss., Oxford University, 1967–8).

51. Gruffydd Aled Williams, 'The Welsh Content of Christ Church MS 184', *Christ Church Library Newsletter* 10 (forthcoming).

52. Carleton Brown, ed., *Poems by Sir John Salusbury and Robert Chester* (London and Oxford: Kegan Paul, Trench, Trübner & Co. and Humphrey Milford, Oxford University Press, 1914). For a study of Anglo-Welsh cultural interaction at Lleweni, see Gruffydd Aled Williams, 'Dwy Lenyddiaeth, Dau Fyd: Diwylliant yn Llyweni yng Nghyfnod y Dadeni', *Llên Cymru* 40 (2017): 40–76.

53. NLW MS 5390D, 141.

PART III

*

REVOLUTION AND INDUSTRY

13

Revolution, Culture, and Industry,
c. 1700–1850

PAUL O'LEARY

Different narratives – sometimes intertwined, sometimes mutually exclusive – have at various times framed our understanding of Wales in the eighteenth and early nineteenth centuries. All seek to make sense of a non-state people and its culture in a period when the country lacked both its own governmental framework and a major urban centre within its boundaries to provide a focus for national life. Consequently, some historians have framed this period in terms of developments such as the rise of Protestant Nonconformity or a national cultural renaissance, while others have emphasized various forms of transformative change: the Industrial Revolution, the impact of the Atlantic revolutions of the late eighteenth century, and the emergence of mass political movements.[1]

While some historians see the period in terms of the formation of communal identities (especially those of class and nation), others have underlined the emergence of the idea of individuality and the self. Prys Morgan finds at this time the origins of 'a fractured consciousness – a rift between the collective and the individualistic' that is often associated with a later period.[2] Indeed, the general picture that emerges is one of diversity, contradiction, and contingency – the hallmarks of an emergent modernity. This historical overview emphasizes the diverse developments in economy, society, and culture that occurred over the eighteenth and the first half of the nineteenth centuries, with the aim of identifying the sometimes contradictory cross-currents that shaped the lives of its inhabitants at that time.

A key contradiction was the assimilation of Wales to mainly pre-modern English institutions of government and civic life, while at the same time exhibiting a distinctive linguistic and cultural character and a burgeoning modern industrial economy. It is possible to discern both the lineaments of an unreformed *ancien régime* and the beginnings of modern industrial society in this period. These opposites co-existed, often in uncomfortable ways.

Unlike the parliamentary unions with Scotland (1707) and Ireland (1800), Wales had been assimilated to the English state in the sixteenth century, and consequently all the key structures of official life – law, poor law, and the Church – were English. This position was underlined when the Court of Great Sessions, the only distinctive legal institution in Welsh life, was abolished in 1830.

Power and Land

In the eighteenth century Wales had a small (albeit growing) population that was dispersed fairly evenly across the country. In 1700 the population was about 390,000, rising to around 450,000 half a century later. The distinctive pattern of urbanization consisted of mainly small towns, with English towns such as Bristol, Liverpool, Chester, and Shrewsbury acting as regional 'capitals'. It is in this context that we must see London as the de facto capital city of Wales, the centre of political and cultural life and the hub of political and economic ambitions. Small towns in Wales provided limited opportunities for the growing middle classes, and consequently it was in London that major Welsh social, cultural, and philanthropic institutions were established, often with aristocratic patronage. These included the Honourable and Loyal Society of Antient Britons (1716), the Honourable Society of Cymmrodorion (1751), and the Gwyneddigion Society (1770). The first invented ritual of the new eisteddfodic movement, the *gorsedd* of bards, which had been fashioned by the eccentric radical Edward Thomas (Iolo Morganwg), was held on Primrose Hill in London in 1789.

Wales in this period was predominantly a rural society in which land conferred status and power. Rural society resembled a pyramid with power tightly concentrated at the apex, resting in the hands of perhaps twenty-five to fifty squires in each county. Parliamentary politics was controlled by about thirty to forty landed families. Among them, Sir Watkin Williams-Wynn (1772–1840) of Wynnstay in north-east Wales was known colloquially as the 'prince of Wales'. Below these social elites, farming was largely small-scale and many farms were self-sufficient family units. Walter Davies observed of north Wales in 1811 that 'Several of the lower kind of farmers, and their dependants, have their tables as scantily supplied with the luxuries of salted bacon, butter and cheese, as even those of the paupers they are forced to relieve.' Davies called their houses 'the habitations of wretchedness'.[3] Comments like these are evidence of the limited resources and precariousness of agricultural society. There is little evidence of an 'agricultural revolution' in Wales in the eighteenth century, although flickers of change were observable towards the century's end. In 1796 Thomas Pennant of Flintshire claimed that 'Every great farmer seems now to have taken the early part of his education in Change-Alley.'[4] By the early nineteenth century, substantial farmers could afford to commission paintings by artists such as Hugh Hughes.[5]

The landless rural poor occupied a precarious space in eighteenth-century Wales.[6] Enclosure of common lands reduced the resources available when times were hard and exposed this social group to the punitive attitudes of the local magistracy. The vicissitudes of the agricultural economy and periodic subsistence crises made the poor the least enviable group in rural society. These conditions increased the movement of people out of the countryside.

Crises and Customs

Food riots and other disturbances were indicators of wider social tensions. Seven men were killed following an attack on food stores in the towns of Caernarfon and Carmarthen in the 1750s, while the years 1794–6 and 1800–1 were particularly riotous, occurring as they did at a time when the price of corn increased faster than wages. As the poor spent 60 per cent of their earnings on bread, the increase in prices caused extensive hardship. However, economic conditions only go so far in explaining such unrest. According to E. P. Thompson, the poor operated according to a 'moral economy', in which attitudes to food prices (and much else) were determined by ill-defined but influential ideas of community justice.[7] These ideas were representative of a deep divide between patrician and plebeian cultures, the one monopolizing political power and the other channelling protest. The power of ideas of popular justice can be gauged by the extent of unrest in 1795 – 'the year of the housewives' revolt' – when the iron town of Merthyr Tydfil was briefly occupied by an insurgent crowd. Such ideas stood in opposition to the increasingly dominant market economy that was progressively recalibrating social and economic relationships. The clash between different conceptions of economy continued to shape relationships in rural society at least until the middle of the nineteenth century.

The 1790s was a decade of transition and particular tension. According to Gwyn A. Williams, the rural districts of mid and north Wales experienced their 'first crisis of modernization' in that decade.[8] This crisis found expression in the remarkable myth of the existence of Welsh-speaking Indians in North America. The context for this engagement with North America was the wars between Britain and France of 1793–1815, which accelerated the crises of modernization. Nevertheless, loyalism outstripped radicalism during that war, as shown by popular support for organizations like the militia and the Volunteers.

Most radicals who had been inspired by the ideals of the American and French revolutions now either recanted or made a public show of doing so. Others, like Morgan John Rhys, emigrated to the USA, where he founded a Welsh settlement along progressive lines. At home, anxiety bred xenophobia and distrust. The French military incursion at Fishguard in 1797 was tangible evidence of an invasion threat to Wales, and it was used by groups such as the Methodists to establish their loyal credentials. Memorials to military heroes were erected across Wales, such as the Navy Temple at Monmouth in 1800.

Beliefs, Knowledge, and Mentalities

The official religion of Wales – the Church of England – was the institution of social elites and of a decreasing proportion of other Welsh people. However, it is from within that church that the movement known as the 'Methodist Revival' began from about 1735.[9] This socially and politically conservative evangelicalism was dominated by Calvinistic theology. The revival ended in the late 1790s, although its influence on Wales led to the founding of the Calvinistic Methodist denomination in 1811, and its activities revitalized old dissenting denominations, such as the Baptists and the Independents. Meanwhile, migration to the USA enabled the creation of transatlantic religious networks among the Baptists and Methodists.

For many people, literacy was acquired in the context of organized religion. The Anglican rector Griffith Jones established circulating schools in the 1740s in which thousands were taught to read the Bible, and these schools are credited with making the majority of people functionally literate in Welsh by the end of the century. This initiative was taken forward by the Methodist preacher Thomas Charles, who initiated a Sunday school movement in the late 1780s. However, for some people books and reading meshed with older mentalities and practices – such as witchcraft and magic – in less predictable ways.[10] Welsh was the language of the majority in this period, but English was increasingly visible in public life.

The dispersed population and the lack of a national capital meant that the newspaper press was slow to develop. During the eighteenth century, the lack of a domestic press entailed dependence on newspapers produced in

England.[11] Periodicals, especially those of a religious nature, were published, and the country acquired its first Welsh-language political periodical in *Y Cylchgrawn Cyn-mraeg* (1793–4), edited by the Baptist radical Morgan John Rhys, but domestic newspapers were a product of the first decade of the nineteenth century. The first of these, *The Cambrian*, was published in Swansea from 1804, and it is significant that its title spoke to wider ambitions than those of the town alone. Swansea – the largest Welsh town by 1801 – was a commercial centre with international networks centred on the local copper industry. Its middle classes established scientific institutions, especially the Royal Institution of South Wales from 1835, and in 1848 the town was visited by the annual conference of the British Association.[12] Science is a neglected facet of Welsh culture. Even at the same time as Nonconformity was expanding in the middle of the nineteenth century, geology and the emerging theory of evolution (co-formulated by Alfred Russel Wallace, who had taught science classes at Neath in the 1840s) was undermining its epistemological foundations.

As Wales developed into a site of literary and artistic tourism in the eighteenth century, a particular type of knowledge about the country was produced in the form of 'tours' and landscape painting. Authors such as William Gilpin, Daniel Defoe, and Michael Faraday – as well as painters such as Paul Sandby, Julius Caesar Ibbetson, and J. M. W. Turner – created powerful literary and visual representations of the country and its people. Artists who 'discovered' Wales and were preoccupied with ruins and the 'primitive' painted picturesque and romantic landscapes that rejected modern life, but these were not the only visual representations of Wales to be produced during this period. Urban and industrial society and the new social classes it created were also memorialized by artists; moreover, in the 1830s and 1840s photography combined science and art to allow the recording of the present in an entirely new way. This development was signalled by Henry Fox Talbot's book, *The Pencil of Nature* (1844).

The recovery of the Welsh past that had begun in eighteenth-century London continued among 'patriotic' Anglican social elites in Wales in the 1830s and 1840s, including such luminaries as Lady Llanover and Lady Charlotte Guest, who celebrated Welsh musical and literary heritage, as shown by the publications of the Welsh Manuscripts Society from 1837. New histories were written, and from 1846 archaeological inquiry was published in the Cambrian Archaeological Association's periodical, *Archaeologia Cambrensis*. Antiquarianism filled the gap created by the absence of a Welsh university. As well as religious writings and antiquarian scholarship, however, an increasing body of 'useful' knowledge that was related to secular developments in contemporary society appeared in Welsh during the 1840s and 1850s.

Industry, Empire, and Slavery

Wales was integrated in international trading networks and the country was implicated in developing imperial relationships. The Welsh benefited both directly and indirectly from slavery and the slave trade, which was conducted principally through Bristol and Liverpool. James Rogers from Pembrokeshire, for example, became one of Bristol's most successful slave traders; between 1785 and 1793 he was the second most important slave trader in Bristol, and the twelfth most important across the British Isles. Thomas Williams ('the Copper King') of Anglesey was intimately involved in the African trade, while Swansea's copper industry produced copper bracelets that were used for buying slaves in Africa and copper sheets that protected the bottoms of slave ships in tropical waters. In 1781 Richard Pennant took control of slave plantations in Jamaica, from which money flowed to north Wales to be invested in the slate industry and the building of Penrhyn Castle. The slave trade provided economic opportunities for both seamen and traders.

Opposition to the slave trade was mainly on religious grounds (although not all Christians opposed it), and in the 1790s there were about twenty petitions to parliament from Wales demanding abolition. Abolition of the slave trade (i.e. the buying and selling of slaves) was made illegal in 1807, although slavery continued in British territories until the 1830s. Such campaigns had implications for an emerging consumer culture, as luxury goods such as sugar and rum were products of slave economies. While some Welsh people benefited from slavery in the West Indies, individuals returning to Wales following service in the East India Company ('nabobs') brought wealth from Asia to buy opulent properties, land, and luxury goods at home. Furthermore, Welsh men and women were compromised by other engagements with empire, not least through missionary work in India, Madagascar, and elsewhere.

Fortunes accrued from slavery were used by some Bristol merchants to invest in the metallurgical industries of south Wales. From the 1770s the iron industry received a major boost from such investment, a spur that was intensified during the wars with France in 1793–1815, when the metallurgical industries benefited hugely from the demands of a war economy. British patriotism during the French wars was not selfless: war and loyalism brought material benefits to industrialists and workers alike, albeit not in equal measure. Cyfarthfa Iron Works, for example, gained a reputation for good quality naval cannon, a fact recognized when Admiral Nelson visited the works in 1802. Industry adjusted to a peace-time economy more successfully after 1815 than did agriculture, and by 1851 the iron-producing centre of Merthyr Tydfil was the largest town in Wales. By the 1840s coal had become the powerhouse of industry in the south and in the north-east, whereas the second marquis of Bute developed the port of Cardiff and laid the foundations for the town's future growth as a global coal-exporting port. In fact, we can understand the Industrial Revolution in terms of a fundamental change in the energy base of society that, in turn, sustained technological and demographic growth.

Rebellion, Riot, and Reform

The post-war economic disruption after 1815 was intensified by the effects of the eruption of Tambora volcano on Sumbawa Island in Indonesia which devastated European agriculture, leading to 1816 being known as 'the year without a summer'. It is a reminder of the interrelatedness of Wales not only with an international economy but also with a global ecosystem. The decades after 1815 created a divide in Welsh society, between the fortunes of agriculture and those of industry. This occurred against a background of unprecedented demographic growth, with the population doubling in the first half of the nineteenth century, from about 586,000 in 1801 to 1.16 million in 1851, mainly as a result of net immigration into Wales from workers, mostly from England, seeking employment in the industrial towns.

The benefits of industrialization percolated downwards unevenly in the form of employment and access to a mass consumer culture, but relentless manual labour and the exploitation of men, women, and children was the dark side of industrialization. Government inquiries catalogued the shockingly brutalizing effect of such work on young lives, while unplanned urban development with inadequate sanitation and poor water supply created disease-ridden environments. The most dramatic consequences were the cholera 'visitations' of 1832 and 1849, but other diseases were more prevalent. In this context, the Public Health Act of 1848 was a more significant milestone than political reform.

Nevertheless, protest movements emerged and mass protest and political agitation dominated the 1830s and 1840s. This is usually portrayed as the emergence of class-consciousness among working people. The Reform Crisis of 1831–2 witnessed riots at Carmarthen and an armed uprising at Merthyr Tydfil, but the Reform Act of 1832 enfranchised only the male middle classes and defined women as being outside the political nation. Disillusionment with this result and with the social and economic conditions of the 1830s led to the creation of the first mass political movement, Chartism. The unsuccessful armed Chartist revolt at Newport in November 1839 ensured that industrial south Wales was seen as a hotbed of sedition. In rural Wales the long agricultural depression after 1815 caused widespread discontent and precipitated mass protests between 1839 and 1844. In these years the cross-dressing male protesters of the Rebecca movement mobilized community solidarity to attack profiteering practices in the regulation of roads through the charging of tolls. The imposition of martial law was seriously canvassed in 1843. A French writer believed that only a novelist such as Sir Walter Scott could do justice to the disturbances, and, indeed, the events were fictionalized in French in a serialized romantic novel in 1844.[13]

Government responses to social unrest in the 1830s and 1840s were focused on a combination of repression and obtaining systematic knowledge about this unruly society. That knowledge was used to implement piecemeal reform and systems of control. The reports of the Education Commissioners of 1847, the notorious 'Blue Books', deployed colonial stereotypes to devalue the Welsh language and depict the people as an uncivilized multitude in need of anglicization. This was also a gendered view, with women identified by the commissioners as being particularly immoral. These reports embody the creation of 'authoritative' knowledge as part of a process of discipline and control. They demonstrate one of the key contradictions of the position of Wales in British society: it was a beneficiary of empire while, at the same time, its language and culture were 'othered' by metropolitans. The contradictions of this 'subaltern imperialism' (as it might be described) were never fully resolved, but they became more visible because of the emergence of a distinctively Welsh public sphere that found expression in a diverse print culture by the 1840s.

Nation and Peoples

By the late 1840s the period of mass revolts was over, notwithstanding a brief flurry of agitation in 1848. As the age of rail transport, the telegraph, and the mass newspaper press dawned, the parameters of Welsh life changed decisively.[14] Industrial capitalism changed experiences of time, as clock time became the dominant way of partitioning the day and increasingly determined the rhythms of life and work. One commentator claimed that railways 'will gradually break down national peculiarities' and that, in another fifty years, south Wales would be '"revolutionized" in a peaceful sense'.[15] Wales was, indeed, revolutionized by the transformative power of new types of communication in the middle of the nineteenth century, but the prediction of the gradual 'break down [of] national peculiarities' – a theme much favoured by English observers – was considerably wide of the mark. Just as the invention of Britain as a national community was facilitated by dramatic changes in the speed and extent of communication, so was the re-imagining of Wales.[16] In 1845 Léon Faucher, a French economist and politician, could write that although Wales had no separate political existence from England, 'the principality is still a nation' ('la principauté est encore une nation'). 'We have treated the Welsh as English,' he wrote, 'and they are something else entirely; their legal status does not correspond with their actual condition.'[17] That claim would be confirmed in the second half of the nineteenth century.

Nevertheless, ideas of nationality in a non-state nation were problematic. The events of the 1840s led to the creation of a powerful myth of 'the Nonconformist nation'; in 1843, for example, it was claimed that 'everyone knows that Nonconformists are the body of the Welsh people' ('gŵyr pawb mai Ymneillduwyr ydyw y corff o bobl Cymru').[18] Sometimes statements of this kind have been mistaken for descriptions of statistical reality, whereas more properly they should be seen as a rhetorical positioning of Nonconformity vis-à-vis the Anglican Church; this rhetoric was intended to legitimize one tradition of Protestantism and delegitimize the other. Following a series of religious revivals in the first half of the century, a census demonstrated that Nonconformists accounted for approximately 80 per cent of worshippers in Wales in 1851; but about half the population did not attend a place of worship at that time. Sectarian divisions within Protestantism increasingly developed along a church-chapel alignment from mid-century, although anti-Catholicism was one virulent antagonism that provided a focus of unity. The demarcation of identity boundaries came up against the diverse reality of Welsh society, whether in religious terms (Protestant, Catholic, Jew, unbelievers), in-migration from Ireland and England, or in the varied ways in which individuals attempted to understand their world. Increasingly frequent anti-Irish riots between 1826 and 1850 were a sign of how ethnic diversity caused tensions.

In 1850 some Welsh people lived in an agrarian society that would have been recognizable to their forebears in 1700, whereas a substantial and growing minority now lived in a technologically advanced, and culturally and linguistically diverse, urban society. Those who migrated from one to the other had experience of both realities. At the end of this period, therefore, the complex counter-currents that characterized Welsh life intensified, rather than diminished, under the impact of increasing urbanization and industrialization.

Notes

1. Geraint H. Jenkins, 'Wales in the Eighteenth Century', in *A Companion to Eighteenth-Century Britain*, ed. H. T. Dickinson (Oxford: Oxford University Press, 2002), 392–402; Philip Jenkins, 'Between Two Revolutions: Wales, 1642–1780', in *The People of Wales: A Millennium History*, ed. Gareth Elwyn Jones and Dai Smith (Llandysul: Gomer Press, 1999), 83–110; Neil Evans, 'As Rich as California: Opening and Closing the Frontier in Wales 1780–1870', in *The People of Wales*, ed. Jones and Smith, 111–44; Prys Morgan, 'From a Death to a View: The Hunt for the Welsh Past in the Romantic Period', in *The Invention of Tradition*, ed. Eric Hobsbawm and Terence Ranger (Cambridge: Cambridge University Press, 1983), 43–100.

2. Prys Morgan, 'A Private Space: Autobiography and Individuality in Eighteenth- and Early Nineteenth-Century Wales', in *From Medieval to Modern Wales: Historical Essays in Honour of Kenneth O. Morgan and Ralph A. Griffiths*, ed. R. R. Davies and Geraint H. Jenkins (Cardiff: University of Wales Press, 2004), 160–74; Russell Davies, *Hope and Heartbreak: A Social History of Wales and the Welsh, 1776–1871* (Cardiff: University of Wales Press, 2005).

3. Walter Davies, *The Agriculture and Domestic Economy of North Wales* (London: Sherwood, Neely and Jones, 1811), 83, 357.

4. Thomas Pennant, *The History of the Parishes of Whiteford and Holywell* (London: B. and J. White, 1796), 246.

5. Peter Lord, *The Visual Culture of Wales: Imaging the Nation* (Cardiff: University of Wales Press, 2000).

6. David W. Howell, *The Rural Poor in Eighteenth-Century Wales* (Cardiff: University of Wales Press, 2000).

7. E. P. Thompson, *Customs in Common* (London: Merlin Press, 1991).

8. Gwyn A. Williams, *In Search of Beulah Land: The Welsh and the Atlantic Revolution* (London: Croom Helm, 1980), 39–40.

9. Derec Llwyd Morgan, *The Great Awakening in Wales*, trans. Dyfnallt Morgan (London: Epworth Press, 1988).

10. Richard Suggett, *A History of Magic and Witchcraft in Wales* (Stroud: History Press, 2008).

11. Marion Löffler, *Welsh Responses to the French Revolution: Press and Public Discourse, 1789–1802* (Cardiff: University of Wales Press, 2012).

12. Louise Miskell, 'Intelligent Town': An Urban History of Swansea, 1780–1855* (Cardiff: University of Wales Press, 2006).

13. [John Lemoine], 'Lettres sur les affaires extérieures: troubles dans le pays de Galles – Rebecca et ses filles', *Revue des Deux Mondes* 3 (1843): 1031; 'Le mystère de Rebecca: épisodes des derniers troubles de la principauté de Galles', *Revue Britannique*, 5th series, 19–20 (1844): 160–99, 403–33.

14. Paul O'Leary, *Claiming the Streets: Processions and Urban Culture in South Wales, c. 1830–1880* (Cardiff: University of Wales Press, 2012).

15. *Cardiff and Merthyr Guardian*, 24 July 1847.

16. Paul O'Leary, 'The Languages of Patriotism in Mid-Nineteenth Century Wales', in *The Welsh Language and Social Domains in the Nineteenth Century*, ed. Geraint H. Jenkins (Cardiff: University of Wales Press, 2000), 533–60.

17. Léon Faucher, 'Études sur l'Angleterre: les classes inférieures', *Revue des Deux Mondes* 11 (1845): 40–53.

18. 'Idwal', 'Yr Eglwys Wladol', *Y Dysgedydd* 22 (1843): 256.

14

Antiquarianism and Enlightenment in the Eighteenth Century

MARY-ANN CONSTANTINE

Testun gwylofain ydyw adrodd helbulon a gorthrymderau'r *Cymru* ym mhob Oes a gwlâd er pan gymmyscwyd y Iaith yn Nhŵr *Babel*.[1]

(It is a tearful matter to recount the trials and oppressions of the Welsh people through all ages and in all lands since the language was first mixed in the Tower of Babel.)

In 1716 a twenty-three-year-old clergyman named Theophilus Evans published *Drych y Prif Oesoedd* ('The Mirror of the First Ages'), an ebullient history of the Welsh people from the earliest times. From the post-Troy arrival of Brutus on British shores, and through fierce but invariably doomed resistance to wave upon wave of subsequent invasions, Evans tells the story of a nation battling to preserve its linguistic and religious identity. Packed with bold similes and stirring dialogue (techniques borrowed from his classical sources), he brings the distant past vividly into the present to reconnect his audience with their antique and honourable lineage. In a nice inversion of the age-old modesty topos, Evans tells his readers that everything else to be read on the subject is a tissue of lies, and that he has gone to immense personal trouble in writing this book. If they don't like it, he says, 'gosodent y Bai arnynt eu hunain, nid arnaf i' ('let them put the blame on themselves, and not me').[2]

Readers did like it. A revised and much expanded version of the work appeared in 1740, and from then on it continued to be read and reprinted well into the nineteenth century, with some twenty-one editions appearing by 1902.[3] *Drych y Prif Oesoedd* shaped the way many people understood the Welsh past and influenced later writers such as Iolo Morganwg – who, though he would have no truck with the Galfridian 'lies' of the Brutus story, found the notion of Welsh Protestantism as the continuation of the original British Christianity highly congenial. Evans also had a profound and more immediate influence on his own grandson and namesake, Theophilus Jones, who would, nearly a century on, publish another important historical work, a dense, painstakingly researched, two-volume *History of the County of Brecknock* (1805–9).

More than one critic has noted that eighteenth-century Wales is rather nicely book-ended by the two Theophiluses, and that some of the period's distinctive cultural features and developments are played out in the differences and the similarities between them.[4] From Evans's bold story of a nation written in lively Welsh, to Jones's dense account of a single county written in English, we move from confidence in the sufficiency of classical texts and native tradition to explain the past (Tacitus, Caesar, Giraldus, Geoffrey), into a world where sources are many and varied – where buildings, objects, landscape features, and oral testimony all combine with written evidence to create a layered summoning of place through centuries. What both writers share, however, is an intense relationship with the deep past, and a belief, whatever the language of the publication, that Welsh is both the vehicle and the guardian of a particular quality of ancientness.

Given that both men are in some sense historians rather than writers of literature as we tend to understand it now, the assertion of a shared curiosity about Britain's past might seem rather underwhelming. The past, after all, is what historians 'do'. Nevertheless, quite apart from the difficulty of deciding where history writing ends and creative writing begins (accounts of *Drych y Prif Oesoedd* tend to note rather patronizingly that it is now 'no longer read as history' but can be safely approached as one of the period's literary triumphs), an obsession with the early Welsh past is the driving force behind much eighteenth-century Welsh literature, however broadly or narrowly defined. This chapter aims to give a general sense of how certain key themes run through a broad nexus of texts and genres, and suggests that a distinctively eighteenth-century concern to collect and connect with the past helped Welsh writers in both languages to develop ideas about national literary history. The antiquarian movement and contemporary literary production are powerfully intertwined.[5]

Ancient Britons in a New British State

As in the early modern period, the need to explore and proclaim the antiquity of Welsh tradition was born of recent political pressures. It was in part a response to the Act of Union with Scotland in 1707, which made 'Britannia' a single entity for the first time since the Roman conquest and entailed a certain amount of repositioning in Wales's relationship with the rest of the United Kingdom. In 1715, a year after the succession of George I and the start of the

Hanoverian dynasty, the Society of Ancient Britons was formed amongst the London Welsh, partly for charitable purposes (providing bursaries for Welsh apprentices, founding what would become the Welsh School at Gray's Inn), but also, very clearly, to mark the distance between the loyal and Protestant Welsh and the more volatile – and Catholic – Scottish and Irish. The fact that Queen Caroline's birthday fell conveniently on 1 March allowed for demonstrative expressions of support for the Crown coupled with Welsh patriotic sentiment through parades and ceremonies, as well as through poems and sermons in Welsh and English.[6]

Most early eighteenth-century 'Ancient Britons' understood that Wales had a unique role in the British project, being the 'First Inhabitants' of the island and the preservers of a primitive form of Christianity which bypassed 'popish' history altogether. Some accounts stressed an early intermingling of blood (and even, surprisingly, of language) with the invading Saxons, and most took for granted the inherent Welshness of the post-Tudor monarchy. Nehemiah Griffith's poem *The Leek* presented to the queen and the Ancient Britons in 1717, is a good example of how even the Welsh/Saxon conflicts of the early British past might be reconfigured to strengthen bonds in the present, creating a carefully positioned and thoroughly contemporary anti-Jacobite allegory.[7] Even outside the London-centred Welsh networks, an anglophone Welsh writer such as Wrexham-based Jane Brereton could put native history to good loyalist use and find in those waves of Roman and Saxon conquest a kind of providential purification process which would result in Hanoverian British civility.[8] Not all eighteenth-century Ancient Britons viewed the past with such equanimity, however: the St David's Day sermons of the scholar-preacher Moses Williams drew rather on the traditional 'British histories' (*brudion*, or *brytiau*) of the popular Welsh-language almanacs and ballads, to recall with anger the perfidies of the Saxon conquest and bemoan the loss of Welsh territories and the modern encroachment of English. But whether loyal or resistant, the literature of this period appears constantly responsive to and in negotiation with English/British perceptions of what Wales and the Welsh might signify.[9]

Behind the buoyant language of the *Drych*, then, are several underlying anxieties, most of which intensify in the course of the century. A key factor is the question of religion and the position of the Anglican Church in Wales, increasingly in competition with, and then threatened by, the rise of Nonconformism, and in particular a brand of Calvinist Methodism which would come by the nineteenth century to be perceived as peculiarly Welsh. Language, too, is an issue. Welsh remained the country's majority language for most of the eighteenth century, but the literate classes (not only the London Welsh, but many of the native gentry) chose increasingly to speak and write in English – though many existed comfortably enough in both. Seen from within a Welsh-language perspective, such shifts mark the onset of significant anglicization and even at the time were viewed with despair as part of a broader narrative of linguistic decline. Yet the collisions and compromises of biculturalism were far from unproductive, and this is an aspect of eighteenth-century Welsh literature which has received little recognition from either side.

The year of union, 1707, saw a different kind of gathering-together of the diverse cultures of the British Isles with the publication of Edward Lhuyd's *Archaeologica Britannica*. An extraordinary polymath, Lhuyd (1660–1709) pursued studies into botany, geology, antiquities and philology, and became keeper of the Ashmolean museum in Oxford.[10] The *Glossography*, which formed the first part of a much larger projected work, brought together examples of Cornish, Breton, Welsh, Scots-Gaelic, Irish, and Manx, outlining the linguistic affinities between them and giving scientific form to the concept of an original Celtic language. The notion of a shared Celtic inheritance linking the western peripheries (and, following the theories of the Breton writer Paul Pezron, emphasizing an original Celtic culture throughout Europe) ran directly counter to the prevailing politico-religious fault lines, which set a Protestant Hanoverian Britishness against the Catholic fringe.[11] Although 'Celticism' did not really gather ideological impetus until the nineteenth and twentieth centuries, the idea of a British 'Celtic' past would both enrich and complicate relations between England and Wales throughout the eighteenth century.

Much of Lhuyd's material was the result of an extraordinary four-year tour begun in 1697, taking in every county in Wales and parts of northern Ireland, Scotland, southern Ireland, Cornwall, and Brittany (where he was briefly arrested and imprisoned as a spy). Lhuyd's impact on Welsh intellectual life reverberates down the century, from the widespread influence of his antiquarian researches, many of which fed directly into Edmund Gibson's edition of Camden's *Britannia* (1695),[12] to more specific and significant points of contact: in the bitter cold winter of 1775, the young stonemason Edward Williams, who would be better known as the bard Iolo Morganwg, wrote to ask his father to send his precious copy of the *Archaeologica* down to Faversham in Kent, where midnight studies into 'British' etymologies were helping him endure his English exile. Lhuyd's early death in 1709 was a bitter loss to many branches of scholarship, and the vast collection of material he left behind, though extensively mined from his manuscripts, was never fully exploited.

Among the contributors to the *Glossography* was Moses Williams, who had been one of Lhuyd's assistants at the Ashmolean. One of Williams's own schemes was an ambitious but unsuccessful attempt to gather together the earliest known Welsh manuscript texts and get them printed. His *Proposals for Printing by Subscription a Collection of Writings in the Welsh Tongue, to the Beginning of the Sixteenth Century* (1719) sounded a note of frustration and alarm that would ring through Welsh literature for decades to come:

> The great Distance of the several Libraries, where Welsh manuscripts are preserved, and the Difficulty of Access to some of them, have been no small Hindrance to the Improvement of the History of the Ancient Britains [sic], as well as to a competent Knowledge of their Language, so necessary to an Understanding of British Antiquities: Nor can it be denied that all Manuscripts (whether in publick Places or private Hands) are liable to be embezzled or destroyed.[13]

'Welsh Augustans' and the Mid-Century Celtic Revival

That desire to get early manuscript material into print becomes something of an eighteenth-century leitmotif. And yet conscious as authors were of the fragility of their manuscript inheritance (and familiar as many were with stubborn or shamefully neglectful gentry owners of valuable texts), the literary 'scene' was still markedly manuscript-based. Although the last two decades of the century would see a sharp rise in the volume of Welsh printed works, the continued predominance of a culture of lending and copying, alongside the presence of local *eisteddfodau,* means that questions of literary prestige and influence cannot simply be tracked through successive publications. Reputations could still be made in eighteenth-century Wales without going into print, and authors from a surprisingly broad range of social classes participated in the creation of a literary tradition.[14] Copying manuscripts also kept writers and composers of poetry in touch, not only with their peers but with an earlier literary inheritance.[15]

Nevertheless, the early medieval material became increasingly opaque, and the collapse of the old bardic system of poetic patronage had broken the continuity of key strands in the literary tradition. While poets from Gwynedd to Glamorgan still practised, and handed on, the more complex and tightly prescribed forms of the *canu caeth* (strict-metre poetry), poetic output moved increasingly towards the looser, often song-based, metrics of the *canu rhydd* (poetry and song in free metres).[16] By the middle of the century, attempts to recover the beginnings of Welsh literature begin to feel like a form of salvage. An early such attempt was Lewis Morris's slim anthology *Tlysau yr Hen Oesoedd* ('Gems of Past Ages', 1735), printed on Morris's own letterpress in Holyhead and primarily aimed at literate Welsh speakers. Brief captions to the Welsh texts teasingly offered non-Welsh speakers glimpses (but no translations) of 'Things which very few English readers have any Knowledge of, except our Antiquaries, our MSS having never been made publick, and in a great measure destroyed, by the Folly of some, and the Envy of others.'[17] The anthology itself is a curious mixture; snippets of 'druidic verses' (the gnomic *Eira Mynydd* stanzas) rub shoulders with entertaining anecdotes and various triadic pearls of wisdom attributed to Taliesin, 'father of bards'. Morris seems to have intended the *Tlysau* to appear regularly, but only the one issue ever appeared. The devotion proclaimed on its title page to 'Cywreinrwydd yr Hên Frutaniaid' ('the intricate beauties of the Ancient Britons') would, however, focus his energies for much of his life. Many of his ideas were gathered into his unpublished *magnum opus*, the 'Celtic Remains', which was deposited in the library of the Welsh School after his death, to become another potent instance of manuscript material exerting influence on subsequent generations.

Lewis was the eldest of four brothers, sons of an Anglesey cooper and farmer. Of the four, only William remained at home, working for the Customs at Holyhead and pursuing an interest in botany. Lewis settled in Cardiganshire, where he acted as steward for the Crown, fighting numerous battles with local squires over rights to lead mines; he was also a surveyor and produced naval charts of the Welsh coast. John joined the navy and died in action in 1740; and Richard, who had moved to London in 1722, finally obtained a post as a clerk in the navy office, where he was excellently placed to be a purveyor of news and information, and rose to a position of rank. It was Richard who, in 1751, founded the Honourable Society of the Cymmrodorion ('First Inhabitants'), which professed aims more avowedly cultural than the Society of Ancient Britons and had stronger connections with literary communities in Wales; they helped to sponsor several publications and continued to support the Welsh School in London.

The letters between the Morris brothers are acknowledged classics of eighteenth-century Welsh literature.[18] Lively, gossipy, they mix commentary on national politics with the latest news of their fruit trees, their children, their cats; they catalogue, in exhaustive detail, their illnesses and frustrations;

they can be lewd and wickedly funny. Above all they are brilliantly bilingual, punning and playing a kind of verbal hide-and-seek – so that shifts in mid-sentence from English to Welsh often reveal more than just a change of language.

Early in 1760, for example, Lewis Morris read extracts from the newly published 'Fragments of Ancient Poetry' printed anonymously in the *Gentleman's Magazine*: they were the precursors of the more extensive, and hugely successful, Ossianic poetry of James Macpherson. Morris curtly dismissed them, twice over, as 'but a modern song . . . Nid fel cywyddau ac awdlau'r Britaniaid' ('Not like the poems and odes of the Britons').[19] The words *cywydd* and *awdl* here are precise, and essentially untranslatable, terms from Welsh poetic tradition and reinforce his point. Later he would complain:

> In gods name what title has such stuff to be called Poetry without rhyme or numbers and mostly by oral tradition and yet in the highlands of North Britain this is called versification. Irish all over and bombast![20]

'North Britain' is a sharp reminder of the Act of Union of 1707; 'Irish', of course, is quite simply used here as a term of abuse. The Morrises' response to the 'Ossian crisis', which provoked both sceptical and enthusiastic interest in literature in the Celtic languages generally, was to retaliate with home-grown scholarship. The first scholarly edition of Welsh medieval texts was the work of a talented but ill-starred member of their circle, the clergyman Evan Evans ('Ieuan Brydydd Hir').[21] *Some Specimens of the Poetry of the Antient Welsh Bards* (1764) – a complicated tripartite text in English, Latin, and Welsh – offered texts from the Age of the Princes (1100–1300) and attempted an overview of Welsh poetry from the sixth to the sixteenth century. Though *Specimens* was partly driven by Evans's anger at the neglect of a national literature at 'great risque of mouldering away',[22] his presentation of early Welsh poetry to an English-speaking readership was defensive, polite, and cautious, stressing the difficulty of translation and interpretation across the centuries. The Latin dissertation contained the first ever published translation of a few stanzas of a text now considered the foundation of Welsh literary tradition – the newly rediscovered 'epic Poem in the British called *Gododin*, equal at least to the Iliad, Aeneid or Paradise Lost'.[23]

Evans, who corresponded with the likes of Daines Barrington, Thomas Gray, and Thomas Percy, was an important conduit for knowledge of Welsh texts amongst English literati with antiquarian interests, and can be credited with a key role in the eighteenth-century Celtic revival in English literature.[24]

Its most famous production, perhaps, was Gray's ode 'The Bard' (1757), which ventriloquized, for generations to come, the ultimate act of bardic Welsh resistance to the conquering forces of Edward I:

> Dear lost companions of my tuneful art,
> Dear, as the light that visits these sad eyes,
> Dear, as the ruddy drops that warm my heart,
> Ye died amidst your dying country's cries—
> No more I weep. They do not sleep.
> On yonder cliffs, a grisly band,
> I see them sit, they linger yet,
> Avengers of their native land:
> With me in dreadful harmony they join,
> And weave with bloody hands the tissue of thy line.[25]

Gray's poem – in English, by an Englishman – staged the dramatic (and perfectly non-historical, though many preferred to believe otherwise) massacre of the Welsh poets by an English king, and the defiant suicide of the 'Last Bard'. From the 1760s it became another 'tearful' episode in the traditional list of oppressions against the Welsh, and 'Edward the Bardicide', as Iolo Morganwg called him, loomed large in the minds of Welsh writers who had somehow to negotiate the supposed death of a poetic tradition while keeping it very much alive.[26] Though Gray's poem did end up as a set text for translation into Welsh at an eisteddfod in 1798, it is arguable that the 'bardomania' of the 1760s and beyond was an inherently anglophone phenomenon, a form of tradition-creation for an audience eager to exoticize Welsh landscapes and the Welsh past. The theme – a defiant figure in a craggy north Welsh landscape – lent itself perfectly to visual interpretation, inspiring dramatic paintings by Thomas Jones, Philippe de Loutherbourg, William Blake, and John Martin.[27] De Loutherbourg's *Welsh Bard* would become especially widely known after it was used as the frontispiece to another work of antiquarian recovery, Edward Jones's *Musical and Poetical Relicks of the Welsh Bards* (1784), an influential collection of poems and songs which would reappear as the much-expanded *Bardic Museum* of 1802.

Evan Evans was himself a fine poet. One of his best-known pieces is the short sequence of *englynion* composed after visiting Basaleg, the ruined hall of Ifor Hael, patron of the fourteenth-century poet Dafydd ap Gwilym:

> Llys Ifor hael, gwael yw'r gwedd, – yn garnau
> mewn gwerni mae'n gorwedd;

drain ac ysgall mall a'i medd,
mieri lle bu mawredd.

Yno nid oes awenydd, – na beirddion,
    na byrddau llawenydd,
nac aur yn ei magwyrydd,
na mael, na gŵr hael a'i rhydd.

I Ddafydd gelfydd ei gân – oer ofid
    roi Ifor mewn graean;
mwy echrys fod ei lys lân
yn lleoedd i'r dylluan.

Er bri arglwyddi byr glod, – eu mawredd
    a'u muriau sy'n darfod;
lle rhyfedd i falchedd fod
yw teiau ar y tywod.[28]

(The hall of Ifor Hael, ill-looking
stone-heap in a meadow,
gone under brambles and the curse of thistle;
briars where once was glory.

The muse does not sing there – there are no poets
no tables loaded with delight;
no gold inside its precinct
no bright armour, no generous giver.

And for Dafydd the crafter of song – cold grief,
as Ifor goes under the earth;
what horror that his bright hall
is now a place for owls.

Though lords shine with transient glory,
their greatness, these walls, must collapse.
Astonishing that pride should come to lie
In houses on the shingle.)

This is one of the century's loveliest poems, perfectly balanced between a
native medieval tradition (the dark, ruined halls of the Cynddylan stanzas in
the Llywarch Hen sequence) and the contemporary English mode of ruins
and retrospection. It reads, indeed, like a lyrical, elliptical version of John
Dyer's much earlier evocation of these same themes in his description of the
ruined castle on the slopes of 'Grongar Hill' (1727):

And there the pois'nous adder breeds,
Conceal'd in ruins, moss, and weeds;
While, ever and anon, there falls
Huge heap of hoary moulder'd walls.
Yet time has seen, that lifts the low,
And level lays the lofty brow,
Has seen this broken pile complete,
Big with the vanity of state;
But transient is the smile of Fate!
A little rule, a little sway,
A sunbeam in a winter's day,
Is all the proud and mighty have
Between the cradle and the grave.[29]

After his death in 1789, Evan Evans's superb manuscript collection went to Paul Panton of Anglesey, where, at the turn of the century, it would be extensively mined by the editors of the *Myvyrian Archaiology* (1801–7).

There were other literary hopes for the period, and the energetic Morrises nurtured many of them, both intellectually and financially. They included poets such as Robert Hughes (Robin Ddu o Fôn), whom Lewis attempted to bring into his household as a youth, 'i wneuthur Merddin neu Daliesin o honaw, ond fe naccaodd ei rieni ei ollwng' ('to make a Myrddin or a Taliesin of him, but his parents refused to let him go').[30] And in 1752 Lewis Morris had written to Evan Evans of another discovery:

> I propose to you a correspondent, a friend of mine, an Anglesey man, who will be glad of your acquaintance and I dare say *you* of *his*. Especially when you have seen some of his performances. His name is *Gronow* Owen . . . He is but lately commenced a Welsh poet, and the first ode he ever wrote was in Imitation of your ode on Melancholy, having no Grammar to go by. His 'Cywydd y Farn fawr' is the best thing I ever read in Welsh.[31]

Goronwy Owen (1723–69), an Anglican curate and schoolmaster, became known for his ambitious Miltonic poems on grand subjects in the neoclassical tradition. A key figure in what Saunders Lewis identified as a 'School of Welsh Augustans', his poetry is a striking demonstration of the ways in which native Welsh traditions at this point offered an especially close fit with dominant trends in English: most notably in the poetry of praise and lament, but also the more conversational modes.[32] He is, or perhaps was, considered one of Wales's most accomplished poets, although his high, often obscure, style ('excessively admired and imitated in the nineteenth century')[33] has not weathered particularly well. Nevertheless, there is a sweeping energy to pieces like 'Cywydd y Farn Fawr' ('Cywydd on Judgment Day'), his major attempt at the required Welsh epic, which was published, with extensive annotations and comments, in the Morrises' 1763 anthology *Diddanwch Teuluaidd*:

> Rhoir gawr nerthol, a dolef
> Mal Clych, yn entrych y Nef
> Llef mawr, goruwch llif Mor-ryd
> Uwch dyfroedd Aberoedd Byd
> Gosteg a roir, ac Ust! Draw
> Dwrf Rhaiadr; darfu'r rhuaw:
> Angel a gân, hoywlan lef
> Felyslais nefawl oslef.[34]

> (A huge shout goes up, a cry
> Like bells in highest Heaven;
> A great voice over the flow of oceans,
> Above the waters of the world's estuaries
> Proclaiming a silence and Hush! Yonder
> The rush and roar of waterfall is stilled:
> An angel sings, a clear-bright sound,
> Sweetvoiced, the tones of heaven.)

Great things were expected of Goronwy Owen, but like Evan Evans he had a frustrated career within the Anglican Church and failed to secure a living in Wales. He eventually obtained a post teaching Latin at a grammar school in Virginia and emigrated with his family in 1756; his wife and youngest child would die on their gruelling three-month journey to America. Apart from an elegy written on the death of Lewis Morris in 1766, Owen contributed nothing further to Welsh literature. He married twice more, purchased a tobacco and cotton plantation in Brunswick County, and died there in 1769.

Literary Histories, Bardic Voices, and a Sense of Place

The conscious shaping of a deep-rooted literary tradition in Welsh continued with the publication by Rhys Jones (Blaenau) of another anthology, *Gorchestion Beirdd Cymru* (*Triumphs of the Welsh Poets*, 1773, 2nd edn 1864), known as 'Y Bais Wen' ('The White Petticoat') because of its extra-wide margins. The volume focused principally on poetry of the mid-fifteenth to the mid-sixteenth centuries but did include one or two examples of the much older poems. Though these early medieval texts were increasingly obscure, Welsh-language poets could still claim a direct lineage to the *cynfeirdd*, 'early poets' (at this period a rather nebulous cluster of works ascribed to Taliesin, Aneirin, Llywarch Hen, and Myrddin), and hence to a 'British' literary tradition preceding anything available to English writers. Eighteenth-century English literary history effectively began with Chaucer; *Beowulf* would not be published before 1815. Thus, though in practice most poets were exploring the twelfth-century *cywydd* form and were doubtless more influenced by the fourteenth-century Dafydd ap Gwilym than by any of the supposedly sixth-century founding fathers, that sense of continuity in a native language predating Roman, Anglo-Saxon, and Norman conquests remained as potent in the latter half of the century as it had been for Theophilus Evans:

[E]r ein gorchfygu gan y Rhufeiniaid a'r Saeson yr ŷm yn cadw ein hiaith . . . os nid yn berffaith-gwbl, etto yn burach nag un genhedl yn y bŷd. *Eu Hiaith a gadwant eu Tir a gollant*, eb'r Myrddin.[35]

(Though conquered by the Romans and the Saxons we still keep our language . . . if not wholly intact, yet purer than any other nation in the world. *Their Language they shall keep; their Land they shall lose*, said Myrddin.)

For Welsh writers in English – who had no linguistic equivalent of lowland Scots to signal their non-Englishness – writing 'Welshness' was often a matter of tapping into this British tradition by invoking these early bards, Taliesin in particular. One of the more unusual exponents of the bardic voice was the writer Anne Penny, born Anne Hughes to a clerical family in Bangor, who spent her married life in England. Her *Poems, with a Dramatic Entertainment* appeared in 1771 and encompassed an eclectic mix of classical and Celtic subjects, with versions of Ossianic 'Fragments' among them. The volume opens, however, with two pieces versified from the *Specimens* of Evan Evans, 'Taliesin's Poem to Elphin' and 'An Elegy on Neest, by Einion'. It also contains a poem in praise of Thomas Gray, underlining yet again the extent to which, in the anglophone Welsh tradition at least, his ode was accepted as speaking, not about Wales, but for Wales:

> O! Taliesin, guide my Hand
> Attune the trembling Strings, inchant the Lay
> That dares attempt to carol Gray
> Thou long-lost Homer of my native land . . .[36]

Penny's is a distinctive female voice in an overwhelmingly male tradition of this type of bardic invocation, although, as Elizabeth Edwards shows in this volume, she would be followed in the Romantic period by Felicia Hemans. It is perhaps not, on reflection, surprising to find a female writer tapping into a bardic literary history in this way, since there can have been very little else for her to 'inherit'. As Cathryn Charnell-White has shown, extant work by contemporary Welsh-language women writers likewise offers few clues as to how (or indeed whether) they may have framed an alternative sense of literary tradition.[37] Like much of the men's poetry, their work is both social and sociable, declaring friendship, love, or gratitude, and expressing Christian values of loss or resignation in the face of death. 'Taliesin's Poem to Elphin', the first poem in Anne Penny's collection, gained a significantly wider audience when, apropos of a supposed tradition linking the bard Taliesin to the area around Llyn Geirionydd, a lake near Conwy, it reappeared a few years later in Thomas Pennant's second Welsh Tour, the *Journey to Snowdon* (1781). The fact of its inclusion, and the shift in context from a fairly modest collection of poems printed by subscription to a work of prose with a far wider circulation, deserves some consideration here. By the 1790s travel writing would become one of the most avidly read genres in Britain; Pennant himself was to some extent responsible for this, along with writers like William Gilpin, whose *Observations on the River Wye* (1782) opened up a picturesque southern counterpart to Pennant's more alpine north. Due in part to the rather uneasy status of travel writing within traditional literary canons, Pennant has been largely overlooked as a Welsh author: there are nonetheless good grounds for seeing his *Tours* as among the most influential literary productions of the period, helping to shape perceptions of Wales, Welsh culture, and Welsh history on both sides of the border well into the following century.[38]

Thomas Pennant of Downing (1726–98) was in many ways a natural successor to Edward Lhuyd – a product of the Enlightenment, a keen naturalist and antiquarian, with a national and international correspondence network which included Joseph Banks, Richard Gough, Gilbert White of Selborne, Simon Pallas, and the Swedish botanist Carl Linnaeus. Known as the author of *British Zoology* (1761–6) and *Synopsis of Quadrupeds* (1771), his successes as a travel writer came after publishing accounts of two journeys into Scotland undertaken in 1769 and 1772. Working closely with the Reverend John Lloyd of Caerwys, he began gathering material for his *Tours in Wales* shortly after, and they appeared in three volumes between 1778 and 1783. The style of the tours can best be described as omnivorous, taking in everything from castles and stately homes to mines and fisheries, waterfalls and rock formations: passages of lyrical enthusiasm for the grandeur of Snowdonian landscapes rub shoulders with relentlessly detailed reckonings of the genealogies of local gentry. These rich and crowded narratives would be used extensively as a source for writers not only of other tours and of histories but of place-focused poems such as Anna Seward's 'Llangollen Vale' (1795) and Richard Llwyd's *Beaumaris Bay* (1800), of Gothic novels with Welsh settings, and collections of 'national song'.[39]

'Welsh travels' had enjoyed a certain vogue back in the earlier decades of the eighteenth century, but they were a different animal altogether. Often ascribed to famous authors, these satirical accounts of (probably fictional) travels into deepest Wales played lively variations on the theme of Cambrian crudeness, all leeks and toasted cheese, filthy peasants with pedigrees stretching back to Adam, and an 'inarticulate' language 'more like the Gobbling of Geese or Turkies than the Speech of rational Creatures':[40]

> Tis a Tongue (it seems) not made for every mouth; as appears by an Instance of one of our Company, who, having got a Welsh polysyllable into his throat, was almost choak'd with Consonants; had we not, by clapping him on the back, made him disgorge a guttural or two, and so saved him.[41]

The landscape is also the object of amused scorn:

> The Country is mountainous, and yields pretty handsome clambering for Goats, and hath Variety of Precipice to break one's Neck; which a Man may sooner do than fill his Belly, the Soil being barren, and an excellent Place to breed a Famine in.[42]

By the end of the century, of course, the polarities were quite reversed. Those same barren mountains would come to be seen as fastnesses protecting an ancient tongue, with both items now recalibrated as things of beauty and mystery (although in practice, of course, travellers often still found the former dreary, and the latter frustratingly opaque). Welsh landscapes, both sublime and picturesque, join medieval Welsh literature and legend as the other significant and enduring export of the century into English consciousness. The inspiration for a wealth of texts and images from Wordsworth's meditations on the Wye above Tintern Abbey to Turner's castles and seascapes, Welsh hills and coasts, rivers, ruins, and woodlands became established, once and for all, as essential subjects for the creative arts. It has been suggested, interestingly, that an intense response to landscape is not a recognizable feature of Welsh-language writing until reabsorbed, via English, in the nineteenth century.[43] It is tempting to counter this with such poignant evocations of place as Evan Evans's 'Llys Ifor Hael', or Goronwy Owen's longing for and celebration of his native Ynys Môn (Anglesey), but there may be some truth in the notion that (for want of a better word) a 'Romantic' aestheticizing gaze is not generally part of the Welsh repertoire; it may even be that the very different relationship between the visual arts and poetry in Wales explains why there is no equivalent to John Dyer's early injunction to 'Draw the Landskip bright and strong'.[44] The nature of the differences in various types of 'place' poetry in the two languages, and the reasons behind those differences, certainly merit further critical exploration.

It fell to the second Theophilus to point up the superficiality of most travellers' responses to his native land, as they appeared in the torrent of Welsh tours published at the end of the century. His lengthy, anonymous, and highly irritated critique of some half a dozen recent tourist accounts of Wales appeared in the *Cambrian Register* in 1799; it was followed up by further biting comments in his *History of Brecknockshire* on the 'mosquito genus called tourists, which has of late infested the principality'.[45] Jones's accusation against these writers, that they are 'epidemically in the habit of asserting facts without foundation and inferring without data',[46] goes to the heart of the struggle over representations of Welsh culture in the two languages, and from 'insider' and 'outsider' perspectives. Jones's particular criticism is that of a local historian with a sharp eye for the particular and a concomitant distaste for generalizations about 'Wales' and 'Welsh customs'. His grandfather's wide-shot history of the Cymry as a *cenedl* ('people / nation / race') has evolved into an Enlightenment-style accumulation of information based on the careful observation of people in their communities – in their natural habitats, as it were. Yet as Hywel Davies rightly observes, Jones, who accuses Mrs Morgan of 'moon-blindness' in her account of dazzling white Welsh cottages, could turn a blind eye himself to things which undermined his own counter-narrative. One intriguing example of this is his scathing refutation of Samuel Pratt's assertion of a general Welsh belief in fairies, an assertion based on Pratt's encounter with a 'clergyman' who had written a book on the subject. In strenuously denying the existence of such a figure, Jones overlooked (or suppressed his knowledge of) the work of the extraordinary Pontypool preacher Edmund Jones, *Yr Hen Proffwyd,* who had indeed published detailed accounts of supernatural encounters in his parish and throughout Wales in 1771 and 1780.[47]

Edmund Jones is one of the century's more idiosyncratic writers, and deserves to be better known; he has been called 'the first author to give Wales an extensive and representative account of its strange and supernatural underbelly, the like of which England and some European countries has possessed for many years'.[48] An Independent minister, the product of Old

Dissent, he believed (as did many of his contemporaries in other denominations) that spirits and apparitions were tangible proof of God's working in the
world, and took it upon himself to collect and catalogue as many such
encounters as he could obtain, either from personal experience or from
trustworthy, religious-minded witnesses. His folklore, as Adam Coward has
observed, is distinguished by an '"Enlightened" empirical epistemology'
which seeks to persuade 'by sheer weight of examples'[49] and foregrounds
the importance of observation, accuracy, and authority. Jones's style is thus
marked by an irresistible matter-of-factness. It is the voice of the natural
historian – field notes inflected with the cadences of the Bible – and is a world
away from the saccharine tones and neatly structured narratives of many
nineteenth-century folk tales:

> About the year 1757, David Griffith (a carpenter in the parish of Caerwent)
> was going from his work. Being a little past the river rheen, he was suddenly
> and exceedingly terrified by a sound in the air – like the braying of an ass, but
> more disagreeable (something hellish and more tangible in the sound). To
> add to his terror, he saw a dark roller, rolling by his side, and passing on to a
> hedge before him. It made such a noise as if all the hedges about were tore to
> pieces – so amazed and terrified and confounded he was. (Who, in his case,
> would not have been so?) He knew not how he went home. When he came
> to light, he fainted and became as a dead man, and was ill about a fortnight
> after that.[50]

Conclusion

Jones's odd narratives occasionally contain directly reported speech in Welsh
or use local names for certain phenomena (e.g. cŵn annwn or cyhyraeth for the
ghostly hounds and the noise of the sky-hunt). They are yet another reminder
of how Welsh literature in this period reflects a transaction between the two
languages. The process is especially notable for its flow in both directions, the
eighteenth century being one of the few periods when Welsh-language
material can be said to have directly impacted on the English literary tradition. The journey made by the medieval Welsh poem to Elphin, through its
various incarnations in both manuscript and print, is in some ways symptomatic of the fortunes of Welsh literature in the course of the century. From
the sober dual-language text of Evan Evans to the versified, expanded, and
English-only effusion of Anne Penny's collection and its (spurious, if delight-
ful) relocation, via Pennant, to the banks of Llyn Geirionydd, we can see how
the processes of antiquarian recovery and contemporary creativity were

linked, and how a native literary tradition came to be re-imagined in another language.

The social reality of that transaction, however, was less inspiring. Welsh lost much ground in the course of the century, as rapid industrialization drastically altered the linguistic shape of traditional communities and economic hardship forced many to emigrate. For every anglophone poet trying on bardic robes for size, there was a Welsh writer lamenting the passing of the old patrons and decrying a growing language rift between the classes that left Welsh poets increasingly stranded:

> Gwayw i anhyf go anhoff,
> 'Go out away! Get ye off!'
> Dyna araith dyn oeredd;
> Difenwi'r iaith, dwfn oer wedd.[51]

> (A sharp insult to the modest, unloved [poet]:
> *'Go out away! Get ye off!'*
> That is the speech of an unfeeling man
> Belittling the language; deep and cold his looks.)

(The joke here being that the unpleasant *Sais*, did he but know it, is turning the Welsh bard away in pretty plausible *cynghanedd*.)

Welsh and English-language writers did not, however, drift inexorably apart. In the turbulent political climate of the 1790s, a new generation of writers and antiquarians, bilingual inheritors of an already complex dual literary tradition, would set about renewing its forms and modes of expression in some quite astonishing ways.

Notes

1. Theophilus Evans, *Drych y Prif Oesoedd* (Amwythig: John Rhydderch, 1716), 17. The second edition of 1740 expands this idea more aggressively to suggest that recording the history of the Cymry is not merely a tearful business but an unpleasant and shameful one (*salw a chwith*), since they were forever rebelling against God. For Evans see *Theophilus Evans (1693–1767): Y Dyn, ei Deulu, a'i Oes*, ed. Geraint H. Jenkins (Aberystwyth: Adran Gwasanaethau Diwyllianol Dyfed, 1993).
2. Evans, *Drych* (1716), 'At y Darllenydd'.
3. Eryn M. White, 'A Tale of Two Mirrors: Forming an Identity for the Calvinistic Methodist Church of Wales', in *Religion, Identity and Conflict in Britain: From the Restoration to the Twentieth Century*, ed. Stuart J. Brown, Frances Knight, and John Morgan Guy (London: Ashgate, 2013), 81–92 (at 85).

4. Prys Morgan, 'Y Ddau Theophilus: Sylwadau ar Hanesyddiaeth', *Taliesin* 19 (1969): 36–45; Glanmor Williams, 'Romantic and Realist: Theophilus Evans and Theophilus Jones', *Archaeologica Cambrensis* 140 (1991): 17–27.

5. For earlier treatments of this period, see Branwen Jarvis, ed., *A Guide to Welsh Literature c. 1700–1800* (Cardiff: University of Wales Press, 2000); Prys Morgan, *The Eighteenth Century Renaissance* (Llandybïe: Christopher Davies, 1981).

6. Sarah Prescott, *Eighteenth-Century Writing from Wales: Bards and Britons* (Cardiff: University of Wales Press, 2008), 1–28. See also Rhys Kaminski-Jones, 'True Britons: Ancient British Identity in Wales and Britain, 1680-1815', PhD thesis, University of Wales (2017).

7. Ian Atherton, 'Commemorating Conflict and the Ancient British Past in Augustan Britain', *Journal for Eighteenth Century Studies* 36, 3 (2013): 377–93. My thanks to Rhys Kaminski-Jones for this reference.

8. Prescott, *Bards and Britons*, 29–56.

9. See Bethan M. Jenkins, *Between Wales and England: Anglophone Welsh Writing of the Eighteenth Century* (Cardiff: University of Wales Press, 2017).

10. Frank Emery, *Edward Lhuyd F.R.S, 1660–1709* (Cardiff: University of Wales Press, 1971); Dewi W. Evans and Brynley F. Roberts, eds., *Archæologia Britannica: Texts and Translations* (Aberystwyth: Celtic Studies Publications, 2007). Transcriptions of many of Lhuyd's letters are available through *Early Modern Letters Online*, http://emlo.bodleian.ox.ac.uk (search under 'Lhwyd') (accessed 15 November 2017).

11. For theories of language in the period, see Caryl Davies, *Adfeilion Babel: Agweddau ar Syniadaeth Ieithyddol y Ddeunawfed Ganrif* (Caerdydd: Gwasg Prifysgol Cymru, 2000); for the creation of a 'Protestant Britain', see Linda Colley, *Britons: Forging the Nation 1707–1837* (New Haven and London: Yale University Press, 1992). This work is nuanced by, e.g., Colin Kidd's 'Integration: Patriotism and Nationalism', in *A Companion to Eighteenth Century Britain*, ed. H. T. Dickinson (Oxford: Oxford University Press, 2002), 369–80.

12. For a detailed account of Lhuyd's involvement with *Britannia*, see John Cramsie, *British Travellers and the Encounter with Britain 1450–1700* (Woodbridge: Boydell Press, 2015), 335–91.

13. Moses Williams, *Proposals (s.l., s.n, 1719)*, 1.

14. See Mary-Ann Constantine, '"British Bards": The Concept of Laboring Class Poetry in Eighteenth-Century Wales', in *A History of British Working Class Literature*, ed. John Goodridge and Bridget Keegan (Cambridge: Cambridge University Press, 2017) 101–15.

15. Catherine McKenna, 'Aspects of Tradition Formation in Eighteenth-Century Wales', in *Memory and the Modern in Celtic Literatures*, ed. Joseph Falaky Nagy, CSANA Yearbook 5 (Dublin: Four Courts Press, 2006), 37–60.

16. Examples of both poetic traditions for this period can be found in two anthologies: *Blodeugerdd Barddas o Ganu Caeth y Ddeunawfed Ganrif*, ed. A. Cynfael Lake (Cyhoeddiadau Barddas, 1993); E. G. Millward, ed., *Blodeugerdd Barddas o Gerddi Rhydd y Ddeunawfed Ganrif* (Cyhoeddiadau Barddas, 1991).

17. Lewis Morris, *Tlysau yr Hen Oesoedd* (Caergybi, 1735), 2.

18. John H. Davies, ed., *The Letters of Lewis, Richard, William and John Morris of Anglesey (Morrisiaid Môn) 1728–1765*, 2 vols. (Aberystwyth: privately printed, 1907–1909); Hugh Owen, ed., *Additional Letters of the Morrises of Anglesey (1735–1786)*, 2 vols. (London: The Honourable Society of Cymmrodorion, 1947, 1949).

19. Davies, ed., *Letters*, vol. II, 273.

20. Owen, ed., *Additional Letters*, vol. II, 467; see Mary-Ann Constantine, 'Ossian in Wales and Brittany', in *The Reception of Ossian in Europe*, ed. Howard Gaskill (London: Thoemmes, 2004), 67–90.

21. Gerald Morgan, *Ieuan Fardd* (Caernarfon: Gwasg Pantycelyn, 1988). His work is thoughtfully discussed in Prescott, *Bards and Britons*, 57–83.

22. Evan Evans, *Some Specimens of the Poetry of the Antient Welsh Bards* (London: R. and J. Dodsley, 1764), iii.

23. Lewis Morris to Edward Richard, 1758; cited in Ffion Llywelyn Jenkins, 'Celticism and Pre-Romanticism: Evan Evans', in *A Guide to Welsh Literature*, ed. Jarvis, 114.

24. See Jenkins, 'Celticism'; Edward D. Snyder, *The Celtic Revival in English Literature 1760–1800* (Cambridge, MA: Harvard University Press, 1923); Arthur Johnston, *Enchanted Ground: The Study of Medieval Romance in the Eighteenth Century* (London: Athlone Press, 1964).

25. Thomas Gray, 'The Bard', *Odes by Mr Gray* (Strawberry Hill: R. and J. Dodsley, 1757), 15, ll. 39–48.

26. See Mary-Ann Constantine, *The Truth Against the World: Iolo Morganwg and Romantic Forgery* (Cardiff: University of Wales Press, 2007), 122–4. 'Bardic' resistance in Scotland and Ireland is explored in Katie Trumpener's *Bardic Nationalism: The Romantic Novel and the British Empire* (Princeton: Princeton University Press, 1997).

27. Peter Lord, *The Visual Culture of Wales: Imaging the Nation* (Cardiff: University of Wales Press, 2000), 156; Sam Smiles, *The Image of Antiquity: Ancient Britain and the Romantic Imagination* (New Haven and London: Yale University Press, 1994), 55–62.

28. 'Llys Ifor Hael', in *Blodeugerdd Barddas o Ganu Caeth*, ed. Lake, 65; my translation.

29. John Dyer, 'Grongar Hill', in *Selected Poetry and Prose*, ed. John Goodridge (Nottingham: Trent Editions, 2000), 12, ll. 80–92.

30. William Morris to Richard Morris, May 1762, in Davies, ed., *Letters*, vol. II, 477.

31. Owen, ed., *Additional Letters*, vol. I, 224.

32. Saunders Lewis, *A School of Welsh Augustans* (Wrexham: Hughes, 1924); Branwen Jarvis, *Goronwy Owen* (Cardiff: University of Wales Press, 1986).

33. Dafydd Johnston, *A Pocket Guide to the Literature of Wales* (Cardiff: University of Wales Press, 1994), 61.

34. Goronwy Owen, *Diddanwch Teuluaidd* (Llundain: Williams Roberts, 1763), 79, ll. 37–44 (reproduced without annotations; my translation, with kind assistance from Dafydd Johnston). For an edited version, see *Blodeugerdd Barddas o Ganu Caeth*, ed. Lake, 93–7.

35. Evans, *Drych* (1716), 17–18.

36. Anne Penny, *Poems, with a Dramatic Entertainment* (London: Printed for the Author, 1771), 134.

37. Cathryn A. Charnell-White, *Beirdd Ceridwen: Blodeugerdd Barddas o Ganu Menywod hyd tua 1800* (Llandybïe: Gwasg Dinefwr, 2005), 390.

38. Mary-Ann Constantine and Nigel Leask, eds., *Enlightenment Travel and British Identities: Thomas Pennant's Tours in Scotland and Wales* (London: Anthem Press, 2017). For the surge in British travel writing, see Malcolm Andrews, *In Search of the Picturesque: Landscape Aesthetics and Tourism in Britain 1760–1800* (Aldershot: Scolar Press, 1989).

39. Mary-Ann Constantine, '"To Trace Thy Country's Glories to their Source": Dangerous History in Thomas Pennant's Tour in Wales', in *Rethinking British Romantic History, 1770–1845*, ed. Porscha Fermanis and John Regan (Oxford: Oxford University Press, 2014), 121–43.

40. [John Torbuck], *A Collection of Welsh Travels, and Memoirs of Wales. Containing I. The Briton Describ'd, or a Journey thro' Wales* ... [London: J. Torbuck, 1740], 10.

41. Ibid., 61–2.

42. Ibid., 45. For enduring Welsh stereotypes, see Peter Lord, *Words with Pictures: Welsh Images and Images of Wales in the Popular Press, 1640–1860* (Aberystwyth: Planet, 1995).

43. Glyn Tegai Hughes notes that 'the single most striking feature of Welsh literature in the eighteenth century, at least before Iolo Morganwg, is the almost complete absence of the landscape': 'Life and Thought', in *A Guide to Welsh Literature*, ed. Jarvis, 19; Prys Morgan suggests that 'such sentiments were unthinkable in the eighteenth century': 'From Death to a View: The Hunt for the Welsh Past in the Romantic Period', in *The Invention of Tradition*, ed. Eric Hobsbawm and Terence Ranger (Cambridge: Cambridge University Press, 1992), 87.

44. Dyer, 'Grongar Hill', 10, l. 14.

45. Hywel Davies, 'Wales in English Travel Writing 1791–8: The Welsh Critique of Theophilus Jones', *Welsh History Review* 23, 3 (2007): 86.

46. Ibid.

47. Edmund Jones, *A Geographical, Historical, and Religious Account of the Parish of Aberystruth: In the County of Monmouth* (1779); *A Relation of Apparitions of Spirits in the Principality of Wales* (1780).

48. John Harvey, introduction to Edmund Jones, *The Appearance of Evil: Apparitions of Spirits in Wales*, ed. John Harvey (Cardiff: University of Wales Press, 2003), 8.

49. Adam N. Coward, 'Edmund Jones and the Pwcca'r Trwyn', *Folklore* 126 (2015): 182.

50. Jones, *The Appearance of Evil*, 96. Jones's prose, incidentally, reads like an innocent prefiguring of the heavy satirical style of the twentieth-century Caradoc Evans.

51. The poet is Edward Jones, Bodfari: cited in *Blodeugerdd Barddas o Ganu Caeth*, ed. Lake, xv.

15

Romantic Wales and the Eisteddfod

ELIZABETH EDWARDS

Bridging Cultures: An Overview

Among the Romantic-period material at the National Library of Wales is a miscellaneous collection of poems and pamphlets from the 1790s, bound together in a single volume shelf-marked 'Castell Gorfod Amryw 6'. Some of the better-known pieces in this volume include the 1790 St Asaph eisteddfod prize-winning essay on 'Rhyddid' ('Liberty') by the Montgomeryshire cleric Walter Davies ('Gwallter Mechain', 1761–1849); a series of eisteddfod prize-winning odes (*awdlau*) by the Caernarvonshire weaver and schoolmaster David Thomas ('Dafydd Ddu Eryri', 1759–1822); and *Seren Tan Gwmmwl* ('The Cloud-hidden Star'), a Painite political tract by the Denbighshire poet and pamphleteer John Jones ('Jac Glan-y-Gors', 1766–1821). Also in the volume, but far less familiar in this company, are works such as Richard Powell's *Awdyl ar Dymhorau y Vlwyzyn* ('An Awdl on the Seasons'), written in modish orthography for the 1793 Bala eisteddfod; John Roberts's *Awdyl ar Destyn y Gwyneddigion* (?1801), a call to cultural and artistic revival in Wales, beginning 'Deffro Awenwawd' ('Awaken Muse'); and *Beaumaris Bay: A Poem* (1800) by 'the Bard of Snowdon', Richard Llwyd (1752–1835).

The collection is brief and highly selective, perhaps assembled by chance, since not all of these pieces are predictable bedfellows. But as a rapid overview of the period, it provides a useful starting point for a discussion of it, introducing a range of literary forms and political ideas and including work in both of the languages of Romantic Wales. Incorporating pieces written from virtually opposite political perspectives, it demonstrates the breadth of prose works being produced in 1790s Wales, from Walter Davies's politically cautious and loyalist 'account of Welsh liberty through the Tudor Union',[1] to Jac Glan-y-Gors's Welsh adaptation of English radical thought. By including the work of David Thomas, it illustrates the strict-metre poetry judged the best of its day and sets it alongside examples of Welsh poetry that represent a much larger body of work, now forgotten. In the case of Llwyd's *Beaumaris Bay*, a long poem indebted to eighteenth-century antiquarianism, the Welsh cultural revival, and the topographical verse tradition in English, it includes the landmark publication of a poet whose contemporary reputation as an anglophone writer reached all of Wales and travelled beyond it.

Some of the writers mentioned above have recently become more prominent and better understood as a result of revisionist accounts of the Romantic period in Wales.[2] Based on textual editing and literary-historical recovery, these accounts draw on lesser-known or hard-to-find texts, including manuscripts, and printed material that has tended to be viewed as ephemera, such as newspaper and periodical writing, to produce a wider and more detailed literary landscape for Enlightenment and Romantic Wales.[3] Such work has added weight to the idea that Welsh literary history should be studied through its two languages, in contrast to earlier accounts that treated Welsh-language material only, or mainly examined cultural exchanges and the movement of people and ideas in terms of Wales and anglophone writing.[4] This overview of Romantic Wales builds, therefore, on developments in a critical process that is enabling 'a genuinely comparative account of the Welsh- and English-language poetic traditions in Wales and the role played by translating and translations in bridging what has been seen as two completely separate linguistic cultures'.[5]

As the miscellaneous nature of the texts in the National Library of Wales bound volume suggests, this period in Welsh literary history needs to be understood in terms of the variety of its forms and the influences behind them – from medieval metrical conventions to English classicism, the mid-century 'graveyard school' of poetry, the ballad revival, and contemporary popular culture. It also needs to be seen in the light of a spectrum of political difference, while the language question arches over the period not just in terms of the need to read Romantic Wales bilingually, but because this is an important phase of linguistic change in terms of concepts, ideas, and neologisms. However, range is not the only issue here: points of contact and connection are equally and vitally important. That the language in which works were published is not the whole story is nicely illustrated by the relationship between Jac Glan-y-Gors's radical pamphlets in Welsh and the English-language political public sphere that influenced him, or the tide of Welsh-language medieval poetry that rises into *Beaumaris Bay* from long footnotes on almost every page. There are obvious bridges, too, in the writings of those who composed poetry in both English and Welsh, as did

David Thomas, while the way in which Romantic Wales was not strictly bound by one language or the other can be seen in the wider work of its writers, especially their reading lives and correspondence networks.[6]

Using the themes above as a foundation for approaching the period, this chapter traces Welsh literary history between 1789 and the mid-nineteenth century through the development of Wales's first (and most enduring) literary-artistic public institution, the *eisteddfod* (a bardic gathering; literally a sitting or session). Revitalized and re-imagined in the 1790s, it expanded into local regions throughout Wales by the 1820s, before entering a period of increasingly aristocratic patronage and anglicization from the 1820s to the 1840s. The reconceptualization of the eisteddfod from its original, medieval form, along with the emergence of parallel new movements such as the *gorsedd* (also a gathering of bards, the separate development of which is discussed below), as both a focal point for Welsh national revival and a vehicle for political opposition reveal the ways in which the format of the bardic meeting was one of the most potent and productive cultural bridges of this period.

'A General Freedom'? The Eisteddfod after 1789

In a recent introduction to Welsh-language poetry written in the 1790s in response to the French Revolution, Cathryn Charnell-White has made the case that it is not necessarily the use of the Welsh language but the role and status of the poet in Wales, and his bardic identity, developed and sustained over centuries, that most clearly characterizes responses to events in France as specifically Welsh. 'What marks out the chorus of conservative and radical voices as Welsh' in this period, she argues, 'is the way in which they fulfil the prescribed role of the poet and adhere to the genres and conventions of their native poetic traditions, both strict- and free-metre.'[7] The second element in identifying the specificity of the Welsh responses is their location within what Charnell-White describes as a 'well-defined bardic sphere', an existing system of networks and lines of connection drawn across Wales by exchanges of letters and literary manuscripts.[8] That long-standing, relatively stable Welsh bardic network was boosted in the late eighteenth century by the re-emergence of the eisteddfod movement. The medieval eisteddfod was an event at which bards were required to demonstrate (usually before their patrons) their professional skills, especially their mastery of legal knowledge and traditional wisdom. Despite going almost unrecorded in the period between the twelfth century and the celebrated meetings held at

Carmarthen around 1453 and Caerwys in 1523 and 1567, it survived in a scaled-down form to be held sporadically in eighteenth-century north Wales as what were known as *eisteddfodau'r almanaciau* ('the almanac eisteddfods').[9] The year 1789, however, saw the first step in a transformation of the movement's status when it came under the patronage of an influential London-Welsh grouping, the Gwyneddigion Society (founded in 1770): the event held at Bala in September 1789 was sponsored by the Gwyneddigion.

The timing of the alliance between the eisteddfod and its new sponsors stands out because it coincides so suggestively with the French Revolution. The Gwyneddigion Society was founded, its members claimed in 1789, on principles of 'Freedom in Church and State'. By the time of the St Asaph eisteddfod in the following year, the set theme on which poets had to compose their verse was 'Rhyddid', 'Liberty', as we have seen in the 'Castell Gorfod Amryw 6' collection; however, with certain exceptions, discussed below, it would be wrong to connect the revitalization and recreation of Welsh cultural forms with political revolution. The revival of the eisteddfod instead follows, and continues, the longer process of cultural revival in eighteenth-century Wales outlined by Mary-Ann Constantine in the previous chapter of this volume. Yet the importance of the themes of recovery and (re)invention in the period generally cannot be overstated. At the end of the eighteenth century, Wales was underdeveloped relative to the rest of Britain, with, as Geraint H. Jenkins has shown, no clear cultural centre, populous capital city, scientific academies, or 'Welsh universities to train young scholars in the craft of writing history and to help them recover and sustain the memory of the nation'.[10] Building on decades of literary and antiquarian discovery that either took place within or was closely tied to eighteenth-century Wales, the eisteddfod partly addresses this gap in the nation and provides a pathway from the earlier eighteenth-century cultural revival towards Victorian Wales.

That work of reclaiming the Welsh literary past cannot be easily separated from late eighteenth-century perceptions of Welsh status and patriotism. Geraint H. Jenkins reads the manuscript collecting and editorial work of the Morris circle and the London Welsh as a boost to national confidence, which emerged in the period alongside developments in industrial and agrarian life in Wales, as well as in trade, urbanization, and communications (as outlined by Paul O'Leary in this volume). 'As the economy became more productive and diverse,' Jenkins argues, 'signs of cultural change and renewal also became increasingly apparent.'[11] It is more difficult, perhaps, to measure qualitative change in Wales in terms of attitude and mood, but it may be the case that 'Celticism offered an opportunity ... to hark back to a time of supreme poetic confidence, when royal poets sang in royal courts without doubting the supremacy of the song or of the tradition from which it sprang.'[12] In a pattern that would only become clearer with the passage of time, the eisteddfod offered opportunities and points of entry for writers, many of whom came from modest backgrounds: David Thomas was a weaver, and later a schoolmaster, Richard Llwyd was a domestic servant, while Edward Williams ('Iolo Morganwg', 1747–1826), a pivotal figure in Romantic Wales discussed below, worked as an itinerant stonemason.

A new confidence about place and political conviction can arguably be felt in the writing of David Thomas, speaking on behalf of a region, if not a nation, in his 'Awdl ar Rhyddid' ('An Awdl on Liberty'). In this poem Thomas depicts liberty as a strictly defined concept, bounded by religious belief ('nad rhyddid treiddiol – i bechu / Yn groes i Iesu, Iôn grasurol', 'this is not a general freedom to sin / contrary to Christ, gracious Lord', ll. 17–18) and defending and preserving a largely peaceful status quo ('Ffrwyth rhyddid, trefnid di-roch, / Yw llwyddiant oll, a heddwch', 'the fruits of liberty, quiet order, / are complete success and peace', ll. 67–8) that figures as a notably British quality ('Nu fu gwlith un fendith fwy / I Frydain, le dyfradwy', 'there never was any greater dew of blessing upon / Britain, well-watered place', ll. 110–11).[13] Thomas's concern in the poem for British unity structures the landscapes around Snowdonia within a wider archipelagic context connecting Wales, Scotland, and England, but he similarly maps north-west Wales as a haven of loyalism for moderate patriots in his English-language poetry, as in 'The Banks of the Menai' (1792):

> The rural scene, the prospect bright,
> Rush now spontaneous on my sight:
> Here nature's works, how beauteous and how great,
> where the wise patriots find a sweet retreat![14]

Pieces such as this, or the 1790 St Asaph submissions on 'Rhyddid', display 'simple institutional loyalism', though it is important to stress that writers such as Thomas and Walter Davies are part of the wider conservative and defensively patriotic response in Britain to the French Revolution.[15] In their Welsh context, however, these writers' seemingly Burkean emphasis on maintaining the authority and stability of the state, or on religious loyalty, may also be characteristic of their exceptional position within that response. Historians of the vernacular Welsh poetic tradition point to its 'inherent conservatism' and tendency to support the place of the Welsh within the

British state.[16] In terms of poetic form, 'Awdl ar Rhyddid' sits safely within Welsh neoclassicism, rather than seeking innovation, as Cathryn Charnell-White points out: 'Its opening *invocatio* to the goddess of liberty echoes the classical poets of Greece and Rome, while literary allusions direct the reader's attention to the Ancients of the native Welsh bardic tradition: Aneirin, Gwalchmai, Dafydd Benfras and others.'[17] That said, Thomas is perhaps bolder in Welsh than in English, as in his unexpected inversion of the liberty theme in 'Awdl ar Rhyddid' in a passage declaring 'Iawn gloi dewrion ein gwladwriaeth, / Rhag bradwriaeth' ('it is right to lock up brave men of our state / for fear of treason', ll. 134–5). In lines written months if not years before alarmism about revolution and reform took hold in mid-1790s Britain, Thomas anticipates and writes himself into the reactionary pressure that would attempt, and largely succeed, to close down political debate.

'Britania's [*sic*] Ancient Bards Appear': Iolo Morganwg and the *Gorsedd*

Rhyddid/liberty, arguably the concept that best sums up the controversies of the 1790s, recurs in competing forms across the decade. From the St Asaph eisteddfod in 1789, it reappears as the theme at the first of Iolo Morganwg's *gorsedd* meetings, held at Primrose Hill in London in June 1792. Understood today as an integral part of the modern eisteddfod and as a spectacle of druidic pageantry, the *gorsedd* as invented by Iolo in the 1790s was a very different affair. Iolo maintained that it was an ancient institution whose full title was *Gorsedd Beirdd Ynys Prydain* ('Meeting/Gathering of the Bards of the Island of Britain'), but its composition, the timing of its emergence, and the ambitious claims he made for it all signal the shaping influence of contemporary contexts.

The word's various possible meanings bring out different aspects of the organization Iolo was seeking to establish: *gorsedd* can denote a mound of earth or hillock, a throne, a repository for weapons, and a 'court, hall, dwelling place; court of law, judicial assembly, tribunal, session, judge's seat; assembly, [or] gathering'.[18] The polysemous nature of the word conveys the way in which the 1790s *gorsedd* was conceived as a visible (the 'hillock' definition applies here) and accountable public body that would cultivate Welsh cultural nationalism and provide a platform for Iolo's political ideas. At the centre of that vision of an institution that would concentrate attention on Welsh culture and its survival, and express radical-oppositional political thought, was the figure of the bard, whose traditional role as the remembrancer and legislator of his society was the mechanism by which both of these aims were imagined possible. There are clear parallels with the eisteddfod in that the *gorsedd* was also a bardic gathering involving the performance of poetry. But Iolo Morganwg's *gorsedd* was founded from the outset on political principles reaching to a deeper level than could be said of the revived eisteddfod.

That it was possible to flesh out a political system via the figure of the bard was a direct result of the extent to which antiquarianism had become set in the eighteenth-century literary imagination. The poetry of James Thomson (1700–48), and later Thomas Gray (1716–71) and James Macpherson (1736–96), developed the druid-bard as an emblem of oppositional Whiggism; building on and reacting to their writings, by the late 1780s Iolo had invented a comprehensive bardo-druidic vision that classed the druids as the aboriginal ancestors of the Welsh bards.[19] Not least because he claimed this position for himself, Iolo has often been seen as the definitive 'last bard', the sole survivor and representative of a lost tradition.[20] And yet, as Mary-Ann Constantine has shown, Iolo also drew on that sense of the druids as forerunners of the modern Welsh bard for much of his rhetorical authority: as much the first, and therefore most authentic, as the last of his race.[21]

Much of that authoritative vision was sketched out in a publication that appeared in 1792, *The Heroic Elegies and Other Pieces of Llywarç [Llywarch] Hen*, an edition and translation of the ninth-century verse cycle by the translator and lexicographer William Owen Pughe. More important in terms of the *gorsedd* was the preface that ran before the poetry, which functioned as a manifesto for Iolo's bardic scheme. This preface became a well-known piece, reprinted and quoted elsewhere.[22] But it also raised suspicions almost as soon as it appeared, on account of both its implicit political allegiances and its historical validity: the *Critical Review*, for instance, welcomed the appearance of *Llywarch Hen* but was sceptical about the authenticity of the sources that Iolo and William Owen Pughe had worked from, complaining that they had breached the antiquarian and historical method by not referencing them:

> [A] modern author's assertions meet with no credit, as indeed they deserve none … all learned men and accurate thinkers, expect to know where the manuscripts used are; what is their antiquity; and what reasons can be assigned for affixing them to any particular period.[23]

The novelist Edward 'Celtic' Davies (1756–1831) went further, drawing specific links between Iolo's bardism and the values resonating from the French Revolution:

I do not recollect to have seen this doctrine, in its full extent, promulgated by any code, before a certain period of the French Revolution, when the *meek* Republicans of Gaul, and their modest partisans in other countries, joined the *indefeasible right of equality* with the *inviolable duty of peace*, and impressed them upon the orderly subjects of every state; whilst they themselves were preparing for every species of injury to civil society. But whencesoever this fallacious principle took its rise, it certainly did not belong to the *Druids*, or to the *Bards*, without great limitation.[24]

Edward Davies was right to be unconvinced: as Damian Walford Davies has shown, the *Llywarch Hen* preface is a coded article of Jacobin sympathy, with 'a politicized agenda that located the ideals of liberty, equality and peace as the surviving body of a specifically Welsh (and Glamorgan-based) Bardic philosophy of which such figures as [Iolo] and Pughe appear as incarnations and guardians'.[25] As the more administrative or constitutional meanings of *gorsedd* – assembly, tribunal – suggest, Iolo's *gorsedd* was the first small step towards 'a utopian republic, established on the principles of social equality, common property, public accountability and a bold, freethinking search after "Truth"'.[26]

By the time Iolo re-imagined them as liberty-guarding Welsh bards, druids had long embodied historical resistance as the heroic (if ultimately doomed) opponents of the invading Romans in the first millennium. Although the French Revolution undoubtedly transformed the representational possibilities of the bard, the mid- to late-century Celtic revival coincided with a period of rising calls for political reform that must also be acknowledged as the crucible in which the concept of the bard was formed. The question of America's break from Britain brought democratic politics to the centre of contemporary debate, not least via influential Welsh thinkers such as Richard Price, who defended popular sovereignty in *Observations on the Nature of Civil Liberty* (1776), and David Williams, later advisor to the new French state, who argued for an improved system of parliamentary representation in *Letters on Political Liberty* (1782; translated into French in 1783).[27] However, the French Revolution brought the example of republicanism much closer to home and intensified political debate in Wales, as in Britain more generally. The responses of radical clerics and rational Dissenters briefly but powerfully transformed the nature of Welsh public discourse, giving rise to a series of radical Welsh-language periodicals whose short-lived nature attests, at least in part, to the state-sponsored repression of oppositional voices.[28] American independence prepared the ground for the political discourse surrounding the French Revolution, but as emblems of resistance, egalitarianism, freedom, and peace, the bard and his collective *gorsedd* perhaps uniquely find their moment in the wake of 1789.

The very real possibilities of intimidation and persecution as the counter-revolutionary reaction to events in France took shape also meant that concealment or disguise became a necessity for radical-sympathizing Welsh writers, rather than a theatrical spectacle. Conservative opinion, and mobilization on the ground, was quick to emerge in Britain: loyalist associations were appearing in Wales by the autumn of 1792, and just over a year after the initial meeting of the *gorsedd*, the 'Scottish Martyrs' – key figures in the Scottish reform movement – were convicted of sedition and sentenced to transportation.[29] Iolo himself claimed that he had been the victim of surveillance and had had his papers searched, while the mainly Welsh-language 'clandestine meetings, coded messages and druidic moots' in which he was involved were objects of suspicion to the conservative authorities throughout the 1790s.[30] Yet the concept of the bard is double-edged. A distrusted figure in some quarters, he also distances the suspected subject from political engagement, as does the sociable and cultural format of the bardic assembly, whether in the form of the eisteddfod or the *gorsedd* (which was not, it must be said, exclusively revolutionary in tone: David Thomas's 'The Banks of the Menai' was publicly declaimed at the September 1792 meet). At a wider British level, the increasingly reactionary nature of politics in the 1790s meant that radicalism was a belief system needing more to be masked than embellished or exaggerated.

The *gorsedd* was also an inspiring context for Iolo: a place in which, drawing on history and myth, he could invent and play out alternative fictional worlds. At times, the philosophy and ceremony of bardism supplied the main theme of his writing, as in 'Ode on the Mythology of the Ancient British Bards', one of the closing pieces in his 1794 collection, *Poems, Lyric and Pastoral*, and unpublished works such as 'Bardic Institutes Written at Carn Moesen', which depicts blue-robed bards ('dip'd in heav'n's ethereal blue') as figures of universal peace and benevolence:

> Meek sons of Peace to nature dear
> Britania's [*sic*] ancient Bards appear,
> Meet in gay ^{wide} circles on the green,
> Where nought invades the solemn ^{sacred} scene
> Of bloodful war, of dinful strife,
> Or aught that swells the storms of life
> Or aught that gilds the soot of art
> Or hides from truth each canker'd heart

That hides from man his deep disgrace
Derived from fashions lustful _{wanton} race.
. . .

and whilst they bid all discord cease
hear them proclaim the laws of peace.
The blest commands of love divine
And truth, eternally benign,
Truth that displays unchanging right
In the meridian blaze of light.[31]

Intensely pacifist and critical of contemporary society in general, this poem emphasizes the tendency towards the abstract and gestural in Iolo's poetry, but as Cathryn Charnell-White points out, '[s]ome of [his] most radical works were composed for Gorsedd meetings'. Among these are Welsh-language poems on Rhita Gawr, a giant who slays despots and makes a cloak from their beards, his Painite 'Breiniau Dyn' ('Rights of Man'), and anti-monarchical addresses to peace:

Rhyfel yn gawr sy'n rhwyfaw
Fal tonnau'r aig, fal draig draw;
. . .
Gorchest cethin brenhinoedd
Yw'r cyfan i'w gân ar goedd . . .[32]

(The giant, war, has dominion over us
like the ocean's waves, like a dragon yonder;
. . .
The savage exploits of kings
is all war proclaims . . .)

Considering his reputation both in his own time and today, Iolo Morganwg is the writer most conspicuously absent from the 'Castell Gorfod Amryw 6' collection, and one of the strongest cultural bridges in Romantic Wales.[33] He is also one of the most contentious figures of Welsh history – arguably 'the most remarkable and most complicated figure in the whole history of Welsh literature' – because he was also a brilliant forger whose additions to the corpus of medieval poetry went unidentified for over a century.[34] By making his forged texts inseparable from the surviving works of fourteenth-century poets like Dafydd ap Gwilym, Iolo corrupted and obscured the genuine tradition and misled those who followed him – a move that some later scholars have been unable to excuse.[35]

Forgery can, however, be seen as an extension of the reworked past that underpinned the *gorsedd*. Iolo saw little, up to and including forgery, as off-limits because, as Geraint H. Jenkins observes, he perceived 'that the function of history was to re-create a past to suit the needs of the present'.[36] But both Iolo's forgeries and his reinvention of a past that met the needs of his own time also highlight tensions within the Celtic revival. The cultural confidence that came with regaining the past needs to be weighed against the way in which working through that past exposed the perceived injustices and stress points of Welsh history.[37] Alan Liu has argued that to be Welsh at the turn of the nineteenth century 'was to be aware in every moment of the relation between *then* and *now* – specifically of a continuity of calamity so embedded in prehistorical and irrecoverable tradition that calamitous change ... seemed as fixed in the Welsh character as the *longue durée* lay of the land itself'.[38] Iolo's writing career is arguably a product of that new cultural assurance and sense of lack simultaneously, evident on the one hand in the supreme confidence with which he successfully forged the Welsh tradition, and, on the other, in the gaps, as he perceived them, that made forgery seem necessary. It is for this reason that the brilliantly colourful Glamorgan depicted in his forged medieval *cywyddau*, in his political pastorals and historical essays, should be seen, like Sir Walter Scott's Scotland, as one of the great creations of the Romantic period.[39]

'A World Within Itself'? 1819 and Beyond

In the surveillance atmosphere of the 1790s, it was almost inevitable that the enigmatic rites and rebellious, levelling language of the *gorsedd* would attract attention.[40] The first *gorsedd* of the bards to be held in Wales, rather than London, took place at Stalling Down in Glamorgan in 1795. But just a couple of years later, with fears of a French invasion at a peak, the *gorsedd* appeared increasingly alarming to the state authorities, not least in the wake of the unsuccessful French landing at Fishguard in February 1797. A meeting held on Garth Mountain in 1798 was closely watched by the Glamorgan Yeomanry, in an episode described by Damian Walford Davies as 'proof that the *gorsedd* was taken seriously by the authorities as a Jacobin threat and as a dangerous paradigm for reform'.[41]

Iolo had been privately battling against espionage and state-sponsored suppression in his unpublished writings since at least 1794, as in poems such as 'Church and King rampant or Satan let loose for

a thousand years', which laments the near-impossibility of sustaining
political opposition:

> Our feet are every where beset
> By wily spies an odious clan
> How lies conseald th' informer's ^{oppressor's} net
> for those who seek the rights of man . . .[42]

Even in the pressurized atmosphere of 1794, Iolo had still been able to channel
his ideas through the *gorsedd*, but the contemporary context in the later 1790s
meant that further development of his bardic assembly became almost
impossible. Though they met in the wide open-air spaces of Glamorgan,
Iolo and his fellow bards found themselves in ever-tighter political spaces: the
'Gagging Acts', passed late in 1795, restricted public meetings as part of the
institutional suppression of the discussion of reform in Britain. After
a clandestine *gorsedd* held at Dinorwig in 1799, meetings of the eisteddfod
and the *gorsedd* were suspended until the end of the French wars, but the pace
of change after 1815 was fast. By 1818, the first provincial Cambrian Society
had been established in Dyfed by a group of literary Anglican clergymen; it
was with the support of this society that a milestone eisteddfod was held in
Carmarthen in July of the following year. This event stands out because it
incorporated the *gorsedd* into the eisteddfod and enduringly linked the two
institutions as a result. Yet within the conservative Anglican framework of
the post-1815 eisteddfod, the *gorsedd*'s cultural and ceremonial force far out-
weighed its deep-set radical values, which had become difficult to see, let
alone sustain, in the post war period.[43]

This was the overall direction the eisteddfod would now take: 1819 marked
the beginnings of a new cultural momentum located in Wales rather than
London, even though long-held connections, and tensions, between Wales
and London continued into the 1820s. Like the *gorsedd* previously, London
hosted the eisteddfod for an expatriate Welsh community and also acted as
a cradle for its development. Events in London contributed, for instance,
towards the continuing reinvention of the Welsh past, as in Felicia Hemans's
'The Meeting of the Bards', a poem written for and performed at the 1822
London eisteddfod. The published version of the poem included a preface
quoting *The Heroic Elegies . . . of Llywarch Hen* that emphasized the bardic
ritual of the *gorsedd*:

> The Gorseddau, or meetings of the British bards, were anciently ordained to
> be held in the open air, on some conspicuous situation, whilst the sun was

above the horizon; or, according to the expression employed on these occasions, 'in the face of the sun, and in the eye of the light'.[44]

Hemans's portrait of the 'conspicuous' and illuminated nature of proceedings, along with the descriptions of blue-robed bards and sheathed swords (both symbolizing peace) that follow, suggest how deeply a depoliticized version of Iolo Morganwg's 1790s mythmaking had soaked into the cultural landscape of 1820s Wales. Though she was born in Liverpool, Hemans, later the best-selling female poet of the nineteenth century, grew up in north Wales and wrote a significant body of poetry on Welsh themes, including the song texts for John Parry's ('Bardd Alaw', 1776–1851) *A Selection of Welsh Melodies* (1822). Huw Meirion Edwards has suggested that patriotic nostalgia for an idealized past is the keynote of 1820s literature from Wales.[45] This is true of Hemans's songs for *Welsh Melodies*, though the collection's retrospective register of mourning – at the level of the lyrics, if not the often upbeat music – also creates an impression of cultural continuity through the Welsh past.[46]

Hemans's work of voicing the bard in the early 1820s in works mainly addressing an English-speaking audience highlights the theme of anglicization that grew through the eisteddfod movement of the 1820s. The Welsh gentry had become increasingly anglicized during the eighteenth century, as Glyn Tegai Hughes points out:

> By the end of the century even the minor gentry, even in the west, had retreated from Welsh (although some continued to subscribe to Welsh books), and by doing so exacerbated the sharp division already inherent in the social structure.[47]

The eisteddfod of course became, in time, a genuinely national institution. But in the 1820s, it was shaped by the local and national elites – the Welsh local gentry and English aristocracy – who acted as its patrons. The 1819 Carmarthen event, for example, was 'convened under the joint patronage of the Lord of Dynevor and George III', in a move that inaugurates what Cathryn Charnell-White sees as 'a trajectory of increasing Britishness and imperialism' in the nineteenth-century eisteddfod movement.[48]

At this point in time it was not clear to contemporaries whether a London-metropolitan or native version of the eisteddfod would prevail, as Ffion Mair Jones shows in a discussion of the cultural work of the clergyman and song collector John Jenkins ('Ifor Ceri', 1770–1829).[49] The language question, however, clarifies the nature of the cultural struggle between Wales and London, which largely turned on the relative status of the Welsh and English languages within the eisteddfod context. Glyn Tegai Hughes argues that the former now seemed 'backward-looking, relying on the "authority" of a garbled account of the past for its legitimacy', while the latter was 'forward-looking and fuelled by a belief that Welsh talent would out on a much wider stage when expressed in the major mode'.[50] For some, the London-facing culture of English-language Wales seemed the path to modernity and advancement – aspirations that could hardly be helped by a poorly understood home-grown phenomenon like Iolo Morganwg's crypto-republican bardism. The metropolitan artistic world also influenced the eisteddfod in other ways. By the mid-1820s, fashionable theatrical music (as opposed to traditional Welsh forms) had begun to play such a major role in *eisteddfodau* that John Jenkins privately questioned whether the 'honor of their [the Welsh gentry's] country and the moral and social worth of its Inhabitants [would] be best promoted' by discontinuing them altogether.[51] At the very least, Jenkins felt, the eisteddfod needed a major overhaul that would restore its 'literary character' and concern for preserving Welsh manuscripts for the nation.

At the same time, however, a new literary character of a different nature was being forged in Wales as a direct result of the eisteddfod. The establishment of Cambrian Societies throughout Wales in 1818–19, and London in 1820, and the expanded eisteddfod movement they helped to foster, played a major part in the continuing development of a Welsh public sphere in terms of print culture. Efforts to enlarge a Welsh-language public sphere by means of periodicals had faltered in the 1790s, but by the 1820s collections of poetry and prose that crossed boundaries of place and time had begun to appear. Volumes appeared 'containing full accounts of the eisteddfodau together with a number of the prize-winning compositions in poetry and prose', among them *Awen Dyfed* ('The Muse of Dyfed', 1822), *Ffrwyth yr Awen* ('Fruits of the Muse', 1823), and *Eos Dyfed* ('The Dyfed Nightingale', 1824). As a result, 'For the first time,' Hywel Teifi Edwards observes, 'a public appraisal of a substantial body of eisteddfod literature was possible.'[52] Beyond the eisteddfod, parallel efforts to pull together a body of anglophone Welsh writing can be seen in publications such as *The Cambrian Register* (published in three volumes, 1796–1818) and *The Cambrian Wreath* (1828), in which Iolo Morganwg, Richard Llwyd, and Felicia Hemans feature prominently. Some publications mixed Welsh- and English-language material in varying degrees, as in *The Cambro-Briton* (1821–2), which featured Welsh poetry with translations, or the 'deliberately cheap, accessible anthology, aimed at the followers of the Provincial Eisteddfodau', *Ceinion Awen y Cymmru* (1831), which ranged from Dafydd ap Gwilym to translations of Byron, Bishop Heber, and Felicia Hemans.[53]

This mixing aside, the Welsh language continued to present the eisteddfod, and Welsh literary culture in general, with difficult questions. What direction should the nation's literature take? What was the role of the poet, and the purpose of his or her work? In the 1820s, as in the 1790s, the expanded eisteddfod was still an important route by which aspiring writers could take part in the artistic life of the nation, and yet, as Hywel Teifi Edwards has shown, the literary culture of Wales lacked widespread support in spite of the institution's increasing prominence. The changing nature of the eisteddfod itself – including its turn to the English language, or to polite and fashionable music – was part of the problem. 'How the Victorian *prifardd* [chief poet] came to find himself relegated in the very institution within which, as tradition dictated, he was properly to hold pole position,' Edwards observes, 'is a matter central to our understanding of the exigent state of nineteenth-century Welsh literature in general.'[54]

While John Jenkins kept his thoughts about the eisteddfod to himself, the status of the Welsh, and particularly Welsh-language literature, was a point that William Owen Pughe was prepared to debate in public in the 1820s. In March 1828, Pughe wrote to the editor of *The Scotsman* in protest at the 'want of information in respect to the state of Wales' in an article that had appeared in its pages shortly before. Pughe's letter was a catalogue of Welsh literary achievements, from its almanacs, dictionaries, and grammars to its history of poetry (crowned by the production of *The Myfyrian Archaiology* between 1801 and 1807) and lively contemporary periodical culture and book trade. The editor responded by admitting his ignorance of Welsh affairs, but also by attributing that ignorance to the insulating or distancing effects of the Welsh language:

> The mis-statements and the want of information so remarkably prevalent respecting Wales, show in a striking point of view the influence of a strange language in isolating the inhabitants of a district from the neighbourhood and fellow-subjects. Wales, like the High-lands, forms a world within itself of which, speaking in a moral & political sense, the Saxon population of Britain knows less than it does of New York or Pensylvania [*sic*].[55]

Attitudes such as this, with their latent suggestions of a lack of civility common to Wales and Highland Scotland, reveal the wider 'undermining of the Welsh language as a national language fit to respond to the transformation of Welsh society in an imperial Britain which adopted "Progress" and

"Success" as its bywords'. The logical end result, Hywel Teifi Edwards argues, was the 'denigration of Welsh poetry as a largely useless product, which inevitably led to what can only be called a crisis of confidence'.[56]

This sense of Welsh as a redundant or problematic language for poetry would not have been helped by long-running disagreements over form that applied specifically to that genre. For the highly influential Goronwy Owen in the eighteenth century, poetry was the space for 'a highly-wrought and specialized form of language' distinct from prose, but even this definition proved controversial.[57] The complex patterns of alliteration and rhyme that comprise *cynghanedd* had seemed prison-like to the English poet Anna Seward when she encountered it in the 1790s as a result of her friendship with David Samwell:

> Eminently to the honour of Wales, and calculated to fan the flame of genius, is that patriotic institution [the eisteddfod] which allots a silver medal to the best poem in its native language. But I am sorry to find that its poetic composition has such an absurd shackle. To make alliteration an indispensable duty, which is but an ornament, and ought never to be used with studied profuseness, is strange indeed. Your bards should combine to cast away such tyrannous fetters.[58]

It would be easy to dismiss Seward's views as those of an outsider, but her sense of the imagination in strict-metre chains was also felt within Wales. The Welsh-language poet and self-educated shoemaker's apprentice (later Anglican clergyman) John Blackwell ('Alun', 1797–1840) similarly characterized strict-metre poetry as a 'bardic Bastile' in an essay on the Welsh language for the 1824 Welshpool provincial eisteddfod.[59]

By the early nineteenth century, popular genres such as the ballad, the hymn, and the carol had flourished in ways that challenged the authority of strict-metre poetry. The eisteddfod was, however, still a particular focal point for the disputes over poetic form known as 'brwydr y mesurau' ('the battle of the metres') that spanned the eighteenth and nineteenth centuries. Eighteenth- and nineteenth-century Welsh poetry generally draws on a long and arguably restrictive tradition of imitation, but for Huw Meirion Edwards, the eisteddfod's prescriptive approach to style and subject matter means that '[a]lmost inevitably, much of the period's more enduring poetry was composed beyond the confines of stifling eisteddfodic convention'.[60] Critics agree that the nineteenth-century eisteddfod movement produced little poetry of lasting worth, and yet, in a period of rapid change within Britain and in terms of empire, the genre must also be seen as a 'shaper and signifier of national aspirations, as the voice of individual and communal experience which needed an audience if it was to resonate'.[61]

That attempt to make Welsh-language poetry part of the fabric of the nineteenth-century nation would have to survive challenging times, as the eisteddfod became the means of channelling national aspirations in a different sense in the 1830s. The last provincial eisteddfod, held at Cardiff in 1834, was followed by ten *eisteddfodau* held in Abergavenny between 1835 and 1853 under the patronage of Augusta Hall (Lady Llanofer) and the Abergavenny Cymreigyddion Society. The outstanding literary production of this period was not Welsh-language poetry but Lady Charlotte Guest's English translation of medieval legends and Arthurian stories, published in collected form in 1849 as *The Mabinogion*. Drawing on the work of William Owen Pughe, and with the help of key eisteddfod figures such as Thomas Price ('Carnhuanawc', 1787–1848) and John Jones ('Tegid', 1792–1852), Guest's enduring translation opened up Welsh culture to a new international audience.[62] Though Augusta Hall strongly supported the Welsh language – in 1867 she would note that 'every *soul* had as absolute a right to the use of his own language as the beasts and birds'[63] – and though the *eisteddfodau* she presided over argued 'for a wider recognition of the value of Welsh as an old European language worthy of scholarly study', these events were 'engulfed' in English.[64] They were also held under the auspices of a body, the Abergavenny Cymreigyddion, that 'more than any other society, sustained bardism's momentum'.[65] As in the 1820s, however, this phase of the eisteddfod's development did not go unchallenged in the 1840s, not least by the young Merthyr Tydfil chemist Thomas Stephens (1821–75), who called for a rational corrective to the imagined past popularized by Iolo Morganwg and his followers. Stephens openly criticized the Abergavenny eisteddfod as an 'empty show' in a series of letters to the *Cambrian* newspaper in 1842 that led to a public dispute involving leading cultural figures such as Iolo Morganwg's son Taliesin Williams (1787–1847) and Thomas Price.[66] Stephens's efforts aside, however, the bardic custom that was now interlaced with the eisteddfod – a national institution from 1861 onwards – would not be understood as fictionalized, and nor would Welsh be confirmed as its primary language, until well into the twentieth century.

Notes

1. Cathryn Charnell-White, ed., *Welsh Poetry of the French Revolution 1789–1805* (Cardiff: University of Wales Press, 2012), 57.

2. The poetry of David Thomas ('Dafydd Ddu Eryri') has been edited and discussed in the broader context of the 1790s, as has John Jones's ('Jac Glan-y-Gors') polemical prose, while Richard Llwyd's poetry has been collected and edited in a single volume. See respectively Charnell-White, *Welsh Poetry*, 230–73; Marion Löffler (with Bethan Jenkins), ed., *Political Pamphlets and Sermons from Wales 1790–1806* (Cardiff: University of Wales Press, 2014), 111–90; Elizabeth Edwards, ed., *Richard Llwyd: Beaumaris Bay and Other Poems* (Nottingham: Trent Editions, 2016).

3. For selections from the periodical and newspaper press, see Marion Löffler, *Welsh Responses to the French Revolution: Press and Public Discourse, 1789–1802* (Cardiff: University of Wales Press, 2012). Charnell-White, ed., *Welsh Poetry*, and Elizabeth Edwards, ed., *English-Language Poetry from Wales 1789–1806* (Cardiff: University of Wales Press, 2013), both draw extensively on manuscript sources.

4. See, for example, Branwen Jarvis, ed., *A Guide to Welsh Literature c. 1700–1800* (Cardiff: University of Wales Press, 2000), which discusses Welsh-language material only, and Damian Walford Davies and Linda Pratt, eds., *Wales and the Romantic Imagination* (Cardiff: University of Wales Press, 2007), which focuses on Wales and anglophone cultural exchanges.

5. Sarah Prescott, 'Review of *English-Language Poetry from Wales*, ed. Elizabeth Edwards', *International Journal of Welsh Writing in English* 2, 1 (2014): 211.

6. See, for example, Geraint H. Jenkins, Ffion Mair Jones, and David Ceri Jones, eds., *The Correspondence of Iolo Morganwg*, 3 vols. (Cardiff: University of Wales Press, 2007).

7. Charnell-White, ed., *Welsh Poetry*, 2.

8. Ibid.

9. Cathryn Charnell-White, *Bardic Circles: National, Regional and Personal Identity in the Bardic Vision of Iolo Morganwg* (Cardiff: University of Wales Press, 2007), 120–1.

10. Geraint H. Jenkins, 'Historical Writing in the Eighteenth Century', in *A Guide to Welsh Literature*, ed. Jarvis, 23.

11. Ibid., 26–7.

12. Ffion Llewellyn Jenkins, 'Celticism and Pre-Romanticism: Evan Evans', in *A Guide to Welsh Literature*, ed. Jarvis, 113.

13. See Charnell-White, ed., *Welsh Poetry*, 230–49 for the full text of the poem in Welsh, with an English translation.

14. Edwards, ed., *English-Language Poetry from Wales*, 76.

15. Charnell-White, ed., *Welsh Poetry*, 36. For the wider British context, see also Mark Philp, ed., *Resisting Napoleon: The British Response to the Threat of Invasion, 1797–1815* (Aldershot: Ashgate, 2006).

16. Charnell-White, ed., *Welsh Poetry*, 28–9.

17. Ibid., 11.

18. Charnell-White, *Bardic Circles*, 119.

19. See Marilyn Butler, 'Romanticism in England', in *Romanticism in National Context*, ed. Roy Porter and Mikuláš Teich (Cambridge: Cambridge University Press, 1988), 37–67, and Dafydd Moore, 'James Macpherson and "Celtic Whiggism"', *Eighteenth-Century Life* 30, 1 (2006): 1–24.

20. Jenkins, 'Historical Writing', 33.

21. Mary-Ann Constantine, *The Truth Against the World: Iolo Morganwg and Romantic Forgery* (Cardiff: University of Wales Press, 2007).

22. See, for example, a section titled 'Religious Tenets, and Discipline, of the British Bards. [From Owen's Translation of the Heroic Elegies, and other Epistles of Llwyarç Hen]', in *The New Annual Register . . . For the Year 1793* (London: G. G. and J. Robinson, 1794), 155–64.

23. *The Critical Review; or Annals of Literature*, vol. 9 (London: A. Hamilton, 1794), 169.

24. Quoted in Damian Walford Davies, *Presences that Disturb* (Cardiff: University of Wales Press, 2002), 166.

25. Ibid., 160.

26. Ibid., 162.

27. Whitney R. D. Jones, *David Williams: The Anvil and the Hammer* (Cardiff: University of Wales Press, 1986).

28. Marion Löffler describes the trajectory of three 1790s Welsh-language radical periodicals, including the threats levelled against some of their editors, in *Welsh Responses to the French Revolution*.

29. Hywel M. Davies, 'Loyalism in Wales 1792–1793', *Welsh History Review* 20, 4 (2001): 687–716.

30. Geraint H. Jenkins, '"A Very Horrid Affair": Sedition and Unitarianism in the Age of Revolutions', in *From Medieval to Modern Wales: Historical Essays in Honour of Kenneth O. Morgan and Ralph A. Griffiths*, ed. R. R. Davies and Geraint H. Jenkins (Cardiff: University of Wales Press, 2004), 175–96.

31. NLW MS 13117E.

32. Edward Williams ('Iolo Morganwg'), 'Cywydd Gorymbil ar Heddwch' ('A Cywydd Invoking Peace'), in *Welsh Poetry*, ed. Charnell-White, 184–5, ll. 17–19, 31–2. See 154–61 for the text of 'Breiniau Dyn'.

33. In the introduction to his 1809 song collection, *A Selection of Welsh Melodies* ('Observations on the Present State of Music and Poetry'), John Parry – not necessarily an obvious supporter of Iolo – judged him the 'first among the bards of the present day (or of many centuries back) as uniting with a first-rate poetical genius, an intimate acquaintance with our ancient history, manners, and customs, as well as the sciences in general'. His modern standing as by some way the most significant Welsh writer of the period has been assessed by the AHRC-funded project, *Iolo Morganwg and the Romantic*

Tradition in Wales, www.iolomorganwg.wales.ac.uk (accessed
17 August 2017).

34. Ceri W. Lewis, 'Iolo Morganwg', in *A Guide to Welsh Literature*, ed. Jarvis, 127.

35. See Marion Löffler, *The Literary and Historical Legacy of Iolo Morganwg 1826–1926* (Cardiff: University of Wales Press, 2007), 130–49.

36. Jenkins, 'Historical Writing', 33.

37. The complex response of the poet and antiquarian Evan Evans to the poetry of Thomas Gray is a good example of this duality. See Sarah Prescott, *Eighteenth-Century Writing from Wales: Bards and Britons* (Cardiff: University of Wales Press, 2008), 57–83.

38. Alan Liu, *Local Transcendence: Essays on Postmodern Historicism and the Database* (Chicago: University of Chicago Press, 2008), 89 (emphasis original).

39. The point is made by G. J. Williams: 'Nid cwbl amhriodol fyddai cymharu Morgannwg Iolo Morganwg a Sgotland Syr Walter Scott – y mae'n un o greadigaethau mawr y cyfnod rhamantaidd yng Nghymru' ('It would not be entirely inappropriate to compare the Glamorgan of Iolo Morganwg with the Scotland of Sir Walter Scott – it is one of the great creations of the Romantic period in Wales'), *Iolo Morganwg* (Caerdydd: Gwasg Prifysgol Cymru, 1956), 320.

40. On the culture of repression and surveillance of the 1790s, see Kenneth R. Johnston, *Unusual Suspects: Pitt's Reign of Alarm and the Lost Generation of the 1790s* (Oxford: Oxford University Press, 2013).

41. Davies, *Presences that Disturb*, 167.

42. Edwards, ed., *English-Language Poetry from Wales*, 128.

43. Marion Löffler documents how quickly radicalism fell away in 1790s Wales: 'By October 1796 . . . the Welsh attempt to create a radical periodical press was over . . . The first decade of the nineteenth century belonged to Welsh-language periodicals founded by Methodists, loyalists, patriots and eisteddfod enthusiasts, not to radical Wales' (*Welsh Responses to the French Revolution*, 52).

44. Felicia Hemans, 'The Meeting of the Bards', *The Works of Mrs Hemans*, 7 vols. (Edinburgh and London: Blackwood and Cadell, 1839), V, 29.

45. Huw Meirion Edwards, 'The Lyric Poets', in *A Guide to Welsh Literature c. 1800–1900*, ed. Hywel Teifi Edwards (Cardiff: University of Wales Press, 2000), 108.

46. For a discussion of Hemans's lyrics as expressing a resistant Welsh nationalism, see Elizabeth Edwards, '"Lonely and Voiceless Your Halls Must Remain": Romantic-era National Song and Felicia Hemans's *Welsh Melodies* (1822)', *Journal for Eighteenth-Century Studies* 38, 1 (March 2015): 83–97.

47. Glyn Tegai Hughes, 'Life and Thought', in *A Guide to Welsh Literature*, ed. Jarvis, 5.

48. Charnell-White, ed., *Welsh Poetry*, 33.

49. Ffion Mair Jones, '"To Know Him Is to Esteem Him": John Jenkins, Ifor Ceri 1770–1829', *Montgomeryshire Collections* 99 (2011): 53–82.
50. Hughes, 'Life and Thought', 36.
51. Quoted in Jones, '"To Know Him Is to Esteem Him"', 79.
52. Hywel Teifi Edwards, 'The Eisteddfod Poet: An Embattled Figure', in *A Guide to Welsh Literature*, ed. Edwards, 30.
53. Edwards, 'The Lyric Poets', 110.
54. Edwards, 'The Eisteddfod Poet', 26–7.
55. William Owen Pughe to Pryce Buckley Williams, 24 May 1828, NLW MS 1885B, fols. 12–13.
56. Edwards, 'The Eisteddfod Poet', 35.
57. Branwen Jarvis, 'Goronwy Owen: Neoclassical Poet and Critic', in *A Guide to Welsh Literature*, ed. Jarvis, 94.
58. Anna Seward to David Samwell, 31 June 1791, *Letters of Anna Seward: Written Between the Years 1784 and 1807*, 6 vols. (Edinburgh: Archibald Constable, 1811), III, 83.
59. Quoted in Edwards, 'The Lyric Poets', 101.
60. Ibid., 97.
61. Edwards, 'The Eisteddfod Poet', 35.
62. Rachel Bromwich, '"The Mabinogion" and Lady Charlotte Guest', *THSC* (1986): 127–41.
63. Jane Aaron, *Nineteenth-Century Women's Writing in Wales: Nation, Gender and Identity* (Cardiff: University of Wales Press, 2007), 67.
64. Edwards, 'The Eisteddfod Poet', 37.
65. Charnell-White, *Bardic Circles*, 156.
66. Marion Löffler with Hywel Gethin Rhys, 'Thomas Stephens and the Abergavenny Cymreigyddion: Letters from the *Cambrian* 1842–3', *National Library of Wales Journal* 34, 4 (2009), online only, www.llgc.org.uk/fileadmin/fileadmin/docs_gwefan/amdanom_ni/cylchgrawn_llgc/cgr_erth_XXXIVr h4_2009_2.pdf (accessed 17 August 2017).

16

Popular Poetry, Methodism, and the Ascendancy of the Hymn

E. WYN JAMES

The eighteenth century is one of the great turning points in Welsh history. It was a century of 'awakenings' which saw the beginnings of far-reaching demographic, cultural, economic, and political changes that would transform Wales and Welsh life. These included a revival of interest in the language, literature, antiquities, and traditions of Wales, a great expansion in popular education, increasing political radicalization, and the beginnings of major industrial developments and urbanization.

A central element in these developments was religion. The period from the mid-eighteenth century onward saw marked changes in religious adherence and patterns of worship, stemming largely from the 'Methodist Revival' that began in around 1735. In 1700, Wales was a thinly populated country of about 390,000 inhabitants, with a mainly rural economy, where loyalty to the gentry and the established Anglican Church went almost unquestioned, and with only about 5 per cent of the population adhering to Nonconformist groupings such as the Independents (or Congregationalists) and the Baptists. By 1850 the population had trebled, with burgeoning industrial communities (in the south-east in particular), a significant growth in radicalism, and much political and social unrest; and for every Anglican there were by then almost four people attending worship at Nonconformist chapels, which had been opening at an average of one every eight days between 1800 and 1850. As a result, the second half of the nineteenth century would see a cultural hegemony in Wales that was primarily Liberal in political allegiance and Nonconformist in religion. 'Chapel-building mania' meant that Nonconformist chapels became a dominant architectural feature in every town and village throughout the country, and it was partly because of the enthusiastic hymn-singing which characterized the life of those chapels that by the mid-1870s Wales had become known as 'the Land of Song'.[1]

During the hundred or so years from the middle of the eighteenth century, Wales experienced at least fifteen major evangelical revivals, not to mention many more localized awakenings.[2] Crucially, these religious revivals were conducted mainly through the medium of Welsh, the only language of most of the population at that time. Under these influences, Christian worship became increasingly characterized by fervent preaching and by ardent, extemporary prayer and praising, together with other expressions of religious ecstasy and 'enthusiasm'; eighteenth-century Welsh Methodists were given the nickname 'Welsh Jumpers' because of their practice of leaping for joy in their meetings.[3] Methodism began as a renewal movement within the Anglican Church, but by the early nineteenth century the Welsh Calvinistic Methodists had become a Nonconformist denomination. Furthermore, the 'enthusiasm' that marked Methodist worship gradually spread to the older Nonconformist denominations, meaning that by the first half of the nineteenth century a common theological and experiential ethos – Calvinist and evangelical – had come to characterize Welsh Nonconformity in general.

A core element in the expression of this experiential evangelical faith was the hymn. From the very beginnings of the Methodist Revival, hymns and hymn-singing were a central element in the expression of the beliefs and emotions of those who came under the influence of these evangelical revivals. This led to a veritable explosion in hymn-writing and the creation of what would become a large and extremely influential body of popular verse; it has been estimated, for example, that over 3,000 hymns were produced in Welsh in the half century between 1740 and 1790.

This corpus of evangelical hymnody is one of the great highlights of Welsh literature and an important precursor of the romantic lyric poetry which flourished in Welsh in the nineteenth and early twentieth centuries. These evangelical hymns represent a major new departure in Welsh literature and popular culture, for they are to a large degree a new kind of religious expression in song, a new genre to satisfy a new depth of personal religious experience. At their best, they are characterized by passion, vigour, and a lyrical beauty and combine effectively the theological and the experiential, the objective and the subjective.

Popular Culture and Methodism

In January 1695 the young poet from Penllyn, Siôn Dafydd Laes, was on his deathbed. He was perhaps the last poet to be wholly dependent for his livelihood on the patronage of the gentry, and he has become a symbol of the final faltering breaths of the rich bardic tradition of medieval Wales.[4] However, that bardic tradition would in fact persist into the eighteenth century, albeit in a modified and much weakened and impoverished state, and upheld now by amateurs from among the lower orders of society (mainly artisans, small farmers, and sextons), who lacked the poetic craftsmanship and artistry of the professional bards at the height of that tradition. Huw Morys ('Eos Ceiriog', 1622–1709), a farmer from Pontymeibion in the Ceiriog Valley and the most prominent poet of the seventeenth century, is an important transitional figure in the recasting of the bardic tradition in this period. He wrote poems in *cynghanedd* in the traditional strict metres, but although patronized to an extent by the gentry he was not dependent on them for his living and he also wrote poetry for a wider social spectrum. As such, he may be regarded as a forerunner of the *beirdd gwlad*, 'country poets', of north-east Wales who would gather regularly in taverns from the early eighteenth century onward to practise their craft. It is from these gatherings of *beirdd gwlad*, or *eisteddfodau* as they began to be called, that the modern *eisteddfod* movement started to develop, after the London Welsh society, the Gwyneddigion, a significant number of whose members came from north-east Wales, began sponsoring such gatherings from 1789 onward.[5]

Huw Morys not only continued to write traditional strict-metre poetry but was also a key figure in the development of a new genre in Welsh poetry often called *canu rhydd cynganeddol* (free-metre poetry in *cynghanedd*) or *canu carolaidd* (carol poetry) which would prove extremely popular during the eighteenth century and the first half of the nineteenth century among the *beirdd gwlad* of north-east Wales in particular. *Canu rhydd*, free-metre poetry, appears to have existed side by side with poetry written in *cynghanedd* in the strict metres during the Middle Ages, but because of its lower status very little was committed to writing until the sixteenth century. However, with the decline of the bardic order and growing English influences, free-metre poetry becomes increasingly prominent and large quantities of such poems begin to be put to paper. The metres of that poetry fall into two broad categories. Some are in traditional Welsh strict metres, but without *cynghanedd*, while others were written in metres which allowed them to be sung to the popular tunes of the day.[6] Free-metre poetry without *cynghanedd* was predominant in south Wales throughout the early modern period, but increasingly, from the middle of the seventeenth century onward, the poets of north-east Wales, with Huw Morys as a crucial figure among them, grafted *cynghanedd* onto free metres, creating a very sensuous and sonorous effect, especially when those poems were sung on the popular tunes for which they were set, where 'the articulations of the stanza coincided with the articulations of the air, the music of the tune bringing out the music of the *cynghanedd*, and the rhymes continually answering one another'.[7]

Hundreds of ballads and carols in this intricate style, abounding in assonance and alliteration, were written for popular consumption by the poets of north-east Wales during the 200 years from the mid-seventeenth to the mid-nineteenth centuries.[8] Many of these same poets would also compete on strict-metre poetry at the *eisteddfodau*, and from among them also came the authors of the rustic plays known as *anterliwtiau*, 'interludes', which probably developed out of the morality plays of the sixteenth century. This again was a genre pioneered by Huw Morys and was at its strongest in north-east Wales in the eighteenth century. These amateur folk plays were frequently performed in fairs and markets, in farmyards and in tavern yards, with a waggon or a makeshift platform serving as a stage. In structure they normally included a main 'story-line' together with a traditional sub-plot involving the stock characters of the Fool and the Miser, and another characteristic of these metrical plays is that the spoken verse was interspersed with eight or nine songs in the intricate ballad style of the period, some of which came to have a life of their own, free from their original context.[9] About forty of these *anterliwtiau* have survived in print and manuscript, with almost all of their authors emanating from north-east Wales.[10] Among them were Jonathan Hughes (1721–1805), Llangollen; Thomas Edwards ('Twm o'r Nant', 1739–1810); Huw Jones (d. 1782), Llangwm, and Ellis Roberts ('Elis y Cowper', *c.* 1712–89), all of whom were also prolific poets in the *canu rhydd cynganeddol* style and familiar figures in the bardic network that gathered at *eisteddfodau* and in taverns and was such a central component in the lively folk culture which characterized that part of Wales in that period.

It is often claimed that the Methodists killed off this older folk culture. However, while it is true that the spiritual awakenings of the period were a crucial element in the major cultural changes that were afoot, and that the culture which developed as a result of the evangelical revivals would gradually become dominant by the middle of the nineteenth century, other factors were also at work. It has been argued that the folk literature of the eighteenth century which was pioneered by Huw Morys and others did not represent a new beginning but was actually the final phase of a traditional Welsh bardic culture which had been in gradual, terminal decline since at least the middle of the seventeenth century as the gentry patrons became increasingly anglicized.[11] While the growth of Methodism probably accelerated its demise, that traditional, predominantly rural, community folk culture was already becoming increasingly regarded as 'old-fashioned' as the eighteenth century progressed, under the influence

E. WYN JAMES

of modernity, urbanization, and industrialization, not to mention the
growth of an individualism linked to romanticism and radicalism. The
cultural changes that were afoot were more complicated, therefore, than
simply a clash between Methodism and an older, more 'carefree' folk
culture.

Nevertheless, it is true that the growth of Methodism was a key factor in
those changes. It is said that, in the second half of the eighteenth century,
there were two events that could draw a large crowd in north Wales, namely
an *anterliwt* performance and a Methodist sermon. However, by the end of
the century the *anterliwt*'s popularity was going into steep decline, in contrast
with Methodism and evangelical Nonconformity, which were increasingly
winning hearts and minds and would become the cultural hegemony in
Wales by the middle of the nineteenth century.[12] Twm o'r Nant, the greatest
of all *anterliwt* writers, became increasingly attracted to Methodism, and it is
symbolic of the ascendancy of the new evangelical counter-culture that
Twm's last public appearance was in the 'big seat' in a Calvinistic
Methodist chapel at Tremadog in February 1810, listening to a sermon by
Thomas Charles of Bala (1755–1814), the foremost leader of the second
generation of Welsh Calvinistic Methodists, in the company of some of the
most powerful Methodist preachers of the day, including John Elias (1774–
1841), who would become the commanding leader of the next generation of
Welsh Calvinistic Methodists.[13]

The Emergence of the Hymn

While the Protestant Reformation saw an outpouring of hymns and hymn-
singing in Germany, this was not the case in Britain, where the Reformers
followed Calvin rather than Luther in his emphasis that God was so majestic
that only the words of God himself were sufficiently exalted to praise him in
public worship. As a result, while Calvinists encouraged congregational
singing in the vernacular as part of church worship, they believed that the
appropriate texts for doing so were paraphrases of Scripture, and metrical
psalms in particular. Some metrical psalms had been produced in Welsh in
the medieval period,[14] but the coming of Protestantism and the affording of
official status to Welsh as a language of public worship by Act of Parliament
in 1563 (which led to the translation of the Bible and the Book of Common
Prayer into Welsh) generated new attempts to create metrical versions of the
Psalms in Welsh, some in strict-metre poetry and others in free metres. These
culminated in the metrical psalter of Edmwnd Prys, first published in 1621.[15]

Edmwnd Prys (1543/4–1623) was a prominent cleric, a noted scholar, and a talented poet in both strict and free metres, and his metrical psalter has been described 'as a work of great literary merit and as a landmark within Welsh free metre poetry';[16] indeed one leading critic has gone so far as to call it possibly the finest metrical psalter produced in Europe in the Reformation period[17] – a significant claim given the huge popularity of the genre across northern Europe in that period. These metrical psalms proved extremely popular. They were virtually the only songs used in public worship by both Anglicans and Nonconformists for over two centuries, and some are still sung today.

Other popular religious poems that began to multiply in Welsh from the sixteenth century onward are what might be called 'sermons in song'. Partly in order to counteract the dearth of preaching in the established Anglican Church, various types of carol literature of a religious nature start to appear in manuscript and then in print from the sixteenth century onwards. Initially, the word *carol* in Welsh could refer to any song in free metre, but there was an increasing tendency to use it for songs associated with seasonal customs and the ecclesiastical year.[18] In style, the religious free-metre poems of the early modern period are generally simple and direct, without the intricacies of the traditional strict-metre poetry, but also without much of its artistry. Their concern is not so much with craftsmanship as with the message, and their function is mainly social, didactic, and devotional, exhorting the community to piety, prayer, and penitence rather than giving expression to a range of personal spiritual experiences. For the most part, they use a standard Welsh rather than dialect, but tend towards colloquial rather than literary forms and do not hesitate to use English loanwords. Although generally mediocre, this free-metre verse possesses a certain melodiousness and sprightliness, and at its best can produce memorable poetry, such as the Christmas carol written in 1621 by Risiart Dafydd, probably a gamekeeper at Margam, which portrays the Incarnation as a ladder of sturdy, faultless rungs joining heaven and earth,[19] and the poem by Tomas Llywelyn (*fl.* 1580–1610) of Rhigos which takes the form of a dream where the church and the tavern debate their respective merits, with the tavern arguing that it is more like paradise than the church, because it is always full of every pleasure and delight.[20]

The best known of the religious carols of the period are the *plygain* carols, since the tradition of singing them during the Christmas season still persists today, albeit in a modified form.[21] As the name *plygain* (from the Late Latin *pullicantiō*; 'cockcrow') suggests, they were originally sung in church services early on Christmas morning. They are essentially long sermons in song. Although they express wonder at the mystery of the God-man and his Incarnation, rather than concentrating on the Christmas story itself, they tend to centre on Christ's atonement on the cross, exhorting to repentance, faith, and godly living, and they frequently encompass the whole of the redemption story from Adam's Fall in the Garden of Eden to the joys of heaven. It is said that the first person to have written a *plygain* carol was Wmffre Dafydd ab Ifan, the sexton of Llanbryn-mair, who died in 1646,[22] and it was especially, although not exclusively, in north-east Wales that these carols flourished from the mid-seventeenth century until the mid-nineteenth century, written in the complex *canu rhydd cynganeddol* style, full of assonance and alliteration, that had been pioneered in that part of Wales by Huw Morys and others in the seventeenth century.

A type of carol popular in south-east Wales between the first half of the sixteenth century and the middle of the seventeenth was the *cwndid*, many of which were religious, moral, and didactic in nature;[23] while another type of religious carol, the *halsing*, was popular in south-west Wales between the Restoration and the Methodist Revival.[24] The most popular and influential of all the authors of Welsh religious free-metre poetry of the early modern period was Rhys Prichard (1579?–1644/5), a Puritan-inclined Anglican clergyman from Llandovery in north Carmarthenshire, who was referred to by some of his contemporaries as *y cwndidwr du*, 'the black *cwndid* writer'.[25] The use of poetry for popular instruction is clearly demonstrated by the way Prichard turned sections of devotional books into simple, memorable verse so as to make their contents more accessible for the largely illiterate population of the day.[26] He wrote thousands of verses. Some are single stanzas, but many form longer poems, often running into tens of verses. This large corpus of religious verse was wide-ranging in subject matter, from doctrinal to devotional, and from the cautionary to the exhortative, and included verses to be recited on all manner of occasions and in all sorts of contexts, for example while dressing in the morning, or before going courting, or at Communion, or in childbirth. While Prichard's aim was to compose catchy verse for popular consumption rather than elevated poetry, he had the ability to create striking imagery, as in this stanza from a long poem entitled 'Cofiwch Angau', 'Remember Death':

> Ni cheir gweled mwy o'n hôl
> Nag ôl neidir ar y ddôl;
> Neu ôl llong aeth dros y tonne
> Neu ôl saeth mewn awyr dene.

(Nothing of our trace remains
more than the track of a snake across a meadow,
or the wake of a ship at sea,
or the thin flight of an arrow through the air.)[27]

Vicar Prichard used a limited number of metres. Most of his stanzas are quatrains, with the vast majority in the four-stressed-line metre that was commonly used for the *hen benillion* (literally the 'old stanzas'), the large body of popular traditional folk verses which are sometimes also called *penillion telyn*, 'harp stanzas', since singing them to harp accompaniment was a common form of entertainment at social gatherings. Although frequently written in the first person singular, most of these *hen benillion* are anonymous and are very difficult to date with any accuracy, but in atmosphere they belong to a pre-urban, pre-Methodist Wales. They began being collected in earnest in the eighteenth century by antiquarians who recognised their literary worth,[28] but some are at least as old as the sixteenth century, and the fact that religious reformers like Vicar Prichard adopted the genre is indicative of its popularity in oral tradition in the seventeenth century.

Despite the predominance of metrical psalms and carol literature, hymns were not entirely neglected in the pre-Methodist period. Some Anglicans, such as Rowland Vaughan (*c.* 1590–1667) and Ellis Wynne (1671–1734), turned their hand to writing the occasional hymn,[29] but it is among the Puritans and their Nonconformist successors that the congregational hymn really began to take its first faltering steps. Some of the Welsh Puritans, such as the fiery Vavasor Powell (1617–70), enthusiastically encouraged hymn-singing, both in private devotions and in congregational worship. Powell wrote some hymns himself, but although he spoke Welsh and composed prayers in Welsh, his hymns are almost all in English, which emphasizes the English influences that pervaded much of the Puritan movement in Wales. Here are the opening lines of one of his poems, 'A Hymn on the Sabboth Day':

> The rest of rests to me is Christ, in whom I do rejoyce;
> His day a Sabboth is to me; 'Tis not mine but his choice.
> He rose and rested on that day, to shew his work was done.
> His blest example is my Rule, his Candle is my Sun . . .[30]

But generally it was the psalms that dominated congregational worship among Puritans and Nonconformists. Many of the poems described as 'hymns' were intended mainly as expressions of an individual's piety and tended as a result to be more personal and poetical than is usual in congregational hymns. The most prominent composer of devotional poetry was the mystical Puritan, Morgan Llwyd (1619–59). A prose writer of the first order, Llwyd was uneven as a poet – indeed, it could be argued that he is at his most poetical in his prose – but some of his poetry is noteworthy, in particular his sensuous paraphrase of parts of the first and second chapters of the Song of Solomon: 'Fy Nuw, cusana fi â'th fin. / Melysach yw dy serch na'r gwin. / Di yw anwylyd f'enaid i . . .' ('My God, caress me with those lips of Thine. / Much sweeter is thy love than wine. / Thou art the darling of my soul . . .').[31] His poems also include some metrical psalms, and, like Rhys Prichard, he too wrote devotional and didactic verse in the manner of the *hen benillion*. Morgan Llwyd was probably the most steeped in Welsh culture of all the Welsh Puritan leaders, and although many of his poems are in English, this may explain why his Welsh-language poetry is generally superior to his English verse.[32]

While Nonconformists normally favoured the use of psalms in congregational worship, there was one main exception. Because Christ and his disciples had sung 'an hymn' (Matthew 26:30) at the Last Supper, this was seen as scriptural warrant for singing a hymn during the Communion service. This connection between hymn-singing and the Lord's Supper may be seen clearly in the small collections of Welsh hymns which began to be published by Nonconformists by the early eighteenth century. The first of these was a collection of six sacramental hymns by Thomas Baddy (d. 1729), a Nonconformist minister in Denbigh, appended to his 1703 Welsh translation of Thomas Doolittle's *A Treatise Concerning the Lord's Supper*. Then almost immediately, in 1705, James Owen (1654–1706), a Nonconformist minister based in Shrewsbury, published *Hymnau Scrythurol* ('Scriptural Hymns'), which included hymns to be used at the sacraments of the Lord's Supper and baptism, together with some for use on the Lord's Day. Three or four similar collections appeared during the next twenty years or so, including a further collection of eleven hymns by Thomas Baddy appended to his metrical version of the Song of Solomon, published in 1725.[33] Scriptural paraphrasing was a commonplace of these early eighteenth-century hymn collections, with the Song of Solomon featuring prominently, for, as one historian has emphasized, '[Thomas Baddy] and his colleagues were especially enamoured of the Song of Solomon, which not only formed a popular cornerstone for many hymns, but also stood in its own right as a collection of love poems that revealed Christ's love for his church and his people.'[34] This reflects the increasingly Christocentric nature of Nonconformist worship in the late seventeenth and early eighteenth centuries, which continues into the Methodist period. The hymns in these early Nonconformist collections tend to be doctrinal and objective in nature, and while one cannot claim that they have any great literary merit, they represent a significant step forward in Welsh-language hymnody.

William Williams of Pantycelyn (1717–1791)

In early eighteenth-century Wales, the worship of both Anglicans and Nonconformists tended, in the main, to be rather sedate and introverted, but, as has already been indicated, the situation would change radically with the outbreak of the evangelical awakening commonly known as the 'Methodist Revival'. While they remained technically members of the established Anglican Church, from the outset the Methodist converts met together in *seiadau* (or 'society meetings'; the singular form is *seiat*, deriving from the English word, 'society'), where they would share their spiritual experiences and put them under the microscope, which is why they were called *seiadau profiad*, 'experience meetings'. The Methodist *seiat* can in many ways be regarded as the cradle of the Welsh congregational hymn. The *seiadau* would begin with the singing of a hymn, and those present would often continue singing, praying, and praising for hours after the meeting had formally concluded. Initially they made use of existing religious verse, such as the metrical psalms of Edmwnd Prys and the hymns of Nonconformists, but very soon some of the Methodist leaders began to write hymns themselves in order to meet the demand from the society meetings and to give expression to the shared, yet intensely personal experiences of the Methodist converts. By the early 1740s small printed collections of hymns had begun to be published for the use of the Methodist societies, and a number of manuscript compilations have also survived from the same period.[35]

Although some of these early efforts are not without merit, none were totally successful in expressing 'in verse the essential zeal and individual sense of salvation and intimacy with Christ that characterized the revival'.[36] But then, in 1744, there appeared from a printing press in Carmarthen what was, at first sight, an ephemeral penny-pamphlet entitled *Aleluia*, containing nine hymns. This was the first venture into print by the greatest of all Welsh hymn-writers and one of the creators of modern Welsh literature, namely William Williams of Pantycelyn. William Williams is usually referred to in Welsh cultural circles as 'Williams Pantycelyn' or simply as 'Pantycelyn', after the name of the farm where he spent most of his adult life, near the busy market town of Llandovery in north Carmarthenshire, a major junction on the drovers' roads from west Wales to southern England. Born in 1717 and dying in 1791, his life spans the eighteenth century, and in many ways Williams is the embodiment of the profound changes in the religious life of Wales that occurred during that period.[37]

He was born into a Nonconformist family and went to study at a dissenting academy near Hay in Breconshire. On his way home from the academy to his lodgings one day in 1737 or 1738, he experienced evangelical conversion upon hearing the fervent young Methodist leader, Howel Harris (1714–73), preaching in Talgarth churchyard. Life would never be the same again. Rather than becoming a doctor, as he had intended, Williams now set his sights on being a physician of souls. However, his Methodist conversion made him look towards the Anglican ministry rather than the Nonconformity of his upbringing, and he served in the Llanwrtyd area for a few years in the early 1740s as curate to Theophilus Evans (1693–1767), author of the extremely influential *Drych y Prif Oesoedd*, 'The Mirror of the First Ages', 'the most widely read history book in Welsh in the eighteenth and nineteenth centuries', with at least twenty editions having appeared by 1900.[38] Theophilus Evans was vehemently opposed to Methodism, and the Anglican authorities refused to confer full priest's orders on Williams; thus in 1743 he left his curacy in order to devote himself entirely to the Methodist cause. Williams Pantycelyn would become one of the most able Methodist leaders of his generation. From his home-base at Pantycelyn, he travelled extensively throughout Wales for almost fifty years – over 2,500 miles annually on horseback – shepherding the Methodist flock and evangelizing. Little wonder, then, that images of travel and pilgrimage occur so frequently in his hymns.

Williams was a prolific writer. Between 1744 and his death in 1791, he published over ninety books and pamphlets, almost all in Welsh. A wide variety of material flowed from his pen. In addition to his hymns, he wrote two epic poems, both around 5,500 lines in length. One, entitled *Golwg ar Deyrnas Crist* ('A Prospect of Christ's Kingdom'), is a panoramic, cosmic overview of the history of the world, from the eternal decrees which preceded creation up until the end of time; while the other, *Bywyd a Marwolaeth Theomemphus* ('The Life and Death of Theomemphus'), focuses on the spiritual experiences of a representative (albeit larger-than-life) Methodist convert from cradle to grave.[39] Over thirty funeral elegies form a substantial body of verse that provides important insights into the development and ethos of the Methodist Revival in Wales. Williams also wrote eight original prose works and published a number of translations into Welsh of works by authors on both sides of the Atlantic, demonstrating that while Williams devoted his time and efforts almost entirely to ministering in Wales and through the Welsh language, he was at the same time part of an international evangelical network.

The common factor which links all of his writings is that they were produced for utilitarian reasons. They are the work of a born, if rather undisciplined, literary genius, spurred on by the need to provide practical literature for Methodist converts, to help them understand their spiritual experiences and to build them up in their faith. For example, among his original prose works are a treatise on jealousy (which he compares to a crocodile tearing its prey into pieces), a discussion on the stewardship of material wealth, and a volume of marriage guidance. His conviction that ignorance was the breeding ground for prejudice, sectarianism, and bigotry was the stimulus for his most ambitious literary project, his encyclopaedic *Pantheologia*, a 654-page volume on the history of the religions of the world, published in parts over a period of almost twenty years between 1762 and 1778–9. Not only is this volume brim-full of information about the various faiths and belief systems, but it also contains much about the history, geography, and customs of the lands in which those faiths were to be found. It is a volume which shows Pantycelyn to be an heir of 'enlightenment' as well as 'enthusiasm'.

It is difficult to overemphasize the importance of this literary corpus and its influence on the religious and cultural life of Wales. Through it Williams Pantycelyn became the predominant literary voice of the Methodist Revival in Wales and one of the most significant figures in Welsh literature in the modern period. With Williams, said the literary critic, Kathryn Jenkins, 'for the first time in Welsh literature a preoccupation with spiritual experience and personal salvation became the main topic of poetry'.[40] She could also say that, whereas 'there had been very little discussion of women's experiences and emotions' in Welsh literature prior to Williams, he was 'the first author to give women a central role in some of his works'.[41] Pantycelyn's original prose works, although works of practical theology, were also examples of creative writing, since they took the form of a dialogue or correspondence between fictional characters, frequently with Latin or Greek names. Interestingly, the major Welsh literary critic, Saunders Lewis (1893–1985), describes one of these works as the first attempt in Welsh to create a novel.[42] He made even more eye-catching claims. Williams, he argued, represented a break with the traditional classical aesthetic of Welsh literature and as such was the first modern poet and the first Romantic poet, not only in Wales but possibly in the whole of Europe.[43]

Despite the significance of Pantycelyn's literary corpus as a whole, and his epics and original prose works in particular, pride of place must be given to his hymns. He wrote over 850 hymns in Welsh, publishing them regularly in books and pamphlets between 1744 and 1787, and he is rightly regarded as 'the father of the Welsh congregational hymn'.[44] In addition, Pantycelyn wrote just over 120 hymns in English, bringing his total output to almost 1,000 hymns,[45] and the English adaptation of one of his Welsh hymns, 'Guide me, O thou great Jehovah', is among the best-known and most popular hymns in the English-speaking world. Written primarily for the use of the Methodist community, his hymns cover the whole range of evangelical Christian experience and are a balanced blend of the theological and the experiential. In style, Williams Pantycelyn mixes literary Welsh (and in particular that of the majestic Renaissance translation of the Bible) with the Welsh of the marketplace to develop a new, supple poetic diction with which to explore and express the world of the soul and the self that had opened to the converts of the revival. The hymns abound with scriptural allusions and imagery and make extensive use of typology – a technique which draws the Methodist believer of the eighteenth century dramatically and dynamically into the biblical narrative.[46]

As can be seen in Williams's best-known English hymn, 'Guide me, O thou great Jehovah', one of the most prominent of these images, which draws especially on the Exodus story in the Old Testament, is that of the believer as a pilgrim, travelling through the barren wilderness of this world towards his heavenly home. He prays for divine guidance and protection on that journey, through all the trials and temptations that he must face, until he lands 'safe on Canaan's side' of Jordan, the river of death. Such imagery is by no means the exclusive preserve of Williams Pantycelyn, of course, but what is distinctive is what might be described as a fusion of local and biblical landscapes,[47] for side by side with the imagery of travelling through a desert, through a 'barren land', in Pantycelyn's hymns the pilgrim 'also meets with streams and floods, and with a succession of steep hills and threatening crags which belong unmistakeably to the landscape of Wales'.[48] The other main image in Pantycelyn's hymns, drawing in this case especially on the Song of Solomon, is that of Christ as Lover and Beloved, and of the Saviour as Bridegroom.[49] An intense love for Christ and a deep longing for heaven run through Pantycelyn's hymns, and that is primarily because heaven means, above all else, being with Christ. Indeed to Williams, Christ is heaven; and it is the passion of personal redemption which pervades his work, and ultimately the passion for the Redeemer himself, which makes Williams Pantycelyn the great hymn-writer that he is.

By way of example, let us consider one of Pantycelyn's most famous hymns, first published in 1764 and described by John Morris-Jones (1864–1929), Professor of Welsh at Bangor, as one of the most perfect lyrics in the Welsh language. Here it is in full with a literal English translation:

Mi dafla' 'maich oddi ar fy ngwar	I cast my burden from off my shoulders
Wrth deimlo dwyfol loes;	as I feel divine anguish;
Euogrwydd fel mynyddau'r byd	guilt like the world's mountains
Dry yn ganu wrth dy groes.	turns to song at thy cross.
Os edrych wnaf i'r dwrain draw,	If I look to the east yonder,
Os edrych wnaf i'r de,	if I look to the south,
Ymhlith a fu, neu ynteu ddaw,	among those who have been, or are yet
'Does tebyg iddo Fe.	to come,
	there is no one like Him.
Fe rodd ei ddwylo pur ar lled,	He stretched his pure hands wide,
Fe wisgodd goron ddrain,	He wore a crown of thorns,
Er mwyn i'r brwnt gael bod yn wyn	so that the filthy might be white
Fel hyfryd liain main.	like lovely fine linen.
Esgyn a wnaeth i entrych ne'	He ascended into highest heaven
I eiriol dros y gwan;	to intercede for the weak;
Fe sugna f'enaid innau'n lân	He will draw up my soul fully
I'w fynwes yn y man.	to his bosom before long.
Ac yna caf fod gydag Ef	And there I shall be with Him
Pan êl y byd ar dân,	when the world goes on fire,
Ac edrych yn ei hyfryd wedd,	and gaze into his lovely countenance,
Gan' harddach nag o'r bla'n.	a hundred times more beautiful than
	before.

In structure the hymn develops robustly from sin to salvation. Pilgrimage is suggested by the oblique reference in the first verse to the scene in John Bunyan's *Pilgrim's Progress* where the burden of sin is loosed from off the shoulders of the pilgrim as he approaches a wayside cross. The cross of Christ is literally at the heart of this hymn, being depicted in the middle verse; and the biblical allusion to Revelation 19:8 ('for the fine linen is the righteousness of saints') gives further depth to that depiction. But although he is not actually referred to once by name in the hymn, it is the Saviour himself, and the matchless beauty of the Beloved, which is central to the hymn from start to finish. The emphasis is on the visual, and while such gazing means that there is an objectivity at work to a degree, the mood is extremely subjective throughout. In the original Welsh the rhythms and word patterns combine to create an evocative atmosphere and a consummate whole. Each verse is a single sentence which develops effortlessly, reaching a climax in the last line; and like movements in a symphony, each verse not only reaches its own climax but leads on from verse to verse to the ultimate climax where the believer is in highest heaven gazing on the Beloved's unsurpassable countenance.

In addition to his great influence on the literature and religion of modern Wales, it is also worth emphasizing Pantycelyn's wider impact, including on the growth of radicalism. As can be seen in his pamphlet, *Aurora Borealis* (1774), and in his influential English hymn, 'O'er those gloomy hills of darkness', Williams Pantycelyn was a postmillennialist; that is, he believed that there would be an extended period – the 'Millennium', or 'Thousand Years' – prior to Christ's Second Coming when the Christian gospel and social justice would hold sway throughout the world. By the end of the eighteenth century many evangelicals, including Pantycelyn, believed that this millennial dawn was imminent. This gave much impetus to the powerful Protestant overseas missionary movement that arose in that period, as well as movements for social reform, such as the campaign to abolish the slave trade. It is significant that Williams Pantycelyn was the first person to condemn the transatlantic slave trade in print in Welsh in 1762, and in 1779 he translated the first slave narrative to appear in Welsh.[50]

Despite the steep decline in formal religion in Wales, Williams Pantycelyn's influence has not totally evaporated. His hymns still form the core of Welsh-language hymnody, as is seen by the fact that he is the author of 87 out of the 872 hymns in the interdenominational Welsh hymnal, *Caneuon Ffydd* ('Songs of Faith', 2001). At every international rugby match, the Welsh crowd regularly roars Williams's 'Feed me till I want no more', to the strains of the hymn-tune, *Cwm Rhondda*. Indeed, given the familiarity of so many Welsh people with Pantycelyn's hymns, until fairly recently at least, it could be claimed that no-one over the past 200 years or so has had more influence on the minds and world-view of the Welsh than William Williams of Pantycelyn.

Hymn-Writing after Williams Pantycelyn

A number of hymn-writers began to emerge from Williams Pantycelyn's shadow by the middle of the eighteenth century, some with only a handful of items to their name, while others are more sustained and substantial in output. Particularly noteworthy are Morgan Rhys (1716–79) and Dafydd William (1720/1–94), who were both schoolmasters, and Dafydd Jones (1711–77), the drover from Caeo whose translations of Isaac Watts's psalms and hymns supplanted Edmwnd Prys's metrical psalms in the worship of Nonconformist congregations.[51] Most of these hymn-writers were from south Wales, with a good number coming from within a seven-mile radius of Llandovery, the home town of Williams Pantycelyn, and of Rhys Prichard in the previous century. In this body of evangelical verse, one meets the same themes, imagery, and expressions time and again, and hymn-writers echo one another to varying degrees. This is not surprising given that they are part of the same religious movement and reflect the discourse and diction of the *seiat* meetings, which were strongly characterized by biblical and experiential language; and between them, these hymn-writers 'created a tribal idiom' and gave to their readers 'a commonly shared imagination'.[52]

As the influence of the revival movement spread gradually throughout Wales and across denominations, significant hymn-writers began to appear in other parts of the country, and by the early nineteenth century the centre of hymn production had moved to north Wales – the contemplative David Charles (1762–1834) of Carmarthen (brother of Thomas Charles of Bala) and the melancholy Thomas William (1761–1844) of Bethesda'r Fro in the Vale of Glamorgan were the last major hymn-writers from south Wales until the centre of hymn-writing returned to Carmarthenshire around the turn of the twentieth century with authors such as Elfed (H. Elvet Lewis; 1860–1953) and Nantlais (W. Nantlais Williams; 1874–1959). Among the most notable hymn-writers of the first half of the nineteenth century are Robert ap Gwilym Ddu (Robert Williams; 1766–1850), Pedr Fardd (Peter Jones; 1775–1845), and Ieuan Glan Geirionydd (Evan Evans; 1795–1855). The fact that all three have bardic names is significant. Most authors of hymn texts in the second half of the eighteenth century were hymn-writers first and foremost, although they also produced elegies and some other religious poetry. However, in the case of nineteenth-century hymn-writers, the focus has changed and they are generally poets who write hymns as part of a wider and more varied body of work, which often included strict-metre as well as free-metre poems; and the emergence of these poet-hymnists is indicative of the fact that the heirs of the revival movement of the eighteenth century were becoming increasingly mainstream in Welsh cultural life. The hymns of this period tend to be more polished and restrained in style and more doctrinal in tone, and while the focus is still mainly on the spiritual experiences of the individual, there is a wider range of subject matter, often relating to the corporate life of the community of believers and reflecting the increasing institutionalization of chapel culture as the nineteenth century proceeded.

As Welsh Nonconformity grew numerically and became more institutionalized, there were increasing efforts to reform congregational singing; the fervent, spirited, and rather unruly style of singing which had evolved under revival influences gradually gave way to a more disciplined hymn-singing in four-part harmony. The 1860s was an important decade in the reform of congregational singing and saw the development of the extremely popular *cymanfa ganu*, 'hymn-singing festival', movement, the wide adoption of the Tonic Sol-fa system (a letter-notation system which allowed people with little formal education to become musically literate fairly easily), and the adoption of a more elevated style in hymn-tunes, inspired in part by the German chorale. If the period between the powerful Llangeitho Revival of 1762 and the widespread 1859 Revival may be labelled 'the golden age of the Welsh hymn', the period from the 1860s to the 1920s may be regarded as 'the golden age of the Welsh hymn-tune', since it witnessed the emergence of a number of notable hymn-tune composers from working-class backgrounds who would provide memorable tunes for the great hymn-texts of classical Welsh evangelical hymnody; and some of their hymn-tunes, such as *Aberystwyth* and *Cwm Rhondda*, remain popular world-wide down to the present day.[53]

Ann Griffiths (1776–1805)

While the female voice was audible enough in the singing of hymns from the earliest days of the Methodist Revival, the writing of hymn-texts was mainly a male preserve, judging from the material that has survived in print and manuscript. The work of about thirty female hymn-writers has survived in Welsh from the eighteenth and nineteenth centuries.[54] Many of these have only a handful of stanzas to their name, and only a few of their hymns remain in congregational use today, but among them there is one outstanding figure, the only person to come near to rivalling Williams Pantycelyn as Wales's greatest hymn-writer, namely Ann Griffiths (1776–1805), or Ann Thomas as she was known until her marriage in 1804.[55]

Williams Pantycelyn and Ann Griffiths are very different in many ways. His life spanned much of the eighteenth century, while she lived for only twenty-nine years, dying in 1805 following childbirth. Williams had a prominent leadership role in the Methodist movement, journeying regularly the length and breadth of Wales for almost half a century from his farm in

Carmarthenshire, whereas Ann Griffiths lived her life in comparative obscurity on her family's farm, Dolwar Fach, in the parish of Llanfihangel-yng-Ngwynfa in northern Montgomeryshire, and probably travelled not much further than the 25-mile journey to Bala to sit at the feet of her mentor, Thomas Charles, an intellectual giant whose catechism and encyclopaedic scriptural dictionary would count among the most influential writings in Welsh for generations.[56] Williams Pantycelyn was a prolific author, while all that has survived of Ann Griffiths's work is just over seventy stanzas and eight letters. Williams's aim was to create a body of hymns that would give expression to the range of spiritual conditions found among evangelical believers, whereas Ann Griffiths composed her verses, often during periods of intense meditation, in order to articulate her deepest thoughts and feelings, and shared only some of them with others.[57] Although Williams Pantycelyn did not attend university, at his dissenting academy he received a good grounding in the classics, in English literature, and in the works of the English Puritan divines. In contrast, Ann Griffiths had very little formal education, although she could read and write Welsh and seems to have had some fluency in English, especially in the written language.

Whereas Williams Pantycelyn received a Nonconformist upbringing, Ann Griffiths and her immediate family were faithful members of the Anglican Church until the conversion of most of them to Methodism. Prior to her conversion, Ann Griffiths was an enthusiastic participant in the popular folk culture that characterized north-east Wales in her day. Her immersion in the vibrant bardic culture of the day is confirmed by the survival of a substantial manuscript volume of poetry which once belonged to her family and which contains poems by people such as Gwerfyl Mechain, Huw Morys, Twm o'r Nant, and Huw Jones of Llangwm, together with the work of local poets. She herself signed her name (as Ann Thomas) in that book in 1796, the year that witnessed the first steps of her conversion to Methodism, a watershed which would see her turn her back completely on the popular culture that had captivated her up to that point.[58]

If Methodism brought an earnestness to Welsh life and culture, together with a stricter morality and a heightened awareness of being part of a cosmic drama, it also created closely knit religious communities and networks where members could 'express their spiritual experiences and emotional troubles', and find solace and encouragement; and it planted in those members 'certain moral values and devotional habits which became an intrinsic part of their daily lives'.[59] Moreover, Methodism was 'novel and exciting'. While it engendered vehement opposition in some quarters, for others, especially among the young, it was an 'attractive religion', partly because of 'its emphasis on soul-searching preaching, intimate fellowship and fervent hymn-singing', and 'it brought enormous spiritual joy and satisfaction to thousands of Welsh people'.[60] All these aspects are reflected in the hymns and letters of Ann Griffiths, who would certainly say that, rather than changing mirth for misery, her conversion to Methodism meant that she had exchanged a superficial merriment for a much deeper joy, which was often expressed ecstatically in her life and work.

It is possible that most, if not all of Ann Griffiths's hymns were composed between 1802 and 1804, and it seems that many of them started life as single stanzas. However, in what has survived of her work, there are some sequences of stanzas which appear to form organic entities, although it is possible that, in a number of those cases, the hymn grew verse by verse over a period of time. The longest of her hymns, the seven-stanza 'Rhyfedd, rhyfedd gan angylion' ('Wonderful, wonderful to angels'), has been described by Saunders Lewis as 'one of the majestic songs in the religious poetry of Europe':[61]

Rhyfedd, rhyfedd gan angylion,
    Rhyfeddod fawr yng ngolwg
      ffydd,
Gweld Rhoddwr bod, Cynhaliwr helaeth
    A Rheolwr pob peth sydd,
Yn y preseb mewn cadachau
    A heb le i roi ei ben i lawr,
Ac eto disglair lu'r gogoniant
    Yn ei addoli'n Arglwydd mawr.

Pan fo Sinai i gyd yn mygu
    A swn yr utgorn uwcha' ei radd,
Caf fynd i wledda tros y terfyn
    Yng Nghrist y Gair heb gael fy lladd;
Mae ynddo'n trigo bob cyflawnder,
    Llond gwagle colledigaeth dyn;
Ar yr adwy rhwng y ddwyblaid
    Gwnaeth gymod trwy ei offrymu
      ei hun.

Wonderful, wonderful to angels,
    a great wonder in the eyes of faith,
to see the Giver of being, the abundant
    Sustainer
    and Ruler of everything that is,
in the manger in swaddling clothes
    and with nowhere to lay his head,
and yet the bright host of glory
    worshipping Him as great Lord.

When Sinai is altogether in smoke,
    and the sound of the trumpet at its
    loudest,
I can go to feast across the boundary
    in Christ the Word without being
    slain;
in Him all fullness dwells,
    enough to fill the gulf of man's
    perdition;
in the gap between the two parties
    He made reconciliation through his
    self-offering.

Efe yw'r Iawn fu rhwng y lladron,
  Efe ddioddefodd angau loes,
Efe a nerthodd freichiau ei ddienyddwyr
  I'w hoelio yno ar y groes;
Wrth dalu dyled pentewynion,
  Ac anrhydeddu deddf ei Dad,
Cyfiawnder, mae'n disgleirio'n danbaid
  Wrth faddau yn nhrefn y cymod
    rhad.

He is the Satisfaction that was between
    the thieves,
  it was He who suffered the pains of
    death,
  it was He who gave to the arms of his
    executioners
    the power to nail Him there to the
    cross;
while paying the debt of brands plucked
    out of the burning,
  and honouring his Father's law,
righteousness shines with fiery blaze
    as He pardons within the plan of the
    free reconciliation.

O! f'enaid, gwêl y fan gorweddodd
  Pen brenhinoedd, Awdwr hedd,
Y greadigaeth ynddo'n symud,
  Yntau'n farw yn y bedd;
Cân a bywyd colledigion,
  Rhyfeddod fwya' angylion nef;
Gweld Duw mewn cnawd a'i gydaddoli
  Mae'r côr, dan weiddi 'Iddo Ef!'

O my soul, behold the place where lay
    the chief of kings, the Author of
    peace,
all creation moving in Him,
  and He dead in the tomb;
song and life of the lost,
  greatest wonder of the angels of
    heaven;
the choir sees God in flesh and worships
    Him together,
  crying out 'Unto Him!'

Diolch byth, a chanmil diolch,
  Diolch tra bo ynwy' i chwyth,
Am fod gwrthrych i'w addoli
  A thestun cân i bara byth;
Yn fy natur wedi ei demtio
  Fel y gwaela' o ddynol-ryw,
Yn ddyn bach, yn wan, yn ddinerth,
  Yn anfeidrol wir a bywiol Dduw.

Thanks for ever, and a hundred thou-
    sand thanks,
  thanks while there is breath in me,
because there is an object to worship
  and a theme for a song to last for ever;
in my nature, tempted
  like the lowest of human kind,
a babe, weak, powerless,
  infinite true and living God.

Yn lle cario corff o lygredd,
 Cyd-dreiddio â'r côr yn danllyd fry
I ddiderfyn ryfeddodau
 Iechydwriaeth Calfari;
Byw i weld yr Anweledig,
 Fu farw ac sy'n awr yn fyw;
Tragwyddol anwahanol undeb
 A chymundeb â fy Nuw.

Yno caf ddyrchafu'r Enw
 A osododd Duw yn Iawn,
Heb ddychymyg, llen, na gorchudd,
 A'm henaid ar ei ddelw'n llawn;
Yng nghymdeithas y dirgelwch,
 Datguddiedig yn ei glwy',
Cusanu'r Mab i dragwyddoldeb
 Heb im gefnu arno mwy.

Instead of carrying a body of corruption,
 penetrating ardently with the choir
  above
into the endless wonders
 of the salvation wrought on Calvary;
living to see the Invisible,
 who was dead and now is alive;
eternal inseparable union
 and communion with my God.

There I shall exalt the Name
 which God set forth to be a
  Propitiation,
without imagination, curtain, or covering,
 and with my soul fully in his likeness;
in the fellowship of the mystery
 revealed in his wounds,
I shall kiss the Son to all eternity,
 and never turn from Him any more.[62]

The double note of wonder – 'Rhyfedd, rhyfedd' – which is struck at the outset resounds throughout the whole of Ann's work. The chief source of her amazement is the fathomless mystery of the God-man, Jesus Christ, while another source of the paradoxes that abound in her work is the juxtaposition between her sinfulness and the holy law of God. On the cross, she says, in the third verse, righteousness shone with fiery blaze as Christ honoured his Father's law; or as she says in another hymn: 'My sorrowful soul, on remembering [the spiritual battle won by Christ], leaps for joy; it sees the law held in honour and its great transgressors going free; the Author of life put to death and the great Resurrection buried.'[63]

As Saunders Lewis has emphasized, Ann Griffiths is a poet of passionate contemplation, and her work is the fruit of deep meditation in Scripture. She immersed herself in the Bible, in all its parts, both Old Testament and New, and as a result one finds in her work a profusion of biblical quotations and allusions drawn from all parts of Scripture, which clearly underline the breadth of her scriptural knowledge and her great debt to the Bible as a source text. The second verse of 'Rhyfedd, rhyfedd gan angylion', for example, not only makes typological use of the narrative in the book of Exodus, when God gave the Ten Commandments on mount Sinai, but it also includes direct references to, or echoes of, passages from the books of Isaiah, Ephesians, John, Colossians, Psalms, Ezekiel, and Hebrews, and all that in just one eight-line stanza.[64] Indeed, if we neglect to consider Ann's work in biblical light, we not only lose strata of meaning and significance but are also in danger of misunderstanding and misinterpreting her work. For example, the implied eroticism at the close of 'Rhyfedd, rhyfedd gan angylion' – 'I shall kiss the Son to all eternity' – is significantly qualified when one realizes that it is a reference to Psalm 2:12 – 'Kiss the Son, lest he be angry' – where the kiss is one of homage.

The density in which biblical references occur in Ann Griffiths's work augments the atmosphere of intensity which pervades her hymns and which sets her apart from other hymn-writers. This intensity, which reflects the depth of spiritual experience from which her verses emanate, together with such expressions as 'eternal inseparable union and communion with my God' in verse six of 'Rhyfedd, rhyfedd gan angylion' and 'I was content to give all that I possessed, be it good or bad, for the Son in a marriage union' in one of her letters[65] have led to her being frequently labelled, if controversially, as a 'mystic'. Definitions of 'mysticism' vary, but what is clear is that the matter of union with Christ is central to Ann Griffiths's thought and emotions. One symbol she uses to convey union with him is that of the image of Christ being imprinted on her, like an impression made on wax. Paradoxically, this symbol by which Ann Griffiths conveys her union with Christ also emphasizes the fact that they are at the same time two distinct entities.

Continuing Significance

Although Williams Pantycelyn and Ann Griffiths are very different in many ways, there is also much that is similar. They are both evangelicals who lived through periods of profound spiritual experiences and fervent emotion. For both, the central source text is the Bible; both were Calvinist in doctrine; there is a balance in both between the objective and the subjective, between head and heart, light and heat; and both return again and again to the same basic themes: an acute awareness of the majesty of God and of their own frailty and waywardness; the centrality of the cross of Christ in the plan of salvation; and a deep longing – a longing to be holy, a longing for heaven, and above all, a longing for Christ, the Beloved.

Methodism and evangelical Nonconformity created a large body of litera-ture in Welsh. It was wide-ranging and included poetry, sermons, biogra-phies, theological expositions, biblical commentaries, and various types of devotional, educational, and periodical literature; but as has already been suggested, one of its highlights was the remarkable corpus of evangelical hymns that emerged over the hundred years between the mid-eighteenth and the mid-nineteenth centuries, and the work of Williams Pantycelyn and Ann Griffiths in particular. It is a corpus which is one of the pinnacles of Welsh literature and a body of work of international standing; it also laid the foundations for a tradition of hymn-writing and hymn-singing which remains a distinctive element in Welsh popular culture to the present day.

Notes

1. E. Wyn James, 'The Evolution of the Welsh Hymn', in *Dissenting Praise: Religious Dissent and the Hymn in England and Wales*, ed. Isabel Rivers and David L. Wykes (Oxford: Oxford University Press, 2011), 263–4.

2. D. Geraint Jones, *Favoured with Frequent Revivals: Revivals in Wales 1762–1862* (Cardiff: Heath Christian Trust, 2001).

3. For a discussion of this phenomenon and the opposition to such energetic worship, see R. Geraint Gruffydd, 'The Revival of 1762 and William Williams of Pantycelyn', in *Revival and its Fruit*, by Emyr Roberts and R. Geraint Gruffydd (Bridgend: Evangelical Library of Wales, 1981), 19–40.

4. Daniel Huws, 'Siôn Dafydd Laes: Seren Wib o Fardd', in *Blodeuglwm*, ed. Rhidian Griffiths (Aberystwyth: Aberystwyth Bibliographical Group, 2016), 47.

5. Hywel Teifi Edwards, *Yr Eisteddfod* (Llys yr Eisteddfod Genedlaethol, 1976), 17–34; Hywel Teifi Edwards, *The Eisteddfod*, Writers of Wales (Cardiff: University of Wales Press, 1990), 10–15; G. J. Williams, *Agweddau ar Hanes Dysg Gymraeg*, ed. Aneirin Lewis (Caerdydd: Gwasg Prifysgol Cymru, 1969), 124–47.

6. On this free-metre poetry and its metres, see T. H. Parry-Williams, ed., *Canu Rhydd Cynnar* (Caerdydd: Gwasg Prifysgol Cymru, 1932); Gwyn Williams, *An Introduction to Welsh Poetry* (London: Faber and Faber, 1953), chapter 8; R. Geraint Gruffydd, ed., *A Guide to Welsh Literature c. 1530–1700* (Cardiff: University of Wales Press, 1997), chapters 2–4; Phyllis Kinney, *Welsh Traditional Music* (Cardiff: University of Wales Press, 2011), chapter 2.

7. Thomas Parry, *A History of Welsh Literature*, trans. H. I. Bell (Oxford: Clarendon Press, 1955), 231.

8. For example, around a thousand ballad pamphlets, each normally containing two or three songs, have survived from the eighteenth century, with the vast majority of them being printed in north Wales and the Marches. For this ballad and carol literature, see R. Geraint Gruffydd, *Llenyddiaeth y Cymry: Cyflwyniad Darluniadol. Cyfrol 2: O tua 1530 i tua 1880* (Llandysul: Gwasg Gomer, 1989), 62, 64; W. Rhys Nicholas, *The Folk Poets*, Writers of Wales (Cardiff: University of Wales Press, 1978), 16–21; Geraint H. Jenkins, *Literature, Religion and Society in Wales, 1660–1730* (Cardiff: University of Wales

Press, 1978), 154–8, 161–4; Phyllis Kinney, 'The Tunes of the Welsh Christmas Carols', *Canu Gwerin (Folk Song)* 11 (1988): 28–57, and 12 (1989): 5–29; Tegwyn Jones, 'Welsh Ballads', in *A Nation and its Books: A History of the Book in Wales*, ed. Philip Henry Jones and Eiluned Rees (Aberystwyth: National Library of Wales, 1998), chapter 20; Mary-Ann Constantine, ed., *Ballads in Wales* (London: FLS Books, 1999); Thomas Parry, *Baledi'r Ddeunawfed Ganrif* (Caerdydd: Gwasg Prifysgol Cymru, 1935, 1986).

9. For an example, see E. Wyn James, 'An "English" Lady among Welsh Folk: Ruth Herbert Lewis and the Welsh Folk-Song Society', in *Folk Song: Tradition, Revival, and Re-creation*, ed. Ian Russell and David Atkinson (Aberdeen: Elphinstone Institute, University of Aberdeen, 2004), 273–4.

10. On the *anterliwt* and its authors, see Dafydd Glyn Jones, 'The Interludes', in *A Guide to Welsh Literature c. 1700–1800*, ed. Branwen Jarvis (Cardiff: University of Wales Press, 2000), chapter 10, and the items cited in the bibliography there.

11. Prys Morgan, *The Eighteenth Century Renaissance* (Llandybïe: Christopher Davies, 1981), chapter 1; Parry, *Baledi'r Ddeunawfed Ganrif*, chapters 5 and 6; G. J. Williams, 'Traddodiad Llenyddol Dyffryn Clwyd a'r Cyffiniau', *Transactions of the Denbighshire Historical Society* 1 (1952): 28–32.

12. It should be emphasized, however, that the older traditional folk culture did not die out completely but remained as a sub-culture, sufficiently strong for remnants of it to be collected orally at the beginning of the twentieth century by the newly formed Welsh Folk-Song Society.

13. E. Wyn James, 'Rhai Methodistiaid a'r Anterliwt', *Taliesin* 57 (1986): 14. On John Elias, see R. Tudur Jones, *John Elias: Prince Amongst Preachers* (Bridgend: Evangelical Library of Wales, 1975).

14. *Gwassanaeth Meir*, ed. Brynley F. Roberts (Caerdydd: Gwasg Prifysgol Cymru, 1961). This work also included Welsh translations of some Latin hymns.

15. On these metrical versions of the Psalms, see Gruffydd Aled Williams, 'Mydryddu'r Salmau yn Gymraeg', *Llên Cymru* 16, 1–2 (1989): 114–32. On Edmwnd Prys, see Gruffydd Aled Williams, *Ymryson Edmwnd Prys a Wiliam Cynwal* (Caerdydd: Gwasg Prifysgol Cymru, 1986); A. M. Allchin, *Praise Above All: Discovering the Welsh Tradition* (Cardiff: University of Wales Press, 1991), 25–9.

16. Sally Harper, 'Tunes for a Welsh Psalter: Edmwnd Prys's *Llyfr y Psalmau*', *Studia Celtica* 37 (2003): 221. Prys's psalter was the first printed book in Welsh to contain music notation.

17. R. Geraint Gruffydd, *Y Ffordd Gadarn: Ysgrifau ar Lên a Chrefydd*, ed. E. Wyn James (Pen-y-bont ar Ogwr: Gwasg Bryntirion, 2008), 164.

18. Sally Harper and Alan Luff, 'Welsh Carols', in *The Canterbury Dictionary of Hymnology*, www.hymnology.co.uk/w/welsh-carols (accessed 17 September 2017); Brinley Rees, *Dulliau'r Canu Rhydd 1500–1650* (Caerdydd: Gwasg

Prifysgol Cymru, 1952), chapter 1; David Jenkins, 'Carolau Haf a Gaeaf', *Llên Cymru* 2, 1 (January 1952): 46.

19. *Blodeugerdd Barddas o'r Ail Ganrif ar Bymtheg (Cyfrol 1)*, ed. Nesta Lloyd (Cyhoeddiadau Barddas, 1993), 78–9. The hymn-writer, Dafydd William (1720/1–94), who taught in circulating schools in the Margam area, uses the same imagery in one of his hymns; see E. Wyn James, 'Dafydd William, Llandeilo Fach: An Eighteenth-Century Glamorgan Hymn-Writer', *Morgannwg* 47 (2003): 17–20.

20. Glanmor Williams, *Grym Tafodau Tân* (Llandysul: Gwasg Gomer, 1984), 164–79.

21. On the development of the *plygain* carol tradition, see Roy Saer, *'Canu at Iws' ac Ysgrifau Eraill/'Songs for Use' and Other Articles* (Cymdeithas Alawon Gwerin Cymru/Welsh Folk-Song Society, 2013).

22. Enid Roberts, *Braslun o Hanes Llên Powys* (Dinbych: Gwasg Gee, 1965), 65–6.

23. According to Ifor Williams ('Lexicographical Notes', *BBCS* 3, 2 (May 1926: 127)), the word *cwndid* derives ultimately from the Middle Latin *conductus*, referring to 'a sort of motet, sung while the priest was proceeding to the altar'. On the *cwndid* (pl. *cwndidau*), see 'Hopcyn' (Lemuel J. Hopkin James) and 'Cadrawd' (T. C. Evans), *Hen Gwndidau, Carolau, a Chywyddau, Being Sermons in Song in the Gwentian Dialect* (Bangor: Jarvis & Foster, 1910); Ceri W. Lewis, 'The Literary History of Glamorgan from 1550 to 1770', in *Glamorgan County History. Vol. IV: Early Modern Glamorgan*, ed. Glanmor Williams (Cardiff: Glamorgan County History Trust, 1974), 566–76.

24. According to *Geiriadur Prifysgol Cymru*, the word *halsing* (pl. *halsingod, halsingau*) is a borrowing from the English *ha(i)lsing*, meaning 'greeting, salutation'. On the *halsing*, see Geraint Bowen, 'Yr Halsingod', *THSC* (1945): 83–108; Jenkins, *Literature, Religion and Society in Wales*, 158–61. Some of the tunes for the *cwndid* and the *halsing* are discussed in *Merêd: Detholiad o Ysgrifau Dr Meredydd Evans*, ed. Ann Ffrancon and Geraint H. Jenkins (Llandysul: Gwasg Gomer, 1994), chapter 15.

25. G. J. Williams, *Traddodiad Llenyddol Morgannwg* (Caerdydd: Gwasg Prifysgol Cymru, 1948), 121. On Rhys Prichard, see Nesta Lloyd, 'Late Free-Metre Poetry', in *A Guide to Welsh Literature c. 1530–1700*, ed. Gruffydd, 114–19; Jenkins, *Literature, Religion and Society in Wales*, 150–4; R. Brinley Jones, *'A Lanterne to their Feete': Remembering Rhys Prichard 1579–1644, Vicar of Llandovery* (Porth-y-rhyd: Drovers Press, 1994).

26. Nesta Lloyd, '"Yr Ymarfer o Dduwioldeb" a Rhai o Gerddi Rhys Prichard', *Y Traethodydd* 150 (1995): 94–106.

27. Welsh text in *Cerddi'r Ficer: Detholiad o Gerddi Rhys Prichard*, ed. Nesta Lloyd (Cyhoeddiadau Barddas, 1994), 166; English translation in Emyr Humphreys, *The Taliesin Tradition* (Bridgend: Seren Books, 1989), 59.

28. The first to do so seems to have been Lewis Morris (1701–65). As indicated in
    the extensive discussion on the *hen benillion* in a letter he wrote in 1738, he
    believed some of these verses to be very ancient, embodying the 'remains of
    druidical Learning'; see *Additional Letters of the Morrises of Anglesey (1735–1786)*,
    ed. Hugh Owen (London: Honourable Society of Cymmrodorion, 1947), 74,
    77. Lewis Morris patterned a number of his own poems on the *hen benillion*.
    On the *hen benillion*, see T. H. Parry-Williams, ed., *Hen Benillion*, 3rd edn
    (Llandysul: Gwasg Gomer, 1965); Glyn Jones, trans., *A People's Poetry*
    (Bridgend: Seren, 1997); Tegwyn Jones, ed., *Tribannau Morgannwg* (Llandysul:
    Gwasg Gomer, 1976).

29. James, 'The Evolution of the Welsh Hymn', 236. Although he is remembered
    primarily as an exceptional prose writer, Ellis Wynne composed a metrical
    psalm and a number of hymns and carols. For a complete collection of his
    poems, see *Cerddi'r Bardd Cwsg*, ed. Dafydd Glyn Jones (Bangor: Dalen
    Newydd, 2014).

30. [Edward Bagshaw], *The Life and Death of Mr. Vavasor Powell* (London: *s.n.*,
    1671), 95. On Vavasor Powell's hymn-singing, see R. Tudur Jones, 'The
    Healing Herb and the Rose of Love: The Piety of Two Welsh Puritans
    [Vavasor Powell and Morgan Llwyd]', in *Reformation, Conformity and Dissent*,
    ed. R. Buick Knox (London: Epworth Press, 1977), 159–61.

31. The English translation is in M. Wynn Thomas, *Morgan Llwyd*, Writers of
    Wales (Cardiff: University of Wales Press, 1984), 22. For a discussion of this
    poem, see R. M. Jones, *Llên Cymru a Chrefydd* (Abertawe: Christopher Davies,
    1977), 322–40.

32. Approximately eighty poems by Llwyd have survived, about half in English
    and half in Welsh. They are included in the three volumes of his collected
    works, *Gweithiau Morgan Llwyd* (1899, 1908, 1994). A selection of twenty-eight
    are in *Cerddi Morgan Llwyd*, ed. Dafydd Glyn Jones (Bangor: Dalen Newydd,
    2016).

33. For details of these early Nonconformist collections, see M. H. Jones,
    'Casgliadau Argraffedig o Emynau cyn "Aleluia" Pantycelyn (1744)', *Journal of
    the Historical Society of the Presbyterian Church of Wales* 14, 1 (March 1929): 3–9;
    R. Tudur Jones, *Congregationalism in Wales*, ed. Robert Pope (Cardiff:
    University of Wales Press, 2004), 83–4, 87–8, 91.

34. Jenkins, *Literature, Religion and Society in Wales*, 150.

35. For details of these printed and manuscript collections, see Gomer M.
    Roberts, *Y Pêr Ganiedydd*, vol. II (Aberystwyth: Gwasg Aberystwyth, 1958),
    20–40.

36. Derec Llwyd Morgan, 'Williams, William [known as William Williams
    Pantycelyn] (1717–1791)', *Oxford Dictionary of National Biography* (Oxford:
    Oxford University Press, 2004).

37. For a good introduction in English to Williams and his work, see Glyn Tegai Hughes, *Williams Pantycelyn*, Writers of Wales (Cardiff: University of Wales Press, 1983). See also Eifion Evans, *Bread of Heaven: The Life and Work of William Williams, Pantycelyn* (Bridgend: Bryntirion Press, 2010); H. A. Hodges, *Flame in the Mountains: Williams Pantycelyn, Ann Griffiths and the Welsh Hymn*, ed. E. Wyn James (Talybont: Y Lolfa, 2017); and Kathryn Jenkins, 'Williams Pantycelyn', in *A Guide to Welsh Literature c. 1700–1800*, ed. Jarvis, 256–78, which includes a bibliography. Among important discussions in Welsh are: Saunders Lewis, *Williams Pantycelyn* (Llundain: Foyle's, 1927; new edn with introduction by D. Densil Morgan, Caerdydd: Gwasg Prifysgol Cymru, 2016); Kathryn Jenkins, *Cân y Ffydd: Ysgrifau ar Emynyddiaeth*, ed. Rhidian Griffiths (Caernarfon: Cymdeithas Emynau Cymru, 2011); Glyn Tegai Hughes, *'Yr Hen Bant': Ysgrifau ar Williams Pantycelyn* (Talybont: Y Lolfa, 2017). The Welsh literary journal *Llên Cymru* produced a special issue on Williams Pantycelyn (17, 3–4, 1993). The collection *Meddwl a Dychymyg Williams Pantycelyn*, ed. Derec Llwyd Morgan (Llandysul: Gwasg Gomer, 1991), includes a comprehensive bibliography by Huw Walters of writings on Williams Pantycelyn and his work.

38. See E. Wyn James, '"The New Birth of a People": Welsh Language and Identity and the Welsh Methodists, *c.* 1740–1820', in *Religion and National Identity: Wales and Scotland c. 1700–2000*, ed. Robert Pope (Cardiff: University of Wales Press, 2001), 23. See also chapter 14 in this volume.

39. Eifion Evans, *Pursued by God: A Selective Translation with Notes of the Welsh Religious Classic Theomemphus* (Bridgend: Evangelical Press of Wales, 1996), provides English metrical translations for about a third of the verses of the poem, together with a linking commentary covering the omitted verses.

40. Jenkins, 'Williams Pantycelyn', 273.

41. Ibid., 265; see also Kathryn Jenkins, 'Pantycelyn's Women, Fact and Fiction: An Assessment', *Journal of Welsh Religious History* 7 (1999): 77–94.

42. Lewis, *Williams Pantycelyn*, 59; cf. 159, 220.

43. Ibid., 17, cf. 29–30, 106; but cf. Hughes, *Williams Pantycelyn*, 39–40, where it is argued that this can only be claimed if Romanticism is viewed 'as some vague philosophical tendency'.

44. Kathryn Jenkins, '"Songs of Praises": The Literary and Spiritual Qualities of the Hymns of William Williams and Ann Griffiths', *The Hymn Society of Great Britain and Ireland Bulletin* 15, 5 (1998): 98.

45. His English hymns are reprinted in *Songs of Praises: English Hymns and Elegies of William Williams Pantycelyn 1717–1791*, ed. R. Brinley Jones (Felin-fach: Llanerch, 1991).

46. Hughes, *Williams Pantycelyn*, 86–98; Jenkins, 'Williams Pantycelyn', 275–6.

47. Rowan Williams, 'Tirwedd Ffydd', *Bwletin Cymdeithas Emynau Cymru* 4, 1–2 (2008–9): 8.

48. Hodges, *Flame in the Mountains*, 96.
49. See especially the discussion in R. M. Jones, *Cyfriniaeth Gymraeg* (Caerdydd: Gwasg Prifysgol Cymru, 1994), chapter 3.
50. E. Wyn James, '"Blessèd Jubil!"': Slavery, Mission and the Millennial Dawn in the Work of William Williams of Pantycelyn', in *Cultures of Radicalism in Britain and Ireland*, ed. John Kirk, Michael Brown & Andrew Noble (London: Pickering & Chatto, 2013), 95–112.
51. On these hymn-writers and their context, see Brynley F. Roberts, 'The Literature of the "Great Awakening"', in *A Guide to Welsh Literature c. 1700–1800*, ed. Jarvis, 282–98; Derec Llwyd Morgan, *The Great Awakening in Wales*, trans. Dyfnallt Morgan (London: Epworth Press, 1988), 273–5.
52. Morgan, *The Great Awakening in Wales*, 272, 280.
53. For these musical developments, see James, 'The Evolution of the Welsh Hymn', 262–4, and the references there.
54. On women and the Welsh hymn in the eighteenth and nineteenth centuries, see Eryn M. White, 'Women in the Early Methodist Societies in Wales', *Journal of Welsh Religious History* 7 (1999): 95–108; E. Wyn James, 'Merched a'r Emyn yn Sir Gâr', *Barn* 402–3 (1996): 26–9; Jane Aaron, *Nineteenth-Century Women's Writing in Wales: Nation, Gender and Identity*. 2nd edn (Cardiff: University of Wales Press, 2010), 13–24.
55. Discussions in English on Ann Griffiths's life and work include A. M. Allchin, *Ann Griffiths: The Furnace and the Fountain* (Cardiff: University of Wales Press, 1987); Dorian Llywelyn, '"The Fiery, Blessed Ann": Experience and Doctrine in the Spirituality of Ann Griffiths', *Spiritus* 9 (2009): 217–40; R. M. Jones, 'Ann Griffiths and the Norm', in *A Guide to Welsh Literature c. 1700–1800*, ed. Jarvis, 305–27, which includes a bibliography. Discussions in Welsh include R. Geraint Gruffydd, 'Ann Griffiths: Llenor', *Taliesin* 43 (1981): 76–84; J. R. Jones, 'Ann Griffiths', *Llên Cymru* 8, 1–2 (1964): 33–41; Jones, *Cyfriniaeth Gymraeg*, chapter 4; Dyfnallt Morgan, ed., *Y Ferch o Ddolwar Fach* (Caernarfon: Gwasg Gwynedd, 1977). The standard edition of Ann Griffiths's work is *Rhyfeddaf Fyth . . . : Emynau a Llythyrau Ann Griffiths*, ed. E. Wyn James (Y Drenewydd: Gwasg Gregynog, 1998). Translations of her hymns and letters into English by H. A. Hodges are to be found in Hodges, *Flame in the Mountains*, and by Alan Gaunt and Alan Luff in *Ann Griffiths: Hymns and Letters* (London: Stainer & Bell, 1999).
56. See D. Densil Morgan, ed., *Thomas Charles o'r Bala* (Caerdydd: Gwasg Prifysgol Cymru, 2014).
57. Only one verse and one letter survive in Ann Griffiths's own hand, most of the extant verses having been transmitted orally by Ann to Ruth Evans, a close spiritual confidante who was a maid-servant at Dolwar Fach. Ruth in turn recited the verses to her husband, John Hughes (1775–1854), who recorded the verses in his copy-book and also made copies of seven letters

Ann had sent to him. For more detail on the transmission and publication of her hymns and letters, see E. Wyn James, 'Cushions, Copy-books and Computers: Ann Griffiths (1776–1805), her Hymns and Letters and their Transmission', *Bulletin of the John Rylands Library* 90, 2 (2014): 163–83; E. Wyn James, 'Ann Griffiths: O Lafar i Lyfr', in *Chwileniwm: Technoleg a Llenyddiaeth*, ed. Angharad Price (Caerdydd: Gwasg Prifysgol Cymru, 2002), 54–85.

58. E. Wyn James, 'Ann Griffiths: Y Cefndir Barddol', *Llên Cymru* 23 (2000), 147–70.

59. Geraint H. Jenkins, 'The New Enthusiasts', in *The Remaking of Wales in the Eighteenth Century*, ed. Trevor Herbert and Gareth Elwyn Jones (Cardiff: University of Wales Press, 1988), 51, 43.

60. Ibid., 50, 43.

61. Saunders Lewis (trans. H. A. Hodges), 'Ann Griffiths: A Literary Survey', in Hodges, *Flame in the Mountains*, 155.

62. English translation by H. A. Hodges, in Hodges, *Flame in the Mountains*, 268–9.

63. Ibid., 237.

64. For a detailed listing of the extensive scriptural quotations and allusions in the hymns and letters of Ann Griffiths, see Hodges, *Flame in the Mountains*, 309–20.

65. Ibid., 219.

17

Travel, Translation, and Temperance: The Origins of the Welsh Novel

KATIE GRAMICH

Prose tales were an important part of the Welsh medieval tradition, but modern prose fiction in Welsh did not begin to appear until the nineteenth century. Even then, some of the earliest Welsh-language novelistic texts were translations from English texts. It was not until the late nineteenth century that the Welsh-language novel established itself as a distinctive genre.

Fiction in English set in Wales or dealing with Welsh life and characters developed earlier; it was well established by the later eighteenth century. Interestingly, one of the earliest such texts was also a translation – from the French: *Tideric Prince de Galles* by De Curli was published in Paris in 1677 and an English translation appeared in London in 1678, under the title *Tudor, A Prince in Wales: An Historical Novel in Two Parts*; a new translation of the text appeared in 1751 under the title, *The Life and Amours of Owen Tideric Prince of Wales*. By this time Wales was becoming established as a setting for a number of English-language novels, ranging from Gothic romances to sentimental and didactic fiction (as critics such as Jane Aaron, Moira Dearnley, and Sarah Prescott have shown).[1] Perhaps the heyday of the early anglophone Welsh novel was the 1790s when, in the hands of women writers such as Anna Maria Bennett, Isabella Kelly, Ann Howell, Mary Robinson, Emily Clarke, and Isabella Lansdell, Wales became the setting *à la mode* for affective tales of young women in peril and old families fallen on hard times.

The Life and Amours of Owen Tideric, Prince of Wales, otherwise Owen Tudor, published in London in 1751, is anonymous, but the publisher is named as William Owen, which suggests perhaps some genuine Welsh credentials. The reissued novel has a clear political purpose; in the wake of the defeat of the Jacobites in 1745, it aims to emphasize the unity of what it calls 'the several sorts of people that inhabit the islands of Britain and Ireland' who are actually 'unit[ed] in our present royal family'.[2] The novel is at pains to emphasize that it is a 'true history', and not a 'romance', concerning Owen Tudor, described as 'descendant of Cadwallader, King of the Ancient Britons' (5). In this way, the fifteenth-century Welsh prince is used as a symbol of *British* unity. However, once the novel begins, it is the 'amours' of Owen which take pride of place – it is, basically, a love story concerning Owen Tudor and Princess Catherine of France, who undergo many tribulations before they are eventually married in a secret ceremony. The writing is quite natural and sometimes astonishingly intimate, as we get an insight into Owen's and Catherine's internal conflicts, thoughts, and feelings. Finally, their secret marriage is discovered, Catherine dies, and Owen himself is decapitated.

This early text begs many fundamental questions, including 'is it a novel?' and 'is it Welsh?' Throughout the text, Owen Tudor's specifically Welsh identity is emphasized, though the novel is not set in Wales but primarily in France. The idea of providence is important, underpinning the political theme which suggests that the events of the novel lead inevitably to the present allegedly united state of the British Isles. As a novel, it is almost there – it is a long narrative very like what one would nowadays think of as an historical novel; it has distinctive characters, intrigue, long passages of lively direct speech; and, above all, insights into the thoughts and feelings of the main protagonists. But it is not really a Welsh novel, since Owen's Welshness is simply declared and not enacted.

Another candidate for the earliest Welsh novel also has French connections and settings; it is a novel by Penelope Aubin, published in London in 1721 and entitled *The Life of Madam de Beaumount, a French Lady: who lived in a cave in Wales above fourteen years undiscovered* . . ..[3] In the preface to this tiny book, we are informed that 'Wales, being a Place not extremely populous in many Parts, is certainly more rich in Virtue than England, which is now improved in Vice only' (vii). The novel is set near Swansea, which is described as a 'Sea-Port in Wales, in Glamorganshire' where 'dwelt a Gentleman whose Name was Mr Lluelling [*sic*]' (9). The year is 1717 and Mr Lluelling comes across 'a Maid of exquisite Beauty' in a nearby cave (11). Belinda and her mother turn out to be French refugees fleeing from religious persecution. Mr Lluelling is a virtuous 'Antient Briton' who immediately declares his love for Belinda and marries her. However, he is not a particularly intelligent hero (especially in contrast to the sharp and resourceful Madam de Beaumont herself, who is always donning male disguises and escaping from impregnable fortresses). In fact, Mr Lluelling is stupid enough to leave his new wife in the care of his dastardly 'cousin-German', Mr Charles Owen Glandore, who has been corrupted by studying the law in London and who immediately tries to rape Belinda. Belinda evades that fate but is incarcerated, and even when she escapes, her difficulties are compounded because everyone she meets speaks only Welsh and she cannot make herself understood. Eventually Belinda and Mr Lluelling are happily reunited and they go to live together in Normandy.

This is much closer to a Welsh novel than *Owen Tideric* in that it displays a clear knowledge of Welsh geography, culture, and customs, including variations in the prevalence of Welsh speaking in different parts of Wales. The focus is on adventure and excitement; it also features a great deal of travel – to France, Sweden, Muscovy, Tartary, and Ireland, with not a few shipwrecks and kidnappings en route. Penelope Aubin was born in London and her father was a French officer; she published seven novels in the 1720s, along with some translations from the French.[4] The author was not a Welsh novelist, then, but she was using Wales as an interesting backdrop for her racy text, as so many English writers were to do towards the end of the eighteenth century and early in the nineteenth.

One prominent example of such a writer was Thomas Love Peacock (1785–1866), whose relationship with, and literary use of, Wales was much richer than that of Aubin or his Romantic contemporaries. Married to a Welshwoman, Jane Gryffydh of Maentwrog, Peacock spent considerable time in Wales, and Welsh tropes recur in his novels, particularly in *The Misfortunes of Elphin* (1829).[5] Nevertheless, he also wrote non-Welsh texts and, according to Meic Stephens, 'his fame rests on those of his works with English settings', such as *Crotchet Castle* (1831) and *Gryll Grange* (1860–1).[6] To an extent, Peacock may be regarded as one of the first English authors to exhibit signs of an elective Welsh identity, a phenomenon repeated in the case of the Somerset-born Anne Beale who settled near Llandeilo and wrote a number of fully fledged Welsh novels in the mid- to late nineteenth century, including *Rose Mervyn of Whitelake* (1879), based on the Rebecca Riots. Beale first came to Wales as a governess for the three children of a local curate in 1840 at the age of twenty-five. In her 1844 travel book, *The Vale of the Towey*, she describes her first arrival in Wales like this:

> When I came hither, a stranger, I was struck by the loveliness of the country, as well as by the character, manners, and language of its primitive inhabitants ... I was going into Wales for the first time, and ... the novelty and beauty of the scenery, together with the pure mountain air, dispelled whatever feelings of sadness had seized upon me ... I had not expected to be at once so much 'at home' as I felt myself when I arrived at my journey's end, nor had I anticipated the warmth and friendliness of manner that characterize the Welsh, who are neither distant nor cold, but easily approachable.[7]

It is clear from her writing that Beale was immediately attracted to her new environment and, in effect, fell in love with the place and its people, using them as subjects for much of her prolific later literary work, which appeared from the 1840s to the 1890s. Beale's local following is indicated by the enthusiastic treatment given to her in an 1858 book on *Llandeilo Vawr and its Neighbourhood, Past and Present* by Gwilym Teilo. In a section subtitled 'Eminent Characters', Beale is afforded a six-page encomium in which she is described as 'accomplished', 'amiable', and 'gifted', while her work in *The Vale of the Towey* is praised as 'display[ing] great powers of description, and of giving colour to natural objects'.[8] 'The setting of the book,' Teilo explains, is 'a village in this immediate neighbourhood, and the characters, so wittily portrayed, are its inhabitants. The delineations of some of them,' he adds, 'are as true to nature as artistic skill could daguerrotype them' (46). Yet even in her most positive representation of Welshness, in the 1876 novel *The Pennant Family*, as Dearnley points out, 'her emphasis is on the need for love and understanding between the indigenous population and the "interloper"', which, as Dearnley observes, 'points inexorably, in this novel, to a continued process of anglicization'.[9] In fact, Beale's attitude towards Welsh betrays some ambivalence; like Matthew Arnold some thirty years later, Beale seems to approve of anglicization while at the same time waxing lyrical about 'the grand old Welsh language'.[10]

One of the aspects of Welsh life which prevents Beale from identifying wholeheartedly with her adoptive home is the fact that she is separated from the 'Welsh peasantry' by a class divide. Maintenance of her class position is clearly quite important for Beale – she cannot afford to 'go native' completely because she cannot afford to compromise her status as a gentlewoman. Perhaps this is particularly acute on account of her original, rather ambivalent status as a governess – neither quite of the gentlefolk, nor yet a servant (interestingly, the 1844 census lists Anne Beale separately from the three servants of the household). Beale observes that many of the people she calls 'the Welsh peasantry' are 'miserably poor', but she blithely goes on to say that 'my business is not with them', indicating unmistakeably her class difference.[11] Similarly, the adjectives 'primitive' and even 'primeval' are frequently used by Beale in describing both the landscape of the Towey valley and its inhabitants. Though we might regard this use of language as indicating a supercilious attitude towards Wales, it is evident that the adjectives are actually used positively in order to valorize place and people, but they also serve to underline their alterity. At the same time, she is perfectly prepared to claim possession of a Welsh identity, in her telling usage of the first-person plural, for instance, in describing Llandeilo as 'our town' (50) and referring to the habits of 'we country-folk' (63).

Beale's construction of Welshness is not untypical for the later nineteenth century: while she is an enthusiastic admirer of Welsh difference and, to a degree, a participant in that different culture, she is also a proud Briton and an upholder of empire. She constructs an autobiographical narrative of identity in which she 'came hither, a stranger' but was surprised not only by the unexpected grandeur of the landscape but by the friendliness of the natives. Unlike the English Romantic travellers who preceded Beale in their journeys to Wales in search of sublime scenery, Beale clearly becomes intensely interested in the people of Wales, hence the change of title from *The Vale of the Towey* to *Traits and Stories of the Welsh Peasantry*. This is not to deny that Beale's ideology is imperialist, but it is to suggest that Beale's construction of a Welshness in which she herself had a role probably meant that she saw herself as the defender of the 'proud Cambrians' rather than their detractor. Beale was, therefore, more integrated into and engaged with Welsh cultural life than was Peacock, whose association with major Romantic figures such as Shelley meant that his fame was greater in English and metropolitan literary circles. These borderline cases make particularly acute the question of how to define 'the Welsh novel', and it is tempting to do so partly by reference to readership and subject position, rather than the author's birthplace, nationality, or even the contents and style of their works.

Anne Beale, like Peacock, also published novels with no overt Welsh connections, particularly in later life when she moved away from Wales to settle in London. In doing so, she was emulating the practice of earlier women writers, notably Anna Maria Bennett. In the heyday of the Romantic tourist in the 1780s and 1790s, Bennett was one of the few among the dozens of writers who used Wales as an exotic backdrop in the period to have an insider perspective, since she was of Welsh birth and parentage. Bennett's two Welsh novels, *Anna, or Memoirs of a Welch Heiress* (1786) and *Ellen, Countess of Castle Howel* (1794), draw on the author's Welsh background – she was born Anna Maria Evans, the daughter of a Merthyr Tydfil grocer.[12] Her two Welsh-set works express a decided anxiety and ambivalence about Welsh identity and the fraught relationship between England and Wales. Both her Welsh novels also feature 'nabobs' or ex-colonials and engage with ideas about colonialism and empire, asking implicitly where Wales fits in to the idea of British sovereign rule.[13] Bennett was exceptionally popular and famous in her lifetime – *Anna* sold out on the day of publication and her work was translated into French and German. In determining the label best suited for works such as those of Bennett, Beale, and Peacock, perhaps the now unfashionable term 'Anglo-Welsh' is the most appropriate to indicate the cultural hybridity which is evident in their texts and which tends to get overlooked when they are seamlessly amalgamated, as they have been, into an English literary mainstream.

Contemporary with Anna Maria Bennett was Edward 'Celtic' Davies, whose only published novel, *Elisa Powell, or Trials of Sensibility* (1795), is an entertaining and stylishly written epistolary work. The author was a Welsh curate and antiquarian like his narrator, Henry Stanley, and the novel opens very much like a travel narrative, with Stanley writing to his English friend, James Wilson, also a clergyman, about the delights of the Welsh rural town of 'B' (probably Brecon) where he has recently moved. He even refers explicitly to travel narratives: 'You may recollect that we have admired the landscapes of the principality, as exhibited to us in the tours of Wyndham, Gilpin, and others?'[14] But he is not in Wales as a tourist – he has bought a Welsh estate and begins to interact with his farmer-tenants, who turn out to be clever, industrious, and eloquent, even if some of them do speak broken English. Stanley himself is decidedly pro-Welsh and emphasizes their descent from the 'ancient Britons' (22). Davies creates some memorable Welsh characters in this novel, including the incorrigible flirt, Maria Jones, and the eccentric antiquarian, Dr Pemberton, who is always vainly seeking 'the grave of Lywelyn' (38). The second part of the novel unfortunately focuses on the vapid heroine, Elisa Powell, who causes mayhem wherever she goes because men *will* fall in love with her. At the end of the novel, the modern reader is glad to see her expire, still writing letters. This is very much a Welsh novel of sensibility, in vogue in England at the time: Davies adopts a sophisticated and urbane voice and attempts to bridge the gap between Wales and England by presenting a positive picture of Welsh culture to his English correspondent and, presumably, the English reader.

If *Elisa Powell* is somewhat influenced by the travel narrative, Llewellin Williams's *The Journal of Llewellin Penrose, a Seaman*, first published in London in 1815, is a travel book *tout court*. This text has sometimes been called 'the first American novel' because its author almost certainly wrote the book when he was living in America in the 1770s, but the manuscript was not published until many years later in London, when the author, now an old man down on his luck, left it to a John Eagles, whose son finally published it.[15] The book is a first-person account of a shipwreck and many years' sojourn in what is probably the Mosquito Coast in Costa Rica. It appears to be a true story – the descriptions of the flora and fauna and the author's encounters with the native peoples are astonishingly detailed. But is it a *Welsh* novel? At the outset the narrator tells us, 'Llewellin Penrose is my name; I was born in Caerphilly, in Glamorganshire, in the month of May 1725.'[16] In fact there still is a village called Penrhos near Caerphilly, so the author, Llewellin Williams, may well have practised the time-honoured custom in Wales of adopting the name of one's birthplace instead of an all-too-common surname. Llewellin soon runs away to sea, though: sailing from Bristol, his ship is taking coal from Neath to Cork in Ireland. But after this first trip, Llewellin's journeys become much more ambitious and far-ranging until he is shipwrecked in the West Indies. The rest of the narrative concerns what he does on this shipwrecked coast for the next twenty-eight years. There are few overt Welsh traces in the text, but Llewellin does call the sons he has with Luta, his native wife, Owen, Morgan, and Rees, distinctively Welsh names. When his fourth child, a girl, is born, he calls her 'America'. These names may indicate the changing identity of the author himself. The narrator is ardently anti-slavery and exceptionally sympathetic towards the native peoples he meets, often contrasting them with Europeans and showing how the natives are often superior to so-called 'civilized' people.

Very unlike the passionate seriousness of *Llewellin Penrose* is the flippantly sardonic 1828 novel *The Adventures and Vagaries of Twm Shon Catti* by T. J. Llywelyn Prichard, which is a comic novel through and through. It is a mock-biography of the eponymous Cardiganshire folk hero, sometimes known as the Welsh Robin Hood. Early on in the text, the reader is informed:

> Catti, the mother of Twm, lived in the most unsophisticated manner at Llidiard-y-Fynnon ... This little farm was their father's freehold property, but provokingly situate in the middle of the vast possessions of Squire Graspacre, an English gentleman-farmer, who condescendingly fixed himself in the principality with the laudable idea of civilizing the Welsh. The most feasible mode of accomplishing so grand an undertaking, that appeared to him, was, to dispossess them of their property, and to take as much as possible of their country into his own paternal care. The rude Welsh, to be sure, he found so blind to their own interests, as to prefer living on their farms to either selling or giving them away, to profit by his superior management.[17]

The author, Llywelyn Prichard, was quite a character himself – born in Builth Wells, he later made a living as a strolling player, then married and opened a bookshop in Builth and began to publish his own works in verse and prose. He lost his nose in a duel and ended up destitute in a Swansea dosshouse.

This is a curriculum vitae far removed from those of the respectable Nonconformist ministers who wrote a good deal of the Welsh-language literature of the nineteenth century. *Twm Shon Catti* has a strong claim to be the first genuinely Welsh novel in English, although it clearly owes a good deal to English comic novelists like Fielding and Sterne. But the perspective is unmistakably Welsh: Prichard undertakes to tell Twm Shon Catti's story because the Welsh folk hero has been stolen and misrepresented on the English stage in a bastardized version. The novel is virulently anti-Methodist; at one point the narrator laments, 'Before methodism spread its puritanic gloom over Wales . . . mirth and minstrelsy, dance and song, games and rural pastimes, were the order of the day' (ch. IV). But the main focus is Twm, who defies the squire and goes on the run, hiding out in a cave; his wanderings and adventures all feature Twm outwitting highwaymen, landlords, and parsons and escaping again to his cave, often disguised as a woman. Prichard's hero has a happy ending, marrying the Lady of Ystrad Ffin and becoming mayor of Brecon. The text is littered with Welsh words and translations of Welsh poems; clearly, Prichard was bilingual and keen to show the beauties of Welsh culture to an anglophone readership.

But what was Welsh-language culture itself producing at this time? As Prichard's embittered reflections on Methodism suggest, there was certainly a strong prejudice against the novel in the Nonconformist culture of Wales, which a number of critics cite as a factor in the late emergence of the novel in Welsh. Indeed, the suspicion about the morality of the novel, partly because it quite literally told lies, meant that there was some uncertainty over what to call the new genre in Welsh. The novel was referred to by various names including *ffug-chwedl*, *ffug-hanes*, and *ffug-draith* ('false-fable', 'false-story', and 'false-narrative'), terms which suggest the anxiety of Welsh readers about the novel's propriety. Advertisements placed by booksellers in nineteenth-century journals frequently take pains to underline the wholesomeness and moral virtue of the novels on sale. In Welsh-speaking Wales the dominant genres were still poetry and religious writing, especially hymns and sermons, along with biographies of Nonconformist ministers.

One text sometimes referred to as the first Welsh-language novel is *Y Bardd, neu, Y Meudwy Cymreig* ('The Bard or The Welsh Hermit') by William Ellis Jones, who went by the bardic name of 'Cawrdaf', which was published in Carmarthen in 1830. However, few critics in the field are content with the designation of this text as 'the first Welsh novel'. And it is easy to see why. It is an unstable, hybrid text, which owes a great deal to the work of the seventeenth-century Puritan preacher, John Bunyan, especially his allegorical narrative, *The Pilgrim's Progress* (1678–84). Cawrdaf's primary purpose is religious and didactic; he takes his fictional poet on a series of journeys, led by the personified figure of Providence, to meet a range of people whose lives and tribulations serve to teach moral lessons. In the preface the author describes his book as having 'dull hollol newydd o addysgu' ('an entirely new method of teaching').[18] Nevertheless, the lengthy narrative does have many of the trappings of an adventure story along the lines of *Robinson Crusoe* or *Llewellin Penrose*. There is a first-person narrator, shipwrecks, love affairs, misunderstandings, banishments, class conflicts, and journeys to exotic locations. However, the didactic intention is inescapable.

Perhaps one of the most interesting aspects of the text is the list of subscribers, which is four pages long and gives a glimpse of the potential readership for this new phenomenon – a novel in Welsh. Thus, we know, for example, that R. Griffiths, a wheelwright from Holyhead, was a subscriber, also R. Rees, a grocer from Machynlleth, and Miss M. Jones, a dressmaker from Llanrwst. The range of occupations and classes is wide, starting from the bishop of St David's and Sir Thomas Mostyn, Bart., and encompassing rectors, solicitors, drapers, millers, and butchers. Joiners and printers are particularly well represented. Most of the women subscribers are unmarried but a few are, and some also have an occupation, e.g. Mrs Williams, printer, Aberystwyth, who may well have been buying multiple copies for resale.

Y Bardd is very different from its English-language namesake, *The Bard; or, The Towers of Morven*, a novel by Evan Jones published in London in 1809. Jones begins his novel with grandiloquent gusto; his white-bearded bard sits on a north Welsh mountain-top in the midst of a storm, playing his harp and singing, an image evidently influenced by the recently invented *gorsedd* (or 'gathering') of the bards popularized by Iolo Morganwg.[19] The plot is complicated and feverishly Gothic: the hero, Idwal, falls in love with the bard's daughter, Elfleda, but is challenged by the evil warrior, Ithel Vaughan, who desires her for himself. A good Gothic heroine, Elfleda is kidnapped and incarcerated in Caer Cerrig, situated 'high over the impending precipice of Moelvaur, on the highest summit of the stupendous mountain Snowdon'.[20] While imprisoned, Elfleda has horrid dreams of sexual violation: 'Suddenly she found herself in the grasp of a ruffian who, with unrelenting ferocity, brandished in one hand a naked dagger over her defenceless head, whilst his other wandered in rude freedom over the sacred beauties of her person' (76). Attempting to escape, Elfleda finds her way down a dark corridor where 'ten thousand venomous reptiles dragged their slimy length over the green surface of the humid walls, and marked their track in fetid excretions'; avoiding the slime, Elfleda is confronted by the 'horrid phantom' of the murdered Mysanwy and then, groping about in the gloom, places her hand on a 'cold, clammy substance' which turns out to be 'the starting eye of a putrid corpse' (83). There is much titillation of which Cawrdaf's Welsh-language bard would most certainly disapprove. Nevertheless, Evan Jones's novel is emphatically Welsh. The London printers appear to have had difficulties with some of the Welsh place-names, and here and there they have been corrected by hand in Cardiff University Library's Special Collections copy: for example, 'Cwrn' has been corrected to 'Cwm' and 'crrw' changed to the correct spelling, 'cwrw', and then footnoted as 'ale' – possibly these corrections are by the author himself (7). As in Cawrdaf's *Y Bardd*, there is copious interpolated verse, much of it telling legendary Welsh tales. In comparison with Cawrdaf's Welsh-language novel, Jones's novel is much more clearly an entertainment and a risqué one at that, but it is nevertheless overtly pro-Welsh in its political message, and it contains a wealth of Welsh words, places, and legends. Both novels have religious points to make and both take the reader on exhaustive travels around Welsh landscapes. Jones is, however, imitating English and Scottish models in his experiment with the new form, while Cawrdaf is, he believes, creating a new form for the instruction of his fellow Welshmen, though it undoubtedly borrows from the sermon, the allegory, and the travel narrative.

Several critics have argued that the real breakthrough for the Welsh-language novel was Gwilym Hiraethog's text, *Aelwyd f'Ewythr Robert* ('Uncle Robert's Hearth'), an 1853 translation (one of several which appeared at the time) of Harriet Beecher Stowe's *Uncle Tom's Cabin*, first published in 1852.[21] Gwilym's text was really an adaptation which tells Beecher Stowe's story within a frame set in a Welsh family's house; it proved enormously popular and showed sceptical Nonconformists that the novel could be a force for good – in this case for the abolition of slavery – rather than an agent of corruption. The initial illustration in *Aelwyd f'Ewythr Robert* depicting the hearthside scene of storytelling is also suggestive of the reception of the novel in this period – the texts would be read aloud and shared communally, thus including even those in the community who may have been illiterate. It is also notable that a large proportion of later nineteenth-century novels in both Welsh and English were first published serially in magazines, mirroring the practice of English writers such as Charles Dickens and Elizabeth Gaskell and, again, facilitating a communal reading experience.

With the enormous success of the Welsh translations of *Uncle Tom's Cabin*, *eisteddfodau* in Wales were soon setting competitions for the *ffug-hanes* with moral subjects. In 1854, for instance, Merthyr Tydfil's Cymmrodorion eisteddfod set as a subject for its *ffug-hanes* competition 'The Reformed Drunkard', and there were six competitors. The winner was Lewis William Lewis, writing under the pen name 'Llew Llwyfo' and his winning novel, *Llewelyn Parri neu Y Meddwyn Diwygiedig* ('Llewelyn Parry or the Reformed Drunkard') was published in 1855. The author, who suggests that he is himself a former drunkard, says in the preface, 'Y mae nofel Gymraeg yn beth newydd ar y ddaear' ('A novel in Welsh is something new on the face of the earth'), and goes on to acknowledge that many people will condemn this work simply because it is a novel, the name alone being enough to frighten some narrow-minded people; however, he hopes they will change their minds when they actually read it, seeing that it is intended to do good.[22]

Temperance novels became very common in Welsh towards the end of the century. Both male and female authors wrote them and, as Dafydd Jenkins has pointed out, they are not in the end of much literary interest because they are wholly predictable in terms of character and plot.[23] Nevertheless, as late as 1905 William J. Griffiths published a temperance novel with the irresistible title *O'r Pwlpud ... I'r Crogbren* ('From the Pulpit to the Gallows').[24] Cardiff University Library's Special Collections edition is bound together with a number of other texts which are all religious in character: sermons, biographies of ministers, and an account of the 1904–5 Evan Roberts religious revival. This indicates that for the owner of this volume, at least, the novel was an emphatically religious form.

Another temperance novel is John Thomas D. D.'s *Arthur Llwyd y Felin* ('Arthur Lloyd of the Mill'), first published in 1879 and republished posthumously in Liverpool in 1893 in a handsome illustrated edition. This novel is unremittingly didactic and presents a sentimental picture of rural Wales. Its opening sentence is: 'Mewn llannerch anghysbell a neillduedig yn nghilfach cwm cul, ac yn cael ei gylchynu o bob tu gan fân fryniau ... a moelydd, gorweddai pentref bychan gwylaidd a diaddurn' ('In a remote and secluded glade in a nook of a narrow valley and surrounded on all sides by hills and mountains lay a humble and unadorned little village').[25] This is undistinguished writing but good fodder for the parodist, as demonstrated when a truly talented Welsh writer emerges a few years later and immediately begins to mock this kind of didactic sentimentalism. It is no accident that the first novel by Daniel Owen (1836–95), *Y Dreflan* ('The Small Town'), first published in Treffynnon in 1881, is emphatically urban in setting and its opening paragraph seems to be an explicit mockery of the start of *Arthur Llwyd y Felin* and its like:

Na feddylied y darllenydd am fynyd mai rhyw bentref amhoblog a dinôd
ydyw y Dreflan; oblegid pe felly, prin y byddai yn werth i mi ysgrifennu, nac
iddo yntau ddarllen, dim o'i hanes. Y mae ein Treflan o chwech i saith mil
o drigolion, er y dywed y rhai a ddeuant o Liverpool a Manchester yma eu
bod yn dyfod i'r 'wlad'; a phan ânt yn ôl, meant yn dywedyd eu bod yn
myned i'r 'dref'. Gyda llaw, mae clywed Dic-Sion-Dafyddion o'r trefydd
mawrion yn siarad fel hyn yn fy mlino nid ychydig.

(Let the reader not imagine for a minute that Y Dreflan is some insignificant
and sparsely populated village; for if it were, it would hardly be worth my
writing or him reading about it. Treflan has six to seven thousand inhabitants, though those who come here from Liverpool or Manchester say
they're coming to the 'country' and that they're going to 'town' when
they go back there. By the way, listening to every Tom, Dick, and Harry
from the cities talking like that irritates me not a little.)[26]

This is Daniel Owen's first novel and one is immediately struck by his
confident voice. His is an opinionated and lively narrator who uses normal
vernacular Welsh and thankfully has no wish to preach to the reader. Owen
was apprenticed to a tailor and later set up in business on his own in his home
town of Mold in north-east Wales. He did attend the Methodist training
college in Bala for a few years, but Daniel Owen's great forte is being able to
mock Methodist society gently from within. He is an insider and his four
novels and one collection of short stories are all about Welsh life, centring
upon the chapels. He clearly loves the novel form and has a natural storyteller's facility – his work atones for all those dreary temperance tracts, and it
often does so by using exactly the same kinds of settings and materials.
Indeed, his own first foray into print was as a translator into Welsh of an
American temperance novelette which rejoiced in the title *Ten Nights in a Bar
Room*.[27] His second novel, *Hunangofiant Rhys Lewis: Gweinidog Bethel*
('The Autobiography of Rhys Lewis, Minister of Bethel Chapel'), published
in Wrexham in 1885, is a parody of those countless hagiographic biographies
of ministers that came hot off the presses of nineteenth-century Wales. Owen
was strongly influenced by English novelists such as Dickens, Thomas Hardy,
and George Eliot, but his material is exclusively and distinctively Welsh.
Owen's work was immediately popular and translated into other languages,
including English, which is a nice instance of repaying one's literary debts.

As a comic novelist, Daniel Owen had one unique forerunner, his namesake, but no relation, David Owen, who wrote under the pen-name 'Brutus'.
Brutus seems to have been a defrocked priest, or rather a Baptist minister
who was sacked for embezzlement. He then started writing for and editing

Welsh journals, including the Anglican periodical *Yr Haul* ('The Sun'), for which he wrote a series of mock biographies just a few years before Daniel Owen. Unfortunately, Brutus never finished his rambling, repetitive, serialized masterpiece *Wil Brydydd y Coed* ('Will, the Bard of the Trees'), published between 1863 and 1865, for he died in 1866. *Wil Brydydd y Coed* was published as a separate volume posthumously and it still remains readable and humorous today.[28] Wil, a kind of Welsh Candide, takes it into his head to become a preacher, but he is ridiculously ignorant and his sermons are nonsensical though he takes in his gullible congregations, who think he is a very deep thinker indeed. Clearly, Brutus has an axe to grind against the chapels, not unlike Caradoc Evans some fifty years later. Again, this is an insider's critique. Brutus knows what a sermon should sound like, having preached not a few in his time, so his parodies of sermons, in both Welsh and English, are things of hilarious beauty.

The macaronic tendencies of Brutus are a reflection of an increasingly bilingual society in Wales. Some writers took advantage of this by publishing in both Welsh and English. Isaac Craigfryn Hughes is a case in point. Craigfryn was a coal miner from Quakers Yard and his most popular work was *Y Ferch o Gefn Ydfa*, which also appeared in English as *The Maid of Cefn Ydfa*, both published in Cardiff in 1881.[29] It is difficult to overemphasize the enormous popularity of this romance, based on a folk tale and ballad about a real woman, Ann Maddocks, and her doomed love for the poet, Wil Hopkin. By 1938 the English version had reached its thirty-first edition, and a new edition was published as late as 1979. When Gwyn Jones wrote an essay on what he called the 'first forty years' of Anglo-Welsh literature, he explicitly condemned *The Maid of Cefn Ydfa* as the kind of lamentable sentimental dross that the new industrial novelists – and Caradoc Evans – were writing against.[30] Gwyn Jones's judgement is emphatically gendered. *The Maid of Cefn Ydfa*, despite the fact that its author was not only a man but a former collier, is too 'feminine' for him, its affective conventions too cloying.

Those very romance conventions were also employed by many Welsh women writers, including Mary Oliver Jones, author of *Y Fun o Eithinfynydd* ('The Girl from Eithifynydd') published in Caernarfon in 1894.[31] This novel is a posthumous publication by a Welshwoman who lived in Birkenhead and was an important contributor to Welsh periodicals in the last decades of the nineteenth century. The novel is based on the pseudo-life of the medieval poet Dafydd ap Gwilym and his love for Morfudd, the maid of Eithinfynydd of the title. It is a historical romance originally published serially in O. M. Edwards's journal, *Cymru*. It is a lively and readable novel with a high proportion of direct speech, bringing the characters alive. The characters speak normal, vernacular Welsh, not an artificially archaic language. It is set in Wales and the places and place-names are recognizable to a modern reader. Mary Oliver Jones shows a skill and an ease with the novel form and with writing in a natural language, which are indices of how far the novel has come since the stilted lessons of Cawrdaf's *Y Bardd* some fifty years previously.

Towards the turn of the century, in both languages, there sprang up a new generation of women novelists, notably 'Allen Raine', a writer from west Wales who became a publishing phenomenon after her first novel, *A Welsh Singer*, was published by Hutchinson in London in 1897.[32] From then until her death in 1906, she became the voice of Wales for an English and American readership who bought her novels in their hundreds of thousands. It is only in the last few years that Allen Raine has begun to be written back into the narrative of Welsh literary history, owing to the prejudice of earlier critics like Gwyn Jones who dismissed her work with contempt, calling it a 'sandcastle dynasty'.[33] Another important Welsh writer of the *fin de siècle* was Amy Dillwyn, though she followed the pattern of earlier writers like Anna Maria Bennett and Anne Beale in publishing only some Welsh-set novels, while her other works were more metropolitan and designed to appeal to an English audience. Nevertheless, her 1880 novel, *The Rebecca Rioter*, is emphatically Welsh and both formally and thematically daring.[34] In the Welsh language, too, there were important new female voices, such as 'Gwyneth Vaughan', the pseudonym of Annie Harriet Hughes, who published, for example, *O Gorlannau y Defaid* ('From the Sheepfolds') in Carmarthen in 1905. Even more distinctive and lively was the first-person narrative of Winnie Parry's *Sioned*, published in Caernarfon in 1906.[35] The confidence of these writers with the form and with using a natural, non-artificial language shows that the Welsh novel had come of age.

Many early prose works in Welsh – devotional works, prayer books, and sermons – were published in London, but when Welsh-language fiction began to appear in the nineteenth century, it was predominantly published by presses in Wales itself. This is an important difference from the Anglo-Welsh fiction of the time which was, overwhelmingly, published in London. Clearly these differences might also suggest a different readership. So, for example, while Daniel Owen, undoubtedly the most important early novelist in the Welsh language, had his works published in Treffynnon, his native Mold, and in Wrexham, his anglophone counterpart, Allen Raine, had all her novels published in London and New York. Nevertheless, there were some

Welsh writers who published English fiction in Wales and a number of authors who published fiction in both languages, such as Craigfryn, discussed above.

It was a slow start for the Welsh-language novel, then, especially for women writers, but by the early twentieth century it was well established and had produced at least one first-class writer in Daniel Owen. One of the reasons that the Welsh-language novel initially did not flourish or produce work of literary value was that many of its early proponents were clergymen, who were wary of the genre itself. This was a reflection of the fact that a large proportion of the educated population of Wales in the nineteenth century was associated with the chapels: virtually every ambitious young man of the *gwerin* ('folk') wanted to be a preacher. But preachers want to preach, and the novels they wrote reflected this fact. It is significant that when a major novelist does spring into being in Welsh-language culture, he is a tailor, not a preacher. And above all, by the end of the nineteenth century Welsh women writing in both languages began to write novels. Unlike the early Welsh women writers, like Anna Maria Bennett who really had no choice but to make a name for herself in England as a British novelist, writers like Winnie Parry, Gwyneth Vaughan, and Allen Raine could return to Wales and write unmistakably Welsh novels often centred upon women and everyday life. In the course of the nineteenth century, Wales had undergone a huge demographic and linguistic shift, for in the early part of the century as few as 10 per cent of the population of Wales could speak English, but by the end of the century only about half the population could speak Welsh. If the early anglophone Welsh novel's Welsh credentials were sometimes dubious, at the threshold of the twentieth century English began to be the mother tongue of an increasing proportion of the Welsh population. At the same time, south Wales became one of the powerhouses of the new industrial world, creating the conditions for a new flowering of Welsh fiction in English. Joseph Keating's industrial novel, *Son of Judith*, published at the turn of the century,[36] could be seen as the harbinger of this new body of literature; but the story of the twentieth-century Welsh industrial novel is one which will be explored elsewhere in this volume.

Notes

1. See Jane Aaron, *Nineteenth-Century Women's Writing in Wales: Nation, Gender, and Identity* (Cardiff: University of Wales Press, 2007); Moira Dearnley, *Distant Fields: Eighteenth-Century Fictions of Wales*

(Cardiff: University of Wales Press, 2001); Sarah Prescott, *Eighteenth-Century Writing from Wales: Bards and Britons* (Cardiff: University of Wales Press, 2008).

2. De Curli, trans. anonymous, *The Life and Amours of Owen Tideric, Prince of Wales, otherwise Owen Tudor : who married Catharine, Princess of France and widow of our great King Henry V, from which marriage descended Henry VII, Henry VIII, Edward VI, Queen Mary, and Queen Elizabeth, all of whom had from him the surname Tudor; and from him likewise are descended, by the eldest daughter of Henry VII, the present royal family of Great Britain, France and Ireland: first wrote in French and published many years since at Paris, and now translated into English* (London: William Owen, 1751), x.

3. Penelope Aubin, *The Life of Madam de Beaumount, a French Lady : who lived in a cave in Wales above fourteen years undiscovered, being forced to fly France for her religion, and of the cruel usage she had there : also her lord's adventures in Muscovy, where he was a prisoner some years : with an account of his returning to France, and her being discover'd by a Welsh gentleman, who fetch'd her lord to Wales, and of many strange accidents which befel them, and their daughter Belinda, who was stolen away from them, and of their return to France in the year 1718* (London: E. Bell, J. Darby, A. Bettesworth, F. Fayram, J. Pemberton, J. Hooke, C. Rivington, F. Clay, J. Batley, E. Symon, 1721).

4. Dearnley, *Distant Fields*, 12.

5. Thomas Love Peacock, *The Misfortunes of Elphin* (London: Thomas Hookham, 1829).

6. Meic Stephens, ed., *The New Companion to the Literature of Wales* (Cardiff: University of Wales Press, 1998), 573.

7. Anne Beale, *The Vale of the Towey or, Sketches in South Wales* (London: Longman, Brown, Green, and Longmans, 1844), vii, 2, 9.

8. William Davies ('Gwilym Teilo'), *Llandeilo-Vawr and its Neighbourhood, Past and Present* (Llandeilo: D. W. & G. Jones, 1858), 46.

9. Moira Dearnley, '"I Came Hither, A Stranger": A View of Wales in the Novels of Anne Beale (1815–1900)', *New Welsh Review* 1, 4 (1989): 29.

10. Dearnley, *Distant Fields*, 29.

11. Anne Beale, *Traits and Stories of the Welsh Peasantry* (London: George Routledge, 1849), 22. (This was a reissue of *The Vale of the Towey* with a new title and preface.)

12. Jane Aaron, *Welsh Gothic* (Cardiff: University of Wales Press, 2013), 25. See Anna Maria Bennett, *Anna: or, Memoirs of a Welch Heiress*, 4th edn (London: Minerva Press, 1796), and Maria Bennett, *Ellen, Countess of Castle Howel: A Novel* (London: Minerva Press, 1794).

13. Francesca Rhydderch, 'Dual Nationality, Divided Identity: Ambivalent Narratives of Britishness in the Welsh Novels of Anna Maria Bennett', *Welsh Writing in English: A Yearbook of Critical Essays* 3 (1997): 1–17.

14. Edward 'Celtic' Davies, *Elisa Powell, or Trials of Sensibility: A Series of Original Letters, Collected by a Welsh Curate* (London: printed for G. G. and J. Robinson, 1795), 3.

15. See Llewellin Williams, preface to *The Journal of Llewellin Penrose, a Seaman* (London: J. Murray, 1815), and Terry Breverton, ed., *The First American Novel* (Cowbridge: Glyndwr, 2007).

16. Williams, *The Journal of Llewellin Penrose*, 2.

17. T. J. Llewelyn Prichard, *The Adventures and Vagaries of Twm Shon Catti, Descriptive of Life in Wales: Interspersed with Poems* (Aberystwyth: John Cox, 1828). The novel is available online at www.gutenberg.org/files/40419/404 19-h/40419-h.htm
    (Ch. II) (accessed 20 September 2017).

18. W. E. Jones ('Cawrdaf'), preface to *Y Bardd, neu, y Meudwy Cymreig: yn cynnwys teithiau difyr ac addysgiadol y bardd, gyda rhagluniaeth* (Carmarthen: J. L. Brigstocke, 1830).

19. See Chapter 15 in this volume on the invention of the *gorsedd*.

20. Evan Jones, *The Bard: or, The Towers of Morven; a Legendary Tale* (London: Printed for the author and sold by R. Dutton, 1809), 52.

21. William Rees ('Gwilym Hiraethog'), *Aelwyd f'Ewythr Robert: neu, Hanes Caban f'Ewythr Tomos* (Denbigh: Thomas Gee, 1853).

22. Lewis William Lewis ('Llew Llwyfo'), *Llewelyn Parri: neu, Y Meddwyn Diwygiedig; yn gosod allan echryslonrwydd bywyd y meddwyn a bendithion llwyrymwrthodiad: [y ffughanes buddugol yn Eisteddfod y Cymrodorion Dirwestol, Nadolig 1854]* (Merthyr Tydfil: Rees Lewis, 1855), iii.

23. Dafydd Jenkins and Morfydd E. Owen, 'Y Nofel Gymraeg Gynnar', in *Rhyddid y Nofel*, ed. Gerwyn Wiliams (Caerdydd: Gwasg Prifysgol Cymru, 1999), 42.

24. William J. Griffiths, *O'r Pwlpud . . . i'r Crogbren: ffug-chwedl ddirwestol* (Bangor: Evan Thomas, 1905).

25. John Thomas, *Arthur Llwyd y Felin* (Liverpool: John Edwards, 1893), 5.

26. Daniel Owen, *Y Dreflan: ei phobl a'i phethau* (Treffynnon: P. M. Evans, 1881), 1.

27. See John Rowlands, *Ysgrifau ar y Nofel* (Caerdydd: Gwasg Prifysgol Cymru, 1992), 13.

28. David Owen ('Brutus'), *Wil Brydydd y Coed: cofiant Siencyn Bach y Llwywr a chofiant Dai Hunandyb*, 3rd edn (Carmarthen: Spurrell, 1896).

29. Isaac Craigfryn Hughes, *Y Ferch o Gefn Ydfa: chwedl hanesyddol o'r ddeunawfed ganrif* (Cardiff: Western Mail, 1881); Isaac Craigfryn Hughes, *The Maid of Cefn Ydfa: An Historical Novel of the 18th Century* (Cardiff: Western Mail, 1881).

30. Gwyn Jones, *The First Forty Years: Some Notes on Anglo-Welsh Literature* (Cardiff: University of Wales Press, 1957), 9.

31. Mary Oliver Jones, *Y Fun o Eithinfynydd: neu, Helyntion carwriaethol Cymru fu* (Caernarfon: Cwmni'r Wasg Genedlaethol Gymreig, *c.* 1894). For the original poem by Dafydd ap Gwilym, see *DG.net*, poem 157, www .dafyddapgwilym.net (accessed 20 September 2017).

32. Anne Adaliza Puddicombe ('Allen Raine'), *A Welsh Singer* (London: Hutchinson, [1897] 1906). See also, by the same author, *Torn Sails: A Tale of a Welsh Village* (London: Hutchinson, 1898), *By Berwen Banks: A Novel* (London: Hutchinson, 1899), *Garthowen: A Story of a Welsh Homestead* (London: Hutchinson, 1900), *A Welsh Witch: A Romance of Rough Places* (London: Hutchinson, 1902), *Queen of the Rushes: A Tale of the Welsh Revival* (London: Hutchinson, 1906; repr. Dinas Powys: Honno, 1998). For a discussion of Raine, see Katie Gramich, *Twentieth-Century Women's Writing in Wales: Land, Gender, Belonging* (Cardiff: University of Wales Press, 2007), 34ff.; Sally Jones, *Allen Raine* (Cardiff: University of Wales Press, 1979).

33. Jones, *The First Forty Years*, 9.

34. Amy Dillwyn, *The Rebecca Rioter*, ed. Katie Gramich (Dinas Powys: Honno, [1880] 2001).

35. Annie Harriet Hughes ('Gwyneth Vaughan'), *O Gorlannau y Defaid* (London and Carmarthen: David Nutt, and Spurrell & Son, 1905); Winnie Parry, *Sioned* (Caernarfon: Swyddfa Cymru, 1906; repr. Dinas Powys: Honno, 1988).

36. Joseph Keating, *Son of Judith: A Tale of the Welsh Mining Valleys* (London: G. Allen, 1900).

PART IV

★

THE TRANSITION TO MODERNITY

18

The Modern Age, c. 1850–1945

CHRIS WILLIAMS

The application of steam to the facilitation of intercourse, is a fact of the highest importance, and is fraught with blessings, which but few can as yet adequately appreciate.

Monmouthshire Merlin, 22 June 1850

The 'modern age' arrived in Wales in 1850. Not in all of Wales, but in enough for the development to be significant. The occasion was the opening, on 18 June, of the South Wales Railway, connecting London with Swansea via Gloucester. The arrangement of connecting coach services meant that henceforth travellers might leave towns in Pembrokeshire early in the morning and arrive in London or Birmingham the same evening. Travel to 'every spot most famed for beauty or grandeur', whether in south or north Wales, 'hitherto known to the great mass of the public only by description or reading, the pencil of the painter, or the book of the tourist', would now be possible, according to Newport's *Monmouthshire Merlin*.[1] The railway would benefit commerce, stimulate industry, and act as a 'herald' of social 'peace and concord'. In importance it would 'far outweigh that memorable EIGHTEENTH OF JUNE' (the anniversary of the battle of Waterloo), dissolving 'the barriers and lines of demarcation' between Wales and England and facilitating the import of agricultural produce from Ireland. The railway was proof of 'the triumphs of science, of the progress of the mind, of the power of co-operation'.[2] Later it was argued that the railway would broaden the horizons of the Welsh people: 'To be a Taffy will be no longer to be a semi-civilized being ... hidden among his own wild mountains and glens ... he will become one of the great human family.'[3]

In the century that followed the coming of the South Wales Railway (extended to Neyland in 1856 and enhanced by the opening of the Severn tunnel in 1886), Wales was transformed demographically, linguistically, economically, socially, and politically. In addition, by the end of the Second

World War, 'Wales' as a concept, or as, if you prefer, an 'imagined commu-nity', enjoyed much more of a presence than it had in 1850, even if the destiny of the Welsh nation remained an open question.[4] Throughout, Wales was not necessarily the automatic or primary point of reference for the people of Wales – there were the complementary and competing identifications of region (most obviously 'south Wales'), of the wider British national frame-work (which could lead both Welsh and non-Welsh to use the words 'English' and 'England' in inclusive ways), and of the British empire (home to many Welsh migrants). But becoming 'one of the great human family', as the *Merlin* put it, did not entail the loss of a sense of Welshness. On the contrary, it has been argued that this was the century in which a sense of Wales was clearly reborn.[5]

Life

Between 1850 and 1945 the size of the Welsh population more than doubled. The 1851 population census recorded Wales as home to 1,163,139 people. The 1951 census counted 2,598,675 people in Wales, down from the 1921 high of 2,656,474. Rapid bursts of growth were seen in the 1880s and in the first decade of the twentieth century (when the population grew by a fifth). Although there was substantial migratory movement in and out of (and within) Wales, this population growth was driven predominantly by natural increase. In common with the rest of mainland Britain, Wales experienced a demographic transition from a pre-industrial situation in which high birth rates were offset by high death rates, through a period where birth rates (driven by increasing nuptiality) rose as death rates declined (less dramati-cally), thence to a position where lower birth rates and lower death rates were the norm. The crude birth rate for Wales has been estimated at 32.2 (births per 1,000 people) in 1850, falling to 17.1 by 1945. The crude death rate (deaths per 1,000 people) fell across the same period from 20.2 to 13.2, although it is the decline in the infant mortality rate (deaths per 1,000 births) that is a more consistent indicator of improving conditions, falling from 120.3 in 1850 to 54 in 1945 (even then substantially higher than the England and Wales average). The marriage rate (per 1,000 people) rose from 16.2 in 1850 to 19.6 in 1945 and the average age of marriage fell. More people lived longer: in 1951 42.5 per cent of the Welsh population was 40 years of age or more, whereas in 1851 the percentage had been only 24.6. In the middle of the nineteenth century, 46 per cent of the Welsh were under 20, but by 1951 that was down to 29 per cent.[6]

If there were, then, many more Welsh people in 1945 than in 1850, it was also the case that they were distributed across Wales rather differently. Together the counties of Glamorgan and Monmouth comprised 17 per cent of the total area of Wales. Already in 1851 they were home to a third of the Welsh population. By 1921 that had risen to 64 per cent, falling slightly by 1951. Within the south-east, industrial settlements, towns, and eventually cities housed an increasing proportion of people. In 1851 the iron town of Merthyr Tydfil was the largest urban settlement in Wales, with a total of 46,378 inhabitants. By 1951 Cardiff (which had been a city since 1905 and which would be identified formally as Wales's capital in 1955) housed 243,632 people, and Swansea 160,988. The most characteristic urban form was, however, that of the mining valleys. According to Philip N. Jones, here 'settlement of a scale and density comparable to the great coalfields of Western Europe [was] imposed upon an environment initially almost as wild, difficult and uninviting as that of the Appalachian Mountains of the eastern United States'.[7]

Such growth in the south-east was achieved in part by natural increase, but also by net inward migration up to the outbreak of the First World War. By contrast, the rural counties of Brecon, Pembroke, and Montgomery suffered sustained net out-migration throughout the period covered here. Wales, as a human society, changed shape, becoming 'bottom-heavy' in ways that sometimes challenged traditional notions of Welsh nationality. Overall, and despite significant in-migration from the west of England and Ireland especially, during the century after 1850 a net outflow of people was the general experience (the exception being 1901–11) as the Welsh moved to English industrial towns and cities or migrated abroad to destinations including the USA, Canada, and Australia. After the First World War, the economic depression was responsible for net out-migration from Wales of 442,000 between 1920 and 1939, with the southern industrial areas particularly hard hit.

Radical demographic growth and internal redistribution of the Welsh population was accompanied by another major transformation: anglicization. The absence of census figures measuring the prevalence of the Welsh language before 1891 does not prevent one from getting a strong sense of the dramatic nature of this change. According to the 1891 census, 30 per cent of the Welsh people were monolingual Welsh speakers, and a further 24 per cent were able to speak both Welsh and English. Even at this stage, and despite the fact that over half the Welsh could speak Welsh, English was the majority tongue, with 70 per cent able to converse in it. The following sixty years saw the near-total erosion of Welsh monolingualism (the 1951

census records just 41,155) and the decline of the total speaking Welsh at all to
27 per cent. Monoglot English speakers were in a majority in Wales from the
1901 census onwards. This national picture was heavily regionally differen-
tiated, with the counties of Anglesey, Caernarfon, Cardigan, Carmarthen,
and Merioneth remaining (progressively beleaguered) bastions of the Welsh
language. Urbanization was not an unmitigated disaster for the Welsh
language: 68 per cent of Merthyr's and 46 per cent of Swansea's population
was Welsh-speaking in 1891, but in the long run the language of the streets in
south Wales was English: only 4 per cent of Cardiffians were Welsh speakers
by 1951. By 1945 Welsh life was lived longer and by many more people, but
largely in the south-east, in urban settings, and through the English language.

Work

The main reason for the shifts in Welsh demography sketched above was that
between 1850 and 1914 Wales had become one of the world's industrial
powerhouses. The potential had already been there in the early decades of
the nineteenth century, as the often complementary industries of coal, iron,
copper, and tinplate stimulated industrialization in and around Merthyr
Tydfil, the Swansea and Neath valleys, Newport, and Cardiff.
The discovery of steam coal reserves in the central Glamorgan coalfield
from the mid-1840s propelled the process forward at a rate of knots only
equalled by Royal Navy vessels, themselves fuelled by Welsh coal. In 1854,
the south Wales coalfield produced 8.5 million tons of coal, and by 1913,
57 million tons, one-fifth of all Britain's coal, the bulk of it for export. With
industrial growth tied umbilically to the expansion of the British empire (and
its conflicts) and the spread of overseas trade, Wales saw swathes of its
landscape transformed by the building of mines, works, roads, and railways.
Population growth on a phenomenal scale followed the spread of highly
intensive manual industry, with the prospects of high earnings drawing
young men and their families in from rural areas.

In the second half of the nineteenth century, coal clearly outstripped iron,
which had been the motor force of eighteenth-century Welsh industrialization, but iron and steel, along with other metal trades including copper and
tinplate, remained vital to the industrial profile of localities including Merthyr
Tydfil and the 'heads of the valleys' to its east, the lower Swansea valley, and
Llanelli. Overall, south Wales became 'amongst the most buoyant growth
centres in the world for industrial production . . . Only the Ruhr in Germany
and the industrial sectors of the eastern United States rivalled south Wales as

a centre of heavy industry.'[8] Elsewhere significant pockets of industry developed around slate mining and quarrying in the north-west (nine-tenths of all British production coming from Caernarfonshire and Merionethshire), and coal, iron, and steel in the north-east on Deeside and around Wrexham.

This was, then, an industrial experience, but a lopsided one. The manufacturing sector, for example, was relatively weak. Between 1851 and 1911 only 23 per cent of Welsh jobs were in manufacturing industry, compared with a British average of 33 per cent. Over half of the Welsh workforce was in 'primary' production sectors (most obviously agriculture and coal mining) in 1851, and that had only fallen to 44 per cent by 1911. According to the 1921 census, 39 per cent of all occupied males in Glamorgan and Monmouthshire worked in mining and quarrying. The problem with the almost mono-industrial nature of the coalfield, as John Williams put it, was that mining is inherently transitory, and 'there is no necessity for an economy based on mining to give rise to a continuing industrial society'.[9] Contemporaries were aware of this problem. For the Barry Dock News of 28 July 1893, 'The industries upon which Barry depends for its existence are very few. The export of coal, ship repairing, the management of the dock and railways and the building trades are practically the whole. There is no import trade worth speaking of.' The same was true of the entire south Wales coastal belt: the prosperity that made possible the civic grandeur of Edwardian Cardiff rested on narrow and insecure foundations.

The skewed nature of the Welsh economy meant that the gender division of labour in Wales was more extreme than in many other parts of Britain. In 1921, 87.7 per cent of adult men were economically active, but only 21.2 per cent of women. Women were disproportionately over-represented in the poorly paid, casualized sectors of the economy. Apart from agricultural work and domestic service, women were found in the clothing industries, in commercial and financial occupations, and in clerical and sales work, with some representation in the professions (especially nursing and teaching). Heavy industrial work was available only in some industries, such as tinplate. Female paid workers were typically young and single rather than mature and married, and many such working lives were halted by marriage, only to be restarted by widowhood.

The structural imbalance of the Welsh economy was unforgivingly revealed during the decades between the world wars. Markets for Welsh coal shrank, and mine closures were the result. The loss of earning power in major industries exacerbated the problem for ancillary trades and the consumer market. Male employment in mining and quarrying across Wales fell from 274,682 in 1921 to 110,000 in 1951. In agriculture the workforce declined from 95,480 to 79,457. Unemployment soared, reaching an all-Wales peak of 37.5 per cent in 1932, much higher than the British average of 22.2 per cent. Towards the end of the 1930s, there was some attempt to address the problem as new industrial estates were opened (such as Treforest in 1938) and there was increased activity in metal manufacturing and engineering (new steel-works being opened at Ebbw Vale, also in 1938), but it was the rearmament mini-boom before the Second World War that brought respite to most industrial settlements rather than any dramatic change in direction.

One dimension of the Welsh industrial scene that remained constant, irrespective of whether the economy was in rude health or listing badly, was its often challenging workplace relations. Coal mining, in particular, enshrined contestation and dispute through the nature of its wage-bargaining processes, and the concentration of large numbers of workers whose com-mon interests were often perceived to be more important than any levels of internal status or remunerative differentiation meant that there was plenty of raw material both for clashes with authority and for the development of a strong trade union tradition. Distinct traditions and experiences were characteristic of the railways, the docks, and the iron and steel industries, but these did not distract from the overall impression that the Welsh industrial worker was more than ready to articulate grievances and to act on them with frequency. Landmark and highly dramatic disputes such as those of 1898, 1921, and 1926 should therefore be seen as part of a much broader pattern of industrial friction, which lent weight to a gathering momentum behind the emerging labour movement and a desire for legal protection and parliamentary representation from the late nineteenth cen-tury onwards, and which translated into a more ambitious programme for political change by the time of the First World War. As one government report explained, in 1917, 'All [miners'] movements initiated . . . during recent years, consciously or unconsciously, are directed towards the overthrow of the present capitalist system.'[10]

Belief

Socialism and militant trade unionism in Wales, so pronounced a feature of the first half of the twentieth century, were not, however, what distinguished Welsh society during the second half of the nineteenth century. The 1851 religious census provided clear evidence that Protestant Nonconformity was the majority religious preference in Wales, outnumbering the established

Anglican Church by about four to one.[11] In the course of the next seventy years, a sustained campaign was fought and won for the disestablishment (and disendowment) of the church, culminating in the Welsh Church Act of 1914 (implemented 1920). Disestablishment was not only a campaign fought on the issue of freedom of religious expression, or indeed to rectify those legal and civil disadvantages under which Nonconformists had sometimes laboured. It became an issue of much wider import: resonant with the desire for the recognition of Welsh nationality and Welsh distinctiveness, expressive of a fierce pride in Welsh-language culture and cultural heritage, and (ultimately) a test case for both Welsh Liberal politicians and Liberal governments. Milestones on the way to its achievement included the Welsh Sunday Closing Act of 1881 (the first modern piece of legislation to recognize Wales, excluding Monmouthshire, as a discrete entity) and a vigorous campaign involving civil disobedience against the Education Act of 1902. Whatever else Welsh Liberal politicians were divided on (including the question of home rule for Wales in the 1890s), they could unite on the need to secure disestablishment.

Wales was never, entirely, a 'Nonconformist nation', as it housed substantial minorities of both Anglicans and Roman Catholics. But the 1904–5 religious revival could give the impression that Nonconformist fervour had a particularly Welsh tinge, and the hold of religion among Welsh-speaking communities tended to be stronger than among their English-language counterparts. Ultimately the impact of anglicization, alongside general secularizing trends, destabilized the place of religious discourse at the centre of Welsh public life, but its centrality in the period before the First World War is indisputable.

Nonconformity was, then, a political issue, championed by the Liberal party in Wales. From the 1860s onwards, Welsh politics diverged from the British pattern of alternating Liberal/Conservative equilibrium, as first the Liberals (and then, from 1922, the Labour party) achieved hegemony. Conservative voters existed, but the nature of the British electoral system meant that the Tories could expect to win at best only a scattering of seats in Wales. The voting system itself, as in Britain generally, was not fully democratic until adult women gained the franchise on the same basis as men in 1928, but Welsh politics remained dominated by men until well after the Second World War. The first female MP for a Welsh constituency was Megan Lloyd George, elected Liberal for Anglesey in 1929. She was still the only female MP in Wales in 1945.

Megan was the daughter of David Lloyd George, Wales's most accomplished modern politician (Liberal MP for Caernarfon Boroughs, 1890–1945). Despite an early attachment to the cause of home rule, Lloyd George personified a Welsh national distinctiveness harnessed to the enabling power of the British state. As chancellor of the exchequer after 1908, he drove through radical changes to taxation, old age pensions, and social security in the teeth of livid opposition from Conservatives and peers. His anti-imperialist credentials established by a principled 'pro-Boer' stance during the South African war (1899–1902), he threw his energies behind the war effort against Germany in 1914 and emerged as the pre-eminent war leader of his generation, becoming prime minister in 1916 and seeing Britain through to victory in 1918. Architect of the Paris Peace settlement of 1919, Lloyd George remained in office (at the head of a predominantly Conservative coalition) until 1922. In 1919 he was lauded by the *Welsh Outlook* as 'the greatest Welshman yet born'.[12]

Lloyd George's Wales was, by the time he left office, being replaced by one more heavily influenced by the political and industrial concerns of the Welsh working class. Much of the energy of Labour politicians in the 1920s and 1930s was occupied by the immediate and pressing concerns of the economic downturn that gripped Wales's heavy industries. Again, the remedy sought was that of the power of the British state to intervene constructively in economic and social affairs, although with Labour forming only two minority governments (1924, 1929–31) opportunities were scarce. Whether 'Wales' was a meaningful context for most elected Welsh politicians was uncertain: for many its relevance was limited to issues of language and culture, especially the granting of disestablishment. Campaigns for Wales to be represented in cabinet, as Scotland had been since 1892, came to nothing, and although Welsh nationalism took on a new form with the foundation of Plaid Genedlaethol Cymru (the 'National Party of Wales') in 1925, its achievements were scant and its profile highly controversial. Rather, it was the British context that was clearly dominant in Wales during the first half of the twentieth century. Laws were made in Westminster, there was no all-Wales political forum, and it was the British state that fought and won two world wars, with the active compliance of the vast bulk of the Welsh people on both occasions.

At the beginning of 1945, with victory in the Second World War confidently anticipated if not yet within reach, Keidrych Rhys, editor of the literary magazine *Wales*, cited the comments of Denys Val Baker that 'the war has made the Welsh realise that they are a nation with a country, a people, a culture and a tradition *different* from England's to fight for. There is a new wave of national feeling among our people.'[13] Rhys himself was less sanguine, writing that 'fortunately or unfortunately, a country only gets the literature and politicians it deserves' and suggesting that 'Wales to-day could aptly be described as the Land of Frightened People.'[14] With wartime conditions still in existence, it was understandable that Rhys's mood was anxious. Would peacetime bring substantial progress in terms of industrial reconstruction and enhanced social justice, or might it instead see a return to the often desperate conditions of the 1930s? Great Britain's place and status in the post-war world, let alone that of Wales, could hardly be taken for granted in the context of the rise of the superpowers of the United States and Soviet Union and the tremors passing through the structures of the British empire. Wales, during the previous century, had experienced multiple and transformational changes. What was certain, in 1945, was that more change was in the offing. Denys Val Baker was right to say that the Welsh had a stronger sense of themselves as a distinct nation than had been so before 1939, but what that might translate into in political or cultural terms (spheres partly under the democratic control of the Welsh themselves), let alone economic (largely beyond such control), was difficult to predict.

If there is one moment in 1945 which marks the beginning of a new era in the history of Wales (and the history of the United Kingdom), then it is neither 8 May (Victory in Europe day) nor 15 August (Victory over Japan day), but rather 26 July, when the general election results were declared. Across Britain, Clement Attlee's Labour party took 48 per cent of the popular vote and 393 seats (of a total of 640) in the House of Commons. In Wales the outcome was more emphatic, if also (given pre-war voting patterns) more predictable: 58 per cent of the vote and 25 of 36 seats. The first majority Labour government formed in the wake of this landslide victory had significant Welsh representation in the form of George Hall (MP for Aberdare) as Secretary of State for the Colonies, Aneurin Bevan (Ebbw Vale) as Minister of Health, Ted Williams (Ogmore) as Minister of Information, James Griffiths (Llanelli) as Minister of National Insurance and Hilary Marquand (Cardiff East) as Secretary for Overseas Trade.[15] Between 1945 and 1948 this government implemented a radical programme extending public ownership and building the structures of what has come to be known as the 'welfare state', delivering on the promises its elected representatives had been making to Labour voters since before the previous world war. The lives working people in Wales could live after 1945 would be significantly different from those they had endured before.

Notes

1. *Swansea Herald*, cited in the *Monmouthshire Merlin*, 15 June 1850.
2. *Monmouthshire Merlin*, 22 June 1850.
3. *Monmouthshire Merlin*, 5 October 1850.
4. Benedict Anderson, *Imagined Communities* (London: Verso, 1983).
5. Kenneth O. Morgan, *Rebirth of a Nation: Wales, 1880–1980* (Oxford: Clarendon Press, 1981).
6. Unless otherwise specified, statistics for this chapter are taken from the relevant tables in John Williams, ed., *Digest of Welsh Historical Statistics* (Cardiff: Welsh Office, 1985).
7. Philip N. Jones, *Colliery Settlement in the South Wales Coalfield, 1850–1926* (Hull: University of Hull, 1969), 32.
8. Morgan, *Rebirth of a Nation*, 59.
9. John Williams, *Was Wales Industrialised?* (Llandysul: Gomer Press, 1995), 24.
10. Cd.8668, Commission of Enquiry into Industrial Unrest, No. 7 Division, *Report of the Commissioners for Wales, Including Monmouthshire* (1917), 24.
11. David Hempton, *Religion and Political Culture in Britain and Ireland* (Cambridge: Cambridge University Press, 1996), 50.
12. Kenneth O. Morgan, *Modern Wales: Politics, Places and People* (Cardiff: University of Wales Press, 1995), 361.
13. Keidrych Rhys, 'Editorial', *Wales* 4–6 (1945): 4.
14. Ibid., 5, 6.
15. In addition, Arthur Jenkins (Pontypool) was Parliamentary Secretary to the Minister of Education, Ness Edwards (Caerphilly) was Parliamentary Secretary to the Minister of Labour, and Arthur Pearson (Pontypridd) was Comptroller of the Household.

19

T. Gwynn Jones and the Renaissance of Welsh Poetry

ROBERT RHYS

T. Gwynn Jones (1871–1949)

The opening lines of T. Gwynn Jones's *cywydd* 'Hydref' ('Autumn') exemplify the sonorous mastery of *cynghanedd* and strict-metre poetry which so enchanted his contemporary audience:

> Gwelais fedd yr haf heddyw,
> Ar ŵydd a dail, hardded yw
> Ei liwiau fyrdd, olaf ef,
> Yn aeddfedrwydd lleddf Hydref.[1]

> (I saw the summer's grave today,
> On trees and leaves
> how beautiful its last, myriad colours
> in the melancholy ripeness of Autumn.)[2]

Written in 1906, just four years after Gwynn Jones had won the chair at the National Eisteddfod for his epoch-defining *awdl* 'Ymadawiad Arthur' ('The Passing of Arthur'), this poem offered a poetic vision of the ambiguities and paradoxes of life in a style which came to appeal more to contemporary readers than the turgid regurgitations of moral certainty which had characterized, and perhaps blighted, Welsh poetry in the late nineteenth century. There was also the faintest echo of the body of English poetry with which Jones and his successors were acquainted, and to which they were indebted. 'Hydref', with its echoes of Keats's 'Ode to Autumn', and 'Ymadawiad Arthur', with its debt to Tennyson, and through Tennyson to Malory, are two striking examples of the historical irony whereby a resurgent Welsh nationalist poetry often drew inspiration from English poetry.[3]

Gwynn Jones became a leading protagonist, 'a towering presence'[4] in the established and largely undisputed narrative of early twentieth-century

Welsh-language poetry. The story told is one of renaissance and renewal, a rejection of 'the last century', and the creation of a golden age the like of which had not been seen since medieval times. Wales 'has witnessed an outburst of splendid poetry', it was typically claimed in 1917, 'which, judged by any standard, whether imaginative insight, sensitiveness to beauty of colour, form, and music, or technical craftsmanship and artistry in words, has reached a level of achievement unsurpassed at any period in her literary history.'[5] The poet and essayist T. H. Parry-Williams captured the thrill of the new in a sonnet recollecting his response as a student to reading a volume of lyrics published by two young poets, W. J. Gruffydd and R. Silyn Roberts, in 1900:[6]

> Ei Horas a'i Gatwlws ar y llawr,
> Yntau ar newydd win yn feddw fawr.
>
> (His Horace and Catullus on the floor,
> he was drunk on new wine.)

The 'renaissance' was never regarded as a purely aesthetic one, devoid of wider contexts. Gwynn Jones himself emphasized the role of a new scholarship, coming out of Oxford and then the new colleges of the University of Wales, in editing and disseminating the classics of medieval literature, and poetry in particular, which was such an inspiration to generations of poets: 'In Oxford, or on the Continent, were trained a few young Welshmen who had inherited the old literary tradition, and it was with the return of those men to Wales that the new epoch really began.'[7] The most significant of these was John Morris-Jones, whose own poetry heralded a new movement and whose position as Professor of Welsh and frequent National Eisteddfod adjudicator allowed him to promote new standards and principles.[8] Gwynn Jones's pseudonym in the 1902 competition was 'Tīr n-ōg', pointing us to the wider Celtic revival, to his many Celtic connections, and to his labours as translator and interpreter of Irish poetry.[9]

Of the many tribute poems published after Jones's death in 1949, two terse couplets by T. H. Parry-Williams indicate his standing within his cultural community. The poem was titled simply 'Bardd' ('Poet'):

> Canodd ei gerdd i gyfeiliant berw ei waed;
> Canodd hi, a safodd gwlad ar ei thraed.
>
> Canodd ei gân yn gyfalaw i derfysg Dyn;
> Canodd hi, ac nid yw ein llên yr un.[10]

(He sang his poem to the seething accompaniment of his
   own blood;
he sang it, and a nation stood on its feet.

He sang his song as a counter-melody to Man's turmoil,
He sang it, and our literature is no longer the same.)

This evokes Gwynn Jones's railing against philistinism and Mammon-wor-
ship, his despair and cynicism regarding the condition of humanity, evident
long before the trauma of the First World War, the lament to a departed
glory, 'Y Nef a Fu' ('The Heaven that Once Was'), written between 1901 and
1903, being a prime example. Parry-Williams acknowledges his transformative role in giving his readership a majestic body of work to take pride in and
celebrate as a new pinnacle in Welsh-language literature. Some of his most
famous passages, the three *hir-a-thoddaid* towards the end of 'Ymadawiad
Arthur', for instance, with their idealized evocation of *Ynys Afallon* ('The Isle
of Avalon'), could not fail to resonate with the aspiring nation-builders of the
century's first decade. Saunders Lewis argued that its contemporary context,
the rise of a nationalist movement within the Liberal Party in Wales, made
this the most significant of Jones's works.[11] In this century M. Wynn Thomas
has argued that its greatness can be attributed to its underlying ambiguities
and concerns, reading it as 'the sunset song' of the Cymru Fydd movement.
The final couplet to this day crystallizes the continuing crisis of 'Y Gymru
Gymraeg' ('Welsh-Speaking Wales'), as well as the entire Welsh nation:[12]

Bedwyr yn drist a distaw
At y drin aeth eto draw.

(Bedwyr, sad and quiet,
Turned once more to the battlefield.)

Could it be that the complexities of Jones's vision were sometimes overlooked? Were the sublime technical mastery and enchanting images a mixed
blessing, sense being submerged by a beautiful style?[13] 'Madog', arguably
Jones's greatest poem, based on a traditional story of a Gwynedd prince
setting out in search of a better land, was a stylistic tour de force, combining
elements of the *englyn unodl union* and elegiac couplet. Jones had accused
critics of being 'so busy with the consideration of accessories' when discussing R. Williams Parry's spectacular 1910 Eisteddfod success, 'Yr Haf' ('The
Summer'), that its true significance had not dawned upon them.[14] Jones
similarly felt that his audience in 1917 failed to grasp its contemporary thrust

as an anti-war poem, despite its author's prominent public stance as a
pacifist.[15]

The cluster of three mellifluous cross-rhyming lyrics composed in 1920,
'Rhos y Pererinion', 'Ynys Enlli', and 'Ystrad Fflur', suggest rejection of
present circumstances and a yearning for escape. They represent in miniature
the dynamic at work in his acclaimed longer poems, the imagination creating
idealized worlds where the need for escapism and an alternative world is a
critique of contemporary society. At Ystrad Fflur, Strata Florida Abbey in
Ceredigion, he sees 'angof angau prudd/ Ar adfail ffydd', 'the oblivion of
melancholy death on the ruin of faith' – and yet when he walks here amidst
the dead, removed from the world and its burden, he finds peace from his
pain:

> Ond er mai angof angau prudd
> Ar adfail ffydd a welaf,
> Pan rodiwyf ddaear Ystrad Fflur,
> O'm dolur ymdawelaf.[16]

> (But though I see upon faith's ruins
> Sad death's oblivion,
> When I walk the earth of Ystrad Fflur
> It eases me of pain.)

In 'Ynys Enlli' the poet contemplates Bardsey Island, visible from
Aberystwyth, morbidly wondering whether it would not be better to be as
the 20,000 saints reputedly buried there than to be oppressed by the world's
treachery and tumult: 'Na byw dan frad y byd na'i fiwch', 'living beneath the
world's treachery and its tumult'.[17] In the case of these lyrics, the perceived
discord between sound and sense surely contributes to a richer experience for
the reader. In his poetry, as D. Gwenallt Jones wrote in his elegy to him, he
forged the perfect nation of his dreams, *creadigaeth hiraeth* – longing's
creation.[18]

Gwynn Jones sometimes sang in a plainer style; a late twentieth-century
critic would express regret that the poet had not developed the realist,
colloquial mode employed most strikingly in the ballad 'Pro Patria', published in 1913 but not included in the canon which Jones created of his own
work in published volumes in 1932 and 1934.[19] Narrated by a soldier in the
Boer War, it underlines the brutalizing effect of war with a scene of gang
rape. In 1934–5 he published under a nom de plume a series of *vers libre* poems
in which he experimented with *cynghanedd* outside the traditional strict
metres. These poems, eventually published as *Y Dwymyn* ('The Fever'),

made it harder for readers to ignore the poet's voice.[20] The vision is unmistakably sombre although the style and diction are not markedly more modern or informal. The opening poem, 'Y Saig' ('The Feast'), addresses the remains on a salmon platter. The dead fish is invited to reflect on the absurdity of what passes as advanced cultural civilization in catching a fish and preparing it as a gastronomic feast. The false teeth and the eyes under false glasses of the 'land animal' ('pryfyn tir') which craves the fish will soon be food himself to smaller animals. 'And isn't that funny?' the salmon is asked, with the poem closing with the poet's own answer – 'Diau: Chwardd' ('For certain. Laugh'). This cynical commentary on contemporary civilization, with the fragments of a fish centre stage, strike a modernist note. Responses to T. Gwynn Jones have grappled with the terms 'traditional', 'romantic', and 'modernist' in their relationship to the work of one who made such extensive use of medieval tale and Celtic myth, often expressed in archaic diction. This literature has been reviewed by Jerry Hunter who has suggested that the ruins and fragments found in his work, as well as his use of allegory, invite us to read him in the light of Walter Benjamin's writing on the aesthetics of modernism.[21] 'His poetry,' wrote John Rowlands, 'is an oblique comment on the crumbling world he was living in.'[22] Jones's development in the long poems can be seen as moving 'from the easy solution of "Ymadawiad Arthur", through the agnostic pessimism of "Madog", to the harsh self-sacrificial honour of "Argoed"'.[23] But Rowlands also believes that the features of the poet's style 'tend to dull the impact of his work'.[24] This perceived obliquity nevertheless has the potential of making the texts fertile reading grounds for contemporary critics; an example is Peredur Lynch's exposition of the significance of 'Argoed', set in Gaul under Roman occupation, as a commentary on the linguistic state of Wales in the 1920s.[25]

R. Williams Parry (1884–1956)

When R. Williams Parry published *Yr Haf a Cherddi Eraill* ('The Summer and Other Poems'), in 1924, he closed his acknowledgements with reference 'to the example of my literary master, T. Gwynn Jones'.[26] In 1970 John Gwilym Jones closed his introduction to a new edition of Williams Parry's first volume, *Yr Haf a Cherddi Eraill*, by referring to it as a timely tribute to one of our greatest poets; indeed, he added, 'Tybed nad y mwyaf oll?' ('Perhaps the greatest of them all?').[27] This statement would have been regarded as contentious at the time, but not as outrageous as it would be now. R. Williams Parry had been a star in the poetic firmament since his 1910

Eisteddfod poem had captured a generation already tuned to a new melody by T. Gwynn Jones. Its cultural impact was astonishing: 'From one end of the country to the other young men learnt passages off by heart.'[28] A few years later, another Welsh poet, Hedd Wyn, died in the battle of Pilkem Ridge at the end of July 1917, before he could be chaired at the National Eisteddfod in Birkenhead. Williams Parry wrote a series of *englynion coffa* (elegiac stanzas), which expressed the feeling of a national sense of loss and became common and lasting cultural currency. The sumptuous romanticism of the Eisteddfod poem has been pared to the bone to register death. And we find no gesture towards hope based on Christian doctrine and experience:

> Y bardd trwm dan bridd tramor – y dwylaw
> Na ddidolir rhagor:
> Y llygaid dwys dan ddwys ddôr,
> Y llygaid na all agor![29]

> (Grave the bard underground overseas, hands
> That will never unclasp;
> Keen eyes beneath a closed lid,
> Eyes unable to open.)

This turn away from archaic diction and medieval literary and mythic allusion towards a less florid style was taken by more than one of the major poets of the beginning of the century. Landmark poems in Williams Parry's evolution included 'Adref' ('Homewards'), originally published in 1917, with its rejection of the romantic medievalism which had brought the poet his renown as well as a commitment to a more honest agenda based on his own time and experience;[30] and also 'Yr Hwyaden' ('The Duck'), his pastiche of the style of 'Yr Haf' and located in his first volume immediately following it, a clear acknowledgement of the need to move to a degree of defamiliarizing his poetic language.[31]

John Gwilym Jones also points us to one of the reasons for the poet's appeal to mid-twentieth-century critics. He was the poet of paradox and ambiguity, states best resolved by a poetic imagination with metaphor in a foregrounded role. The New Criticism found in Williams Parry's texts ideal material. Ambiguity indeed was more than a literary device; it was a world-view for a generation who did not share the Christian convictions of previous generations. Like T. Gwynn Jones, Williams Parry can be regarded as post-Christian or secular – a dramatic departure from the consensus of centuries. In his poetry, J. Gwilym Jones argued, 'he realized, like all honest people, that there is in life an unavoidable complexity'.[32]

Williams Parry agreed with the realistic biblical stance on the fragile brevity of life but made that a reason to celebrate earthly delights, in the natural world in particular, rather than to devalue them as belonging to the temporal things which pass away: 'It's not that we need fewer sacred hymns, but more songs in praise of the soil.'[33] 'Y Llwynog' ('The Fox') is a consummate expression of this artistic credo, combining 'sensitive observation and exquisite command of language'.[34] Adopting a disciplined, more concrete vocabulary than in many of his other sonnets, his aim is to capture the experience of suddenly meeting a fox on a mountainside with photographic detail and clarity. Having located the event in time and place and intimated that the call of the wild has trumped that of the church bells, the fox itself, 'ei ryfeddod prin' ('rare wonder'), appears. The moment of mutual paralysis is captured before the fox departs, like 'a shooting star':

> Llithrodd ei flewyn cringoch dros y grib;
> Digwyddodd, darfu, megis seren wib.[35]

> (Across the hillcrest slipped his russet fur;
> He flared, he faded, like a shooting star.)

The transient, fleeting moment of wonder is worthy of celebration, and it is the poet's calling to do so. It is a mark of the poem's continuing attraction that one of the most comprehensive treatments of a single poem, including a review of previous critical literature and illuminating correspondences with other poets, appeared in 2000.[36]

A similar experience, that of seeing a hare on a mountain, is recorded in 'Y Peilon' ('The Pylon').[37] Here the poet depicts his own journey towards a more balanced and nuanced view of the relationship between nature and technology. Earlier poems had presented these as incompatible. 'Eifionydd', one of his most popular poems, follows Gwynn Jones on the escapist route, away from the scars and sounds of progress and industry to a rural avenue.[38] His fears that the construction of electricity pylons would have a disastrous effect on wildlife are allayed by seeing a hare set off on its zig-zag route from the pylon base. The poem's artistic achievement is modest but assured, enabled by cohesive use of figurative language in applying words from the 'natural' sphere – planting, skeleton, ribs, roots – to the pylon, thus using metaphor as synthesizing agent and preparing the ground for the reversal of the image/referent order in the closing simile, when the hare is described as one of the pylon's bolts of lightning:

O'r eithin wrth ei fôn fe wibiodd pry'
Ar garlam igam-ogam hyd y mawn,
Ac wele, nid oedd undim ond lle bu;
Fel petai'r llymbar llonydd yn y gwellt
Wedi rhyddhau o'i afael un o'i fellt.[39]

(A creature darted from the gorse at its base
Off to the peat at helter-skelter pace,
And look, not a thing was there but where he'd been;
As if the quiet lubber in the grass
Has unleashed a single lightning flash.)

This poem was composed in 1940, at the end of a turbulent decade. The poet's unease regarding his working conditions as a lecturer at Bangor, and his conviction that this could be attributed to a philistine academic community, had led him to declare that he would go on strike as a poet. When his friend Saunders Lewis was dismissed from his post by University College Swansea in the aftermath of the Penyberth Bombing School case without receiving the support of some prominent Welsh scholars, he saw it as a confirmation that the same forces were at work against Lewis. His muse was fired by what he saw as the injustice done to Lewis and by the apathy shown by many to his plight. As a result the poet 'was triggered ... to flirt with *engagement*'[40] in a small cluster of poems, in particular 'J. S. L.' (Saunders Lewis's initials) and the heavily allusive 'Cymru 1937' ('Wales 1937'), both sonnets in which the poet's passion was reflected in the break with the conventional ten-syllable line; both were angry, passionate, controversial. But he struggled with the concept of political poetry which addressed contemporary social woes, regarding it as a dereliction of the muse's chief duty, which was to remind humankind of the wretched woe of the human condition. This view was expressed in two sonnets he sent to Aneirin ap Talfan (Aneirin Talfan Davies), joint editor of the new socially committed monthly periodical, *Heddiw* ('Today'), entitled 'Marwoldeb' ('Mortality') and 'Propaganda'r Prydydd' ('The Poet's Propaganda').[41]

Whatever his reservations about the turn towards commitment, his responses to the Saunders Lewis controversy were part of it, and 1936 came to be considered a watershed in Welsh-language literature and culture, used, for instance, as a dividing line by R. M. Jones in a two-volume study.[42] John Gwilym Jones's suggestion in the 1970 foreword to *Yr Haf* was soon overtaken in the critical arena by two book-length studies of the poet, testimony to his status at that time.[43] But it was Alan Llwyd who tackled the R. Williams Parry myth head on, following T. Emrys Parry in drawing attention to the 'endless' echoes of other poets in his work, in particular English ones,[44] and opening his 1984 study with the statement that R. Williams Parry is the greatest myth in our literature.[45]

D. Gwenallt Jones (1899–1968)

David James Jones, known by his nom de plume Gwenallt or D. Gwenallt Jones, studied under T. Gwynn Jones when the latter was professor of Welsh at Aberystwyth, later being appointed a lecturer in the same department. His early work, including poems written during his college years which have only recently come to light, echoed that of the older poet.[46] A revealing glimpse of the renaissance is afforded by a story Gwenallt told of Gwynn Jones lecturing on a specific type of strict-metre poem, the *cywydd gofyn*. The lecturer entered the next class to find half a dozen poems in the genre composed by his students and pinned to the blackboard, which he then proceeded to read aloud and review.[47] Inspired to master the strict metres, Gwenallt went on to win the National Eisteddfod chair in 1926 and 1931, but it was during the 1930s that he developed his own distinctive voice. A careful curator and interpreter of his spiritual and poetic pilgrimage, in one of his later poems, 'Y Drws' ('The Door'), Gwenallt used the Aberhenfelen myth from the Second Branch of the *Mabinogi* for this purpose. His generation's dalliance with medievalism and Romanticism is portrayed as an amnesiac, aestheticized rejection of social responsibility. When the door to Aberhenfelen was opened, however, they heard the cry of the world in its pain and the red bark of the industrial dust.[48] The fetish of the self would be replaced with an unapologetic social commitment to nation and church. Underpinned by Saunders Lewis's concurrent writings, this turn towards social engagement and towards a consciously Christian world-view once more was a crucial one in defining Welsh-language modernism, or at least arguably its most influential version. This new stance demanded new diction, fresh imagery, different rhythms; the conventions of the more facile lyrical poetry, which featured prominently in the influential school curriculum anthology *Telyn y Dydd*, would be displaced by a rougher, more disruptive poetic.[49] When the magazine *Heddiw* first appeared in 1936, it included a new poem by Gwenallt with the same title, 'Heddiw' ('Today'), highlighting the poet's conscious role as contemporary prophet. Published in his 1939 collection *Ysgubau'r Awen* ('The Sheaves of the Muse'), under the title 'Ar Gyfeiliorn' ('Adrift'), this intense jeremiad portrayed Welsh society as being economically destitute and spiritually bankrupt. The second stanza is new, as Christine James has noted, within Gwenallt's own poetic development, in its depiction of an industrial community in depression: the Romantic palette is finally set aside and a new, almost journalistic mode is adopted:[50]

Dynion yn y deheudir heb ddiod na bwyd na ffag
A balchder eu bro dan domennydd ysgrap, ysindrins, yslag:
Y canél mewn pentrefi'n sefyllian, heb ryd na symud na swn,
A'r llygod boliog yn llarpio cyrff y cathod a'r cwn.[51]

(Men in the south of Wales without food or drink or a fag,
The glory of their countryside under scrapheap, cinders, slag,
The canal in villages dawdling, no ford, no movement, no sound,
And the big-bellied rats devouring the corpses of cat and hound.)

Any formalist assessment of Gwenallt's impact can identify the new, foregrounded elements, including a modern diction, a severe imagery, a less predictable metre, and a rediscovered Christian conviction. Saunders Lewis described him as the only major new poet to emerge between the wars, and one who heralded a new age, for the days of the lonely poet who drew his material from his own emotional life were numbered.[52] Gwenallt himself relished the role, distancing himself from an outdated Romanticism with a savage, sarcastic attack on a collection of poems by Bangor college poets which clung to an obsession with mortality.[53]

Gwenallt was born in Pontardawe in Glamorganshire to a family who had migrated, like so many others, from rural Carmarthenshire to 'Eldorado'r trefi' ('the Eldorado of the towns'). But he spent his summers with family in the old county, and he writes of both industrial and rural experiences. His graphic images of industrial life, many of them found in the opening sequence of *Eples* ('Leaven', 1951), created a dominant perception of him as an industrial poet. And the strong visual element inspired A. M. Allchin to draw a parallel with the work of a group of south Wales painters from the same background as the poet.[54] The belief that Christian faith alone brings fulfilment is expressed in the sonnet 'Sir Forgannwg' ('Glamorganshire'), from the 1939 volume *Ysgubau'r Awen*. How empty the lives of the working men, says the poet, their faces covered by coal dust as a symbol of their personalities suppressed under the capitalist system; neither has their plight been relieved by political agitation. But the sestet claims that the change from working weekday clothes to Sunday best is symbolic of a spiritual transfiguration:

Y Sul a rydd amdanynt ddillad glân
Ac yn eu hwyneb olau enaid byw
Tynnir y caets o waelod pwll i'r nef
Â rhaffau dur Ei hen olwynion Ef.[55]

(Yet Sunday puts upon them spotless clothes,
The light of living souls within their faces,
The cage is hauled to heaven from the pit
By his ancient winch's ropes of steel.)

'The apt and highly striking metaphorical climax'[56] is but one example of his exquisite way with the device. Another is found in 'Gwlad Adfeiliedig' ('Ruined Land' or 'Waste Land'), his lament for the depopulation of the rural areas, with the ironic implication that the industrial communities, for a time at least, grew fat at their expense:

Tynnwyd yr hufen gan y dur a'r glo
A gado'r llefrith glas mewn llestr a phair.[57]

(The cream has been taken by the steel and coal
Leaving the skimmed milk in dish and pitcher.)

Gwenallt is often a poet of unambiguous declarations and polarized contrasts; readers can respond by appreciating the techniques used in processing strong theological and social convictions into song, or by accepting the challenge to disagree, to read against the grain, to deconstruct in order to draw attention to inconsistencies.[58] Differing interpretative communities have made his poems contested sites, and not all critics accept the validity of deconstructive readings.[59] Given the scale of the industrial and social changes to Welsh society, it may be that indifference has become a more common response than disagreement. In preparing a comprehensive annotated edition of Gwenallt's work, Christine James was aware that the world described in the poems was a *terra incognita* for the modern audience.[60] We cannot replicate the reading conditions of the mid twentieth century, when writers from Welsh-speaking valley communities such as Bryan Martin Davies and Dafydd Rowlands were directly inspired by him. But the edition of his complete poems as well as a biography are significant developments, as is the renewed interest in his religious poetry, evidenced by the volume of literary criticism, *Sensuous Glory*.

Waldo Williams (1904–1971)

The Pembrokeshire poet Waldo Williams was also an admirer of T. Gwynn Jones, regarding him as one of the greatest Welsh poets and the one to whom he owed a debt above all others.[61]

No poet's stock has risen more after his death than that of Waldo Williams. This owes something to the mythologized persona of the pacifist who endured jail terms for his beliefs while being regarded also as a lovable eccentric and national prophet.[62] His work displays an uneven progression from derivative lyric to allusive and challenging verse. With many of the poems grounded in his native Pembrokeshire, the terrain became an arena for competing values and ideologies. The proliferation of military sites on his native hearth, the gunnery range at Castle Martin, the munitions dump at Trecŵn, the aerodromes at Brawdy and near St David's fired his muse; he set against them the *gwerin*, or common people, blinded and deluded though they might be by a coercive state, and the land itself, Puncheston Common, Plumstone rock, and above all the Preseli mountain range. Introductions to a small selection of poems will give an indication of the powerful resonances and anguished tensions found in his work, and may also help us to appreciate why Jason Walford Davies, one of Waldo's chief interpreters and professor of Welsh in John Gwilym Jones's old department at Bangor, is of the opinion that Waldo is 'arguably the finest Welsh-language poet of the twentieth century'.[63]

'Ar Weun Cas-mael' ('On Puncheston Moor') was published on 2 April 1942 after the poet had resigned his post as headmaster of Puncheston School. Apparently misled by his director of education to think that his decision to register as a conscientious objector would result in automatic dismissal, Waldo applied and got a post at Botwnnog County School. His exile from the territory which he believed to be a vessel for values of brotherhood was traumatic. The stance he adopted seems to be one of determined resistance and hope. But from the outset the harbingers of hope for his solitary ramble on the moor are in the natural world, not within the local community. The gorse bushes and skylark are invested with social and spiritual significance. The bushes hold 'the flame of faith'; the lark possesses the true muse and is the community's hope. After the first two verses the poem takes a turn towards apostrophe, and the final five stanzas are in this strain. Isolated and marginalized by his pacifist stance, the poet addresses the natural symbols, adding to their significance their gift for flourishing in adverse circumstances. Apostrophe plays a role in Waldo Williams's poetry, and the theory of lyric expounded by Jonathan Culler would find no shortage of corroborative texts in the Welsh poet's work. 'To apostrophize,' argues Culler, 'is to will a state of affairs, to attempt to bring it into being by asking inanimate objects to bend themselves to your desire.'[64] This describes Waldo's position; and the field of apostrophic address is enlarged to include the terrain which acts as a stage for the harbingers. The acres of Puncheston moor (and Wales through synecdoche) are *llwm*, poor or bare, hiding their true value from the world's gaze. The moor's inhospitable terrain and climate is a 'magwrfa annibyniaeth barn' ('a nursery of independence of thought'). Its *genius loci* is invoked, as the force which has inspired this community to live in brotherhood and to express independence of thought:

> O! Gymru'r gweundir gwrm a'r garn,
> Magwrfa annibyniaeth barn,
> Saif dy gadernid uwch y sarn
> O oes i oes.
> Dwg ninnau atat; gwna ni'n ddarn
> O'th fyw a'th foes.[65]

> (O! Wales of the cairn and the dark moorland,
> Nursery of independence of judgement,
> Above the rubble your strength will stand
> From age to age.
> Draw us to you: make us a part
> Of your life and ways.)

'Trecŵn', site of the munitions dump only a few miles from Puncheston, is where men serve 'the false power' of militarism. The *genius loci* alone can elevate a barbaric society from 'our caves'. The poet-prophet, feeling alienated from his own people, can only turn to the moor and its inspiration, asking that he be inspired to be a 'true' poet like William Wordsworth's skylark, 'To the kindred points of heaven and home!' Despite its jaunty, Burns-derived metre and superficial cheer, this poem has strong undercurrents of alienation and frustration.

'Preseli' was composed in 1946 in response to the War Office's intention to commandeer a large area on the Preseli hills for military purposes. Waldo Williams saw this as a direct attack on the landscape and values that formed his world-view. But his was not now a lone voice; as a poet in exile, teaching at Kimbolton School in Huntingdonshire, he wrote to support a vigorous campaign being waged in Pembrokeshire against the Government's proposals.[66] 'My people', as he refers to them in this poem and elsewhere,

377

now meet his idealized expectations of them, rallying behind local leaders in a successful campaign, a faithful expression of 'independence of thought' worthy of inclusion in a roll of honour which included early Quakers and Baptists as well as the 'Daughters of Rebecca', who campaigned against unjust taxes in the nineteenth century. The prophetic stance expressed is less strained, therefore, and the poet asserts with confidence his debt to his community, its people as well as its terrain. The call to resistance uttered in the final stanza of five has long transcended its specific historical context and become a rallying cry for many acts of communal struggle:

> Hon oedd fy ffenestr, y cynaeafu a'r cneifio:
> Mi welais drefn yn fy mhalas draw.
> Mae rhu, mae rhaib drwy'r fforest ddiffenestr.
> Cadwn y mur rhag y bwystfil, cadwn y ffynnon rhag y baw.[67]

> (This was my window, the harvesting and the shearing.
> I beheld order in my palace there.
> A roar, a ravening is roaming the windowless forest.
> Let us guard the wall from the beast, keep the well-spring free
>   of the filth.)

'Geneth Ifanc' ('A Young Girl') is a profoundly evocative poem, displaying technical dexterity in its use of half rhymes and variations of rhythms and line lengths. It was written after a visit to Avebury Museum in Wiltshire. Struck by the skeleton of a child discovered at a prehistoric village on Windmill Hill, the poet was moved to re-imagine her community. The poem can be read also as a delayed elegy to his sister Morvydd Moneg, who died at the age of thirteen in 1915. At the risk of oversimplifying, the four stanzas of 'Geneth Ifanc' could be said to proclaim four intertwined aspects of Waldo's work: mysticism, brotherhood, compassion, and prophetic vision. The poet's ability to transcend the limits of the temporal is articulated here, and this imaginative transportation is driven by the sight of the Avebury skeleton, which sends him on an empathetic return journey to her community:

> Geneth ifanc oedd yr ysgerbwd carreg;
> Bob tro o'r newydd mae hi'n fy nal.
> Ganrif am bob blwyddyn o'm hoedran
> I'w chynefin af yn ôl.[68]

> (A young girl, once, this skeleton of stone,
> Each time she takes hold of me anew.
> I go back every year of my life
> A hundred to her homestead.)

He has been persuaded that this community was one of peace. His belief, confirmed in 1956 in one of the definitive statements of his convictions, 'Brenhiniaeth a Brawdoliaeth' ('Kingship and Kinship'), was essentially that wars and strife on the scale found during his lifetime had not always been a feature of human society.[69] His optimistic view of human nature had been awakened or confirmed by the experience recollected in his major poem, 'Mewn Dau Gae' ('In Two Fields'). It had been validated by contemporary anthropological views held by W. J. Perry and G. Eliot Smith, both cited in the article.[70] The poet enthusiastically embraced the notion of a 'Golden Age of Peace' (discredited by later scholarship) as one which matched his own appreciation of the communal patterns observed in the agricultural communities of Pembrokeshire:

> Rhai'n trigo mewn heddwch oedd ei phobl,
> Yn prynu cymorth daear â'u dawn;
> Myfyrio dirgelwch geni a phriodi a marw,
> Cadw rhwymau teulu dyn.

> (Dwellers in peace were her people,
> Purchasing earth's sustenance with their skill.
> Pondering the mystery of birth and marriage and death,
> Preserving the bonds of the family of man.)

Waldo's personal life was punctuated by trials and losses.[71] Periods of illness blighted his professional and artistic progress; his wife died after two years of marriage in 1943. An intense identification with those who suffer loss and tribulation is seen in some poems, a notable example being 'Almaenes' ('German Woman').[72] In 'Geneth Ifanc' the reader acquainted with biographical knowledge cannot but sense that the skeleton of the young girl represents the sister who had begun to teach the boy Waldo to write poetry. Her voice, it is said, was no longer in the mountain – 'Ni bu ei llais yn y mynydd mwy'. The ambiguity prompts the reader to call to mind possible connections between the blue stones of the Preseli and Neolithic monuments in Wiltshire, as well as an early poem in which Waldo celebrated a joyous childhood on the mountain with his siblings; and even to hear an echo of a traditional stanza, 'Mi a glywais fod yr hedydd/ Wedi marw ar y mynydd' ('I've heard that the skylark has died on the mountain'), thus connecting both the lost girls to a recurring symbol of hope in the poet's work and setting up the rejection of despair and celebration of lives proclaimed in the visionary final stanza:

> Dyfnach yno oedd yr wybren eang,
> Glasach ei glas oherwydd hon;
> Cadarnach y tŷ anweledig a diamser
> Erddi hi ar y copâu hyn.

> (Deeper there was the wide sky,
> Bluer its blue because of her.
> Stronger the invisible and timeless house
> Because of her on these hill-tops.)

R. Geraint Gruffydd cites this last stanza as an example of Waldo being stimulated by other texts, finding a clear echo of a poem by A. S. J. Tessimond. Jason Walford Davies followed this trail and found more correspondences between Waldo's work and material published in *The Penguin New Writing* in 1944.[73]

Dail Pren ('Leaves of the Tree') is the only volume of poetry for adults which Waldo Williams published during his lifetime.[74] The title is a phrase from Revelation 22:2, 'and the leaves of the tree were for the healing of the nations', indicating that his pacifist vision was undimmed. His poem 'Mewn Dau Gae' ('In Two Fields'), first published in the weekly press in the months prior to its inclusion in the volume, is regarded as a climax to his poetic career, although he was to compose some important poems between 1956 and his death in 1971. It is an open, evocative text, recreating his boyhood experience of being convinced of the reality of brotherhood and projecting a vision of peace which awaits the coming of 'y Brenin Alltud' ('the Exiled King'). The poem has been widely discussed and explicated.[75] The critical community formed around it reminds us that the 'renaissance' in Welsh-language poetry in the twentieth century depended on a symbiotic relationship with a new circle of literary critics.

Gwyn Thomas (1936–2016)

Gwyn Thomas was raised in the slate quarrying town of Blaenau Ffestiniog in north-west Wales. The important social centres of his upbringing were the chapel and the cinema, which act as complementary sources in his work, one of the factors which led to a wide range of stylistic registers and subject matter.[76] Gerwyn Wiliams has convincingly shown that a mere list of poem titles is enough to prove how Gwyn Thomas expanded the field of Welsh-language poetry to include, among other things, the world of children and popular American culture.[77] When the young scholar-poet published his accomplished first volume, *Chwerwder yn y Ffynhonnau* ('Bitterness in the Wells'), in 1962, few could have envisaged the path his poetic career would have taken.

Joseph Clancy has drawn attention to the unaffected, ordinary poetic voice found in his work: 'He is, in short, "one of us", an amiable ordinary man busy "living a life" and making what sense of it he can. He is not, apparently, a poet – though only a poet who cherishes language and shapes it with the skill of Gwyn Thomas could give him so plausible a voice and place us so firmly in his presence.'[78]

A presence which is familiar, therefore, not 'towering' or mystical, and this is reflected in his work. Gwyn Thomas eschewed any move towards opaque expression, often providing his readers with explanatory footnotes. He was dismissive of much critical and theoretical writing, once stating that half the practitioners of twentieth-century literary theory couldn't write and tied themselves up in jargon. 'Busnes esbonio yw esbonio,' he maintained, 'the business of explication is to explicate'.[79] This bluff no-nonsense approach could lead to an accusation of lazy anti-intellectualism, but it also accords with his rare intellectual confidence as an artist and scholar. It is a confidence and composure displayed in his own language and people; there is no need to create an impression, no need for approval or reassurance. Convinced that scholarship and poetry alike should communicate in the media age, he wrote, for example, an accessible textbook on early and medieval Welsh-language poetry, *Y Traddodiad Barddol* ('The Poetic Tradition').[80] As a poet, if not a consciously avant-garde, experimental modernist, he was nevertheless a modernizer and a popularizer. Gerwyn Wiliams, discussing aspects of his relationship with American culture, calls his muse 'democratic'.[81] Although an able maker of images, seeing his native slate town of Blaenau Ffestiniog as 'yn freichled o dref ar asgwrn o graig' ('a bracelet town on the bone of a rock'), and the kingfisher as 'cryman asbri' ('sickle of brio'), he gradually moved towards drawing less attention to his own inventiveness, cutting out the ostentatiously 'poetic'. He would aim at releasing the latent power of 'ordinary' words and ostensibly moribund symbols such as *niwl* (fog), *nos* (night), *haul* (sun), and *gwyn* (white, blessed). How to do this? The old familiar devices will do, rhyme, rhythm, and consonance, but on the poet's terms, and always with focused artistic intent. Rhyme is central, but its deployment unconventional, very often without regular stanza patterns; a couplet to close a *vers libre* poem, for instance. Of the poets considered here, he is the only one not to write a body of work in *cynghanedd* and the strict metres or to serve an apprenticeship learning that craft. But there are individual lines of *cynghanedd*, used sparingly and on the poet's terms. 'Morlo' ('Seal') describes the experience of seeing a seal in the sea off Fishguard; the encounter has echoes of Williams Parry's with the fox; the harmony between man and animal is conveyed through the closing line 'Yn Abergwaun un bore gwyn' ('in Fishguard one blessed morning').[82] His poetry is striking for its avoidance of cliché, empty rhetoric, everything we call in Welsh *barddonllyd* – affectedly or pseudo-poetic. Devices, patterns of cohesion, and internal deviation are never random.[83] Some poems take the form of a triad, an opening statement being followed with an antithesis leading to a concluding synthesis. 'Gwylanod' ('Seagulls') opens with a series of four metaphors conveying the brilliant whiteness of the gulls flying between us and the sun. They then descend as scavengers on a refuse tip before ascending once more:

> Codi i ddolennau'r purdeb,
> Y torchau amlwyn troellog
> Yng ngwregys disglair yr heulwen:
> Gwylanod mewn goleuni.[84]

> (Rising to the links of purity,
> The multiple twining white twists
> In the sunshine's brilliant belt:
> Seagulls in sunlight.)

Presented with more metaphors impressing upon them the sunny purity of the scene in the sky above, readers are now aware that the picture has been compromised by the description of the seagulls' eating habits. The closing line again uses *cynghanedd* to suggest closure, but this time with a degree of cynical irony.

Gwyn Thomas was a prolific poet, publishing twenty volumes over the period 1962–2013. The title he gave of one of his later volumes, *Murmuron Tragwyddoldeb a Chwningod Tjioclet* ('Murmurings of Eternity and Chocolate Bunnies'), typifies a poet for whom intimations of mortality were rarely absent but who would insist on celebrating the joys of everyday life – with his children, and then his grandchildren in particular – as well as satirizing life's many absurdities.[85]

Conclusion

In my afterword to a two-volume collection of critical essays by various authors discussing forty-four Welsh-language poets of the twentieth century,

I found that I could not deny the period its assessment of itself as a golden age.[86] We return to Parry-Williams on Gwynn Jones, 'Canodd hi, a safodd gwlad ar ei thraed' ('He sang it, and a nation stood on its feet'). The nation indeed stood on its feet in wonder, in celebration, but also in response to a call to duty. Throughout the century the poetic community was energized and renewed by literary movements and political shocks, and it consolidated itself by establishing journals and anthologies.[87] A new awakening in strict-metre poetry led to the establishment of a poetry society, Y Gymdeithas Gerdd Dafod, in 1976. Its most prominent figure, Alan Llwyd, has been cited regularly in this chapter, but it is as a poet whose technical mastery puts him on a par, at least, with the most accomplished of his predecessors, including T. Gwynn Jones, that his greatness lies.[88] In 2017 he was fulfilling the traditional social function of the bard, publishing greetings and elegies in the press but also on his Facebook page to an appreciative following. The momentum generated by a poetic renaissance of the last century continues in this one.

Notes

1. T. Gwynn Jones, *Caniadau* (Wrecsam: Hughes a'i Fab, 1934), 175–6.
2. Translations into English are by the author unless otherwise attributed.
3. Saunders Lewis, '*Morte d'Arthur* a'r *Passing of Arthur*', in *Meistri a'u Crefft*, ed. Gwynn ap Gwilym (Caerdydd: Gwasg Prifysgol Cymru, 1981), 203–8; M. Wynn Thomas, 'Seisnigrwydd "Ymadawiad Arthur"', *Y Traethodydd* (Gorffennaf 2012): 142–65.
4. John Rowlands, 'Introduction', in *The Bloodaxe Book of Modern Welsh Poetry*, ed. Menna Elfyn and John Rowlands (Tarset: Bloodaxe Books, 2003), 18.
5. Edgar Jones, 'Some Aspects of Modern Welsh Poetry', *Welsh Outlook* 4, 3 (1 March 1917): 97–103.
6. T. H. Parry-Williams, 'Madrondod', in *Casgliad o Gerddi*, ed. J. E. Caerwyn Williams and Amy Parry-Williams (Llandysul: Gwasg Gomer, 1987); W. J. Gruffydd and R. Silyn Roberts, *Telynegion* (Bangor: Jarvis & Foster, 1900).
7. T. Gwynn Jones, 'Modern Welsh Literature', *Welsh Outlook* (1 January 1914): 19.
8. See Allan James, *John Morris-Jones*, Writers of Wales (Cardiff: University of Wales Press, 1987); Allan James, *John Morris-Jones*, Cyfres Dawn Dweud (Caerdydd: Gwasg Prifysgol Cymru, 2011). For reference to his role as forerunner to T. Gwynn Jones and his importance within the literary renaissance, see Robert Rhys, 'Welsh Literature in the Nineteenth Century', in *The Welsh Language and its Social Domains 1801–1911*, ed. Geraint H. Jenkins (Cardiff: University of Wales Press, 2000), 265–91 and Dafydd Johnston, 'The Literary Revival', in *A Guide to Welsh Literature c. 1900–1996*, ed. Dafydd Johnston (Cardiff: University of Wales Press, 1998), 1–21.

9. See Llŷr Gwyn Lewis, 'Cyfieithiadau T. Gwynn Jones a Tadhg O Donnchadha o Farddoniaeth Gymraeg a Gwyddeleg', *Ysgrifau Beirniadol 33* (Bethesda: Gwasg Gee, 2014): 11–46; Gwynn ap Gwilym, 'Rhagymadrodd', in *Cyfres y Meistri 3: T. Gwynn Jones*, ed. Gwynn ap Gwilym (Llandybïe: Christopher Davies, 1982), 11–37. Tir na-n Og, literally 'land of youth', is an early Irish term for the otherworld or fairy-land.

10. Parry-Williams, *Casgliad o Gerddi*, 132.

11. Lewis, '*Morte d'Arthur* a'r *Passing of Arthur*'.

12. Thomas, 'Seisnigrwydd "Ymadawiad Arthur"'.

13. Derec Llwyd Morgan, *Barddoniaeth T. Gwynn Jones* (Llandysul: Gwasg Gomer, 1972), 44–5.

14. Jones, 'Modern Welsh Literature', 21.

15. D. J. Bowen, 'Madog', in *Cyfres y Meistri 3: T. Gwynn Jones*, ed. Gwynn ap Gwilym, 391–2; T. Gwynn Jones, 'Madog', in *Caniadau*, 87–104.

16. Jones, *Caniadau*, 192; the translation is from Clancy, *Twentieth Century Welsh Poems*, 13.

17. Jones, *Caniadau*, 190–2.

18. 'T. Gwynn Jones', in *Cerddi Gwenallt: Y Casgliad Cyflawn*, ed. Christine James (Llandysul: Gwasg Gomer, 2001), 155–8.

19. John Rowlands, 'Dau Lwybr T. Gwynn Jones', *Y Traethodydd* 148 (1993): 69–87; T. Gwynn Jones, 'Pro Patria', *Y Beirniad* 3 (1913): 1–7; for a translation of extracts from 'Pro Patria', see Elfyn and Rowlands, eds., *The Bloodaxe Book of Modern Welsh Poetry*, 36–9.

20. T. Gwynn Jones, *Y Dwymyn 1934–35* (Aberystwyth: Gwasg Aberystwyth, 1944); see also David Jenkins, *Thomas Gwynn Jones* (Dinbych: Gwasg Gee, 1973), 310–48.

21. Jerry Hunter, 'T. Gwynn Jones', *Taliesin* 98 (1997): 37–54.

22. Glyn Jones and John Rowlands, *Profiles: A Visitor's Guide to Writing in Twentieth-Century Wales* (Llandysul: Gomer Press, 1980), 13.

23. Ibid.

24. Ibid., 14.

25. Peredur I. Lynch, 'Refferendwm 1979, Cerddi Ianws a Thopos "Cymry Taeog"', *Ysgrifau Beirniadol 30* (Bethesda: Gwasg Gee, 2011): 78–109.

26. R. Williams Parry, *Yr Haf a Cherddi Eraill* (Bala: R. Evans a'i Fab, 1924).

27. R. Williams Parry, *Yr Haf a Cherddi Eraill* (Dinbych: Gwasg Gee, 1970), 16.

28. Emyr Humphreys, *The Taliesin Tradition* (Bridgend: Seren, 1989), 205.

29. Williams Parry, *Yr Haf a Cherddi Eraill* (1924), 103; Clancy, trans., *Twentieth Century Welsh Poems*, 46.

30. *Yr Haf a Cherddi Eraill* (1924), 24; *Cerddi R. Williams Parry: Y Casgliad Cyflawn*, ed. Alan Llwyd (Dinbych: Gwasg Gee, 1998), 5.

31. *Cerddi R. Williams Parry*, 48–52; first published in *Welsh Outlook*, September 1919. For a bibliography of his works, see Bedwyr Lewis Jones, *R. Williams*

Parry: 'Ar y Daith ni Phara', ed. Gwyn Thomas (Caerdydd: Gwasg Prifysgol Cymru, 1997), 165–80.

32. Williams Parry, Yr Haf a Cherddi Eraill (1970), 14.

33. Translated from the Welsh, 'Pridd y Ddaear', in Rhyddiaith R. Williams Parry, ed. Bedwyr Lewis Jones (Dinbych: Gwasg Gee, 1974), 27–36; see also Bedwyr Lewis Jones, Robert Williams Parry, Writers of Wales (Cardiff: University of Wales Press, 1972).

34. Clancy, trans., Twentieth Century Welsh Poems, xxxiii.

35. R. Williams Parry, Yr Haf a Cherddi Eraill (1924), 22; Clancy, trans., Twentieth Century Welsh Poems, 47.

36. Jason Walford Davies, 'Gwisga'r Awen Liwiau Hynod: "Y Llwynog"', Llên Cymru 23 (2000): 171–91.

37. Cerddi R. Williams Parry, ed. Alan Llwyd, 138.

38. Ibid., 72.

39. Ibid., 138; Clancy, trans., Twentieth Century Welsh Poems, 57.

40. Rowlands, 'Introduction', in The Bloodaxe Book of Modern Welsh Poetry, 19.

41. See Alan Llwyd, Bob: Cofiant R. Williams Parry (Llandysul: Gwasg Gomer, 2013), 319–79.

42. R. M. Jones, Llenyddiaeth Gymraeg 1902–1936 (Cyhoeddiadau Barddas, 1987); Llenyddiaeth Gymraeg 1936–1972 (Llandybïe: Christopher Davies, 1975). Jones revisited the period in Mawl a Gelynion ei Elynion: Hanfod y Traddodiad Llenyddol Cymraeg (Cyhoeddiadau Barddas, 2002).

43. Jones, R. Williams Parry; T. Emrys Parry, Barddoniaeth Robert Williams Parry: Astudiaeth Feirniadol (Dinbych: Gwasg Gee, 1973).

44. Alan Llwyd, Cyfres y Meistri 1: R. Williams Parry (Abertawe: Christopher Davies, 1979), 16–27.

45. Alan Llwyd, R. Williams Parry (Caernarfon: Gwasg Pantycelyn, 1984), 3.

46. Alan Llwyd, Gwenallt (Talybont: Y Lolfa, 2016), 85–132.

47. Ibid., 99.

48. D. Gwenallt Jones, 'Y Drws', in Cerddi Gwenallt, ed. James, 200.

49. Annie Ffoulkes, ed., Telyn y Dydd, 4th edn (Caerdydd: William Lewis, 1929).

50. Christine James, 'Tirluniau Dychymyg Gwenallt', in Cawr i'w Genedl, ed. Tegwyn Jones and Huw Walters (Llandysul: Gwasg Gomer, 2008), 217–44.

51. Cerddi Gwenallt, ed. James, 72; Clancy, trans., Twentieth Century Welsh Poems, 96–7.

52. Saunders Lewis, review of D. Gwenallt Jones, Cnoi Cil, in Baner ac Amserau Cymru, 10 February 1943, 7; quoted in Robert Rhys, 'D. Gwenallt Jones', in Y Patrwm Amryliw: Cyfrol 1, ed. Robert Rhys (Cyhoeddiadau Barddas, 1997), 155–163.

53. D. Gwenallt Jones, 'Beirdd yr Angau', Heddiw (Gorffennaf 1938): 348–50.

54. A. M. Allchin and D. Densil Morgan, trans. Patrick Thomas, *Sensuous Glory: The Poetic Vision of D. Gwenallt Jones* (Norwich: Canterbury Press, 2000), 12–14.

55. *Cerddi Gwenallt*, ed. James, 113.

56. Densil Morgan, in *Sensuous Glory*, 59.

57. *Cerddi Gwenallt*, ed. James, 68; Clancy, trans., *Twentieth Century Welsh Poems*, xx.

58. For example, John Rowlands, *Cnoi Cil ar Lenyddiaeth* (Llandysul: Gwasg Gomer, 1989), 70–8; M. Wynn Thomas, 'Pwys Llên a Phwysau Hanes', in *Sglefrio ar Eiriau*, ed. John Rowlands (Llandysul: Gwasg Gomer, 1992), 1–21.

59. Densil Morgan, in *Sensuous Glory*, 66–8.

60. *Cerddi Gwenallt*, ed. James, xlviii–xlix.

61. 'Sgwrs â Bobi Jones', in *Waldo Williams: Rhyddiaith*, ed. Damian Walford Davies (Caerdydd: Gwasg Prifysgol Cymru, 2001), 91–6.

62. For a bilingual introduction to his life and work, see Alan Llwyd, *Stori Waldo Williams: Bardd Heddwch / The Story of Waldo Williams: Poet of Peace* (Cyhoeddiadau Barddas, 2010).

63. Jason Walford Davies, 'Myned Allan i Fanfrig Gwreiddiau: Waldo Williams a The Penguin New Writing', *THSC* 19 (2013): 148–68. The words quoted are from the English summary, 167.

64. Jonathan Culler, *Theory of the Lyric* (Cambridge, MA and London: Harvard University Press, 2015), 215–16.

65. Waldo Williams, *Waldo Williams: Cerddi 1922–1970*, ed. Alan Llwyd and Robert Rhys (Llandysul: Gwasg Gomer, 2014), 247–8; Clancy, trans., *Twentieth Century Welsh Poems*, 127.

66. See Hefin Wyn, *Battle of the Preselau: The Campaign to Safeguard the 'Sacred' Pembrokeshire Hills* (Maenclochog: Clychau Clochog, 2008).

67. *Waldo Williams: Cerddi 1922–1970*, ed. Llwyd and Rhys, 253; Clancy, trans., *Twentieth Century Welsh Poems*, 129.

68. *Waldo Williams: Cerddi 1922–1970*, ed. Llwyd and Rhys, 246; Clancy, trans., *Twentieth Century Welsh Poems*, 134.

69. *Waldo Williams: Rhyddiaith*, ed. Walford Davies, 304–11.

70. R. Geraint Gruffydd, '"Geneth Ifanc": Rhai Sylwadau', in *Cof ac Arwydd: Ysgrifau Newydd ar Waldo Williams*, ed. Damian Walford Davies and Jason Walford Davies (Cyhoeddiadau Barddas, 2006), 136–42.

71. For a full biography, see Alan Llwyd, *Waldo* (Talybont: Y Lolfa, 2014).

72. Robert Rhys, '"Ni Thraetha'r Môr ei Maint": Cerddi "Almaenig" Waldo Williams yn 1946', *Llên Cymru* 34 (2011): 226–36.

73. Gruffydd, '"Geneth Ifanc": Rhai Sylwadau', 141–2; Walford Davies, 'Myned Allan i Fanfrig Gwreiddiau'.

74. Waldo Williams, *Dail Pren* (Aberystwyth: Gwasg Aberystwyth, 1956).

75. These include: Bedwyr Lewis Jones, 'Mewn Dau Gae', in *Cyfres y Meistri 2: Waldo Williams*, ed. Robert Rhys (Abertawe: Christopher Davies, 1981), 149–59; Dafydd Elis Thomas, 'Mewn Dau Gae', in *Cyfres y Meistri 2: Waldo Williams*, ed. Rhys, 160–7; Gwyn Thomas, 'Mewn Dau Gae', in *Dadansoddi 14* (Llandysul: Gwasg Gomer, 1984), 54–63; Ned Thomas, 'Waldo Williams: In Two Fields', in *Poetry in the British Isles*, ed. Hans-Werner Ludwig and Lothar Fietz (Cardiff: University of Wales Press, 1991), 253–66; Damian Walford Davies, 'Mapping Partition: Waldo Williams' "In Two Fields" and the 38th Parallel', in *Cartographies of Culture* (Cardiff: University of Wales Press, 2012), 172–202.

76. Thomas describes his upbringing in *Bywyd Bach* (Caernarfon: Gwasg Gwynedd, 2006) and *Yn Blentyn yn y Blaenau* (Caernarfon: Cyngor Sir Gwynedd, 1981).

77. Gerwyn Wiliams, 'Yr Ianci o'r Blaenau: Golwg ar Gerddi Gwyn Thomas', in *Gweledigaethau: Cyfrol Deyrnged yr Athro Gwyn Thomas*, ed. Jason Walford Davies (Cyhoeddiadau Barddas, 2007), 242–68.

78. 'Preface', in Gwyn Thomas, *Living a Life: Selected Poems 1962–82*, selected and introduced by Joseph P. Clancy with translations by Joseph P. Clancy and Gwyn Thomas (Amsterdam: Scott Rollins for Bridges Books, 1982), 7–8.

79. Gwyn Thomas, 'Hugh Bevan (1911–1979)', *THSC* (1993): 99–114.

80. Gwyn Thomas, *Y Traddodiad Barddol* (Caerdydd: Gwasg Prifysgol Cymru, 1976).

81. Wiliams, 'Yr Ianci o'r Blaenau'.

82. Gwyn Thomas, *Enw'r Gair* (Dinbych: Gwasg Gee, 1972), 49.

83. His poem 'Sbaeneg Park Sinema' is a superb example; for a detailed discussion, see Robert Rhys, 'Dysgu Darllen', in *Sglefrio ar Eiriau*, ed. Rowlands, 151–71.

84. Thomas, *Enw'r Gair*, 47; the translation is by Joseph P. Clancy, in Gwyn Thomas, *Living a Life: Selected Poems 1962–1982*, 51.

85. Gwyn Thomas, *Murmuron Tragwyddoldeb a Chwningod Tjioclet* (Cyhoeddiadau Barddas, 2010).

86. Rhys, 'Ôl-ymadrodd', in Rhys, ed., *Y Patrwm Amryliw: Cyfrol 2* (2006), 299–307.

87. I discuss the significance of anthologies in 'Ôl-ymadrodd'. See also Chapter 30 in this volume.

88. For a history of the first twenty-five years of Y Gymdeithas Gerdd Dafod and a bibliography of Alan Llwyd's work up to 2003, see Huw Meirion Edwards, ed., *Alan* (Cyhoeddiadau Barddas, 2003); see also Jones, *Mawl a Gelynion ei Elynion*, 315–70.

Industrial Fiction

STEPHEN KNIGHT

Towards Industrial Fiction

English novelists were dealing with industry in fiction from the early nine-teenth century, whether from a liberal distance, like Charles Dickens and Elizabeth Gaskell, or with sympathetic involvement, like the Chartist novel-ists Ernest Jones and Thomas Wheeler. Welsh fiction was much later to engage with the theme,[1] in part because the novel itself was slower to emerge in Wales in either of the country's languages, but also because the thrust of literary liberalism was dominated by the Nonconformist chapels and the earliest novels focused on moral discourse like Daniel Owen's *Rhys Lewis* (1885) or local historical myth like Isaac Hughes's *The Maid of Cefn Ydfa* (1881), both originally appearing in Welsh.[2] Rev. John Jenkins, for example, who wrote as 'Shôn Shincyn', worked in the iron industry in the 1790s, owned a press by 1819, and wrote widely about his world, but very likely saw the novel as an English and bourgeois form and never engaged with it.[3]

After a late start, Welsh writers took enthusiastically to the industrial form and a range of novels, in both English and Welsh, from determinedly leftist through family-focused and woman-focused to nostalgic and conservative, have made Wales one of the major international producers of industrial fiction. A number of early women writers reference the industrial world in their fiction,[4] though only Irene Saunderson (see below) focused in generic terms on industrial fiction. The first narrative dealing with Welsh industry itself appears to be *Little Johnny* (1891) by John Protheroe, who started work in a colliery aged seven and a half in the 1860s: Jonathan Evans suggests it was written for use in Nonconformist Sunday schools,[5] and it may have stimu-lated the first industrial writer of importance in Wales, Joseph Keating, who was a miner underground for six years from 1883 when he was twelve. He later worked for newspapers and started writing fiction in the 1890s with some short stories in *Young Wales* and other local magazines; his work then began to appear in magazines sold in England and the United States. An anthology, *Adventures in the Dark*, was published in 1906 by the *Western Mail*, by which time Keating had published two novels in England. The short stories are realistic in setting, including the dangers of mining, but as Evans notes, they often focus on issues of superstition and folklore and do not engage in any political or even reportage style with industrial realities.[6]

When he turned to novels, Keating also used unpolitical models. In *Son of Judith* (1900), after a pit explosion the hero leads to safety both a distressed lady visitor and the man who is, unknown to him, his father: adventure and romance are the dominant modes. The novel does include a substantial amount of mining material, which probably influenced Allen Raine, a successful producer of popular and sometimes fairly serious romances set in Wales. Her novel *A Welsh Witch* (1902) 'features not only scenes in a Glamorganshire coalmine but a mine disaster'[7] – yet this is not a major thread of the novel, nor does industry recur in Raine's later work. Keating's second novel, *Maurice* (1905), is subtitled *A Romance of Light and Darkness*, but the romance between Jethro and Olwen is secondary to the focus on Maurice, a child whose part of south Wales is reached by the growing coal industry. Much of the novel is to do with family and place, and chapter XVI is a powerful version of the 'boy's first day down a coal-mine' theme (already found in *Little Johnny*), but silver-spoon romance emerges when Maurice is revealed as the long-lost son of an Irish aristocrat. After that, Keating avoided industry for some time, but returned to it in *Flower of the Dark* (1917) – the title itself seems to refer to the symbolic final sequence of Emile Zola's major industrial novel *Germinal*. Romance is still strong, and the English audience seems in mind: the hero is a skilful manager risen from the ranks, with the Anglo-Saxon name Osla; he helps the beautiful Aeronwy, daughter of a mine-owner, maximize her income before marrying her, with a cross-generic murder mystery along the way.

Keating had some early followers. Irene Saunderson, the wife of a south Wales doctor, gave a demotic voice and sympathetic representation to the travails of colliers in *A Welsh Heroine* (1911), but her brave working-class girl finally marries the noble English officer who leads his troops against the striking miners. Differently directed away from politics is D. Miles Lewis's *Chapel: The Story of a Welsh Family* (1916), a saga with Keatingesque excitements about a mine-owning family whose curious surname, Chapel, roots them and their eventual survival in the Nonconformist domain of value.

Rhys Davies, the son of a shopkeeper in Blaenclydach in the Rhondda, offers a more complex withdrawal from political confrontations. Davies's work often sees coalfield life as degrading rather than politically stimulating,[8] and in both his autobiography, *Print of a Hare's Foot* (1969), and the autobiographical novel *Tomorrow to Fresh Woods* (1941), he writes negatively about the strikes of 1910–11. His first novel, *The Withered Root* (1927), puts family in the foreground, as is common in Welsh fiction, but here not positively. The son is a miner who moves away from home and industry to become a preacher, and the novel is essentially personal not political: in his autobiography Davies said it described 'warfare between religious spirit and carnal flesh, with spirit a heavy loser'.[9]

Though based in London and seen as combining moral and aesthetic qualities – D. H. Lawrence admired his work – Davies often returned to the industrial world, though rarely in political terms. In *Count Your Blessings* (1932), the central figure is a girl who leaves a mining village for a Cardiff brothel, finally returning with both money and regrets. Less displaced is *The Red Hills* (also 1932): the hero works an old-fashioned surface mine near a new-style deep pit: his own vigour, and his passionate women, rescue him from the mean-minded vengeance of the industrial villagers. Davies was more political in his trilogy about the evolution of 'Glan Ystrad' from rural peace to the 1930s. The first in the sequence, *Honey and Bread* (1935), shows industry assaulting both an innocent world and a landowning family, while the second, *A Time to Laugh* (1937), realizes late nineteenth-century conflict on the coalfield. The treatment is largely anti-mine owner, but Davies locates the book's focal intelligence in a doctor, one of the family who once owned the pastoral valley. He sympathizes with the workers, yet finally, watching the unemployed as they dance around a bonfire, he tells his beautiful wife it is 'a time to laugh', 'with all this wealth'.[10]

The last of the trilogy, *Jubilee Blues* (1938), uses Cassie, a rural domestic worker, as a personal and basically apolitical focus. She inherits money from her master and with it her husband opens a valleys pub – she is as exploited as the miners whose injuries and starvation she sympathetically observes, before finally returning to the country. Davies was inherently idealist rather than political, feeling that the miners' resistance re-enacted ancient Welsh responses to invaders; he admired the old-world radical eccentric Dr William Price of Llantrisant, who appears in *Tomorrow to Fresh Woods*, and is described in Davies's autobiography as 'a descendant of the warrior-bards ... instead of foreign soldiers he had coal-owners and iron-masters to grapple with'.[11]

Industrialism Accepted

Jack Jones was a Merthyr Tydfil miner who turned to writing when out of work, but unlike Keating, he did not follow middle-class patterns. His first novels *Rhondda Roundabout* (1934) and *Black Parade* (1935) seem in title and form close to popular culture like theatre or circus: the texts are essentially cavalcades of local life. But he also has a clear sense of radical politics and creates strong women characters – the original title of *Black Parade* was 'Saran', for its central female figure. This was his first-written but second-published novel, heavily cut for publication, a rambling family saga reaching from the development of the local coal industry around 1870 to the years when trade weakened and conflict grew before the First World War. *Rhondda Roundabout* was evidently more acceptable to the English publisher, Faber and Faber, where T. S. Eliot was working. Against *Black Parade* it is shorter, modern rather than historical, and focused on a single hero, including his romance. Dan Price, BA, is a Nonconformist preacher, who supports Labour and wins the heart of a charming shop girl. There is political activity, but it blurs into comedy – the potential Communist ogre is a huge drinker known as Dai Hippo.

The novels were quite successful and opened Jones's path to more serious social and political writing, especially in his major socio-political survey, *Bidden to the Feast* (1938). Longer and fuller-plotted, this offers much data, about mining, sanitation, immigration, and the Merthyr district in general. It deals politically with the 1890s hauliers' strike and the post-boom deterioration in the valleys, but includes other themes – emigration, mercantile activity, the family and its emotional meanings. Elements of emotive populism are already present, through which Jones may have been responding to commercial publishing. Glyn Jones, who knew Jack Jones well, reports that, in the mid-thirties, an English publisher rejected the manuscript of 'Behold They Live' as too gloomy.[12] Jack Jones's later work is politically weaker, with sentimental novels about the Welsh diaspora (*Off to Philadelphia in the Morning*, 1947), Cardiff social and business life (*River out of Eden*, 1951), or simply valleys nostalgia (*Choral Symphony*, 1955).

The first Welsh novelist to accept the industrial world for itself and account for it in political, if also emotive, terms, Jones has been generally disregarded as a less than serious artist – Dai Smith described him, a little belittlingly, as 'the most successful purveyor of South Wales realism'.[13] But Jones had importance as the first writer to give a direct account of ordinary life in the Welsh industrial context. *Bidden to the Feast* especially was well received, with many readers and reprints, and his work provided a sense of conviction and immediacy. His autobiography, *Unfinished Journey* (1937), struck an especially strong chord among people aware of both their past mobility and their uncertain present direction.

Jones's work is a striking contrast to that of the factually oriented Bert Coombes, whose family immigrated for work from England. In *These Poor Hands* (1939), he gives a plain, searching account of a miner's life and he provided further detail in *Those Clouded Hills* (1944); the often anthologized short story 'Twenty Tons of Coal' is widely recognized as a quiet revelation of the experience of a miner's life. Research on Coombes's manuscripts by Bill Jones and Chris Williams has shown much care went into *These Poor Hands*, and he completed, but never published, a good deal of other fiction, now published as *With Dust Still in His Throat* (1999).[14] Coombes's adoption of a quiet, even recessive and English-style authorial voice makes him very different from the characteristically powerful, flamboyant voice of the Welsh writers, typified by Jack Jones and continued, in a more politically conscious and sophisticated form, by Lewis Jones.

Lewis Jones's novel sequence *Cwmardy* (1937) and *We Live* (1939) has a prominent place among international industrial fiction. Both documentary-like and strongly leftist, responding to a time when Wales was gripped by a sense of the need for radical action, Jones also wrote for an English audience who were now aware of and concerned about what was happening in Wales: Storm Jameson called it 'the finest socialist novel I have ever read'.[15] Welsh traditions of narrative are also strong in Jones's work. Family is the centre of *Cwmardy*, with an emotionally strong mother and a father who is big, honest, and somewhat limited, or as the locals would say, *twp*. The son moves towards politics both by instinct and by the influence of a slightly old-world union leader, and especially his daughter. As with her, Lewis Jones, like Jack Jones, gives women a strong role, though not always a happy one: Len's sister dies in childbirth, and Jones deploys the motif of the lost sister, so common in Welsh fiction.[16]

The stark political events in and around Tonypandy from about 1900 to the mid-1930s are recounted through *Cwmardy* and *We Live*. The central figure, Len Roberts, is not physically strong, but is both studious and an instinctive leader and speaker, realizing in this the concept that true revolution comes from the rank and file's instinctive political awakening and their work-place combination – an idea central to the anarcho-syndicalism that was strong in the south Welsh coalfield and essentially opposed the idea of centralized power dear to the Communist Party line that Jones officially espoused.[17]

Socialism is essentially seen as international, and Len, with little backing in the valley, resists in *Cwmardy* the call to support the First World War; in *We Live* he journeys to Spain to fight, and dies there. Jones himself died from a heart attack, apparently through his energetic action on behalf of the Spanish government and its international cause, and he did not live to complete the second novel, though his notes were the basis of the conclusion, where the local political collectivity, with the surviving Roberts family prominent, realizes its continuing vitality in a pro-Spain march of 'common unity'.[18] Jones's plans included a third novel where the returning Welsh soldiers from Spain played a major part in the battle for a socialist British state. The most political of all the Welsh industrial novelists, Lewis Jones's reputation has internationally survived to the present as a writer with a conscious sense of radical purpose.

Industrialism Distanced: Welsh-Language Fiction

Industry existed in Wales outside the south-east, and it was not only handled in English. The major Welsh writer Kate Roberts produced *Traed mewn Cyffion* (1936, translated as *Feet in Chains*), set in the slate-quarrying region of Gwynedd in north-west Wales but primarily realizing its impact on working-class family experience. Jane Gruffydd marries into the quarrying world and tends her children, but they disperse – the daughter into town life, two sons becoming teachers: one is killed in the war and a third son leaves for south Wales. Both he and the surviving teacher are politicized, but that is for the future. The war is seen as a destructive modernism parallel to the industrial disaster of the great strike in the slate fields, and, as Ned Thomas comments, Roberts 'shows the social forces converging on the domestic situation'.[19]

A later novel which traces the emotive impact of his native north-western industrial context is Caradog Prichard's *Un Nos Ola Leuad* (1961, translated both as *Full Moon* and as *One Moonlit Night*). Prichard, who worked as an English-language journalist in Cardiff and London, was, as Harri Pritchard Jones reports, long tormented by the notion that his father had been a *bradwr*, a 'traitor', or scab, in the great slate-field strike of 1900–3.[20] *Un Nos Ola Leuad* is a young man's biography that communicates powerfully the sense of personal and social instability generated on the slate fields. The hero's isolative degeneration symbolizes the disintegrating social and ethical structures of the world of the slate industry: the novel transcends the usual politics of the industrial novel and suggests how intense and poetic the form can become.

T. Rowland Hughes, also born in the north Wales slate-quarrying region, became a broadcaster-writer in south Wales: several of his novels refer to industry. The third, *Wiliam Jones* (1944), starts in the northern quarries, and then in 1935 Wiliam moves south, both to industrial strife and the rich communal and religious life of the valleys, before, like Hughes himself, working for the BBC. Two other novels, *O Law i Law* (1943, translated as *From Hand to Hand*) and *Y Cychwyn* (1947, translated as *The Beginning*), used the slate- mining context, but as little more than a backdrop for closely observed personal and familial narratives.

More central to the industrial tradition is Hughes's *Chwalfa* (1943, translated as *Out of Their Night* – though 'chwalfa' means something like 'dispersal', 'disaster', even 'total defeat'). Focused on the great slate strike, it is basically a history of heroic but failed labour resistance, and Hughes realizes both courage and oppression, and also the complex human reasons for strike breaking.

The audience for these Welsh industrial novels was not large, but, apparently because of their language-restricted and so specialized audience, the novels are able to project an intensity and seriousness that were dispersed in the case of Jack Jones, at least in part by the marketing interests of his English publishers. The most striking example of a Welsh author whose politicized account of industry became in that external context substantially diluted is Gwyn Thomas.

Industrialism Distanced: English

From Barry, south Wales, after studying Spanish at Oxford, Thomas entered *Sorrow for Thy Sons* (1986) for a 1937 competition for a Depression novel by the leftist London publisher Gollancz, but his bleak account of three brothers and a desperate Rhondda community was rejected. In his autobiography *A Few Selected Exits*, Thomas says that the writing was found impressive, but unduly negative.[21]

Focused on the period's fierce responses to the stringent means test laws, the novel has no trace of an upbeat ending: the hope-starved central figure finally leaves the valley; one brother, a deeply radical mischief-maker, remains; so does the third, who promulgates the values of the shop he works in. Thomas never repeated this bitter political realism, later producing fluent, witty writing in fiction and journalism, and matching media performances, including attacks on the Welsh language movement. Later fiction can retain elements of dissent. 'Oscar', a novella in *Where Did I Put my Pity?*

(1946), is a fable with political edge: the hero finally oversees the death of the brutal coal-tip owner Oscar; Raymond Williams's introduction to *All Things Betray Thee* (1986) praised it as a novel that preserves a political historical force through its romanticized tone and title.

Thomas's later novels and short stories tend to be dismissed as crowd-pleasing lightweight material, stripped of his original leftist conviction. But his work is better understood in the light of postcolonial criticism.[22] If *Sorrow for Thy Sons* was too Welsh and left for a semi-radical publisher, *All Things Betray Thee* (1949) was thought by another London publisher, Michael Joseph, to be a possible successor, much sought at the time, to the crowd-pleasing Richard Llewellyn (discussed below). Responding to an essentially colonized position, Thomas's later work offers a postcolonial hybrid voice, combining native Welsh themes such as ogres, sovereignty-symbolizing women, and communal values with a satiric awareness of colonizing oppression, and also stylistically mixing, in challenging ways, a traditionally imaginative Welsh rhetoric with the demotic structures of the colonizing language – postcolonialists call this verbal challenge 'abrogation'. The texts that achieve this complex hybridity most successfully are not so much industrial as post-industrial: in *The World Cannot Hear You* (1951) and *The Thinker and the Thrush* (written by 1948 but not published until 1988), the sage, witty group of friends who collectively narrate the novels (a very unusual communal literary formation) no longer have industrial work and observe ironically the world of south Wales, its dreams and its complicities. In a complexity also recognizable in the postcolonial context, Thomas was also notoriously hostile to full-blown nativism in the form of the Welsh language, which had been abandoned in his own family.

Reflecting in both engaged and displaced mode on the history of industrial colonialism, *All Things Betray Thee*, Thomas's major single achievement, deals with the foundational events of Welsh radicalism, the popular resistance at Merthyr in 1831 and the Chartist attack on Newport in 1839 – yet the very setting is given an ironically romanticized English name, Moonlea. Christopher Meredith described the novel as 'a sort of Ruritania with class war',[23] but critics have seen the symbolically realized strength of the novel. Raymond Williams felt that by resisting the English pressure towards 'a fiction of private lives',[24] and so 'writing at an effectively legendary distance', Thomas was allegorizing the industrial struggle;[25] Dai Smith, finding the book 'great', sees in the role of the harpist an allegory of the position of the leftist writer in the 1940s.[26] If Thomas is, as Williams and Smith suggest, acting essentially as a symbolist, it is not hard to see in the same mode a self-projection of the author in Lewis, the young and eventually vengeful miner of 'Oscar' – Thomas had, or claimed to have, an uncle called Oscar, whom his autobiography describes as 'a cantankerous jeweller' from Mountain Ash.[27]

Political depths are at times suggested in his other books, which might seem primarily entertaining. Thomas's favourite term for his valley characters, 'voters', must remind readers of the positive possibilities of democracy, and a recurrent setting, Mynydd Coch ('Red Mountain'), seems to have some radical implication. More generally Glyn Jones felt that no-one could miss 'the powerful underthrob of compassion' in the stories,[28] and Katie Jones saw a consistent background of 'the underlying struggle of landlord/coal owner against worker'.[29] Howard Fast, the American Marxist novelist, was a great admirer of Thomas's work; as Golightly has recorded, they maintained a warm and distinctly left-wing correspondence through the Cold War years,[30] and in *Literature and Reality* Fast described *All Things Betray Thee* (under its American title *Leaves in the Wind*) as 'one of the best achievements in socialist realism that we know in modern Western literature'.[31]

Glyn Jones called Gwyn Thomas 'the *cyfarwydd* of the working class',[32] and this term, meaning 'traditional storyteller', refers both to his compelling verbal skills and to his volatile imagination. By far the most verbally gifted of the writers to realize the Welsh industrial context, Gwyn Thomas seems to have been basically unsuited to realist fiction, too subtle and multiple in his responses to accept the inherent political and moral directness of the form – as he said in his autobiography, 'my bardic name was ambivalence'.[33] The continuing audience for his work – evident in successful reprints and lively public interest in talks about him – suggests that the anti-colonial tensions he generated, for the spirit but against the form of traditional industrial fiction, have given his work a dynamic hybridized quality.

A less imaginative account of the socio-political context appeared in Gwyn Jones's *Times Like These* (1936), presenting life in the southern valleys from 1920 to the collapse of the Labour Government in 1929. The protagonist experiences unemployment, but also the death of his wife, and this is not primarily a politically focused story: Raymond Williams commented that, in this novel, 'the family, always important in the Welsh tradition, becomes the only structure of real value, but it is more a refuge than a means of rectifying the situation'.[34] The novel also includes 'the sympathetic portrayal of middle-class characters',[35] including a colliery agent and a Newport businessman. Overall, it is a sombre and somewhat passive account, a novel of exposition rather than engagement, and Jones did not return to the industrial theme, moving on to a distinguished literary and scholarly career.

The last-dated Welsh industrial novel of the thirties, Richard Llewellyn's *How Green Was My Valley* (1939), withdraws fully from industrial engagement into conservative sentimentalization. Like its title, the story avoids the motifs of the Welsh industrial tradition, eschewing painful social politics for the tasteful pleasures of nostalgia. A highly skilled piece of book-making, very effectively reworked in John Ford's 1941 film, the novel's success in England exploited the attractions of quaint regionality, absorbing the challenging political dramas of the pre-war period through Welsh stereotypes and the charm of personal achievement, from brickyard songsters to a handsome young schoolboy. The setting is a mining village, there is industrial trouble, but, as if a reverse of *Cwmardy*, the big father ultimately leads the strike-breakers. Raymond Williams pithily called it 'the export version of the Welsh industrial experience',[36] and two recent essays have described both its inner speciousness[37] and its highly skilful placing in the market by its publisher.[38]

Dai Smith contrasts the novel's rave reviews in England with Keidrych Rhys's trenchant headline in the literary journal *Wales*, 'Ignore this Trash', and notes that little about real work or actual union activity is represented in the novel.[39] Similarly inauthentic is the author's pseudonym: born Vivian Lloyd to Welsh parents living in London (though he always claimed to have been born in St David's, deep in south-west Wales), he wrote under a name so Welsh-seeming it has an extra double l, correctly Llewelyn: this was, with some ironic appropriateness here, the name of the last Celtic prince of Wales, who died in 1282 and has been replaced by English princes since 1301. Not all the novel's romance was the author's creation: he planned to call it 'Slag', which would have cast a more negative general light, yet the publisher's chosen saccharine title does match much of the text. Llewellyn went on to merchandise his technique more fully in three sequels: the much later last title appears to relish the industrial emptiness of modern Wales, *Green, Green, My Valley Now* (1975).

In the same genre of regional nostalgia, Michael Gareth Llewelyn wrote the popular *The Aleppo Merchant* (1945), which, with its rural images and village pubs, seems like a strain-free version of Rhys Davies's *Jubilee Blues*, even more detached from the industrial context. Llewelyn also produced a mining saga with a focus on politics and education, *To Fame Unknown* (1949), but in the less politically aware post-war context its serious tone and lack of nostalgic whimsy apparently made it less well received. Also in the 'How Green' tradition are novels by Alexander Cordell, an English army officer who retired to Wales, his mother's country, and produced fluent historical melodramas of Welsh industry, starting with *Rape of the Fair Country* (1959).

Cordell was judged a 'more than competent historian' by Chris Williams,[40] but the hyperbolic tone of the novels and the consistent use of clichés of language and behaviour separate them from the actuality of industrial experience: Raymond Williams called them 'headline novels'.[41] Their success appears to have stimulated historical romances by woman writers, like *The Smouldering Hills* (1996) by Celia Jones, set in Dowlais, *A Fierce Flame* by Tydfil Thomas (1997), set in Merthyr, and the successful Swansea-based series by Iris Gower beginning with *Copper Kingdom* (1983), dealing with the development of the metallic industries in the late nineteenth century and extending through six novels to *Black Gold* (1988), set during the general strike of 1926. Gower's melodramatic series is notable for combining familiar masculine industrial dramas with a credible, if also highly coloured, account of the way women lived, survived, and sometimes triumphed in the difficult industrial world.

Memorializing Industrialism

Not all post-war industrial reminiscences were unserious. Menna Gallie's *Strike for a Kingdom* (1959) was received patronizingly by *The Times Literary Supplement* as 'Fresh and beguiling from the land of her fathers'[42] but is in fact an unsentimental account of politics and gender focusing on the 1926 general strike, set in a fictional version of Gallie's native Ystradgynlais. It centres, as if having limited confidence in the political genre itself, on a mysterious death but is much more than crime fiction: the mine-manager 'has been murdered by economic conditions'.[43] Gallie strongly deploys a woman's voice – humour and gossip are central – and she emphasizes the effect of politics upon the social context, especially on women. In *The Small Mine* (1962), she concentrates more on human relations in the context of a pit village than humour and politics. She thought this her best work,[44] and Aaron shows how the central event is enriched with social symbolism: 'This is the story not so much of an individual death as of a representative Valley community, and in particular its womenfolk, as they struggle to come to terms with the sudden catastrophic loss.'[45] Gallie's other Welsh-related novel, *Man's Desiring* (1960), withdraws, essentially autobiographically, from the industrial tradition into another area of characteristically Welsh labour, offering a saga of a collier lad who becomes a young academic, like her own husband, with whom she moved away from Wales.

A non-Welsh viewpoint brings a more analytic tone to *The Adventurers* (1960), the only novel by the London-based leftist historian Margot

Heinemann. About post-war political commitment and largely set in Wales, it traces the movements of Dan Owen, who resists conscription into the mines during the Second World War, as he – and especially his mother – have higher aspirations. He becomes a successful and somewhat cynical journalist in London, but the book increasingly revisits his home, Abergoch (Heinemann no doubt knew this meant 'red estuary'), to explore the growing problems of both the coal industry and the left itself.

Equally retrospective and political, but based in traditional discourses – male, political, and Welsh-language – is *The Angry Vineyard* (1975) by Rhydwen Williams, which appeared first in English and was then published in Welsh, as were his other emotive historical treatments of past industry, the series named *Cwm Hiraeth* (*Valley of Yearning*) and his powerful novel *Amser i Wylo* (*A Time to Weep*) about the 1913 Senghenydd mine disaster, published just after the 1984 miners' strike. In his only English novel (*The Angry Vineyard*), Williams interweaves fact and fiction to realize the dramatic events and political contexts of the Merthyr Rising of 1831 and focuses, in particular, on the execution of Dic Penderyn: he comments that the novel is 'a testimony to certain values that have outlived the ironmasters and their industries and most of the acrid wastes they left behind'.[46]

Raymond Williams has addressed the decline of heavy industry and the subsequently changing politics in Wales in two essays[47] and also, in varying degrees, five novels. *Border Country* (1960), *Second Generation* (1964), and *The Fight for Manod* (1979) deal in a loose sequence with the 1926 strike, the Welsh diaspora into English industry, and the recent possibility of new-style industries and social forces in Wales – while incrementally locating these dramas in the context of European political and cultural thought familiar from his scholarly writing. Two other novels deal to a considerable degree with Welsh politics and people, but in different time frames: in *The Volunteers* (1978) Williams writes of a dystopic near future, but in *Loyalties* (1985) his focus is firmly on the past. Written in a style and tone more intellectual than emotive, and so bringing a new note to Welsh industrial fiction, the novels have a recurrent concern with an increasingly dispossessed Welsh working class, from the defeated railway strikers of *Border Country* and the expatriate car workers of *Second Generation*, to the noble but sidelined artisans of *Loyalties*: the emphasis is conceptual, primarily negative, and, as Gwyneth Roberts noted, distinctly masculine.[48]

Williams's fullest and most modern-focused statement about Wales is *The Fight for Manod*, where industry is based in electronics and information, and old structures of political organization seem almost irrelevant in a Europe-oriented country much changed from the world of the great strike, which both he and his narrator left behind in *Border Country*. *The Volunteers* is primarily a politically chilling and well-developed piece of near-futurism, but old-style industrial action offers lasting value as miners picket a coal-depot and troops move in. Industry provides only a memorial context in *Loyalties*, which reviews various forms of leftism but seems, like the strikers of 1984, when it was being written, to achieve no more than a dead end. The unfinished 'Black Mountains Trilogy' never reached the industrial dwellers in the region, and ultimately Williams, like Gwyn Thomas and Menna Gallie, offered a rich, reflective, but essentially retrospective view of the industrial world of Wales, with the exception of what seems now his most persuasively present-oriented work, *The Fight for Manod*.

Post-Industrialism

Recent writers have explored the aftermath of industry in areas long dependent on it. Christopher Meredith's *Shifts* (1988) explores and contextualizes the south Wales steel industry with an emphasis on negative change, as the novel realizes industrial, social, and therefore personal disintegration, leaving one man to move around, including to England, in casual work, another to look intermittently into local history, and his wife simply to drift, largely without recourse. Less psycho-social in its explorations is John L. Hughes's *Before the Crying Ends* (1986), a modernist realization of life without work in Pontypridd. A bold reversal of collier heroics is Duncan Bush's *Glass Shot* (1991), which uses a psycho-thriller mode to assert its position as a negative reflex of industrial fiction. The anti-hero can find only trivial sub-industrial work as a tyre-fitter, and his derailed energies flow over into violence and malice. His position is symbolized when, passing in his large car a pit where a few last miners are on strike, his glance at them is distant, disconnected.

Other post-industrial writers retain some reverence, along with much regret, even anger, about the industrial past. Ron Berry, who worked in a Rhondda pit, used the industrial backdrop for novels of male self-discovery, like *Hunters and Hunted* (1960) or *Flame and Slag* (1968), but not long before he died in 1997 he published his major industrial novel *This Bygone* (1996), which can be ironic about politics – the hero goes into small-time mine ownership – but also memorially realistic: John Pikoulis commented that 'only in Lewis Jones's *Cwmardy* has pit life been so authentically realized'.[49] In the same mood, but less energetic, is *The Drift* (1974) where Aldryd Haines tells a 1950s story of a young miner's awakening interest in politics and education. Robert

Morgan has published several collections of retrospective mining stories, and *In the Dark* (1994) offers calm, biting vignettes of valley life. Other authors have dealt with the end of the mining industry in Wales; Tom Davies's *Black Sunlight* (1986) updates the Jack Jones-esque saga to the 1980s, climaxing in 1984 with no way forward for characters or community, in spite of a mystical element focused on a charismatic disabled character. *Dark Edge* (1997), by Roger Granelli, deals more directly with the final confrontation by making his collier hero half-brother to a thuggish, even sociopathic, policeman. Russell Celyn Jones's well-received novel *An Interference of Light* (1995) symbolizes the situation with a northern focus by relocating the great slate-fields strike to the late 1930s, as if southern and coal-focused, but also becoming a personalized meditation – as in the title, which emotionally generalizes a slate miner's technique for judging rock.

Much as women like Roberts and Gallie remembered evaluatively the industrial world they had known, Catherine Merriman, in *State of Desire* (1996), retains positivity from the industrial past. Part of a young widow's personal reawakening is to fight against an environmentally destructive plan for open-cast mining in the southern uplands, so imagining a modern world where women can resist modern industrial blight and also suggesting more positively than most of Merriman's male parallels that the commitment and resistance of the industrial novel can continue in the present. A more general sense of the difficult social and personal aftermath of industrialism broods in the vigorous restlessness of recent south-eastern Welsh novels like Des Barry's realization of male anxiety through nostalgia, *A Bloody Good Friday* (2002), Rachel Trezise's intense female parallel *In and Out of the Goldfish Bowl* (2000), and John Williams's mix of eulogy and elegy for a past industrial community in *Cardiff Dead* (2000).

Setting aside the inauthenticities of Llewellyn and the undue sentimentalism of Cordell and Gower, the industrial novel in Wales successfully overcame many challenges, such as combatting the attitudes of English publishers and accommodating the varied and changing tastes of audiences. Among the international versions of the form, the Welsh contribution is one of the fullest, most varied, and most forcefully creative of a consciousness both national and political: David Bell has spoken of 'the predominance of Welsh writers among the miner novelists'.[50]

Apart from its substantial extent, the Welsh tradition is notable for a number of things – its recurrent radical vigour; the extent to which it internalizes the viewpoint within the working class, without outsiders interfering as interpreters; the recurrent emphasis on the creative and evaluative role of women; the marked and unusual degree to which rural themes are involved; the crossover into Welsh-language fiction; the variety of voices, from popular through political to reflective and intellectual. The achievement of the Welsh industrial novel is – with an authentic touch of democracy and social spirit – communally broad and mobile, not individualistically private or self-indulgently static. Of about twenty major landmarks in the international industrial novel, that is, novels which define the possibilities and test the limits of the form, the Welsh writers can claim to have provided at least a quarter, a contribution involving novels that have set world standards – the human commitment of Jack Jones, the communal leftism of Lewis Jones, the moving power of Kate Roberts, the complex postcolonialism of Gwyn Thomas, the emotive wit of Menna Gallie, the intellectual seriousness of Raymond Williams. Industrial fiction has been one of the most productive industries of Wales.

Notes

1. H. Gustav Klaus, 'Under the Sway of Coal', *New Welsh Review* 39 (1997): 29.
2. See Chapter 17 in this volume for a discussion of these novels.
3. Jonathan Evans, 'People, Politics, and Print: Notes Towards a History of the English-Language Book in Industrial South Wales up to 1900' (PhD diss., Cardiff University, 2010), 91–6.
4. Kirsti Bohata and Alexandra Jones, 'Welsh Women's Industrial Fiction, 1880–1910', *Women's Writing* 24, 4 (2017): 499–516.
5. Evans, 'People, Politics, and Print', 278.
6. Ibid., 282–7.
7. Katie Gramich, introduction to *Queen of the Rushes* by Allen Raine (Dinas Powys: Honno, 1998), 5–6.
8. Stephen Knight, '"Not a Place for Me": Rhys Davies's Fictions and the Coal Industry', in *Decoding the Hare: Essays on Rhys Davies*, ed. Meic Stephens (Cardiff: University of Wales Press, 2001), 54–70.
9. Rhys Davies, *Print of a Hare's Foot* (London: Heinemann, 1969), 119.
10. Rhys Davies, *A Time to Laugh* (London: Heinemann, 1937), 432.
11. Davies, *Print of a Hare's Foot*, 27.
12. Glyn Jones, *The Dragon Has Two Tongues: Essays on Anglo-Welsh Writers and Writing* (London: Dent, 1968), 93.
13. Dai Smith, *Wales: A Question for History* (Bridgend: Seren, 1999), 174.
14. See Bill Jones and Chris Williams, *B. L. Coombes*, Writers of Wales (Cardiff: University of Wales Press, 1999); Bert Coombes, *With Dust Still in his Throat*, ed. Bill Jones and Chris Williams (Cardiff: University of Wales Press, 1999).
15. Storm Jameson, quoted in David Bell, *Ardent Propaganda: Miners' Novels and Class Conflict* (Umea: Umea University Press, 1995), 87.

16. Stephen Knight, *A Hundred Years of Fiction: From Colony to Independence* (Cardiff: University of Wales Press, 2004), 69–70.

17. Stephen Knight, 'Anarcho-Syndicalism in Welsh Industrial Fiction', in *'To Hell with Culture': Anarchism in Twentieth Century British Literature*, ed. H. G. Klaus and S. Knight (Cardiff: University of Wales Press, 2005), 51–65.

18. Lewis Jones, *We Live* (London: Lawrence and Wishart, 1939, 1978), 334.

19. Ned Thomas, *The Welsh Extremist: A Culture in Crisis* (London: Gollancz, 1971), 65.

20. Harri Pritchard Jones, introduction to *One Moonlit Night* by Caradog Prichard, trans. Philip Mitchell (Edinburgh: Canongate, 1995), ix.

21. Gwyn Thomas, *A Few Selected Exits* (London: Hutchinson, 1968; repr. Bridgend: Seren, 1989), 180.

22. See Stephen Knight, 'The Voices of Glamorgan: Gwyn Thomas's Colonial Fiction', *Welsh Writing in English* 7 (2001–2): 16–34.

23. Christopher Meredith, 'Two from the Heart', review of *All Things Betray Thee* by Gwyn Thomas, *Planet* 59 (1986): 98–9.

24. Raymond Williams, introduction to *All Things Betray Thee* by Gwyn Thomas (London: Lawrence and Wishart, 1986), vi.

25. Raymond Williams, *The Welsh Industrial Novel: Inaugural Gwyn Jones Lecture, 1978* (Cardiff: Cardiff University College Press, 1979), 18.

26. Dai Smith, 'The Early Gwyn Thomas', *THSC* (1985): 72–3.

27. Thomas, *A Few Selected Exits*, 41.

28. Jones, *The Dragon Has Two Tongues*, 121.

29. Katie Jones, 'Review of *Selected Stories* by Gwyn Thomas', *New Welsh Review* 3 (1988): 75.

30. Victor Golightly, '"We, Who Speak for the Workers": The Correspondence of Gwyn Thomas and Howard Fast', *Welsh Writing in English* 6 (2000): 67–88.

31. Howard Fast, *Literature and Reality* (New York: International, 1950), 51.

32. Jones, *The Dragon Has Two Tongues*, 123.

33. Thomas, *A Few Selected Exits*, 226.

34. Williams, *The Welsh Industrial Novel*, 13–14.

35. James A. Davies, 'Kinds of Relating: Gwyn Thomas (Jack Jones, Lewis Jones, Gwyn Jones) and the Welsh Industrial Experience', *Anglo-Welsh Review* 86 (1987): 74.

36. Williams, *The Welsh Industrial Novel*, 17.

37. Ian A. Bell, 'How Green Was My Valley?', *Planet* 73 (1992): 3–9.

38. John Harris, 'Not Only a Place in Wales', *Planet* 73 (1992): 10–15.

39. Dai Smith, 'Myth and Meaning in the Literature of the South Wales Coalfield', *Anglo-Welsh Review* 25 (1975): 30.

40. Chris Williams, 'Master of a Lost Past', *Planet* 121 (1997): 13.

41. Williams, *The Welsh Industrial Novel*, 19.

42. Anon, 'Wales 2, Hungary 1', review of *Strike for a Kingdom* by Menna Gallie, *Times Literary Supplement*, 20 February 1959, 102.

43. Menna Gallie, *Strike for a Kingdom* (London: Gollancz, 1959), 167.

44. Angela Fish, 'Flight-Deck of Experience', *New Welsh Review* 18 (1992): 62.

45. Jane Aaron, foreword to *The Small Mine* by Menna Gallie, Honno Classics series, 2nd edn (Dinas Powys: Honno, 2000), vi.

46. Rhydwen Williams, *The Angry Vineyard* (Swansea: Christopher Davies, 1975), 10.

47. See Williams, *The Welsh Industrial Novel*, and also 'Working Class, Proletarian, Socialist: Problems in some Welsh Novels', in *The Socialist Novel in Britain*, ed. H. Gustav Klaus (Brighton: Harvester, 1982), 110–21.

48. Gwyneth Roberts, 'The Cost of Community: Women in Raymond Williams's Fiction', in *Our Sisters' Land: The Changing Identities of Women in Wales*, ed. Jane Aaron *et al.* (Cardiff: University of Wales Press, 1994), 214.

49. John Pikoulis, 'Word-of-Mouth Cultures Cease in Cemeteries', *New Welsh Review* 34 (1996): 14.

50. Bell, *Ardent Propaganda*, 10.

21

From Nonconformist Nation to Proletarian Nation: Writing Wales, 1885–1930

M. WYNN THOMAS

'Standing out pre-eminently as the most remarkable phenomenon in the National Life of Wales during recent years', declared W. George Roberts exultantly in 1903, 'is the overwhelming, almost magical, power of Nonconformity.' A year later, Evan Roberts was to demonstrate the seemingly irresistible potency of this magic when his religious revival (1904–6) electrified attention worldwide. No-one could have imagined what was shortly to come – the bewilderingly rapid disintegration of a seemingly impregnable socio-religious hegemony. Even as late as December 1916, this powerful nineteenth-century chapel culture would seem to have reached the jubilant apogee of its influence when its favourite son, David Lloyd George, became prime minister of an imperial Britain. Who then could possibly have believed that, a mere couple of decades later, anglophone writers would be celebrating their supposed recent liberation from the 'dark chapels, squat as toads' that had lent 'an appearance of grey gloom to Welsh life'?

Indeed, the emergence in Wales, during the inter-war decades of the early twentieth century, of an arresting anglophone literary culture may be usefully regarded as a determined revolt against the chapel past by a brash young generation of writers and intellectuals. Produced and empowered by a newly established secularizing system of state secondary schooling, these were intent on wresting control of social discourse and ideology from a supposedly sclerotic religious ministerial elite. Implicated in their struggle were other features of modern Wales's great age of convulsive change (roughly spanning a couple of decades each side of the century divide). Most notable of these was the radically transformative culture shift that had accompanied the creation, in the southern coalfield society, of a new, cosmopolitan industrial society. In its prime, it could legitimately pride itself on marching in the very vanguard of global progress, and the self-confidence thus generated was duly manifested in innovative cultural creativity.

But such gains were inevitably shadowed by linguistic and cultural loss: the 1901 census revealed that, for the first time in a millennium and a half of history, Wales had become a predominantly English-speaking country. This alarming contraction of the aboriginal Celtic language may have served to trigger the spectacular period of creativity that followed, resulting in a body of twentieth-century writing in Welsh to rival that of the golden age of the late Middle Ages. Many of these writers reacted even earlier than their anglophone contemporaries against the constrictive values and conventions of Nonconformity. It would be another half century before Welsh-medium education would be sponsored by the state, but some young intellectuals had been introduced to the wealth of their cultural past at an Oxford that had famously followed Matthew Arnold's advice to establish a prestigious pioneering Chair in Celtic. A few had also made their way to great continental universities such as Freiburg and the Sorbonne.

Modelling their work on the most progressive 'scientific' continental scholarship in such fields as philology, lexicology, and textual studies, a new cadre of highly gifted university scholars regularized and modernized Welsh orthography and grammar and began painstakingly to construct a reliable understanding of Welsh *barddas* (the ancient strict-metre tradition) on the basis of a rigorous editorial examination of the fragmentary corpus of key manuscript remains. Although strictly academic in provenance, this great enterprise of scholarship was to enable a remarkable modern renaissance of Welsh-language poetry, with towering figures such as John Rhys (a pioneering Celtic philologist), John Morris-Jones (a magisterial grammarian), and Ifor Williams (the supreme authority on early Welsh poetry) becoming culture heroes for the first generation of Welsh-language writers ever to receive an advanced formal education in the long, illustrious history of their own literary inheritance.

By the beginning of the twentieth century, therefore, creative writers in Welsh were well equipped to modernize their ancient culture, and they proceeded to do so to profoundly transformative effect. Not that you would ever have known that from the explosively subversive work of Caradoc Evans, the Welsh-speaking Fleet Street journalist from the rural west who seemed to libel mainstream Welsh-language culture unforgivably when he portrayed his chapel background, in a collection of short stories provocatively entitled *My People* (1915), as avaricious, repressively patriarchal, morally grotesque, and sexually gross, as well as otherwise monstrously deformed. Lethally unfair yet selectively accurate, like all great satire, this exposé of the dark underworld of chapel society outraged smugly pious

Welsh-language society even as the new anglophone Wales of the heavily industrialized south found welcome confirmation in it of its own superior, progressive, socio-political character. The result was a *Kulturkampf* between modern Wales's two linguistic cultures that became the bane of national life for two-thirds of the twentieth century.

Evans's most brilliant 'modernist' invention – the grotesquely misshapen, pseudo-biblical English that is the spoken vernacular of his disturbingly claustrophobic world – served as an important template for Anglo-Welsh writing for several decades to come, while his home in Aberystwyth became, by the early thirties, a site of pilgrimage for such rising stars of a new 'Anglo-Welsh' culture as Glyn Jones and his friend, Dylan Thomas. They, along with their many notably gifted contemporaries, were to be memorably dubbed 'the sons of Caradoc' by a later generation that regarded *My People* as the indubitable *fons et origo* of Wales's English-language literature. Only of late has this highly influential (and controversially gendered) model of sudden cultural emergence been severely challenged. Developing research has revealed a much more prolonged, rich, and complex history in Wales of anglophone literary production that, as it gained critical mass, gradually consolidated around the turn of the nineteenth and twentieth centuries into distinctive cultural form, although it was the 1930s before it was able to produce a whole generation of striking talent.

The dark brilliance of Evans's savagely satiric caricatures has, however, obscured the fact that Welsh Nonconformity, whose unsavoury underside had been mercilessly revealed by his distorting lens, had, in fact, produced during the decades preceding the First World War what may reasonably be considered the first body of creative work in English deliberately focused on a distinctively Welsh cultural phenomenon – the Nonconformist nation. The origins of a modern body of Welsh writing in English (as distinct from previous desultory publication) may therefore persuasively be traced back not, as popularly supposed, to the anti-chapel writing of *My People* but rather to a dozen or so novels – and some poetry – sponsored by the very chapel culture Evans had attacked.

And interestingly enough, Welsh-language fiction can be traced back to the very same source and to much the same period. The first Welsh-language novelist – probably still to this day his country's most gifted writer of fiction – was Daniel Owen of Mold. His fidelity to the magisterial, all-encompassing Nonconformist culture in which he had been raised and which he had hoped to serve as a minister did not prevent him from even-handedly displaying its weaknesses in a series of powerful, immensely popular novels, memorable as much for the Dickensian richness of their vivid, quirky characterizations and humorous vignettes as for their profound engagement with contemporary crises of faith and morality.

Religious doubts, deriving not least from recent scientific discoveries, are voiced most powerfully through the agonized discussions that the intelligent, laboriously self-educated, young miner Bob has with his pious mother, Mari Lewis, in Owen's masterly fictional autobiography of a young minister, *Rhys Lewis* (1885). But Bob's arguments are offset not so much by Mrs Lewis's responses as by the quiet integrity and principled human sympathy of her character, attributes that testify eloquently to the sterling qualities of her steadfast faith. And, like all Owen's novels, *Rhys Lewis* overflows with characters whose loveable idiosyncrasies of conduct and speech turned them into instant heroes of the folk culture of the day. Such is Wil Bryan, the mischievous youngster, irrepressibly irreverent but invariably good natured, one of whose pranks is silently to advance the hour hand of the chapel clock to shorten the tedium of prayers. Having disobediently taken another clock to pieces, he is dismayed to discover, after guiltily reassembling it, that he still has one tell-tale piece left over. Memorably endearing too, is Tomos Bartley, an old man the simple probity of whose faith is encapsulated in his homely turns of pungent phrase, and matched by his total humble devotion to his cheerfully monosyllabic wife Barbara, his soul-mate and oracle. Characters like Bryan and Bartley enabled Owen implicitly to expose the mealy-mouthed 'humbug' (Wil Bryan's scathing term) of the chapel establishment, their assiduous promotion of social status and respectability, and systematic practice of hypocrisy. And through the ultimately tragic character of the monstrous Captain Trefor, he traced in *Enoc Huws* (1891) the career of a petty industrial entrepreneur whose mastery of religious cant and carefully cultivated façade of ostentatious piety enabled him to gull the credulous into sinking their life's savings in his ruinously empty lead mine.

In the introduction to *Enoc Huws,* Daniel Owen wrote feelingly about attempts such as his to capture in fiction the previously unrecorded values and conventions that distinguished Welsh Nonconformity. Eager to draw these qualities to the attention of English readers, a number of novelists broadly contemporary with Owen, but lacking his genius, attempted to 'translate' this distinctive Welsh culture into English. Most successful, perhaps, was Eleazar Roberts, whose *Owen Rees* (1893) is an important social record of the religious life of the Liverpool Welsh, at a time when 60,000 had migrated to the city from Wales and established more than fifty substantial chapels there. Already aware that Welsh Presbyterianism (Calvinistic

Methodism) was under serious threat from modern life, Roberts tried to convey the value of such sanctified institutions as the *seiat* (confessional fellowship meeting), the *sasiwn* (grand regional convention), the sermon, and the chapel meeting, along with such key rites as admission to, and expulsion from, membership. His young minister hero, Owen, has both to deal with the challenges of Darwinism, Christian Socialism, and incipient psychoanalysis and to effect the transition from narrow Calvinism to the new, progressive form of faith consistent with the disclosures of the 'Higher Criticism' of German theological scholarship.

The work of an insider, *Owen Rees* contrasts strikingly with well-meaning attempts by outsiders such as William Edwards Tirebuck in his collection of stories *Jenny Jones and Jenny* (1896) to capture the ethos of the Welsh chapel. There he deals in a humorously sympathetic manner with the quaint ways of the much-vaunted Welsh *gwerin* (pious ordinary folk), that great central myth of Welsh Nonconformity which Caradoc Evans was so savagely to debunk. Though scarcely more than a string of homilies and anecdotes, David Davies's *Echoes from the Welsh Hills* (1883) was, along with its sequel *John Vaughan and his Friends* (1897), a conscious attempt to manufacture an export-version of this myth, and Davies makes much of the great moral example of chapel-going that Wales sets for the rest of the United Kingdom, in an introduction whose national self-satisfaction is echoed in *Among the Mountains: or Life in Wales*, published (probably in 1867) by 'Ceredig' (W. D. Richards). This is an unappetising tale about a humble young Welshman whose progress to wealth as a Liverpool shopkeeper is attributed entirely to his conspicuous piety. While such novels were composed with an English readership in mind, *Llangobaith* (1886), by Erasmus B. Jones, published as it was in Utica, New York State, aimed its chapel propaganda at an American market.

A half century after the appearance of *Among the Mountains*, a novel like Margam Jones's *The Stars of the Revival* (1910) continued nostalgically to peddle the worn, shop-soiled myth of a golden age of the Welsh chapels, the passing of which A. P. Thomas had already mourned in his 1896 novel, *In the Land of the Harp and the Feathers*. Sentimentally recalling the 'devout old-world Welsh people', 'dear [and] old-fashioned', Thomas despaired of the 'half and half Christians' of his own time by whom those old-stagers had been replaced. The only poet to attempt to capture this passing world in verse was William Parry ('Gwilym Pont Taf'), author of *The Old Welsh Evangelist* (1893) and *Welsh Hillside Saints* (1896). Combined, these texts serve as an epic verse chronicle of the socio-religious world of Welsh Nonconformity – Parry's poem on the 'The Association' ('Sasiwn') alone stretches over 160 boringly conventional pages. Wales is hymned throughout as a latter-day Palestine, its landscape sanctified by the chapels dotted 'Among the hills that rise like sentinels, / The calm, majestic guardians of the land', evidence that the Lord has 'revealed thyself among our hills, / Thy splendours gleamed among our stubborn rocks; / Thy glory showered on our ancient rills'.

The myth of the chapel *gwerin* is again tediously prominent in *Gwen Penri: A Welsh Idyll* (1899), by John Bufton, an author from Mold like Daniel Owen. But the novel also concentrates, to much better effect, on the struggle of the New Woman – in this case a young female undergraduate – for an acknowledged place within the traditional patriarchal structure of the chapel. Moreover, Gwen is tellingly a student of science, and so the novel turns into an interesting allegory of the developing new marriage between science and theology. Even more effective a portrayal of a New Woman is that of Nancy in Sara Maria Saunders's short story, 'Nancy on the Warpath'. First by outspoken word and then through daring deed, she forces her father-in-law, an autocrat of hearth and chapel, to yield to her feisty will. And as for the challenge of the new learning to the chapels, this is dealt with again in allegorical fashion in Margam Jones's *Angels in Wales* (1914), a novel which outlines the relationship between three children educated 'according to the tastes of their mothers. One was sent to Babylon [Love and Passion], the other to Jerusalem [Religious faith] and the third to Athens [Wisdom and Learning].'

By the end of the nineteenth century, then, Welsh Nonconformity had become fully conscious of the threatening encroachments of a new dispensation, and the adjustments it consequently made both to its theology and to its practices is the subject of Walter Gallichan's *The Conflict of Owen Prytherch* (1905) and T. Marchant Williams's *The Land of My Fathers* (1889). The latter is preoccupied with the attempt of the more progressive chapels to break with their strict Calvinist inheritance and to liberalize in tune with the times. The most powerful threat to Nonconformist hegemony came, however, not in the form of science or the new theology but in the form of politics. From the early 1890s onwards, Wales became increasingly enthralled by the astonishing advance to positions of political influence of the young political and intellectual vanguard associated with the confident Young Wales / Cymru Fydd movement, itself headed by two emergent luminaries, the tragically short-lived Tom Ellis (eventually to become chief Liberal whip) and, of course, the mercurial, magnetic, (and amoral) Lloyd George. Loose, uneasy alliance though it was of several different ideological factions, Cymru Fydd in its youthful prime was the militant expression of an unprecedented politicization of Welsh cultural identity and had as its goal the creation of a Welsh parliament, subordinate to an 'imperial' parliament at Westminster. During Cymru Fydd's heyday, both old-school Nonconformists and their bitter rivals, the conservative and unionist Welsh Anglicans, tended to agree; the chapels had become little more than the Welsh Liberal Party at prayer. The high-point of *The Ethics of Evan Wynne* (1913), by D. Hugh Pryce, is the mental breakdown the novel's eponymous hero suffers as a consequence of championing the chapels and supporting their campaign for the disestablishment in Wales of the state church of England. He is duly healed by the ministrations of his gentle, devotedly Anglican wife.

The absorbing Palace of Westminster soap opera of the manoeuvrings of the charismatic young leaders of the new Welsh liberalism is the subject of Beriah Gwynfe Evans's comic caricature of a novel, *Dafydd Dafis: Sef Hunangofiant Ymgeisydd Seneddol* (1898). This fantastical tale tracks the political education of an innocent named Dafydd, a native of rural Cardiganshire who has made his fortune selling milk in London, in the weird ways and wiles of the Commons. He acts throughout in comically abject obedience to the instructions of his ambitious, enterprising, and entertainingly scheming wife, the formidable Claudia. Evans's novel was in many ways a device for educating the large, recently enfranchised segment of the Welsh male population that was unfamiliar with the arcane grammar of political life. It was also propaganda for the radical reforming liberalism of Lloyd George and his progressive Welsh associates.

Little more than a sequence of political *tableaux vivants*, *Dafydd Dafis* exemplifies skills Evans had developed as an author of popular dramas about Welsh history and that were again evidenced when, in 1911, he scripted a national pageant to celebrate the inauguration of the prince of Wales. But the most culturally noteworthy of such popular spectacles was the bizarre national pageant of Wales enthusiastically performed in 1909 by an amateur cast of 5,000 against the backdrop of Cardiff Castle. It included one thousand 'fairies' forming a living map of Wales, Cardiff City soccer team dressed up as medieval Welsh soldiers to storm a castle, and Lord Tredegar, hero of the Charge of the Light Brigade, incongruously starring as Wales's greatest anti-English hero, Owain Glyn Dŵr. A charade of history it may have been, but it was solemnly staged to advertise one of the important cities of Empire – most of the steam coal that powered both the Merchant and the Royal Navy was at this time exported from Cardiff and Barry docks. The pageant was therefore designed to advertise the new Wales's total allegiance to the imperial enterprise, in line with the ideology of the pageant master, one of the most outrageously colourful figures in modern Welsh cultural history. An adventurer and mercenary, 'Owen Rhoscomyl' published derring-do novels such as *Old Fireproof* (1906), *A Scout's Story* (1908), and *Lone Tree Lode* (1913) based on his life as Indian tracker, buffalo hunter, soldier in the Boer War, and one of Roosevelt's legendary 'rough riders' in Cuba. Yet another novel, *The Jewel of Ynys Galon* (1895), may well have been based on the brief flirtation he had with piracy.

Rhoscomyl's obsession with the 'manly' military prowess of the Welsh was in part a reaction against the 'soft power' version of the nation promoted by the Young Wales movement in the wake of the calamitous defeat, at a stormy meeting of 1896 in Newport, of Lloyd George's pet political project – the establishment of a parliament for Wales. From that wreckage there eventually emerged the one literary masterpiece of the period, in the form of T. Gwynn Jones's 'Ymadawiad Arthur' (1902), a magnificent revival of the great medieval strict-metre poetic tradition that heralded the second golden age of Welsh literature that was to follow.[1] It was a postcolonial reclamation of Arthur, a legendary figure long lost by Wales to the English who had – most recently thanks to Tennyson – refashioned him into a central hero of their own nationalist ideology. In his *awdl*, Jones concentrated on the tragic story of Arthur's fateful defeat at Camlan, and his mournful retirement to Afallon (Avilion), a magical location specifically identified in 'Ymadawiad Arthur' as the sanctuary of collective national memories and of traditions there kept permanently available for recovery and regeneration. At once an unforgettable record of the crisis of modern Welsh-language culture and an important exemplar and enabler of that culture's capacity for reinvention and renewal, Jones's masterpiece is also a moving meditation, when it focuses on the return of Arthur's magical sword Caledfwlch (Excalibur) to the Lady of the Lake, on the diminished powers for self-defence that were left to a Welsh-language Wales mortally threatened by the nation's new anglophone culture. And there seems no doubt that shadowing the dramatization in 'Ymadawiad Arthur' of the moment of the hero's fateful loss of supernatural powers are T. Gwynn Jones's memories of the 1896 defeat of that modern Arthur, David Lloyd George, in Newport, at the hands of aggressive spokesmen for the new anglophone Wales of the industrial south.

By far the most powerfully effective servant of Young Wales's core ideology of cultural nationalism was the prodigally versatile and prodigiously industrious O. M. Edwards (1858–1920). With all the authority and expertise of the brilliant young Oxford don he was, Edwards set about delivering a remarkable programme of publications with the explicit aim of restoring a cultural memory of nationhood whose long absence had allowed the Welsh to become purely local and tribal in their allegiances. The compendious popular journals he produced in the grand Victorian manner (particularly *Cymru*, 1891–1920) aimed both to capture the colour and texture of this patchwork quilt of myriad local allegiances and to foster a sense of over-arching national identity – an identity that Edwards, a confirmed and sophis-ticated Europhile, firmly placed in a wider, continental context.

A visionary patriot and inspirational educator, 'O. M.', as he came to be affectionately called, produced periodicals, memoirs, travelogues, readable histories of Wales, a charming autobiography, and popular editions of Welsh classics. His *Cartrefi Cymru*, a profile of the humble homes of leading figures of the Welsh cultural past that created a modern rural landscape of national memory, itself became an instant popular classic. On a conservative estimate, Edwards authored two dozen books, launched and edited seven periodicals – his *Cymru'r Plant* (1892–1920) brought children's literature in Wales into being – and initiated and managed seven series. Invariably produced with the general reader in mind, his works testified to Edwards's trust in the naturally cultivated *gwerin* of rural Welsh-speaking Wales. When, however, he launched his periodical *Wales* (1894–7) in an attempt to reach the new, anglophone Welsh proletariat of the heavily populated industrial valleys, his failure (a cultural parallel to that of Lloyd George at Newport) highlighted the limits both of his natural constituency and of his visionary cultural nationalism.

One of Edwards's students at Balliol was Edward Thomas who, following decades of tedious reviewing and prose writing, was to briefly develop, between 1914 and his death in action in 1917, into a hauntingly talented, potentially major poet. Influentially characterized by F. R. Leavis as at once definitively 'modern' and quintessentially English, Thomas's hallmark 'lim-inal' sensibility may alternatively be understood as symptomatic of his chronic crisis of self-identification. Although born and raised in London, he was of Welsh parentage and was exposed to Welsh-language culture during visits throughout childhood, adolescence, and early manhood to his father's immediate and extended family. Such an experience undoubtedly sensitized him to that intense aliveness to the interpenetration of land and people over millennia that distinguished the visionary cultural nationalism of his Oxford tutor, O. M. Edwards, whose influence – not least on Thomas's anti-imperial dream of local, deep-rooted Englishness – has as yet barely been explored. As Andrew Webb has recently emphasized, O. M. had intended for Thomas a career either as an academic or as schoolteacher in Wales, and when he published *Wales* in 1901, Edwards received a passionately enthusiastic letter from Thomas declaring his admiration for it 'because I am Welsh'. In a late letter, he could still dream of settling with his family in Wales at war's end.

Particularly relevant in connection with Thomas is Edwards's evocative sense of his Wales as a national community of richly differentiating geo-social localities steeped in history and legend, strong echoes of which may be heard in the many prose works so lovingly limning the sedimented human and natural geography of southern England that Thomas produced before the war, as again during it in his signature poem 'Lob'. But Thomas's nostalgia for settled place was always that of a psychologically unsettled, permanently displaced person, whose journey in search of psychic origins ended ominously only in 'an avenue dark, nameless, without end', and whose quest for the quintessence of self led only to a confrontation with his eternal doppelgänger ('The Other'). Even the grounded localism with which he is so often credited turns out, on closer inspection, to be liable to subsidence – 'Adlestrop', for instance, may appear to valorize the idyllic 'embeddedness' of a little English rural station, but it opens by emphasizing that the experience comes only in and as a fleeting moment in transit, a fragile respite snatched in an interval of modern rail travel. In his poetry Thomas is always a lonely peregrine soul – the list of gifts he yearns to give his wife heartbreakingly concludes with 'And my self, too, if I could find / Where it lay hidden and it proved kind.' As for his prose, it veers often away from England and into a Wales with whose contemporary industrial self (visited, for instance, in 'Swansea town') he shows he is as familiar as with the ancient, legendary past and lovely landscape he celebrates in *Beautiful Wales*. No wonder he was so impatient with the vogue for the mistily, mystically 'Celtic' that had gripped the England of his day like a brief cultural spasm.

His aliveness to the contemporary also found issue, as Andrew Webb has noted, in contributions to the Cardiff-based literary journal *Nationalist*.[2] There he published two fictional sketches infused with the kind of patriotism sponsored by the Young Wales movement. Indeed, his writings at the turn of the century featured many of the preoccupations of Cymru Fydd – the return of Arthur, the recovery of Welsh folklore, folksong and legend, and the seminal cultural attempt to reconnect with the great strict-metre bardic tradition. Far from proving ephemeral and superficial, these interests were to enter into the very marrow of Thomas's imagination, affecting his constructions of Englishness and even finding issue in his remarkable poetry in the form not merely of occasional references but of settled habits of allusion and indeed of writing. Webb has persuasively pointed to important instances where the mature Thomas adopted a variety of Welsh metrical forms and literary genres (such as vaticinatory poetry), adapting them for creative use in his mature English poems. And Thomas's sympathies with outsiders, manifest in his early championing of Irish and American literature as in his openness to gay and lesbian writing, may owe something to his personal experience of psycho-cultural marginality.

That sensation of being ever on the outside was also felt by two other prominent Welsh anglophone writers of the period, both from the border county of Monmouthshire. Arthur Machen shared Thomas's sense of uneasy, but creatively fruitful, suspension between two cultures, while W. H. Davies was a figure in transit virtually from childhood, and ever subject to the 'fever of restlessness' which may well have been what attracted Thomas to his case. Davies's vagabond native disposition is neatly encapsulated at the beginning of *Autobiography of a Supertramp* (1908) where he recalls a trip he made to Bristol as a tiny boy, in the company of his Cornish mariner grandfather, aboard a vessel named *The Welsh Prince*. Wales was never more than an embarkation point for Davies, who seems to have been untroubled by issues of cultural identity, happy to be labelled English when necessary. Having received minimal education and having left home so young, he was never exposed to the new discourse of anglophone Welshness being developed under the auspices of some elements of Young Wales. Very much his own man, he disarms his reader from the beginning of his *Autobiography* with his guileless readiness to confess to thieving in his youth, and as his picaresque adventures riding the rails all over America unfold the supertramp begins, in his artful innocence, to foreshadow the figure of Chaplin's immortal tramp.

What the appeal of the open road was to American writers from Whitman to Kerouac, the lure of the railroad was to Davies. But while capitalizing on the myth of the United States as the benign land of freedom through self-sufficiency, he also slyly punctures it. His colourful brotherhood of tramps mirrors American society itself in favouring hustlers, con-men, predators, and opportunists. He evokes the legend of the western cattlemen only to expose their casual cruelties; he condemns the dark violence of a southern lynch-mob by reporting it with all the cunning artlessness of Mark Twain in *The Adventures of Huckleberry Finn*, only to betray his own racism by describing African Americans as a 'not very intelligent race'. After all, Davies was no naïf. Although he profitably impersonated a rural ruminant in his popular Georgian pastoral poetry ('What is this life if, full of care, / We have no time to stand and stare?'), he had in fact been raised an urban urchin left pretty much to his own devices in the cosmopolitan dockland areas of a booming port in what came to be styled 'American Wales'.

No wonder he responded so readily to the magnetic pull of the real America – as Christopher Harvie has demonstrated, at this time the great ports and seaboard cities dotting both sides of the Atlantic were the power-houses of the new industrial civilization and had much more in common with each other than they shared with their respective national hinterlands. And Davies's carefully censored and sanitized traveller's tales (he can primly pass over the details of 'a week's debauchery') found a ready audience in an Edwardian England, one of whose favourite texts was, like Davies's auto-biography, a fantasy of homosocial freedom – Kenneth Grahame's *Wind in the Willows*, in which Mr Toad so memorably submits to the lure of the open road. At bottom, Davies is a petit-bourgeois bohemian very much to the taste of his respectable Edwardian readers – he could be so insouciant and invete-rate a tramp for the first five years only because he was secure in the knowledge that at home he had a 'small estate' of a hundred pounds left him by his grandmother.

Unlike Davies, Arthur Machen (Arthur Llewelyn Jones) treated the limbo-land of his border county of Monmouthshire (Gwent) as an alembic for brewing dark fictions. The countryside around his native Caerleon, some-time location of a legionary fort in the border regions of an atavistic Wales, seemed to him from childhood haunted by a sinister glamour he came to associate with the presence of the great god Pan. The sleep of reason produces monsters, noted Goya, and in Machen's 'horror' fiction, dark forces arise not only from the natural world but from the human unconscious as if in sneering mockery of late nineteenth-century bourgeois society's naïve faith in the forces of progress – science, empire, rational religion (Machen's particular *bête noire* was the complacently rational temper of the Anglican Church to which he, like his clerical father, belonged). Not the least enduring interest of his work is the way it provided the cultural aspirations and anxieties of his age with feverishly heightened narrative shape and symbolic expression. Into the nightmare forms of his demonic *femmes fatales* were crammed the sexual fears aroused at the *fin de siècle* by the dangerously liberated figure of the New Woman. Females in his fiction are particularly susceptible to libidinous possession by Pan, and through them this shape-shifting creature of a border imagination is able to insinuate himself into the very heart of 'tenebrous London' itself, the seat of empire – the city having been founded on the site of an ancient pre-Roman Celtic settlement. 'Sexual deviance' seems to be a signature characteristic of those possessed by the

satyr. As for Machen's arrogantly meddling scientists, those nineties descendants of Frankenstein whose experiments exposed the human brain to the
invasion of evil, they eerily anticipated the era of psychoanalysis and of
neurosurgery. And the sinister powers of many of his characters are attributed to their mixed, and therefore indeterminate, racial origins at the very
time that empire was giving rise to fears that the white race might be running
the risk of taint by miscegenation. There is plenty of insolently casual racial
prejudice in Machen, and in 'The Shining Pyramid' this found disturbing
fictional issue as he merged anxiety about the influx of 'foreigners' through
the booming port of Newport with pseudo-anthropological ideas common at
the time connecting the supposedly pre-Celtic 'Iberian' population of Wales
with stories of the sinister 'little people'. In this story they are imagined as
periodically emerging from the darkness of their underground existence to
practise unspeakable rites at night in the 'bowl' of Caerleon's ancient Roman
amphitheatre.[3]

One central duality of Machen's imagination is highlighted if one compares one of his most popular fictions, 'The Bowmen,' with his own commentary on it. Written in the wake of the British retreat from Mons
(August 1914), this story about the return of the legendary bowmen of
Agincourt to assist the modern army was avidly mistaken for fact by
a traumatized public. But the response of the author of this classic modern
myth to its extraordinary success was sceptical. For him it demonstrated how
susceptible was an age besotted with a narrow rationalism to the blandish-
ments of the wildest kinds of superstitious fantasies. Hence, the irrational
cults of Madame Blavatsky, Mahatmas, psychics, theosophy, Freemasonry,
and the Order of the Golden Dawn (to many of which the early Machen had
felt ambivalent attraction). It confirmed his view that only by reconnecting
itself with its roots as an authentic mystery religion could the Christianity in
which he himself believed, the site of a higher reason, rescue both itself and
the age from their respective illusions.

In his commentary he homed in on an interesting distortion of the
historical facts about Agincourt that had been deliberately introduced into
his story. In reality those famous longbow men had not been English: 'they
were mercenaries from Gwent, my native country, who would appeal to
Mihangel and to saints not known to Saxons – Teilo, Iltyd [sic], Dewi,
Cadwaladyr [sic] Vendigeid'. Why did this matter? Because for Machen, the
roots of the High Anglicanism of rite, symbol, and mystery, whose 'priests
were called to an awful and tremendous hierurgy' in which he believed, were
to be found not in the early post-Augustinian church of the Saxons but in the

early Celtic Church of his native Wales. And so, by choosing to misrepresent those bowmen as English in his story, Machen seems to have been sardonically implying that his readers, the contemporary Anglo-Saxon inhabitants of imperial England, would prefer to be consoled by false superstitions (such as his own fake legend) than spiritually enlightened by a 'Celtic' truth. It is one of those intriguing occasions when Machen briefly assumes the character of a postcolonial writer. Always content to label himself an 'English' writer, he took a comfortably contributionist view of his Welshness, sharing Arnold's opinion that the privilege of the impractical 'Celtic' Welsh was to enrich English cultural identity with a primitive poetic otherworldliness. But, in Machen, that Celtic unearthliness frequently took on a quite un-Arnoldean threatening character.

Like Arnold, he wanted to bring a redeeming 'Celtic' influence to bear on the narrowly rational, practical, and functional 'Anglo-Saxonism' of imperial England. This wish was born of his early subversive dreams, while being educated as a son of empire at Hereford Public School, of returning home to Caerleon, in whose Romano-Celtic past lurked presences that confounded the gospel of the 'civilizing' power of the Classics he was taught at English public school. His late novel *The Secret Glory* (1923) traces precisely such a narrative, albeit in a lurid light. Subject to bullying and worse away at school in the Midlands, the young Welshman Ambrose Meyrick entertains ecstatic visions of escape to the 'faery hills and woods and valleys of the West', the realms of an 'old faith' that originated in such locations as 'the cell of Dewi . . . in the City of the Legions'. During the last decades of his life, Machen devoted much ink to the claim that the legend of the holy grail (which he recognized as a medieval fiction) was a distorted recollection of an ancient Celtic truth: the body of Christ had been laid in a mystic altar subsequently entrusted by the patriarch of Jerusalem to the care of Dewi Sant, the ascetic Celtic monk who was to become patron saint of Wales.

Dewi became for the later Machen the light twin of the dark Pan, a symbol of the benign, ecstatic aspects of those supra-rational and supernatural 'Mysteries' whose sinister form was that of the satyr. 'Sorcery and sanctity,' he wrote, 'are the only realities. Each is an ecstasy, a withdrawal from the common life' ('The White People', 113). His late obsession with Dewi's church found strong fictional form in *The Great Return* (1915), a work that remains one of his best because the mysteries in which it deals are conjured up with much less opulent period portentousness than in many of his more celebrated horror stories.

Yet the latter continue to appeal to popular taste, as they in turn had originated in part from the late Victorian taste for melodrama with a strong decadent flavour. Thus, the novella *The Great God Pan* (1894) features a series of interlinked stories tracing the growing disbelieving fascination of strong-minded bachelors, men of reason, science and public affairs, with the baleful metamorphosis from seductive woman to seductive woman of some neb-ulous, darkly numinous force that degrades men in the act of destroying them. The inaugural motif of *The Great God Pan*, in the form of an innocent young nature-loving girl claimed, and hideously changed, by infernal sub-terranean primal forces and reduced to a seething corruption, is repeated in 'The Shining Pyramid', a short story also indebted to the deductive detective format popularized by Conan Doyle (whose Holmes has his own occult aspects).

Machen's gift for conjuring ominous, Rackham-like landscapes of 'unctu-ous' roots, writhing trees and lush insinuating succulents, of 'wild domed hills and darkling woods' and 'occult valleys', is displayed to advantage in his masterly short novel *The Hill of Dreams*. Its leisurely, discursive, digressive opening neatly offsets the slowly fomenting inner drama as the 'Celt' within the hero Lucian begins to stir. Reluctantly recognizing that even women are not devoid of the sordid cruelty and malice he sees abroad, he withdraws into phantasmagoric recreation of ancient life in all its lush erotic sensuousness in the Roman amphitheatre town of Caermaen, luxuriating, like Huysmans, in becoming 'lord of his own sensations'. This narcissistic process is repeated, after an interval, in a London the dreary desultoriness of whose monotonous streets and boarding houses Machen expertly captures as the urban landscape darkens towards an apocalyptic vision of ordinary lewd, sordid vulgarity. At the long climactic conclusion of the novel, Lucian escapes from this death in life through confronting, in fevered dream of his early years, the inter-linked ecstasy and horror of the kind of transcendent, visionary experience of which Machen himself was such a devout votary. But, unlike the cannier Machen, Lucian falls prey, in the process, to the dark energies that he, as an authentic writer, has inescapably had to tap in himself.

Whereas both Davies and Machen had gravitated to London in search of success, Allen Raine (Anne Adaliza Puddicombe) became a best-seller after returning to her native coastal region of west Wales. And indeed, her popular romances may themselves be classified partly as regional fiction because much of their widespread appeal lay in their local colour. But in this, as in other, respects, Raine had a gift for creative compromise that allowed her to breathe the life of current concerns into the deadening formulae of both the regional and the romance novel without inconveniencing, and thus alienating, the traditional readership of those genres. While *Queen of the Rushes* (1906), one of the best of her eleven novels, conventionally divides its female leads into the wild, wilful, and passionate (Nance) and the quiet and tractable (Gwenifer), with the plot duly favouring the latter, it shrewdly uses this familiar device to highlight such pressing contemporary issues as women's lack of social voice. Traumatized as a child by seeing her mother drown, Gwenifer remains mute for much of the novel until thoroughly socialized by a conventional marriage, while the licence given Nance to bear public witness to, through participation in, the legendary Evan Roberts's evangelical revival of 1904–5 proves deeply troubling to her masterful young husband who rightly comes to associate it with her (unconsummated) infatuation with a dashing young sea captain. And as so often in romance, wild nature – here the sea-soaked coastal landscape of a wind-lashed west Wales – becomes the wild zone of unregulated female energies. Viewed through a postcolonial lens, Raine, whose affectionate, unpatronizing attachment to her natal district is everywhere unmistakeable in her writing, could be said to reclaim for 'native' use the romance form that, in the hands of late eighteenth-century English female novelists, had sometimes exploited a seemingly culture-free Wales as a conveniently primitive, exotic setting.

Even in Raine's work, the Welsh language, suggested by quaint additions and adjustments to standard spoken English, is implicitly (if sympathetically) treated as the language of chapel and peasantry. Yet by the time *Queen of the Rushes* was published, a great renaissance of sophisticated Welsh-language literary culture was already under way, heralded by T. Gwynn Jones's 'Ymadawiad Arthur'. 'Yr Haf' ('The Summer'), by R. Williams Parry, a lavishly gifted rising star, is one of a suite of poems that, in this period, reset the thermostat of Welsh-language poetry by raising its body temperature. It is a filigree of sensuous celebration of the passionate sensibility of youth, and on publication it shocked staid chapel-goers with its manifesto for hedonism as much as it delighted a young generation with its stylized erotic poetic. Within a few years of its debut in 1910, it had also acquired a poignant patina, seeming in retrospect to be the innocent defiant swansong of Edwardian Wales. Modelled on several of Dafydd ap Gwilym's classic poetic debates between elderly killjoy moralists with eyes only for the afterworld and youth giddily content with the sensuous cornucopia of nature and flesh, it was also a virtuosic revelation of *cynghanedd*'s power to eroticize the Welsh language.

One of the poets to capitalize on Williams Parry's breakout from the dreary pious didacticism of late nineteenth-century poetry was his cousin T. H. Parry-Williams, whose 'chromatic' *awdl* of 1915 was a product of his exposure to modernist art while studying first in Freiburg and then in Paris. The medium, he had there learned, could be the message, and in his poem 'Eryri' he explored an exile's spectrum of moods by deconstructing the landscape of his native Snowdonia into a Fauvist kaleidoscope of shifting colours. But content could also still pack a punch, as another gifted young poet, Gwenallt, demonstrated when he wrote 'Y Sant' ('The Saint'). The poem included such a frenzied carnival of the senses that the eisteddfod adjudicators jibbed at publishing it even while conceding its originality. Culturally game-changing though this body of poetry proved to be in its day, all three poets were to radically overhaul their style before later entering their prime, abandoning their early lushness to display widely different talents. Williams Parry added some cool steel and occasional rough political edge to his naturally warm romantic sensibility, while Parry-Williams perfected a casual, low-key, colloquial style of throw-away 'versifying', ostensibly flippant but delicately flavoured with complex ironies. As for Gwenallt, pain at the human degradation of the beloved workforce of his native industrial Swansea valley (his own father was burned to death when an overhead crucible of molten metal spilled its load) eventually resulted in remarkable poems in which lines strung taut by anger hummed with outrage.

In many of their cases, this change in the whole temper and tenor of their poetry was precipitated by the First World War, in which some 40,000 young Welsh men lost their lives and Lloyd George earned the accolade of 'architect of victory'. The only work of stature to have been born directly of the carnage was Gwynn Jones's *Madog*, a long narrative poem heavy with self-protective, conservative, neo-medieval ornament, yet infiltrated by an ominous modern nihilism. It features a young Welsh's prince's flight from a fratricidal world in search of a blessed isle whose very existence is left indeterminate as he is drowned before ever sighting it. The poem fore-shadowed the disillusioned post-war poet's withdrawal into a world of his own in several powerful poems exquisitely fashioned out of Welsh tradition. The response of his fellow-pacifist, the equally disillusioned and psychically wounded Parry-Williams, was diametrically opposite. As noted above, he favoured an anti-bardic verse that disclaimed any pretence to the prestige of grand poetic affirmation while being riddled with an unsettlingly elusive scepticism. Parry-Williams's startlingly innovative personal essays of teasing rumination darkened into whirlpools of equivocation suited to life after

Freud and an Einsteinian universe riddled with relativism. His cousin Williams Parry served in an artillery company while composing some remarkable memorial verses. One – to the young poet Hedd Wyn, who was killed in action – permanently affected the Welsh mind. In the stark chiselled clarity of its dignified restraint, this *englyn* sequence seemed to resemble a classical epigram and treated the death, in a dark trench, of a Welsh-speaking lad from remote rural Gwynedd as an instance of sense-lessly enforced terminal exile.

Shock waves from a distant front came in the form of a curt English telegram to the monoglot Welsh Roberts family in Gwynedd, announcing a son's death from dysentery following his initial wounding at Salonica. That revelation of class and cultural injustice and of the *terribili* of life was never forgotten by one of the daughters, Kate Roberts (1891–1985) who, in 1923, announced her arrival as a remarkable fiction talent with the publication of *O Gors y Bryniau*, a collection of typically terse short stories. Most of the other dozen volumes, duly seasoned with tartness, which she published before her death over sixty years later, were likewise to bear stern, unflinching witness to the epic stoicism of the austere slate-quarrying communities of north-west Wales, whose women, in particular, displayed formidable resilience. Her incomparable mastery of the richly dialectal Welsh of this mountainous area of thin stony soil and subsistence smallholdings enabled her to capture the elusive emotional tonalities of human relations in tight-knit communities besieged by circumstance, as well as to excavate their deep infrastructure. Hers was no static, self-enclosed society but one undergoing radical change. The year-long lock-out at the Penrhyn quarries in 1896 and subsequent heroic three-year strike from 1900 to 1903 had heralded the slow decline of the north Wales slate industry that once could boast it 'roofed the world'. The result was widespread poverty. Quietly registering the results at the level of family and neighbourhood, Roberts's early stories, their prose stripped to the bare bone of life in straitened circumstances, powerfully record a repertoire of survival strategies, including reluctant migration to Liverpool, the States, or to the equally 'foreign', briefly booming, districts of the coal-mining south, and touchingly desperate investment in the opportunities provided by education.

Since the naked loneliness of individual souls is a central theme in Roberts's great stoical work from the outset, it is not surprising that she began to write when teaching in the largely anglicized south Wales coalfield, isolated alike from her native location and (in a sense) from her mother tongue. She can thus ironically be considered an honorary member of that first generation of writing talent belatedly emerging from the dense heterogeneous population of the south-eastern industrial valleys on the eve of the First World War. Traditional English fictional genres proved unequal to the challenge of mediating the experience of these remarkable raw mining settlements, as is evident from the unsuccessful attempt made by the sometime miner Joseph Keating, in his pioneering *Son of Judith* (1900), to marry vivid (if carefully censored) vignettes of the colliers' dangerous life underground to the highly marketable conventional machinery of the romance novel. A year later, when Keir Hardie became Wales's first Labour MP, it was left to R. M. Thomas in *Trewern* to trace the roots of rapidly increasing labour unrest back to the Merthyr Rising and Chartist movements of the 1830s, while in 1911 Charles Ellis Lloyd explored the impact of the new secular gospel of Socialism and the growing attractions of Syndicalism in *Love and the Agitator*.

As the society of the south Wales coalfield came under ever-increasing economic pressure, so a hitherto supposed mutuality of interest between owners and workers was replaced by a new, radically unionized, culture of militant confrontation. This ominous transformation in labour relations is the theme of J. O. Francis's *Change* (1913), a powerful and accomplished three-act play in the Galsworthy mould that enjoyed passing success in its day both in London and in New York. It centres on relations between two generations of a single mining family, the father being a relic of the old world of labour quiescence, while his son Lewis is a committed union activist provoked into a potentially violent clash with the troops sent in during a strike to protect local blacklegs. His life is saved by his gentle, pacific brother Gwilym, who loses his own life in the process, thus branding Lewis as Cain in his father's fiercely unforgiving eyes. In this play, therefore, the development of proletarian consciousness and the worsening of labour conditions culminate in both class and intergenerational conflict that leads to domestic tragedy.

Contemporary with *Change* were culturally controversial Welsh-language plays by D. T. Davies and W. J. Gruffydd. Highlighting fractures in the hegemonic control of the chapels, this social issues theatre broadly in the Ibsenist tradition seemed to promise a burgeoning of Welsh and Anglo-Welsh drama comparable to the efflorescence of Anglo-Irish drama on Dublin's Abbey Theatre stage; and one particularly venturesome young writer, destined to become one of the towering intellectual figures and creative talents of twentieth-century Wales, found this an enticing possibility. Saunders Lewis was born in Wallasey, the son of a distinguished Nonconformist minister, and raised there in an affluent bourgeois Welsh-speaking home. His studies for a degree in English at Liverpool University were interrupted by wartime service as an officer in Flanders and Cyprus, an experience that led to a lifelong love of French and European culture that included a deep interest in writers of the right such as Barrès and Maritain, a notable Thomist and Christian humanist. As a young incipient nationalist, Lewis was so excited by the role of Anglo-Irish drama in preparing the way for the anti-colonial Easter Rising of 1916 that four years later he wrote *The Eve of Saint John*, a fantastical Welsh folk comedy modelled on the resolutely anti-realist works of Synge and Yeats.[4]

The relative failure of this interesting early experiment helped convince Lewis that, lacking its own distinctively idiomatic variant of standard English, Wales could never match Ireland in producing a genuinely indigenous anglophone literature of its own. Thereafter his creative genius was placed entirely at the service of the Welsh language upon whose survival, he became convinced, a viable modern Welsh nationhood depended. Reluctantly persuaded that the language could be saved only by political means – he has been colourfully styled Wales's de Gaulle and a little Welsh Lenin – he joined a handful of other leading young intellectuals in 1925 to form Plaid Cymru (the National Party of Wales). Informing its ideology was the nostalgic vision, brilliantly advanced by Lewis in a series of clinically incisive publications, of Wales as an ancient European nation. Its culture had, he argued, reached its zenith in the fourteenth and fifteenth centuries when a unique corpus of strict-metre poetry (*barddas*) was supported by an enlightened native social élite of minor gentry (yeomanry and squierarchy) and underwritten by Catholic values held in common with the whole of Europe. Lewis deplored the collectivist anglocentrism of the British socialism fervently embraced by what he saw as the degraded rootless proletariat of the anglophone industrial valleys. And he also despised the fading British liberalism of Nonconformist Wales whose promotion of economic individualism and social ambition had resulted only in a crass materialistic philistinism and the cynical political opportunism of a Lloyd George who had abandoned Wales for Britain and empire.

The theatre offered the young Lewis a forum for consolidating his nostalgic conservative vision of a regulated and graduated society. Set in the early nineteenth century, his *Gwaed yr Uchelwyr* ('The Blood of the Gentry', mischievously mistranslated by some reviewers as 'The Blood of the Highbrows') celebrated the sterling qualities of an old Welsh yeoman family. Its loss of status has, it seems, in no way weakened its fierce fidelity to ancestral land now largely in the possession of English or Scottish arrivistes, nor lessened its sense of social obligation. It is this *noblesse oblige* that prompts the family's young daughter, Luned, to reject true love in a self-sacrificial gesture deliberately reminiscent of the Corneillean tragedy Lewis so revered.

Lewis's mistrust of the unfettered individualism promoted by liberal capitalism found strikingly complex creative expression in *Monica* (1930), a revolutionary novella whose frank treatment of the turbulent sexual desires of women as much as men provoked social outrage. It brought prostitution and syphilis directly into the respectable bourgeois milieu of a suburban Swansea whose underworld of lurking fantasy and frustration it thus exposed. The novella is a powerful distillation of Lewis's ambivalent feelings about the liberated New Woman, admiration and sympathy darkening into disapproval. In her headlong disregard of kinship ties, marriage vows, and social bonds, Monica (a wistful fantasist like Emma Bovary) is reminiscent of Blodeuwedd. The latter is the figure from the Mabinogion out of whose socially disruptive legend (the tragically transgressive struggle for sexual fulfilment and authentic self-realization of a woman created out of flowers to satisfy a prince) Lewis had begun, in 1923, to fashion a remarkable verse drama resonant with contemporary relevance. It would not be completed until 1948.

The aggravated tensions in this period between women's awakening sensibility and their dependent social position also received memorable attention from Dorothy Edwards in two singular short story collections, *Rhapsody* (1927) and *Winter Sonata* (1928). Disconcertingly dispassionate in tone while vaguely sinister with foreboding, her stylishly enigmatic fiction includes studies in variant forms of male narcissism and possessiveness, frequently centring on claustrophobic instances of psycho-social control. With their faintly abstracted air, the stories can seem puzzlingly full of non-sequiturs and inconsequentialities, and in many of them musical performance provides a code for subtle emotional transactions between the sexes. A desolating air of isolation and loneliness haunts several of them. 'Cultivated People', for example, delicately traces the web of unspoken relations between a gifted German musician and three of her acquaintances – a bachelor and a married couple. A frustrated émigrée unhappily content with her own company, Miss Wolf finds herself the reluctant object of both men's admiration, to the cold fury of the husband's neglected wife. The delicate mysteriousness of these narratives is enhanced by natural descriptions that occasionally resemble Chirico's paintings in their sensuous vacuity: 'A cart came slowly up the hill, pulled by a white horse walking uncertainly on the loose stones of the road' (164).

In retrospect, the tragically short-lived Edwards can be viewed as a forerunner of the remarkable generation of talent to emerge from south Wales during the thirties. Another such harbinger was Rhys Davies, who by contrast went on to a lengthy, distinguished career of fifty years as a polished prolific novelist and internationally recognized master of fastidiously crafted short stories. A native of Blaenclydach, a minor tributary valley of the Rhondda Fawr, Davies was a boy of nine when the epochal Tonypandy riots erupted in 1910. And no sooner had he left home for London in 1921 than his valley was desolated by the General Strike of 1926 and the protracted industrial action of the heroically resistant miners. Yet his writerly imagination remained largely impervious to these epic events in labour history that so indelibly marked the minds of his younger contemporaries Idris Davies, Glyn Jones, Gwyn Jones, Lewis Jones, and Gwyn Thomas. Unlike them, he was not interested in recording the momentous period when his Rhondda 'was a major factor in the industrialization of the planet'. All his life Davies was to be a natural loner, an elegant misfit destined, not least by his homosexual orientation, to haunt the margins of any established group or society.

The son of a shopkeeper, Rhys Davies was indifferent to the proletarian sympathies of other, politically committed, writers of his age and background, and he cherished the aesthetic detachment he believed timely, permanent departure from the 'dour valley' of his upbringing had granted him. Insulated by a protective and carefully protected distance that lent disenchantment to his writer's eye and turned his turbulent native valley into a still 'form restrictive as an urn', he could return to the Rhondda in cool imagination. This he proceeded to do in his very first novel, The Withered Root (1927), a lurid portrayal of a Welsh preacher's guilty descent into carnality and terminal mental derangement that was indebted both to the Grand Guignol theatre, then enjoying a brief vogue in London, and to the Gothic grotesqueries of Caradoc Evans's seminal collection My People.

Indeed, The Withered Root is clearly a melodramatic account of the great Evan Roberts Revival of 1904–6, as viewed through the distorting lens of Caradoc Evans's calculatedly defamatory fiction, and so involves a discursive socio-cultural deformation that neatly allegorizes the major change, during the period with which this chapter has been concerned, from the image of Wales as a Nonconformist nation to that of Wales as a socialist proletarian nation. Not only did writers play a crucial role in the formation of both of these images but the displacement of the one by the other was a fraught process that, while obviously powered by historical circumstances, was also textually mediated both in Welsh and in English by authors such as Caradoc

Evans and R. Williams Parry, and by Rhys Davies, whose novel *The Withered Root* can usefully be read as a seminal instance of the literal writing off, by an aggressive emergent class of creative writers, of the residual class of preachers who had been masters of the word, and therefore of the social world, for much of the previous century. Henceforth it would be Dylan Thomas, Saunders Lewis, and their contemporaries who would be the new lords of language in both Welsh and English.

Notes

1. T. Gwynn Jones's poem 'Ymadawiad Arthur' ('The Passing of Arthur') won the chair at the National Eisteddfod held in Bangor in 1902. It was subsequently published as part of a collection of his verse, *Ymadawiad Arthur a Chaniadau Ereill* (Caernarfon: Cwmni y Cyhoeddwyr Cymreig, 1910).
2. Andrew Webb, *Edward Thomas and World Literary Studies: Anglocentrism and English Literature* (Cardiff: University of Wales Press, 2013).
3. Arthur Machen, *The Great God Pan, The Shining Pyramid, The White People,* Library of Wales (Cardigan: Parthian, 2010). See also Susan Aronstein's discussion of Arthur Machen's 'fantasy fiction' in Chapter 31 of this volume.
4. For further discussion of Saunders Lewis's work as a dramatist and writer, see Chapter 26 in this volume.

22

The Short Story in the Twentieth Century

MICHELLE DEININGER

In his well-known exploration of a model of the short story, Edgar Allan Poe underlined the importance of 'unity of effect or impression' and thereby set in motion an aesthetic categorization of the form that is still influential today. In many ways, however, this model does not fit the short story as it has flourished in Wales. Indeed, the term 'short story' is perhaps representative of a historical product of the late nineteenth century onwards, characterized by the well-wrought and atmospheric stories of Hawthorne and Poe and their literary descendants. The short story in Wales is as enmeshed in constructions of national identity and the scars of industrialization as the Victorian novel was for England. Through language which is lithe and vivid, it profoundly engages with Welsh experience, from the hearth to the coal-field, and has become, throughout its development in the twentieth century, a genre for exploring belonging, loss, childhood, and alienation.

The term 'short fiction' is perhaps more appropriate than 'short story' in the context of Wales, accommodating anything from the lightly drawn sketch to the industrial autobiography. These terms are used interchangeably in this chapter, but always with the sense of inclusivity that the broader term of short fiction suggests. In many respects, the tradition of oral poetry and its lyrical evocation of experience, handed down through Welsh-speaking society, helps to explain the adoption of the short story genre by so many Welsh authors, whether writing in Welsh or English and however indirect their relationship to the Welsh language. The short story, with its focus on the suppleness of language, seems closer to this traditional verse form than to the novel.

The dominance of English in the modern short fiction of Wales is partly a result of changes to educational policy in Wales at the end of the nineteenth century. The Westminster-led reform of Welsh education, specifically the 1889 Education Act, ensured that, irrespective of the language spoken at home, all children would be educated in English, a change which had far-reaching effects on literary production in Wales. Before this shift in legislative policy, the notorious findings of the 'Blue Books', or the *Reports of the Commissioners of Inquiry into the State of Education in Wales* (1847), had already laid the groundwork for the promotion of English-language education and its supposedly 'civilizing' properties. The legacy of the racist, ill-informed, and derogatory language of the Blue Books would reverberate through women's writing, in particular, in representations which challenged the reports' negative depiction of Welsh women. However, the first half of the twentieth century, often referred to as the heyday of the short story in Wales, is associated mainly with the work of male writers from working-class areas who deployed the form to explore the harsh realities of life in the increasingly industrialized valleys. Writers such as Caradoc Evans (1878–1945) and Glyn Jones (1905–95) would be part of this first wave of English-educated writers from Welsh-speaking families.

In accounts of the anglophone literature of the twentieth century in Wales, Evans and his controversial collection *My People* (1915) looms large. Glyn Jones, writing in his influential book *The Dragon Has Two Tongues* (1968, 2001) and drawing upon the work of Gwyn Jones, notes: 'For anyone to have spoken about the Anglo-Welsh short story before 1915, when *My People* appeared, would have been almost an impossibility.'[1] Until the 'flowering' of the mid-1930s, Gwyn Jones himself called Evans 'the most important figure of the Anglo-Welsh literary movement',[2] a movement that Raymond Garlick originally defined as 'writing in the English language by a Welshman'.[3] While this definition and its focus on male writers has shifted somewhat with the introduction of the phrase 'Welsh writing in English', the term 'Anglo-Welsh' can still be useful to identify this group of writers who experienced this fracture from their mother tongue. What this chapter aims to achieve is to survey the evocative and extremely well-crafted writing of some key Anglo-Welsh short-fiction writers, as well as evaluating the impact of anthologies and drawing on some examples of Welsh-language fiction. At the same time, there will be a recurring focus on female proponents of the form, drawing attention to writers whose contribution has not yet been fully recognized.

The Politics of Anthologizing

Women have traditionally been excluded from a history of short fiction in Wales. This has occurred for a number of reasons: their choice of genre (often the romance or rural-based domestic fiction), their focus on the minutiae of female experience, a lack of sustained publishing in anthologies, and the politics of national identity, especially if these women were not originally born in Wales. Tony Brown, one of the few critics to engage fully with the form, examines women writers included in Jane Aaron's path-breaking anthology *A View Across the Valley: Short Stories by Women from Wales, c. 1850–1950* (1999), commenting that there is 'nothing . . . of industrialism, nothing about the huge shifts from the boom years at the end of the nineteenth-century to the disasters of the 1930s, nothing of the struggles of working-class families to survive'.[4] Yet, in many respects, the shifts that Brown underlines are registered repeatedly in the short stories of this period by both men and women, from the fictions of Allen Raine (1836–1908) onwards.

The way in which a nation's literature is anthologized is often a marker of its confidence; at the same time, it can put forward to the world a vision which is distorted. From the 1930s onwards, there were popular editions of anglophone Welsh short stories, beginning with Faber's *Welsh Short Stories* in 1937. Alongside some now familiar names, such as Gwyn Jones and Dylan Thomas, this collection features a significant amount of writing by women, including Siân Evans, Eiluned Lewis, Allen Raine, Kate Roberts, and Dorothy Edwards, as well as two novellas – Hilda Vaughan's *A Thing of Nought* and Margiad Evans's *Country Dance*. After this initial volume, several other important anthologies were published, including collections edited by Gwyn Jones for Penguin (1940) and Oxford University Press (1956). Blackwood-born Gwyn Jones (1907–99), a graduate of University College, Cardiff, and editor of *The Welsh Review*, was himself an important proponent of the Welsh short story, including three collections: *The Buttercup Field* (1945), *The Still Waters* (1948), and *Shepherd's Hey* (1953). Yet, while Jones's edited anthologies drew attention to texts which would have gone unnoticed by a more general readership, particularly outside Wales, they also had their drawbacks. Jane Aaron, for example, has emphasized that the endemic lack of recognition women writers have traditionally encountered is 'partly the consequence of the inconsistent manner in which they have been treated by former editors of Welsh short story anthologies'.[5] It was not until the publication of Aaron's *A View Across the Valley* (1999) that perceptions of women's contribution to the short story form altered significantly, at least in some circles. Aaron drew attention to the many voices that were developing the form from the middle of the nineteenth century onwards. Particular examples include Somerset-born but Llandeilo-based writer Anne Beale's 'Mad Moll', a standalone piece from the hybrid travelogue-cum-romance, *The Vale of the Towey* (1843), and the work of Welsh-language activist, Sara Maria Saunders, in her interconnected tales of village life in *Welsh Rural Sketches* (1896–9).

Re-visioning the Canon: Caradoc Evans, Allen Raine, and Marginality

Any account of the short story would, of course, be remiss if it did not, at some point, discuss Caradoc Evans's infamous collection *My People* (1915). At the time, the stories were strikingly different and, as has been documented substantially in criticism since its publication, inflammatory, and, to some, offensive then and now. *My People*, with its idiosyncratic characterization of patriarchal rural families and its heavy-handed biblical overtones, certainly provided the next generation of short story writers with a model to explore Wales and its culture, Rhys Davies being no exception in his early stories. However, it would be misleading to say this was the only viable model available to writers. If newspapers of the late nineteenth and early twentieth centuries are any indicator of taste, the short story was already immensely popular in Wales. *The Cardiff Times and South Wales Weekly News*, for instance, heavily advertised its forthcoming publication of Allen Raine's 'Gibbet and Cross', a story of greed and the frailty of human relationships, written a matter of weeks before the author's death.[6] Raine's reputation was infamously savaged by Caradoc Evans and her writing deemed an ephemeral 'sandcastle dynasty'. It is here that the politics of genre become significant – Raine was a writer of sentimental romances, of stories which focused on human relationships, romantic love, and emotion, which were regarded as a marginal subdivision of an already marginal form.

The short story in the twentieth century, as a whole, has often been associated with experiences that are, in some sense, marginal, written in a genre which deals with loss, loneliness, exile, and dispossession. Tony Brown explores the relationship between marginality and Welsh identity in the short story, drawing upon the work of Frank O'Connor and Clare Hanson. In *The Lonely Voice* (1962), O'Connor emphasizes the lack of a hero in the short story and the recurring feature of the 'submerged population group'.[7] Clare Hanson pushes O'Connor's original ideas further:

> The short story is a vehicle for different kinds of knowledge, knowledge which may be in some way at odds with the 'story' of dominant culture. The formal properties of the short story – disjunction, inconclusiveness, obliquity – connect with its ideological marginality and with the fact that the form may be used to express something suppressed/repressed in mainstream literature.[8]

Hanson's further claim, that 'the short story is or has been notably a form of the margins, a form which is in some sense ex-centric, not part of official or "high" cultural hegemony', seems significant if we look at fields of literature that have been traditionally overlooked or neglected by the mainstream, especially a field such as Welsh writing in English. Raine's 'Home, Sweet Home', for example, is an emotive critique of both the institutions of the state and the family in failing to care adequately for the elderly, infirm, and mentally ill, especially women. Raine's 'Flow on, Thou Shining River' is another subtly political story which examines the impact of industrialization on women's experience. The elderly Hughes sisters, Miss Lavinia and Miss Mary Ella, live at no. 10, Glenarth Road, Carny-coed, looked after by their servant. Raine quickly draws attention to the difference between the admittedly sentimentalized Carny-coed of the past, 'a little sleepy country town, nestling in the trees, and surrounded by sunny meadows, where the soft-flowing river made continual music', and the 'smoky blot upon the landscape' it becomes, where 'furnaces roared, steam-engines puffed, and the throb of machinery filled the air', disrupted by the discovery of a coal seam running beneath the town.[9] The story is a work of mourning for a way of life that has come to an end. The two women seek self-induced exile in London when their village changes beyond recognition, returning years later to the other side of town, their beloved house now the site of a warehouse. While Raine does, at times, make use of overblown and excessively senti-mental language, we cannot sweep her aside as Caradoc Evans did; she should be recognized as a transitional yet foundational short story writer who articulated, through the romance, many of the key concerns and pre-occupations of the women writers who would come after her.

The Short Story in Welsh: D. J. Williams and Kate Roberts

The Welsh-language short story has a distinct trajectory and separate history compared to that of its anglophone sister. Two authors with a considerable output of translated stories, D. J. Williams (1885–1970) and Kate Roberts (1891–1985), who were also friends, bridge the divide between the two traditions, allowing both Welsh and English readers a glimpse into their rich imaginative worlds. While D. J. Williams was born earlier than the other male writers considered in this chapter, his influence on Welsh writing, including the genre of the short story, has been profound and long-lasting. Born in Rhydcymerau, Carmarthenshire, his experiences included both work as a collier and in education at the University College of Wales, Aberystwyth and then Jesus College, Oxford, and a career in teaching. He was a founding member of Plaid Cymru, with Saunders Lewis and Lewis Valentine, and spent nine months in Wormwood Scrubs (1936–7) for setting fire to some of the huts of the Bombing School at Penyberth, near Pwllheli, as a political protest. Williams's endeavours in the short story were extensive, including his trilogy of short stories, *Storïau'r Tir* ('Stories of the Land', 1936, 1941, 1949). As in his important work *Hen Dŷ Ffarm* ('The Old Farmhouse', 1953), first published in Welsh and then translated into English eight years later through the UNESCO scheme for raising awareness of the literature of smaller countries, Williams is consistently focused on what he calls his *milltir sgwâr*, or 'square mile', of home and community. In 'A Good Year' ('Blwyddyn Lwyddiannus'), published in the Faber anthology a year after its publication in *Storïau'r Tir Glas* ('Stories of the Green Land', 1936), he explores the highs and lows experienced by Rachel, who has been widowed for fifteen years and must rely on the annual sale of her cow's calf to provide the rent on her home, Pant y Bril. Alive to the way poverty affects older women, as is Kate Roberts, Williams deftly engages lyrical prose to evoke Rachel's burgeoning sense of hope, as she sees 'young growth, on currant bush, gooseberry, and the red rose climbing up the house. She looked at it all, this miracle of sudden birth, as if she saw it for the first time, unconsciously drawing it all into her own life.'[10] There is an unremitting devotion to Wales which spills out of Williams's writing, even in translation. In *Hen Dŷ Ffarm*, he writes: 'Although I have spent three quarters of my life far out of sight of it, and have lived in a kind and engaging society, my heart has never once left its homeland.'[11] In contrast, 'The Mecca of the Nation' features a cunning guest-house landlady, Catherine Lloyd, and her guest, Mr Dogwell Jones, QC, an aspiring MP. Williams carefully juxtaposes the political scheming of Jones with his landlady's domestic manipulations, including pumping Jones for free legal advice over late-night coffee and chocolates, only to scrupulously include these on his itemized bill. As a whole, the story gives some indication of the range of Williams's subject matter, as well as underlining his nationalist political beliefs.

The publication of Kate Roberts's *A Summer Day* (1946) marks the first substantial volume of her work to be available to an English-speaking readership. As certain stories had already been published in *Life and Letters Today*, *The Welsh Review*, and the Faber and Penguin anthologies, these publications suggest, as Katie Gramich notes, that 'Roberts's work was already gaining a reputation both in Wales and England at the time.'[12] Joseph P. Clancy's edition, *The World of Kate Roberts* (1991), with its careful and sensitive translations, opens up Roberts's work further, enabling the English-speaking reader the opportunity to explore the richness of her work. While Roberts is rightly renowned as a short story writer, she is best known for her evocation in all her fiction, short stories and novels, of the inner and domestic lives of women, especially from working-class backgrounds. She is especially sensitive to the way poverty shapes and (de)forms experience, and often writes of the implications of financial insecurity in old age, or, as Clancy puts it, 'what the struggle against poverty reveals of human nature and the human condition'.[13] One of Kate Roberts's best-known stories is 'The Quilt', taken from her 1937 collection, *Ffair Gaeaf* ('Winter Fair'). The quilt of the title is one of the few items Ffebi Williams holds onto when her husband is made bankrupt, losing the business, their house, and most of their possessions. When Ffebi first sees the quilt, an image of luxury in a world punctuated by creeping poverty, it is the kind which makes 'everyone's mouth water', made of 'thick white wool, with stripes across it, stripes of every colour'.[14] It is, just like Rhys Davies's depiction of the silk garment, in 'Nightgown' (discussed below), an item so beautiful that it offers Ffebi a means to transcend her poverty, if only temporarily. At the end of the story, Ffebi is desperately clutching the quilt as the house is cleared of all its furniture, herself also a symbol of an era now passed.

Glyn Jones, Education and Alienation

Turning now to one of the major proponents of the anglophone short story in Wales, Glyn Jones (1905–95) was born in Merthyr Tydfil to a Welsh-speaking family. While this was a working-class area, Jones was not himself of this class, as his father was employed in a clerical role in the Post Office. He was educated in English, trained as a teacher at St Paul's College, Cheltenham, and worked in the slums of Cardiff. His 1937 collection, *The Blue Bed*, proved him to be a subtle and innovative writer. He wrote particularly eloquently from the viewpoint of the child, something which is especially clear in a story such as 'The Boy in the Bucket', which explores the inner imaginative life of Ceri, a boy who falls asleep in chapel and dreams he is travelling in one of the containers, transported by overhead wires, which carry dirt away from the colliery. Jones's attention to detail in his creation of characters using warmth and wry humour is apparent from the outset, from Barachaws ('bread-and-cheese') the roadman, 'clearing the metallic phlegm out of his throat for the singing', to Jones the dayschool teacher who has 'scabs in his hair and ... go[es] behind the blackboard to pick them off'.[15] As Tony Brown argues in his introduction to the *Collected Stories*, Jones was compelled 'towards loving compassionate at-one-ness with others in the community, however disreputable, however unattractive'.[16]

Jones's emphasis on the symbiosis of humanity and the landscape is apparent in a story such as 'I Was Born in the Ystrad Valley', in which he describes the houses built next to the river which runs down the valley as 'long rows of grey streets spiney with vertebral chimneys'.[17] However, in this story it is protagonist Wyn's insights regarding his education and relation to literature that are especially striking. The disorienting effects of a university education result in the some-what bitterly comic label of a 'collier's son with the outlook of a French aesthete' (4). In speaking of the literature he is taught, he realizes, in hindsight, that 'I know, rather with thankfulness than with disappointment and bitterness, that I am an outsider, that this literature was not written for me or for anyone like me' (5). It is this separation and loneliness, ideas which are directly related to Frank O'Connor's thesis about 'submerged population groups', which in many ways articulate the experience of writers who, if not exactly working-class themselves, knew first-hand how a middle-class, English education provided them with a profound sense of alienation.

While a university education, for the most part, is a fairly common feature of the experience of the male writers discussed in this chapter, for women it is less so, and this impacts upon their imaginative opportunities. The alienated academic, for example, is not often found in the short stories of women, aside from women writers based in Wales but not born there. These women often explore this experience through the eyes of a male character, such as in Bertha Thomas's Oxford-educated Elwyn Rosser in 'The Way He Went' or Emily Pearson Finnemore's disaffected schoolmaster in 'The Ghost of Aunt Ann'. Kathleen Freeman, a Birmingham-born, Cardiff-based academic is one of the few women writers to explore this position fully. Alienation, in Freeman's academic fictions, derives from a lack of meaningful relationships rather than from scholarship. In the case of Miss Bellamy, in 'The Fraying of the Thread', this lack imbues her with 'a certain restlessness – a sense of loss' while she experiences 'joy in [her] work'.[18] In studying, Miss Bellamy has 'been able to devote [her] whole energies to learning, and to avoid trivial daily intercourse with [her] kind' (198), a rare opportunity for women generally.

Beyond the Valleys: Rhys Davies, Dylan Thomas, Alun Lewis, and Leslie Norris

As we have seen, writing from the 1930s onwards is often characterized by loss and exile, whether in the form of a character's experiences or in the fact of the writer being physically away from home at the time of composition. Rhys Davies (1901–78) is perhaps one of the most prolific and important short story writers of the twentieth century. Born in Blaenclydach, in the Rhondda valley, Davies was, from the outset, an outsider: 'a grocer's son in a coal-mining community ... a Welshman who left Wales to write about his homeland from London ... gay in, initially, a heavily masculine and homo-phobic context, and, later, in a freer but still repressive, London'.[19] Although Davies had no higher education, he read voraciously and was influenced in his early years by Caradoc Evans and D. H. Lawrence, the latter of whom he met. Collections of his stories include *The Things Men Do* (1936), *A Finger in Every Pie* (1942), *The Trip to London* (1946), *Boy with a Trumpet* (1949), *The Darling of her Heart* (1958), and *The Chosen One* (1967). One of Davies's most haunting stories is 'Nightgown', a tale of Mrs Rees, wife of Walt and mother of five sons, who all work in the pits. Once she has given up hope of having a daughter, she is left with the recurrent trials of trying to feed and wash these men, but they suck the life out of her as fast as they empty the kitchen cupboards. When she spots a beautiful silk nightgown in the draper's window, she decides to have a little something for herself and scrimps for just under a year to pay for it. The nightgown is, like Ffebi's quilt, an emblem of beauty in a masculinized world which is a relentless cycle of poverty and hard work. When Mrs Rees dies, mainly from malnutrition, she is dressed in the nightgown and is transformed. However, her husband is so oblivious that he thinks the nightgown is part of the medical benefits they receive from paying insurance and promptly starts to look for a second wife to fill her place. Women, Davies seems to be arguing, are interchangeable and replaceable in this brutal vision of working-class Wales.

Another prolific contemporary of the period, Dylan Thomas (1914–53) may not need much introduction. However, it is important to note that he was born in Swansea and, like Glyn Jones, though he witnessed poverty, he was actually part of the middle classes, due to his father's profession as a senior English master at Swansea Grammar School. Thomas was also one of the few male short story writers to avoid the burden of teaching as a career. Famous for his collection *Portrait of the Artist as a Young Dog* (1940), Thomas wrote numerous stories which stretch the fabric of language to its very limits, as well as capturing, with exquisite word-play, the perspective of childhood. One of his popular anthologized stories, 'A Story', plays on the fact that nothing much actually happens in the narrative, which opens with:

> If you can call it a story. There's no real beginning or end and there's very little in the middle. It is all about a day's outing, by charabanc, to Porthcawl, which, of course, the charabanc never reached, and it happened when I was so high and much nicer.[20]

Another memorable story is 'Extraordinary Little Cough', the title of which plays on the surname of one of the children featured, George Hooping. At the beginning of the story, Thomas manages to encapsulate the almost limitless expanse of childhood imagination within a few lines, following the potentially tragic trajectory of the children's apple cores, from catching in a bicycle wheel to an imaginary hanging as punishment for accidentally killing the cyclist, who, thankfully, avoids being hit by a lorry. A few lines cannot do Thomas justice, but his literary legacy lives on with sufficient vigour for him to remain always in print and frequently read, studied, anthologized, and broadcast.

Acclaimed war poet Alun Lewis (1915–44) was born in Cwmaman, near Aberdare, and attended the University College of Wales, Aberystwyth, and the University of Manchester. Unsuccessful in his ambition to be a journalist, he earned a living through supply teaching. Despite having pacifist sympathies, he enlisted with the Royal Engineers and was posted to India and later Burma, where he died from a bullet wound to the head, fired from his own gun. These military years spurred Lewis into writing some of his finest war poetry, as well as a collection of short stories, *The Last Inspection* (1943). His posthumous collection, *In the Green Tree* (1948), includes two of his most memorable Indian-set stories, 'Ward "O" 3 (b)' and 'The Orange Grove'. The former follows the interconnected experiences of a group of wounded soldiers, from various ranks and social classes, waiting to hear if they will be allowed by the medical board to go home, while the latter story focuses on the journey of Staff-Captain Beale, who is scouting out an area of central India for an army exercise during a period of extreme civil unrest after the arrest of Gandhi and Nehru. As his driver leaves him to find eggs for their meal, he feels, in a rendering of isolation typical of Lewis, 'all the loneliness of India about him and he knew he had never been more alone'.[21] One of his Welsh-set stories which repays further reflection is 'The Housekeeper', a story which closely details the life of Myfanwy, mother to two boys, Mervyn and Jackie, wife to an unemployed husband, Penry, and carer to her husband's elderly mother, whose life is 'like being caught in a winding belt in the colliery, going round and round, never getting loose . . . '[22] Penry's unhealthy obsession with the sow, which dies giving birth, is the nightmarish reversal of D. J. Williams's life-providing calf. The dead sow is a physical reminder of the pointless and painful frustrations of their lives. There are, as with many of the other stories discussed in this chapter, glimpses of dark humour. When Mervyn confesses to his mother that he has seen 'Granny [with] her head in the gas oven again' (105), his mother advises him to 'leave her to it' if he catches her again.

Leslie Norris (1921–2006) was, at first, known for his poetry, but his reputation as a short story writer grew with the publication of his two collections, *Sliding* (1978) and *The Girl from Cardigan* (1988). 'Waxwings', for example, published in *Sliding*, was awarded the Katherine Mansfield prize for its quality. Norris was born, as were so many of the key male writers of the century, in Merthyr Tydfil, and taught in both England and the United States. While he wrote extensively about his homeland in his prose and poetry, he did not return to live in Wales again after 1948. As a result, Norris is often seen as a figure of exile, writing about his Welsh roots but never returning to them. In some respects, the lyricism of his writing and his repeated return to Wales in the pages of his fictions parallel the more recent work of Canadian-born contemporary writer Tristan Hughes, who was brought up on Anglesey and frequently writes about childhood, as well as exile and belonging, in his short fiction and novels.

Both of Leslie Norris's short story collections draw extensively upon his childhood in Merthyr before the Second World War and often deploy a child narrator. The title story of *Sliding* demonstrates Norris's keen eye for the materiality of childhood from the perspective of Bernard, from an image of a frozen tap in the yard which has an irreverent 'tongue of glass pok[ing] out of its mouth' to a boy called Albert Evans whose inner thighs are 'chafed raw' from the cold, covered in painful, 'weeping cracks'.[23] In 'The Girl from Cardigan', unemployment is rife, so Selwyn's mother leans on her cousin, a town councillor, to find Selwyn a job. The story is comically observed, never more so than at the point when Selwyn takes over the distribution of stationery supplies and begins to write 'neatly and ostentatiously' in a blue notebook, recording every item the councillors take.[24] In fact, these are 'meaningless ciphers' (10) which Selwyn uses to lever himself into a higher-level position. The story critiques the small-minded politics of the local council but also draws attention to the way power is formed through outward shows of wealth and status, such as Selwyn's new clothes, shoes, and haircuts.

Exile and Community: Dorothy Edwards, Margiad Evans, and Lynette Roberts

As we turn to women writers from the 1920s onwards, similar preoccupations begin to emerge – of loneliness, exile, and dislocation. Perhaps one of the richest and yet most introspective collections to have come out of the 1920s is Dorothy Edwards's *Rhapsody* (1927). Christopher Meredith, in his foreword to the Library of Wales edition, notes the predominance of 'extremely con-trolled studies of constrained desire, loneliness and incomplete relationships' in her stories.[25] Again, we are reminded of the loneliness which, as Frank O'Connor argued, defines many modern short stories. Claire Flay writes eloquently of Edwards's position within Welsh culture and her relationship with form: 'Doubly marginalized as a woman and as a Welsh writer, debarred from the patriarchal leisured society that she chose to depict and the male-dominated work-class society from which she came, the short story became Edwards's chosen vehicle.'[26] One of her most famous stories, 'The Conquered', explores gendered power relations with great subtlety and is also the only story to have a distinctly Welsh setting. The story interweaves the physical remnants of Roman colonization with psychological conquest. The English narrator, Frederick Trenier, visits his aunt 'on the borders of Wales', where his flirtations with a Welsh neighbour, Gwyneth, come to nothing.[27] As one of the recurrent images of the story is the Roman road which runs close to the aunt's property, the story is an exploration of the damage caused by imperialist and patriarchal attitudes, most obviously to women. The fact that most of Edwards's stories are narrated by a male voice suggests that she was attempting to deconstruct patriarchal ideology from within. As a whole, Edwards's stories seem to be about the transitory nature of human relationships and the failure to make meaningful connections, and it is this aspect of her writing which aligns her with a modernist tradition.

Lynette Roberts (1909–1995), in some respects, pushes the boundaries of Welsh identity to its most generous limits. Born in Argentina to Welsh parents, Roberts attended art school in London before she married Keidrych Rhys, a significant Welsh literary journalist, editor, and poet, and began her life in Llanybri, Carmarthenshire, during the Second World War. Roberts's stories are brief vignettes and are more like snapshots of rural life than a sustained exploration. Her seven short stories form a preface to the essay 'An Introduction to Village Dialect' (1944), in which she 'endeavour[ed] to prove that [contemporary Welsh dialect] has both a tradition and a root' and traces a variety of sayings and folkloric traditions through texts from various periods of Welsh history.[28] While Patrick McGuinness has argued that her poetry constitutes a 'cosmopolitan's claim to a rooted culture that is also a culture of rootedness', her short fiction has similar preoccupations.[29] 'Tiles', the second of 'Seven Stories', begins in the middle of a discussion between the narrator, who is unwell, and her neighbour, Rosie. Rosie lights a fire, using traditional materials (called 'pele'), and then attempts to scour the floor, prompting the narrator to complain about having floorboards instead of tiles, as 'almost every cottage has them but mine'.[30] The conversational exchange between the narrator and Rosie prompts Rosie to recollect the practice of inscribing patterns on tiled floors, which could be read as an act of preservation for customs and traditions now passing, mirrored by Roberts's interest in fading architectural styles and practices. Roberts's pared-back style and use of a collage of voices recalls the practices of modernist classics such as T. S. Eliot's *The Waste Land*. Her poetry has been examined by Laura Wainwright for its modernist preoccupations, not only with exile and marginality, but for the creative possibilities a liminal Anglo-Welsh identity could offer.[31] Her short fictions require a similar exploration, which takes into account her multifaceted identity.

Margiad Evans is another important outsider in the history of women's writing in Wales. Having spent some of her childhood on the Welsh border, in Herefordshire, Evans fell in love with the country, its landscapes and traditions. The adoption of the name 'Margiad Evans' over her real name of Peggy Eileen Whistler gives some indication of her desire to align herself with Welsh culture, even if she could not or did not want to belong fully to it. The tension between English and Welsh identities is played out with particular violence in *A Country Dance,* a novella in essence, although its inclusion in the 1937 Faber anthology underlines its familial relationship to the short story. The stories in her collection *The Old and the Young* (1948) are exquisite, lyrical pieces which explore landscape and the imagination in ways which point towards neo-romanticism. Clare Morgan, for example, sees Evans as 'bas[ing] her relation with the Welsh border, that doubly liminal land ... on the Neo-Romantic ideals of sublimity, wholeness and transcendence'.[32] At the same time, Evans is alive to the almost overwhelming emptiness of the landscape, an atmosphere of loneliness that she evokes especially convincingly in 'People of his Pasture' and with some humour in 'The Old Woman and the Wind'. What all three writers share is an ability to weave elements of the past, whether personal histories or grand narratives of civilization or mythology, into tightly constructed narratives of the present, with the precision of poetry. Later in the century, in the 1970s, writers such as Elizabeth

Baines and Ivonne Piper would demonstrate a similar ability to push language to its utmost, rewriting their respective landscapes and communities through an ecofeminist lens.[33] In the 1980s and 1990s, short story collections published by Leonora Brito, Catherine Merriman, Clare Morgan, Siân James, and Glenda Beagan changed the direction of the form further, exploring issues such as race, female identity, ageing, and Welsh-language learning. Brito stands out, in particular, as a voice of the experience of Welsh people of colour, an area of Welsh writing in English that deserves to take a much more central position in our understanding of the history of the form.

Other Forms of Knowledge: Queer Desire in the Short Story

As Clare Hanson has argued, the short story can be a potent genre for different types of knowledge which call into question established social norms. One area of Welsh women's short fiction which has attracted the least attention to date is the queer short story. If Welsh female short fiction writers are marginalized, then Welsh lesbian subjectivity is even more so, especially as lesbian identity and desire are so heavily coded that they remain virtually unseen. The character of Ruth in Dorothy Edwards's 'The Conquered' is a case in point; once 'very lively and something of a tomboy' (45) and described as more 'like her father' (51), Ruth has now 'become very quiet' (45) and conforms to the expectations of her gender. This depiction might now be recognized as a portrayal of a submerged lesbian identity. Female characters in queer short fiction are, again, often isolated and alienated – from themselves, their communities, and wider friendship networks. Kathleen Freeman's Miss Bellamy, the scholar in 'The Fraying of the Thread', remarks that she has 'met with so little genuine friendliness in my life' (198) in a way which poignantly foreshadows the language of Dorothy Edwards's suicide note. Margiad Evans's well-known story 'A Modest Adornment' explores the lesbian relationship between Miss Plant and Miss Ada Allensmoore, who seem completely unsuited to live together, through the intrusion of a neighbour, Mrs Webb, another outsider. In later twentieth-century writing, Siân James's 'A Most Moderate Lust' features a wife and her husband's lover forming a relationship without him, while Deborah Kay Davies's 'Kissing Nina' charts the rejection of teenage lesbian desire for heterosexual conformity. Twenty-first-century Welsh writers such as Kate North would take the queer short story to a new level again. In 'The Largest Bull in Europe', North challenges the constraints of gender conventions through using a female, first-person narrator who only ever refers to her partner as 'you'. In many ways, the disorienting narrative voice of North's story links back to Kathleen Freeman's techniques. Freeman often refrains from using cues to denote who is speaking so that, in a story such as 'The Mistake', from *The Intruder and Other Stories* (1926), the reader could initially ascribe dialogue concerning a female love interest, who tragically died, to the male character rather than the actual speaker, Miss Hilomax.

Queer history in Wales is gradually beginning to receive more critical attention, not least with the publication of Huw Osborne's edited collection of scholarly essays, *Queer Wales* (2016), and Norena Shopland's *Forbidden Lives: LGBT Stories from Wales* (2017). The history of the queer short story in Wales will undoubtedly benefit from the republication of many forgotten or under-read authors in Parthian's queer short story anthology edited by Kirsti Bohata, Huw Osborne, and Mihangel Morgan, which brings together queer Welsh short fiction from the nineteenth century to the present. Some of Kathleen Freeman's short stories feature in this anthology, while *The Intruder and Other Stories* is due for republication in the Honno Classics imprint. The wider availability and renewed interest in these highly significant literary and cultural works mark a shift in the way Wales looks back at its queer history, not now with shame but with pride.

Conclusion

The impact of language loss through changes to education policy at the end of the nineteenth century remains a defining moment in the development of anglophone short fiction in Wales. The fracture caused by this abrupt disconnection from a rich tradition marks the work of so many of the writers in this chapter, from underlying imagery to the very subject matter of the stories themselves. The recurrent focus on home and community, itself a mainstay of the Welsh-language short story, suggests that writers in English embraced these kinds of images as a recompense for this loss. As this chapter has also argued, it is vital that we recognize the way in which women writers have shaped the anglophone tradition, including those who made Wales their home and fashioned the short story in their own distinctive way. The politics of anthologizing remains a pressing issue, not least for women's writing, especially as we move further away from the political and cultural events that shaped the previous century. One of the most recent anthologies of twentieth-century short fiction, edited by Dai Smith for the Library of Wales series, reaffirms that the tales worth retelling are those that concern male, working-class experience, especially in the industrialized valleys. The paucity of female-authored content (only five women authors are represented out of forty-two stories) sits uncomfortably with the editor's declaration that his aim is to 'touch upon the lives of Wales in the past one hundred years' without being an 'objective survey'.[34] His hope that the edition will serve 'as a definition' (xvi) of the form suggests otherwise. This kind of editorial decision-making pushes women writers to the margins of their own history, in an imprint which is designed to record, preserve, and advertise the wealth of anglophone Welsh writing to the world.

From the 1937 Faber collection to Smith's most recent editorial endeavours, we have been reading the Welsh short story too narrowly. We need to think in terms of short fictions, in both languages, which encompass the numerous facets of the genre, short fictions which have sprung from every stratum of Welsh society. How many modern readers have encountered the carefully delineated Pembrokeshire coastlines of the forgotten Lilian Bowen-Rowlands in the 1890s, or the harrowing mining stories of the equally over-looked Phyllis M. Jones in the late 1960s? The quality of the writing of such little-known and under-read authors speaks for itself, but without preservation and revitalization through the publication of accessible editions, these names will be lost from our cultural memory. A genre which speaks so distinctly to the lived experience of its people, as well as the changing nature of Welsh cultural identity, deserves a far more prominent place in our literary history. When the history of the twenty-first-century short story is written, it is to be hoped that erasure and exclusion play no part in its construction.

Notes

1. Glyn Jones, *The Dragon Has Two Tongues: Essays on Anglo-Welsh Writers and Writing*, ed. Tony Brown, rev. edn (Cardiff: University of Wales Press, 2001), 51.

2. Gwyn Jones, *Background to Dylan Thomas and Other Explorations* (Oxford: Oxford University Press, 1992), 84.

3. Raymond Garlick, *An Introduction to Anglo-Welsh Literature* (Cardiff: University of Wales Press, 1972), 9.

4. Tony Brown, 'The Ex-centric Voice: The English-Language Short Story in Wales', *North American Journal of Welsh Studies* 1, 1 (2001): 29–30.

5. Jane Aaron, introduction to Aaron, ed., *A View Across the Valley* (Dinas Powys: Honno, 1999), xiv.

6. Allen Raine, 'Gibbet and Cross', *The Cardiff Times and South Wales Weekly News*, 3 October 1908.

7. Frank O'Connor, *The Lonely Voice: A Study of the Short Story* (Hoboken: Melville House, 2004), 17.

8. Clare Hanson, *Re-reading the Short Story* (Basingstoke: Macmillan, 1989), 6.

9. Allen Raine (see Puddicombe), 'Flow on, Thou Shining River', in *All in a Month and Other Stories* (London: Hutchinson & Co, 1908), 74.

10. D. J. Williams, 'A Good Year', trans. Wyn Griffiths, in *Twenty-Five Welsh Short Stories*, ed. Gwyn Jones and Islwyn Ffowc Elis (Oxford: Oxford University Press, 1971), 225–6.

11. D. J. Williams, *Hen Dŷ Ffarm / The Old Farmhouse*, trans. Waldo Williams (Llandysul: Gomer Press, 2001), 68.

12. Katie Gramich, *Kate Roberts* (Cardiff: University of Wales Press, 2011), 77.

13. Joseph Clancy, introduction to *The World of Kate Roberts* (Philadelphia: Temple University Press, 1991), xii.

14. Kate Roberts, 'The Quilt', in *The World of Kate Roberts*, 79.

15. Glyn Jones, 'The Boy in the Bucket', in *The Collected Stories of Glyn Jones*, ed. Tony Brown (Cardiff: University of Wales Press, 1999), 215.

16. Tony Brown, introduction to *The Collected Stories of Glyn Jones*, lvii.

17. Glyn Jones, 'I Was Born in the Ystrad Valley', in *The Collected Stories of Glyn Jones*, 3.

18. Kathleen Freeman, 'The Fraying of the Thread', in *The Intruder and Other Stories* (London: Jonathan Cape, 1926), 199.

19. Huw Edwin Osborne, *Rhys Davies* (Cardiff: University of Wales Press, 2009), 3.

20. Dylan Thomas, 'A Story', in *Collected Stories* (London: Phoenix, 2000), 347.

21. Alun Lewis, 'The Orange Grove', in *The Second Penguin Book of Welsh Short Stories*, ed. Alun Richards (London: Penguin, 1994), 136.

22. Alun Lewis, 'The Housekeeper', in *Collected Stories* (Bridgend: Seren, 1995), 101.

23. Leslie Norris, 'Sliding', in *Collected Stories* (Bridgend: Seren, 1996), 13.

24. Leslie Norris, 'The Girl from Cardigan', in *The Girl from Cardigan* (Bridgend: Seren, 1988), 10.

25. Christopher Meredith, foreword to *Rhapsody*, by Dorothy Edwards (Cardigan: Parthian, 2007), ix.

26. Claire Flay, *Dorothy Edwards* (Cardiff: University of Wales Press, 2011), 25.

27. Dorothy Edwards, 'The Conquered', in *Rhapsody* (Cardigan: Parthian, 2007), 45.

28. Lynette Roberts, 'An Introduction to Village Dialect', in *Lynette Roberts: Diaries, Letters and Recollections*, ed. Patrick McGuinness (Manchester: Carcanet, 2008), 107.

29. Patrick McGuinness, introduction to *Lynette Roberts*, ed. McGuinness, xii.

30. Lynette Roberts, 'Tiles', in *Lynette Roberts,* ed. McGuinness, 96.

31. Laura Wainwright, '"Always Observant and Slightly Obscure": Lynette Roberts as Welsh Modernist', *Almanac* 16 (2012): 187–225.

32. Clare Morgan, 'Exile and the Kingdom: Margiad Evans and the Mythic Landscape of Wales', *Welsh Writing in English: A Yearbook of Critical Essays* 6 (2000): 113.

33. See Michelle Deininger, 'Pylons, Playgrounds, and Power Stations: Ecofeminism and Landscape in Women's Short Fiction from Wales', in *Ecofeminism in Dialogue*, ed. Douglas A. Vakoch and Sam Mickey (Lanham: Lexington, 2018), 45–60.

34. Dai Smith, introduction to vol. I of *Story: The Library of Wales Anthology,* 2 vols. (Cardigan: Parthian, 2014), xv.

23

Welsh Modernist Writing in Wales and London

GERAINT EVANS

Modernist writing has often been characterized as an essentially metropolitan phenomenon, visible in the great cities of the world: London before the Great War, Paris after it, and New York as the century matured. This idea grew out of a canonical paradigm in the mid-twentieth century which prioritized the work of a group of modernist writers from America, France, and England, whose work came to define literary modernism and which was most visibly codified by Cyril Connolly in one hundred 'key books' as *The Modern Movement*.[1] In recent decades a broader understanding of literary responses to the phenomenon of modernity has led to a more inclusive sense of literary modernisms, and the challenge of re-theorizing the literature of Wales – and of other postcolonial cultures – has been very productive.

In the early twentieth century, writers from Wales who were writing in English faced some difficult choices. Did they follow the lead of some Irish writers such as Wilde, Joyce, and Beckett by seeking to make a career in London or Paris, or did they attempt to forge a new literature by writing in new ways and creating new audiences through publishing in Wales?[2] What London, Paris, and New York all share is that they are the hubs of an economic and cultural power which is predicated on a colonial infrastructure that nations like Wales and Ireland do not possess. Amongst the 'four nations' of Britain and Ireland, Wales, in the early twentieth century, was furthest from the metropolitan paradigm of modernity, having no centre of commerce which was comparable to Dublin in Ireland or Edinburgh and Glasgow in Scotland. It is therefore no surprise that modernity finds different expressions in Wales, particularly in Welsh.[3] One of the most interesting writers to address this issue is Raymond Williams, whose view of Wales from the 'border country' was based on a highly theorized understanding of postcolonial literary production. In his posthumously published essays on the politics of modernism, he argues that 'the metropolitan interpretation of its own processes as [universal processes]' produces a highly selective paradigm of modernism and one which needs to be critiqued when dealing with non-metropolitan or postcolonial literary production.[4]

One apparent difference between the literature of Wales in the two languages during this period is that writing in Welsh tends to be more politically radical than writing in English but that political radicalism is not always linked to the formal characteristics of modernism which make it easier to place David Jones and Dylan Thomas in an international context. Writers such as Lynette Roberts and Dorothy Edwards are more interesting in this respect, and provide an alternative to the work of David Jones and Dylan Thomas, whose careers might be seen as evidence of the same phenomenon in Wales which can be seen in Irish writing, most famously in the careers of Joyce and Beckett: it was possible to be part of the modern world in Swansea or Dublin, but it was difficult to be a modernist writer without living in London or Paris.

The Beginnings of Welsh Modernism

In her critical biography of the early career of T. H. Parry-Williams (1887–1975), *Ffarwél i Ffreiburg* ('Farewell to Freiburg'), Angharad Price examines Parry-Williams's experience as a young scholar.[5] His career was a model of outward-looking mobility. After a first degree and an MA at the University College of Wales in Aberystwyth (1905–9), he took a B.Litt. at Jesus College, Oxford (1909–11) and a PhD at Freiburg University (1911–13) before spending almost a year at the École des Hautes Études at the Sorbonne in Paris (1913–14). At Freiburg, a modern European university which was alive with the spirit of modernism, Parry-Williams was part of a student body that included Martin Heidegger and Walter Benjamin. When he moved to Paris after completing his Freiburg thesis, he found himself in the most vibrant city in Europe. At the end of the Belle Époque, this was the Paris of Picasso and Proust, of Debussy, Ravel and Stravinsky, and of Apollinaire and Gertrude Stein. It was here that Parry-Williams began to write under the influence of modernity, beginning a long poem called 'Y Ddinas' ('The City'), which he completed in Aberystwyth the following year, and which Angharad Price argues convincingly was the first truly modernist poem in Welsh. But when Parry-Williams left Paris in the early months of the First World War, returning to a lectureship in Welsh at Aberystwyth, he seemed to turn his back on the iconoclastic modernism of metropolitan Paris, returning to more traditional forms of poetry, particularly to sonnets and to stanzas composed in rhyming couplets without *cynghanedd*.

But in his prose writing in the decades which followed, he pioneered a new style of prose essay – part memoir, part travelogue, part philosophical medita-tion – which came to be his most characteristic mode of writing. What he achieved in these essays and in the mature poetry, through his exploration of alienation, isolation, and the struggle between intellect and emotion, are new forms of modernist writing which remain anchored in the Welsh literary tradition but attest to the shock of modernity. These are modernist modes of literary production which are salient outside the metropolis.

This search for modernist modes of expression within a literary commu-nity which valued traditional styles of writing overlapped with a major revival of interest in traditional poetry. Added to that, the dominant ideal of political and social organization in Welsh nationalist politics for most of the early twentieth century was the organic, Welsh-speaking rural commu-nity, an ideal which often informs the textual fabric of literary production. In Welsh-language prose, this idea of the rural linguistic community as a cultural ideal finds some of its most influential expression in the short stories of Kate Roberts and in the work of D. J. Williams. 'D.J.', as he was invariably known, had grown up in rural Carmarthenshire and his stories and prose memoirs bridged the divide between radical yearning and conservative nostalgia. He wrote a series of short stories about rural Wales which were published in 1936, 1943, and 1949 and which form a trilogy, a selection of which was later published as *Storïau'r Tir* ('Stories of the Land').[6] These stories celebrate the cohesion of Welsh rural society and promote, in parti-cular, the idea of *cymeriad*, the extraordinary character whose personality exemplifies the brilliance of their community. This interest in character and a writing style which combined formal precision with rich dialect helped to make D. J. Williams and Kate Roberts the most popular short story writers in Welsh in the middle of the twentieth century.

D. J. Williams's interest in the uniqueness of the disappearing characters of Welsh rural life can perhaps be seen at its sharpest not in the stories but in three volumes of memoirs, the earliest of which was called *Hen Wynebau* ('Old Faces', 1934).[7] Williams memorializes some of the characters of his native district just as the way of life which they represent is disappearing. While his portraits are affectionate, they are never sentimental, and although Williams is writing mainly about people rather than places, his work is congruent with English portraits of disappearing rural life from earlier in the century from writers such as Ford Madox Ford and Edward Thomas.[8] The best known of these portraits is the first in the volume, Dafydd 'r Efailfach ('Dafydd of the Small Forge'), who is introduced as 'yr unig ddyn maes o'r cyffredin yn yr Hen Ardal' ('the only out-of-the-ordinary person in the Old District').[9] Dafydd is a labourer, small of stature and illiterate. His distinction lies in his spoken language. He is a famous storyteller, a fastidious describer of people and events: 'meistr yr union air' ('the master of the exact word'), and Williams's implication is that the source of his own mastery of language is not the universities of Wales and Oxford or his love of English Romantic poetry and French short stories but the example of this unlettered Flaubertian, who exemplified the virtues of *le mot juste* while living entirely in the rural community where he was born and earning his living as a labourer. D.J. is unambiguous in his praise: he was a true artist and nobody, outside the plays of J. M. Synge, ever spoke as brilliantly as this man. He never worried about learning to read and rejoiced in living in the moment, requiring nothing from life except his food and drink and the right to hold a mirror up to nature. The Shakespearean reference is not accidental, as the portrait goes on to describe how his artistry, although based on the spoken word, extended even into the physical comedy of his daily life so that even the act of packing tobacco into a pipe became a captivating performance. And in relating a story, he never searched for a word, he would just find it, in the moment, seeing again the events he was relating as if they were alive before him, so that the whole lexicon of language and dialect danced at his service. And as he reached the climactic moment of the anecdote, he would enunciate that one perfect word in a way which print cannot capture. It was 'fel petai rhyw frêc yn pwyso'n otomatig ar rhithm ei barabl' ('as if some brake pressed automatically on the rhythm of his speech'), so that the perfect timing of the delivery added the smack of laughter to the end of the story.[10]

Formally and thematically these memoirs and stories look back to Hardy's *Wessex Tales* (1888) and to the cabinet of human curiosities which is Joyce's *Dubliners* (1914), but in their adherence to a rural ideal they capture a mid-century reluctance to embrace the urban experimentalism of modernist writing. In Ireland, similar tensions are still being explored by Seamus Heaney in the late 1960s when he writes about the disappearance of the rural crafts in Ireland in poems such as 'The Forge' and 'Thatcher'.[11] And while these ideas were widely explored by writers in Wales in the middle quarters of the century, it is characteristic of Saunders Lewis that he should push the idea further than most other writers or critics. In conversation with D. J. Williams for a series of radio talks which were published as *Crefft y Stori Fer* ('The Craft of the Short Story', 1949), Lewis says:

Mae'n hyfryd eich clywed chi'n canmol diwylliant cymdeithas eich hen ardal. Cas gennyf i'r syniad sy mor gyffredin mai peth llyfr yw diwylliant. Fe all cymdeithas wledig anllythrennog fod yn fwy diwylliedig na llawer cymdeithas lythrennog ac yn well magwrfa i artist, ei hiaith yn lanach a mwy byw, a'i safonau'n uwch a'i thraddodiadau'n gyfoeth iddi . . .[12]

(It's wonderful to hear you praising the culture of the society of your old district. I hate the idea which is so common that culture is about books. A rural, illiterate community can be more cultured than many literate communities and a better nursery for artists, its language cleaner and more alive, and its standards higher and its traditions a treasure for it . . .)

In the 1960s and 1970s, perhaps under the influence of the renewed ruralist fervour of the language movement, a new desire for the authenticity of rural memoirs led to the republication of D. J. Williams's *Hen Wynebau* and the appearance of a number of similar books such as *Pigau'r Sêr* (1969) and *Maes Mihangel* (1974) by J. G. Williams (1915–87), and the posthumously published *Hunangofiant Gwas Ffarm* ('The Autobiography of a Farm Servant', 1977) by Fred Jones Y Cilie (1877–1948).[13] This genre of writing had a devoted readership, but none of these later books had the impact of Williams's originals and his idea of 'y filltir sgwâr' ('the square mile') continues to resonate in Welsh literature and politics today.

From Ruralism to Modernism

In his volume of memoirs *Hen Dŷ Ffarm* ('The Old Farmhouse', 1953), D.J. writes about the first six years of his life 'o gwmpas y nyth'('around the nest') and describes the idea of 'y filltir sgwâr', or square mile, which he argues is the origin of community and from which all future abstractions around the idea of nationalism must inevitably grow:

I mi, dyma fro y broydd, y godidocaf ohonynt oll. Dysgais ei charu, mi gredaf, cyn dysgu cerdded. Ni theithiais y darn yma o wlad erioed – o Fwlch Cae Melwas i Fwlch Cefen Sarth ac o Graig Dwrch i'r Darren Fowr – heb deimlo rhyw gynnwrf rhyfedd yn cerdded fy natur – cynnwrf megis un yn teimlo penllanw ei etifeddiaeth ddaearol ac ysbrydol yn dygyfor ei enaid. Dyma wlad fy nhadau mewn gwirionedd . . .[14]

(For me, this is the country of all countries, the most majestic of them all. I learned to love it, I believe, before learning to walk. I never travelled this part of the country – from Bwlch Cae Melwas to Bwlch Cefen Sarth and from Craig Dwrch to Darren Fawr – without feeling some extraordinary agitation creeping through my nature – the agitation of one who feels the high tide of his earthly heritage stirring his soul. This, truly, is the land of my fathers . . .)

He goes on to argue that it is 'Y brogarwch cyfyng hwn . . . a'i ganolbwynt yn "y filltir sgwâr" yn Hen Ardal fach fy mebyd', 'this narrow love of place, with its centre in "the square mile" of the Old District of my childhood', which is the basis of his nationalism. This idea, that abstract loyalties grow out of personal attachments and experiences, is central to the idea of cultural nationalism which characterizes Welsh writing, in both languages, through-out the century. For writers in Welsh in particular, the phrase 'y filltir sgwâr' becomes shorthand for the value of community in the fight against the colonial infrastructure of government and economy which many saw as being essentially unchanged since the Acts of Union, passed between 1536 and 1543, had created the new state of 'England and Wales'.[15] In the middle years of the 1960s, when the Welsh language movement and political nation-alism were beginning to gain momentum, the significance of some of these ideas for Welsh literary and political life was explored by D. Gwenallt Jones (1899–1968), the scholar and poet who published as Gwenallt. In an influential essay called 'Y Fro: Rhydcymerau' ('The District: Rhydcymerau'), published in a *festschrift* for D. J. Williams, Gwenallt argued that D.J.'s masterwork was the first three chapters of *Hen Dŷ Ffarm* together with the best portraits in *Hen Wynebau* but that poverty and economic policies had already undermined the rich Welsh culture of the farming life which D.J. so admires.[16] He also suggests – perhaps as an antidote to the cult of nostalgia – that it was only his escape from the farming life through education that had allowed D.J. the critical distance and the leisure to write about it. Gwenallt had already memorialized the district himself in a poem called 'Rhydcymerau' which was collected in his third volume of poems, *Eples* ('Leaven'), in 1951. Gwenallt takes the whole rural idyll of D.J.'s square mile, bounded as it is by the romantic nomenclature of the fields and farms which define it, and within a formally modernist poem provides a new and apocalyptically political con-text to the post-war innovation of the planned rural economy:

> Plannwyd egin coed y Trydydd Rhyfel
> Ar dir Esgeir-ceir a meysydd Tir-bach
> Ger Rhydcymerau.[17]

> (The saplings of the third war have been planted
> On the land of Esgeir-ceir and the fields of Tir-bach
> Near Rhydcymerau.)

Between the bookends of this new realpolitik, Gwenallt brilliantly describes the march of the generations in his own family. His grandmother, whose face was like the vellum of a medieval manuscript and whose spoken Welsh was a time-capsule of Welsh eighteenth-century puritanism. His grandfather and his uncle, 'Nwncwl Dafydd', who both farmed and lived in a vibrant culture of poetry and learning and raised a generation of poets, deacons, ministers, and teachers. And all that now remains are the forestry commission trees, lifeless forests of pinewood: 'Coed lle bu cymdogaeth, / Fforest lle bu ffermydd', 'Trees where once was community, forest where there were farms'. And at its heart, in the lair of the English Minotaur, lie the remains of Welsh culture:

Ac yn y tywyllwch yn ei chanol hi
Y mae ffau'r Minotawros Seisnig;
Ac ar golfenni, fel ar groesau,
Ysgerbydau beirdd, blaenoriaid, gweinidogion ac athrawon Ysgol Sul
Yn gwynnu yn yr haul,
Ac yn cael eu golchi gan y glaw a'u sychu gan y gwynt.

(And in the darkness of the centre
In the den of the English Minotaur
On columns, as if on crosses,
The skeletons of poets, deacons, ministers and
Sunday School teachers
Bleaching in the sun
And being washed by the rain and dried by the wind.)

Gwenallt is a central figure in the complex representation of a Welsh industrial experience which often uses rural life as a descriptive contrast, and he is one of the key writers whose search for appropriate literary forms led to the development of new kinds of Welsh modernist poems. In his poetry, especially in the mature collection *Eples*, he finds, in poems such as 'Rhydcymerau' and 'Y Meirwon', 'The Dead', a modernist poetic voice which has all the brash clarity of a political rallying cry while retaining the lyrical beauty of the rhythms of Welsh speech. He generally wrote in free verse, without the use of *cynghanedd*, but the directness of his poetic vision spoke to the heart of political aspiration in a Wales brought to life by the politics of language and a desire for political self-determination.

Gwenallt's Welsh poetry addresses many of the same concerns and issues that stand out in the work of Idris Davies, the politically strident poetic voice of industrial south Wales in the 1930s and 1940s. Both poets write to the

urban/rural dichotomy which could still be mapped onto successive generations of workers in many parts of Wales. In *The Angry Summer* (1943) and
Tonypandy (1945), Davies writes movingly about the effects of the alienation
of industrial production in south Wales on the cohesion of industrial communities and celebrates the cultural richness of life in the Welsh valleys.[18]
The sequence of fifty short, untitled poems which make up *The Angry Summer*
are one of the best literary responses to the General Strike of 1926, and to the
hardships suffered by industrial workers between the wars.

Idris Davies was also writing in English about an industrial life which was still
being lived in Welsh in pockets of industrial south Wales.[19] His focus, however,
is on the class struggle and the dignity of working families, particularly in the
valleys of the south east. The great poetic sequence in Welsh which addresses
these themes is *Sŵn y Gwynt Sy'n Chwythu* (1952), 'The Sound of the Wind that's
Blowing', by J. Kitchener Davies. This unusual *pryddest* was not an eisteddfod
piece but was commissioned for BBC radio by Aneirin Talfan Davies. The
sequence was written to be performed as a dramatic monologue and explores
the growth and development of the central character from his childhood in rural
Cardiganshire to his search for meaning – or perhaps his despair – in the
industrial wasteland of the Rhondda.[20] On first publication, after the broadcast,
a preface by Gwenallt described it as one of the great Welsh poems of the
century and its most spiritual sections invite comparison with Waldo Williams's
much-admired poem 'Mewn Dau Gae' ('In Two Fields', 1956).[21]

By the time the issue of linguistic survival has overtaken the debate about
class and poverty in the work of poets such as R. S. Thomas and Gerallt Lloyd
Owen, a similar congruence of literary purpose once again unites the work of
these two great Welsh writers, writing in the two languages of Wales. Their
respective volumes, *Not That He Brought Flowers* (1969) and *Cerddi'r Cywilydd*
('Poems of the Shame', 1972), capture a political mood that fluctuates
between defiance and despair. In *Cerddi'r Cywilydd*, Gerallt Lloyd Owen's
much anthologized poem 'Fy Ngwlad' ('My Country') begins with an address
to Llywelyn ap Gruffydd, the last independent Prince of Wales who was
killed in the watershed of 1282:

> Wylit, wylit, Lywelyn,
> Wylit waed pe gwelit hyn.
> Ein calon gan estron ŵr,
> Ein coron gan goncwerwr,
> A gwerin o ffafrgarwyr
> Llariaidd eu gwên lle'r oedd gwŷr.[22]

(You would cry, you would cry, Llywelyn,
You would cry blood if you saw this,
Our hearts owned by foreigners,
Our crown held by a conqueror,
And a favour-loving people
Meekly smiling, where once were men.)

Writing in his poem 'Reservoirs' about the flooding of Welsh valleys to create a water supply for English cities, R. S. Thomas confides that 'There are places in Wales I don't go', and that the 'serenity' of the reservoir's 'expression / Revolts me'. He complains that he cannot escape from 'the putrefying of a dead / Nation' and concludes that English culture is 'elbowing our language / Into the grave that we have dug for it.'[23] There is nothing surprising about the merciless invective of this poem's denunciation when it is read alongside the work of Gerallt Lloyd Owen.

Writing Back from the Metropolis

The Welsh-language poets of the early and mid-century, for whom living and publishing in Wales was generally the only practical option, would come to be seen as part of a new golden age of Welsh poetry, with poets such as Robert Williams Parry, D. Gwenallt Jones, and Waldo Williams writing the political and cultural aspirations of a nation into poems which would adorn the posters of political radicalism in the 1960s and 1970s. In the same half century, many Welsh writers in English would build a career through the international publishing houses of London. Caradoc Evans was one of the first to find an international readership for fiction about life in rural Wales through living and publishing in London, although in Wales he was always a controversial figure and critical opinion remains divided. His first three collections of stories, *My People* (1915), *Capel Sion* (1916), and *My Neighbours* (1919) describe a hauntingly ugly world of distorted religion in which greed, lust, and envy are the main attributes of 'the peasantry of west Wales'.[24] His characters also speak in a highly stylized English calque of the west Wales dialect of Evans's youth:

> Silah Penlon was a doltish virgin. People who were bound to
> Capel Sion said to her mother:
>   'Large is the Big Man's curse upon you, Becws Penlon.'
>   'What for do you speak wild, people bach?' answered Becws.
> 'Wench fach very tidy is the wench fach.'[25]

The dialogue of Caradoc Evans's characters attempts to convey Welsh speech in English and this innovation, together with his rejection of bourgeois realism, a sometimes naturalistic narrative mode, and the use of exaggerated, even grotesque motifs of behaviour led many critics of Welsh writing in English to see him as a founding figure whose work looks forward to some of the modernist narratives of the mid-century. Other critics find his use of caricature too unsettling and argue that it creates a non-Welsh reading position which invites mockery and ridicule.[26] A few years after the appearance of these three collections of stories, Caradoc Evans's reputation for betraying his own people and for describing them as venal peasants was settled for good in the minds of many of the London Welsh, some of whom strongly objected to his satirical comedy *Taffy*, which opened at the Prince of Wales theatre in February 1923.[27] The dialogue in this play and in these early stories is certainly nothing like the vibrant and poetic Hiberno-English speech which J. M. Synge had pioneered in *The Playboy of the Western World* (1907), a play which depicts the spiritually and linguistically rich lives of the otherwise impoverished inhabitants of the west coast of Ireland.

In the decades which followed, Vernon Watkins, Dylan Thomas, Rhys Davies, David Jones, and many others would achieve a world readership through the international distribution which came from being published in London. Dylan Thomas would court the literary worlds of London and New York from a base in west Wales, while Vernon Watkins lived a more secluded life in Swansea and the Gower. Other writers, such as David Jones and Rhys Davies, would write about Wales while living and working almost exclusively in London.

For writers who explored the idea of Welshness from a metropolitan base, the motif of the return journey is a constant theme, particularly so in English, where the narratives of social and geographic mobility are most numerous. One of the best-known examples is Dylan Thomas's autobiographical play for radio, *Return Journey* (1947), in which the poet returns for three days to south Wales, 'searching for the Swansea he knew as a boy and a young man'.[28] The play was a great success and Vernon Watkins, writing in the *Times Literary Supplement* some years later, describes it as 'the most moving . . . the most intimate, the most strictly autobiographical of all [his] talks, and the most Welsh'.[29] But to a large extent this is the Welshness of nostalgia, and part of its success is that the dramatic frame story speaks to exiles everywhere of a longing to return to a world that cannot be regained.

These literary journeys of rediscovery, in which the critical distance of the double life seems to illuminate the old world, are not confined to writers returning from London, and within Wales itself there are return journeys which speak to those who have moved away in a different sense. Vernon Watkins spent his whole working life in the Gower and Swansea of his childhood, but his poem 'Returning to Goleufryn' contains many of the elements of the literary 'return journey' while being characteristic of Welsh writing in English from the middle of the twentieth century. Modernist in appearance, the poem looks backwards to earlier traditions in which the growth of the poet's mind was the main theme, and the purpose of the narrative was to illustrate the changed state of the modern world. There is the sense of mobility or exile, implied by the conscious act of return, and that return is contextualized by a sparkling image of idyllic childhood in a rural Carmarthenshire which was 'lovely ... sunny ... alive with blind-petalled blooms'. The poem captures a reflective moment of young-adult realization which signifies a coming of age while glossing for its readers both the family context and the languages of childhood: 'Returning to Goleufryn ... Returning to my grandfather's house ... Goleufryn, the house on the hill.'[30]

Vernon Watkins was a childhood friend of Dylan Thomas, one of the Swansea 'Kardomah Boys', and they shared the childhood experience of family holidays in rural Carmarthenshire, experiences which they later explored in their published writing. But there is a distinction to be made here between Watkins's continuing sense of himself as a Welsh writer writing in and about Wales and Dylan Thomas's more compartmentalized literary life in which the Wales of his childhood is explored in the prose work, often with a non-Welsh focalization for a non-Welsh audience, while his poems are largely written within the contemporary discourse of English poetry. Watkins stands apart from his childhood friend, and much of his work has more in common with some of the Welsh-language poets such as Gwenallt and Euros Bowen.

M. Wynn Thomas has argued persuasively that Vernon Watkins and Euros Bowen can be read as European poets whose fundamental poetic impulses are symbolist in nature and whose work is representative of a non-metropolitan modernist paradigm in mid-century Welsh writing.[31] Euros Bowen is one of the most formally modernist of the Welsh-language poets. He delights in the image-based poetry and metrical experimentation of *Des Imagistes*, the seminal anthology of imagist poetry edited by Ezra Pound in 1914, but he generally writes in a loose version of *cynghanedd* which he called *cynghanedd rydd* ('free cynghanedd'):

Eira ddoe ar y ddaear
Yn anadl yn y nos yn deilio'n hael
Ar ofalon y daith yng nghalon dyn.[32]

(Yesterday's snow on earth,
The breath of night in generous bloom
over the ways of care in the heart of man.)

This example is taken from *Poems* (1974) in which he provides his own English translations or English versions of a selection of earlier poems, with the Welsh and English texts appearing on facing pages of the book. Some are in full *cynghanedd*, some in free *cynghanedd*, and some in free verse, but all use elements of a modernist poetics to an extent that is unusual in traditional strict-metre poetry of the mid-twentieth century. Here is the opening of his poem 'Drych / Mirror':

O graffu,
          ffotograffig
yw llonyddwch y llyn heddiw :

Coed distaw,
caeau eto yw ei wastad,
gro glan yn warrog o'r goleuni,
ffram a llwybrau
wedi eu fframio oll obry,
dan y graig wedyn yn grefft.[33]

(The lake today,
if you observe,
is a photographic calm :

Still trees,
a reflection of fields,
banks of shingle in the light,
farms and paths
all framed there,
a pattern of shapes under the hill.)

This mixture of free verse and bardic discipline sounds like a contradiction, but it represents a deeply thoughtful response to the challenge of modernity from a poet who also cherished his inherited tradition. In a note to his final, posthumous collection of poems, *Lleidr Tân*, 'Fire Thief' (1988), he says that he does this because we have to honour and observe the cultural past rather than just imitating it. He argues that using the twenty-four traditional metres

from the late Middle Ages is a poetic form of vain repetition but that free
cynghanedd allows a poet, even a modernist poet, to acknowledge the past
while writing in the present: 'Mae Cynghanedd Rydd yn osgoi sythu'n stiff
yng nghwpwrdd rhew yr ystrydebol' (*Cynghanedd Rydd* is the way to avoid
stiffening up in the ice-box of cliché').[34]

Modernist Prose in English and Welsh

T. H. Parry-Williams's experience of being liberated to write in new ways
about Welsh life while living in Freiburg and Paris is itself one of the great
motifs of international modernism. Many of the great English language
writers of the early twentieth century – Joyce and Beckett, Pound and
Eliot, Mansfield and Conrad – are writers working in exile and living or
publishing in international centres of cultural production such as Paris or
London. A few Welsh-language writers followed this pattern, including the
London-based newspaper editor Caradog Prichard, but most Welsh-language
writers lived and published in Wales. Saunders Lewis, the most internationalist of Welsh writers, was often trapped between the two paradigms. A
strong advocate of writing in Welsh and publishing in Wales, he agonized
over accepting the commission to produce the 'Writers of Wales' volume on
his close friend David Jones because it might be 'a betrayal' which could 'set a
bad example for Welsh writers'.[35] He also complained to friends about the
parochialism of Wales. Feeling that his BBC radio talk 'Tynged yr Iaith' ('The
Fate of the Language') had been a flop, he wrote to David Jones that he
wished he could 'get back to Italy, stay there, and hear no more ever of
Wales'.[36] For most Welsh-language writers, however, the desire to live and
work in Welsh and the need to find Welsh publishers and to build a Welsh
readership meant that a life lived in Wales was the only life they could
imagine.

For writers in English the situation could be more complicated. David
Jones (1895–1974) had grown up in London and apart from extended periods
working in Eric Gill's artistic communities in Ditchling and Capel-Y-Ffin in
the Black Mountains, he would spend most of his working life there.[37] A
generation earlier Edward Thomas, whose family connections with Wales
were even stronger than those of David Jones, would write one of the finest
early novels about the Welsh diaspora. Set in south London and a fictionalized Laugharne in west Wales, *The Happy-Go-Lucky Morgans* (1913) explores
the cultural and linguistic identity of the Morgan family, whose lives in the
semi-rural south London suburb of Balham in the late nineteenth and early

twentieth centuries is a translated reflection of their lives in the riverside town of Abercorran in Carmarthenshire, to which they ultimately return. In its use of a multi-perspective narrative, the use of memory as a means of exploring identity, and the non-narrative representation of moments of existence, *The Happy-Go-Lucky Morgans* stands alongside Joyce's *Portrait of the Artist* (1916) as an early-century modernist exploration of individual and community in a multilingual world which stands on the brink of modernity. Another writer for whom the move to London became permanent was Rhys Davies (1901–78), who grew up in Blaenclydach near the Rhondda but moved to London in his early twenties. A prolific writer, whose best work appeared in the 1930s and 1940s, Rhys Davies used Welsh and English settings for his fiction, but in his *Honey and Bread* trilogy he uses the industrial valleys of his youth.[38] In these novels he extends the style of D. H. Lawrence's early novels to explore the dehumanizing effects of industrial capitalism in south Wales.[39]

The pre-eminent modernist of Welsh writing in English is David Jones. The most visible of the Welsh modernists within the metropolitan, internationalist paradigm, his work spans the middle quarters of the century and links the London modernism of T. S. Eliot with the Welsh radicalism of Saunders Lewis. Jones came from a Welsh family but lived most of his life in London, exploring in both writing and painting the conjunction of traditions which made London the historical and literary capital of 'the Island of Britain' whose lore and tradition begin – for Jones – with the folkloric elements of the *Mabinogion* and which is still visible in the Celtic place-names of the Thames basin.

Jones began studying drawing and painting at the Camberwell Art School and, after serving in the First World War as a private with the Royal Welch Fusiliers, he returned to studying at the Westminster School of Art. By the end of the war he was working as an official artist and his early career is mostly concerned with the visual arts. It is in his long prose poem about the war, *In Parenthesis* (1937), that he finds his feet as a writer. Jones was published by Faber throughout his career, and in T. S. Eliot he found an early champion. In the anonymous blurb for the wrapper of the first edition of *In Parenthesis*, Eliot recognizes the book as 'an early epic'. It is 'not a "war book"' so much as a distillation of the essence of war books ... one of the strangest, most sombre and most exciting books that we have published'.[40] When the book was reissued in a new edition in 1961, the new preface, this time signed by Eliot, confirms and enhances his opinion of the work. Eliot says that he was proud to share the responsibility for having published it in 1937: 'On reading the book in typescript I was deeply moved. I then regarded it, and I still regard it, as a work of genius.'[41] Eliot was not alone. In *Ways of Escape* (1980) Graham Greene describes it as one of 'the great poems of the century'. W. H. Auden, reviewing the first American publication of the book, calls it 'the greatest book about the First World War'. And for Tom Dilworth, Jones's biographer, *In Parenthesis* is simply 'the best book on war in English, it may be the greatest work of British literature between the wars'.[42] Jones writes in the modernist style of Eliot and Pound, but to their cultural canvas Jones adds a Brythonic Celticity which he sees as the link back to Rome, with modern Welsh reminding us daily of our European and Christian heritage. The seven sections of *In Parenthesis* take epigrams from the *Gododdin*, the Old Welsh poem whose origins lie in the tribal wars of post-Roman Britain. This is the Britain of Arthur, and the sense of antiquity which the *cyfarwydd*, the storytelling poet of medieval Wales, brought to his fireside reminiscences is given to the Welsh soldier in the 'Great Boast' which is the central set piece of Part 4, 'King Pellam's Launde':

> This Dai adjusts his slipping shoulder straps, wraps close his
> Misfit outsize greatcoat – he articulates his English with an
> alien care.
> My fathers were with the Black Prinse of Wales
> At the passion of
> The blind Bohemian king.
> They served in these fields,
> It is in the histories that you can read it . . .[43]

Jones's other long poem, *The Anathémata: Fragments of an Attempted Writing* (1952), is focused on London, again with elements from early Welsh literature designed to interpose Brythonic Welshness between Rome and Tudor England. What is often regarded as his finest poem on a Welsh subject was published in the year of his death in 1974. 'The Sleeping Lord' elaborates the idea of Arthur sleeping in a cave, waiting to be summoned to save his country, an image which captures the essence of postcolonial opposition which is the basis of so much of the literature of Wales in the later twentieth century. Tracing the topography of Wales through Arthurian place-names, the narrative voice wonders whether there is a gigantic warrior slumbering in the landscape or whether the 'sleeping lord' might be the country itself:

> Does the land wait the sleeping lord
> or is the wasted land
> that very lord who sleeps?[44]

In all of Jones's work as a writer, and in much of his later work as an artist, there is the sense of his artistic identity which is organically composed of all the elements which he writes about: Welsh, English, Cockney, Brythonic, and Catholic. The anxiety about identity politics which characterizes so much of postcolonial literature is replaced in Jones's work by a bold act of subversion and assimilation. Writing in the complex allusive style of high modernism, Jones retains the bedrock of Latinity which he sees as fundamental to European culture, but he adds to it the language, history, literature, and mythology of what he sees as a Brythonic Celticity. In a letter written to Saunders Lewis in October 1971, Jones rehearses the arguments for cultural continuity over two millennia and declares of the Welsh that 'we are the heirs of Romanity. How can we think of Meirionydd without thinking of Marianus, or Padarn Beis Rhudd without recalling Paternus.'[45] In the first half of the twentieth century, there were a number of Welsh-speaking writers who wrote in English. What is remarkable about David Jones is that he is one of the first to explore the idea that Welshness in English is predicated on Welsh-language culture, even for monolingual English speakers living in London. That idea, which becomes mainstream in the final decades of the twentieth century, was radical and challenging in the literary world of the 1930s.

A number of other writers in this period also use the early history of Wales to imply continuity or to create a more coherent sense of nation. In a series of novels published in the 1930s, John Cowper Powys (1872–1963) uses Welsh locations and characters to explore a magical exoticism which owes more to Matthew Arnold than to Jones's idea of the Welsh as the inheritors of Brythonic Romanity. In *A Glastonbury Romance* (1932), *Maiden Castle* (1937), and *Morwyn* (1937), Powys uses characters from medieval Welsh tradition, such as Urien and Pwyll, to add textual complexity to English modernist novels whose focalization is rarely Welsh. Glastonbury itself is a powerful symbol of English appropriation where the figure of Arthur operates as an assimilated remnant of Welshness in a modern English town. Powys's historical romance *Owen Glendower* (1940) has a clearer Welsh focalization and his historical novel *Porius*, which he believed to be his masterpiece, is significantly located in the same Arthurian world of sub-Roman Britain which Jones explores in 'The Sleeping Lord'.[46] Completed in 1949 and first published in an abridged form in 1951, the reconstructed complete edition was published in 2007. The story unfolds during one week in October 499 and is set in and around a Roman fort in north Wales. The son of a Brythonic prince in Edeyrnion is under threat from the Saxons led by Colgrim, and Arthur, who is called Emperor of Britain, comes to their assistance, sending the magicians Nineue, Medrawd, and Myrddin Wyllt. However, while Powys thought of *Porius* as his chief work of fiction, it is also characteristic of all his work in being mainly concerned with the psychology of myth and the dynamics of personal relationship. This makes his work quite different to that of most Welsh writers of the period, writers for whom the personal has become inescapably political.

If David Jones is the English-language writer whose work most successfully combines the textual strategies of modernism with an exploration of Welsh identity, then the Welsh-language prose writer whose work most fully explores the modernist mode of writing is Caradog Prichard (1904–80). As a young writer Prichard wrote mainly poetry and worked almost exclusively in Welsh. In his early twenties he won the crown at the National Eisteddfod, which was held in Caergybi in 1927, a feat which he repeated in 1928 (Treorci) and 1929 (Liverpool). These three poems were collected with his other early work in 1937 in *Canu Cynnar* ('Early Poems'), a volume which contains an early reference to the theme of his greatest novel in being dedicated to 'holl ddeiliaid Ysbyty'r Meddyliau Claf yn Ninbych' ('all the inmates of the Hospital for Sick Minds in Denbigh').[47] He began working as a journalist, first in Caernarfon and then in other towns in Wales, before moving to London, where he lived for the greater part of his life, working as a journalist and newspaper editor.[48]

In his mature work Prichard turns to fiction and finds a different mode of writing, which builds on the strategies of international modernist writing, using non-linear naturalism and the rich dialect of his native Bethesda to create fictional paradigms of small-town industrial north Wales. In the 1960s and 1970s, he published short stories and a remarkable autobiography called *Afal Ddrwg Adda* ('Adam's Bad Apple', 1973), but his major work of fiction is the novel *Un Nos Ola Leuad* ('One Full Moon', 1961). The novel is an exploration of madness and identity, set in a Welsh-speaking quarry community which can be read as a fictionalized portrait of Bethesda. The novel has a complex structure and is packed with sparklingly original characters such as Wmffra Tŷ Top ('Humphrey Top House'), whose unselfish acts of kindness brighten the childhood of the unnamed Boy who is the central character. Some of the other less malign characters include the wonderfully named Harri Bach Clocsia ('Harry Little Clogs'), Bob Car Llefrith ('Bob Milk Cart'), Ffranc Bee Hive ('Frank Bee Hive'), and the reformed alcoholic Wil Colar Startsh ('Will Starch Collar'), whose return from a night of drinking in the

Blue Bell is interrupted by a voice in a wheel of fire calling on him to repent: 'Tro'n ôl, bechadur, tro'n ol' ('Turn back, sinner, turn back').[49]

The novel follows the final day in the life of the unnamed central character on his release from incarceration in the asylum where he has spent most of his life. As he retraces the journeys of his childhood in the streets of his home town, he recalls the characters, scenes, and voices of his final days of freedom leading up to the key moment of his life, when he killed Jini Bach Pen Cae ('Little Jini Top Field'), in an explosion of rage and confused sexuality. Moonlight is one of the main images in the novel, signifying both the periodic madness of the 'lunatics' who inhabit the village and the monthly rhythms of a female sexuality which has little expression in a world still governed by the bigotry of puritanism. Most significantly, the moonlight suggests the illumination of self-knowledge, the memory of actions and responsibilities from which the unnamed Man can never escape.

A political reading of the novel is that madness and criminality are the by-products of poverty and that it is the political failure to address that causal relationship which leads to medical incarceration being used as an instrument of social control. In the opening scene of the novel, the Boy is asked where he had been, getting up to mischief and 'gyrru pobol y pentre ma o'u coua' ('driving the people of this village out of their minds'). And even at this early stage the Boy has a simple answer: 'Nid ni sy'n u gyrru nhw o'u coua, nhw sy'n mynd o'u coua' ('It's not us who are driving them out of their minds. It's them who are going out of their minds').[50] But no heed is ever paid to the insight of the innocent witness and the cycle of poverty, madness, and incarceration continues unchecked against a background of violence and death as the Boy hears about the suicide of Yncl Now Moi, 'Moi's Uncle Owen', who hanged himself in the lavatory and Gryffudd Ifas Braich, 'Griffith Evans from Braich', who was killed at the quarry, leaving the Boy to wonder if Gryffudd Ifas would still have his scar in heaven.[51]

The incarceration of first the Boy's mother and then the Boy himself creates a continuity of social failure and institutional retribution that dramatically culminates in the Man's inability to continue living after his release. He and his mother are destroyed by the experience of separation and by their loss of liberty, but their cases are not simple parallels. The Boy is locked up for killing Jini Bach Pen Cae, but his mother is innocent of any crime. She is herself a victim, first of poverty, then of repeated sexual assault and then of incarceration. The dramatic parallel of their treatment reveals the misogyny of their social condition: he commits a sexualized crime while his mother is the victim of sexual crime, but both end up in an asylum. This pattern of misogyny is repeated throughout the story: Harri Bach Clocsia is a well-known flasher, but it is the sexually precocious girls, Catrin Jên Lôn Isa ('Catrin Jane Lower Lane') and Jini Bach Pen Cae, who are briefly incarcerated in an effort to control their behaviour. It is on her release, still unrepentantly curious about life and sex, that Jini embarks on a final tryst with the Boy, which this time leads to her death. Whether or not the Boy and Jini are too young to be criminally responsible and whether or not Harri Bach and the Boy's mother are too damaged to be redeemed, the story makes it clear that there are gender-based distinctions at work in the different treatments they receive.

All the characters in *Un Nos Ola Leuad* display the poetic brilliance of a vibrant spoken language and make this extraordinary novel a Welsh counterpart to the great Irish modernists: James Joyce (1882–1941), Máirtín Ó Cadhain (1906–1970), and Flann O'Brien (1911–1966). As in Joyce's *Ulysses* (1922), O'Brien's *At Swim-Two-Birds* (1939), and Ó Cadhain's Irish-language masterpiece *Cré na Cille* ('The Dirty Dust', 1949), the textual complexity, verbal invention and densely crafted social observation work together to suggest that all lives are the potential subjects of art. The Man in Prichard's *One Full Moon* is in many ways the literary child of Leopold Bloom, the original sexually and religiously compromised modernist hero. As in Bloom's journey, the journey of the Man back to his childhood home encompasses a life within a day, a life that is framed by the symbolically rich full moon. This also has been a life of heroic struggle, an Odyssean journey back to an idealized home and a life that metonymizes the struggle of people for whom institutionalized poverty and organized religion conspire to limit the possibility of escape.

Notes

1. Cyril Connolly, *The Modern Movement: 100 Key Books from England, France and America 1880–1950* (London: Andre Deutsch and Hamish Hamilton, 1965).
2. For an account of how some of these issues have been discussed in relation to Irish modernist writing, see Carol Taaffe, 'Irish Modernism', in *The Oxford Handbook of Modernisms*, ed. Peter Brooker *et al.* (Oxford: Oxford University Press, 2010), 782–96.
3. For an account of urban development in Britain and Ireland, see Hugh Kearney, *The British Isles: A History of Four Nations* (Cambridge: Cambridge University Press, 1985, rev. edn 2012).
4. Raymond Williams, *The Politics of Modernism: Against the New Conformists*, ed. Tony Pinkney (London: Verso, 1989), 47.

5. Angharad Price, *Ffarwél i Ffreiburg: Crwydriadau Cynnar T. H. Parry-Williams* (Llandysul: Gwasg Gomer, 2013).

6. D. J. Williams, *Storïau'r Tir* (Llandysul: Gwasg Gomer, 1966); the original collections were called *Storïau'r Tir Glas* (1936), *Storïau'r Tir Coch* (1941), and *Storïau'r Tir Du* (1949).

7. D. J. Williams, *Hen Wynebau* (Aberystwyth: Gwasg Aberystwyth, 1934).

8. See, for example, Ford Madox Hueffer [Ford], *The Heart of the Country* (London: Alston Rivers, 1906) and Edward Thomas, *The South Country* (London: Dent, 1909).

9. Williams, *Hen Wynebau*, 9; the translation is mine, as are all subsequent translations unless otherwise noted.

10. Ibid., 13

11. Seamus Heaney, *Door into the Dark* (London: Faber, 1969), 19–20.

12. Saunders Lewis, ed., *Crefft y Stori Fer* (Llandysul: Y Clwb Llyfrau Cymreig, 1949), 22–35; the five conversations were broadcast during the winter of 1947–8 in a series called *Cornel y Llenor* ('The Writer's Corner').

13. J. G. Williams, *Pigau'r Sêr* (Dinbych: Gwasg Gee, n.d. [1969]); J. G. Williams, *Maes Mihangel* (Dinbych: Gwasg Gee, 1974); Fred Jones, *Hunangofiant Gwas Ffarm* (Abertawe: John Penry, 1977).

14. D. J. Williams, *Hen Dŷ Ffarm* (Aberystwyth: Gwasg Aberystwyth, 1953), 48.

15. See Chapter 8 in this volume.

16. D. Gwenallt Jones, 'Y Fro: Rhydcymerau', in *D. J. Williams, Abergwaun: Cyfrol Deyrnged*, ed. John Gwyn Griffiths (Llandysul: Gwasg Gomer, 1965), 116–26.

17. *Cerddi Gwenallt: Y Casgliad Cyflawn*, ed. Christine James (Llandysul: Gwasg Gomer, 2001), 148.

18. For a broader discussion of Gwenallt and Idris Davies, see Daniel Williams, 'Welsh Modernism', in *The Oxford Handbook of Modernisms*, ed. Peter Brooker *et al.*, 805–10.

19. On Idris Davies and the Welsh language, see Dafydd Johnston, 'Idris Davies a'r Gymraeg', in *Diffinio Dwy Lenyddiaeth Cymru*, ed. M. Wynn Thomas (Caerdydd: Gwasg Prifysgol Cymru, 1995), 96–119.

20. James Kitchener Davies, 'Sŵn y Gwynt Sy'n Chwythu', in *Gwaith James Kitchener Davies*, ed. Mair I. Davies (Llandysul: Gwasg Gomer, 1980), 15–26.

21. Waldo Williams, *Waldo Williams: Cerddi 1922–1970*, ed. Alan Llwyd and Robert Rhys (Llandysul: Gwasg Gomer, 2014), 249. See also Chapter 19 in this volume.

22. Gerallt Lloyd Owen, *Cerddi'r Cywilydd* (Caernarfon: Gwasg Gwynedd, 1972), 22.

23. R. S. Thomas, *Not That He Brought Flowers* (London: Rupert Hart-Davies, 1969), 26.

24. Caradoc Evans, *My People: Stories of the Peasantry of West Wales* (London: Andrew Melrose, 1915).

25. Caradoc Evans, 'The Pillars of Sion', in *Capel Sion* (London: Melrose, 1916), 61.

26. See Belinda Humphrey, 'Prelude to the Twentieth Century', in *A Guide to Welsh Literature*, vol. VII: *Welsh Writing in English*, ed. M. Wynn Thomas (Cardiff: University of Wales Press, 2003), 41–5.

27. See John Harris, 'Novel to Play: The Trials of *Taffy*', in *Seeing Wales Whole*, ed. Sam Adams (Cardiff: University of Wales Press, 1998), 25–55.

28. Dylan Thomas, 'Return Journey', in *The Broadcasts*, ed. Ralph Maud (London: Dent, 1991), 177–89.

29. Vernon Watkins, 'Dylan Thomas and the Spoken Word', *Times Literary Supplement* (19 November 1954): 731.

30. Vernon Watkins, 'Returning to Goleufryn', in *The Lady with the Unicorn* (London: Faber, 1958), 15–16.

31. M. Wynn Thomas, 'Symbyliad y Symbol: Barddoniaeth Euros Bowen a Vernon Watkins', in *Diffinio Dwy Lenyddiaeth Cymru*, ed. Thomas, 170–94.

32. Euros Bowen, 'Eira Ddoe / Yesterday's Snow', from *Poems* (Llandysul: Gomer Press, 1974), 56–7; the English versions are also by Euros Bowen.

33. Euros Bowen, 'Drych / Mirror', from *Poems*, 92–3.

34. Euros Bowen, *Lleidr Tân* (Caernarfon: Gwasg Gwynedd, 1989), 97.

35. NLW MS, letter from Saunders Lewis to David Jones, 13 December 1969.

36. NLW MS, letter from Saunders Lewis to David Jones, Easter Sunday 1962; the BBC radio broadcast was on 13 February 1962 and is now thought of as the catalyst which created the Welsh language movement and led to important legislative change in the legal status of the language.

37. See Thomas Dilworth, *David Jones: Engraver, Soldier, Painter, Poet* (London: Cape, 2017).

38. Rhys Davies, *Honey and Bread* (London: Putnam, 1935); *A Time to Laugh* (London: Heinemann, 1937); *Jubilee Blues* (London: Heinemann, 1938).

39. For a well-theorized account of industrial fiction in Wales, see Stephen Knight, *A Hundred Years of Fiction: From Colony to Independence* (Cardiff: University of Wales Press, 2004).

40. David Jones, *In Parenthesis* (London: Faber, 1937). All references are to this edition.

41. T. S. Eliot, 'A Note of Introduction', in *In Parenthesis* (London: Faber, 1961), vii.

42. See Graham Greene, *Ways of Escape* (London: Bodley Head, 1980), 28; W. H. Auden, 'The Geste Says This and the Man who Was on the Field . . .', *Mid-Century Review 39* (1962): 12; Dilworth, *David Jones: Engraver, Soldier, Painter, Poet*, 192.

43. Jones, *In Parenthesis*, 79.

44. David Jones, 'The Sleeping Lord', in *The Sleeping Lord* (London: Faber, 1974), 96.

45. NLW MS, letter from David Jones to Saunders Lewis, 12 October 1971.
46. See Herbert Williams, *John Cowper Powys* (Bridgend: Seren, 1997), 143.
47. Caradoc Prichard, *Canu Cynnar* (Wrecsam: Hughes a'i Fab, 1937), [v].
48. See Menna Baines, *Yng Ngolau'r Lleuad: Ffaith a Dychymyg yng Ngwaith Caradog Prichard* (Llandysul: Gwasg Gomer, 2005).
49. Caradog Prichard, *Un Nos Ola Leuad* (Dinbych: Gwasg Gee, n.d. [1961]), 40.
50. Ibid., 7.
51. Ibid., 18, 20.

24

The Poetry Revolution: Dylan Thomas and His Circle

WILLIAM CHRISTIE

Had the ardent nationalist and co-founder of Plaid Cymru, Saunders Lewis, had his way, there would have been no place in a history of Welsh literature for Wales's best-known writer. Born 27 October 1914 and reared in the anglicized suburb of Uplands in Swansea, Dylan Thomas spoke and wrote only in English and remained a determined monoglot throughout his short life, attempting no other languages, least of all Welsh. 'There is nothing hyphenated about him. He belongs to the English,' declared Lewis in a famous address to the Urdd Graddedigion Prifysgol Cymru Cangen Caerdydd (Guild of Graduates of the University of Wales, Cardiff branch) in 1938 entitled 'Is There an Anglo-Welsh Literature?'[1] Lewis, a lecturer at the University College in Swansea and linguistic essentialist who advocated an organic, Welsh-speaking society, was discussing the first issue of Keidrych Rhys's ground-breaking Anglo-Welsh literary journal, *Wales*, which in the summer of 1937 had opened with an experimental short story by Thomas entitled 'Prologue to an Adventure'. Though Thomas himself was sceptical about the idea of an Anglo-Welsh literature, which struck him as at best irrelevant and at worst apologetic, he was friends with Keidrych Rhys (and best man at his wedding) and actively supportive of the enterprise.

Rhys's choice of Thomas as an opening flourish for a journal that would circulate and celebrate English-language writing by Welsh authors can be understood as a recognition of the importance of Thomas to this newly self-conscious cluster of talented young writers (Idris Davies, Nigel Heseltine, Alun Lewis, Glyn Jones, Lynette Roberts, Vernon Watkins, Rhys Davies), and a shrewd marketing strategy at the same time. Though only twenty-two, Thomas was already a name amongst the poetry writers and readers of both Wales and England, and had been since the publication, not long after his twentieth birthday, of an astonishingly original first volume, *18 Poems* (1934). 'From that day,' wrote William Empson, 'he was a famous poet.'[2]

18 Poems

In *18 Poems*, Thomas had offered the reading public a selection of the strikingly idiosyncratic poems he had been cultivating in school exercise books since the age of fifteen.[3] Throughout his adolescence, and especially after – having left Swansea Grammar School at the age of sixteen – he threw in his job as a journalist at the *South Wales Evening Post* after a year and a half in December 1932, Thomas had little else to engage or distract him other than writing long letters to his London literary correspondent and lover, Pamela Hansford Johnson, occasional rehearsals for the amateur Little Theatre in Mumbles, and meetings with artistic friends. His time had been spent writing – 'fluently and furiously', in the words of James A. Davies[4] – and what he wrote he entered into his famous notebooks. Though he would eventually sell the notebooks in 1941, effectively renouncing them as a resource for future publications, poems drafted or written during this brief period would comprise nearly half the *Collected Poems* that Thomas brought out in 1952, the year before he died.

What the notebook poems bear witness to is 'Thomas's poetic self-making between the ages of fifteen and nineteen', to quote John Goodby.[5] From the beginning of the fourth notebook in August 1933, the poems take on the gnomic tone, dense anatomical imagery, regular thrusting rhythm, and complex aural patterning typical of Thomas's so-called 'process poems', as he explores the implication of the human body and its parts in a universal cycle of life and death and the impersonal processes, weathers, heavens, tides, and times of an indifferent universe.

> A process in the weather of the heart
> Turns damp to dry; the golden shot
> Storms in the freezing grave.
> A weather in the quarter of the veins
> Turns night to day; blood in their
> suns
> Lights up the living worm.
>
> A process in the eye forewarns
> The bones of blindness; and the
> womb
> Drives in a death as life leaks out.[6]

Fourteen of the notebook poems found their way into *18 Poems*, seven of them written during a prodigiously fertile period of just over six weeks.

Within the brief period of eight months represented by this last notebook, Thomas had created a corpus.

The publication of 18 Poems was a London affair, and the person most responsible for launching Thomas's professional career was the eccentric fifty-year-old poet, Victor Neuburg, who ran Poet's Corner, a regular show-case for aspiring poets established in the *Sunday Referee* newspaper in April 1933. Not only did Neuburg's (and Hansford Johnson's) support enable Thomas to gain confidence and extend his circle of London contacts, but Poet's Corner awarded him its major literary prize in the form of sponsorship of a first volume of poems, to be jointly published with David Archer of Parton's Bookshop, off Red Lion Square in Holborn. The 'landscape of arty-literary London' was managed from a comparatively small area, according to Valentine Cunningham, for whom Parton Street, Red Lion Square, func-tioned as a 'kind of epicentre'.[7] Parton put up £20, the *Sunday Referee* £30, and 18 Poems by Dylan Thomas appeared on 18 December 1934 for 3s. 6d.

The first collection, *18 Poems*, met with an admiration mounting to enthu-siasm from the critical reviewers. The *Adelphi, The Spectator, New Verse, European Quarterly*, and the *Times Literary Supplement* all published favourable reviews.[8] 'Mr. Thomas's habit of translating human experience into the terms of physiology and the machine, and his vivid sense of the correspondence between the forces informing the macrocosm and the microcosm', wrote the anonymous reviewer in the *Times Literary Supplement*, 'result in some power-ful as well as surprising imaginative audacities.'[9] Even those who found the poems baffling – and this would become a critical issue with the publication of Thomas's next two volumes – were willing to credit him with the creation of a new and exciting language.

The best-known and most anthologized of the process poems is 'The force that through the green fuse drives the flower', copied out or composed on 12 October 1933 and sent to Victor Neuburg at the *Sunday Referee*, where it appeared on 29 October, two days after the poet's nineteenth birthday:

> The force that through the green fuse drives the flower
> Drives my green age; that blasts the roots of trees
> Is my destroyer.
> And I am dumb to tell the crooked rose
> My youth is bent by the same wintry fever.
>
> The force that drives the water through the rocks
> Drives my red blood; that dries the mouthing streams
> Turns mine to wax.

> And I am dumb to mouth unto my veins
> How at the mountain spring the same mouth sucks.[10]

Cosmic, elemental, 'primitivistic in its self-hypnotic incantation', according to M. L. Rosenthal, it 'brings chanter and listener face to face with the appalling destructive force with which the unity of all nature is bound up'.[11] 'The force that through the green fuse drives the flower' is and does all these things, but we should be careful not to allow the 'self-hypnotic incantation' to mask a no less characteristic irony and subtle self-qualification. The poem rather explores than asserts a pantheistic union between man and nature through a quintessential life-and-death force. For all the speaker of the poem may share with 'the crooked rose', he cannot make himself heard. The phrase 'I am dumb to tell' is repeated five times as a refrain, an impasse that unwittingly distinguishes language-using animals like humans from an inarticulate natural world. We are reminded of the foliate head in medieval iconography, choking on its natural appendages. The lines become an ironic lament on behalf of humanity for its inability to communicate *to* nature its intuition of unity *with* nature. A division persists, in other words, if only in the human ability self-consciously to reflect on and express a shared process, and a shared mortality.

Thomas was the first to insist that his poetry was neither spontaneous in origin nor ceremoniously hypnotic in intention, taking obsessive care with the choice and development of his images. If he identified 'a very much overweighted imagery that leads too often to incoherence' as one of the 'main faults' of his writing in a letter to his publisher in December 1935, at the same time he defended himself vehemently against the charge of writing an irrational and unintelligible surrealism: 'every line *is* meant to be understood'.[12] Nevertheless, amid the social and political turmoil of the 1930s, poems like 'The force that through the green fuse drives the flower' offered the poetry-reading public excitement, even something like hope. For all the images of decay and death in the process poems, there was an unmistakable vitality marking their strong rhythms, sonorous music, and elemental landscapes and mindscapes, their compounds and coinages. 'Dylan Thomas was a language changer like certain other strong individualists before him,' writes Barbara Hardy, naming Shakespeare, Dickens, Hopkins, and Joyce.[13] Compellingly, Thomas's first lines shock and disorient: 'I see the boys of summer in their ruin', 'Where once the twilight locks no longer', 'Light breaks where no sun shines', 'Before I knocked and flesh let enter', and so on. The diction is familiar enough, and so, too, is the grammar and syntax (though this is not always the case), but we have to strain to make sense of it, to allow familiar structures to accommodate the unfamiliar, grammatically and conceptually. It is the same with Thomas's characteristic inversion of clichés and stock phrases: 'once below a time', 'fall awake', 'a grief ago', 'dressed to die', 'the stations of the breath'. The impulse to rattle or rearrange the verbal props upon which we rely in order to force them on our consciousness and to compel us to rethink the world through these modifications was a reflex reaction with Thomas: he does it in poetry, he does it in his radio features and familiar letters.

No less characteristic was Thomas's attention to the sounds of words: '"Drome", "bone", "doom", "province", "dwell", "prove", "dolomite" – these are only a few of my favourite words, which are insufferably beautiful to me. The first four words are visionary; God moves in a long "o".'[14] Again and again, Thomas attributed his urge to write to a love of the sounds words made:

> these words were, to me, as the notes of bells, the sounds of musical instruments, the noises of wind, sea, and rain, the rattle of milk-carts, the clopping of hooves on cobbles, the fingering of branches on a window pane, might be to someone, deaf from birth, who has miraculously found his hearing. I did not care what the words said, overmuch, nor what happened to Jack & Jill & Mother Goose and the rest of them; I cared for the shapes of sound that their names, and the words describing their actions, made in my ears; I cared for the colours the words cast on my eyes.[15]

'A poem on the page,' therefore, 'is only half a poem.'[16] As far as Thomas's reading his own poetry out loud was concerned, 'I think that one of the magical things,' said Aneirin Talfan Davies, one of Thomas's producers when the poet worked as a writer and broadcaster for the BBC, 'is that he has made people believe that they understand his poetry. He has insinuated the meaning into the reading.'[17] Whether magic or sleight of hand, what it sounded like made sense.

What Thomas was *not* doing, moreover, only reinforced his attraction for his early readers. Densely figurative, he was *not* subtly expository; visionary, it seemed, not worldly; strange, certainly, but that came as a relief, and he was sensual instead of being intellectual. If the poems were often obscure, they were not erudite, hieratic, allusive – having none of the cultured élitism of the Modernists, in other words, or of the Oxford Marxists. 'The Audenesque convention is early ended,' wrote Desmond Hawkins, reviewing *18 Poems* in *Time and Tide* on 9 February 1935, 'and I credit Dylan Thomas with being the first considerable poet to break through fashionable limitation and speak an unborrowed language, without excluding anything that has preceded him.'[18] Alive or dead, in sickness or in health, there is nothing more democratic than the human body picked clean of its clothes and culture:

> Light breaks where no sun shines;
> Where no sea runs, the waters of the heart
> Push in their tides;
> And, broken ghosts with glow-worms in their heads,
> The things of light
> File through the flesh where no flesh decks the bones.

In a letter to Pamela Hansford Johnson of November 1933, Thomas famously defended the anatomical preoccupations of his experimental poems:

> The body, its appearance, death, and diseases, is a fact, sure as the fact of a tree. It has its roots in the same earth as the tree. The greatest description I know of our own 'earthiness' is to be found in John Donne's Devotions, where he describes man as earth of the earth, his body earth, his hair a wild shrub growing out of the land. All thoughts and actions emanate from the body. Therefore the description of a thought or action – however abstruse it may be – can be beaten home by bringing it onto a physical level. Every idea, intuitive or intellectual, can be imaged and translated in terms of the body, its flesh, skin, blood, sinews, veins, glands, organs, cells, or senses.
>   Through my small, bone-bound island I have learnt all I know, experienced all, and sensed all. All I write is inseparable from the island.'[19]

It was not long before a bold, sometimes grotesque anatomical imagery and cannibalized Christian mythology became recognized as Thomas's signature. If the reviewers of 18 Poems missed some of the wit and self-irony, the jokes and literary allusions, the appeal of these early poems is hardly surprising. How long he would be able to enforce that notice was another matter. Just prior to the publication of 18 Poems, Thomas had left Swansea to try and settle in London, beginning a pattern of migrating between Wales and London that would last his whole life – a pattern punctuated by extended stays in Hampshire, the Cotswolds, and Oxfordshire, brief visits to Ireland, Italy, Czechoslovakia, and Iran, and, in his final years, extended tours of the United States. In Wales, until the war at least, he shared the company of a group of talented creative friends now known collectively as the 'Kardomah boys'. Opposite the newspaper offices of the South Wales Evening Post where Thomas had worked in Castle Street, Swansea, the Kardomah café had been converted from a Congregational chapel. Here, throughout late adolescence and early adulthood, Thomas met regularly with a group that at different times included his oldest and closest friend, the composer, scholar, and writer, Daniel Jones; poet and fellow journalist, Charles Fisher; the painter, Fred Janes, who would commute between Swansea and his London art school and share digs with Thomas in London; another painter, Mervyn Levy, whom Thomas had known since his primary school days and with whom he would also occasionally live in London; the Englishman, Tom Warner, another musician, who became a schoolmaster; Wynford Vaughan-Thomas, later a war correspondent as well as a travel writer and broadcaster; the poet and novelist, John Prichard, and Thomas's close friend and regular correspondent on poetic matters, the poet, Vernon Watkins.

In London, on the other hand, Thomas developed the extraordinarily punitive regime of drinking and socializing for which he is infamous, and which only intensified during the reading tours he conducted across the United States in the last four years of his life. Eventually, this intense and sometimes self-destructive sociability would drain his poetic creativity. Once his poetry had brought him to the attention of the public, Thomas extended his London social circle and professional contacts. Cyril Connolly invited him over to meet Anthony Powell, for example, and, on another occasion, Evelyn Waugh and Desmond MacCarthy.[20] Thomas, however, was never entirely comfortable meeting and conversing with established writers of an educated, upper-class background. As a result, many of his London friends came from regional England, Ireland, Scotland, and the Commonwealth countries: Australia, New Zealand, South Africa, Canada. And, of course, from Wales, which would remain the source of his security and creativity.

This was especially the case with the friendship begun on one of Thomas's 'bolthole' visits to Swansea in March 1935 with the poet, Vernon Watkins, eight years his senior and a practising Christian with a job in a bank, who wrote rather than drank in the evenings. After the heady days of Thomas's epistolary courtship of Pamela Hansford Johnson, there were few people with whom he would discuss poetry in any detail. Daniel Jones would always share his confidence, but in his lifetime it was only Watkins with whom Thomas would maintain a close friendship centred on the shared craft of poetry. Of the two poets, interestingly, Watkins was the more defensive about his work, even though it would be some years before the publication of his own first volume, *The Ballad of the Mari Lwyd* (1941). Their closeness and Watkins's admiration for Thomas has meant that, of all the Welsh poets writing in English during and after Thomas, Watkins is the one in whose work Thomas's influence is most manifest. Having said that, Watkins's poetry was never as congested as Thomas's and the influence did not last. Watkins went on to publish four more volumes of original poetry in his own lifetime, and after his death at the age of sixty-one, in 1967, a number of others followed.

One issue over which the two friends fell out was that of Thomas's growing obscurity in his writing. More and more, with the poetry written after the publication of 18 *Poems*, the reader struggles with an impenetrably heterogeneous and proliferating imagery of the dialectical kind Thomas would later describe to the apocalyptic poet, Henry Treece:

> A poem by myself *needs* a host of images, because its centre is a host of images. I make one image – though 'make' is not the word; I let, perhaps, an image be 'made' emotionally in me and then apply to it what intellectual and critical forces I possess – let it breed another, let that image contradict the first, make, of the third image bred out of the other two together, a fourth contradictory image, and let them all, within my imposed formal limits, conflict.[21]

Even by Modernism's standards, much of Thomas's poetry is difficult, and how far 'every line *is* meant to be understood', as he assured J. M. Dent, remains a moot point. 'Are you obscure?' he asked Glyn Jones: 'But, yes, all good modern poetry is bound to be obscure.'[22] Later, Thomas would begin to doubt the high Modernist exclusiveness with which he had embraced his vocation as a young poet. The poems of the early years in London represent experiments in excess, testing how far he could develop challengingly obscur-antist practices before alienating both his reader and himself.

The Stories and Poetry of the Middle Years

It was the same with the short stories that Thomas wrote over the course of a year between late 1933 and late 1934. The continuities between the process poems and these dark fables are striking: the same impassioned rhetoric and rhythm; the same dark, sensuous imagery; the same heavily laden Christian symbolism; the same fantastic settings – except that the stories, because of their settings, the presence of characters, and their limited narrative devel-opment, are a more obviously melodramatic development of the 'gothic-grotesque' tradition in which he is working: 'His Freudian and revolutionary impulses, sexual and religious obsessions, dark wordplay and sardonic wit,' writes John Goodby, 'work through Nonconformist repressions and an abject social reality.'[23] The young Dylan, who delighted in horrifying himself with tales and films of vampires and werewolves, embraces more openly in the stories than he does in the poems the blood and the body parts, the monstrosity, and the sexual taboos never far away from the gothic: incest, idiocy, insanity, rape, crucifixion, stillbirth. 'The Burning Baby', for example, is a typically dark, anti-clerical tale of the ritual burning of a stillborn child, the offspring of an incestuous relationship between a Nonconformist rural minister, Rhys Rhys, and his willing daughter.[24] Out of biblical as well as Welsh mythology, Thomas would fashion a nightmare version of rural west Wales as a fictional place he called Jarvis Valley, a grotesque, adolescent version of the Welsh anti-pastoral of Caradoc Evans and William Faulkner's Yoknapatawpha.

Though its violence is less explicit than in the stories, the poetry written immediately after *18 Poems* is dense in its choice and pattern of imagery, yoking multiple, often heterogeneous images together 'uncompromisingly', to quote Walford Davies:[25]

> Altarwise by owl-light in the halfway-house
> The gentleman lay graveward with his furies:
> Abaddon in the hang-nail cracked from Adam,
> And, from his fork, a dog among the fairies,
> The atlas-eater with a jaw for news,
> Bit out the mandrake with tomorrow's scream.
> Then, penny-eyed, that gentleman of wounds,
> Old cock from nowheres and the heaven's egg,
> With bones unbuttoned to the halfway winds,
> Hatched from the windy salvage on one leg,
> Scraped at my cradle in a walking word
> That night of time under the Christward shelter,
> I am the long world's gentleman, he said,
> And share my bed with Capricorn and Cancer.

A chorus of complaint began to sound in the critical establishment. The otherwise sympathetic Desmond Hawkins in *The Spectator*, for example, argued that Thomas had been 'less successful at subduing his material to communicable form'.[26] The *Times Literary Supplement* reviewer found much that was 'baffling', the *London Mercury* 'a mere riot of noise'.[27] For some of these critics the diagnosis was clear: Thomas was a surrealist, his poetry at best irrational and absurd, at worst 'psychopathological nonsense' (to quote Geoffrey Grigson).[28]

Though Thomas's reputation was salvaged by an effusive and hyperbolic review by Edith Sitwell in the widely read *Sunday Times*, it did not end there.

A reference in Sitwell's review to the necessary 'difficulty' of Thomas's poetry – 'largely the result of the intense concentration of each phrase, packed with meaning' – provoked an avalanche of letters 'on the pros and cons of modern poetry', twenty of which were printed over the following two months.[29] The upshot of this high-profile public debate was that, after 750 copies of *Twenty-Five Poems* (1936) sold immediately, a second, third, and fourth impression were required, which meant that 3,000 copies were soon sold, 'making it one of the more successful poetry books of the 1930s', to quote Andrew Lycett, with figures at least comparable with W. H. Auden and John Betjeman.[30]

Watkins recalls that Thomas preferred his more recent and more difficult poems at the time of publication, but they were taking him much longer to compose, and he was soon prompted, though not without misgivings, to abandon the imagistic overload which was alienating many of his readers:

> I'm almost afraid of the once-necessary artifices and obscurities, and can't, for the life or death of me, get any real liberation, any diffusion or dilution or anything, into the churning bulk of the words; I seem, more than ever, to be tightly packing away everything that I have and know into a mad-doctor's bag, and then locking it up.[31]

The review of *Twenty-Five Poems* in the *New Statesman* ended by agreeing that Thomas was a 'really original poet', but 'for the moment, perhaps', the poet was 'wondering which way to turn'.[32]

However uncertain Thomas may have been about his style, he was already established. When Keidrych Rhys published 'Prologue to an Adventure' in *Wales* in June 1937, Thomas (soon to be married to Caitlin Macnamara) could number among his friends and supporters (besides Edith Sitwell and Cyril Connolly) William Empson and Stephen Spender, and the following year T. S. Eliot, John Masefield, and Walter de la Mare were writing wholeheartedly to support what turned out to be an unsuccessful application to the Royal Literary Fund.[33]

Some of the creative effort that was not going into poems in 1938 and 1939 was going into writing stories very different in form and atmosphere from the crepuscular extravaganza with which he had been testing the tolerance of the reading public. In these new stories, using a child's-eye narrative perspective, Thomas recovered and reshaped luminous incidents and episodes from his own Swansea and Carmarthenshire childhood. 'A Visit to Grandpa's', written during the winter of 1937–8 and published in the *New English Weekly* in March 1938, became the first of a series of ten that, in April 1940, came out as *A*

Portrait of the Artist as a Young Dog.[34] Thomas soon added 'One Warm Saturday' and 'The Peaches'. In 'The Peaches',[35] Thomas uses his Aunt Ann and Uncle Jim Jones's struggling farm, Fernhill, as the setting for a moving story of a paid holiday undertaken by a boy from a wealthy city family. The child who tells the story is himself an urban visitor to this strange world of rural subsistence – both part of, and not part of, the family of his poor relations, for whom a tin of peaches represents the height of refinement. In a closely observed, class-calibrated fable, Thomas is able to satirize the folly of Nonconformist enthusiasm in the narrator's cousin, Gwilym, while at the same time figuring it as one of many distorted voices in the awkward conversation going on in Welsh society between different historical sensibilities and social classes. Thomas moves beyond adolescent self-obsession to a vision of the artist as an almost cruelly observant, privileged child and youth around whom an interpretable world of characters and events unfolds.

It is indicative of the relativities within Thomas's workload that his next volume, *The Map of Love*, which appeared on 24 August 1939, should have included seven prose stories alongside sixteen poems. Like *Twenty-Five Poems*, the collection moves uncertainly in different directions. The stories revert to his more overtly symbolic and surrealistic narrative style, and the selection of poems mixes recent nativity and birthday poems – 'A saint about to fall', 'If my head hurt a hair's foot', 'Twenty-four years' – with others that extensively rework early notebook entries: 'How shall my animal', 'Once it was the colour of saying', and the moving and popular elegy written for his aunt, Ann Jones: 'After the funeral'. As for its reception, the volume hardly had one: it appeared just eight days before the outbreak of the Second World War.

Deaths and Entrances

Throughout most of the war, Thomas enjoyed his first regular income since working for the *South Wales Evening Post* as a school-leaver, becoming a documentary film writer for Strand Films. This, combined with family crises and a prolonged uncertainty about his poetry meant that the years 1939–44 were lean ones. Thomas did, however, compose a handful of war elegies that were occasional in ways his poems had rarely been. The best known was inspired directly by the Blitz and distinguished by having its own title – 'A Refusal to Mourn the Death, by Fire, of a Child in London' – which hints at the public nature of the enterprise. Indeed, the title alone contains the paradox on which the poem turns: its very formality and gravitas (like that of the poem), not to mention the pathos guaranteed by its simple narrative details, belie its resolution not to mourn. To refuse *is* to mourn:

> Never until the mankind making
> Bird beast and flower
> Fathering and all humbling darkness
> Tells with silence the last light breaking
> And the still hour
> Is come of the sea tumbling in harness
>
> And I must enter again the round
> Zion of the water bead
> And the synagogue of the ear of corn
> Shall I let pray the shadow of a sound
> Or sow my salt seed
> In the least valley of sackcloth to mourn
>
> The majesty and burning of the child's death.

The war elegies return to the pulpit for their ministration and to the Bible for their language: Dylan Thomas as his great uncle, the bard and Nonconformist preacher, Gwilym Marles.

> Deep with the first dead lies London's daughter,
> Robed in the long friends,
> The grains beyond age, the dark veins of her mother,
> Secret by the unmourning water
> Of the riding Thames.
> After the first death, there is no other.

However ambiguous its categorical ending – after the first death, there is eternal life? after the first death, there is nothing? if there is no other death, why is this a 'first'? – the poet-priest would appear to have something authoritative, something ceremonial, something consolatory to offer the congregation, his readers.

The devastation from air raids in and around Swansea early in 1941 saw the resurrection of Swansea in Thomas's literary imagination, especially the Swansea of his childhood. When the 1940s brought Thomas work in the more popular media of radio and propaganda films – in radio features like 'Reminiscences of Childhood', for example, 'A Child's Christmas in Wales', and 'Return Journey' – we witness him turning to Wales and to the past, plundering his own childhood as he had done in the stories of *A Portrait of the Artist as a Young Dog*. What we get after 1941, however, is nostalgia – usually, but not always, self-ironic and framed as an indulgence – a nostalgia that will soon become a characteristic part of

Thomas's engagement with the new and larger public represented by the audience of the BBC, where his writing and recording commitments were increasing every year.

Nostalgia will also become an integral part of a revised poetic. As early as December 1933, Thomas can be found writing to Hansford Johnson that 'one day I hope to write something altogether out of the hangman's sphere, something larger, wider, more comprehensible, and less self-centred'.[36] Readers of Thomas's next and fourth volume of verse, *Deaths and Entrances* (1946), a product of the poet's second and final period of sustained creative activity at New Quay in 1944–5, were greeted by more accessible imagery and heard a very different music. Begun for his twenty-seventh birthday in 1941, 'Poem in October' occupied Thomas until his 'thirtieth year to heaven' in 1944:

> It was my thirtieth year to heaven
> Woke to my hearing from harbour and neighbour wood
> And the mussel pooled and the heron
> Priested shore
> The morning beckon
> With water praying and call of seagull and rook
> And the knock of sailing boats on the net webbed wall
> Myself to set foot
> That second
> In the still sleeping town and set forth.

It was as if a light broke on the landscape of his memory and his imagination was invaded by a wider, more inclusive pathos. Intricately patterned by its sounds, 'Poem in October' has an almost flawless syllabic count of 9, 12, 9, 3, 5, 12, 12, 5, 3, 9 in each stanza. The turnings of memory, the season, and the landscape in the poem are mirrored in the intricate turnings of the rhythm and assonance.

> A springful of larks in a rolling
> Cloud and the roadside bushes brimming with whistling
> Blackbirds and the sun of October
> Summery
> On the hill's shoulder,
> Here were fond climates and sweet singers suddenly
> Come in the morning where I wandered and listened
> To the rain wringing
> Wind blow cold
> In the wood faraway under me.

Not that this scrupulous attention to prosodic detail was new. Thomas's craftsmanship, careful to the point of obsessiveness, is characteristic of all his work, early *and* late. For all its apparent spontaneity, an early poem like 'If I were tickled by the rub of love', for example, has a syllabic patterning (10, 10, 10, 10, 10, 10, 6) as flawlessly consistent as that of 'Poem in October'. 'I am a painstaking, conscientious, involved and devious craftsman in words,' wrote Thomas in the document which would become 'Poetic Manifesto'.[37] He was, to quote Chris Baldick, 'the most dedicated practitioner both of half-rhyme and of pararhyme'.[38]

What *was* new was what the poet called 'a lovely slow lyrical movement',[39] more open syntax, and accessible imagery. 'The strange compelling imagination of his work in the 1930s seems far away when we read "Poem in October" or "Fern Hill",' as James Davies has said, 'the latter are beautiful, disconcerting, but less intense, perhaps less original'.[40] Perhaps. The jury is out and has been ever since Thomas embarked on his new style. Many critics feel, with William Empson and Walford Davies, that it was in the 'density' of Thomas's process poems that 'the trapped ambiguities and contradictions of experience' were 'most effectively and affectively caught', in Davies's words.[41] But there are ambiguities and contradictions lurking beneath the lilting surface of lyrics like 'Fern Hill', which can look with characteristic ambivalence both before and after, and simultaneously indulge and ironize a rhapsodic escapism and nostalgia. The poems of *Deaths and Entrances* were different from the early poems, but they were still inimitably Dylan Thomas: 'The conversation of prayers', 'A Refusal to Mourn', 'Poem in October', 'This side of truth', 'The hunchback in the park', 'A Winter's Tale', 'In my craft or sullen art', 'Fern Hill', to name the better known from amongst twenty-five remarkably various poems.

No less than *18 Poems, Deaths and Entrances* won an immediate and responsive audience. J. M. Dent began by printing 3,000 copies and then had to reprint another 3,000 a month later,[42] and with one or two exceptions the volume was critically acclaimed. 'Mr Thomas must simply be regarded as a phenomenon,' wrote the anonymous reviewer in *The Listener*, summing up the critical reaction: 'He writes, and the result is a poetry that has all the marks of greatness.'[43] Again, as in 1934, the British public was entranced by a new voice, in this case one that seemed overwhelmingly positive after the experiences of the war.

Under Milk Wood

When Thomas re-created provincial Wales for his famous radio 'play for voices', *Under Milk Wood*, the busy memory and detailed observation of the *Portrait* stories were enlivened by a rich blend of fantasy, satire, and comic gusto – as well as genuine affection. And were enlivened, of course, by poetry: 'Love the words' was the one piece of directorial advice he had to offer the cast at the first full performance of *Under Milk Wood* in New York in May 1953.[44] It is this, before anything else, that establishes a continuity between Thomas's best-known work and the strikingly idiosyncratic forms he entered into his notebooks in the early 1930s.

There is no single original either for the town of Llareggub in which the play is set or for any one of its characters. 'It's a lyrical – & <sometimes> slapstick – picture of a small <Welsh> town-that-never-was,' as Thomas told an audience when reading from the work in the lead up to its first performance.[45] Its characterizations are informed as much by Thomas's reading as they are by the people he met, and any adequate genealogy would have to include, along with Shakespeare and Dickens and James Joyce – 'Joyce is there in the characters,' writes Barbara Hardy, 'he's there in the time scheme, he's there in the dream fantasy, he's there in the narrative monologues, he's there in the fun and flow'[46] – writers such as Caradoc Evans, T. F. Powys, Stella Gibbons, and Edgar Lee Masters's *Spoon River Anthology* (1915).

Thomas's manuscript notes give us some idea of what was behind his choice of title:

> The lust & lilt and <lather & crackle> of the
> bird-praise <& body of> Spring with its breasts full of
> rivering May-milk, means, to that lordly
> fish-head <nibbler>, nothing but
> another nearness to the
> slashing
> tribes and navies of the
> Last Dark Day who'll sear &
> pillage down Armageddon
> Hill to his <double> locked
> <rusty-> shuttered tick tock
> dust scribbled shack at
> the bottom of the
> town in [love *crossed out*] that has fallen
> head over bells in love.

And I'll never have such loving again
hums & longs
pretty Polly.[47]

The lines confirm the role of Polly Garter, with her babies and unapologetic sexuality, as tutelary spirit of the piece. Polly rules under Milk Wood as Artemis/Diana, the mother-goddess of the ancient world, an eternally young, untamed girl nourishing life with many breasts. Indeed, she is the Earth herself, her breasts mountains, her body a dwelling place for all living creatures. Every incident, every relationship, every aside in this pastoral fantasy is shaped by *eros*, and never more so than when characters abstain or abominate. Indeed, the sexual instinct is most active in its repression, for the town offers a gallery of portraits in which sex is most remarkable in its frustration, displacement, or flat denial, from Mr Mog Edwards's obsession with money to 'Mrs Ogmore-Pritchard's terrible death-waiting loneliness' (in Thomas's arresting manuscript note to himself), refusing to have boarders breathe all over her furniture.

The only work of Sigmund Freud that Thomas admitted having read was *Interpretation of Dreams*,[48] but there can be no doubt that the works of most relevance to his imagination were *Mourning and Melancholia* and *Beyond the Pleasure Principle*. With its cast of over seventy characters, many of them with a Dickensian distinctiveness and memorability, *Under Milk Wood* is a comic opera busy with idiosyncratic life – a busyness and vitality symbolized and generated by an inventive orchestration and imagery. At the same time, however, the vitality of Llareggub is frequently exposed as the defensive strategy of a people 'born to die', as the Rev. Eli Jenkins quietly reminds the audience, invoking Thomas's affinity with Dean John Donne, whose symbols and harbingers of death in *Devotions Upon Emergent Occasions* pervade the early poetry.

Thomas and Wales

In the long prologue to his *Collected Poems*, written and published a year before he died, Thomas traced the tides of his life through their full cycle. At the still centre and crucial turning point of the poem's tidal ebb and flow – in which the first of a hundred and two lines rhymes with the last, the second with the second last, and so on, until they meet in a rhyming couplet in the middle – we come to the line 'To Wales in my arms', which is also the poem's buried dedication. At the outset of Thomas's writing life, provincial Wales had been everything socially smug and sexually repressive to the young poet, and he had coped by exaggerating his own alienation and adopting a number of different poses. In spite of the fame he achieved and his longed-for escape to London, however, Thomas still found himself gravitating back to Wales.

Robert Pocock recalled having 'only once heard Dylan express an opinion of Welsh nationalism. He used three words. Two of them were Welsh Nationalism.'[49] On the issue of his own Welshness or the Welsh affinities of his poetry, Thomas countered Saunders Lewis's exclusive linguistic purism with a vocational purism of his own, in which the poet moved to protect his art against the contamination of politics. He was not oblivious to 'the erosion of the political and cultural traditions of post-war Wales' and 'prolonged economic depression' that motivated and informed the Welsh nationalist movement[50] – indeed, there is evidence of his awareness in occasional poems and most acutely in the *Portrait* stories. His obligation, however, at least as Thomas saw it, was to himself and to his art.

This was and is unlikely to satisfy the nationalists, or indeed those critics who want to know about Thomas's attitude to Wales or about the Welsh roots of Thomas's literary expression and practices, the critics for whom the Welshness (or not) of his poetry turns into questions of interpretation and value. Addressing the Scottish PEN in September 1948, Thomas was characteristically facetious: 'Regarded in England as a Welshman (and a waterer of England's milk), and in Wales as an Englishman, I am too unnational to be here at all. I should be living in a small private leper house in Hereford or Shropshire, one foot in Wales and my vowels in England.'[51] At the same time, however, he expressed a genuine ideal of what is now called transnationality, one that avoided the reductive essentialism of nationalist thinking.

The fact remains that all of Thomas's best poetry was written in Wales, and all his best stories and radio features set in Wales. His 'links with Welsh writers', moreover, 'despite Thomas's own reservations about many of them and a general indifference to the idea of "Anglo-Welsh" writing, became a significant element in his literary career', as James Davies points out.[52] As for the Welshness (or not) of Thomas's poetry, again, it is best to avoid too categorical an approach to the question. 'I'm not influenced by Welsh bardic poetry,' he wrote to Stephen Spender, 'I can't read Welsh.'[53] This much we know to be true, just as we know that it has not stopped critics writing, sometimes persuasively, of characteristically Welsh rhythms and verse forms in his work. On one occasion, Thomas himself warned a would-be editor: '"I dreamed my genesis" is more or less based on Welsh rhythms, & may seem, rhythmically, a bit strange at first.'[54] At the same time, as his friend, Glyn

Jones, pointed out, Thomas always 'felt the need for some sort of discipline to his verse'.[55] Only rarely did he flirt with traditional verse forms – with the sonnet in the half-rhymed 'When all my five and country senses see', 'Among those Killed in the Dawn Raid was a Man Aged a Hundred', and 'Lie Still, Sleep Becalmed', as well as in the 'Altarwise by owl-light' sequence, and most famously (and most effectively) with the repetitive villanelle form in 'Do not go gentle into that good night'. Yet Thomas wrote no poem without imposing often punitive technical limits on himself.

Does this make him a Welsh poet? Aneirin Talfan Davies certainly thought so: 'Dylan's whole attitude is that of the Medieval bards. They gave themselves tasks. He said he knew nothing about Welsh bardic poetry, but I often talked to him about it. You have to be wary of Dylan – he was always laying false trails.'[56] There are, moreover, other kinds of Welshness and other ways of approaching these Welsh affinities. Roland Mathias draws attention to the various ways in which the tone, rhythm, and idiom of Thomas's poetry could be seen to derive from the Welsh-speaking chapel culture of south-west Wales.[57] Insofar as the language of any poet will be found, like DNA, to carry traces of an incomprehensively complex inheritance, the interpretation of these and other correspondences requires tact and circumspection. 'He would call himself a Welsh poet writing English poetry, because Welsh was in his blood' – so Vernon Watkins, who, like Thomas, disapproved of the term 'Anglo-Welsh' that was becoming fashionable during his time. 'You can be wholly Welsh, and write only English poetry. And that's what Dylan did.'[58]

Notes

1. Saunders Lewis, *Is There an Anglo-Welsh Literature?* (Cardiff: Guild of Graduates of the University of Wales, 1939), 5. Lewis, it has to be said, later changed his attitude to Thomas.
2. William Empson, 'The Collected Dylan Thomas', in his *Argufying: Essays on Literature and Culture*, ed. John Haffenden (London: Hogarth Press, 1988), 393.
3. Four of these 'notebooks' are still extant (there is a gap between July 1932 and January 1933). Held in the Poetry Library of the State University of New York, Buffalo, they were first made available to the public in 1967 in an edition by Ralph Maud.
4. James A. Davies, *A Reference Companion to Dylan Thomas* (Westport, CT: Greenwood Press, 1998), 25.
5. John Goodby, *The Poetry of Dylan Thomas: Under the Spelling Wall* (Liverpool: Liverpool University Press, 2013), 52.

6. Dylan Thomas, *Poet in the Making: The Notebooks of Dylan Thomas*, ed. Ralph Maud (London: Dent & Sons, 1968), 262.

7. Valentine Cunningham, *British Writers of the Thirties* (Oxford: Oxford University Press, 1988), 108, 109.

8. For a history of Thomas's critical reception, see Davies, *A Reference Companion to Dylan Thomas*, 243–336.

9. *Times Literary Supplement*, 13 March 1935, 163.

10. All quotations from the poems Thomas published in his own lifetime are from *The Collected Poems of Dylan Thomas: The New Centenary Edition*, ed. John Goodby (London: Weidenfeld and Nicolson, 2014).

11. M. L. Rosenthal, *The Modern Poets* (New York: Oxford University Press, 1965), 210.

12. Dylan Thomas, *Collected Letters*, ed. Paul Ferris, rev. edn (London: Dent, 2000), 232.

13. Barbara Hardy, *Dylan Thomas: An Original Language* (Athens and London: University of Georgia Press, 2000), 52.

14. Thomas, *Collected Letters*, 90.

15. From an interview with Thomas in 1951 known as 'Poetic Manifesto', in *Early Prose Writings*, ed. Walford Davies (London: Dent, 1971), 154.

16. 'The Festival of Spoken Poetry', in Dylan Thomas, *The Broadcasts*, ed. Ralph Maud (London: Dent, 1991), 198.

17. David N. Thomas, ed., *Dylan Remembered*, vol. II: *Interviews by Colin Edwards, 1935–1953* (Bridgend: Seren / Poetry of Wales Press, 2004), 148.

18. Desmond Hawkins, 'Review of *18 Poems* by Dylan Thomas', *Time and Tide* 16, 6 (1935): 206.

19. Thomas, *Collected Letters*, 57.

20. Andrew Lycett, *Dylan Thomas: A New Life* (Woodstock and New York: The Overlook Press, 2003), 108; Paul Ferris, *Dylan Thomas: The Biography*, 2nd edn (London: Dent, 1999), 112.

21. Thomas, *Collected Letters*, 328–9.

22. Thomas, *Collected Letters*, 122.

23. Goodby, *The Poetry of Dylan Thomas*, 240, 241.

24. Dylan Thomas, *Collected Stories*, ed. Walford Davies (London: Phoenix, 2000), 36–41.

25. Walford Davies, *Dylan Thomas* (Milton Keynes: Open University Press, 1986), 18.

26. Desmond Hawkins, quoted in Lycett, *Dylan Thomas*, 136.

27. See Davies, *A Reference Companion to Dylan Thomas*, 246, 292.

28. Geoffrey Grigson, quoted in Davies, *A Reference Companion to Dylan Thomas*, 293.

29. Davies, *A Reference Companion to Dylan Thomas*, 292.

30. Lycett, *Dylan Thomas*, 136.

31. Thomas, *Collected Letters*, 249. Watkins's comments as quoted in *Collected Poems*, 195.

32. As quoted in Ferris, *Dylan Thomas*, 133.

33. Thomas, *Collected Letters*, 377, n. 2.

34. Thomas, *Collected Stories*, 143–8.

35. Ibid., 127–42.

36. Thomas, *Collected Letters*, 94.

37. Reprinted in Thomas, *Early Prose Writings*, 158.

38. Chris Baldick, *The Oxford English Literary History*, vol. X: *The Modern Movement (1910–1940)* (Oxford: Oxford University Press, 2004), 79.

39. Thomas, *Collected Letters*, 581.

40. Davies, *A Reference Companion to Dylan Thomas*, 68.

41. Walford Davies, *Dylan Thomas: The Poet in His Chains*, The W. D. Thomas Memorial Lecture (Swansea: University College of Swansea, 1986), 26.

42. Constantine Fitzgibbon, *The Life of Dylan Thomas* (London: Dent & Sons, 1965), 302, 314.

43. Anon., quoted in Davies, *A Reference Companion to Dylan Thomas*, 296.

44. See Colin Edwards's interview with Sada Thompson and Nancy Wickwire, in *Dylan Remembered*, ed. Thomas, vol. II, 226.

45. University of Texas at Austin, Harry Ransom Center, Dylan Thomas Collection.

46. Hardy, *Dylan Thomas: An Original Language*, 57.

47. Harry Ransom Center, Dylan Thomas Collection.

48. Dylan Thomas, 'Answers to an Enquiry', *New Verse*, 11 October 1934, reprinted as Appendix 4 in Thomas, *Collected Poems*, 227.

49. Robert Pocock, quoted in Fitzgibbon, *The Life of Dylan Thomas*, 10.

50. Kenneth O. Morgan, *Rebirth of a Nation: Wales, 1880–1980* (Oxford: Clarendon Press, 1981), 210.

51. Dylan Thomas, quoted in E. W. Tedlock, ed., *Dylan Thomas: The Legend and the Poet* (London: Heinemann, 1960), 8.

52. Davies, *A Reference Companion to Dylan Thomas*, 36.

53. Thomas, *Collected Letters*, 953.

54. Ibid., 161–2.

55. Glyn Jones, in *Dylan Remembered*, ed. Thomas, vol. II, 48.

56. Aneirin Talfan Davies, quoted in Ferris, *Dylan Thomas*, 104–5.

57. Roland Mathias, *A Ride Through the Wood: Essays on Anglo-Welsh Literature* (Bridgend: Poetry Wales Press, 1985), 72.

58. Vernon Watkins, in *Dylan Remembered*, ed. Thomas, vol. II, 62.

PART V

*

THE PATH TO NATIONHOOD
IN THE LATE TWENTIETH
CENTURY

25

Debating Nationhood, c. 1945–2000

SEÁN AERON MARTIN AND MARI ELIN WILIAM

In 1955 Cardiff was formally recognized as the capital of Wales, a symbolic celebration of civic nationhood for a 'stateless' nation. However, this suggestive ascendancy of urban and industrial Wales challenged historically established notions of Welshness, particularly due to Cardiff's location in what later became labelled by political scientist Denis Balsom as 'British Wales'. Balsom's 'Three Wales Model', a construct which indicated varying political and cultural identities, split the nation, roughly, into Plaid Cymru's 'Y Fro Gymraeg' ('The Welsh Heartland') in the west, Labour's south 'Welsh Wales' coalfields, and the Conservative 'British Wales' of the east.[1] This partition, although rudimentary, was nonetheless a powerful concept and broadly represented three different 'national' responses to the challenges facing post-war Wales. Concurrently, the continued retreat of the old 'Liberal' nation under the spectre of modernity created cultural space for differing expressions of Welshness, which was often, as this chapter argues, fraught with tension and contested interpretations of the meaning of Wales. Nevertheless, following decades of necessary conflict and compromise, by the turn of the millennium a reconstituted nationhood had asserted itself within the Welsh consciousness.

'Affluence' and Crisis: Economic Identities

Claims to Welsh nationhood, albeit couched in cultural terms, have often been embedded in Wales's economic viability and control of its resources.[2] However, the very idea of a Welsh 'economy' or of 'traditional' Welsh industry has historically been a nebulous one, obscured by the macroeconomic British picture and the segmented nature of the Welsh economic base. Arguably, assertions of Welsh economic distinctiveness were further undermined in the post-war period, with the contraction of some of its archetypal industries and the growth (and then withdrawal) of interventionist, centralized government planning, as well as the impact of affluence and technological modernization.[3]

Reconstruction was inevitably the watchword in the aftermath of the Second World War, and this had particular salience in many Welsh communities, such as the Rhondda, where monolithic dominance by heavy industries had led to devastation during the Great Depression.[4] The narrative of 'never again' saw post-war austerity counterbalanced by the Attlee administration's expansion of the welfare state, the establishment of the NHS, and the nationalization of key utilities and industries. Although these were 'British' policies, driven by state centralization, they were also viewed as having a radical 'Welsh' socialist hue, particularly due to the presence of two Welsh Labour figures – Aneurin Bevan and Jim Griffiths – in key reforming ministries.

Coal nationalization in 1947 held a special poignancy, as it seemingly heralded the class victory of the miners, and signalled their emergence from the 'cataclysmic' shadow of the inter-war years.[5] However, the extent of this 'new dawn' is questionable, as the coming decades under the National Coal Board saw not only pit closures but also the national trauma of the 1966 Aberfan Disaster.[6] This epitomized the pre-Thatcherite decline of 'King Coal' in Wales, already mired in state neglect, double-standards, and environmental degradation.

Nationalization could have provided an economic backbone to Welshness in the era of the supposed post-war consensus. However, with a few exceptions, such as the creation of the Wales Gas Board in 1949, the nationalized industries reinforced the splintering of Wales and augmented east–west links across Offa's Dyke, as opposed to north–south cooperation within Wales.[7] There were complaints from Conservatives that nationalization and planning were prioritizing centralization over localism, and for Welsh nationalists they were insidious and deliberate threats to Welsh identity.[8] Similar concerns were iterated by the cross-border draw of Wales's main transport links. In *Border Country* Raymond Williams described the rail-map with 'arteries, held in the shape of Wales' but 'running out' into England, and Thomas Firbank wrote in the 1950s that geography had shaped Wales into 'pockets which, even to-day, were almost watertight'.[9] Topographically, the landscape was inimical to constructing a north–south road, and in the post-1945 decades the spread of the car inevitably saw two new east–west arteries developing: the M4 along the south Wales corridor to London, and the A55 strengthening the ties between north Wales and the north-west of England.

The car encapsulated the shapeshifting nature of identity in the age of the so-called 'affluent society'. It eased the passage of commuters, visitors, and, ultimately, longer-term migration between England and Wales, enabling social changes such as suburbanization, the profusion of 'second homes' in rural areas, and an increasingly fluid cultural and linguistic mix.[10] However, improved mobility also sustained the budding of a tourist industry, and a Welsh Tourist Board had emerged by the 1950s, with the purpose of 'selling' Wales as a distinctive 'package'; albeit a package that flagged a sentimental, Welsh-doll impression of a nation.[11]

Tourism also created service-sector employment, often providing rural areas decimated by depopulation – partially driven by agricultural mechanization – with much needed diversification. However, such modernization could lead to contested claims on Welsh land and rurality, as schemes such as the development of nuclear power stations in north-west Wales during the 1950s and 1960s became subject to seemingly existential debates framed around 'bread' versus 'beauty'.[12] These were often emblematic of contrasting elite and grassroots perceptions of tradition and modernity in the 'battle for Welshness'.[13]

Undoubtedly change was encroaching into the economy in post-1945 Wales, much of it driven by varying degrees of regional planning. The 1945 Distribution of Industry Act directed investment to areas most in need, in particular the deprived south Wales coalfield.[14] By the mid-1960s, such funnelling was made under the auspices of the Welsh Office and, later, the Welsh Development Agency, adding a Welsh tinge to what was still essentially regional planning for Wales.

However, even though there was nominal 'full employment' in Wales during the 1950s and 1960s, and diversification towards manufacturing and the service sector, much of the new work provided was low-paid, low-skilled, or state-dependent.[15] There remained significant pockets of unemployment during this period, and Wales was, relatively, one of the poorest parts of Britain. Out of twelve UK regions, it had the second lowest output per head between the 1960s and 1990s, and the switch from its over-reliance on heavy industry to over-reliance on government intervention was exposed by the economic melange of the 1970s.[16] According to sympathetic economic analyses during the 1970s, the roots of Welsh problems lay in the 'internal colonialism' and 'uneven development' of the British state, which sidelined Wales to a 'satellite position' in England's orbit.[17] The twin impact of de-industrialization and post-1979 Thatcherism's 'rolling back of the frontiers of the state' sounded the death knell of the coal industry and had particularly pernicious results in a region disproportionately dependent on government intervention as its mainstay.

Whilst most people in Wales could indulge in the 'British' material gains of affluence and consumerism in the post-1945 period and benefited from the safety net of the welfare state, its 'traditional' staple industries were withering away, and with it their established communitarian cultures of Welshness. National pride had been invested in Wales's geological riches, and industrial valleys carved into a rural hinterland were defining features of a stereotypical Welsh landscape and a south-Walian collective 'valleys' identity.[18] Indeed, agriculture and slate quarrying, along with coal mining, were considered quintessentially 'Welsh' in their respective corners of Wales, but the defining story of these sectors in the post-1945 period was their haemorrhaging of workers, reaching its apogee in the aftermath of the 1984–5 Miners' Strike – final proof of the evaporation of the classless, Welsh *gwerin* myth of the past.[19]

Although Welsh industrial communities had no monopoly on economic distress in the 1980s, with similar decimation widespread across many parts of the UK, arguably, if any Welsh economic distinctiveness is sensed in the latter half of the twentieth century, it is one predicated on the distinctiveness of decline. While there was a reconfiguration of the economy in Wales post-1945, unearthing a 'Welsh economy' in an age that embraced centralization, globalization, and an unbridled free market capitalism is, ultimately, a futile task. Nonetheless, economic failure did raise questions about power and accountability, linking into political debates on 'who governs Wales'. Feelings of economic victimization also stimulated more interest in democratic devolution, in the belief that Wales could control its economy 'from within' better than suffering ideological vagaries 'from without'.[20]

'A Process not an Event': Welsh Devolution

This 'democratic deficit' is pivotal to much of the discourse surrounding Welsh devolution, allowing the public to endorse the sudden shift of power from Westminster to Cardiff and laying the future foundations of Wales as a political nation. However, Welsh administrative decentralization had been gradually developing throughout the twentieth century, gathering pace in the post-war era, when Wales could boast seventeen departments devolved from Westminster.[21] Most of this was achieved under the Conservative governments of the 1950s who, like the Labour party, recognized the demand for an outlet for Welsh political aspirations.[22] Indeed, Harold Wilson's Labour government of 1964, reacting to this national sentiment and pressure from elements within the party in Wales, created a secretary of state for Wales on their return to power.[23] In truth, this post held little real influence, being merely an extension of the position of minister for Welsh affairs created by Churchill's government in 1951. Moreover, since there was a considerable overlap between other ministries, some senior Labour cabinet members questioned its purpose.[24] Nevertheless, it was the symbolism of the post which was arguably most significant: possessing a seat in cabinet and a credible portfolio, Wales could point to the new Welsh secretary as a manifestation of the nation's growing importance within the Union. Furthermore, the Welsh Office's remit, while initially rather minimal, gradually increased as administrative devolution steadily continued, contributing to the creation of what Johnes has labelled a 'proto Welsh state'.[25]

Nonetheless, these modest developments were purely functional and did not necessarily translate into growing support within either major party for any form of political separatism. Wilson's approach towards Wales was no different from that of the Conservatives, which, in effect, married rational and political motivations together, while transferring very little actual power. Moreover, the Labour leadership was acutely suspicious of any overt expressions of Welsh national aspiration and only moderated its stance as a pragmatic reaction to the perceived 'rise of nationalism', following Plaid Cymru leader Gwynfor Evans's by-election victory in 1966 and a period in which the party's electoral ascent seemed to threaten Labour's south Wales heartlands. This, combined with similar gains for the Scottish National Party (SNP), necessitated the party to establish the Crowther-Kilbrandon Royal Commission on the Constitution in 1969. Undeniably a delaying mechanism, it nonetheless recommended a legislative assembly for Wales, particularly thrusting the issue into the fore once Labour's precarious return to government in 1974 made it dependent on nationalist support in the Commons. Labour's official commitment to Welsh devolution was clearly an exercise in political expediency.[26]

Meanwhile, public opinion on the matter was equally misleading. While devolution advocates could point to significant levels of approval among the public, this enthusiasm proved to be fickle. Crucially, it evaporated when combined with a decline in living standards.[27] Put simply, ideological support for devolution was severely lacking in 1979 and could only be buttressed by a sound economic forecast, which, during that turbulent decade, could not be offered.[28] Consequently, its overwhelming rejection, with almost 80 per cent voting against, was a crushing disappointment to Welsh nationalists.[29] Furthermore, the referendum campaign itself led to a re-emergence of age-old debates – between and even within Welsh Labour and Plaid Cymru – on what defined 'Welshness', exposing the linguistic, cultural, and political divisions embedded in Welsh society. Indeed, the intensely vicious war of words in the run-up to 1979 implied that there were, in fact, two nations within Wales's geographical expanse.[30] The idea of a unified 'Welsh' identity remained an extremely fragile paradigm which could be deconstructed with disturbing ease. Therefore, the devolution referendum of 1979 was a profoundly traumatizing experience for both traditional 'parties' of Wales: uncovering the divisions inherent in Welsh Labour, its rejection also precipitated the fall of the Callaghan government, while the nature of the defeat shattered Plaid's illusory 'Party for Wales' status. In the end, with the Conservative party's subsequent election victory, including impressive gains in Welsh constituencies, it seems that the referendum was a clear triumph for 'British Wales'.[31]

Thatcher is often cited as a crucial if unwitting architect of Welsh devolution. Although this may be an accurate assessment, her contribution was not, as some have suggested, altogether negative. Her controversial policies and insensitive approach certainly helped to define Wales as a nation in opposition to 'Thatcherism'[32] and also converted former sceptics, such as Labour MP Ron Davies, to the benefits of devolution by defining the measure as a means of protecting Wales from future bursts of Thatcherite policies while also overcoming the so-called 'democratic deficit'.[33] On the other hand, as Thatcher gave little thought to Wales,[34] she allowed her various Welsh secretaries of state considerable freedom of action, leading to a Welsh Office that undoubtedly possessed a 'Welsh' agenda.[35] This, combined with continued administrative decentralization, inadvertently prepared the political ground for Welsh devolution in the following decade. Thus, Thatcher's eleven years in power made a double, unintended contribution to the development of a Welsh political nationhood: it created a broad form of Welsh nationalism based on 'anti-Toryism', a trend that would take Welsh Conservatives years to reverse, while also providing the practical rationale for seeing Wales as a distinct political entity.[36]

The opportunity to express this distinction would arrive following the Labour election landslide of 1997, providing Wales with a chance to put the demons of 1979 to rest with a second referendum on devolution, an issue the Labour Party had kept as a manifesto commitment throughout its years in opposition. However, it is again questionable how genuinely committed the New Labour leadership were to the cause, and difficult not to view their pro-devolutionary rhetoric as merely a ploy in Tony

Blair's propaganda-induced '100 days' proclamation. Blair himself, holding deep reservations on the issue, only reluctantly adopted it from his predecessor, the late John Smith, and was unable to abandon it due to pressure from certain sections of the party.[37] Once more, it seems that expediency shaped their approach. Nevertheless, one cannot argue that, without New Labour's support during the referendum campaign, hollow though it might appear, devolution would certainly have remained in obscurity. What is more, the cross-party support, consisting of Labour, Plaid Cymru, and the Liberal Democrats, emphasized a new degree of unity and optimism in Wales on a matter that had previously torn the nation asunder.

In contrast, the response of the public was decidedly mute. The disappointingly low turnout revealed Welsh apathy, while simultaneously delegitimizing the pro-devolutionists' pursuit of democratic accountability. Worse still, the result itself – a wafer-thin majority of just 0.6 per cent – brought up new fears of a 'divided nation'.[38] Nonetheless, one cannot fail to notice the change in Welsh public opinion – with a swing of nearly 30 per cent, it seemed that the trauma of 1979 had finally been resolved, and Wales could look to the future with hope.[39]

It would be easy to dismiss devolution as a purely empty political gesture, a continuation of the British state's tokenistic approach to Wales throughout the modern era. Unlike the Scottish Parliament, the new Welsh Assembly gained no tax-raising powers, initially merely assuming the responsibilities of the civil service, with critics deriding it as a 'glorified county council'.[40] However, it was arguably the symbolism of this gesture that was most crucial – after decades of laborious campaigning, finally here was a legitimate political arena where the direction of Welsh politics could be determined: a political 'institute' which Wales could point to as an expression of its nationhood.

The Dragon Has Two Tongues? Language and Modernization

In 1967, the nationalist philosopher J. R. Jones argued that a savage language divide was tearing Wales apart, leading him to ponder if such rupturing was the only option in asserting Welsh language rights.[41] This highlights the incongruities of delineating Welsh nationhood through a language prism: on the one hand, the Welsh language has been considered the foundation stone of Welsh national distinctiveness, but on the other, much language discourse in the post-1945 period conveyed an unhomogenized tribalism, stemming from varying responses to its decline.

Statistically, the Welsh language was wilting in the post-1945 period. By 1961 the percentage of the population who spoke the language had halved to around a quarter of the population since the turn of the century, as historical mentalities about English as the language of 'progress' blended with rural depopulation, in-migration, and Anglo-American cultural modernization to create a noxious linguistic mix.[42] For essentialist nationalists, whose concept of Welsh nationhood rested on possession of a 'national' language, this was catastrophic.[43]

Plaid Cymru's constitutional methods seemed inadequate in the face of such language depletion. In 1962, Saunders Lewis, a Plaid dissident by that stage, demanded a 'revolution' predicated on civil disobedience to save the language and restore its dignity.[44] This led to the establishment of Cymdeithas yr Iaith Gymraeg, the Welsh Language Society, which instigated law-breaking campaigns, such as the road-sign daubing protest, to highlight the language's servile position. Others, such as the Free Wales Army and Meibion Glyndŵr, saw physical force nationalism, or at least the threat of it, as the only option.[45]

However, language activists were in the minority, and even though unthreatening St David's Day and National Eisteddfod-type patriotism enjoyed cross-party support, the campaigns of the 1960s radicalized the discourse surrounding the Welsh language, edging it from a 'safe' cultural sphere into contentious political terrain.[46] This was epitomized by the vicious mutual suspicion of the 1970s devolution debate, where Welsh Labour's 'Gang of Six' catastrophized an assembly that would, they claimed, be overrun with Welsh speakers, while pro-devolutionists, particularly from Plaid Cymru, bitterly accused these detractors of being 'anti-Welsh'.[47] Attitudes towards the language did not split evenly along party lines either: the 'red dragon/red flag' question within the Labour Party showed internal fissures and differing priorities on language as well as devolution.[48] It would also be a fallacy to construe 'Welsh speakers' as a harmonic grouping: 'natural' Welsh speakers who felt no urge to 'rescue' the language were often far more prone to the vehemence of the language brigade than disengaged non-Welsh speakers.[49]

Nonetheless, in the 'official' domain, the Welsh language found far greater shelter in the post-1945 period than it had experienced for centuries. Welsh Language Acts passed in 1967 and 1993 gave it legislative protection, acknowledging its 'equality' with English in the public sector, thus embodying the notion of a bilingual nation and making Welsh an occupational skill. Welsh-language education was on a forward march, with the proliferation of Welsh-language primary schools being followed by an expansion in the secondary sector from the 1950s onwards.[50] This turned the spectre of the Blue Books on its head, as the language's cultural capital made it an attractive prospect for generating upwards social mobility in more anglicized parts of Wales. However, old stigmas die hard, and in the Welsh-language heartlands, it struggled to shake off its grassroots legacy of being a marker of 'low socio-economic status'.[51]

In fact, all of this was merely a protective shell: although it enshrined Welsh as a 'paper' language and raised its profile, its contribution towards the 'living' virility of the language was more ambiguous. Such defensive mea-sures, after all, stemmed from fears about language decay, and this falloff was by no means restricted to traditionally anglicized parts of 'British' and 'Welsh Wales'. Unprecedented demographic changes meant that the credibility of 'Y Fro Gymraeg' as a space that represented the spiritual essence of Welshness was in peril.[52] This perceived violation of the Welsh countryside was most infamously mythologized by the Tryweryn controversy, as the 1965 submer-sion of the pastoral, Welsh-speaking village of Capel Celyn to provide water for Liverpool stimulated outrage at 'English' exploitation and Welsh national impotence.[53]

But attempts to preserve a bucolic, Welsh-speaking past were increasingly anachronistic, particularly in an age of accelerating secularization and ubi-quitous cultural changes. Television was viewed by many nationalists as an opportunity to make the Welsh language and the notion of Wales relevant for a modern age. But it was also a threat that led Welsh children to become 'quietly English' in their own homes.[54] Campaigns for Welsh-language broadcasting proved contentious, breeding resentment that precious televi-sion time was 'wasted' on a provision that the majority of the population could not follow.[55] The establishment of S4C in 1982, a notable victory in the annals of language campaigners, resolved the debate but crystallized the linguistic divide by creating a separate enclave for broadcasting in the Welsh language. Additionally, another 'victory', the battle for bilingual road signs, was a rather pyrrhic triumph: although Welsh place-names were now 'flagged' on a daily basis, it was predominantly an empty gesture, simulta-neously 'exotic' yet ultimately 'banal', masking the realities of language erosion.[56]

Of course, for the majority in Wales, the Welsh language flitted only occasionally into their peripheral vision, and they felt no need to artificially construct or protect their national identity. Even though the 1969 investiture of Charles as Prince of Wales engendered protest from a minority, overall Welsh speakers and non-Welsh speakers alike, from the grassroots to the elite, indulged unquestioningly in a ceremonial that celebrated the coexistence of Welshness and monarchical Britishness.[57]

Although the 2001 census showed a slight increase in the numbers of Welsh speakers, barely 20 per cent claimed knowledge of the language at the turn of the twenty-first century. Whilst it was making a limited comeback in parts of eastern and urban Wales, it was losing its grip as a community language in the north and west, and failing to make inroads as a social language beyond the school gates.[58] If a uniform 'national' language is a precondition of a nation state, then perhaps only one of the dragon's two tongues satisfied that criterion at the end of the twentieth century.

Nation of the Mind: Wales and Rugby

If the pursuit of a distinct linguistic nationhood was a fruitless endeavour which led Wales into a bitterly divided cultural cul-de-sac, then expressions of Welsh national identity would have to be sought from other avenues. Arguably, one of the most successful of these has come in the form of Wales's 'national sport', rugby. Indeed, rugby has offered modern Wales an alternative pathway to venting national sentiment, allowing the creation of a shared sense of identity and national cohesion, which Benedict Anderson alludes to in his definition of nations as 'imagined political communities'.[59] During the post-war era, rugby has, for Wales, become one of the primary expressions of this imagined community.[60]

It is ironic that the most politically and economically unstable decade in post-war British history should hold such reverence in Wales's popular psyche. During the 1970s, Welsh rugby witnessed a much celebrated 'golden age', which captured the imagination of the public and created national heroes from such gifted players as Barry 'King' John to Phil Bennett, and of course the immortal Gareth Edwards.[61] However, this is hardly surprising, given the turbulence of the times. In an era marked by industrial decline, political impotence, and perceived national malaise, where would the nation turn to for heroes? One answer could be the world of rugby: a stage on which Welsh humiliations could be reversed and national pride restored; a stage on which national unity could be maintained while Welsh society remained hopelessly split; and for a small and stateless nation, a stage that provided real 'tangible evidence' of Wales's existence. Moreover, the varied composition of the national fifteen arguably offered socially and culturally diverse members of Welsh society a share in the team's success. Comprised of manual workers, miners, and members of the professional and middle classes, while also including a mixture of English and Welsh speakers, this was the Welsh nation as it wished to be represented: transcending class barriers and demonstrating national unity in the face of fierce internal conflict. Thus, the Welsh public could rally behind this seemingly 'classless' and culturally diverse national team, who became the dominant northern hemisphere rugby nation, winning numerous Five Nations Championships and, significantly, contributing to successful British and Irish Lions tours.[62]

Wales's fixation with its national sport was, at times, a source of great consternation among the nation's more politically minded nationalists. Their own, more assertive agitation for political self-determination and protection of the language was met by a largely indifferent public reaction, while 'Match Day' witnessed a considerable surge in Welsh pride and national sentiment. This was perfectly encapsulated in the traumatizing rejection of devolution in 1979, at a time when ironically the national team was at the zenith of its sporting powers, leading some partisan observers to castigate rugby's stultifying effect on Welsh political consciousness.[63] These national events, therefore, became safe spaces to assert the nation's Welshness, obviating the need to translate it into the political sphere, much to the chagrin of Welsh nationalists.[64]

The weakness of Welsh political nationhood, perceived to be in perpetual decline following the trauma of 1979 and exposed yet again under Thatcher and the acceleration of de-industrialization during the 1980s, was mirrored by a dearth in Wales's national sport – confirmation, for some, that rugby and nationhood were indeed inextricably linked. This was further exacerbated by the end of the decade with the introduction of professionalism, a move which robbed Wales of a certain amount of dignity that amateurism – itself a tremendously fluid term – seemed to offer, while also rendering it utterly incapable of competing with its wealthier neighbour England for sporting glory.[65]

However, what goes down, it seems, must come up. Following Labour's victory in 1997, and Wales's narrowly successful devolution campaign the same year, an air of self-confidence and optimism seemed to return to the nation, and this was again demonstrated on the rugby field, with a successful bid to host the Rugby World Cup, and an historic win over the 'old Saxon oppressor' in 1999, offering hope to Welsh hearts.[66] This intertwining of sports and nationhood was reinforced with the construction of the

Millennium Stadium. Built for the 1999 World Cup, it dominates the Cardiff city skyline, and arguably the Welsh psyche. Furthermore, its prominence within Welsh national consciousness highlights the important role rugby has played in cultivating a form of nationhood acceptable to the Welsh people, while its iconic status both within and beyond Wales's border points to a burgeoning civic nationhood. The implication is clear – however small or insignificant it might be in other political and cultural arenas, Wales is still a rugby nation. And while some might frown at its tokenism, in this modern world of small victories, who is to contest which form of nationhood takes precedence?

The post-1945 period was characterized by the uneven development of Welsh nationhood, with key signifiers, such as economic and political identity, waxing and waning in an atmosphere of reconstruction and crisis. Ironically, these diverse responses to modernity shaped a more uniform sense of Welsh national belonging. The Welsh language, for example, withdrew in its heartlands but witnessed a tentative revival beyond these borders, while rugby became an increasingly powerful conduit for national cohesion. Through these expressions of nationhood, primarily moderate in nature, Welsh identity was thus renegotiated, enabling a greater degree of reciprocation between the contested 'Three Nations' of Wales. Whether this led to a truly 'distinctive' Welshness, or instead to a reworked accommodation with a 'British' world, would remain to be seen in the post-devolutionary landscape.

Notes

1. Denis Balsom, 'The Three-Wales Model', in *The National Question Again: Welsh Political Identity in the 1980s*, ed. John Osmond (Llandysul: Gomer Press, 1985), 1–17.
2. See, for example: Edward Nevin, *The Social Accounts of the Welsh Economy 1948–1956* (Aberystwyth: University of Wales Press, 1957); Gwynfor Evans, *Wales as an Economic Entity: A Reply* (Cardiff: Plaid Cymru, 1960).
3. Martin Johnes, *Wales Since 1939* (Cardiff: University of Wales Press, 2012), 35–95.
4. Hilda Jennings, *Brynmawr: A Study of a Distressed Area* (London: Allenson & Co., 1934).
5. Keith Gildart, *North Wales Miners: A Fragile Unity, 1945–1996* (Cardiff: University of Wales Press, 2002), 21–64.

6. A coal tip engulfed the local school, leading to 144 deaths, the majority of them children. Ian McLean and Martin Johnes, *Aberfan: Government and Disasters* (Cardiff: Welsh Academic Press, 2000).

7. For example, the Electricity Act of 1947 formed the Merseyside and North Wales Electricity Board (MANWEB), isolating south Wales as a separate entity and reinforcing the sense that technological advancement was not an all-Wales endeavour.

8. Captain Peter Thorneycroft, *The Welsh Tory*, November, 1947; National Library of Wales, Papers of Undeb Cymru Fydd, C. F. Matthews to T. I. Ellis, 10 February 1958, Folder 200 'Trydan'.

9. Raymond Williams, *Border Country* (Cardigan: Parthian, 2006), 8; Thomas Firbank, *A Country of Memorable Honour* (London: Harrap, 1953), 210.

10. Council for Wales and Monmouthshire, *Second Memorandum by the Council on its Activities* (London: HMSO, 1953); Chris Bollom, *Attitudes and Second Homes in Rural Wales* (Cardiff: University of Wales Press, 1978); John W. Aitchison and Harold Carter, 'Yr Iaith Gymraeg 1921–1991: Persbectif Geo-ieithyddol', in '*Eu Hiaith a Gadwant?' Y Gymraeg yn yr Ugeinfed Ganrif*, ed. Geraint H. Jenkins and Mari A. Williams (Cardiff: University of Wales Press, 2000), 43–5.

11. D. Morgan Rees, 'A View of Welsh Tourism', *Wales* 47 (1960): 35–7.

12. Ministry of Power, *Report of Public Inquiry Concerning Proposals to Construct a Nuclear Power Station at Trawsfynydd* (London: HMSO, 1958).

13. Pyrs Gruffudd, 'The Battle of Butlin's: Vulgarity and Virtue on the North Wales Coast, 1939–1949', *Rural History* 21, 1 (2010): 75–95.

14. For example, the building of factories such as Hoover in Merthyr, and the establishment of a new steel plant at Port Talbot in 1951.

15. Gareth Rees and Teresa L. Rees, eds., *Poverty and Social Inequality in Wales* (London: Croom Helm, 1980).

16. Leon Gooberman, *From Depression to Devolution: Economy and Government in Wales, 1934–2006* (Cardiff: University of Wales Press, 2017), 220.

17. Michael Hechter, *Internal Colonialism: The Celtic Fringe in British National Development, 1536–1966* (London: Routledge and Kegan Paul, 1975), 302; Leopold Kohr, *Is Wales Viable?* (Llandybïe: Christopher Davies, 1971), 43.

18. See Hywel Teifi Edwards, *Arwr Glew Erwau'r Glo: Delwedd y Glowr yn Llenyddiaeth y Gymraeg 1850–1950* (Llandysul: Gwasg Gomer, 1994), and Dai Smith, *Aneurin Bevan and the World of South Wales* (Cardiff: University of Wales Press, 1993).

19. Agriculture and mining and quarrying were the two sectors employing the highest number of males in Wales in 1911. Digest of Welsh Historical Statistics 1700–1974, 'Labour', http://gov.wales/statistics-and-research/diges t-welsh-historical-statistics/?tab=previous&;lang=en (1985) (accessed

28 February 2017); Prys Morgan, 'The Gwerin of Wales: Myth and Reality', in *The Welsh and Their Country*, ed. I. Hume and W. T. R. Pryce (Llandysul: Gomer Press, 1986), 134–50.

20. On the Miners' Strike, see, for example, Hywel Francis, *History on our Side: Wales and the 1984–85 Miners' Strike* (Ferryside: Iconau, 2009).

21. Wil Griffith, 'Devolutionist Tendencies in Wales, 1885–1914', in *Debating Nationhood and Governance in Britain, 1885–1945: Perspectives from the Four Nations*, ed. Duncan Tanner et al. (Manchester: University of Manchester Press, 2006), 89–117; Vernon Bogdanor, *Devolution in the United Kingdom* (Oxford: Oxford University Press, 1999), 158.

22. See, for example, John Graham Jones, 'The Parliament for Wales Campaign, 1950–56', *Welsh History Review* 16 (1992): 207–36; Huw T. Edwards, *Hewn from the Rock: The Autobiography of Huw T. Edwards* (Cardiff: Western Mail Press, 1967), 125–32.

23. James Griffiths, *Pages from Memory* (London: Dent & Sons, 1969), 164–5.

24. Richard Crossman, *The Diaries of a Cabinet Minister*, vol. I: *Minister of Housing, 1964–66* (London: Hamilton Ltd. & Cape Ltd, 1975), 117.

25. Johnes, *Wales Since 1939*, 218.

26. For Labour attitudes on Welsh devolution, see Andrew Edwards, 'A "Monkeys Tea Party"? Division, Discord and the Development of Labour's Policy on Devolution, 1966–79', in *Cof Cenedl XXIV*, ed. Geraint H. Jenkins (Llandysul: Gwasg Gomer, 2009), 161–89.

27. Bodleian Library, Opinion Research Centre, The Scope for Conservative Advance in Wales, CCO/180/32.

28. Andrew Edwards and Duncan Tanner, 'Defining or Dividing the Nation? Opinion Polls, Welsh Identity and Devolution, 1966–1979', *Contemporary Wales* 18 (2006): 54–71.

29. James Lewis, 'Wales Votes No to Assembly by Four to One', *The Guardian*, 3 March 1979, 2.

30. Arfon Gwilym, 'Ymgyrch y Celwyddau' ('The Lying Campaign'), *Y Cymro*, 27 February 1979, 13; R. Merfyn Jones and Ioan Rhys Jones, 'Labour and the Nation', in *The Labour Party in Wales, 1900–2000*, ed. Duncan Tanner, Chris Williams, and Deian Hopkin (Cardiff: University of Wales Press, 2000), 257–8.

31. John Osmond, 'Mr Morris and the Elephant: The Referendum, the Election, and the Future of Welsh Politics', *Planet* 48 (1979): 2–8.

32. Hywel Francis, 'Mining: The Popular Front', *Marxism Today* (1985): 12.

33. Bogdanor, *Devolution*, 196; Ron Davies, *Devolution: A Process Not an Event* (Cardiff: Institute of Welsh Affairs, 1999), 4.

34. 'Wales' and 'Welsh Nationalists' are each mentioned *once* in her memoirs, Margaret Thatcher, *The Downing Street Years* (London: HarperCollins Publishers, 1999), 289, 602.

35. Bangor University Archive, Cymru 2000 Collection, Peter Walker interviewed by Merfyn Jones, 2–4.

36. Dylan Griffiths, *Thatcherism and Territorial Politics: A Welsh Case Study* (Aldershot: Avebury, 1996), 53–4.

37. Tony Blair, *A Journey* (London: Random House, 2007), 251.

38. Glyn Mathias, 'The Ballot Bites Back', *Planet* 125 (1997): 17–20.

39. 'Wales Says Yes', *Western Mail*, 19 September 1997, 1.

40. For coverage of this debate, see Kevin Morgan and Geoff Mungham, *Redesigning Democracy: The Making of the Welsh Assembly* (Bridgend: Seren, 2000).

41. J. R. Jones, *A Raid i'r Iaith Ein Gwahanu?* (Aberystwyth: Cymdeithas yr Iaith, 1978), 5.

42. Aitchison and Carter, 'Yr Iaith Gymraeg 1921–1991', 42. For contemporary reports, see, for example, Home Office, *Rural Wales* (London: HMSO, 1953); Colin Rosser and Christopher Harris, *The Family and Social Change: A Study of Family and Kinship in a South Wales Town* (London: Routledge and Kegan Paul, 1965).

43. For a delineation of Welsh nationalist thought, see Richard Wyn Jones, *Rhoi Cymru'n Gyntaf: Syniadaeth Plaid Cymru* (Caerdydd: Gwasg Prifysgol Cymru, 2007).

44. Saunders Lewis, *Tynged yr Iaith* (London: BBC, 1962).

45. Dylan Phillips, *Trwy Ddulliau Chwyldro? Hanes Cymdeithas yr Iaith Gymraeg, 1962–1992* (Llandysul: Gwasg Gomer, 1998); Wyn Thomas, *Hands Off Wales: Nationhood and Militancy* (Llandysul: Gomer Press, 2013).

46. Ned Thomas, *The Welsh Extremist: A Culture in Crisis* (London: Victor Gollancz, 1971).

47. Many accounts from the period outline the linguistic tension, e.g. Elystan Morgan, *Atgofion Oes* (Talybont: Lolfa, 2012), 264, and also emphasize its gradual dissipation – Paul Flynn, Welsh Grand Committee, 23 January 2013, col. 49, www.publications.parliament.uk/pa/cm201213/cm general/wgrand/130123/pm/130123s01.htm (accessed 15 March 2017).

48. This was far from being a static, two 'camps' division. See the ambivalence in Aneurin Bevan, 'The Claim of Wales', *Wales* 25 (1947): 151–3. Also, Andrew Edwards and Mari Elin Wiliam, 'The Red Dragon/Red Flag Debate Revisited: The Labour Party, Culture and Language in Wales, 1945 – c. 1970', *Welsh History Review* 26 (2012): 105–27.

49. The editorial in *Barn*, September 1979, blamed Welsh speakers, not 'the English', for rejecting devolution.

50. Flintshire Archives, Flintshire Education Committee Minutes, 1955–6, FC/2/56; W. Gareth Evans, 'Y Wladwriaeth Brydeinig ac Addysg Gymraeg 1914–1991', in *'Eu Hiaith a Gadwant?'*, ed. Jenkins and Williams, 346–8.

51. Glyn Williams, Ellis Roberts, and Russell Isaac, 'Language and Aspirations for Upward Social Mobility', in *Social and Cultural Change in Contemporary Wales*, ed. Glyn Williams (London: Routledge and Kegan Paul, 1978), 204.

52. For a summary of these concerns and responses, see Simon Brooks and Richard Glyn Roberts, eds., *Pa beth yr aethoch allan i'w achub?* (Llanrwst: Gwasg Carreg Gwalch, 2013).

53. Gwynfor Evans, *Save Cwm Tryweryn for Wales* (Cardiff: Plaid Cymru, 1956); Hywel M. Griffiths, 'Water Under the Bridge? Nature, Memory and Hydropolitics', *Cultural Geographies* 21 (2014): 449–74.

54. 'Welshman's Notebook', *Wrexham Leader*, 26 January 1951.

55. Jamie Medhurst, *A History of Independent Television in Wales* (Cardiff: University of Wales Press, 2010), 61–75.

56. For an outline of the campaign, see Peter Merriman and Rhys Jones, '"Symbols of Justice": The Welsh Language Society's Campaign for Bilingual Road Signs in Wales, 1967–1980', *Journal of Historical Geography* 35 (2009): 350–76.

57. John Ellis, *Investiture: Royal Ceremony and National Identity in Wales, 1911–1969* (Cardiff: University of Wales Press, 2008).

58. Office for National Statistics, *Census 2001: Report on the Welsh Language* (London: HMSO, 2004).

59. Benedict Anderson, *Imagined Communities* (London: Verso, 1991).

60. Gareth Williams, '"The Dramatic Turbulence of Some Irrecoverable Football Game": Sport, Literature and Welsh Identity', in *Sport in the Making of Celtic Cultures*, ed. Grant Jarvie (London: Leicester University Press, 1999), 55–70.

61. Clem Thomas and Geoffrey Nicholson, *Welsh Rugby: The Crowning Years, 1968–1980* (London: Collins, 1980).

62. David Smith and Gareth Williams, *Fields of Praise: The Official History of the Welsh Rugby Union, 1881–1981* (Cardiff: University of Wales Press, 1980), 407–58.

63. Nigel Jenkins, *Song and Dance* (Bridgend: Poetry Wales Press, 1981), 43.

64. Martin Johnes, 'Eighty-Minute Patriots? National Identity and Sport in Modern Wales', *The International Journal of the History of Sport* 17 (2000): 93.

65. David Smith and Gareth Williams, 'Beyond the Fields of Praise', in *More Heart and Soul: The Character of Welsh Rugby*, ed. H. Richards, Phil Stead, and Gareth Williams (Cardiff: University of Wales Press, 2000), 205–32.

66. 'Gorfoledd' ('Jubilation'), *Y Cymro*, 14 April 1999, 1.

26

The Legacy of Saunders Lewis

TUDUR HALLAM

Writer, politician, language campaigner, and public intellectual, Saunders Lewis (1893–1985) continues to exert a ghostly presence over contemporary British politics and the future of the Welsh nation. Yet the Wales of today falls somewhat short of the one Lewis himself envisaged and failed to realize. His vision of making Welsh in Wales as strong as English in England seems particularly distant. On the other hand, as the governance structures of Wales continue to develop, his vision for a devolved Welsh government and for the political empowerment of Wales still haunts its corridors of power. Moreover, if one considers that Lewis's main achievement was the politicization of the language, every statement made by any politician or activist regarding the Welsh language continues, consciously or unconsciously, to work within the cultural discourse which Saunders Lewis presented so forcefully in his political and literary writings, summed up in his assertion that 'Wales without the Welsh language will not be Wales', for the language is more important than self-government.[1]

As his biographer, T. Robin Chapman, has noted, Lewis's legacy of influence is for the most part indirect, subliminal, 'almost subconscious'.[2] Mythologized by poets such as R. Williams Parry, Gerallt Lloyd Owen, and R. S. Thomas, demonized by those opposed to all things Plaid Cymru (the Welsh nationalist party), the mention of his name continues to act upon the Welsh psyche as a haunting reminder that a nation 'grimly dedicated to the hopeful extinction of its own language' must be 'slightly sub-normal, masochistic and white-livered'.[3] To this day, no serious critic in the broad field of Welsh cultural studies can ignore Lewis's seminal works as politician, literary critic, poet, novelist, and playwright. Gwyn Alf Williams, the Marxist historian, once remarked in a critical letter to Lewis's daughter that although he stood at 'the opposite pole of the political spectrum', he recognized in Lewis 'a genius, a marvellous writer, a man utterly committed to Wales who has, virtually by himself, reshaped Welsh history'.[4]

Recent studies have sought to discuss Lewis's plays, literary criticism, politics, and private life in detail. Richard Wyn Jones's book, *The Fascist Party in Wales? Plaid Cymru, Welsh Nationalism and the Accusation of Fascism*, sought to look more closely at the man, his policies, and the way others tainted him with accusations of fascism. The author did so precisely because Lewis remains for the most part more myth than man, more of an imagined ideal than a written manifesto.[5] He stood for Wales, for political self-determination, and, being the extreme radical conservative that he was, he envisaged a polity for Wales, in Welsh. While some aspects of his economic policies seemed very crude, especially for people brought up in the mining valleys of south Wales, for whom Lewis's policy of de-industrialization in the 1930s was offensive, the fact that he stood up for Wales at all and saw in its language a vehicle suitable for the mass-media age of technological advancement and science – not just literature – is, for others, nothing short of visionary and heroic.

Although privately educated in English, and although English literature was his chosen subject of study at the University of Liverpool, English in a sense remained a language of inauthenticity for Lewis. English, the language of Lewis's education and of several close friendships, not to mention his courtship and marriage, always, to an extent, belonged to others, as it did in some ways to Dylan Thomas too, being 'his parents' second and acquired language'[6]. But whereas Thomas had no immediate linguistic alternative, Lewis, who had lost his mother and had been raised by his aunt, increasingly came to appreciate the necessity of his mother tongue, 'the only language in which I can cope with creative work fairly well'.[7] Welsh, the language of family and of religious worship – Lewis's father was minister to a Welsh Methodist congregation in Wallasey, on the Wirral peninsula – is described by Lewis in 1922 as 'a simple language, easy to learn, lovely to speak, a civilised language too, spoken by a large and increasing population'.[8] He understood that a sense of 'being', or *Dasein*, to use Heidegger's term – our being here, feeling alive – requires a sense of authenticity which is only achieved when *Dasein* 'makes up its own mind, is its own person, or true to its own self'.[9] One might suggest that such an existentialism and a need for authenticity, especially when coupled with elements of psychoanalysis (such as an inferiority complex) and postcolonial theory (such as the concepts of mimicry and hybridity) best explain Lewis's insistence, from the outset, on the centrality of the Welsh language to Wales and to Welsh politics. As Thomas Mann observed, a remark quoted by Lewis in a short letter to *The Observer* entitled 'Mother Tongue': 'Language is the guarantee of a community that cannot be forsworn.'[10]

The Politician

In a comparative study of literature in Britain, Stephen Wade credits Lewis with initiating 'a totally new literature of regional consciousness'.[11] Not so, I would argue, for Lewis, a Welshman, born and educated in England, did not think of Wales in regional terms. Lewis saw Wales not as a region of Britain but as a distinct nation, which had its own regional varieties. This is not to say that his nationalism was devoid of a British context, or that he did not appreciate the political interplay of the part in relation to the whole. For example, in 1931, in what came to be known as 'The Banned Wireless Talk', censored by the BBC in 1930 as 'the talk was calculated to inflame Welsh sympathies', Saunders Lewis argued that Welsh nationalism would 'bring a new method and a new force to the life of Great Britain, and England as well as Wales will benefit from our vigour and from our new and better-found comradeship'.[12]

Lewis did not argue that Wales should be regarded as a whole in itself. From the outset he condemned outright that form of materialist nationalism which seeks to make international concerns, and, moreover, our common bonds of humanity, subservient to the absolute authority of the individual state. Such a materialist nationalism, he argued, was the enemy of civilization, and one of Lewis's most memorable statements is this: 'Let us not ask for independence for Wales. Not because it is not practical, but because it is not worth having.'[13]

Although he sought not to put Wales first and all others second, as material nationalists do, regionalizing Wales via assimilation into the English way of life was never an option for him. Wales has its own history as well as its own language, a rich and long-standing literary and popular culture – which Lewis referred to as 'civilization' – and a people whose language and customs attest to their distinctiveness. For these reasons, Lewis argued for home rule (W. *ymreolaeth*): not independence, not unconditional freedom, but 'enough freedom to establish and protect civilisation in Wales'.[14] He recognized that Wales's central problem was its regional status within England, and that a Welsh civilization could not be developed 'as long as Wales considered itself part of England, involved in England's political life, acknowledging that London and London's Parliament is the epicentre of its life'.[15]

Lewis's post-war generation had learned the failures of Welsh liberalism and its once-radical movement *Cymru Fydd*, literally 'Wales to Be' but known in English as Young Wales. No more could one be satisfied with being a proud patriot in literary and cultural terms alone, making rousing speeches in one's mother tongue at the National Eisteddfod before returning to England in order to disappear headlong into the dominant culture of London and the political framework of Westminster, in which Wales had hardly any voice. Such liberalism leads not to a balanced cultural exchange between two distinct and diverse nations, but rather to the lesser's subservient assimilation into the larger, and, as Stephen Wade suggests, to regionalism. In what has become known as the Act of Union of England and Wales (1536), the latter of the two countries was recognized in order to be reduced: 'incorporated, united and annexed to and with this his Realm of *England*'.[16]

In 1922, having returned from the war in France an Irish sympathizer and a Welsh nationalist, and having completed his studies in English, and to a lesser degree French, at the University of Liverpool, Lewis was appointed as lecturer in Welsh at the University of Wales College Swansea, in the town where his father and aunt now lived. At this point, he had not completely turned his back on the possibility of writing for Wales in English, and had he, or, perhaps more influentially, his mentor at Liverpool University, Professor Oliver Elton, not faintly praised the experimental language of Lewis's first play, *The Eve of St John* (1921), calling it 'a pretty and interesting thing', then who knows what might have become of the young Anglo-Welsh playwright.[17] That said, Lewis was now for the first time living in Wales, and his comparative studies in Welsh literature had really just begun. By 1925 and the publication of his seminal text, a piece of literary criticism on the fifteenth-century poet Dafydd Nanmor – a text which owes as much to Oliver Elton as it does to Emrys ap Iwan or Maurice Barrès – Lewis saw that the future of Wales, and any sense of its entitlement to govern, was dependent upon a new reading and appreciation of the nation's distinct cultural past, understood as a golden age of creativity to be replicated in the present. In that year, he agreed to became one of the founding members of a new political movement, Plaid Genedlaethol Cymru, known today as Plaid Cymru, the Party of Wales, on the condition that Welsh would be its internal language of business. In later life, Lewis as writer and editor continued to champion the party's cause in both languages, and, indeed, his famous lecture to the Guild of Graduates of the University of Wales, 'Is There an Anglo-Welsh Literature?' (1939), is as suggestive as it is dismissive of the possibility of such a literature. Nevertheless, in so far as he himself campaigned to make Welsh the civic language of governance in Wales, Lewis sought to overturn a centuries-old monolingual policy of English homogenization and, along with it, a subservient Welsh mentality.

Lewis was the party's president in its foundational period, from 1926 to 1939. Its *telos* was, and to some extent still is, self-determination, 'to be responsible for civilization and the means of social life in our part of Europe'.[18] Nevertheless, the elitist in Lewis ensured that he is understandably seen as an awkward father-figure for the left-of-centre party which Plaid Cymru has become. This is why, at best, his legacy comes and goes: felt, unquantified, at times a real force, but more often, distant and phantom-like.

Lord Dafydd Wigley, former leader of Plaid Cymru from 1991 to 2000, has argued that Lewis was in a sense 'above politics, as he did not seek power, but rather endeavoured to awaken a nation'.[19] Such an observation alludes to the fact that Lewis's legacy, powerful though it is in many ways, is not a story of political success. At best he was an awkward politician, aloof and academic, too aristocratic in his ideals, too Catholic a nationalist for many non-conformists; a brilliant literary philosopher but one desperately lacking the common touch which might have advanced the nationalist cause in the 1930s. In a famous interview in 1961, Lewis himself acknowledged a sense of abject failure as he reflected upon his public life.[20] He had hoped radically to change the political landscape of Wales, as had been done in Ireland, a country which served both as an inspiration and a model in so many ways for Lewis and his party, far more so than France. Yet, as he took stock of his life, it seemed to Lewis that the party which he had co-established in Wales in 1925 had at best achieved the type of impact one might expect from a well-organized pressure group.

This is not to say that the party failed to make any impact on UK politics. For example, referring to the creation of the Welsh Office in 1965 and the new government post of Secretary of State for Wales, Lewis noted that 'Welsh nationalists of an ardent optimism claim that only they have put the Right Honourable James Griffiths [the first Secretary of State] where he now is.'[21] The degree to which Lewis and others in his party actually influenced Welsh political development and Welsh political thinking is, of course, 'a matter of petty dispute'.[22] Similarly, it is impossible to quantify Lewis's impact as regards his party's ambitious campaign in the 1930s, as it sought to persuade the British Broadcasting Corporation to create a separate service for Wales. The BBC was reluctant to use the Welsh language, as such a development would, to the anglocentric mind, only 'serve propaganda purposes'.[23] What cannot be denied, however, is that Lewis, both as president of Plaid Genedlaethol Cymru and as a member of the University of Wales Council's delegation to the BBC, played a key role in changing the BBC's policy and practice.[24] He did so, of course, alongside many others, yet he seemed to have realized more than most that broadcasting in Wales was not simply a cultural issue but rather a political one, and his writings in this field, visionary and often startling at the time, retain a certain currency in the context of broadcasting and media communications in Britain.

The Language Campaigner

In Lewis's own lifetime, Welsh powerlessness was perhaps most apparent in the 1950s, when the Welsh-speaking valley of Capel Celyn was drowned. Known most commonly as 'Tryweryn', the name of the river dammed to create the new reservoir which would supply water to the city of Liverpool, this one word, 'Tryweryn', continues to act as a symbol of Welsh powerlessness within the British state. All but one of the Members of Parliament from Wales voted against the creation of the dam and the drowning of the valley; all but one still constituted a minority at the UK Parliament in London. Annexed and assimilated into England's political system of control over Welsh affairs, this episode exposed the inability of the Welsh MPs to act as stewards of their own land and their own people. Wales's voice, though expressed and recorded in London, simply did not matter.

Lewis's response to Tryweryn was to craft a radio lecture in which the classical rhetorical structures of *exordium, probationes, confirmatio, narratio, refutatio*, and *peroratio* work together so beautifully and so persuasively that those listening to his lecture's *amplificatio* in 1962 felt inclined to form a movement, a new pressure group, committed to changing the fate of the Welsh language in Wales. Thus Cymdeithas yr Iaith ('The Welsh Language Society'), which is still active and effective today, was called into action, leading to peaceful, non-violent protest and civil disobedience against the rule of the land, and often to imprisonment. As exemplified by the 2012 television documentary presented by Adam Price (former Member of Parliament for Plaid Cymru and later Assembly Member and party leader), Lewis's lecture continues to act as a rallying cry against the possible death of the language.

Though Lewis had long retired from the political scene in 1962 – indeed, nearly twenty years had passed since he bitterly failed to win the 1943 parliamentary by-election for the House of Commons constituency of University of Wales – this famous radio lecture, *Tynged yr Iaith* ('The Fate of the Language'), should be regarded as one of his greatest political accomplishments. Lewis had long held the sociolinguistic views presented in the lecture, but such was its immediate impact on its audience that it is rightly regarded as a seminal text of historical importance. *Tynged yr Iaith* foresaw the death of the language and called for radical intervention. It is a powerful, emotive text, as evocative as the famous graffiti mural of 'Cofia Dryweryn' ('Remember Tryweryn') overlooking the village of Llanrhystud south of Aberystwyth. Lewis points the finger not only at the colonizing English but also at the subservient, indifferent Welsh. Written directly with Tryweryn in mind, the event which highlighted Plaid Cymru's inability to act as effective stewards for Wales, the lecture's political impact was second only to Lewis's involvement in another contentious case of land appropriation in Wales some twenty-five years earlier.

Whereas 'Tryweryn' floods the mind with images of a deluge sweeping aside a Welsh valley, its inhabitants, and their way of life, the word 'Penyberth' conjures up images of a blaze of political protest, the flames of Welsh civil disobedience, and the sight of Saunders Lewis and two others, D. J. Williams and Lewis Valentine, standing in a criminal court accused of an act of arson at a newly established military base in the Llŷn Peninsula in north-west Wales. This political act of protest, for which the perpetrators readily took responsibility, gave Saunders Lewis the opportunity to explain his actions and advance the cause of Plaid Genedlaethol Cymru at the trial in Caernarfon. This took place in 1936, 400 years since the first of the Acts of Union were enacted by Henry VIII. Addressing the judge in English, for the Crown's representative could not speak the language of the accused, nor did they under the Acts of Union have the right to expect him to, Lewis explained that their action was the only one available to them, as 'all democratic and peaceful methods of persuasion had failed to obtain even a hearing for our case'. Indeed, the then Prime Minister, Stanley Baldwin, had refused to meet a delegation from Wales, though they represented the concerns of 500,000 people. Thus, 'when we saw clearly the whole future of Welsh tradition threatened as never before in history', since establishing a military base and aerodrome in the Llŷn Peninsula would anglicize and militarize one of 'the essential homes of Welsh culture, idiom, and literature', the three men chose to invoke the process of law, appealing not to the law of the British anglo-centric state but rather to 'the universal moral law', trusting 'a jury of their countrymen' at Caernarfon Court, believing not only in their 'justice as a jury, but also in [their] courage'.[25]

When the Caernarfon Court was unable to reach a verdict, the case was transferred to the Old Bailey in London, thus highlighting the colonial, incorporated framework which Lewis and his fellow countrymen opposed and sought to change. The three Welshmen were sentenced to nine months' imprisonment in Wormwood Scrubs prison in London, and Lewis was permanently dismissed from his academic post as a lecturer in Welsh at University College Swansea. On their release, however, they were welcomed as heroes by large crowds in Caernarfon, and though it has taken some time for Swansea University to acknowledge Lewis's stature as one of the architects of modern Wales, its Graduation Programme, produced for each graduate and graduation ceremony, lists his appointment as a lecturer in Welsh in 1922 as one of its most notable achievements. Similarly, in 2016, Swansea Council unveiled a blue plaque to commemorate Lewis's association with the city, with Councillor David Hopkins, Lord Mayor of Swansea, describing him as 'instrumental in a movement to stop the decline of the Welsh language and restore pride in Welsh culture'.[26]

The Writer and Critic

While he was in Wormwood Scrubs, Lewis and his two fellow inmates received the warden's permission to listen to *Buchedd Garmon* (1937), a radio play which Lewis had written between the two court cases, following a commission by the newly established 'Welsh region' of the BBC. Years later, in 1957, Lewis would cast a critical eye, or rather a critical ear, over the play, especially its long, poetical speeches.[27] It is little wonder that the author of *Siwan* (1956), a play in which every word and act seems most purposeful and interconnected, and in which the poetry itself is all the more naturalistic and powerful for its understatement, would criticize the rhetorical exuberance of the earlier play. Nevertheless, while the play might not be the equal of Lewis's best, it has an energy and a directness which immediately engages the audience. Ioan Williams has argued that *Buchedd Garmon* 'may be read as an expression of everything that Saunders Lewis said in the court at Caernarfon'.[28] Set in the first half of the fifth century following the Roman withdrawal from Britain, King Emrys (the Welsh form of the Romano-British name Ambrosius) serves as Lewis's surrogate character. His call is Lewis's call. His fight against internal heretics and external barbarians mirrors that of Lewis's party in twentieth-century Britain:

> Garmon, Garmon
> Gwinllan a roddwyd i'n gofal yw Cymru fy ngwlad,
> I'w thraddodi i'm plant
> Ac i blant fy mhlant
> Yn dreftadaeth dragwyddol;
> Ac wele'r moch yn rhuthro arni i'w maeddu.
> Minnau yn awr, galwaf ar fy nghyfeillion,

Cyffredin ac ysgolhaig,
Deuwch ataf i'r adwy,
Sefwch gyda mi yn y bwlch,
Fel y cedwir i'r oesoedd a ddel y glendid a fu.[29]

(Garmon, Garmon,
My country Wales is a vineyard entrusted to my care,
To pass down to my children
And to my children's children
An inheritance for ever;
And behold the swine rushing to despoil it.
Now I call on my friends,
Scholars and laymen,
Come and stand with me in the breach,
To preserve the beauty that is past in the ages that are to come.)

The speech is reminicent of King Henry's famous speech in Act III, Scene 1 of Shakespeare's *Henry V*, 'Once more unto the breach, dear friends, once more', and Lewis knew that it is by such words that nations are called into being.

Buchedd Garmon serves to reinforce Lewis's view that literature was as important for the future of Wales as any of his political speeches, even as a defendant in the court in Caernarfon. Never did he argue, however, that literature should be used as a crude propagandist tool; indeed, he despised the notion of literature as propaganda and saw the playwright's tendency to preach as one of the main weaknesses of Welsh drama. Kate Roberts, one of the few Welsh literary figures who also wrote political journalism, was admired by Lewis as 'she rigidly shuts the door on the least breath of propaganda in her stories and novels'.[30] Instead, he saw a vibrant literary culture, producing the kind of literature which can move an audience both intellectually and emotionally – like the works of Shakespeare, Sophocles, Racine, or Corneille, to name four of Lewis's favoured authors – as fundamental to the development of political structures that would promote and support Welsh culture. This is why Lewis sought not only to obtain a broadcasting service for Wales but also to encourage creative writers to be productive. Val Gielgud, former Head of Productions at the BBC, once remarked that Wales's claim, along with Scotland and Northern Ireland, to 'reasonable representation in the broadcasting field' was irrefutable, simply because of 'the undeniable existence of an endemic national drama'.[31]

While Gielgud's remark does not at all represent the original position of his predecessors at the BBC, it is nevertheless entirely in tune with Lewis's reasoning. Welsh literary classics, such as the poetry of Taliesin and Aneirin, the stories of the *Mabinogi,* and the *cywyddau* of Dafydd ap Gwilym, no less than the work of twentieth-century writers such as Kate Roberts and Alun Cilie, serve as a reminder that there once existed a Welsh polity and a Welsh nation which opposed English rule and the anglicization of its people. As Lewis reasoned, in his banned wireless talk:

> Even the mere existence to-day of a distinct Welsh culture and of national institutions of any kind implies that Wales had once a political entity also, and whether we know it or not we are the heirs of the past. You cannot artificially encourage the language and literature and arts of a people and at the same time refuse them any economic and political recognition. The thing isn't possible. If you will the existence of a Welsh National Orchestra, National Museum, National Eisteddfod, university, literature, and architecture, you are willing the existence of a Welsh nation, and you are therefore willing a Welsh Government and political machinery.[32]

The key words here are 'recognition' and 'existence'. To exist, or more importantly, to be recognized as existing, would be the ultimate goal for the new political party: 'the only way to extraversion and normality,' as Dafydd Glyn Jones put it.[33] A 'final word' in Lewis's seminal lecture, *Egwyddorion Cenedlaetholdeb* ('The Principles of Nationalism') is given to '[t] his: that Britain and Europe and every country recognise the value and importance of [Welsh] civilisation, recognise that it has a part to play and a contribution to make in the world, and afford it therefore a seat in the League of Nations'.[34]

In his speech at the courthouse at Caernarfon in 1936, Lewis explained that his own political awakening was as a result of his literary studies in Welsh. The literary renaissance of the twentieth century, the rediscovery by professional scholars of a literary tradition which could rival, as Lewis often argued, the greatness of Shakespeare, was fostering not only new literary standards but also a desire to create the strong political and educational structures which might best sustain and promote a culture whose literary tradition was 'great and classical' as regards its 'seriousness of function in society', yet 'unique and subtle and richly expressive' in its particular forms.[35] In a famous essay on the fifteenth-century poet Dafydd Nanmor, in which the critic as much as the poet in Lewis extols the merits of *perchentyaeth* ('house ownership'), we find the seeds of Lewis's economic policy of distributing property among the masses. This essay, published in 1925 in the newly established periodical *Y Llenor,* is one of Lewis's seminal texts, an essay which redefined the parameters of literary criticism in Wales. No more would the critic reduce the words of a literary text to etymological study or historical commentary, but rather, in a more creative manner, they would discuss its poetics and value and, furthermore, evaluate its meaning and relevance to contemporary life. Once described by the poet and critic D. Gwenallt Jones as 'the best piece of literary criticism ever written in Welsh',[36] Lewis's essay fused together aspects of English New Criticism and Welsh Nonconformist expository writing, combining the style of criticism which his English professor, Oliver Elton, had favoured at Liverpool University with the close, contextual readings which would have underpinned his father's Welsh Methodist sermons.

In effect, 'Dafydd Nanmor' ushered in the age of modern Welsh cultural studies, and though Lewis himself had the utmost respect for his scholarly predecessor, the critic, poet, and grammarian, John Morris-Jones, Lewis is generally credited for being the first to interpret the true significance of the Welsh literary tradition. His mentor at Liverpool, Oliver Elton, respected 'the affair of textual editing, of linguistics, and of [establishing] the Shakespeare canon', and yet, according to Elton, the critic's main concern should be 'what we think of Shakespeare and find in him, and what, after all, he is to us'.[37] It was this sense of putting 'us' (W. *ni*), into Welsh literature, and doing so with a sense of urgency, that caught Lewis's readers by surprise and made them his captives. Professor G. J. Williams, who subsequently appointed Lewis as senior lecturer in Welsh at Cardiff in 1957, praised him for being 'the first' to read Welsh literature in its European context, and to see in such poets as Dafydd Nanmor a contemporary message for the future of Wales.[38] Lewis could convincingly debate the date of the *Mabinogi* with the best of medieval scholars, but it was his sense of adaptation and renewal, his ability to tell the story anew as critic and creative writer, that made Lewis an early forerunner to modern screenwriters and producers.

'Welsh literature' as a discipline of study and field of social activity would therefore be a very different thing were it not for Lewis's seminal contributions in this field. What he sought primarily was to create for the Welsh that sense of *métier* which he saw as characteristic of French thought, when a celebrated body of literary work informs a common sense of literary values in the public. To this end, not only did Lewis write essays of note on 'nearly every important author in the history of Welsh literature',[39] he was the first to explain the merits of an author's work to the public, and why these authors mattered now. And he, more than any other critic, best explained the significance of the medieval Welsh literary tradition, seeing in the work of the sixth-century poet, Taliesin, a panegyric verse that 'belongs to the main stream of European literature', a poetry which became 'the foundation of the entire Welsh poetic tradition for a thousand years, right up to the sixteenth century'.[40] Within that tradition, 'essentially creative' from the outset,[41] one sees artistic developments of note, especially in the work of Dafydd ap Gwilym, who in 'a turning aside from the tradition of heroic panegyric' embraced 'the continental and classical modes of *jongleur* and *trouvère*' and sang 'out of moments of experience, realized with swift intensity, accidents, and occasions for incandescence'.[42]

At times, Lewis lacked the patience of a meticulous medievalist, but nevertheless, as evidenced by Dafydd Johnston's high regard for Lewis's work in his *Llên yr Uchelwyr* (2005), as far as explaining the poetic excellence of the Welsh literary tradition is concerned, his is one of the most convincing and authoritative voices. Consider, for example, the new edition of another of Lewis's seminal texts, *Williams Pantycelyn* (1927), published in 2017 to celebrate the hymn writer's third centennial. Lewis's text, which sought to canonize Pantycelyn – styling him as no longer the author of all-too-familiar Welsh hymns, but rather as one of the first in Europe to express the sentiments of the Romantic movement – has itself been retrieved as canonical, one of the masterpieces of Welsh literature in the twentieth century. Echoing R. Geraint Gruffydd's assessment of Lewis's most important essays on Welsh literature – 'that they themselves are literary works'[43] – D. Densil Morgan's edition is a testament to Lewis's longevity as a creative literary critic.

In the 1980s and 1990s, Lewis's canon-formation project faced a number of intellectual challenges from Marxist, feminist, and postmodernist critics. Accused of 'inventing' the literary tradition, one imagines Lewis's delight at the sight of such vibrant philosophical debate in Welsh, energized by the philosophical literature of France, the United States, and other countries. John Rowlands, who famously deconstructed many of Lewis's individual essays, analysing his authoritative style and essentialist discourse, remarked that Lewis, nevertheless, 'somehow' manages 'to rise like a phoenix from the ashes'.[44] That, I believe, is as a result of two things. Firstly, there is the ability of individual poems and stories from all periods of the Welsh literary tradition – 'Enaid Urien ap Rheged', 'Ystafell Cynddylan', *Branwen Ferch Llyr, Culhwch ac Olwen*, 'Marwnad Llywelyn ap Gruffudd', 'Llys Owain Glyn Dŵr', 'Trafferth Mewn Tafarn', 'Henaint', 'Marwnad Siôn y Glyn', 'Wele'n sefyll rhwng y myrtwydd', *Enoc Huws*, 'Ymadawiad Arthur', 'Cymru 1937', 'Y Cwilt', *Un Nos Ola Leuad*, 'Mewn Dau Gae', to name but a few – to continue to move the reader both intellectually and emotionally in the present day. Secondly, there is the way in which such individual artefacts were presented so creatively and imaginatively by Lewis himself, who saw these canonical texts collectively as composing the nation's on-going story, to be retold and reused to inspire new beginnings, but always to be celebrated one at a time by means of comparative poetics, contextual insight, and a creative critic's ability to grasp the reader's attention through hyperbole, metaphor, and imagery. Lewis's collected essays as literary critic, *Meistri'r Canrifoedd* (1973) and *Meistri a'u Crefft* (1981), and in the broader but closely related fields of political and cultural studies, *Ysgrifau Dydd Mercher* (1945), *Canlyn Arthur* (1986), and *Ati Wŷr Ifainc* (1986), testify to his variety of interests as a prolific socio-political and philosophical writer.

The Teacher

When adjudicators at the National Eisteddfod praise a new poet for being as irreverent and brilliant as, for example, Dafydd ap Gwilym, that sense of *métier* for which Lewis worked so tirelessly seems to be at play. Lewis's vision, however, was that such a *métier* should not only be the preserve of a few professional scholars and literary critics, but rather the understanding from which all schoolchildren in Wales might feel a sense of joy and self-worth and aspire to great, creative things, not necessarily as poets. The medieval Welsh literary tradition, inasmuch as the word *traddodiad* ('tradition') implies both delivery and transmission, was designed as a set of working texts to be interpreted, enacted, and performed to a live audience, and though the guild of the professional poets died out in the sixteenth century, Welsh literature of the modern period, as evidenced by Lewis's own writing on post-Reformation and twentieth-century authors, came to establish itself as a vibrant subject of intellectual study, capable of stimulating the ablest of minds in the schools and universities of Wales in the twentieth century.

This was not always the case. In 1945, in an essay in which he articulates a sincere respect for the accomplishments of Welsh poetry in English – 'this poetry in English is the most important thing to be produced in Wales during the [second world] war'– Lewis bemoans the current standards of poetry in Welsh.[45] Whilst those who studied English literature attained a sense of literary grandeur, especially through the study of 'great plays' by writers such as Shakespeare, the 'baby food' offered to those in the Welsh class unsurprisingly produced malnourished poets of mediocre ability, and Lewis above all despised mediocrity. Lewis believed that the Welsh literary tradition, when it is well taught, inspires competition and creativity, creates a Rhys Iorwerth or a Caryl Lewis, gives a Bobi Jones an incentive to learn and to live in Welsh. At times, Lewis's sense of tradition is too isolationist, too organic. In reality, multilingual authors, such as Lewis himself, of course, need not confine their sources of inspiration to Welsh alone, nor should they, but as a subject of study, in a bilingual land where only a minority are bilingual, Lewis managed to explain the grandeur of Welsh literature, to modernize it as a subject of study and to welcome others to it.

Above all, he dismissed the long-standing myth that the Welsh language would only keep its speakers enslaved 'under the hatches', being ill-equipped to act as a medium of education.[46] In many respects, education was at the heart of Lewis's nationalism. The party sought to address and counteract feelings of national inferiority which, to some extent, Lewis himself had experienced as a 'fearfully Welsh and timid' student in an English educational system.[47] In Wales, as is true of many imbalanced bicultural situations, one language is stigmatized and continually reduced whilst another, more dominant and privileged, is perpetually reinforced. Not until 2010 did such a thing as a new Welsh-medium educational strategy emerge in Wales, and Lewis's comparative analysis seems as relevant now as it did in 1945: 'There is hardly today a country in Europe, with the exception of Wales, where the nation's particular language is taught as a "subject", as if it were foreign.'[48]

Though perhaps not its immediate audience, it is as a school textbook that several generations of Welsh schoolchildren remember Lewis's novel *Monica* (1930). It achieved little by way of critical recognition for the best part of twenty years, even though it caused quite a stir in 1930 due to its risqué subject matter. Delicately written, *Monica* subsequently became a curriculum favourite for schools, giving way eventually to other texts. Dedicated to the eighteenth-century Welsh hymn writer, William Williams Pantycelyn – which in itself enforces the idea of a *renaissance* and a living tradition – it develops the theme of loveless marriage, and, in very much an understated tone, presents the life of a woman who steals away her sister's fiancé, marries him, and dominates him sexually until that fantasy is interrupted and ruined by pregnancy. Though lust, prostitution, and venereal disease lack the literary shock appeal they once had – and in some respects, the characterization through dialogue in Lewis's later novel, *Merch Gwern Hywel* (1964), seems more authentic and captivating – *Monica* was an important attempt by Lewis to contribute something current and alive in the way of creative prose, at a time when prose, with the emerging exception of Kate Roberts, seemed to lack the energy of the best poets, such as T. Gwynn Jones, R. Williams Parry, or T. H. Parry-Williams. Though he placed a great emphasis on tradition, one must remember that Lewis, no less so than T. S. Eliot, was primarily a modernist.

The Playwright

It has been argued that Lewis's 'most important contribution to Welsh literature was as a dramatist'.[49] His canonicity in this field is unparalleled, and his significance to Welsh-speaking audiences is comparable to that of Shakespeare among English-speaking audiences, Racine and Corneille for French-speaking audiences, and Bertolt Brecht for German-speaking audiences. Lewis's plays, now regarded as twentieth-century classics, continue to be performed by national and community theatre companies, and *Siwan*, arguably his theatrical masterpiece, has secured for itself a canonicity which few literary texts enjoy within any national school curriculum. Theatr Genedlaethol Cymru, a separate body from National Theatre Wales, has performed a number of Lewis's plays since its inception in 2003, including *Esther* in 2006, one of the company's most successful early productions, praised by critic Gareth Miles for its 'gripping story, authentic message, interesting characters and powerful language'.[50] In many respects, Lewis's most notable plays, especially *Blodeuwedd* (1948), *Siwan* (1956), and *Esther* (1960), set the standard by which others must succeed. He remains arguably Wales's greatest dramatist, and as his translator into English, Joseph P. Clancy, once argued, 'In the absence of a strong native tradition, he may almost be said to have invented a dramatic literature for Welsh-speaking Wales, drawing eclectically upon chiefly European models, traditional and modern, to create theatrical works of art for a culture that for much of his career had no professional theatre.'[51] In one sense, Theatr Genedlaethol Cymru, whether or not it continues to produce Lewis's plays regularly, exists as a direct result of what he achieved as a playwright and what he envisaged for Wales as a politician – a theatrical forum of debate and dreams which would do for Wales what the Abbey Theatre did for Ireland, and what Shakespeare did for England.

Five or six of his plays stand out as modern classics worthy of study, and more importantly, performance. Although Lewis himself might not have admired every aspect of Theatr Genedlaethol Cymru's 2012 production of *Blodeuwedd* (1948) – often he bemoaned the lack of professional standards of acting – this production confirmed the play's stature as one of Lewis's finest works. First performed in 1948, *Blodeuwedd* develops the story of the woman made of flowers, taken from the Fourth Branch of the *Mabinogi*. It is a grand Racinean play, and at times, Blodeuwedd's sense of self-disgust comes close to that of Phèdre's. It precedes Lewis's advance towards a more naturalistic theatre, but, in the hands of a gifted classical actress, Blodeuwedd is a masterful, captivating creation. In many ways, its theme is the central theme of Lewis's novel, *Monica*, for Blodeuwedd, born of flowers and not of flesh, can but live in the here and now, enslaved by her nature and her lust. Dismissed by her husband, she is left alone and yields to the temptations of another, only to be betrayed by him. Lust, demanding immediate ecstasy, leads only to ruin, and the forces of social responsibility (aided by wizardry) deny the individual all sense of personal pleasure or agency. The third act – a play within a play – is one of Lewis's best. Action, dialogue, and character-ization are all in harmony, whereas in previous attempts, and in subsequent comedies, Lewis failed to interweave these elements successfully. Here, however, words become weapons, used to conceal and reveal intentions, entrusted with the power to move others, both on stage and in the audience. To speak, let alone to confess, is itself a dangerous act. François Hédelin's principle of French neoclassical theatre, 'parler c'est agir', 'to speak is to act', seems an apt description of Lewis's drama, as action-in-words is concentrated on the psychological conflict of characters struggling to make sense of their surroundings and each other.[52]

The poetry of *Blodeuwedd* leads to the poetical speech of *Siwan* (1956), which in turn transforms into the prose of *Esther* (1960) and the plays of twentieth-century European Wales, *Gymerwch chi Sigarét?* (1956), *Brad* (1958), and *Cymru Fydd* (1967). Myth and history give way to more recent and contemporary events, and, as has been said of Shakespeare, 'so ruthless an experimenter', one is struck by the range of Lewis's subject matter as playwright.[53] The short play *Yn y Trên* (1965) is existentialist and somewhat absurd in its design, though the dialogue craft of the more conventional plays is nevertheless present. These, I would argue, are Lewis's most successful plays, among which *Siwan* is arguably the finest. Described by Lewis as a poem, but perhaps in the French theatrical sense of the word, the play has been an established school curriculum text for many years. Its power, however, lies in its performance. Only in performance is the theatricality of the text realized and experienced, as 'the action gobbles up the audience'.[54] Only in performance does Siwan – the illegitimate daughter of King John of England, the wife of Llewelyn the Great, aspiring Prince of Wales – become the most intriguing voice and captivating figure. In her tenderness and disbelief in Act I, her madness and grief in Act II, her strength and aspirations in Act III, a Welsh audience recognizes in Siwan its own desperate sense of inauthenticity, frustration, and desire, forever identified as the 'other' of English rulers and contesting Welsh men.

Prior to being held hostage by the play's power, one might be forgiven for thinking that Alis's lengthy description of Gwilym Brewys's hanging in Act II might be a case of 'abandoning the directness of drama for the indirectness of narrative', but nothing could be further from the truth. 'Another dramatist taking up this story might have chosen to present a wider range of characters, with greater movement and event rather than dialogue,' suggests Ioan Williams.[55] That might very well be the case, but, in performance, the play's concentration on one main protagonist, the effect of her words on others and of others' on her, continually draw the audience towards the stage, as if caught in a continual, emotional close-up. Littering the stage with a wider range of characters would only have produced the effect of 'beaucoup d'agitation'.[56]

Siwan, a character in conflict with herself as much as anyone else, is tragically moving and touches one's soul. Married politically to a husband who conceals his love for her, she unwittingly seeks a moment of authentic joy in another lover's arms. Enraged by his wife's betrayal, Llywelyn, the husband, not to be calmed or controlled by the arguments of his political advisors, jeopardizes the entire future of Wales by hanging the French baron, Gwilym Brewys. A year passes before he confesses his sin – he has always loved his wife and never told her. He begs her to return, as his trusted aid and advisor, and, moreover, as his wife. This she does, but only on her terms. *Siwan* is as perfect a play as one could hope to write. It achieves that essential quality of theatre, which is often lost in the 'stage opening, the powerful light and shade, the number of feet between [audience] and players', i.e. 'intimacy'.[57] The plot is simple and deep. The action could not be otherwise. Through a variety of linguistic techniques, including deixis, imperative verbs, imagery, silence, and an understated sense of rhythm in individual lines and dialogue, one is drawn to a character who wants to enjoy the simplicities of life, not as a monarch, but as a woman, one who wants to exist, and to be recognized as existing, by another, but for herself.

Saunders Lewis the poet also merits recognition here, perhaps even more so for his accomplishments as a leading modernist. His voice is unrepentantly raw and direct, revealing a playwright's desire to expose the naked truth by means of disturbing images and striking word combinations. The social imagery is especially grotesque and somewhat surreal in Lewis's most memorable and perhaps controversial poems, 'Y Dilyw 1939' (published in 1942) and 'Golygfa Mewn Caffe' (published in 1940). Powerful in as much as they are strange and disturbing, the language is coarse, the standpoint unsympathetic, the form, a controlled and controlling *vers libre*, the most quoted line, anti-Semitic. Metaphors and similes captivate the mind; imagery abounds in a nightmarish verse. Although Richard Wyn Jones has demonstrated that anti-Semitism was not an integral or even an important part of Lewis's world-view, this 'single stanza of poetry' has for others been enough 'to establish guilt'.[58]

Other poems, such as 'Llygad y Dydd yn Ebrill', a nature poem displaying Lewis's ability to write in the traditional rules of *cynghanedd*, and 'I'r Lleidr Da', a religious poem in metre and rhyme, testify to Lewis's broad range as a poet, but, though not prolific, he excelled as a modernist in *vers libre*. Two other poems in particular, 'Gweddi'r Terfyn' and 'Mair Fadlen', have confounded critics, the former for its ambiguity of faith in the face of death, the latter for its deep, dramatic appeal. Indeed, R. M. Jones has suggested that 'Mair Fadlen' might be the language's greatest twentieth-century poem.[59] Its powerful opening first verse might be seen as indicative of Lewis's attempts to enter the female mind, though of course, in his plays, a strong character such as Iris seems to speak for herself from the start and, more often than not, the female protagonist either out-thinks or out-performs her male counterparts. Here too, despite the narrator's hyperbolic generalization, is a specific metaphor and a detailed study of an individual woman's pain:

> Am wragedd ni all neb wybod. Y mae rhai,
> Fel hon, y mae eu poen yn fedd clo;
> Cleddir eu poen ynddynt, nid oes ffo
> Rhagddo nac esgor arno. Nid oes drai
> Na llanw ar eu poen, môr marw heb
> Symud ar ei ddyfinder. Pwy – a oes neb -
> A dreigla'r maen oddi ar y bedd dro?[60]

> (About women no one can know. There are some,
> Like this one, whose pain is a locked sepulchre;
> Their pain is buried in them, there is no fleeing
> From it and no casting it off. No ebb
> Nor tide of their pain, a dead sea without
> Movement upon its depth. Who – is there anyone –
> Who will take away the stone from this sepulchre?)

Conclusion

In many ways, the play *Siwan* stands as a metonym for the multi-stranded vision of Saunders Lewis. The character of Siwan wants for herself what Lewis sought for Wales – a sense of authenticity in another's recognition, in her own time, on her own terms – but whereas Lewis the engaged politician remained oddly removed from the people of Wales, Siwan enthralls an audience and draws them into the psychological complexities of her delicate, deliberate character. She speaks to the future of Wales, not as Lewis did in 1931, in terms of a 'strong, manly independence and . . . an ancestral pride', but rather, as a newcomer and as a woman, concerned for the wellbeing of her child and what she herself has worked for with others, a future in Wales, where such notions as self-determination and the normality of the Welsh language are taken for granted. While Siwan epitomizes many of those qualities which made Lewis inaccessible to others – aristocracy, Catholicism, elitism – she, as much as Alis, her maid, is sympathetic and engaging. *Siwan's* appeal lies in our ability to eavesdrop 'upon the secrets of the mighty', who, surprizingly and reassuringly, are as frail and troubled as ourselves.[61] Indeed, when performed imaginatively by competent actors to a live audience, *Siwan* has perhaps more potential than Lewis's political writing to awaken that love of Wales and desire for cultural authenticity which motivated the achievements of Saunders Lewis.

Notes

1. Saunders Lewis, *Meistri'r Canrifoedd: Ysgrifau ar Hanes Llenyddiaeth Gymraeg*, ed. R. Geraint Gruffydd (Caerdydd: Gwasg Prifysgol Cymru, 1973), 127.
2. T. R. Chapman, *Un Bywyd o Blith Nifer: Cofiant Saunders Lewis* (Llandysul: Gwasg Gomer, 2006), 384.
3. Saunders Lewis, 'Towards a Scientific Language', in *Western Mail*, 16 January 1965, 7.
4. Personal letter from Gwyn A. Williams to Mair Saunders Jones, dated 21 July 1984 (Aberystwyth, National Library of Wales).
5. Richard Wyn Jones, *The Fascist Party in Wales?: Plaid Cymru, Welsh Nationalism and the Accusation of Fascism* (Cardiff: University of Wales Press, 2014).
6. Tudur Hallam, '"Curse, Bless, Me Now": Dylan Thomas and Saunders Lewis', *Journal of the British Academy* 3 (2015): 238.
7. Saunders Lewis, 'Mother Tongue' in *The Observer*, 22 March 1959, 4.

8. Saunders Lewis, *Letters to Margaret Gilcriest*, ed. Mair Saunders Jones, Ned Thomas, and Harri Pritchard Jones (Cardiff: University of Wales Press, 1993), 486.

9. M. Inwood, *Heidegger: A Very Short Introduction* (Oxford: Oxford University Press, 2000), 27.

10. Lewis, 'Mother Tongue', 4.

11. S. Wade, *In My Own Shire: Region and Belonging in British Writing 1840–1970* (Westport and London: Praeger, 2002), 54.

12. Saunders Lewis, *The Banned Wireless Talk on Welsh Nationalism* (Caernarvon: Swyddfa'r Blaid Genedlaethol, 1931), 8.

13. Saunders Lewis, *Egwyddorion Cenedlaetholdeb* (Machynlleth: Evan Jones, 1926), 4.

14. Ibid., 6.

15. Ibid., 7.

16. *The UK Statute Law Database*, Parliament of England (1535), 'An Acte for Lawes and Justice to be ministered in Wales in like fourme as it is in this Realme' / 'Laws in Wales Act 1535 (repealed 21.12.1993)'. See Chapter 8 for a discussion of the Acts of Union of 1536 and 1543 which united England and Wales into a single polity.

17. Oliver Elton, letter to Saunders Lewis (1921), in *Letters to Margaret Gilcriest*, 460–1.

18. Lewis, *Egwyddorion Cenedlaetholdeb*, 4.

19. Dafydd Wigley, 'Saunders Lewis, Plaid Cymru ac Ewrop', lecture delivered in Penarth, 19 November 2015.

20. Saunders Lewis and Aneirin Talfan Davies, 'Dylanwadau: Saunders Lewis mewn Ymgom ag Aneirin Talfan Davies', *Taliesin* 2 (1961): 5–18.

21. Saunders Lewis, 'Welsh Literature and Nationalism' (1965), in *Presenting Saunders Lewis*, ed. Alun R. Jones and Gwyn Thomas (Cardiff: University of Wales Press, 1973), 143.

22. Lewis, 'Welsh Literature and Nationalism', 143.

23. The Regional Director, E. R. Appleton's objections to broadcasting in Welsh were quoted in 'Copi o'r memorandwm a gyflwynwyd gan Blaid Genedlaethol Cymru i'r Pwyllgor Seneddol ar Ddarlledu, Mai 30, 1935', *Y Ddraig Goch* 9.7 (Gorffennaf [July] 1935): 6. 'Wales, of her own choice, is part of the British Commonwealth of Nations, of which the official language is English. When His Majesty's Government decided to form a corporation for the important function of Broadcasting, it was natural that the official language be used throughout. To use the ancient languages regularly, – Welsh, Irish, Gaelic and Manx, would be either to serve propaganda purposes or to disregard the needs of the greatest number ... If the extremists who desire to force the language upon listeners in the area, whether they will or not, were to have their way, the official language would lose its grip.'

24. The Welsh-language television channel, S4C, began broadcasting in 1982, after years of lobbying from within Wales and elsewhere. See Chapter 32 in this volume for the wider context of broadcasting in Wales.

25. All quotations in this paragraph are from Saunders Lewis, 'The Caernarfon Court Speech' (1936), repr. in Presenting Saunders Lewis, ed. Jones and Edwards, 115–26.

26. 'Blue plaque unveiled for Saunders Lewis', www.swansea.gov.uk/article/ 29164/Blue-plaque-unveiled-for-Saunders-Lewis (accessed 10 September 2017). On 19 November 2015 a blue plaque was also unveiled on Lewis's former home in Westbourne Road, Penarth. This was the occasion of Dafydd Wigley's lecture, quoted above.

27. Saunders Lewis, 'Drama ar gyfer Gŵyl Ddewi', Radio Times, 22 February 1957 [produced for 24 February – 2 March], 9.

28. Ioan Williams, A Straitened Stage: A Study of the Theatre of J. Saunders Lewis (Bridgend: Seren Books, 1991), 50.

29. Saunders Lewis, Buchedd Garmon (1937), repr. in Ioan M. Williams, ed., Dramâu Saunders Lewis: Y Casgliad Cyflawn, 2 vols. (Caerdydd: Gwasg Prifysgol Cymru, 1996), I, 139, my translation.

30. Lewis, 'Welsh Literature and Nationalism', 144.

31. Val Gielgud, British Radio Drama 1922–1956: A Survey (London: Harrap, 1957), 28.

32. Lewis, 'The Banned Wireless Talk on Welsh Nationalism', 8.

33. Dafydd Glyn Jones, 'His Politics', in Presenting Saunders Lewis, ed. Jones and Thomas, 33.

34. Lewis, Egwyddorion Cenedlaetholdeb, 7–8.

35. Lewis, 'The Essence of Welsh Literature' (1947), in Presenting Saunders Lewis, ed. Jones and Thomas, 158.

36. D. Gwenallt Jones, 'Beirniadu Beirniad', Y Llenor 12 (1933): 32.

37. Oliver Elton, Modern Studies (London: Arnold, 1907), 79.

38. G. J. Williams, 'Cyfraniad Saunders Lewis fel Ysgolhaig Cymraeg', in Saunders Lewis: Ei Feddwl a'i Waith, ed. P. Davies (Dinbych: Gwasg Gee, 1950), 123.

39. R. G. Gruffydd, 'Rhagymadrodd', in Saunders Lewis, Meistri'r Canrifoedd, ed. R. G. Gruffydd (Caerdydd: Gwasg Prifysgol Cymru, 1973), ix.

40. Saunders Lewis, 'The Essence of Welsh Literature' (1947), repr. in Presenting Saunders Lewis, ed. Jones and Thomas, 150.

41. Ibid., 150.

42. Saunders Lewis, 'Dafydd ap Gwilym' (1963), repr. in Presenting Saunders Lewis, ed. Jones and Thomas, 161–3.

43. Gruffydd, 'Rhagymadrodd', in Meistri'r Canrifoedd, x.

44. John Rowlands, Saunders y Beirniad (Caernarfon: Gwasg Pantycelyn, 1990), 22.

45. Saunders Lewis, 'Diwylliant yng Nghymru', in *Ysgrifau Dydd Mercher* (Llandysul: Y Clwb Llyfrau Cymraeg, 1945), 101; my translation.

46. R. R. W. Lingen, *Reports of the Commissioners of Inquiry into the State of Education in Wales: Carmarthen, Glamorgan, Pembroke* (London: Parliamentary Committee of Council on Education, 1947), 3.

47. Lewis, *Letters to Margaret Gilcriest*, 342.

48. Lewis, 'Diwylliant yng Nghymru', 102; my translation.

49. Meic Stephens, ed., *The New Companion to the Literature of Wales* (Cardiff: University of Wales Press, 1998), 434.

50. Gareth Miles, 'Yn y Crochan', *Barn* 522/523 (Gorffennaf/Awst 2006): 96; my translation.

51. Joseph P. Clancy, 'Translator's Preface', in *The Plays of Saunders Lewis: Translated from the Welsh by Joseph P. Clancy* (Llandybïe: Christopher Davies, 1985), vol. I, 7.

52. François Hédelin, Abbé d'Aubignac, *La Pratique du théâtre*, ed. by Pierro Martino (Alger, Paris, Carbonel: Champion, 1927), 282.

53. Harold Bloom, *Shakespeare: The Invention of the Human* (London: Fourth Estate, 1999), 722.

54. Gwenan Mared, 'Atgyfodi Clasur', *Barn* 545 (Mehefin 2008): 55.

55. Williams, *A Straitened Stage*, 114.

56. Hédelin, *La Pratique du théâtre*, 246. The French phrase is difficult to translate precisely; literally 'too much agitation', but perhaps in the sense of 'too much excitement', too much going on.

57. W. B. Yeats, 'Certain Noble Plays of Japan', in *Essays and Introductions* (London and Basingstoke: Macmillan, 1961), 222.

58. See Jones, *The Fascist Party in Wales?* It is worth noting that Lewis deliberately extols the virtues of the Jewish Protagonist in his play *Esther* (1960).

59. R. M. Jones, *Mawl a Gelynion ei Elynion: Hanfod y Traddodiad Llenyddol Cymraeg: Cyf. 2: Amddiffyn Mawl* (Cyhoeddiadau Barddas, 2002), 171.

60. Saunders Lewis, 'Mair Fadlen' in *Siwan a Cherddi Eraill* (Llandybïe: Llyfrau'r Dryw, [1956]), 24–6; the translation quoted here is by Gwyn Thomas, 'Mary Magdalen', in *Presenting Saunders Lewis*, ed. Jones and Thomas, 191. See also Clancy's translation in *Selected Poems of Saunders Lewis: Translated from the Welsh by Joseph P. Clancy* (Cardiff: University of Wales Press, 1993), 23.

61. David Maskell, *Racine: A Theatrical Reading* (Oxford: Clarendon, 1991), 48.

27

R. S. Thomas, Emyr Humphreys, and the Possibility of a Bilingual Culture

ANDREW WEBB

Overview

From the 1940s to the 1960s, the anglophone Welsh writers Emyr Humphreys and R. S. Thomas registered through their work the emergence of a possible bilingual culture in Wales. The aim of this chapter is to assess the contribution of these writers to more recent debates about the cultural potential of bilingualism in Wales. The chapter expands upon Daniel G. Williams's recent distinction between 'tribal' and 'multicultural' representations of Welshness in order to identify some of the characteristics of a specifically Welsh bilingual culture. It then traces these characteristics through the mid-twentieth-century work of Humphreys and Thomas. It finds that both authors construct intended Welsh readerships from two groups: English-language readers who are fluent in Welsh; and English-language readers who, while not necessarily fluent in Welsh, are nonetheless familiar with the linguistic and cultural complexity of modern Wales. Both writers effectively engage in a process of nation building, by speaking to these groups and 'othering' metropolitan English-language readers with no experience or knowledge of Wales's linguistic complexity. The chapter goes on to show how both authors – in different ways – record the historical demise of a Welsh-language culture centred on Nonconformist, agricultural communities and raise the possibility that an emergent bilingual society – registered in a representation of Wales's linguistic complexity, of Welsh-language acquisition, of Welsh-language modernity, and technologically networked communities – would one day take its place.

The Emergence of Bilingualism in Twentieth-Century Wales

The main function of the novelist, suggests Emyr Humphreys, is 'to perpetuate the language of the tribe'.[1] One writer who does so, he points out, is the Welsh-language author Kate Roberts: according to Humphreys, she 'dominate[s] the continuing consciousness of her tribe'.[2] This tribal view of Welsh-language culture and the responsibilities of its writers towards it draws a parallel with the work of the poet R. S. Thomas. In his much anthologized poem 'Welsh History', Thomas writes of 'a people' who

> fought, and were always in retreat,
> Like snow thawing upon the slopes
> Of Mynydd Mawr; and yet the stranger
> Never found our ultimate stand
> In the thick woods, declaiming verse
> To the sharp prompting of the harp.[3]

The speaker of Thomas's poem identifies with the Welsh, depicting them in racial and cultural terms as a tribe. They are a 'people [. . .] / Clinging stubbornly to the proud tree / Of blood and birth'. They are 'always in retreat', falling back to an 'ultimate stand' of 'verse' and 'harp', a set of traditions – bound up with the Welsh language – that remain impenetrable to the 'stranger'. The role of the poet, it would seem, is one of 'declaiming verse' to the gathered tribe: making the culture's last stand.

Daniel G. Williams has discussed the tendency, even among writers open to linguistic difference and cultural pluralism, to represent the Welsh-language community as a 'tribe'.[4] Williams argues that presenting Welsh-language culture in this way – as a 'closed culture, inaccessible to others', 'the key to an inner sanctum' – is 'potentially disastrous'.[5] While, in typical postcolonial fashion, it usefully counters the metropolitan reader's expectation of an 'other' that is transparent and open to the metropolitan gaze, it also suggests that Welsh is a culture that is shut off from incomers.[6] For Williams, this threatens to equate language, which is always 'learnable', with race, a category that can never be acquired, and to present Welsh as a closed system. The Welsh language can then be represented not as 'a mode of communication' but instead as a 'symbolic marker of ethnicity' and a 'constraint on communication between peoples', the point at which 'it becomes easy to wish that it should disappear'.[7] Williams suggests, rather bleakly, that this is 'perhaps, the likeliest future' for Welsh-language culture.[8] Indeed, his work remains haunted by the 'nightmarish possibility' that bilingualism is merely a 'way-station in the journey from Welsh monolingualism to English monolingualism'.[9] However, Williams also imagines an alternative direction of travel, based on the continuing 'possibility of a bilingual culture'.[10] In order for this to happen, it is essential, he argues, for Welsh to resist the drift towards tribal status, to insist on its own role as 'the crucible for multicultural citizenship', and not to cede that status to the English language. He goes on to trace some of the features of an emergent bilingual space within Welsh literature, suggesting that it first emerged in the work of R. S. Thomas, Emyr Humphreys, and Margiad Evans, before focusing on its more recent, fuller expression in the work of Menna Elfyn and Gwyneth Lewis.[11] Their work, suggests Williams, 'mediate[s] between, and meditate[s] upon' the linguistic boundaries that have dominated modern Welsh culture.[12]

Williams places great emphasis on the Welsh language as a key marker in a modern, civic Welsh identity. The keyword here is civic: the future of the Welsh language depends on its representation as a language of modernity, in particular as an acquirable aspect of national identity, one that can be fostered through the education system and learned by incomers.[13] There is clear recent evidence of its success in this regard. Since 1962, when Saunders Lewis, arguably the most significant Welsh-language public intellectual of the twentieth century, delivered 'Tynged Yr Iaith' ('The Fate of the Language') – a seminal lecture in which he warned that, unless action were taken, Welsh would die out in the twenty-first century – the number of children attending Welsh medium primary schools has increased fourteen-fold.[14] As a result, in the second decade of the twenty-first century, the Welsh language is no longer the preserve of the old, its numbers declining with the passing of each generation, but is now increasingly spoken by young people, even in areas with little recent history of Welsh. In Wales as a whole, the 1991 census recorded that, for the first time in a century, knowledge of Welsh was more widespread among children than it was among the population as a whole, a key marker of the language's future. The proportion of Welsh speakers has declined in its strongholds – areas of the north or west like Gwynedd and Carmarthenshire – while it has grown in border areas like Alyn in the north-east, as well as Gwent and Cardiff in the south-east.[15] The raw census data, which suggests that, in the first two decades of the twenty-first century, the Welsh language is spoken by roughly 20 per cent of Wales's population, masks this generational shift in the preponderance of Welsh. While there are ongoing and vigorous debates about the competence and linguistic significance of these new generations of Welsh speakers, the cultural impact of this change on our understanding of Welsh-language and bilingual culture is becoming clear. Modernizing trends that were evident in Welsh-language culture prior to this expansion in educational provision have accelerated. Welsh is incontestably a language of modernity, no longer predominantly associated with Nonconformist or agricultural ways of life that have long been in decline, but with a vibrant culture that is evident across all aspects of modern life. Welsh is also now a language of government, which is remarkable given its centuries-long exclusion from the corridors of power. It is also a language of opportunity and aspiration: the ability to speak Welsh, once seen as a hindrance to 'getting on' in the world – to the extent that many parents did not pass the language on to their children – is now seen as essential to an individual's job prospects in many parts of Wales.

These changes shape the possibility of a bilingual future. While the remaining areas in which Welsh is a majority language need support, it is important to recognize that the majority of Welsh-language communities are, and will be, networked groups of speakers, fluent in both English and Welsh, living – for the most part – in regions in which English is the majority language. These communities embody a complex Welsh linguistic inheritance in which national identity is associated not only with the Welsh language but also with versions of the English language that the Welsh have made their own, and into which Welsh-language culture may be translated. The continuing viability of these communities depends on political support for measures including the expansion of Welsh-language education; support for incomers to learn Welsh; for the principle of bilingualism and the visibility of the language so that it is possible, for those who wish to do so, to live through the medium of Welsh; the embrace of new technologies that enable geographically dispersed groups of Welsh speakers to communicate to each other; and, perhaps above all, on the establishment of job opportunities in order to enable Welsh speakers to remain in Wales.[16]

Today, a genuine bilingual culture remains a work in progress, and it faces many obstacles before it can be realised. In the mid-twentieth century, while its shape was far from clear (and the tools to achieve it even less so), I want to suggest that the emergent characteristics of a modern, bilingual Welsh culture are nonetheless evident. What is at stake in my argument, then, is the historical rootedness of the 'possibility of a bilingual culture'. I have taken as my subject matter the work of R. S. Thomas and Emyr Humphreys, the pre-eminent poet and novelist respectively of anglophone Wales in the second half of the twentieth century. My contention, first and foremost, is that – in spite of the 'tribal' view of Welsh culture set out at the beginning of this chapter – both writers actually privilege and encourage a bilingual readership in two senses of the word: firstly, English-language readers fluent in Welsh and familiar with its literature; secondly, English-language readers, who even if not fluent in Welsh, are nonetheless distinct from an English readership in their experience and knowledge of Welsh culture, its linguistic complexity, and its use of a distinctively Welsh, English-language discourse. R. S. Thomas's hostility towards the idea of a bilingual Wales – expressed both in his correspondence and through his depictions of the idealized past of a tribal Welsh-language community, and its modern-day descendants like Iago Prytherch – can be contextualized as an attempt to preserve a residual Welsh-language culture during a period of domination. On a deeper, formal level, his poetry and prose nonetheless establish the space for a bilingual culture. In the case of Humphreys, his novels of the 1950s and 1960s signal the end of an inward-looking, Nonconformist, agricultural Welsh-language community, a way of life that – he suggests – has become unbearable and ill-equipped for the modern world. They also show the possibility that an emergent bilingual society would one day replace this culture, a hope registered in his novels' representation of linguistic complexity in Wales, of language acquisition, of Welsh-language modernity, of engagement with modern technology as a means of developing networked communities.

R. S. Thomas (1913–2000)

R. S. Thomas was born in Cardiff in 1913 and brought up in an English-speaking environment in Holyhead on Anglesey. From there, he went to Bangor University, and became an Anglican priest, ministering in the border areas of Chirk and Tallarn Green in Flintshire; in Manafon, Montgomeryshire from 1942 to 1954; in Eglwysfach, near Aberystwyth, until 1972, when he moved to Aberdaron in the Llŷn. He died in 2000, having published twenty-five collections of English-language poetry in his lifetime, as well as five substantial pieces of autobiographical prose in Welsh, and numerous essays and articles in both languages.

It can certainly be argued that Thomas's work has little to contribute to the possibility of a bilingual Wales. As 'Welsh History' suggests, it often depicts a tribal Welshness, characterized by its focus on 'relics' of the past, on dying aspects of rural culture, on its essentialist depiction of the Welsh language as the last refuge of an otherwise defeated 'race'. The alternative vision of a bilingual Wales was one to which Thomas remained hostile. In a 1968 letter to the writer and critic Raymond Garlick, Thomas declared that, 'I'm afraid I can't think like you about bilingualism, although I realize that rationally speaking one tends to get outargued.'[17] This view does not soften with age. Thomas's later years are characterized by what Jason Walford Davies has described as 'increasing ... Welsh-languageness'.[18] At one point, he withdrew from a nationalist rally on learning that he was expected to speak in English, pointing out that:

> Despite all the difficulties and criticism and accusations of being unrealistic, I tend to side with Saunders [Lewis] on this question. After the initial boost to the Welsh ego, bilingualism means the end of Welsh as a creative language.[19]

Even Thomas's most discussed poetic creation – the character of Iago Prytherch, sheep farmer, and 'ordinary man of the bald Welsh hills' – seems to fit into this uncompromising rejection of bilingualism, conforming instead to a tribal conception of Welsh-language identity. Prytherch is first named in 'A Peasant', published in *The Stones of the Field* (1946), and is a recurrent presence in Thomas's poetry over the next two decades. 'A Peasant' closes with the following lines:

> Yet this is your prototype, who, season by season
> Against siege of rain and the wind's attrition,
> Preserves his stock, an impregnable fortress
> Not to be stormed even in death's confusion.
> Remember him, then, for he, too, is a winner of wars,
> Enduring like a tree under the curious stars.[20]

Prytherch, it would seem, is a character straight out of a pre-industrial age, portrayed as a timeless figure, 'impregnable' to the forces of modernity, valued for his qualities of endurance. He is also a 'prototype' whose example will lead his people back to the promised land of pre-industrial, rural Welsh nationhood. As Tony Brown has pointed out, he is as much a product of myth as the result of a real encounter, but he is nonetheless emblematic of the association, in Thomas's mind, between Welshness and a rural culture which survives the intrusions of the modern world.[21]

There is a shift over time in Thomas's representation of Welsh rural culture. The 1945 essay 'The Depopulation of the Welsh Hill Country' depicts the last generation of upland farmers above Manafon as a mythical Welsh version of a Yeatsian Irish peasantry unaffected by – indeed, defined against – modernity, albeit that, by then, they are 'the shadows of what their fathers were'.[22] By 1968, in his essay *The Mountains*, Thomas writes of them firmly in the past tense –

'They have gone now; the cuttings are deserted; *yr hafotai* in ruins' – but their memory is still idealized, as they move 'with their flocks from *yr hendre*, the winter house, to *yr hafod*, the sheiling', where they 'swap[ped] *englynion* over the peat cutting'.[23] So, while it seems that Thomas increasingly accepts that his tribal conception of Welsh rural identity has no basis in present reality, it nonetheless remains a cornerstone of his imagined nation.

It is perhaps inevitable that such an understanding of Welshness is associated with the past:

> There is no present in Wales,
> And no future;
> There is only the past,
> Brittle with relics,
> Wind-bitten towers and castles
> With sham ghosts;
> Mouldering quarries and
> mines;
> And an impotent people,
> Sick with inbreeding,
> Worrying the carcase of an old song.[24]

Writing in 1972, Dafydd Elis Thomas suggests that such lines from 'Welsh Landscape', published in *An Acre of Land* (1952), with their explicit focus on the 'relics' of the 'past', are in keeping with the 'wholly historical' nationalism to be found in Thomas's poetry.[25] Present-day concerns of the Welsh people – including 'unemployment, migration, non-democratic government, lack of economic development [and] linguistic injustice' – simply do not feature; instead, Thomas's vision of Wales revolves around the heroes of the past, epitomized by Owain Glyn Dŵr, a figure in whom 'history and myth merge', and whose heroics are repeatedly contrasted with 'the current gutlessness of the Welsh people'.[26]

And yet, there are ways in which Thomas's work suggests the possibility of an emergent bilingual culture. Before we consider this, we need to contextualize Thomas's depiction of a tribal, rural Welsh identity, and we can do this by turning to Raymond Williams. In his essay 'Welsh Culture', Williams identifies a moment in history of 'real independence': a point at which people possess 'a new confident sense of their present and future', when they 'know [. . .] the past as past', as a 'shaping history', and see their present moment as one of 'new and active creation'.[27] But he also points to another phase in the history of a dominated culture: an 'earlier stage' during which 'real independence' is not possible, in which there is instead 'a fixation on the past, part real, part mythicized because the past in either form is one thing they can't take away from us'.[28] Williams's insights here offer a way of reading Thomas's poetry. Thomas's focus on the past – to the point, as we have seen in 'Welsh Landscape', where he denies the possibility of a Welsh future or present – might well be described as a 'fixation'. His focus on the resistance of Owain Glyn Dŵr, for example, certainly alights on a point in Welsh history when an empirical narrative meets popular legend. Similarly, his creation of Iago Prytherch is an attempt to construct a myth of Welsh identity centred on 'an ordinary man of the bald Welsh hills'. As myths with their origins in history – resistance to fifteenth-century English rule, or resistance to sweeping modernity – they are 'form[s] of the past that cannot be taken away' and might be understood, then, as efforts to preserve Wales's threatened identity at a time of change. It offers a way of contextualizing what might otherwise be seen as a conservative, even reactionary, politics.

There are ways, however, in which Thomas's work may be characterized as emergent, anticipating the possibility of a bilingual culture. Indeed, in spite of his occasional pronouncements to the contrary, his writing career is unarguably bilingual. His earliest prose efforts in Welsh, 'Adar y Plwyfi' ('Birds of the Parishes') and 'Adar y Gaeaf' ('Winter Birds'), began to appear in Y Llan, the magazine for the Church in Wales, as early as 1945, with short prose articles appearing in Y Fflam from the following year.[29] With the exception of an English-language review published in The Dublin Magazine in 1941, and a letter printed in Keidrych Rhys's journal Wales in 1944, Thomas's Welsh-language prose publication is therefore synchronous with its English-language prose equivalent, and it actually predates the 1946 publication of his first English-language poetry collection.

While the synchronicity of Thomas's English- and Welsh-language writing is important, it is equally significant that, from the start of his career, Thomas's work investigates what it means to be writing Wales in English. His most pressing concern in the 1940s, as Brown has argued, is the question of how he could be a Welsh poet while not yet being able to write poetry in the language.[30] The question of what it meant to be an 'Anglo-Welsh' writer, to use the term then in use, had also been raised by Saunders Lewis in response to the 1937 appearance, in Keidrych Rhys's pioneering new journal Wales, of a number of young anglophone Welsh poets. In a 1938 lecture, 'Is There an Anglo-Welsh Literature?', Saunders Lewis famously argued – with reference to Dylan Thomas, one of the journal's contributors – that there was no such thing as an anglophone Welsh literature.[31] As Brown has shown, the issue was still 'under active debate' within the pages of Wales when it was relaunched in 1943.[32] Writers including W. Moelwyn Merchant, H. Idris Bell, and Wyn Griffith offered a range of views on the role of the English-language Welsh writer. Rhys, in his editorial to the second issue of the relaunched journal, suggested that anglophone Welsh writing was 'a stage on the way back to the use of Welsh for literature'.[33] Thomas, therefore, was part of the first generation for whom these concerns became a central, much discussed, feature of their work across the two languages.

Thomas's own answer to the question of identity raised in this period is ambiguous, even politic. He clearly identifies a nascent anglophone Welsh tradition but suggests, in line with Lewis and Rhys, that 'for all we know, our movement may simply be a phase in the re-cymrification of Wales'.[34] There is an ambiguity in the phrase 'for all we know' which suggests that the role of this new anglophone Welsh literary tradition was not yet clear in his mind. In a 1952 essay, 'Llenyddiaeth Eingl-Gymreig' ('Anglo-Welsh Literature'), published in Y Fflam, he repeats the idea that anglophone Welsh literature is 'a means of rekindling interest in the Welsh-language culture, and of leading people back to the mother-tongue'.[35] Elsewhere, Thomas suggests that anglophone Welsh writing has inherited the mantle of Welsh-language literature and that its future direction and role is more open. In a 1946 essay, 'Some Contemporary Scottish Writing', he suggested that 'the mantle of writers like T. Gwynn Jones and W. J. Gruffydd is falling not upon younger Welsh writers, but upon those of us who express ourselves in the English tongue'.[36] He even instructs English-language Welsh writers to

> discover Welsh history. Secondly, steep yourself in the Welsh literary tradi-
> tion. Thirdly, become acquainted with Welsh geology, geography, natural
> history and all other aspects of life here. And finally write out of that full
> knowledge and consciousness in English – if you can.[37]

The instruction here certainly fulfils the first of the aims he set out in Y Fflam – anglophone Welsh writing is here a 'means of rekindling interest in the Welsh-language culture' – but there is no indication that it will 'lead . . . people back to the mother tongue'. Indeed, the end result of developing an anglophone Welsh literature in 'full knowledge and consciousness' of its Welsh-language forebear is unclear. What we know is that Thomas is concerned to carve out a space for an English-language Welsh literature whose future role in Welsh society cannot be predicted.

Thomas is innovative in the way his work shifts from one language to the other and back again. In his autobiographical essay 'Y Llwybrau Gynt' ('Former Paths'), first published in Welsh in 1972, Thomas looks back to the beginning of his writing career, when he was a curate at Tallarn Green in Hanmer, Flintshire, in the anglicized corner of north-east Wales. He recalls looking west to the 'hills of Wales' and decides to 'set about learning Welsh, in order to be able to return to the true Wales of my imagination'.[38] Here we have an English-language translation of a Welsh-language narrative, itself written thirty years after the event, of Thomas's decision to learn Welsh. To narrate this turning point, as well as his earlier English-language life, in Welsh, is in effect to rewrite those years in his newly-acquired language. By the time we read it in English, it has crossed back and forth over Wales's internal linguistic border several times. These are then re-translated back into English. The same could be said of the four autobiographical essays written between 1972 and 1990 – 'Y Llwybrau Gynt' ('Former Paths'), 'Hunanladdiad y Llenor' ('The Creative Writer's Suicide'), *Neb* ('No-one') and *Blwyddyn yn Llŷn* ('A Year in Llŷn') – all written in Welsh, and subsequently translated, by others, into English. As Geraint Evans argues, by writing in this way, Thomas effectively creates a bilingual readership.[39] Those with a knowledge of the Welsh-language prose develop a fuller understanding of the English-language poetry. The success of Thomas's work in the anglophone sphere led to the translation into English of many of his prose texts. As Evans suggests, this brought Welsh-language literature to a wider international audience and drew attention to the correspondence between Welsh-language and anglophone Welsh traditions.[40]

There are other aspects to the bilingualism here. Those Welsh-language prose readers are introduced to an English-language poetry that is thoroughly imbued with references and allusions to classic Welsh literature. 'Hiraeth', for example, published in his first collection *Stones of the Field* (1946), refers to 'Ceridwen's bowl' as an image of possible national rebirth.[41] 'Winter Retreat', from the same first collection, refers to the Twrch Trywth in the *Mabinogion* story 'Culhwch ac Olwen'. Jason Walford Davies has drawn attention to the full extent of Thomas's engagement with the Welsh-language literary tradition. He has identified depictions of key figures including Saunders Lewis, Ann Griffiths, Twm o'r Nant, and Gwenallt, among others.[42] The more subtle references to Welsh-language literature in Thomas's poetry include allusions to stories from the *Mabinogion*; to early *englynion* poetry in 'Border Blues' ('Eryr Pengwern, penngarn llwyt heno'); to the unworldly fifteenth-century poet Siôn Cent; to a *cywydd* by the satirist-poet Siôn Tudur, the source of the title of Thomas's second collection, *An Acre of Land*; to Welsh folk verse (the line 'Sŵn y galon fach yn torri', or 'the sound of the little heart breaking', is the epigraph to *The Minister*); to Dafydd ap Gwilym in numerous poems; to Iolo Goch; to more contemporary writers including Dewi Emrys, Saunders Lewis, Gwenallt, Waldo Williams, and R. Williams Parry. As Walford Davies points out, taken as a whole, the allusions to the Welsh-language literary tradition pull 'against the heroic ideal expressed in Aneurin and Taliesin', suggesting instead their author's empathy with the 'shattering tragedy of their struggle'.[43] The same pattern of influence is evident in respect of Thomas's appropriation of Welsh prosodic techniques. In a 1947 BBC radio broadcast, Thomas admitted to 'long pondering over the question of Anglo-Welsh writing', thoughts that had been 'responsible for certain experiments of mine both in subject matter and technique'.[44] In the same broadcast, he gives 'The Welsh Hill Country', the first poem from the 1952 collection *An Acre of Land*, as an example of a poem with 'characteristically Welsh internal rhyme and alliteration':[45]

> Too far for you to see
> The fluke and the foot-rot and the fat maggot
> Gnawing the skin from the small bones[46]

Here, then, the internal rhyme of 'too' and 'you' is paralleled in 'gnaw' and 'small', while the hard, plosive sounds of 'f' and 't' sculpt the opening, lending a material, gristly quality to the language that reflects the subject matter. There is a hint of *cynghanedd* in the repetiton of 'f' and 't' across the two halves of the second line. Indeed, in the same year that *An Acre of Land* was published, Thomas gave lectures in Scotland on the history of Welsh-language literature.[47] Brown shows that, in 'Wales' from *Song at the Year's Turning*, Thomas engages with the main techniques of *cynghanedd*: internal rhyme, assonance, and consonantal alliteration:

> Above the clatter of the broken water
> The song is caught in the bare boughs;
> The very air is veined with darkness – hearken!
> The brown owl wakens in the wood now.[48]

Here, the 'b', 'c', and 't' sounds of 'Above the clatter' are repeated in the second half of the line, 'broken water', an arrangement that recalls *cynghanedd*. At its most innovative, Thomas's poetry develops the formal aspects of both languages in a way that creates a new kind of poetry: one that anticipates the linguistic shifts of later poets like Gwyneth Lewis. As Walford Davies has shown, 'A Welsh Ballad Singer' plays with the echoes between the two languages in its depiction of Twm o'r Nant, the eighteenth-century composer. Thomas's own poem begins:

> Thomas Edwards – Twm o'r Nant
> If you prefer it – that's my name,
> Truth's constant flame purging my heart
> Of malice and mean cant.[49]

This is a reworking of Twm o'r Nant's own words,

> Thomas Edwards yw fy enw
> Ond Twn o'r nant mae cant yn fy ngalw

> (Thomas Edwards is my name
> But Twn o'r Nant is what hundreds call me),

where the Welsh-language internal rhyme of 'Nant' and 'cant' (meaning a hundred) is reworked into the English version in which 'Nant' is end-rhymed with 'cant', meaning pious hypocrisy.[50]

There are different kinds of bilingualism at play here. While those with a knowledge of Welsh-language literature certainly have the fullest understanding of the text, those same bilingual readers are also challenged in their conception of literature from Wales. They discover a literature that is imbued with Welsh literary references and prosodic techniques, and informed by a biography that is written in Welsh, and yet written in the English language. In this sense, while the surface attitudes and implicit political views expressed in Thomas's poetry serve to reinforce a tribal conception of Welsh-language culture, its form, language, and cultural references work against any single language-based notion of the Welsh 'tribe'. But there is a second category of intended reader here too. In addition to the fully bilingual reader who appreciates the references to Welsh-language literary culture, Thomas's poetry also speaks to those English-language readers with an awareness of Wales's linguistic complexity. These are the non-Welsh speakers who, while not necessarily sympathizing with Thomas's politics, nonetheless understand the pressures on identity that come from being part of a Welsh society historically divided along linguistic lines. The opening of 'Welsh Landscape',

> To live in Wales is to be conscious
> At dusk of the spilled blood
> That went in to the making of the wild sky[51]

is an appeal to Welsh readers defined not by their race, or language, but by their home address. What unites such readers is their consciousness of the divisions and violence that form Welsh history. This will not speak – at least not in the same way – to monoglot English readers who do not 'live in Wales', and who are not presumably aware of Wales's cultural complexity. The same is true of a poem like 'Welsh' in which, after declaring 'I'm Welsh, see; / A real Cymro', the speaker – an English-speaking Welsh person – admits:

> Only the one loss.
> I can't speak my own
> Language – Iesu.
> All those good words;
> And I outside them.[52]

While the tone, the implied conflation of language with identity, and the use of an adopted narrative voice to condemn itself are all rather offensive, the intended readership nonetheless combines those on both sides of Wales's internal linguistic border. The poem may be provocative and divisive, but it still serves as the focal point around which readers from both of Wales's linguistic traditions can meet. The readers who are outside the orbit of the poem's intended readership are those who are unaware both of Wales's linguistic complexity and of the bitterness and division that this poem will provoke. The possibility of a bilingual culture is present both in the poem's intended readership, and the linguistic divide upon which it meditates.

Before I turn to Emyr Humphreys, there are two further points to make about Thomas's decision to learn Welsh back in the early 1940s. As Brown points out, this decision was taken in a bourgeois context in which English was seen as the language of social advancement, and Welsh 'the badge of the uncultured and backward-looking'.[53] Taken before political support for adult education programmes, Thomas's decision makes him a pioneer of an adult language movement that would later become an important platform of a bilingual culture. It is also worth noting the location in which Thomas made his decision – Flintshire, north-east Wales.

> And from there, some fifteen miles away, I saw at dusk the hills of Wales rising, telling as before of enchanting and mysterious things. I realised what I had done. That was not my place, on the plain amongst Welshmen with English accents and attitudes. I set about learning Welsh, in order to be able to return to the true Wales of my imagination.[54]

Thomas's association of the 'hills' in the west with 'true Wales' can be read retrospectively as the moment which anticipates his subsequent life journey through Manafon, Eglwysfach, and Aberdaron to the most Welsh-speaking part of Wales. In other words, we might read this in a way that reinforces the association of the Welsh language with its heartlands in north and west Wales. But the text is doing more. The 'true Wales of my imagination' is not only a geographical space. It is also a moment of nascent possibility associated with the decision to learn Welsh and, significantly, one that takes place in Flintshire 'amongst Welshmen with English accents and attitudes'. In this sense, the 'true Wales of my imagination' represents not only the romanticized 'return' to the 'tribe' in the 'hills of Wales' but also the sowing of a possible bilingual culture among English-speaking Welsh people in the 1940s on the plains of Flintshire.

Emyr Humphreys (b. 1919)

Flintshire is the home county of Emyr Humphreys, who was born in 1919 and brought up in Trelawnyd, near Prestatyn. With his English-speaking upbringing – he attended the village school at which his father taught, and then grammar school in Rhyl – he could have been one of Thomas's 'Welshmen with English accents'. And, like the older poet, Humphreys too recalls 'the view from the border', looking west from Flintshire towards 'the romantic attraction of Snowdonia in the distance'.[55] From this corner of Wales, Humphreys went on to study history at the University of Wales, Aberystwyth, from 1937 to 1939, where he – again like Thomas – taught himself Welsh as a young adult. He was a conscientious objector in the Second World War, working on farms in Pembrokeshire, south-west Wales, and Caernarvonshire in the north-west, before working, immediately after the war, in Italy. He then worked as a teacher in London, before returning to Wales in 1951 to work as a drama producer for the BBC, and then in 1965 as a lecturer at University of Wales, Bangor, before retiring to work as a writer in 1972. Since *The Little Kingdom*, his first novel, published in 1946, Humphreys has published twenty-one novels in English, including the seven-volume 'The Land of the Living' series, and culminating in *The Shop* (2005). Other English-language work includes numerous short stories, articles, works of non-fiction (including *The Taliesin Tradition*, first published in Welsh in 1983 and translated into English in 1989), poetry collections, and a *Collected Poems*, published in 1999. This has appeared alongside Welsh-language material including novels, poetry, translations, radio, and television drama.

Humphreys's novel, *A Man's Estate*, published in 1955, registers the historical end of the once-hegemonic Liberal, Nonconformist elite at the centre of Welsh-language agricultural communities. In an echo of Caradoc Evans, the novel presents this demise as the destruction of an inward-looking, corrupt, patriarchal – and even incestuous – society. The plot is premised on the return of Philip Esmor-Elis, a researcher at an English university, to the Elis family home in the north Wales community of Pennant. Philip has been exiled since birth, brought up by his aunt in London, but is heir to Y Glyn, the Elis estate, an inheritance he now wants to claim in order to continue with his research. The Elises are a wealthy, Welsh-speaking, middle-class, Liberal farming family at the centre of the local community.

Over the course of the novel, this archetypal Welsh-language community and its principal family are shown to be at their point of collapse. A rather sensationalist ploy portrays an inward-looking – one might even say tribal – community that is imploding both under external pressure – the enlistment of its young into the British Army, or the return of its exiles – and internal stresses – social mores and patriarchal structures which have exploited its inhabitants to breaking point. Readers learn that the late Elis Felix Elis, Philip's father and the local Liberal MP, had been killed by Philip's mother, Mary, who is also the local magistrate: having discovered that Elis had fathered a child, Ada, by the housekeeper, Mary denied her husband water when he had pneumonia. Following her husband's death, Mary then gave away their son, Philip, and married the chapel deacon, Vavasor, by whom she had another son, Dick. When Ada became pregnant by Dick, Vavasor – worried about what the community will think – forced Dick to enlist in the army, where he was killed during the First World War. Ada, who is broken by the loss of her lover, is then sexually exploited by one member of the community after another – in return for the money and status that would enable her to start a hotel business. Meanwhile, Hannah, Philip's devout Nonconformist sister, who keeps house for her mother and uncle, is effec- tively a prisoner in her own home.[56] As M. Wynn Thomas has remarked, *A Man's Estate* is concerned with the 'cultural, emotional and sexual repression' associated with a 'residual and stagnant Nonconformist society' then coming to an end.[57]

There are several ways, however, in which *A Man's Estate* registers the possibility of a bilingual culture. When one of the characters remarks that '[i]t delighted him to talk familiarly with Dr Pritchard. He used the "ti" as if it were a privilege', a bilingual readership is privileged, not only in the way that the Welsh word features in the English-language text, but also in the cultural knowledge that intended readers are implicitly expected to possess.[58] This text speaks both to those fluent in Welsh and to those English-language Welsh readers who are aware of the linguistic complexity of their culture. By contrast, the monoglot English-language reader who approaches the text without an awareness of, or interest in, Wales's linguistic complexity stands outside the text's intended readership. These readers confront the fact that the novel's subject matter is a Welsh culture that has both been translated *into* English and developed its own version *of* English. The later translation of the novel into Welsh, *Etifedd Y Glyn* ('The Heir of Y Glyn') adds another layer of bilingual complexity to this picture: here, after all, is a text which translates a Welsh-language culture into English, helping to construct a Welsh English-language discourse as it does so, which is then re-translated back into Welsh. The linguistic border within Wales is crossed and re-crossed in the effort to build a bilingual readership. By the same token, the border between this readership and an English-language readership that is not interested in Wales is strengthened. As Humphreys writes, 'It became clear to me by about the middle fifties that the subject that interested me, that gave me a reason for writing, was not a subject that interested the reading public outside Wales.'[59] It is important to recognize the genuine bilingualism implied here: as Humphreys writes elsewhere, 'To be Welsh is to know Welsh whether in Gwynedd or in Gwent, *whether in Welsh or in English.*'[60] His work therefore speaks to two groups of bilingual readers: those who speak Welsh and English, and those English-language readers with a knowledge of Welsh culture, who are conscious of Wales's linguistic richness. The intended readership that is 'othered' is one that does not participate in this bilingualism: an English-language readership that is 'not terribly interested in knowing about Wales'.[61]

The novel meditates upon some of the characteristics and consequences of Wales's historic language divide in a way that a novel intended for 'the reading public outside Wales' would not. The prominence given to the character of Philip – his return to Pennant is the device on which the plot hangs – suggests the text's concern to address Wales's complex linguistic and cultural inheritance. Philip's bilingual upbringing is complicated by his rejection of Welshness. He describes his return to Wales as 'a journey I have never wanted to make' and remains an outsider to the inward-looking community (230). His arrival heralds the destruction of the old Nonconformist community, as represented by the older generation of Elis, Mary, and Vavasor. Philip's bilingualism, mobility, scientific job, and complex cultural inheritance make him an early representative of an emergent force in Welsh culture; he is both a harbinger of the returning exile and a symbol of a Welsh-language culture that – in its Liberal, Nonconformist, agricultural form – is no longer self-sufficient. However, Hannah, who has never left the farm, is able to see him only in ways that emerge from a residual Nonconformist culture. He is an epoch-changing 'Saviour' (54); she wills him to 'claim [his] inheritance, beautiful and dangerous, to destroy and restore' (31). This suggests both the desire of some of those within the community to bring an inward-looking, patriarchal culture to an end and the difficulty of those brought up in such a community to describe what comes next. It suggests a Welsh culture going through discontinuous change and fracture. Its capacity to adequately represent such change is hindered by Humphreys's use of a mythical pattern to structure the plot as tragedy.

As Diane Green has shown, *A Man's Estate* is a reinterpretation of the Orestes–Electra myth, a view endorsed by Humphreys.[62] A son returns to his place of birth, only to discover that his mother has killed his father, and that his half-sister Ada was made pregnant by his half-brother Dick, who has been sent to his death by his own father. While this structure contributes to the novel's representation of a tragically imploding culture, it also serves to de-historicize its subject matter, focusing instead on family relations, and inhibiting its capacity to represent wider historical forces. To the extent that it allows engagement with history, this use of myth lends itself to the representation of residual elements in society. Humphreys's 1958 novel, *A Toy Epic*, drops such overt mythical patterning, enabling a deeper engagement with the historical forces that have shaped Welsh society. This novel also adopts a slicker use of multi-vocal narrative, shifting more quickly from one character's perspective to the next. The paradoxical effect of this more fragmented style is the depiction of a cultural plurality that could not occur in *A Man's Estate*, where the characters are still framed in terms of their insider or outsider status.

A Toy Epic depicts three boys – Michael, Iorwerth, and Albie – growing up in Flintshire in the 1930s. Michael, the son of a bilingual Church in Wales rector, Iorwerth, the son of a Welsh-speaking farmer, and Albie, the child of a bilingual bus driver are brought together when they pass the entrance exam for Llanrhos Grammar School. The text registers the conflict between visions of the Welsh language: one in which it is the key to an inner Welsh sanctum that is inextricably associated with a Nonconformist, agricultural community; and another in which it marks an emergent bilingualism. The text depicts the former – represented through the character of Iorwerth – as the unchanging essence of Wales, but it does so in a way that also critiques such an easy representation. Michael, at the end of the novel, undergoes a conversion to the Welsh nationalist cause, describing Iorwerth as 'the soul of Wales', and dedicates his life to 'people like Iorwerth who among us all is its

[Wales's] most direct heir'.[63] Iorwerth certainly sees himself as heir to a separate Welsh tradition: 'inwardly firm in my own upbringing and persuasion' while 'conforming outwardly' to the appearance expected of a grammar school boy (67). As the only pupil to take the entrance exam in Welsh, he describes his subsequent school career as that of an 'Israelite in Babylon, resistant to foreign influences, and careful of my household gods' (67).

Iorwerth's character represents a tribal view of Welsh identity as a linguistic community – rooted in farming and Nonconformism – that continues to survive under the surface of an ever-encroaching, English-speaking modernity. By the novel's end, after several temptations – a university scholarship, becoming a doctor, enlistment – Iorwerth returns home to his father and the farm on which he grew up. His emphatic declaration – 'My father, I am coming home to be with you. I shall never be far away from you again as long as we live' (121) – can be read in literal or religious terms as one possible future for the Welsh-language community: a rejection of modernity, of social mobility, and a return to the tribe in pursuit of a role as the 'soul of Wales'. This tribal view is critiqued within the text. Firstly, it is ventriloquized mainly through Michael, and not simply attributable to Humphreys, as M. Wynn Thomas has rightly pointed out.[64] Secondly, the text foregrounds 'Iorwerth's shortcomings in his capacity as heir to a culture', as M. Wynn Thomas also points out.[65] His efforts are 'doomed to fail' as a result of the 'great culture-shift' that has taken place.[66] There is no indication that his retreat to the farm on which he was born will enable Welsh-language culture to flourish in the given historical circumstances. Instead, the formal construction of the text itself serves to critique the tribal view of Welsh culture and to register the emergent shoots of a bilingual culture.

Most significantly, any tribal view of Welsh-speaking, rural, Nonconformist Wales as the nation's 'soul' is immediately undermined by the language in which the novel is published – English – and by the bilingual process of its construction. As early as 1941, Humphreys wrote sections in English, and then almost two decades later, in 1958, translated some of them into Welsh and broadcast them on the radio as *Y Tri Llais* ('The Three Voices'), before publishing them as a Welsh-language novel of the same name later that year. *A Toy Epic*, also published in 1958, is close to its Welsh-language predecessor (minus an opening chapter in which there is a dream sequence). In its incubation, construction, and readership, then, the novel is a bilingual affair.

This bilingualism is also the subject matter of the text. The text registers the localized complexity of language use in this part of north-east Wales in the 1920s and 1930s. Michael's father, a rector in the Church in Wales, is bilingual, and takes church services in both languages; his mother is English speaking but understands enough Welsh to follow the playground conversations of her son; the maid is Welsh speaking but brings up Michael and his sister to speak English, declaring that 'only old Methodies spoke Welsh all the time' (19). A similarly complex picture is evident in the case of Iorwerth. His experiences in the Methodist chapel – in Welsh – are relayed to readers in English, with key Welsh words left untranslated (31). Similarly, he is the only one to take his grammar school entrance exam in Welsh, while his subsequent education happens through English (40). Albie's father, a bus driver, speaks Welsh, but his mother does not, while Albie listens to the radio to get a 'cultivated English accent' (78). The intended readership is Welsh and falls into two groups: either fluent in English and Welsh; or fluent in English and familiar with the linguistic and cultural complexities of Wales. The readership for which the text is not intended is a monoglot English one without any knowledge of such matters.

A Toy Epic registers a linguistic complexity that anticipates what would happen to other parts of Wales later in the twentieth century. The insistence, in the opening line, that this is 'one of the four corners of Wales' is a corrective reminder to all those critics and cultural commentators who see Wales in binary terms: Wales cannot simply be divided into the predominantly English-speaking industrialized areas of the south and east, and the predominantly Welsh-speaking areas of the north and west. Indeed, one of the reasons that the novel speaks to subsequent generations is that the linguistic complexity evident in north-east Wales in the 1920s and 1930s was to become a familiar aspect of everyday life in all parts of Wales, not only in areas like the Rhondda which have long been linguistically complex, but also in formerly monoglot urban areas like Cardiff where a significant Welsh-speaking population has become established, and even in formerly monoglot Welsh-speaking areas of the north and west where English is also now increasingly heard. If, as Raymond Williams later argued, all of Wales is now a border, we should not be surprised that it is in areas of linguistic rupture like Flintshire where the signs of a representative bilingual culture first emerge.

The modernist device of narrating the novel entirely through the voices of Michael, Iorwerth, and Albie undermines any notion of linguistic tribalism. As M. Wynn Thomas points out, it is not Iorwerth, but 'the three boys together who are a "potent symbol of Wales"' in the way they together represent the nation's cultural divisions.[67] The idea that the Welsh-speaking, rural, Nonconformist culture alone speaks for Wales is already a thing of the past. Even Michael's description of Iorwerth as '[Wales's] most direct heir' suggests exploration of a complex inheritance of Welsh-language identity rather than any straightforward possession of it in the present. Instead, the novel registers how the Welsh-speaking, rural, Nonconformist culture has come under pressure from wider societal change. For example, when Iorwerth's father is too ill to farm, he finds that the workers that they would previously have employed to do the work have emigrated to the new seaside towns, or to English cities in search of work. They have no choice but to employ Jacob, a worker who is known to drink, a decision which raises a conflict within themselves between their need to get the farm work completed and their role as upholders of the Nonconformist tradition (92). In this way, the text registers a culture under so much historical pressure that its constituent elements – the agricultural and Nonconformist strands – are in conflict with each other, even within the same character.

Although *A Toy Epic* clearly signals the end of a Welsh-speaking, Nonconformist, rural hegemony and suggests the possible emergence of a bilingual culture, it is also structured by the present impossibility of such a culture. The novel examines three characters as they are shaped by one of the institutions that render genuine bilingualism impossible: a selective school system that insists on English as the sole point of access to modernity, and which restricts the Welsh language to a role as the medium of a declining rural, Nonconformist culture. Selection for Llanrhos County Grammar School is the event that brings the three main characters of Iorwerth, Michael, and Albie together and is the premise on which the subsequent *bildungsroman* is based. However, its chronological structure is a limiting factor. The narratives offered by the three characters never escape the very institution – the English-language grammar school – which polices and conditions Welsh culture's access to modernity and limits the possibility of bilingualism. In this way, the novel is limited in its capacity to critique the historical conditions that underpin it. Nonetheless, in its focus on selective anglophone education as the gateway to modernity, *A Toy Epic* anticipates a key concern of the later language movement and identifies the institution on which hopes for a bilingual future rest.

Outside the House of Baal, published in 1965, depicts the life of J. T. Miles, from his childhood and youth in north-east Wales at the end of the nineteenth century, through his brief period as a blacksmith, and then his career as a minister through the First World War, through the depression in south Wales in the 1930s, to his old age in north-east Wales in the post-war period up to the 1960s. One key difference with *A Toy Epic* is the Faulkner-esque, non-chronological arrangement of the sections. It is not a 'coming of age' novel. Instead, the narrative juxtaposes sections describing J. T.'s old age against those that describe his younger days. The result is a novel that, to a greater extent than *A Toy Epic*, is able to investigate the historical conditions that underpin the characterization. The discontinuity and fractures of twentieth-century Welsh history are brought to the fore.

The novel – like its two predecessors discussed above – registers the end of Liberal Nonconformist Wales. By his old age in the post-war period, J. T.'s Nonconformist discourse is one that no one else shares. His nephew Norman simply 'doesn't understand' the Bible-informed advice given by J. T. on how to cope with a family crisis,[68] and when he makes a joke to a young man about 'a dove descending', the man looked at him 'as if J. T. had spoken in a foreign language' (394). J. T., in retirement, is a man suffering from depression and 'an overwhelming sense of failure' (381). He learns that Bayley Lewis, one of the religious figures that inspired him as a young man, had hanged himself (380). None of his three children – Ronnie, a lecturer in an English university, Thea, a globe-trotting actress, and Vernon, a probation officer, also based outside of Wales – shares his Nonconformist beliefs. J. T. speaks only to himself, muttering 'Behold thy gods, O Israel' under his breath at the sight of the lorry delivering barrels of beer to the nearby pub, the ironically named The House of Baal (63). This pub, at the centre of the housing estate in which J. T. now lives, is a symbol of the final inversion of Nonconformist discourse. A 'cross between castle and cathedral', and complete with its stained-glass windows, it has replaced the religious institutions that were formerly at the centre of community (155). The name, unmoored from its biblical origins, now indicates a place of drinking, an activity against which Welsh Nonconformism once defined itself, and against which the Welsh Liberal establishment achieved the legal milestone of the first Wales-only law of the modern period.

Outside the House of Baal also registers the end of a viable, self-supporting, politically Liberal, agricultural community. The narrative is centred on Argoed in north-east Wales, a 'farm, with its house in the centre like an ancient stronghold spread over the crown of the hill' (30), inhabited, at the turn of the twentieth century, by the siblings, Lydia, Kate, Dan Llew, Griff and Ned, and their 'pa' who is a farmer and local 'leader of the nonconformists [*sic*]' (32). The novel charts the demise of Argoed, and the form of Welsh identity that it represents. At the hands of Wynne Bannister, the man Kate marries after her father's death, and Dan Llew, who sees Argoed through his estate agent's eyes, Argoed ceases to function as a working farm. Its land is broken up or rented out, its buildings re-mortgaged. By the end of the novel, Argoed is a faint memory, transposed as the name of Dan Llew's new bungalow on the coastal plain; Dan Llew has become a tragic figure in old age, reduced in his dementia to walking back up the hill to the old farmhouse in search of his long-dead father (212). J. T. and his sister-in-law Kate live at 8 Gorse Avenue, on a new estate built around a pub, just off the coast road and yards from a holiday village, all built on land that was once part of Argoed. It is no wonder that J. T. declares that 'Times have changed. This isn't the place I used to know' (155). Indeed, by the end of the novel, north Wales has become a place from which he is utterly alienated. His final decision to go to Anglesey by taking a 'mystery tour of North Wales' is sadly apt, epitomizing the way in which his own country has been appropriated for consumption by tourists, mystified and exoticized in a way that he finds incomprehensible (399).

There are several ways in which *Outside the House of Baal* registers some of the characteristics of an emergent bilingual Welsh culture. It is a novel that is concerned with the question of how to narrate Welsh history from the 1890s to the 1960s. Its fractured, non-chronological narrative structure – episodes taken out of sequence from the life of a Welsh-speaking, Nonconformist minister, the last of his kind – is in many ways aptly suited to the task of constructing a historical narrative. It anticipates the postcolonial viewpoint established by Ngugi wa Thiong'o in a Kenyan context: he theorizes the process by which a dominated culture constructs its own historical narrative as 'a painful re-membering, a putting together of the dismembered past to make sense of the trauma of the present'.[69] The absence of familiar reference points certainly renders J. T.'s old age traumatic. The text begins the process of 're-membering' a Welsh historical narrative, one that departs quite significantly from British history: for example, it speaks far more critically of the impact of the world wars, both of which cause devastating loss of life and accelerate a decline in religious belief in Wales, and in the viability of its agricultural and linguistic communities. The novel also dramatizes the act of reaching back beyond Nonconformism to a deeper resource of Welsh identity. Over the course of the day, J. T. learns that he has inherited the stopwatch of Ifan Cole, the smith with whom he worked before being called to minister, and it becomes increasingly important to J. T. that he must go to Anglesey to claim his inheritance. It is as if he needs to go back to a time in his life prior to his Nonconformist turn, to a more profound resource of Welsh identity – found in the labour and comradeship of his one-time fellow smith. The watch that he must retrieve becomes a symbol of the mode of time that he, and, by implication, a decimated Welsh culture, must recover and restart.[70] In these ways, the novel is a 'painful re-membering': it carries out the essential work of cultural transmission, both across languages and across the historical rupture represented by the end of Welsh Liberal Nonconformism.

The novel is of course written in English and translates a Welsh-language culture into English. Those familiar with Welsh-language culture will recognize intertextual allusions to it: the name, Argoed, for example, recalls T. Gwynn Jones's poem of the same name. The occasional Welsh word and phrase is inserted into the text in a way that privileges both the reader fluent in Welsh and the English-language reader who, while not fluent in Welsh, is nonetheless familiar with a bilingual environment. In this way, its intended readership is similar to that of the previous novels. For example, when Kate asks her niece to speak more slowly – 'remember English is my second language' (361) – the novel speaks directly to two kinds of Welsh reader: the reader who is fluent in English and Welsh, and the non-Welsh speaker who is nevertheless familiar with Wales's linguistic code-switching. The reader who is 'othered' here is the one for whom Kate's reminder – that for some on these islands, English is a second language – comes as a shock.

The text registers the complexity of linguistic change within the post-war community. J. T.'s son, Ronnie, represents one extreme: a Welsh speaker prepared to sacrifice his language in order to get on in the world. As a soldier in the Second World War, he rejects Wales as 'an open-air museum', declaring his intention to go where 'the future is shaped' (324). Sure enough, as a lecturer at an English University in the years after the war, Ronnie maintains a pejorative view of Wales, accusing J. T. of wanting 'to become a spiritual Red Indian living in a language reservation', of being a member of 'a tribe of gentle Nonconformists who played happily in their native hills, safe in the custody of a great empire' (371). This view masks a set of complexities: on the one hand it allies the Welsh language community with colonized First-Nation Americans, and on the other hand, it accuses the Welsh of silent complicity in the British empire. It fails to realize any value in the Welsh language, but, above all, it also fails to recognize the linguistic potential of the Wales in which J. T. now lives. In this Wales, J. T. and Kate, who are Welsh speakers, live on Gorse Avenue, a street they share with, among others, Mrs Box, an English-speaking incomer to Wales who runs a bed and breakfast business from her home (149). Mr Wilson, an incomer from Manchester, runs the Blue Corner Stores where J. T. buys his cereal (150). But when Mr Ellis, a former college friend of J. T., comes into the shop, or when he meets Mrs

Pickering on the way home, the dialogue switches between English and Welsh depending on who is involved in the conversation (151). In these ways, the text registers the social complexity of linguistic change and the emergence of new Welsh-language communities within increasingly English-speaking areas.

Humphreys has written that the Welsh-language movement is not explicitly depicted in his work until *Bonds of Attachment*, published in 1991, and that it appears 'in embryonic form' only in *National Winner*, published in 1971.[71] However, *Outside the House of Baal* does register the emergent Welsh-language movement, revitalized by Saunders Lewis in 1962, and soon, in 1971, to be positioned by Raymond Williams in the vanguard of the global New Left, along with civil rights movements in the USA and Ulster.[72] Miss Pickering is an adult Welsh learner, determined to acquire the language that her mother, from the border town of Oswestry, did not learn (175). She is an early example of the success of attempts by *Cymdeithas yr Iaith* (The Welsh Language Society) to encourage new generations to learn Welsh. She is also an active campaigner, trying to prevent the 'wicked' changes of Welsh names to English names: 'fancy calling it the Greenhill Estate' (214). J. T. is also part of this movement: he has a similar attitude to the loss of the house name Argoed: 'All the past is in a name, he said. What else is there left?' (248).

Finally, the novel anticipates the use of new technologies to bring together geographically disparate communities of Welsh speakers. Humphreys has written of his interest in the relation between older forms of social organization like the family, and 'the newer forms of technology'.[73] At one point, J. T. is asked by John Henry, Kate's nephew, to record a message for relatives in South Dakota (378). It is clear that this is seen as a possible response to the geographical dispersal of Welsh-language speakers: 'I'm doing what I can to keep the old Argoed breed together' (381). The text registers the possibility of using technology to bring together people who have been forced apart by the forces of modernity: 'the distance between us is annihilated by this device', says J. T., anticipating the ways in which Welsh-language networks would emerge, owing their existence to new technologies, and establishing new possibilities of a bilingual culture (382).

Conclusion

The emergent signs of a genuinely bilingual culture are inscribed into the forms, linguistic interplay, and subject matter of the mid-twentieth-century work of R. S. Thomas and Emyr Humphreys. Both authors acquired their 'bilingual brain . . . by dint of effort', to quote Humphreys, and use their new-found position to construct a new Welsh readership for their work: one that includes those fluent in Welsh, as well as those English speakers who, while not fluent in Welsh, are aware of their nation's linguistic complexity. It is the English-language readers from beyond Wales's border who are rendered 'other' in the privileging of this intended readership, which constitutes the expanded and welcoming 'tribe' on which the possibility of a bilingual culture rests.

Notes

1. Emyr Humphreys, 'Notes on the Novel', *New Welsh Review* 35 (1996–7): 10; repr. in Humphreys, *Conversations and Reflections*, ed. M. Wynn Thomas (Cardiff: University of Wales Press, 2002), 227.

2. Emyr Humphreys, 'Under the Yoke', *New Welsh Review* 3 (1998): 9; repr. in Humphreys, *Conversations and Reflections*, 77.

3. R. S. Thomas, *Collected Poems* (London: Dent, 1993), 36.

4. Daniel Williams, *Wales Unchained: Literature, Politics and Identity in the American Century* (Cardiff: University of Wales Press, 2015), 142–3.

5. Ibid., 143.

6. Ibid., 144.

7. Ibid., 145–6.

8. Ibid., 147.

9. Ibid., 154.

10. Ibid., 147.

11. Ibid., 148–50.

12. Ibid., 150.

13. The future prospects of the Welsh language do not depend on the preservation of Welsh-language communities associated with religious Nonconformism or agricultural ways of life, important as these have been to the survival of the Welsh language into the twentieth century. In recording the importance of Nonconformist and agricultural communities to the survival of the Welsh language, we should not forget the work of Brinley Thomas, who has shown that the industrialization of the south Wales valleys, far from contributing to the decline of the Welsh language, actually helped save it. The establishment of Welsh-language communities in the western coalfield ensured that migrants from the Welsh-speaking rural hinterland could maintain their language, which adapted to the modern, industrial era.

14. In 1962, 3,795 pupils attended Welsh-medium primary schools; fifty years later, in 2012, the figure was 52,336, with a further 16,492 attending bilingual

schools. See Janet Davies, *The Welsh Language: A History* (Cardiff: University of Wales Press, 2014), 125.

15. Davies, *The Welsh Language*, 159. See also Geraint H. Jenkins, ed., *'Let's Do Our Best for the Ancient Tongue': The Welsh Language in the Twentieth Century* (Cardiff: University of Wales Press, 2000). Welsh is still a minority language in Cardiff – of its ninety-eight primary schools, eighty-one are English medium – but these figures nonetheless suggest that the Welsh language is becoming increasingly established in Wales's capital city.

16. The latter presents a problem that has not yet been properly addressed. It is certainly well recognized that economics has exercised a decisive influence on the language's well-being in different parts of Wales. For example, the recent growth of the Welsh-language community around Cardiff is associated with the jobs brought by the devolved institutions and new opportunities for a bilingual middle class. On the other side of the coin, the historical decline in the Welsh-speaking populations of Gwynedd and Ceredigion can be partly attributed to the loss of jobs in sectors such as slate quarrying and agriculture, in which the workforce was mainly Welsh speaking. With an estimated 5,000 Welsh speakers a year leaving Wales in search of work in the decade up to 2013, it is clear that the possibility of a genuine bilingualism rests partly on the creation of job opportunities to allow those coming through the Welsh-medium education system to remain within Welsh-language networks (see, for example, Davies, *The Welsh Language*, 168).

17. R. S. Thomas, *Letters to Raymond Garlick 1951–1999*, ed. Jason Walford Davies (Llandysul: Gomer Press, 2009), 71.

18. Jason Walford Davies, 'A Corresponding Voice', introduction to *Letters to Raymond Garlick 1951–1999*, by R. S. Thomas, ed. Walford Davies, xlv.

19. Thomas, *Letters to Raymond Garlick 1951–1999*, 83.

20. Thomas, *Collected Poems*, 4.

21. Tony Brown, *R. S. Thomas*, Writers of Wales (Cardiff: University of Wales Press, 2006), 14.

22. R. S. Thomas, *Selected Prose*, ed. Sandra Anstey (Bridgend: Poetry of Wales Press, 1983), 22.

23. Ibid., 105.

24. Thomas, *Collected Poems*, 37.

25. Dafydd Elis Thomas, 'The Image of Wales in R. S. Thomas's Poetry', *Poetry Wales* 7, 4 (1972): 60.

26. Ibid., 61–2.

27. Raymond Williams, 'Welsh Culture', in *Who Speaks for Wales? Nation, Culture, Identity*, ed. Daniel Williams (Cardiff: University of Wales Press, 2003), 9.

28. Ibid.

29. See Thomas, *Selected Prose*, for a bibliography of Thomas's prose across English and Welsh.
30. Brown, *R. S. Thomas*, 27.
31. See Saunders Lewis, 'Is There an Anglo-Welsh Literature?' (Caerdydd: Cangen Caerdydd, Urdd Graddedigion Prifysgol Cymru, 1939). This was a position from which Saunders Lewis was later to retreat.
32. Brown, *R. S. Thomas*, 27.
33. Keidrych Rhys, editorial in *Wales* 2 (1943), 2.
34. Thomas, *Selected Prose*, 28.
35. Ibid., 41–2.
36. Ibid., 26.
37. R. S. Thomas, 'Anglo-Welsh Literature', *The Welsh Nationalist* (December 1948), 3.
38. R. S. Thomas, *Autobiographies*, trans. Jason Walford Davies (London: Dent, 1997), 10.
39. Geraint Evans, 'Crossing the Border: National and Linguistic Boundaries in Twentieth-Century Welsh Writing', *Welsh Writing in English: A Yearbook of Critical Essays* 9 (2004): 127.
40. Ibid., 123–35.
41. R. S. Thomas, *Stones of the Field* (Carmarthen: Druid Press, 1946), 34.
42. Jason Walford Davies, '"Thick Ambush of Shadows": Allusions to Welsh Literature in the Work of R. S. Thomas', *Welsh Writing in English* 1 (1995), 78.
43. Ibid., 105.
44. R. S. Thomas, 'The Poet's Voice', BBC radio broadcast, 21 August 1947. Quoted in Brown, *R. S. Thomas*, 34.
45. Ibid.
46. Thomas, *Collected Poems*, 22.
47. R. S. Thomas, *Neb* (Caernarfon: Gwasg Gwynedd, 1985), 45.
48. R. S. Thomas, *Song at the Year's Turning* (London: Hart-Davis, 1955), 47.
49. Ibid., 79.
50. For a fuller consideration of the Welsh-language literary references in Thomas's poetry, see Walford Davies, '"Thick Ambush of Shadows": Allusions to Welsh Literature', and Walford Davies, *Gororau'r Iaith: R. S. Thomas a'r Traddodiad Llenyddol Cymraeg* (Caerdydd: Gwasg Prifysgol Cymru, 2000).
51. Thomas, *Collected Poems*, 37.
52. Ibid., 129.
53. Brown, *R. S. Thomas*, 8.
54. Thomas, *Autobiographies*, trans. Walford Davies, 10.
55. Humphreys, *Conversations and Reflections*, 3.
56. For a gendered reading of *A Man's Estate*, see chapter 6 of Linden Peach, *The Fiction of Emyr Humphreys* (Cardiff: University of Wales Press, 2011).

57. M. Wynn Thomas, foreword to *A Man's Estate* by Emyr Humphreys (Cardigan: Parthian, 2006), x.

58. Emyr Humphreys, *A Man's Estate* (Cardigan: Parthian, 2006), 302. All subsequent references to this text are in parentheses in the body of the text.

59. Humphreys, *Conversations and Reflections*, 133–4.

60. Emyr Humphreys, 'Chasing Shadows', *Arcade* 7 (1981): 21, italics added.

61. Humphreys, *Conversations and Reflections*, 133.

62. Diane Green, *Emyr Humphreys: A Postcolonial Novelist?* (Cardiff: University of Wales Press, 2009), 59.

63. Emyr Humphreys, *A Toy Epic* (Bridgend: Seren, 1989), 116. All subsequent references to this text are in parentheses in the body of the text.

64. M. Wynn Thomas, afterword to *A Toy Epic* by Emyr Humphreys (Bridgend: Seren, 1989), 138.

65. Ibid., 134.

66. Ibid.

67. Ibid., 138.

68. Emyr Humphreys, *Outside the House of Baal* (Bridgend: Seren, 1965; repr. 1996), 386. All subsequent references to this text are in parentheses in the body of the text.

69. Ngugi wa Thiong'o, *Decolonising the Mind: The Politics of Language in African Literature* (London: J. Currey, 1986), 3.

70. For a fuller consideration of the representation of 'Welsh Time' in *Outside the House of Baal*, see chapter 8 of Peach, *The Fiction of Emyr Humphreys*.

71. Humphreys, *Conversations and Reflections*, 188–9.

72. Raymond Williams, 'Who Speaks for Wales?', in *Who Speaks for Wales? Nation, Culture, Identity*, ed. Daniel Williams (Cardiff: University of Wales Press, 2003), 4.

73. Humphreys, *Conversations and Reflections*, 7.

28

Inventing Welsh Writing in English

DIANA WALLACE

The late twentieth-century shift from 'Anglo-Welsh literature' to 'Welsh writing in English' is more than a trivial change of literary critical nomenclature. It maps a movement from the initial identification of a relatively narrow early canon of literature in and about Wales in English, which was male-dominated and inward-looking, to the acknowledgement of a wider and more diverse body of writing which could take its place as a major literature in its own right on an international stage. Taking its cue in part from the new postcolonial theories, the rejection of the term 'Anglo-Welsh' was based on the recognition that, in Stephen Knight's words, 'It refuses Welsh status to Welsh people who, not speaking Cymraeg, nevertheless do not feel at all English.'[1] If the formulation 'Welsh writing in English' is linguistically clumsy, as a critical concept it has proved open, flexible, and inclusive. Indeed, that very clumsiness might be said to have its uses in drawing attention to the complexities involved in negotiating any discussion of a national literature which comes out of a colonial and/or postcolonial situation and thus involves both tension with the imperial nation and what M. Wynn Thomas has usefully called 'internal difference'.[2] Such tensions are most acute, of course, in the relationship between the two languages of Wales. The invention of 'Welsh writing in English' as a theory and a category which foregrounds these issues allows us to re-read and reassess mid-century writing in Wales, as well as the writing which emerged in the 1980s and 1990s.

Resistance to the term 'Anglo-Welsh' as a politically problematic term was evident from the outset. Saunders Lewis's question in 1938 – 'Is There an Anglo-Welsh Literature?' – and his equally contentious conclusion that there was no such separate literature[3] opened a heated debate which ran right through the twentieth century. Asked in 1939, 'Do you consider yourself to be an Anglo-Welsh writer?' George Ewart Evans's answer was: 'I don't like the category – Anglo-Welsh. It suggests an artificial Babu – fusion of cultures, etc . . . For a writer whose writing is Wales, not merely about Wales – "Welsh" I think should be the term.'[4] Asked the same question in 1946, R. S. Thomas answered firmly, 'No! A Welsh writer.'[5] Nevertheless the term persisted; as late as 1997 Dannie Abse edited an anthology entitled *Twentieth Century Anglo-Welsh Poetry.*[6]

Despite early objections, in the mid-century context 'Anglo-Welsh' provided an easily understandable term which enabled the project of building a critical canon around the writers of the 'first flowering'. The W. D. Thomas memorial lecture, 'The First Forty Years: Some Notes on Anglo-Welsh Literature', given by Professor Gwyn Jones in 1957, marked a crucial moment in the identification of a tradition of writers who were mainly working-class men from the south Wales valleys.[7] Glyn Jones begins *The Dragon Has Two Tongues: Essays on Anglo-Welsh Writers and Writing* (1968) by noting what he terms the 'necessity [for] the invention of a literary term to denote writers like those represented in *Modern Welsh Poetry* [the anthology edited by Keidrych Rhys in 1944], i.e. Welshmen [*sic*] who write, whether poems, stories, novels or plays, in English'.[8] To distinguish these from the writers who write in Welsh, he proposes 'reluctantly . . . to follow custom and call them "Anglo-Welsh"'.[9] Later he qualifies this to define an Anglo-Welsh writer as 'a Welsh man or woman who writes *about* Wales in English'.[10] Subject matter and place here become a crucial part of the definition. As Jones admits, the writers he chooses to focus on – Caradoc Evans, Jack Jones, Gwyn Thomas, Huw Menai, Idris Davies, Dylan Thomas – were those for whom he felt a particular affinity. The canon he establishes is primarily (like that of Gwyn Jones) based in working-class industrial south Wales, deriving from a Nonconformist tradition, and overwhelmingly male.

Post-War Prose: Looking Backwards

In contrast to the dynamism of the 1930s and 1940s, the post-war decades have been seen as an 'empty' period.[11] Tony Conran argues that a decade after the war, the Anglo-Welsh poetry scene was 'in ruins'.[12] The death of Dylan Thomas in 1953 appeared to leave a vacuum. Idris Davies and Alun Lewis were dead; Lynette Roberts stopped publishing poetry, while Glyn Jones and Emyr Humphreys had turned to the novel; *The Welsh Review* ceased publication in 1948, and *Wales* in 1949. It was left to R. S. Thomas to emerge after the death of Vernon Watkins in 1967 as the new figurehead for Anglo-Welsh poetry. A lack of jobs meant that the post-war generation of writers were going into 'exile': T. Harri Jones took a post in Australia in 1959, while Danny Abse, John Ormond, John Tripp, Sally Roberts Jones, and Conran himself all went to London.[13] Yet this picture of exhausted stasis overlooks the fact that these years are rich in prose. Both Roland Mathias and Raymond Williams note a brief fashion in the English market for Welsh fiction in the 1950s.[14] This period is also notable for autobiography and memoir, often in un-canonical or hybridized genres, which do not fit into the traditional accounts of Anglo-Welsh literature.

For established writers, this was often a period of retrospection. Both Emyr Humphreys and Glyn Jones produced classic *Bildungsromane* which drew on their own formative experiences – notably Humphreys's *A Toy Epic* (1958) and Jones's *The Valley, The City, The Village* (1956) and *The Island of Apples* (1965).[15] The motif of the development of a young man growing up within the specificity of a Welsh place and people has a key significance in Anglo-Welsh criticism at this point. By beginning *The Dragon Has Two Tongues* with an autobiographical chapter, Glyn Jones positioned his own experience and background as 'characteristic of those of a number, even a majority of modern Anglo-Welsh writers' in a way which may have inadvertently helped to exclude other narratives.[16] As Harri Webb noted in 'Synopsis of the Great Welsh Novel', the narrative perspective of the 'sensitive boy who never grows up' became one of the clichés of the form, along with the drowned valley, the Welsh Mam, and the colliery explosion.[17] Webb's conclusion – 'One is not quite sure / Whether it is fiction or not' – indicates the fluid relationship between fiction and autobiography here.

A rather different approach to this autobiographical theme is Dannie Abse's semi-fictionalized account of growing up Welsh and Jewish in Cardiff during the Second World War: *Ash on A Young Man's Sleeve* (1954). Writing back from London, Abse recalls:

> This was all a long time ago: I was ten years high and lived in South Wales. Everything was different, more alive somehow. The landscape and the voices were dramatic and argumentative. Already I knew the chapels and the pubs and the billiard halls and the singing.[18]

The south Wales 'landscape' here, however, is a middle-class urban environment thirty miles distant from the valleys themselves, and even further from the uplands of rural Wales. This urban landscape is shadowed by the darkening of the wider European context, with its horrifically personal implications for the Jewish-Welsh Abse. This is most frighteningly figured in the surreal passage where Cardiff station transforms into the scene of the Holocaust: 'The voice over the crackling loudspeaker shouted, "All change at Auschwitz-Dachau." . . . Near the Refreshment Room stood a hygienic-looking shed containing a few gas chambers.'[19] While the middle-class urban setting may have contributed to the critical neglect of this text, Abse's concern with hybridity and duality within an international context looks forwards to the diversity of 'Welsh writing in English'.

Other generically hybrid autobiographical texts which sit uneasily within the paradigms being produced by mid-century Anglo-Welsh criticism include Rhys Davies's unreliable autobiography, *Print of a Hare's Foot* (1969), which encompasses as iconic figures both Dr William Price and D. H. Lawrence.[20] The latter was, like Davies himself, from a working-class mining community and writing at an oblique angle to the mainstream of modernism. Even more difficult to categorize is Margiad Evans's poetic account of her epilepsy and late motherhood in *A Ray of Darkness* (1952).[21] Evans's concern with autobiography and memory and their relationship with place is sharply intensified by the awareness of her illness. Place, landscape, and the relationship between self and community are again central to Brenda Chamberlain's poetic memoir of living on Ynys Enlli (Bardsey Island) – 'the home of my heart', as she called it – in *Tide Race* (1962).[22] This fusion of memoir, poetry, folklore, legend, and anthropology, illustrated with Chamberlain's evocative drawings, has been described by Tony Brown and M. Wynn Thomas as 'a neglected minor classic of woman's search for selfhood'.[23] Davies, Evans, and Chamberlain are all writers whose texts inscribe and explore their status as outsiders whether through gender, nationality, or sexuality.

A more mainstream figure, Raymond Williams was producing during this period the literary and cultural criticism which was to make him a key figure in the New Left, including *Culture and Society* (1958) and *The Long Revolution* (1961). Alongside these, however, he was also writing fiction based on his own experience of a working-class childhood on the borders of Wales in his trilogy, *Border Country* (1960), *Second Generation* (1964), and *The Fight for Manod* (1979). *Border Country* is another retrospective text concerned with identity, community, and belonging. The London-based academic Matthew Price returns to south Wales to visit his ill father, a former railway signalman, and the novel flashes back to incidents in the past, most crucially the class conflicts of the General Strike of 1926.[24] Through this engagement with his father, the history of his community, and the landscape where he grew up, Matthew (or Will, as he is called in Glynmawr) reaches a *rapprochement* with his own divided identity. Williams's attempt at what Daniel G. Williams calls 'substantiating a new realism' in *Border Country* was underpinned by his left-wing politics.[25] However, as Katie Gramich notes, he was less sympathetic to the burgeoning gender politics of the 1960s: 'The feminist revolution is not envisaged as being part of the cultural revolt for which [Williams] calls.'[26]

While the theoretical paradigms offered by the concept of Welsh writing in English have enabled us to begin revisiting the work of women writers in this period – including Brenda Chamberlain, Margiad Evans, and Hilda Vaughan – this is still an under-researched area. Lynette Roberts's *The Endeavour: Captain Cook's First Voyage to Australia* (1954),[27] for instance, is an extraordinary reconstruction of Cook's discovery of the east coast of Australia, which appears at first glance to have nothing to do with Wales. Yet it offers a complex examination of the early process of colonization and the politics of naming, as Cook '[takes] possession of [Australia] in the name of his Majesty', naming 'the whole Eastern coast . . . "New Wales"'.[28] Like Eiluned Lewis's equally neglected *The Leaves of the Tree* (1953) or the late work of Elizabeth Inglis-Jones, Roberts's text offers fertile ground for future feminist and postcolonial readings.

The 'Second Flowering': Writing 'for Wales'

In 1967 an editorial in *Poetry Wales* by Meic Stephens heralded a 'second flowering' of 'Anglo-Welsh' poetry by a new generation of writers – including Harri Webb, Tony Conran, John Ormond, Leslie Norris, John Tripp, Raymond Garlick, Roland Mathias, and Sally Roberts – alongside established poets such as Dannie Abse, R. S. Thomas, and Glyn Jones.[29] This revitalization was fostered by a range of new publications and organizations that provided a platform for Anglo-Welsh writing. Meic Stephens had founded Triskel Press in 1963 and *Poetry Wales* in 1965, while *Dock Leaves*, founded by Raymond Garlick in 1949, was renamed *The Anglo-Welsh Review* in 1958, and Ned Thomas founded *Planet* in 1970. In London, Bryn Griffiths had founded the Guild of Welsh Writers in 1965, with members including John Tripp, Sally Roberts, and Leslie Norris. Two important anthologies foregrounded the vigour of this new generation. Bryn Griffiths's *Welsh Voices: An Anthology of New Poetry from Wales* (1967) included nineteen poets, of whom only one (Sally Roberts) was female.[30] John Stuart Williams and Meic Stephens's more extensive *The Lilting House: An Anthology of Anglo-Welsh Poetry 1917–1967* (1969), with an introduction by Raymond Garlick, included forty-three poets, of whom four were female (Brenda Chamberlain, Lynette Roberts, Alison J. Bielski, and Sally Roberts).[31] Alongside these, Tony Conran published *The Penguin Book of Welsh Verse* (1967), which made Welsh poetry in translation more available to the English-reading public.

The context for what Roland Mathias called this 'sociological air-change'[32] was an increased affluence in the 1960s, despite the decline of Welsh heavy industry, which led to the return of some of the writers who had gone into exile. This was accompanied by significant moves towards a more independent identity for Wales. Protests against the drowning of Cwm Tryweryn, Saunders Lewis's radio talk *Tynged yr Iaith* ('The Fate of the Language'), and the subsequent formation of Cymdeithas yr Iaith Gymraeg (the Welsh Language Society) in 1962 all indicated an increased national consciousness. A Secretary of State for Wales was appointed in 1964 and the Welsh Office was established in Cardiff in 1965. Following the Welsh Language Act of 1967, more schools began to use Welsh as a medium for education. In 1967 the Arts Council for Wales was established, with Meic Stephens appointed as the first director of its Literature Committee. Through its funding initiatives, the Arts Council 'profoundly altered the institutional base of Welsh publishing and ... significantly influenced output'.[33]

For Meic Stephens, what distinguished this new generation of Anglo-Welsh poets was a nationalist consciousness. His *Poetry Wales* editorial provided a manifesto for Anglo-Welsh poetry:

> [B]efore a poet writing in English can fully justify his position as Anglo-Welsh, he needs either to write about Welsh scenes, Welsh people, the Welsh past, life in contemporary Wales, or his own analysis of all these, or else attempt to demonstrate in his verse those more elusive characteristics of style and feeling which are generally regarded as belonging to Welsh poetry.[34]

Raymond Garlick, in the introduction to *The Lilting House,* suggests that 'some of [these poems] are Welsh in this fullest sense, that not only are they written by Welshmen or about Wales – they are written *for Wales'*.[35] If writing 'for Wales' was the political imperative, Jeremy Hooker, in a review of *The Lilting House,* also notes that 'one distinguishing feature of the Anglo-Welsh poet is his [sic] concern with the past and his sense of tragic disconti-nuity between past and present'.[36]

The exemplary 'Anglo-Welsh poet' of this generation, Tony Conran argues, is Harri Webb, who was 'political, witty, determinedly middle-brow, rooted in the valleys yet also committed to Wales as a whole'.[37] Webb's *The Green Desert* (1969) gives poetic voice to his nationalist politics, but the Wales of these poems is one of past glories, now disinherited, and 'Caught between two languages, / Both dying'.[38] In 'The Boomerang in the

Parlour', Webb compares the Australia his father visited as a young man, 'a clean new empty country', with Wales:

> [. . .] a land whose memory
> Has not begun, whose past has been forgotten
> But for a clutter of nightmares and legends and
>   lies.
> This land, too, has a desert at its heart.[39]

The desert image is repeated in 'Israel' where Wales is offered the example of the Jews who, having survived the war, have 'tuned in to Maccabeus':

> The mountains are red with their
>   blood,
> The deserts are green with their seed.
> Listen, Wales.[40]

While Israel's deserts are regenerating, Webb suggests that Wales's 'desert' is green, yet only in the sense of being rural and depopulated.

Webb also offered a sardonic interrogation of what was becoming orthodoxy in the arts. His Caradoc-Evansian 'Cywydd o Fawl' ('Praise Poem') on the effects of the Arts Council on writing in Wales lambasted the 'pounds, they have, many thousand' to give to the 'bards respectable', and the poets' supine acquiescence: 'Tongue we all, bards Welsh, Ta!'[41] Although harsh, this chimes with Conran's argument that the 'reservation' effect of economic subsidization by the Welsh Arts Council led to a lack of challenge, and to an excessive emphasis on Welsh subject matter in the poetry of this period.[42]

Unease over the definition and meaning of 'Anglo-Welsh' became increasingly evident, as John Davies's 'How to Write Anglo-Welsh Poetry' of 1977 indicated:

> First, apologise for not being able
> to speak Welsh. Go on: apologise.
> Being Anglo-*anything* is really tough;
> any gaps you can fill with sighs.[43]

'[G]et some roots,' he advised, 'juggle names like / Taliesin and ap Gwilym,' 'Spray place-names around', and 'A quick reference to cynghanedd / always goes down well.' In a subsequent *Poetry Wales* editorial which began wearily, 'So it's "Anglo-Welsh poetry again"', J. P. Ward argued that the recent period of Anglo-Welsh poetry 'seems over'.[44] By the summer 1977 editorial, however, he was enumerating the names of a new group of poets who had begun to publish in the 1970s – including Tony Curtis, Duncan Bush, Sheenagh

Pugh, Steve Griffiths, Jon Dressel, Robert Minhinnick, and Nigel Jenkins, along with Gillian Clarke, Ruth Bidgood, and Peter Finch – and whose work seemed to him to represent the 'latest wave' in what he now called 'Welsh poetry in English'.[45] Ultimately though, it was the devastating effect of the no-vote in the 1979 referendum on devolution in Wales (20.26% voted in favour, 79.74% against) which sounded the final knell for many of the 'second flowering' generation. Harri Webb saw this as the end of an era: 'I don't believe that writing in English about Wales matters very much anymore. Anglo-Welsh literature is, more or less, a load of rubbish,' he said in 1985.[46]

A Female Flowering: Welsh Women's Writing in English

Both the first and the second flowerings of Anglo-Welsh literature were overwhelmingly male affairs. This left a dearth of role models for women, as Gillian Clarke recorded:

> I threw my first poems in the bin because I was unaware they were poems. I suppose it was because I hadn't read anything in print that was like what I was writing. I think we do need models, and I was both Welsh and a woman. The world wasn't interested in either.[47]

The development of feminism after 1968 created an environment which encouraged women writers to find their voice (whether or not they identified as feminist), locating themselves in relation to both nationality and gender. What Jeremy Hooker has called 'the release of energy in women's writing and the shaping of new forms and apprehensions of reality that resulted' was hugely significant for women writers in Wales, as elsewhere.[48] Gillian Clarke and Ruth Bidgood both began to publish in the early 1970s and their work, together with that of writers such as Hilary Llewelyn-Williams, 'functioned so as to make room for women within a male-dominated Welsh culture which had previously seemed reluctant to include the feminine'.[49]

As editor of *The Anglo-Welsh Review* from 1975 to 1984, Clarke published and drew attention to women's poetry. An editorial in 1979 noted the way in which women writers 'often disappear into obscurity' and attributed this partly to women's disinclination to strive for fame, but also to the critical under-valuation of the domestic and familiar, which at that time were more likely to be women's subjects.[50] In 1982, in response to the assertion that there were 'almost no women writers in Wales', Clarke noted, 'How unready are such Welsh writers as Ruth Bidgood, Jean Earle, Sally Roberts Jones or

Sheenagh Pugh to push their reputations forward, how their places on the stage are taken by men with smaller talents than theirs.'[51] Many of these women started their poetic careers later in life. For Ruth Bidgood it was a move to the mid-Wales village of Abergwesyn, at first in the mid-1960s as a family holiday home and then full-time in 1974, which kick-started her career as a poet. Her first collection, *The Given Time* (1972), opened what was to become a sustained and detailed engagement with this rural area. The title poem of that collection meditates on 'the broken shape' of an abandoned house, 'lapped / By the first waves of forest-land':

> The house has lost its life, not yet identity –
> It is known hereabouts, stories are still told,
> Of men who lived there. Silent, it poses questions,
> Troubles me with half-answers, glimpses, echoes.[52]

Bidgood's poems tell the 'stories' of such abandoned houses and give a voice to those who occupied them (both male and female) and have been forgotten. They both celebrate and mourn the particularities of this specific landscape and its history. Matthew Jarvis has helpfully characterized Bidgood within the Welsh-language tradition of *canu bro* ('poetry of place') as 'a poet of a community in its place'.[53] Taken as a whole, he argues, her body of work constitutes 'a mid-Wales epic' which is 'one of the most important and substantial achievements of Anglo-phone Welsh poetry since its revival in the 1960s'.[54]

Like Bidgood's, Clarke's poetic career began relatively late and was enabled by a move back to west Wales around 1984. As M. Wynn Thomas recognized, 'Clarke's poetry consistently tries to redress the balance – of the historical record, in social arrangements, or cultural life – in favour of previously slighted female experience.'[55] Her important long poem *Letter from a Far Country* (1982) offers a sensitive engagement with the gendering of 'country' as both rural landscape and nation. The landscape of Wales is explicitly gendered in a way which reclaims it for women:

> As I write I am far away.
> First see a landscape. Hill country
> essentially feminine,
> the sea not far off.[56]

The poem celebrates women's domestic activity – 'counting / folding, measuring, making, / tenderly laundering cloth', or making 'Jams and jellies of blackberry / crabapple, strawberry, plum'.[57] Such preserves are a form of art as 'Familiar days are stored whole / in bottles.'[58] Yet Clarke contrasts this with 'the male right to the field' – as a young girl carrying tea out to the men, she finds that the corn stalks have scraped her ankles 'raw and bleeding' as poppies.[59] Now the shifting of gender roles means that the new generation of women 'are leaving' – what, she asks, will this mean in terms of Welsh culture?

> Will the men grow tender and the children strong?
> Who will teach the Mam iaith and sing them songs?
> If we adventure more than a day
> Who will do the loving while we're away?[60]

Attentive to both the importance of tradition in maintaining Welsh culture – 'the Mam iaith' ('mother tongue') – and the need for change, Clarke's poem negotiates a delicate balance between the two, 'preserving' the best of the past while making room for the new.

Through poems which rewrote Welsh myth, gave voice to silenced women, or recovered the lost history of Welsh Nonconformist women, the work of poets such as Bidgood, Clarke, and Llewelyn-Williams was, as Jane Aaron and Wynn Thomas argue, crucial in 'making Welshness a concept with which more women could identify' during this period.[61] If the flowering of Welsh women's poetry in English was late in starting in the twentieth century, it produced a particularly rich and varied body including the voices of poets as diverse as Sally Roberts Jones, Jean Earle, Christine Evans, Sheenagh Pugh, and Catherine Fisher.

As with women's poetry, the energy released by the women's movement proved enabling for some Welsh women writers of fiction, most notably Siân James. Her fine historical novel, *A Small Country* (1979), looks back to the First World War from a feminist and nationalist perspective to foreground the point of view of Welsh men *and* women. Brother and sister, Catrin and Tom Lewis of Hendre Ddu, both find their lives transformed by the war: Catrin puts aside her ambitions to be an artist, while Tom joins up. It is this experience which makes Tom, paradoxically, intensely aware of his Welsh nationality and the 'language and culture of our unimportant small country':

> I had hardly thought of myself as Welsh before . . . Now I think of myself as the product of a different society, not better, not worse but with a completely different history . . . How well worth preserving these differences seem to be. When I think of the civilisation we're fighting for, I can only think of the patch I know best.[62]

Like Clarke, James is looking to the past to understand what to value in the present. Furthermore, Katie Gramich has drawn attention to the important intertextual relationship between *A Small Country* and Kate Roberts's *Traed mewn Cyffion* ('Feet in Chains', 1936), in which James's novel revisits the gender roles of the earlier novel, by one of the greatest Welsh-language writers, in the light of feminism.[63] It would be easy to mistake James's work for middlebrow 'women's romance', since she writes about typically female subjects – sexuality and midlife crisis in *Storm at Arberth* (1994), late motherhood in *Second Chance* (2000) – but, like Clarke's poetry, James's exploration of gender issues is deeply embedded within her concern for Welsh culture and community.

A very different writer, the wickedly satirical but conservatively Catholic Alice Thomas Ellis (Anna Haycraft) was notoriously anti-feminist. Brought up in north Wales, Ellis's memoir *A Welsh Childhood* (1990) claims that she 'never felt truly at home anywhere but in Wales'.[64] For Ellis, however, Wales is a space of 'Celtic mist', legends, tragic histories, and eccentric characters, where 'all the layers of the past have been fractured and splintered together'.[65] Celtic Christianity and the pagan supernatural coexist in the haunted present. The Tylwyth Teg ('fairy folk') and Cŵn Annwn ('hounds of Annwn', or the otherworld) 'may still be around', she writes; 'The knockers certainly are, for I've heard them.'[66] This Arnoldian 'othering' of Welsh culture is reflected in her first novel, *The Sin Eater* (1977). The Irish Catholic Rose (an undeniably 'tough' woman) is 'enthralled' when she believes she witnesses the custom of sin-eating: '"Did you see that?" she kept saying, "Did you see? The *cwpan y meirw*, the cup of death. Some loony aboriginals and the Welsh are the only people who ever did that, and the aborigines have stopped."'[67] As Jane Aaron argues, the connection here between aboriginal and Welsh cultures is suggestive, since it positions both as colonized peoples who project their own sense of inferiority and self-loathing onto a scapegoat.[68] (The fact that Rose is both Irish and Catholic adds further layers.)

Ellis and James take radically different approaches to Welsh culture, but together with Bernice Rubens, Mary Jones, Glenda Beagan, Clare Morgan, and Catherine Merriman they represent a post-1968 generation of Welsh women whose fiction engages in one way or another with the changes brought by feminism. The establishment of Honno, the Welsh women's press, in 1986 was particularly important in publishing new work by Welsh women, as well as reprinting neglected classics. Arguably, however, the most vibrant flowering of Welsh women's fiction comes after devolution in the 2000s.

Towards Devolution: Writing a Diverse Wales in English

In the two decades prior to the millennium, Welsh writing in English became an increasingly diverse and plural field with writers looking outwards towards the international stage. Critically, the spread of postcolonial theories offered a way out of the 'Anglo-Welsh' impasse by helping to situate 'Welsh writing in English' within a global context of national literatures which included an anglophone element, notably Irish, Scottish, Canadian, American, Australian, and South African writings in English. Margaret Atwood's proposal in *Survival: A Thematic Guide to Canadian Literature* (1972) – 'Let us suppose in short that Canada is a colony'[69] – offered a way of thinking about the literatures of many countries forced to use the language of the oppressor. In 'Welsh Culture' (1975), Raymond Williams argued that 'To the extent we are a people, we have been defeated, colonized, penetrated, incorporated', and he recognized 'the signs of a post-colonial culture'.[70] Many resisted this approach – in 1991 Ned Thomas noted that 'in the Anglo-Welsh world it is still a provocation to offer an analysis of our literature as "colonial", and Anglo-Welsh writers often reveal the symptoms unconsciously.'[71] Indeed, he suggested that although Anglo-Welsh critics were often deploying similar ideas to those mooted by Atwood, 'the sharper discourse which actually *called* the Welsh situation colonial came only from critics strongly identified with the Welsh language such as Bobi Jones and myself'.[72] Nevertheless, it seems to have been partly what Jane Aaron calls 'the influence of a slow immersion in postcolonial theory'[73] which facilitated the invention of Welsh writing in English. The relaunch of *Anglo-Welsh Review* in 1988 as *New Welsh Review* was one indication of this shift.

The rise of Welsh writing in English as an academic subject had begun with a course on Anglo-Welsh writing established by Raymond Garlick as part of Welsh studies in Trinity College, Carmarthen in 1971, and a BA course entitled 'Literature in Twentieth-Century Wales' at Aberystwyth University established in 1977 by Ned Thomas (who took up his lectureship there in 1970) with Robin Young and Jeremy Hooker. In 1984, M. Wynn Thomas and James Davies developed the first MA in Modern Welsh Writing in English at University College, Swansea. This year also saw the founding of the Association of Welsh Writing in English (AWWE), with its first conference held in 1986.

The poets who began publishing in the 1970s (including Tony Curtis, Robert Minhinnick, Nigel Jenkins, Steve Griffiths, Sheenagh Pugh, Jon

Dressel, and Christine Furnival) were distinguished from the 'second flower-ing', J. P. Ward suggested, by being less nationalistic and more plural in their subject matter: 'The confidence of identity,' he argued, 'enables cultural diversification.'[74] Some actively distanced themselves from the previous generation. Robert Minhinnick, who edited *Poetry Wales* from 1997 to 2008, argued that the 'creators and apologists for '"Anglo-Welsh Literature" were an unworldly and unWelsh group of academics and writers, anaemically deferential to the Welsh language' who 'backed us into a literary cul-de-sac from which we have ... only just emerged'.[75] Similarly, Tony Curtis stated: 'My personal reaction over the last few years has been against all that nationalist stuff.'[76]

Despite Curtis's disavowal of 'that nationalist stuff' and the international outlook of his historical narrative poems (such as 'Soup', about the Holocaust, or 'The Death of Richard Beattie-Seaman in the Belgian Grand Prix, 1939'),[77] his oeuvre exemplifies the complexities of this period. Bobi Jones suggests that 'the colourful density' of Curtis's language, his poems about particular individuals, his loyalty to place, class solidarity, and elegizing all draw him towards the Welsh tradition.[78] Curtis's poems about his family, for instance, particularly a moving sequence of poems about his father in *Preparations*, are firmly located in place, mainly in Pembrokeshire. His poems often move out from the personal and local to global history, as in 'Crane-flies', where his son's distress over other boys pulling the wings off flies is linked to television pictures of 'the Phalange massacres in Beirut – / mangled corpses parcelled in sheets'.[79] War and death are key themes in Curtis's work, and these connect him not only to Dannie Abse but also to the preoccupation with green and peace politics in the work of writers such as Robert Minhinnick, Nigel Jenkins, and several women writers.[80] An interest in art and ekphrasis is another strong element, as in the sequence *The Deerslayers*, which takes its inspiration from a folio of photo-graphs by Les Krim, or the collaboration with surreal collagist John Digby in *The Arches* (1998).[81] Indeed, Tony Conran suggests that Curtis's work may be more exemplary of his generation than it initially appears: 'In finding his imagination's roosting place in the tragedies of Nazi Germany and other avenues of death, [Curtis] may have come nearer to the quick of Welsh sensibility than we realise.'[82]

Within the overall context of a country struggling with the effects of post-industrialization and Thatcherite politics, the events of the 1980s – the Falklands War, the Miners' Strike of 1984–5, Greenham Common, the activities of Meibion Glyndŵr, the Campaign for Nuclear Disarmament (CND) – increasingly politicized many writers. In Mary Jones's gothic and allegorical *Resistance* (1985), English-speaking Welshwoman Ann Thomas, suffering from cancer of the jaw and recently made redundant, escapes to a mid-Wales hotel where she finds herself badly disorientated.[83] The dilapidated hotel itself, with its labyrinthine corridors and ominously wooden fire escape, situated within a rat-infested and decaying landscape, figures both Ann's internal psychological state and that of the Welsh nation in decline. Initially alienated by the Welsh-speaking and all-male clientele, who are in fact a group of Welsh nationalists planning a bomb-attack, Ann becomes increasingly drawn to their leader Aled. Moreover, the novel repeatedly links Ann's cancer with the English language in Wales as an evasive and malignant force.[84] As the title suggests, this is a novel about modes of resistance, remembering, and survival – 'Cofia Dryweryn' ('Remember Tryweryn') and 'Cofia Abergele' ('Remember Abergele') exhort the local graffiti-[85] – but the ambiguous ending offers no easy answers. Jones's bringing together of nationalist and gender concerns is also a feature of other works in this period, such as Catherine Merriman's *State of Desire* (1996), where the widowed Jenny becomes involved in the fight against a local open-cast mine, or the work of Glenda Beagan.

Another writer deeply influenced by the political climate of this period is poet and novelist Christopher Meredith, who made his name with *Shifts* (1988). A formally sophisticated novel which vividly renders the south Wales valleys dialect, *Shifts* depicts the effects of de-industrialization on the lives of four characters in a declining steel town. Meredith's second novel, *Griffri* (1991), was radically different in tone and setting, a historical novel told in the first person by a court poet in the twelfth century, when the Normans were colonizing Gwent. Yet the two novels are linked in a way which connects the decline of the present back to the trauma of colonization in Wales's past. In *Shifts*, it is the discovery of Welsh history that enables the cuckolded Keith to take some control of his life, partly through learning Welsh.[86] In *Griffri*, Meredith complicates this solution. As *pencerdd* ('chief poet'), Griffri's function is to be 'keeper of memories, the lister of the dead . . . who affirms the road you choose'.[87] Yet the novel repeatedly shows the difficulties of ordering the chaos of a traumatized present into historical narrative: 'These summaries are bound to be a kind of lie,' Griffri acknowledges, 'but what else is there?'[88] In an important postcolonial reading, Kirsti Bohata argues that *Griffri* explores the violence of cultural exchange within the process of colonization, both through the Norman appropriation of territory, power, and myth and through the Welsh adoption of Norman practices of blinding and castrating prisoners.[89] In perhaps the most disturbing scene in the novel, Howel ap Iorwerth blinds and castrates his own cousin, Owain Pencarn.[90] Griffri himself comes to recognize his own complicity in the violence. By foregrounding Griffri's position as court poet (or 'paid-arselicker'),[91] Meredith interrogates the uses of poetry and the place of the artist within a fragmented and fractured culture and community.

Meredith's *Shifts* has been described by Stephen Knight as an 'automatic choice on most courses in Welsh literature',[92] and this comment in itself indicates the development of a new canon of Welsh writing in English over the last two decades of the twentieth century. The establishment of the first academic journal in the field – *Welsh Writing in English: A Yearbook of Critical Essays*, edited by Tony Brown, with Jane Aaron and M. Wynn Thomas as associate editors – was a key moment in consolidating this. With an editorial signalling the importance of engagement with recent thinking about 'postcolonial literatures and issues of national/cultural identity', the contents of the first volume in 1995 set out its stall unequivocally by including essays on neglected women writers alongside a feminist reading of Raymond Williams's novels, a postcolonial approach to the relationship between the two literatures of Wales, and work on the more canonical Dylan Thomas and R. S. Thomas.[93] Following the 'yes' vote in the 1997 referendum on devolution, the creation of the National Assembly for Wales in 1999 gave an important political impetus to the writing, publishing, and teaching of Welsh writing in English. By 2007, Welsh writing in English was taught in all but two Welsh higher education institutions and included an increasing diversity of theories, and an exciting plurality of writers and texts.

Notes

1. Stephen Knight, *A Hundred Years of Fiction: From Colony to Independence* (Cardiff: University of Wales Press, 2004), xv.
2. M. Wynn Thomas, *Internal Difference: Twentieth-Century Writing in Wales* (Cardiff: University of Wales Press, 1992).
3. Saunders Lewis, *Is There an Anglo-Welsh Literature?* (Caerdydd: Urdd Graddedigion Prifysgol Cymru / University of Wales Guild of Graduates, 1939). Originally delivered as The Annual Lecture, 10 December 1938.
4. George Ewart Evans, 'Answer to Questionnaire', *Wales* 1, 8/9 (1939): 225.
5. R. S. Thomas, 'Replies to "Wales" Questionnaire 1946', quoted by Tony Brown, in *R. S. Thomas*, Writers of Wales (Cardiff: University of Wales Press, 2006), 32.
6. Dannie Abse, ed., *Twentieth Century Anglo-Welsh Poetry* (Bridgend: Seren, 1997).

7. Gwyn Jones, *The First Forty Years: Some Notes on Anglo-Welsh Literature*, The W. D. Thomas Memorial Lecture (Cardiff: University of Wales Press, 1957).

8. Glyn Jones, *The Dragon Has Two Tongues: Essays on Anglo-Welsh Writers and Writing*, ed. Tony Brown, rev. edn (Cardiff: University of Wales Press, 2001), 6.

9. Ibid.

10. Ibid., 192; emphasis added.

11. Roland Mathias, *Anglo-Welsh Literature: An Illustrated History* (Bridgend: Poetry Wales Press, 1987), 105, 106.

12. Tony Conran, *Frontiers in Anglo-Welsh Poetry* (Cardiff: University of Wales Press, 1997), 177.

13. Ibid., 217.

14. Knight, *A Hundred Years of Fiction*, 167.

15. Emyr Humphreys, *A Toy Epic* [1958] (Bridgend: Seren, 1989); Glyn Jones, *The Valley, The City, The Village* [1956] (Cardigan: Parthian, 2009), and *The Island of Apples* [1965] (Cardiff: University of Wales Press, 1992).

16. Jones, *The Dragon Has Two Tongues*, 9.

17. Harri Webb, *The Green Desert: Collected Poems 1950–1969* (Llandysul: Gomer Press, 1969), 34.

18. Dannie Abse, *Ash on a Young Man's Sleeve* [1954] (London: Penguin, 1982), 11–12.

19. Ibid., 127.

20. Rhys Davies, *Print of a Hare's Foot* [1969] (Bridgend: Seren, 1998).

21. Margiad Evans, *A Ray of Darkness* (London: Arthur Barker, 1952). For perceptive accounts of this text, see the essays in Kirsti Bohata and Katie Gramich, eds., *Rediscovering Margiad Evans: Marginality, Gender and Illness* (Cardiff: University of Wales Press, 2013).

22. Brenda Chamberlain, *Tide-Race* [1962] (Bridgend: Seren, 2007), 16.

23. Tony Brown and M. Wynn Thomas, 'The Problems of Belonging', in *A Guide to Welsh Literature*, vol. II: *Welsh Writing in English*, ed. M. Wynn Thomas (Cardiff: University of Wales Press, 2003), 189.

24. Raymond Williams, *Border Country* [1960] (Cardigan: Parthian, 2006).

25. Daniel G. Williams, 'Writing Against the Grain: Raymond Williams' *Border Country* and the Defence of Realism', in *Mapping the Territory: Critical Approaches to Welsh Fiction in English*, ed. Katie Gramich (Cardigan: Parthian, 2010), 225.

26. Katie Gramich, 'The Fiction of Raymond Williams in the 1960s: Fragments of an Analysis', *Welsh Writing in English: A Yearbook of Critical Essays* 1 (1995): 63.

27. Lynette Roberts, *The Endeavour: Captain Cook's First Voyage to Australia* (London: Peter Owen, 1954).

28. Ibid., 224, 225.

29. Meic Stephens, 'The Second Flowering', *Poetry Wales* 3, 3 (1967): 2–9.

30. Bryn Griffiths, ed., *Welsh Voices: An Anthology of New Poetry from Wales* (London: Dent, 1967), v.

31. John Stuart Williams and Meic Stephens, eds., *The Lilting House: An Anthology of Anglo-Welsh Poetry 1917–1967* (London and Llandybie: Dent and Christopher Davies, 1969). Notably, Emyr Humphreys refused to be included because he objected to the term 'Anglo-Welsh' (*The Lilting House*, xv).

32. Mathias, *Anglo-Welsh Literature*, 107.

33. Jane Aaron and M. Wynn Thomas, '"Pulling You Through Changes": Welsh Writing in English Before, Between and After Two Referenda', in *Welsh Writing in English*, ed. Wynn Thomas, 278. See also Chapter 30 in this volume for the broader context of funding support for Welsh publishing.

34. Stephens, 'The Second Flowering': 7.

35. Raymond Garlick, introduction to *The Lilting House*, ed. Williams and Stephens, xxi; emphasis added.

36. Jeremy Hooker, *The Presence of the Past: Essays on Modern British and American Poetry* (Bridgend: Poetry Wales Press, 1987), 157.

37. Tony Conran, 'Poetry Wales and the Second Flowering', in *Welsh Writing in English*, ed. Wynn Thomas, 230.

38. Webb, 'Thanks in Winter', in *The Green Desert*, 45.

39. Webb, *The Green Desert*, 29.

40. Ibid., 59. Judas Maccabeus was the revolutionary who led the Jews against the Seleucid Empire in the second century BC.

41. Ibid., 43.

42. Conran, 'Poetry Wales and the Second Flowering', 252.

43. John Davies, 'How to Write Anglo-Welsh Poetry', *Poetry Wales* 11, 4 (1976): 22–3.

44. J. P. Ward, editorial in *Poetry Wales* 12, 3 (1977): 3.

45. J. P. Ward, editorial in *Poetry Wales* 13, 1 (1977): 5, 7.

46. Harri Webb, *Western Mail* interview [April 1985], quoted in Brian Morris, *Harri Webb* (Cardiff: University of Wales Press, 1993), 103.

47. Gillian Clarke, quoted by David T. Lloyd, in 'Interview with Gillian Clarke', in *Writing on the Edge: Interviews with Writers and Editors of Wales*, ed. David T. Lloyd (Amsterdam and Atlanta: Rodopi, 1997), 145.

48. Jeremy Hooker, 'Ceridwen's Daughters: Welsh Women Poets and the Uses of Tradition', *Welsh Writing in English: A Yearbook of Critical Essays* 1 (1995): 131.

49. Aaron and Thomas, 'Pulling You Through Changes', 288.

50. Anonymous, editorial in *The Anglo-Welsh Review* 65 (1979): 1.

51. Gillian Clarke, editorial in *The Anglo-Welsh Review* 70 (1982): 3.

52. Ruth Bidgood, 'The Given Time', in *New and Selected Poems* (Bridgend: Seren, 2004), 13.

53. Matthew Jarvis, *Ruth Bidgood* (Cardiff: University of Wales Press, 2012), 130.

54. Ibid.

55. M. Wynn Thomas, 'Place, Race and Gender in the Poetry of Gillian Clarke', in *Dangerous Diversities: The Changing Faces of Wales*, ed. Katie Gramich and Andrew Hiscock (Cardiff: University of Wales Press, 1998), 16.

56. Gillian Clarke, 'Letter from a Far Country', in *Selected Poems* (Manchester: Carcanet, 1985), 53.

57. Ibid., 56, 57.

58. Ibid., 57.

59. Ibid., 58.

60. Ibid., 64.

61. Aaron and Thomas, 'Pulling You Through Changes', 288.

62. Siân James, *A Small Country* [1979] (Bridgend: Seren, 1999), 172.

63. Katie Gramich, *Twentieth-Century Women's Writing in Wales: Land, Gender, Belonging* (Cardiff: University of Wales Press, 2007), 166.

64. Alice Thomas Ellis, *A Welsh Childhood* [1990] (London: Penguin, 1992), 5.

65. Ibid., 40.

66. Ibid., 18.

67. Alice Thomas Ellis, *The Sin-Eater* (London: Duckworth, 1977), 100.

68. Jane Aaron, *Welsh Gothic* (Cardiff: University of Wales Press, 2013), 190–1.

69. Margaret Atwood, *Survival: A Thematic Guide to Canadian Literature* [1972] (Toronto: McClelland and Stewart, 2004), 45.

70. Raymond Williams, 'Welsh Culture' [1975], in *Who Speaks for Wales? Nation, Culture, Identity*, ed. Daniel Williams (Cardiff: University of Wales Press, 2003), 9.

71. Ned Thomas, 'Sinking into the Landscape: Notes on Anglo-Welsh Literature and Australia', in *The Historical and Cultural Connections and Parallels Between Wales and Australia*, ed. Gavin Edwards and Graham Sumner (Lewiston, Queenston, and Lampeter: Edward Mellen, 1991), 103.

72. Ned Thomas, 'Parallels and Paradigms', in *Welsh Writing in English*, ed. Wynn Thomas, 318.

73. Personal communication, July 2015. See also Jane Aaron, 'Forming the Subject: The Genesis of Welsh Writing in English as an Academic Discipline', *The Association of Welsh Writing in English* (May 2017), www.awwe.org/forming-the-subject.html (accessed 14 December 2017).

74. Ward, editorial in *Poetry Wales* 13, 1: 6–7.

75. Robert Minhinnick, 'My Petition to the Zoo Keeper', *Planet* 90 (1992): 15–16.

76. Tony Curtis, quoted by David T. Lloyd, in 'Interview with Tony Curtis', in Lloyd, ed., *Writing on the Edge*, 113.

77. Tony Curtis, *New and Selected Poems* (Bridgend: Seren, 1986), 26, 23.

78. Bobi Jones, 'The Demise of the Anglo-Welsh', *Poetry Wales* 28, 3 (1993): 16 (originally published as 'Tranc yr Eingl-Gymry' in *Barddas*, Ebrill 1992).

79. Curtis, *New and Selected Poems*, 111.

80. Aaron and Thomas, 'Pulling You Through Changes', 291.

81. Curtis, *The Deerslayers*, published in *New and Selected Poems*, 67–72. Tony Curtis and John Digby, *The Arches* (Bridgend: Seren, 1998).

82. Conran, *Frontiers in Anglo-Welsh Poetry*, 274.

83. Mary Jones, *Resistance* (Belfast: Blackstaff, 1985).

84. Kirsti Bohata, '"Unhomely Moments": Reading and Writing Nation in Welsh Female Gothic', in *The Female Gothic: New Directions*, ed. Diana Wallace and Andrew Smith (Basingstoke: Palgrave, 2009), 189–90.

85. Jones, *Resistance*, 102. On the political and cultural significance of Tryweryn, see Chapter 26 in this volume. Abergele in north Wales was the place where two Welsh nationalists were killed by a bomb they were carrying on the evening before the investiture of Prince Charles as Prince of Wales in Caernarfon in 1969.

86. Christopher Meredith, *Shifts* [1988] (Bridgend: Seren, 1997), 127.

87. Christopher Meredith, *Griffri* [1991] (Bridgend: Seren, 1994), 9.

88. Ibid., 177.

89. Kirsti Bohata, *Postcolonialism Revisited*, Writing Wales in English (Cardiff: University of Wales Press, 2004), 146–57.

90. Meredith, *Griffri*, 209.

91. Ibid., 9.

92. Knight, *One Hundred Years of Fiction*, 180.

93. Editorial in *Welsh Writing in English: A Yearbook of Critical Essays* 1, 1 (1995): 3–4.

29

Exile and Diaspora: Welsh Writing
Outside Wales

MELINDA GRAY

What is 'Welsh writing outside Wales'? If it has sometimes been difficult to define writing within the borders of Wales as 'Welsh', then the theoretical questions raised by this new query will surely bring back into focus the anxieties of identity which have been hashed out in the scholarship on Welsh culture from the 1980s on; they should also, however, allow us to appreciate how far those debates and discussions have moved us along. In the last fifteen years, the argument is increasingly made for recognition of the variety and heterogeneity of Welsh writing. Thus, Ned Thomas cautions that the canon of Welsh writing in English is still under negotiation, that an agreement on 'criteria' has yet to be reached, but he also suggests 'comparative treatment' as a promising way forward.[1]

Other authors emphasize the hybridity of both Welsh- and English-language literary traditions in Wales, and they identify a growing trend for recognition and acceptance of diversity in Welsh culture. These and a number of other studies have helped to lay the theoretical foundations for this essay by giving us the tools for understanding cultural tensions and differences within Welsh culture, so that, as Kirsti Bohata has written, 'difference – and *différence* – is perceived as central', allowing 'a productive internal discourse' rather than divisiveness.[2] The study of Welsh literature in such places as the United States and Patagonia is 'embryonic', to borrow Ned Thomas's term, and so the writing surveyed here does not constitute an exhaustive list, and the terms of inclusion are necessarily flexible.[3]

Common themes in this literature are the experiences of migration and diaspora. Stephen Constantine has written that, etymologically, diaspora simply means 'a scattering', and yet the word has accrued other meanings, in particular with respect to its association with the Old Testament, namely 'a sense of expulsion and exile from home, of loneliness and isolation in culturally alien places, and of a desire to return'. Diaspora can foreground 'the difference between . . . overseas migrants and their hosts'.[4] As a close study of this literature soon discovers, migration and the experience of living away from Wales has inspired not only attention to differences but also many efforts to create and establish meaningful continuities and exchanges.

Writing from outside Wales may give special prominence to problems of belonging, and yet the writers discussed in this chapter cannot be considered political exiles in a strict sense; many, even in the nineteenth century, returned to Wales on visits, if not to resettle or retire there. Most historical research supports the idea that neither Welsh emigrants nor their descendants viewed themselves as true exiles from Wales. They departed Wales in search of employment and freedoms greater than those they had had, and they tended to do well in their adoptive lands. The memory of what was left behind has served as powerful inspiration for many a migrant writer, as in the following nineteenth-century Welsh poem from Vermont:

> Rhaid gadael Gwlad fy Nhadau – i eraill,
>   A morio trwy'r tonau;
> Er hyn mae hon yn parhau,
> Yn nôd fy nymuniadau.[5]

> (I must leave to others the Land of my Fathers
>   And sail across the sea;
> And yet it is unceasing
> As the object of my desire.)

Twentieth-century and contemporary Welsh diaspora writing offers many glimpses of the perplexities of hybridity and hyphenated identities, for instance in Leslie Norris's poem 'Belonging'. The setting of this poem could be Utah, where Norris, born in Merthyr Tydfil, Glamorgan in 1921, spent the last twenty years of his life teaching at Brigham Young University. Here the speaker has just finished reading from his work, and he is approached by an old man, 'someone's / Grandfather' with faded eyes who offers up for inspection a family tree:

> 'I'm Welsh,' he said. I read his
> Pedigree. Bentley, Lawrence, Faulkner,

> Graydon, no Welsh names. I nodded,
> Gave back his folded pride, shook
> My head in serious admiration. Belonging,

> After all, is mostly a matter of belief.
> 'I should have known you anywhere,' I said,
> 'For a Welshman.' He put away his chart,

Shook hands, walked into the foreign light,
I watched him go. Outside, the sprinklers,
Waving their spraying rainbows, kept America green.[6]

In the 'America' of this poem – where the lawns are green because we want them to be and we make them so – belonging can be 'mostly a matter of belief', and people who have lived here for generations can still be Welsh. The speaker, however, stands apart, in the dimness, beyond the reach of 'the foreign light' into which the old man disappears. In fact, for Norris himself, 'belief' may not have been so easy a solution to problems of belonging, as interviews with him suggest.

In general, the writing under consideration in this chapter offers a variegated perspective on Welsh migration and diaspora, in which loneliness, loss, and recognition of difference coexist with engagement and productive re-workings of identity. Writing outside Wales often has something to say about multiple belongings. This chapter will not try to settle questions of belonging (i.e. is this text Welsh or American or Australian?); instead, it recognizes that as these questions are framed by the writers and texts identified here, they are productive, expanding the possibilities for the notion of 'Welsh writing'.

The Nineteenth Century

From the middle decades of the nineteenth century, there was significant emigration from Wales to the British colonies, to Patagonia, and, more than anywhere else, to the United States. Emigrant communities first borrowed and later set up their own printing presses, and they published journals, newspapers, pamphlets, and books. Both seeking to maintain connections with their old lives, with families and friends left behind, and helping to shape communities in their new homes, their cultural and literary productions illuminate the mid- and later nineteenth century as a golden age for Welsh writing outside Wales. But a profound shift in poetics at the end of the nineteenth century ensured that most of this earlier literature was forgotten or discounted as unreadable. Scholarly studies have tended to focus primarily on the historical and sociological interest of nineteenth-century Welsh emigrant writing rather than its literary aspects, though there are notable exceptions, primarily with regard to Welsh writing from the United States.[7] While much of what was published is long out of print, the advent of digitization has made some of this material more widely available than it ever was.

A considerable body of nineteenth-century emigrant writing in Welsh and English is preserved on the pages of journals and newspapers. Many periodicals were edited by religious leaders and some were affiliated with particular denominations (Methodist, Congregationalist, and Baptist), and yet, considered altogether and over time, they published an impressive variety of writing: sermons, biographies, essays on religious matters, hymns, poetry and other literature, coverage of current affairs, news from Wales, from the country of publication, and some world news. Bill Jones has made a case for the literary value of the correspondence printed in these journals.[8]

The United States was home to the earliest and most extensive Welsh periodical press from 1838, when the monthly journal *Y Cyfaill o'r Hen Wlad yn America* ('The Friend from the Old Country in America') published its first issue. The weekly newspaper *Y Drych* ('The Mirror') ran for more than half a century. There were English-language journals such as *The Cambrian: A Magazine for the American Welsh*, which appeared monthly from 1880 to 1919. Over the course of the nineteenth and early twentieth centuries, more than forty Welsh newspapers and periodicals were published in the United States.[9] In the second half of the nineteenth century, Australia and Patagonia each had a periodical press in Welsh. In Victoria, Australia, where there was a vibrant Welsh community from 1851, two Welsh newspapers were published: *Yr Australydd* ('The Australian', 1866–72) and *Yr Ymwelydd* ('The Visitor', 1874–6), each of which carried sermons, essays, poetry, and some fiction.[10] There was a Welsh settlement in Patagonia from 1865, and in 1878 *Ein Breiniad* ('Our Privilege') saw a brief run there; it was the first printed newspaper in any language in Patagonia. First published in 1891, *Y Drafod* ('The Discussion') was edited by Eluned Morgan from 1893; it carried news from Wales and Argentina together with a variety of other writing. Glyn Williams has described *Y Drafod* as 'a cultural newspaper which has no party political allegiance, nor is it the expression of a single class. One of its main functions has been to serve as an outlet for Welsh literary expression in the settlement.'[11] *Y Drafod* continues today in Spanish and Welsh.[12] In London, late in the century, a bilingual English and Welsh newspaper was established by Thomas John Evans. Evans edited *The London Kelt* from 1895, through mergers with various other publications, until 1916.[13]

Poetry was broadly appreciated in the United States at this time and often appeared on the pages of American journals. Nineteenth-century Welsh emigrant periodicals often printed poems, and some had a poet's corner with a designated poetry editor, for Welsh poetry was an institution, nurtured by chapel and eisteddfod culture. In 1872, Congregationalist minister and poet

R. D. Thomas published *Hanes Cymry America* ('A History of the American Welsh') which included, among many catalogues of eminent Welsh Americans, two lists of poets that gave the names, and sometimes the bardic names, of more than 150 poets and five female poets (*barddonesau*), together with the city or town in which the poet was living.[14] Thomas's lists show that poets were scattered across the country, clustered where there were Welsh churches and more substantial settlements of Welsh people. Scranton, PA alone was home to 'over fifty recognized Welsh bards' in the 1860s and 1870s.[15] The poems published by these poets were formal competition poems – poems produced in the context of eisteddfodau – religious poems, elegies, political poems, and poems of social commentary, some of them relating to specific historical moments, such as the American Civil War, as Jerry Hunter has shown. Much of this poetry was formally and linguistically conventional, drawing on Nonconformist theologies and Victorian iconography, and it resonated with aspects not only of Welsh but also of English and American traditions.

From early on, American journals welcomed the work of many women writers to their pages, of whom one of the most gifted and uniquely prolific was Laura Griffiths (d. 1863) of Prospect, NY. Griffiths lived most of her life in a lively Welsh community north of Utica, NY where she was a maid, serving for a time in the household of a respected Congregationalist minister. Married but with no children of her own, she raised the orphaned children of her brother. Between 1845 and 1863, she published about fifty poems, mainly in the Congregationalist journal *Y Cenhadwr Americanaidd* ('The American Messenger') which was edited and published by Rev. Robert Everett from his home in nearby Steuben. Many of Griffiths's poems are elegies for family and friends, but she also published playful celebrations of marriage and salutations on the birth of a child; verses written on behalf of her church, thanking a sister parish for the gift of Communion vessels; and a religious poem on Christ's earthly incarnation. In one poem published late in 1862, near the end of her own life, Griffiths took on a topic of national significance, namely President Lincoln's intention to issue an Emancipation Proclamation that would put an end to slavery. Published tributes to her at the time of her death in 1863 made it clear that Griffiths held a position of respect within her community. Another female poet who published frequently in *Y Cenhadwr* over the course of twenty years was Rebecca Jones. Born in a village outside Utica, she was an invalid and lived in her father's house until her death in 1874. Her fascination with current American ideas and writing culminated in her last published work, translations into Welsh of poems by her contemporaries, Alice and Phoebe Cary.

Writing in Welsh was a choice for Jones, as it was increasingly for Welsh writers in the United States in the later part of the century.

A smaller number of Welsh poets succeeded in publishing volumes of poetry in the United States. A remarkable early book of verse in English is *Wales, and Other Poems* (1839) by Maria James (1793–1868). At the outset, her story is very similar to those of the Welsh women who were publishing their poetry in the journals: as a child she had emigrated with her family to a quarry in New York, learned her first words of English on the transatlantic crossing, and became a servant in the home of a prominent American Methodist family. Here her path diverged, for she was educated together with the young daughter of the family, who encouraged her literary efforts and helped publish her book, which garnered praise from both Welsh and American audiences; the latter expressed interest in her as a rare example of a working-class woman with literary talent. In 1848 her poems were included in two anthologies of poetry by American women. Later on, her work seems to have been discounted by American anthologists as too much 'of its time', too conventional to stand out. More recently her work has reappeared in an anthology of nineteenth-century Welsh women's writing.[16]

It was expensive to publish a volume of poetry in the United States and often these projects were financed by subscription, or by the poets themselves. A number of the Welsh poets who managed to do so had first established themselves in Wales. One, Lewis William Lewis (Llew Llwyfo, 1831–1901), had won top prizes at national and local *eisteddfodau* in Wales and was also known as a singer and as an early novelist. Lewis travelled and worked in the United States for a relatively brief period of six years during which he travelled through the States, singing and competing in American *eisteddfodau*, briefly edited an American journal, and published two volumes of his work in Utica, in 1868 and 1871.[17] The first, as Lewis confesses in his preface, had been rejected by a prominent Welsh publisher who apologized that Lewis's poems were 'too good, too ponderous, too lacking in the comic element' to sell. Lewis defends himself by arguing that the life he knew was serious, full of hard work and tribulation. He set his mind on the more liberal outlook of the Americans ('rhyddfrydedd yr Americaniaid') and paid an American publisher to print and sell his book, including many of the poems that won him eisteddfod fame. Only one poem appears specifically to address his American market, a 'national hymn' ('Emyn Genedlaethol') for the Welsh of America.[18] A second author of a volume of poetry, Rowland Walter (Ionoron Glan Dwyryd, 1819–1884), left Blaenau Ffestiniog for the quarries of Vermont in the mid-1850s after publishing his first book in Wales. Walter made an arrangement similar to Lewis's with the same Utica publisher and in 1872 brought out *Caniadau Ionoron* ('Songs of Ionoron'). While this volume opens with a series of formal competition odes (*awdlau*), it also collects many poems that record the poet's associations with the Welsh in Vermont. Eirug Davies notes that one volume of poetry, published in Chicago in 1877, includes 'a detailed ... Welsh metrical treatise'.[19] Welsh American journals also published instruction in Welsh metrics to assist budding poets.

The disruptive experiences of emigration and the proliferation of Welsh publications in America opened the door to different kinds of writing. What was likely the first original novel ever serialized in a Welsh-language periodical appeared in an American newspaper, *Y Drych a'r Gwyliedydd* ('The Mirror and Sentinel'), between 12 April 1856 and 4 April 1857, 'Y Carcharor ym Mhatagonia' ('The Prisoner in Patagonia').[20] Translation was a means by which nineteenth-century writers could introduce new kinds of writing into Welsh, as when Robert Everett published Welsh translations of *Uncle Tom's Cabin*, Harriet Beecher Stowe's extremely popular anti-slavery novel, in serial instalments in *Y Cenhadwr* in 1853, and then as a book in 1854.[21]

At least one more novel appeared in the pages of *Y Drych* in 1870, and in the same year, *Yr Australydd*, the Australian Welsh newspaper, serialized 'Cymro yn Awstralia' ('A Welshman in Australia').[22] In the 1880s and 1890s, the novels of Daniel Owen (1836–1895), written in Welsh in Wales, fostered a broader interest in and acceptance of the novel form in Welsh, and following Owen's death in 1895 the American press put out a call for Welsh novelists. The 1896 eisteddfod of Middle Granville, NY awarded a prize for the best submission on the theme of the importance of learning by the hearth ('Dylanwad Addysg yr Aelwyd') to R. R. Williams of L'Anse, Michigan. Published in 1897, Dafydd Morgan's narrative of Welsh immigration and settlement, of tensions between tradition and progress, shares the interests of both American and Welsh fiction of its time.[23]

In the same period, Margaret Evans Roberts (1833–1921) was a writer who succeeded in bringing new ideas to the Welsh in the United States. Having emigrated from Carmarthenshire in 1861, she lived in Iowa and in Scranton, and wrote hundreds of essays for *Y Drych* from the 1870s until 1911 on 'a dazzling array' of subjects including the theory of evolution, of which she was an early proponent, science, religion, temperance, and women's rights. Her significant public presence extended from the page to the podium, where she lectured and engaged skilfully in debate. While her subjects stirred controversy among her readers, she was also praised, as Bill Jones has written, for 'her bravery in challenging entrenched orthodoxies and promoting new ideas in the fields of feminism and science'.[24]

The man who took over editorship of *Y Drych* in this period and kept it for a quarter century, through the First World War, was Dafydd Rhys Williams (1851–1931), a writer and journalist who emigrated to the United States in 1883. By this time, the Welsh-language press in the United States was shrinking as immigration from Wales slowed and literary tastes changed. Citing the earlier work of historian Emrys Jones, Bill Jones has noted that 'the American-born children of Welsh immigrants rebelled not only against the Welsh language but against religion itself. They embraced new "worldly" cultural values which the older generation frowned upon.'[25] In the spirit of renewal, Williams wrote in 1908 of his mission to reinvigorate Welsh publishing by 'bringing into the language some other sorts of books' ('dwyn i'r iaith ryw fath o lyfrau heb yr uchod') than the volumes of religious commentary, hymnbooks, songbooks, and poetry ('yr holl gyfrolau yn esboniadau, llyfrau emynau, llyfrau canu, awdlau ac englynion') which were the staples of the Welsh-language press.[26] Williams published eight volumes of his essays, plays, and short fiction between 1896 and 1913.

In 1913, Sam Ellis, a retired schoolteacher in Utica, published a single collection of stories full of nostalgia for rural nineteenth-century Wales; the last of these, the only one of the stories that is in English, is a parable of immigration and consequent exile from old values. A Welsh prospector in the California gold fields strikes it rich, only to discover late in life that his increase in means has made it impossible to return to the happier ways of his youth in rural Wales.[27] Ellis's stories speak from a moment of crisis, when Welsh-language writing and culture in the United States was in precipitous decline and on the verge of extinction. Bill Jones has offered a bleak rendition of this situation in his book about Scranton, where, during the late nineteenth and early twentieth centuries, 'the thriving Welsh-language culture which had characterized the "Welsh Athens of America" waned and virtually disappeared'.[28]

On the whole, however, scholars have represented the process of Welsh assimilation in the United States as relatively untroubled, and that, as historian Ronald Lewis writes, 'Americanization was the result of a two-way process whereby the Welsh increasingly participated in the dominant culture and mainstream Americans accepted them.'[29] The notion of a 'two-way process' is one that could help to explain the work of Elizabeth Owen, whose two volumes of poetry appeared in Denver, following the First World War. Owen's first book, *Odes of Odd Moments*, appeared in 1922, and it was followed by a collection in Welsh, *Briwsion Barddonol* ('Poetic Fragments'), in 1927. The two collections are remarkably similar (though one is not a translation of the other): the poet's language in both books is old-fashioned and colloquial; and both books include patriotic poems and war poems, elegies, celebrations, and many other poems relating to the poet's life in Denver. The very publication of the volumes may be understood as a kind of nostalgia for Welsh culture, or, more precisely, for nineteenth-century Welsh culture in the United States.

William Dean Howells (1837–1920), the novelist and 'Dean of American letters' from Ohio whose father had emigrated from Hay-on-Wye in the early nineteenth century, can be understood as having had a place in the story of the turn-of-the-century transition in Welsh writing in the United States. As Daniel Williams has shown, Howells's interest in his ethnic heritage took him on three visits to Wales in the 1880s and 1890s and helped to shape his argument, radical at the time, for the essential heterogeneity of American culture and 'the cultural independence of American literature'.[30] In an essay from 1897 about writers who left the United States for other places, Howells wrote that 'the literary spirit is the true world-citizen and is at home everywhere . . . Literary absenteeism . . . is not peculiarly an American vice or an American virtue. It is an expression or a proof of the modern sense which enlarges one's country to the bounds of civilization.'[31] One could say the same for those nineteenth-century writers who left Wales for other places, offering from afar new perspectives on Welsh identity.

The Twentieth Century and Beyond

In 1986, the poet Tony Curtis wrote that 'writing in Wales, as far as the majority of outsiders are concerned . . . means Dylan Thomas'. The global outpouring of tributes to Dylan Thomas in 2014, the centenary year of his birth, suggests that this view still holds for many outside Wales.[32] Born in Swansea, south Wales, Thomas spent much of the 1930s and 1940s in the Fitzrovia district of London, where he participated in a literary scene that included other Welsh writers and artists. The poet first visited New York in 1950 and spent much of the following three years travelling around the States on reading tours, one of the first poets to do so. He was working on his radio play *Under Milk Wood* during his last visit to the United States in 1953 and died shortly afterwards in New York. Much has been written about how he captivated audiences with his exuberant style, his powerful Welsh voice, his humour, sensuality, and love of words. The story of Thomas's early demise has sometimes seemed to eclipse the reputation of his poetry. Centenary exhibitions and performances such as those at the Dylan in Fitzrovia Festival in London, the Melbourne Writers' Festival, The Poets' Theatre in Cambridge, MA (where Thomas gave his first reading from *Under Milk Wood*), and at the 92Y Poetry Center in New York (where the play was first read onstage with other actors) testify to this poet's unique legacy outside Wales.

Among the young Welsh poets of Dylan Thomas's generation, both Leslie Norris (1921–2006) and T. Harri Jones (1921–1965) left Wales in order to find employment and spent the latter part of their lives far away from their birthplaces in south Wales. Each was deeply influenced by Thomas's distinctive work. T. Harri Jones spent his earliest years in the village of Cwm Crogau, Powys, where he heard Welsh spoken but learned only English from his mother. The natural settings of his childhood gave shape to many of his poems. His study of English literature at Aberystwyth was interrupted by the Second World War, and he spent formative years serving in the Royal Navy. After the war, he completed his degree and then left for England, where he taught and published a first volume of poetry. In 1959, he left the UK for the University of Newcastle in New South Wales, Australia, where he was a lecturer until his accidental death by drowning in 1965. Jones published three volumes of poetry from Australia and a monograph on Dylan Thomas. His poems explore themes of love and sexuality, and while some proclaim the poet's hedonistic delight in his new Australian life and the pleasure he took in family and friends, a number of others speak of guilt and the bitterness of exile. Perhaps as a consequence of his removal from Wales, his conflicted Welsh identity, and his early death, Jones's work has sometimes fallen between the cracks; he is not as well known in either Wales or Australia as some of his contemporaries.

In an interview conducted in 1991, Leslie Norris described first learning to write poetry as a boy: 'Dylan Thomas's verse stung me into poetry.'[33] Like Thomas, Norris wrote both poetry and short stories, and, like T. Harri Jones, much of his work drew on the natural landscapes of his childhood. From 1948 Norris lived outside Wales, studying and piecing together a teaching career in England while winning awards for his poetry. Norris started to build an international readership by publishing work in *Poetry Wales*, *The New Yorker*, and *The Atlantic Monthly*. In 1985, the poet moved to Utah where he was poet-in-residence at Brigham Young University until his death in 2006. Norris thrived in the United States, publishing two further volumes of poetry and a second collection of stories, as well as stories for children and translations from German of Rainer Maria Rilke's poetry. He gained a devoted following among his students and readers. In the same interview from 1991, when he had been living in the United States for the better part of a decade, Norris affirmed that his poetry was known in Wales and that he was recognized there 'as an Anglo-Welsh poet', and yet he was clearly uncomfortable with the perceived limitations of this designation. While Norris may have felt himself to be 'truly ... a Welshman', as he declared, his writing explored other influences and affinities, giving rise to his insistence that he was 'probably ... an English poet writing in the mainstream of the English tradition'.[34] Recent consideration of Norris's work understands his development of themes of loss, memory, and the ambivalence of identity in relation to multiple literary traditions: English, Welsh, and American.[35]

The literary careers of many Welsh writers have been meaningfully shaped by periods spent living outside Wales; Norris chose to stay in the United States, many others have returned to Wales. Poet John Davies (b. 1944) spent three years in the 1980s living and teaching in Michigan, Utah, and Seattle. As Tony Curtis has suggested, the cultural collisions experienced during those years may have felt familiar to a poet raised in industrial south Wales in the 1940s and 1950s, and they provided him with material for many of the poems in *The Visitor's Book* (1985), *Flight Patterns* (1991), and *Dirt Roads* (1998).[36] The first poet laureate of Wales, Gwyneth Lewis (b. 1959), has written about the perspective afforded her by living away from Wales. She has described a crucial moment in her life when, having completed a degree in English literature at the University of Cambridge, she found herself trapped between two languages and two traditions, unable to choose, and therefore silenced. The opportunity to study at Harvard University offered her a way forward; there she met Seamus Heaney, who set an example as one who 'had made himself at home in a global tradition without losing his grasp of his own native culture' ('wedi ymgartrefi mewn traddodiad byd-eang, heb golli gafael ar ei ddiwylliant cynhenid ef ei hun').[37] Lewis is a singular example of a Welsh writer able to move successfully between languages and traditions on the world stage, but there are many other Welsh writers for whom living outside of Wales has granted an important perspective.

Throughout the twentieth century, the cities and universities of England offered to writers employment and publishing opportunities that were unavailable in Wales, with London being a particular attraction. The 'London Welsh' had been an identifiable group since at least the late eighteenth century, producing writers who often had an ambivalent relationship with Wales.[38] Modernist poet and artist David Jones (1895–1974), author of *In Parenthesis* (1937), was born in London to Welsh parents and lived his entire life in London but was constantly drawn to the literary traditions of Wales. Others Welsh writers in London were Caradoc Evans (1878–1945), author of the short story collection *My People* (1915), Caradog Prichard (1904–1980), author of the classic Welsh novel *Un Nos Ola Leuad* ('One Moonlit Night', 1961), and Dannie Abse (1923–2014), the prolific Welsh-Jewish poet and doctor who was born in Cardiff and lived most of his life in London. Welsh novelist and academic Raymond Williams (1921–88) spent his life at Oxford and Cambridge universities, but he drew on material from his childhood in a village near Abergavenny for *Border Country* (1960) and other novels. Williams was a Welsh nationalist and member of Plaid Cymru whose pioneering work in cultural studies and essays on exile and identity have shaped the interests of contemporary Welsh writers such as Daniel Williams.[39] Contemporary Welsh-language poet Ifor ap Glyn was born and raised in London and has twice won the crown (the prize awarded to the best *pryddest*, or free-metre poem) at the National Eisteddfod. Together with other Welsh poets, he has participated in the Smithsonian Folklife Festival held in Washington, DC, where he has taught Welsh poetic composition. His collection *Cerddi Map yr Underground* ('Songs of the Underground Map', 2001) includes a cycle of poems commissioned by the BBC about the London Welsh School and 'Map yr Underground', a poem that traces an ancient Welsh belonging in London by drawing on the medieval Welsh tradition of the otherworld, Annwn, in order to read the familiar map of the London Tube as a shared tribal path, a '*Songlines* Llundain'.[40]

One of the most important loci for literary exchange with Wales in the twentieth century is Patagonia. The Welsh Patagonian settlement, led by a group of pioneers who set sail from Wales in 1865, was from the outset imagined as a way to nurture the Welsh language and its culture at a time when these were perceived to be losing ground in Wales, and also in the United States. Largely because of the remoteness of the settlement and the Welsh settlers' resistance to governance by Argentina, the Welsh language held a stronger course in Patagonia than it did in the United States, and only over the course of the twentieth century was there gradual assimilation to Argentina and the Spanish language. Even so, there remains a high degree of bilingualism in Welsh and Spanish in Patagonia and the association between Wales and Patagonia is still generating a rich body of writing.

Born aboard ship en route to the new settlement in Patagonia, Eluned Morgan (1870–1938) travelled to Wales a number of times, for education and work. She was a leader among the Welsh in Patagonia, where she helped to set up a school, and she became the first woman to edit a Welsh-language newspaper (*Y Drafod*, 'The Discourse', from 1893). Among other works, she published two volumes of travel writing related to Patagonia, *Dringo'r Andes* ('Climbing the Andes', 1904) and *Gwymon y Môr* ('Seaweed', 1909) that found an eager readership in Wales. R. Bryn Williams (1902–1981), a prolific Welsh writer born in Patagonia, published a biography of Eluned Morgan in 1948 as well as numerous other books about Welsh Patagonian culture. The BBC radio adaptations of his novels from the 1950s to the 1970s, tales of adventure and romance, helped to shape the sensibility of a generation in Wales, as Gareth Miles has described.[41] Saunders Lewis, renowned Welsh literary critic and writer and founder of the Welsh national party, Plaid Cymru, had high regard for Eluned Morgan and her work. In a famous radio broadcast of 1962, 'Tynged yr Iaith' ('The Fate of the Language'), Lewis argued that, in Wales, the Welsh language was on the verge of dying out altogether, and he held up, as a model for Wales, the Welsh Patagonian colony's struggle to keep and protect its native language and culture, setting off what Esther Whitfield has called 'a reanimation' of the idea of Welsh Patagonia for the twenty-first century.[42]

The historical and cultural associations between Wales and Patagonia are fertile ground for comparative study. Esther Whitfield's essays begin this project and offer a sense of the extensive Spanish-language writing from Welsh Patagonia, beginning with Carlos Bertomeu's foundational 1943 novel *El valle de la esperanza* ('The Valley of Hope').[43] Bertomeu's historical romance is the first of many novels that focus on the nineteenth-century settlers of Patagonia and on the voyage of the *Mimosa*, the ship that carried the first group of Welsh colonists to Patagonia in 1865. Others are Phyllis Owen's *Mimosa: A Narrative Based on Fact* (1995); Sian Eirian Rees Davies's *I Fyd Sy Well* ('To a Better World') which won the Daniel Owen prize at the National Eisteddfod in 2005; Carlos Dante Ferrari's *El riflero de Ffos Halen* ('The Rifleman of Ffos Halen', 2005), which has been translated into Welsh; and Mónica Soave's *El botón de nácar* ('Pearl Button', 2005). A number of memoirs by early settlers or their descendants have been recently published or reissued, among them Fred Green's *Pethau Patagonia* ('Patagonian Things', 1984) and Elvey MacDonald's *Llwch* ('Dust', 2009).[44] Hazel Charles Evans's novel *Glas* ('Blue', 2006) calls up a more modern world, while a volume of poetry arising from the Welsh association with Patagonia is *Eldorado* by Iwan Llwyd and Twm Morys (1999).

From the 1960s and onwards, novels from the United States have offered many versions of a historical or mythical Welsh past. Howard Thomas, a writer based in Utica, NY published two novels, now long out of print: *The Singing Hills* (1964) and *The Road to Sixty* (1966). Both stories unfold in the Welsh American communities north of Utica, in the mid-nineteenth century, which Thomas identifies as a time of transition for Welsh settlers working out how to keep Welsh traditions alive while becoming American. Shannon Kay Penman has had more lasting success with her vividly detailed historical novels set in twelfth- and thirteenth-century Wales. The popularity of the trilogy that begins with *Here Be Dragons* (1985) led to the design of a website partially funded by the North Wales Tourism Partnership which helps readers to find and visit the sites described in Penman's books.[45] C. W. Sullivan has written about the American fantasy novelists who have made use of material from the *Mabinogion* and other medieval Welsh tales.[46] Among those Sullivan mentions are Evangeline Walton, Lloyd Alexander, whose series of novels beginning with *The Book of Three* (1964) was adapted to film by Disney, and Nancy Bond. Susan Cooper, an English writer with family ties to mid-Wales who has long made her home in the United States, won both the Newbery Honor and the Newbery Award for books in *The Dark Is Rising Sequence* (1965–77), two of which are set in Wales. Kathryn Davis's *The Walking Tour* (1999) is a more recent literary novel that also makes use of material from the native Welsh medieval tales. Born in England to Welsh and Chinese parents, Peter Ho Davies moved to the United States to study creative writing in the early 1990s and stayed. His novel *The Welsh Girl* was long-listed for the Booker Prize in 2007. Reviewed in the *New York Times* as a 'counterwar novel,' a description which encourages consideration of it in relation to an important strand of Welsh anti-war writing, the story is set in the Welsh countryside during the Second World War.[47] American scholars have also published translations of Welsh literature: Patrick K. Ford's edition and translation of the *Mabinogion* first appeared in 1977 and was reissued by the publisher in 2008; Joseph P. Clancy has published a number of anthologies of translations of Welsh poetry, both medieval and modern; and John K. Bollard has recently published editions of Welsh medieval tales and poetry in which his translations appear together with photography of Welsh landscapes.

David Lloyd is an American writer and director of Creative Writing at Le Moyne College in Syracuse, NY who grew up in a Welsh family in Utica. Lloyd's poetry, fiction, and scholarship demonstrate his deep engagement with Wales and Welsh literary traditions. In *Boys* (2004), a collection of short fiction, the adolescent protagonist of the title story is the grandson of a Welsh immigrant. Some of the importance of Lloyd's anthology, *Other Land: Contemporary Poems on Wales and Welsh American*

Experience (2009), lies in its terms of inclusion, for this, as Lloyd writes, is a broad collection of 'poets with an American background who have written in sustained and considered ways about the Welsh culture, landscape, and people ... in some cases over the course of a lifetime'.[48] The volume presents a selection of Lloyd's own poems together with the work of nine others such as Sarah Kennedy, whose poems are based on eighteenth-century domestic manuscripts from the National Library of Wales; Jon Dressel, a poet with Welsh and German roots, based in Saint Louis, MO, who has also lived in Wales; and Joseph P. Clancy, an American scholar, translator, and poet who has lived in Wales since his retirement from teaching in New York.

Lloyd's anthology includes a number of poems by Denise Levertov (1923–1997), one of the most respected American poets of her generation. Levertov was born in England and educated at home by her parents, a Welsh mother and Russian Jewish father who had converted to Anglicanism and become a priest. She married an American, and after moving to the United States after the war, in 1948, she published many volumes of poetry which, over the course of her career, won a number of prestigious awards. In the 1960s, during the Vietnam War, she became an anti-war crusader and activist, and she often wrote consciousness-raising poetry that reflected her political positions and social views. Welsh poet Menna Elfyn has written about her own early discovery of American women poets whose worlds were not limited to poetry; among these was Levertov, who was discovering her Welsh roots.[49] Levertov visited Wales and wrote both memoirs and poems in collections, including *Life in the Forest* (1978) and *Candles in Babylon* (1982), about the strength of her relationship to her Welsh mother and the importance of family stories from Wales.

Notes

1. Ned Thomas, 'Parallels and Paradigms', in *A Guide to Welsh Literature*, vol. VII: *Welsh Writing in English*, ed. M. Wynn Thomas (Cardiff: University of Wales Press, 2003), 310–26.
2. Kirsti Bohata, *Postcolonialism Revisited*, Writing Wales in English (Cardiff: University of Wales Press, 2004), 157.
3. Thomas, 'Parallels and Paradigms', 310.
4. Stephen Constantine, 'British Emigration to the Empire-Commonwealth since 1880: From Overseas Settlement to Diaspora?', *The Journal of Imperial and Commonwealth History* 31, 2 (2003): 17.

5. 'Awdl – Gwlad fy Nhadau' ('Ode – Land of my Fathers'), in Rowland Walter (Ionoron Glan Dwyryd), *Caniadau Ionoron: Yn Cynnwys Awdlau, Cywyddau, Englynion a Phenillion* (Utica, NY: T. J. Griffiths, 1872), 101.

6. Leslie Norris, *The Complete Poems*, ed. Meic Stephens (Bridgend: Seren, 2008), 222.

7. See, for example, the work of Jerry Hunter in 'Y Traddodiad Llenyddol Coll' ('The Lost Literary Tradition') in *Taliesin* 118 (2003): 13–44; and Hunter, *Sons of Arthur, Children of Lincoln: Welsh Writing from the American Civil War* (Cardiff: University of Wales Press, 2007); and also Esther Whitfield, 'Mordecai and Haman: The Drama of Welsh America', in *American Babel: Literatures of the United States from Abnaki to Zuni*, ed. Marc Shell (Cambridge, MA: Harvard University Press, 2002), 93–116.

8. Bill Jones, 'Writing Back: Welsh Emigrants and their Correspondence in the Nineteenth Century', *North American Journal of Welsh Studies* 5, 1 (2005): 23–45. See also Alan Conway, *The Welsh in America: Letters from the Immigrants* (Minneapolis: University of Minnesota Press, 1961).

9. Idwal Lewis, 'Welsh Newspapers and Journals in the United States', *National Library of Wales Journal* 2, 3–4 (1942): 124–30.

10. William David Jones and Aled Jones, 'The Welsh World and the British Empire, *c.* 1851–1939: An Exploration', *Journal of Imperial and Commonwealth History* 31, 2 (2003): 57–81.

11. Glyn Williams, *The Welsh in Patagonia: The State and the Ethnic Community* (Cardiff: University of Wales Press, 1991), 248.

12. W. Brooks, 'Welsh Print Culture in Y Wladfa' (PhD diss., Cardiff University, 2012), 115–19 for poetry in *Ein Breiniad* ('Our Privilege'); and 147–8 for literature in *Y Drafod*.

13. John Evans, 'Thomas John Evans', *Dictionary of Welsh Biography*, http://wbo.llgc.org.uk/en/s-EVAN-JOH-1863.html (accessed 15 November 2017).

14. R. D. Thomas (Iorthryn Gwynedd), *Hanes Cymry America/Cyflawn Olygfa ar Gymry America*, 2 vols. (Utica, NY: T. J. Griffiths, 1872), I, 57–60 and II, 42–3.

15. William D. Jones, *Wales in America: Scranton and the Welsh 1860–1920* (Cardiff: University of Wales Press, 1993), 87.

16. Maria James's poems are included in Caroline May, ed., *The American Female Poets* (Philadelphia: Lindsay and Blakiston, 1848); Rufus Wilmot Griswold, ed., *The Female Poets of America* (Philadelphia: Henry C. Baird, 1848); and Katie Gramich and Catherine Brennan, eds., *Welsh Women's Poetry 1460–2001: An Anthology* (Dinas Powys: Honno, 2003), 96–102.

17. Llew Llwyfo (Lewis William Lewis), *Gemau Llwyfo: sef detholion o brif cyfansoddiadau a chaneuon* (Utica, NY: T. J. Griffiths, 1868), and *Y Creawdwr: Cerdd Ddysg; hefyd Cerdd Goffa gan Dewi Dinorwig* (Utica, NY: T. J. Griffiths, 1871).

18. Llwyfo, *Gemau Llwyfo*, 5–6, 274.

19. Eirug Davies, 'Celtic Languages in North America, Welsh', in vol. I of *The Celts: History, Life and Culture*, ed. John T. Koch (Santa Barbara, CA: ABC-CLIO, 2012), 169. The volume of poetry Davies refers to is Richard Prichard, *Blodau'r Gorllewin* (Chicago: R. R. Meredith a'i Feibion, 1877).

20. Aled Jones and Bill Jones, *Welsh Reflections: Y Drych & America 1851–2001* (Llandysul: Gomer Press, 2001), 25–6, 155. On the serial novel in the Welsh-language press, see Aled Gruffydd Jones, *Press, Politics and Society: A History of Journalism in Wales* (Cardiff: University of Wales Press, 1993), 193.

21. On the Welsh translations of *Uncle Tom's Cabin*, see Melinda Gray, 'Uncle Tom's Welsh Dress: Ethnicity, Authority and Translation', in *Beyond the Difference: Welsh Literature in Comparative Contexts*, ed. Alyce von Rothkirch and Daniel Williams (Cardiff: University of Wales Press, 2004), 173–85; and Jerry Hunter, *I Ddeffro Ysbryd y Wlad: Robert Everett a'r Ymgyrch yn erbyn Caethwasanaeth Americanaidd* (Llanrwst: Gwasg Carreg Gwalch, 2007), 177–85.

22. R. Owen, 'David Lloyd Davies (Dewi Glan Peryddon)', Dictionary of Welsh Biography, http://yba.llgc.org.uk/en/s-DAVI-LLO-1881.html (accessed 12 November 2017); and Jones and Jones, 'The Welsh World and the British Empire', 69.

23. Melinda Gray, 'Language and Belonging: A Welsh-Language Novel in Nineteenth-Century America', in *Multilingual America: Transnationalism, Ethnicity, and the Language of American Literature*, ed. Werner Sollors (New York: New York University Press, 1998), 91–102.

24. Bill Jones, 'Margaret E. Roberts', in *Making it in America: A Sourcebook of Eminent Ethnic Americans*, ed. Elliott Robert Barkahn (Santa Barbara, CA: ABC-CLIO, 2001), 315–16; also Jones and Jones, *Welsh Reflections*, 74–5.

25. Jones, *Wales in America*, 109.

26. Dafydd Rhys Williams, *Llyfr Pawb* (Utica, NY: T. J. Griffiths, 1908), 13–14.

27. Sam Ellis, *Ann y Foty yn Mynd i'r Môr* (Utica, NY: T. J. Griffiths, 1913).

28. Jones, *Wales in America*, 106.

29. Ronald L. Lewis, *Welsh Americans: A History of Assimilation in the Coalfields* (Chapel Hill: University of North Carolina Press, 2008), 307–8.

30. Daniel Williams, 'From Hay-on-Wye to the Haymarket Riots: William Dean Howells and Wales', *New Welsh Review* 64 (2004): 57.

31. William Dean Howells, 'American Literature in Exile', in *Literature and Life: Studies* (New York and London: Harper and Brothers, 1902), 204–5.

32. Tony Curtis, 'Grafting the Sour to Sweetness: Anglo-Welsh Poetry in the Last Twenty-Five Years', in *Wales, the Imagined Nation: Studies in Cultural and National Identity*, ed. Tony Curtis (Bridgend: Poetry Wales Press, 1986), 100.

33. Stan Sanvel Rubin and Bruce Bennett, 'A Sound Like a Clear Gong', transcript of a conversation that took place on 9 October 1991, in *An Open*

World: Essays on Leslie Norris, ed. Eugene England and Peter Makuck (Columbia, SC: Camden House, 1994), 15.

34. Rubin and Bennett, 'A Sound Like a Clear Gong', 20.

35. See the essays in Daniel Westover, ed., *Leslie Norris*, triple special issue, *Literature and Belief* 29 and 30, 1 (2010).

36. Curtis, 'Grafting the Sour to Sweetness', 119.

37. Gwyneth Lewis, 'Byw Mewn Bydoedd Cyfochrog', in *Gweld Sêr: Cymru a Chanrif America*, ed. M. Wynn Thomas (Caerdydd: Gwasg Prifysgol Cymru, 2001), 205.

38. See Peter Daniels, *In Search of Welshness: Recollections and Reflections of London Welsh Exiles* (Tal-y-bont: Y Lolfa, 2011); Emrys Jones, ed., *The Welsh in London 1500–2000* (Cardiff: University of Wales Press on behalf of the Honourable Society of Cymmrodorion, 2001).

39. See Raymond Williams,*Who Speaks for Wales? Nation, Culture, Identity*, ed. Daniel G. Williams (Cardiff: University of Wales Press, 2003).

40. Ifor ap Glyn, *Cerddi Map yr Underground* (Llanrwst: Gwasg Carreg Gwalch, 2001), 8–9.

41. Gareth Miles, 'Dylanwad Patagonia ar y Meddwl a'r Dychymyg Cymreig', *Taliesin* 125 (2005): 97–102; and see also Esther Whitfield, 'Empire, Nation and the Fate of a Language: Patagonia in Argentine and Welsh Literature', *Postcolonial Studies* 14, 1 (2011): 85.

42. Whitfield, 'Empire, Nation', 80.

43. See ibid.; and Esther Whitfield, 'Welsh-Patagonian Fiction: Language and the Novel of Transnational Ethnicity', *Diaspora: A Journal of Transnational Studies* 14, 2/3 (2005): 333–48.

44. See Geraldine Lublin, 'Fred Green a'r "Cyfeillgarwch Parhaol" rhwng y Cymry a Brodorion Patagonia', *Taliesin* 133 (2008): 81–92.

45. See 'Princes of Gwynedd', http://princesofgwynedd.com (accessed 15 September 2017).

46. C. W. Sullivan III, '*Y Mabinogion* a Ffuglen Ffantasi America' in *Gweld Sêr*, ed. Thomas, 99–116. See also Chapter 31 in this volume.

47. Richard Eder, 'Crosscurrents of Identities: British Soldiers, German Soldiers, and a Welsh Barmaid', *Books of the Times*, 2 May 2007, www.nytimes.com /2007/05/02/books/02eder.html (accessed 24 November 2017).

48. David Lloyd, ed., *Other Land: Contemporary Poems on Wales and Welsh-American Experience* (Cardigan: Parthian, 2008), ix.

49. Menna Elfyn, 'America: Cymhlethdod o Achlysuron' in *Gweld Sêr*, ed. Thomas, 77.

30

Literary Periodicals and the Publishing Industry

LISA SHEPPARD

In her 1928 lectures at Girton and Newnham Colleges, Cambridge, Virginia Woolf insisted that 'a woman must have money and a room of her own if she is to write fiction'.[1] The 'room', as well as referring to a literal space where a woman could write free from her duties as wife and mother, has a more figurative meaning, too: a place in the literary tradition or, perhaps more importantly, her own tradition of women's writing upon which to draw, and space to develop, explore new themes and publish. In short, she must have a literary identity. With this, as well as the necessity of access to financial assets, in mind, one might easily apply Woolf's comments to the situation faced by Welsh writers at various times during the twentieth and twenty-first centuries, both female and male, writing fiction, poetry, and literary criticism, in both Welsh and English. Whereas medieval poets turned first to the Welsh princes and then the nobility for sponsorship, from the mid-twentieth century, writers, as well as the literary presses and periodicals that have published their work, and the literary festivals that have supported them, have been sponsored by a variety of grants, subsidies, and funding bodies. While their predecessors participated in a tradition of praise for their patrons, this chapter will argue that modern authors, poets, and critics have had to challenge various conventions, practices, and agendas (literary or otherwise) in order to make 'room' for certain bodies of literature, new styles of writing, and approaches to criticism, as well as a particular means of national cultural expression. Ironically, while sponsorship has helped carve out this space, the vital support such funding provides has at times been under threat, and Welsh literature, its authors and institutions, has faced pressure to demonstrate the relevance and viability of its work.

The first section of this chapter will focus on Welsh publishing houses, particularly the development of those presses publishing Welsh writing in the English language, providing a home-grown outlet for anglophone writers who had previously had to turn to the London scene to get their work into print. The section will discuss how these developments created a space for a literature for and of English-speaking Wales, as well as the carving out of a space for Welsh writing in English in the literary tradition of Wales. The chapter's second section will examine literary periodicals in both languages and their roles in shaping, but also challenging, the Welsh literary tradition. It will focus in particular on women's contributions, as well as the Welsh-language periodical *Tu Chwith* and its attempts to create a space for new, experimental voices in literature and criticism who could not find an outlet elsewhere. The third section of the chapter will focus on literary festivals, concentrating for the most part on the annual National Eisteddfod and the platform, the literal and metaphorical 'llwyfan', it provides for Welsh-language literature. A constant theme throughout each section will be the financial support that is essential to the continuation of the literary ventures discussed. As the chapter will demonstrate, this funding has on occasion been under threat for various reasons, but the Welsh literary scene's ability to adapt during the late twentieth and early twenty-first centuries has meant that important steps have been taken to help ensure Welsh literature in both languages will have the money and the room to thrive in the future.

A Literature of their Own? The Development of Welsh Presses Publishing in English

This section will concentrate on Welsh literary presses, and particularly the development of English-language presses in Wales. In doing so, it will examine how this enabled anglophone Wales to develop a literature of its own: free of the demands of London publishers, authors were able not only to write what they wanted but also to write for a Welsh audience and provide anglophone Wales with a literature that spoke to them and their experiences. It will discuss, too, the challenges posed by a relatively small audience in Wales and to what extent the publication of English-language texts in Wales has allowed anglophone writers to participate in a Welsh literary tradition in which their place has often been questioned.

When we consider the history of Wales's literary presses in the 1800s and 1900s, it seems that the place of Welsh-language literature in Welsh life was cemented by the many publishing houses that developed throughout the period. By the end of the nineteenth century, there were high levels of literacy among the Welsh public and Welsh-language presses had developed to satiate the market for reading material. Thus, despite the fact that the number of Welsh speakers declined throughout most of the twentieth century, from the beginning of the period they were serviced by presses publishing the work of Welsh(-language) authors, and others would be established throughout the century. Gwasg Gomer (Gomer Press) was established in 1892 in Llandysul on the Cardiganshire-Carmarthenshire border and is run to this day by the same family, publishing work by some of the Welsh language's foremost contemporary writers, including Tony Bianchi, Catrin Dafydd, and Mererid Hopwood. Even before that, Thomas Gee established Gwasg Gee (Gee Press) in 1808, which was bought in the 1930s by the renowned author Kate Roberts and her husband Morris Williams. Gwasg Gee continued to publish until 2001. Gwasg y Lolfa (Y Lolfa Press) was established in 1967 by Robat Gruffudd, son of Welsh-language authors J. Gwyn Griffiths and Kate Bosse-Griffiths, during an 'exciting period of fun and protest'.[2] It was the unofficial publisher of Cymdeithas yr Iaith Gymraeg (The Welsh Language Society), and by now, along with Gomer Press, it is the main publisher of Welsh-language literature. Along with Gwasg Carreg Gwalch (Carreg Gwalch Press), established in 1980 by the poet Myrddin ap Dafydd, these presses and others have ensured that there have been publishers to whom Welsh-language writers can turn throughout the twentieth century and at the beginning of the twenty-first.

Although originally established to publish Welsh-language material, both Gomer and Y Lolfa have published English-language works for many years, many of them written by Welsh authors or authors with a connection to Wales.[3] Presses such as Seren (established in 1981 as the publishing imprint of the literary periodical, *Poetry Wales*), Parthian (established in 1992), and Cinnamon Press (established in 2005) are among the foremost publishers of English-language writing in Wales, but Welsh authors writing in English have not always been so well served by home-grown presses. The authors often acknowledged as the founding mothers and fathers of modern Welsh writing in English generally had to turn to London-based presses in order to get their work published. The location of publication is a significant factor in the discussion of the anglophone Welsh literature produced between the end of the nineteenth century and the middle of the twentieth century. The lack of means of literary production in English in Wales in this period, as well as the want of associated societies and practices (such as reviews, literary scholarship, and so on) raised questions regarding the 'Welshness' of Welsh writing in English, questions which still affect the field today.

Saunders Lewis's 1938 lecture, 'Is There an Anglo-Welsh Literature?', is probably the best known of these ruminations upon the national affiliation of literature in the English language written in or about Wales. Lewis suggests that there is no 'body of compositions in the English language that may be called a separate literature having its peculiar traditions and character, and acknowledged as Anglo-Welsh'.[4] One reason he gives is that the so-called 'Anglo-Welsh' writers do not write for their fellow compatriots – they are 'déracinés'.[5] The question of who was the intended audience of writing in English about Wales is one that has continued to receive attention from critics. In his seminal study of twentieth-century Welsh writing in English, *A Hundred Years of Fiction*, Stephen Knight begins by foregrounding this issue:

> In 1900, Welsh fiction in English was basically a way for English readers to tour Wales without leaving the armchair. There were collections of stories about travel, topography and the quaint, even mysterious, habits of the natives; there were novels where visiting characters and readers alike could be excited by beauty and strangeness, but never surrender their English values; there were historical novels to laud, in a safe past, the military spirit of this country which was now subservient to England; there was even the beginning of a fiction of industry, though nothing yet like the radical challenge to appear thirty years ahead. Most of this fiction produced in London, often in handsome formats, partly by Welsh writers, in some way validated the colonial presence of the English and their language in Wales by shaping the views given of Wales and the Welsh people in terms of English attitudes and various forms of condescending curiosity.[6]

According to Knight, at the turn of the twentieth century anglophone writing about Wales was mainly intended for an English audience, or readers with an arguably colonialist attitude towards Wales. He also suggests that there is a relationship between the values and sentiments expressed in such works, their usual readers, and the fact that they are published in London. In the sense that these texts were written only 'partly by Welsh writers', published in England, and appealed to 'English values' or 'English attitudes', one might be forgiven for asking to what extent this body of literature can be called 'Welsh'.

For Saunders Lewis, there was no question as to which nation Anglo-Welsh literature belonged to – speaking of Dylan Thomas, he declared, 'There is nothing hyphenated about him. He belongs to the English.'[7] His main objection to the 'déracinés' of Anglo-Welsh writers was that, unlike their Anglo-Irish counterparts, they were unable to draw upon Welsh traditions as these had not generally taken root in anglophone Welsh society. Although Lewis makes no specific reference to the fact that authors had to turn to London publishers to see their work in print, it is not difficult to see how this situation could be partly responsible for the links he sees between

Welsh writers, the literary traditions and communities of England, and the lack of comparative traditions and communities in English-speaking Wales.

Given these deficiencies, one might also ask to what extent Anglo-Welsh literature in this period belonged to the Welsh, in terms of being read by the people of Wales. The anglophone Welsh author Rhys Davies himself commented upon the relationship of his own English-language writing to London publishers and to Welsh readers, describing both relationships in negative terms. He begins his 1933 essay, 'Writing About the Welsh', thus:

> It is not a pleasant job to write stories of the Welsh people. Writing in English, one is published in London and one has to battle with the ancient recoil of the English from Welsh life. Across the border in Wales, books – and especially novels – are looked upon as frivolous unnecessary things that cost money to obtain, that frequently encourage sin and blasphemy and provoke indolence, that sometimes even dare to criticise the purity of Welsh life. There, who needs a book beyond the Bible? . . . The Welsh look upon all other books with disfavour.[8]

For Davies, then, the Welsh author writing in English in this period suffers doubly – his subject is unappreciated by his English publisher and his medium is vilified by his compatriots. In referring to the Welsh in the third person throughout, one assumes he is addressing a non-Welsh audience, and, most interestingly, it would seem he is trying to persuade their 'neighbours' of their 'charms'.[9] It is perhaps most telling that, in doing so, he reiterates some of the colonial stereotypes Knight identifies in earlier examples of writing about Wales.[10] Although Wales's positive attributes (singing, David Lloyd George, beauty spots, and seaside resorts) are noted and the English reprimanded for thinking of the Welsh as dishonest, Davies himself refers to the 'miniature nationality' of the Welsh and describes them as 'still bucolic and simple', 'beautifully child-like', 'seldom ambitious to conquer the world', but also 'immoral and shocking'.[11] By stating at the end that enduring and unspoilt qualities such as these are what compel him to write about Wales, it would seem that his work might, as Knight suggests in relation to texts at the turn of the twentieth century, be written solely for English readers and with English imaginings of Wales in mind.

It could be argued, however, that Davies's essay is an example of what postcolonial theorists like Homi Bhabha would term 'mimicry', the process by which a colonial subject mimics the colonizer until they appear to be 'almost the same but not quite'.[12] Bhabha argues that the colonial subject's mimicry of their masters ultimately produces a 'slippage' – a difference despite the similarity – that threatens the entire colonial project.[13] Davies's clichéd assertion that the Welsh 'will abuse you and beat you out of the place with leeks as tall as a policeman's truncheon' should you do anything but flatter them draws attention to the other stereotypical images of Wales repeated in the essay and casts doubt upon them. Davies, then, appears to 'play both games simultaneously', to borrow Katie Gramich's phrase – that is, his writing addresses both Welsh and English audiences at once.[14] A number of anglophone Welsh authors, including Dannie Abse, Alun Richards, and Bernice Rubens, have written poetry and fiction which, although read and appreciated by wider British audiences, address Welsh audiences too and demonstrate in many cases an allegiance to Wales. While these writers published their work for the most part in the second half of the twentieth century, we can arguably attribute a similar quality to earlier writers and works, too, such as Amy Dillwyn's *The Rebecca Rioter* (1880) and Allen Raine's *A Welsh Singer* (1897). Having asserted that English-language writing about Wales produced by London publishers at the turn of the twentieth century was directed in the main towards English audiences, Knight subsequently goes on to argue that Raine's work challenged this practice. He notes that her work 'realised a real, if partial, separate identity and value for a Welsh social culture' and 'test[ed], even inherently resist[ed], the constraints of English colonial publishing practices'.[15]

In considering the effect of the lack of home-grown publishers on anglophone Welsh writing and its sense of belonging to a Welsh literary culture and tradition, we must also take into account its effect on the content of the work and the career of the author. Saunders Lewis hinted at this in his aforementioned lecture when he noted, 'Not literature only, as a thing, must suffer when there are wrongs in the social body, but the writers of imagination must suffer in their minds and powers.'[16] Discussing the reception of Dylan Thomas's early works, Ned Thomas echoes the Kenyan writer Ngũgĩ wa Thiong'o's discussion of African writers' contributions to English literature, as he argues that: 'They are said to bring a new vitality to the language. They are praised not for being transparent but for being painted differently. Is that a good thing? It's not good for the individual writers. They make a name, but they may then have to live up to having this special exotic quality, rather than pursuing their interaction with their own societies.'[17] Knight goes so far as to argue that this arrangement had a detrimental, and sometimes deathly, effect on Welsh writers and readers alike:

It directed Dylan Thomas away from potent modernist fiction, delayed the career of Gwyn Thomas, contributed to the tragic death of Dorothy Evans, denied readers a substantial number of novels by rejection and influenced in negative ways a whole series of major writers, from Jack Jones to Emyr Humphreys.[18]

Knight gives further attention to the delayed career of Gwyn Thomas, the Rhondda-born novelist, dramatist, and schoolteacher. Discussing the rejection of Thomas's first novel, *Sorrow for Thy Sons*, by Victor Gollancz in 1937, Knight notes, quoting from Dai Smith's 1986 introduction to the novel, that it was refused in part because 'it crucially lacked "the relief of beauty that Rhys Davies can give"'.[19]

Even with the establishment of periodicals such as *Poetry Wales* in 1965 and of institutions such as the Welsh Arts Council in 1967 (both of which owe much to the poet and critic, Meic Stephens), many of the problems faced by Anglo-Welsh writers in terms of claiming their place in the Welsh literary tradition persisted. Poet, critic, and founder of the influential periodical *Dock Leaves*, Raymond Garlick, noted in an interview in 1990, 'One odd thing about this Anglo-Welsh business in Wales is that it's as though every generation of writers has to do it all over again.'[20] The many articles that appeared in Welsh periodicals throughout the latter half of the twentieth century discussing the status of Anglo-Welsh writing seem to testify to this.[21]

The problem of finding a Welsh readership remained too. Despite the relatively stable history of Welsh-language publishing in Wales, one might argue that authors in Welsh as well as English in Wales face difficulties in finding readers. In a 1995 essay entitled 'Writing on the Edge of Catastrophe', Welsh-language author Wiliam Owen Roberts declared, 'The population of Wales i[s] about 2,500,000. Out of this, about 400,000 to 500,000 speak Welsh. This includes everyone and as a writer that's my entire possible audience. The percentage of people who actually read literature in Welsh must be anyone's guess.'[22] Ned Thomas has argued that the situation for anglophone Welsh writers is comparatively worse. Discounting for a moment the possible world-wide audience for Welsh writing in English, he argues: 'In theory [in Wales] there are half a million Welsh speakers and three million English speakers ... So there should be six times the audience [for anglophone Welsh writing], but all the evidence is that there isn't six times the audience, indeed there isn't sometimes half the audience for a book in English in Wales that there is for a book in Welsh.'[23]

In recent decades the way in which Welsh writing in English, particularly prose fiction, has been produced has undergone a significant change. For Knight, by the turn of the twenty-first century, even more important than the increasing number of Welsh authors writing in English is the fact that the majority of this body of literature is being published in Wales.[24] Since its establishment, the Welsh Arts Council, and more recently, Literature Wales and the Welsh Books Council, have subsidized individual authors, presses, and literary periodicals. This and the establishment of Wales-based presses publishing English-language literature have made it easier for writers to choose to publish in Wales and to lessen any decrease in income they might incur by not working with wealthier presses further afield. The importance of this funding to authors writing in Wales, and the opportunity it provides to work with Wales-based presses, was demonstrated in 2016, when the Welsh Government proposed reducing the Welsh Books Council's funding by 10.6 percent in 2016–17. The decision was reversed when hundreds of authors, academics, and readers signed letters of protest, arguing that home-grown publishing was essential to a vibrant national literary culture.[25]

The development of anglophone Welsh presses does not mean that contemporary Welsh authors no longer turn to London-based presses; some of the period's most successful and well-known offerings have been published in London, including Trezza Azzopardi's *The Hiding Place*, published in 2000 by Picador, and John Williams's *Cardiff Dead*, published in the same year by Bloomsbury. Unlike their predecessors at the turn of the twentieth century, however, these authors' depictions of their native Wales are far from romantic and mysterious. Rather than depicting their homeland as an untouched wilderness, these novels, set in Cardiff and tracing the city's changing faces during the second half of the twentieth century up to the post-devolutionary period, present the reader with characters who struggle to keep pace with a Wales that has undergone dramatic changes over the course of their lives. Nor does the Wales of these novels offer an escape to the reader – these are tales of poverty, dysfunctional families, and industrial decline, abusive fathers in Azzopardi's case, and drugs and gangs in that of Williams. Azzopardi's and Williams's Wales is not isolated, quaint, or backwards either – their Cardiff is a multicultural city, their characters multi-ethnic, and their stories internationally connected.

In addition to these successful London-published titles, many English-language volumes have appeared from Wales-based presses. Seren Books, founded in 1981 and based in Bridgend, offers a range of fiction and poetry from well-known writers such as Sheenagh Pugh and Dannie Abse, as well as helping to advance the careers of younger authors including Christopher Meredith, Francesca Rhydderch, Mike Jenkins, and Owen Sheers. The press also publishes a quarterly poetry magazine, *Poetry Wales*, founded in 1965, which gives poets further opportunity to share their work. Amongst its more recent successful ventures are the book series, 'New Stories from the Mabinogion', where authors including Fflur Dafydd, Gwyneth Lewis, and Lloyd Jones re-imagine and relocate the famous medieval Welsh prose tales in a range of different temporal and geographical settings; and the 'Seren Classics' series which, as well as reissuing original Seren texts such as Meredith's *Shifts* (1989), enables texts such as Caradoc Evans's infamous *My People* (1915) and works by Rhys Davies, Margiad Evans, and Gwyn Thomas, previously published across the border, to be published in Wales at last.

Another English-language press which plays a central role in the current development of Welsh writing in English is the Cardigan-based Parthian, established in 1992 by Richard Lewis Davies. In addition to publishing many international authors, Parthian has published work by some of contemporary Welsh writing in English's most influential and important voices including Rachel Trezise, Stevie Davies, Deborah Kay Davies, Cynan Jones, and Tristan Hughes. It is also responsible for publishing the 'Library of Wales' series under the general editorship of Dai Smith, a series which was commissioned following the Welsh Assembly Government's Culture, Welsh Language and Sport Committee's review of Welsh Writing in English (2004).[20] The series brings back into print novels and short story collections, many of which were originally published by London presses, including the works of Gwyn Thomas, Arthur Machen, Dorothy Edwards, and Raymond Williams. As well as providing contemporary authors with an opportunity to publish new work in Wales, these presses are concerned with illuminating Welsh writing in English's past and creating links with the Welsh language tradition in order to claim anglophone literature as part of Wales's literary heritage.

A Voice of their Own: Reframing the Discussion and Challenging Convention in Literary Periodicals

Prior to developments such as the establishment of the Welsh Arts Council and literary subsidies from the Welsh government, literary periodicals provided anglophone authors with their best opportunity to have their work published in Wales. Literary periodicals such as Keidrych Rhys's *Wales* (1937) or Gwyn Jones's *The Welsh Review* (1939), which appeared prior to the Second World War, created, according to Malcolm Ballin, 'a presumption that there is a need within Wales for at least one periodical that will give publishing opportunities for Welsh writers in English while facilitating debate on literary and social topics'.[27] During the second half of the twentieth century and into the new millennium, this need was met by three titles in particular: *Poetry Wales*, *Planet*, and *The New Welsh Review* (as this final title is currently known). Meic Stephen's *Poetry Wales* first appeared in 1965 at a time when '[w]e were very few in number who had any interest in what we called Anglo-Welsh literature', and *Planet* was first published in 1970, edited by Ned Thomas.[28] Established in 1988, *The New Welsh Review* may appear to be youngest of the three, but it is a new incarnation of *The Anglo-Welsh Review* (1958), which itself was a reinvention of *Dock Leaves*, established by Raymond Garlick and Roland Mathias in 1949. The increased 'Welshness' of the title over time might signal an increased confidence in claiming that identity, or a determination to contribute to a national literature. But it also signals an ability to adapt to the changing nature of the anglophone Welsh literary scene and to bring it within an institutional framework.

Turning to the periodicals of the Welsh-language literary scene, it might be tempting to think of these Welsh-language publications as more conservative, simply because they serve a minority language community. Of course, some of them are affiliated with what can be termed the Welsh-language literary 'establishment'; these include the Welsh Academy's *Taliesin*, established by the poet Gwenallt (David Jones) in 1961 (which ran until 2016), and *Barddas*, the magazine of Y Gymdeithas Gerdd Dafod (the society for traditional Welsh strict-metre poetry), which was established in 1976 under the editorship of the *Prifeirdd*, 'chief poets', Alan Llwyd and Gerallt Lloyd Owen. On occasion, however, Welsh-language literary periodicals have challenged the literary status quo. Two periodicals in particular, *Y Traethodydd* ('The Essayist') and *Tu Chwith* ('Inside Out'), did this by giving, respectively, a voice to women and a forum for new, experimental voices, with both groups making a significant contribution to the development of Welsh-language literature and criticism.

At first glance, *Y Traethodydd* might appear to be the most conservative of all current Welsh periodicals. It is the journal of the Presbyterian Church in Wales, and, having been established in 1845, it is the longest-published periodical in the Welsh language, offering quarterly articles about theology, philosophy, history, and literature, as well as occasional poems and short fictional pieces. In 1986, however, an issue of *Y Traethodydd* appeared, guest-edited by Kathryn Curtis, Marged Haycock, Elin ap Hywel, and Ceridwen Lloyd-Morgan, which focused on women's writing, women's history, and feminist literary criticism, and included interviews with female authors and poets. This significant moment in the journal's history was part of a pioneering endeavour in Welsh literary circles to rediscover and promote women's voices against the backdrop of what could be described as an overwhelmingly male literary tradition in both languages. A year later, Honno Press was established with the aim of publishing contemporary women's writing and rediscovering the forgotten female voices of Wales in English and Welsh, a project which arguably reached its peak in 2003 with the publication of *Welsh Women's Poetry 1460–2001*, the first bilingual anthology of female-authored poetry from Wales, edited by Catherine Brennan and Katie Gramich.

The challenge *Y Traethodydd*'s venture constituted to the established literary scene in Wales was highlighted by the publication a year later of *Blodeugerdd Barddas o Farddoniaeth Gymraeg yr Ugeinfed Ganrif* ('An Anthology of Twentieth-Century Welsh-Language Poetry', 1987), edited by Alan Llwyd and Gwynn ap Gwilym. The anthology is mainly remembered for causing what Gerwyn Wiliams has described as the 'Anthological Scandal of the Century', as it contained very few examples of work by women and ignored completely the work of Menna Elfyn, arguably the best-known contemporary Welsh-language poet.[29] Alan Llwyd defended these editorial decisions by claiming, 'It was not our job to search for Marxist poets and Feminist poets. Our job was to search for worthy poems, not second rate or clueless poems about some fashionable or popular topics at the time . . . it is not our fault that not one great Marxist poet or one great Feminist poet has come to light in Wales.'[30] The continuing need for interventions such as those made by *Y Traethodydd* and Honno is perhaps further demonstrated by the output of the Library of Wales series, which, like Llwyd's comments, might hint at the androcentric nature of some Welsh canon-forming activities. The series is dominated by male writers, and its short story anthologies, *Story: I* and *Story: II* (both published in 2014 and edited by Dai Smith), contain eighteen stories by women as opposed to forty-two by men. The role of periodicals more generally in symbolically challenging a historically male-dominated literary tradition is confirmed by the wealth of female editors who have run English- and Welsh-language literary periodicals in recent years. From 2000 until the publication of its final issue in 2016, *Taliesin* was edited by women (Manon Rhys and Christine James from 2000 to 2009, and Siân Melangell Dafydd and

Angharad Elen from 2009 to 2016), and the most recent resident editors of *Tu Chwith* were Rhiannon Marks and Elin Angharad (2011–13). Zoë Skoulding began editing *Poetry Wales* in 2008, and Nia Davies took on this role in 2014; *Planet* has been edited by Emily Trahair since 2012, and before that was edited by Jasmine Donahaye from 2010; and *New Welsh Review* has had a female editor since 2002 (Francesca Rhydderch from 2002 to 2008, Kathryn Gray from 2008 to 2011, and Gwen Davies since 2011).

Alan Llwyd's comments in response to the criticism directed at *Blodeugerdd o Farddoniaeth Gymraeg yr Ugeinfed Ganrif* gave fuel to other Welsh literary voices that have until relatively recently been obscured. The rejection of 'Marxist' and 'Feminist' voices, and the focus on poetry that was deemed 'worthy' is indicative of the mistrust towards more modern schools of literature and critical theory within Welsh-language literary circles until the closing decades of the twentieth century. The establishment of the periodical *Tu Chwith* in 1993 by students at Aberystwyth University sought to rectify this issue. Taken from Iwan Llwyd's crown-winning poem, 'Gwreichion' ('Sparks'), at the 1991 National Eisteddfod, the periodical's title, which has the sense of being 'inside-out', 'back-to-front', or even 'left-field', was indicative of its original aim to turn the Welsh literary tradition and the way it was studied on its head. In their first editorial, written as two separate texts presented side by side, Simon Brooks and Elin Llwyd Morgan signalled their commitment to literary theory and the promotion of innovative creative and critical writing which would challenge the hegemony of Welsh intellectual, cultural, and literary institutions.[31] *Tu Chwith* was symptomatic of wider changes in Welsh-language literature throughout the late 1980s and early 1990s. These developments can be analysed as a reaction to the disappointment of the overwhelming rejection of devolved government for Wales in the 1979 referendum, and the subsequent realization that new literary voices and ideas were now needed to challenge, deconstruct, and transform the dominant images and icons of Welsh life reified by the literary and cultural establishment.

It was not easy for these new voices to be heard, however. In 1982, Iwan Llwyd Williams and Wiliam Owen Roberts, who would become two of the most prominent contributors to this new mode of writing in Welsh, high-lighted the issue of access. They argued that the relatively small community of writers, readers, and critics in Wales meant that it was all too easy for 'one particular opinion or perspective regarding our poetry' to dominate, and this had indeed already taken place, in their opinions.[32] They describe the difficulty of finding something new to say when forced to write within the confines of what they term 'the select tradition':

> Creating poetry that is relevant in the Welsh language is by now painful and very hard work. Very often poets feel it is an act of necrophilia. Discovering new images is by now difficult, with the language itself contracting. It is much easier to stick to the tradition's means of expression (e.g., cywydd, awdl, englyn); the tradition's images; the tradition's legends; the tradition's myths, the tradition's diction; the tradition's nostalgia, without once doubting the validity of it all ... It is an impossibly difficult task, in this situation, for young poets to discover their own voices and means of expression, and those of their society. Indeed, how can they create images and diction that interpret the true reality of their lives in the present historical epoch, when prominent critics, the educational system (school and university) and to a great extent, eisteddfodic adjudication, continue to promote that which we consider to be 'the myth of the select tradition'.[33]

Despite the opportunities for reinvention, revision, or even iconoclasm that a well-documented and familiar canon can offer writers wishing to experiment, Williams and Roberts demonstrate that this very canon often meant authors would face criticism for failing to follow the well-trodden literary path.

Although it first appeared eleven years after Williams and Roberts were writing, one of *Tu Chwith*'s founding aims was to address this issue, 'to present writers who have not published work before, or writers who want to venture in a new direction in their literary careers'.[34] It would focus on prose, publishing only bold poetry that was unlikely to be accepted for publication by other Welsh language periodicals.[35] *Tu Chwith*'s editors implied that other Welsh literary magazines should be added to Williams and Roberts's list of the institutions which maintained the homogeneity of the tradition. Later in the first issue, they challenged one of the editors of another of these periodicals, Gerwyn Wiliams of *Taliesin*, regarding his desire for his publication to be 'a mirror for the wealth and diversity of our cultural universe'.[36] To *Tu Chwith*, merely reflecting the cultural scene rather than taking a specific editorial stance meant nothing more than solidifying the existing hegemonic approach to writing and criticism.

Like Williams and Roberts, too, the editors of *Tu Chwith* identified the need for a more varied critical approach to Welsh literature, and this seems to be the editors' main concern. Its co-editor, Simon Brooks, wrote scathingly on this topic, arguing that 'criticism in Wales continues to fatten on a mindset which is rooted in the intellectual fads of the past ... There is a desperate need to find alternative intellectual foundations and to adopt postmodernism as the conceptual system that will stimulate our contemporary cultural approach.'[37] In his view, critics had not engaged with postmodern and poststructural ideas as boldly as literary authors had done. The period between the publication of Williams and Roberts's article and the first issue of *Tu Chwith* was one of postmodernist experimentation with form and genre, particularly in the field of the novel, which saw the publication of ground-breaking texts which engaged with, deconstructed, and laughed at the tradition. These included Wiliam Owen Roberts's *Bingo!* (1985); *Y Pla* ('The Plague', 1987), which deconstructed the sentimental Welsh historical novel; Robin Llywelyn's allegorical *Seren Wen ar Gefndir Gwyn* ('A White Star on a White Background', 1991); and Mihangel Morgan's *Dirgel Ddyn* ('Mysterious Man', 1993), whose main female character shared her name with the eighteenth-century hymn writer, Ann Griffiths. These texts' engagement with postmodernist, poststructuralist, and Marxist ideas was largely new in the Welsh context.[38] Whilst creative writers were deconstructing the tradition, *Tu Chwith* saw the need to 'redefine the essence of our critical foundations'.[39]

The reaction amongst other Welsh literary circles to these dismantlings and redefinitions arguably provides further evidence that such a platform was needed and perhaps goes some way to explaining why relatively few attempts at engaging with critical theory have been made in the Welsh context, even to this day. Whilst the reaction to the aforementioned postmodern fiction in Welsh was mixed, as Angharad Price has documented,[40] those who attempted to use contemporary literary theory were the subject of fierce criticism. The opposition intensified with the publication of *Sglefrio ar Eiriau* ('Skating on Words'), in 1992, edited by John Rowlands, a series of critical engagements with Welsh literature grounded in different literary theories, which was itself compiled as a response to the unrepresentative *Blodeugerdd* edited by Alan Llwyd and Gwynn ap Gwilym and their editorial policy of selecting poems based on their 'quality and standard'.[41] In response to Rowlands's volume, Llwyd described the field of critical theory as 'a pile of complexity and confusion', calling its proponents 'alleged critics' and accusing them of 'literary Stalinism'.[42] Brooks has argued that the reactions of Llwyd and other anti-theorists (many of whom are well-regarded poets and authors in their own right) who describe critical theory as 'futile', 'incomprehensible', 'false', and 'untrue' are grounded in their particular view of the Welsh nation and language:[43]

> This response [i.e. the negative response to theory] is a reaction against the putative threat to a complete Welsh world. A perfect world, an ideal world that faces annihilation from outside. Here are authors who have sought refuge in Welsh-language literature, and very often in *cynghanedd* ... Welsh-language literature is a place for a soul to find peace. The intractable interference of theory in this refuge is almost psychological violence.[44]

Considered in a different light, it is possible to read *Tu Chwith*'s attempt to redefine Welsh critical foundations as an attempt to redefine the foundations of 'Welshness'. The result was to help diversify the voices that spoke of and for Wales and broaden the stories Wales told about itself.

It is important to remember that *Barddas*, too, was and is an important magazine in its own right, a forum which has given a voice to poets writing in *cynghanedd* and in the strict metres unique to Wales. Ironically, in light of Brooks's challenge to those who sought a refuge in Welsh literature and *cynghanedd*, it is *Barddas* which is the last remaining of three long-running and influential Welsh literary magazines. In 2015 *Taliesin* did not secure funding from the Welsh Books Council for publication beyond 2016 and has subsequently ceased production. After having its funding from the Welsh Books Council withdrawn in 2011, *Tu Chwith* continued for a while, but no new issue has appeared since August 2014. The guest editors of that issue, Gruffudd Antur and Elis Dafydd, refer to *Tu Chwith*'s uncertain future going forwards due to lack of funds, by quoting Elin Llwyd Morgan's original 1993 editorial where she warns that financial conditions mean there can be no guarantee that the journal can enjoy a prolonged run.[45] It appeared that Welsh-language periodical publishing was in a dire situation until two new magazines were established in 2016. One of these was *Y Stamp*, an online and print publication edited by students which attempts to follow in the footsteps of *Tu Chwith*. The other was *O'r Pedwar Gwynt* ('From the Four Winds'), which has since provided an injection of energy and intellectualism to the genre of Welsh periodicals. The ambitious editorial vision of critic Sioned Puw Rowlands and author Owen Martell is demonstrated by their inclusion of exciting literary pieces, insightful literary criticism, and political discussion. *O'r Pedwar Gwynt* offers a challenge to the Welsh reading public to engage with new ideas, which may prove vital in shaping the future of a devolved Wales. The periodical's initial success, combined with that of *Y Stamp*, suggests a brighter future ahead for Welsh periodical publishing than could have been imagined in the early 2010s.

A 'Llwyfan' of their Own: The Eisteddfod and Welsh Literary Festivals and Awards

Whilst the debates surrounding the relevance of literary theory to the Welsh context are worthy of exploration, that they exist at all will come as no surprise to those familiar with the highlight of the literary calendar in Wales, the National Eisteddfod. Held annually during the first week of August at different locations from year to year, this event is the focal point for Welsh literary creation and criticism. Literary entries, be they novels, short stories, microfiction, long *awdlau* or *pryddestau*, or the four-line *englyn un odl union*, are judged anonymously, and audiences wait with bated breath for the judges to announce whether anyone has been deemed worthy of winning. Given these circumstances it is perhaps unsurprising that some critics of Welsh literature prefer the liberal humanist approach of considering the 'quality' of the work and search for 'excellent poems',[46] rather than engaging in, for example, feminist or Marxist critiques. That is not to say, though, that the literature produced for *eisteddfodau* is not current, or experimental, or varied. The nation's interest in literature and the diversity of work created there can be attributed partly to the many local *eisteddfodau* held across the country, and to the Urdd Eisteddfod (the annual eisteddfod for the Urdd Gobaith Cymru, the Welsh League of Youth) and Young Farmers' Eisteddfod (also for young people), all of which provide fertile grounds for the development of new writing talent. Whilst literary events such as the Hay Festival, held annually in the border town of Hay-on-Wye, may bring international attention and feature the giants of world literature, the National Eisteddfod and its pavilion are the focal point of the literary calendar when Welsh-language writing, criticism, and publishing take centre stage.

The history of the Eisteddfod has been well documented by literary historians such as Hywel Teifi Edwards and Alan Llwyd, and an account of the eisteddfod tradition, from the one held by the Lord Rhys of Deheubarth in Cardigan Castle in 1176, to Iolo Morganwg's invention of the Gorsedd of the Bards, to the establishment of the National Eisteddfod in the modern sense in the latter half of the nineteenth century, is beyond the scope of this chapter.[47] Llwyd's interesting study of the early days of the modern National Eisteddfod until 1918 explores the festival's identity as 'Prifysgol y Werin', the 'University of the *Gwerin*', that is, the mainly rural, Welsh-speaking, Nonconformist folk, where one could receive a literary education of sorts without having to venture across the border to Oxford or Cambridge, or to one of the newly established University Colleges at Lampeter (1822) and

Aberystwyth (1872). Llwyd notes how, ironically, the modern National Eisteddfod, first held in 1881 in Merthyr Tydfil, was instigated in the main by the educator Sir Hugh Owen and others, 'British imperialists' rather than 'Welsh nationalists',[48] in order to:

> present an image of Wales as a respectable, responsible, decent nation, and a capable nation that possessed a natural and innate inclination for the arts: to turn the nation in to a respectable and valuable member of the Empire.[49]

Llwyd argues that this attempt was halted by the Welsh people, particularly the most patriotic among them, and the Gorsedd, which was, and still is, committed to the Welsh language.[50] Subsequent years saw the Gorsedd and the newly established university colleges of Wales wrangle for control of the Eisteddfod, particularly during Professor John Morris-Jones's attempts to overhaul the kinds of topics set for competitions in the early twentieth century. Given this recent history of Wales's main literary festival, it is little wonder that opposition towards literary theory, perceived to be too intellectual, is voiced by the traditionalists of the Welsh literary scene and that the polarization of 'academic' readers and, albeit well-read, 'lay' readers permeates the responses to some of the recent prize-winning works.[51]

The nickname 'Prifysgol y Werin' may seem rather apt if one considers how the lifestyles and values of the *gwerin* seem to permeate some of the National Eisteddfod's literary adjudications, but many other instances do much to disprove the idea that adjudications are necessarily old-fashioned or puritanical. It might be tempting to hold the strictures of Nonconformism responsible for the criticism faced by Gwenallt in 1928 for his *awdl*, 'Y Sant' ('The Saint'), for example, which, as Hywel Teifi Edwards explains, depicted 'his subject's struggle with his libido'.[52] One judge, John Morris-Jones himself, condemned it as 'a heap of filth'[53] and the Chair was not awarded to Gwenallt. Two years previously, however, Gwenallt had won the Chair for another *awdl*, 'Y Mynach' ('The Monk'), in which 'carnal desires' were a theme.[54] In 1924 too, Prosser Rhys famously won the crown with his *pryddest* 'Atgof' ('Remembrance'), which depicted homosexual relations. These inconsistencies point towards a far more complex relationship between the Eisteddfod and its main audiences. The same changeable attitudes can be seen in the idea that the Eisteddfod and Welsh literature are essentially rural phenomena, or that Welsh poets are more suited to writing about rural life. In 1978, there was much opposition to the Eisteddfod being held at Cardiff that year, and when no entry to the Chair competition, on the theme of 'Y Ddinas' ('The City') was deemed worthy of winning, some commentators discussed the events in an apocalyptic tone. Alan Llwyd, for example, opened his editorial to the first issue of *Barddas* published in the wake of the Eisteddfod by exclaiming 'Atal y Gadair!' – 'The withholding of the Chair!'[55] Llwyd and Gwynn ap Gwilym went on to argue that *cynghanedd* was essentially a rural craft incompatible with urban life and that it was unacceptable to expect rural poets to write about the city.[56] Others, such as John Rowlands, took a more holistic view of Cardiff's 1978 Eisteddfod and declared it 'llwyddiant diamheuol o safbwynt llenyddol' – 'an undoubted success from a literary point of view' – despite no poet being deemed worthy of the highest accolade in Welsh-language literature.[57]

Placing the concerns of commentators in 1978 in their historical context, one can argue that they are in some sense a product of their time: Mudiad Adfer ('The Restoration Movement') had been established by Cymdeithas yr Iaith Gymraeg ('The Welsh Language Society') to protect Wales's Welsh-speaking heartlands from rising levels of in-migration; the journey to 1979's devolution referendum was under way, and with it the defining, challenging, and criticizing of certain concepts and perceptions of Wales and Welshness, particularly those related to the Welsh language which was increasingly confined to areas of west and north-west Wales. Simon Brooks's argument regarding the tendency of some authors and critics to seek refuge from change and uncertainty in the Welsh language and its literary traditions are to some extent an echo of Hywel Teifi Edwards's comments that Eisteddfod adjudications have demonstrated 'a reluctance to force the language into testing situations' and that the choice of competition themes shows a tendency to '[keep] to the beaten track of well-trodden Welsh concerns'.[58] But the literature produced by competitors often refuses the confines prescribed by others. As far back as 1915, T. H. Parry-Williams won the crown for a *pryddest* on the theme of 'Y Ddinas' ('The City'), and at the 2008 National Eisteddfod, held in Cardiff, Hywel Griffiths's 'Stryd Pleser' ('Pleasure Street') received the same accolade for a poem celebrating the Welsh capital's vibrant Welsh-speaking community. Even those who miss out on awards due to linguistic concerns are not resigned to obscurity. One example is the original manuscript for Llwyd Owen's controversial novel, *Ffawd, Cywilydd a Chelwyddau* ('Fate, Shame and Lies'), which was denied victory in the Daniel Owen Memorial Prize at the 2005 Eisteddfod because of its use of non-standard language (which, it could be argued, is merely the speech of its Cardiff-born narrator), despite judges describing the author as the competition's 'greatest genius'.[59] Owen's revised manuscript (which retained its narrator's distinctive Cardiff Welsh) was subsequently published by Y Lolfa and signalled the beginning of a successful career for its author; it has also contributed significantly to the continuing development of a genre of fiction about young Welsh speakers living and working in Cardiff.

In response to the charge that writers are reluctant to explore new themes and forms, one need only look to 2002's National Eisteddfod, held at Tyddewi (St David's), to see how Welsh poets and authors have managed to respond creatively and ingeniously to topics grounded in traditional themes and rules. Myrddin ap Dafydd won the Chair with a sequence of poems on the theme of 'Llwybrau' ('Paths' or 'Routes'), in which he experimented with *cynghanedd* and combined old metres to create new ones; Angharad Price won the Prose Medal for her postmodern interpretation of the Welsh tradition of memoir writing, *O! Tyn y Gorchudd* ('O, pull off the veil'), a hymn title framing an imaginary autobiography of an aunt, Rebecca Jones, who had died as a young girl; and in the Crown competition, Aled Jones Williams claimed the prize with his experimental prose poem in response to the theme of 'Awelon' ('Breezes') about a person undergoing cancer treatment, a text which comprised small separate poems in boxes and ended challengingly with a single comma in a box.

Not only do the seemingly conservative rules and expectations fail to stifle writers' creativity and innovation, in many ways some of them, particularly the language rule, seem absolutely necessary if literature in a minority culture such as that of Welsh is to thrive and if its best authors are to receive the credit they deserve. The National Eisteddfod is the only literary competition at a nationwide level that gives a platform – a 'llwyfan', one might say – solely to Welsh-language literature written by people of all ages and backgrounds. Other major British literary prizes, such as the Man Booker or the coveted places on the *Granta* list of new writers, are open only to those who write in English. There is, of course, a need to recognize the successes of anglophone writers, as Wales does with its bilingual Book of the Year awards, and could do still more to promote Welsh authors writing in English. These prizes, however, all too often claim that their shortlisted authors represent 'the future of literature in Britain', seemingly without entertaining the possibility that literatures in other languages, native or imported, exist in today's Britain, let alone have a role in its tomorrow. In this sense, one could even argue that the Eisteddfod's prizes are some of the most inclusive of British literary awards – authors are not required to come from certain countries (as was the case until 2014 with the Man Booker), and, grouping all competitions together, Eisteddfod entrants are not limited in genre or form.

Recent conversations about 'modernizing' the National Eisteddfod seem conveniently to forget these positive points and to ignore the practices of the wider arts scene in Wales and the rest of the United Kingdom. Whilst it is true that, as Hywel Teifi Edwards notes, eisteddfodic practices demonstrate a reverence for tradition,[60] it does not necessarily follow that this is synonymous with being outmoded. In 2012, while Education and Skills Minister for the Welsh Government, Leighton Andrews, announced the establishment of a Task and Finish Group to explore ways in which the Eisteddfod could be updated, including making it more appealing to those who do not speak Welsh. The biggest collective opposition to this review was produced by none other than *Tu Chwith*, whose young contributors responded to the Task and Finish Group's assignment in an Eisteddfod-themed issue.[61] Guest editor Llŷr Gwyn Lewis noted that 'possibly, the Task Group's biggest weakness is its lack of young voices' – that is, representatives of the young people experiencing the Maes (the 'field' on which the National Eisteddfod is held) independently for the first time, the young musicians trying to get themselves noticed, the children collecting freebies from the stands, and the young writers bringing a contemporary feel to traditional literary activities.[62] The response from *Tu Chwith* is significant, not only because it demonstrates that young people want a say in the future of this old institution but also because their comments question in particular what could be deemed the most revisionist of the Task and Finish Group's considerations, namely the possibility of holding the festival at one site each year, and making it more appealing to non-Welsh speakers.

The question of language is one that has received much attention as the Task and Finish Group have undertaken their review. Welsh speakers are familiar with the charge that their language is exclusive or 'middle class' and that their culture must adapt and become more open and accessible. Some, however, have expressed a concern that the Eisteddfod's core audience and contributors (Welsh speakers), and its entire *raison d'être* of promoting Welsh-language literature and culture across Wales, are being forgotten. Llŷr Lewis encapsulates this predicament when he says, 'As with every other element of Welsh-language life, it must be ensured that the Eisteddfod is not something for a faction of the ubiquitous "middle class". But woe betide us too if we disregard that class completely.'[63] Simon Brooks has ruminated on this issue, comparing the Eisteddfod to other festivals that celebrate a particular marginalized culture or way of life such as Cardiff's gay community's Mardi Gras, the Traveller Community's Appleby Fair, or Black History Month. He argues that while festivals such as these must welcome participation from those whom they do not necessarily immediately represent, 'it is a completely different matter ... to argue that the Mardi Gras should be changed to make heterosexual people feel more comfortable, or to worry that Black History Month doesn't feature enough white faces.'[64] Although Leighton Andrews gave his reassurance that the language rule used in the Eisteddfod's competitions would not change, it is understandable that the review caused concern about what role Welsh-language literary and musical competitions might have if the Eisteddfod 'Maes' was to become more bilingual. Presented in 2013, the review's recommendations did not make specific reference to increasing the bilingualism of the festival, although it does specify that it should aim to 'attract visitors from all corners of the world'.[65] In relation to the National Eisteddfod's importance, Brooks argues that 'every culture needs its own space'.[66] As the Eisteddfod develops over the coming years, time will tell how it manages to strike a balance between attracting visitors from a variety of backgrounds, whilst also engaging and representing its core Welsh-speaking audience.

Conclusion

Throughout this chapter Welsh literature's search for a platform, be it with presses, periodicals, or festivals, has been a constant theme. So too has the threat some of these important and embattled platforms have faced. There is scope, however, for a discussion of how the support given to Welsh literature by these types of literary activism could be increased. The Hay Festival, for example, is comparable to the Eisteddfod in the sense that it is an annual literary and cultural festival but conducted through the medium of English rather than Welsh. While some have argued that the festival deserves Welsh government funding on the basis that it provides a platform for Welsh writing in English,[67] it could also be argued that the internationally renowned writers it succeeds in attracting – Toni Morrison and Salman Rushdie are among recent starring guests – tend to overshadow Wales's own anglophone literature and culture showcased at the festival. There is scope for celebration and indeed hope for the future, with the introduction of aspects of Welsh writing in English to GCSE and A-Level curricula in Wales. Interventions in publishing, such as those made by the Library of Wales series, have ensured that texts are available for study as well as creating a sense of an existing body of literature that is worthy of attention at a national level. The challenge will be ensuring that students' interest is maintained and that material to enhance their studies continues to be available. The vital work done by the Association for Welsh Writing in English, established in 1984, is worthy of note here, as its members strive to promote Wales's anglophone literature (and the study of many aspects of Welsh life in both languages) to those engaged in the secondary and higher education sectors, as well as the world of publishing, policy, and heritage. The work done by another Welsh press, the University of Wales Press, has been invaluable in this respect too, with its critical series in both Welsh and English: 'Y Meddwl a'r Dychymyg Cymreig' ('The Welsh Mind and Imagination'), established in 1995 under the editorship of John Rowlands and most recently edited by Gerwyn Wiliams; and 'Writing Wales in English', established in 2004, edited then by M. Wynn Thomas and currently by Kirsti Bohata and Daniel G. Williams. Both these series, supported by many other titles in Welsh and English, provide rich and often innovative engagements with Welsh literature across a broad range of themes, genres, and time periods. One only has to look at the Bibliography in this volume to see the enormous contribution made by the University of Wales Press to supporting and publishing Welsh literature of all periods in both languages.

As is the case with many other outlets, however, these series and publications (as well as those of other presses, and academic journals too), which provide the basis for scholarship in the field of what has been termed 'Wales Studies', are threatened financially. In 2013, the Higher Education Funding Council for Wales (HEFCW) announced that the funding for publications in the field of Wales studies, upon which presses like the University of Wales Press depend, would come to an end in 2016.[68] Whilst there is much to be positive about regarding the current state of Welsh literary culture, further challenges lie ahead, not only for creative authors but for literary critics and academic writers too. While some of Wales's medieval poets would travel the country in search of a paying audience, there is work to be done to ensure that today's writers and critics do not have to wander too far from the hard-won outlets for Welsh literary expression in order to find an audience and the financial support that is essential to their continued development.

Notes

1. Virginia Woolf, 'A Room of One's Own', in *A Room of One's Own / Three Guineas*, ed. Michèle Barrett (London: Penguin, 1993), 3.
2. *Y Lolfa*, 'History of Y Lolfa', www.ylolfa.com/en/ycwmni.php (accessed 5 June 2017).
3. Catrin Dafydd's *Random Deaths and Custard* (2007) and its sequel *Random Births and Lovehearts* (2015), along with her Welsh-language writing, are published by Gomer, and Tony Bianchi's *Bumping* (2010), set in his native

Northumberland, is published by Alcemi, the English-language publishing wing of Y Lolfa.

4. Saunders Lewis, *Is There an Anglo-Welsh Literature?* (Caerdydd: Cangen Caerdydd, Urdd Graddedigion Prifysgol Cymru, 1939), 5.

5. Ibid., 11.

6. Stephen Knight, *A Hundred Years of Fiction: From Colony to Independence* (Cardiff: University of Wales Press, 2004), xi.

7. Lewis, *Is There an Anglo-Welsh Literature?*, 5.

8. Rhys Davies, 'Writing About the Welsh', in *Ten Contemporaries*, ed. John Gawesworth (London: Joiner and Steele, 1933), 41.

9. Ibid., 42.

10. Knight, *A Hundred Years of Fiction*, xi.

11. Davies, 'Writing About the Welsh', 41–52.

12. Homi K. Bhabha, *The Location of Culture* (London and New York: Routledge, 1994), 86.

13. Ibid.

14. Katie Gramich, 'Both In and Out of the Game: Welsh Writers and the British Dimension', in *A Guide to Welsh Literature*, vol. VII: *Welsh Writing in English*, ed. M. Wynn Thomas (Cardiff: University of Wales Press, 2003), 255.

15. Knight, *A Hundred Years of Fiction*, 25.

16. Lewis, *Is There an Anglo-Welsh Literature?*, 13.

17. Ned Thomas, quoted in David T. Lloyd, 'Interview with Ned Thomas', in *Writing on the Edge: Interviews with Writers and Editors of Wales* (Amsterdam and Atlanta, GA: Rodopi, 1997), 16. See also Ngũgĩ wa Thiong'o, *Decolonising the Mind: The Politics of Language in African Literature* (London: James Currey, 1986).

18. Knight, *A Hundred Years of Fiction*, xi–xii.

19. Ibid., 94.

20. Raymond Garlick, quoted in David T. Lloyd, 'Interview with Raymond Garlick', in *Writing on the Edge*, 24.

21. For a detailed overview of when and where articles such as these appeared, see Malcolm Ballin, *Welsh Periodicals in English 1882–2012* (Cardiff: University of Wales Press, 2013).

22. Wiliam Owen Roberts, 'Writing on the Edge of Catastrophe', in *Peripheral Visions: Images of Nationhood in Contemporary British Fiction*, ed. Ian A. Bell (Cardiff: University of Wales Press, 1995), 77.

23. Thomas quoted in Lloyd, 'Interview with Ned Thomas', in *Writing on the Edge*, 17.

24. Knight, *A Hundred Years of Fiction*, xi.

25. For the full text of three such letters signed *en masse* by Welsh authors, academics, and publishers, see *WalesArtsReview.org*, www.walesartsreview .org/wbc-cuts/ (accessed 16 December 2017).

26. See Welsh Assembly Government, *Welsh Writing in English: A Review* (Culture, Welsh Language and Sport Committee, 2014).

27. Ballin, *Welsh Periodicals in English*, 93.

28. Meic Stephens, quoted in David T. Lloyd, 'Interview with Meic Stephens', in *Writing on the Edge*, 32.

29. Gerwyn Wiliams, 'Sbecian ar Dir Newydd', *Barn* 302 (1988): 6. This and all subsequent translations of Welsh-language texts in this chapter are mine.

30. Alan Llwyd, 'Golygyddol', *Barddas* 135-7 (Gorffennaf/Awst/Medi 1988): 12.

31. Elin Llwyd Morgan and Simon Brooks, 'Prolog', *Tu Chwith* 1 (1993): 5-7.

32. Iwan Llwyd Williams and Wiliam Owen Roberts, 'Myth y Traddodiad Dethol', *Llais Llyfrau* (October 1982): 10.

33. Ibid., 10-11.

34. Morgan and Brooks, 'Prolog', 5.

35. Simon Brooks, 'O Tel Quel i Tu Chwith', *Tu Chwith* 1 (1993): 5-6.

36. Gerwyn Wiliams, quoted in Anon., 'Y Cyfnodolyn Cymodlon: Cyfweliad â *Taliesin*', *Tu Chwith* 1 (1993): 71.

37. Brooks, 'O Tel Quel i Tu Chwith', 5-6.

38. Cf. Caradog Prichard, *Un Nos Ola Leuad* (Dinbych: Gwasg Gee, 1961).

39. Brooks, 'O Tel Quel i Tu Chwith', 6.

40. See Angharad Price, *Rhwng Gwyn a Du: Agweddau ar Ryddiaith Gymraeg y 1990au* (Caerdydd: Gwasg Prifysgol Cymru, 2002).

41. Llwyd, 'Golygyddol', *Barddas* 135-7: 14.

42. Alan Llwyd, 'Golygyddol', *Barddas* (Jul/Aug 1992): 6-12.

43. Simon Brooks, '"Yr Hil": Ydy'r Canu Caeth Diweddar yn Hiliol?', in *Llenyddiaeth Mewn Theori*, ed. Owen Thomas (Caerdydd: Gwasg Prifysgol Cymru, 2006), 7-8.

44. Brooks, '"Yr Hil": Ydy'r Canu Caeth Diweddar yn Hiliol?', 9.

45. Gruffudd Antur and Elis Dafydd, 'Golygyddol', *Tu Chwith* 40 (2014): 9.

46. Llwyd, 'Golygyddol', *Barddas* 135-7: 14.

47. See Chapter 15 in this volume for an account of the eisteddfod and the *gorsedd* in the eighteenth century.

48. Alan Llwyd, *Prifysgol y Werin: Eisteddfod Genedlaethol 1900-1918* (Cyhoeddiadau Barddas, 2008), 14.

49. Ibid., 15.

50. Ibid.

51. See, for example, Price, *Rhwng Gwyn a Du*, for an analysis of the response to Robin Llywelyn's Prose Medal-winning novel of 1992, *Seren Wen ar Gefndir Gwyn* (Llandysul: Gwasg Gomer), which led to the polarization of the Welsh reading public in precisely these terms.

52. Hywel Teifi Edwards, *The Eisteddfod*, Writers of Wales (Cardiff: University of Wales Press, 1990), 45.

53. John Morris-Jones, quoted in Edwards, *The Eisteddfod*, 45.

54. Edwards, *The Eisteddfod*, 45.

55. Alan Llwyd, 'Golygyddol', *Barddas* 22 (Medi 1978): 2.

56. Ibid., 2–3; also Gwynn ap Gwilym, 'Cymraeg y Pridd a'r Concrit', *Barn* 203–4 (1979): 259–64.

57. John Rowlands, 'Wrth Fynd Heibio', *Barn* (Medi 1978): 323.

58. Edwards, *The Eisteddfod*, 43.

59. Elfyn Pritchard, Bethan Mair, and Catrin Puw Davies, 'Gwobr Goffa Daniel Owen', in *Cyfansoddiadau a Beirniadaethau Eisteddfod Genedlaethol 2005, Eryri a'r Cyffiniau*, ed. J. Elwyn Hughes (Llandybïe: Gwasg Dinefwr ar ran Llys yr Eisteddfod, 2005), 99.

60. See Edwards, *The Eisteddfod*.

61. See *Tu Chwith* 39 (Haf 2013).

62. Llŷr Gwyn Lewis, 'Golygyddol', *Tu Chwith* 39 (Haf 2013): 8.

63. Ibid.

64. Simon Brooks, 'Dyfodol yr Eisteddfod', *Barn* 598 (Tachwedd 2012): 4.

65. National Eisteddfod Task and Finish Group, 'Report and Recommendations of the National Eisteddfod Task and Finish Group', October 2013 (Welsh Language Division, Department for Education and Skills, Welsh Government), 31. Available at http://gov.wales/docs/dcells/publications/131 023-report-and-recommendations-national-eisteddfod-task-and-finish-group-en.pdf (accessed 15 December 2017).

66. Brooks, 'Dyfodol yr Eisteddfod', 4.

67. Ibid.

68. For a discussion of what impact this might have on the study of Welsh life, including the study of Welsh literature in both languages, see M. Wynn Thomas, 'The Future of Welsh Studies', website of the University of Wales Press, 15 February 2014, www.uwp.co.uk/the-future-of-welsh-studies/ (accessed 16 Decemeber 2017).

'Beyond the Fields We Know': Wales and Fantasy Literature

SUSAN ARONSTEIN

Mapping the Territory

Fantasy narratives begin with a map, a representation of the world the reader is about to enter; this map designates the borders of the territory, inscribes the landscape, identifies major cities, and marks ethnic and political divisions. Maps are an invitation to enter and explore. They delineate the space, marking landmarks and topographies, but leave the direction to the traveller, the details to the chronicler. Think of the chapter that follows as a map to, rather than a chronicle of, the world of Welsh fantasy literature. It will set the borders of the territory – and, as we know, territorial borders are arbitrary limits, often subject to dispute – leaving, like all maps, others unmarked, and locating divisions. As the mapmaker, I have tried to provide an accurate sketch of my subject, but it is only a sketch. Others might dispute my borders; redraw my landscape; feature other cities.[1]

Some might say that any map to the realm of Welsh fantasy is a medieval one, inscribed by early Welsh tales set in what Jeffrey Gantz, in his introduction to the *Mabinogion,* calls 'the mystic Celtic past of has been and never was'.[2] In their view, these tales of an enchanted Otherworld that lies, to use Lord Dunsany's famous phrase, just 'beyond the fields we know', have not been *adapted to* fantasy but have *always-already been* fantasy.[3] This concept of a magical, mystical medieval Welsh literature, however, is not medieval at all; it is, rather, a by-product of the nineteenth century's invention of the 'Celts' and the 'Celtic'. Beginning with the Romantics, writers and thinkers turned from the modern industrial and urban world to find inspiration in a Celtic past and present associated with the natural and the supernatural, with sprites and fairies, thus sparking an interest in Celtic landscape, litera- ture, and lore at the same time that they cemented colonialist associations between the so-called Celtic margins – Wales, Scotland, Cornwall and Ireland – and the pre-urban, pre-industrial, pre-rational past.

If the Romantics invented the Celtic landscapes with their fairy forests, magical mountains, and enchanted lakes, Matthew Arnold invented the people and literatures that landscape produced. Arnold coined the term 'Celtic Magic' to designate an inherent connection between the Celt and his/her landscape: 'the infinite life of Nature, her weird power and her fairy charm . . . the fairy-like loveliness of Celtic nature. Magic is the word to insist on.'[4] Like the Romantics' construction of Celtic landscapes, however, the connection Arnold makes here between the Celts and the fairy realm of nature is not free from political and ideological agendas, or without cultural consequences. On the one hand, it appears to romanticize and valorize the Celts' association with the natural and the magical; on the other, it codes them as primitive and superstitious, backward and non-rational. As such, Arnold's treatise contributed to what Helen Fulton identifies as a 'fundamentally English colonialist ideology whose strategy [was] to construct the alterity of Wales and Ireland as subaltern cultures and to evaluat[e] the Celts in much the same way as Joseph Conrad evaluated the Africans, that is as the whimsical and almost dangerously enticing "other" of the soberly and politically astute Anglo-Saxons'.[5]

Fulton's analogy between Arnold's construction of the 'Celt' and Conrad's construction of the 'African', between fairies and the racial Other, is also found in nineteenth-century discussions of elves and faeries, which often euhemerized them as stemming from a branch of the evolutionary tree that included the newly discovered African Pygmies.[6] Regardless of whether they were euhemerized as an alternate branch on the evolutionary tree, the last of a pre-Celtic race, the descendants of the druids, or perceived as spirits, elementals, or relics of a more magical time, fairies manifested the persistence of the primitive in 'alternative and autonomous worlds' found in 'the remote Celtic areas, the increasingly diminishing, though still wild regions of Cornwall, Wales, Scotland, and of course, Ireland'.[7]

This nineteenth-century coding of the Celtic lands as a land out of the misty past, the home of supernatural beings, enchantments, and wonders, a place set aside from modernity and progress, an alternative to the rational, industrialized, and urban centres of economic and political power was a two-edged sword. For some, these lands preserved a lost ideal, a past full of wonder, spiritual and transcendent truths, and a connection to the natural to which we must return. For others, they harboured the atavistic, a primitive world opposed to progress, rationality, beauty, and truth, whose grotesque

inhabitants erupted into an unsuspecting present. For natives and nationalists, this construction of Celtic lands and heritage could serve both as 'part of
a special and thus precious ethnic and national heritage' and as an image to
embrace and capitalize on.[8] For the colonists, both those who longed for the
lost realm of Faerie, and those who feared its primitive rites, it served to
appropriate and marginalize the people who inhabited those lands.

Celtic fantasy stems from this appropriation and marginalization of the
Celts and serves as a counterpart to the fantasy narratives founded in
a nineteenth-century medievalism that valorized kings and knights, hierarchy
and chivalry – and, above all, an orderly society in which everyone from
rulers and lords to women and peasants knew their place. Tales rooted in
nineteenth-century visions of this chivalric, Anglo-European Middle Ages –
stretching from William Morris's *The Wood Beyond the World* (1894) and *The
Well at the World's End* (1896), through Tolkien's *Lord of the Rings* (1954–5), to
its many descendants – are set in an ultimately rational and patriarchal world
of kings and battles, heroes and quests. Those that rise from the same era's
invention of a misty Celtic ever-present past, however, take place in a land of
'green and burning trees in which anything can happen', a realm saturated
with the mystical and the numinous, characterized by what Helen Fulton
identifies as 'magical naturalism'. In these worlds 'the fantastic is
a naturalized form of reality', and magic is not agential, not the result of
spells and charms, but innate, simply *there*.[9] Their 'common elements'
include, according to a popular fantasy website, not kings and heroes, but
'pagan religions, druids, [and] matriarchal societies'.[10]

Welsh fantasy is a subgenre of Celtic fantasy; thus, our map will inscribe
a topography that includes enchanted forests, haunted hills, mystical lakes,
and shimmering realms in the mist, inhabited by fairies and pagans, druids
and goddesses. Within this topography, I draw four divisions – think of them
as generic kingdoms – although, as with all such divisions, the borders
between them are not as firm as the map might suggest: the land of the
Mabinogion, Haunted Hills, Cosmic Battlefields, and Celtic Realms. Within
each of these realms, I will sketch a few representative textual-cities, mostly
focusing on those that are either founded in Welsh legends and traditions or
set in an enchanted Wales. Both the land of the *Mabinogion* and Haunted Hills
are ancient kingdoms, and I have traced their histories – a move from the
explorations of Celtic Magic and Celtic primitivism of the late nineteenth and
early twentieth centuries, through a post-Tolkien turn to epic concerns, to
a New Age-tinged focus on a return to wonder and mysticism. Cosmic
Battlefields and Celtic Realms are relatively new kingdoms, scions of the

old, but very much rooted in twentieth-century concerns: power and identity, gender and race.

The Story as It Should Have Been: 'Recovering' the *Mabinogion*

The invention of Wales as an enchanted land, home to fairies and spiritual
wonders, was aided by the translation and dissemination of the medieval
Welsh tales that, courtesy of Lady Charlotte Guest, came to be collectively
known as the *Mabinogion*.[11] First published as a bilingual edition in seven
volumes between 1838 and 1845, reissued in a three-volume set in 1849, and in
an English-only edition in 1877, Guest's work, which made the Welsh tales
available for the first time to a non-Welsh-speaking audience, was immensely
popular in both England and the United States, where Sidney Lanier adapted
it as part of *The Boys' Library of Legend and Chivalry* (1881).

Guest and Lanier found in the *Mabinogion* a testimony to a primitive, wild,
lawless people, a curious tradition to be preserved and compared, less than
favourably in Lanier's case, to Thomas Malory's *Morte Darthur* and continental romances. Kenneth Morris, writing in the early twentieth century, however, found not a primitive past but mystical and spiritual truths, and rather
than seeking, as did Guest and Lanier, to preserve and transmit an ancient
text, Morris purports to recover a lost one. He presents his *The Fates of the
Princes of Dyved* (1914) as a restoration of the 'pristine purpose' of the Welsh
tales that reignites 'their day star' from the dim 'rushlight' preserved by Guest
and Lanier.[12] This 'rushlight,' Morris argues, contains corrupted fragments of
'The Story of the Soul, leading it from the first freedom of Gwynfyd, down
into the depths of Abred and incarnation, to the gates of that path of freedom,
and then onward to the heights'; his version of the *Mabinogion*, he promises,
will recover the true story of Pwyll and Rhianon:[13]

> Man comes in contact with that inward and divine light which is to make
> a god of him at last ... She will take queenhood in the Island of the
> Mighty ... in Dyfed, he will share his throne with her, will become as it
> were her disciple; since she is the brightest and most beautiful vision of his
> days.[14]

Morris's theosophical 'restoration' of the Four Branches is an ingenious
work, liberally reworking plot, drawing on several Welsh motifs and myths,
and beautifully echoing Guest's style to create a new myth centred on Pwyll's
journey to wisdom and immortality. The story of Pwyll and Rhianon,

Pryderi's quest for the lost birds of Rhianon, Rhianon's penance, Madog's thwarted conquest of Dyved, and the final restoration of the faithful to youth and vigour is cast as an allegory, but Morris's prose also paints an enchanted Otherworld of mists and shadows, with 'glamor in it, and wonder, and the whole of the shadowy beauty of the world': the transformation of Rhianon's enchanted hall into a place of sorrow where 'there was no hue nor beauty left in the plates of pearl and amethyst, nor in the drinking-horns of polished diamond; the best of them might have been of tin-garnished lead'; an enchanted maiden, 'her white fingers twinkling and wandering over the strings of a harp, bringing out of them such music as he had never attained the hearing of during his whole life'; a hall 'suddenly filled with light and music; three bright jewels of song fluttered among the rafters, more light-giving than the moon of heaven'.[15] Inspired by nineteenth-century constructions of Celtic magic and leavened with occult mysticism, Morris's work stands as the first example of a post-medieval, Celticized fantasy world.

It was not, however, a popular success; nor was the next novel based on the Four Branches, Evangeline Walton's 1936 version of the tale of Math, Gwydion, Arianrhod, Lleu Llau Gyffes, and Blodeuwedd, published under the unfortunate title of *The Virgin and the Swine*, and while the medieval Welsh tales continued to circulate in translations and children's editions, it was 1964 before another author turned to them for inspiration and created a new myth. Set in a land that their author insists 'is not Wales' and yet closely resembles it, and taking characters and motifs straight from the *Mabinogion*, Lloyd Alexander's *Chronicles of Prydain* pentalogy tells a tale that owes more to Tolkien in tone, theme, and world-view, than it does to its Welsh roots.[16] The series follows the adventures of Taran of Caer Dallben and his companions as they seek to fend off the armies of Arawn, lord of Annuvin, who threatens the freedom of Prydain. In its depiction of an epic conflict between the forces of beleaguered good and absolute evil, its band of unlikely heroes, and its portrayal of Gwydion as more stoic-hero-Aragorn than magician Son of Don, the *Chronicles* transform the magical Otherworld of Wales into an epic, rather than a Celtic fantasy. In addition, its tale of an assistant pig-keeper who through wits and courage and hard work learns that it is character and not birth that makes the man at the same time that he ends up with the princess and the kingdom is, as many have noted, stamped, 'made-in-America.'

The first book in the series, *The Book of Three*, introduces the major characters – Taran, the assistant pig-keeper, who dreams of a more adventurous life; Dallben, the distracted wizard/druid; Arawn, who has 'stolen all things of advantage to men'; the semi-divine House of Don, which has protected men from his evil reach; and our unlikely companions, a headstrong Princess, a puckish creature named Gurgi (a sort of benevolent Gollum), and a would-be bard with a flair for poetic invention. As he searches for his missing oracular pig, Taran learns the virtues of bravery, patience, and loyalty; the companions defeat the Horned King and his armies of Cauldron-Born, zombie warriors brought back from the dead; and Taran returns to Caer Dallben, concluding, Dorothy-like, that 'there is no place like home'. The second novel, *The Black Cauldron,* again sends Taran against the Cauldron-Born as the warriors of Prydain seek to snatch the Cauldron from Arawn's hands. Here, he comes up against his own pride and desperate longing for heroic fame and worth, as he deals with the contemptuous Prince Efnisien, who is determined to keep the pig-keeper in his place and is forced to give up a magical brooch that bestows foresight and wisdom in the service of the larger quest. The companions again triumph, setting the stage for the series' next two books, *The Castle of Llyr* and *Taran Wanderer,* which diverge slightly from the epic plot to recount coming-of-age adventures for both Eilonwy, who at the end of *The Castle of Llyr* agrees to go off and learn how to be a princess, and Taran, who at the end of *Taran Wanderer* finally internalizes that it is who he is, not to whom he was born, that matters. The final book, *The High King,* returns to the conflict between Arawn and the men of Prydain. This is where Taran comes into his own, as it is he, and not Gwydion, who wields the sword Dyrnwyn to overcome the Lord of Death. The age of enchantment is at an end – all magic passes from Prydain, the House of Don departs for the Summer Country, and the series concludes as the former assistant pig-keeper becomes the high king.

Although Alexander's retelling of the *Mabinogion* transposes Welsh figures – Gwydion, Arianrhod, Arawn, and Efnisien among others – and motifs – the cauldron of rebirth, the wandering craftsman, books of wisdom, castles taken back by the sea, to name a few – into the *Chronicles,* he recasts them into a new form: one with a beginning, a middle, and an end, logical transitions, and clear-cut good and evil. As he does so, he creates a coherent myth that – from the point of view of our modern expectations about narrative – makes the Welsh originals seem fragmentary, mere echoes of Alexander's tale of Arawn and the Sons of Don, a story that ends as Wales is poised to transform into a modern anglicized and Americanized civilization.

Alexander's de-Celticization of the *Mabinogion* is in keeping with the fantasy genre as it developed in the wake of J. R. R. Tolkien and

C. S. Lewis, whose writings dominated the genre in the years following the Second World War. While both authors incorporate Celtic names and motifs – the elven realms of Lothlorien, Narnia's Otherworld, the departure of the elves from the world of men – neither Tolkien nor Lewis write Celtic fantasy. Both Middle Earth and Narnia are places of law and absolutes, of men and kings. There is no room in either for shifting borders, mystical uncertainty, unruly nature, and feminine power. The works of Tolkien and Lewis, however, led to the rediscovery of our next – and very different – retelling of the *Mabinogion*. Their popularity proved that there was an audience for fantasy literature, and publishers began to seek out works to market to this audience. The most influential of the fantasy lines to stem from this 1960s revival was the Ballantine Adult Fantasy series, which 'discovered' the ill-fated *The Virgin and the Swine* and made Evangeline Walton's work, originally written in the 1930s, a product of the 1970s, when Lin Carter came across a copy of her retelling of the Fourth Branch. A quest to find the novel's author ensued and when Betty Ballantine finally found Walton in Tucson, she also found 'a dream come true': Walton had finished her retelling of the Four Branches, in spite of the fact that her publisher had refused to look at 'any more material on the subject', and was still in possession of the supposedly unsaleable manuscripts. Ballantine published them, to critical and popular acclaim, in four volumes, including the original novel, now renamed *The Island of the Mighty*, between 1970 and 1974.[17]

Walton, as does Kenneth Morris, presents her version of the *Mabinogion* as a return to the 'real' tale behind the Welsh text, consistently referencing the medieval text within her telling – amplifying, explaining, correcting, and presenting her narrator as someone who has privileged access to the events chronicled in it. As she does so, Walton, like Alexander, seems to recover the myth those tales only partially recount:

> The fiery, passionate, and very immediate accounts of real men and women ... set in a time when belief in the gods of air and earth, of fire and water, were vast, inexplicable realities in a world pregnant with magic, a world of marvels and wonders, teeming with strange creatures who might well be denizens of strange other landscapes, and who almost certainly would have monstrous arcane powers.[18]

In addition to embodying Welsh/Celtic fantasy's essential characteristic – that sense of a world 'pregnant with magic' and 'teeming with strange creatures' – Walton's 'recovery' of the Four Branches of the *Mabinogi* introduces some of the genre's most prominent concerns: the passing of magic and wonder as the world grows old, the transition between the old and the new, and the conflict between a masculine, patriarchal view of the world and a feminine view associated with nature and freedom.

For Walton, the stories of Pwyll and Rhiannon, Branwen and Efnisien, Pendaron and Pryderi, Gwydion and Math, Lleu and Blodeuwedd are all the story of the conflict between the Old Tribes, who worship the goddess and forgo property, fatherhood, and the ownership of women, and the New Tribes, influenced by the evil that comes from the east, with their 'Man-Gods,' and 'The Father who claims all power, and soon will overturn and break the Cauldron of Rebirth itself.' In her version of the tale, the tragedies that bring the enchantment of the Island of the Mighty to an end all revolve around the adoption of the ways of the east: Branwen's marriage ('The first marriage ever made for reasons of state-craft'),[19] Arianrhod's obsession with perceived virginity, Gwydion's with fatherhood, Blodeuwedd's creation as an object and possession. All of which will lead, as the blessed head of Bran warns his men, to a world in which the 'injustice of the East' – the creation of women as property – will prevail:

> And out of that constant injustice will rise continually more evils to breed wars and fresh injustice until men forget that there was ever a world at peace. When humankind lets one half of humankind be enslaved, it will be long and long, even when that slavery wanes, before freedom is respected and nation ceases to tear nation; before the world unlearns the habit of force.[20]

In this vision of the coming of the new age, Walton recovers a very different *Mabinogion* to that of either Morris or Alexander. In Morris, the forces of 'good' triumph, and the soul ascends; in Alexander, good triumphs, and modernity begins; for Walton, modernity also begins, but it stems from the triumph of evil and leads to slavery and war.

These Haunted Hills: Re-Enchanting the Modern World

While the *Mabinogion,* in all of its versions, is set in Gantz's 'mystic Celtic past of has been and never was',[21] the fantasy works we will discuss here are all set in their author's present, a present haunted, for better or worse, by that same mystic Celtic past. We begin in the nineteenth century with the son of a Welsh clergyman, Arthur Machen, who found both terror and transcendence in the hills and valleys of his boyhood, exemplifying the nineteenth century's splitting of the fairy world between the atavistic and the ideal, the grotesque and the numinous. This split makes Machen a curious figure: both a decadent writer, who penned schlock tales of supernatural horror, and a spiritual author, who composed transcendent narratives of spiritual grace.

In his horror tales Machen, drawing on the identification of the fairies as the remnants of an earlier race, represents the persistence of the past in the present as bestial, irrational, and dangerous. Tales of fairies and demon lovers cloak dreadful secrets, orgies, and human sacrifice. In 'The White People', an old nurse takes her young charge to a secret pool, where 'out of the water out of the wood came two wonderful white people', 'to play and dance, and sing', and, ultimately, lure the girl through forbidding landscapes and queer and intoxicating countries – familiar from the erotically charged, forbidden tales her nurse has told her – to her death. 'Such traditions', we are warned, 'as that girl had listened to in her childhood are still existent in occult and unabated vigour' in 'the west' of 'ancient woods', 'wild, domed hills', and 'ragged land'.[22] It is to this west that the narrator of 'The Shining Pyramid' travels in order to solve the mystery of a missing girl from Croesyceiliog whom the locals claim has 'gone with the fairies'. Here, he finds mysterious flint designs, 'mystic hanging woods', and a 'circular depression, which might well have been an old Roman amphitheatre', to which 'the country people are afraid to come . . . it is supposed to be a fairies' castle'. The girl has indeed 'gone with the faeries', to be raped and sacrificed by 'things made in the form of men, but stunted like children, hideously deformed, the faces with almond eyes burning with evil and unspeakable lusts'. The narrator explains that he had tracked down the solution to this mystery through the hint offered by 'the old name of fairies, "the little people" . . . and the very probable belief that they represent a tradition of the prehistoric Turanian inhabitants of the country, who were cave dwellers', adding, 'I don't regret our inability to rescue the wretched girl. You saw the appearance of those things that gathered thick and writhed in the Bowl; you may be sure that what lay bound in the midst of them was no longer fit for earth.'[23]

These are but two tales of the many in which Machen depicts a wild Welsh landscape marked with the signs of atavistic races and traditions, lurking in the 'places beneath the hills', haunting the present. In these tales, the past threatens the present, and nothing good can be found in old traditions and lore. In others of Machen's tales, however, it is the present that is demonized, while Welsh landscapes and tales offer their confused and haunted protagonists respite and redemption. These tales sacralize this landscape, setting it apart from the modern and mundane. In them, the enchanted hills and valleys of Wales point to a larger truth, a 'secret glory': not fairies, but saints, not erotic trysts, but grail masses. Machen's 1922 novel *The Secret Glory* provides a counterpart to 'The White People' and 'The Shining Pyramid'. Introduced as either the tale of 'a saint who had lost his way in the centuries' or an account 'of an undeveloped lunatic', *The Secret Glory* recounts the adventures of Ambrose Meyrick. Exiled in the flat and industrial modern landscape surrounding his English public school, Ambrose dreams of Norman arches and remembered medieval tales:

> A man passed by a familiar wall one day, and opening a door before unnoticed, found himself in a new world of unsurmised and marvellous experiences. Another man shot an arrow farther than any of his friends and became the husband of the fairy.[24]

As he 'watches the dreary land grow darker and darker', knowing that he 'had been driven from great and unspeakable joys into miserable exile and banishment', a vision transports Ambrose to the Welsh fairylands of his youth. The light of a silver star and the sound of a silver trumpet reveal a hidden well, from which he drinks, filling 'his soul and body . . . with a flood of great joy'. And 'he was no longer in that weary land of grey ploughland and dun meadow . . . He was on a hillside, lying on the verge of a great wood . . . Far in the east, a vast wall of rounded mountain rose serene towards the sky. All about him was the green world of leaves.' Here, Ambrose is caught up in the secret glory of the grail, and this vision stays with him through all the years of his exile, as his 'soul revisit[s] the fairy hills and woods and valleys of the west', where long ago his father had taken him to see the grail, and on 'strange pilgrimages over the beloved land' to visit 'deep wells in the heart of the wood, where a few broken stones, perhaps, were the last remains of a hermitage'.[25]

Ambrose's life and career are haunted by his visions of the grail, visions inextricably tied to his longing for the enchanted landscape of Wales. 'Every little wood,' he writes, 'every rock and fountain, and every running stream of Gwent were hallowed for me by some mystical and entrancing legend.'[26] In the end, these visions lure Ambrose completely away from the modern, compelling him to take up his place in the past, becoming the final keeper of the 'Celtic cup', charged with returning it to the east, where he is killed by 'infidels' 'enraged by the shining rapture of his face'. 'Ambrose Meyrick gain[s] the Red Martyrdom and achieve[s] the most glorious Quest and Adventure of the Sangraal.'[27]

Machen's depiction of a Welsh landscape haunted, for good or ill, by a legendary past establishes a vision of Wales as a land where the past still lives – or comes to life, as it does in Alan Garner's 1967 novel *The Owl Service*, born, Garner writes, out of an essential link between the land and the legend:

> We went to stay at a house in a remote valley in North Wales. Within hours of arriving I knew that I had found the setting for the story, or the setting had found me … The sensation of finding, not inventing, a story continued. It was all there, waiting, and I was the archaeologist picking away the earth to reveal the bones.[28]

These bones tell a story in which the present is doomed to repeat the tragedy of the past, where the tale of Lleu, Blodeuwedd, and Gronw lurks beneath the surface of the supposedly modern valley – a dinner service hidden in the attic, a painting covered by plaster. This persistence of the past in the present is captured in the language itself. Huw the farmhand explains the rock with a hole in it to the English boy vacationing at the farmhouse: 'There is a man being killed at that place … He is standing on the bank of the river, see, and the husband is up there on the Bryn with a spear: and he is putting the stone between himself and the spear, and the spear is going right through the stone and him.'[29] The story that should be in the past (the one found in the *Mabinogion*, which Gwyn, son of the Welsh cook, has been taught is 'the clear-running spring of Celtic genius', 'our national heritage', and which the English vacationers dismiss as 'short stories. Fine if you like that sort of thing – wizards and blood all over the place') is 'still happening'.

The Owl Service, like 'The White People,' and 'The Shining Pyramid', finds only tragedy in the haunting of Wales; the tales of the past threaten the life and sanity of the young people caught up in them. Becoming Blodeuwedd ruined Gwyn's mother's life, as she fled in the wake of his father's – Lleu's – accidental murder at the hands of Huw/Gronw, and now the story seems destined to repeat itself in Allison, Roger, and Gwyn even as the residents of the valley look passively on. 'They are the three who suffer every time,' Huw insists, 'for in them the power of this valley is contained, and through them the power is loosed.'[30] The tale of *The Owl Service* is the tale of needing to make a clean break from the past, to banish it to the realm of stories – to move on into the present. And while the Welsh can see this – 'she wants to be flowers, and you make her owls, and she is at the hunting' – it takes the sensible English boy to break the spell and save them: 'Is that all it is? … Flowers. Flowers, Ali … You're not birds. You're flowers.'[31]

The Owl Service finds a tragic connection to the past in the haunted landscape of Wales, where stories refuse to be told in the past tense. For Roger, Gwyn, and Allison, redemption lies in a successful transition to the modern world. Charles De Lint's *Moonheart* (1984) has a more complex relationship with the past – one that incorporates both the anti-modernism of Machen's grail tales and the call to exorcise the past and move into the future of Garner's haunting myth. *Moonheart* translates the Otherworld – along with Taliesin – across the ocean and to the New World, where it shimmers not beyond the fields we know, but in the streets of modern Ottawa. The plot centres around a group of musicians, writers, artists, and 'other misfits' who occupy Tamson house – an odd structure that seems out of time and out of place and that, indeed, as we find out, straddles the border between the modern world and the enmeshed Otherworlds of the faeries (both the elves of the Celts and the 'mysteries' of the New World's native tribes) – and the evils that stalk them, ranging from misguided constables, through a corrupt business man and his thugs, to Mal'ek'a – the 'Dread that Walks Nameless'. De Lint's depiction of the Otherworld as a place where time is 'like an eddy or a whirlpool' and space can be traversed by thought – a vanishing place retreating from, yet contiguous with, twentieth-century Ottawa – depicts an enchanted world accessible to those who follow 'The Way': a distinctly New-Age cocktail of theosophy, invented Celtic mysticism, and eastern thought that hints at the transformative possibilities of mystical truths in much the same manner as Machen does in *The Secret Glory*.

The ins and outs of *Moonheart*'s extremely complex plot do not lend themselves to summary; suffice to say that, in the end, Mal'ek'a is defeated, the protagonists have progressed on 'The Way', and the sanctity of the Otherworld has been preserved, at the same time that the cycle of vengeance, begun when Taliesin cursed Maelgwn's druids as he set off for the New World, has been brought to a close. As this plot plays out, the novel redeems the past, looks towards the future, and preserves a space for magical naturalism – and with it, for the soul's journey to its higher purpose – within an urban landscape, suggesting that our modern cities are as haunted, and as enchanted, as the mountains and valleys of Wales.

Cosmic Battlefields: The Light and the Dark

While Machen, Garner, and De Lint all turn to a view of reality in which the borders between 'this' world and 'that' are thin, where the past intrudes upon – or co-exists with – the present to chronicle personal journeys, other fantasy writers have blended this 'Celtic' view of the relationship between this world and the Otherworld with a cosmic battle between absolute good and absolute evil. The most well known of these writers is Susan Cooper, whose *The Dark Is Rising Sequence* of five novels (1965–77) sets the final battle between the Light and the Dark in a modern Britain saturated with the past, as the 'Old Ones' of the Light seek the magical talismans that will allow them to defeat the Dark before it enslaves the world. All of the novels in this sequence draw on Celtic motifs – the grail, enchanted harps, an otherworld that hovers on the borders of modern Britain, druids / magicians who can transcend temporal and physical boundaries – and most of them are set in the 'Celtic borders' of Cornwall and Wales. Any of them could serve as an exemplar of Celtic fantasy; however, I will focus my discussion here on the fourth book in the sequence, *The Grey King* (1975), which unfolds in a remote Welsh landscape, riddled and haunted by the past.

The minute that Will Stanton enters the Welsh valley to which he has been sent to convalesce, he experiences 'a strange new feeling of enclosure, almost of menace' and feels 'he was in a part of Britain like none he had ever known before: a secret enclosed place, with a power hidden in its shrouded centuries at which he could not begin to guess'.[32] In 'this unfamiliar land of green valleys and dark misted mountain peaks', Will carries out his quest against the Dark.[33] As he does so, Cooper inscribes the landscape of Wales with supernatural and cosmic significance – as a stronghold of the Dark – and locates mythic narratives within it. In this valley, the pendragon returns: not Arthur himself, but his son, Bran, brought forward in time by Merlin to grow up in this remote valley; here, the legendary Sleepers lie beneath an enchanted lake; here, within the caverns of the mountain itself, and yet outside of time and space, the Lords of the High Magic hold court. Against this background of myth and magic, Will and Bran fight off the forces of the Dark embodied in the Grey King, the *Brenin Llwyd*, made manifest in 'the grey-white cloud [that] hung ragged round the highest hills'.[34] They find a harp of gold and wake Arthur's Sleepers, who rise 'high over the lake and away', reinforcements for the Light.[35] The book ends as Bran accepts his destiny, the Grey King flees the valley, and the stage is set for the final battle between the Light and the Dark.

The Grey King received the first Tir na n-Og award (presented by the Welsh Books Council) for an English-language book with 'an authentic Welsh background'. Interestingly enough, this authentic background relies not on realism, but on magical naturalism – on etching the landscape of Wales with legends – placed in the service of a cosmic mythology. In the end, however, this mythology concludes, as do so many tales about the defeat of darkness, with the closing of the borders between an otherworld and the world of the here and now, in 'real' Wales. 'Drake is no longer in his hammock, nor is

Arthur somewhere sleeping,' Merriman/Merlin tells the children who have aided the Light in its quest, 'because the world is yours and it is up to you.'[36] Enchantments, he continues, 'will retreat into the hidden places of your minds, and you will never again know any hint of it except in dreams'.[37] The sequence concludes with 'five children [standing] on the roof of Wales looking out over a golden valley and the blue sea' at a view that, if no longer magical, is still 'worth the climb'.[38]

Cooper places her cosmic battle in our own world; Guy Gavriel Kay, on the other hand, transports many of the same Celtic/Welsh themes and motifs to an otherworld in the *The Fionavar Tapestry* (1984–6), written in the wake of the author's stint editing Tolkien's *Silmarillion*. Not surprisingly, given Kay's recent immersion in Middle Earth, these novels are grounded in what feels like a very Christian world-view, consisting of a multiverse of otherworlds created by 'The Weaver', and threatened by Rakoth, an evil whose shadow, we are told, is known in all of the worlds of the Weaver. In all worlds, the children of the Weaver must confront Rakoth; in some they are successful; in others, Rakoth prevails. Fionavar, however, is the first of all worlds, and, as it goes in Fionavar, so it will echo throughout the multiverse. The *Tapestry* begins as five Canadian students are called to Fionavar, where centuries ago an alliance of humans and the *lios alfar* (elves – Kay had been reading *a lot* of Tolkien) had defeated and bound Rakoth. While *The Summer Tree*, the first book in the series, primarily deals with the political divisions and power struggles within and among the various races and kingdoms of Fionavar, the novel ends as Rakoth frees himself, and the trilogy turns to the realm's second battle to defeat Rakoth and thus save all the worlds of the Weaver from falling under his shadow.

The Fionavar Tapestry is a kind of Narnia-meets-Middle Earth, but the world of Fionavar is more 'Celtic' than either, not only in its names and motifs – Pwyll, the Sleepers, the Wild Hunt, elven enchantments, Cafall, the raid on Annuvin, the Cauldron-Born – but also in its magical naturalism: the gods and their offspring walk the woods, myths become real, time and space collapse. This Celticized secondary world provides a stage where the mythic struggle can reach resolution, and Arthur – raised from his sleeping place under Glastonbury Tor in our world, to fight again in Fionavar – can be freed from his endless cycle of resurrection and penance. This time he 'lives to see the end': Camlann is won, evil banished, and all of the worlds preserved from darkness. Arthur, Guinevere, and Lancelot sail off together to the west, the borders between worlds are sealed, and 'the Five' and the people of Fionavar are left to move forward into the present.

Celtic Realms

As we have seen, in most Celtic fantasy novels – and certainly in those inflected by a Tolkien-inspired struggle between the forces of good and evil – the Celtic, even the idealized Celtic, is in the end relegated to the past, sent, however reluctantly, to the enchanted lands in the west, so that modernity can begin. Even in those novels, such as Machen's, in which the enchanted realm figures as a true world opposed to the physical one of shadows and deceit that most men know, that world is still seen as other, apart, outside of time – and he who would enter it does so by forsaking his body – by achieving, as does Ambrose Meyrick, 'the Red Martyrdom'.

I want to close this survey of Welsh literature and fantasy with a series that seeks to break this pattern: Patricia A. McKillip's *Riddle-Master*, which, although it neither explicitly adapts Welsh literature nor is set in an imagined Wales, comes I believe the closest to the 'Celtic spirit' as it was imagined and defined by Matthew Arnold, and then co-opted, through Robert Graves's *The White Goddess*, by New-Age thinkers. In her preface to the 1999 reissue of the *Riddle-Master* trilogy (originally published between 1976 and 1979), McKillip describes an artistic journey that began with Tolkien – 'the riddling, the underground waters and caves, the sense of destiny, prophecy inherent in the myth of the return of the king' – and ended in 'the rich and strangely unmined possibilities for female heroes, which glittered with color and a wealth of tales for the taking'.[39] At the end of this journey, McKillip finds the High One's realm, and the story of the passing of an age that leaves enchantments intact.

The High One's realm exemplifies magical naturalism. In it, dead kings bargain with the living for their crown, land-rulers can feel the corn growing in their fields, powerful beings come out of the sea to take the shape of dead traders, and wizards can shape the wind. In this realm, two heroes, Morgan of Hed and Raederle of An, flee their destiny – a destiny that demands that they accept the lawless past, the shapelessness, that is their heritage. McKillip's work is cyclical rather than teleological; it contains no absolute good or evil; it ends in a land that is still enchanted, with a king whose destiny is not to rule, a woman who finds her power, and a romance of equals not bound by marriage. In this, *Riddle-Master* comes closer to the feel of Welsh tales – or at least our concept of them – than, with the possible exception of Evangeline Walton's works, any of the works explicitly based on the Celtic materials.

Mapping a Fantasy Wales

Tony Curtis begins his introduction to *Wales: The Imagined Nation* with an epigraph from one of his poems, 'Pembrokeshire Seams', inspired by the words of the historian Gwyn A. Williams:

> Wales is a process.
> Wales is an artefact which the Welsh produce.
> The Welsh make and remake Wales
> day by day, year by year, generation after
> generation
>   if they want to.[40]

As we have seen in this chapter, however, Wales has been made and remade not just by the Welsh but also by many others with their own desires and agendas: English and American, theosophist and Rosicrucian, New-Age fantasist and feminist. In this remaking, Wales has become a Celtic fantasy world, and Welsh tales and mythology, proto-fantasy. This creation of a popular fantasy Wales does indeed preserve the 'Welsh mythic tales' 'as the surviving remnants of a once proud culture'[41] and provide 'a common space for romantics, tourists, scholars, and nationalists in which they can congregate, speak, and imagine the world to be different, a mythic space [that] can be shared and appropriated and fantasized about'.[42] However, this shared and fantasy space is not an empty space free for utopic visions; its realms are haunted by other imaginings and other visions, many of which perpetuate Matthew Arnold's relegation of the Welsh and Wales to a fantasy past, a relegation that is still not without its cultural consequences; thus, while we travel its enchanted roads, we must also remember that this Wales is a fantasy and not Wales itself.

Notes

1. I am not the first to attempt to draw this map, and my effort owes much to C. W. Sullivan III's *Welsh Celtic Myth in Modern Fantasy* (Westport, CT: Greenwood Press, 1989); the Spring 1990 issue of the *New Welsh Review*, dedicated to children's literature; Donna R. White's *A Century of Welsh Myth in Children's Literature* (Westport, CT: Greenwood Press, 1998); Kath Filmer-Davies's *Fantasy Fiction and Welsh Myth: Tales of Belonging* (London: Macmillan, 1996); and Audrey L. Becker and Kristin Noone, eds., *Welsh Mythology and Folklore in Popular Culture* (Jefferson, NC: McFarland & Company, 2011). However, I seek to expand the terrain covered by these earlier maps to include not just works that specifically invoke Welsh myths

and characters but also ones that are grounded in a more general sense of 'Celtic Magic' invented in the nineteenth century.

2. *The Mabinogion*, trans. Jeffrey Gantz (Harmondsworth: Penguin, 1976), 10.

3. Edward Plunkett, Lord Dunsany, consistently uses this phrase to locate Elfland in his 1924 novel, *The King of Elfland's Daughter*, and Lin Carter adopted it as the title for his collection of Dunsany's short stories, published by Ballantine in 1972.

4. Matthew Arnold, *The Study of Celtic Literature* (London: David Nutt, 1910; first published 1867), 133–37, cited by Helen Fulton, 'Magic and the Supernatural in Early Welsh Arthurian Narrative: *Culhwch ac Olwen* and *Breuddwyd Rhonabwy*', *Arthurian Literature* 30 (2013), 4.

5. Fulton, 'Magic and the Supernatural', 3–4.

6. I am indebted here to Carole Silver's discussion in *Strange and Secret Peoples: Fairies and Victorian Consciousness* (New York: Oxford University Press, 1999), chapter 4.

7. Silver, *Strange and Secret Peoples*, 149.

8. Ibid.

9. Sullivan, *Welsh Celtic Myth in Modern Fantasy*, 10; Fulton, 'Magic and the Supernatural', 25.

10. Anonymous, 'Celtic Fantasy', Best Fantasy Books, http://bestfantasybooks .com/celtic-fantasy.html (accessed 13 December 2017).

11. I use here and throughout this discussion the title given to the Welsh narratives by Lady Charlotte Guest, because, although the academic world has corrected Guest, the fantasy authors I discuss persist in using Guest's title.

12. Kenneth Morris, *The Fates of the Princes of Dyved* (London: Theosophical Book Company, 1914); electronic edition, 2000, www.theosociety.org/pasadena/ dyfed/fates-hp.htm (accessed 13 December 2017).

13. I adopt here and throughout my discussion of *The Fates of the Princes of Dyved* Morris's spelling, 'Rhianon'.

14. Morris, *The Fates of the Princes of Dyved*.

15. Ibid.

16. Lloyd Alexander, *The Chronicles of Prydain*, 5 vols. (New York: Henry Holt & Co., 1964–8); Kindle ebook edition, 2014.

17. *The Virgin and the Swine*, based on the Fourth Branch of the *Mabinogi*, was published in Chicago by Willett, Clark & Co. in 1936, and later renamed as *The Island of the Mighty*. The four volumes in the series, based on the Four Branches of the *Mabinogi*, are: *Prince of Annwn* (New York: Ballantine, 1974); *The Children of Llyr* (New York: Ballantine, 1972); *The Song of Rhiannon* (New York: Ballantine, 1973); *The Island of the Mighty* (New York: Ballantine, 1972). The books were retold by Evangeline Walton and republished as a single volume under the title

The Mabinogion Tetralogy (London: Overlook Duckworth, 2012); Kindle ebook edition, 2003.

18. Betty Ballantine, 'Introduction', *The Mabinogion Tetralogy*, Kindle ebook.
19. Walton, *Mabinogion Tetralogy: The Children of Llyr*, chapter 2.
20. Ibid, chapter 7.
21. *The Mabinogion*, trans. Gantz, 10.
22. Arthur Machen, 'The White People', in *The Great God Pan, The Shining Pyramid, The White People*, Library of Wales (Cardigan: Parthian, 2010), 111–66. 'The White People' was first published in 1904.
23. Arthur Machen, 'The Shining Pyramid', in *The Great God Pan*, 77–110. 'The Shining Pyramid' was first published in 1895.
24. Arthur Machen, *The Secret Glory*, in *The Caerleon Edition of the Works of Arthur Machen*, vol. IV (London: Martin Secker, 1923), 50. *The Secret Glory* was first published in 1922.
25. Machen, *The Secret Glory*, 73.
26. Ibid., 173.
27. Ibid., 250. These are the closing lines of the book. For another discussion of Machen's fiction, see Chapter 21 in this volume.
28. Alan Garner, 'Postscript', *The Owl Service* (London: Collins, 1967, 1998), 222.
29. Garner, *The Owl Service*, 43.
30. Ibid., 99.
31. Ibid., 218.
32. Susan Cooper, *The Grey King* (Harmondsworth: Penguin, 1975, 1977), 19.
33. Ibid., 36.
34. Ibid., 22.
35. Ibid., 183.
36. Susan Cooper, *Silver on the Tree* (Harmondsworth: Penguin, 1977, 1979), 282.
37. Ibid., 283.
38. Ibid., 284.
39. Patricia A. McKillip, *Riddle-Master: The Complete Trilogy* (New York: Ace Books, 1999), v–vi.
40. Tony Curtis, ed., *Wales: The Imagined Nation – Studies in Cultural and National Identity* (Bridgend: Poetry Wales Press, 1986), 7.
41. Filmer-Davies, *Fantasy Fiction and Welsh Myth*, 26.
42. Becker and Noone, eds., *Welsh Mythology and Folklore in Popular Culture*, 3.

32

Theatre, Film, and Television in Wales in the Twentieth Century

JAMIE MEDHURST

The Wales of stereotype, leeks, daffodils, look-you-now-boyo rugby supporters singing Max Boyce songs in three-part harmony while phoning mam to tell her they'll be home for tea and Welsh cakes has gone.[1]

All cultures that want to survive need to represent themselves to the wider world and to themselves[2]

This chapter aims to consider the role played by three major cultural forms that provided a platform for playwrights and authors in twentieth-century Wales. There is no doubt that theatre, film, and television have played, and continue to play, a vital part not only in creating what Hazel Walford Davies calls 'alternative worlds' but also in reflecting and defining who we are to ourselves and to others.[3] They have been at the heart of the nation-building project, to the extent that the historian the late Dr John Davies argued in his authoritative historical account of the BBC in Wales that contemporary Wales was an artefact created by broadcasting.[4] To that one might wish to add theatre and film.

Wales in the twentieth century was, in the words of a former chairman of the Independent Television Authority, 'an awkward area' for those outside of the country trying to make sense of the complex national identity.[5] There were (and still are to a large degree) a series of binary opposites with which one had to contend: two languages, one ancient and indigenous, the other alien but the language of the state; two cultural traditions; a rural, some might say regressive or 'old fashioned' way of life, and an urban, progressive, and supposedly modern way of life; a culture that was, at its heart, Nonconformist, and one that was deemed to be secular. These were the perilous seas that had to be navigated by writers and dramatists producing theatre, film, and television for the 'home' audience, but also for an increasingly international audience.

A chapter such as this can only hope to offer a snapshot or provide an overview of such a large area. However, there were clear themes which emerged during the century with regard to the place and role of these three forms. Although the chapter takes each 'area' in turn, the structure is not to suggest that theatre, film, and television were mutually exclusive in any way. Indeed, as the century progressed, so the boundaries between the media blurred in terms of writing and acting. Together, the three areas offer an insight into the complex, interweaving issues of nationhood, national identity, language, and culture in the twentieth century.

Theatre

> Theatre is a part of a binding social process. It creates and reinforces a common identity in a public act. In effect theatre says: 'This is who we are, these are the things that worry us, these are our neighbours, these are our gods, our dreams, this is how we live and this is our language.' Theatre reflects social reality in ways that poetry and the novel cannot, and there is a subterranean tunnel that connects theatre and the social consciousness.[6]

Whilst it may be disingenuous to argue, as Carl Tighe does, that Wales 'has almost no theatre history to speak of', it would be true to say that prior to the twentieth century, the theatrical tradition in Wales was not as strong as that of its larger neighbour. Certainly, the Theatre of the Interlude (*Theatr yr Anterliwt*) was prevalent during the late eighteenth and early nineteenth centuries, its most notable proponent being Twm o'r Nant (1739–1810). These 'satirical, celebratory, moralistic and indecent' plays, as Ioan Williams refers to them, flourished in rural Wales but became victims of the rise of the Methodist movement which perceived any form of theatre to be ungodly and immoral.[7] It could be argued, therefore, that theatre and drama in Wales was a twentieth-century phenomenon, and it was not until the second decade of the twentieth century that a full theatre tradition started to emerge, thanks in large part to the support and patronage of Lord Howard de Walden (1880–1946).[8] In 1911, de Walden offered an annual prize of £100 at the National Eisteddfod for the best play in Welsh or English suitable for a touring company in Wales. 'This invitation,' argues Anwen Jones, 'encapsulates the moment at which Wales stepped forward into the new cultural arena of a Welsh national theatre.'[9] Ioan Williams sees the emergence of the Welsh National Theatre Company, which came as a result of the efforts of de Walden and his associates, as marking the start of a drama movement in Wales which lasted until the immediate post-war period.[10] During this period, and in particular during the inter-war period, attempts were made to develop the movement into a platform for launching a National Theatre for Wales. However, for the time being, the period was marked by amateur theatre and could be described as a 'golden age' for amateur drama with, at one point, around 500 companies in Wales. Playwrights such as John Oswald (J. O.) Francis (1882–1956) and Richard Griffith (R. G.) Berry (1869–1945) benefited from the patronage of de Walden and produced plays such as Francis's *Change* (1913) and *Cross Currents* (1923). If writers writing in English were predicting political, cultural, and societal change, as Francis was doing, then the dominant theme of pre-Second World War writing in Welsh was the hypocrisy within the Welsh-language chapel-going population.[11]

Described by Elan Closs Stephens as 'a period rich in confusion and contradiction', the 1950s and 1960s witnessed the demise of the amateur dramatic tradition, partly because of the rise of television (see below) but also because of the development of a professional, text-based national theatre which itself had to face an increasing threat from television.[12] This post-war period in Welsh drama saw the emergence of what Ioan Williams terms a 'Theatre of National Consciousness'.[13] There was a move away from drama as conceived by playwrights such as Emlyn Williams, whose *The Corn Is Green* (1938) appeared on Broadway in 1940 and was then a successful film, to greater experimentation with verse drama. The master of this genre form and one of the dominant forces in twentieth-century theatre and literature was Saunders Lewis (1893–1985).[14] By mid-century, Lewis was acknowledged to be one of the leading dramatists and critics of the period. He was also a major figure in Welsh culture and politics, having been a founding member and later president of the Welsh Nationalist Party, Plaid Cymru, between 1926 and 1939. He had also been arrested and imprisoned (along with teacher D. J. Williams and Baptist minister Lewis Valentine) for an arson attack on the RAF bombing school at Penyberth in 1936 on pacifist and nationalist grounds. Two of his key plays of the post-war period, *Blodeuwedd* (1948) and *Siwan* (1956), draw on Welsh myth and history, the former based on the tale of the girl made from flowers in the Fourth Branch of the *Mabinogi*, the latter on the daughter of King John of England who married Prince Llewelyn the Great of Wales (Llywelyn ap Iorwerth). Further plays such as *Gymerwch chi Sigaret?* (1956), *Brad* (1958), and *Esther* (1960) are all considered as part of the canon of Welsh-language drama, just as the work of T. S. Eliot features in the canon of English-language verse and prose. Commenting on Lewis's contribution, Elan Closs Stephens argues that

> his range and energy, the prolific abundance of plays and critical studies, testify to his energy; more importantly, the quality of his writing testifies to

a need to reformulate Welsh political thought either through action or through drama.[15]

The period after the Second World War and the 1970s also saw the work of John Gwilym Jones (1904–88) and Gwenlyn Parry (1932–91) being performed not only on the stage but increasingly on radio and television. Parry's stage plays, which include *Saer Doliau* (1966), *Ty ar y Tywod* (1968), *Y Ffin* (1973), and *Y Tŵr* (1978), have had a lasting impact on theatre in Wales and, as Roger Owen has argued, brought the Theatre of the Absurd to Welsh audiences for the first time.[16]

The 1960s heralded a period of enhanced support for theatre in Wales. In 1962, the British Arts Council established a Welsh Committee which, in turn, formed the Welsh Theatre Company/Cwmni Theatr Cymru under the directorship of Warren Jenkins. The company produced and performed across Wales, predominantly in the English language. Welsh-language theatre developed as a partnership between the company and the BBC, the key figure in this respect being Wilbert Lloyd Roberts, head of drama at the BBC. Based in Bangor, Roberts pulled together a group of talented actors, including Cefin Roberts, and the company went from strength to strength. In 1971, the company gained a substantial grant from the Welsh Arts Council (established in 1967) which allowed it to commission work from writers such as Eigra Lewis Roberts and Emyr Humphreys, and in 1974 the company commissioned a play from Saunders Lewis for the princely sum of £500.[17]

The 1970s and 1980s saw Welsh theatre develop in interesting and exciting ways. Across the country, theatres were built in association with universities (Theatr y Werin in Aberystwyth and the Sherman Theatre in Cardiff in 1973, Theatr Gwynedd in Bangor in 1975) or at the instigation of local authorities (Theatr Clwyd in Mold in 1976). At the same time as this physical manifestation of a confidence in Welsh theatre, the form itself was moving into a phase characterized by Eugenio Barba's notion of a 'Third Theatre'. As Ioan Williams has noted, 'New Welsh theatre practice in the seventies related more directly to social and cultural circumstances in a rapidly changing world than either the "first" established theatre, or the "second" theatre of the avant-garde.'[18] In addition to radical theatre companies which produced experimental, site-specific, and essentially devised theatre, such as the Cardiff Laboratory Theatre, Moving Being, and Brith Gof (established by Mike Pearson and Lis Hughes Jones in 1981), there were those companies which provided an outlet for new writers in Wales such as Made in Wales (from its establishment in 1981 until its closure in 1999), Theatr Bara Caws, and Cwmni Theatr Hwyl a Fflag.

The theatre of the 1970s and 1980s was concerned with the contemporary, not with what Williams calls the 'fictionalized other space of dramatic literature'.[19] Community theatre and theatre for young people and schools developed and characterized an evolving Welsh theatre, led by companies such as Theatr Gorllewin Morgannwg and Cwmni Cyfri Tri, which, in 1989 when it merged with Cwmni Theatr Crwban, became Arad Goch, one of the leading producers of theatre for young people under the artistic directorship of Jeremy Turner.[20] In Welsh-language theatre, the three-year secondment of Emily Davies from a lectureship in the department of Drama at the University College of Wales, Aberystwyth (as it was then) to the artistic directorship of Cwmni Theatr Cymru proved to be an inspired move. Davies wanted to create a new style of Welsh acting and new Welsh audiences, and for the company to allow new playwrights to develop. To a large degree, her vision was fulfilled. However, despite Emily Davies's undoubted vision and skill, and despite the talented group of actors and writers she had gathered, the company folded in 1984 following a series of meetings and rescue packages.[21]

There is no doubt that these companies, emerging as they did in a changing Wales, did a great deal to modernize Wales, the Welsh identity, and the Welsh theatrical audience. This paved the way for writers such as Dic Edwards and Ed Thomas, who continued to throw off the last vestiges of an 'old', stereotypical Wales in their writing. Thomas's 'new Wales' is 'fast, maverick and imaginative, and innovative and inventive in its aim to be a small, interesting country within a European context, a country where the albatross of Britain has finally fallen from its neck'.[22]

In evaluating a century of Welsh drama in 1996, Elan Closs Stephens remarked that 'so far, for a small country working against the odds, the theatrical track record has been a remarkable affirmation of the will to live'.[23] In the post-devolutionary era, with two national theatres in good health (the English-language National Theatre Wales, founded in 2010, and the Welsh-language Theatr Genedlaethol Cymru, founded in 2003) and a pool of inventive and highly creative writers, the will not only to live, but to invent and reinvent itself, appears to be stronger than ever.

Film

> Film was never made to feel very welcome in Wales. As a two or three year old infant, stinking slightly of gin and the sweat of the fairground, it ran slap up against Evan Roberts and the [religious] Revival of 1904–5, and was severely mauled. It survives, but remains retarded to this day.[24]

Just as eighteenth-century Methodism had considered theatre as ungodly and antithetic to Wales and its cultural traditions, so the religious revival of 1904–5 stifled the early years of film in Wales. There were some notable filmic events, however, in these pre-Hollywood days. The film pioneer Arthur Cheetham, from Rhyl, started producing films in the final years of the nineteenth century, although one of the highlights of his career was undoubtedly filming the visit of William Cody ('Buffalo Bill') to Rhyl in 1903. The Edwardian film-makers Mitchell and Kenyon also visited north Wales and in 1906 filmed the Wales versus Ireland football match in Wrexham, which remains the oldest remaining international game to be filmed. Another film pioneer, William Haggar, produced Wales's first fiction narrative film in 1905, and in 1918 Maurice Elvey directed the biographical film *The Life Story of David Lloyd George*, a masterpiece of silent cinema lasting two and a half hours. Having been missing presumed lost forever, it was rediscovered in 1994 and restored two years later.

The 1920s witnessed the peak of silent cinema (and the introduction of the 'talkie' in 1927). Films and cinema-going were grasping the public imagination, causing one commentator to note that, by 1926, 'the cinemas are certainly more numerous than the theatres and possibly more numerous than the churches'.[25] The films being watched in Wales's 250 cinemas at the end of the decade were mainly American, leading to the political scientist, Alfred Zimmern, to describe the country as 'American Wales'.[26] It was in the 1930s that Wales began to make its mark in filmic terms. British mainstream films at this time tended to portray Wales as being 'devoid of industry or factory disputes, and entirely populated by shepherdesses, gypsies and lovelorn swains prone to romantic quests. Harsher realities rarely intruded into these rustic or Ruritanian-style idylls'.[27] However, films such as *Today We Live* (1937) and *Eastern Valley* (1937) featured the industrial mining communities of south Wales and portrayed a harsher, more realistic way of life.[28] The major film of the 1930s from the standpoint of Wales in British mainstream cinema was *The Citadel* (1938), directed by King Vidor. The film drew critical acclaim and praise from film critics, in particular for the way in which the film offered a real sense of life in London and south Wales. In many ways a 'social problem film', for which Vidor was known, the film 'offered a fuller view of South Wales than any other previous feature film'.[29] The 1930s also witnessed the first Welsh-language feature film, *Y Chwarelwr* ('The Quarryman', 1935). Directed by Sir Ifan ab Owen Edwards (founder of the Welsh League of Youth, Urdd Gobaith Cymru), the film explored the harsh realities of life for men working in the slate quarries of north Wales.

Hollywood and Ealing Studios hit Wales in the 1940s. *The Proud Valley* (1940) and *How Green Was My Valley* (1941) provided images of Wales which were to endure (for better or worse) for decades. As John Humphrys has stated:

> We are defined in the English mind by our national caricature. The daftest cliché in the film director's manual – coal dust covered men singing in perfect harmony as they trudge back to the cottages from the pit – may fade away now the pits have closed. But don't bank on it ... And why must they all have IQs of 10 but be very very cunning? And why must half the characters sound as though they're Peter Sellers imitating a doctor from Madras?[30]

Ealing Studios' *The Proud Valley* was essentially a vehicle for singer Paul Robeson and, as Dave Berry has noted, it was the nearest Ealing Studios came to producing a radical film.[31] Robeson had performed in the south Wales valleys in the 1930s, raising money for the Spanish Civil War, and the film was a box office success in the valleys and in Cardiff. In contrast to *The Proud Valley*, *How Green Was My Valley*, directed by John Ford, is seen by many as being overly nostalgic for a mythical Wales that never was and, to use Peter Stead's phrase, 'pure Hollywood schmaltz'.[32] Based on Richard Llewellyn's novel, the film won five Oscars but attracted criticism for its lack of reality and over-sentimentalization of the harsh realities of a mining community.

The harsh realities of the Second World War were the topic of a key documentary film, produced, directed, and scripted by poet, artist, and film-maker Humphrey Jennings in 1943. *The Silent Village* was set in the mining village of Cwmgiedd in the Swansea valley and effectively transposed the tragic events of the 1942 Nazi massacre of the Czech village of Lidice to Cwmgiedd. The Welsh villagers 'played' the parts of the Czech villagers and the scenes of the women and children being taken away to camps whilst the men of the village were lined up against a wall, singing the Welsh national anthem defiantly before being shot by firing squad are amongst the most powerful in any film. This moving, poignant film has none of the crass, hectoring propaganda that one might associate with the films of, for example, Leni Riefenstahl, but the message of the film resonated widely across mining communities and beyond.

Another Welsh writer who worked on propaganda film during the war period was Dylan Thomas. The Ministry of Information drew on his writing skills in films such as *Wales: Green Mountain, Black Mountain* (1942) and *These Are the Men* (1943). Many have described Thomas as a war poet in a similar vein to Jennings, and there is no doubt that the films produced by both have a poetic, lyrical feel to them.

Emlyn Williams's film *The Last Days of Dolwyn* (1949), which he wrote and directed, was significant for a number of reasons. Firstly, it dealt with the politically sensitive topic of the drowning of a Welsh community in order to provide water for Liverpool, and secondly, it featured a considerable amount of Welsh-language dialogue, which had not been seen or heard in mainstream British cinema until this point. In the same year, Ealing Studios released *A Run for Your Money* based on an original story by the Welsh actor Clifford Evans and starring Meredith Edwards and Donald Houston. In a film which relies heavily on clichés, Twm and Dai, two cheery, innocent Welsh miners, travel to London to see a Wales versus England rugby international (what else?). They are soon distracted by what the big, bad city has to offer and find themselves yielding to various temptations, lost in the metropolis. Interestingly, Dave Berry suggests that *A Run for Your Money* provided a template for later films, notably the BBC's *Grand Slam*, written by Gwenlyn Parry and directed by John Hefin in 1978.[33] Berry also summarizes Ealing Studios' attitude in its filmmaking endeavours:

> Ealing had no truck with angst. They specialized in benign caricatures and presented a Britain more or less at ease with itself. The Welsh were treated no more condescendingly by the studio than anyone else, but they were patronized: even when they displayed native nous and their integrity enabled them to triumph over alien skullduggery, we were left in no doubt that it was a victory for innocence and a fundamental lack of judgement.[34]

But what of post-war Welsh film, films from Wales produced by Welsh directors and scriptwriters? According to Wil Aaron,

> For twenty years, between 1950 and 1970, the Welsh film scene, apart of course, from television films, was a barren, arid, empty desert ... the heavy hand of television, a worthy successor to Evan Roberts, battered the poor retarded Welsh film industry into the ground once more.[35]

There is no doubt that the new medium of television impacted upon the development of film in Wales during the 1950s and 1960s. With increasing numbers of people investing in television sets, the new entertainment medium, entering as it did the very heart of the home, beat film hands down. There were exceptions, particularly in the Welsh language with the release of *Yr Etifeddiaeth* in 1949, a film by John Roberts Williams, then editor of the Welsh-language weekly newspaper, *Y Cymro*. In 1951, as part of the Welsh contribution to the Festival of Britain, Paul Dickson's *David* was released. Described as 'a masterpiece in miniature' by Dave Berry, the film focuses on the life, work, and community of an Ammanford caretaker and is full of compassion and pathos.[36]

As the 1960s and 1970s progressed, and as television tightened its grip on the viewing population, 'not only were the indigenous shoots of a Welsh cinema crushed, but the mighty bastions of Hollywood – the Odeons and Ritzses and Coliseums – also began to crack and fall apart'.[37] Yet there were also signs of hope, such as Jack Howells's Oscar for his film for the ITV company for south Wales, TWW (Television Wales and West), on Dylan Thomas in 1963, and the opening of the Film School in Newport in 1966.

Increased public expenditure on film in Wales (albeit very modest sums) came in the form of the establishment of the Welsh Film Board, Y Bwrdd Ffilmiau Cymraeg, in 1971, and the Welsh Arts Council Film Sub-Committee. The former had responsibility for the funding and development of Welsh-language film, although its emphasis was, as Wil Aaron and Kate Woodward have both noted, more on using film as weapon in the fight to save the Welsh language as opposed to promoting film as art.[38] The 'Bwrdd' came to an end in 1986, much of its remit and *raison d'être* having been taken over by S4C, the Welsh-language television channel.

During the 1970s a more radical Welsh filmic voice was also coming to the fore, for example in the work of Karl Francis, who later went on to become head of drama at BBC Wales for a short period. Francis's *Above Us the Earth* (1977) focused on the impact of a pit closure on individuals and a community. Francis went on in the 1980s to direct *Milwr Bychan / Boy Soldier* (1986), a powerful film dealing with issues around national identity, Welshness, and a British soldier serving in Northern Ireland (played by Richard Lynch). The film, like Stephen Bayly's *Rhosyn a Rhith / Coming up Roses* (1986), was shown to critical acclaim in the West End. On a more local level, Chapter Arts Centre in Cardiff established itself as a creative hub for community filmmakers during the 1980s and gained funding from the newly formed Channel 4 in order to develop the work.

As the century drew to a close, Welsh film-makers produced two Oscar-nominated films – *Hedd Wyn* (1992) and *Solomon a Gaenor* (1998) – and in a flurry of post-devolutionary activity, a number of influential Welsh films were released. Marc Evans directed *House of America* (1997), based on Ed Thomas's play, which dealt with contemporary Welsh issues (an American company threatening a west Wales community with plans for open cast mining) in a way which split critical opinion as to its merits.[39] In the same year *Twin Town*, directed by Kevin Allen, hit the screens and became the most commercially successful film focusing on Wales since *How Green Was My Valley*. However, the film was as far removed from Richard Llewellyn's portrayal as could be imagined:

> The traditional family so central in *How Green Was My Valley* has now become dysfunctional, and big sister no longer hankers for the love of a preacher man, for she's far too busy working as a receptionist in a massage parlour by day and doing tricks for bent bobbies by night. On the other side of the divide the coal masters, scab labour in tow, have been displaced by villainous businessmen and cocaine-dealing undercover cops at the top of the food chain in the pre-millennium undergrowth.[40]

In 1999, Justin Kerrigan's *Human Traffic* bid farewell to the 'old' Wales for good, using Cardiff as a backdrop for a vibrant, energetic, and affectionate film on youth and club culture. Evan Roberts would no doubt be turning in his grave.

Television

Although the BBC's regular television service began from Alexandra Palace in north London on 2 November 1936, its initial reach was to a small band of 'lookers-in' within a thirty mile or so radius of the transmitter. The outbreak of the Second World War in September 1939 resulted in the immediate shutdown of the fledgling service, which eventually reopened on 7 June 1946. Despite the BBC's wishes, post-war expansion of television was slow due to the lack of capital funding available in a time of austerity, and in 1947–8 television accounted for only one tenth of the BBC's total expenditure; even by 1950 the budget for television was only half that of the (radio) Home Service.[41] By May 1949, the total number of television licences had reached only 140,850.[42] Nevertheless, by November 1949, a five-year plan for the extension of the television service had been published by the BBC and on 17 December of that year the Sutton Coldfield transmitter opened near

Birmingham, bringing BBC television programmes to the Midlands for the first time.

Television transmitters, however, are not renowned for their respect for national boundaries and so those living on the eastern border of Wales in possession of a television set were able to receive the programming. Thus, television came to Wales effectively in the relaying of programmes from London via the Midlands. It was not until August 1952 that the first BBC television transmitter on Welsh soil was opened in Wenvoe in the Vale of Glamorgan. Yet despite being physically located in Wales, the transmitter served not only south Wales but also the west of England (the areas surrounding Bristol and Bath), due to the nature of the airwaves and the aforementioned 'lack of respect'. By 1954 over thirty-four hours of television per week were being broadcast in Wales, and by 1959 half the households in Wales possessed television licences.[43]

Radio had proved to be a fertile ground for quality drama in Wales during the 1950s and 1960s, broadcasting the work of Saunders Lewis, John Gwilym Jones, Emyr Humphreys, and W. S. Jones ('Wil Sam') amongst others. Elan Closs Stephens has shown that between 1955 and 1972 the drama department at BBC Wales produced 117 radio plays 'of note, that is a high literary standard', in addition to children's serials, features, and other programmes.[44] Much of the credit for this must go to Aneirin Talfan Davies, the BBC's head of programmes in Wales, who was determined to foster native Welsh playwrights.[45]

During television's early post-war development, and prior to the establishment of BBC Wales in 1964, it was not uncommon to see Welsh drama, produced by the BBC in Wales, being transmitted on network television across the UK. Under the direction of Dafydd Gruffydd and D. J. Thomas (who had moved from radio to television), writers such as Elaine Morgan (*Without Vision*), Emlyn Williams (*The Light of the Heart*), and Eynon Evans (*Winning Ways*) were all given the opportunity to reach a wide audience on the increasingly popular medium of television in the late 1950s.[46] But television is an expensive medium and drama is an expensive genre to produce, and so with limited resources (for drama in both English and Welsh languages) and limited hours in which to broadcast (as laid down by the Government), the BBC was unable to sustain a programme of drama production for a long period, particularly as television was about to become increasingly competitive with the advent of the advertising-funded rival to the BBC, Independent Television.

Independent Television (ITV) first came to Wales in 1958, when Television Wales and West (TWW) began to broadcast from its Pontcanna Studios in Cardiff, although viewers in north Wales could see ITV via Granada Television in Manchester from 1956. However, during the period of its licence (1958–68), TWW made little impact in terms of television drama, focusing resources instead on light entertainment – popular programmes which would attract large audiences in both languages. The ITV regulator, the Independent Television Authority (ITA), was concerned about the lack of indigenous drama, as a letter from Lyn Evans, the ITA's Regional Officer, to John Baxter, TWW's Managing Director in 1964, shows:

> My committee have on several occasions drawn attention to the absence of drama productions in the Welsh language on independent television. They feel that there is plenty of talent among Welsh people in this field and that some effort ought to be made to exploit it.[47]

By July 1964, the ITA had requested that TWW should be required to produce 'four dramatic productions a year' and that these should be a mix of Welsh-language and English-language Welsh-interest productions.[48] On St David's Day 1965, TWW broadcast R. G. Berry's *Dwywaith yn Blentyn*, but by July the company was noting the difficulties in finding good Welsh drama to broadcast. Just as Howard de Walden had done in 1911, TWW launched a competition with a prize for the best half-hour television drama. Three plays were submitted, by J. R. Evans, Wil Sam, and Gwenlyn Parry, and at the end of the year the company transmitted a Welsh translation of Chekhov's *The Bear*.[49]

Meanwhile, with the creation of BBC Wales in February 1964, Wales now had five hours of English-language programming and seven of Welsh per week, opting out of the UK network at various points during the day. The additional hours allowed the BBC drama department to develop its playwrights, who included Gwenlyn Parry, Michael (Meic) Povey, and Rhydderch Jones. Parry went on to work with BBC Wales head of drama, John Hefin, to create the BBC's longest-running soap opera, *Pobol y Cwm*, in October 1974, and the unforgettable *Grand Slam* in 1978. Povey became one of Wales's leading actors and playwrights across theatre, film, and television, including writing for HTV Wales's south Wales-based soap opera *Taff Acre* (1981). Rhydderch Jones, with Parry, penned the classic Welsh-language sitcom starring Ryan Davies and Guto Roberts, *Fo a Fe* (1970–7).

The 1980s saw Welsh-based drama on the UK network, notably John Hefin's masterly *The Life and Times of David Lloyd George* written by Elaine

Morgan, and the serial *District Nurse*, which starred Nerys Hughes. The advent of S4C in November 1982 heralded a new era in television drama, not least as all Welsh-language output that had previously been on BBC Wales and HTV was now on the one channel. It also stimulated the growth of an independent production sector, not only in Cardiff and environs but in west and north Wales as well.

The final decade of the century was a problematic one in terms of ensuring that Wales-based productions reached an audience outside the country itself. At the BBC, Steve Blandford argued that 'the BBC London drama hierarchy's reluctance to support and develop Welsh work certainly suggests an inherent prejudice'. He went on to quote Alan Clayton, a former head of drama at HTV Wales, who suggested that the root of the problem lay not only in London but within Wales also: 'For years, there has been a marked lack of self-belief in Welsh writing and directing talent both in Wales and London. There is a perception within Wales that works deriving from Wales won't be sexy enough in London. This feeling has led to compromise and apathy.'[50] There were attempts to counter this trend, the most notable, perhaps, being HTV Wales's project *Nuts and Bolts*. Instigated by Pete Edwards, then head of Drama Development at HTV Wales, and broadcast in 1999–2002, the drama serial took a raw, gritty look at life in and around Merthyr Tydfil. Edwards took the unprecedented decision to mix professional and amateur actors in workshops to add to the authenticity of the drama.[51] Despite interest from the ITV2 network and a late night showing on that channel, the serial was pulled after four seasons, mainly due to a lack of commitment from the London-based ITV network.

Conclusion

Theatre, film, and television in Wales in the twentieth century not only provided fertile territory for the development of Welsh writers and actors but played a key role in the creation and circulation of cultural meanings, speaking to the country itself but also beyond its borders. As the century progressed, and increasingly from the 1970s onwards, these three key areas, components of the so-called cultural industries, moved away from representations of the old Wales as described by Ed Thomas at the beginning of this chapter to more edgy, socially relevant, and challenging portrayals of the country – in both languages. At the same time, however, it was proving increasingly difficult for broadcasters based in, and controlled from, London to take Welsh writing seriously. In this sense, it is difficult not to view the final years of the century through the prism of postcolonialism. Perhaps the final word should go to the country's pre-eminent cultural theorist, Raymond Williams, for his words underpin this consideration of a century of theatre, film, and television in Wales:

> If there is one thing to insist on in analysing Welsh culture it is the complex of forced and acquired discontinuities: a broken series of radical shifts, within which we have to mark not only certain social and linguistic continuities but many acts of self-definition by negation, by alternation and by contrast.[52]

Notes

1. Ed Thomas, 'The Welsh: A Land Fit for Heroes (Max Boyce Excluded)', *The Observer*, 20 July 1997, 16.
2. Steve Blandford, ed., *Wales on Screen* (Bridgend: Seren, 2000), 15.
3. Hazel Walford Davies, Introduction to *State of Play: Four Playwrights of Wales*, ed. Hazel Walford Davies (Llandysul: Gomer Press, 1998), xvii.
4. John Davies, *Broadcasting and the BBC in Wales* (Cardiff: University of Wales Press, 1994), back cover.
5. Charles Hill, *Behind the Screen: The Broadcasting Memoirs of Lord Hill of Luton* (London: Sidgwick and Jackson, 1974), 48.
6. Carl Tighe, 'Theatre (or Not) in Wales', in *Wales: The Imagined Nation*, ed. Tony Curtis (Bridgend: Poetry Wales Press, 1986), 242.
7. Ioan Williams, 'Towards National Identities: Welsh Theatres', in *The Cambridge History of British Theatre*, vol. III, ed. Baz Kershaw (Cambridge: Cambridge University Press, 2004), 242. See also Chapter 16 in this volume for the *anterliwt* tradition in eighteenth-century Wales.
8. For a critical examination of de Walden's contribution, see Hazel Walford Davies, 'Howard de Walden a Mudiad y Theatr Genedlaethol Gymreig, 1911–14', and 'Howard de Walden a Chwaraedy Cenedlaethol Cymru, 1927–40', both in *Y Theatr Genedlaethol yng Nghymru*, ed. Hazel Walford Davies (Caerdydd: Gwasg Prifysgol Cymru, 2007), 1–46 and 47–128 respectively. See further Walford Davies's article, '"The Country of My Heart": Lord Howard de Walden and Wales', THSC 20 (2014): 18–36.
9. Anwen Jones, *National Theatres in Context: France, Germany, England and Wales* (Cardiff: University of Wales Press, 2007), 151.
10. Williams, 'Towards National Identities', 246.
11. See Elan Closs Stephens, 'A Century of Welsh Drama', in *A Guide to Welsh Literature, c. 1900–1996*, ed. Dafydd Johnston (Cardiff: University of Wales Press, 1998), 239–42.

12. Elan Closs Stephens, 'Drama', in *The Arts in Wales 1950–1975*, ed. Meic Stephens (Cardiff: Welsh Arts Council, 1979), 240.

13. Williams, 'Towards National Identities', 243.

14. For a comprehensive collection of all Saunders Lewis's drama together with valuable critical commentary, see Ioan M. Williams, ed., *Dramâu Saunders Lewis: Y Casgliad Cyflawn*, vols. I and II (Cardiff: University of Wales Press, 1996, 2000).

15. Stephens, 'A Century of Welsh Drama', 249.

16. For a detailed critical study of Parry's work, see Roger Owen, *Gwenlyn Parry* (Cardiff: University of Wales Press, 2013).

17. Jones, *National Theatres in Context*, 203.

18. Williams, 'Towards National Identities', 262.

19. Ibid., 263.

20. For an analysis of the work of Arad Goch, see Roger Owen, *Ar Wasgar: Theatr a Chenedligrwydd yn y Gymru Gymraeg, 1979–1997* (Caerdydd: Gwasg Prifysgol Cymru, 2003), 176–81.

21. Lisa Lewis, 'Cwmni Theatr Cymru ac Emily Davies, 1982–4', in *Y Theatr Genedlaethol yng Nghymru*, ed. Walford Davies, 208–51.

22. Walford Davies, ed., *State of Play*, 117.

23. Stephens, 'A Century of Welsh Drama', 268.

24. Wil Aaron, 'Film', in *The Arts in Wales 1950–1975*, ed. Stephens, 297.

25. B. Ifor Evans, 'Wales and the Cinema', *Western Mail*, 16 October 1926, 6.

26. See Peter Miskell, *A Social History of the Cinema in Wales, 1918–1951: Pulpits, Coal Pits and Fleapits* (Cardiff: University of Wales Press, 2006), 4–6.

27. Anon., *Welsh Film History: 1930–39* (2010), www.bbc.co.uk/wales/arts/sites/film/pages/history-1930–1939.shtml (accessed 13 December 2017).

28. It is important to note that the 1930s saw the emergence of the British Documentary Movement under the aegis of John Grierson, who later went on to help establish the Film School in Newport. The GPO Film Unit films, such as Alberto Cavalcanti's *Coal Face* (1935) and Arthur Elton and Edgar Anstey's *Housing Problems* (1935), took a similar approach.

29. Peter Stead, 'Wales in the Movies', in *Wales: The Imagined Nation*, ed. Curtis, 169.

30. John Humphrys, 'Time to Blow All the Coal-Dust Clichés Away', *Western Mail*, 20 March 1996, 13.

31. David Berry, *Wales and Cinema: The First Hundred Years* (Cardiff: University of Wales Press, 1994), 166.

32. Stead, 'Wales in the Movies', 172.

33. Berry, *Wales and Cinema*, 215.

34. Ibid., 214. For a full and critical assessment of the portrayal of Wales and her people on screen, see Gwenno Ffrancon, *Cyfaredd y Cysgodion:*

Delweddu Cymru a'i Phobl ar Ffilm 1935–1951 (Caerdydd: Gwasg Prifysgol Cymru, 2003).

35. Aaron, 'Film', 298.
36. Berry, *Wales and Cinema*, 249.
37. Aaron, 'Film', 302.
38. Ibid., 306; Kate Woodward, *Cleddyf ym Mrwydr yr Iaith? Y Bwrdd Ffilmiau Cymraeg* (Caerdydd: Gwasg Prifysgol Cymru, 2013).
39. Blandford, *Wales on Screen*, 66.
40. Darryl Perrins, 'This Town Ain't Big Enough for the Both of Us', in *Wales on Screen*, ed. Blandford, 152.
41. Andrew Crisell, *An Introductory History of British Broadcasting*, 2nd edn (London: Routledge, 2002), 80.
42. General Post Office Archive, Post 69/45.
43. Davies, *Broadcasting and the BBC in Wales*, 199.
44. Stephens, 'A Century of Welsh Drama', 247.
45. Davies, *Broadcasting and the BBC in Wales*, 271–2.
46. I am grateful to Dr Billy Smart of the University of Reading for sharing information with me on lost and forgotten television drama. The information derives from an AHRC-funded research project at RHUL, 'The History of Forgotten Television Drama'.
47. National Library of Wales, Huw T. Edwards Papers, A3/25, letter from Lyn Evans to John Baxter, 29 January 1964. For further details of concerns over drama on TWW, see Jamie Medhurst, *A History of Independent Television in Wales* (Cardiff: University of Wales Press, 2010), 151–3.
48. Medhurst, *A History of Independent Television*, 152.
49. Ibid., 153.
50. Blandford, *Wales on Screen*, 137.
51. Ibid., 141.
52. Raymond Williams, 'Wales and England', in *Who Speaks for Wales? Nation, Culture and Identity*, ed. Daniel G. Williams (Cardiff: University of Wales Press, 2003), 20.

PART VI

★

AFTER DEVOLUTION

33

The Dragon Finds a Tongue:
Devolution and Government in Wales Since 1997

KEVIN WILLIAMS

A devolved Wales stumbled into existence in the early hours of the morning of 19 September 1997. By a very small margin, Wales voted for the transfer of powers to a National Assembly. As the rain drizzled down, the Labour Secretary of State Ron Davies described devolution 'as a process, not an event'.[1] Since then Davies's words have been regularly used to describe the emergence of the National Assembly for Wales and the development of a national polity. The ambivalence of the Welsh people has ensured that the process of giving life to the devolved structures has been slow. It has taken place against a background of profound change in Welsh society which is eroding many of the distinctive characteristics of Welsh life that had been embedded since the late nineteenth century. De-industrialization and economic transformation and, more recently, the forces of globalization are undermining the social basis of Welsh identity. Growing uncertainty pervades what it means to be Welsh, at the very moment when the country has the first real chance to build its own distinct national community.

Institutional Change

The institutional arrangements for a devolved Wales were laid down by a series of legislative acts after 1997. The first was the Government of Wales Act in 1998, which established the National Assembly. Section 2 of the Act outlined the powers to be devolved, which included responsibility for health, education, transport, environment, language and culture, agriculture, and tourism. The assembly's powers outlined in the Act were less extensive than those conferred on the Scottish Parliament (which was also established following a referendum in 1997). The assembly did not have primary law-making authority; it could only make delegated legislation within its areas of devolved competence. The National Assembly officially opened in Cardiff in May 1999. Many complained that it had no more power than the former

Welsh Office in London and drew attention to difficulties over funding. There was considerable confusion over the assembly's initial powers, and the evolution of the body has been characterized by the continual effort to clarify, streamline, and acquire more powers.[2]

The Richard Commission was established in 2002 to assess the further devolution of power, and it recommended in 2004 that the National Assembly should be transformed 'into a full-fledged legislative assembly with primary legislative powers on all matters not explicitly reserved to Westminster'.[3] The deliberation that followed the Commission's recommendations was characterized by three factors: it was dominated by Labour Party concerns; it took place behind closed doors and away from public scrutiny; and most of the key decisions were made in London, not Wales.[4] As a result, many of the recommendations of the Commission attracted criticism. The Government of Wales Act passed in 2006 extended the legislative powers of the assembly and created a separate executive, the Welsh Assembly Government (WAG). The 2006 rebalancing is described as the introduction of 'a scheme of quasi-legislative devolution',[5] as considerable power was retained by Whitehall and Westminster with the secretary of state exercising more influence than his or her counterpart in Scotland. This reflected the ambivalence within elite Labour circles about the process of devolution.

The outcome of the 2007 assembly election brought about a coalition between Plaid Cymru and Labour, which further propelled the search for more powers. Many, including some Labour grassroots activists, argued that, in spite of the 2006 Act, the assembly remained 'beholden to MPs to grant the necessary authority'.[6] Carwyn Jones, who replaced Rhodri Morgan as first minister in 2009, had always complained that devolution in Wales was 'a mess' due to the original decision to award the assembly 'limited powers in devolved areas'.[7] Tidying this up was important and a referendum on increasing the law-making powers of the National Assembly took place on 3 March 2011. In response to the question: 'Do you want the assembly now to be able to make laws on *all* matters in the twenty subject areas it has powers for?', a majority of those who turned out to vote said 'yes'. Wales's political leaders were ecstatic. Carwyn Jones referred to 'the year that Wales truly came of age',[8] while Plaid Cymru leader Ieuan Wyn Jones asserted that it marked 'the beginning of a new era of Welsh devolution . . . and the rest of the world can now sit up and take notice of the fact that our small nation, here on the western edge of the continent of Europe, has demonstrated pride in who we are, and what we all stand for'.[9]

Within months of the referendum, a new body was established by the Tory Welsh Secretary Cheryl Gillan to review the assembly's fiscal powers, and the further possibility of extending the assembly's powers. The Commission on Devolution in Wales, better known as the Silk Commission, published two reports in 2012 and 2014 which recommended the assembly have increased responsibility for financial and tax matters as well as policing, transport, and energy. A time frame of ten years to achieve these changes was suggested, with the possibility of a further referendum to gain public consent. More controversially, Silk put forward the view that the number of representatives in the National Assembly should be increased. The key Silk recommendation, however, was that Wales should move to a 'reserved powers' model, in which powers reserved to the UK Government are listed, with all others being devolved. This would, the commission argued, give greater clarity about what is and is not devolved, and would bring Wales into line with the arrangements in Scotland and Northern Ireland.

The growth of the institutional apparatus of devolution and the increase in governmental and legislative activity in Cardiff Bay has happened against a backdrop of fewer Welsh people bothering to participate in the politics of Wales. In the 2011 referendum, just over 35 per cent of the population of Wales turned out, less than the number who had participated in the previous referendum and assembly elections. The growing acceptance of devolution and the National Assembly reflected in opinion polls and surveys has not been matched by more participation in electoral politics. Disillusionment with politics is manifest throughout the British Isles, but the tentative way in which many in Wales have responded to the new structures contrasts sharply with what has happened in Scotland. Many people across Wales have experienced a sense of isolation from what is happening in Cardiff Bay. Polls since 2007 have found that the majority of people in Wales do not believe that the assembly looks after all parts of the country equally.[10] This contrasts with the promises made in the 1997 referendum campaign of a political process that would be 'inclusive' of all parts and peoples of Wales.

A New Politics

Ron Davies, in the lead-up to the 1997 referendum, promised a 'new' and more 'inclusive' politics for a devolved Wales. He stated later that the principle of inclusivity was the essential foundation of the whole devolution enterprise.[11] To this end, a system of voting that included proportional representation (PR) was adopted for assembly elections. Assembly members were elected by a combination of 'first past the post' and a regional vote for a party. PR was deemed necessary to gain cross-party support essential to legitimate constitutional change. It was also politically expedient, in light of the strong opposition to devolution inside Labour. There was bitter infighting in the party in Wales prior to the 1997 referendum.[12] Several Welsh Labour MPs were prominent opponents of the plan for constitutional change, but their opportunities to campaign during the referendum for a 'no' vote were curtailed by the Labour whips.

Following the narrow outcome of the 1997 referendum, Davies sought to make overtures to a broader political community in Wales, as well as attract Labour candidates for the assembly who reflected a wider range of experience and background. Efforts were made to encourage such candidates, but in spite of many responding to these calls the Wales Labour Party 'failed to select candidates from a wide range of professional backgrounds', and half of Labour's candidates were drawn from 'the usual suspects', predominantly former local government councillors, and no one from the private sector found their way onto the candidates list.[13]

The efforts to develop a new type of politics can be said to have died with Ron Davies's walk on the wild side of Clapham Common.[14] His departure as secretary of state for Wales ushered in the return to the tribal politics that has resonated throughout Welsh political history. This time, however, it took a relatively unusual form in the battle between Alun Michael and Rhodri Morgan. It was unusual in the sense that no one was quite sure why the Blair administration had decided to oppose Morgan's claim to lead Welsh Labour. Popular in Wales, Morgan appeared to have alienated the prime minister, who supported Michael for the Welsh secretary's job in the face of the overwhelming backing Morgan enjoyed amongst Labour activists and voters.[15] London Labour used the union block vote to 'parachute' their man Michael in to the post. Morgan's defeat was achieved with the support of the Welsh Labour Executive.[16] Michael's short-lived tenure after Labour's success at the 1999 assembly elections was 'marked by rigid central control by the First Secretary and excessive deference to Millbank and Whitehall'.[17] Inclusiveness was redefined to mean backing 'Team Wales', which was translated into total support for Alun Michael and his ministers. Anti-Morgan rhetoric in the London press and within Labour Party circles in London and Cardiff was vituperative. Much was made of Morgan's 'untidy house' and his allegedly bizarre sense of humour.[18] Morgan had the last laugh when Alun Michael resigned following a vote of no confidence in the assembly in 2000. His resignation was followed by his rapid return to the safety of the ministerial corridors in London.[19]

On taking office, Morgan attempted to pursue a policy of putting 'clear red water' between Wales and London. For the first minister this referred to the notion that Wales's political values were 'more community-minded, more collectivist and for some more Socialist than those of England'. Putting aside discussion of the validity of this assertion, the struggle became part of a broader dispute between 'old' and 'new' Labour, with Morgan, in Roy Hattersley's words, representing the democratic socialism that had characterized the party.[20] In a speech to the National Centre for Public Policy in 2002, Morgan appeared to repudiate the basic ideology of New Labour.[21]

The commitment to inclusivity remained until 2011, in the form of a coalition government which encouraged co-operation between Wales's political parties. Such collaboration represented political expediency and came to an end with Labour's success in the 2011 assembly elections when the party won thirty seats and was able to govern alone. 'Inclusiveness' continued to be part of the discourse, figuring in policy documents coming out of Cardiff Bay, but it was now little more than a rhetorical device. Paul Chaney and Ralph Fevre had correctly concluded a decade earlier that 'the cut and thrust of party politics, factionalism within parties and the personal style of key AMs during the Assembly's first two years mean that there is little evidence for an enduring "inclusive" style of conducting "new" devolved politics'.[22] This is not to say that there were no achievements to emerge from the politics of inclusivity.

The representation of women in the assembly was a notable success. Following the 1999 elections the assembly had the second highest proportion of women representatives in Europe, and between 2003 and 2007 half of the AMs were female. The means by which Labour increased its representation of women was not without controversy. For the first National Assembly elections, Labour adopted a 'twinning policy' to bring about gender balance. Neighbouring constituencies were 'twinned' to decide on one male and one female candidate between them, to ensure equal representation. Women-only shortlists caused considerable consternation amongst the Labour rank and file. In certain constituencies it led to rebellion, such as in Blaenau Gwent which saw former Labour minister Peter Law leave the party, to win as an independent MP in the 2005 general election. By 2011 the proportion of women AMs had declined, leading to the charge that 'both the Labour Party in Wales and Plaid Cymru have retreated from previous strong positions on gender balance'.[23]

The building of devolved structures was accompanied by the promises made by many politicians that the assembly would transform the nature of politics in Wales and that they would, in a spirit of inclusiveness, work together for the betterment of Wales. These words have not been matched by the practices and performance of Wales's politicians and political parties. This is the result of many factors, including the complexity of the Welsh devolution settlement, the failure to effectively inform the Welsh public about the work of the National Assembly, and above all the weakness of Welsh civil society.

Welsh Civil Society

The 'lamentable condition' of civil society in Wales has often been described as a major obstacle to the development of devolved structures.[24] People in Wales are generally not used to participating in a Welsh policy process, and the early union of Wales and England meant that distinctive Welsh institutions are absent or under-developed compared to Scotland and Ireland. The lack of separate legal and education systems and the under-development of a Welsh press and media have led to a weak civil society. What has developed is 'disunited' and 'insufficiently Welsh',[25] and it is not national. A vibrant civil society led the push to devolution in Scotland, while in Wales devolution is seen as the impetus to develop a civil society. This was summed up by Wales's most indefatigable campaigner for devolution at the very outset. John Osmond looked to the assembly to 'reinforce and give substantive civic meaning to the national dimension of the country's identity'.[26] The function of the assembly was to build the national structures that had eluded the Welsh, and to do this it meant growing a civic culture that was national and open to everyone to participate in.

Such aspirations have had to confront the statist inclinations of Welsh Labour. There were early efforts to galvanize public engagement and participation. In keeping with the commitment to inclusivity, the assembly government announced the need to develop a partnership with the voluntary sector, the objective of which was to create 'a civil society which offers equality of opportunity to all its members regardless of race, colour, sex, sexual orientation, age, marital status, disability, language preference, religion, or family/domestic responsibilities'.[27] The assembly approved a set of consultative networks aimed at different sectors of civil society, including the Wales Council for Voluntary Action (WCVA), Disability Wales, the Interfaith Council for Wales, and the All Wales Ethnic Minority

Association (AWEMA). However, as these arrangements were put into practice it became apparent that the interaction was on the assembly's terms. Inclusion was quickly transmogrified into incorporation. Graham Day notes that 'responsiveness towards the full diversity of Welsh society has been overshadowed by notions of acting together as "Team Wales", carrying connotations of consensualism, assimilation, and the suppression of differences'.[28]

Incorporation is manifest in the way in which the basic levers of power have been taken into the assembly's orbit. The Welsh Development Agency (WDA) was the most high-profile casualty of the 'bonfire of the quangos' that was ignited by the assembly government. It was taken over by the assembly in 2006 – along with the Welsh Tourist Board, and Education and Learning Wales (ELWA) – as part of the centralization of control of the economic levers of power. More surprising, perhaps, has been the way in which the assembly has tried to exert control in other fields, including the arts and culture. In 2005, at the time of the opening of Wales Millennium Centre, Rhodri Morgan announced that a number of Wales's leading arts bodies and enterprises, including the Welsh National Opera, Academi, and Theatre Clwyd, would be taken under the direct control of the assembly. 'Artsgate' – as the political furore around this announcement was dubbed by some – included the sacking of the chair of the Welsh Arts Council and the expression of strong concerns about the threat to artistic freedom.[29] The proposal was defeated when the opposition parties in the assembly got together to force the government into consultations which eventually led to a reconsideration of the policy.

Democratic Deficit

The assembly's interventions into various aspects of Welsh life reflect the weakness of civil society, but they also have to be seen against the backdrop of anxieties about the 'democratic deficit' in Wales. AMs have. since the 1997 referendum, expressed concerns about the lack of public knowledge of decisions made in Cardiff Bay, which is seen as impeding the development of Welsh democracy. The absence of indigenous media is at the forefront of these concerns and has been the subject of numerous reports since the Welsh Affairs Committee set up an inquiry into 'Broadcasting and the National Assembly', prior to the first assembly elections.[30] The problem of 'getting the Welsh message' across was identified at the outset of the devolution process. The Select Committee attributed the low turnout at the 1997 referendum to the lack of Wales-based newspapers and the limited reach of Welsh broadcasting. The under-development of online media in Wales has been seen subsequently as further hindering the efforts of the assembly to communicate with the citizens of Wales. Numerous ways of tackling the dependence on London-based media have been put forward with the suggestions of Presiding Officer Rosemary Butler in 2013 among the most recent.[31] Butler and her predecessors emphasize similar themes: the anglocentric approach of the London media, the structural weaknesses of the media in Wales, and the paucity of media coverage of Welsh politics and policy. These themes were reiterated at a conference hosted by the assembly about the BBC's relationship with Wales in April 2014.[32] London-based media is an easy target for such bashing, and some argue it enables AMs and ministers to avoid addressing the assembly's failure to develop a coherent communication policy.

The assembly has made numerous ad hoc efforts to further its engagement with the people of Wales. Central to these has been using advances in media technology to improve coverage and interaction with voters, including a focus on hyper-local media. This resembles the debate in the 1970s and 1980s when the *papurau bro* (local papers) were seen as a means to respond to the declining coverage of Welsh affairs in the national UK press. Spearheaded by the photocopier and the fax, such publications – mostly in Welsh – were seen as helping to keep local communities informed. In the digital world, the emphasis is on bloggers and tweeters and local newspapers online; it is the online world that connects the local to the national and beyond. Such outlets do provide coverage of the assembly and Welsh Government plans, proposals, and policies. How much is a matter of opinion. Professor Ian Hargreaves believes that Wales has 'got more chance in the new media configuration than it had in the old one which was dominated by traditional print media'.[33] However, the extent to which new media can contribute to building national coverage depends on the communications infrastructure in Wales and people's ability to access and use the technologies. Blogging comes with an information health warning; it is opinion-oriented, often simply commenting on the news in the mainstream media or responding to the rumour and gossip in Cardiff Bay. Bloggers do not usually generate stories, are not bound by any rules for the dissemination of information, and often speak to a small audience. Tweeters feed off the online world to establish a conversation which combines hard fact and uninformed speculation. Local newspapers in Wales – on or offline – tend to reflect a 'gap' that many across Wales perceive between local communities and the national policy-making.

Whatever the problems locally, it is at the national level that major challenges confront the communication process. The assembly's failure to develop a communications policy or strategy is a reflection of several factors. Three perhaps are worth emphasizing: the sensitivity of assembly members and ministers to critical scrutiny, the failure to devolve broadcasting, and the emphasis placed on the 'creative' industries as business enterprises. Relations between the media and the assembly have been troubled since the outset. Alun Michael set the tone when he called on broadcasters to 'report constructively' and provide 'mature discussion', believing that failure to do so would 'be letting Wales down', while his successor Rhodri Morgan was more outspoken, accusing the Welsh broadcast media of being 'undoubtedly hostile' to devolution with their 'flip, glib, quick cynical' judgements.[34] Criticism has been levelled at successive Welsh administrations for their reticence to appear in the media. According to one columnist, assembly ministers give the impression 'they are hermit crabs, seemingly scared of facing questions about what they are (or are not) doing'.[35] Limited appearances contribute to the lack of knowledge of who in government is responsible for what. This reticence is explained by some commentators as a lack of confidence amongst Wales's political leaders. A limited pool of talent and low levels of remuneration are the tired clichés used to account for the lack of leadership. Structural obstacles around policy and identity are perhaps more significant.

One structural problem that has inhibited the assembly's efforts to communicate effectively is the centralized nature of British broadcasting. In the absence of indigenous newspapers, broadcasting plays a crucial role in shaping Welsh life; so important that Wales's most loved historian believed that modern Wales is an 'artefact created by broadcasting'.[36] Since devolution British broadcasters have struggled to address the matter of broadcasting, which is central to any country's effort to foster its own political institutions and conduct its own politics. Changes in commercial broadcasting have seen the number of dedicated hours for Welsh programming shrink. The BBC has invested more in its nation-regions, and with the shift of resources out of Britain's capital city it has sought to redress the London-centric bias that has characterized the corporation since its inception as a public service in 1927. However, much of this is a matter of production investment, while most of the decisions about news, political, and drama coverage are still made by commissioners and editors in London. The situation in Wales is complicated by the existence of two broadcasting communities, one imagining Wales through the Welsh language and the other through the English language. The growing problem of funding S4C is contributing to the ever-increasing gap in spending on Welsh- and English-language radio and television services. The decline in English-language broadcasting was described by the Welsh Affairs Committee in 2009 as 'bleak', and it requested that the government 'urgently consider ... ways to address the shortfall'.[37] The Scottish Government's call to have broadcasting devolved[38] has not been matched by the Welsh Government, and the Silk Commission recommended that it should remain the responsibility of London. Given the importance of broadcasting to building devolved structures, the limited public protest from the industry, politicians, and civil society about this state of affairs is surprising.

Most of the discussion that has surrounded broadcasting, the media, and more generally the creative industries in Wales has centred on their economic importance. Assembly debates can be characterized by statements about how many jobs particular start-up projects have brought to local communities in Wales. The economic importance of these industries in Wales must not be underestimated, but there is a tendency amongst policymakers in Wales to focus on the creative industries as businesses, neglecting their contribution to the representation of Wales.[39] It is perhaps easier to assess these industries in terms of jobs created, investment attracted, and skills imparted. Their cultural contribution is less easy to calculate. A thriving creative sector in economic terms will not necessarily contribute – or could even be detrimental – to the representational needs of Wales. Perhaps the more pertinent question here is what the representational needs of Wales are in the post-devolution age.

New Sense of Identity

The establishment of the National Assembly has 'undoubtedly changed both the concept and the reality of "Wales" as a political and, arguably, a cultural and social place',[40] and it is not surprising that discussion about Welsh national identity has figured prominently. Traditional confusion and contention over what it is to be Welsh has not significantly changed since devolution. The efforts during the last fifteen years to blend the peoples who live within the geographical confines of an area called Wales – or Cymru, depending on your linguistic affiliations – into a national community have exposed the fragility of Welsh national identity. Nation building has been characterized by a variety of efforts to regenerate or reconfigure 'Welshness'. Some have sought to promote historic Welsh values by wrapping themselves in the past. Some have attempted to brand Wales with a new identity such as the short-lived 'Cool Cymru', which celebrated the work of certain cultural producers in the Welsh creative industries. Some particularly have attempted to promote a 'new progressive civic national identity'.[41] These different approaches underline the assessment that 'while the Welsh are sure that they are Welsh, there is no shared idea about what precisely Wales is or who is Welsh'.[42] Growing support for the assembly and more visibility for Wales in British and international affairs has not corresponded with a greater sense of being Welsh. According to Richard Wyn Jones and Roger Scully, 'the people of Wales did become more Welsh in their desired centre of government in the first decade of devolution', but 'in their basic sense of national identity they became no more Welsh at all'.[43] The notion of a Welsh national identity remains fractured by a diffuse sense of locality, language, and culture.[44]

The historian Gwyn Alf Williams concluded his seminal work *When Was Wales?* by declaring that it is becoming ever more difficult to imagine Wales as a unified entity.[45] He was writing in the political context of Thatcherism and the remaking of the British state in the 1980s. The erosion of many of the features of modern Welsh identity that had emerged towards the end of the nineteenth century was already apparent. The decline of the Welsh language, the decay of Nonconformist religion, and the demise of the coal and steel industries were contributing to the increasing difficulties of defining what brings 'Welsh' people together, beyond the emotional spasms felt when Wales plays its national game. Williams's pessimism is resisted by many today who point to the revival of the language and development of Wales-only institutions. However, the capacity to re-imagine Welsh identity since devolution has been shaped by new factors, factors beyond what is happening in Wales and Britain, which lend credence to Williams's words. The media and communications revolution, globalization, multiculturalism, and Britain's place in Europe pose a challenge to how we understand what it means to be Welsh in the contemporary world. Numerous communities in Wales are now exploring their sense of belonging to Wales.[46] The emergence of new and different articulations of Welsh identity challenges not only the perception of being Welsh at this time, but also the meaning of 'Welshness' in the future and the past. Rather than make the boundaries of the imagined community of

Wales clearer, devolution has accentuated the fragile and fractured nature of Welsh identity.

Notes

1. See Ron Davies, *Devolution: A Process Not an Event* (Cardiff: Institute of Welsh Affairs, 1999).
2. See Martin Johnes, *Wales Since 1939* (Manchester: Manchester University Press, 2012), 422–3.
3. C. Jeffrey, 'The Report of the Richard Commission: An Evaluation', Briefing no.12, June 2004.
4. See Alan Trench, *Old Wine in New Bottles? Relations Between London and Cardiff After the Government of Wales Act, 2006* (UCL: Constitution Unit, 2007), 10. Also published under the same title in *Contemporary Wales* 20, 1 (2007): 31–51.
5. Richard Rawlings, 'Hastening Slowly: The Next Phase of Welsh Devolution', *Public Law* (2005): 824–52.
6. Nicholas Davies and Darren Williams, *Clear Red Water: Welsh Devolution and Socialist Politics* (London: Francis Boutle, 2009), 54.
7. Carwyn Jones, *The Future of Welsh Labour* (Cardiff: IWA, 2004), 20.
8. Carwyn Jones, 'Speech to Labour Party Conference', Liverpool, 26 September 2011.
9. Ieuan Wyn Jones, interviewed by BBC News, 'Wales Says Yes in Referendum Vote', 4 March 2011.
10. Johnes, *Wales Since 1939*, 424.
11. Graham Day, 'Chasing the Dragon? Devolution and the Ambiguities of Civil Society in Wales', *Critical Social Policy* 26, 3 (2006): 646.
12. See P. Flynn, *Dragons Led by Poodles: Inside Story of a New Labour Stitch Up*, (London: Politico's Publishing Co., 1999); Kevin Morgan and Geoff Mungham, *Redesigning Democracy: The Making of the Welsh Assembly* (Bridgend: Seren, 2000).
13. Kevin Morgan, *Towards Democratic Devolution: The Challenge of the Welsh Assembly*, Papers in Planning and Research 171 (Cardiff: Department of City and Regional Planning, Cardiff University, 1999).
14. Ron Davies resigned as secretary of state for Wales in 1998 following an assault on him by a man he met on Clapham Common in south London. In 2004, he resigned from the Labour Party.
15. For a discussion of Labour's internal battles, see Andy McSmith, 'Boyos in the Back Room Slay a Dragon', *The Guardian*, 14 February 1999.
16. Morgan and Mungham, *Redesigning Democracy*, 129.
17. Paul Chaney and Ralph Fevre, 'Ron Davies and the Cult of "Inclusiveness": Devolution and Participation in Wales', *Contemporary Wales* 14, 1 (2001): 40.

18. See, for example, B. Clement, 'The Saturday Profile: Rhodri Morgan, MP for Cardiff West: The Clown Prince of Wales', *The Independent*, 13 February 1999.

19. For a discussion of the resignation, see Alys Thomas and Martin Laffin, 'The First Welsh Constitutional Crisis: The Alun Michael Resignation', *Public Policy and Administration* 16, 1 (2001), 18–31.

20. Roy Hattersley, 'A Comrade in Cardiff', *The Guardian*, 30 December 2002.

21. Rhodri Morgan, 'Clear Red Water', speech given at The National Centre for Public Policy, Swansea, 11 December 2002. For a transcript, see the Socialist Health Association website, www.sochealth.co.uk/the-socialist-health-association/sha-country-and-branch-organisation/sha-wales/clear-red-water/ (accessed 15 December 2017).

22. Chaney and Fevre, 'Ron Davies and the Cult of "Inclusiveness"', 41.

23. Joyce McMillan and Ruth Fox, *Has Devolution Delivered for Women?* (Edinburgh/London: British Council Scotland/Hansard Society, 2010), 7.

24. Day, *Chasing the Dragon*, 643.

25. Ibid., 644.

26. John Osmond, ed., *The National Assembly Agenda* (Cardiff: Institute of Welsh Affairs, 1998), 1.

27. Welsh Assembly Government, ch. 2, para. 2.7 (2000), quoted in Day, *Chasing the Dragon*, 647.

28. Day, *Chasing the Dragon*, 651.

29. Brian Logan, 'Arts Funding Row Breaks Out in Wales', *The Guardian*, 7 February 2006.

30. Welsh Affairs Committee, 'Broadcasting and the National Assembly', HMSO, 1999.

31. National Assembly for Wales, 'Addressing the Democratic Deficit – Presiding Officer to Outline Assembly's Actions', news item, 7 November 2013.

32. For discussion and speeches, see 'Perthynas y BBC â Chymru / The BBC's relationship with Wales', YouTube (2014), www.youtube.com/watch?v=LdrxIWo9bEs&feature=youtu.be&list=PLAiwHW5TKfkGakUCQjuZWxjeb4SRriPg2 (accessed 14 December 2017).

33. BBC News Online, 'Ian Hargreaves Says Citizen Journalism Has a Big Role in Wales' (5 May 2013), www.bbc.co.uk/news/uk-wales-22419883 (accessed 14 December 2017).

34. Kevin Williams, 'An Uneasy Relationship: The National Assembly and the Press and Media', in *Building a Civic Culture*, ed. Barry Jones and John Osmond (Cardiff: Institute of Welsh Affairs, 2003).

35. Graham Henry, 'Welsh Government Needs to Step up to the Plate on Media Appearances', *Wales Online* (29 June 2014), www.walesonline.co.uk/news/news-opinion/welsh-government-needs-step-up-7341495 (accessed 14 December 2017).

36. John Davies, *Broadcasting and the BBC in Wales* (Cardiff: University of Wales Press, 1994).

37. House of Commons, Welsh Affairs Committee, *English Language Television Broadcasting in Wales*, Eleventh Report of Session 2008–9 (London: Stationery Office Limited, 2009), 3.

38. The all-party Smith Commission in Scotland could not agree on the devolution of broadcasting, although it supported the Scottish government having a greater say in the operation of the BBC and a formal consultative role in the renewal of the BBC Charter.

39. Steve Blandford, 'Wales and the Question of the "Creative Industries"', *North American Journal of Welsh Studies* 7 (2012): 1–17.

40. Katie Gramich, *Twentieth Century Women's Writing: Land, Gender, Belonging* (Cardiff: University of Wales Press, 2007), 183.

41. For example, Leanne Wood, 'Greening the Welsh Dragon', in *Breaking Up Britain: Four Nations after a Union*, ed. Mark Perryman (London: Lawrence and Wishart, 2007), 86.

42. Richard Haesly, 'Identifying Scotland and Wales: Types of Scottish and Welsh National Identities', *Nations and Nationalism* 11, 2 (2005): 256.

43. Richard Wyn Jones and Roger Scully, *Wales Says Yes: Devolution and the 2011 Welsh Referendum* (Cardiff: University of Wales Press, 2012), 71.

44. For a discussion of national identity in the Celtic nations of the UK in the post-devolution era, see Arthur Aughey, Eberhard Bort, and John Osmond, *Unique Paths to Devolution: Wales, Scotland and Northern Ireland* (Cardiff: Institute of Welsh Affairs, 2011); Haesly, 'Identifying Scotland and Wales', 243–63; B. Taylor and K. Thomson, eds., *Scotland and Wales: Nations Again?* (Cardiff: University of Wales Press, 1999); W. Houseley, Kate Moles, and Robin Smith, 'Identity, Brand or Citizenship: The Case of Post-Devolution Wales', *Contemporary Wales* 22, 1 (2009): 196–210.

45. Gwyn A. Williams, *When Was Wales? A History of the Welsh* (Harmondsworth: Penguin, 1985), 304.

46. For example, see Charlotte Williams, Paul O'Leary, and Neil Evans, eds., *A Tolerant Nation? Revisiting Ethnic Diversity in a Devolved Wales* (Cardiff: University of Wales Press, 2015); Marco Giudici, 'Discourses of Identity in Post-Devolution Wales: The Case of the Welsh-Italians', *Contemporary Wales* 25 (2012): 227–46; Graham Day, H. Davis, and A. Drakakis-Smith, '"There's One Shop You Don't Go Into if You Are English": The Social and Political Integration of English Migrants in Wales', *Journal of Ethnic and Migration Studies* 36, 9 (2010): 1405–23.

34

'Amlhau Lleisiau'n Llên':
Birth and Rebirth in Welsh-Language Literature, 1990–2014

LLŶR GWYN LEWIS

Whilst the literature of the 1990s, a key and extremely productive period in Welsh-language literature, has been charted to a greater degree than more recent material, it has been done mostly through the medium of Welsh. An English-language summary of the period, therefore, as attempted in this chapter, is long overdue.

More challenging is an attempt to survey literature from around the time of devolution onwards, for two main reasons. Firstly, the material still retains a novelty that makes it difficult to tease out the dominant narratives and trends within the literature of the period. This is related to the second difficulty, namely that Welsh-language literature has flourished and proliferated to a degree that summarizing the texts since c. 2000 can seem little more than an exercise in selective list-making. For that reason, the chapter attempts to view recent literary activity in a broader comparative context along with the key texts of the 1990s.

Living Life on the Edge, 1990–1997

The stark reality of the decline of the Welsh language was spelled out in no uncertain terms when the results of the 1991 census were published. When it was announced that only 18.6 per cent of the population spoke Welsh, a reduction once again from 18.9 per cent in 1981, for many this was the next step in a long decline from the failures of the devolution referendum of 1979. There remained, however, an optimism that a new Wales might be born from the ashes of the old, but it required to be sung into existence. Myrddin ap Dafydd and Iwan Llwyd were two young poets who stepped forward to snatch the chair and the crown respectively at the 1990 National Eisteddfod.

Myrddin ap Dafydd's 'Gwythiennau' ('Veins'), after the elegies of the 1980s, was a heartfelt paean to fatherhood. Birth and rebirth, rather than death, became the focus. A series of scenes follows the conception of Rhys – a nod to the pseudonym of one of Meibion Glyndŵr's leaders, Rhys Gethin[1] – and his mother's hopes and fears for him in a decade of insecurity and worry. Though Iwan Llwyd was more concerned, in one way, with the past and with the 1979 referendum, his poem 'Gwreichion' ('Sparks'), too, is preoccupied with rebirth and regeneration. The main sense within these precise, evocative poems is one of hope and regeneration. Referring to Bruce Chatwin's writings on aboriginal songlines, 'Gwreichion' proclaims that through knowing and reviving their own songlines, the Welsh may again 'sing' themselves into being.

Many of this generation of writers were influenced by postmodernist aesthetics and poststructuralist theory which had reached Welsh universities in the 1980s. Llwyd, along with Wiliam Owen Roberts, his erstwhile peer at University College Aberystwyth, in articles called 'Myth y Traddodiad Dethol' and 'Mae'n bwrw yn Toremolinos' published in *Llais Llyfrau* in 1982 and *Y Faner* in 1984, argued that the prevailing myth of a continuous but selective Welsh literary tradition was a construct that had been created and perpetuated by scholars such as Saunders Lewis, whom they called a 'critical vampire'.[2] Realism, these articles claimed, did not reflect reality, and neither could it while it stubbornly adhered to an anachronistic literary tradition. They argued for the reinvention and reappropriation of the tradition with a view to commentating on, and shaping, the Wales of the present and the future. Their willingness to approach the fragments of the tradition, not with reverent awe but with a view to dissecting, pulling apart, and subverting the motifs and illusions of the canon with a cacophony of various voices, was something that Welsh-language writing had not yet seen.[3]

Roberts sought to realize this in *Y Pla* (1987), his fictional account of the fourteenth century, venerated in the canon as a time when Welsh nobility and poets coincided to produce a glut of poetry which represented the golden age of Welsh literature.[4] He rewrote the period from the standpoint of the serfs, portraying elements such as church corruption, bestiality, and drunkenness which contradicted its Saundersian depiction. *Y Pla*'s author revels in intertextuality, anachronism, and grotesquery in equal measure. Events echo globally here, too, as the spread of Islam and the Black Death across Europe are traced in the story of Ibn al Khatib. Violence looms around every corner, and the belief that change and upheaval must inevitably come, and soon, grips the reader.

Though Roberts published only one volume of prose during the 1990s, it is alongside authors such as Mihangel Morgan, Robin Llywelyn, and Angharad

Tomos that he is most often viewed.[5] For he was one of the leading writers of what was already by 1993 being called a 'small renaissance' of prose writing in Welsh.[6] The first true harbinger of that renaissance was Robin Llywelyn who, with his two novels *Seren Wen ar Gefndir Gwyn* (1992) and *O'r Harbwr Gwag i'r Cefnfor Gwyn* (1994), swept aside the slate dust and concocted fantasy worlds where fantastically named characters roamed fictional landscapes under the threat of the displacement of war or exile for the sake of love. Ostensibly allegorical but never overtly or entirely so, the novels dazzled, bewildered, and enchanted readers in equal measure, immersing them in their dreamlike 'Celtic' worlds which verge on the science-fictional and the filmic. As Katie Gramich noted, 'There is an unbroken *continuum* between the legends and the story and dreams: this is magical realism with an unmistakably Welsh accent.'[7]

Films, too, play an important part in the work of another of this new generation: Mihangel Morgan, purveyor of outcast iconoclasm who set many of his early works in marginalized urban settings. Through surreal locations, marginalized characters, and myriad cultural references, Welsh and otherwise, works such as *Dirgel Ddyn* (1993) present a new and irreverent viewpoint to Welsh-language literature, killing a few sacred cows (such as Nonconformism) along the way. He is, as John Rowlands famously declared, an iconoclast who 'does everything that the national and literary metanarrative forbids'.[8] Later works such as *Melog* (1997) are among the most concentrated efforts in Welsh to question the very nature of reality and of truth. Mihangel Morgan is an author of the margins. His is in many ways a doubly- or perhaps even triply-marginalized perspective: urban, Welsh-speaking, gay.[9]

Other prominent writers, such as Angharad Tomos, a language campaigner who was jailed for her activism, shared these attributes with Morgan. As Tony Bianchi noted, 'Their subjects are most often constituted as exiled narrators in a world of redundant or ambiguous meanings.'[10] Tomos's highly lyrical *Titrwm* (1994), as well as Manon Rhys's *Cysgodion* (1993), demonstrate that postmodernism in this sense was also a mode through which female experiences might be charted and explored in new and exciting ways.

In poetry, *Cilmeri*, Gerallt Lloyd Owen's classic third collection, was published in 1991. But the poets who came to prominence in the 1990s were, though certainly strongly influenced by him and others, markedly different in their approach to poetry. They sought to popularize the medium through live performances and innovative television programmes;

collectively they developed the *cywydd* form into a tool of public communication, *cywyddau cyhoeddus*. This new wave produced a stunning variety of voices, including Meirion Macintyre Huws, Nia Powell, and Tudur Dylan Jones, playfully dubbed by Ceri Wyn Jones 'criw *takeaway* yr Awen'.[11]

Despite their accomplishments, Simon Brooks complained in the radical literary magazine *Tu Chwith*: 'There is a new aesthetic "movement" afoot in prose, but poetry still lags behind, mostly because of *cynghanedd*'s grip. I think that *cynghanedd* is stuck to realism, though the idea of taking a genre like *cynghanedd* from the Middle Ages and turning it inside out could be very exciting.'[12] Dafydd Johnston commented in a review of a collection of *cywyddau*, 'It's interesting to note that postmodernist methods can be found in the works of the two poets who stand out as unique voices in this collection, namely Emyr Lewis and Twm Morys ... the whole point of [Lewis's poem] "Malu" is that it is an example of the disappearance of the author – a sophisticated critical joke.'[13] In terms of subject matter, too, Llion Elis Jones said of Emyr Lewis that '[a]s in the work of another of his fellow wayfarers, Iwan Llwyd, this sense of unrest and of constant movement is a continuous accompaniment to the poems, reflecting, perhaps, the culture of a generation that turned its back on the anxiety surrounding a lack of roots in a specific region, an anxiety that has been so prevalent in this century's literature'.[14]

Iwan Llwyd's 'You're not from these parts?' addresses the collective sense of displacement in a more head-on manner, highlighting the irony of the enquiry, in English, by a pub landlord in Ceredigion after the narrator had greeted him in Welsh. He admits that, no, he isn't, technically speaking, but that he still feels a sense of belonging to the area through his adopted occupation as itinerant poet: 'achos mae pob taith eilwaith yn gwlwm / â'r ddoe sy'n ddechreuad, â fory ers talwm.'[15] This sense is evident too in the 'haring', or 'sgwarnogi', of Twm Morys's poetry in his first volume, *Ofn fy Het*:[16] 'This is not a longing (not for a place, in any case), but an impression (a false one, perhaps) of not belonging anywhere. This is the image of the itinerant minstrel. And that is very ironic, considering the vivacity of the oral Llŷn dialect that he has and which enriches his poems.'[17]

These examples highlight many shared attributes: the influence of the medieval minstrel-poets and the adoption of their methods and journeys as patterns to follow; the highly oralized (and stylized) idiom of the poetry; and the way in which poets reconcile their sense of uprootedness and displacement in the present by taking recourse to medieval stories, poems, and customs in a fittingly fragmentary manner.

Authors and poets shared other concerns, too; many engaged in what might be described as a project of oralizing literary language, or of drawing attention to the problematic nature of the dominant mode of formal literary Welsh employed almost uniformly since John Morris-Jones's orthographizing of the language. Wiliam Owen Roberts's narratives employ a colloquial oral Welsh which unsettles narratorial authority in the texts; Angharad Tomos's *Titrwm* highlights the artificial nature of highly formal Welsh and draws out the tension between the written and the spoken; in Manon Rhys's *Cysgodion*, the tension is between different dialects of spoken Welsh. Robin Llywelyn and Twm Morys, certainly, recreated a language in print that was consistently nearer the spoken Welsh of Llŷn, Eifionydd, and Arfon in north-west Wales than had been attempted before. Indeed, it might even be argued that they 'out-spoke' spoken Welsh by producing a highly idiomized version which contained fewer anglicisms than that spoken by most today. This ensured two things in particular: firstly, readers were constantly reminded that they were reading *Welsh* literature.[18] Secondly, through their register these texts signalled a departure from a great deal of the previous literature of the twentieth century, with its formal, standardized written Welsh, and pointed back to earlier examples of Welsh literature such as Ellis Wynne, and even the *Mabinogi*. As Roberts and Llwyd had implored, writers began to 'look again continously at different epochs in our literature, and to *reimagine* them in the light of our age and its needs'.[19] As Dafydd Johnston comments: 'Oddly enough from one aspect, postmodernism is much less rebellious than modernism in its relationship with tradition. The postmodernist does not reject tradition, but receives it happily and treats it whimsically.'[20] Freed from the fetters of orthodox Nonconformism and nationalism, the new literature of the 1990s nonetheless brazenly asserted its inherent Welshness.

Postmodernist considerations of boundaries, space, and exile become inevitably bound up, in a Welsh context, with anxieties over the popular and cultural perceptions that the language is 'losing ground'.[21] Welsh speakers feel themselves to be dislocated subjects, the threat of finding oneself in a state of exile within one's own habitat a constant and ever-present one. For this reason, a curious characteristic of postmodernism as a literary mode is that its tenets are at once entirely suitable and complete anathema to the Welsh context.[22]

It has been argued that the startling newness of Llywelyn's, Roberts's, and Mihangel Morgan's work can be attributed to the way in which they seemed collectively to suggest that realism was no longer an available mode through which to explore the Welsh speaker's experience.[23] They employed postmodernist devices in order to imagine and construct new spaces within which the increasingly bilingual nature of Wales might be problematized or even transcended. They also played postmodernist games in order to subvert and distort the Welsh literary tradition and the old image of a rural, Nonconformist Wales.

It is of course problematic to label a handful of authors, often with quite disparate aims and methods, and sometimes criticizing each other's works, under the same movement of postmodernism. While a handful of authors were engaging in the exploration and experimentation described here, others persisted with what Katie Gramich called an 'attenuated realism'.[24] Aled Islwyn, Eirug Wyn, and Bethan Gwanas are particularly bright examples of gifted authors who had no truck in particular with postmodernism, but who are admired and read widely. Indeed, much of the critical debate surrounding the prose writing of the 1990s pitched a handful of experimental, 'elite' authors against more traditional, 'popular' authors, or the so-called 'common reader'.[25]

There did indeed grow a robust critical atmosphere during the 1990s, especially centred around Aberystwyth. Simon Brooks and others founded *Tu Chwith*, a journal which espoused postmodern, poststructuralist standpoints and which set about looking at the world with 'trais a therfysg tu chwith allan' ('violence and upheaval inside out'), a motto lifted from Iwan Llwyd's 'Gwreichion'. *Taliesin*, too, became a radical and highly important forum of literary discussion during the period, especially under the joint editorship of Gerwyn Wiliams and the late John Rowlands. Indeed Rowlands's towering influence, presiding spirit, and unerring *chwaeth* (taste) can be felt over the vast majority of the avant-garde literary activity of the 1990s.

Perhaps in order to distance itself from accusations of the kind exemplified above, however, a distinctive feature of Welsh-language postmodernism was that it often denied its own existence. As commentators such as Jerry Hunter and Richard Wyn Jones argued,[26] the way in which postmodernism, and associated critical schools such as poststructuralism, questioned and refuted the idea of any kind of absolute truth or *telos* was not a game that authors who, as Wiliam Owen Roberts claimed, were 'writing on the edge of catastrophe' could afford to play.[27] There was an underlying ideological stance to many of these texts: Roberts's works written from a Marxist standpoint, for example, or Angharad Tomos's overtly nationalist aims. But as Katie Gramich suggests, 'post-modernist experimentation is *not* incompatible with political commitment'.[28] Rejoicing in the dizzying freedom offered by the nihilism of postmodernism, but also faced with the prospect of linguistic ground disappearing beneath their feet – 'crebachu'n un car bychan', as Emyr Lewis puts it – writers sought in various ways to transcend boundaries of place and genre, through fluid, mobile, and chameleonic means, in order to re-imagine Welshness anew.[29]

From Freedom to Reality, 1998–2004

The new Wales that authors had been dreaming and imagining for so long was about to be realized in political terms. That most central of historical aims, Welsh independence, became a possibility, indeed a reality following the narrow victory of the 'yes' campaign in the 1997 referendum for Welsh devolution. The prevailing tone of Welsh literature for at least a century had been guarded, negative. The language's death had seemed almost inevitable, but that could change with a form of self-determination. Welsh writing gathered a confidence and exuberance unfelt for decades. Grahame Davies's 'Mae'n gêm o ddau fileniwm' is a typically wry expression of this new-found confidence, and the collection in which it was published, *Cadwyni Rhyddid* (2001), is one of the most direct poetic responses to the notion that Wales finally may have been 'free'. Perhaps the most apparent indicator of a new-found freedom is a nation's liberty to satirize itself, as Davies does in his collection: 'There is something much more than a naïve enmity towards the city. This is a poet who includes himself within the satire.'[30] Another author who thrives on the satirical possibilities offered by devolution and its effects is Robat Gruffudd, most notably in novels such as *Carnifal* (2004) and *Afallon* (2012), and the poetry collection *A Gymri di Gymru?* (2009).

Emyr Lewis's *Amser Amherffaith* (2004) strikes a more confident tone than that of his earlier *Chwarae Mig* (1995). In 'Aberglasne', there is a reclamation of land, a re-grounding and renaming: 'rhoi enw'n ôl i dir neb, rhoi enw a gwarineb'.[31] The poem concludes that a restoration of order can release the potential of a more unbridled freedom: 'Yn rhydd nawr y cerddwn ni / drwy Aberglasne'r glesni; / a rhwng meini gerddi gwâr / ymryddhau'r ŷm o'r ddaear'.[32] *Ymryddhau*; freeing oneself; this is one of the collection's central tenets, and nowhere is this better represented than in 'Rhyddid', a sequence of poems which won the 1998 Eisteddfod crown.[33] They revel in their cosmopolitan atmosphere, exploring Cardiff as a natural locus of Welsh-language poetry. The freedoms of the sequence centre on time and play on the Welsh term for the imperfect tense, or 'imperfect time', within which,

Lewis persuades us, we can dream, imagine, and dance. These are highly personal poems, but they also speak of a new sense of optimism and freedom.

This confidence manifested itself in other ways too; many poets turned outwards to face the world and broader concerns. Llion Jones engages wryly and entertainingly with the effects of technology – television, the internet – on our lives;[34] Gerwyn Wiliams, since the mid-nineties, has offered a Welsh perspective on the ever-growing, ever-shrinking 'global village'.[35] Myrddin ap Dafydd's chair-winning 'Llwybrau' (2002), too, was a nod to that global village and the way in which it interacts with smaller communities; it was also a metrical tour de force which dragged the *cynghanedd* into the twenty-first century with aplomb.

The role of language in a civic Wales was also being reconfigured. As Geraint Evans notes, Gwyneth Lewis 'is unusual in Welsh writing for having created an equally significant reputation for writing poetry in Welsh and English'.[36] Her ease in moving between the two languages, and her eagerness to project different voices and differing viewpoints within and between them, came to fruition in striking form in *Y Llofrudd Iaith* (1999).[37] In this volume, Lewis approaches anew the 'death' of language, suggesting that if it can die, it is possible for someone to kill it. Post-mortem and murder inquiry rolled into one, various suspects – including the poet, the farmer, and the archivist – are interviewed by a detective named 'Carma'. The volume casts Welsh as 'mother' tongue in order to explore themes of 'relation, loss and responsibility': 'What are represented by them [the volume's characters] are indifference, rural economic hardship, and a fundamental change in the nature of the community.'[38]

Female writers would proliferate in the Wales of the new millennium. The *Barddas* anthology of twentieth-century poetry, published in 1987, had been criticized for its almost complete disregard for female Welsh poets, the prolific Menna Elfyn in particular.[39] A decade later, however, it would have been nigh on impossible to ignore the distinct and confident female voices in prose and in poetry, not least among them Mererid Hopwood and Karen Owen whose mastery of *cynghanedd* belies the perception of that craft strictly as a male domain.[40] In 2001, Mererid Hopwood became the first woman to win the National Eisteddfod chair with 'Dadeni' ('Rebirth'), a tender and lyrical *awdl* narrating a mother's words to her infant son, meditating on the way in which her identity is shaped to a great degree by her motherhood. In her son, she is complete ('yn ei goflaid, rwy'n gyflawn') because she sees that 'Fy hanes yw dy hanes di'.[41] He is a 'fi arall – / hwn yr un a fydd ar ôl'.[42] The mother is now complete, and yet other: 'deall mai arall wyf mwy'.[43]

When the infant dies, conversely, she is '[y] ferch nad yw'n ferch na'n fam'.[44]
What is the 'Dadeni', however, in this personal, tender tale of grief and loss?
In the italicized epilogue, the narrator admits

> ... *Mae fy neges a'i hanes hi yn hen,*
> *y mae'n hŷn na'r stori*
> *ddistaw hon: dy ddewis di*
> *dy hunan yw'r dadeni.*[45]

(My burden, and its history, is old,
it's older than this quiet story:
the rebirth is up to you yourself.)

Italicized and set apart from the main body of the poem which greets the
child itself, this epilogue turns to the reader to offer this challenge. The three
judges were bewildered, seeing no relevance or need for it.[46] The *awdl* was
also criticized by one reviewer in the wake of the 2001 Eisteddfod:

> I have trouble fathoming, in the case of Mererid Hopwood and Elfyn
> Pritchard, how two parents who were fortunate enough to raise healthy
> children could go about imagining that their children had died ... Choosing
> such a theme says something about the Welsh psyche at the beginning of
> a new century and new millennium that I'm not entirely happy with.[47]

But '[Y] mae'n hŷn na'r stori / ddistaw hon'; birth and rebirth may be
metaphors for the nation here. If so, is the suggestion that no sooner had
the baby of devolution been born than it had already begun to wane and
sicken? In this metaphorical context the direct challenge of the epilogue
makes more sense, and it cannot be entirely a coincidence that the title of
Angharad Price's study of 1990s fiction, *Rhwng Gwyn a Du* (2002), published
the following year, echoes a line from this *awdl*, when the mother asserts: 'yn
y darn rhwng gwyn a du / mae egin pob dychmygu'.[48] Here again is that
circle of birth, death, and rebirth made possible through the imagination.

Another young writer, Owen Martell, emerged onto the literary scene
with *Cadw dy Ffydd, Brawd* (2000).[49] The novel exudes a new-found confidence in its willingness to engage with Anglo-American hegemonies, drawing them into the scope of Welsh-language writing. Rather than writing from
a situation of excitement, of exploring uncharted ground in cultural and
political terms, however, Martell's Dafydd Gilley finds himself caught up in
a life of cliché, false starts, and disappointment. The grip of the American
dream – the aim throughout the novel is to get to Chicago – and its attendant
ennui instigate a 'philosophical discussion on the Welsh's position. It is

a novel about Wales, and about an individual who lives outside Wales.'[50] Gilley is nourished, buoyed, by film-like images of himself and of his possible life: but that illusion is subverted if not shattered at the end. 'Dafydd doesn't have the confidence to be a person. He is so lifeless. But Dafydd Gilley, despite his characteristically modern condition, is determined not to remain in the mire.'[51]

Some persisted in their optimism for longer. In his novel *Rhaid i bopeth newid* (2004), Grahame Davies offers a challenge to devolved Wales by juxtaposing the devoted selflessness of Simone Weil's self-sacrificial life with the gradual realization of a language campaigner living in rural north Wales that her combative and outdated methods – protest, petitions, slogans, and adversarial radio debates – are no longer as effective as they had been. The novel's turning point comes when a conservative politician engages in some behind-the-scenes machinations at the Assembly in order to help her endeavours to pass a property law which protects Welsh-speaking communities. The implication is that, in a post-devolution Wales, 'everything', including even the means of securing the language's future, 'has to change'. It is a cautionary yet exultant tale.

But as other texts suggest, the devolution dream had already begun to fall apart at the seams. The Welsh Assembly brought its own set of challenges to Welsh-language culture: a renewed sense of Welsh civic identity made many uneasy following centuries of the centrality of the language to the national *esprit de corps*. Others quickly saw that devolution is, as the cliché goes, a process rather than an event. It is perhaps too easy to see the devolution referendum of 1997 and the subsequent establishment of the Welsh Assembly in 1999 as historic moments of rebirth and regeneration. Not even the results of the 2001 census, which suggested a rise in the number of Welsh speakers, were able to sustain the confidence of writers for too long: in the same year, a Plaid Cymru councillor, Seimon Glyn, dared to suggest that a sustained influx of people coming to live in largely Welsh-speaking communities was having a detrimental effect on the linguistic make-up of those places by failing to learn the language and pricing local buyers out of the market. Though he was labelled a racist by some in Welsh civil society, elsewhere Glyn's calls fell on more favourable ears, echoing a dawning realization that Welsh-speaking communities were still under threat – perhaps even more so, some argued, than before devolution.[52]

Perhaps the most significant novel written in Welsh in the new millennium to date is Angharad Price's *O! Tyn y Gorchudd*, winner of the prose medal at the 2002 Tyddewi Eisteddfod. Conceived as the fictional autobiography of Price's great aunt, her lyrical and haunting prose portrayed a learned rural family, and their trials, tribulations, and courage in the face of adversity. The novel depicted a family and community of the kind that was, even during the early twentieth century, rapidly disappearing, a decline which, in the light of the vehement reactions to Cymuned's campaigns and the violent twist at the end of the novel, was rendered even more starkly poignant. Indeed, Price herself went so far as to suggest that the novel was, in part, written as a response to recent events, and the disappearance of the life portrayed in the novel, due to an array of economical, technological, and demographic reasons.[53]

The response can be detected in poetry, too. Twm Morys's second published collection, *2* (2002), sees a regression from the playfulness of his first collection, *Ofn fy Het* (1995) to a more earnest diction and an eagerness to assume the mantle of *bardd gwlad*. The first poem in the collection, 'Dod adre', sets the tone, as the narrator admits 'Blinais ar wib olwynion', stating his desire to take root, to become more static.[54] Here Morys harbours a desire to see his world narrowing 'yn un nodyn, un edau'.[55] The journey, the undulation and crossing of borders and boundaries which underlined the poet's mission during the nineties now holds no appeal: the poet's role can only be understood as a part of a rooted community. The only way to 'read the map properly' is to dot it with pins indicating all the *lieux de mémoire* of a people: 'y mannau lle bu pwll / a chwarel a ffwrnais', or 'Lle bu Gwydion a Lleu a Brân, / lle bu tri yn cynnau tân'.[56] Place must be imbued with meaning once more, as Morys yearns for the time 'rhwng bod ein gwlad yn rhydd, a'n hiaith yn mynd i'w gilydd'.[57]

Then, in 2004, came a startling novel from a young author who was not, as Angharad Price and Twm Morys were, closely associated with Cymuned, the lobby group founded in 2001 to campaign on behalf of Welsh-speaking rural communities. This was a different kind of rural Wales, but in *Martha, Jac a Sianco* (2004) Caryl Lewis brought a south-west agricultural community to life, by focusing on the lives of three siblings struggling to make ends meet on the family farm and trying resolutely to adapt to a quickly changing, and anglicizing, world. The novel combines tender, humorous portrayals of the three with a more caricatured version of Judy, the English gold-digger. Throughout there is a sinister sense of degradation which almost echoes Caradoc Evans. But this is balanced with a tenderness that demonstrates the way in which Lewis has grasped a key element of the Welsh experience for decades and portrayed it as she saw it, changing and yet somehow stubbornly static, at the beginning of a new century.

English-language fiction and writing elsewhere has also, of course, made a similar return to more traditional modes of narrative. As critics, too, have begun to ask what comes 'after theory', so authors, dizzied by their brief flirtation with the abyss, have duly taken a step back from the brink. The brink for Welsh-language writing, however, was still worryingly near. For so long, the answer to the continuing decline of Welsh speakers had been 'independence', 'freedom', 'political autonomy'. 'Rhaid i bopeth newid' ('everything needs to change'), Grahame Davies had suggested, but many writers were already asking whether anything indeed had. Something did, however, change nonetheless. The seeds of a different approach to writing literature in Welsh may have been sown with the likes of *O! Tyn y Gorchudd*, *Martha, Jac a Sianco*, and Mererid Hopwood's 'Dadeni': a more conciliatory, considered, and perhaps more mature mode of writing, which moved away from the exuberance of postmodernism but retained its subversive and questioning nature.

Surfing, Not Drowning, 2005–2014

In 2011, Angharad Price surveyed the preceding decade's fiction and found very few direct literary responses to, and portrayals of, the devolution process. Most writers, it seemed, did not deem it worthy of especial mention or attention.[58] In light of this, Price ventured to ask:

> Are the Welsh, by instinct or custom, more comfortable in discussing national failure rather than success? Does the literary-historical metanarrative mean that it's easier to grieve than to celebrate in Welsh literature, or easier to feel *hiraeth* instead of facing the possibilities of the present and of the future?[59]

Another, more provocative, question is whether such an insipid and uninspiring process as devolution has done anything in order to merit a creative response: 'Many novelists suggested that the devolution process itself has not been dramatic enough to inspire creativity.'[60]

As Simon Brooks has noted, however, a direct response is not necessarily the only possibility. Claiming that the decade following devolution was a golden age for Welsh prose, he remarks: 'What has happened is that Welsh-language prose has responded to devolution. A crop of excellent books has appeared. They don't discuss politics per se, but they all discuss social commentary in some way or other. It's difficult to imagine this kind of discussion about Welsh communities if devolution hadn't happened.'[61] In novels such as Dewi Prysor's *Lladd Duw* (2010), *Creigiau Aberdaron* (2010) by Gareth F. Williams, and Angharad Price's *Caersaint*, Brooks claimed, 'there is a mature discussion about problems faced by real communities in Wales today'.[62]

Caersaint (2010) portrays a town that closely resembles Caernarfon, which still retains a high percentage of Welsh speakers from diverse backgrounds and class. The idea of having a Welsh-speaking protagonist from an ethnic minority background (Jaman, or Jamal, who has a Muslim father) is entirely plausible in such a setting. The town embodies an ideal, though by no means idealized, post-devolution Wales, which debates issues and tensions of civic, multicultural identity, through the medium of an idiomized, natural Welsh.[63]

Perhaps one result of devolution was to free Welsh authors to write of a wider array of subjects, people, and situations. Increasingly, the Welsh experience in the wider world is a viewpoint which is being explored and mined for the benefit of literature. A particularly gifted marauder through space and time is the virtuosic Jon Gower, whose heady combinations of fantasy, travel, and touches of postmodernism in texts such as *Y Storïwr* (2011) and *Dala'r Llanw* (2009) ensure that his readers never know what to expect from one work to the next. With the proliferation of authors, certain genres emerge and develop, too: the works of Llwyd Owen, Dewi Prysor, Alun Cob, and others, for example, build on the foundations laid by such authors as Geraint V. Jones in opening up the crime fiction and thriller genres in Welsh.

Authors experiment frequently with form and genre too. The most significant playwright of recent times, Aled Jones Williams, won the Eisteddfod crown in 2002 for a ground-breaking prose poem, charting a cancer sufferer's experience with a postmodern collage of stream-of-consciousness fragments. Annes Glynn won the prose medal in 2004 for *Symudliw*, a collection of flash fiction, a form which since Robin Llywelyn's *Dŵr Mawr Llwyd* (1995) has gained ground to become a regular feature of recent prose. This readiness to push the boundaries of form, perhaps most evident in Aled Jones Williams's various plays, poems, and novels, which all somehow transcend the boundaries of their genres, echoes what Declan Kiberd has called in the context of early twentieth-century Ireland 'the search for a national style'.[64]

Endeavouring to relate experiences completely removed from Wales and Welsh characters are Wiliam Owen Roberts's two mammoth offerings, *Petrograd* (2008) and *Paris* (2013), the first two parts of an epic trilogy which charts the trials and tribulations of one family during the Communist

Revolution and its aftermath. In its sheer scale and ambition, the project is impressive. Similarly monumental is Gareth F. Williams's *Awst yn Anogia* (2014), a portrayal of Crete during the Second World War; such works are significant for broadening, once again, the canvas of what can be written in Welsh.

These outward-looking novels, as well as Robin Llywelyn's *Un Diwrnod yn yr Eisteddfod* (2004), which is strikingly different from his other works in its more traditionally realist setting and structure, highlight a tendency already mentioned in this chapter. It is indicative of a sense that the onus is now on the Welsh themselves to debate and negotiate the reality of post-devolution Wales. Realist as it may be, however, fiction cannot now escape a painful awareness of its own fragility and its own artifice. Mihangel Morgan's later works remain plagued by many of the same questions regarding the nature of reality, but they are now rendered potent and pertinent for the individual and the community in novels such as *Pantglas* (2011) and *Cestyll yn y Cymylau* (2007). Works such as Tony Bianchi's *Cyffesion Geordie Oddi Cartref* (2010), Gareth Miles's *Y Proffwyd a'i Ddwy Jesebel* (2007), or Siân Melangell Dafydd's *Y Trydydd Peth* (2009) signalled new and fruitful directions for Welsh-language literature, offering a compromise between the Scylla of a strained return to 1990s postmodernism or magical realism, and the Charybdis of an oblivious and stubborn adherence to an outdated social realism.

The turn towards realism also suggests that a continuing anxiety about the disappearance of language remains at the heart of Welsh writing. Since many of the policies which can influence language use, most notably in education, are controlled from Cardiff in post-devolution Wales, it is more difficult to identify a clear 'outside' enemy who can be blamed for all linguistic woes. Failures of the assembly government or the Welsh Language Commissioner, much like other bodies before them, to tackle such thorny issues as migration into the Welsh 'heartlands', and the attendant flow outwards, or the so-called 'brain drain' bring the problem of declining language use closer to home.

It is perhaps surprising how few Welsh-language writers have felt comfortable publishing in English as well as in Welsh. Yet it becomes less so when one considers the case of Menna Elfyn, who has encountered criticism for publishing her work, increasingly extensively, with facing-page translations. Critics such as Robert Rhys have suggested that 'there is some weight to the argument that the translators are the editors that the poet has needed since the beginning of her career'.[65] Others have drawn attention to how these editions seem to marginalize the original language of composition. As Angharad Price notes, 'the truth is that the bilingual volume disturbs the Welsh-language poetry'.[66] Price also emphasizes, however, that when the translations are disregarded, 'there is some truly splendid Welsh poetry here',[67] poetry that plays with the accepted norms of grammar and vocabulary in a unique manner.

As Geraint Evans suggests, 'One of the main sites of struggle in modern Wales has been the language of composition for writers, artists and academics. Should it be Welsh or should it be English or could it, perhaps, be both?'[68] Writers such as Llwyd Owen, Lloyd Jones, Tony Bianchi, and Fflur Dafydd have increasingly undertaken the translation of their own work themselves. Fflur Dafydd has asserted that her novel *Twenty Thousand Saints* (2008) is based on her earlier Welsh-language prose medal winner, *Atyniad* (2006), but that the work was adapted and changed to a great degree during the process.[69] Others, like Gwyneth Lewis, have composed original works in both languages. Owen Martell's latest novel, *Intermission* (2013), is an example of his English-language fiction, as are Catrin Dafydd's novels *Random Deaths and Custard* (2007) and *Random Births and Love Hearts* (2015). Jon Gower, too, writes extensively in two languages.

This might be a reflection upon, and acceptance of, increasingly 'bilingual' social and literary networks.[70] In the case of authors such as Martell, Gower, and Catrin Dafydd, it is a natural reflection of their hybrid linguistic backgrounds. On the other hand, Fflur Dafydd has suggested that whilst writing in Welsh is to her as natural as breathing, writing in English was a highly politicized undertaking.[71] Indeed Twm Morys went as far as refusing to have his work translated for the *Bloodaxe Book of Modern Welsh Poetry* in 2003, asking why the onus is constantly on Welsh-language poets to translate their work into English, rather than vice versa.[72]

Is there a difference, then, between translation and a more politically acceptable willingness or ability to write different works in Welsh and in English? Twm Morys himself in his first volume included a handful of accomplished English-language *cywyddau*, suggesting that he, at least, sees an important distinction here. Interestingly, Menna Elfyn herself has argued in the past: 'I believe, then, that it is still important to raise a generation of poets who will sing monolingually in Welsh at the end of the [twentieth] century. There is a clear difference between translating work and creating in English.'[73]

It might be argued in fact that novels such as Llwyd Owen's, set mostly in and around Cardiff, need no translating, because the admixture of various registers and languages in the work reflects accurately the world in which and for which he writes. Especially at the beginning of his career, Owen was criticized by some for this macaronic approach; in order to be properly 'representative', perhaps an even more macaronic approach to novel writing is needed: as Angharad Price remarks, 'Traditional realism will be bound to betray the reality of the Welsh language. And realists who do not wish to include extensive pieces of English will be bound to portray a world which is, empirically speaking, unreal.'[74] But if this is to be done, it must be attempted from both sides, as it were, of that great linguistic divide, else it is a compromise that will result in decimation.

Authors and poets have also broadened their horizons in terms of the ways in which they approach questions of language. The appearance of literature which has ecological concerns at its heart is notable in this regard and can be regarded as mirroring, or conflating with, concerns for the language. Notable examples are Lloyd Jones's *Y Dŵr* (2009) and Lleucu Roberts's *Annwyl Smotyn Bach* (2008). In *Y Dŵr*, life on a Welsh farm is threatened by a rising lake which has already engulfed large parts of the country. The fact that the young Huw retreats to a world of books and stories in order to make sense of the creeping starvation and desolation around him, and that his sister Mari creates and reconstructs stories from the family's past, and ultimately with Nico finds salvation for them through these myths, is a suggestion of the importance and potency of stories and of literature in such a world.

In Guto Dafydd's recent poem 'Llanw', composed following the violent storms of 2014 which caused considerable damage to Aberystwyth's seafront, the narrator admits: 'Pan soniem am y llif yn merwino'r wlad / a'r môr yn cnoi a llyncu'r tir o'n gafael, / doedden ni ddim o ddifri'.[75] Now the threat is suddenly all too real. This ecological turn exposes the emptiness of the original rhetorical construct. In *Y Dŵr*, and in Dafydd's 'Llanw', natural disasters, the all-too-palpable results of climate change, come to fulfil the abstractions of previous generations. 'Fesul tŷ nid fesul ton / Y daw'r môr dros dir Meirion', Gerallt Lloyd Owen had warned.[76] But here, metaphor is transformed to potent reality, and the possibility that the sea's tide may arrive concomitantly with, or even before, a 'tide of Englishness', becomes alive.

Emerging, as it were, on the other side of disaster, Jerry Hunter's incredibly inventive *Ebargofiant* (2014) is set in a post-apocalyptic landscape and written in a newly orthographized and defamiliarizing Welsh which explores the need not only to recreate self and society following ecological disaster, but also language, and relates how recreating language is an essential component of recreating self. Elsewhere, too, the sometimes militant nature of attempts to save the language, and the linguistic tools employed in that campaign, are called into question or modified. Ifor ap Glyn's 'Terfysg', which won the crown in 2013, is one example of the way in which census results of 2001 and 2011 have tended to generate a much more lively and direct response than the devolution process itself. In these poems, however, the emphasis is on persuasion, education, compromise, and reconciliation as the most appropriate tools of language restoration, rather than the old methods of protest and aggression.

Taking their cue mainly from the diction and form of the preceding generation, Hywel Griffiths, Rhys Iorwerth, and Guto Dafydd are among those who have won the major prizes at the Eisteddfod, with many others such as Iwan Rhys and Eurig Salisbury coming tantalizingly close. Some, like Simon Brooks, have claimed that this generation is yet to respond to devolution, and moreover that they have as yet failed to emerge from the towering shadow of the previous generation.[77] The allure of the popular radio series, *Talwrn y Beirdd*, remains strong, along with the Stomp, a Welsh-language version of the poetry slam which was popularized by Eirug Wyn and others at the turn of the century and which garnered large audiences, numbering in the hundreds, in the annual Eisteddfod event. Some commentators have suggested that the *Talwrn* and, to a lesser degree, the Stomp, however, are in part responsible for a certain uniformity of voices and lack of experimentation; Alan Llwyd went as far as to suggest, when reviewing a collection of the *Talwrn*'s highlights in 2013, that this was the 'age of the great loosening of Cerdd Dafod', and that popular performance poetry was to blame.[78]

Tudur Hallam elsewhere has analysed both Griffiths's and Salisbury's, as well as Aneirin Karadog's, first volumes of poetry, arguing that only now are they beginning to find their own 'voice' or 'essence', and that traces of their different and differing styles can already begin to be detected.[79] This is a difficult task, however, when much contemporary poetry is characterized by irony, self-doubt, and the search for meaning, rather than the ideological certainty of the past. Perhaps the poet of this generation who most skilfully combines detailed attention to craft with genuine and sometimes heart-rending poetic expression is Rhys Iorwerth. His subjects range from love poetry, which moves from the drunken to the tender with unerring ease, to profound explorations of the tension between the lively Welsh-language scene of which he was a part in Cardiff and the call of his native Caernarfon, to more political concerns regarding, once again, the disappearance of language and the inept inertia of the Welsh Government in getting to grips with this.[80]

The poetic scene burgeons, and there are gifted poets such as Christine James, Dafydd John Pritchard, Siân Northey, Mari George, and Huw Meirion

Edwards on whom there is no room to expound here but whose works demonstrate the polyphonic nature of Welsh poetry today. An illustration of how two generations of poets have influenced each other and have begun to seek ways out of the post-devolution impasse can be found in the works of the winners of the chair and the crown at the 2014 National Eisteddfod.

Guto Dafydd, winner of the crown in 2014, embraces and acknowledges the creative possibilities of 'writing on the edge of catastrophe' or, as he sees it, surfing on the crest of a wave of destruction.[81] In 'Trydar', traditional rural communities have been stripped of their populations. The trees are bare, 'Trydar' proclaims, but we own the sky, pointing towards new forms of communication, new lines of belonging and of partaking in Welsh-language communities.[82] Yet Guto Dafydd's poetry often belies its own cocksure proclamations. So immersed in his own tradition is he that he can point to the exile of the court poet Dafydd Nanmor when discussing the ecological threat to the Traeth Mawr at Porthmadog or compare the chance existence of personal relationships with the survival of the Red Book of Hergest.[83] The tradition is being reappropriated, reworked, and reapplied, to refreshingly new ends.

Ceri Wyn Jones's lyrical virtuosity and mastery of wry, Cardigan-tinged strict-metre poetry are evident in his collection *Dauwynebog* (2007), and his chair-winning *awdl* of 2014, 'Lloches' ('Refuge'), confronts the duality of contemporary Welsh life. Decried by one judge, Alan Llwyd, as a macaronic travesty, it is nevertheless a poem which should be lauded for availing itself of the various tones and registers available to the bilingual Welsh speaker today.[84] Through them Jones addresses many questions that his hometown of Cardigan, Wales, and Welsh speakers have to face and answer, rather than persist with old dichotomies. 'Lloches' challenges us to confront and to attempt to dismantle that easy 'us/them' dichotomy which prevents everyone from moving forwards. Jones asserts that, like it or not, places like Cardigan belong to 'them' as much as they do to 'us', if not more so: the castles themselves are emblems of that.

Postscript

In many ways, the literature of the past twenty-five years or so can be seen as a golden age in Welsh-language literature, though the immediate future seems slightly unclear. The default mode of writing in Welsh for more than a century has been politically tinged and written with the painful and ever-present awareness that there may not even be a literature and readership in Welsh in the discernibly near future. The postmodernism which prevailed in European and American literature during the 1990s was well suited to the sense of chaos, subversion, and unease with which the writers wished to engage: it was a fortunate meeting which allowed a bright young generation of writers and critics to create their own unique kind of postmodernism on the edge of a precipice.

Once the nation had been afforded a semblance of 'significance' in the form of self-government, it became more difficult to continue with the postmodernist project. This momentous event had to be addressed, and meaning had to be inscribed on it. That Welsh-language writers as a whole have been unable to do so successfully remains a matter of debate. Though critics have begun to ask about new directions in writing,[85] they are difficult to discern because the same preoccupations prevail: loss of language, the feeling that one is an exile in one's own country. It is perhaps time to reconsider the either/or distinction inherent in Saunders Lewis's famous claim that securing the future of the language is more important than self-government. The strong, flourishing, and expanding nature of Welsh writing in English is another issue which complicates the Welsh-language situation. The welcome growth of such an identifiably Welsh literature in a dominant tongue could be deemed to nullify the urgency and the necessity for a Welsh-language literature, for so many centuries the only mode of expression available to the population of Wales. Many feel threatened by this; other writers, as we have seen, strive to build bridges, to connect, and to bring the 'two tongues' of the dragon nearer.

For our literature to begin travelling in new directions, it is necessary to find new, subtle, and complex means of dealing with the neo-liberal, apathetic, and, to an extent, apolitical mire in which we write. This requires new idioms which go beyond an ironic and quiescent self-criticism and a dependence on national memory and past glories, idioms which engage with the language and experience of the new century, looking outwards while acknowledging the past. How Welsh-language writers will respond to the UK's decision to leave the EU, for example, remains to be seen, though the results of the 2016 referendum on EU membership seem initially to have been received with the same air of despondency, disappointment, and anger that met the 1979 devolution referendum.

Some writers may come to see this period of political upheaval as an opportunity for cultural change and yet another wave of regeneration/rebirth. The critical milieu of Welsh-language writing seems to be gathering strength once again, with the appearance of new periodicals such as *O'r*

Pedwar Gwynt and *Y Stamp*, and even a podcast, *Clera*, dedicated to Welsh-language poetry. Along with these new spaces has emerged a younger generation of politically engaged and gifted writers, such as Elan Grug Muse, who writes in both Welsh and English and embeds her work in new media as well as print. Novels such as Catrin Dafydd's *Gwales* (2017) look to the political future with a mixture of apprehension and hope, while Guto Dafydd's *Ymbelydredd* (2016) has brought autofiction to its fullest realization yet in Welsh. This novel, with its metropolitan and European outlook intertwined with highly personal meditations on the human body's frailty, acquired a sizeable audience of admirers after winning the Daniel Owen memorial prize in 2016. Alys Conran's English-language *Pigeon* (2016), meanwhile, whose protagonists converse mainly in Welsh and which was translated by Siân Northey and simultaneously published in its Welsh version, has done more perhaps than any other recent work of fiction to enable a dialogue between Welsh and English that speaks for a bilingual nation.

Notes

1. 'Meibion Glyndŵr' ('the Sons of [Owain] Glyndŵr') is a reference to the rebel who led an uprising against the English Crown in the early years of the fifteenth century. It is the name of a nationalist protest group active in the last two decades of the twentieth century which targeted holiday homes owned by English people who were not resident in Wales.

2. 'Fampir beirniadol.' Iwan Llwyd Williams and Wiliam Owen Roberts, 'Myth y Traddodiad Dethol', *Llais Llyfrau* (October 1982): 11. See also Wiliam Owen Roberts and Iwan Llwyd Williams, 'Mae n bwrw yn Toremoltnos', *Y Faner* (14 December 1984), 6–7. In this chapter, Welsh quotations have been presented in English (author's translations) with the original Welsh in the notes.

3. An interesting discussion of these articles can be found in Guto Dafydd, 'Her newydd yr hen siwrneiau', in *Awen Iwan*, ed. Twm Morys (Cyhoeddiadau Barddas, 2014), 41–73. It should also be noted that other developments were afoot during the period which preceded the literary renaissance of the nineties. These included the forum on literary criticism held at Aberystwyth in 1988, 'Deialog '88', and the issue of *Y Traethodydd* in 1986 dedicated to discussing feminist literary criticism. See Chapter 30 in this volume.

4. Wiliam Owen Roberts, *Y Pla* (Bangor: Annwn, 1987).

5. *Bingo!*, a reinterpretation of the diaries of Franz Kafka, came in 1985, and *Y Pla* was published in 1987.

6. 'Mae yna deimlad ar led ein bod yn cael rhyw ddadeni bychan mewn rhyddiaith Gymraeg ar hyn o bryd . . . Oes metaffuglen yw hon, efallai, lle

mae realaeth naïf wedi'i disodli gan dechneg hunangyfeiriadol sy'n fodd
i archwilio drysni'r oes fodern.' John Rowlands, 'Cystadleuaeth y Fedal
Ryddiaith: Beirniadaeth John Rowlands', in *Cyfansoddiadau a Beirniadaethau
Eisteddfod Genedlaethol Frenhinol Cymru*, ed. J. Elwyn Hughes (Llandybïe:
Gwasg Dinefwr dros Lys yr Eisteddfod Genedlaethol, 1993), 90.

7. 'Mae 'na *continuum* didoriad rhwng y chwedlau a'r stori a'r breuddwydion:
   dyma realaeth hudol gydag acen ddigamsyniol Gymraeg.' Katie Gramich,
   'O'r Seren Wen i'r Cefnfor Gwyn', *Taliesin* 87 (October 1994): 106.

8. 'Drylliwr delwau yw Mihangel Morgan, fandal o lenor sy'n gwneud popeth
   y mae'r metanaratif cenedlaethol a llenyddol yn ei wahardd.' John Rowlands,
   'Chwarae â Chwedlau: Cip ar y Nofel Gymraeg Ôl-fodernaidd', in *Rhyddid
   y Nofel*, ed. Gerwyn Wiliams (Caerdydd: Gwasg Prifysgol Cymru, 1999), 181.

9. See the comments by Simon Brooks, 'Diaspora y Nofel', review of *Y Sêr yn eu
   Graddau, Barn* 454 (2000): 46.

10. Tony Bianchi, 'Aztecs in Troedrhiwgwair: Recent Fictions in Wales', in
    Peripheral Visions: Images of Nationhood in Contemporary British Fiction, ed. Ian
    A. Bell (Cardiff: University of Wales Press, 1995), 72.

11. 'The Muse's takeaway crew.' Ceri Wyn Jones, 'Cywyddau Cyhoeddus', in
    Cywyddau Cyhoeddus 2, ed. Myrddin ap Dafydd (Llanrwst: Gwasg Carreg
    Gwalch, 1996), 10.

12. 'Mae "symudiad" esthetaidd newydd ar gael ym maes rhyddiaith ond mae
    barddoniaeth yn dal ar ei hôl hi a hynny'n bennaf oherwydd gafael
    y gynghanedd. Dwi'n meddwl bod y gynghanedd yn gaeth wrth realaeth er
    y gall y syniad o godi genre fel y gynghanedd o'r canol oesoedd a'i throi
    wyneb-i-waered fod yn gyffrous iawn.' Simon Brooks and Wiliam
    Owen Roberts, 'Trafodaeth a gaed yn sgil rhai sylwadau a wnaethpwyd am
    waith Denis Diderot', *Tu Chwith* 2 (Summer 1994): 71.

13. 'Mae'n ddiddorol nodi fod dulliau ôl-fodernaidd i'w gweld yng ngwaith
    y ddau fardd sy'n sefyll allan fel lleisiau unigryw yn y casgliad hwn, sef
    Emyr Lewis a Twm Morys ... holl bwynt y gerdd ["Malu"] yw ei bod yn
    enghraifft o ddiflaniad yr awdur – jôc feirniadol soffistigedig.'
    Dafydd Johnston, 'Traddodiad Cyfoes', review of *Cywyddau Cyhoeddus*,
    Taliesin 88 (1994): 117.

14. 'Fel yng ngwaith un arall o'i gyd-fforddolion, Iwan Llwyd, mae'r ymdeimlad
    hwn o aflonyddwch a symud parhaus yn gyfeiliant cyson i'r cerddi ac yn
    ddrych efallai o ddiwylliant cenhedlaeth a gefnodd ar yr ymboeni am ddiffyg
    gwreiddiau mewn bro neu ardal benodol, y pryder hwnnw a fu mor amlwg
    yn llenyddiaeth y ganrif hon.' Llion Elis Jones, 'Cameleon, nid brân', review
    of *Chwarae Mig, Taliesin* 93 (Spring 1996): 101.

15. 'Because every journey is again a knot / between yesterday's beginning, and
    the tomorrow of long ago.' Iwan Llwyd, 'You're not from these parts?', in
    Be 'di Blwyddyn rhwng Ffrindia? Cerddi 1990–99 (Talybont: Gwasg Taf, 2003), 35.

16. For a detailed discussion of this method of 'haring' in Morys's work, see Sioned Puw Rowlands, *Hwyaid, Cwningod a Sgwarnogod: Esthetig Radical Twm Morys, Václav Havel a Borumil Hrabal* (Caerdydd: Gwasg Prifysgol Cymru, 2006), 40–3.

17. 'Nid hiraeth sydd yma (nid am le, beth bynnag), ond argraff (camargraff, efallai) o beidio â pherthyn yn unman. Dyma ddelwedd y clerwr crwydrad. Ac mae hynny'n eironig iawn o ystyried y bwrlwm o iaith lafar Llŷn sydd ganddo ac sy'n cyfoethogi'i gerddi.' Dafydd Johnston, 'Yr Ôl-fodernydd Cyndyn', review of *Ofn fy Het, Taliesin* 94 (Summer 1996): 121.

18. 'Rhaid cofio bod hanfod hollol Gymreig i'r nofel . . . Mae'r ffactor Gymreig yn ei gosod ar wahân i unrhyw nofel ôl-fodernaidd arall a ddarllenais.' Bethan Mair Hughes, 'Nid gêm Nintendo yw hyn, ond bywyd!', *Tu Chwith* 1 (1993): 43.

19. 'Ailedrych yn barhaol ar wahanol epocau yn ein llenyddiaeth, a'u *hail-drosi* yng ngoleuni ein hoes a'n hanghenion.' Roberts and Williams, 'Mae'n bwrw yn Toremolinos', 7.

20. 'Yn ddigon rhyfedd ar un olwg, mae ôl-foderniaeth yn llawer llai gwrthryfelgar na moderniaeth yn ei pherthynas â thraddodiad. Nid ymwrthod â thraddodiad a wna'r ôl-fodernydd, ond ei dderbyn yn llawen a'i drin yn wamal.' Johnston, 'Yr Ôl-fodernydd Cyndyn', 119.

21. Tony Bianchi notes that in contemporary Welsh writing in English there are found 'preoccupations with boundaries of time, space and identity in a period of profound change; with the signs by which these boundaries are less and less adequately recognized; and with the dislocated subject seeking, through these uncertainties, a stable habitation.' Bianchi, 'Aztecs in Troedrhiwgwair', 45.

22. Cf. 'Breuo parhaus a phellgyrhaeddol y gymuned Gymraeg el lilaidi yn ystod chwarter olaf yr ugeinfed ganrif. Dyna brofiad diasporig, *disparate* ac ôl-fodern os buo 'na un erioed.' ('The continuous and far-reaching unravelling of the Welsh-language community during the last quarter of the twentieth century. There's a diasporic, disparate and post-modern experience if ever there was one.') Brooks, 'Diaspora y Nofel', 44.

23. See Angharad Price, *Rhwng Gwyn a Du* (Caerdydd: Gwasg Prifysgol Caerdydd, 2002), 128.

24. Katie Gramich, 'The Welsh Novel Now', *Books in Wales* (1995): 5.

25. See Price, *Rhwng Gwyn a Du*, 8–41.

26. Richard Wyn Jones and Jerry Hunter, 'O'r chwith: pa mor feirniadol yw beirniadaeth ôl-fodern?', *Taliesin* 92 (Gaeaf 1995): 9–32.

27. Wiliam Owen Roberts, 'Writing on the Edge of Catastrophe', in *Peripheral Visions: Images of Nationhood*, ed. Bell, 77.

28. Gramich, 'The Welsh Novel Now': 3.

29. 'Shrivelling into one tiny car.' Emyr Lewis, 'M4', *Chwarae Mig* (Cyhoeddiadau Barddas, 1995), 56.

30. 'Mae yna lawer mwy na rhyw elyniaeth naif tuag at y ddinas. Dyma fardd sydd yn cynnwys ef ei hun yn y dychan.' Evans Dylan Foster, 'Bardd Treganna', review of *Cadwyni Rhyddid*. *Barn* 464 (Medi 2001): 38.

31. 'To give no man's land back its name, / give a name and give gentility.' Emyr Lewis, 'Aberglasne', in *Amser Amherffaith* (Llanrwst: Gwasg Carreg Gwalch, 2004), 42.

32. 'Freely now do we walk / through Aberglasne's greenery; / and between the stones of civilized gardens / we are freeing ourselves from the earth.' Ibid.

33. Ibid.

34. Llion Jones, *Pethe Achlysurol* (Cyhoeddiadau Barddas, 2007). See, in particular, his 2000 chair-winning sequence, 'Rhithiau' (13–21). Significant also was the publication in 2002, following a conference on the same subject, of Angharad Price, ed., *Chwileniwm: Technoleg a Llenyddiaeth* (Caerdydd: Gwasg Prifysgol Cymru, 2002). This was a collected volume of articles and essays that signalled the possibilities and advantages of the relationship between literature and technology and prefiguring a decade that has seen the Welsh language carve out a space for itself on the internet and on social media.

35. See, for example, 'Pentref', in *Cydio'n Dynn* (Talybont: Y Lolfa, 1997), 28.

36. Geraint Evans, 'Crossing the Border: National and Linguistic Boundaries in Twentieth-Century Welsh Writing', *Welsh Writing in English: A Yearbook of Critical Essays* 9 (2004): 129.

37. Gwyneth Lewis, *Y Llofrudd Iaith* (Cyhoeddiadau Barddas, 1999).

38. 'Perthynas, colled a chyfrifoldeb . . . yr hyn a gynrychiolir ganddynt [cymeriadau'r 'nofel'] yw difrawder, cyni economaidd cefn gwlad, newid sylfaenol yn natur y gymdeithas.' Dafydd Pritchard Jones, 'Y Llofrudd', review of *Y Llofrudd Iaith*, *Barn* 443/4 (Ionawr 2000): 87.

39. A summary of the various reviews of *Blodeugerdd Barddas o Farddoniaeth Gymraeg yr Ugeinfed Ganrif* (1987), as well as a fierce and reactionary response to them, can be found in Alan Llwyd's editorial in *Barddas* 135–37 (Gorffennaf/Awst/Medi 1988): 12–15. For a balanced survey of the 'scandal' engendered by the anthology, see Rhiannon Marks, *Pe Gallwn, Mi Luniwn Lythyr: Golwg ar Waith Menna Elfyn* (Caerdydd: Gwasg Prifysgol Cymru, 2013), 29–35.

40. See Myrddin ap Dafydd, Hilma Lloyd Edwards, Tudur Dylan Jones, Karen Owen, Ceri Wyn Jones, Mererid Hopwood, Twm Morys, and Emyr Lewis, 'Y Gynghanedd: Crefft Dynion?', *Tu Chwith* 9 (Gwanwyn 1998): 127–32.

41. 'My history is your history.' Mererid Hopwood, 'Dadeni', in *Cyfansoddiadau a Beirniadaethau Eisteddfod Genedlaethol Cymru 2001*, ed. J. Elwyn Hughes (Llandybïe: Gwasg Dinefwr ar ran Llys yr Eisteddfod, 2001), 17.

42. 'Another me – a me who will remain.' Ibid.

43. 'I understand that I am now an other.' Ibid., 18.

44. 'The girl who is neither girl nor mother.' Ibid., 19.

45. Ibid., 20.

46. See the judges' comments in *Cyfansoddiadau*, ed. Hughes (2001), 1–15.

47. 'Rydw i'n cael anhawster dirnad, yn achos Mererid Hopwood ac Elfyn Pritchard, sut y gall dau riant a fu'n ddigon ffodus i fagu plant iach fynd ati i ddychmygu eu bod nhw wedi colli plant ... Mae dewis thema o'r fath yn dweud rhywbeth nad ydw i'n hapus yn ei gylch am psyche cenedl y Cymry ar gychwyn canrif a milflwydd newydd.' Vaughan Hughes, 'Ieuan Wyn a Chwedlau Eraill', *Barn* 464 (Medi 2001): 27.

48. 'In the part between black and white is the root of all imagining.' Hopwood, 'Dadeni', 17.

49. Owen Martell, *Cadw dy Ffydd, Brawd* (Llandysul: Gwasg Gomer, 2000).

50. 'Trafodaeth bur athronyddol am safle'r Cymry. Mae'n nofel am Gymru, ac am unigolyn sydd yn byw y tu allan i Gymru.' David Greenslade, 'Edrych am Rachel', review of *Cadw dy Ffydd, Brawd*, *Barn* 448 (Mai 2000): 49.

51. 'Does gan Dafydd mo'r hyder i fod yn berson. Mor ddifywyd ydyw. Ond nid yw Dafydd Gilley, er ei gyflwr nodweddiadol o fodern am aros mewn pydew.' Ibid.

52. 'Anodd bellach ydi peidio â dod i'r casgliad fod holl drywydd sefydliadol a meddyliol y Gymru Newydd yn ddinistriol inni. Mae'r Gymru Newydd yn ddall i iaith a diwylliant a chymuned' ('It's difficult by now not to come to the conclusion that the entire institutional and intellectual direction of the New Wales is destructive to us. The New Wales is blind to language and culture and community'). Simon Brooks, editorial in *Barn* 458 (Mawrth 2001): 7. See also Simon Brooks, ed., *Llythyrau at Seimon Glyn* (Talybont: Y Lolfa, 2001).

53. 'I do feel strongly that we need to draw attention to the fact that this [is] a way of life that is under extreme pressure at the moment.' Angharad Price interviewed by Fflur Dafydd, 'Re-writing Autobiography', *New Welsh Review* 60 (Summer 2003): 28.

54. 'I have become tired of the rush of wheels.' Twm Morys, 2 (Cyhoeddiadau Barddas, 2002), 15.

55. 'Into one note, one thread.' Ibid.

56. 'The places where there was a pit, a quarry and a furnace'; 'Where Gwydion, Lleu and Brân were, where three kindled a fire.' Ibid., 38.

57. 'Between having our country free, and our language falling in on itself.' Ibid., 51.
58. Angharad Price, '"Dim oll"? Ymateb Nofelwyr Cymraeg i Ddatganoli', *Llên Cymru* 34 (2011): 237–47.
59. 'A yw'r Cymry, o reddf neu o arfer, yn fwy cyfforddus wrth drafod methiant yn hytrach na llwyddiant cenedlaethol? A yw'r metanaratif llenyddol-hanesyddol yn golygu ei bod yn haws galaru na dathlu mewn llenyddiaeth Gymraeg, neu'n haws hiraethu nag wynebu posibiliadau'r presennol a'r dyfodol?' Ibid., 241.
60. 'Cafwyd gan sawl nofelydd awgrym nad yw'r broses ddatganoli ei hun wedi bod yn ddigon dramatig i ysbrydoli creadigrwydd.' Ibid., 243.
61. 'Beth sydd wedi digwydd yw bod rhyddiaith Cymraeg wedi ymateb i ddatganoli. Mae cnwd o lyfrau gwych wedi ymddangos. Dy'n nhw ddim yn trafod gwleidyddiaeth fel y cyfryw, ond maen nhw i gyd yn trafod sylwebaeth gymdeithasol mewn rhyw ffordd neu'i gilydd. Mae hi'n anodd dychmygu'r math yna o drafodaeth ar gymunedau Cymreig heb fod datganoli wedi digwydd.' Simon Brooks, 'Barddoniaeth gyfoes yn "aflwyddiannus"', *Golwg* 23 (21 April 2011): 8. Later, Brooks comments, 'Ar hyn o bryd mae gennym ni gnwd o lyfrau a nofelau gwych yn ymddangos yn y Gymraeg. A dw i'n credu bod hynny yn digwydd, y safon mor uchel, mor gyson, am y tro cyntaf yn ein diwylliant' ('Right now we have a crop of excellent books and novels appearing in Welsh. And I think this is happening, to such a consistently high standard, for the first time in our culture'). Simon Brooks, 'Oes aur rhyddiaith Gymraeg', *Golwg* 23 (14 July 2011): 6. See also Price, *Rhwng Gwyn a Du*, 168.
62. '[Mae] yna drafodaeth aeddfed am broblemau sy'n wynebu cymunedau go iawn yn y Gymru sydd ohoni.' Brooks, 'Barddoniaeth gyfoes', 8.
63. As Price herself noted in an interview for *Barn*, 'Mae o'n fy niflasu i weithiau, clywed pobl yn sôn am y gogledd, neu'r gorllewin, fel rhyw lefydd Cymreig hen ffasiwn, mewnblyg, sydd â rhyw obsesiwn efo purdeb diwylliannol ac ati. 'Di hynny ddim yn wir o gwbl. Mae Caernarfon, er enghraifft, yn lle cosmopolitan ers canrifoedd lawer – ymhell cyn Caerdydd!' ('I get fed up, sometimes, hearing people talk about the north or the west as if they are old-fashioned introverted Welsh places which have an obsession with cultural purity and all the rest. It's not true at all. Caernarfon, for example, has been a cosmopolitan place for centuries – long before Cardiff!'). Menna Baines, 'Y Saint yn eu Gogoniant', interview with Angharad Price, *Barn* 566 (Mawrth 2010): 34. I am grateful to my colleague Dr Lisa Sheppard for various talks and discussions regarding *Caersaint* and Tony Bianchi's text. Her work has greatly informed the nature of my comments here.

64. Declan Kiberd, *Inventing Ireland: The Literature of the Modern Nation* (London: Jonathan Cape, 1995), 116.

65. 'Mae cryn nerth i'r ddadl mai'r addaswyr yw'r golygyddion y bu'r bardd eu hangen ers dechrau ei gyrfa.' Robert Rhys, 'Menna Elfyn', in *Y Patrwm Amryliw*, vol. II, ed. Robert Rhys (Cyhoeddiadau Barddas, 2006), 244.

66. 'Y gwir amdani yw fod y gyfrol ddwyieithog yn mennu ar y farddoniaeth Gymraeg.' Angharad Price, 'Y cyfieithwyr yn flaena', review of *Cusan Dyn Dall*, *Barn* 460 (Mai 2001): 41.

67. 'Mae yma farddoniaeth Gymraeg wirioneddol ysblennydd.' Ibid.

68. Evans, 'Crossing the Border': 123.

69. Fflur Dafydd, 'Author's Notes: *Twenty Thousand Saints*', *Western Mail*, 18 October 2008.

70. Indeed, Fflur Dafydd went so far as to suggest that 'moving to write in English was something that was influenced by devolution' ('yr oedd "symud i sgwennu yn Saesneg yn rhywbeth gafodd ei ddylanwadu gan ddatganoli"'). Fflur Dafydd to Angharad Price, in Price, 'Dim oll?', 245. Dafydd also noted, a decade on from devolution, that writing in English was something that writers could do 'without being criticized' ('heb gael eu beirniadu am droi i'r Saesneg').

71. 'I mi mae sgwennu yn y Gymraeg fel anadlu. Gweithred wleidyddol ydy ysgrifennu yn Saesneg.' Fflur Dafydd, 'Tu ôl i'r Llên', *Taliesin* 148 (Gwanwyn 2013): 114.

72. Twm Morys, 'A Refusal to be Translated', *Poetry Wales* 38, 3 (2003): 55. For a detailed discussion of the debate surrounding translation that ensued, see Marks, *Pe Gallwn, Mi Luniwn Lythyr*, especially chapter 18, written in English (183–98).

73. 'Credaf, felly, ei bod hi'n bwysig o hyd i fagu cenhedlaeth o feirdd a fydd yn canu yn uniaith Gymraeg ar ddiwedd y ganrif. Mae yna wahaniaeth clir rhwng cyfieithu gwaith a chreu yn y Saesneg.' Menna Elfyn, 'Beirdd y Tafodau Fforchiog', *Barddas* 226 (February 1996): 11. See also the discussion, ahead of its time perhaps, on a new fashion of writing in both languages that was prompted by this article, in *Barddas* 228 (April 1996): 10–14.

74. 'Bydd realaeth draddodiadol yn rhwym o fradychu realiti'r Gymraeg. A bydd realyddion na fynnant ddefnyddio talpiau helaeth o Saesneg yn rhwym o bortreadu byd sydd – yn empiraidd – yn afreal.' Price, *Rhwng Gwyn a Du*, 128.

75. 'When we spoke of the flood coming to agitate the country / and the sea biting and swallowing the land away from us, / we weren't being serious.' Guto Dafydd, *Ni Bia'r Awyr* (Cyhoeddiadau Barddas, 2014), 14.

76. 'House by house, not wave by wave / is how the sea will come over Meirionydd.' Gerallt Lloyd Owen, 'Tryweryn', *Cilmeri a Cherddi Eraill* (Caernarfon: Gwasg Gwynedd, 1991), 48.

77. 'Yn gyffredinol, dw i ddim yn credu bod yr ymateb yma i wleidyddiaeth y Gymru ddatganoledig newydd yn amlwg yn ein barddoniaeth ... dydi hi ddim yn ymddangos bod barddoniaeth wedi bod yr un mor ffyniannus â rhyddiaith ers datganoli.' Brooks, 'Barddoniaeth gyfoes', 8.

78. 'Daeth oes y llacio mawr ar Gerdd Dafod bellach.' Alan Llwyd, review of *Pigion Talwrn y Beirdd 12*, *Taliesin* 148 (2013): 94.

79. Tudur Hallam, 'R/hanfodoli', in *Ysgrifau Beirniadol* 31 (Bethesda: Gwasg Gee, 2013), 49–91. Hallam discusses, mostly, Hywel Griffiths's *Banerog* (Talybont: Y Lolfa, 2009).

80. Rhys Iorwerth, *Un Stribedyn Bach* (Llanrwst: Gwasg Carreg Gwalch, 2014).

81. Dafydd, *Ni Bia'r Awyr*, 9.

82. Ibid., 61.

83. Ibid., 28–9; 42–3.

84. Alan Llwyd, 'Beirniadaeth Alan Llwyd', in *Cyfansoddiadau a Beirniadaethau Eisteddfod Genedlaethol Cymru*, ed. J. Elwyn Hughes (Llandybïe: Gwasg Dinefwr ar ran Llys yr Eisteddfod, 2014), 6–11.

85. See Price, 'Dim oll?'; Tony Bianchi, 'Tri'n Hawlio Terra Nullius', *Barddas* 327 (Awst 2015), 47–9.

35

Writing the Size of Wales

ALICE ENTWISTLE

For as long as it has been represented, Wales has been imaged. As sheep, boar's head, dragon, old woman. As fierce, poor, mountainous, wet; musical, industrious. As morally derelict; as saved, by its chapels and ministers, its coal and rugby. As small: with just over 3 million inhabitants, Wales hosts barely 5 per cent of the UK's total populace. The protagonist of Lloyd Jones's 2006 novel *Mr Cassini* dubs its cultural locale 'a corner store in a supermarket age'.[1]

Curiously, however, this apparently diminutive territory can figure large. In the soundbite age, Wales has come into possession of its own evaluative-figurative purpose. Its surface area – of *c.* 8,000 square miles, bounded by nearly 800 miles of coastline – is freely and frequently used to measure the territorialized extent or effect of some piece of global news: sometimes to mark progress or empowerment but more often, as Jones's character also observes, to dramatize loss:

> Almost everything in the world is measured in Wales units now. Part of the ice-cap melted away last year and they said it was three times the size of Wales. If some of the rainforest is chopped down it's five times the size of Wales. It's an international unit of measurement. A measure of disaster, usually.
>   *(253)*

It is a question of scale. In the words of Raymond Williams, 'Smallness . . . is a shape we are carrying.'[2] That said, as Gaston Bachelard observes, 'Values become condensed and enriched in miniature.'[3]

Long-running scholarly debates about the nature and reach of Welshness only relatively recently homed in on the complex topos of Wales itself. Yet political devolution in 1997 foregrounded a *basso continuo* tuned for centuries to the Welsh people's fiercely self-protective interest in the national *bro* (very loosely, 'environs' or 'region').[4] Hence Hywel ap Owain Gwynedd's twelfth-century paean to his country's 'foreshore and her mountains, her castle near the woods and her cultivated land, her water meadows, her valleys and her

fountains, her white seagulls and gracious women ... her woodland, her
heroes and their homes ... I love all her *broydd* to which my valour entitles
me, all the wide wasteland and the wealth that hides there.'[5] If, as Tony
Conran observes, there was little sense of Wales as a geographical whole
prior to this, the importance of territory to a people 'passionately devoted to
their freedom and to the defence of their country' was not lost on Giraldus
Cambrensis.[6]

'The presiding spirit of Welsh history has been the shape-shifter Gwydion
the Magician, who always changed his shape and always stayed the same,'
wrote Gwyn Alf Williams in his influential and polemical history *When Was
Wales?*[7] Arguably, it was the appearance of that book, shortly after the people
of Wales had overwhelmingly rejected political devolution in the referendum
of 1979, which helped to tilt the national discourse more self-consciously
towards geopolitics. And yet Wales's most ancient songs and stories preceded
by centuries the so-called 'spatial turn' in Welsh literature which articulates
the poststructuralist 'recognition that position and context are centrally and
inescapably implicated in all constructions of knowledge'.[8] In its modern
forms, the 'spatial turn' plays on the perception that 'all kinds of hybrids are
being continually recast by processes of circulation within and between [a]
universe of spaces through a continuous and largely involuntary process of
encounter'.[9] This chapter concurs with Damian Walford Davies that 'different spaces of writing have profound consequences for the contours of
literary form'.[10] Landscape is one among many routes into the geo-cultural
problematic of space. Generally proximal, visible, and experiential, socio-
historically and culturally it is also an obvious one. Certainly, writers in
today's Wales savour the potential of the seemingly immemorial 'lie' of
their land, 'a realm in which, in the spirit of the legendary tales of *The
Mabinogion*, all is by no means what it superficially seems'. Nigel Jenkins
goes on: 'For millennia the inhabitants of these 8,000 square miles have used
and sometimes abused, shaped and remoulded the land they have lived on, as
the land in turn has shaped them and helped fashion their distinctive
culture.'[11]

Late twentieth-century literary and cultural critics found in cartography a
malleable critical trope. Poised literally, metaphorically, and performatively
between here and there, between empirical and imaginative, determinism
and dialogic, textual and exegetical modes, maps have been used to represent
all kinds of spatialities, across many disciplinary fields. Walford Davies
declares that the 'culturally plural, historicized cartographic paradigm is of
crucial importance in the critical and cultural project of defining the

Welshness (variously conceived) of Welsh writing in English'.[12] In recent years, Wales's literary ecology has been 'mapped' through its borders, regions, and topography; its towns and villages, old houses and monuments; its geographies of gender, industry, cultural practices and identity-groups; of language-use, current events, historical and ancient stories.[13]

In the new millennium, it would seem that 'everything is mappable'.[14] Or is it? Nigel Thrift distils from the complex of space four foundational principles which call this assumption into question:

> The first is that everything, but everything, is spatially distributed, down to the smallest monad ... Second, there is no such thing as a boundary. All spaces are porous to a greater or lesser degree ... Third, every space is in constant motion. There is no static and stabilized space ... Fourth, there is no one kind of space. Space comes in many guises: points, planes, parabolas; blots, blurs and blackouts. Some want to have it that the meeting is the thing. Others that it is scaling. Others that it is emergence. Others that it is translation.[15]

Amid what Marc Augé calls the overabundances of 'supermodernity', the two-dimensional map surely compromises space which it can graph only 'with equal value everywhere and in all directions. It is uniform and it is neutral.'[16] Likewise cartography's habit of 'precise and permanent separation [and] spatial fixing' betrays a determining 'urge towards classification, order, control and purification', which sits uneasily with the poststructural emphases 'of connectivity, networked linkage, marginality and liminality, and the transgression of linear boundaries and hermetic categories – spatial "flow" – which mark experience in the late twentieth-century world'.[17] Indeed, simply in the transfer between actual and representative which its 'graph'-ing enacts, cartography distorts. As Mark Monmonier observes, since 'the map must use symbols that almost always are proportionally much bigger or thicker than the features they represent ... to present a useful and truthful picture, an accurate map must tell lies'.[18]

For Henri Lefebvre, space is at once materially (and conceptually) productive, and simultaneously produced. Doreen Massey refines Lefebvre's proposition with her own much-quoted contention that space is 'always under construction ... in the process of being made. It is never finished, never closed. Perhaps we might imagine space as a simultaneity of stories-so-far.'[19] Massey's construction of space as an inexhaustibly multidimensional narrative has anchored various literary-geographical studies of the cultural (socioeconomic and historical-political) dialectics linking author, text, reader, and context(s). That said, Massey's silent elision of any distinction between concrete and abstract notions of space also underlines the challenges of theorizing a concept which – for Kant, like time – necessarily precedes any conceiving of it. In that paradox, Massey's abstract (discursive), material (linguistic), and spatio-textual domain suggests an equivalence of space and 'genre'.

This chapter argues that the dialogical abstract-concrete spaces of literary genre and form are products of both the geographies and the cultures in and from which a textual construct emerges. Drawing on theorized concepts of 'space' and 'place', I read genre as space and the page as a web of associated and disassociated places edged by an infinitely regressive zone of encounter. However, as 'a means of production [space] is also a means of control . . . it escapes in part from those who would make use of it'.[20] Some literary texts from Wales speak as resonantly in their failure to fashion a cultural-political 'palimpsest' of contemporary Wales as others do in producing a new creative text-territory of the landscape.[21]

Literary Spaces: Genre as Landscape

The problematics of genre have distracted literary and other critics for centuries. As John Frow reflects, 'Genre is neither a property of (and located "in") texts, nor a projection of (and located "in") readers; it exists as a part of the relationship between texts and readers.'[22] Certainly, after Derrida's deconstruction of its signifying bounds, literary genre is surely implicated in John Wylie's definition of landscape as 'a milieu of meaningful cultural practices and values, not simply a set of observable material cultural facts'.[23] If genre discourse has yet to mobilize the topographical metaphors it evokes, like landscape it begs definition as 'both the phenomenon itself *and* our perception of it'; like landscape, genre is 'not just about *what* we see [or encounter], but about *how we look* [or read]'.[24]

In retrospect, the first decades of Wales's new century have been marked by a startling degree of literary invention. A generation of new millennial novelists announced themselves by worrying – in various moods – at certain exclusive-seeming 'givens' of their cultural (and generic) milieu. The mid-century south Wales of Emyr Humphreys, Gwyn Thomas, and Ron Berry, memorably refurbished by Chris Meredith in *Shifts* (1988), is deftly unpicked among Cardiff's diverse cultures by Trezza Azzopardi (*The Hiding Place*, 2000) and John Williams's compendious, mixed-mode *The Cardiff Trilogy* (2006), in the riotous Merthyr demotic of Des Barry's *A Bloody Good Friday* (2002) and the off-kilter humour of Meredith's *A Book of Idiots* (2012), set in the Valleys. Alys Conran's adeptly macaronic tour de force *Pigeon* (2016) follows a trail blazed (in dialect use as much as episodic form) by Niall Griffiths (*Grits*, 2000; *Sheepshagger*, 2001; and *Stump*, 2003) in tilting the protest westwards and into a rural landscape rich in a collective sense of cultural-linguistic loss and shame which buries pride as well as answers. Worthy of Caradoc Evans, Griffiths's mountainous north is as unremittingly – Gothicly – bleak as the Aberystwyth satirized in Malcolm Pryce's darkly comic detective fiction (*Aberystwyth Noir*, 2001–11), a town enervated by hopeless parochialism. These, and novels by Stevie Davies, Patrick McGuinness, Cynan Jones, Tristran Hughes, Tom Bullough, and – more mutedly, from her London base – Sarah Waters, along with the short stories of Rachel Trezise, Tessa Hadley, Tyler Keevil, and Francesca Rhydderch (to shortchange a vibrant and expanding scene), exceed, refuse, or subvert conventional expectations by bringing genre and place into conversation.

Among this host of inventive fictions published in the first decade of Wales's new century, Lloyd Jones's *Mr Cassini* is a virtuosic example of generic self-disruption. This is not simply a story told by a number of voices, each in its own way embedded, each in its own way embedding numerous others. A narrative landscape which divides and subdivides in time is also spatially disorienting: we learn that it has taken place over a single week only in the last of its three main parts, entitled 'Reality'. The chapters announce their own tidal rhythm in a dialogic structure which washes performatively (in its alternating voices) to and fro over the same liminal, beach-like strand. At the same time, the work is both contextualized by and played out in strata of intersecting stories which seem at first barely related; each of them looks different depending on the narrative frame in which we encounter them. Amid this seemingly reflexive fluidity, the overarching narrative – the poignantly familiar story of a man left by time and various kinds of loss to (re)parent himself – is (belatedly) justified in explicitly concrete terms and metaphorically concrete 'grounds':

> *Come on then Dad. I've put a very long story between you and me, a very long trail of words. Look at all the paragraphs. Look at all the sentences. Look at all the words and letters between you and me.* And his father would have to step on every single letter, as if he were crossing stones in a very wide river, before he got to him . . .   (270; *emphases original*)

Mr Cassini's interest in its own self-undoing and disorienting arrangement persists among the many kinds of material – formal, figurative, thematic, psychic, philosophical – in, through and with which it is uttered. Fascination with water obtrudes: 'What made it move? A sacred power? *Flowing water is a magician's hinge, the passage between two worlds*, says Iain Sinclair' (60; emphases original). Sea, fjords, lakes, ponds, wells, springs, trapped in rain, ice, snowflakes: water, if it is not always fluvial, throughout disrupts the allure of pattern, especially numerical. Negotiating between water and number, slipping from unconsciousness (Part 1 is entitled 'Dream') through the semi-willed liminality of 'Day Dream' (Part 2) into the 'Reality' (Part 3) on which it closes, like its 'real-life' protagonist the text is poised between a conflicted and unresolved desire to cede control both to flux and fixity. A seven-day 'journey through time and space', originating in the flight of seven swans through the seven colour bands of the rainbow (13), is governed in other ways by this and other reputedly magic numbers, not least the seven years it takes the (eponymous) Cassini space-probe to reach the seven rings of Saturn:

> The number seven is my number as they say; since I seem to choose it before all other numbers in draws and lotteries, I will use it too in my quest for personal discovery. There are no more than seven basic plots to the human story ... They say that the human body undergoes a complete change of cells every seven years.
>
> (21)

The book's three separate parts comprise in total fourteen chapters; with its prologue, Part 1 falls into seven discrete elements, doubling the sum of the other two parts. In some ways the formalities of a dizzying technical and imaginative achievement only reinforce the depth of unreliability which its disoriented readers are asked to plumb:

> *Everything is happening now. The past and the future, too. All that has happened and all that will happen is happening now. Without beginning, middle or end, the performance is continuous and ever-happening. Whatever has been in the past and whatever will be in the future is happening now, all at the same time.*
>
> (193–4; emphases original)

Rooted in the landscape and terrain of Wales, *Mr Cassini* makes its cultural context seem incapable of containing its own energies and resonances. The text's self-orbiting form, rhizomatically shaping and reshaping itself and our experiences of it, grows or spills compromisingly out of the polyphonic multiply-arcing narrative by which it might normally be contained or mapped. It misbehaves; it subverts by exceeding the limits of its own generic landscape.

Strangely for its size and garrulity, this novel is elegiac. Typically, elegy poses an intellectual and emotional challenge which formally – materially – it cannot answer. There is never the space. Elegy must build itself on and out of a silence it can neither ignore nor fill. Likewise Duxie, trapped like his story between past and future, is always enthralled

> by the word on the page, by the fact that the sea of white around each letter is sometimes more meaningful – more emancipating? – than the words them-selves. Books as liquid charts, slopping from one hand to the next. Sentences as sea-bound glaciers with their story meanings trapped inside them, debris. Memories as terminal moraines. Each page a white mist, a spell upon the land, crowded with words which have forgotten their childhoods.   (208)

Such moments adroitly remind us that the white spaces and words etched in and on it make any page a bewitching terrain. If its edges make 'the island of the page' a usefully self-delimiting arena of signification, this is perhaps especially so for the lyric poem, longest-lived form of creative expression in a Wales which still cherishes it.[25] Even today, the lyric poem in Wales is 'a genre of poetry perhaps most commonly circulated primarily in print, and read, whether silently or aloud, from the page [and enjoying] a significant and independent life *on* the page'.[26]

The Page as Space and Place

Straightforwardly constructed as 'space made meaningful by human agency', 'place' has to do with the processes of representation and evaluation: 'Place is also a way of seeing, knowing, and understanding the world.'[27] Accordingly, 'In practice, all space is anthropological, all space is practised, all space is place.'[28] Self-evidently, most text-spaces constitute material places; what written expression does not depend to some extent on emplacement to achieve itself? To tweak the words of Susanne Langer, 'we say a [text is about] a place, but [materially] it *is* a place.'[29]

Arguably, as for the place so for the page, a material topos designated both place and space. As Walter Ong explains, 'Print is comfortable only with finality. Once a letterpress forme is closed, locked up . . . and the sheet printed, the text does not [readily] accommodate changes'; print culture likewise 'tends to feel a work as "closed", set off from other works, a unit in itself'.[30] Rendering language visual, 'print locks words into position' to be nuanced by the ways in which 'typographical space is present to the psyche' (121). Although Ong illustrates this with the radical spatialities of concrete poetry, any poetic construct 'interacts with the visually and kinaesthetically perceived space around [it]' and 'plays with the absolute limitations of textuality' (129).

This is particularly the case in Wales where, as in other multilingual cultures, questions of identity and difference are complicated by language use. As Gillian Clarke puts it, 'Living in a land with two languages is a delicate situation. There's no moment of life in Wales that hasn't got that edge.'[31] The bilingual Gwyneth Lewis responds to the delicacies of her cultural-linguistic situation with circumspection: 'With small communities, if there's a strong feeling of belonging, there's an equally strong feeling of not belonging. I suppose I always want to question where that line is drawn.'[32] The implication is that such a line, if it is to be 'drawn' at all, should be disputable; mobile. It is perhaps a sign of cultural-creative devolution that some very fine recent poetry seems more inclined to de-territorialize different psycho-imaginative states than rehearse the national or ethnographic anxieties which impelled their predecessors. One of the most ambitious works of the last decade, Lewis's epic *A Hospital Odyssey* (published in the same year as *Mr Cassini*) discerns in poetry an equili-brium ('particles aren't billiard balls, things, / but notes, all matter a coherent song / ... / harmonics on a musical scale played by the universe')[33] which explains the curative properties of her own work's formal architecture: 'It's a hospital, / this place I'm constructing line by line, / ... Words are my health, / the struggle to hear and transcribe the tune / ... the only work that can make me immune / to lying' (59). Anchored in this characteristic sense of ethical duty, Lewis's questing examination of a Dantesque National Health Service she both honours and lampoons touches on her cultural-political context only at its close, in the resolving help of a spectral Aneurin Bevan (Book 10).[34] The hospital made by Lewis's epic in stanza, page, and book silently calls attention to the socio-economic Wales which shadows her narrative, pathologizing a sense of cultural dispossession and complacency which are as corrupting as any social malaise.

The facing-page dual-language texts favoured by Menna Elfyn (like Gwyneth Lewis, a Welsh-speaking writer) shape a different formal response to the same cultural-linguistic situation. Few poets are more creatively energized than Elfyn by the politics of language use in Wales. Elfyn's con-tentiously translated poems spill out of their own linguistic and material limits, in the twin cultural/political and authorial provenances of each double-page spread. The macaronic self-doubling title of *Murmur* translates as 'murmur' or 'whisper', but in Welsh contains a punning reference to 'wall-wall', a duality which lightly confirms that even 'a word is a meeting place'.[35] The strong intertextual connotation of the word *murmur* in Welsh poetic usage also takes us back to the golden age of Welsh poetry through the famous lyric by T. Gwynn Jones which describes the abbey at Ystrad Fflur, 'Strata Florida', the burial place of Dafydd ap Gwilym:

> Mae dail y coed yn Ystrad Fflur
> Yn murmur yn yr awel,
> A deuddeng Abad yn y gro
> Yn huno yno'n dawel.[36]

> (The leaves of the trees in Ystrad Fflur
> Are murmuring in the air,
> And twelve Abbots in the grove
> Sleep there quietly.)

This word's multiple meeting places deftly gesture at both the cultural barriers raised and reinforced by language use and the will to undermine them by 'murmur'-ing against or beneath them while striving (in stuttering or defective speech) for linguistic self-control:

> *Mur-mur,*
> *waliau yw seiniau*
> *yr heniaith.*
> *Deallwn beth yw 'shibboleth',*
> *Yr 's' yn amlwg ar ein tafodau,*
> *Yr 'sh' sh' 'sh',*
> *siars mai iaith tawelwch yw.*

> (Wall-wall,
> Walls are sounds
> of the old tongue.
> We understand 'shibboleth',
> The 's' is clear on our lips;
> The 'sh', 'sh', 'sh',
> A warning that it's the language of silence.)

The concluding part of this important sequence links these observations with the medical condition to which its epigraph points, charging the whole with unashamed emotion:

> *Byw gyda churiadau a wna bard,*
> *yn gyson o afreolus:*
> *lubb-dupp, a'i alaw*

yn cario
goslef a llef sy'n llifo
at gwynion holl fydrau ei waed.

(Poets live with beats,
consistently irregular;
lubb-dupp, its melody
carries a pitch that flows
through all the heartaches
and metre of the blood.)[37]

In contrast with the strong sense of place and linguistic history which we find in the work of Gwyneth Lewis and Menna Elfyn, works by Wales-identifying or Wales-associated poets such as Matthew Francis (*Mandeville*, 2008; *Muscovy*, 2013), Pascale Petit (*What the Water Gave Me*, 2010), Samantha Wynne Rhydderch (*Banjo*, 2012), and Damien Walford Davies (*Judas*, 2015) throw a highly performative and multiple lyric voice – all are expert monologists – well beyond Wales's own geo-historical environs. Spatio-linguistic mechanisms help these volumes release a suggestively anachronistic version of their place and moment from the cultural-material dimensions of the page. Jemma L. King destabilizes the space/place of the page more immediately. The twenty-six models in King's *The Undressed* (2014) protest – in a collection juxtaposing each new lyric with a mostly page-sized erotic photograph of its nineteenth-century European subject – against a tradition of abuse in which they unwillingly conspire. The paginary economies of a beautifully balanced collection focus attention on the warped representational processes of an art which layers exposure upon exposure (embodied, technological, economic, and moral); gaze upon gaze (of lens, photographer, model, consumer, poet, and reader), disturbingly perpetuated in and by its aestheticizing. Does the collection revile, subvert, or reinscribe the traducing of the pictured women?

King's poetic space-places reiterate the silences which impropriety necessitates: as each picture ends at – or is interrupted by – the frame which controls (corset-like, more than one poem implies) the representation of its subject-object, so is the white space governing the lines and stanzas of each poem interrupted by all the stories (of naivety and pride, innocence and shame, avarice and even love) they tell. The texts slip dialogically between the equivalently visual forms of text and photograph, between the pages each version occupies, and among the male–female power-relations they utter. What is, bitterly, for Karla 'just a body, receptacle – vehicle', Lydia turns into gleeful 'hex': 'We moon creatures in our silks / can skin men in minutes.'[38]

The 'talk' between portrait and poem (echoed between model and photographer, life and representation, subject and poet) compounds the reading experience, loosing the bounds of each page, each image, each text.

In its formalities the lyric construct is rendered a (poetic) place, bordered by its shaping morphologies – of stanza, end-rhyme, rhythm and line-ending – and located in its framing page-space. Massey argues that a place's 'particularity' emerges not 'through counterposition to the other which lies beyond, but . . . [in] the mix of interconnections to that beyond'.[39] As a poet who mines the connections between immediate and beyond, Ruth Bidgood might agree. Not a Welsh speaker, Bidgood figures the mid-Walian landscape which offers its dwellers context, shelter, and sustenance as an expressive non-linguistic 'language' of itself; a non-verbal matrix in which belonging and alienation are interleaved. Poem after poem in Bidgood's award-winning *Time Being* (2009) presents the remote uplands and hidden valleys of her local environs as texts to be read, geomorphological pages in which layers of vegetation, habitation, survival, and loss have been laid down over aeons, in a process of continual growth, erosion, and overwriting. A guarded poetics rereads landscape as a kind of atemporal extra-linguistic meeting place of the actual and the possible:

> For miles the land unfolded
> its flaws, beauties, logic, enigmas,
> contradictions, in unemphatic
> shadowless diversity, like yet unlike a map;
> closer than any map could be
> to those who dug, fenced, coppiced, levelled here,
> bypassed, bridged, laid stone on stone,
> changed and pulled down and built again.[40]

A 'land' always slipping from the attempt to situate it silently mocks the poet's as well as the map's definitive purposes. Line after 'unemphatic' line of this poem manifestly fails to contain the vectors of time, energy, and purpose it strives to depict. In the culturally and formally conditioned domain of the lyric poem, exclusions can seem more than coincidentally significant. In spatio-material terms, the page proscribes all kinds of creative, imaginative, and indeed aesthetic potential; and yet from its (conventional) location – the page – the lyric poem / event simultaneously connects and converses with its own poetic, literary, and aesthetic contexts and heritage. Ian Davidson remarks, 'The shape on the page is produced by the poem.'[41] And, we might say, vice versa; the signifying life ('shape') of any poem inheres in the dialectical relationship between its form and its paginary context. As Tim

Cresswell remarks, 'Issues of boundedness and rootedness and connections are ... used in complicated ways by people.'[42] The spatially mediated decisions distinguishing a text from the uninscribed page – de Certeau's *une espace propre* – throw the concrete/abstract event of the poem into literal relief.

On Edge

> The edges of one place are sources for the edges of other places, generative contours for entire place-worlds.[43]

Cultural theorists view edges with suspicion, perhaps because they signify the kind of deterministic thinking which poststructuralism refutes. Limits exclude even as they confine. The 'energetic ontology' posited by Thrift grants 'the importance of physical presences and absences (as well as linguistic presences and absences) in producing breaks, lacunae and emissions [*sic*] which interrupt and transmute encountering'.[44] In the spaces they open up, gaps and breaks produce edges. However, these ruptures and occlusions remain spaces of conjunction: of juxtaposition, differentiation, and the deferral of meaning.

Part-Estonian, part-Cornish émigré Philip Gross seems drawn to the borders and edges, thematic, linguistic, local, and geo-social, which resonate in the inter-cultural, inter-familial stories and scenarios his poems study, whether or not they draw on the south Wales he has lived and worked in for some twenty-five years. Latterly, a writer with a taste for collaborating has turned to the dislocated processes of site-specific expression. *A Fold in the River* (2015), a layered study of the river Taff, was produced in concert with artist Valerie Coffin Price, whose sepia, discreetly collagistic watercolours frame, trail across, tangle, and converse with the poems and prose fragments scattered through a self-aware textual terrain. In some ways the book extends the thematic of Gross's award-winning *The Water Table* (2010), compelled by the enormous seaway of the Bristol Channel. One of Cardiff's two chief rivers, the lower reaches of the Taff connect Wales's capital city with the knotted geology and industrial history of the Rhondda Cynon Taff Valley system.

Shifting between textual and visual modes, among the spaces and zones in which these meet, *A Fold* strings together its elliptical verbal and visual elements – entranced by the smell, sound, and feel, as well as the sight of water – in ways which interrogate the differing media and forms of text and picture. The book's dual aesthetic 'folds' literally out of itself into the illustrated double-page spreads across which texts and watercolour images (often embedding traces of manuscript notes) wind. The generative page itself is thus called, performatively, into view as a place of proliferating utterance all its own. 'The Stain' appears, in lines reminiscent of William Carlos Williams's triadic foot, on the left-hand side of a double-page spread. Across the rest meanders the delicate, attenuated image of a (staining) watercolour much like a pen-and-ink map of a river's course, apparently clipped from the notebook in which it was originally painted (across several folds). Read in this interpene-trating context, text and image edge up against, seep into and through, each other in a visual, aesthetic, and culturally specific dialogue which frames the work and its co-producers against the dynamic immaterialities of the river:

> 'The Stain'
>
> It spreads – one touch
>   of water; and the ink
>   lets go –
> as if the paper wants this, physically.
>   It bleeds
> like damp through plaster;
>   as a worry-dream
>   you can't
> recall persists; a smudge-print on the day . . .   (A Fold 18–19)

Interweaving its authors' separate kinds of creative idiom, this literally fluvial text-art somehow taps a Heraclitean dynamism which can only elude its representation, adeptly destabilizing its own material, formal, and generic bounds. And yet the planar course of the tiny telescoped river the volume reproduces, wandering as words and image across and between the pages it populates, also gestures at the spatial bio-mathematical rhythms of fractal science; the infinitely regressive mathematical phenomenon which renders edges impossible: 'A fractal is a geometric built from a shape that repeats on multiple scales . . . each little piece of one looks much like the whole thing; the distinction between scales fades away.'[45] A book which unfixes its own defining outline, which folds and unfolds itself literally and metaphorically out of the bio-environs it seeks to conjure, cast in miniature, in its own textual flux, seems informed by the fractal science which calls certain kinds of edge – finitude – into question.

Another writer who is drawn to the self-iterating fractal, Zoë Skoulding shifts us from the text-like river of a river-like text to the illimitable inter-iorities of the corporeal. Skoulding's supple lyrics tease out the dialectic linking an inseparable external world with the porous sensory human intelligence it saturates, figuring the body as a polysemous topos, constituting, in the words of the philosopher Elizabeth Grosz:

> an assemblage of organs, processes, pleasures, passions, activities, behaviors [sic] linked by fine lines and unpredictable networks to other elements, segments, and assemblages ... a series of surfaces, energies, and forces, a mode of linkages, a discontinuous series of processes, organs, flows, and matter ... a set of operational linkages and connections with other things, other bodies. The body is not simply a sign to be read, a symptom to be deciphered, but also a force to be reckoned with.[46]

Unrestingly conscious of their immaterialities, Skoulding's poems invariably foreground their failure to textualize the fleeting neuro-physical responses on which their own existence ironically depends. On the other hand, as 'Exchange' observes, in the virtual multidimensional networks embedding and embedded in contemporary experience, the textual traces of an evanescent 'voice / lost in reconstructions of itself' is perhaps all that can be rescued of the edgeless, unsituated body such traces mediate:

> I can hardly contain myself
> I run through cables
> stretch my fingers into white
> noise over landscapes[47]

This kind of exfoliating lyric self-construction speaks to and about a cultural-political existence and experience constituted in the 'chips, wires and signals of proliferating forms of communication' which have long interested a lively-minded poet.[48] However, Skoulding's corporeal idiom also recalls Paul Rodaway, for whom human sensory intelligence produces a 'multi-sensual hyper-real geography'.[49] Situated in the relatively new domain of perceptual geography, Rodaway reflects that 'Perception – as a combination of sensation and cognition – is inclusive of both passive encounter with environmental stimuli and active exploration of that environment, as the body moves through space and time interacting with a world' (12). Situationist-influenced psychogeography of course knows and gently mocks this recognition, specifically in the urban environments traversed in Skoulding's superb *Remains of a Future City* (2008). *The Museum of Disappearing Sounds* (2013) interiorizes the non-visual but spatially sensitive faculties of touch, sound, and scent, in poems which move from the notionally civic public space of its impossible eponymous museum, through the public/private capsule of the railway carriage into the anonymous yet profoundly intimate world of the work's concluding sequence 'The Rooms'.

The five 'exhibits' of the opening title sequence examine the unemplaced perceptual space-places produced by and in aural stimuli and response. Throughout the text, conventional tercet and quatrain forms are punctured by spatial gaps which are silent in their vacancy. The left-hand margins of the exhibits shift to and fro around *caesurae* figured (performatively) as mute blocks of white space; requiring some kind of aural and visual pause, they invite us to listen to the ways in which each is filled.

As charged as any Elizabethan love song, 'exhibit 4' obliquely identifies the self-splintering 'vibrations' of a telephonic voice – elusive as it 'shimmers on the end of the line' – with birdsong. At once part of and separate from that natural context, the speaker's excitement and anxiety seem somehow to have been absorbed by the very technology which has ruptured the moment of connection it initiated:

> breath hops and starts
>   is this is this is this is this is this
> I vanish in lossy comprehension . . .
>
> the rhythms that cradle us
> turn to an I-you stammer of ringtones
> on the nervous system's high whine[50]

Such lyrics reconceive the spatio-material breaks of line, stanza, and page as zonal realms of irruption and co-incidence; neither poem nor page seem any more 'edged' than the undecideable human body which (reciprocally) produces and is produced in each zone, as the fourteen poems – chambers – of 'The Rooms' attest. The first, 'Room 321', unequivocally links the actual, apparently delimited, spaces of human and textual experience, and the reciprocal, radar-like border-crossing processes of signification and response in which each 'event', poetic and sensory/cognate, unobtrusively undoes the margins of the other:

>   It's here that everything
> is happening twice
>   once in the body
> and once in the words for it
>   and there's no
> escaping that song in your head
>   the one
> that was in the room and is now in you

In persistently constructing text and self as mutually embodied forms of expression as well as consumption, Skoulding delineates almost carelessly the profoundly expressive 'textualized body' which Grosz posits as 'page or material surface, possibly even a book of interfolded leaves ... ready to receive, bear and transmit meanings, messages or signs, much like a system of writing ... a text which is as complicated and indeterminate as any literary manuscript' (117). The trope of the body-as-text propels us again, and appositely, into a material yet illimitable domain which seems for the literary reader more satisfyingly, more fluidly, morphological than any map. To read an idiom like Skoulding's is not simply to be immersed in a formally realized contemporary experience in which virtual and material, bodied and unbodied, actual and simulated commingle. It is also to encounter the inclusive and exclusive, edged and unedged domain of the text-page as textile or fabric on which, as in woven cloth, 'images are never imposed ... their patterns are always emergent ... implicit in a web which makes them immanent to the processes from which they emerge'.[51]

Conclusion

The small-scale, formally conceived but simultaneously permeable textual terrain of the poetic space-place invites us to sense in the space/place/text of Wales 'a process not a product, a relationship not an acquisition'.[52] Fraying the possibilities of genre, form, page, and authorship, some of Wales's most suggestive recent literary achievements emerge from and project a national/cultural space-place whose size and shape will always evade the generic or literary will to determine and confine it. In literary forms redolent of a contemporary 'not/quite' world poised (for Thrift) 'permanently in a state of enunciation, between addresses, always deferred', Wales's bolder writers are etching a new 'not/quite' version of their literary-cultural imaginary onto – without ever quite erasing – the richly patterned fabric of their creative and historical environs.[53] Their texts ambivalently re-inscribe and at the same time elude their own paginary space-places, in a 'palimpsestuous' process of literary sedimentation and erasure. Tirelessly dismantling the stuff of their own genres and forms, such texts suggestively fail to figure – to scale up or down – the cultural landscape of a post-millennial Wales which remains persistently bigger than it seems.

Notes

1. Lloyd Jones, *Mr Cassini* (Bridgend: Seren, 2006), 283.
2. Raymond Williams, 'The Arts in Wales', in *Who Speaks for Wales: Nation, Culture Identity*, ed. Daniel G. Williams (Cardiff: University of Wales Press, 2003), 12.
3. Gaston Bachelard, *The Poetics of Space*, trans. Maria Jolas [1969] (Boston: Beacon Press, 1994), 150.
4. I am perhaps impertinently re-scaling a generally localized signifier for the national context. Ned Thomas notes that 'a term of social rather than physical geography, an area with subjectively perceived borders, and perhaps embracing people as much as land' is one of those words 'linguistically Celtic in origin . . . recorded as in continuous use from early medieval times; and [probably] current long before that, as the existence of the word *bro* in Breton testifies'. See Thomas, 'Bro: Welsh Keywords', *Planet: The Welsh Internationalist* 207 (2012): 82, 85.
5. Emyr Humphreys, *The Taliesin Tradition* (Bridgend: Seren, 2000), 14. For the original poem, see *The Oxford Book of Welsh Verse*, ed. Thomas Parry (London: Oxford University Press, 1962), no. 22; translation by Joseph P. Clancy, *Medieval Welsh Poems* (Dublin: Four Courts Press, 2003), 136–7.
6. Tony Conran, *Welsh Verse*, 3rd edn (Bridgend: Seren, 1986), 38; Gerald of Wales, *The Journey Through Wales and the Description of Wales*, trans. Lewis Thorpe (London: Penguin, 1978), 233.
7. Gwyn A. Williams, *When Was Wales? A History of the Welsh* (Harmondsworth: Penguin, 1985), 6.
8. Denis Cosgrove, ed., *Mappings* (London: Reaktion Books, 1999), 7.
9. Nigel Thrift, 'Space', *Theory, Culture and Society* 23, 2–3 (2006): 139.
10. Damian Walford Davies, *Cartographies of Culture: New Geographies of Welsh Writing in English* (Cardiff: University of Wales Press, 2012), 16.
11. Nigel Jenkins, 'The Lie of the Land', in *Footsore on the Frontier: Selected Essays and Articles* (Llandysul: Gomer Press, 2001), 13.
12. Walford Davies, *Cartographies of Culture*, 15.
13. See among numerous other studies, Jane Aaron, Henrice Altinck, and Chris Weedon, eds., *Bordering Gender Studies* (Cardiff: University of Wales Press, 2010); Katie Gramich, *Twentieth-Century Women's Writing in Wales: Land, Gender, Belonging* (Cardiff: University of Wales Press, 2007); Katie Gramich, ed., *Mapping the Territory: Critical Approaches to Welsh Fiction in English* (Cardigan: Parthian, 2010); Matthew Jarvis, *Welsh Environments in Contemporary Poetry* (Cardiff: University of Wales Press, 2008).
14. Walford Davies, *Cartographies of Culture*, 206.
15. Thrift, 'Space', 140–1.

16. Marc Augé, *Non-Places*, trans. John Howe (London and New York: Verso, 1995), 88; Edward Relph, *Place and Placelessness* (London: Pion, 1976), 24–5.

17. Cosgrove, ed., *Mappings*, 4–5.

18. Mark S. Monmonier, *How to Lie With Maps* (Chicago: University of Chicago Press, 1996), 1.

19. Doreen Massey, *For Space* (London: Sage, 2005), 9.

20. Henri Lefebvre, *The Production of Space*, trans. Donald Nicholson-Smith (Oxford: Blackwell, 1991), 26.

21. Sarah Dillon, *The Palimpsest: Literature, Criticism, Theory* (London: Bloomsbury, 2007), 3.

22. John Frow, *Genre* (London and New York: Routledge, 2006), 102.

23. Jacques Derrida, 'The Law of Genre', in *Modern Genre Theory*, ed. David Duff (Harlow: Longman, 2000), 219–31; John Wylie, *Landscape* (London and New York: Routledge, 2007), 5.

24. Wylie, *Landscape*, 7.

25. Michel De Certeau, *The Practice of Everyday Life*, trans. Steven Rendall (Berkeley, Los Angeles and London: University of California Press, 1984), 135.

26. Marion Thain, ed., *The Lyric Poem: Formations and Transformations* (Cambridge: Cambridge University Press, 2013), 2 (emphasis added).

27. Tim Cresswell, *Place: An Introduction* (Chichester: John Wiley & Sons, 2015), 12, 18.

28. Nigel Thrift, *Spatial Formations* (London: Sage Publications, 1996), 47.

29. From Susanne Langer, *Feeling and Form: A Theory of Art* (New York: Scribner, 1953), quoted in Relph, *Place and Placelessness*, 29.

30. Walter J. Ong, *Orality and Literacy: The Technologizing of the Word* (London: Methuen, 1982), 132, 133.

31. Gillian Clarke, 'Gillian Clarke', in *Writing on the Edge: Interviews with Writers and Editors of Wales*, ed. David T. Lloyd (Amsterdam and Atlanta, GA: Rodopi, 1997), 9.

32. Gwyneth Lewis, 'Gwyneth Lewis', in *In Her Own Words: Women Talking Poetry and Wales*, ed. Alice Entwistle (Bridgend: Seren, 2014), 109.

33. Gwyneth Lewis, *A Hospital Odyssey* (Tarset: Bloodaxe Books, 2010), 147.

34. See also Gwyneth Lewis, *Sunbathing in the Rain: A Cheerful Book on Depression* (London and Philadelphia: Jessica Kingsley, 2007), 94; Entwistle, ed., *In Her Own Words*, 114.

35. Malcolm Allchin, quoted in Jeremy Hooker, *Imagining Wales: A View of Modern Welsh Writing in English* (Cardiff: University of Wales Press, 2001), 195.

36. T. Gwynn Jones, *Caniadau* (Wrecsam: Hughes a'i Fab, 1934), 192; translated by Geraint Evans.

37. Menna Elfyn, '*Murmuron*' / 'Murmurs', in *Murmur* (Tarset: Bloodaxe, 2010), 61, 65.

38. Jemma L. King, *The Undressed* (Cardigan: Parthian, 2014), 28, 59.

39. Doreen Massey, *Space, Place and Gender* (Cambridge: Polity Press, 1994), 5.

40. Ruth Bidgood, 'Reading a Landscape', in *Time Being* (Bridgend: Seren, 2009), 44–6.

41. Ian Davidson, *Ideas of Space in Contemporary Poetry* (Basingstoke: Palgrave Macmillan, 2007), 4.

42. Cresswell, *Place*, 113.

43. Edward S. Casey, 'Do Places Have Edges? A Geo-Philosophical Enquiry', in *Envisioning Landscapes, Making Worlds: Geography and the Humanities*, ed. Stephen Daniels *et al.* (London: Routledge, 2011), 67.

44. Thrift, *Spatial Formations*, 31.

45. George Musser, *The Complete Idiot's Guide to String Theory* (New York: Alpha / Penguin, 2008), 207.

46. Elizabeth Grosz, *Volatile Bodies: Toward a Corporeal Feminism* (Bloomington, IN: Indiana University Press, 1994), 120.

47. Zoë Skoulding, 'Exchange', in *Remains of a Future City* (Bridgend: Seren, 2008), 15.

48. Zoë Skoulding, *Contemporary Women's Poetry and Urban Space: Experimental Cities* (Basingstoke: Palgrave Macmillan, 2013), 213.

49. Paul Rodaway, *Sensuous Geographies: Body, Space and Place* (London: Routledge, 1994), 178.

50. Zoe Skoulding, 'The Museum of Disappearing Sounds', in *The Museum of Disappearing Sounds* (Bridgend: Seren, 2013), 8.

51. Sadie Plant, 'Shuttle Systems', in *Networks: Documents of Contemporary Art*, ed. Lars Bang Larsen (Cambridge, MA and London: MIT and Whitechapel Gallery, 2014), 24.

52. Noragh Jones, 'Rhiannon, Mabon and Me', in *Discovering Welshness*, ed. Fiona Bowie and Oliver Davies (Llandysul: Gomer Press, 1992), 121.

53. Thrift, *Spatial Formations*, 289.

Afterword

GERAINT EVANS AND HELEN FULTON

The story of Welsh literature is richer and more dynamic than seems possible from a small country that thinks like a nation but has never been a state. Our sense of the dynamism of Welsh literature comes in part from the range of voices in this book – voices of writers whose work has meant a great deal to us (Dafydd ap Gwilym, T. Gwynn Jones, David Jones, Saunders Lewis, Gwyneth Lewis, to name just a few) but also the voices of our contributors, whose collective understanding of the power and endurance of Welsh literature gives this volume its energy.

What emerges from these many voices is a sense of Welsh literature as historically important, a literature that has always faced outwards towards the rest of Britain, Europe, and indeed the wider world, while at the same time defining a national culture. It is a literature that has always worked in more than one language, with Welsh, Latin, French, and English speaking to each other in different combinations at different times, just as other languages continue to arrive in Wales and inflect its literary culture.

It is also a literature that, like many world literatures, articulates both colonial and postcolonial subjectivities. There has been some resistance, inside and outside Wales, to the view that Wales was a colony of empire and can therefore be regarded as having developed a legitimate postcolonial sensibility; some have argued that Wales has been too complicit with British imperialism to claim a postcolonial status.[1] But the literary evidence of imperialism as a dominant and often oppressive force in Welsh cultural life – alongside political evidence such as the Acts of Union – is a pervasive theme of our book. As Kirsti Bohata has written, 'The case of Wales is an excellent example of how postcolonial paradigms may be employed ... to reveal the ways in which the Welsh have been subjected to a form of imperialism over a long period of time, while also acknowledging the way the Welsh have been complicit in their own subjugation and in the colonization of others.'[2] This dual subjectivity, famously theorized by Homi Bhabha, is evident in Welsh literature throughout its long history.[3] The tenth-century prophetic poem *Armes Prydein* ('The Prophecy of Britain') rails against the colonizing power of Athelstan's kingdom, while Iolo Goch, writing in the fourteenth century, praises his colonial masters, Roger Mortimer, earl of March (d. 1398), and the English king, Edward III. In the early modern centuries, antiquarians worked to recuperate manuscripts and translations in Welsh while basing themselves in the London heartland of imperial power.

The double subjectivity is even more evident after the industrial expansions of the late nineteenth century when a colonized Welshness began to be expressed in the language of the colonizer. Early twentieth-century examples of Welsh writing in English often seemed to be addressed to monoglot English readers who, whether they lived in Wales or not, identified with a dominant English culture in which Wales and the Welsh were the 'other'. William Christie, writing in this volume, has described Saunders Lewis's remarks about Dylan Thomas as someone who, because he did not speak or write in Welsh, 'belonged to the English', and this is indeed how Dylan Thomas continues to be regarded by many Welsh writers and critics. Thomas is an ambivalent figure precisely because his work formed a key moment of transition in Welsh literary history, when Welsh writing in English came to acquire the same postcolonial doubleness and ambiguity as Welsh writing itself. Another key figure in that same moment of transition is David Jones, the artist and writer who formed a deep and intimate friendship with Saunders Lewis and sought advice from him on Welsh words and phrases which he then worked into his writing and into the group of art works which Jones called painted inscriptions. David Jones is an important figure in the story of the literature of Wales because he was one of the first major writers in English who took as his starting point the idea that nobody could make meaningful art about Wales – especially monolingual English speakers like himself who were living in London – without understanding something of the history and culture of Welsh Wales. The method which Jones developed of working in English while being enveloped in an awareness of Welsh-language history is one of the great shifting moments of Welsh writing in English and one which was almost without precedent in London in the early twentieth century when he published his magnificent poetic memoir of the First World War, *In Parenthesis* (1937).

From the point of view of literary production, perhaps the most significant political movement in twentieth-century Wales, led by Cymdeithas yr Iaith, the Welsh Language Society, and enacted – albeit reluctantly at times – by Westminster governments, has been the drive towards bilingualism. Policies supporting Welsh-medium education, bilingual governance and administration, and Welsh-language media have created, as Andrew Webb writes in this volume, two readerships in Wales for Welsh writing in English: 'English-language readers who are fluent in Welsh; and English-language readers who, while not necessarily fluent in Welsh, are nonetheless familiar with the linguistic and cultural complexity of modern Wales.' This is, indeed, the 'empire writing back': not only is there a new confidence among Welsh writers that they are addressing themselves to 'insiders' who understand their cultural perspective, but such texts also construct 'outsiders', often but not always located outside Wales, who are linguistically and geographically marginalized. Through the emergence of bilingualism as a dominant cultural force, Welsh writing and Welsh writing in English find themselves occupying the same postcolonial terrain.

There is another key issue which underlies much of this volume and that is the means by which literature is made available to readers, whether in the form of manuscripts, printed books, websites, or e-books. Any national literature is only as robust as its publishing industries, as Lisa Sheppard has shown comprehensively in her chapter in this volume. The reclamation of Welsh writing as a national literature arguably began with the first printing press to be set up legally in Wales, by Isaac Carter in 1718, an innovation which led to the astonishingly rich world of Welsh-language printing which helped to make literacy in Welsh the dominant experience in Wales for the next two centuries.[4] But despite the proliferation of local publishers and local and national periodicals, it was not until the late nineteenth and early twentieth centuries, with the establishment of Gwasg Gomer (1892) and the University of Wales Press (1922), that Welsh authors had access to publishers whose institutional stability created reliable structures of national distribution. At the present time, funding for Welsh publishers remains dependent on organizations such as the Welsh Arts Council, the Welsh Books Council, and the reconfigured University of Wales, while London-based publishers are beginning to recognize that there is a potentially global audience for Welsh writing outside Wales. Within Wales, audiences, especially for Welsh-language writing, remain enthusiastic but relatively small, and funding is a constant challenge. The emergence of digital and online publishing, especially e-books, may yet offer a solution, if production quality and reader experience can be maintained, but the quality of that experience may be crucial in a country where a discriminating reading public has an instinctive understanding of the difference between texts and books and an abiding love of a well-made book.

The structure of our book has deliberately emphasized the symbiotic relationships between politics, economics, social developments, technological change, and cultural production. The history of Welsh literature is therefore a reflex of the history of Wales itself, and the future of one depends on the future of the other. Reading the last few chapters of this book, there can be no doubt that the devolution of government in 1999 has transformed political and cultural life in Wales. Throughout the middle decades of the twentieth century, when political devolution was still a dream rather than an expectation, the literary ideal for writers in Welsh was the organic Welsh-speaking community of rural Wales. The Wales of D. J. Williams, Kate Roberts and Saunders Lewis, even the Wales of R. S. Thomas, was a rural country of culturally conservative Welsh speakers, but almost overnight, following devolution in 1999, the dominant setting for new Welsh fiction became urban, with Welsh life in Cardiff being the key motif. In this, as in much else, the work of the Cardiff-based writer Sion Eirian was ahead of its time. His best work has straddled the worlds of theatre, film, and television, but his 1979 novella *Bob yn y Ddinas* ('Bob in the City') explored the desolate world of an unemployed steel worker who moves from his native Clwyd to Cardiff, a place which initially seems to him a metropolis of opportunity.[5]

Since 2000 there has been an explosion of new writing, in Welsh, in English, and in both languages together, which is fully engaged with millennial issues common to most of Europe. Welsh literature, including film and television, is now a significant commercial industry in Wales and forms a key part of what is known as 'Wales Studies', defined by the Learned Society of Wales as 'the intellectual exploration, explanation, and understanding of all things relating to Wales and its relations with the wider world'.[6] Produced both inside and outside Wales, defining itself as inclusive rather than exclusive, Welsh literature today has the capability, in at least two languages, to mediate national preoccupations for an international audience. This is the history of Welsh literature: multilingual, many-voiced, and constantly shapeshifting.

Notes

1. This view was first expressed by Bill Ashcroft, Gareth Griffiths, and Helen Tiffin in their ground-breaking book, *The Empire Writes Back: Theory and Practice in Post-Colonial Literatures* (London: Routledge and Kegan Paul, 1989). For different viewpoints in the debate, see Stephen Knight, *A Hundred Years of Fiction: From Colony to Independence* (Cardiff: University of Wales Press, 2004); Dai Smith, 'Psycho-Colonialism', *New Welsh Review* 66 (2004), 22–9;

Kirsti Bohata, *Postcolonialism Revisited*, Writing Wales in English (Cardiff: University of Wales Press, 2004).

2. Bohata, *Postcolonialism Revisited*, 5.

3. Homi Bhabha, *The Location of Culture* (London and New York: Routledge, 1994). Bhabha uses terms such as 'mimicry' and 'doubling' to describe ways in which colonized cultures attempt to align themselves with their colonizers. See also Chapter 30 in this volume.

4. Isaac Carter first set up his press in Newcastle Emlyn, Cardiganshire, before moving to Carmarthen seven years later. See Eiluned Rees, *Libri Walliae: A Catalogue of Welsh Books and Books Printed in Wales, 1546–1820* (Aberystwyth: National Library of Wales, 1987).

5. Sion Eirian, *Bob yn y Ddinas* (Llandysul: Gomer, 1979).

6. The Learned Society of Wales / Cymdeithas Ddysgedig Cymru, www.learnedsociety.wales/our-projects/welsh-studies/ (accessed 15 December 2017).

Bibliography

Manuscripts

Aberystwyth, National Library of Wales
David Jones Collection
Folder 200 'Trydan'
Great Sessions Records, Wales 4/1/2/36
Huw T. Edwards Papers. A3/25
NLW 15
NLW 1885B
NLW 13117E
NLW 3054D
NLW 5269D
NLW 5276D
NLW 5390D
Peniarth 1, *Llyfr Du Caerfyrddin* ('The Black Book of Carmarthen')
Peniarth 2, *Llyfr Taliesin* ('The Book of Taliesin')
Peniarth 4–5, *Llyfr Gwyn Rhydderch* ('The White Book of Rhydderch')
Peniarth 6
Peniarth 7
Peniarth 68
Peniarth 76
Peniarth 112
Peniarth 178, part ii.
Austin, Texas, The University of Texas at Austin, Harry Ransom Center
Dylan Thomas Collection
Bangor, Bangor University Archives
Cymru 2000 Collection
Wiliam Cynwal Papers, BMSS/119
Cardiff, Central Library
Cardiff 2.81, *Llyfr Aneirin* ('The Book of Aneirin')
Cardiff 2.114 (formerly 7)
Cardiff 2.39 (formerly 21)
Cardiff 2.40 (formerly 26)

Hawarden, Flintshire, Flintshire Record Office
  Flintshire Education Committee Minutes (1955–56) FC/2/56
Kew, The National Archives
  SP 1/113
  SP 15/127/258
London, British Library
  Add. 29
  Add. 23986
  Add. 31094
  Add. 70109
  Cotton Cleopatra E.iv
  Cotton Cleopatra E.v
  Egerton 2623
  Lansdowne 11
  Harley 280
  Harley 420
London, The Postal Museum
  Post 69/45
Oxford, Bodleian Library
  Conservative Party Archive, CCO/180/32
Oxford, Jesus College
  14
  111, 'Llyfr Coch Hergest' ('The Red Book of Hergest')

Primary Sources

Aaron, Jane, ed. *A View Across the Valley*. Dinas Powys: Honno, 1999.

Abse, Dannie. *Ash on a Young Man's Sleeve*. 1954; repr. Harmondsworth: Penguin, 1982.
  ed. *Twentieth Century Anglo-Welsh Poetry*. Bridgend: Seren, 1997.

Alexander, Gavin, ed. *Sidney's 'The Defence of Poesy' and Selected Renaissance Literary Criticism*. London: Penguin Books, 2004.

Alexander, Lloyd. *The Chronicles of Prydain*. 5 vols. New York: Henry Holt & Co., 1964–8.
  The Book of Three. New York: Henry Holt and Co., 1999.

Aneirin: Y Gododdin. Ed. and trans. A. O. H. Jarman. Llandysul: Gomer Press, 1988.

Annales Cambriae. Ed. John Williams (ab Ithel). London: Longman, Green, Longman, and Roberts, 1860.

Anon. 'Le mystère de Rebecca: épisodes des derniers troubles de la principauté de Galles'. *Revue Britannique*, 5th series, 19–20 (1844): 160–99, 403–33.

ap Dafydd, Myrddin, ed. *Cywyddau Cyhoeddus* 2. Llanrwst: Gwasg Carreg Gwalch, 1996.

ap Glyn, Ifor. *Holl Garthion Pen Cymro Ynghyd*. Talybont: Y Lolfa, 1991.
  Cerddi Map yr Underground. Llanrwst: Gwasg Carreg Gwalch, 2001.

Armes Prydein: The Prophecy of Britain from the Book of Taliesin. Ed. Ifor Williams, trans. Rachel Bromwich. Dublin: Dublin Institute for Advanced Studies, 1972.

Arnold, Matthew. *On the Study of Celtic Literature* [1867]. In *Lectures and Essays in Criticism: The Complete Prose Works of Matthew Arnold*, ed. R. H. Super. 11 vols. Ann Arbor MI: University of Michigan Press, 1960–77, III: 291–386.

Aubin, Penelope. *The life of Madam de Beaumount, a French lady : who lived in a cave in Wales above fourteen years undiscovered, being forced to fly France for her religion, and of the cruel usage she had there : also her lord's adventures in Muscovy, where he was a prisoner some years : with an account of his returning to France, and her being discover'd by a Welsh gentleman, who fetch'd her lord to Wales, and of many strange accidents which befel them, and their daughter Belinda, who was stolen away from them, and of their return to France in the year 1718*. London: E. Bell, J. Darby, A. Bettesworth, F. Fayram, J. Pemberton, J. Hooke, C. Rivington, F. Clay, J. Batley, E. Symon, 1721.

Yr Australydd (1866–72).

Baldwin, Elizabeth, Lawrence M. Clopper, and David Mills, eds. *Records of Early English Drama: Cheshire Including Chester*. 2 vols. London and Toronto: The British Library and University of Toronto Press, 2007.

Bartrum, Peter C., ed. *Welsh Genealogies 300–1400*. 8 vols. Cardiff: University of Wales Press, 1974.

ed. *Welsh Genealogies 1400–1500*. 18 vols. Cardiff: University of Wales Press, 1983.

Barry, Des. *A Bloody Good Friday*. London: Cape, 2002.

BBC News Online. 'Ian Hargreaves Says Citizen Journalism Has Big Role in Wales'. 5 May 2013. www.bbc.co.uk/news/uk-wales-22419883.

Beale, Anne. *The Vale of the Towey or, Sketches in South Wales*. London: Longman, Brown, Green, and Longmans, 1844.

Traits and Stories of the Welsh Peasantry. London: George Routledge, 1849.

Bennett, Anna Maria. *Anna: or, Memoirs of a Welch Heiress*. 4th edn. London: Minerva Press, 1796.

Ellen, Countess of Castle Howel: A Novel. London: Minerva Press, 1794.

Bennett, J. A. W. and G. V. Smithers, eds. *Early Middle English Verse and Prose*. 2nd edn. Oxford. Oxford University Press, 1968.

Berry, Ron. *Flame and Slag*. London: Allen, 1968.

Hunters and Hunted. London: New Authors, 1960.

This Bygone. Llandysul: Gomer Press, 1996.

Bertomeu, Carlos. *El valle de la esperanza: una historia de Gales y Chubut – novela*. Buenos Aires: El Ateneo, 1943.

Bianchi, Tony. *Bumping*. Talybont: Alcemi, 2010.

Cyffesion Geordie Oddi Cartref. Llandysul: Gwasg Gomer, 2010.

Bidgood, Ruth. *New and Selected Poems*. Bridgend: Seren, 2004.

Time Being. Bridgend: Seren, 2009.

Blair, Tony. *A Journey*. London: Random House, 2007.

Blodeugerdd Barddas o Ganu Caeth y Ddeunawfed Ganrif. Ed. A. Cynfael Lake. Cyhoeddiadau Barddas, 1993.

Blodeugerdd Barddas o Ganu Crefyddol Cynnar. Ed. Marged Haycock. Cyhoeddiadau Barddas, 1994.

Blodeugerdd Barddas o Gerddi Rhydd y Ddeunawfed Ganrif. Ed. E. G. Milward. Cyhoeddiadau Barddas, 1991.

Blodeugerdd Barddas o'r Ail Ganrif ar Bymtheg. Cyfrol I. Ed. Nesta Lloyd. Cyhoeddiadau Barddas, 1993.

Borges, Jorges Luis. *Labyrinths.* Harmondsworth: Penguin, 1970.

Bowen, Euros. *Poems.* Llandysul: Gomer Press, 1974.

Lleidr Tân. Caernarfon: Gwasg Gwynedd, 1989.

Bowen, Lloyd, ed. *Family and Society in Early Stuart Glamorgan: The Household Accounts of Sir Thomas Aubrey of Llantrithyd, c. 1565–1641.* Cardiff: South Wales Record Society, 2006.

Branwen uerch Lyr. Ed. Derick Thomson. Dublin: Dublin Institute for Advanced Studies, 1961.

Brenhinedd y Saesson or the Kings of the Saxons: BM Cotton MS. Cleopatra B v and the Black Book of Basingwerk, NLW MS. 7006. Ed. and trans. Thomas Jones. Cardiff: University of Wales Press, 1971.

Brenhinoedd y Saeson, 'The Kings of the English', A D 682–954: Texts P, R, S in Parallel. Ed. David Dumville. Basic Texts for Medieval British History 1. Aberdeen: University of Aberdeen Department of History, 2005.

Breudwyt Maxen Wledic. Ed. Brynley F. Roberts. Dublin: Dublin Institute for Advanced Studies, 2005.

Brut Dingestow. Ed. Henry Lewis. Caerdydd: Gwasg Prifysgol Cymru, 1942.

Brut y Brenhinedd, Llanstephan MS. 1 Version, Selections. Ed. Brynley F. Roberts. Dublin: Dublin Institute for Advanced Studies, 1971.

Brut y Tywysogyon, or The Chronicle of the Princes: Peniarth MS. 20 Version. Ed. and trans. Thomas Jones. Cardiff: University of Wales Press, 1952.

Brut y Tywysogyon, or The Chronicle of the Princes: Red Book of Hergest Version. Ed. and trans. Thomas Jones. Cardiff: University of Wales Press, 1955.

Bufton, John. *Gwen Penri: A Welsh Idyll.* London: Elliot Stock, 1899.

Bush, Duncan. *Glass Shot.* London: Secker and Warburg, 1991.

Calendar of Ancient Correspondence Concerning Wales. Ed. J. Goronwy Edwards. Cardiff: University of Wales Press, 1935.

Calendar of Ancient Petitions Relating to Wales. Ed. William Rees. Cardiff: University of Wales Press, 1975.

Calendar of the Clenennau Letters and Papers in the Brogyntyn Collection. Ed. T. Jones Pierce. National Library of Wales Journal Supplement series IV, Pt 1. Aberystwyth: National Library of Wales, 1947.

Calendar of State Papers Domestic. London: HMSO, 1856–.

Calendar of Wynn of Gwydir Papers, 1515–1690. Ed. John Ballinger. Aberystwyth: National Library of Wales, 1926.

The Cambrian: A Magazine for the American Welsh (1880–1919).

The Cambridge Juvencus Manuscript Glossed in Latin, Old Welsh, and Old Irish: Text and Commentary. Ed. Helen McKee. Aberystwyth: CMCS Publications, 2000.

Campbell, Sarah. '"The Strong Man" and its Contexts: An Edition, Translation and Study of a Medieval Welsh Morality Play'. PhD diss., Catholic University of America, 2004.

Canu Aneirin. Ed. Ifor Williams. Caerdydd: Gwasg Prifysgol Cymru, 1938.

Canu Llywarch Hen. Ed. Ifor Williams. Caerdydd: Gwasg Prifysgol Cymru, 1935, repr. 1990.

Cardiff and Merthyr Guardian, 24 July 1847.

The Cardiff Times and South Wales Weekly News, 3 October 1908.

Carpenter, E. *Eskimo Realities*. New York: Holt, Rinehart and Winston, 1973.

Cd.8668. Commission of Enquiry into Industrial Unrest. No. 7 Division. *Report of the Commissioners for Wales, Including Monmouthshire.* 1917

Y Cenhadwr Americanaidd (1840–1901).

Chamberlain, Brenda. *Tide-Race.* 1962; repr. Bridgend: Seren, 2007.

Chaucer, Geoffrey. *The Riverside Chaucer.* Ed. Larry Benson. Boston: Houghton Mifflin, 1987.

The Chronicle of Adam Usk, 1377–1421. Ed. and trans. C. Given-Wilson. Oxford: Oxford University Press, 1997.

Chronicon Adæ de Usk, A D 1377–1421. Ed. and trans. E. M. Thompson. 2nd edn. London: Henry Frowde, 1904.

Churchyard, Thomas. *The Worthines of Wales.* London: G. Robinson for Thomas Cadman, 1587.

Chwedleu Seith Doethon Rufein. Ed. Henry Lewis. Caerdydd: Gwasg Prifysgol Cymru, 1958.

Clancy, Joseph P., ed. *The World of Kate Roberts.* Philadelphia: Temple University Press, 1991.

    trans. *The Earliest Welsh Poetry.* London: Macmillan, 1970.

    trans. *Twentieth Century Welsh Poems.* Llandysul: Gomer Press, 1992.

    trans. *Medieval Welsh Poems.* Dublin: Four Courts Press, 2003.

Clarke, Gillian. *Selected Poems.* Manchester: Carcanet, 1985.

Clement, B. 'The Saturday Profile: Rhodri Morgan, MP for Cardiff West: The Clown Prince of Wales'. *The Independent,* 13 February 1999.

Conran, Alys. *Pigeon.* Cardigan: Parthian, 2016.

Coombes, Bert. *These Poor Hands.* London: Gollancz, 1939.

    Those Clouded Hills. London: Cobbett, 1944.

    With Dust Still in his Throat. Ed. Bill Jones and Chris Williams. Cardiff: University of Wales Press, 1999.

Cooper, Susan. *The Dark Is Rising Sequence.* New York: Margaret K. McElderry Books, 2010.

Cordell, Alexander. *Rape of the Fair Country.* London: Gollancz, 1959.

Council for Wales and Monmouthshire. *Second Memorandum by the Council on its Activities.* London: HMSO, 1953.

The Critical Review; or Annals of Literature. Vol. 9. London: A. Hamilton, 1794.

Crossman, Richard. *The Diaries of a Cabinet Minister.* Vol. I: *Minister of Housing, 1964–66.* London: Hamilton Ltd. & Cape Ltd, 1975.

Culhwch and Olwen: An Edition and Study of the Oldest Arthurian Tale. Ed. Rachel Bromwich and D. Simon Evans. Cardiff: University of Wales Press, 1992.

Curtis, Tony. *New and Selected Poems.* Bridgend: Seren, 1986.

Curtis, Tony, and John Digby. *The Arches.* Bridgend: Seren, 1998.

Y Cyfaill o'r Hen Wlad yn America (1838–69).

Cyfranc Lludd a Llefelys. Ed. Brynley F. Roberts. Dublin: Dublin Institute for Advanced Studies, 1975.

Cyfreithiau Hywel Dda yn ôl Llyfr Blegywryd. Ed. Stephen J. Williams and J. Enoch Powell. 2nd edn. Cardiff: University of Wales Press, 1961.

Cyfres Beirdd y Tywysogion. Ed. R. Geraint Gruffydd. 7 vols. Cardiff: University of Wales Press, 1991–6.

Dafydd ap Gwilym: His Poems. Trans. Gwyn Thomas. Cardiff: University of Wales Press, 2001.

Dafydd ap Gwilym.net. www.dafyddapgwilym.net.

Dafydd ap Gwilym: The Poems. Trans. R. M. Loomis. Binghamton, NY: Center for Medieval and Early Renaissance Studies, State University of New York, 1981.

Dafydd, Catrin. *Random Deaths and Custard*. Llandysul: Gomer Press, 2007.

Random Births and Lovehearts. Llandysul: Gomer Press, 2015.

Gwales. Talybont: Y Lolfa, 2017.

Dafydd, Fflur. 'Author's Notes: *Twenty Thousand Saints'*. *Western Mail*, 18 October 2008.

Dafydd, Guto. *Ni Bia'r Awyr*. Cyhoeddiadau Barddas, 2014.

Ymbelydredd. Talybont: Y Lolfa, 2016.

Dante Ferrari, C. *El riflero de Ffos Halen*. Buenos Aires: Ediciones Escritores Argentinos de Hoy, 2003.

Davies, Ceri, ed. *Rhagymadroddion a Chyflwyniadau Lladin, 1551–1640*. Cardiff: University of Wales Press, 1980.

Davies, D. T. *Ble Ma Fa?* Aberystwyth: Gwasg y Ddraig Goch, 1914.

Davies, David. *Echoes from the Welsh Hills: or Reminiscences of the Preachers and People of Wales*. London: Alexander and Sheaphard, 1883. Reissued London: Passmore, [1888].

John Vaughan and his Friends, or More Echoes from the Welsh Hills. London: Simpkin, Marshall, Hamilton, Kent & Co, 1897.

Davies, Edward 'Celtic'. *Elisa Powell, or Trials of Sensibility: A Series of Original Letters, Collected by a Welsh Curate*. London: printed for G. G. and J. Robinson, 1795.

Davies, Idris. *The Angry Summer: A Poem of 1926*. London: Faber, 1943.

Tonypandy. London: Faber, 1945.

The Complete Poems. Ed. Dafydd Johnson. Cardiff: University of Wales Press, 1994.

Davies, James Kitchener. *Gwaith James Kitchener Davies*. Ed. Mair. I. Davies. Llandysul: Gwasg Gomer, 1980.

Davies, John. *Microcosmos: The Discovery of the Little World, with the Government Thereof*. Oxford: Joseph Barnes, 1603.

Antiquae Linguae Britannicae, nunc communiter dictae Cambro-Britannicae, a suis Cymraecae vel Cambricae, ab aliis Wallicae,Rudimenta. London: John William, 1621.

Davies, John. 'How to Write Anglo-Welsh Poetry'. *Poetry Wales* 11, 4 (1976): 22–3.

The Visitor's Book. Bridgend: Poetry Wales Press, 1985.

Flight Patterns. Bridgend: Seren, 1991.

Dirt Roads. Bridgend: Seren, 1998.

Davies, John H., ed. *The Letters of Lewis, Richard, William and John Morris of Anglesey (Morrisiaid Môn) 1728–1765*. 2 vols. Aberystwyth: privately printed, 1907–9.

Davies, Peter Ho. *The Welsh Girl*. New York: Mariner Books, 2007.

Davies, Rhys. *The Withered Root*. London: Holden, 1927. Cardigan: Parthian, 2007.

Count Your Blessings. London: Putnam, 1932.

The Red Hills. London: Putnam, 1932.

Honey and Bread. London: Putnam, 1935.

A Time to Laugh. London: Heinemann, 1937.

Jubilee Blues. London: Heinemann, 1938.

Tomorrow to Fresh Woods. London: Heinemann, 1941.

Print of a Hare's Foot. London: Heinemann, 1969; repr. Bridgend: Seren, 1998.

Davies, Ron. *Devolution: A Process Not an Event*. Cardiff: Institute of Welsh Affairs, 1999.

Davies, Sian Eirian Rees. *I Fyd Sy Well*. Llandysul: Gwasg Gomer, 2005.

Davies, Tom. *Black Sunlight*. London: Macdonald, 1986.

Davies, W. H. *Autobiography of a Supertramp*. London: Fifield, 1908; Cardigan: Parthian, 2013.

Davies, Walter. *The Agriculture and Domestic Economy of North Wales*. London: Sherwood, Neely and Jones, 1811.

Davis, Kathryn. *The Walking Tour*. New York: Mariner Books, 1999.

De Curli. *The Life and Amours of Owen Tideric, Prince of Wales, otherwise Owen Tudor : who married Catharine, Princess of France and widow of our great King Henry V, from which marriage descended Henry VII, Henry VIII, Edward VI, Queen Mary, and Queen Elizabeth, all of whom had from him the surname Tudor; and from him likewise are descended, by the eldest daughter of Henry VII, the present royal family of Great Britain, France and Ireland: first wrote in French and published many years since at Paris, and now translated into English*. Translated anonymously. London: William Owen, 1751.

Digest of Welsh Historical Statistics (1700–1974). 'Labour'. Chapter 2. Released 1985. http://gov.wales/statistics-and-research/digest-welsh-historical-statistics/?tab=previous&lang=en.

Dillwyn, Amy. *The Rebecca Rioter*. Ed. Katie Gramich. 1880; repr. Dinas Powys: Honno, 2001.

Donovan, P.J., ed. *Cywyddau Serch y Tri Bedo*. Caerdydd: Gwasg Prifysgol Cymry, 1982.

Drych Kristnogawl. Ed. Geraint Bowen. Cardiff: University of Wales Press, 1996.

Dunsany, Lord, Edward Plunkett. *The King of Elfland's Daughter*. New York and London: G. P. Putnam, 1924.

Beyond the Fields We Know. Ed. Lin Carter. Ballantine Adult Fantasy. New York: Ballantine, 1972.

Dyer, John. *Selected Poetry and Prose*. Ed. John Goodridge. Nottingham: Trent Editions, 2000.

Edwards, Dorothy. *Rhapsody*. Cardigan: Parthian, 2007.

Winter Sonata. Dinas Powys: Honno, 2011.

Edwards, Huw T. *Hewn from the Rock: The Autobiography of Huw T. Edwards*. Cardiff: Western Mail Press, 1967.

Edwards, Owen M. *Cartrefi Cymru*. Ed. Thomas Jones. Wrecsam: Hughes a'i Fab, 1962.

ed. *Cymru* (1891–1920).

ed. *Cymru'r Plant* (1892–1920).

Eirian, Sion. *Bob yn y Ddinas*. Llandysul: Gwasg Gomer, 1979.

Elfyn, Menna. *Murmur*. Trans. Elin ap Hywel, Joseph Clancy, Gillian Clarke, Damian Walford Davies, and Paul Henry. Tarset: Bloodaxe, 2010.

Elfyn, Menna, and John Rowlands, eds. *The Bloodaxe Book of Modern Welsh Poetry*. Tarset: Bloodaxe, 2003.

Ellis, Alice Thomas. *The Sin-Eater*. London: Duckworth, 1977.

A Welsh Childhood. London: Penguin, 1992.

Ellis, Sam. *Ann y Foty yn Mynd i'r Môr*. Utica, NY: T. J. Griffiths, 1913.

The Elucidarium and Other Tracts in Welsh from Llyvyr Agkyr Llandewivrevi. Ed. J. Morris Jones and John Rhŷs. Oxford: Oxford University Press, 1894.

Englynion y Beddau: The Stanzas of the Graves. Ed. and trans. John K. Bollard, photography by Anthony Griffiths. Llanrwst: Gwasg Carreg Gwalch, 2015.

Entwistle, Alice, ed. *In Her Own Words: Women Talking Poetry and Wales*. Bridgend: Seren, 2014.

Evans, B. Ifor. 'Wales and the Cinema'. *Western Mail*, 16 October 1926, 6.

Evans, Beriah Gwynfe. *Dafydd Dafis: Sef Hunangofiant Ymgeisydd Seneddol*. Wrecsam: Hughes a'i Fab, 1898.

Evans, Caradoc. *My People: Stories of the Peasantry of West Wales*. London: Andrew Melrose, 1915.

    Capel Sion. London: Melrose, 1916.

    Taffy: A Play of Welsh Village Life in Three Acts. London: Melrose, n.d. [1923].

Evans, Evan. *Some Specimens of the Poetry of the Antient Welsh Bards*. London: R. and J. Dodsley, 1764.

Evans, George Ewart. 'Answer to Questionnaire'. *Wales* 1, 8–9 (1939): 225.

Evans, Gwynfor. *Save Cwm Tryweryn for Wales*. Cardiff: Plaid Cymru, 1956.

Evans, Hazel Charles. *Glas*. Llanrwst: Gwasg Carreg Gwalch, 2006.

Evans, Margiad. *A Ray of Darkness*. London: Arthur Barker, 1952.

Evans, Meredydd. *Merêd: Detholiad o Ysgrifau Dr Meredydd Evans*. Ed. Ann Ffrancon and Geraint H. Jenkins. Llandysul: Gwasg Gomer, 1994.

Evans, Theophilus. *Drych y Prif Oesedd*. Amwythig: John Rhydderch, 1716; repr. Caerdydd: Gwasg Prifysgol Cymru, 1961.

Faucher, Léon. 'Etudes sur l'Angleterre: les classes inférieures'. *Revue des Deux Mondes* 11 (1845): 40–53.

Ffoulkes, Annie, ed. *Telyn y Dydd*. 4th edn. Caerdydd: William Lewis, 1929.

Finch, Annie, ed. *After the New Formalism: Poets on Form, Narrative and Traditions*. Ashland: Story Line Press, 1999.

Flynn, Paul. Welsh Grand Committee, col. 49. 23 January 2013. www.publications .parliament.uk/pa/cm201213/cmgeneral/wgrand/130123/pm/130123s01.htm.

Francis, Hywel. 'Mining: The Popular Front'. *Marxism Today* (February 1985): 12.

Francis, J. O. *Change: A Glamorgan Play in Four Acts*. Aberystwyth: Gwasg y Ddraig Goch, 1913.

Freeman, Kathleen. *The Intruder and Other Stories*. London: Jonathan Cape, 1926.

Galar y Beirdd: Marwnadau Plant / Poets' Grief: Medieval Welsh Elegies for Children. Ed. and trans. Dafydd Johnston. Cardiff: Tafol, 1993.

Gallichan, Walter. *The Conflict of Owen Prytherch*. London: Watts & Co., 1905.

Gallie, Menna. *Strike for a Kingdom*. London: Gollancz, 1959.

    Man's Desiring. London: Gollancz, 1960.

    The Small Mine. London: Gollancz, 1962; 2nd edn with foreword by Jane Aaron, Honno Classics, Dinas Powys: Honno, 2000.

Garlick, Raymond, and Roland Mathias, eds. *Anglo-Welsh Poetry, 1480–1980*. Bridgend: Poetry Wales Press, 1984.

Garner, Alan. *The Owl Service*. London: Collins, 1967, 1998.

Geoffrey of Monmouth. *The Historia regum Britannie of Geoffrey of Monmouth*. Ed. Neil Wright and Julia Crick. 5 vols. Cambridge: D.S. Brewer, 1984–91.

    History of the Kings of Britain: An Edition and Translation of the De gestis Britonum [Historia Regum Britanniae]. Ed. Michael D. Reeve, trans. Neil Wright. Woodbridge: Boydell Press, 2007.

Gerald of Wales. *The Journey Through Wales and The Description of Wales.* Trans. Lewis Thorpe. Harmondsworth: Penguin, 1978.

Gildas: The Ruin of Britain and Other Works. Ed. Michael Winterbottom. London: Phillimore & Co, 1978.

The Gododdin of Aneirin: Text and Context from Dark-Age North Britain. Ed. and trans. John T. Koch. Cardiff: University of Wales Press, 1997.

The Gododdin: The Oldest Scottish Poem. Trans. K. H. Jackson. Edinburgh: Edinburgh University Press, 1969.

Gower, Iris. *Copper Kingdom.* London: Century, 1983.

   Black Gold. London: Century, 1988.

Gramadegau'r Penceirddiaid. Ed. G. J. Williams and E. J. Jones. Caerdydd: Gwasg Prifysgol Cymru, 1934.

Granelli, Roger. *Dark Edge.* Bridgend: Seren, 1997.

Graves, Alfred Perceval, trans. *Welsh Poetry Old and New in English Verse.* London: Longmans, Green, 1912.

Gray, Thomas. *Odes by Mr Gray.* London: Strawberry Hill, for R. and J. Dodsley, 1757.

Green, Fred. *Pethau Patagonia.* Caernarfon: Cyhoeddiadau Mei, 1984.

Greene, Graham. *Ways of Escape.* London: Bodley Head, 1980.

Griffiths, Ann. *Hymns and Letters.* Trans. Alan Gaunt and Alan Luff. London: Stainer & Bell, 1999.

   Rhyfeddaf Fyth . . . Emynau a Llythyrau Ann Griffiths. Ed. E. Wyn James. Y Drenewydd: Gwasg Gregynog, 1998.

Griffiths, Bryn, ed. *Welsh Voices: An Anthology of New Poetry from Wales.* London: Dent, 1967.

Griffiths, Hywel. *Banerog.* Talybont: Y Lolfa, 2009.

Griffiths, James. *Pages from Memory.* London: J. M. Dent & Sons, 1969.

Griffiths, William J. *O'r Pwlpud . . . i'r Crogbren: ffug-chwedl ddirwestol.* Bangor: Evan Thomas, 1905.

Griswold, Rufus Wilmot, ed. *The Female Poets of America.* Philadelphia: Henry C. Baird, 1848.

Gross, Philip, and Valerie Coffin Price. *A Fold in the River.* Bridgend, Seren, 2015.

Gruffydd, Elis. *Cronicl o Wech Oesoedd.* NLW MSS 5276D and 3054D, 1552.

Gruffydd, R. Geraint, ed. '*Englynion y Cusan* by Dafydd ap Gwilym.' *Cambrian Medieval Celtic Studies* 23 (1992): 1–6.

Gruffydd, W. J., and R. Silyn Roberts. *Telynegion.* Bangor: Jarvis & Foster, 1900.

Guto'r Glyn.net. Aberystwyth: Centre for Advanced Welsh and Celtic Studies, 2013. www.gutorglyn.net.

Gwaith Bleddyn Fardd a Beirdd Eraill Ail Hanner y Drydedd Ganrif ar Ddeg. Ed. Rhian M. Andrews, N. G. Costigan (Bosco), Christine James, Peredur I. Lynch, Catherine McKenna, Morfydd E. Owen, and Brynley F. Roberts. Cyfres Beirdd y Tywysogion, vol. VII. Caerdydd: Gwasg Prifysgol Cymru, 1996.

Gwaith Casnodyn. Ed. R. Iestyn Daniel. Aberystwyth: Canolfan Uwchefrydiau Cymreig a Cheltaidd, 1999.

Gwaith Cynddelw Brydydd Mawr, I. Ed. Nerys Ann Jones and Ann Parry Owen. Cyfres Beirdd y Tywysogion, vol. III. Caerdydd: Gwasg Prifysgol Cymru, 1991.

Gwaith Cynddelw Brydydd Mawr, II. Ed. Nerys Ann Jones and Ann Parry Owen. Cyfres Beirdd y Tywysogion, vol. IV. Caerdydd: Gwasg Prifysgol Cymru, 1995.

Gwaith Dafydd ap Gwilym. Ed. Thomas Parry. Caerdydd: Gwasg Prifysgol Cymru, 1952.

Gwaith Dafydd Llwyd o Fathafarn. Ed. W. Leslie Richards. Caerdydd: Gwasg Prifysgol Cymru, 1964.

Gwaith Dafydd y Coed a Beirdd Eraill o Lyfr Coch Hergest. Ed. R. Iestyn Daniel. Aberystwyth: Canolfan Uwchefrydiau Cymreig a Cheltaidd, 2002.

Gwaith Einion Offeiriad a Dafydd Ddu o Hiraddug. Ed. R. Geraint Gruffydd and Rhiannon Ifans. Aberystwyth: Canolfan Uwchefrydiau Cymreig a Cheltaidd, 1997.

Gwaith Gruffudd ap Dafydd ap Tudur, Gwilym Ddu o Arfon, Trahaearn Brydydd Mawr ac Iorweth Beli. Ed. by N. G. Costigan (Bosco), R. Iestyn Daniel, and Dafydd Johnston. Aberystwyth: Canolfan Uwchefrydiau Cymreig a Cheltaidd, 1995.

Gwaith Gruffudd ap Maredudd. Ed. Barry J. Lewis and Ann Parry Owen. 3 vols. Aberystwyth: Canolfan Uwchefrydiau Cymreig a Cheltaidd, 2003, 2005, 2007.

Gwaith Gruffudd Gryg. Ed. Barry J. Lewis and Eurig Salisbury. Aberystwyth: Canolfan Uwchefrydiau Cymreig a Cheltaidd, 2010.

Gwaith Gruffudd Llwyd a'r Llygliwiaid Eraill. Ed. Rhiannon Ifans. Aberystwyth: Canolfan Uwchefrydiau Cymreig a Cheltaidd, 2000.

Gwaith Guto'r Glyn. Ed. John Llywelyn Williams and Ifor Williams. Caerdydd: Gwasg Prifysgol Cymru, 1939.

Gwaith Hywel Dafi. Ed. A. Cynfael Lake. 2 vols. Aberystwyth: Canolfan Uwchefrydiau Cymreig a Cheltaidd, 2015.

Gwaith Lewys Glyn Cothi. Ed. Dafydd Johnston. Caerdydd: Gwasg Prifysgol Cymru, 1995.

Gwaith Llywarch ap Llywelyn 'Prydydd y Moch'. Ed. Elin M. Jones and Nerys Ann Jones. Cyfres Beirdd y Tywysogion, vol. V. Caerdydd: Gwasg Prifysgol Cymru, 1991.

Gwaith Llywelyn Brydydd Hoddnant, Dafydd ap Gwilym, Hillyn ac Eraill. Ed. Ann Parry Owen and Dylan Foster Evans. Aberystwyth: Canolfan Uwchefrydiau Cymreig a Cheltaidd, 1996.

Gwaith Llywelyn Goch ap Meurig Hen. Ed. Dafydd Johnston. Aberystwyth: Canolfan Uwchefrydiau Cymreig a Cheltaidd, 1998.

Gwaith Llywelyn Fardd I ac Eraill o Feirdd y Ddeuddegfed Ganrif. Ed. Kathleen Anne Bramley, Nerys Ann Jones, Morfydd E. Owen, Catherine McKenna, Gruffydd Aled Williams, and J. E. Caerwyn Wiliams. Cyfres Beirdd y Tywysogion, vol. II. Caerdydd: Gwasg Prifysgol Cymru, 1994.

Gwaith Madog Benfras ac Eraill o Feirdd y Bedwaredd Ganrif ar Ddeg. Ed. Barry J. Lewis. Aberystwyth: Canolfan Uwchefrydiau Cymreig a Cheltaidd, 2007.

Gwaith Siôn Tudur. Ed. Enid Roberts. 2 vols. Caerdydd: Gwasg Prifysgol Cymru, 1981.

Gwaith Tudur Aled. Ed. T. Gwynn Jones. Caerdydd: Gwasg Prifysgol Cymru, 1926.

Gwassanaeth Meir. Ed. Brynley F. Roberts. Caerdydd: Gwasg Prifysgol Cymru, 1961.

Gwilym, Arfon. 'Ymgyrch y Celwyddau' ('The Lying Campaign'). *Y Cymro*. 27 February 1979, 13.

Haines, Aldryd. *The Drift*. Llandybïe: Christopher Davies, 1974.

Hardy, Thomas. *Wessex Tales: Strange, Lively and Commonplace*. London: Macmillan, 1988.

Heaney, Seamus. *Door Into the Dark*. London: Faber, 1969.

Hechter, Michael. *Internal Colonialism: The Celtic Fringe in British National Development, 1536–1966*. London: Routledge and Kegan Paul, 1975.

Heinemann, Margot. *The Adventurers*. London: Lawrence and Wishart, 1960.

Hemans, Felicia. *The Works of Mrs Hemans*. 7 vols. Edinburgh and London: Blackwood and Cadell, 1839.

Hen Gerddi Gwleidyddol, 1588–1660. Cardiff: Cymdeithas Llên Cymru, 1901.

Historia Gruffud vab Kenan. Ed. D. Simon Evans. Cardiff: University of Wales Press, 1977.

Historia Peredur vab Efrawc. Ed. G. W. Goetinck. Cardiff: University of Wales Press, 1976.

Home Office. *Rural Wales*. London: HMSO, 1953.

'Hopcyn' (Lemuel J. Hopkin James) and 'Cadrawd' (T. C. Evans). *Hen Gwndidau, Carolau, a Chywyddau, Being Sermons in Song in the Gwentian Dialect*. Bangor: Jarvis & Foster, 1910.

Hopwood, Mererid. 'Dadeni'. In *Cyfansoddiadau a Beirniadaethau Eisteddfod Genedlaethol Cymru, 2001*, ed. Hughes, 16–20.

House of Commons, Welsh Affairs Committee. *English Language Television Broadcasting in Wales*. Eleventh Report of Session 2008–9. London: Stationery Office Limited, 2009.

Howells, William Dean. *Literature and Life: Studies*. New York and London: Harper and Brothers, 1902.

Hueffer, Ford Madox. *The Heart of the Country*. London: Alston Rivers, 1906.

Hughes, Annie Harriet ('Gwyneth Vaughan'). *O Gorlannau y Defaid*. London and Carmarthen: David Nutt, and Spurrell & Son, 1905.

Hughes, Garfield H., ed. *Rhagymadroddion 1547–1659*. Caerdydd: Gwasg Prifysgol Cymru, 1976.

Hughes, Isaac Craigfryn. *Y Ferch o Gefn Ydfa: chwedl hanesyddol o'r ddeunawfed ganrif*. Cardiff: Western Mail, 1881.

   The Maid of Cefn Ydfa: An Historical Novel of the 18th Century. Cardiff: Western Mail, 1881.

Hughes, John L. *Before the Crying Ends*. London: Bodley Head, 1986.

Hughes, T. Rowland. *O Law i Law*. Llundain: Foyle, 1943. Trans. Richard Ruck as *From Hand to Hand*. London: Methuen, 1950.

   Wiliam Jones. Aberystwyth: Gwasg Aberystwyth, 1944. Trans. Richard Ruck, *William Jones*. Aberystwyth: Gwasg Aberystwyth, 1953.

   Chwalfa. Aberystwyth: Gwasg Aberystwyth, 1946. Trans. Richard Ruck as *Out of their Night*. Aberystwyth: Gwasg Aberystwyth, 1954.

   Y Cychwyn. Aberystwyth: Gwasg Aberystwyth, 1947. Trans. Richard Ruck as *The Beginning*. Llandysul: Gomer Press, 1967.

Humphreys, Emyr, *Outside the House of Baal*. Bridgend: Seren, 1965, repr. 1996.

   'Chasing Shadows'. *Arcade* 7 (1981): 19–22.

   A Toy Epic. Bridgend: Seren, 1989.

   'Under the Yoke'. *The New Welsh Review* 3 (1998): 9–13.

   Conversations and Reflections. Ed. M. Wynn Thomas. Cardiff: University of Wales Press, 2002.

   A Man's Estate. Cardigan: Parthian, 2006.

Humphrys, John. 'Time to Blow All the Coal-Dust Cliches Away'. *Western Mail*, 20 March 1996, 13.

Iolo Goch: Poems. Ed. and trans. Dafydd Johnston. Llandysul: Gomer Press, 1993.

Iorwerth, Rhys. *Un Stribedyn Bach*. Llanrwst: Gwasg Carreg Gwalch, 2014.

Jacobs, Nicolas, ed. *Early Welsh Gnomic and Nature Poetry*. London: Modern Humanities Research Association, 2012.

James, Maria. *Wales, and Other Poems*. New York: John S. Taylor, 1839.

James, Sian. *A Small Country*. 1979, repr. Bridgend: Seren, 1999.

Jeffrey, C. *The Report of the Richard Commission: An Evaluation*. Devolution Briefings no.12. Birmingham: ESRC Devolution Programme, 2004.

Jenkins, Nigel. *Song and Dance*. Bridgend: Poetry Wales Press, 1981.

Jones, Carwyn. *The Future of Welsh Labour*. Cardiff: IWA, 2004.

Speech to Labour Party Conference. Liverpool, 26 September 2011.

Jones, Celia. *The Smouldering Hills*. Cardiff: Castan, 1996.

Jones, Ceri Wyn. 'Cywyddau Cyhoeddus'. In *Cywyddau Cyhoeddus 2*, ed. ap Dafydd, 10–11.

'Lloches'. In *Cyfansoddiadau a Beirniadaethau*, 2014, ed. Hughes, 16–23.

Jones, David. *In Parenthesis*. London: Faber, 1937.

The Anathemata: Fragments of an Attempted Writing. London: Faber, 1952.

The Sleeping Lord and Other Poems. London: Faber, 1974.

Jones, D. Gwenallt. *Eples*. Aberystwyth: Gwasg Aberystwyth, 1951.

Cerddi Gwenallt: Y Casgliad Cyflawn. Ed. Christine James. Llandysul: Gwasg Gomer, 2001.

Jones, Edmund. *A Geographical, Historical, and Religious Account of the Parish of Aberystruth: In the County of Monmouth*. Trevecka, 1779.

A Relation of Apparitions of Spirits in the Principality of Wales, 1780.

The Appearance of Evil: Apparitions of Spirits in Wales. Ed. John Harvey. Cardiff: University of Wales Press, 2003.

Jones, Erasmus. *Llangobaith*. Utica, NY: Thomas J. Griffiths, 1886.

Jones, Evan. *The Bard: or, The Towers of Morven; A Legendary Tale*. London: Printed for the author and sold by R. Dutton, 1809.

Jones, Fred. *Hunangofiant Gwas Ffarm*. Abertawe: John Penry, 1977.

Jones, Glyn. *The Valley, the City, the Village*. London: Dent, 1956.

The Island of Apples. 1965; repr. Cardiff: University of Wales Press, 1992.

The Collected Stories of Glyn Jones. Ed. Tony Brown. Cardiff: University of Wales Press, 1999.

Jones, Gwenan, ed. *A Study of Three Welsh Religious Plays*. Bala: The Bala Press, 1939.

Jones, Gwyn. *Times Like These*. London: Gollancz, 1936.

The Walk Home. London: Dent, 1962.

Jones, Gwyn, and Islwyn Ffowc Elis, eds. *Twenty-Five Welsh Short Stories*. Oxford: Oxford University Press, 1971.

Jones, Ieuan Wyn. 'Wales Says Yes in Referendum Vote'. Interview. *BBC News*. 4 March 2011.

Jones, J. Gwynfor, ed. *The History of the Gwydir Family*. Llandysul: Gomer Press, 1990.

Jones, J. R. *A Raid i'r Iaith Ein Gwahanu?* Aberystwyth: Cymdeithas yr Iaith, 1978.

Jones, Jack. *Rhondda Roundabout*. London: Faber and Faber, 1934.

Black Parade. London: Faber and Faber, 1935.

Unfinished Journey. London: Hamilton, 1937.

Bidden to the Feast. London: Hamilton, 1938.

Off to Philadelphia in the Morning. London: Hamilton, 1947.

River Out of Eden. London: Hamilton, 1951.

Choral Symphony. London: Hamilton, 1955.

Jones, Lewis. *Cwmardy*. London: Lawrence and Wishart, 1937.

　We Live. London: Lawrence and Wishart, 1939, 1978.

Jones, Llion. *Pethe Achlysurol*. Cyhoeddiadau Barddas, 2007.

Jones, Lloyd. *Mr Cassini*. Bridgend: Seren, 2006.

Jones, Margam. *The Stars of the Revival*. London: John Long, 1910.

　Angels in Wales. London: John Long, 1914.

Jones, Mary. *Resistance*. Belfast: Blackstaff, 1985.

Jones, Mary Oliver. *Y Fun o Eithinfynydd: neu, Helyntion Carwriaethol Cymru Fu*. Caernarfon: Cwmni'r Wasg Genedlaethol Gymreig, *c.* 1894.

Jones, Russell Celyn. *An Interference of Light*. London: Viking, 1995.

Jones, T. Gwynn. *Ymadawiad Arthur a Chaniadau Ereill*. Caernarfon: Cwmni y Cyhoeddwyr Cymreig, 1910.

　'Pro Patria'. *Y Beirniad* 3 (1913): 1–7.

　Caniadau. Wrecsam: Hughes a'i Fab, 1934.

　Y Dwymyn 1934–35. Aberystwyth: Gwasg Aberystwyth, 1944.

Jones, T. Harri. *The Collected Poems of T. Harri Jones*. Ed. Julian Croft and Don Dale-Jones. Llandysul: Gomer Press, 1987.

Jones, Thomas, ed. '*Cronica de Wallia* and Other Documents from Exeter Cathedral Library MS. 3514'. *Bulletin of the Board of Celtic Studies* 12 (1946): 27–44.

Jones, W. E. ('Cawrdaf'). *Y Bardd, neu, y Meudwy Cymreig: yn cynnwys teithiau difyr ac addysgiadol y bardd, gyda rhagluniaeth*. Carmarthen: J. L. Brigstocke, 1830.

Joyce, James. *A Portrait of the Artist as a Young Man*. London: Egoist, 1916.

　Ulysses. Paris: Shakespeare & Co., 1922.

Keating, Joseph. *Son of Judith: A Tale of the Welsh Mining Valleys*. London: G. Allen, 1900.

　Maurice: A Romance of Light and Darkness. London: Chatto and Windus, 1905.

　Adventures in the Dark. Cardiff: Western Mail, 1906.

　Flower of the Dark. London: Cassell, 1917.

Kedymdeithyas Amlyn ac Amic. Ed. Patricia Williams. Caerdydd: Gwasg Prifysgol Cymru, 1982.

King, Jemma L. *The Undressed*. Cardigan: Parthian, 2014.

Klausner, David, ed. *Records of Early English Drama: Herefordshire and Worcestershire*. Toronto: University of Toronto Press, 1990.

　'The Statute of Gruffudd ap Cynan/Statud Gruffudd ap Cynan'. *Welsh Music History/ Hanes Cerddoriaeth Cymru* 3 (1999), 282–98.

　Records of Early Drama: Wales. London and Toronto: The British Library and University of Toronto Press, 2005.

Kyffin, Maurice. *The Blessedness of Brytaine, or a Celebration of the Queenes Holyday*, 1587. Facsimile. London: Honourable Society of the Cymmrodorion, 1885.

The Law of Hywel Dda: Law Texts from Medieval Wales. Ed. and trans. Dafydd Jenkins. Llandysul: Gomer Press, 1986.

Legendary Poems from the Book of Taliesin. Ed. and trans. Marged Haycock. 2nd edn. Aberystwyth: CMCS Publications, 2015.

Lemoine, John. 'Lettres sur les affaires extérieures: troubles dans le pays de Galles – Rebecca et ses filles'. *Revue des Deux Mondes* 3 (1843): 1031.

Levertov, D. *Life in the Forest*. New York: New Directions, 1978.

Candles in Babylon. New York: New Directions, 1982.

Lewis, Alun. *Collected Stories*. Bridgend: Seren, 1995.

Lewis, D. Miles. *Chapel: The Story of a Welsh Family*. London: Heinemann, 1916.

Lewis, E. A. *The Welsh Port Books (1550–1603)*. Cymmrodorion Record Series 12. Cardiff: University of Wales Press, 1927.

Lewis, Emyr. *Chwarae Mig*. Cyhoeddiadau Barddas, 1995.

Amser Amherffaith. Llanrwst: Gwasg Carreg Gwalch, 2004.

Lewis, Gwyneth. *Y Llofrudd Iaith*. Cyhoeddiadau Barddas, 1999.

Sunbathing in the Rain: A Cheerful Book on Depression. London and Philadelphia: Jessica Kingsley, 2007.

A Hospital Odyssey. Tarset: Bloodaxe Books, 2010.

Lewis, James. 'Wales Votes No to Assembly by Four to One'. *The Guardian*, 3 March 1979, 2.

Lewis, Lewis William ('Llew Llwyfo'). *Llewelyn Parri: neu, Y Meddwyn diwygiedig; yn gosod allan echryslonrwydd bywyd y meddwyn a bendithion llwyrymwrthodiad*. Merthyr Tydfil: Rees Lewis, 1855.

Gemau Llwyfo: sef detholion o brif cyfansoddiadau a chaneuon. Utica, NY: T. J. Griffiths, 1868.

Y Creawdwr: Cerdd Ddysg; hefyd Cerdd Goffa gan Dewi Dinorwig. Utica, NY: T. J. Griffiths, 1871.

Lewis, Saunders. *The Eve of Saint John: A Comedy of Welsh Life*. Newtown: Welsh Outlook, 1920.

Egwyddorion Cenedlaetholdeb. Machynlleth: Evan Jones, 1926.

Monica. Aberystwyth: Gwasg Aberystwyth, 1930.

The Banned Wireless Talk on Welsh Nationalism. Caernarfon: Swyddfa'r Blaid Genedlaethol, 1931.

Ysgrifau Dydd Mercher. Llandysul: Y Clwb Llyfrau Cymraeg, 1945.

Siwan a Cherddi Eraill. Llandybïe: Llyfrau'r Dryw, [1956].

Tynged yr Iaith. London: BBC, 1962.

Meistri'r Canrifoedd: Ysgrifau ar Hanes Llenyddiaeth Gymraeg. Ed. R. Geraint Gruffydd. Caerdydd: Gwasg Prifysgol Cymru, 1973.

Presenting Saunders Lewis. Ed. Alun R. Jones and Gwyn Thomas. Cardiff: University of Wales Press, 1973.

The Plays of Saunders Lewis: Translated from the Welsh by Joseph P. Clancy. 4 vols. Llandybïe: Christopher Davies, 1985–6.

Letters to Margaret Gilcriest. Ed. Mair Saunders Jones, Ned Thomas, and Harri Pritchard Jones. Cardiff: University of Wales Press, 1993.

Selected Poems of Saunders Lewis: Translated from the Welsh by Joseph P. Clancy. Cardiff: University of Wales Press, 1993.

Dramâu Saunders Lewis: Y Casgliad Cyflawn. Ed. Ioan Williams. 2 vols. Caerdydd: Gwasg Prifysgol Cymru, 1996, 2000.

Lewis, Saunders, and Aneirin Talfan Davies. 'Dylanwadau: Saunders Lewis mewn Ymgom ag Aneirin Talfan Davies'. *Taliesin* 2 (1961): 5–18.

Lhuyd, Edward. 'Letters of Edward Lhuyd'. *Early Modern Letters Online*. http://emlo .bodleian.ox.ac.uk.

Lingen, R. R. W. *Reports of the Commissioners of Inquiry into the State of Education in Wales: Carmarthen, Glamorgan, Pembroke*. London: Parliamentary Committee of Council on Education, 1947.

The Llandaff Charters. Ed. Wendy Davies. Aberystwyth: National Library of Wales, 1979.

Llewelyn, Michael Gareth. *The Aleppo Merchant*. London: Murray, 1945.

　　To Fame Unknown. London: Murray, 1949.

Llewellyn, Richard. *How Green Was My Valley*. London: Joseph, 1939.

　　Green, Green, My Valley Now. London: Joseph, 1975.

Lloyd, Charles Ellis. *Love and the Agitator*. London: Century Press, 1911.

Lloyd, David. *Boys: Stories and a Novella*. Syracuse: Syracuse University Press, 2005.

　　ed. *Other Land: Contemporary Poems on Wales and Welsh-American Experience*. Cardigan: Parthian, 2008.

Lloyd-Morgan, C. and K. Hughes, eds. *Dringo'r Andes a Gwymon y Môr gan Eluned Morgan*. Dinas Powys: Honno, 2001.

Llwyd, Iwan. *Be 'di Blwyddyn rhwng Ffrindia? Cerddi 1990–99*. Talybont: Gwasg Taf, 2003.

Llwyd, Iwan, and Twm Morys. *Eldorado*. Llanrwst: Gwasg Carreg Gwalch, 1999.

Llwyd, Morgan, *Cerddi Morgan Llwyd*. Ed. Dafydd Glyn Jones. Bangor: Dalen Newydd, 2016.

　　Gweithiau Morgan Llwyd o Wynedd. 3 vols.: vol. I ed. T. E. Ellis, Bangor: Jarvis & Foster, 1899; vol. II ed. John H. Davies, Bangor: Jarvis & Foster, 1908; vol. III ed. J. Graham Jones and Goronwy Wyn Owen, Caerdydd: Gwasg Prifysgol Cymru, 1994.

Llyfr Aneirin: Ffacsimile. Ed. Daniel Huws. Aberystwyth: Llyfrgell Genedlaethol Cymru, 1989.

Llyfr Du Caerfyrddin. Ed. A. O. H. Jarman. Caerdydd: Gwasg Prifysgol Cymru, 1991.

Llyfr Gwyn Rhydderch: Y Chwedlau a'r Rhamantau. Ed. J. Gwenogvryn Evans and Bobi Jones. Caerdydd: Gwasg Prifysgol Cymru, 1977.

Llyfr Iorwerth: A Critical Text of the Venedotian Code of Medieval Welsh Law. Ed. Aled Rhys William. Cardiff: University of Wales Press, 1960.

Logan, Brian. 'Arts Funding Row Breaks Out in Wales'. *The Guardian*, 7 February 2006.

The London Kelt (1895–1904).

The Mabinogi. Trans. John K. Bollard. Llandysul: Gomer Press, 2006.

The Mabinogi and Other Medieval Welsh Tales. Trans. Patrick K. Ford. Berkeley and Los Angeles: University of California Press, 1977.

The Mabinogion: From the Llyfr Coch o Hergest and Other Ancient Welsh Manuscripts. Ed. and trans. Lady Charlotte Guest. 3 vols. London: Longman, Brown, Green and Longmans; Llandovery: W. Rees, 1849.

The Mabinogion. Trans. Lady Charlotte Guest. London: Dent, 1906.

The Mabinogion. Trans. Gwyn Jones and Thomas Jones. London: Dent, 1949.

The Mabinogion. Trans. Jeffrey Gantz. Harmondsworth: Penguin, 1976.

The Mabinogion. Trans. Sioned Davies. Oxford: Oxford University Press, 2008.

MacDonald, Elvey. *Llwch: hunangofiant*. Talybont: Y Lolfa, 2009.

Machen, Arthur. *The Hill of Dreams*. London: Grant Richards, 1907; Cardigan: Parthian, 2010.

　　The Great Return. In *The Caerleon Edition of the Works of Arthur Machen*, vol. VII. London: Martin Secker, 1923.

The Angels of Mons. London: Simpkin Marshall, 1915.

House of Souls. Stratford: Ayer, 1922.

The Secret Glory. In *The Caerleon Edition of the Works of Arthur Machen*, vol. IV. New York: Alfred Knopf, 1922; London: Secker, 1923.

'The Shining Pyramid'. In *The Shining Pyramid and Other Stories by Welsh Authors*, ed. Sam Adams and Roland Mathias, 2–25. Llandysul: Gomer Press, 1970.

The Great God Pan, The Shining Pyramid, The White People. Library of Wales. Cardigan: Parthian, 2010.

Manawydan uab Llyr. Ed. Ian Hughes. Cardiff: University of Wales Press, 2007.

Martell, Owen. *Cadw dy Ffydd, Brawd*. Llandysul: Gwasg Gomer, 2000.

'Marwnad Cynddylan'. In *Bardos: Penodau ar y Traddodiad Barddol Cymreig a Cheltaidd, cyflwynedig i J. E. Caerwyn Williams*, ed. R. Geraint Gruffydd, 10–28. Caerdydd: Gwasg Prifysgol Cymru, 1982.

Math uab Mathonwy. Ed. Ian Hughes. Dublin: Dublin Institute for Advanced Studies, 2013.

May, Caroline, ed. *The American Female Poets*. Philadelphia: Lindsay and Blakiston, 1848.

McKillip, Patricia A. *Riddle-Master: The Complete Trilogy*. New York: Ace Books, 1999.

Meredith, Christopher. *Shifts*. Bridgend: Seren, 1988.

Griffri. 1991, repr. Bridgend: Seren 1994.

Merriman, Catherine. *State of Desire*. London: Macmillan, 1996.

Miles, Gareth, trans. *Y Gaucho o'r Ffos Halen*. Llanrwst: Gwasg Carreg Gwalch, 2004.

Ministry of Power. *Report of Public Inquiry Concerning Proposals to Construct a Nuclear Power Station at Trawsfynydd*. London: HMSO, 1958.

Monmouthshire Merlin, 15 June 1850.

22 June 1850.

5 October 1850.

Morgan, Rhodri. 'Clear Red Water'. Speech given at The National Centre for Public Policy, Swansea. 11 December 2002.

Morgan, Robert. *In the Dark*. Llandysul: Gomer Press, 1994.

Morgan, William. *Y Beibl Cyssegr-lan 1588*. Facsimile. Aberystwyth: National Library of Wales, 1987.

Morris, Kenneth. *The Fates of the Princes of Dyved*. London: Theosophical Book Company, 1914; electronic edn, 2000, www.theosociety.org/pasadena/dyfed/fates-hp.htm.

Morris, Lewis. *Tlysau yr Hen Oesoedd*. Caergybi, 1735.

Morys, Twm. 2. Cyhoeddiadau Barddas, 2002.

'A Refusal to be Translated'. *Poetry Wales* 38, 3 (2003): 55.

Musser, George. *The Complete Idiot's Guide to String Theory*. New York: Alpha/Penguin, 2008.

Myvyrian Archaiology of Wales. Ed. Owen Jones, Edward Williams ('Iolo Morganwg'), and William Owen Pughe. 3 vols. London: The Gwyneddigion Society, 1801–7.

National Assembly for Wales. 'Addressing the Democratic deficit – Presiding Officer to Outline Assembly's Actions'. News release. 7 November 2013.

Assembly Cynulliad. 'Perthynas y BBC â Chymru / The BBC's Relationship with Wales'. *YouTube*. 7 April 2014. www.youtube.com/watch?v=LdrxIWo9bEs&feature=youtu .be&list=PLAiwHW5TKfkGakUCQjuZWxjeb4SRriPg2.

National Statistics/Ystadegau Gwladol. 'National Survey for Wales, 2014: Headline Results, 2013–14, Revised'. https://gov.wales/docs/statistics/2014/140530-national-survey-wales-2013-14-headline-results-revised1-en.pdf.

Nennius: British History and the Welsh Annals. Ed. and trans. J. Morris. History from the Sources: Arthurian Period Sources 8. London: Phillimore, 1980.

The New Annual Register . . . For the Year 1793. London: G. G. and J. Robinson, 1794.

Norris, Leslie. *The Girl from Cardigan.* Bridgend: Seren, 1988.

    Collected Stories. Bridgend: Seren, 1996.

    The Complete Poems. Ed. Meic Stephens. Bridgend: Seren, 2008.

O'Brien, Flann. *At Swim-Two-Birds.* London: Longman, 1939.

Ó Cadhain, Máirtín. *Cré na Cille* (1949). Trans. Alan Titley as *The Dirty Dust.* New Haven: Yale University Press, 2015.

Ofcom. 'Internet Citizens 2014: Use of Selected Citizen-Related Online Content and Services'. Research Document. 27 November 2014.

Office for National Statistics. *Census 2001: Report on the Welsh Language.* London: HMSO, 2004.

Owein, or Chwedyl Iarlles y Ffynnawn. Ed. R. L. Thomson. Dublin: Dublin Institute for Advanced Studies, 1968.

Owen, Daniel. *Y Dreflan: ei phobl a'i phethau.* Treffynnon: P. M. Evans, 1881.

    Hunangofiant Rhys Lewis: Gweinidog Bethel. Wrecsam: Hughes a'i Fab, 1882–5; repr. Cardiff: University of Wales Press, 2000. Trans. Stephen Morris as *Rhys Lewis: Minister of Bethel.* Mold: Brown Cow, 2015.

    Profedigaethau Enoc Huws. Wrecsam: Hughes a'i Fab, 1891; repr. Caerdydd: Hughes a'i Fab, 1995. Trans. Les Barker as *The Trials of Enoc Huws.* Mold: Brown Cow, 2010.

Owen, David ('Brutus'). *Wil Brydydd y Coed: cofiant Siencyn Bach y Llwywr a chofiant Dai Hunandyb.* 3rd edn. Carmarthen: Spurrell, 1896.

Owen, Elizabeth. *Odes of Odd Moments.* Denver: Bradford-Robinson Printing Co., 1922.

    Briwsion Barddonol. Denver: publisher unknown, 1927.

Owen, George. *The Description of Penbrokshire.* Ed. Henry Owen. 4 vols. London: Cymmrodorion Record Series, 1892–1936.

Owen, Gerallt Lloyd. *Cerddi'r Cywilydd.* Caernarfon: Gwasg Gwynedd, 1972.

    Cilmeri a Cherddi Eraill. Caernarfon: Gwasg Gwynedd, 1991.

Owen, Goronwy. *Diddanwch Teuluaidd.* Llundain: William Roberts, 1763.

Owen, Hugh, ed. *Additional Letters of the Morrises of Anglesey (1735–1786).* 2 vols. London: The Honourable Society of Cymmrodorion, 1947, 1949.

Owen, Phyllis M. *Mimosa: A Narrative Based on Fact.* Bridgend: D. Brown and Sons, 1995.

The Oxford Book of Welsh Verse. Ed. Thomas Parry. London: Oxford University Press, 1962.

Parry, Glyn. *A Guide to the Records of Great Sessions in Wales.* Aberystwyth: National Library of Wales, 1995.

Parry, R. Williams. *Yr Haf a Cherddi Eraill.* Bala: R. Evans, Gwasg y Bala, 1924; 2nd edn Dinbych: Gwasg Gee, 1970.

    Cerddi R. Williams Parry: Y Casgliad Cyflawn. Ed. Alan Llwyd. Dinbych: Gwasg Gee, 1998.

Parry, William. *The Old Welsh Evangelist, and Other Poems.* Bristol: William F. Mack, 1893.

    Welsh Hillside Saints. Manchester: J. Roberts and Sons, 1896.

Parry, Winnie. *Sioned*. Caernarfon: Swyddfa Cymru, 1906; repr. Dinas Powys: Honno, 1988.

Parry-Williams, T. H. ed. *Canu Rhydd Cynnar*. Caerdydd: Gwasg Prifysgol Cymru, 1932.

    ed. *Rhyddiaith Gymraeg: Y Gyfrol Gyntaf, Detholion o Lawysgrifau, 1488–1609*. Caerdydd: Gwasg Prifysgol Cymru, 1954.

    ed. *Hen Benillion*. 3rd edn. Llandysul: Gwasg Gomer, 1965.

    Casgliad o Gerddi. Ed. J. E. Caerwyn Williams and Amy Parry-Williams. Llandysul: Gwasg Gomer, 1987.

Peacock, Thomas Love. *The Misfortunes of Elphin*. London: Thomas Hookham, 1829.

Pedeir Keinc y Mabinogi. Ed. Ifor Williams. Caerdydd: Gwasg Prifysgol Cymru, 1930, 1951.

Penman, Shannon Kay. *Here Be Dragons*. New York: Holt, Rinehart and Winston, 1985.

Pennant, Thomas. *The History of the Parishes of Whiteford and Holywell*. London: B. and J. White, 1796.

Penny, Anne. *Poems, with a Dramatic Entertainment*. London: printed for the author, 1771.

Penry, John. *A Treatise Containing the Aequity of an Humble Supplication . . . in the Behalf of the Countrey of Wales*. Oxford: Joseph Barnes, 1587.

    The Notebook of John Penry, 1593. Ed. Albert Peel, *Camden Society*, 3rd series, LXVII. London: Royal Historical Society, 1944.

    Three Treatises Concerning Wales. Ed. David Williams. Cardiff: University of Wales Press, 1960.

The Poems of Taliesin. Ed. Ifor Williams, trans. J. E. Caerwyn Williams. Dublin: Dublin Institute for Advanced Studies, 1968.

The Poetry of Llywarch Hen. Ed. and trans. Patrick K. Ford. Berkeley: University of California Press, 1974.

Powel, David. *The Historie of Cambria, Now Called Wales*. London: R. Newberie and H. Denham, 1584.

Powys, John Cowper. *Porius*. London: MacDonald, 1951; London: Duckworth, 2007.

Pryce, D. Hugh. *The Ethics of Evan Wynne*. 1913.

Prichard, Caradog. *Canu Cynnar*. Wrecsam: Hughes a'i Fab, 1937.

    Un Nos Ola Leuad. Dinbych: Gwasg Gee, 1961. Trans. Menna Gallie as *Full Moon*. London: Hodder and Stoughton, 1973. Also trans. Philip Mitchell as *One Moonlit Night*. Edinburgh: Canongate, 1995.

Prichard, Rhys. *Cerddi'r Ficer: Detholiad o Gerddi Rhys Prichard*. Ed. Nesta Lloyd. Cyhoeddiadau Barddas, 1994.

Prichard, Richard. *Blodau'r Gorllewin: yn cynnwys awdlau, cywyddau, ac englynion, yn nghydag eglurhad ar y gynghanedd gymreig*. Chicago: R. R. Meredith a'i Feibion, 1877.

Prichard, T. J. Llewelyn. *The Adventures and Vagaries of Twm Shon Catti, Descriptive of Life in Wales: Interspersed with Poems*. Aberystwyth: John Cox, 1828. www.gutenberg.org/files/40419/40419-h/40419-h.htm.

Prise, John. *Historiae Britannicae Defensio/A Defence of the British History*. Ed. and trans. Ceri Davies. Oxford: Bodleian Library, 2015.

Prophecies from the Book of Taliesin. Ed. and trans. Marged Haycock. Aberystwyth: CMCS Publications, 2013.

Protheroe, John. *Little Johnny*. Cardiff: self-published, 1891.

Pryce, D[aisy] Huw. *The Ethics of Evan Wynne*. London: Everett and Co., 1913.

Puddicombe, Anne Adaliza ('Allen Raine'). *A Welsh Singer*. 1897; repr. London: Hutchinson, 1906.

   Torn Sails: A Tale of a Welsh Village. London: Hutchinson, 1898.

   By Berwen Banks: A Novel. London: Hutchinson, 1899.

   Garthowen: A Story of a Welsh Homestead. London: Hutchinson, 1900.

   A Welsh Witch: A Romance of Rough Places. London: Hutchinson, 1902.

   Queen of the Rushes: A Tale of the Welsh Revival. London: Hutchinson, 1906; repr. Dinas Powys: Honno, 1998.

   All in a Month and Other Stories. London: Hutchinson, 1908.

Raine, Allen. See Puddicombe, Anne Adaliza.

Randolph, Thomas. *The Muses' Looking Glass*. London, STC: 20694#, 1638.

Rees, William ('Gwilym Hiraethog'). *Aelwyd f'Ewythr Robert: neu, Hanes Caban f'Ewythr Tomos*. Denbigh: Thomas Gee, 1853.

Rhys, Siôn Dafydd ('Rhæsus, Joannes Davides'). *Cambrobrytannicæ Cymraecæve Lingvae Institvtiones et Rvdimenta*. London: Thomas Orwin, 1592.

Richards, Alun, ed. *The Second Penguin Book of Welsh Short Stories*. Rev. 2nd edn. London: Penguin, 1994.

Richards, W. D., 'Ceredig'. *Among the Mountains: or Life in Wales*. Ebbw Vale: J. Davies and London: J. Clarke, [n.d., post 1867].

Roberts, Eleazar. *Owen Rees: A Story of Welsh Life and Thought*. London: Elliot Stock, 1893.

Roberts, Kate. *O Gors y Bryniau*. Wrecsam: Hughes a'i Fab, 1926.

   Traed Mewn Cyffion. Aberystwyth: Gwasg Aberystwyth, 1936. Trans. Idris Walter and J. I. Jones as *Feet in Chains*. Denbigh: Jones, 1977.

Roberts, Lynette. *The Endeavour: Captain Cook's First Voyage to Australia*. London: Peter Owen, 1954.

   Lynette Roberts: Diaries, Letters and Recollections. Ed. Patrick McGuinness. Manchester: Carcanet, 2008.

Roberts, Wiliam Owen. *Y Pla*. Bangor: Annwn, 1987.

Rowland, Jenny, ed. and trans. *Early Welsh Saga Poetry. A Study and Edition of the Englynion*. Cambridge: D. S. Brewer, 1990.

   ed. and trans. *A Selection of Early Welsh Saga Poems*. London: Modern Humanities Research Association, 2014.

Rowlands, John. 'A Critical Edition and Study of the Welsh Poems Written in Praise of the Salusburies of Lleweni'. DPhil diss., Oxford University, 1967–8.

Salesbury, William. *A Dictionary in Englyshe and Welshe moche necessary to all suche Welshemen as wil spedly learne the englyshe tongue*. London: John Waley, 1547.

   A playne and a familiar Introduction teaching how to pronounce the letters in the Brytish tongue. London: Henry Denham, 1567.

   Oll Synnwyr pen Kembero ygyd. Ed. J. Gwenogvryn Evans. Bangor and London: Jarvis & Foster and J. M. Dent & Co., 1902.

   Kynniver Llith a Ban. Ed. John Fisher. Cardiff and Oxford: University of Wales Press Board and Humphrey Milford, Oxford University Press, 1931.

   Llyfr Gweddi Gyffredin 1567. Facsimile. Ed. Melville Richards and Glanmor Williams. Cardiff: University of Wales Press, 1965.

Saunders, Sara Maria. 'Nancy on the Warpath'. In *A View Across the Family: Short Stories by Women from Wales, c. 1850–1950*, ed. Jane Aaron, 14–26. Dinas Powys: Honno, 1999.

Saunderson, Irene. *A Welsh Heroine*. London: Lynwood, 1911.

Seward, Anna. *Letters of Anna Seward: Written Between the Years 1784 and 1807*. 6 vols. Edinburgh: Archibald Constable, 1811.

Skene, William Forbes. *The Four Ancient Books of Wales*. 2 vols. Edinburgh: Edmonston and Douglas, 1868.

Skoulding, Zoë. *Remains of a Future City*. Bridgend: Seren, 2008.

    Contemporary Women's Poetry and Urban Space: Experimental Cities. Basingstoke: Palgrave Macmillan, 2013.

    The Museum of Disappearing Sounds. Bridgend: Seren, 2013.

Smith, Dai, ed. *Story: The Library of Wales Anthology*. 2 vols. Cardigan: Parthian, 2014.

Smith, Logan Pearsall, ed. *The Golden Grove: Selected Passages from the Sermons and Writing of Jeremy Taylor*. Oxford: Clarendon Press, 1930.

Soave, Mónica. *El botón de nácar: Historias en la historia de los colonos galeses en la Patagonia*. Buenos Aires: Ediciones Simurg, 2005.

Somerset, J. A. B., ed. *Records of Early English Drama: Shropshire*. Toronto: University of Toronto Press, 1994.

Songs of Praises: English Hymns and Elegies of William Williams Pantycelyn 1717–1791. Ed. R. Brinley Jones. Felin-fach: Llanerch, 1991.

Statutes of the Realm. Ed. Alexander Luders et al. 11 vols. London: Dawsons of Pall Mall, 1810–28.

Statutes of Wales. Ed. Ivor Bowen. Leipsic: T. Fisher Unwin, 1908.

Stradling, John. *The Storie of the Lower Borowes of Merthyrmawr*. Ed. Henry J. Randall and William Rees. South Wales and Monmouthshire Record Society Publications 1. Cardiff: William Lewis, 1932.

T. B. *The Rebellion of Naples, or the Tragedy of Massanello*. London, Wing B199. 1649.

Testament Newydd. London: Henry Denham for Humfrey Toy, 1567.

Testament Newydd William Salesbury. Caernarfon: Robert Griffith, 1850.

The Text of the Book of Llan Dâv. Ed. J. Gwenogvryn Evans. Aberystwyth: National Library of Wales, 1979.

Thatcher, Margaret. *Downing Street Years*. London: Harper Collins Publishers, 1999.

Thomas, Alfred P. *In the Land of the Harp and the Feathers: A Series of Welsh Idylls*. London: H. R. Allenson, 1896.

Thomas, Dylan. 'Answers to an Enquiry'. *New Verse*, 11 October 1934.

    Under Milk Wood: A Play for Voices. New York: New Directions, 1954.

    Poet in the Making: The Notebooks of Dylan Thomas. Ed. Ralph Maud. London: Dent & Sons, 1968.

    Early Prose Writings. Ed. Walford Davies. London: Dent & Sons, 1971.

    The Broadcasts. Ed. Ralph Maud. London: Dent & Sons, 1991.

    Collected Letters. Ed. Paul Ferris. Rev. edn. London: Dent, 2000.

    Collected Stories. Ed. Walford Davies. London: Phoenix, 2000.

    The Collected Poems of Dylan Thomas: The New Centenary Edition. Ed. John Goodby. London: Weidenfeld and Nicolson, 2014.

Thomas, Ed. 'The Welsh: A Land Fit for Heroes. (Max Boyce Excluded)'. *The Observer*, 20 July 1997, 16.

Thomas, Edward. *Beautiful Wales*. London: A. & C. Black, 1905.

    Poems. New York: Holt, 1917.

The South Country. London: Dent, 1909.

The Happy-Go-Luck Morgans. London: Duckworth, 1913.

The Annotated Collected Poems. Ed. Edna Lonley. Tarset: Bloodaxe, 2008.

Thomas, Gwyn (1913–1981). *Where Did I Put My Pity?* London: Progress, 1946.

All Things Betray Thee. London: Joseph, 1949; with an introduction by Raymond Williams, London: Lawrence and Wishart, 1986.

The World Cannot Hear You. London: Gollancz, 1951.

A Few Selected Exits. London: Hutchinson, 1968; repr. Bridgend: Seren, 1989.

Sorrow for Thy Sons. London Lawrence and Wishart, 1986.

The Thinker and the Thrush. London: Lawrence and Wishart, 1988.

Thomas, Gwyn (1936–2016). *Chwerwder Yn Y Ffynhonnau*. Dinbych: Gwasg Gee, [1961].

Enw'r Gair. Dinbych: Gwasg Gee, 1972.

Living a Life: Selected Poems 1962–1982. Selected and introduced by Joseph P. Clancy with translations by Joseph P. Clancy and Gwyn Thomas. Amsterdam: Scott Rollins for Bridges Books, 1982.

Thomas, Howard. *The Singing Hills: A Story About Welsh Settlers in Upstate New York*. Prospect, NY: Prospect Books, 1964.

The Road to Sixty. Prospect, NY: Prospect Books, 1966.

Thomas, John. *Arthur Llwyd y Felin*. Liverpool: John Edwards, 1893.

Thomas, R. D. *Hanes Cymry America / Cyflawn Olygfa ar Gymry America*. Utica, NY: T. J. Griffiths, 1872.

Thomas, R. M. *Trewern*. London: T. Fisher Unwin, 1901.

Thomas, R. S. *The Stones of the Field*. Carmarthen: Druid Press, 1946.

'Anglo-Welsh Literature'. *The Welsh Nationalist* (December 1948): 3–8.

An Acre of Land. Newtown, Mont.: Montgomeryshire Printing Co., 1952.

Song at the Year's Turning. London: Hart-Davis, 1955.

Not That He Brought Flowers. London: Rupert Hart-Davis, 1969.

Selected Prose. Ed. Sandra Anstey. Bridgend: Poetry of Wales Press, 1983.

Neb. Caernarfon. Gwasg Gwynedd, 1985.

Collected Poems. London: Dent, 1993.

Autobiographies. Trans. Jason Walford Davies. London: Dent, 1997.

Letters to Raymond Garlick 1951–1999. Ed. Jason Walford Davies. Llandysul: Gomer Press, 2009.

T[homas], S[imon]. *Hanes y Byd a'r Amseroedd*. London: D. Lloyd, 1721.

Thomas, Tydfil. *A Fierce Flame*. London: Minerva, 1997.

Thomson, R. L. 'Iarlles y Ffynnon: The Version in Llanstephan MS 58'. *Studia Celtica* 6 (1971): 57–89.

Tirebuck, William Edwards. *Jenny Jones and Jenny*. Wrexham: Hughes and Son, 1896.

[Torbuck, John]. *A Collection of Welsh travels, and memoirs of Wales. Containing I. The Briton describ'd, or a journey thro' Wales: ... II. A trip to North-Wales, by a Barrister of the Temple. III. A funeral sermon, preach'd by the Parson of Langwillin. IV. Muscipula; or the Welsh mouse-trap, a poem. The whole collected by J. T. a mighty Lover of Welsh Travels*. London: John Torbuck, 1740.

Trezise, Rachel. *In and Out of the Goldfish Bowl*. Cardiff: Parthian, 2000.

Trioedd Ynys Prydein: The Triads of the Island of Britain. Ed. and trans. Rachel Bromwich. 4th edn. Cardiff: University of Wales Press, 2014.

The Triumph Tree: Scotland's Earliest Poetry AD 550–1350. Ed. T. O. Clancy. Edinburgh: Canongate, 1999.

Troelus a Chresyd o Lawysgrif Peniarth 106. Ed. W. Beynon Davies. Caerdydd: Gwasg Prifysgol Cymru, 1976.

Vaughan, Arthur Owen (Owen Rhoscomyl). *The Jewel of Ynys Galon*. London: Longmans, Green & Co., 1895.

Old Fireproof: Being the Chaplain's Story. London: Duckworth and Son, 1906.

A Scout's Story. London: Duckworth, 1908.

Vita Griffini Filii Conani: The Medieval Latin Life of Gruffudd ap Cynan. Ed. and trans. Paul Russell. Cardiff: University of Wales Press, 2005.

'Wales says Yes'. *Western Mail*, 19 September 1997, 1.

Walter Map. *De nugis curialium: Courtiers' Trifles*. Ed. and trans. M. R. James, rev. C. N. L. Brooke and R. A. B. Mynors. Oxford: Oxford University Press, 1983.

Walter, Rowland. *Caniadau Ionoron: Yn Cynnwys Awdlau, Cywyddau, Englynion a Phenillion*. Utica, NY: T. J. Griffiths, 1972.

Walton, Evangeline. *The Mabinogion Tetralogy*. London: Overlook Duckworth, 2012.

Watkins, Vernon. *The Lady with the Unicorn*. London: Faber, 1948.

Webb, Harri. *The Green Desert: Collected Poems 1950–1969*. Llandysul, Gomer Press, 1969.

Welsh Affairs Committee. 'Broadcasting and the National Assembly'. HMSO, 1999.

Welsh Assembly Government. *Welsh Writing in English: A Review*. Culture, Welsh Language and Sport Committee. 2014.

'Welshman's Notebook'. *Wrexham Leader*, 26 January 1951.

Wilde, Oscar. *De Profundis: The Ballad of Reading Gaol and Other Writings*. Ware: Wordsworth, 1999.

Wiliams, Gerwyn. *Cydio'n Dynn*. Talybont: Y Lolfa, 1997.

Williams, D. J. *Hen Wynebau*. Aberystwyth: Gwasg Aberystwyth, 1934.

Hen Dŷ Ffarm. Aberystwyth: Gwasg Aberystwyth, 1953. Trans. Waldo Williams as *The Old Farmhouse*. Llandysul, Gomer Press, 2001.

Storïau'r Tir. Llandysul: Gwasg Gomer, 1966.

Williams, Dafydd Rhys. *Llyfr Pawb*. Utica, NY: T. J. Griffiths, 1908.

Williams, Ieuan M., ed. *Humphrey Llwyd, Cronica Walliae*. Cardiff: University of Wales Press, 2002.

Williams, Gruffydd Aled, ed. *Ymryson Edmwnd Prys a Wiliam Cynwal*. Caerdydd: Gwasg Prifysgol Cymru, 1986.

Williams, J. G. *Pigau'r Sêr*. Dinbych: Gwasg Gee, 1969.

Maes Mihangel. Dinbych: Gwasg Gee, 1974.

Williams, John, ed. *Digest of Welsh Historical Statistics*. Cardiff: Welsh Office, 1985.

Williams, John. *Cardiff Dead*. London: Bloomsbury, 2000.

Williams, John Stuart, and Meic Stephens, eds. *The Lilting House: An Anthology of Anglo-Welsh Poetry 1917–1967*. London and Llandybïe: Dent and Christopher Davies, 1969.

Williams, Moses. *Proposals*. Pamphlet. s.l., s.n, 1719.

Williams, Raymond. *Border Country*. London: Chatto and Windus, 1960; repr. Cardigan: Parthian, 2006.

Second Generation. London: Chatto and Windus, 1964.

The Volunteers. London: Eyre Methuen, 1978.

The Fight for Manod. London: Hogarth, 1979.

Loyalties. London: Hogarth, 1985.

Williams, R. B. *Bandit yr Andes*. Caerdydd: Hughes a'i Fab, 1950.

Y March Coch. Llandysul: Gwasg Gomer, 1954.

Croesi'r Paith. Llandybïe: Llyfrau'r Dryw, 1958.

Eluned Morgan: Bywgraffiad a Detholiad. Aberystwyth: Y Clwb Llyfrau Cymraeg, 1948.

Williams, Rhydwen. *Cwm Hiraeth: Y Briodas*. Llandybie: Llyfrau'r Dryw, 1969.

Cwm Hiraeth: Y Siol Wen. Llandybïe: Llyfrau'r Dryw, 1970.

Cwm Hiraeth: Dyddiau Dyn. Llandybïe: Llyfrau'r Dryw, 1973.

The Angry Vineyard. Abertawe: Davies, 1975.

Amser i Wylo: Senghenydd, 1913. Abertawe: Christopher Davies, 1986.

Williams, T. Marchant. *The Land of My Fathers*. London and New York: Longmans, 1889.

Williams, Waldo. *Dail Pren*. Aberystwyth: Gwasg Aberystwyth, 1956.

Waldo Williams: Rhyddiaith. Ed. Damian Walford Davies. Caerdydd: Gwasg Prifysgol Cymru, 2001.

Waldo Williams: Cerddi 1922–1970. Ed. Alan Llwyd and Robert Rhys. Llandysul: Gwasg Gomer, 2014.

Williams, W. Prichard, ed. *Deffyniad Ffydd Eglwys Loegr a gyfieithwyd i'r Gymraeg o Ladin yr Esgob Jewel yn y flwyddyn 1595, gan Maurice Kyffin*. Bangor: Jarvis & Foster, 1908.

Williams, William ('Llewellin Penrose'). *The Journal of Llewellin Penrose, a Seaman*. London: J. Murray, 1815.

Woolf, Virginia. 'A Room of One's Own'. In *A Room of One's Own/Three Guineas*, ed. Michèle Barrett, 3–103. London: Penguin, 1993.

Wylie, John. *Landscape*. London and New York: Routledge, 2007.

Wynne, Ellis. *Cerddi'r Bardd Cwsg*. Ed. Dafydd Glyn Jones. Bangor: Dalen Newydd, 2014.

Yeats, W. B. *Essays and Introductions*. London and Basingstoke: Macmillan, 1961.

Ystorya Bown de Hamtwn. Ed. Morgan Watkin. Caerdydd: Gwasg Prifysgol Cymru, 1958.

Ystorya de Carolo Magno. Ed. Stephen J. Williams. Caerdydd: Gwasg Prifysgol Cymru, 1930.

Ystorya Gereint uab Erbin. Ed. R. L. Thomson. Dublin: Dublin Institute of Advanced Studies, 1997.

Ystoryaeu Seint Greal. Ed. Thomas Jones. Caerdydd: Gwasg Prifysgol Cymru, 1992.

Secondary Sources

Aaron, Jane. 'A National Seduction: Wales in Nineteenth-Century Women's Writing'. *New Welsh Review* 27 (Winter, 1994): 31–8.

Nineteenth-Century Women's Writing in Wales: Nation, Gender and Identity. Cardiff: University of Wales Press, 2007, 2010.

Welsh Gothic. Cardiff: University of Wales Press, 2013.

'Forming the Subject: The Genesis of Welsh Writing in English as an Academic Discipline'. *The Association of Welsh Writing in English* (May 2017). www.awwe .org/forming-the-subject.html.

Aaron, Jane, Henrice Altinck, and Chris Weedon, eds. *Gendering Border Studies*. Cardiff: University of Wales Press, 2010.

Aaron, Jane, Teresa Rees, Sandra Betts, and Moira Vincenelli, eds. *Our Sisters' Land: The Changing Identities of Women in Wales*. Cardiff: University of Wales Press, 1994.

Aaron, Jane, and M. Wynn Thomas. '"Pulling You Through Changes": Welsh Writing in English Before, Between and After Two Referenda'. In *Welsh Writing in English*, ed. M. Wynn Thomas, 278–309.

Aaron, Jane, and Chris Williams, eds. *Postcolonial Wales*. Cardiff: University of Wales Press, 2005.

Aaron, Wil. 'Film'. In *The Arts in Wales*, ed. Stephens, 297–308.

AHRC Research Project. 'Iolo Morganwg and the Romantic Tradition in Wales'. Aberystwyth: Centre for Advanced Welsh and Celtic Studies, 2001–2008. www.wal es.ac.uk/en/CentreforAdvancedWelshCelticStudies/ResearchProjects/Completed Projects/IoloMorganwgandtheRomanticTraditioninWales/IoloMorganwgFullerDe scription.aspx.

Allchin, A. M. *Ann Griffiths: The Furnace and the Fountain*. Cardiff: University of Wales Press, 1987.

Praise Above All: Discovering the Welsh Tradition. Cardiff: University of Wales Press, 1991.

Allchin, A. M., and D. Densil Morgan, trans. Patrick Thomas. *Sensuous Glory: The Poetic Vision of D. Gwenallt Jones*. Norwich: Canterbury Press, 2000.

Allen, Richard. *Quaker Communities in Early Modern Wales: From Resistance to Respectability*. Cardiff: University of Wales Press, 2007.

Anderson, Benedict. *Imagined Communities*. London: Verso, 1983.

Andrews, Malcolm. *In Search of the Picturesque: Landscape Aesthetics and Tourism in Britain 1760–1800*. Aldershot: Scolar Press, 1989.

Anon. 'Celtic Fantasy'. Best Fantasy Books. http://bestfantasybooks.com/celtic-fantasy .html.

Anon. 'Y Cyfnodolyn Cymodlon: Cyfweliad â *Taliesin*'. *Tu Chwith* 1 (1993): 70–6.

Anon. 'Wales 2, Hungary 1'. Review of *Strike for a Kingdom* by Menna Gallie. *Times Literary Supplement*, 20 February 1959, 102.

Anon. 'Welsh Film History: 1930–39'. 5 March 2010. www.bbc.co.uk/wales/arts/sites/fil m/pages/history-1930–1939.shtml.

Antur, Gruffudd, and Elis Dafydd. 'Golygyddol'. *Tu Chwith* 40 (2014): 5–9.

ap Dafydd, Myrddin, Hilma Lloyd Edwards, Tudur Dylan Jones, Karen Owen, Ceri Wyn Jones, Mererid Hopwood, Twm Morys, and Emyr Lewis. 'Y Gynghanedd: Crefft Dynion?' *Tu Chwith* 9 (Gwanwyn 1998): 127–32.

ap Gwilym, Gwynn. 'Cymraeg y Pridd a'r Concrit'. *Barn* 203–4 (1979): 259–64.

ed. *Cyfres y Meistri 3: T. Gwynn Jones*. Llandybïe: Christopher Davies, 1982.

ed. *Meistri a'u Crefft*. Caerdydd: Gwasg Prifysgol Cymru, 1981.

Armstrong, R., and T. Ó hAnnracháin, eds. *Christianities in the Early Modern Celtic World*. Basingstoke: Palgrave, 2014.

Aronstein, Susan. 'When Arthur Held Court in Caer Llion: Love, Marriage, and the Politics of Centralization in *Gereint* and *Owein*'. *Viator* 25 (1994): 215–28.

'Becoming Welsh: Counter-Colonialism and the Negotiation of Native Identity in *Peredur vab Efrawc*'. *Exemplaria* 17 (2005): 135–68.

Ashcroft, Bill, Gareth Griffiths, and Helen Tiffin. *The Empire Writes Back: Theory and Practice in Post-colonial Literatures*. London: Routledge and Kegan Paul, 1989.

Atherton, Ian. 'Commemorating Conflict and the Ancient British Past in Augustan Britain'. *Journal for Eighteenth Century Studies* 36, 3 (2013): 377–93.

743

Atwood, Margaret. *Survival: A Thematic Guide to Canadian Literature.* 1972; repr. Toronto: McClelland and Stewart, 2004.

Auden, W. H. 'The Geste Says This and the Man Who Was on the Field . . .' *Mid-Century Review* 39 (1962): 12–13.

Augé, Marc. *Non-Places.* Trans. John Howe. London and New York: Verso, 1995.

Aughey, Arthur, Eberhard Bort, and John Osmond. *Unique Paths to Devolution: Wales, Scotland and Northern Ireland.* Cardiff: Institute of Welsh Affairs, 2011.

Bachelard, Gaston. *The Poetics of Space.* Trans. Maria Jolas. Boston: Beacon Press, 1994.

Bagshaw, Edward. *The Life and Death of Mr Vavasor Powell.* London: *s.n.*, 1671.

Baines, Menna. *Yng Ngolau'r Lleuad: Ffaith a Dychymyg yng Ngwaith Caradog Prichard.* Llandysul: Gwasg Gomer, 2005.

'Y Saint yn eu Gogoniant'. Interview with Angharad Price. *Barn* 566 (Mawrth 2010): 33–4.

Baldick, Chris. *The Oxford English Literary History.* Vol. X: *The Modern Movement (1910–1940).* Oxford: Oxford University Press, 2004.

Ballin, Malcolm. *Welsh Periodicals in English 1882–2012.* Cardiff: University of Wales Press, 2013.

Balsom, Denis. 'The Three-Wales Model'. In *The National Question Again,* ed. Osmond, 1–17.

Barkahn, E. R., ed. *Making it in America: A Sourcebook of Eminent Ethnic Americans.* Santa Barbara, CA: ABC-CLIO, 2001.

Bartrum, P. C. 'Was There a British "Book of Conquests"?' *Bulletin of the Board of Celtic Studies* 23 (1986): 1–5.

A Welsh Classical Dictionary: People in History and Legend up to About AD 1000. Aberystwyth: National Library of Wales, 1993.

Becker, Audrey L., and Kristin Noone, eds. *Welsh Mythology and Folklore in Popular Culture.* Jefferson, NC: McFarland, 2011.

Beier, A. L., and R. Finlay, eds *London 1500–1800: The Making of a Metropolis.* London: Longman, 1986.

Bell, David. *Ardent Propaganda. Miners' Novels and Class Conflict.* Umeå: Umeå University Press, 1995.

Bell, H. I. *The Development of Welsh Poetry.* Oxford: Clarendon Press, 1936.

Bell, Ian A. 'How Green Was My Valley?' *Planet* 73 (1992): 3–9.

ed. *Peripheral Visions: Images of Nationhood in Contemporary British Fiction.* Cardiff: University of Wales Press, 1995.

Beresford, M. W. *New Towns of the Middle Ages: Town Plantation in England, Wales and Gascony.* London: Lutterworth, 1967.

Berry, Dave. *Wales and Cinema: The First Hundred Years.* Cardiff: University of Wales Press, 1994.

Bevan, Aneurin. 'The Claim of Wales'. *Wales* 25 (1947): 151–3.

Bhabha, Homi K. *The Location of Culture.* London and New York: Routledge, 1994.

Bianchi, Tony. 'Aztecs in Troedrhiwgwair: Recent Fictions in Wales'. In *Peripheral Visions:* ed. Bell, 44–76.

'Tri'n Hawlio Terra Nullius', *Barddas* 327 (Awst 2015), 47–9.

Blandford, Steve. 'Wales and the Question of the "Creative Industries"'. *North American Journal of Welsh Studies* 7 (2012): 1–17.

ed. *Wales on Screen.* Bridgend: Seren, 2000.

Blasing, Mutlu Konuk. *Lyric Poetry: The Pleasure and Pain of Words*. Princeton: Princeton University Press, 2007.

Blayney, Peter W. M. *The Stationers' Company and the Printers of London*. 2 vols. Cambridge: Cambridge University Press, 2013.

Bloom, Harold. *Shakespeare: The Invention of the Human*. London: Fourth Estate, 1999.

Boddy, G. W. 'Players of Interludes in North Yorkshire in the Early Seventeenth Century'. *North Yorkshire Record Office Publications* 7, 1 (1976): 95–130.

Bogdanor, Vernon. *Devolution in the United Kingdom*. Oxford: Oxford University Press, 1999.

Bohata, Kirsti. *Postcolonialism Revisited*. Writing Wales in English. Cardiff: University of Wales Press, 2004.

'"Unhomely Moments": Reading and Writing Nation in Welsh Female Gothic'. In *The Female Gothic: New Directions*, ed. Wallace and Smith, 180–95.

Bohata, Kirsti, and Katie Gramich, eds. *Rediscovering Margiad Evans: Marginality, Gender and Illness*. Cardiff: University of Wales Press, 2013.

Bohata, Kirsti, and Alexandra Jones. 'Welsh Women's Industrial Fiction, 1880–1914'. *Welsh Women's Writing, 1536–1914* (2017): 499–516.

Bollard, J. K. 'The Structure of the Four Branches of the *Mabinogi*'. *Transactions of the Honourable Society of Cymmrodorion* (1974–5): 250–76.

'Traddodiad a Dychan yn *Breuddwyd Rhonabwy*'. *Llên Cymru* 13 (1980): 155–63.

'The Role of Myth and Tradition in the Four Branches of the *Mabinogi*'. *Cambridge Medieval Celtic Studies* 6 (1983): 67–86.

trans. 'Myrddin in Early Welsh Tradition'. In *The Romance of Merlin: An Anthology*, ed. Peter Goodrich, 13–54. New York: Garland, 1990.

Bollom, Chris. *Attitudes and Second Homes in Rural Wales*. Cardiff: University of Wales Press, 1978.

Boutcher, Warren. 'Vernacular Humanism in the Sixteenth Century'. In *The Cambridge Companion to Renaissance Humanism*, ed. Kraye, 189–202.

Bowen, D. J. 'Graddedigion Eisteddfodau Caerwys, 1523 a 1567/8'. *Llên Cymru* 2 (1952–3): 129–34.

'Ail eisteddfod Caerwys a chais 1594'. *Llên Cymru* 3 (1954–5): 139–61.

'Y Cywyddwyr a'r Dirywiad'. *Bulletin of the Board of Celtic Studies* 29 (1980–2): 453–96.

'Madog'. In *Cyfres y Meistri 3: T. Gwynn Jones*, ed. Gwynn ap Gwilym, 391–2.

Bowen, Geraint. 'Yr Halsingod'. *Transactions of the Honourable Society of Cymmrodorion* (1945): 83–108.

ed. *Y Traddodiad Rhyddiaith yn yr Oesau Canol*. Llandysul: Gwasg Gomer, 1974.

Bowen, Ivor. *The Statutes of Wales*. London and Leipsic: T. Fisher Unwin, 1908.

Bowen, Lloyd. *The Politics of the Principality: Wales, c. 1603–1642*. Cardiff: University of Wales Press, 2007.

Bowie, Fiona, and Oliver Davies, eds. *Discovering Welshness*. Llandysul: Gomer Press, 1992.

Bradshaw, Brendan, and Peter R. Roberts, eds. *British Consciousness and British Identity: The Making of Britain, 1533–1707*. Cambridge: Cambridge University Press, 1998.

Breeze, Andrew. 'Did a Woman Write the Four Branches of the Mabinogi?' *Studi Medievali* 38, 2 (1997): 679–705.

The Origins of the Four Branches of the Mabinogi. Leominster: Gracewing, 2009.

Breverton, Terry, ed. *The First American Novel*. Cowbridge: Glyndwr, 2007.

Bromwich, Rachel. 'Celtic Dynastic Themes and the Breton Lays'. *Études Celtiques* 9 (1960): 439–74.

    Matthew Arnold and Celtic Literature: A Retrospect, 1865–1965. Oxford: Oxford University Press, 1965.

    '"The Mabinogion" and Lady Charlotte Guest'. *Transactions of the Honourable Society of Cymmrodorion* (1986): 127–41.

    'Dwy Chwedl a Thair Rhamant'. In *Y Traddodiad Rhyddiaith yn yr Oesau Canol*, ed. Bowen, 143–75.

Bromwich, Rachel, A. O. H. Jarman, and Brynley F. Roberts, eds. *The Arthur of the Welsh: The Arthurian Legend in Medieval Welsh Literature*. Cardiff: University of Wales Press, 1991.

Brooker, Peter, Andrzej Gasiorek, Deborah Longworth, and Andrew Thacker, eds. *The Oxford Handbook of Modernisms*. Oxford: Oxford University Press, 2010.

Brooks, Simon. 'O Tel Quel i Tu Chwith'. *Tu Chwith* 1 (1993): 5–6.

    'Diaspora y Nofel'. Review of *Y Sêr yn eu Graddau*. *Barn* 454 (2000): 45–6.

    Editorial. *Barn* 458 (Mawrth 2001): 6–9

    '"Yr Hil": Ydy'r Canu Caeth Diweddar yn Hiliol?' In *Llenyddiaeth Mewn Theori*, ed. Thomas, 1–38.

    'Barddoniaeth gyfoes yn "aflwyddiannus"'. *Golwg* 23 (21 April 2011), 8.

    'Oes aur rhyddiaith Gymraeg'. *Golwg* 23 (14 July 2011), 6.

    'Dyfodol yr Eisteddfod'. *Barn* 598 (Tachwedd 2012): 4.

    ed. *Llythyrau at Seimon Glyn*. Talybont: Y Lolfa, 2001.

Brooks, Simon, and Richard G. Roberts, eds. *Pa beth yr aethoch allan i'w achub?* Llanrwst: Gwasg Carreg Gwalch, 2013.

Brooks, Simon, and Wiliam Owen Roberts. 'Trafodaeth a gaed yn sgil rhai sylwadau a wnaethpwyd am waith Denis Diderot'. *Tu Chwith* 2 (1994): 61–76.

Brooks, W. 'Welsh Print Culture in Y Wladfa'. PhD diss., Cardiff University, 2012.

Brown, Carleton, ed. *Poems by Sir John Salusbury and Robert Chester*. London and Oxford: Kegan Paul, Trench, Trübner & Co. and Humphrey Milford, Oxford University Press, 1914.

Brown, Stuart J., Frances Knight, and John Morgan Guy, eds. *Religion, Identity and Conflict in Britain: From the Restoration to the Twentieth Century: Essays in Honour of Keith Robbins*. Farnham: Ashgate, 2013.

Brown, Tony. 'The Ex-centric Voice: The English-Language Short Story in Wales'. *North American Journal of Welsh Studies* 1, 1 (2001): 25–41.

    R. S. Thomas. Writers of Wales. Cardiff: University of Wales Press, 2006.

Brown, Tony, and M. Wynn Thomas. 'The Problems of Belonging'. In *Welsh Writing in English*, ed. Thomas, 165–202.

Bryant-Quinn, M. Paul. 'To Preserve our Language: Gruffydd Robert and Morys Clynnog'. *Journal of Welsh Religious History* 8 (2000): 17–34.

Buckler, W. E. 'On the Study of Celtic Literature: A Critical Reconsideration'. *Victorian Poetry* 27, 1 (Spring 1989): 61–76.

Bullock-Davies, Constance. *Professional Interpreters and the Matter of Britain*. Cardiff: University of Wales Press, 1966.

Butler, Marilyn. 'Romanticism in England'. In *Romanticism in National Context*, ed. Porter and Teich, 37–67.

Bynum, Caroline Walker. 'Metamorphosis, or Gerald and the Werewolf'. *Speculum* 73, 4 (1998): 987–1013.

Metamorphosis and Identity. New York: Zone Books, 2001.

Cam, Helen Maud. *Law-Finders and Law-Makers in Medieval England: Collected Studies in Legal and Constitutional History*. London: Merlin Press, 1962.

Carey, John. 'A British Myth of Origins?' *History of Religions* 31 (1991): 24–38.

Carson, Angela. 'The Structure and Meaning of *The Dream of Rhonabwy*'. *Philological Quarterly* 53 (1974): 289–303.

Casey, Edward S. 'Do Places Have Edges? A Geo-philosophical Enquiry'. In *Envisioning Landscapes, Making Worlds*, ed. Daniels *et al.*, 65–73.

Certeau, Michel de. *The Practice of Everyday Life*. Trans. Steven Rendall. Berkeley, Los Angeles, and London: University of California Press, 1984.

Chandler, Kirstie. 'The Humour in *Breuddwyd Rhonabwy*'. *Studia Celtica* 36 (2002): 59–71.

Chaney, Paul, and Ralph Fevre. 'Ron Davies and the Cult of "Inclusiveness": Devolution and Participation in Wales'. *Contemporary Wales* 14, 1 (2001): 29–49.

Chapman, T. R. *Un Bywyd o Blith Nifer: Cofiant Saunders Lewis*. Llandysul: Gwasg Gomer, 2006.

Charles-Edwards, Gifford. 'The Scribes of the Red Book of Hergest'. *National Library of Wales Journal* 21 (1979–80): 246–56.

Charles-Edwards, Thomas. 'The Date of the Four Branches of the Mabinogi'. *Transactions of the Honourable Society of Cymmrodorion* (1970–1): 263–98.

'The Authenticity of the *Gododdin*: An Historian's View'. In *Astudiaethau ar yr Hengerdd, Studies in Old Welsh Poetry*, ed. R. Bromwich and R. B. Jones, 44–71. Cardiff: University of Wales Press, 1978.

The Welsh Laws. Cardiff: University of Wales Press, 1989.

'The Textual Tradition of Medieval Welsh Prose Tales and the Problem of Dating'. In *150 Jahre 'Mabinogion'*, ed. Maier and Zimmer, 23–40.

'The Date of *Culhwch ac Olwen*'. In *Bile ós Chrannaib: A Festschrift for William Gillies*, ed. Wilson McLeod *et al.*, 45–56. Ceann Drochaid: Clann Tuirc, 2010.

Wales and the Britons, 350–1064. Oxford: Oxford University Press, 2012.

Charles-Edwards, Thomas, Morfydd E. Owen, and Paul Russell, eds. *The Welsh King and his Court*. Cardiff: University of Wales Press, 2000.

Charnell-White, Cathryn A. *Beirdd Ceridwen: Blodeugerdd Barddas o Ganu Menywod hyd tua 1800*. Llandybïe: Gwasg Dinefwr, 2005.

Bardic Circles: National, Regional and Personal Identity in the Bardic Vision of Iolo Morganwg. Cardiff: University of Wales Press, 2007.

ed. *Welsh Poetry of the French Revolution 1789–1805*. Cardiff: University of Wales Press, 2012.

Chrimes, S. B. *Henry VII*. 2nd edn. New Haven: Yale University Press, 1999.

Cichon, Michael. 'Eros and Error: Gross Sexual Transgression in the Fourth Branch of the Mabinogi'. In *The Erotic in the Literature of Medieval Britain*, ed. Amanda Hopkins and Cory James Rushton, 105–15. Woodbridge: D. S. Brewer, 2007.

Clancy, Joseph P. *Other Words*. Cardiff: University of Wales Press, 1999.

Clancy, Thomas O. 'The Kingdoms of the North: Poetry, Places, Politics'. In *Beyond the Gododdin*, ed. Woolf, 153–76.

Clarke, Gillian (unsigned). Editorial. *The Anglo-Welsh Review* 65 (1979): 1.

Editorial. *The Anglo-Welsh Review* 70 (1982): 3.

Colley, Linda. *Britons: Forging the Nation 1707–1837.* New Haven and London: Yale University Press, 1992.

Connolly, Cyril. *The Modern Movement: 100 Key Books from England, France and America 1880–1950.* London: Andre Deutsch, Hamish Hamilton, 1965.

Conran, Tony. *Welsh Verse.* 3rd edn. Bridgend: Seren, 1986.

　Frontiers in Anglo-Welsh Poetry. Cardiff: University of Wales Press, 1997.

　'Poetry Wales and the Second Flowering'. In *Welsh Writing in English*, ed. Thomas, 222–54.

Constantine, Mary-Ann. 'Ossian in Wales and Brittany'. In *The Reception of Ossian in Europe*, ed. Gaskill, 67–90.

　The Truth Against the World: Iolo Morganwg and Romantic Forgery. Cardiff: University of Wales Press, 2007.

　'"To Trace thy Country's Glories to their Source": Dangerous History in Thomas Pennant's Tour in Wales'. In *Rethinking British Romantic History, 1770–1845*, ed. Fermanis and Regan, 121–43.

　'"British Bards": The Concept of Laboring Class Poetry in Eighteenth-Century Wales'. In *A History of British Working Class Literature*, ed. John Goodridge and Bridget Keegan, 101–15. Cambridge: Cambridge University Press, 2017.

　ed. *Ballads in Wales.* London: FLS Books, 1999.

Constantine, Mary-Ann, and Dafydd Johnson, eds. *'Footsteps of Liberty and Revolt': Essays on Wales and the French Revolution.* Cardiff: University of Wales Press, 2013.

Constantine, Mary-Ann, and Nigel Leask, eds. *Enlightenment Travel and British Identities: Thomas Pennant's Tours in Scotland and Wales.* London: Anthem Press, 2017.

Constantine, Stephen. 'British Emigration to the Empire-Commonwealth Since 1880: From Overseas Settlement to Diaspora?' *The Journal of Imperial and Commonwealth History* 31, 2 (2003): 16–35.

Conway, A. *The Welsh in America: Letters from the Immigrants.* Minneapolis. University of Minnesota Press, 1961.

Cooper, Helen. *The English Romance in Time: Transforming Motifs from Geoffrey of Monmouth to the Death of Shakespeare.* Oxford: Oxford University Press, 2004.

Cosgrove, Denis, ed. *Mappings.* London: Reaktion Books, 1999.

Coward, Adam N. 'Edmund Jones and the Pwcca'r Trwyn'. *Folklore* 126 (August 2015): 177–95.

Cowley, F. G. *The Monastic Order in South Wales, 1066–1349.* Cardiff: University of Wales Press, 1977.

Cramsie, John. *British Travellers and the Encounter with Britain 1450–1700.* Woodbridge: Boydell Press, 2015.

Cresswell, Tim. *Place: An Introduction.* Chichester: John Wiley & Sons, 2015.

Crisell, Andrew. *An Introductory History of British Broadcasting.* 2nd edn. London: Routledge, 2002.

Culler, Jonathan. *Theory of the Lyric.* Cambridge, MA and London: Harvard University Press, 2015.

Cunningham, Valentine. *British Writers of the Thirties.* Oxford: Oxford University Press, 1988.

Currie, Oliver. 'Reappraising the Role of Sixteenth-Century Bible Translations in the Development of Welsh Literary Prose Style'. *Translation Studies. Special Issue: Translation in Wales* 9, 2 (2016): 152–67.

Curtis, Tony, ed. *Wales: The Imagined Nation: Studies in Cultural and National Identity.* Bridgend: Poetry Wales Press, 1986.

Dafydd, Fflur. 'Re-writing Autobiography'. *New Welsh Review* 60 (Summer 2003): 24–9.
'Tu ôl i'r Llên'. *Taliesin* 148 (Gwanwyn 2013): 110–14.

Dafydd, Guto. 'Her newydd yr hen siwrneiau'. In *Awen Iwan*, ed. Morys, 41–73.

Daniel, Iestyn. 'The Date, Origin and Authorship of "The Mabinogion" in the Light of *Ymborth yr Enaid'*. *The Journal of Celtic Studies* 4 (2004): 117–52.

Daniel, Iestyn, Marged Haycock, Dafydd Johnston, and Jenny Rowland, eds. *Cyfoeth y Testun: Ysgrifau ar Lenyddiaeth Gymraeg yr Oesoedd Canol.* Caerdydd: Gwasg Prifysgol Cymru, 2003.

Daniels, Peter. *In Search of Welshness: Recollections and Reflections of London Welsh Exiles.* Talybont: Y Lolfa, 2011.

Daniels, Stephen, Dydia DeLyser, J. Nicholas Entrikin, and Doug Richardson, eds. *Envisioning Landscapes, Making Worlds: Geography and the Humanities.* London and New York: Routledge, 2011.

Davidson, Ian. *Ideas of Space in Contemporary Poetry.* Basingstoke: Palgrave Macmillan, 2007.

Davies, Andrew. '"The Gothic Novel in Wales" Revisited: A Preliminary Survey of the Wales-Related Romantic Fiction at Cardiff University'. *Romantic Textualities: Literature and Print Culture, 1780–1840.* Issue 2 (August 1998, revised 18 February 2013). www.romtext.org.uk/articles/cc02_no1/.

Davies, Caryl. *Adfeilion Babel: Agweddau ar Syniadaeth Ieithyddol y Ddeunawfed Ganrif.* Caerdydd: Gwasg Prifysgol Cymru, 2000.

Davies, Ceri. *Latin Writers of the Renaissance.* Cardiff: University of Wales Press, 1981.
Welsh Literature and the Classical Tradition. Cardiff: University of Wales Press, 1995.
ed. *Dr John Davies of Mallwyd: Welsh Renaissance Scholar.* Cardiff: University of Wales Press, 2004.

Davies, Ceri, and John E. Law, eds. *The Renaissance and the Celtic Countries.* Oxford: Blackwell Publishing, 2005.

Davies, Edward. *The Mythology and Rites of the British Bards.* London: J. Booth, 1809.

Davies, Eirug. 'Celtic Languages in North America, Welsh'. In *The Celts*, ed. Koch, 168–9.

Davies, Grahame. Review of *Dauwynebog*. BBC Cymru: Llais Llên. 17 November 2014. www.bbc.co.uk/cymru/adloniant/llyfrau/adolygiadau/750-dauwynebog.shtml.

Davies, Hywel. 'Loyalism in Wales 1792–1793'. *Welsh History Review* 20, 4 (2001): 687–716.
'Wales in English Travel Writing 1791–8: The Welsh Critique of Theophilus Jones'. *Welsh History Review* 23, 3 (2007): 65–93.

Davies, James A. 'Kinds of Relating: Gwyn Thomas (Jack Jones, Lewis Jones, Gwyn Jones) and the Welsh Industrial Experience'. *Anglo-Welsh Review* 86 (1987): 72–86.
A Reference Companion to Dylan Thomas. Westport, CT: Greenwood Press, 1998.

Davies, Janet. *The Welsh Language: a History.* Cardiff: University of Wales Press, 2014.

Davies, John. *Broadcasting and the BBC in Wales.* Cardiff: University of Wales Press, 1994.

Davies, John Reuben. *The Book of Llandaf and the Norman Church in Wales.* Woodbridge: Boydell and Brewer, 2003.

Davies, Lowri, and Alun Jones. 'Dyn Blin o Lŷn'. Interview between Davies and Jones. *Barn* 436 (Mai 1999): 44–8.

Davies, Morgan T. 'The Rhetoric of Gwilym Ddu's *Awdlau* to Sir Gruffydd Llwyd'. *Studia Celtica* 40 (2006): 155–72.

Davies, Nicholas, and Darren Williams. *Clear Red Water: Welsh Devolution and Socialist Politics*. London: Francis Boutle, 2009.

Davies, R. R. *Lordship and Society in the March of Wales, 1282–1400*. Oxford: Clarendon Press, 1978.

　Conquest, Co-existence, and Change: Wales 1063–1415. Oxford and New York: Oxford University Press, 1987; repr. as *The Age of Conquest: Wales 1063–1415*. Oxford: Oxford University Press, 1991, 2000.

　The Revolt of Owain Glyn Dŵr. Oxford: Oxford University Press, 1995.

　The First English Empire: Power and Identities in the British Isles 1093–1343. Oxford: Oxford University Press, 2000.

Davies, R. R., and Geraint H. Jenkins, eds. *From Medieval to Modern Wales: Historical Essays in Honour of Kenneth O. Morgan and Ralph A. Griffiths*. Cardiff: University of Wales Press, 2004.

Davies, Rhys. 'Writing about the Welsh'. In *Ten Contemporaries*, ed. John Gawesworth, 41–52. London: Joiner and Steele, 1933.

Davies, Russell. *Hope and Heartbreak: A Social History of Wales and the Welsh, 1776–1871*. Cardiff: University of Wales Press, 2005.

Davies, Sioned. '*Pedeir Keinc y Mabinogi*: A Case for Multiple Authorship?' In *Proceedings of the First North American Congress of Celtic Studies*, ed. G. MacLennan, 443–59. Ottawa: University of Ottawa, 1988.

　Crefft y Cyfarwydd. Cardiff: University of Wales Press, 1995.

　'Written Text as Performance: The Implications for Middle Welsh Prose Narratives'. In *Literacy in Medieval Celtic Societies*, ed. Pryce, 133–48.

　'Performing *Culhwch ac Olwen*'. *Arthurian Literature* 21 (2004): 27–51.

　'"O Gaer Llion I Benybenglog". Testun Llanstephan 50 o Iarlles y Ffynnon'. In *Cyfoeth y Testun*, ed. Daniel *et al.*, 326–48.

Davies, Sioned, and Peter Wynn Thomas, eds. *Canhwyll Marchogion: Cyd-destunoli Peredur*. Caerdydd: Gwasg Prifysgol Cymru, 2000.

Davies, Walford. *Dylan Thomas*. Milton Keynes: Open University Press, 1986.

　Dylan Thomas: The Poet in his Chains. The W. D. Thomas Memorial Lecture. Swansea: University College of Swansea, 1986.

Davies, Wendy. 'Braint Teilo'. *Bulletin of the Board of Celtic Studies* 26 (1974–6): 123–37.

　An Early Welsh Microcosm: Studies in the Llandaff Charters. London: Royal Historical Society, 1978.

　Wales in the Early Middle Ages. Leicester: Leicester University Press, 1982.

　'The Latin Charter-Tradition in Western Britain, Brittany and Ireland in the Early Mediaeval Period'. *In Ireland in Early Mediaeval Europe: Studies in Memory of Kathleen Hughes*, ed. D. Whitelock *et al.*, 258–80. Cambridge: Cambridge University Press, 1982.

Davies, William ('Gwilym Davies'). *Llandeilo-Vawr and its Neighbourhood, Past and Present*. Llandeilo: D.W. & G. Jones, 1858.

Davis, Nicholas. 'The Meaning of the Word "Interlude": A Discussion'. *Medieval English Theatre* 6, 1 (1984): 5–15.

Day, Graham. 'Chasing the Dragon? Devolution and the Ambiguities of Civil Society in Wales'. *Critical Social Policy* 26, 3 (2006): 646.

Day, Graham, H. Davis, and A. Drakakis-Smith. '"There's One Shop You Don't Go Into if You Are English": The Social and Political Integration of English Migrants in Wales'. *Journal of Ethnic and Migration Studies* 36, 9 (2010): 1405–23.

Dearnley, Moira. 'I Came Hither, A Stranger: A View of Wales in the Novels of Anne Beale (1815–1900)'. *The New Welsh Review* 1, 4 (Spring 1989): 27–32.

Distant Fields: Eighteenth-Century Fictions of Wales. Cardiff: University of Wales Press, 2001.

Deininger, Michelle. 'Pylons, Playgrounds, and Power Stations: Ecofeminism and Landscape in Women's Short Fiction from Wales'. In *Ecofeminism in Dialogue*, ed. Douglas A. Vakoch and Sam Mickey, 45–60. Lanham: Lexington, 2018.

Deleuze, Gilles, and Felix Guattari. *A Thousand Plateaus: Capitalism and Schizophrenia*. Trans. Brian Massumi. London and New York: Continuum, 2004.

Derrida, Jacques. *Of Grammatology*. Trans. Gayatri Chakravorty Spivak. Baltimore and London: Johns Hopkins University Press, 1976.

On the Name. Ed. Thomas Dutoit. Redwood: Stanford University Press, 1995.

Modern Genre Theory. Ed. David Duff. Harlow: Longman, 2000.

Dickinson, H. T., ed. *A Companion to Eighteenth-Century Britain*. Oxford: Oxford University Press, 2002.

Dillon, Sarah. *The Palimpsest: Literature, Criticism, Theory*. London: Bloomsbury, 2007.

Dilworth, Thomas. *David Jones: Engraver, Soldier, Painter, Poet*. London: Cape, 2017.

Diverres, A. H. 'Iarlles y Ffynnawn and Le Chevalier au Lion: Adaptation or Common Source?' *Studia Celtica* 16–17 (1981–2): 144–62.

Duff, David. *Modern Genre Theory*. Harlow: Longman, 2000.

Dumville, David N. 'Early Welsh Poetry: Problems of Historicity'. In *Early Welsh Poetry*, ed. Roberts, 1–16.

'The Origins of Northumbria: Some Aspects of the British Background'. In *The Origins of Anglo-Saxon Kingdoms*, ed. Steven Bassett, 213–22. Leicester: Leicester University Press, 1989.

'The Welsh Latin Annals'. In *Histories and Pseudo-Histories of the Insular Middle Ages*, vol. III, 461–7. Aldershot: Variorum, 1990.

Duncan, Nancy, ed. *Bodyspace: Destabilising the Geographies of Gender and Sexuality*. London: Routledge, 1996.

Dunshea, Philip. 'The Meaning of Catraeth: A Revised Early Context for Y Gododdin'. In *Beyond the Gododdin*, ed. Woolf, 81–114.

Edel, Doris. 'The Catalogues in Culhwch ac Olwen and Insular Celtic Learning'. *Bulletin of the Board of Celtic Studies* 30 (1983): 253–67.

Eder, Richard. 'Crosscurrents of Identities: British Soldiers, German Soldiers, and a Welsh Barmaid'. *Books of the Times*. 2 May 2007. www.nytimes.com/2007/05/02/books/02eder.html.

Edwards, Andrew. 'A "Monkey's Tea Party"? Division, Discord and the Development of Labour's Policy on Devolution, 1966–79'. *Cof Cenedl XXIV* (2009), ed. Jenkins, 161–89.

Edwards, Andrew, and Duncan Tanner. 'Defining or Dividing the Nation? Opinion Polls, Welsh Identity and Devolution, 1966–1979'. *Contemporary Wales* 18 (2006): 54–71.

Edwards, Andrew, and M. E. Wiliam. 'The Red Dragon/Red Flag Debate Revisited: The Labour Party, Culture and Language in Wales, 1945 – c. 1970'. *Welsh History Review* 26 (2012): 105–27.

Edwards, Dana. 'Media and the Memory in Wales Interview with Robert Bevan'. 23 February 2011. www.mediaandmemory.co.uk/contributors/contributor.php?id=cac00343.

Edwards, Elizabeth. '"Lonely and Voiceless your Halls Must Remain": Romantic-Era National Song and Felicia Hemans's *Welsh Melodies* (1822)'. *Journal for Eighteenth-Century Studies* 38, 1 (March 2015): 83–97.

ed. *English-Language Poetry from Wales 1789–1806*. Cardiff: University of Wales Press, 2013.

ed. *Richard Llwyd: Beaumaris Bay and Other Poems*. Nottingham: Trent Editions, 2016.

Edwards, Gavin, and Graham Sumner, eds. *The Historical and Cultural Connections and Parallels Between Wales and Australia*. Welsh Studies. Vol. 4. Lewiston, Queenston, and Lampeter: Edward Mellen, 1991.

Edwards, Huw M. *Dafydd ap Gwilym: Influences and Analogues*. Oxford: Oxford University Press, 1996.

'The Lyric Poets'. In *A Guide to Welsh Literature c. 1800–1900*, ed. Edwards, 97–125.

ed. *Alan*. Cyhoeddiadau Barddas, 2003.

Edwards, Hywel Teifi. *Yr Eisteddfod*. Llys yr Eisteddfod Genedlaethol, 1976.

The Eisteddfod. Writers of Wales. Cardiff: University of Wales Press, 1990.

ed. *Cwm Tawe*. Llandysul: Gwasg Gomer, 1993.

Arwr Glew Erwau'r Glo: Delwedd y Glowr yn Llenyddiaeth y Gymraeg 1850–1950. Llandysul: Gwasg Gomer, 1994.

'The Eisteddfod Poet: An Embattled Figure'. In *A Guide to Welsh Literature c. 1800–1900*, ed. Edwards, 24–47.

ed. *A Guide to Welsh Literature c. 1800–1900*. Cardiff: University of Wales Press, 2000.

Edwards, J. G. *The Principality of Wales, 1267–1967: A Study in Constitutional History*. Caernarfon: Caernarvonshire Historical Society, 1969.

Elfyn, Menna. 'Beirdd y Tafodau Fforchiog'. *Barddas* 226 (February 1996): 10–11.

'America: Cymhlethdod o Achlysuron'. In *Gweld Sêr*, ed. Thomas, 74–82.

Eliot, T. S. 'A Note of Introduction'. In *In Parenthesis* by David Jones. London: Faber, 1961.

Ellis, John. *Investiture: Royal Ceremony and National Identity in Wales, 1911–1969*. Cardiff: University of Wales Press, 2008.

Elton, Oliver. *Modern Studies*. London: Arnold, 1907.

Emery, Frank. *Edward Lhuyd F.R.S, 1660–1709*. Cardiff: University of Wales Press, 1971.

Empson, William. *Argufying: Essays on Literature and Culture*. Ed. John Haffenden. London: Hogarth Press, 1988.

England, Eugene, and Peter Makuck, eds. *An Open World: Essays on Leslie Norris*. Columbia, SC: Camden House, 1994.

Entwistle, Alice. *Poetry, Geography, Gender: Women Rewriting Contemporary Wales*. Cardiff: University of Wales Press, 2013.

Evans, Dewi W., and Brynley F. Roberts, eds. *Archæologia Britannica: Texts and Translations*. Aberystwyth: Celtic Studies Publications, 2007.

Evans, Dylan Foster. 'Bardd Treganna'. Review of *Cadwyni Rhyddid*. *Barn* 464 (Medi 2001): 38–9.

Evans, Eifion. *Pursued by God: A Selective Translation with Notes of the Welsh Religious Classic Theomemphus*. Bridgend: Evangelical Press of Wales, 1996.

— *Bread of Heaven: The Life and Work of William Williams, Pantycelyn*. Bridgend: Bryntirion Press, 2010.

Evans, Geraint. 'Crossing the Border: National and Linguistic Boundaries in Twentieth-Century Welsh Writing'. *Welsh Writing in English: A Yearbook of Critical Essays* 9 (2004): 123–35.

— 'William Salesbury and Welsh Printing in London Before 1557'. In *Authority and Subjugation in Writing of Medieval Wales*, ed. Kennedy and Meecham-Jones, 251–66.

— 'Wales and the Welsh Language in Andrew Borde's *Fyrst Boke of the Introduction of Knowledge*'. *Studia Celtica* 42 (2008): 87–104.

— 'A Lost Seventeenth-Century Welsh Book Rediscovered in Paris'. *Transactions of the Honourable Society of Cymmrodorion* 15 (2009): 28–40.

— 'The Authorship of *Drych Cydwybod* [?1616]'. *Transactions of the Honourable Society of Cymmrodorion* 17 (2011): 1–13.

Evans, Gruffydd Glyn. 'Yr Anterliwt Gymraeg'. *Llên Cymru* 1 (1950–3): 83–96; 2: 224–31.

Evans, Gwynfor. *Wales as an Economic Entity: A Reply*. Cardiff: Plaid Cymru, 1960.

Evans, H. T. *Wales and the Wars of the Roses*. 2nd edn. Stroud: Sutton, 1998.

Evans, John. 'Thomas John Evans'. In *Dictionary of Welsh Biography*. http://wbo.llgc.org.uk/en/s-EVAN-JOH-1863.html.

Evans, Jonathan. 'People, Politics, and Print: Notes Towards a History of the English-Language Book in Industrial South Wales up to 1900'. PhD thesis, Cardiff University, 2010.

Evans, Neil. 'As Rich as California: Opening and Closing the Frontier in Wales 1780–1870'. In *The People of Wales*, ed. Jones and Smith, 111–44.

Feather, John. *A History of British Publishing*. 2nd edn. Abingdon: Routledge, 2006.

Faletra, Michael A. *Wales and the Medieval Colonial Imagination: The Matters of Britain in the Twelfth Century*. New York: Palgrave Macmillan, 2014.

Fast, Howard. *Literature and Reality*. New York: International, 1950.

Fermanis, Porscha, and John Regan, eds. *Rethinking British Romantic History, 1770–1845*. Oxford: Oxford University Press, 2014.

Ferris, Paul. *Dylan Thomas: The Biography*. 2nd edn. London: Dent, 1999.

Ffrancon, Gwenno. *Cyfaredd y Cysgodion: delweddu Cymru a'i phobl ar ffilm 1935–1951*. Caerdydd: Gwasg Prifysgol Cymru, 2003.

Fietz, Lothar. 'Topos/Locus/Place: The Rhetoric, Poetics and Politics of Place, 1500–1800'. In *Poetry in the British Isles: Non-Metropolitan Perspectives*, ed. Ludwig and Fietz, 15–30.

Filmer-Davies, Katherine. *Fantasy Fiction and Welsh Myth: Tales of Belonging*. Basingstoke: Palgrave, 1999.

Findon, Joanne, Sarah Sheehan, and Westley Follett, eds. *Gablánach in scélaigecht: Celtic Studies in Honour of Ann Dooley*. Dublin: Four Courts Press, 2013.

Firbank, Thomas. *A Country of Memorable Honour*. London: Harrap, 1953.

Fish, Angela. 'Flight-Deck of Experience'. *New Welsh Review* 18 (1992): 60–4.

Fitzgibbon, Constantine. *The Life of Dylan Thomas*. London: Dent & Sons, 1965.

Flay, Claire. *Dorothy Edwards*. Cardiff: University of Wales Press, 2011.

Fletcher, Anthony, and Diarmaid MacCulloch. *Tudor Rebellions*. 5th edn. Harlow: Pearson Longman, 2008.

Flynn, P. *Dragons Led by Poodles: Inside Story of a New Labour Stitch-up*. London: Politico's Publishing Co., 1999.

Ford, Patrick K. 'Prolegomena to a Reading of the Mabinogi: *Pwyll* and *Manawydan*'. *Studia Celtica* 16–17 (1981–2): 110–25.

'*Branwen:* A Study of the Celtic Affinities'. *Studia Celtica* 22–23 (1987–8): 29–41.

Fox, Adam, and Daniel Woolf, eds. *The Spoken Word: Oral Culture in Britain, 1500–1850*. Manchester: Manchester University Press, 2002.

Francis, Hywel. *History on our Side: Wales and the 1984–85 Miners' Strike*. Ferryside: Iconau, 2009.

Franklin, Caroline. 'Wales as Nowhere: The Tabula Rasa of the "Jacobin" Imagination'. In *Footsteps of Liberty and Revolt*, ed. Constantine and Johnson, 11–33.

Friedman, Susan Stanford. *Mappings: Feminism and the Cultural Geographies of Encounter*. New Jersey: Princeton, 1998.

Frow, John. *Genre*. London and New York: Routledge, 2006.

Fulton, Helen. *Dafydd ap Gwilym and the European Context*. Cardiff: University of Wales Press, 1989.

'Trading Places: Representations of Urban Culture in Medieval Welsh Poetry'. *Studia Celtica* 31 (1997): 219–30.

'Cyd-destun Gwleidyddol *Breudwyt Ronabwy*'. *Llên Cymru* 22 (1999): 42–56.

'Cultural Meanings in the *Mabinogi*'. In *Origins and Revivals: Proceedings of the First Australian Conference of Celtic Studies*, ed. G. Evans, B. Martin, and J. Wooding, 437–52. Sydney: Centre for Celtic Studies, University of Sydney, 2000.

'The *Mabinogi* and the Education of Princes in Medieval Wales'. In *Medieval Celtic Literature and Society*, ed. Helen Fulton, 230–47. Dublin: Four Courts Press, 2005.

'The *Encomium Urbis* in Medieval Welsh Poetry'. *Proceedings of the Harvard Celtic Colloquium* 26 (2006): 54–72.

'Magic and the Supernatural in Early Welsh Arthurian Narrative: *Culhwch ac Olwen* and *Breuddwyd Rhonabwy*'. *Arthurian Literature* 30 (2013): 1–26.

'Owain Glyndŵr and the Prophetic Tradition'. In *Owain Glyndŵr: A Casebook*, ed. Michael Livingston and John K. Bollard, 475–88. Liverpool: University of Liverpool Press, 2013.

'Gender and Jealousy in *Gereint uab Erbin* and *Le Roman de Silence*'. *Arthuriana* 24.2 (2014): 43–70.

'Originating Britain: Welsh Literature and the Arthurian Tradition'. In *A Companion to British Literature*, ed. Robert DeMaria, Heesok Chang, and Samantha Zacher, 308–22. Oxford: Wiley-Blackwell, 2014.

'Translating Europe in Medieval Wales'. In *Writing Europe, 500–1450: Texts and Contexts*, ed. Aidan Conti, Orietta da Rold, and Philip Shaw, 159–74. Cambridge: D. S. Brewer, 2015.

'Ceredigion: Strata Florida and Llanbadarn Fawr'. In *Europe: A Literary History*, ed. David Wallace. 2 vols., I, 438–54. Oxford: Oxford University Press, 2016.

ed. *Dafydd ap Gwilym: Apocrypha*. Llandysul: Gomer Press, 1996.

ed. *A Companion to Arthurian Literature*. Oxford: Wiley-Blackwell, 2009.

ed. *Urban Culture in Medieval Wales*. Cardiff: University of Wales Press, 2012.

Garlick, Raymond. *An Introduction to Anglo-Welsh Literature*. Cardiff: University of Wales Press, 1972.

Gaskill, Howard, ed. *The Reception of Ossian in Europe*. London: Continuum, 2004.

Gielgud, Val. *British Radio Drama 1922–1956: A Survey*. London: Harrap, 1957.

Giffin, Mary. 'The Date of the Dream of Rhonabwy'. *Transactions of the Honourable Society of Cymmrodorion* (1958): 33–40.

Gildart, Keith. *North Wales Miners: A Fragile Unity, 1945–1996*. Cardiff: University of Wales Press, 2002.

Giudici, Marco. 'Discourses of Identity in Post-Devolution Wales: The Case of the Welsh-Italians'. *Contemporary Wales* 25 (2012): 227–46.

Given, James. *State and Society in Medieval Europe: Gwynedd and Languedoc under Outside Rule*. Ithaca, NY: Cornell University Press, 1990.

Goetinck, Glenys. *Peredur: A Study of Welsh Tradition in the Grail Legends*. Cardiff: University of Wales Press, 1975.

'Pedeir Keinc y Mabinogi: Yr awdur a'i bwrpas'. *Llên Cymru* 15 (1987–88): 249–69.

Golightly, Victor. 'Gwyn Thomas's American "Oscar"'. *New Welsh Review* 22 (1993): 26–31.

'"We, Who Speak for the Workers": The Correspondence of Gwyn Thomas and Howard Fast'. *Welsh Writing in English* 6 (2000): 67–88.

Gooberman, Leon. *From Depression to Devolution: Economy and Government in Wales, 1934–2006*. Cardiff: University of Wales Press, 2017.

Goodby, John. *The Poetry of Dylan Thomas: Under the Spelling Wall*. Liverpool: Liverpool University Press, 2013.

Gramich, Katie. 'O'r Seren Wen i'r Cefnfor Gwyn'. *Taliesin* 87 (October 1994): 105–7.

'The Fiction of Raymond Williams in the 1960s: Fragments of an Analysis'. *Welsh Writing in English: A Yearbook of Critical Essays* 1 (1995): 62–74.

'The Welsh Novel Now'. *Books in Wales* (1995): 5.

Twentieth-Century Women's Writing in Wales: Land, Gender, Belonging. Cardiff: University of Wales Press, 2007.

Mapping the Territory: Critical Approaches to Welsh Fiction in English. Cardigan: Parthian, 2010.

Kate Roberts. Cardiff: University of Wales Press, 2011.

Gramich, Katie, and Catherine Brennan, eds. *Welsh Women's Poetry 1460–2001: An Anthology*. Dinas Powys: Honno, 2003.

Gramich, Katie, and Andrew Hiscock, eds. *Dangerous Diversity: The Changing Faces of Wales*. Cardiff: University of Wales Press, 1998.

Grant, Angela. 'Magical Transformation in *Pedeir Keinc y Mabinogi* and *Hanes Taliesin*'. MPhil diss., University of Oxford, 2010.

Grantley, Darryll. *English Dramatic Interludes, 1300–1580*. Cambridge: Cambridge University Press, 2004.

Gray, Melinda. 'Language and Belonging: A Welsh-Language Novel in Nineteenth-Century America'. In *Multilingual America*, ed. Sollors, 91–102.

'Uncle Tom's Welsh Dress: Ethnicity, Authority and Translation'. In *Beyond the Difference*, ed. von Rothkirch and Williams, 173–85.

Green, Diane. *Emyr Humphreys: A Postcolonial Novelist?* Cardiff: University of Wales Press, 2009.

Greene, Graham. *Ways of Escape*. London: Bodley Head, 1980.

Greenslade, David. 'Edrych am Rachel'. Review of *Cadw dy Ffydd, Brawd*. *Barn* 448 (Mai 2000): 49.

Griffith, T. Gwynfor. 'Italian Humanism and Welsh Prose'. *Yorkshire Celtic Studies* 6 (1953–8): 1–26.

Avventure Linguistiche del Cinquecento. Firenze: Le Monnier, 1961.

Griffith, Wil. 'Devolutionist Tendencies in Wales, 1885–1914'. In *Debating Nationhood and Governance in Britain, 1885–1945*, ed. Tanner *et al.*, 89–117.

Griffith, W. P. *Learning, Law, and Religion: Higher Education and Welsh Society, c. 1540–1640*. Cardiff: University of Wales Press, 1989.

Griffiths, Dylan. *Thatcherism and Territorial Politics: A Welsh Case Study*. Aldershot: Avebury, 1996.

Griffiths, H. M. 'Water Under the Bridge? Nature, Memory and Hydropolitics'. *Cultural Geographies* 21 (2014): 449–74.

Griffiths, Ralph A., ed. *Boroughs of Mediaeval Wales*. Cardiff: University of Wales Press, 1978.

'Herbert, William, First Earl of Pembroke (c. 1423–1469)'. In *Oxford Dictionary of National Biography*. Oxford: Oxford University Press, 2014, www.oxforddnb.com/view/article/13053.

Griffiths, Ralph A., and Roger S. Thomas. *The Making of the Tudor Dynasty*. Gloucester: Alan Sutton, 1985.

Grosz, Elizabeth. *Volatile Bodies: Toward a Corporeal Feminism*. Bloomington: Indiana University Press, 1994.

Gruffudd, Pyrs. 'The Battle of Butlin's: Vulgarity and Virtue on the North Wales Coast, 1939–1949'. *Rural History* 21, 1 (2010): 75–95.

Gruffydd, R. Geraint. 'Dau Lythyr gan Owen Lewis'. *Llên Cymru* 2 (1952–3): 36–45.

'Humphrey Lhuyd a Deddf Cyfieithu'r Beibl i'r Gymraeg'. *Llên Cymru* 4 (1956–7): 114–15.

'Awdl Wrthryfelgar gan Edward Dafydd'. *Llên Cymru* 5 (1959): 155–63; 8 (1964): 65–91.

'The Welsh Book of Common Prayer 1567'. *Journal of the Historical Society of the Church in Wales*, 17, 22 (1967): 43–55.

Argraffwyr Cyntaf Cymru: Gwasgau Dirgel y Catholigion adeg Elisabeth. Caerdydd: Gwasg Prifysgol Cymru, 1972.

'In that Gentle Country': The Beginnings of Puritan Nonconformity in Wales*. Bridgend: Evangelical Library of Wales, 1976.

'The Revival of 1762 and William Williams of Pantycelyn'. In *Revival and its Fruit*, by Emyr Roberts and R. Geraint Gruffydd, 19–40. Bridgend: Evangelical Library of Wales, 1981.

'Ann Griffiths: Llenor'. *Taliesin* 43 (1981): 76–84.

'Y Beibl a droes i'w bobl draw': William Morgan yn 1588. London: The British Broadcasting Corporation, 1988.

Llenyddiaeth y Cymry: Cyflwyniad Darluniadol. Cyfrol 2: O tua 1530 i tua 1880. Llandysul: Gwasg Gomer, 1989.

'The Renaissance and Welsh Literature'. In *The Celts and the Renaissance: Tradition and Innovation*, ed. Williams and Jones, 17–40.

'"Geneth Ifanc": Rhai Sylwadau'. In *Cof ac Arwydd: Ysgrifau Newydd ar Waldo Williams*, ed. Walford Davies and Walford Davies, 136–42.

Y Ffordd Gadarn: Ysgrifau ar Lên a Chrefydd. Ed. E. Wyn James. Pen-y-bont ar Ogwr: Gwasg Bryntirion, 2008.

ed. *A Guide to Welsh Literature c. 1530–1700.* Cardiff: University of Wales Press, 1997.

Gruffydd, W. J. 'The Mabinogion'. *Transactions of the Honourable Society of Cymmrodorion* (1912–13): 14–81.

Math vab Mathonwy: An Inquiry into the Origins and Development of the Fourth Branch of the Mabinogi with the Text and a Translation. Cardiff: University of Wales Press, 1928.

Rhiannon: An Inquiry into the First and Third Branches of the Mabinogi. Cardiff: University of Wales Press, 1953.

Folkore and Myth in the Mabinogion. Cardiff: University of Wales Press, 1958.

Haesly, Richard. 'Identifying Scotland and Wales: Types of Scottish and Welsh National Identities'. *Nations and Nationalism* 11, 2 (2005): 243–63.

Hallam, Tudur. '"Curse, Bless, Me Now": Dylan Thomas and Saunders Lewis'. *Journal of the British Academy 3* (2015): 238

Hallam, Tudur, and Angharad Price, eds, *Ysgrifau Beirniadol 32.* Bethesda: Gwasg Gee, 2013.

Hamp, Eric P. 'Mabinogi and Archaism'. *Celtica 23* (1999): 96–110.

Hanson, Clare. *Re-reading the Short Story.* Basingstoke: Macmillan, 1989.

Hardy, Barbara. *Dylan Thomas: An Original Language.* Athens and London: University of Georgia Press, 2000.

Harper, Sally. 'Tunes for a Welsh Psalter: Edmwnd Prys's *Llyfr y Psalmau*'. *Studia Celtica 37* (2003): 221–67.

'Dafydd ap Gwilym, poet and musician'. *Dafydd ap Gwilym.net* (2007). www.dafyddapgwilym.net/essays/sally_harper/index_eng.php.

Harper, Sally, and Alan Luff. 'Welsh Carols'. In *The Canterbury Dictionary of Hymnology.* 2013. www.hymnology.co.uk/w/welsh-carols.

Harris, John. 'Not Only a Place in Wales'. *Planet 73* (1992): 10–15.

'Novel to Play: The Trials of *Taffy*'. In *Seeing Wales Whole*, ed. Sam Adams, 25–55. Cardiff: University of Wales Press, 1998.

Harvey, David. *Justice, Nature and the Geography of Difference.* Cambridge, MA: Blackwell Publishers, 1996.

Hattersley, Roy. 'A Comrade in Cardiff'. *The Guardian*, 30 December 2002.

Hawkins, Desmond. 'Review of *18 Poems* by Dylan Thomas'. *Time and Tide* 16, 6 (1935): 206.

Haycock, Marged. 'Ymddiddan Arthur a'r Eryr'. In *Blodeugerdd Barddas o Canu Crefyddol Cynnar*, ed. Haycock, 297–312. Cyhoeddiadau Barddas, 1994.

'Literary Criticism in Welsh Before c. 1300'. In *The Cambridge History of Literary Criticism.* Vol. II: *The Middle Ages*, ed. A. Minnis and I. Johnson, 333–44. Cambridge: Cambridge University Press, 2005.

'Hanes Heledd Hyd Yma'. In *Gweledigaethau: Cyfrol Deyrnged yr Athro Gwyn Thomas*, ed. Davies, 29–60.

'Living with War: Poets and the Welsh Experience, c. 600–1300'. In *Kings and Warriors in Early North-West Europe*, ed. Jan-Erik Rekdal and Charles Doherty, 24–87. Dublin: Four Courts Press, 2016.

Hédelin, François, Abbé d'Aubignac. *La Pratique du théâtre.* Ed. Pierro Martino. Alger and Paris, Carbonel and Champion, 1927.

Hemming, Jessica. 'Ancient Tradition or Authorial Invention? The "Mythological" Names in the Four Branches'. In *Myth in Celtic Literatures*, ed. Nagy, 83–104.

Hempton, David. *Religion and Political Culture in Britain and Ireland*. Cambridge: Cambridge University Press, 1996.

Heng, Geraldine. *Empire of Magic: Medieval Romance and the Politics of Cultural Fantasy*. New York: Columbia University Press, 2003.

Henry, Graham. 'Welsh Government Needs to Step up to the Plate on Media Appearances'. *Wales Online*. 29 June 2014. www.walesonline.co.uk/news/news-opinion/welsh-government-needs-step-up-7341495.

Henry, P. L. *The Early English and Celtic Lyric*. London: Allen and Unwin, 1966.

Higham, Nick, ed. *Britons in Anglo-Saxon England*. Woodbridge: Boydell, 2007.

Higley, Sarah. 'Perlocutions and Perlections in the Dream of Rhonabwy: An Untellable Tale'. *Exemplaria* 2 (1990): 537–61.

    Between Languages: The Uncooperative Text in Early Welsh and Old English Nature Poetry. University Park, PA: Pennsylvania State University Press, 1993, repr. 2010.

Hill, Charles. *Behind the Screen: The Broadcasting Memoirs of Lord Hill of Luton*. London: Sidgwick and Jackson, 1974.

Hirschi, Caspar. *The Origins of Nationalism: An Alternative History from Ancient Rome to Early Modern Germany*. Cambridge: Cambridge University Press, 2012.

Hobsbawm, Eric, and Terence Ranger, eds. *The Invention of Tradition*. Cambridge: Cambridge University Press, 1983.

Hodges, H. A. *Flame in the Mountains: Williams Pantycelyn, Ann Griffiths and the Welsh Hymn*. Ed. E. Wyn James. Talybont: Y Lolfa, 2017.

Hooker, Jeremy. *The Presence of the Past: Essays on Modern British and American Poetry*. Bridgend: Poetry Wales Press, 1987.

    'Ceridwen's Daughters: Welsh Women Poets and the Uses of Tradition'. *Welsh Writing in English: A Yearbook of Critical Essays* 1 (1995): 128–44.

    Imagining Wales: A View of Modern Welsh Writing in English. Cardiff: University of Wales Press, 2001.

Hopkins, T. J., and Geraint Bowen. 'Memorandwm Morys Clynnog at y Pab Gregori XIII yn 1575'. *Cylchgrawn Llyfrgell Genedlaethol Cymru* 19, 1 (1965): 1–34.

Houseley, W., Kate Moles, and Robin Smith. 'Identity, Brand or Citizenship: The Case of Post Devolution Wales'. *Contemporary Wales* 22, 1 (2009): 196–210.

Howell, David W. *The Rural Poor in Eighteenth-Century Wales*. Cardiff: University of Wales Press, 2000.

Hughes, Bethan Mair. 'Nid gêm Nintendo yw hyn, ond bywyd!' *Tu Chwith* 1 (Ebrill/Mai 1993): 43.

Hughes, Glyn Tegai. *Williams Pantycelyn*. Writers of Wales. Cardiff: University of Wales Press, 1983.

    'Life and Thought'. In *A Guide to Welsh Literature c. 1700–1800*, ed. Jarvis, 1–22.

    'Yr Hen Bant': *Ysgrifau ar Williams Pantycelyn*. Talybont: Y Lolfa, 2017.

Hughes, Ian. 'The King's Nephew'. In *150 Jahre 'Mabinogion'*, ed. Maier and Zimmer, 55–66.

    'The Four Branches of the *Mabinogi* and Medieval Welsh Poetry'. *Studi Celtici* 4 (2006): 154–93.

Hughes, J. Elwyn, ed. *Cyfansoddiadau a Beirniadaethau Eisteddfod Genedlaethol Frenhinol Cymru*. Llandybïe: Gwasg Dinefwr dros Lys yr Eisteddfod Genedlaethol, 1993.

ed. *Cyfansoddiadau a Beirniadaethau Eisteddfod Genedlaethol Cymru, 2001.* Llandybïe: Gwasg Dinefwr ar ran Llys yr Eisteddfod, 2001.

ed. *Cyfansoddiadau a Beirniadaethau Eisteddfod Genedlaethol, 2005, Eryri a'r Cyffiniau.* Llandybïe: Gwasg Dinefwr ar ran Llys yr Eisteddfod, 2005.

ed. *Cyfansoddiadau a Beirniadaethau Eisteddfod Genedlaethol Cymru, 2014, Sir Gâr.* Liandybïe: Gwasg Dinefwr ar ran Llys yr Eisteddfod, 2014.

Hughes, Jonathan. 'Sir Thomas Parry'. In *Oxford Dictionary of National Biography.* Oxford: Oxford University Press, 2004. www.oxforddnb.com / view / article / 21433.

Hughes, Kathleen. 'The Welsh Latin Chronicles: "Annales Cambriae" and Related Texts'. The Sir John Rhŷs Memorial Lecture 1973. *Proceedings of the British Academy* 59 (1973): 233–58; London: Oxford University Press, 1974.

Hughes, Vaughan. 'Ieuan Wyn a chwedlau eraill'. *Barn* 464 (Medi 2001): 26–9.

Hughes, W. J. *Wales and the Welsh in English Literature.* Wrexham: Hughes and Son, 1924.

Hume, I., and W. T. R. Pryce, eds. *The Welsh and Their Country.* Llandysul: Gomer Press, 1986.

Humphrey, Belinda. 'Prelude to the Twentieth Century', in *Welsh Writing in English,* ed. Thomas, 7–46.

Humphreys, Emyr. *The Taliesin Tradition.* Bridgend: Seren, 1989, 2000.

'Notes on the Novel'. *The New Welsh Review* 35 (Winter 1996–7): 9–10.

Hunt, Tony. 'The Art of *Iarlles y Ffynnawn* and the European *Volksmärchen*'. *Studia Celtica* 8–9 (1973): 107–20.

'Some Observations on the Textual Relationship of *Li Chevaliers au Lion* and *Iarlles y Ffynnawn*'. *Zeitschrift für Celtische Philologie* 33 (1974): 93–113.

Hunter, Jerry. 'Moderniaeth T. Gwynn Jones'. *Taliesin* 98 (1997): 37–54.

Soffestri'r Saesson. Caerdydd: Gwasg Prifysgol Cymru, 2000.

'Cyfrinachau ar dafod leferydd: ideoleg technoleg yn yr unfed ganrif ar bymtheg'. In *Chwileniwm: Technoleg a Llenyddiaeth,* ed. Price, 36–53.

'Y Traddodiad Llenyddol Coll'. *Taliesin* 118 (2003): 13–44.

'Taliesin at the Court of Henry VIII: Aspects of the Writing of Elis Gruffydd'. *Transactions of the Honourable Society of Cymmrodorion,* 10 (2004): 41–56.

I Ddeffro Ysbryd y Wlad: Robert Everett a'r Ymgyrch yn erbyn Caethwasanaeth Americanaidd. Llanrwst: Gwasg Carreg Gwalch, 2007.

Sons of Arthur, Children of Lincoln: Welsh Writing from the American Civil War. Cardiff: University of Wales Press, 2007.

Hutton, Ronald. *The Rise and Fall of Merry England: The Ritual Year, 1400–1700.* Oxford: Oxford University Press, 1994.

'Medieval Welsh Literature and Pre-Christian Deities'. *Cambrian Medieval Celtic Studies* 61 (2011): 57–85.

Huws, Byron. 'Manawydan uab Llŷr: A Tale of the Norman Occupation of Deheubarth'. *Transactions of the Honourable Society of Cymmrodorion* (2010): 7–23.

Huws, Daniel. *Medieval Welsh Manuscripts.* Cardiff and Aberystwyth: University of Wales Press and National Library of Wales, 2000.

'Llyfr Coch Hergest'. In *Cyfoeth y Testun,* ed. Daniel et al., 1–30.

'Y Pedair Llawysgrif Canoloesol'. In *Canhwyll Marchogion: Cyd-destunoli Peredur,* ed. Davies and Thomas, 3–4.

Cynnull y Farddoniaeth. Aberystwyth: Canolfan Uwchefrydiau Cymreig a Cheltaidd, 2004.

'Siôn Dafydd Laes: Seren Wib o Fardd'. In *Blodeuglwm*, ed. Rhidian Griffiths, 26–47. Aberystwyth: Aberystwyth Bibliographical Group, 2016.

A Repertory of Welsh Manuscripts and Scribes. 2 vols. Unpublished.

'Idwal', 'Yr Eglwys Wladol'. *Y Dysgedydd* 22 (1843): 256–7.

Ingham, Patricia Clare. 'Marking Time: *Branwen, Daughter of Llyr* and the Colonial Refrain'. In *The Postcolonial Middle Ages*, ed. Jeffrey Jerome Cohen, 225–46. New York: St Martin's Press, 2000.

Inwood, M. *Heidegger: A Very Short Introduction*. Oxford: Oxford University Press, 2000.

Irigaray, Luce. *Elemental Passions*. Trans. Joanna Collie and Judith Still. London and New York: Routledge, 1992.

Jackson, K. H. *Language and History in Early Britain: A Chronological Survey of the Brittonic Languages, First to Twelfth Century* A D. Edinburgh: Edinburgh University Press, 1953.

The International Folk Tale and Early Welsh Tradition. Cardiff: University of Wales Press, 1961.

James, Allan. *John Morris-Jones*. Writers of Wales. Cardiff: University of Wales Press, 1987.

John Morris-Jones. Cyfres Dawn Dweud. Caerdydd: Gwasg Prifysgol Cymru, 2011.

James, Christine. 'Hopcyn ap Tomas a "Llyfrgell Genedlaethol" Ynysforgan'. *Transactions of the Honourable Society of Cymmrodorion* 13 (2007): 31–57.

'Tirluniau Dychymyg Gwenallt'. In *Cawr i'w Genedl*, ed. Tegwyn Jones and Huw Walters, 217–44. Llandysul: Gwasg Gomer, 2008.

James, E. Wyn. '"The New Birth of a People": Welsh Language and Identity and the Welsh Methodists, c. 1740–1820'. In *Religion and National Identity: Wales and Scotland c. 1700–2000*, ed. Robert Pope, 14–42. Cardiff: University of Wales Press 2001.

'Rhai Methodistiaid a'r Anterliwt'. *Taliesin* 57 (1986): 8–19.

'Merched a'r Emyn yn Sir Gâr'. *Barn* 402–3 (1996): 26–9.

'Ann Griffiths: Y Cefndir Barddol'. *Llên Cymru* 23 (2000), 147–70.

'Ann Griffiths: O Lafar I Lyfr'. In *Chwileniwm. Technoleg a Llenyddiaeth*, ed. Price, 54 85.

'Dafydd William, Llandeilo Fach: An Eighteenth-Century Glamorgan Hymn-writer'. *Morgannwg* 47 (2003): 3–23.

'An "English" Lady among Welsh Folk: Ruth Herbert Lewis and the Welsh Folk-Song Society'. In *Folk Song: Tradition, Revival, and Re-creation*, ed. Ian Russell and David Atkinson, 266–83. Aberdeen: Elphinstone Institute, University of Aberdeen, 2004.

'The Evolution of the Welsh Hymn'. In *Dissenting Praise: Religious Dissent and the Hymn in England and Wales*, ed. Isabel Rivers and David L. Wykes, 229–68. Oxford: Oxford University Press, 2011.

'"Blessèd Jubil!": Slavery, Mission and the Millennial Dawn in the Work of William Williams of Pantycelyn'. In *Cultures of Radicalism in Britain and Ireland*, ed. John Kirk, Michael Brown, and Andrew Noble, 95–112. London: Pickering & Chatto, 2013.

'Cushions, Copy-books and Computers: Ann Griffiths (1776–1805), her Hymns and Letters and their Transmission'. *Bulletin of the John Rylands Library* 90, 2 (2014): 163–83.

Jarman, A. O. H. 'The Welsh Myrddin Poems'. In *Arthurian Literature in the Middle Ages*, ed. R. S. Loomis, 20–30. Oxford: Clarendon Press, 1959.

'*Llyfr Du Caerfyrddin*: The Black Book of Carmarthen'. *Proceedings of the British Academy* 71 (1986): 333–56.

'The Merlin Legend and the Welsh Tradition of Prophecy'. In *The Arthur of the Welsh*, ed. Bromwich *et al.*, 117–45.

Jarman, A. O. H., and Gwilym Rees Hughes, eds. *A Guide to Welsh Literature*. Vol. II: *1282–1550*, rev. Dafydd Johnston. Cardiff: University of Wales Press, 1997.

Jarvie, Grant, ed. *Sport in the Making of Celtic Cultures*. London: Leicester University Press, 1999.

Jarvis, Branwen. *Goronwy Owen*. Cardiff: University of Wales Press, 1986.

'Welsh Humanist Learning'. In *A Guide to Welsh Literature c. 1530–1700*, ed. Gruffydd, 135–41.

'Goronwy Owen: Neoclassical Poet and Critic'. In *A Guide to Welsh Literature c. 1700–1800*, ed. Jarvis, 81–103.

ed. *A Guide to Welsh Literature c. 1700–1800*. Cardiff: University of Wales Press, 2000.

Jarvis, Matthew. *Welsh Environments in Contemporary Poetry*. Cardiff: University of Wales Press, 2008.

Ruth Bidgood. Cardiff: University of Wales Press, 2012.

Jenkins, Bethan M. *Between Wales and England: Anglophone Welsh Writing of the Eighteenth Century*. Cardiff: University of Wales Press, 2017.

Jenkins, Dafydd. 'Y Nofel Gymraeg Gynnar'. In *Rhyddid y Nofel*, ed. Wiliams, 29–53.

'*Bardd Teulu* and *Pencerdd*'. In *The Welsh King and his Court*, ed. Charles-Edwards *et al.*, 162–6.

Jenkins, Dafydd, and Morfydd E. Owen. 'The Welsh Marginalia in the Lichfield Gospels. Part I'. *Cambridge Medieval Celtic Studies* 5 (1983): 37–66.

'The Welsh Marginalia in the Lichfield Gospels. Part II: The Surrexit Memorandum'. *Cambridge Medieval Celtic Studies* 7 (1984): 91–120.

Jenkins, David. *Thomas Gwynn Jones: Cofiant*. Dinbych: Gwasg Gee, 1973.

'Carolau Haf a Gaeaf'. *Llên Cymru* 2, 1 (January 1952): 46.

Jenkins, Ffion Llywelyn. 'Celticism and Pre-Romanticism: Evan Evans'. In *A Guide to Welsh Literature c. 1700–1800*, ed. Jarvis, 105–25.

Jenkins, Geraint H. *Literature, Religion and Society in Wales, 1660–1730*. Cardiff: University of Wales Press, 1978.

'The New Enthusiasts'. In *The Remaking of Wales in the Eighteenth Century*, ed. Trevor Herbert and Gareth Elwyn Jones, 43–75. Cardiff: University of Wales Press, 1988.

The Foundations of Modern Wales: Wales 1642–1780. Oxford: Oxford University Press, 1992.

Protestant Dissenters in Wales, 1639–1689. Cardiff: University of Wales Press, 1992.

'Y Gymraeg yn y Cyfnod Modern Cynnar'. In *Y Gymraeg yn ei Disgleirdeb*, ed. Jenkins.

'Wales in the Eighteenth Century'. In *A Companion to Eighteenth-Century Britain*, ed. Dickinson, 392–402.

'Historical Writing in the Eighteenth Century'. In *A Guide to Welsh Literature c. 1700–1800*, ed. Jarvis, 23–44.

'"A Very Horrid Affair": Sedition and Unitarianism in the Age of Revolutions'. In *From Medieval to Modern Wales*, ed. Davies and Jenkins, 175–96.

ed. *Theophilus Evans (1693–1767): Y Dyn, ei Deulu, a'i Oes*. Aberystwyth: Adran Gwasanaethau Diwyllianol Dyfed, 1993.

ed. *The Welsh Language Before the Industrial Revolution*. Cardiff: University of Wales Press, 1997.

ed. *Y Gymraeg yn ei Disgleirdeb: Yr Iaith Gymraeg cyn y Chwyldro Diwydiannol*. Caerdydd: Gwasg Prifysgol Cymru, 1997.

ed. *'Let's Do Our Best for the Ancient Tongue': The Welsh Language in the Twentieth Century*. Cardiff: University of Wales Press, 2000.

ed. *The Welsh Language and its Social Domains 1801–1911*. Cardiff: University of Wales Press, 2000.

ed. *Cof Cenedl XXIV*. Llandysul: Gwasg Gomer, 2009.

Jenkins, Geraint H., Ffion Mair Jones and David Ceri Jones, eds. *The Correspondence of Iolo Morganwg*. 3 vols. Cardiff: Cardiff University Press, 2007.

Jenkins, Geraint H., Richard Suggett, and Eryn White. 'The Welsh Language in Early Modern Wales'. In *The Welsh Language Before the Industrial Revolution*, ed. Jenkins, 45–122.

Jenkins, Geraint H., and Williams, M. A., eds. *'Eu Hiaith a Gadwant?' Y Gymraeg yn yr Ugeinfed Ganrif*. Cardiff: University of Wales Press, 2000.

Jenkins, Kathryn. 'Songs of Praises: The Literary and Spiritual Qualities of the Hymns of William Williams and Ann Griffiths'. *The Hymn Society of Great Britain and Ireland Bulletin* 15, 5 (1998): 98–109.

'Pantycelyn's Women, Fact and Fiction: An Assessment'. *Journal of Welsh Religious History* 7 (1999): 77–94.

'Williams Pantycelyn'. In *A Guide to Welsh Literature c. 1700–1800*, ed. Jarvis, 256–78.

Cân y Ffydd: Ysgrifau ar Emynyddiaeth. Ed. Rhidian Griffiths. Caernarfon: Cymdeithas Emynau Cymru, 2011.

Jenkins, Nigel. *Footsore on the Frontier: Selected Essays and Articles*. Llandysul: Gomer Press, 2001.

Jenkins, Philip. 'Between Two Revolutions: Wales, 1642–1780'. In *The People of Wales*, ed. Jones and Smith, 83–110.

Jennings, Hilda. *Brynmawr: A Study of a Distressed Area*. London: Allenson & Co., 1934.

Johnes, Martin. 'Eighty-Minute Patriots? National Identity and Sport in Modern Wales'. *The International Journal of the History of Sport* 17 (2000): 93–110.

Wales Since 1939. Cardiff: University of Wales Press, 2012.

Johnston, A. F. and Wim Hüsken, eds. *English Parish Drama*. Ludus 1. Amsterdam: Rodopi, 1996.

Johnston, Arthur. *Enchanted Ground: The Study of Medieval Romance in the Eighteenth Century*. London: Athlone Press, 1964.

Johnston, Dafydd. *A Pocket Guide to the Literature of Wales*. Cardiff: University of Wales Press, 1994.

'Traddodiad Cyfoes'. Review of *Cywyddau Cyhoeddus*. *Taliesin* 88 (1994): 116–17.

'Idris Davies a'r Gymraeg'. In *Diffinio Dwy Lenyddiaeth Cymru*, ed. Thomas, 96–119.

'Yr Ôl-fodernydd cyndyn'. Review of *Ofn fy Het*. *Taliesin* 94 (Summer 1996): 119–21.

'Review of *Gwaith Dafydd Benfras ac Eraill o Feirdd Hanner Cyntaf y Drydedd Ganrif ar Ddeg*, ed. N. G. Costigan (Bosco) et al.' *Llên Cymru* 21 (1998): 196–7.

'Monastic Patronage of Welsh Poetry'. In *Monastic Wales: New Approaches*, ed. Janet Burton and Karen Stöber, 177–90. Cardiff: University of Wales Press, 2013.

'Review of *Darogan: Prophecy, Lament and Absent Heroes in Medieval Welsh Literature*, by Aled Llion Jones'. *Cambrian Medieval Celtic Studies* 67 (Summer 2014): 90–3.

ed. *A Guide to Welsh Literature, c. 1900–1996.* Cardiff: University of Wales Press, 1998.

Llên yr Uchelwyr: Hanes Beirniadol Llenyddiaeth Gymraeg, 1300–1525. Caerdydd: Gwasg Prifysgol Cymru, 2015.

Johnston, Kenneth R. *Unusual Suspects: Pitt's Reign of Alarm and the Lost Generation of the 1790s.* Oxford: Oxford University Press, 2013.

Jones, Aled, and Bill Jones. *Welsh Reflections: Y Drych & America 1851–2001.* Llandysul: Gomer Press, 2001.

Jones, Aled Gruffydd. *Press, Politics and Society: A History of Journalism in Wales.* Cardiff: University of Wales Press, 1993.

Jones, Aled Llion. *Darogan: Prophecy, Lament and Absent Heroes in Medieval Welsh Literature.* Cardiff: University of Wales Press, 2013.

Jones, Anwen. *National Theatres in Context: France, Germany, England and Wales.* Cardiff: University of Wales Press, 2007.

Jones, Barry, and John Osmond, eds. *Building a Civic Culture: Institutional Change, Policy Development and Political Dynamics in the National Assembly for Wales.* Cardiff: Institute of Welsh Affairs, 2003.

Jones, Bedwyr Lewis. *Robert Williams Parry.* Writers of Wales. Cardiff: University of Wales Press, 1972.

'Mewn Dau Gae'. In *Cyfres y Meistri 2: Waldo Williams,* ed. Rhys, 149–59.

R. Williams Parry: 'Ar y Daith ni Phara'. Ed. Gwyn Thomas. Caerdydd: Gwasg Prifysgol Cymru, 1997.

ed. *Rhyddiaith R. Williams Parry.* Dinbych: Gwasg Gee, 1974.

Jones, Bill. 'Margaret E. Roberts'. In *Making it in America,* ed. Barkahn, 315–16.

'Writing Back: Welsh Emigrants and their Correspondence in the Nineteenth Century.' *North American Journal of Welsh Studies,* 5, 1 (2005): 23–45.

Jones, Bill, and Chris Williams. *B. L. Coombes.* Writers of Wales. Cardiff: University of Wales Press, 1999.

Jones, D. Geraint. *Favoured with Frequent Revivals: Revivals in Wales 1762–1862.* Cardiff: Heath Christian Trust, 2001.

Jones, D. Gwenallt. 'Beirniadu Beirniaid'. *Y Llenor* 12 (1933): 32.

'Beirdd yr Angau'. *Heddiw* (Gorffennaf 1938): 11–12.

'Y Fro: Rhydcymerau'. In *D.J. Williams, Abergwaun: Cyfrol Deyrnged,* ed. John Gwyn Griffiths. Llandysul: Gwasg Gomer, 1965.

'Breuddwyd Rhonabwy'. In *Y Traddodiad Rhyddiaith yn yr Oesau Canol,* ed. Bowen, 176–9.

Jones, Dafydd Glyn. 'The Interludes'. In *A Guide to Welsh Literature c. 1700–1800,* ed. Jarvis, chapter 10.

Agoriad yr Oes. Talybont: Y Lolfa, 2001.

Jones, Dafydd Pritchard. 'Y Llofrudd'. Review of *Y Llofrudd Iaith. Barn* 443–4 (Ionawr 2000): 87.

Jones, E. D. 'A Welsh *Pencerdd*'s Manuscripts'. *Celtica* 5 (1959): 17–27.

Jones, Edgar. 'Some Aspects of Modern Welsh Poetry'. *Welsh Outlook* 4, 3 (1 March 1917): 97–103.

Jones, Emrys. *The Welsh in London 1500–2000.* Cardiff: University of Wales Press on behalf of the Honourable Society of Cymmrodorion, 2001.

Jones, Ffion Mair. '"To Know Him Is to Esteem Him": John Jenkins, Ifor Ceri 1770–1829'. *Montgomeryshire Collections* 99 (2011): 53–82.

'Welsh Balladry and Literacy'. In *Street Ballads in Nineteenth-Century Britain, Ireland and North America*, ed. David Atkinson and Steve Roud, 105–26. Farnham: Ashgate, 2014.

Jones, Gareth Elwyn. 'Wales 1550–1700: The Historical Background'. In *A Guide to Welsh Literature 1530–1700*, ed. Gruffydd, 1–28. Cardiff: University of Wales Press, 1997.

Jones, Gareth Elwyn, and Dai Smith, eds. *The People of Wales: A Millennium History*. Llandysul: Gomer Press, 1999.

Jones, Glyn. *The Dragon Has Two Tongues: Essays on Anglo-Welsh Writers and Writing*. London: Dent, 1968; repr. ed. Tony Brown. Cardiff: University of Wales Press, 2001.

trans. *A People's Poetry*. Bridgend: Seren, 1997.

Jones, Glyn, and John Rowlands. *Profiles: A Visitor's Guide to Writing in Twentieth-Century Wales*. Llandysul: Gomer Press, 1980.

Jones, Gwilym H. 'The Welsh Psalter, 1567'. *Journal of the Historical Society of the Church in Wales* 17, 22 (1967): 56–61.

Jones, Gwyn. *The First Forty Years: Some Notes on Anglo-Welsh Literature*. Cardiff: University of Wales Press, 1957.

Background to Dylan Thomas and Other Explorations. Oxford: Oxford University Press, 1992.

Jones, Ifano. *Printers and Printing in Monmouthshire and Wales*. Cardiff: William Lewis, 1925.

Jones, J. Gwynfor. *Crefydd, Cenedlgarwch a'r Wladwriaeth: John Penry (1563–1593) a Phiwritaniaeth Gynnar*. Caerdydd: Gwasg Prifysgol Cymru, 2014.

ed. *Wales and the Tudor State: Government, Religious Change and the Social Order 1534–1603*. Cardiff: University of Wales Press, 1989.

Jones, J. R. 'Ann Griffiths'. *Llên Cymru* 8, 1–2 (1964): 33–41.

Jones, John Graham. 'The Parliament for Wales Campaign, 1950–56'. *Welsh History Review* 16 (1992): 207–36.

Jones, Katie. 'Review of *Selected Stories* by Gwyn Thomas'. *New Welsh Review* 3 (1988): 75–7.

Jones, Llion Elis. 'Cameleon, nid brân'. Review of *Chwunu Mig. Taliesin* 93 (Spring 1996): 101–3.

Jones, M. H. 'Casgliadau Argraffedig o Emynau cyn "Aleluia" Pantycelyn (1744)'. *Journal of the Historical Society of the Presbyterian Church of Wales* 14, 1 (March 1929): 1–13.

Jones, Nerys Ann. 'Ffynonellau Canu Beirdd y Tywysogion'. *Studia Celtica* 37 (2003): 81–126.

Jones, Owain Wyn. 'Historical Writing in Medieval Wales'. PhD diss., Bangor University, 2013.

Jones, Philip Henry, and Eiluned Rees, eds. *A Nation and its Books: A History of the Book in Wales*. Aberystwyth: National Library of Wales, 1998.

Jones, Philip N. *Colliery Settlement in the South Wales Coalfield, 1850–1926*. Hull: University of Hull, 1969.

Jones, R. Brinley. *The Old British Tongue: The Vernacular in Wales, 1540–1640*. Cardiff: University of Wales Press, 1970.

'A Lanterne to their Feete': Remembering Rhys Prichard 1579–1644, Vicar of Llandovery. Porth-y-rhyd: Drovers Press, 1994.

William Salesbury. Writers of Wales. Cardiff: University of Wales Press, 1994.

Jones, R. M. ('Bobi'). *Llenyddiaeth Gymraeg 1936–1972*. Llandybïe: Christopher Davies, 1975.

Llên Cymru a Chrefydd. Abertawe: Christopher Davies, 1977.

'Narrative Structure in Medieval Welsh Prose Tales'. In *Proceedings of the Seventh International Congress of Celtic Studies*, ed. D. Ellis Evans, 171–98. Oxford: Oxford University Press, 1986.

Llenyddiaeth Gymraeg 1902–1936. Cyhoeddiadau Barddas, 1987.

'The Demise of the Anglo-Welsh'. *Poetry Wales* 28: 3 (Jan 1993): 14–18. Originally published as 'Tranc yr Eingl-Gymry'. *Barddas* (Ebrill 1992).

Cyfriniaeth Gymraeg. Caerdydd: Gwasg Prifysgol Cymru, 1994.

'Ann Griffiths and the Norm'. In *A Guide to Welsh Literature c. 1700–1800*, ed. Jarvis, 305–27.

Mawl a Gelynion ei Elynion: Hanfod y Traddodiad Llenyddol Cymraeg. Cyf. 2: Amddiffyn Mawl. Cyhoeddiadau Barddas, 2002.

Jones, R. Tudur. *Congregationalism in Wales*. Ed. Robert Pope, new edn. Cardiff: University of Wales Press, 2004.

John Elias, Prince Amongst Preachers. Bridgend: Evangelical Library of Wales, 1975.

'The Healing Herb and the Rose of Love: The Piety of Two Welsh Puritans [Vavasor Powell and Morgan Llwyd]'. In *Reformation, Conformity and Dissent*, ed. R. Buick Knox, 154–79. London: Epworth Press, 1977.

Jones, Richard Wyn. *Rhoi Cymru'n Gyntaf: Syniadaeth Plaid Cymru*. Caerdydd: Gwasg Prifysgol Cymru, 2007.

The Fascist Party in Wales? Plaid Cymru, Welsh Nationalism and the Accusation of Fascism. Cardiff: University of Wales Press, 2014.

Jones, Richard Wyn, and Jerry Hunter. 'O'r chwith: pa mor feirniadol yw beirniadaeth ôl-fodern?' *Taliesin* 92 (Gaeaf 1995): 9–32.

Jones, Richard Wyn, and Roger Scully. *Wales Says Yes: Devolution and the 2011 Welsh Referendum*. Cardiff: University of Wales Press, 2012.

Jones, Sally, *Allen Raine*. Cardiff: University of Wales Press, 1979.

Jones, Tegwyn. 'Welsh Ballads'. In *A Nation and its Books*, ed. Jones and Rees, chapter 20.

ed. *Tribannau Morgannwg*. Llandysul: Gwasg Gomer, 1976.

Jones, T. Gwynn. 'Modern Welsh Literature'. *Welsh Outlook* (1 January 1914): 19.

Jones, T. H. *Dylan Thomas*. Edinburgh: Oliver and Boyd, 1963.

Jones, Thomas. 'A Welsh Chronicler in Tudor England'. *Welsh History Review* 1 (1960): 1–17.

'The Black Book of Carmarthen "Stanzas of the Graves"'. *Proceedings of the British Academy* 53 (1967): 97–137.

et al. 'Nodiadau Cymysg'. *Bulletin of the Board of Celtic Studies* 11 (1944): 137–8.

ed. *Rhyddiaith Gymraeg, Yr Ail Gyfrol: Llawysgrifau a Llyfrau 1547–1618*. Caerdydd: Gwasg Prifysgol Cymru, 1956.

Jones, W. D. *Wales in America: Scranton and the Welsh 1860–1920*. Cardiff: University of Wales Press, 1993.

Jones, Whitney R. D. *David Williams: The Anvil and the Hammer*. Cardiff: University of Wales Press, 1986.

Jones, William David, and Aled Jones. 'The Welsh World and the British Empire, c. 1851–1939: An Exploration'. *Journal of Imperial and Commonwealth History* 31, 2 (2003): 57–81.

Kaminski-Jones, Rhys. 'True Britons: Ancient British Identity in Wales and Britain, 1680-1815'. PhD diss., University of Wales (2017).

Kearney, Hugh. *The British Isles: A History of Four Nations.* Cambridge: Cambridge University Press, 1985, rev. edn 2012.

Kennedy, Ruth, and Simon Meecham-Jones, eds. *Authority and Subjugation in Writing of Medieval Wales.* New York: Palgrave Macmillan, 2008.

Kershaw, Baz. *The Cambridge History of British Theatre.* Vol. III. Cambridge: Cambridge University Press, 2004.

Kiberd, Declan. *Inventing Ireland: The Literature of the Modern Nation.* London: Jonathan Cape, 1995.

Kidd, Colin. 'Integration: Patriotism and Nationalism'. In *A Companion to Eighteenth Century Britain*, ed. Dickinson, 369–80.

Kieckhefer, R. *Magic in the Middle Ages.* Cambridge: Cambridge University Press, 1989.

Kinney, Phyllis. 'The Tunes of the Welsh Christmas Carols'. *Canu Gwerin (Folk Song)* 11 (1988): 28–57, and 12 (1989): 5–29.

   Welsh Traditional Music. Cardiff: University of Wales Press, 2011.

Klaus, H. Gustav. 'Under the Sway of Coal'. *New Welsh Review* 39 (1997): 29–31.

   ed. *The Socialist Novel in Britain.* Brighton: Harvester, 1982.

Klaus, H. Gustav, and Stephen Knight, eds. *British Industrial Fictions.* Cardiff: University of Wales Press, 2000.

   eds. *'To Hell with Culture': Anarchism in Twentieth Century British Literature.* Cardiff: University of Wales Press, 2005.

Klausner, David N. 'Plays and Performing in South Wales'. *Early Theatre* 6, 2 (2003): 57–72.

   'Family Entertainments Among the Salusburys of Lleweni, Denbighshire, and their Circle, 1595–1641'. *Welsh Music History/Hanes Cerddoriaeth Cymru* 6 (2004): 129–54.

   'English Economies and Welsh Realities: Drama in Medieval and Early Modern Wales'. In *Authority and Subjugation in Writing of Medieval Wales*, ed. Kennedy and Meecham-Jones, 213–29.

   '"The Statute of Gruffudd ap Cynan". A Window on Medieval Welsh Bardic Practice'. In *Gablánach in scélaigecht: Celtic Studies in Honour of Ann Dooley*, ed. Findon, Sheehan, and Follett, 265–75.

Knight, Stephen. '". . . the Hesitations and Uncertainties that Were the Truth": Three Women Writers of Welsh Industrial Fiction'. In *British Industrial Fictions*, ed. Klaus and Knight, 163–80.

   '"Not a Place for Me": Rhys Davies's Fictions and the Coal Industry'. In *Decoding the Hare*, ed. Stephens, 54–70.

   'The Voices of Glamorgan: Gwyn Thomas's Colonial Fiction'. *Welsh Writing in English* 7 (2001/2): 16–34.

   A Hundred Years of Fiction: From Colony to Independence. Cardiff: University of Wales Press, 2004.

   'Anarcho-Syndicalism in Welsh Industrial Fiction'. In *To Hell with Culture*, ed. Klaus and Knight, 51–65.

Koch, John T. 'A Welsh Window on the Iron Age: Manawydan, Mandubracius'. *Cambridge Medieval Celtic Studies* 14 (1987): 17–52.

   'Brân, Brennos: An Instance of Early Gallo-Brittonic History and Mythology'. *Cambridge Medieval Celtic Studies* 20 (1990): 1–20.

'The Celtic Lands'. In *Medieval Arthurian Literature: A Guide to Recent Research*, ed. N. J. Lacy, 239–322. New York: Garland, 1996.

Cunedda, Cynan, Cadwallon, Cynddylan: Four Welsh Poems and Britain 383–655. Aberystwyth: Centre for Advanced Welsh and Celtic Studies, 2013.

ed. *The Celts: History, Life and Culture*. 2 vols. Santa Barbara, CA: ABC-CLIO, LLC, 2012.

Kohr, Leopold. *Is Wales Viable?* Llandybïe: Christopher Davies, 1971.

Kraye, Jill, ed. *The Cambridge Companion to Renaissance Humanism*. Cambridge: Cambridge University Press, 1996.

Lambert, Pierre-Yves. 'Magie et pouvoir dans la quatrième branche du *Mabinogi*'. *Studia Celtica* 28 (1994): 97–107.

Langer, Susanne. *Feeling and Form: A Theory of Art*. New York: Scribner, 1953.

Lapidge, Michael. 'The Welsh-Latin Poetry of Sulien's Family'. *Studia Celtica* 8–9 (1973–4): 68–106.

Lapidge, Michael, and Richard Sharpe. *A Bibliography of Celtic-Latin Literature 400–1200*. Dublin: Royal Irish Academy, 1985.

Larrington, Carolyne. *King Arthur's Enchantresses: Morgan and her Sisters in Arthurian Tradition*. London: I. B. Tauris, 2006.

Larsen, Lars Bang, ed. *Networks: Documents of Contemporary Art*. Cambridge, MA and London: MIT Press and Whitechapel Gallery, 2014.

Law, John. 'Actor Network Theory and Material Semiotics'. In *The New Blackwell Companion to Social Theory*, ed. Bryan S. Turner, 141–58. Oxford: Wiley-Blackwell, 2009.

Leckie, R. William. *The Passage of Dominion*. Toronto: University of Toronto Press, 1981.

Lefebvre, Henri. *The Production of Space*. Trans. Donald Nicholson-Smith. Oxford: Blackwell, 1991.

Leighton, Angela. *On Form: Poetry, Aestheticism and the Legacy of a Word*. Oxford University Press, 2007.

Lewis, Barry J. *Welsh Poetry and English Pilgrimage: Gruffudd ap Maredudd and the Rood of Chester*. Aberystwyth: Canolfan Uwchefrydiau Cymreig a Cheltaidd, 2005.

Lewis, Ceri W. 'The Literary History of Glamorgan from 1550 to 1770'. In *Glamorgan County History*. Vol. IV: *Early Modern Glamorgan*, ed. Williams, 566–76.

'The Decline of Professional Poetry'. In *A Guide to Welsh Literature c. 1530–1700*, ed. Gruffydd, 29–74.

'Iolo Morganwg'. In *A Guide to Welsh Literature c. 1700–1800*, ed. Jarvis, 126–67.

Lewis, Gwyneth. 'Byw Mewn Bydoedd Cyfochrog'. In *Gweld Sêr*, ed. Thomas, 204–10.

Lewis, Idwal. 'Welsh Newspapers and Journals in the United States'. *National Library of Wales Journal* 2, 3–4 (1942): 124–30.

Lewis, Llŷr Gwyn. 'Golygyddol'. *Tu Chwith* 39 (Haf 2013): 5–12.

'Cyfieithiadau T. Gwynn Jones a Tadhg O Donnchadha o Farddoniaeth Gymraeg a Gwyddeleg'. *Ysgrifau Beirniadol* 33 (Bethesda: Gwasg Gee, 2014): 21–46.

Lewis, Lisa. 'Cwmni Theatr Cymru ac Emily Davies, 1982–4'. In *Y Theatr Genedlaethol yng Nghymru*, ed. Davies, 208–51.

Lewis, R. L. *Welsh Americans: A History of Assimilation in the Coalfields*. Chapel Hill: University of North Carolina Press, 2008.

Lewis, Saunders. *A School of Welsh Augustans*. Wrexham: Hughes and Son, 1924.

Is There an Anglo-Welsh Literature? Caerdydd: Cangen Caerdydd, Urdd Graddedigion Prifysgol Cymru / Cardiff Branch, Guild of Graduates of the University of Wales, 1939.

'Review of D. Gwenallt Jones, *Cnoi Cil*'. *Baner ac Amserau Cymru* (10 February 1943): 7.

'Damcaniaeth Eglwysig Brotestannaidd'. In *Meistri a'u Crefft*, ed. ap Gwilym, 116–39.

'*Morte d'Arthur* a'r *Passing of Arthur*'. In *Meistri a'u Crefft*, ed. ap Gwilym, 203–8.

Williams Pantycelyn. Llundain: Foyle's, 1927. New edition with introduction by D. Densil Morgan, Caerdydd: Gwasg Prifysgol Cymru, 2016.

'Ann Griffiths: A Literary Survey'. In *Flame in the Mountains*, trans. Hodges, ed. James, 138–59.

ed. *Crefft y Stori Fer*. Llandysul: Y Clwb Llyfrau Cymreig, 1949.

Lindahl, Carl. 'Yvain's Return to Wales'. *Arthuriana* 10 (2000): 44–56.

Lippard, Lucy. *The Lure of the Local: Senses of Place in a Multicultural Society*. New York: The New Press, 1997.

Liu, Alan. *Local Transcendence: Essays on Postmodern Historicism and the Database*. Chicago: University of Chicago Press, 2008.

Lloyd, David T., ed. *Writing on the Edge: Interviews with Writers and Editors of Wales*. Amsterdam and Atlanta, GA: Rodopi, 1997.

Lloyd-Morgan, Ceridwen. 'Narrative Structure in *Peredur*'. *Zeitschrift für Celtische Philologie* 38 (1981): 187–231.

'*Breuddwyd Rhonabwy* and Later Arthurian Literature'. In *The Arthur of the Welsh*, ed. Bromwich *et al.*, 183–208.

'French Texts, Welsh Translators'. In *The Medieval Translator II*, ed. Roger Ellis, 45–63. London: Centre for Medieval Studies, Queen Mary and Westfield College, University of London, 1991.

'Migrating Narratives: *Peredur*, *Owain*, and *Geraint*'. In *A Companion to Arthurian Literature*, ed. Fulton, 128–41.

Lloyd, Nesta. '"Yr Ymarfer o Dduwioldeb" a Rhai o Gerddi Rhys Prichard'. *Y Traethodydd* 150 (1995): 94–106.

'Late Free-Metre Poetry'. In *A Guide to Welsh Literature c. 1530–1700*, ed. Gruffydd, 100–27.

Llwyd, Alan. 'Golygyddol'. *Barddas* 22 (Medi 1978): 2–4.

ed. *Cyfres y Meistri 1: R. Williams Parry*. Abertawe: Christopher Davies, 1979.

R. Williams Parry. Caernarfon: Gwasg Pantycelyn, 1984.

'Golygyddol'. *Barddas* (Gorffennaf/Awst/Medi 1988): 12–15.

'Golygyddol'. *Barddas* (Gorffennaf/Awst 1992): 6–12.

Prifysgol y Werin: Eisteddfod Genedlaethol 1900–1918. Cyhoeddiadau Barddas, 2008.

Stori Waldo Williams: Bardd Heddwch/The Story of Waldo Williams: Poet of Peace. Cyhoeddiadau Barddas, 2010.

Bob: Cofiant R. Williams Parry. Llandysul: Gwasg Gomer, 2013.

'Review of *Pigion Talwrn y Beirdd 12*'. *Taliesin* 148 (2013): 93–7.

Waldo. Talybont: Y Lolfa, 2014.

'Beirniadaeth Alan Llwyd'. In *Cyfansoddiadau a Beirniadaethau Eisteddfod Genedlaethol Cymru, 2014*, ed. Hughes, 6–11.

Gwenallt. Talybont: Y Lolfa, 2016.

Llywelyn, Dorian. '"The Fiery, Blessed Ann": Experience and Doctrine in the Spirituality of Ann Griffiths'. *Spiritus* 9 (2009): 217–40.

Löffler, Marion. *The Literary and Historical Legacy of Iolo Morganwg 1826–1926*. Cardiff: University of Wales Press, 2007.

Löffler, Marion, with Hywel Gethin Rhys. 'Thomas Stephens and the Abergavenny Cymreigyddion: Letters from the *Cambrian* 1842–3'. *National Library of Wales Journal* (May 2009). www.library.wales/fileadmin/fileadmin/docs_gwefan/amdanom_ni/cylchgrawn_llgc/cgr_erth_XXXIVrhif4_2009_2.pdf.

Welsh Responses to the French Revolution: Press and Public Discourse, 1789–1802. Cardiff: University of Wales Press, 2012.

Löffler, Marion, with Bethan Jenkins, eds. *Political Pamphlets and Sermons from Wales 1790–1806*. Cardiff: University of Wales Press, 2014.

Lord, Peter. *Words with Pictures: Welsh Images and Images of Wales in the Popular Press, 1640–1860*. Aberystwyth: Planet, 1995.

The Visual Culture of Wales: Imaging the Nation. Cardiff: University of Wales Press, 2000.

Lublin, Geraldine. 'Fred Green a'r "Cyfeillgarwch Parhaol" rhwng y Cymry a Brodorion Patagonia'. *Taliesin* 133 (2008): 81–92.

Ludwig, Hans-Werner, and Lothar Fietz, eds. *Poetry in the British Isles: Non-Metropolitan Perspectives*. Cardiff: University of Wales Press, 1995.

Luft, Diana. 'The Meaning of *Mabinogi*'. *Cambrian Medieval Celtic Studies* 62 (2011): 57–79.

Lycett, Andrew. *Dylan Thomas: A New Life*. Woodstock & New York: The Overlook Press, 2003.

Lynch, Peredur. 'Refferendum 1979, Cerddi Ianws a Thopos "y Cymry Taeog"'. *Ysgrifau Beirniadol* 30 (2011): 78–109.

MacCana, Proinsias. *Branwen Daughter of Llŷr: A Study of the Irish Affinities and of the Composition of the Second Branch of the Mabinogi*. Cardiff: University of Wales Press, 1958.

Maier, Bernhard. 'Dead Men Don't Wear Plaid: Celtic Myth and Christian Creed in Medieval Irish Concepts of the Afterlife'. In *Writing Down the Myths*, ed. Joseph Falaky Nagy, 109–36. Turnhout: Brepols, 2013.

Maier, Bernhard. and Stefan Zimmer, eds. *150 Jahre 'Mabinogion': deutsch-walisische Kulturbeziehungen*. Tübingen: Max Niemeyer, 2001.

Mared, G. 'Atgyfodi Clasur'. *Barn* 545 (Mehefin 2008): 55.

Marks, Rhiannon. *Pe Gallwn, Mi Luniwn Lythyr: Golwg ar Waith Menna Elfyn*. Caerdydd: Gwasg Prifysgol Cymru, 2013.

Maskell, D. *Racine: A Theatrical Reading*. Oxford: Clarendon Press, 1991.

Massey, Doreen. *Space, Place and Gender*. Cambridge: Polity Press, 1994.

For Space. London: Sage, 2005.

Mathias, Glyn. 'The Ballot Bites Back'. *Planet* 125 (1997): 17–20.

Mathias, Roland. *A Ride Through the Wood: Essays on Anglo-Welsh Literature*. Bridgend: Poetry Wales Press, 1985.

Anglo-Welsh Literature: An Illustrated History. Bridgend: Poetry Wales Press, 1987.

Mathias, W. Alun. 'Llyfr Rhetoreg William Salesbury'. *Llên Cymru* 1 (1950–1): 259–68

Matthew, D. 'Some Elizabethan Documents'. *Bulletin of the Board of Celtic Studies* 6 (1931–3): 70–8.

Matthews, John F. 'Macsen, Maximus, and Constantine'. *Welsh History Review* 11 (1982): 431–48.

McKee, Helen. 'Scribes and Glosses from Dark Age Wales: The Cambridge Juvencus Manuscript'. *Cambrian Medieval Celtic Studies* 39 (2000): 1–22.

McKenna, Catherine. 'The Theme of Sovereignty in *Pwyll*'. *Bulletin of the Board of Celtic Studies* 29 (1980–1): 35–52.

'Learning Lordship: The Education of Manawydan'. In *Ildánach Ildírech: A Festschrift for Proinsias Mac Cana*, ed. John Carey, John T. Koch, and Pierre-Yves Lambert, 101–20. Aberystwyth: Celtic Studies Publications, 1999.

'Revising Math: Kingship in the Fourth Branch of the *Mabinogi*'. *Cambrian Medieval Celtic Studies* 46 (2003): 95–118.

'Aspects of Tradition Formation in Eighteenth-Century Wales'. In *Memory and the Modern in Celtic Literatures*, ed. Nagy, 37–60.

'The Colonization of Myth in *Branwen uerch Lyr*'. In *Myth in Celtic Literatures*, ed. Nagy, 105–19.

'"What Dreams May Come Must Give Us Pause": *Breudwyt Ronabwy* and the Red Book of Hergest'. *Cambrian Medieval Celtic Studies* 58 (2009): 69–99.

'Reading with Rhydderch: Mabinogion Texts in Manuscript Context'. In *Language and Power in the Celtic World*, ed. Anders Ahlqvist and Pamela O'Neill, 205–30. Sydney: Celtic Studies Foundation, University of Sydney, 2011.

McLean, Ian, and Martin Johnes. *Aberfan: Government and Disasters*. Cardiff: Welsh Academic Press, 2000.

McMillan, Joyce, and Ruth Fox. *Has Devolution Delivered for Women?* Edinburgh and London: British Council Scotland and Hansard Society, 2010.

McSmith, Andy. 'Boyos in the Back Room Slay a Dragon'. *The Guardian*, 14 February 1999.

Medhurst, Jamie. *A History of Independent Television in Wales*. Cardiff: University of Wales Press, 2010.

Meredith, Christopher. 'Two from the Heart'. Review of *All Things Betray Thee* by Gwyn Thomas. *Planet* 59 (1986): 98–9.

Merriman, Peter, and Rhys Jones. '"Symbols of Justice": The Welsh Language Society's Campaign for Bilingual Road Signs in Wales, 1967–1980'. *Journal of Historical Geography* 35 (2009): 350–76.

Miles, Gareth. 'Dylanwad Patagonia ar y Meddwl a'r Dychymyg Cymreig'. *Taliesin* 125 (2005): 97–109.

'Yn y Crochan'. *Barn* 522/523 (Gorffennaf/Awst [July/August] 2006): 96.

Millersdaughter, K. 'The Geopolitics of Incest: Sex, Gender and Violence in the Fourth Branch of the *Mabinogi*'. *Exemplaria* 14, 2 (2002): 271–316.

Minhinnick, Robert. 'My Petition to the Zoo Keeper'. *Planet* 90 (1992): 15–16.

Miskell, Louise. *'Intelligent Town': An Urban History of Swansea, 1780–1855*. Cardiff: University of Wales Press, 2006.

Miskell, Peter. *A Social History of the Cinema in Wales, 1918–1951: Pulpits, Coal Pits and Fleapits*. Cardiff: University of Wales Press, 2006.

Monmonier, Mark S. *How to Lie With Maps*. Chicago: University of Chicago Press, 1996.

Moore, Dafydd. 'James Macpherson and "Celtic Whiggism"'. *Eighteenth-Century Life* 30, 1 (2006): 1–24.

Morgan, Clare. 'Exile and the Kingdom: Margiad Evans and the Mythic Landscape of Wales'. *Welsh Writing in English: A Yearbook of Critical Essays* 6 (2000): 98–118.

Morgan, D. Densil, ed. *Thomas Charles o'r Bala*. Caerdydd: Gwasg Prifysgol Cymru, 2014.

Morgan, Derec Llwyd. *Barddoniaeth T. Gwynn Jones*. Llandysul: Gwasg Gomer, 1972.

    Williams Pantycelyn. Llên y Llenor. Caernarfon: Gwasg Pantycelyn, 1983.

    The Great Awakening in Wales, trans. Dyfnallt Morgan. London: Epworth Press, 1988.

    Y Beibl a Llenyddiaeth Gymraeg. Llandysul: Gwasg Gomer, 1998.

    'Williams, William Pantycelyn (1717–1791)'. In *Oxford Dictionary of National Biography*. Oxford: Oxford University Press, 2004. www.oxforddnb.com/view/article/29556.

    ed. *Meddwl a Dychymyg Williams Pantycelyn*. Llandysul: Gwasg Gomer, 1991.

Morgan, Dyfnallt, ed. *Y Ferch o Ddolwar Fach*. Caernarfon: Gwasg Gwynedd, 1977.

Morgan, Elin Llwyd, and Simon Brooks. 'Prolog'. *Tu Chwith* 1 (1993): 5–7.

    'Teulu Tynybraich'. Review of *O! Tyn y Gorchudd*. *Barn* 476 (Medi 2002): 42.

Morgan, Elystan. *Atgofion Oes*. Talybont: Lolfa, 2012.

Morgan, Gerald. *Ieuan Fardd*. Caernarfon: Gwasg Pantycelyn, 1988.

Morgan, Kenneth O. *Rebirth of a Nation: Wales, 1880–1980*. Oxford: Clarendon Press, 1981.

    Modern Wales: Politics, Places and People. Cardiff: University of Wales Press, 1995.

Morgan, Kevin. *Towards Democratic Devolution: The Challenge of the Welsh Assembly*. Papers in Planning and Research 171. Cardiff: Department of City and Regional Planning, Cardiff University, 1999.

Morgan, Kevin, and Geoff Mungham. *Redesigning Democracy: The Making of the Welsh Assembly*. Bridgend: Seren, 2000.

Morgan, Prys. 'Y Ddau Theophilus: Sylwadau ar Hanesyddiaeth'. *Taliesin* 19 (1969): 36–45.

    'Glamorgan and the Red Book'. *Morgannwg: Transactions of the Glamorgan Local History Society* 22 (1978): 42–60.

    The Eighteenth Century Renaissance. Llandybïe: Christopher Davies, 1981.

    'From a Death to a View: The Hunt for the Welsh Past in the Romantic Period'. In *The Invention of Tradition*, ed. Hobsbawm and Ranger, 43–100.

    'The Gwerin of Wales: Myth and Reality'. In *The Welsh and Their Country*, ed. Hume and Pryce, 134–50.

    A Bible for Wales. Aberystwyth: Gwasg Cambria, 1988.

    'A Private Space: Autobiography and Individuality in Eighteenth- and Early Nineteenth-Century Wales'. In *From Medieval to Modern Wales*, ed. Davies and Jenkins, 160–74.

Morris, Brian. *Harri Webb*. Cardiff: University of Wales Press, 1993.

Morys, Twm, ed. *Awen Iwan*. Cyhoeddiadau Barddas, 2014.

Nagy, Joseph Falaky. 'Folklore Studies and the Mabinogion'. In *150 Jahre 'Mabinogion'*, ed. Maier and Zimmer, 91–100.

    ed. *The Individual in Celtic Literatures*. Dublin: Four Courts Press, 1991.

    ed. *Memory and the Modern in Celtic Literatures*. CSANA Yearbook 5. Dublin: Four Courts Press, 2006.

    ed. *Myth in Celtic Literatures*. CSANA Yearbook 6. Dublin: Four Courts Press, 2007.

Nevin, Edward. *The Social Accounts of the Welsh Economy 1948–1956*. Aberystwyth: University of Wales Press, 1957.

Nicholas, W. Rhys. *The Folk Poets*. Writers of Wales. Cardiff: University of Wales Press, 1978.

O'Connor, Frank. *The Lonely Voice: A Study of the Short Story*. Hoboken: Melville House, 2004.

O Hehir, Brendan. 'What Is the *Gododdin*?' In *Early Welsh Poetry*, ed. Roberts, 57–97.

O'Leary, Paul. 'The Languages of Patriotism in Mid-nineteenth Century Wales'. In *The Welsh Language and Social Domains*, ed. Jenkins, 533–60.

    Claiming the Streets: Processions and Urban Culture in South Wales, c. 1830–1880. Cardiff: University of Wales Press, 2012.

Olson, Katharine K. '"Slow and Cold in the True Service of God": Popular Beliefs and Practices, Conformity, and Reformation'. In *Christianities in the Early Modern Celtic World*, ed. Armstrong and Ó hAnnracháin, 92–107.

Olwig, Kenneth R. '*Choras, Chora* and the Question of Landscape'. In *Envisioning Landscapes, Making Worlds: Geography and the Humanities*, ed. Stephen Daniels, Dydia DeLyser, J. Nicholas Entrikin, and Douglas Richardson, 44–54.

Ong, Walter J. *Orality and Literacy: The Technologizing of the Word.* London: Methuen, 1982.

Orchard, Andy. 'Not What it Was: The World of the Old English Elegy'. In *The Oxford Handbook of the Elegy*, ed. Andy Orchard and Karen Weisman, 101–17. Oxford: Oxford University Press, 2010.

Osborne, Huw Edwin. *Rhys Davies.* Cardiff: University of Wales Press, 2009.

    ed. *Queer Wales: The History, Culture and Politics of Queer Life in Wales.* Cardiff: University of Wales Press, 2016.

Osmond, John. 'Mr Morris and the Elephant: The Referendum, the Election, and the Future of Welsh Politics'. *Planet* 48 (1979): 2–8.

    ed. *The National Question Again: Welsh Political Identity in the 1980s.* Llandysul: Gomer Press, 1985.

    ed. *The National Assembly Agenda.* Cardiff: Institute of Welsh Affairs, 1998.

Owen, Roger. 'David Lloyd Davies (Dewi Glan Peryddon)'. *Dictionary of Welsh Biography* http://yba.llgc.org.uk/en/s-DAVI-LLO-1881.html.

    Ar Wasgar: Theatr a Chenedligrwydd yn y Gymru Gymraeg, 1979–1997. Caerdydd: Gwasg Prifysgol Cymru, 2003.

    Gwenlyn Parry. Cardiff: University of Wales Press, 2013.

Padel, Oliver. 'A New Study of the *Gododdin*'. *Cambrian Medieval Celtic Studies* 35 (1998): 45–55.

    'Geoffrey of Monmouth and the Development of the Merlin Legend'. *Cambrian Medieval Celtic Studies* 51 (2006): 37–65.

Page, Sophie, and Catherine Rider, eds. *The Routledge History of Medieval Magic.* London and New York: Routledge, forthcoming.

Parry, Charles. *Supplement to the Catalogue of Welsh Books and Books Printed in Wales 1546–1820.* Aberystwyth: National Library of Wales, 2001.

Parry, T. Emrys. *Barddoniaeth Robert Williams Parry: Astudiaeth Feirniadol.* Dinbych: Gwasg Gee, 1973.

Parry, Thomas. 'Tri chyfeiriad at William Salesbury'. *Bulletin of the Board of Celtic Studies* 9 (1937–9): 108–12.

    Hanes Llenyddiaeth Gymraeg hyd 1900. Caerdydd: Gwasg Prifysgol Cymru, 1953.

    A History of Welsh Literature. Trans. H. I. Bell. Oxford: Clarendon Press, 1955.

    Baledi'r Ddeunawfed Ganrif. Caerdydd: Gwasg Prifysgol Cymru, 1935, 1986.

Patterson, Ian. 'No Man is an I: Recent Developments in the Lyric'. In *The Lyric Poem: Formations and Transformations*, ed. Marion Thain, 217–36. Cambridge: Cambridge University Press, 2013.

Peach, Linden. *The Fiction of Emyr Humphreys.* Cardiff: University of Wales Press, 2011.

Peacock, Molly. 'From Gilded Cage to Rib Cage'. In *After the New Formalism: Poets on Form, Narrative and Traditions*, ed. Annie Finch, 71–8. Ashland, Or.: Story Line Press, 1999.

Perec, Georges. *Species of Spaces and Other Pieces*. Trans. John Sturrock. London: Penguin, 1997.

Perryman, Mark. *Breaking Up Britain: Four Nations After a Union*. London: Lawrence and Wishart, 2007.

Petrovskaia, Natalia. 'Dating *Peredur*: New Light on Old Problems'. *Proceedings of the Harvard Celtic Colloquium* 29 (2009): 223–43.

Medieval Welsh Perceptions of the Orient. Turnhout: Brepols, 2015.

Phillips, Dylan. *Trwy Ddulliau Chwyldro? Hanes Cymdeithas yr Iaith Gymraeg, 1962–1992*. Llandysul: Gwasg Gomer, 1998.

Philp, Mark, ed. *Resisting Napoleon: The British Response to the Threat of Invasion, 1797–1815*. Aldershot: Ashgate, 2006.

Pierce, James. *The Life and Work of William Salesbury: A Rare Scholar*. Talybont: Y Lolfa, 2016.

Pikoulis, John. 'Word-of-Mouth Cultures Cease in Cemeteries'. *New Welsh Review* 34 (1996): 9–15.

Poppe, Erich. '*Owein, Ystorya Bown*, and the Problem of "Relative Distance"'. Some Methodological Considerations and Speculations'. *Arthurian Literature* 21 (2004): 73–94.

'How to Achieve an Optimal Textual Fit in Middle Welsh Clauses'. *Cambrian Medieval Celtic Studies* 68 (2014): 69–100.

Porter, Roy, and Mikuláš Teich, eds. *Romanticism in National Context*. Cambridge: Cambridge University Press, 1988.

Prescott, Sarah. *Eighteenth-Century Writing from Wales: Bards and Britons*. Cardiff: University of Wales Press, 2008.

'Review of *English-Language Poetry from Wales* by Elizabeth Edwards'. *International Journal of Welsh Writing in English* 2, 1 (2014): 209–11.

Price, Angharad. 'Y cyfieithwyr yn flaena'. Review of *Cusan Dyn Dall*. *Barn* 460 (Mai 2001): 40–1.

Rhwng Gwyn a Du: Agweddau ar Ryddiaith Gymraeg y 1990au. Caerdydd: Gwasg Prifysgol Cymru, 2002.

Gwrthddiwygwyr Cymreig yr Eidal. Caernarfon: Gwasg Pantycelyn, 2005.

'"Dim oll"? Ymateb Nofelwyr Cymraeg i Ddatganoli'. *Llên Cymru* 34 (2011): 237–47.

Ffarwél i Ffreiburg: Crwydriadau Cynnar T. H. Parry-Williams. Llandysul: Gwasg Gomer, 2013.

ed. *Chwileniwm: Technoleg a Llenyddiaeth*. Caerdydd: Gwasg Prifysgol Cymru, 2002.

Pritchard, Elyn, Bethan Mair, and Catrin Puw Davies. 'Gwobr Goffa Daniel Owen'. In *Cyfansoddiadau a Beirniadaethau Eisteddfod Genedlaethol 2005, Eryri a'r Cyffiniau*, ed. Hughes, 92–100.

Pryce, Huw, ed. *Literacy in Medieval Celtic Societies*. Cambridge: Cambridge University Press, 1998.

Radnor, Joan. 'Interpreting Irony in Medieval Celtic Narrative: The Case of *Culhwch ac Olwen*'. *Cambridge Medieval Celtic Studies* 16 (1988): 41–59.

Rawlings, Richard. 'Hastening Slowly: The Next Phase of Welsh Devolution'. *Public Law* (2005): 824–52.

Rees, Brinley. *Dulliau'r Canu Rhydd 1500–1650*. Caerdydd: Gwasg Prifysgol Cymru, 1952.

Rees, D. Morgan. 'A View of Welsh Tourism'. *Wales* (New Year 1960): 35–7.

Rees, Eiluned. *The Welsh Book Trade Before 1820*. Aberystwyth: National Library of Wales, 1988.

   Libri Walliae: A Catalogue of Welsh Books and Books Printed in Wales 1546–1820. Aberystwyth: National Library of Wales, 1987.

Rees, Gareth, and Teresa L. Rees, eds. *Poverty and Social Inequality in Wales*. London: Croom Helm, 1980.

Relph, Edward. *Place and Placelessness*. London: Pion, 1976.

Rhydderch, Francesca. 'Dual Nationality, Divided Identity: Ambivalent Narratives of Britishness in the Welsh Novels of Anna Maria Bennett'. *Welsh Writing in English: A Yearbook of Critical Essays* 3 (1997): 1–17.

Rhŷs, John. *Lectures on the Origin and Growth of Religion as Illustrated by Celtic Heathendom*. London: Williams and Norgate, 1888.

Rhys, Keidrych. 'Editorial'. *Wales* 2 (1943): 1–2.

   'Editorial'. *Wales* 4, 6 (1945): 4–6.

Rhys, Robert, ed. *Cyfres y Meistri 2: Waldo Williams*. Abertawe: Christopher Davies, 1981.

   'Dysgu Darllen'. In *Sglefrio ar Eiriau*, ed. Rowlands, 151–71.

   'Welsh Literature in the Nineteenth Century'. In *The Welsh Language and its Social Domains 1801–1911*, ed. Jenkins, 265–95.

   '"Ni Thraetha'r Môr ei Maint": Cerddi "Almaenig" Waldo Williams yn 1946'. *Llên Cymru* 34, 1 (2011), 226–36.

   ed. *Y Patrwm Amryliw*. 2 vols. Cyhoeddiadau Barddas, 1997, 2006.

Richards, H., Phil Stead, and Gareth Williams, eds. *More Heart and Soul: The Character of Welsh Rugby*. Cardiff: University of Wales Press, 2000.

Richards, T. *The Puritan Movement in Wales, 1639 to 1653*. London: National Eisteddfod Association, 1920.

Robert, Gruffydd. *Gramadeg Cymraeg*. Ed. G. J. Williams. Caerdydd: Gwasg Prifysgol Cymru, 1939.

Roberts, Brynley F. 'Un o Lawysgrifau Hopcyn ap Tomas o Ynys Dawe'. *Bulletin of the Board of Celtic Studies* 22 (1967): 223–7.

   'Geoffrey of Monmouth and Welsh Historical Tradition'. *Nottingham Medieval Studies* 20 (1976): 29–40.

   'From Traditional Tale to Literary Story: Middle Welsh Prose Narratives'. In *The Craft of Fiction*, ed. Leigh Arrathoon, 211–30. Rochester, NY: Solaris Press, 1984.

   'Geoffrey of Monmouth, *Historia Regum Britanniae* and *Brut y Brenhinedd*'. In *The Arthur of the Welsh*, ed. Bromwich *et al.*, 97–116.

   'Where Were the Four Branches of the Mabinogi Written?' In *The Individual in Celtic Literatures*, ed. Nagy, 61–73.

   'The Literature of the "Great Awakening"'. In *A Guide to Welsh Literature c. 1700–1800*, ed. Jarvis, 279–304.

   '*Peredur son of Efrawg*: A Text in Transition'. *Arthuriana* 10 (2000): 57–72.

   'Hopcyn ap Tomas ab Einion'. In *Oxford Dictionary of National Biography*. Oxford: Oxford University Press, 2004. www.oxforddnb.com/view/article/48547.

   ed. *Early Welsh Poetry: Studies in the Book of Aneirin*. Aberystwyth: National Library of Wales, 1988.

Roberts, Brynley F., and Morfydd E. Owen, eds. *Beirdd a Thywysogion: Barddoniaeth Llys yng Nghymru, Iwerddon a'r Alban*. Cardiff: University of Wales Press and National Library of Wales, 1996.

Roberts, Enid. *Braslun o Hanes Llên Powys*. Dinbych: Gwasg Gee, 1965.

'Eisteddfod Caerwys 1567'. *Transactions of the Denbighshire Historical Society* 16 (1967): 23–6.

Roberts, Gomer M. *Y Pêr Ganiedydd*. 2 vols. Aberystwyth: Gwasg Aberystwyth, 1949, 1958.

Roberts, Gwyneth. 'The Cost of Community: Women in Raymond Williams's Fiction'. In *Our Sisters' Land: The Changing Identities of Women in Wales*, ed. Aaron et al., 214–27.

Roberts, Helen. 'Court and *Cyuoeth*: Chrétien de Troyes' *Erec et Enide* and the Middle Welsh *Gereint*'. *Arthurian Literature* 21 (2004): 53–72.

Roberts, Peter R. 'The "Act of Union" in Welsh History'. *Transactions of the Honourable Society of Cymmrodorion* (1972–3): 49–72.

'The Welsh Language, English Law, and Tudor Legislation'. *Transactions of the Honourable Society of Cymmrodorion* (1989): 19–76.

'Tudor Legislation and the Political Status of "the British Tongue"'. In *The Welsh Language Before the Industrial Revolution*, ed. Jenkins, 123–52.

'Tudor Wales, National Identity, and the British Inheritance'. In *British Consciousness and Identity: The Making of Britain, 1533–1707*, ed. Bradshaw and Roberts, 8–42.

Roberts, William Owen. 'Writing on the Edge of Catastrophe'. In *Peripheral Visions: Images of Nationhood in Contemporary British Fiction*, ed. Bell, 77–9.

Roberts, William Owen, and Iwan Llwyd Williams. 'Mae'n bwrw yn Toremolinos'. *Y Faner*, 14 December 1984, 6–7.

Roderick, A. J., ed. *Wales Through the Ages*. 2 vols. Llandybïe: Christopher Davies, 1959–60.

Rodaway, Paul. *Sensuous Geographies: Body, Space and Place*. London: Routledge, 1994.

Rodway, Simon. 'The Red Book Text of "Culhwch ac Olwen": A Modernising Scribe at Work'. *Studi Celtici* 3 (2004): 93–161.

'The Date and Authorship of *Culhwch ac Olwen*: A Reassessment'. *Cambrian Medieval Celtic Studies* 49 (2005): 21–44.

'The Where, Who, When and Why of Medieval Welsh Prose Texts: Some Methodological Considerations'. *Studia Celtica* 41 (2007): 47–89.

Dating Medieval Welsh Literature: Evidence from the Verbal System. Aberystwyth: CMCS Publications, 2013.

Rose, Gillian. 'As if the Mirrors Had Bled: Masculine Dwelling, Masculinist Theory and Feminist Masquerade'. In *Bodyspace: Destabilising the Geographies of Gender and Sexuality*, ed. Duncan, 56–74.

Rosenthal, M. L. *The Modern Poets*. New York: Oxford University Press, 1965.

Rosenwein, Barbara H. 'Worrying About Emotions in History'. *American Historical Review* 107, 3 (June 2002): 821–45.

Emotional Communities in the Early Middle Ages. Ithaca, NY: Cornell University Press, 2006.

Rosser, Colin, and Christopher Harris. *The Family and Social Change: A Study of Family and Kinship in a South Wales Town*. London: Routledge and Kegan Paul, 1965.

Rothkirch, Alyce von, and Daniel Williams, eds. *Beyond the Difference: Welsh Literature in Comparative Contexts*. Cardiff: University of Wales Press, 2004.

Rowland, Jenny. 'The Manuscript Tradition of the Red Book *Englynion*'. *Studia Celtica* 18–19 (1983–4): 79–95.

Rowlands, Eurys I. 'Nodiadau ar y traddodiad moliant a'r cywydd'. *Llên Cymru* 7 (1962–3): 217–43.

Rowlands, John. 'Wrth Fynd Heibio'. *Barn* (Medi 1978): 323–5.

Cnoi Cil ar Lenyddiaeth. Llandysul: Gwasg Gomer, 1989.

Saunders y Beirniad. Caernarfon: Gwasg Pantycelyn, 1990.

Ysgrifau ar y Nofel. Caerdydd: Gwasg Prifysgol Cymru, 1992.

'Dau Lwybr T. Gwynn Jones'. *Y Traethodydd* 148 (1993): 69–87.

'Cystadleuaeth y Fedal Ryddiaith: Beirniadaeth John Rowlands'. In *Cyfansoddiadau a Beirniadaethau Eisteddfod Genedlaethol Frenhinol Cymru*, 1993, ed. Hughes, 90–6.

'Chwarae â Chwedlau: Cip ar y Nofel Gymraeg Ôl-fodernaidd'. In *Rhyddid y Nofel*, ed. Wiliams, 161–85.

ed. *Sglefrio ar Eiriau*. Llandysul: Gwasg Gomer, 1992.

Rowlands, Sioned Puw. *Hwyaid, Cwningod a Sgwarnogod: Esthetig Radical Twm Morys, Václav Havel a Borumil Hrabal*. Caerdydd: Gwasg Prifysgol Cymru, 2006.

Rubin, Stan Sanvel, and Bruce Bennett. 'A Sound Like a Clear Gong'. Transcript of a Conversation that Took Place on 9 October 1991. In *An Open World: Essays on Leslie Norris*, ed. England and Makuck, 10–21.

Russell, Paul. 'Scribal (In)consistency in Thirteenth-Century South Wales: The Orthography of the Black Book of Carmarthen'. *Studia Celtica* 43 (2009): 135–74.

Saer, Roy. *'Canu at Iws' ac Ysgrifau Eraill/'Songs for Use' and Other Articles*. Cymdeithas Alawon Gwerin Cymru/Welsh Folk-Song Society, 2013.

Saunders, Corinne. *Magic and the Supernatural in Medieval English Romance*. Cambridge: Cambridge University Press, 2010.

Scott, Kathleen L. *Later Gothic Manuscripts, 1390–1490*. 2 vols. London: Harvey Miller, 1996.

Sessle, Erica. 'Exploring the Limitations of the Sovereignty Goddess Through the Role of Rhiannon'. *Proceedings of the Harvard Celtic Colloquium* 14 (1994): 9–13.

Shell, Marc, ed. *American Babel: Literatures of the United States from Abnaki to Zuni*. Cambridge, MA: Harvard University Press, 2002.

Shopland, Norena. *Forbidden Lives: LGBT Stories from Wales*. Bridgend: Seren, 2017.

Showers, K. *Imperial Gullies: Soil Erosion and Conservation in Lesotho*. Athens, OH: Ohio University Press, 2005.

Siddons, M. *The Development of Welsh Heraldry*. 4 vols. Aberystwyth: National Library of Wales, 1991–2007.

Silver, Carole. *Strange and Secret Peoples: Fairies and Victorian Consciousness*. Oxford: Oxford University Press, 2000.

Sims-Williams, Patrick. 'Some Functions of Origin Stories in Early Medieval Wales'. In *History and Heroic Tale: A Symposium*, ed. Tove Nyberg, I. Piø, P. Meulengracht Sørenson, and A. Trommer, 97–131. Odense: Odense University Press, 1985.

'The Early Welsh Arthurian Poems'. In *The Arthur of the Welsh*, ed. Bromwich *et al.*, 33–72.

'The Submission of Irish Kings in Fact and Fiction: Henry II, Bendigeidfran, and the Dating of the Four Branches'. *Cambrian Medieval Celtic Studies* 22 (1991): 31–61.

'The Death of Urien'. *Cambrian Medieval Celtic Studies* 32 (1996): 25–56.

'The Uses of Writing in Early Medieval Wales'. In *Literacy in Medieval Celtic Societies*, ed. Huw Pryce, 15–38.

'Clas Beuno and the Four Branches of the Mabinogi'. In *150 Jahre 'Mabinogion'*, ed. Maier and Zimmer, 111–27.

Irish Influence on Medieval Welsh Literature. Oxford: Oxford University Press, 2011.

'Powys and Early Welsh Poetry'. *Cambrian Medieval Celtic Studies* 67 (2014): 33–54.

'Dating the Poems of Aneirin and Taliesin'. *Zeitschrift für Celtische Philologie* 63 (2016): 163–234.

Slotkin, Edgar. 'The Fabula, Story, and Text of *Breuddwyd Rhonabwy*'. *Cambridge Medieval Celtic Studies* 18 (1989): 89–111.

Smiles, Sam. *The Image of Antiquity: Ancient Britain and the Romantic Imagination*. New Haven and London: Yale University Press, 1994.

Smith, Dai. 'Myth and Meaning in the Literature of the South Wales Coalfield'. *Anglo-Welsh Review* 25 (1975): 21–42.

'The Early Gwyn Thomas'. *Transactions of the Honourable Society of Cymmrodorion* (1985): 71–89.

Aneurin Bevan and the World of South Wales. Cardiff: University of Wales Press, 1993.

Wales: A Question for History. Bridgend: Seren, 1999.

'Psycho-colonialism'. *New Welsh Review* 66 (2004): 22–9.

Smith, David, and Gareth Williams. *Fields of Praise: The Official History of the Welsh Rugby Union, 1881–1981*. Cardiff: University of Wales Press, 1980.

Smith, J. Beverley. *Yr Ymwybod â Hanes yng Nghymru yn yr Oesoedd Canol/The Sense of History in Medieval Wales*. Inaugural Lecture. Aberystwyth: Coleg Prifysgol Cymru/ University College of Wales, 1991.

'Historical Writing in Medieval Wales: The Composition of *Brenhinedd y Saesson*'. *Studia Celtica* 42 (2008): 55–86.

Smith, Llinos B. 'The Welsh Language before 1536'. In *The Welsh Language Before the Industrial Revolution*, ed. Jenkins, 15–44.

Snyder, Edward D. *The Celtic Revival in English Literature 1760–1800*. Cambridge, MA: Harvard University Press, 1923.

Sollors, Werner, ed. *Multilingual America: Transnationalism, Ethnicity, and the Language of American Literature*. New York: New York University Press, 1998.

Stead, Peter. 'Wales at the Movies'. In *Wales: The Imagined Nation*, ed. Curtis, 161–79.

Stephens, Elan Closs. 'Drama'. In *The Arts in Wales*, ed. Stephens, 239–96.

'A Century of Welsh Drama'. In *A Guide to Welsh Literature, c. 1900–1996*, ed. Johnston, 239–42.

Stephens, Meic. 'The Second Flowering'. *Poetry Wales* 3, 3 (Winter 1967): 2–9.

ed. *The Arts in Wales 1950–1975*. Cardiff: Wales Arts Council, 1979.

ed. *The New Companion to the Literature of Wales*. Cardiff: University of Wales Press, 1998.

ed. *Decoding the Hare: Essays on Rhys Davies*. Cardiff: University of Wales Press, 2001.

Stephenson, David. *The Governance of Gwynedd*. Cardiff: University of Wales Press, 1984. Repr. as *Political Power in Medieval Gwynedd: Governance and the Welsh Princes*. Cardiff: University of Wales Press, 2014.

Sturzer, Ned. 'Inconsistencies and Infelicities in the Welsh Tales'. *Studia Celtica* 37 (2003): 127–42.

'The Purpose of *Culhwch ac Olwen*'. *Studia Celtica* 39 (2005): 145–67.

Suggett, Richard. 'Vagabonds and Minstrels in Sixteenth-Century Wales'. In *The Spoken Word: Oral Culture in Britain, 1500–1850*, ed. Fox and Woolf, 138–72.

A History of Magic and Witchcraft in Wales. Stroud: History Press, 2008.

Suggett, Richard, and Eryn White. 'Language, Literacy, and Aspects of Identity in Early Modern Wales'. In *The Spoken Word: Oral Culture in Britain 1500–1850*, ed. Fox and Woolf, 52–83.

Sullivan III, C. W. *Welsh Celtic Myth in Modern Fantasy*. London: Greenwood Press, 1989.

'Y Mabinogion a Ffuglen Ffantasi America'. In *Gweld Sêr*, ed. Thomas, 99–116.

Taaffe, Carol. 'Irish Modernism'. In *The Oxford Handbook of Modernisms*, ed. Brooker *et al.*, 782–96.

Tanner, Duncan, Chris Williams, and Deian Hopkin, eds. *The Labour Party in Wales, 1900–2000*. Cardiff: University of Wales Press, 2000.

Tanner, Duncan, Chris Williams, Wil Griffith, and Andrew Edwards, eds. *Debating Nationhood and Governance in Britain, 1885–1945*. Manchester: University of Manchester Press, 2006.

Taylor, B., and K. Thomson, eds. *Scotland and Wales: Nations Again?* Cardiff: University of Wales Press, 1999.

Tedlock, E. W., ed. *Dylan Thomas: The Legend and the Poet*. London: Heinemann, 1960.

Thain, Marion, ed. *The Lyric Poem: Formations and Transformations*. Cambridge: Cambridge University Press, 2013.

Thiong'o, Ngũgĩ wa. *Decolonising the Mind: The Politics of Language in African Literature*. London: J. Currey, 1986.

Thomas, Alys, and Martin Laffin. 'The First Welsh Constitutional Crisis: The Alun Michael Resignation'. *Public Policy and Administration* 16, 1 (2001): 18–31.

Thomas, Clem, and Geoffrey Nicholson. *Welsh Rugby: The Crowning Years, 1968–1980*. London: Collins, 1980.

Thomas, Dafydd Elis. 'Mewn Dau Gae'. In *Cyfres y Meistri 2: Waldo Williams*, ed. Rhys, 160–7.

'The Image of Wales in R. S. Thomas's Poetry'. *Poetry Wales* 7, 4 (1972): 59–66.

Thomas, David N., ed. *Dylan Remembered*. 2 vols. Vol. II: *Interviews by Colin Edwards, 1933–1953*. Bridgend: Seren and Poetry of Wales Press, 2004.

Thomas, Gwyn. *Eisteddfodau Caerwys/The Caerwys Eisteddfodau*. Cardiff: University of Wales Press, 1968.

Y Traddodiad Barddol. Caerdydd: Gwasg Prifysgol Cymru, 1976.

Yn Blentyn yn y Blaenau. Caernarfon: Cyngor Sir Gwynedd, 1981.

Dadansoddi 14. Llandysul: Gwasg Gomer, 1984.

'Hugh Bevan (1911–1979)'. *Transactions of the Honourable Society of Cymmrodorion* (1993): 99–114.

Bywyd Bach. Caernarfon: Gwasg Gwynedd, 2006.

Murmuron Tragwyddoldeb a Chwningod Tjioclet. Cyhoeddiadau Barddas, 2010.

Thomas, Isaac. *William Salesbury a'i Destament*. Caerdydd: Gwasg Prifysgol Cymru, 1967.

Y Testament Newydd Cymraeg 1551–1620. Caerdydd: Gwasg Prifysgol Cymru, 1976.

Yr Hen Destament Cymraeg 1551–1620. Aberystwyth: Llyfrgell Genedlaethol Cymru, 1988.

'Translating the Bible'. In *A Guide to Welsh Literature c. 1530–1700*, ed. Gruffydd, 154–175.

Thomas, M. Wynn. 'Ann Griffiths and Morgan Llwyd: A Comparative Study of Two Welsh Mystics'. *Studies in Mystical Literature* 5, 3 (1983): 23–39.

Morgan Llwyd. Writers of Wales. Cardiff: University of Wales Press, 1984.

'Iaith Newid y Byd'. *Golwg* 4 (March 1992): 19–21.

'Pwys Llên a Phwysau Hanes'. In *Sglefrio ar Eiriau*, ed. Rowlands, 1–21.

Internal Difference: Twentieth-Century Writing in Wales. Cardiff: University of Wales Press, 1992.

'Place, Race and Gender in the Poetry of Gillian Clarke'. In *Dangerous Diversities*, ed. Gramich and Hiscock, 3–19.

ed. *DiFfinio Dwy Lenyddiaeth Cymru*. Caerdydd: Gwasg Prifysgol Cymru, 1995.

'Symbyliad y Symbol: Barddoniaeth Euros Bowen a Vernon Watkins'. In *DiFfinio Dwy Lenyddiaeth Cymru*, ed. Thomas, 170–94.

In the Shadow of the Pulpit: Literature and Nonconformist Wales. Cardiff: University of Wales Press, 2010.

'Seisnigrwydd "Ymadawiad Arthur"'. *Y Traethodydd* (Gorffennaf 2012): 142–65.

ed. *Gweld Sêr: Cymru a Chanrif America*. Caerdydd: Gwasg Prifysgol Cymru, 2001.

ed. *A Guide to Welsh Literature*. Vol. VII: *Welsh Writing in English*. University of Wales Press: Cardiff, 2003.

Thomas, Ned. *The Welsh Extremist: A Culture in Crisis*. London: Gollancz, 1971.

'Sinking into the Landscape: Notes on Anglo-Welsh Literature and Australia'. In *The Historical and Cultural Connections and Parallels Between Wales and Australia*, ed. Edwards and Sumner.

'Waldo Williams: In Two Fields'. In *Poetry in the British Isles*, ed. Ludwig and Fietz, 253–66.

'Parallels and Paradigms'. In *Welsh Writing in English*, ed. Thomas, 310–26.

'Bro: Welsh Keywords'. *Planet: The Welsh Internationalist* 207 (2012): 82–8.

Thomas, Owen, ed. *Llenyddiaeth Mewn Theori*. Caerdydd: Gwasg Prifysgol Cymru, 2006.

Thomas, Peter Wynn. 'Middle Welsh Dialects: Problems and Perspectives'. *Bulletin of the Board of Celtic Studies* 40 (1993): 17–50.

'Haenau *Breudwyt Maxen*: Ymarferiad mewn Archaeoleg Destunol'. *Ysgrifau Beirniadol* 23 (1997): 73–98.

'Cydberthynas y Pedair Fersiwn Ganoloesol'. In *Canhwyll Marchogion: Cyd-destunoli Peredur*, ed. Davies and Thomas, 10–50.

Thomas, W. S. K. *Tudor Wales*. Llandysul: Gomer Press, 1983.

Thomas, Wyn. *Hands Off Wales: Nationhood and Militancy*. Llandysul: Gomer Press, 2013.

Thompson, E. P. *Customs in Common*. London: Merlin Press, 1991.

Thorneycroft, Captain Peter. *The Welsh Tory*, November, 1947.

Thrift, Nigel. *Spatial Formations*. London: Sage Publications, 1996.

'Space'. *Theory, Culture and Society* 23, 2/3 (2006):139–46.

Tighe, Carl. 'Theatre (or Not) in Wales'. In *Wales: The Imagined Nation*, ed. Curtis, 241–60.

Times Literary Supplement. Anonymous review of Dylan Thomas, *18 Poems*. 13 March 1935.

Tolstoy, Nikolai. *The Oldest British Prose Literature: The Compilation of the Four Branches of the Mabinogi*. Lewiston, NY, Queenston, and Lampeter: Edwin Mellen Press, 2009.

Trench, Alan. *Old Wine in New Bottles? Relations Between London and Cardiff After the Government of Wales Act, 2006*. London: UCL, Constitution Unit, 2007.

Trumpener, Katie. *Bardic Nationalism: The Romantic Novel and the British Empire*. Princeton: Princeton University Press, 1997.

Valente, Roberta L. 'Gwydion and Aranrhod: Crossing the Borders of Gender in *Math*'. *Bulletin of the Board of Celtic Studies* 35 (1988): 1–9.

Wade, J. *Fairies in Medieval Romance*. Basingstoke: Palgrave Macmillan, 2011.

Wade, S. *In My Own Shire: Region and Belonging in British Writing 1840–1970*. Westport, CT and London: Praeger, 2002.

Wainwright, Laura. '"Always Observant and Slightly Obscure": Lynette Roberts as Welsh Modernist'. *Almanac* 16 (2012): 187–225.

Walford Davies, Damian. *Waldo Williams: Rhyddiaith*. Caerdydd: Gwasg Prifysgol Cymru, 2001.

   Presences that Disturb. Cardiff: University of Wales Press, 2002.

   Cartographies of Culture: New Geographies of Welsh Writing in English. Cardiff: University of Wales Press, 2012.

Walford Davies, Damian, and Jason Walford Davies, eds. *Cof ac Arwydd: Ysgrifau Newydd ar Waldo Williams*. Cyhoeddiadau Barddas, 2006.

Walford Davies, Damian, and Linda Pratt, eds. *Wales and the Romantic Imagination*. Cardiff: University of Wales Press, 2012.

Walford Davies, Hazel. '"The Country of my Heart": Lord Howard de Walden and Wales'. *Transactions of the Honourable Society of Cymmrodorion* 20 (2014): 18–36.

   ed. *Y Theatr Genedlaethol yng Nghymru*. Caerdydd: Gwasg Prifysgol Cymru, 2007.

   ed. *State of Play: Four Playwrights of Wales* Llandysul: Gomer Press, 1998.

Walford Davies, Jason. '"Thick Ambush of Shadows": Allusions to Welsh Literature in the Work of R. S. Thomas'. *Welsh Writing in English: A Yearbook of Critical Essays* 1 (1995): 75–127.

   Gororau'r Iaith: R. S. Thomas a'r Traddodiad Llenyddol Cymraeg. Caerdydd: Gwasg Prifysgol Cymru, 2000.

   '"Gwisga'r Awen Liwiau Hynod": "Y Llwynog"'. *Llên Cymru* 23 (2000), 171–91.

   'Myned Allan i Fanfrig Gwreiddiau: Waldo Williams a *The Penguin New Writing*'. *Transactions of the Honourable Society of Cymmrodorion* 19 (2013): 148–68.

   ed. *Gweledigaethau: Cyfrol Deyrnged yr Athro Gwyn Thomas*. Cyhoeddiadau Barddas, 2007.

Wallace, Diana, and Andrew Smith, eds. *The Female Gothic: New Directions*. Basingstoke: Palgrave, 2009.

Ward, J. P. 'Editorial'. *Poetry Wales* 13, 1 (1977): 3–11

   'Editorial'. *Poetry Wales* 12, 3 (1977): 3.

Watkins, Carl S. *History and the Supernatural in Medieval England*. Cambridge: Cambridge University Press, 2007.

Watkins, Vernon. 'Dylan Thomas and the Spoken Word'. *Times Literary Supplement* (19 November 1954), 731.

Webb, Andrew. *Edward Thomas and World Literary Studies: Anglocentrism and English Literature*. Cardiff: University of Wales Press, 2013.

Welsh, Andrew. 'The Traditional Narrative Motifs in *The Four Branches of the Mabinogi*'. *Cambridge Medieval Celtic Studies* 15 (1988): 51–62.

   'Traditional Tales and the Harmonizing of Story in *Pwyll Pendeuic Dyuet*'. *Cambridge Medieval Celtic Studies* 17 (1989): 15–41.

   'Branwen, Beowulf, and the Tragic Peaceweaver Tale'. *Viator* 22 (1991): 1–13.

   'Manawydan fab Llyr: Wales, England and the "New Man"'. In *Celtic Languages and Celtic Peoples: Proceedings of the Second North American Congress of Celtic Studies, 1989*, ed. Cyril J. Byrne, Margaret Harry, and Pádraig Ó Siadhail, 369–82. Halifax: D'Arcy McGee Chair of Irish Studies, St Mary's University, 1992.

Westover, Daniel, ed. *Leslie Norris*, triple special issue, *Literature and Belief* 29 and 30,1 (2010).

White, Donna R. *A Century of Welsh Myth in Children's Literature*. Westport, CT: Greenwood Press, 1998.

White, Eryn M. 'Women in the Early Methodist Societies in Wales'. *Journal of Welsh Religious History* 7 (1999): 95–108.

  'A Tale of Two Mirrors: Forming an Identity for the Calvinistic Methodist Church of Wales'. In *Religion, Identity and Conflict in Britain: From the Restoration to the Twentieth Century*, ed. Brown *et al.*, 81–92.

Whitfield, Esther. 'Mordecai and Haman: The Drama of Welsh America'. In *American Babel*, ed. Shell, 93–116.

  'Welsh-Patagonian Fiction: Language and the Novel of Transnational Ethnicity'. *Diaspora: A Journal of Transnational Studies* 14, 2/3 (2005): 333–48.

  'Empire, Nation and the Fate of a Language: Patagonia in Argentine and Welsh Literature'. *Postcolonial Studies* 14, 1 (2011): 75–93.

Wiliams, Gerwyn. 'Sbecian ar Dir Newydd'. *Barn* 302 (1988): 5–6.

  'Yr Ianci o'r Blaenau: Golwg ar Gerddi Gwyn Thomas'. In *Gweledigaethau*, ed. Walford Davies, 242–68.

  ed. *Rhyddid y Nofel*. Caerdydd: Gwasg Prifysgol Cymru, 1999.

Williams, Charlotte, Paul O'Leary, and Neil Evans, eds. *A Tolerant Nation? Revisiting Ethnic Diversity in a Devolved Wales*. Cardiff: University of Wales Press, 2015.

Williams, Chris. 'Master of a Lost Past'. *Planet* 121 (1997): 12–18.

  'Problematizing Wales: An Exploration in Historiography and Postcoloniality'. In *Postcolonial Wales*, ed. Aaron and Williams, 3–22.

Williams, Daniel G. 'From Hay-on-Wye to the Haymarket Riots: William Dean Howells and Wales'. *New Welsh Review* 64 (2004): 49–57.

  'Welsh Modernism'. In *The Oxford Handbook of Modernisms*, ed. Brooker *et al.*, 797–816.

  Wales Unchained: Literature, Politics and Identity in the American Century. Cardiff: University of Wales Press, 2015.

  'Writing Against the Grain: Raymond Williams' *Border Country* and the Defence of Realism'. In *Mapping the Territory*, ed. Gramich, 217–43.

  ed. *Slanderous Tongues: Essays on Welsh Poetry In English 1970–2005*. Bridgend: Seren, 2010.

Williams, G. J. *Traddodiad Llenyddol Morgannwg*. Caerdydd: Gwasg Prifysgol Cymru, 1948.

  'Cyfraniad Saunders Lewis fel Ysgolhaig Cymraeg'. In *Saunders Lewis: Ei Feddwl a'i Waith*, ed. Pennar Davies, 121–36. Dinbych: Gwasg Gee, 1950.

  'Traddodiad Llenyddol Dyffryn Clwyd a'r Cyffiniau'. *Transactions of the Denbighshire Historical Society* 1 (1952): 20–32.

  Iolo Morganwg. Caerdydd: Gwasg Prifysgol Cymru, 1956.

  Agweddau ar Hanes Dysg Gymraeg. Ed. Aneirin Lewis. Caerdydd: Gwasg Prifysgol Cymru, 1969, 1985.

Williams, Gareth. '"The Dramatic Turbulence of Some Irrecoverable Football Game": Sport, Literature and Welsh Identity'. In *Sport in the Making of Celtic Cultures*, ed. Jarvie, 55–70.

Williams, Gareth Haulfryn. 'Anterliwt Derwyn Fechan, 1654'. *Caernarvonshire Historical Society Transactions* 44 (1983): 53–8.

Williams, Glanmor. 'Wales and the Reformation'. In *Wales Through the Ages*, vol. II, ed. Roderick, 24–30.

Welsh Reformation Essays. Cardiff: University of Wales Press, 1967.

Grym Tafodau Tân. Llandysul: Gwasg Gomer, 1984.

Harri Tudur a Chymru/Henry Tudor and Wales. Cardiff: University of Wales Press, 1985.

Renewal and Reformation: Wales, c. 1415–1642. Oxford: Oxford University Press, 1987.

'Romantic and Realist: Theophilus Evans and Theophilus Jones.' *Archaeologica Cambrensis* 140 (1991): 17–27.

Wales and the Reformation. Cardiff: University of Wales Press, 1997.

'The Early Stuart Church.' In *The Welsh Church from Reformation to Disestablishment, 1603–1920*, ed. Williams et al., 3–32.

ed. *Glamorgan County History*. Vol. IV: *Early Modern Glamorgan*. Cardiff: Glamorgan County History Trust, 1974.

Williams, Glanmor, and Robert Owen Jones, eds. *The Celts and the Renaissance: Tradition and Innovation*. Cardiff: University of Wales Press, 1990.

Williams, Glanmor, William Jacob, Nigel Yates, and Frances Knight, eds. *The Welsh Church from Reformation to Disestablishment, 1603–1920*. Cardiff: University of Wales Press, 2007.

Williams, Glyn, *The Welsh in Patagonia: The State and the Ethnic Community*. Cardiff: University of Wales Press, 1991.

ed. *Social and Cultural Change in Contemporary Wales*. London: Routledge and Kegan Paul, 1978.

Williams, Gruffydd Aled. *Ymryson Edmwnd Prys a Wiliam Cynwal*. Caerdydd: Gwasg Prifysgol Cymru, 1986.

'Mydryddu'r Salmau yn Gymraeg'. *Llên Cymru* 16, 1/2 (1989): 114–32.

Owain y Beirdd. Aberystwyth: Prifysgol Cymru, 1998.

'Owain Cyfeiliog: Bardd-dywysog?' In *Beirdd a Thywysogion*, ed. Roberts and Owen, 180–201.

'The Poetic Debate of Edmwnd Prys and Wiliam Cynwal' In *The Renaissance and the Celtic Countries*, ed. Davies and Law, 33–54.

'Dwy Lenyddiaeth, Dau Fyd: Diwylliant yn Llyweni yng Nghyfnod y Dadeni'. *Llên Cymru* 40 (2017): 40–76.

'The Welsh Content of Christ Church MS 184'. *Christ Church Library Newsletter* 10, forthcoming.

Williams, Gwyn. *An Introduction to Welsh Poetry*. London: Faber and Faber, 1953.

'*Troelus a Chresyd*: a Welsh Tragedy'. *Transactions of the Honourable Society of Cymmrodorion* (1957): 37–57.

Williams, Gwyn A. *In Search of Beulah Land: The Welsh and the Atlantic Revolution*. London: Croom Helm, 1980.

When Was Wales? A History of the Welsh. Harmondsworth: Penguin, 1985.

Williams, Herbert. *John Cowper Powys*. Bridgend: Seren, 1997.

Williams, Ifor. 'The Computus Fragment'. *Bulletin of the Board of Celtic Studies* 3 (1926–7): 245–72.

'Lexicographical Notes'. *Bulletin of the Board of Celtic Studies* 3, 2 (May 1926): 125–36.

Williams, Ioan. 'Towards National Identities: Welsh Theatres'. In *The Cambridge History of British Theatre*, vol. III, ed. Kershaw, 242–72.

A Straitened Stage: A Study of the Theatre of J. Saunders Lewis. Bridgend: Seren Books, 1991.

Williams, Iwan Llwyd, and Wiliam Owen Roberts. 'Myth y Traddodiad Dethol'. *Llais Llyfrau* (1982): 10–11.

Williams, J. E. Caerwyn. *Geiriadurwyr y Gymraeg yng Nghyfnod y Dadeni*. Caerdydd: Gwasg Prifysgol Cymru, 1983.

Williams, J. E. Caerwyn, and Patrick K. Ford. *The Irish Literary Tradition*. Cardiff: University of Wales Press, 1992.

Williams, John. *Was Wales Industrialised?* Llandysul: Gomer Press, 1995.

Williams, Jon Kenneth. 'Sleeping with an Elephant: Wales and England in the Mabinogion'. In *Cultural Diversity in the Middle Ages*, ed. Jeffrey Jerome Cohen, 173–90. New York: Palgrave Macmillan, 2008.

Williams, Kevin. 'An Uneasy Relationship: The National Assembly and the Press and Media'. In *Building a Civic Culture*, ed. Jones and Osmond, 245–56.

Williams, Mark. *Fiery Shapes: Celestial Portents and Astrology in Ireland and Wales, 700–1700*. Oxford: Oxford University Press, 2010.

'Magic in Medieval Wales and Ireland'. In *The Ashgate Research Companion to Late Medieval Magic*, ed. S. Page, forthcoming.

Williams, Penry, *The Later Tudors: England 1547–1603*. Oxford: Clarendon Press, 1995.

Williams, R. B. *Rhyddiaith y Wladfa*. Dinbych: Gwasg Gee, 1949.

Williams, Raymond. *The Welsh Industrial Novel: Inaugural Gwyn Jones Lecture*. Cardiff: Cardiff University College Press, 1979.

'Working Class, Proletarian, Socialist: Problems in Some Welsh Novels'. In *The Socialist Novel in Britain*, ed. Klaus, 110–21.

Who Speaks for Wales? Nation, Culture, Identity. Ed. Daniel G. Williams. Cardiff: University of Wales Press, 2003.

'Wales and England'. In *Who Speaks for Wales? Nation, Culture, Identity*, ed. Williams, 19–31.

'Welsh Culture'. In *Who Speaks for Wales? Nation, Culture, Identity*, ed. Williams, 5–12.

The Politics of Modernism: Against the New Conformists. Ed. Tony Pinkney. London: Verso, 1989.

Williams, Rowan. 'Tirwedd Ffydd'. *Bwletin Cymdeithas Emynau Cymru* 4, 1–2 (2008–9): 1–12.

Williams, W. 'Sgwrs â Bobi Jones'. In *Waldo Williams: Rhyddiaith*, ed. Walford Davies, 91–6.

Williams, W. Ogwen. 'The Union of England and Wales'. In *Wales Through the Ages*, vol. II, ed. Roderick, 19–23.

Willis, David. *Syntactic Change in Welsh*. Oxford: Clarendon Press, 1998.

Wood, Denis. *The Power of Maps*. New York and London: The Guilford Press, 1992.

Wood, Juliette. 'The Calumniated Wife in Medieval Welsh Literature'. *Cambridge Medieval Celtic Studies* 10 (1985): 25–38.

'Perceptions of the Past in Welsh Folklore Studies'. *Folklore* 108 (1997): 93–102.

'Folk Narrative Influence in Wales at the Beginning of the Twentieth Century: The Influence of John Rhŷs (1840–1916)'. *Folklore* 116 (2005): 325–41.

Wood, Leanne. 'Greening the Welsh Dragon'. In *Breaking Up Britain*, ed. Perryman, 86–94.

Woodward, Kate. *Cleddyf ym Mrwydr yr Iaith? Y Bwrdd Ffilmiau Cymraeg*. Caerdydd: Gwasg Prifysgol Cymru, 2013.

Woolf, A., ed. *Beyond the Gododdin: Dark Age Scotland in Medieval Wales*. St Andrews: Committee for Dark Age Studies, University of St Andrews, 2013.

Wyn, Hefin. *Battle of the Preselau: The Campaign to Safeguard the 'Sacred' Pembrokeshire Hills*. Maenclochog: Clychau Clochog, 2008.

Zeiser, Sarah. 'Bragmaticus omnibus Brittonibus: David, Sulien, and an Ecclesiastical Dynasty in Conquest-Era Wales'. *Proceedings of the Harvard Celtic Colloquium* 31 (2011): 305–20.

'Latinity, Manuscripts, and the Rhetoric of Conquest in Late Eleventh-Century Wales'. PhD diss., Harvard University, 2012.

Index